T0396423

Strangling Aunty: Perilous Times for the Australian Broadcasting Corporation

"In her lament for a sadly diminished national icon, Dr Small describes how in this digital world, the ABC "has left the private box and joined the mosh pit". How "opinion has not only infiltrated fact in news, raised voices drown out 'old' standards of ethics, knowledge and probity". She blames the broadcaster's declining audiences on poor leadership and squandered cultural capital, not politicians or media rivals. Required reading for ABC friends, politicians and, all media students."

—Maurice Newman AC, former Chairman, *Australian Broadcasting Corporation*

"In this engrossing and comprehensive volume, Dr Small uses Pierre Bourdieu's theories to show that Australia's premier public broadcaster, the ABC, has been more effective in holding power to account when it controls its own élite field because that's where it has legitimate authority. She argues for a more empowered, nuanced and proactive mindset to meet the needs of a world seeking neutrality and fact. It's an urgently needed book."

—Dr John Cokley, *CQUniversity*

Virginia Small

Strangling Aunty: Perilous Times for the Australian Broadcasting Corporation

palgrave
macmillan

Virginia Small
University of New South Wales
Australian Defence Force Academy
Canberra, NSW, Australia

ISBN 978-981-16-0775-2 ISBN 978-981-16-0776-9 (eBook)
https://doi.org/10.1007/978-981-16-0776-9

Cover illustration: Richard Milnes / Alamy Stock Photo

This Palgrave Macmillan imprint is published by the registered company Springer Nature Singapore Pte Ltd.
The registered company address is: 152 Beach Road, #21-01/04 Gateway East, Singapore 189721, Singapore

Acknowledgements

Gratitude for the extraordinarily generous and sustaining inspiration from Dr James Warn, Hamish Conroy, Edward Conroy and Patrick Conroy. Louise Kaktiņš and Leon de Bord, thank you.

To the University of New South Wales Canberra, Australian Defence Force Academy (ADFA) School of Business for ongoing support and encouragement, especially former Head of School Professor Michael O'Donnell and Professor of Finance and Deputy Head (Research) Satish Chand.

Thank you to the reviewers Maurice Newman AC and Dr John Cokley, as well as Palgrave Macmillan's anonymous reviewer, for their invaluable feedback and perspicacious observations.

And finally, the generous time, insights and reflection by senior Australian politicians, former ABC senior leaders and former ABC senior staff who agreed to be interviewed for this research. Their confidential contributions are respected and highly appreciated.

This book is dedicated to my father the late Lloyd Small, an ABC audience member, true to the end.

Valerie Small, valete (2020) to my precious mother; and to Marion Edwards (2020), *my* irreplaceable Aunty.

Contents

About the Author

Virginia Small is a visiting fellow at the School of Business at UNSW ADFA, Canberra, and has worked at the *ABC* for over 18 years in a variety of broadcasting roles. Prior to that she was also a finance journalist at the *Sydney Morning Herald* and a money market reporter at *Australian Associated Press*. At the *ABC* she was a respected newsreader and economics journalist and produced and presented a high-rating business program on Radio National. As a news broadcaster and journalist, she gained a day-to-day insight into the goings-on of the *ABC* and the changes of management and its impact. She has a doctoral degree in communication, a master's degree in professional communication and a master's in literature.

List of Images

List of Tables

CHAPTER 1

Institutional Frameworks and Losing the *Field*

1.1 Australia's ABC

This book provides a rigorous and timely analysis of the role of the Australian Broadcasting Corporation (ABC) as a public service broadcaster by examining the impacts of changes and shifting dynamics in the external media environment, key political and business actors as well as the role of the internal staff culture, and the way in which this confluence of forces have begun to strangle the voice of 'Aunty' (aka the ABC). It addresses a gap in the literature where previous publications on the ABC tended to reflect the cognitive scripts of the staff culture, and, as this book reveals, these understandings operate within the *field* and enact its norms in a defensive way, rather than providing a wider perspective as to how the staff culture serves as an actor in the operation of the ABC. Also, this book contributes significantly to the research literature with its rigorous analysis of the ways in which social media have transformed and dislocated the entire professional media environment and assesses the limited understanding that Australia's politicians, ABC management and staff have had of this impact and its ramifications and consequences in terms of the ABC's necessary transitions, where the rush to change has overwhelmed all else. Drawing on Institutional Logics theory and Pierre Bourdieu's *field* theory, this book extends the theoretical framing of the role of a public broadcaster as well as providing a richer understanding of the contested *field*(s)

V. Small, *Strangling Aunty: Perilous Times for the Australian Broadcasting Corporation*,
https://doi.org/10.1007/978-981-16-0776-9_1

in which the public broadcaster operates; and, notes the importance of maintaining its ***cultural capital*** and ***reputational capital*** as vehicles for creditable evolution in the contemporary digitalised media landscape.

The ABC is Australia's only national fully publicly-funded broadcaster public service broadcaster (PSB)/public service media (PSM).[1] Former Chairman, Justin Milne, and past Managing Director, Michelle Guthrie, stated in the 2018 Annual Report, the ABC was capable of doing everything—all to all and: "meets the needs of both niche and mass audiences"[2] referencing online activities plus now 'old-fashion' legacy media—radio and television. This book challenges this pronouncement that it continues to serve equally the niche and mass needs. Its current funding by the Federal Government is a three-year budget of AUD3.16 billion for 2019–2022. It has received what is called triennial funding since 1989. Currently, it serves a population of over 24 million Australians. The budget has grown with the population it serves but has then been reduced some. In reality, Aunty's voice has had several 'choke points'; more recently she came under renewed pressure in 2018 when the Federal Government announced a three-year freeze on its funding indexation, which resulted in cuts to the ABC output with the loss of AUD28 million in 2020–2021 and over AUD41 million in 2021–2022 (Lallo, 2020).[3]

Its first budget in 1932 was A£6900 (described as a "loan" from the Commonwealth Government) plus revenue of A£250,618/1O/ (some of which was revenue from licence fees and orchestra performances etc.). The total amounted to A£257,518/10/or just over what would be today AUD25 million (accounting for inflation) at a time when the population of Australia was 6.5 million people. When the ABC began in 1932, it was on air for 49,133 hours over the financial year (ABC Annual Report 1939–1940) and there were 369,945 radio licenses (and radio licence fees once formed part of its funding structure), equivalent to 5.67% of the population.[4] The bulk of radio programming content then was dedicated to music, its foundational *cultural capital* and it was the early contacts and associations made by its senior management in the music world that formed its reputation as an iconic and unique representative of Australian culture and nationhood. Public Service Broadcasting institutions were established by governments as radio monopolies in early 20th century to control a public good (Scannell, 1997). In Australia, the ABC was formed to disseminate education and culture, although that broad vision has met with overall financial curtailment due to historical waxing and waning interest and support from federal governments. This book does not analyse the vicissitudes of declines and reprieves in ABC budgets. Rather than an economic and financial capital analysis of ABC activity, this book unpacks the accompanying, less quantified, less analysed, but sometimes precipitative decline in its *cultural* and *reputational capitals*.

Today, the ABC provides continuous coverage on multiple platforms with a national radio and television network and an extensive remit of online content, overseas transmissions, including music. Music had been a formative and a highly valued constituent of the content mix for the ABC and much overlooked in recent perspectives on the ABC where news content is assumed to have formed its respected reputation. The ABC has production and transmission operations in all the capital cities of the six states (New South Wales, Victoria, South Australia, Western Australia, Queensland and Tasmania) and two territories (Canberra, Australian Capital Territory and Darwin, Northern Territory). Sydney (NSW) and Melbourne (Victoria) have been considered the two most important offices for the ABC, followed by what is known in-house at the ABC as "the BAPH states"—Brisbane (Queensland), Adelaide (South Australia), Perth (Western Australia) and Hobart (Tasmania). Its prodigious digital offerings via ABC Online offer streamed broadcasting, multi-channels, news pages, apps, podcasts and a range of websites for its programs. The ABC also has a robust social media presence on Twitter and Facebook.

It is worth remembering, however, that from the outset its mission was to be a cultural institution and educator, which aimed to take advantage of its public role, extensive reach and give a nod to its British heritage from the British Broadcasting Corporation (BBC). The first annual report (1932–1933) stated:

> The Commission has realised that it has a certain responsibility in the matter of public education, since it controls a facility for spreading information upon every subject to thousands of citizens.[5]

The first annual report in 1932 added this arresting point about the ABC's role educating Australians:

> One of the conclusions arrived at is that the most satisfactory method of education is the enlargement of interest rather than the mere presentation of information.[6]

Then, in the ABC's 1939–1940 Annual Report the launch of broadcasting to schools was said to:

> Conduce to the building of a better educated democracy. A very important point is that it encourages the intelligent use of broadcast programs. Apart from what the child learns of nature or music or history, he may, under the guidance of the teacher develop his powers of concentration and selection when listening to the spoken word.[7]

Consequently, the ABC's impacts as both cultural and educational institution, especially in its stated Institutional Logics to "concentrate" and "select" "the spoken word" have been profound in Australia and there were noteworthy and serendipitous instances of this. For example, in 2001 the late former President of Indonesia, Abdurrahman Wahid, when a guest at the 40th anniversary party of ABC Television's Foreign Correspondent, an international current affairs program, told the gathering: "I got my English from Radio Australia" (Inglis, 2002).[8] The ABC's Radio Australia, launched in 1939 at the start of World War II, is Aunty's international broadcasting (and online) voice (although it has been diminished considerably in its footprint with waning support from both the ABC and Australian governments). So, while the ABC has always been a major part of Australian media it has also had a unique reach in occupying its own *field* of education, in this case to Papua New Guinea, Asia and South Pacific nations. Radio Australia had given Aunty—and the Australian Government—international impact, regional ascendancy and soft diplomacy. Locally, the ABC developed its goal to teach Australians what they needed to know to be observant citizens of a parliamentary democracy and take an informed opinion to the ballot box, of which compulsory voting was, and still is, a very important adjunct to the ABC's role. Put simply, if everyone votes, everyone needs to know the objective facts. At a time of dramatic change in the traditional media as newspapers, radio and television struggle to compete and maintain audiences with a less regulated, more edgy, booming voiced, 'snatch and grab' emergent digital media field it would seem that nothing could be more beneficial than a clearer understanding of how Australia's major PSM is informing its citizens, and even regional neighbours, through its content as a cultural and educational institution.

This book makes three central assumptions:

1. That the ABC has been a central force in "defining, describing and delimiting what it is possible to say and not possible to say" (Kress, 1985)[9] in discourses on Australia's nationhood and identity, obtaining consensus, creating national idioms and legitimating and upholding its parliamentary democracy and institutions that form the struts of its civil society.
2. That the organisation has been undergoing major changes over many years that have contributed to its decline, subject to a diverse range of pressures that cannot be blamed exclusively and solely on malicious politicians, destructive commercial media actors, or funding cuts.
3. Therefore, that the challenged times of the ABC can also be attributed to a lack of planning and understanding by ABC leadership and governments of the critical need to value and preserve its esteemed reputational and prized experimental status as it made the necessary transition from a PSB to a PSM outfit.

While there is ongoing concern in Australia over the concentration of media ownership in the hands of the few, of far greater concern is that Australians are increasingly inclined to get their news from social media and blogs (Centre for Media Transition, 2020 quoting Fisher et al., 2019),[10] and even though television news is still dominant among consumers, the quality of the news seems to have become irrelevant because "news literacy in Australia is quite low" (ibid.) anyway. Therefore, this inhibits audience discernment and permits variable quality of content.

Allied with this, the taking of content for free from professional media outlets has been causing a crisis in the media for some time. In 2020, the Federal Government made changes that would legislate to compel internet giants pay for the news they plundered and re-platformed. However, it was almost too late to save Australia's only news agency, Australian Associated Press (AAP), which was rescued by philanthropists and investors from closure. It has provided independent, subscription-based news to most newsrooms throughout Australia since 1935. AAP Chairman (and News Corporation Group Executive), Campbell Reid, said "it is a great loss that professional and researched information provided by AAP is being substituted with the un-researched and often inaccurate information that masquerades as real news on the digital platforms" (Mason,

2020a).[11] The consequences of the loss of AAP would have been profound. Firstly, this near collapse of AAP revealed the high degree of piracy carried out by the internet media platforms looting content that had been paid for by news outlets who employed journalists and paid attendant costs such as salaries, rental of premises, electricity bills, staff superannuation, recreation and other leave, tea for the tea room, et cetera; second, it connoted the extraordinary impact of disinformation (fake news) where crowd-sourcing has devalued the individual, investigative, time-consuming work of journalists (Dailey & Starbird, 2014)[12]; third, and allied to this, was how easily the public's sense of genuine news had been violated and perverted; and fourth, the ABC is Australia's only other significant independent news gatherer—albeit even after a shift away from the industrial model of media production. It is a sobering situation for a liberal democracy challenged by autocratic nation states, online security threats as well as what a Brookings Institute report identified as a populist challenge trying to "drive a wedge between democracy and liberalism" (Galston, 2018).[13]

Content that was plucked from Australian media companies had, up until 2020, been available to Google, Facebook and the like for free. It augmented the content on social media where news is sourced widely, as a consequence of this free abundance. The Digital News Report produced by Reuters Institute and Oxford University found that the largest group they surveyed (36%) was educated in the news via social media, 35% did an internet search, while 31% retrieved news from direct entry to a news source (Newman et al., 2016).[14] It showed that news was being curated and filtered by algorithms based on popularity and "hits". No longer is Aunty seen as the singular wise, elder woman who knows what's best for us to know. Australians have moved on. This change in news consumption is dramatic and cannot be underestimated on its ramifications for maintaining an educated and informed society. It has led to a consequential loss in Aunty's monopolistic educational presence in the public sphere. The main questions it prompts for the purposes of looking beyond this research are: "Who are the new online educators?", "What is their information?" and "How do they contribute to a healthy, vibrant liberal democracy?".

The Reuters Institute and Oxford University report pointed out that public service broadcasters around the world were facing questions: about perceived biases, about free news competing with paid content and about whether public funds should continue to pay for public media. Overarching this is the umbrella concern that PSM is now a dated concept anyway by virtue of its 'dated' creation at a time of need after the turn of the twentieth century. All media outfits and their actors, including the PSM, struggle to get eyeballs on their online content. While the Reuters Institute and Oxford University research did not look at Australia's ABC, several points made can be extrapolated to include the ABC. Those surveyed did point out that older broadcasters tended to be considered more reliable, built-up by virtue of their longevity. Sixty-four per cent of Australians said they shared or commented on news; however, the research noted that "sharing and commenting on the news is still largely the province of a small group of dedicated and highly motivated users". These people then become the opinion makers, which deserves further research into the veracity of news and growing resort to experts who inform news reports. Also, and perhaps most challenging, is that everyone is not continuously online reading and sharing news—in other words, not all are online all day, every day. This is an erroneous but concomitant assumption made by politicians of social media where politicians readily chop and change policy, for example, when social media turns hostile towards them. This is another area challenging governments and credible, consistent policy-making.

This book is an effort to bring clarity to controversy, promote informed, respectful discussion and strong support for the ABC, in describing the sort of media world to which it may continue to contribute and thrive. There is no single trope or potted explanation of the ABC because there has been a confluence of forces and activities exerted on the organisation over time and it is only through the enduring tenacity of the institution and the legacy affection of Australians that it survives. The ABC was established to provide cohesion to Australian culture and a sense of Australian identity. Its early mission called the organisation to educate Australians as to who they were and to what they could aspire, culturally and politically. The ABC drew the cultural borders and built bridges of understanding. The ABC defined Australians' place in the world. The organisation was charged with locating and building Australian patriotism, as a unifying concept—not an internally divisive one, and the ABC has had to rise to the challenge of engaging and reflecting a contemporary Australia that moved from a British-based culture to one of the most multicultural, multi-faith nations in the world. On that formidable scale alone, the ABC's task (and Australia's) has been immense and extraordinarily successful. The relationship between the ABC and governments' policies on that could have worked well (mostly). Swiss philosopher Jean Jacques Rousseau described patriotism as something that rises above differences to "the most immediate, accessible form of public-spirited devotion of the common good" (Rousseau, 1762 transl. Gourevitch, 2003)[15] and certainly the mission of the ABC has always been to grow and facilitate an Australian analysis and worldview for the Commonwealth of Australia and in the Australian public interest for the greater good.

An example of this is the ABC's long-standing use of foreign correspondents posted to major overseas cities and world regions. The ABC has been one of Australia's major drivers of identity in supporting Australians finding their place in the world and learning about what mattered to the nation from afar. The ABC has been a good global citizen, implicitly emphasising in its published content that a citizen's first responsibility was to their country (then to the world, as global citizens). The annual broadcasts, and then televising and live-streaming of ANZAC (Australia and New Zealand Army Corp) Day dawn services on 25 April that included Christian prayers, hymns and exhortations, as well as the returned forces' and services' marches through capital cities around Australia is one example of the ABC's explicit duty to country and citizenship. This sharing of what mattered to Australians also forged an Australian identity, ironically through the human loss, destruction, sorrow and fear caused by Australia's military engagements; not just World War I which ANZAC Day commemorates, but all wars and engagements. Over time, the day has become a redolent device in describing unifying Australian narratives and values, thanks to the enduring commitment of the ABC.

Another different example of its support of national interests occurred in 2019 when the ABC announced that its app (application) ABC News was named "Accessible App of the Year" and "Government App of the Year" at the Australian Access Awards. This was the inaugural awards run by the Centre for Accessibility which was a "not for profit" group established to promote digital access for people with disability. The ABC said its news app had "been designed for use by everyone, including viewers with impaired sight, hearing, mobility and cognition" (ABC, 2019a).[16] This was a significant success for a media outfit charged with shepherding the national interest for all Australians. However, this same digital space has created challenges for the public broadcasters, now seeing a period of transition where it is losing *cultural capital*, especially through its raw engagement with and reliance on social media. Therefore, the central problem to be investigated in this book is how the public broadcaster, the ABC, originating and creating its *cultural capital* and *reputational capital* in old media has transitioned to what was once referred to as 'new' media. Ultimately, the research finds it is struggling and Aunty's voice is being strangled.

The genesis of ABC *cultural capital* was in its Institutional Logics articulated at its launch in 1932 to: "provide information and entertainment, culture and gaiety, and to serve all sections and satisfy the diverse tastes of the public" (Inglis, 1983, quoting Lyons).[17] This preceding quote situated the case that the ABC had a primary role as an educator in 1932 as signalled by the Prime Minister, Joseph Lyons' launch speech. While it was allowed to "collect news" (ibid.) it had to support Australian culture as its primary role, not broadcast news. The ABC, therefore, had nascent "artistic legitimacy" (Bourdieu, 1984).[18] It was this that built the audiences and subsequent respect invested in the organisation. Later, it evolved into a unique outfit of news collection and dissemination in Australia remote from the commercial and advertising pressures to sell news (and, therefore, aloof from the pressures of vested interests). It had operated concurrently with commercial media but had also become entrenched as the 'über' media institution playing a dominant role in media, cultural and intellectual life, giving free and universal access to ABC content, funded by licence fees for radio and then television until 1974 when they were ended by the then Labor Prime Minister Gough Whitlam. Universality of access and content has been the basis of the ABC, offering diverse content to cater for all Australian tastes. Now it grapples with algorithms and filter bubbles—a contradictory situation for PSM. In essence, it quests for bespoke content to meet individual interests—yet is required to serve a general audience.

This book makes the claim that the ABC forged its respected position in Australian society because of its initial and sustained status as a purveyor of participatory culture and as an educator in culture. Its reputation for probity and excellence in investigative journalism came much later. But the ABC has been drawing down on its remaining *cultural capital* reserves in recent times amidst claims of inaccuracies, partiality, trivialisation and bias. Journalism augmented the ABC's cultural status, but did not form it, so the deletion of cultural content (this includes in-house drama productions and the decision to avoid covering the 2020 Olympic Games (moved to 2021 because of the Coronavirus pandemic) and platforming strident and legally contentious opinions on social media as representative of all Australian publics are some examples of how it has seriously challenged its status as an Australian icon and institution tasked with being universal—'all to all'. Scannell (2005) said institutions, such as PSMs, faced the challenge of "squaring the circle" (Ibid. p. 141.) of being inclusive while also encouraging differences. Aunty has lost sight of both her universality in her drift from being a reflective institutional broadcaster to an on-demand outfit, motivated to respond to social media as a source of content in the belief it represented issues of concern to the greater good. Yet, research has shown that the practice of using social media as a guide to public opinion is problematised. Specifically, when journalists use personally identifiable data (that individuals may not want published) and, in addition, not all citizens put their voice on social media (Dubois et al., 2020).[19]

Taking the particular as representative of the general compromises the historical concept of the ABC's (and indeed all PSM outfits') universality. To the extent that the literature has argued PSMs demonstrated "a need for a 'public service' algorithm that goes beyond the narrowing down of choice to personal preferences" (Van den Bulck & Moe, 2018). A constant emphasis on probity and thoroughness throughout the ABC's history as an educational and news organisation has been explicit and implicit Institutional Logics in supporting its élite, privileged role and gathering its audiences in the cultural, institutional and educational *fields*. Even the ABC logo and three letters itself[20] exerted institutionalised capital. They were easily recognised and identified with a quality, valued, credentialed organisation: "The ABC is a fine set of initials for a body setting out to enlighten the nation, connoting the beginning of knowledge" (Inglis, 1983 quoting first ABC Chairman Sir Charles Lloyd-Jones).[21] It was renowned for: "accuracy, impartiality, independence and integrity …" and "the pattern I have described seems to recur regardless of technological change" (Chadwick, 2012).[22] But this book argues that cannot be the case, with its digital changes, and chopped activities bringing a loss of public goodwill and decline of its credibility, eroded by an infiltration of opinion and lack of attendance to the needs, best interests and educational aspirations of all Australians. The ABC has relinquished its once powerful role in its media *field* through a lack of planning and lack of respect for what it jettisoned. Attention needed to be paid to: what could be preserved and what needed to change in the monumental shift in media, the challenge of funding cuts and general loss of passion in Australia to support anything 'public'? These were critical concerns for the institution and governments, and both needed to rivet their attention on this question for the sake of the institution as a national asset. The book will examine some diverse case studies, as part of this discussion of the disjuncture between, put simply, the theory of the ABC and what has evolved as practice.

In addressing these concerns, an important part of the institutional analysis of this book situates the ABC in the history and vested purpose of the outfit and situate ongoing institutional changes in the light of these. The Postmaster-General's original oversight of the finances of the ABC reinforced that the "new" medium of radio was to build Australian culture through the communication of information and education (*The Courier Mail*, 1934)[23] via Federal Government influence (Petersen, 1993).[24] According to Petersen (1993) rural Australia was prioritised where "political interest was focused around the demands from country people that ... should have priority access over the new medium" (ibid.). In response to regular complaints that the ABC has become Sydney and Melbourne-focused and regional and rural Australians are unrepresented and left unengaged, the ABC announced in 2020 that it would focus more on these apparently forgotten demographics (FarmOnline & AAP, 2020).[25] This was part of its five year plan announced in 2020. Then in 2021 it announced that it would move 300 of its Sydney staff to a new western Sydney office because the Chair Ita Buttrose said there were "fair" perceptions that the ABC was "too inner-city focused" (Samios, 2021). Communications Minister, Paul Fletcher, who has oversight of the ABC said it was a "good first step" (Ibid). Earlier the ABC (2016)[26] had said: "as Australia's oldest national broadcaster, the ABC has a long connection with, and a deep commitment to, serving all Australian audiences" but admitted in 2019 there were: "some parts of the community that we don't serve as well as we could be" (Duke, 2019a)[27] and that the new focus would be: "people living in Sydney's west ... along with Melbourne's east, Brisbane's south and Perth's south west, and regional cities like Newcastle and Geelong" (ibid.). Earlier, in 2019 the Australian Parliament had amended the *Australian Broadcasting Corporation Act 1983 ABC Charter* to require it to be more representative of regional and national identity as well as the "geographic and cultural diversity of the Australian community" and have two board members with "a substantial connection to, or substantial experience in" regional Australia with the concomitant establishment of a Regional Advisory Council to advise the board and for it to report annually on the number of staff employed in regional and metropolitan areas including the journalist support staff ratio (Parliament of Australia, 2019).[28]

But the ABC's Head of News, Gaven Morris, also revealed that while the ABC "loved" its older audience, it was now looking at "an audience growth strategy" (Duke, 2009a) because of what were described as falling television audiences and static numbers of radio listeners. Morris added none of the ABC's new approaches would mean it was competing with commercial media outlets (Loc. Cit.). Former ABC Chairman, Jim Spigelman, said: "independent surveys have consistently affirmed that about nine in ten Australians believe that the ABC provides 'valuable services' to the Australian community and about half believe that the services are 'very valuable'" (Spigelman, 2013).[29] Past Managing Director, Geoffrey Whitehead, identified these key issues facing the ABC, that also pointed to the evolving participatory media environment: "for radio, how to distribute an existing valuable program content more effectively to more Australians; for television, how to divert more resources into distinctive, entertaining as well as informative Australian content" (Whitehead, 1988).[30]

In terms of Bourdieu's theories of *practice*, *field*, *symbolic power* and *cultural capital*, Aunty has no mastery or legitimacy in the perilous commercial media *field*. It is a *field* that is at odds with her public service, publicly-funded remit. Yet, with the ABC now operating in the commercial *field* the consequence has been that the informed news needed in the public sphere is being strangled in a diverse mêlée of operators scrabbling for "hits" (popularity) and paying subscribers. Commercial news enterprises are businesses run for profit. News is published to sell. The end of the 'rivers of gold' of classified advertisements for newspapers and the shift in advertising online, the promotion of opinion in lieu of facts, and the audience reluctance to pay for editorial content and insatiable hunger for entertaining news that can be shared on social media means competition is relentless and ferocious.

This book argues that the ABC ventured promptly, innocently and wholeheartedly into this digital commercial content *field* without valuing the special nature of its existing *field*, élite *cultural capital* and *reputational capital* that was its unique 'selling point' and access point for all Australians. The ABC must belong in the digital space, prominently, but in the process of wanting to fit-in and be 'liked' in this new *field* means one of two assumptions were made: (1) much of Aunty's *capital* has been devalued because it was considered dated and 'old hat' or, (2) the organisation assumed that its *reputational capital* and *cultural capital* were perennial qualities that would follow it everywhere and anywhere.

According to Bourdieu (1983), however, the *field* had to be "reproduced"—or it would be "lost". So, there should be no surprise that there is "unprecedented hostility" (Meade, 2018a) towards the ABC by News Corporation now that Aunty has placed herself in the commercial *field* and that "the existential threat to the national broadcaster has perhaps never been greater"[31] (ibid.), and growing. Commercial media now finds itself with a fully-publicly subsidised actor in the midst of its sandpit. Research in Europe showed the commercial sector there was not performing as well as the PSM, yet PSM also faced survival challenges (Sehl, 2020).

The literature has identified a gap in understandings of the concepts of "public interest, public good, and public culture" (Tracey, 1998)[32] where the fundamental crisis in public broadcasting is one of, as Tracey (1998) described, "a sense of responsibility to a public as well as a private interest" (ibid.)[33] all precipitated by "a broadband culture" which included "unlimited sources of entertainment" (Loc. Cit.).[34] The painful consequence has been that all public service broadcasters (and public serviced generally) are shrinking and downsizing by being forced to apply the same 'for-profit' private sector management expectations that emerged in the 1980s of: 'efficiencies', 'targets' (Tracey, 1998), 'quotas', 'performance', 'economies of scale', 'outcomes', 'dividends' (and even 'bonuses' and rewards for performance). The once intangible, invisible value of national enrichment and the efficacy of independent public broadcasting have been monetised and traumatised in the process by these 'foreign' expectations. The ethereal, unquantifiable role of the ABC has never been successfully valued against its mammoth contributions to Australia. That is the ultimate tragedy of its present decline. As a once stellar fixture of the Australian media there is blame on two sides—it was taken for granted and it also took itself for granted. As the respected media academic, Professor Paddy Scannell, (2005) said "it is a mark of how far we have lost sight of the essential meaning of broadcasting that it is discussed today in the language of economics and consumer choice and the political rhetoric of citizenship" (Scannell, 2005 p. 142). The citizen is now the consumer.

It is not the objective of this book to speak in detail about matters, incidents and hearsay from within the ABC's past or present, its management, simmering staff conflicts, unhappiness or score-settling. This book is not a polemic, nor is it a nostalgic attempt to idealise and valorise the ABC. Despite the best and well-meaning efforts of various leaders and managements, the ABC was always problematised and challenged. It is also not the objective of this book to re-write the history of the ABC from

1932 to the present. These matters have been addressed ably and in detail by extant grey and academic literature written by ABC historians and former ABC employees. This literature includes: Bolton (1967), Dixon (1975), Inglis (1983, 2006), Thomas (1980), Semmler (1981), Buttrose (1984), Pullan (1986), Whitehead (1988), Davis (1988), Molomby (1991), Petersen (1993), Littlemore (1996), Williams (1996), Dempster (2000), Salter (2007), Scott (2016), O'Brien (2018) and Holmes (2019). Several of these books appear to "set the record straight" or "settle scores" and some contain personalised and anecdotal accounts. Cunningham (2013) said the majority of literature on the ABC had been focused on its history or commentary and this was either defending or attacking the organisation but that "an analysis of its innovation track record may offer a more nuanced pathway" (Cunningham, 2013).[35] It is the intention of this book to address the shortcomings in the literature by contributing to that discussion with a view to the future of Australia's only fully publicly funded, universal media service in an ecology of high-pressure, innovative, niche media and technology.

Therefore, this book does not seek to replicate the magisterial works of Professor Ken Inglis who wrote two books on the history of the ABC. His works encompassed until 2006. Inglis' analyses of the ABC are often anecdotal and personal (especially Inglis, 1983, pp. 45, 87, 65, 116, 149, 256, 331, 398, 415; Inglis, 2006, pp. 126, 239, 295, 342, 393, 462, 468, 492, 514, 522). Instead, this book seeks to take up the story of the ABC, but through a lens that analyses selected aspects of leadership, institution and policies and the key challenges of media technology which have impacted on and will influence the ABC's future. As this text seeks to analyse the organisation using Institutional Logics, it will interrogate management and leadership practices and symbols through language (Thornton et al., 2012a)[36] and Bourdieu's *field* theory using content which is on the public record. It will also pursue themes based on in-confidence interviews with former prime ministers of the Commonwealth of Australia, former ABC Managing Directors, former ABC chairs, former ABC board members and former ABC senior staff. However, all quotes from former political leaders, former chairs, former managers and former staff included in this book have been taken from the public record only. These quotes sometimes reference earlier managers where there are linkages with similar issues, visions and impacts in setting up the role and public expectations of the ABC and how these have been re-interpreted by the ABC in a digitally connected commercial media ecology.

The purpose of this book is to test the claim that when the ABC controlled the élite *field* of media it was far more effective in holding power to account because it had agency in the élite *field*—where power resides. The ABC once had a strong capability in 'jostling' and pressuring politicians and public figures. The ABC insisted on a higher standard of questioning with a researched, knowledge-based approach to topics being interrogated. This book aims to discover a new discernment of how the ABC has functioned as a uniquely Australian 100% taxpayer-funded public service media enterprise, the impact of digitisation and the pervasive in-roads of social media on the organisation. There are diverse forces at work that are strangling the voice of Aunty—a dear, smart, elderly lady who lives in challenging times. This book suggests the way forward and how she may survive it all. The ABC exists in a self-described "digitally-disrupted" age (Hua, 2016). But it could be more aptly be described as a "digitally-disturbed" age with a psychological reference to the perturbations caused by the merger of news with social media and, in addition to this, shackled with a widespread lethargy for the public funding of anything, and new challenges ahead in the aftermath of the Australian (world) economy being trampled by the novel Coronavirus pandemic, which was both a health and economic crisis for the nation (and the world). The consequences of paying for these twin crises means in the future governments, to use the old proverb, will be 'turning coins twice' before spending them. A re-doubled economic restraint by governments may have even more consequences for the ABC, as the downturn in advertising and the economy is having for the traditional commercial media where there have been massive staff losses in an industry already suffering from the targeted and cheaper advertising of digital media (Pascoe, 2020[37]; Mason, 2020b[38]).

1.2 Theories and Methodology Framework: The Main Arguments

This book applies aspects of French sociologist and anthropologist Pierre Bourdieu's *field*, *habitus* and *cultural capital* theories and merges them with Institutional Logics theory in order to provide a methodological framework of analysis. The ABC's *habitus* contributes to the production of meaning and is Bourdieu's (1990) theory of the system of: "durable, transposable dispositions, structured structures predisposed to function as structuring structures" (Bourdieu, 1984)[39] shaped by "vocations", "aspirations" and "expectations" (Bourdieu, 1983).[40] The second methodology of this book, merged with Bourdieu, is Institutional Logics. It has been criticised as having been used to analyse such a broad range of academic content that it lacks specificity and may be a blunt instrument in analysing individual organisations (Lincoln, 1995).[41] Yet, in a publicly funded, public service arts and culture-based organisation the merger of Institutional Logics with Bourdieu's *field* (1983) and cultural production are complementary theories that provide a useful research paradigm because of the dynamic synergies between the two.

Institutional Logics, first described by Friedland and Alford (1991) and Thornton et al. (2012b)[42] said that it had grown to be: "recognised as a core perspective in sociology and organisation theory (Greenwood et al., 2012)".[43] It speaks specifically to the understanding that "construction of a cultural institution's identity is related to the construction of strategic capabilities and resources" (Glynn, 2000).[44] It is hoped that this book will contribute to the body of research to which Institutional Logics has been applied to organisations, including symphony orchestras (Glynn, 2000; Glynn & Lounsbury, 2005),[45] book publishers (Thornton & Ocasio, 1999; Thornton, 2001, 2002) and banking (Marquis & Lounsbury, 2007). This book seeks to offer analysis of the ABC using Institutional Logics and leadership and how cultural challenges and adjustments have been managed in the face of funding cuts and the media revolution of digital media. Institutional Logics "represent frames of reference that condition actors' choices for sense-making" (Thornton et al., 2012b).[46] The book does not take a chronological approach to the ABC. Rather, it selects various incidents and applies them to framework analysis. Thornton et al. (2012b) pointed out there were three aspects to Institutional Logics: principles, practices and symbols and these can be linked with Bourdieu's theories of *logics* and *practice* (ibid.).

This book takes a unique approach providing a different analytical framework to investigate how the ABC has adapted to changing institutional dynamics by adding to the prevailing literature, which is more focused on personal memoirs and reflections. Using Bourdieu combined with Institutional Logics theory it is hoped this will further the literature on analysing public broadcasting organisations by using such methodologies and deepen understandings of the struggles and questionable futures faced by all public service media (PSM), which is at odds with the important role they have fulfilled. It is envisaged that these frameworks will also help describe the use of *fields* in determining outcomes, organisational policy and change within the organisation, and other public broadcasters. It will canvas how the ABC can re-build itself as the élite media organisation and return to being an individuated standard-setter, a flag-bearer within its new *field* of commercial media.

Through a theoretical framework, this book argues:

1. That the key informal networks being assembled in 1932 were a significant group of actors to complement commercial media—intellectuals, musicians, academics, writers—thereby establishing Bourdieu's élite *field* of the ABC which was driven by musical artists and musically—cultivated ABC managers who wanted to bring free quality music to the masses. It was an élite, privileged culture that accomplished it. It was these actors who created the enduring love for the organisation in spite of its role being "subordinated to its commercial competitors" (Jones & Pusey, 2010).[47] The 'poor Aunt of media' became outrageously, joyously rich in *cultural capital* and *reputational capital* through music and learning.
2. And that, therefore, the key actors forming the *habitus* and *cultural practices* through institutional networks built the organisation's Institutional Logics—artistic and entertainment, intellectual and informational. The heydays of ABC, orchestras and the like were embodiments of *social capital* and *cultural capital*. The ABC was based on cultural Institutional Logics, where managers created and mingled in a specific élite *field*, a reputational capital now threatened with a headlong clash with Media Logics[48]—the theory that the media has inherent rules of the game describing how content is made, consumed and iterated. There is destructive tension between the two.
3. The ABC has taken the necessary shift into the commercial digital *field*, bristling and laden with competition, taking with it Media Logics, but forgetting its cultural Institutional Logics background and its immeasurably valuable legacy and reputation. The organisation's shift in *field* from its own élite cultural *field* to the contested, commercial, digitised *field* of news, opinion, commentating, abundant experts and strident voices, occurred in the belief that the ABC could live off its reputation built on what could be described as bourgeois power systems (1984).[49] Yet, this new-found, aberrant belief that bourgeois power systems are toxic and unwanted has damaged and confused the ABC brand—because it formed its reputation within a bourgeois power system. It needed to take pride

in its élite, privileged background and re-value it. While all opinions have always mattered, the ABC's ones mattered most, somehow, because they were argued with knowledge and respectful inclusiveness. It once knew that and held itself erect and disdainful from uninformed opinion, confident in keeping Australians informed. It failed to plan and value this heritage and its critical institutional memory that supported this.

4. The ABC has been pressured on two sides—through technological necessity and funding cuts—to create a vigorous presence in the digital space and has responded with great enthusiasm. It has innovated but also re-created spaces once controlled or patrolled by commercial providers. It has also failed to prepare and update policy and leadership on how it would specifically retain its *cultural capital*. Its management statements imply that everyone knows and loves the ABC and that this would continue into perpetuity. Management and staff brook no criticisms, vastly oversimplifying any attacks (or comments) as part of a Murdoch conspiracy to destroy the ABC. The rush to digitisation presented unplanned challenges for the ABC in an online *field* emboldened with its journalists platforming opinion as if representative of all Australians and their civic society. It is mimicking the less fastidious commercial outfits in this over-reach and losing its distinctiveness.

Using combined aspects of Bourdieu's theories, this book seeks to understand how the ABC built and legitimated its power and how that power is waning and its voice being strangled, yet could be reclaimed. These theoretical frameworks will reveal the structures and practices of the organisation that are usually hidden within the received and normalised operations and *cultural practice* and *habitus* of the organisation by analysing the *field* in which the ABC operated, how it has shifted from that *field* into the digitised and commercialised *field* of media and the role of key actors that illuminate the consequences of that process. It will shed light on how the ABC has managed its transition from being a unique public service broadcaster to a public service media outlet.

This analysis forms a branch of neo-institutional analysis where *field* and actors can be unpacked to nuance understandings of performance, practice, culture and power relations. This segues with Bourdieu's theories of *field*, *social capital* and *cultural capital* and how actors and institutions accumulate this in their *field*. Rather than analysing the organisational result, the neo-Institutional Logics' focus of investigation is process. Institutional Logics offers a means of analysis that "links the actions of actors (organizations) to a larger social structure (the *field*), posits that actors are knowledgeable ('mutual awareness of … a common enterprise'), and suggests that institutions constrain the very actions that produce them ('emergence of … structures of domination')" (Barley & Tolbert, 1997).[50] The once neutral, impartial approach of the organisation has been challenged by media convergence where the discrete siloes of professional media are gone and the *field* of media can now range from an ABC news report to the purchase of a new pair of shoes.

The ABC's transition has tried to amalgamate: opinion, conjecture, binary views and researched information; and, it has proven an awkward mix. While trying to remain a representative voice for all Australians by taking part in strident social media discussions and allegations, it asserts and references legislative, historical expectations, statutory independence and concomitant intentions that it should be 'all to all' to justify its future. This 'all to all' approach of the ABC was challenged by Federal Liberal Government's Mansfield Report "The Challenge of a Better ABC" (1997) in recommending that the ABC reduce its commitment to everyone and focus on regional activities. But its endowment of respect and *cultural capital* that it took with it from its *field* to the new commercial *field* interwoven activities with social media is losing its gloss. Former Managing Director Mark Scott identified that the ABC had "an enormous connection" with the Australian public (Crisp, 2011).[51] Yet it is haunted now by the voice of the emerging anecdotal, if somewhat crude question: "why publicly pay for something when there is so much content out there already?". The shift to digitisation means the ABC has moved from providing a "a public sphere where we can chatter away, building our future" (Funston, 1997),[52] to a clamouring warzone shouting to be heard in a crowded *field* of other actors. What is Aunty to do about her voice? The ABC has shifted from its own distinct *field*, which complemented commercial media, to a living hell. She is in a 'guns loaded and drawn', 'fire at will', open combat with commercial media—and Aunty is not coping well.

The concepts of Institutional Logics theory and Bourdieu's *field*, *habitus* and *cultural capital* theories provide an analytical framework to attain insights into the emerging threats to the democracy it informs and is expected to support; and, how these challenging times may inform broadcasting or Australian public service media policy in the future. Bourdieu said "any *field* has its own rationale for its existence and this explains the value of and legitimates the game" (Bourdieu, in Thomson, 2005), the commercial *field* also has its rationale. This is the doxa of the *field*, or the self-evident truths of the *field*.[53] The ABC rushed into the commercial *field* without taking a new doxa of a new field—place of institutional operation—into account. This book will re-visit some of the history of the ABC and its self-evident truths, but only to contextualise the current perils it faces, or as a means of backgrounding issues being analysed.

This book also argues that instead of its BBC basis being a "cultural straightjacket" (Martin, 2002)[54] it accrued capital successfully in its élite, privileged Australian *field* that gave it the status of being the nation's most respected and loved broadcaster. It is the apparent abandonment of this *field* and pressures from government and the media itself to embrace the digital audiences that has forced the ABC to compete in a hostile and foreign competitive *field* of commercial media. A *field* where it does not belong and to which Aunty arrived leaving her cultural capital in her old *field*—she abandoned her "superannuation fund" of ***cultural capital*** when she left her "ABC *field*". Her ***cultural capital*** turned out to be an impermanent attribute in the rough and tumble of commercial and online media. Aunty is challenged to find the high ground and carve out her own *field* within the *field*, in order to survive. She has to expend much time, planning and effort again if she is to re-build her ***cultural capital.*** Aunty not only took the theoretical field, as a sports reporting outfit, she literally took the field and has been a trail-blazer in terms of sports coverage, breadth of activities covered and the cultivation of knowledgeable presenters. It also was an institution that promoted from within its ranks and Image 1.1 shows how the man who would one day lead the institution began as a golf (sports) reporter in the 1940s. The other man, the sound technician, was also promoted to a leadership role. It was a sign of the prominence with which the ABC sought to place itself in a field that served all tastes and interests in sport.

The ABC's adoption of commercial narratives and formats means the ABC has undergone a loss of differentiation, which had been critical in the past to justifying its funding. It is in pursuit of ABC leaders' new visions of 'relevance' and 'digital story-telling' and 'digital narratives' but without incorporating the hard-won credibility of its past. It is also surprising that the ABC is so shocked by the fierce competition in the ABC's new *field* where it offers its work for free in a monetised *field*. That there is anger and bewilderment about this clash is puzzling because it is simple business economics. It is a market and Aunty is in it. Bourdieu (1983) described *field* as a semi-autonomous sphere of activity where "homologies" (similarities

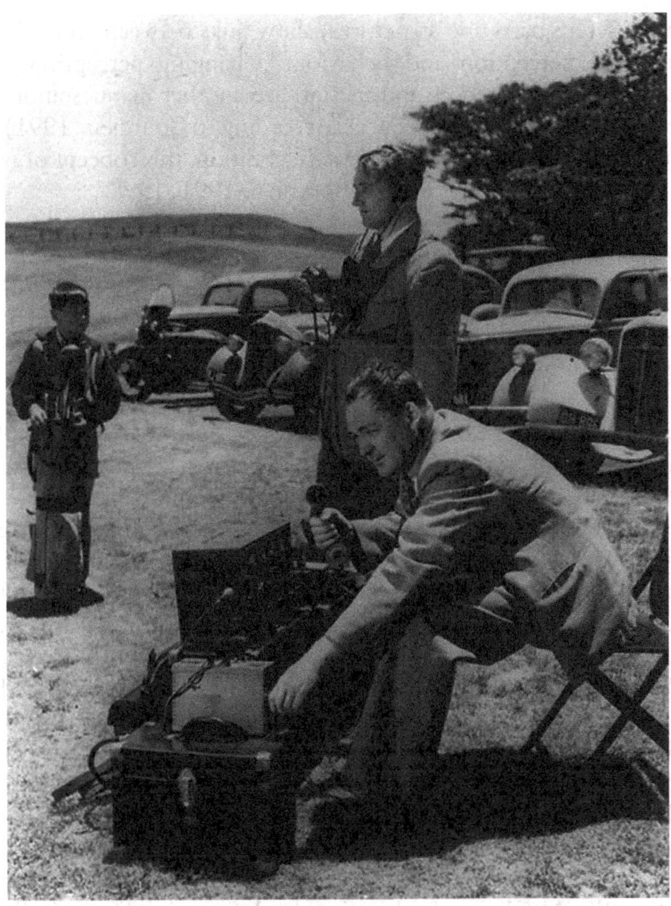

Image 1.1 The ABC takes the *field* (literally): Sporting announcer Talbot Duckmanton standing (with technician Stanley Bancroft seated) providing radio commentary from a Sydney golf course, c. late 1940s. From this relatively simple start, the ABC developed a pivotal role in presenting sports to Australians. Duckmanton became General Manager of the ABC from 1965–1982. Bancroft retired as ABC Supervisor Radio Operation, NSW in 1974 after 50 years' service. Both men's suited attire, while a reflection of the times, also expressed how the institution valued unseen radio. Image courtesy of the National Archives of Australia. NAA: C1748, L17321

between different parts and structures) show links between an institution's place in *field*, perception and behaviour. Changing perceptions of the organisation by its audiences and its staff are another manifestation of the change in *field*, and the consequences. According to Bourdieu (1991), one's position in the *field* shaped one's views. In addition, this concept of *symbolic* power was played out in the media (Bourdieu, 1991, 1998)[55]:

> *On va de plus en plus des univers ou le monde social est decrit-prescrit par la television. La television devient l'arbitre de l'acces a l'existence sociale et politique* [We are going more and more towards a society where the social world is described and dictated by television. Television becomes a referee for an access to social and political life.]. (Bourdieu, 1996)[56]

In summary, Bourdieu was saying television was responsible for inducing a loss of critical thinking. Bourdieu's perception can also be applied to social media, which has supplanted the immediacy of television, and given rise to a surge in online content with an unknown agenda, identities concealed (or fabricated) and information poorly sourced and vetted but shared rapidly nonetheless (Matei et al., 2015).[57] Added to this has been a diminishment of critical thinking where the literature said "the leaf and the branch of social media is visible, but not the tree or the forest" (Smith et al., 2015)[58] and where the landscape of social media can show the ultimate irony of a deeply fragmented riotous, abusive cohort, when its promise was boundless, harmonious, supportive, democratic, socially-networked, cooperative groups and communities.

'Cultural practices', according to Bourdieu (1984),[59] are "highbrow" activities of the élite who go to opera, art galleries, ballet, museums, read books, or are educated to a high(er) level than the general community. Supporting the ABC's quasi-educational role in upholding this élite was the ABC's emphasis on quality music as a "high ABC priority" (Thomas, 1980)[60] from its early years in launching military bands, dance bands, orchestras, choirs, instrumental groups, writing and composition competitions and later eisteddfau. Ironically, well-paid US military servicemen during World War II ("over paid, over sexed and over here") were a large part of ABC audiences for these concerts which helped grow their success among the Australian community during this time and was sustained after the American services had left (ibid.). This was:

> A testimony to the success with which the ABC handled the musical education of Australia, or at least of a certain group of Australians. (Thomas, 1980)[61]

The ABC's *cultural capital* was such that it became a mark of social distinction in Australian life to say you were an avid viewer or listener, naming presenters or programs added to one's personal status and to say "I love the ABC" was an all-encompassing nod to its content and the backflow of *cultural capital* it bestowed on the individual. It indicated you were of the privileged, Australian élite. The ABC acquired Bourdieu's (1986) three forms of cultural capital through these practices: embodied: "embodied long-lasting dispositions of the mind and body" (Bourdieu, 1986),[62] carried out through the logics of the ABC Charter, policies, "this is the way we do things"; objectified: "in the form of cultural goods (pictures, books, dictionaries, instruments, machines, etc.)" (Bourdieu, ibid.) where in the case of the ABC its objects were content, former physical ABC Shops around Australia (shops were closed and moved to online sales in 2015 and this ended altogether in 2018), websites and the logo; and institutionalised: "a form of objectification … it confers entirely original properties on the *cultural capital* which it is presumed to guarantee" (Loc. Cit.) such as the boastful audience members who claim their dedication to the organisation (described previously) as well as the enduring support of the lobby group "Friends of the ABC".

The ABC had given Australians access to informed social positions (Bourdieu, 1984)[63] on music, the arts, intellectual debate. The ABC was never "explicitly demanding"[64] (ibid.) of attention ipso facto—it was not compulsory, or a solo media operator; rather because of the organisation's range of content and vast footprint, it became inevitable (and sometimes through no choice in regional Australia) that many Australians were part of the audience. ABC audiences also became attached by timetabled content and incorporated listening (and viewing) in their daily routines ("I always listen to the 6.00 am news bulletin while I'm getting breakfast", and so on). Australian ABC audiences became loyal followers of content; they religiously watched the investigative television current affairs program "Four Corners" each Monday (and previously Saturday evening, repeated on Sunday), launched in 1961; they listened each morning to the flagship but now defunct 15 minute "7.45 News" bulletin on ABC Radio. In 2020 this bulletin was cancelled as "part of a major overhaul of the national broadcaster" (Worthington & Hitch, 2020).[65] The bulletin divided into 10 minutes of national news and five minutes of state news had been a jewel in the crown of the ABC's *cultural capital*, but it was no longer supported or recognised as such by the organisation. The *cultural capital* of the bulletin had been built up since 1947, when the first independent ABC News bulletin went on air (Inglis, 1983)[66] and with the 7.45 am main bulletin and the major 7.00 pm report "news bulletins were the ABC's most popular offerings" (Inglis, ibid.)[67] with bulletins preceded by The Majestic Fanfare news theme from 1952 (Loc. Cit.), adding classical music heft to the *cultural capital* of the product and:

> introducing bulletins respected for their accuracy, sobriety, and even-handed reporting from the formal arenas of national, state and local politics. The doorkeepers to ABC newsrooms kept out the sensational and the seamy, and rarely let in the warmth or wit. (Inglis, ibid.)

This book furthers research called for by Nick Couldry (2004) who suggested researchers "decentre media research from the study of media texts or production structures" and instead focus on *practices* in and around the media (Couldry, ibid.).[68] To further that aim, the book will analyse theoretical frameworks being applied to this analysis of the "strangling of Aunty" by considering the institutional role of the ABC. Using Bourdieu's (1984) *field*, *practice* and *habitus* theories this chapter will analyse using a degree of exegesis the role of the ABC in *field*, *practice* and *habitus*; and how it once set a standard for educating Australians by providing access to information and arts by acting as gatekeeper of what it considered, as a representative institution, the noteworthy constituent elements of Australianness. The ABC's focus on this was articulated by the Managing Director, David Anderson, who told a 2019 senate estimates committee hearing into the Federal Government's ABC budget freeze for three years (costing the broadcaster AUD83.7 million) that its future depended on localisation:

> One of our priorities for the future is certainly to remain as local as possible ... our role is to reflect the culture and community of the country back to itself. You struggle to do that unless you are local. (Dalzell, 2019)[69]

It signalled a shift from the national to the local, the presumed representative of the national. As a corollary, this book will conduct a prosopographical analysis of what constitutes the Australian élite who have supported the broadcaster and the *field* it occupied because "certain conditions of existence are designated" (Bourdieu, 1984)[70] and then re-enacted, and this process has ensured the survival of the institution funded to be a representative national, rather than local, institution. It will examine how the ABC has negotiated its role as a key member of the Fourth Estate in Australia, and whether the concept of the Fourth Estate is sustainable and credible enough in a digitally-disrupted media. Bourdieu scholars Benson and Neveu (2005)[71] said journalistic agents "possess high volumes of power" (ibid.) and Bourdieu (1998)[72] stated this power was such that:

> The journalistic *field* tends to reinforce the "commercial" elements at the core of all *fields* to the detriment of the "pure". It favors those cultural producers most susceptible to the seductions of economic and political powers, at the expense of those intent on defending the principles and the values of their professions. (ibid.)

In the case of the ABC, it has exercised its power in its *field* through a record of journalism that was incisive, consequential and investigative, for example, and its journalists winning annual Walkley Awards[73] in a peer-awarded acknowledgement of their efforts in grappling with weighty and pertinent national matters that have had complicated and consequential repercussions in confronting destructive power relations and manifestations of corruption, for example.

The ABC has exerted cultural power in other ways. For example, through the insistence on an educated British accent of presenters in organisation's early days, transitioning to educated Australian accents, then general Australian accents. Allied with this early development of the ABC was the management of the spoken word and preference for the British accent among presenters. The late Australian historian Manning Clark said the early ABC promulgated a "dyed in the wool" (Clark, 1995, 1962)[74] British view of the world, its interests and values. The recruitment of male radio presenters in the early days who were expected to wear dinner suits when announcing in the evening was another cultural statement, albeit largely unseen. Cultural assertions will be unpacked later in this chapter. Then, in the appointments of men with knighthoods as chairmen of the ABC from the creation of the Australian Broadcasting Commission in 1932 with Sir Charles Lloyd-Jones to Sir Henry Bland in 1976 (the exception is William Cleary in 1934), and the development of talks by university professors in the earlier years of radio. All with an eye to economic capital in terms of measuring its relevance through audience feedback and later ratings. So, while it has economic capital through a budgetary allocation, it actually obtained its autonomy through its *cultural capital*. It also legitimised its dominance as a public broadcaster through the social capital accrued by its staff and the expertise the organisation gathered in the form of its specialist programs and presenters. Cultural capital was annexed through the high-level connections of its leaders with key international musicians, academics, politicians and supportive and agentic public servants. Major research by DiMaggio (1987) of US arts organisations, including symphony orchestras, theatres and museums, found that "most administrators came from relatively privileged social backgrounds and were notably well educated" (DiMaggio, 1987).[75] And although public arts organisation in the US may have had sponsors and benefactors, there are strong similarities with public cultural organisations, such as the ABC, in that they must be successful, attract audiences and be accountable to the public that subsidises their endeavours with patronage. They must also innovate and provide a public service by anticipating or spotting public need and issues confronting the greater good.

1.3 'Leaving the ABC Building': Pierre Bourdieu, and the Once Exclusive ABC *Field*

Bourdieu's (1977) theories provide an understanding of how power functions, and how it is transmitted and maintained, in this case within an institution. As a consequence, organisations function because staff know 'the rules of the game' of the *field* in which they and the organisation operate. Thomson (2005) described Bourdieu's theories as a "tool kit" for analysis of these rules.[76] Bourdieu (1977) also explained that when an organisation left its *field* and its symbolic capital had changed there was "hysteresis" meaning:

> When the environment with which they are actually confronted is too far distant from that to which they are objectively fitted. (Bourdieu, ibid.)[77]

The preceding diagram (Diagram 1.1) outlines how Power relates to the Journalistic *field through* Doxa (defined in the diagram) as an overriding concern in the drifting rules of the media game, and in the *fields* of journalism, described for the purposes here as being either 'public' or 'commercial'. The knowledge of the *field* is derived from the interaction of the rules of the *field* combined with the institutional ***habitus*** and ***capital*** and, according to Bourdieu, evolves and adapts to external influences. In the case of the diagram, social media and the pressing need to be first has

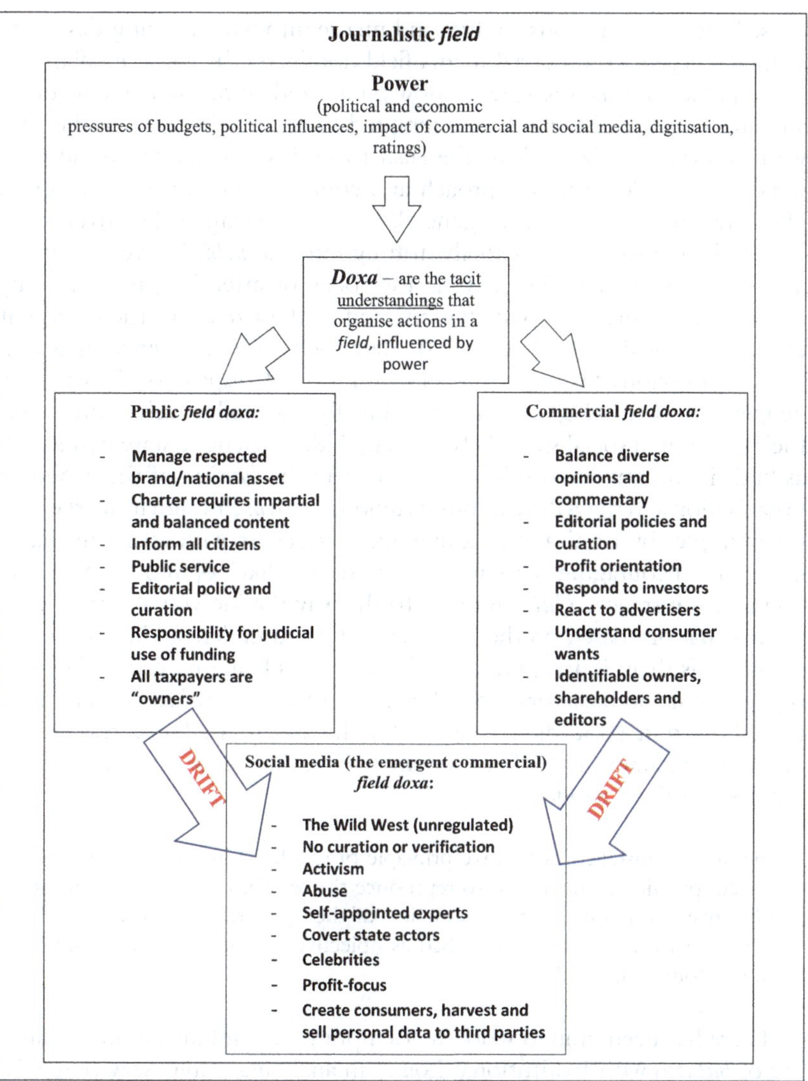

Diagram 1.1 Diagram of the *field* and power. Influences upon the ABC within the Journalistic *field*—(using Bourdieu's field theory interpreted by Small)

caused media institutions to drift and merge into what is being described as the emergent commercial media field dominated by social media. As a consequence of this, the rules of how public and commercial media operate have changed. Media is now tempted to absorb the rules of the wild west of social media; and, in the rush to be first has tended to adopt a sameness in style, ethical approach and content. The preceding diagram illustrates how the media, in general, has acknowledged the advent of a new social media *field* by actually drifting into the *field*. However, for the point of this analysis the ABC is the focus of attention, not shifts by commercial media. The ABC has adapted to the *habitus* of the emergent commercial field. Bourdieu (1990) described *habitus* as encompassing: "the unconscious taking in of rules, values and dispositions", whereby people live in social space, and individually and collectively "internalise their position in social space" (Bourdieu, ibid.).[78] Generic statements such as "this is the way we do this here" indicate the *habitus* of the group or organisation and the ABC exhibits its unique *habitus* through its marketing, for example, by ironically encouraging a sameness with social media in implicitly encouraging staff to contribute, or 'like' opinions and views online, for instance. *Habitus* refers to the way the individual responds to social situations based on their own learning and understanding and what society tells them is acceptable. In this case, it is being used to refer to an organisation and its actors, how they enact their *cultural capital* and how they show *taste* (Bourdieu, 1984)[79] for the arts or academic research or information, for example. They acquire *habitus* through social engagement. *Habitus* is valued habits:

> the durably installed generative principle of regulated improvisations, produced 'practice's which tend to reproduce the regularities immanent in the objective conditions of the production of their generative principle, while adjusting to the demands inscribed as objective potentialities in the situation. (Bourdieu, 1977)[80]

There has been limited work in attempting to combine an understanding of *habitus* with Institutional Logics in analysing public service media, or even Institutional Logics and Bourdieu with other institutions which is "particularly surprising in view of the original debt owed to Bourdieu by institutional theory" (Malsch & Gendron, 2013).[81] There has also been limited research into combining Bourdieu's understandings of practice with analysis of public service organisations aside from the education sphere (Hastings & Matthews, 2015)[82] although in terms of describing the *habitus* of the ABC it is a challenge because the ABC is unique. Hastings and Matthews (2015) said Bourdieu's emphasis on symbolic power may not translate smoothly to an understanding of how the public service functions because "symbolic power in explaining inequities in the distribution of public services may not be immediately obvious" (Hastings & Matthews, ibid.). However, even Bourdieu said "the logic of practice is logical up to the point where to be logical would cease being practical" (Bourdieu & Wacquant, 1992).[83]

This analysis will extend this theoretical gap in applying Bourdieu and Institutional Logics to public service media by analysing the inequity of power distribution within the ABC through staff culture which has at times hijacked the ABC's impartial image and eroded its once more emphatically impartial approach to news. Coupled with this, there has been no analysis of the "hysteresis" manifested by public broadcasters, especially of Aunty. These lags have not only challenged leadership of the ABC but also exposed shortfalls in institutional policy, government policy and legacy protection in preserving ABC independence and institutional memory as a counter ballast to the stunts, stridency and ephemerality of the social media *field*. The ABC's publicly-stated institutional problems focus on three worries: Conservative governments, budgets and Rupert Murdoch. But less is spoken of other actors in the commercial *field* in which the ABC now finds itself mixing, notably the over-bearing, giant social media organisations and their amorphous, octopian social media, their embrace of citizen, participatory journalism and the consequent self-disintegration of ABC independence through its heavy involvement in social media and the (less acknowledged) accompanying doxa of what this research has described as the emergent commercial field which, for the ABC, blends public media with Web 2.0 interactivity and commercial media.

According to the Bourdieusian theoretical schema, a loss of *field* involves erosion of power relationships and *capital*; and this is impacting on the ABC in a diminishment of relevance in tandem with imitation of other content and styles. There has been a failure to value, translate and sustain its power relationships and *capital* in a digital environment. *Field* is "a network, or a configuration, of objective relations between positions" (Bourdieu & Wacquant, 1992)[84] and is Bourdieu's empirical analysis of how power manifests. The ABC accrued and manifested power in its own *field*, and *field* is "a separate social universe having its own laws of functioning independent of those of politics and the economic" (Bourdieu in R. Johnson, 1993).[85] This meant that the ABC had created more than a *field*—it had its own cosmos and held an extraordinarily powerful role in Australian media as a standard-setter, bench-marker, key interpreter of circumstance and authority. The ABC was once the author of Australian culture and civic engagement. This harked back to its policies, *capital* and privilege: "this is the way we do things". This stance was almost incontestable because of the uniqueness of its exclusive *field*. Bourdieu (1990) likened the *field* to sport where players had "a feel for the game" and developed a "mastery acquired by experience of the game".[86] Once having mastered the rules, the symbolic power of the *field* bestowed legitimacy on its players/ actors (and the ABC). Bourdieu's cultural theory of *field* describes *field* as being in constant struggle, and akin to a rugby football *field*—the rules are known, the areas of the *field* are used for specific purposes in the game, players play in positions, rules can be challenged and while there can be "deviations" (e.g., eye-gouging while the referee is not looking) most of the time the rules are clear-cut and known by the players, referees, coaches as well as the eagle-eyed, miss-nothing, designated senior referees and team adviser body—the football crowd (the ABC audience).

Bourdieu (1994)[87] asserted the bourgeoisie established the difference between what is free and what had to be paid for (in contrast to aristocracy and conspicuous spectacle) as they also did for work and recreation, manufacturing and art (ibid.)[88] and indeed public and private media would fit into this paradigm and, therefore, the Australian middle class that created and ritualised the ABC. Bourdieu (1996) spoke of how "the commentator" in creating symbolic goods made an "injection of meaning and value" (ibid.).[89] Bourdieu's (1991) theory of ritualised exchanges means the higher degree of ritual lessens the flexibility in the system. In the light of this theory, it can be shown how profound the disruption damage by digital media has been to professional journalism—in the era of citizen journalism, crowd-sourced news, valued, hyper-linked, tagged, commented, liked and monetised reaction. The ABC has moved to the commercially dominated emergent *field* forgetting how well it (usually) had managed its own special *field*.

Bourdieu (1977) described journalists as having the same cultural capital as bankers, business leaders and managers of states. Yet, unlike their peers, journalists are complex and tormented professionals in that while they are expected to embrace ethical values that prize news as objective, they also write news that has to sell. On reflection, perhaps, not unlike bankers who buy and sell money, yet are challenged similarly by ethics, restraint and the profit motive. Journalists are guided by professional ethical values that dovetail generally with corporate mission statements, but these provide aspiration rather than regulations or law. There is no ultimate, independent body or singular legislation that calls all Australian journalists to account, for example, except for the Journalists' Code of Ethics in Australia and individual news organisations' codes of conduct, mission statements and policies, as mentioned, as well as media laws. ABC journalists are now part of the larger crowd of unindividuated operators who all call themselves journalists, trained or not, vying for attention on social media and craving 'likes' to support their work. Once ABC journalists did not need 'likes'—they just did their public service and were esteemed and self-satisfied with that. That is no longer adequate where social media provokes and supports ambition, careers and popularity. The ABC's abandonment of its own *field* has created new challenges and pressures for ABC journalists in the organisation's rush to get its content online, make itself popular and promote journalists as celebrities and newsmakers. The discrete, detached, remote role of the self-effacing observer journalist has long passed.

The ABC had *cultural capital* and prestige through its agency in its own *field* within Australian society. Its *cultural capital* was mistakenly assumed by its institutional leaders to be an enduring quality, but has proved not so. Since the era of digitisation much of its unique status has declined because its *cultural capital* is not an enduring lifeline in the 'rough and tumble' of the emergent commercial *field*. Bourdieu (1983) warned about the diminishment of *cultural capital* which like the *field*: "the accumulation has to be reproduced with every generation or it is lost" (ibid.)[90] and while the ABC's *cultural capital* had been institutionalised (Bourdieu, 1983): "capital does not exist and function except in relation to a *field*" (Bourdieu & Wacquant, 1992).[91] This book will examine how there exists institutional mechanisms and organisational oversights by which *cultural capital* has been formed and lost. The ABC has had to move away from its special *field* into the crowded, noisy, commercial *field* and within that *field* in Australia one news organisation dominates—*News Corporation*. Lured and pushed by the rise of changed media, cheaper content distribution and bigger audiences, the ABC's prioritisation of digital technology was seen as the most effective way of growing, containing costs and keeping audiences. But in that embrace, it has made missteps by lapsing into commercial opinion-oriented content and digital domains where it is compelled to buy its popularity.

Notwithstanding the received argument that Rupert Murdoch is out to annihilate the ABC, is that it goes unremarked that the ABC is now competing in a very dangerous emergent *field*—and is playing a game Aunty cannot win because she is accountable to every Australian taxpayer, not single owners and ranked shareholders. The *field* ruled by commercial tycoons, like Murdoch, is not a space for our Aunty without her *cultural* and *reputational capitals*—she cannot survive, let along thrive there without it. She was robust in her own *field* of objectivity and aloofness and separation of fact from opinion (impartial); now she has moved into a *field* where the new rules of the game she plays make her completely vulnerable and, worse, compromised. It is no wonder there are increasing attacks on the ABC from the commercially based media—it goes unacknowledged or unobserved that the ABC has placed herself in direct competition for the same space, the same emergent *field*. In theatrical geography, Aunty has left her private box and joined the mosh pit. She needs to reclaim, re-build her reputational capital—as distinct in that emergent commercial digital field.

In addition, *Australian Financial Review* journalist Neil Chenoweth said of Murdoch: "he grew up in Australia in an atmosphere of ritual feuding with other media" (Lieberman, 2007).[92] News Corporation picking fights with Aunty is not new and not going to go away—especially not now. All the complaints about Murdoch's fresh attacks on, or emerging threats to, the ABC (Morton, 2020;[93] Meade, 2020;[94] Meade, 2018b;[95] Rudd, 2018;[96] Flanagan, 2014[97]) have failed to acknowledge this singular and significant issue and it is one of basic business: the ABC has shifted out of its exclusive *field* and into the *field* of the media rabble and there are real institutional consequences for that—political, financial, ideological, competitive, organisational, public service. Then, there are the consequences for all Australians, the Commonwealth of Australia and its democracy, which is the most serious point to be made in this book. All these factors threaten what seems to be a naïve and vulnerable Aunty. The ABC has made the publicly-funded organisation more assailable than ever. Further, the ABC has complicated itself by bringing it into play with content that is rejected as inferior by some of its audience that has traditionally looked to the ABC to delineate fact from opinion and provide discerning 'quality' and prudence. Aunty is over-stretched and needs to consider doing less to permit a return to a higher level of quality. It is an institution that cannot be stretched thinner without compromise. The commercials (all) jostling with her in the *field* argue that the ABC is using public funds to compete in a commercial *field*—and that is the nub of the growing onslaught against the ABC and should not be readily dismissed as "another" attack by Murdoch. Murdoch has been described as having "two fundamental beliefs: One is in free speech, which most people share; the other is in the ideology of free markets" (Flanagan, 2014).[98] This book argues that these beliefs are also shared by the other commercial participants in the emergent commercial field. The commercial field is not built for an 'all for all' approach. Instead, it takes the commercially-oriented Chaucerian approach: "each man for himself (is the only rule)" (Chaucer, 1476)[99] and Aunty is not used, nor institutionally equipped, for that. Traditionally, she has been civic-minded, not profit-minded, and she was never narcissistic; she knew she was fabulous.

ABC audiences' dated expectations of Aunty bound up with quality content needed innovation, yet the divorce from its premium *cultural capital* has been damaging to the brand. It would appear that these "rusted on" ABC supporters with their standards and expectations of what a public broadcaster should be are being overlooked in favour of a youth audience. This search of online youth is also a tortuous route and declines on content quality has proved Aunty to be ignorant of the need to bring her *cultural capital* with her. It is also insulting to youth audiences, Australia's future leaders, that they are believed to be implicitly seeking and deserving of diminished quality news and information mixed with opinion. It shows Aunty's marketing has failed to engage with the essential need to preserve its *cultural capital* accrued by educating generations of 'cradle to grave' Australian audiences from 'Play School', Double J–Triple J, from 'The Argonauts' to Radio National, and to more 'grown-up' programs such as Gardening Australia and the documentaries. ABC programming once started, institutionally, at the beginning of the Australian citizen's life and envisaged its way to the end of that life.

1.4 Institutional Logics Theory: Inaugurating the ABC as "The Gaiety of the Nation"

This is the first use of Institutional Logics combined with Bourdieu to analyse a public broadcaster and the ABC. It is this aspect of the book which offers a new theoretical perspective on public broadcasting and public service media. This methodology permits analysis of "how individual and organizational actors are influenced by their situation in multiple social locations in an interinstitutional system" (Thornton et al., 2012b)[100] where "each institutional order of the inter-institutional system distinguishes unique organizing principles, practices, and symbols that influence individual and organizational behaviour" (ibid.). These principles and practices become the frames of reference that help actors make sense of their *fields*, and following Bourdieu (1983) this sense-making includes the language they use, their motivations and their self-efficacy (Thornton et al., 2012b). This helps shape actors' reasoning and their perceived roles in the institution. This form of analysis of the ABC is pertinent because the ABC is at a crisis point on many levels with the established principles and practices of the organisation either considered dated, or unviable. There has been a loss of translation from 'old' broadcasting media to the emergent digital commercial field.

The opening night of the ABC was a telling and illuminating start for the public broadcaster. The maps of the organisation's future, visions and expectations were rolled out clearly. The whole premise of the ABC had begun as a special privileged space to build Australian culture and create the *field* that accrued its *cultural capital.* The task was even more prodigious because it was to situate Australians as a member of the British Empire, to move Australians onwards from its liminal state as a colonial outpost. It is a good starting point for analysing the Institutional Logics of the ABC and the establishment of its *field* and *habitus* (Bourdieu) because the ABC was not *only* charged with emulating its role model the British Broadcasting Corporation, it was to (paradoxically) build Australian nationhood and "weld the empire" (Lloyd-Jones, quoted in *The Telegraph*, Brisbane, 1932).[101] The first uttered words on the ABC's role and purpose as a government-established broadcaster were set out by the then Prime Minister, Joseph Lyons, in his inauguration speech from Canberra[102] (*researcher's underlined emphasis*):

> Shortly after the British Broadcasting Company began its services in Great Britain the Commonwealth Government took the first steps in the establishment of similar services. Early in 1924 a wider scheme of control was prepared, ensuring the permanency of the service and its gradual extension and improvement. The second stage of progress in the broadcasting service lasted for five years. Two classes of licences were granted by the Postmaster-General-one providing for the establishment and maintenance of stations

> transmitting the main services, which were financed by listeners' licence fees, and the second providing for stations operating for publicity or advertising purposes. Later It appeared to the Government that it was desirable to establish a broadcasting service designed to **serve** the nation as a whole.
>
> This new national service was inaugurated in July, 1929, in Sydney and Melbourne, and later in the other capital cities. A further stage has now been reached, and it has become necessary to devise a new form of control. I take this opportunity of expressing the Government's appreciation of the public-spirited service which those in control of the Australian Broadcasting Company rendered to the public during the time that they provided the programmes (sic). The Government's aim in establishing the Broadcasting Commission has been to provide able and impartial trustees to direct this important national service in the interests of listeners and the public.
>
> Their task will be to provide programmes for entertainment, as well as for information in an acceptable form, having in mind the extremely varied tastes and needs of the community. Broadcasting should be a means of enjoyment for leisure hours and an aid to the culture, as well as to the gaiety of the nation. I have no doubt that the new commission desires enthusiastically to serve all sections and to satisfy the diversified tastes of the public. I am confident that listeners will be quick to appreciate all that is good in the programmes and to realise the high sense of public duty with which the members of the commission face their new responsibilities. I have great pleasure in formally pronouncing the inauguration of the control of the Australian Broadcasting Commission.

In 1932, Charles Lloyd-Jones (knighted in 1951) was the Australian Broadcasting Commission Chairman and spoke in the inaugural broadcast from Sydney along with Country Party Leader Dr Earle Page. The Federal Opposition Leader, James Scullin, was in Melbourne. It was, then, a truly significant broadcast because it linked voices from the major capital cities of Australia, for the first time. Aunty was networked—a thrilling event for the fledgling ABC audience.

The ABC as the primary Australian cultural institution has been influenced by both the formal networking among institutional actors and informal networking. This book will be looking at how networking among actors through the early social networks allowed the formation and dissemination of ***cultural capital*** within the organisation and also provided access to the Australian community in identifying and growing Australia's cultural life. For example, Charles Moses (knighted 1961), the ABC's first Managing Director, mixed socially with conductors and famous artists and encouraged them to tour and visit Australia. This means that Moses, as the formative organisational actor of the ABC, cultivated high culture in the institutional *field* of the ABC and incorporated their artistry, skills and capacities as part of the ABC's agency in its *field*, its *practices* and *habitus*—its reputation. This was because Moses' application of Institutional Logics saw the ABC primarily as a cultural institution. This contrasts dramatically with the ABC's activities today which are information based and where Facebook, Google and Twitter networks the organisation's news as well as attendant opinion, contacts, interpretations and reactions.

Institutional Logics is how an organisation organises itself. It has been defined as:

> The socially constructed, historical patterns of material practices, assumptions, values, beliefs, and rules by which individuals produce and reproduce their material subsistence, organize time and space, and provide meaning to their social reality. (Thornton & Ocasio, 2008)[103]

And there are three levels that can be identified in an organisation: society, *field* and the institution (Thornton et al., 2012b)[104] which link with and support other institutions including: the family, churches, other organisations, the professions (Paterson et al., 2018).[105]

Institutional Logics contributes to macro-organisational theory to address issues that are not readily accessible to economic analysis of macro-organisation theory alone. It focuses on:

> why organisations engage in activities that are legitimate in the symbolic realm rather than the material one; why organisations adopt behaviours that conform to normative demands but conflict with the rational attainment of economic goals or how purely technical or productive objects becomes infused with meaning and significance far beyond their utility value. (Suddaby, 2010)[106]

At the heart of the theory is that social structures and processes can gain meaning in their own right rather than being aimed at specialised ends (Lincoln, 1995).[107] Institutional Logics helps explain why organisations may defy economics and not operate logically, as in the case of the ABC. Looking at the ABC through the lens of Institutional Logics theory can help explain how organisations adopt processes and practices that favour ***meaning*** rather than ***productive value***, inter alia. Herein lies the potential clashes for the ABC pursuing these unmoneyed priorities of meaning and artistic, educational value with successive governments which overlay efficiencies and benchmarks on the ABC's performance, money management and capacity to handle sudden budget cuts. The collision occurs at the point where the cultural institution strives principally to create: *ars gratia artis* (Latin: art for art's sake) and the Federal Government imposes an indexation pause on the ABC's base funding (as in the 2018 Federal Budget). This is not to say the ABC has divided loyalties, split attention or is irresponsible per se; rather, it explains an aspect of Institutional Logics where a company/firm can be expected to be economically prudent while at the same time strive for humanistic or aesthetic outcomes (Amans et al., 2015[108]; Suddaby, 2010),[109] also referred to as "multiple logics" (Amans et al., ibid.), which is particularly relevant for "interdisciplinary collaborations" such as arts-based organisations (Jensen, 2019).[110] This aspect of how the ABC functions institutionally has sometimes been understood poorly by Australian politicians and has created enormous, unplanned dilemmas for management.

This book will analyse how the language used by key actors has shaped perceptions and legitimated practices in ABC media in the light of Institutional Logics. It will explore how that has occurred, in the light of policies and policy shifts. The book will analyse how actors justified artistic pursuits in a financially-challenged organisation. Most organisational research is quantitative; however, the qualitative research for this book has allowed for in-confidence, in-depth interviews and an extensive literature review. Institutional qualitative research helps us understand motivation and intention, which is an aspect being explored in this book although it has been acknowledged by Irving Goffman (1961) that individuals may not be clear on their own motivations sometimes. This book will also look at incidents in the ABC's foreground. It will examine how the institution built its role as the pivotal broadcaster in Australia. Further, Suddaby (2010) acknowledged that research had to "incorporate interpretivist methods that pay serious attention to the subjective ways in which actors experience institutions" (ibid.)[111] Content from interviews can be useful in providing these insights, as can memoirs. Another important aspect of this analysis will follow the use of language by the ABC in regard to speeches by key actors, advertising slogans, the institution's and individuals staff use of Twitter and accompanying responses to complaints from the public, academia, politicians, former staff or other media.

This book will look at the use of language by the ABC that promotes a particular discourse about the organisation and within the ABC. It is a language that denies there are internal problems and projects all organisational problems towards the accusers or "foe". For example, the current way the ABC responds to criticism through denial is a psychological concept which in this instance is used as a defence mechanism "presupposing explicit or implicit accusations" (van Dijk, 1992).[112] The ABC does not engage in acceptance of criticism. Denial, or reconstituted reality, can also be used as an opportunity to neutralise, attack or denigrate criticism. Denial also has links with institutional phenomenon of "groupthink", defined as "defective or dysfunctional group decision making" (Houghton, 2011)[113] where individuals bond in support of the perceived main agenda although this then creates a risk of "stereotyped views of outgroups allowed negative views of the 'enemy' to go unquestioned" (Coates, 2010) and where the literature said group decisions were often suboptimal, anyway in an effort to placate dissent (Mintz & Wayne, 2016).[114] Denial typifies an organisation under siege, as occurs in language used by, and on behalf of, the ABC.

How the ABC describes itself, is how it is, because it is understood that institutional language reveals how an outfit functions and malfunctions (Berger & Luckman, ibid.). In contrast, Varpio et al. (2017) said institutions needed a common language to "enhance transparency" (ibid.). Institutions are constructed by the habitualisation of actors who eventually end up saying: "This is how these things are done" (Berger & Luckmann, 1967)[115] like Bourdieu's *habitus* explained earlier, where language is at the heart of Institutional Logics (ibid.). According to Suddaby (2010)[116] analysis of the use of institutional language also reveals how it relates to the interests of the user, or in this case ABC audiences. For example, when ABC managers make statements to the public, often triggered by staff cuts (and following funding cuts), they use apparent *parrhesia* (blunt, frank talk) but in doing so take a risk, as explained by Michel Foucault, who described it as "dangerous" (Foucault, 1983)[117] because there are unknown consequences with apparent honesty. The tactic is used because ABC managers often want to deliver a message to governments by cloaking it in *parrhesia*, but it is in fact only an apparent truth where other motives have been mobilised. They use this style of speaking to assert organisational concerns because "emotion is integral to institutionalization and de-institutionalization" (Friedland, 2018)[118] in Institutional Logics. Further "Institutional Logics mediates the relationship between language and publics" (Swinehart & Graber, 2012)[119] and Suddaby (2010) said rhetorical strategies showed how institutions legitimated institutional change.[120]

The language used by the ABC describes its *habitus* and how it tries to maintain its institutional supremacy. Bourdieu (1991) said the power of this was such that "by structuring the perception which social agents have of the social world, the act of naming helps to establish the structure of the world, and does so all the more significantly the more widely it is recognised, i.e. authorised" (ibid.).[121] Words published under the banner of the ABC hold great significance, resonance and authority yet the abandonment of its unique *field* lies at the heart of the ABC's crisis—of agency, of trust and of confidence with the public. The ABC has relied on public trust, where trust has been defined in the literature as "one's expectations, assumptions, or beliefs about the likelihood that another's future actions will be beneficial, favorable, or at least not detrimental to one's interests" (Robinson, 1996).[122]

The language used by, and of, the ABC in advertising, policies, management speeches, statements and responses shows how language has shaped the organisation in the past but also how it projects its present and future views. Thornton (2004)[123] said in higher education publishing the interplay of cultural discourses and practices meant "market logics" and "editorial logics" clashed (ibid.); the same could be applied to the ABC where the shift to the emergent commercial field has created a clash with the editorial policies of the institution. Suddaby (2010) said "institutional theorists could and should pay more careful attention to how words are deliberately used to change resource allocations both in the financial and political spheres"[124] adding that there was a "need for institutional theorists to attend to the processes by which institutions are created, maintained and destroyed".[125] There was an absence of language analysis of how individuals influence an organisation (Suddaby, 2010).[126] To further this research recommendation, this book includes knowledge and information gained from structured interviews, which posed the same broad questions to all the anonymous, ABC actor/participant. Through this, the research was able to gain some insights into their agency in influencing the organisation, their close observations of the organisation and their capacity to manage, initiate, influence, interpret, reflect upon or instigate change. There has been a consistency across interviews in asking the same questions of each. However, these broad questions also allowed opportunities to delve into the actors' particular areas of interest, observation or authority. This helped provide rich data and further develop insights into their influence and capacity either within, or without, the organisation.

Institutional Logics analyses how organisations respond, change or sustain stasis and factors influencing this can arise from the individual level, through to teams and outside actors (Corbett et al., 2018).[127] The knowledge structures within an institution are called upon to create responses and this then determines the strategies available to the organisation (ibid.), and provides a method of analysis of a unique institution such as the ABC. The ABC managed a budget of AUD1045.9 million in 2018–2019; however, it can be said to be "non-economically rational" in that its cultural activities and social practices were separate, remote from economic (monetary profit) motivations. Its 'shareholders' are the Australian taxpayers who only seek 'dividends' in being informed, educated and entertained; this is a rare situation for a media corporation where returns cannot fit into a balance sheet but is also a concept of public funding that is falling rapidly into desuetude. It has serious implications for a democracy when public content drifts into an emergent, monetised field.

This book argues that the ABC's survival had been supported by paying close attention to its Charter and developing policies that underpinned its institutional ***habitus*** ("this is the way <u>we</u> do things"), set apart from commercial pursuits, and the aforementioned strategies, which meant that it has had the capacity to attract and educate an élite participatory audience, and build Bourdieu's (1977) ***cultural capital*** and institutional resources. However:

- ongoing funding cuts
- threats of funding cuts
- talk of privatisation/licence fees/subscription fees/selling off/inclusion of paid advertising
- government inquiries
- threats of government inquiries
- staff losses and redundancies
- impending staff losses and redundancies
- threats of staff losses and redundancies
- loss of institutional memory and reputational capital
- loss of legacy knowledge and skills
- tumultuous technological challenges (un-imagined in 1932) requiring the ABC to lead the *field*
- chasing any online audiences, especially youth, everywhere and anywhere

means Australia's biggest, independent, public, national broadcaster, originally threatened by a hostile commercial media, has been destabilised and is being threatened again by commercialism, but differently—and from within and without. Yet when it defends itself the ABC still situates its institutional thinking as if in its own *field*. This is no longer the reality. The ABC now competes with not only all professional media but the wild frontiers of participatory, user-generated, unbridled opinion-focused citizen media, diverse interest and activist groups, advertising, pay-walled content, curated content and competing internet communities of the digital era. Somewhere amongst all that, the Australian citizens of its original remit still exist. In Aunty's new *field*, opinion has not only infiltrated fact in news, opinion is news too, which raises ethical issues of privacy when anything can be news. Raised voices have drowned out "old" standards of ethics, knowledge, reasoned debate, the multiple perspectives of Socratic debate, logic and probity. It has triggered concerns from the audience as to whether it is now truly "their" ABC. Its promotional strapline describes it as "ABC, yours" yet Aunty's esteemed voice is being strangled by paying too much attention to the infinitely splintering, personalised groups of "yours" and not the diverse but unified "us". Allied with this has been the proud political/ideological shift in the ABC towards derogatory, abusive negativity based on personalised criticisms of individuals, society and institutions. This parcelling up of single issues as though representative of the whole has triggered a consequent decline in ABC audience support where there is an identified loss of impartiality. It has also done a disservice to the context and broader ramifications of the issues under analysis. Aunty would have once sniffed at divisiveness, but she is now emboldened by it. This shift was acknowledged by former ABC senior journalist Jonathan Holmes when he blamed management as being inactive in trying to restore the bias balance (Holmes, 2019).[128]

This book promotes the position of Paddy Scannell (1989)[129] that public broadcasting was established as, is, and can continue to be, a "public good and social right". Scannell (1997) said (researcher's underlining):

> I wish to argue for broadcasting in its present form, as a public good that <u>has unobtrusively contributed to the democratization of everyday life</u>, in public and private contexts, from its beginning through to today. (1997)[130]

He said that: "by placing political, religious, civic, cultural events and entertainments in a common domain, public life was equalized in a way that had never before been possible" (ibid.)[131] in creating what he described as: "punctual moments in shared national life" (ibid.).[132] There is a very real sense that, historically, the ABC had represented to Australians the most significant moments in its nation-building and turning points. This was welded to the origins of the organisation, in particular, which was charged with projecting and distilling the essence of Australian nationhood. However, the ABC now offers vastly more than its original 1930s remit of radio. This research argues that the ABC's embrace of online activities, which in commercial media derives income from 'hits', aggregating consumers and on-selling consumers to other organisations, has put the ABC in an invidious situation in a dangerous, emergent *field*. It is well understood in the marketing literature that online intermediaries are not impartial; they are "mediators who shape and supervise market interactions" (Mellet, 2011).[133]

Online activity has a long tail and Aunty no longer controls where her message goes—nor who 'plays' with it. This has serious repercussions for an impartial public outfit. The ABC has a broad footprint to reach Australians of all interests and needs and this originally strengthened the ABC's respected, informational, educational role in Australian culture. It taught Australians who they were. Yet, the threat and reality of funding cuts and concomitant failures to grapple appropriately with the advent and surge of digital media and lack of preservation of the ***reputational capital*** and ***cultural capital*** have meant that the organisation has surrendered its authority as part of its strategy to compete with essential digitisation and drift into its frontier rules. Its privilege, its élitism, were by far its distinguishing qualities features in holding its *field* and reputation against other media. ABC privilege and élitism held other power to account.

1.5 Chapter 2: Managing the ABC

The broad purpose of Chap. 2 is to take an overview of ABC leadership through the lens of Institutional Logics and in the foreground of the role of leadership in the public service. It will not consider each manager of the ABC since its inception, rather it will argue there have been frequent disconnects between management and staff. It also analyses the shifts in culture through management actors. In 2010, the then ABC Chairman Maurice Newman explained: "This is not a five-minute exercise, changing culture and changing attitudes and so on. These are things that take time" (Elliott et al., 2010).[134] Steps taken to manage the digital transition of the

ABC, for instance, have been hampered by a reactive staff culture. In addition, the generally agreed aspiration for the ABC's Managing Director (and other leaders, including the Board) is that it should be true to the Charter, unbiased and that the Managing Director is Editor-in-Chief. To date, this has seemed to be a lightly understood concept in terms of any demonstrated public intervention by management in apparent ABC bias. However, the role of editor-in-chief in the management logics is clear and onerous (Kim, 2018), based on: "the formation of the ideological and thematic line of the publication, and with the planning of the work of the journalistic team, and with representative functions" (Kim, ibid.).[135] In fact, in 2014 Communications Minister Malcolm Turnbull wrote to the ABC Board recommending that the Managing Director, Mark Scott, be relieved of his role as editor-in-chief because the combined role: "creates the impression that the Managing Director is directly in charge of ABC news and current affairs which he is not, and given the wide range of his responsibilities, could not be" (White & Lynch, 2014).[136] This was at a time of funding cuts that Scott was quoted would cause an 8% annual funding reduction (White & Lynch, ibid.).

This chapter will also consider the diligent efforts of Charles Moses, as the ABC's first General Manager, especially in cultivating an élite *field* of actors among musicians, writers, artists who were instrumental in establishing the ABC's *cultural capital*. Moses entertained people at restaurant suppers and attended social functions, dinner parties and performances with the aim of acquiring status for the organisation through his presence and building contacts. Those early actors forged the institutional contacts that would build the ABC's esteemed role in Australian cultural, political, educational and social life. Further to this growth the ABC's status and reputation was built through music—the management and support for its proliferating orchestras, bands and other musical groups.[137] If ABC Managing Directors were to socialise publicly at that level and frequency today, they would be accused of being wasteful, lazy, out of touch (ironically) and élitist. Yet that was once what the ABC did—and did well. The ABC's early years were focused on growing influence among these upper social echelons of Australian society. Later with the support of the ABC's Head of the Concert Department, Charles Buttrose,[138] management built together an influential circle of institutional contacts with the objective of mutually benefiting the growth of an Australian culture, for all Australians. The Institutional Logics of the ABC supported this understanding among managers who (generally) shared the same aspirations to build up resources and practices to educate Australians.

The chapter will also dissect how ABC management fostered the educational capacity of the organisation with the support of Herbert Brookes, the ABC's first Vice-Chairman, and his wife Ivy Brookes, who was exceptionally well connected both as daughter of former Prime Minister Alfred Deakin and as a distinguished violinist. Both the Brookes were generous benefactors in other areas of society. The ABC's early role in establishing classical and contemporary music in Australia was enormous and created caché and self-respect in what was then a nation trying to shed the cloak of a lesser British colonial outpost. The ABC took over where the School of Arts and Mechanics Institutes of the Victorian era left off in growing popular education. The ABC was a triumph.

Another aspect being analysed in this chapter is the growth in the government restraint of public service leadership where there has been a disempowerment by governments, who look over public organisations' shoulders and insist on more control, scrutiny and managerialism. The lessening of autonomy for institutions, such as the ABC, means they are overwhelmed with insecurity and uncertainty. One response to this uncertainly by the ABC has been to place staff on short-term or casual contracts, which allows the institution to respond more quickly to funding cuts. Concomitant with that, the ABC is failing to create staff loyalty, longevity and retain the *reputational capital* accrued by experienced ABC staff. This has complicated rather than solved staffing problems. The economic exigencies mean there is more churning through staff and this then makes it harder for ABC leaders to build confidence in their decisions when their workforce is a changing muster of people. In addition, changed social exigencies means this group must also be benchmarked against cultural quotas. The second response comes from the employees who, quite rightly, now focus on shorter career time horizons, are insecure of work and any long-term ABC planning presented to them by managers is mocked and pushed-back by staff as wishful, unrealistic, or even sinister thinking.

Thirdly, and possibly in response to the latter, ABC managers have been accused of creating a "cone of silence" around decision-making where there can also be identified a disconnect between government media policy and ABC strategy. By and large, its Institutional Logics have confined and cramped decision-making by failing to include stakeholders (the government of the day and its vast publics). A staff culture that is 'siloed' and often opposes management creates challenges for management in considering who from staff to include, and who to exclude, from institutional decisions, although this is problematised/ameliorated by having a staff member on the ABC Board. The ABC is also criticised for lacking a politically representative board, or a politically over-represented board and there have been government moves that tried to redress that, but these subsequently unravelled. Government's 'chop and change' approach to ABC board policy has not helped support ABC institutional leadership and has done serious scaffolding damage to the institution. The impact on the ABC's Institutional Logics of this vacillation by successive governments has been noteworthy and caused an erosion of confidence and agency in the institution in its capacity to manage change and simply trust governments.

This chapter claims that as a public service organisation the ABC's mandate is to provide objective news, information, education and entertainment to all Australians ('all to all') yet this chapter will also analyse how ABC management has also brought itself into ethical conflicts and missteps. For example, there were two incidents in the 1980s the flip-flops in response to government pressure competing with a will to be independent in reporting international conflicts over what was referred to as the "Nyaro Episode" where the Managing Director Geoffrey Whitehead was accused of being silent on the issue, as well as the declared admission of the existence of a "phantom army" of staff by Whitehead. Both suggested a core problem of management/institution disconnect. Similar disjointedness arose during the Managing Directorship of Michelle Guthrie who was confronted with a hostile staff culture, resistant to change. Overall, it suggests that the role and characteristics of management at the ABC are not well understood and, therefore, they are now seen as ineffective, ineffectual actors by both governments and staff. This ongoing situation and debilitated institutional leadership conditions create a major disadvantage for any senior management trying to re-purpose the ABC for digitisation and reclaim, preserve its *reputational capital.*

1.6 Chapter 3: The ABC, "Service for Funding … to Serve, as a Service"

This chapter examines and extends issues relating to ABC staff culture situating staff within the context of the public service and as public servants in Australia and the attendant expectations and roles. The ABC's once Bourdieusian élite staff has evolved into a defensive culture fighting to preserve what was, or what is preferred; and, this will be analysed with examples. ABC staff' special élite status and power within the fluid over-arching *field* of media has also become harder to justify in an era when anyone can be a reporter, commentator, expert or photographer and the brutal truth is that specialisation, professional credentials and legacy knowledge are no longer respected, needed nor affordable. Anyone who has a hand phone can be a reporter and commentator. Literature has expressed concern that the ABC News Division had long regarded itself as separate from the rest of the ABC (Semmler, 1981; Inglis, 1983)[139] and therefore the curtailment of the 07.45 am Radio News bulletin in 2020 may have been "punishment" in the long-standing issue where the News Division sees itself separate, worthy of more separateness from other teams and managers in the ABC. Another interpretation of the decision to end the bulletin was given by a former ABC executive who was quoted that the elimination of the bulletin was: "a political decision to cut something that was high profile and would be noticed by the public and the politicians" (RadioInfo, 2020).[140] Overall, management sometimes struggles with staff that believe it knows better. Yet, when there is churning in management from a variety of institutional/organisational backgrounds, that belief may have some validity vis-à-vis the legacy knowledge of long-term senior staff.

While accumulations of status among ABC staff have supported the ABC's relevance as a *sui generis* élite media organisation, the same areas are now under threat as it struggles not only to keep its distinctive voice, but also to be heard in a strategy-equipped, revenue-driven, emergent commercial *field*. All the while, the ABC travels through a digital future, while retaining an analogue heritage (television, radio) and with all the staff scaffolding and audience expectations that supported that content, unique genres and habitually-timetabled delivery. This chapter argues that, in the pursuit of digital media popularity as a member of the emergent commercial field, the institution has departed from its own unique, impartial public servant *field* and while the digital media *field* is also capable of creating outstanding media, it is a hotchpotch of contributors and certainly not a manifestly élite *field* as the ABC once occupied. From what former leaders and managers have told this research study, the continuity of the organisation has been driven by the loyalty and devotion of its staff to public broadcasting because it understands the ABC is a vital pillar of Australian democracy. However, the role of staff culture is also nuanced and complex because it is also known that: "people tend to bring their own behaviour in line with what they perceive to be the norms of their reference group" (Tankard & Paluck, 2016 in DiMaggio, 2018).[141] So, by implication ABC staff will self-adjust to fit the culture if they are to thrive and survive and research shows staff will comply with the beliefs of the dominant actors in the staff culture.

The undermining and denigration of democratic institutions has become a serious, consequential matter to all Australians and will be discussed, with examples in this chapter. Conflicting with this subversion and depletion of the institutions is the invested belief in 'service' that public institutions embodied, which could be broadly described as selfless service for the greater good. This is a concept important to beginnings and existence of the ABC. Analysis of 'service' occurs frequently in managerial, organisational and institutional literature while at the same time the definition of 'service' was changing (MacInnis, 2005)[142]; consequently there is no one academic definition or understanding of 'to serve' and 'service' (Lau et al., 2011).[143] MacInnis (2005) said the place to start in understanding how service worked in an organisation was to examine its internal culture.[144] Another understanding of service is that it is abstract—something that cannot be physically grasped as: "a time-perishable, intangible experience performed for a customer acting in the role of co-producer" (Fitzsimmons & Fitzsimmons, 2004).[145]

Aunty has always been judged to a higher level of accountability than other media on this basis of service. It is publicly answerable and has occupied a more powerful *field* than other Australian media because it was structured to be free from political influence, therefore independent, and it was envisaged that this positioned it to support Australia's system of constitutional democracy by serving the greater good of the Commonwealth. Its status was enviable. Now it has moved into a *field* over-crowded with formulaic media, and leaving its reputation behind it (or assuming it was immutable and a permanent quality) has converged its factual content with opinion. This shift has been aided by its active use of social media, both by the institution and by its staff. This is a dangerous *field* for a trusted, thoughtful Aunty. She has drifted from a prized exclusive *field* of aloof coverage aimed at serving the general public sphere to an tumultuous marketplace where private is public and the particular has ascendancy over general. But in making the necessary and unavoidable shift to digital media, the ABC has confused this with having to acquire the qualities/traits/values of the miscellaneous emergent commercial digital sphere. It now also competes differently with respected commercial outfits, for example collaborative reporting where joint or multi-actor journalism not only contributes to the needs of commercial outfits, it is shared with the institutional ABC. The ABC now takes up the causes and cudgels of the fragmented, evasive, slippery, online, localised audiences while abandoning its established group of 'all for all' Australian citizens en masse. In this process it has de-intellectualised itself to appeal to these digital groups, and lost sight, or forgotten, the valuable role it served as a public service educator to the Australian nation. Aunty has been seen to "sell-out" her nieces and nephews. Many Australians are not digital hunters or gatherers and these folks have been abandoned, while the pursuit of online issues and "conversations" has created, counter-intuitively, a worrying deficit in democratic debate and discourses. Aunty is satisficing, at best, rather than fulfilling.

This chapter asserts that the shift to a new emergent commercial *field* (and abandonment of its own, exclusive *field*) has brought the ABC into controversy by dabbling in advertising. The now defunct Fairfax News which reformulated as Nine Entertainment in 2018 called out the ABC for its YouTube channels showing advertisements for "Colgate, Cadbury, Dior, Suzuki, Subway, Subaru" and others (Bennett, 2018).[146] The ABC excused this because "in recent years, the ABC has made some of its content available on third-party platforms and services to ensure we remain relevant, engaging and accessible to all Australians by offering them high-quality and distinctive content when and where they want it" (ibid.). So, consorting with commercial advertising is part of its new relevance drive. There is other interesting overlap. ABC Books is in partnership with Rupert Murdoch's publishing company Harper Collins (Cooper, 2009).[147] Yet elsewhere, Murdoch is blamed for any criticism of the ABC by Australian Labor Party (ALP) politicians and by ABC actors, yet criticism about the ABC is only ever from his news outlets' journalists and commentators; there is nothing on the public record from Murdoch personally denigrating the ABC. His employees are accused of being puppets and his entire business described as: "the media company that is the puppet master of our politics and government" (Beecher 2020) and Murdoch's "entire world view is opposed to the principles that underpin the ABC" (Cooper, ibid.). Further, Harding (1979)[148] expressed a direct link in anti-ABC editorial positions between Murdoch and his newspaper *The Australian* in the mid-1970s at the same time as federal funding cuts and the emergence of Melbourne's 'Aunty's Nephew and Nieces' and Sydney's 'Friends of the ABC'. This book argues that frictions and perturbations with the Murdoch empire are nothing new and anger is expended in this direction at the expense of self-reflection and valuing of the essential and vital role of the institution as a separate media outfit is overlooked in preference to this victimhood. The blurring of differences in media offerings and content (Cooper Loc. Cit.) as the ABC blends and re-builds itself into the emergent commercial *field* and as the competition heats up, puts the whole situation with Murdoch (and everyone else) differently and on a bigger scale, yet also requires the ABC as an institution to look back before it moves forward. This will be analysed in this book.

Service has changed in another way. The publics served by public servants have been re-named: customers, or clients, members or subscribers—no longer citizens. Scholars have recently noted that this was not just a linguistic shift but also had an impact on how publics related to services: "a largely ignored social subject is the influence of customers, with whom employees might have intense interactions during their work, especially 'in service' industries" (Cai et al., 2019).[149] ABC audiences are customers now since the ABC has shifted into the emergent commercial digital 'mediasphere'. Social media is a powerful factor in how the ABC operates, its impact, its agency and role—its nomenclature of participants. In turn, ABC staff now have considerable responsibility to interact with the ABC's customers/clients/audiences/subscribers, and this has at times brought about criticism of the ABC. Because of this new approach, "special features of different clients' service needs can make establishment of meaningful solutions challenging" (Manz et al., 2015),[150] which means the ABC is now caught in the commercial customer expectations and as primary stakeholders, these customers are now "the new king" because "content has been dethroned" (QSR web.com, 2015).[151]

The ABC response of re-inventing itself through its audiences/customers by putting the onus on the audience to provide stories, footage and audio means it is now providing media platforms to "town hall" ideas. Institutions use this style of meeting when they want an all of staff meeting and employees can ask random question without notice to the management teams. The question remains, however, has this resulted in a stronger, more loyal relationship between audiences and the national broadcaster when it now competes in the *field* with commercial media—equally reliant on these random audiences/street journalists for content? It also invites the question of the quality of the content as now the gatekeepers and originators have been encouraged to vacate their roles of determining stories in deference to the audience making the editorial choices.

Creating audiences as contributors of content, determining editorial priority and decentralising the organisation are three ways of meeting the challenge of digital media and dwindling funding. But in that process the ABC has had to compromise and surrender its ***cultural capital*** by focusing on the appeal of individual stories created by the audience and individuals and not, necessarily, of benefit or interest to the public at large and service of nationhood. It is a situation where "the routines of news work lead to systemic distortions that label anything threatening to the status quo as illegitimate" (Swartz, 2012)[152] precipitated by a commercial imperative on the internet for news and information. Business logics now clash with journalistic practices in measuring the success of content through easily retrieved data which tracks readers, attaches cookies and guides news towards sensationalism, headlines towards distortion and may substitute for useful public knowledge. It means, "web analytics are exerting a growing influence on individual journalists across the board" (Hanusch, 2017).[153]

In 2004, the BBC released a landmark paper on how it had responded to the challenges of public service media: "Building public value: Renewing the BBC for a digital world".[154] The statement said in regard to the BBC:

> It must apply the test of public value to everything it does—its services, its commercial activities, its scope and scale. The public have a right to expect a very wide breadth of services and content in return for the licence fee, but the BBC's depth of vertical integration and inhouse activity should be based on public rather than its own institutional priorities.[155]

It added the institution was taking a decentralised approach: "the digital world demands a more open, responsive BBC. A BBC which reflects the whole UK in its output and which significantly shifts its broadcasting, production and other operations out of London and into the rest of the UK".[156]

The paper says (researcher's bold type for emphasis):

> "**Broadcasting is a civic art. It is intrinsically public in ambition and effect**. We may experience it individually, but it is **never a purely private transaction.**" Free-to-air broadcasting is what economists call a public good. ... While commercial broadcasters aim to return value to their shareholders or owners, the BBC exists to create public value. ... It says it: "aims **to serve** its audiences not just as consumers, but as members of a wider society, with programmes and **services** which, while seeking to inform, educate and entertain audiences, **also serve wider public purposes***Australian Government, The*. Federal Register of Legislation. ABC Charter, Section 6 ABC Act 1983. [online]. Retrieved 3 January 2020 from https://www.legislation.gov.au/Details/C2018C00079.[157]

While the ABC operates on a much smaller budget and larger footprint that the BBC, as public broadcasters similarities can be drawn. In 2012, ABC Chairman James Spigelman, echoing these sentiments, said in a speech at a RIPE@2012 Conference: "The provision of a bedrock of services (from a trustworthy source, accessible to all Australians without charge and wherever they live, with a degree of certainty that is not now available from other traditional sources) is a fundamental aspect of the public benefit—public value—the ABC delivers" (Spigelman, 2012).[158] The current Managing Director David Anderson said in his first public statement upon being appointed: "I look forward to continuing to lead the ABC and allowing our talented teams to get on with what the ABC does best: serving the Australian people" (Wilson, 2019).[159]

Never before has the ABC been under such a siege: funding has been reduced relative to the size of the Australian population and the reach of the organisation around Australia and overseas has been curtailed. This means actors are placed under new pressures to perform, conform and deliver in the manifest diversity of an emergent commercially-dominated digital media environment. There is also consternation among staff and observers that the ABC is a capital city-based and capital city-focused institution and has lost its capacity to attend to the needs and interests of all Australians—'all to all'. Another criticism from staff and observers is that the ABC is chasing individual causes to appear relevant and please and chase young online media audiences, rather than looking to its public service role for the greater good of Australian society. The idea of the 'the greater good' and the received understandings of the role of the public service will be unpacked in this chapter.

The founding of the BBC and then the ABC in the early twentieth century as acts of public intervention in the market tasked them with providing public communication services. For Australia the ABC arrived not long after Federation of the States in 1901 when Australia became a Commonwealth. When the ABC and earlier the BBC were established they were radio broadcasters only. Since then they have both expanded, with government support (and/or licence fees in the case of the early ABC and the BBC) into other areas of mass, then digital media. The BBC, although funded by licence fees, is facing a fresh challenge of British Government plans to remove the criminal offence from those who do not pay their licence fees, which means licence fee payments will slide—as will BBC funding. The argument for this is that in an age of media abundance there should be no compulsion to tax citizens for a news outlet and that the old funding model was flawed. Both the BBC and ABC have grown from discrete platform broadcasters to embrace the potentialities of new and growing platforms. Yet they struggle with this new *field*.

All of us are impacted upon by the role of institutions, to a greater or lesser extent, and the services they provide. For those few Australians who may not be aware of the ABC, the institution impacts on them too because they are taxed with the rest to pay for the upkeep of the broadcaster. The ABC also influences the debates and understandings of Australianness that swirl around the nation and its Charter states it has must align itself with expectations to do so. As a nation, and as a society, Australians both own the ABC and are responsible for it (Rousseau described this as The Social Compact of "civility" and "beneficence"[160]). The ABC's role "to serve" is carried out by its public servants. The literature on public service said its role was to support the political executive (prime minister and key elected actors) "in the development, implementation and enforcement of government policies"[161]; it also works to support policy and deliver a service (Dickinson et al., 2019).[162]

The ABC exists to serve as Australia's national advocate. This service has changed since the organisation's inception; however, like all other public service media it has had to re-assess its role by looking more closely at the new interests of the audience(s) and how it can maintain its special role as a public broadcaster where it must grow audience participation (Cola & Prario, 2012)[163] yet maintain its relevance and justification for public money. Public institutions serve democracy (Denhardt & Denhardt, 2007)[164]; they are not 'for profit' businesses. Yet, there is limited provision anywhere of one general set of generic principles, or themes, to guide and define public service (ibid.).[165] Public service organisations also operate in an environment where there is eroded respect for institutions; a more demanding, confrontational, fractured public; ubiquitous de-funding pressures; and concurrent contradictory pressures to become 'as efficient' as private enterprises which are based on achieving profits and serving shareholder interests. The understanding that the ABC was a 'service industry' was clear in 1932, when Prime Minister Joseph Lyons launching the broadcaster said:

> the Government's aim in establishing the Broadcasting Commission has been to provide able and impartial trustees to direct this <u>important national service</u> in the interests of listeners and the public … <u>to serve</u> all sections and to satisfy the diversified tastes of the public.[166]

Imbued with the nascent responsibility "to serve" the obligation was reiterated by the first ABC Chairman Charles Lloyd-Jones who told Australians: "the service now belongs to you we are your trustees. It is a service that is not run for profit but purely in the interests of every section of the community."[167] Lloyd-Jones concluded with visionary sentiments: "with sympathy and understanding and by taking our listener into our confidence we hope to succeed". Chancellor of Western Sydney University, Professor Peter Shergold (and former secretary of the Department of Prime Minister and Cabinet) (2017),[168] said that growing distrust of democratic institutions and attacks on Enlightenment values presented a challenge for the public service generally to be more "agile, adaptive and responsive" (ibid., 2017).

The ABC offered three key facets of teaching and learning—expression, participation and reflection; its *cultural practices* and management policies going into the digital space could be expected to support its evolving role in digital media. This book examines the failures in that transition that has strangled Aunty's voice. In 2012, the Managing Director Mark Scott said in a speech that "the ABC had been a pioneer in digital media in Australia"[169] and under its Charter it is required to provide four types of content: "news and current affairs, opinion, topical and factual and performance"[170] and to meet these expectations it had a vast footprint. It has four national radio networks: Radio National, Triple J, News Radio and Classic FM. It has nine metropolitan radio stations in all capital cities as well as the major NSW coastal city of Newcastle (around 160 kilometres north of Sydney). There are 51 regional radio stations. It has digital radio stations Double J, Triple J Unearthed, ABC Kids Listen, ABC Jazz and ABC Country. ABC Extra was established to broadcast special events, such as the 40th anniversary of the Apollo 11 moon landing in 2019. In addition, there is ABC Comedy/Kids (originally ABC2), ABC Me (a channel for school-aged children and includes educational content) and ABC News 24 (a dedicated 24-hour news channel).

Chapter 3 will also explore the conundrum of how to serve and describe audiences, which has been debated since the 1980s (Patriarche & Dufrasne, 2014)[171] because to define audiences, publics or communities "detracts from the true complexity of practices" (ibid.)[172] where there are now "fuzzy boundaries between the public and private space, and greater physical and social closeness between the audience and the performer" (ibid.).[173] Publics and audiences are everywhere but not necessarily accessing PSM content. What the PSMs are finding is that they are attracting older (over 55 years) and educated audiences, while the youth audiences source news from social media such as Facebook and YouTube. PSMs have failed to grow their audiences beyond the reach of their traditional platforms, yet have narrowed their audiences by pursuing individual, personalised stories of people and issues. From a narrow base of individual issues, it has removed its universal relevance by making the assumption that an individual's story is of interest to the general public—where there is no "general public" anyway on the internet. Extrapolating on and moving from the general to a new focus on individual, niche audience needs was never going to be an easy transition. The particular can represent the general, but it is an ambitious leap to make it unilateral. It has also been found that PSM is of less interest to those who are with limited formal education: "this means there is a risk of public service news exacerbating rather than equalising information inequalities" (Schulz et al., 2019).[174]

Research of PSMs in eight countries of Europe (Schulz et al., 2019)[175] showed PSM organisations could no longer lay claim to fulfilling their objective of a universal service, or even close to that. In addition, European PSMs were also no longer trusted news sources for either the politically right, or populist causes. Research found that falling audiences for television and radio meant the model of PSMs had not kept up with fundamental changes in media consumption and "online is therefore key to the future of public service news, and currently public service news provision online falls far short of the ambition of near-universal service" (Schulz et al., 2019).[176] Aunty's voice is being strangled by her own lack of voice and pursuit of niche audiences. She has also sought the voice of others as a substitute for hers.

Schulz et al. (2019) warned in regard to PSM:

> The alternative to this is not the status quo but continued decline and ultimately the very real risk of irrelevance to much of the public – an irrelevance that would undermine the legitimacy of public service media as an institution, leaving them unable to deliver on their public service mission.[177]

The researchers said that with algorithms tied tightly to garnering revenue and advertising, via Google and social media outfits, PSMs have a much harder task in trying to be part of this 'game'. Ultimately, it is agreed that PSMs will decline in relevance and audience reach in the online news mix.[178] Concomitant with that public service news is: "much less widely used among younger audiences than in the wider public" (Schulz et al.,

2019).[179] For example, in studying the BBC audience: "in early 2019 accounted for 63% of all radio listening, and 31% of all linear scheduled television viewing, but just 1.5% of all time spend with digital media". They compared this with Google which consisted of 22% of all time spent with digital media, and Facebook 14% (ibid.).[180]

To meet this challenge, the audience has become so important to the ABC brand that it streams a gate-kept feed from the micro-blogging site, Twitter, of responses from the audience in a ticker format across the bottom of the screen for the duration of the 'Q and A' television debate/discussion panel program. Service industries, of which the ABC is one, must now consider their audiences in delivery of their content as never before.[181] It has the advantage of giving professional journalists an interface with citizen journalists in the creation of content but the significant challenge for the ABC (and indeed all traditional news and information media organisations) is that, to quote Bruns (2012):

> The more users come to rely on Twitter and other social media platforms as a means of discovering what is happening in the world … and move towards a 'news will find me' mentality—the less likely they will be to receive news only from any one specific news outlet.[182]

In addition, a legacy news organisation such as the ABC operates in an area where there is maximum pressure to deliver maximum audience engagement with diminishing resources on scattered platforms and this compromises its service delivery (Bruns, ibid.).[183] There is need for further independent marketing and audience research into this aspect of the ABC. The literature asserted that: "insight regarding nuances of client needs is an important part of provision of effective service"[184] and that these needs changed over time. The ABC has embraced digitisation in order to try to stay "ahead of the game" or at the very least in synchronisation with its audience(s) but this is all happening in its very stressful, strictly undemocratic, new *field* ruled by commercial activity.

1.7 Chapter 4: What Ideas Rule? The Digital Commercial *Field*—Shifting from Private Play*field* to Commercial Mine*field*

This chapter addresses how the ABC communicates ideas and analyses how it uses the technology of her new emergent commercial *field* and the confronting challenges it has posed both to the organisation and to audiences. Aunty once occupied her own, unique, creative, intellectual 'sandpit', pursuing endeavours with which it knew Australians needed to engage. Aunty was free to pursue creative projects that have enriched Australian culture: comedies, investigative journalism, cultural events—all giving her status in her *field* as a benchmark industry standard-setter. She enriched and inspired Australia and created an Australian mindset. The voice of the ABC articulated the ears of Australia and the eyes of the world; it was a "rock of stability … a monolith in Australian cultural life" (Palfreyman, 1993).[185] The value and legacy of this personal creativity of ABC individual actors, the organisation collectively and their combined contribution to the nation is not to be underestimated, nor trivialised by the words 'sandpit' and 'playfield'—terms used here seriously to reflect creative, willing institutional actors focusing, excelling and making a worthy, honest contribution in their own space. And that they did. Not so now. And worse, Aunty has rested on her laurels by believing that all the *cultural capital* she acquired in her previous creative *field* gave a lifelong guarantee of her longevity and rectitude.

Her cultural capital bank account has been filled with past examples of her sense of "Aussie" humour (including comedy programs such as: *Aunty Jack*, *Kath and Kim*, *We Can Be Heroes*, *Utopia etc.*) as well as her sharply-honed civic responsibility and duty (*Four Corners* programs exposing corruption and illegality and triggering numerous royal commissions and political and business resignations and upheavals). Yet, now she is keep drawing down on this capital by referencing past successes, some of which she is now ashamed—for instance, *We Can Be Heroes* is now regarded by the ABC (2020) as racist for the depiction of a Chinese Australian student by a "white" Australian comedian—so she is undermining her own successful judgement, retrospectively. Her current contributions to news and content are proving to be constrained, unsure, self-conscious, light, unrepresentative—or even abusive and offensive. She has lost her *field* and is adrift and unable to find her ground in the emergent commercial *field*. In an organisation that had prided itself on cultivating élite privileged media actors, outstanding and renowned in the *field*, all are now forced to justify their existence and demur from their 'élitism' and 'privilege', now redefined as pejoratives.

In addressing the challenge of the digitisation of media, for example, the ABC has pursued a strategy of active engagement and promotion. The focus of the book will explore examples in this chapter that underpin the shift in strategy towards digitisation, necessitated by new technologies, governments, convergence, as well as the consequences of this engagement with digital media and the implications for the ABC as a national PSM institution. This book argues that in making the necessary switch to digitising its operation and shifting from its own élite content *field*, the ABC now resides in a field already claimed and defended by commercial media. It is populated by actors who have traditionally jostled and competed, had a snide toleration for each other, but possibly a distant respect for the ABC. That has now changed. In shifting to digital media and abandoning the capital of its bespoke privileged élite *field*, the ABC has undermined the important obligations of the ABC as a PSM organisation by compromising its unique authority and credibility, as well as its Charter.

In many ways it is now impossible for the ABC to be 'all for all' when it merges its content in a digital media minefield that is so fractured, fractious, fraught and opinion-heavy. Aunty has departed her safer, prudent, circumspect, élite *field* redolent with its own *cultural capital* and now tries to "sell her wares" without having created a distinguishing space for herself to retain her uniqueness. The ABC leans on the public's prior knowledge of the ABC to continue to support its new directions. In the varied and variously standardised, commercial *field* Aunty either has to fit-in, or face oblivion. The prominence of online opinion demonstrates the chief media operators—the traditional news outlets—have lost their ascendancy. In 2018 the Pew Research Center found that the dominant media operators in the US, for example, were Facebook and YouTube.[186] How the ABC has chosen to create and fixate on unsound, prejudiced distractions and excuses from this fundamental issue will be elaborated in this chapter. The ABC's *cultural capital* was enriching and was not achieved, manifestly and institutionally, by commercial media providers—quality was developed only in parts of the commercial media field because commercial media has never been monolithically one entity in the field, it has represented disparate parts and diverse investments. The ultimate irony is that the ABC's *cultural capital* and *social capital* if retained and nurtured may have been converted to actual capital—increased public funding. The ABC is now spending public funds in pursuit of private opinions but privileging age demographics with value-laden individual expectations and sectional interests, as social media encourages.

Digitisation and conversion from old technologies was essential and in many ways the ABC was a technological leader in Australia. Inglis (2006)[187] said that Managing Director David Hill established a 'multimedia unit' in 1994 to advise him on the how to take the ABC into the digital era (Inglis,

2006). However, this is disputed by Colin Griffith (1996), former acting head of the ABC's Multimedia Unit (from December 1995), who said the unit was established in 1995. In 1995, Managing Director Brian Johns launched ABC Online (Griffith, ibid.; Inglis, ibid.), but the launch was marred by Johns' interest in entering into an online joint venture with a commercial enterprise (Griffith, Inglis, Loc. Cit.). Griffith (1996)[188] said the move into multimedia "presents important opportunities for the ABC to champion Australian information, culture and expression and to extend the role of a public broadcaster". He also cautioned that the ABC needed to "appreciate the fundamentally different landscape of this new media environment compared to those of previous eras" (Griffith, ibid.) because of "fundamentally different creative and narrative demands from those of previous linear media" (Loc. Cit.). Griffith (ibid.) warned:

> The immediate rationale for the ABC's Web presence relates to: • extending the life and utility of programs; • enhancing audience interaction; • marketing and promoting existing services; • using a new distribution system for existing and new audiences. (ibid.)

Further:

> The ABC will seek to play a similar pioneering role as a champion of Australian culture, information and innovation. In addition, the ABC will transfer to this new medium the public broadcasting values that have guided it since its inception. (Loc Cit.)

And added the caveat:

> It cannot simply rely on its reputation and the loyalty of its established audiences. It needs to reinvent its content and support, building existing and attracting new audiences (ibid.).

In 2005, then Managing Director, Mark Scott, launched ABC 2—Australia's first free-to-air digital TV channel but initially so heavily restricted by the government that it screened only time-shifted content. Cooke (2007)[189] predicted that it could become "a new (if not wealthy) home for the work of Australian writers and program makers" (ibid.). The author (2007) asked rhetorically:

> will it mature beyond the infantile developmental norms of mimicry and self-interest to develop a mind, a voice and a personality of its own and ultimately provide a home for original Australian drama, comedy and entertainment? (ibid.)

It has not. It has failed to engage as a 'multicaster' by leaving its "rusted on" Australian generalist constituency behind and becoming waylaid and distracted by the multitude of online opinion and ideas. In 2007, the ABC integrated its New Media and Digital Services division into the mainstream of the organisation (Cooke, 2007). Reduced budgets and fewer staff have also forced Aunty into adopting the ways of commercial content because they are cheaper. Yet, as Jock Given (1998)[190] pointed out broadcasting was not a single technology but a group of cultural practices, institutional practices, language, forms and technologies coalesced into one institutional framework. It was always going to be complicated for the ABC to transition to platforms and the interactivity of Web 2.0. Given (1998) also explained that for operators in the commercial *field* to be competitive their content had to be exclusive and of quality. He questioned whether broadcasters would be able to continue to serve the public interest on that basis. According to former Chairman, James Spigelman (2013),[191] the ABC operates within the multitudinous value-laden expectations of: "process and accountability … and where the values of efficiency and effectiveness may sometimes need to be balanced against other public values such as accessibility, openness, fairness, impartiality, accountability, legitimacy, participation and honesty" (ibid.). Cambridge Dictionary defined "impartial" as: "not supporting any of the sides involved in an argument".[192]

In 2008 ABC catch-up programming was launched with ABC iView. Head of ABC Digital, Arul Baskaran, said this was "over two years ago, long before any of the others made any moves towards catch-up programming" (Brown, 2010).[193] In 2010 the ABC's 24-Hour News channel was launched, in addition to its three other digital channels. Baskaran said one of the biggest challenges for the ABC was capturing the children to teens and young adult audiences (Brown, ibid.). He justified the ABC's activity on Facebook and Twitter as:

> If people aren't talking about you and if you're not listening to what they're saying then eventually you lose relevance and you're dead. (Brown Loc. Cit.)

The assumption with the construction of the ABC's *Q and A* program, for example, was that there was a "growing trend of audiences to surf the net while watching TV. ... We're looking at Apple and learning from them about what you want on TV" (ibid.). The problem with this is that the web is monetised for a consumer market (Ulin, 2009)[194] "putting the fate of media ... in the balance" (Ulin, ibid.).

Social media is also designed on a "flow" basis in a psychological process of gratification where the user becomes a consumer constantly moving from one piece of content to the next (Bolter, 2019)[195] in a superficial process not linked with the formation of public opinion, but instead personal, clannish, consumerist views. The ABC's motivation is to optimise the consumer's exposure to advertisements (ibid.): "applied to politics, flow buries discussion about civic action under endless streams of text, images, and videos" (Bolter, ibid.). As a consequence, news reports become "flow fodder" (Loc. Cit.). Digitisation of media has thus eroded the ground and model of public broadcasting and growing complaints from commercial media about the intrusions and incursions of the ABC (Spigelman, 2013) are obvious and real in spite of ABC denials and veiled accusations of enemies "trying to destroy the ABC". However, to avoid the "market failure" label of the ABC where it has been described as only meeting the needs of the market unmet by commercial operators, it has sought to take them head-on by fully embracing the values and psychological processes of digital media—in this emergent *field*. The elongated debates and discussions that the ABC pioneered are now a memory in favour of snippets and re-ordered ideas that can actually prevent its publics from understanding issues. In this sense the ABC has embraced fully the "digital disruption" of the attention economy, but to its detriment and that of the public it has been tasked to serve which is sometimes left in a state of "digital disorder".

Former Chairman James Spigelman said the ABC moved from a scarce spectrum to an unlimited one and therefore "the editorial role of a trustworthy intermediary to select and organise the abundance of material has become more important, not less" (Spigelman, 2013) and the need for public broadcasters to build social cohesion, never greater. What is argued in this chapter is that understanding the Australian public broadcaster requires reference to its founding origins and the privileged role it was tasked to perform and develop. Therefore, there is an inherent danger in placing the ABC in the generic category of "public broadcaster" with other overseas public broadcasters because there are national differences due to the variety of political issues and communities that existed in their formations. There are similarities but certainly they are not replicas, where even it has been remarked that "the conspicuous lack of a bill of rights, makes Australia a somewhat unusual democracy" (Jones & Pusey, 2010).[196] However, in a generalist context it means that "who controls, consumes, and distributes information is largely determined by who is best able to navigate digital technology" (Owen, 2018).[197] While public broadcasters have been viewed traditionally as "citizen forming" institutions (Nolan, 2006)[198] they now have to create a new role for themselves in diverting 'eyeballs' to their content.

In 2014, Managing Director Mark Scott announced that after hefty funding cuts from the Federal Government the ABC had merged its Innovation Division into an ABC Digital Network Division:

> with the aim of "prioritising our online and mobile expenditure" and "bring our digital designers, UX, digital project managers and developers together". ... It will ensure we are better placed to identify audience trends and respond to them with new and enhanced products and services ... with ABC Digital Network the key to improving the skills of our digital specialists and unlocking a better audience experience. (Scott, 2014)[199]

This statement also signalled that the ABC would focus on "digital newsgathering skills" in the newsrooms (ibid.). This was a shift from traditional and discrete news gathering and journalistic practices. It was justified on the basis of saving money while trying to "achieve deeper and broader audience engagement and relevance" (Scott, ibid.). It means that journalists are fewer in number and chasing online opinions or crafted public relations in lieu of the legacy skills of interviewing individuals 'on' and 'off' the record, cultivating contacts where news reports took time to develop, or sometimes not develop. Time-poor newsrooms have no time for this laborious reporting. For example, the terminal state of 'rounds' that once covered specific aspects of society and government has brought about a substantial loss of civic knowledge of how governments are held accountable in a democracy, coverage of local councils being just one. In addition, the cuts to specialist units at the ABC have included the Science Unit and the loss of its flagship Catalyst program in 2000, even though the Australian Academy of Science told the Federal Government's Mansfield Report into the ABC in 1996: "the ABC is providing a very important public service that would otherwise be largely absent from broadcasting" (ibid.).[200] Sheridan (2020)[201] said: "digital media companies have destroyed the public square except at the national level" and that "the normal mechanisms of democratic deliberation and accountability have been diminished or erased" (ibid.) due to minimised ABC coverage of local and state governments.

There has also been a loss of specialists investigating religion, ethics, business, industry, state governments, trade unions, economics and the media itself and a diminution of dedicated court reporting at all levels in preference to parachuting general journalists into areas of need. According to a confidential briefing document the new emphasis is on reaching "younger and more diverse Australian audiences" with "topical content that's engaging and accessible" (Meade, 2016).[202] National director of the Uniting Church, the Reverend Elenie Poulos, who met with the Managing Director Michelle Guthrie as part of a group of religious representatives expressed concern that:

> Now more than ever we need a well-informed and well-supported conversation about religion and society and we need spaces where those conversations are well informed and the analysis is deep. (Meade, ibid.)

The changes to the way news content is made and distributed are based on analytics—analysis of audience feedback and tracking data, algorithms and clicks—which may also mean that the headline is read, at best. Research in 2003 of UK broadcasters showed that an absence of in-house journalism training, team-work and time pressures means that journalists were less able to attend to quality issues in their content (Ursell, 2003).[203] Patrolling the 'net' is much cheaper for a cash-strapped newsroom. The ABC seems convinced that it is now avoiding what other media outlets do, yet in moving to the emergent commercial field has failed to reconstruct, translate and cherish its once sovereign role in Australian reporting.

ABC board member Fiona Stanley said, Mark Scott made "efforts to take the ABC from digital laggard to leader" (Hyland, 2015)[204] but he was also criticised by editor-in-chief of *The Australian* Chris Mitchell for "abrogating his responsibilities as editor-in-chief" (Hyland, ibid.). This meant that editorial bias and journalists' free hand with opinion both in content and on social media (which have merged) were unchecked and marred the impartial role of the ABC at a time of surging digital growth. Twitter has become normalised throughout journalistic practices (Santana & Hopp, 2016)[205] and can encourage healthy democratic discussions

(Nah & Chung, 2012)[206] but shaping those spaces for PSMs needs close/r planning when impartiality is their ambition. In 2007, ABC's former Head of Arts and Entertainment Courtney Gibson said (2007)[207] the ABC needed to redraw traditional business models and governing structures as well as manage content. Since then, the business model was certainly overhauled, but the content has been delegated to the audience—hence, a content area that is increasingly ungoverned and ungovernable. Further, it chases unbounded horizons with "tell us your story" (an ABC Television program webpage) and elsewhere an invitation from an ABC News page to send story ideas and tip-offs.

This power to control the message and steer the ship of nationhood should be seen as a potential success for the ABC and a separate topic to its digitised online content, yet it has been made problematised and sullied by the infiltration of opinion as news/content. In terms of digital content in general, the outlook was already tough. Aunty subjected herself to a hostile emergent commercial *field* based on Web 2.0 which thrives on 'peer-to-peer' and 'many-to-many' contact. She aids and abets her journalists in bypassing professional media ethics and standards by encouraging her journalists to speak opinions freely on social media, provided they have a disclaimer that it is their views and not the ABC's. In a 2021 update to its social media policy, the ABC created a divide between official ABC social media accounts and staff personal social media accounts. This is problematised, however, because many of the staff social media accounts identify themselves as ABC employees. The role of disclaimers deserves focus here because the literature said that they exonerated neither the journalist, nor the media outlet. There has been diverse research coalescing around the view that it is not a "get out of jail free" card. The feminist literature, for instance, has found that disclaimers were ineffective in supporting women's positive images of themselves (Fardouly & Holland, 2018)[208] while other research has found that disclaimers used by social media companies alerting audiences to fake news did not stop the news being shared and commented upon (Colliander, 2019).[209] This was because of the overwhelming desires of individuals for conformity and to promote themselves on social media (ibid.).

The ABC's social media policy in 2014 (ABC, 2014)[210] requested staff: "do not imply ABC endorsement of your personal views" (re-worded but with a similar intent in the 2021 revisions) and places responsibility with the employee to "'map' yourself carefully, the level of discretion required" according to seniority and role and that "it is advisable that you also add a statement to the effect that any opinions are all your own and not those of the organisation. This will make it clear that you are not speaking on behalf of the Corporation" (Loc. Cit. 2014) and further "the ABC does not take responsibility (including editorial responsibility) for material posted by an individual on their personal social media account" (ibid.). Further, ABC policy appropriates and endorses the corporate culture of Twitter:

> Twitter in particular has an oft-stated and broadly accepted understanding that a retweet is not necessarily an endorsement. (ABC, 2014)

The 2021 revision advises ABC Twitter users to "take steps to remain safe" (2021). However, the new advisory creates a clear delineation between ABC official content tweets and individual, personal tweets (2021). Academic research literature contradicts this hopefulness (Livingston et al., 2020).[211] Journalists' engagement with citizens in sharing and creating opinions is a disconcerting trend in journalism everywhere, but most especially in PSM, which is required to disseminate diverse, representative views with equanimity, and respect. Aunty has complicated herself. This is because there is a theatrical element to performing on social media and a pressure and ambition to build a personal brand (Brems et al., 2017)[212] and garner peer recognition (Powers & Vera-Zambrano, 2018)[213] and this networking (even when disclaimed), inevitably, supports or acknowledges the brand of the news organisation (Brems, ibid.; Lysak et al., 2012[214]).

In addition, to demur from building a brand as an ABC journalist on Twitter is inconceivable, whether it augurs well for the ABC, or not, because ABC management encourages journalists to do so, especially to "live tweet breaking stories on personal accounts" (ABC, 2021). For ABC Policy to deny the link between the ABC journalist and the ABC organisation is fallacious, delusional and proving dangerous because "with the development of social media the individual is placed on a pedestal" (Brems et al. Loc. Cit.) and posts are not ephemeral. They echo. Seemingly vanishing moments of thought and 'on the fly' reaction are "trackable, traceable and permanent" (Demaria, 2015).[215] This is further problematised by the dubious quality of information harvested from social media (Lysak et al., ibid.) anyway. The public relations literature has already identified social media's capacity as an agenda builder with journalists (Lariscy et al., 2009)[216] and is exploiting that opportunity because it has identified journalists as SMIs (Social Media Influencers) (Schifferes et al., 2014).[217] The ultimate point of a disclaimer is for the organisation to avoid litigation in a situation where social media blurs the line between employee and organisation (Mergel & Greeves, 2013).[218] In one way, a disclaimer creates an alert for the reader to create a distance for themselves from the view expressed (which is the ABC's policy objective), but in another way a disclaimer can, counter-intuitively, verify and attest, "I work for the ABC", making it impossible for the reader to separate the view from the institution, the employee from the employer, the opinion from the report. Overlaying this, the social media argy-bargy takes place in a highly competitive *commercial* media field.

The ABC has emerged as a strong competitor in this emergent field overall because to take another example, and in terms of the competitive nature of the commercial *field*, senior Australian media academic, Graeme Turner (2020), pointed out Australian television government policy "has been to ensure that the existing commercial operators were able to address a mass audience of a sufficient scale to ensure viability" yet the arrival of the ABC into the commercial digital *field* and its multifarious offerings has upped the game. It has put the commercial actors at swords' points with the ABC. The ABC has shifted from savvy complementor to competitor. This book will use a socio-constructivist approach to examine how the precipitous shift in *field* has had unplanned, dire consequences for Aunty's voice.

Aspects of the workings of News Corporation in the commercial *field* will be examined in Chap. 4. These include concerns about News Corporations' chasing of tawdry content, pursuing illegal activities to procure news and using its media power to influence governments (Lieberman, 2007).[219] These activities should help the ABC individuate itself. Yet, the ABC resorts to the frequent use of the threadbare phrase "digital disruption" with the implication that it is every person for themselves—media is shifted profoundly for the ABC now it has to compete on the same terrain, even though the ABC is its own media—and also more than media; because it is a public and cultural educator. In Australia, "media" has not been a generic term because there was public media and private media. However, the internet has helped blur and merge public and private. In a federal government regime of declining funding, the ABC has collapsed its model in favour of the popularism and activism of online media as a means of chasing appeal. It has been snagged by an "adapt or die" (Smolkin, 2006)[220] panic that has gripped all news organisations to build websites, platforms and infiltrate social media. Howard Weaver,

Vice-President for News at the US newspaper business McClatchy, said of this challenge: "You can give up, you can hunker down and bleed, or you can fight back".[221] The ABC chose to pursue a fourth option—abandon its unique *field*, forget to translate and transfer its *reputational capital*, and follow the herd.

Over-riding this, for all the promise of democratisation and participation brought by social media it has failed to be truly representative of society. In 2010 Mark Zuckerberg was named "Person of the Year" by Time Magazine because Facebook altruistically and ironically "wants to populate the wilderness, tame the howling mob and turn the lonely, antisocial world of random chance into a friendly world, a serendipitous world" (Grossman, 2010).[222] Letamendia (2017) criticised digital media in that while it may help build awareness of social injustice, it also fell prey to being commoditised and self-referential, thereby preventing any real improvement in people's lives (Letamendia, 2017).[223] As Tucker et al. (2017)[224] argued social media was not about offering a home for democracy so much as a battleground for competing views, and not all of them supportive of a liberal democracy. It is a territory alive with bots, bot-farms and trolls that destabilise discussion, target political leaders and other individuals and derail government policy. Nonetheless, digital media can bring about awareness of previously hidden issues, a voice for the voiceless and positive change. More of the amorphous and tricky role of social media and the troubled and confused relationship with the ABC's professional journalism will be analysed in Chap. 4.

1.8 Chapter 5: Losing the Brand in the Australian Media Landscape—The ABC's Loss of Privilege and Abandonment of Cultural Rituals

This chapter will develop understandings of how the ABC once fortified its *field* and power status with ritual practices and provide illustrations of how that has waned. Couldry (2003) said, "for Bourdieu, rituals are much more than formalizations of otherwise ordinary action: they are *rites of institution*, which institute as natural, and seemingly legitimate, certain key category differences and boundaries".[225] Couldry (2003) explained that ritualisation worked by drawing people or events into categories—"the ritual space of the media".[226] This was done with program schedules, hourly news bulletins and media events (Couldry, 2003) in which could be included the broadcast of royal weddings and even the ones widely listened-to royal Christmas addresses on the ABC—King George VI's Christmas Address on radio (up to 1951) and then Queen Elizabeth II's Christmas Address (from 1952 on radio and from 1957 television, and ongoing). The ABC ritual of playing the "Majestic Anthem" news theme at the start of radio news bulletins began in 1952 replacing Advance Australia Fair (Ward, 2009).[227] It is a conservative, grand ritual alert to the audience to what is considered serious, important content. The tune says: "we are telling you what we sincerely believe you need to know—(now would be a good time to listen)". This was subtle power. The tune itself has *cultural capital* and individuated the ABC as a solitary player in its *field* of information. Interestingly, it is also an élite sign chosen by the ABC under a conservative government in Australian politics when Sir Robert Menzies was the Liberal Party Prime Minister.

Couldry (2003) observed: "Rituals do not so much express order, as naturalise it; they formalize categories, and the differences or boundaries between categories, in performances that help them seem natural, even legitimate".[228] The ABC's Majestic Anthem became part of the ABC's citizens' ritual. Couldry (ibid.) said these media rituals were:

> Formalized actions organized around key media-related categories and boundaries, whose performance frames, or suggests a connection with, wider media-related values.[229]

He stipulated that these rituals were "associated with broader, shared values".[230] Quoting Catherine Bell (text reference not provided):

> The most central quality of ritualisation is how it organizes our movements around space, helps us to experience constructed features of the environment as real and thereby reproduces the symbolic authority at stake in the categorizations on which ritual draws.[231]

Further Couldry (2003)[232] noted that Bourdieu's theory of ritual allowed the concept of power to be examined as part of the approach, where the exertion of power in such instances was subtle, rather than overt and political. Bell (1997)[233] said all ritual had always been a part of human activity (religion, society and culture) and identified ritual in one form as "cultural communication that transmits the cognitive categories and dispositions that provide people with important aspects of their sense of reality".[234] Bell (1997) acknowledged that while the study of ritual began with religion it had expanded into other areas ("evolutionary, sociological, and psychological"[235]). She stated that: "the media and tourist industry are just two of the more prominent forces helping to shape the context for ritual today".[236] She explained that Bourdieu had already identified "values are embodied and reproduced by means of strategies of human 'practice' that are rarely conscious or explicit".[237] They are replicated through ritual.

The role of the media has provided rituals for our lives (Couldry, 2003)[238] by offering us a voice that speaks from the "centre" of the "social world" (Couldry, ibid.).[239] As Bourdieu (1980) pointed out there was a strong co-relation between people who listened to classical music broadcasts, visited art galleries, had knowledge of paintings and "own a record player" (Bourdieu, 1980).[240] He identified three 'tastes' that have distinctive class associations and provide a logic: level 1, Legitimate Taste (lovers of classical music); level 2, Middle-brow Taste ('Rhapsody in Blue' and Renoir paintings); and level 3, Popular Taste (music devalued by popularisation) (ibid).[241] According to Bourdieu (1980), the educational institution, which can include the ABC, does not teach or demand 'cultural practices', rather it exerts an "allocation effect" (ibid.)[242] whereby it bestows acknowledgement and provides access (ibid.) to its audience (to reprise a previous observation on the Majestic Anthem: "now would be a good time to listen"). This was a powerful gate-keeping role for the organisation that has now vanished with the shift of media to the over-run 'wild west' territory of digital content.

This book argues that the ABC has drifted from its exclusive, élite and educational journalism *field* (see Diagram 1.1 previously) and left behind Bourdieu's (1979)[243] *legitimate taste* for *popular taste* in both form and content in an attempt to remain what it defined as relevant by joining the competition and rivalry from online interactive, commercial media. This social media-dominated field boasts greater relevance and certainly provides immediacy but this has infiltrated the way in which journalists and broadcasters report, research and engage with their audience/consumers/Australians. Importantly, and from a parochial perspective, it has changed fundamentally how they speak to/with/for Australians. It has undermined their pre-existing élite *capital* in favour of a *vox populi* approach driven by social media and its attendant commercial media outlets. Hence, the ABC has run headlong into an even bigger clash with *News Corporation*, which considered that it already "owned" the field of commercial media (and probably did) because of its size and extent. Except News Corporation is a commercial media outlet inhabiting the emergent field with the doxa of the commercial *field*, and not from a former public service *field*—debates about media plurality, media monopolies stifling debate, and general news content quality decline in the emergent field notwithstanding. Concerns about deteriorating news quality has been a concern for all respected operators in the commercial field. Relevance and immediacy were once two key areas presided over exclusively by the professional media but this has become blurred by online information. The ABC, at the expense of its own *cultural capital*, rushed to fit-in with digitisation but failed to reflect how it could merge, augment, translate its own exclusive *field* in a media market being deprived of analysis of general, public, commonwealth interests, global issues and has instead been overwhelmed with personal issues and angry groups.

The ABC's own *field* had been buttressed and defined by three key factors. First, its Charter (see Table 1.1) that requires it to provide news, information and entertainment to *all* Australians. Second, its management policies that have instructed it to educate Australia and, so, as a public broadcaster and public servant the ABC has been a primary educator of Australians. Third, the ABC had been sustained by persistent élitist support, encouraged by the ABC's priority to articulate Australian culture, provide educational programming, conduct editorial inquiries and explore ideas and the consequences of facts. It had the job of enculturating Australians, and it did. As Bourdieu and Wacquant (1992) argued all public services were calibrated to the values of the middle class. These public services have also attracted the activists and advocated causes of the middle class. Allied with this was the warning that these powerful social groups could change the rules of the *field* in which the public service played so that they "function to their advantage" (Bourdieu & Wacquant, 1992).[244] In order to "transform" the *field*, these groups have to change "the rules of the game" (ibid.)[245] and change the ABC if necessary. One of the starting points for change would have to be the ABC Charter.

The symbolic power exercised initially by ABC Radio since 1932 and then also by ABC Television can be considered two-tracked. For example, Scannell (2019) said radio (and television) made talk "visible" in two ways—it was "public" and it was "historical" (ibid.).[246] That radio was once live to air, entirely, gave it veracity, proximity and immediacy and "is a pervasive effect of the medium" (Scannell, 1991).[247] It gave the ABC substantial power over a large continent. The unique qualities of live radio

Table 1.1 Charter of the Australian Broadcasting Corporation (Section 6 of ABC Act 1983). Available at: https://www.legislation.gov.au/Details/C2018C00079

1. The functions of the Corporation are:
   a. to provide within Australia innovative and comprehensive broadcasting services of a high standard as part of the Australian broadcasting system consisting of national, commercial and community sectors and, without limiting the generality of the foregoing, to provide:
      i. broadcasting programs that contribute to a sense of national identity and inform and entertain, and reflect the cultural diversity of, the Australian community; and
      ii. broadcasting programs of an educational nature;
   b. to transmit to countries outside Australia broadcasting programs of news, current affairs, entertainment and cultural enrichment that will:
      i. encourage awareness of Australia and an international understanding of Australian attitudes on world affairs; and
      ii. enable Australian citizens living or travelling outside Australia to obtain information about Australian affairs and Australian attitudes on world affairs; and
   b-a. to provide digital media services; and
   c. to encourage and promote the musical, dramatic and other performing arts in Australia.

Note: See also section 31AA (Corporation or prescribed companies to be the only providers of Commonwealth-funded international broadcasting services).

2. In the provision by the Corporation of its broadcasting services within Australia:
   a. the Corporation shall take account of:
      i. the broadcasting services provided by the commercial and community sectors of the Australian broadcasting system;
      ii. the standards from time to time determined by the Australian Communications and Media Authority (ACMA) in respect of broadcasting services;
      iii. the responsibility of the Corporation as the provider of an independent national broadcasting service to provide a balance between broadcasting programs of wide appeal and specialised broadcasting programs;
      iv. the multicultural character of the Australian community; and
      v. in connection with the provision of broadcasting programs of an educational nature—the responsibilities of the States in relation to education; and
   b. the Corporation shall take all such measures, being measures consistent with the obligations of the Corporation under paragraph (a), as, in the opinion of the Board, will be conducive to the full development by the Corporation of suitable broadcasting programs.
3. The functions of the Corporation under subsection (1) and the duties imposed on the Corporation under subsection (2) constitute the Charter of the Corporation.
4. Nothing in this section shall be taken to impose on the Corporation a duty that is enforceable by proceedings in a court.

Australian Government, The. Federal Register of Legislation. ABC Charter, Section 6 ABC Act 1983. [online]. Retrieved 3 January 2020 from https://www.legislation.gov.au/Details/C2018C00079

cannot be replicated through podcasts, for example, which allow podcasters to listen in their own time, in their own way, and in their own place. The old style of broadcasting news bulletins, for example, creates the impression that the news is happening now. Podcasts can be listened to repeatedly. The intimacy of live radio that explored the tension between ephemerality and incandescence through an accompanying nuanced human fragility—hearing a presenter think on their feet, for example, is gone. This change is developed further in this chapter. While the ABC was threatened from the outset, never before has the threat been more intense because of three new reasons: incursions and threats made by digital journalism, an eroding funding base and its own infiltrations into its antipodes of media—the emergent commercial sphere—that operates for profit, not as an exclusive public good. The ABC is experiencing a fierce backlash from commercial media, and its perceived bête noire Rupert Murdoch. It has made these forays into a dangerous *field*. It tracks down elusive audiences via broadband and social media in the commercial *field* as part of its quest for relevance and justification of funding.

1.9 Chapter 6: Political Influences on the ABC—ABC Journalists, Impartial Intermediaries

This chapter seeks to refine understandings of political influences on the ABC, not through polarised depictions of various political parties and who did what to whom, why and how they felt, but rather to consider some of the debates about the role of politics in the institution of the ABC. This will serve to explore whether or not political views and ideologies influence program-making and news coverage. There are renewed questions as to whether the ABC costs "too much" as a publicly funded broadcaster in a crowded commercial *field*. This book argues for a distraction from that defensive debate about political influence and meddling in favour of a more empowered, proactive role and mindset for the ABC to rise to the needs of a quality-challenged news world. This chapter will unpack the enduring cultural role of the organisation that has entrenched it in Australian life where it has built Australian élitism through privileged representation, participation and education. This is a role that could and should sustain the organisation. This book also argues how that status has been eroded through the rush and pressures to digitisation and the reckless abandonment of the reputation acquired in the ABC *field*, the shift of journalism training from the "shop floor" to universities and the pursuit of populist or marginal issues that are being promoted on social media rather than reflecting the more general but profoundly resonant public interests of all Australians. The rise of the celebrity journalist has also pressured ABC journalists into the pursuit of individual popularity that was previously viewed as inappropriate and unwanted, prior to digitisation. Yet, the literature cautioned that new media environments were not liberated frontiers for journalists to roam, rather there were "limits and boundaries" on how they should operate (Carr & Bard, 2018)[248] to sustain their reputations.

The political shifts in organisational language to describe the ABC's corporate vision have occurred over time and, in part, measure this change. For example, in the 1980s the organisation ran promotions on ABC television with the strap line: "It's your ABC". It was an insistence on Australians' cultural ownership of the ABC that helped it accumulate its importance, more so than any vicissitudes of favourable politics, ideologies and funding. Latterly, the use of the pronouns "ours" and "yours" in advertising and promotions is linked more with a defence mechanism to reclaim the past but protect against criticism. It also supports a defensive staff culture and implies an attendant need for its actors to secure status and prominence, where the notion of belonging to "ours" and "yours" gives reflexive endowment of celebrity status and therefore is seen as reinforcing the necessity of the ABC: "we are prominent, therefore you need us, we belong together". Yet, in this whole emphasis on ABC belonging, which generally indicates "cultural, belonging to a religion, a social or professional group, an ideology, or a political party" (Girard & Grayson, 2016),[249] there is no central understanding of where the actual audiences now see themselves as belonging. What are the audience allegiances and how have they been mapped? The disparateness of digital media and its welcome of conversations and stories from those who supply them means Australians are no longer encultured with, or by, the ABC—they are enculturing each other, and this is a significant power shift for a powerful institution to encourage. Australians are in effect educating each other, but are these stories in the larger national interest? It means the task of drawing generalised, applicable meaning from stories is impossible and questions the validity of the ABC's claim to "yours" and "ours", because such Institutional Logics are now beyond the purview of the organisation, merely through its use of language.

The ABC was built by people with a public service ethos—and this research found a striking dissimilarity and diversity of political affiliations among people who support Aunty. Those diametrically opposed to each other, politically, believe as passionately in the ABC as the other. The perpetuated and reiterated belief that the Australian Labor Party (ALP) is the only supporter of the ABC with The National Party a vague supporter and the Liberal Party of Australia definitely not a supporter is wrong. This research does not bear that out. It wildly misrepresents the truth and perpetuating it does damage to the respect and esteem held for the institution. The research found that Aunty has a politically eclectic group of supporters who gaze at it through a partisan lens, certainly, and see things differently, but they see the same institution. And they look with support and concern. For example, alienating certain people and groups has not helped the ABC's cause when regional Australians who vote for the conservative National Party are also fervid ABC supporters and audiences. In fact, the politicised push-back and labelling has disappointed her diverse supporters. On the other hand, it needs to be noted that the ABC has been hypersensitised and upset by partisanship—with political interference by governments in the appointment of board members as rewards for other service, rather than for their devotion to, and profound knowledge of, public broadcasting and the ABC. Recruitments to the board, or management, of folks without public broadcasting knowledge is an ongoing tension.

Staff political priorities have also changed. Journalists now have a priority to build audiences for themselves—and by default their employer. Researching, writing and publishing content is no longer enough—it has to be promoted and marketed by the content creator as well. Where once having a radio news story on the now defunct 07.45 am radio news bulletin was the highpoint of the journalist's day, not only has that opportunity been taken away but news reports now have to have many iterations and platforms to be viable—one "airing" is not enough. Alongside this is the highly contentious belief, mentioned earlier, that social media informs journalists of public opinion with depth, generalisability and quality (Murphy et al., 2014)[250] because it has been found in research that "social media users are not representative of the wider general public" (Murphy et al., ibid.).[251] In cultivating audiences for their content, journalists may only be listening to an echo chamber, each other, fake news, or its ally—filter bubbles. Cultivating contacts over the telephone and keeping a written contact book is now a truly primitive concept in journalism. Yet, in terms of the professional practice and *habitus* its loss means the personal and hidden contact trail can be public, with journalists now obliged to transition towards online profiles to build website traffic. Journalists now reveal their friends. They were walked away from the contact book to become commodified—and commoditise their contacts in the transition. Everyone can be tracked and traced.

This paradox, referred to as "mass-personal" communication (O'Sullivan, 2005),[252] has created two disturbing phenomena with the merger of: private and impersonal, and public and personal. In that process biases, leanings and manipulations are revealed—if only through re-postings, comments, reactions and 'likes'. Even more subtle are the influences of journalists' social bookmarkings to curate favourite websites and links.[253] Indeed, the use of Facebook and Twitter has become part of professional 'practice' (Santana & Hopp, 2016). Not only are ABC journalists building personal brands they augment the corporation's brand and those two are indivisible. It is a situation referred to in the literature as "a double-edged sword" (Lee, 2015)[254] where social media also functions as news platforms merged with personal communication (Lee, ibid.)[255] and arguing that news platforms and personal communication are separate is problematic and unconvincing.

Further, research has shown journalists' social media audience engagement has created negative audience perceptions towards the organisation's news and even the organisation itself (Lee, 2015). As a consequence, this book argues that the ABC has not only shifted its ***field*** but also sacrificed its ***cultural capital*** through the infiltration of opinion in lieu of fact and point-of-view content sharing. The ABC created their ***field*** by setting its own rules of the game—***doxa*** and its content creators' opinions frowned upon. Its new ***field*** is not theirs alone and, in part, the audience is in charge; the giant, profitable internet organisations are also in charge—this pressures content makers to shift towards opinions to accompany and accommodate populist issues in order to appear popular. The ABC struggles with this audience supremacy because not only has it previously been in control, but embedded in its purpose is a primary need to attend to Bourdieu's (1990) middle-class values and expectations of both the public service and its old ABC ***field***. Aunty is bereft. She has had to "kill her darlings" or forget them: these were special to her, especially exclusivity, uniqueness and contemplated, experimental, creative expression in her own time and in her own way. She has had to fit-in with the happening now, anytime is deadline, get 'liked', emergent commercial ***field***. The turf war in the commercial field is apparent and undeniable for a public broadcaster.

Aunty believed in herself and her ***field*** and "belief is thus an inherent part of belonging to a ***field***" (Bourdieu, 1990)[256] because the literary ***field*** "is an independent social universe with its own laws of functioning" (Bourdieu, ibid.)[257] but is also "the economic world reversed" (Loc. Cit.).[258] Cultural production within this *field* must then "not only produce the object of its materiality, but also the value of this object ... artistic legitimacy" (ibid.). The ABC did just that. Bourdieu (1990) said that while artists and writers were dominant they were also dominated by "struggles in the social world" (ibid.)[259] and the ABC has been a site of these struggles. Within the *field* is *doxa*, which "is the relationship of immediate adherence that is established in *practice* between a *habitus* and the *field* to which it is attuned" (Bourdieu, 1990) and "a universe of tacit pre-suppositions that organise action with the *field*" (Benson & Neveu, 2005).[260] According to Bourdieu (2005) journalists belonged to their own journalistic *field*, and in the case of the ABC it once had a more powerful relationship with Australians than with other commercial media, merely because of its public covenant (the Charter).

While ABC ratings remain positive such that it is the most trusted news organisation in Australia by its own measurement, as well as Roy Morgan Research, the Australia Institute and Ipsos. Yet, the ABC's own figures also show a declining trust in the organisation not only by audiences but from within, from staff. In 2017 staff engagement dropped to 46% (52% in 2015), attributed to unhappiness with management (Watkins, 2018).[261] In-house training once supported the *habitus* of the staff (the actors within the *field* of the ABC), so their function became second nature (*habitus*). The Charter is a potent reminder of the responsibility of staff to uphold the ABC's pledge to the Australian people. Although not a legally enforced document, the Charter has subliminal iterations and understanding from Australia's citizens with all the other legal agreements the individual makes in a lifetime. The ABC has had symbolic capital in the three letters of the organisation's name. There was some consternation among staff when it was decided by senior management during the time of Managing Director Michelle Guthrie leadership of a downgrading of the ABC's cultural and economic capital when the 'ABC' letters were dropped in favour of the ABC's accompanying unending wavelength symbol, only. The symbolic capital of the three letters A-B-C plus the wavelength symbol (Lissajous) had given the ABC advantage, prestige and capacity for leverage operating in its *field* because it referenced ABC's respected, reputable content (Image 1.2). The photograph of the Friends of the ABC sticker shows how embedded the ABC has become in Australian culture. It achieved an

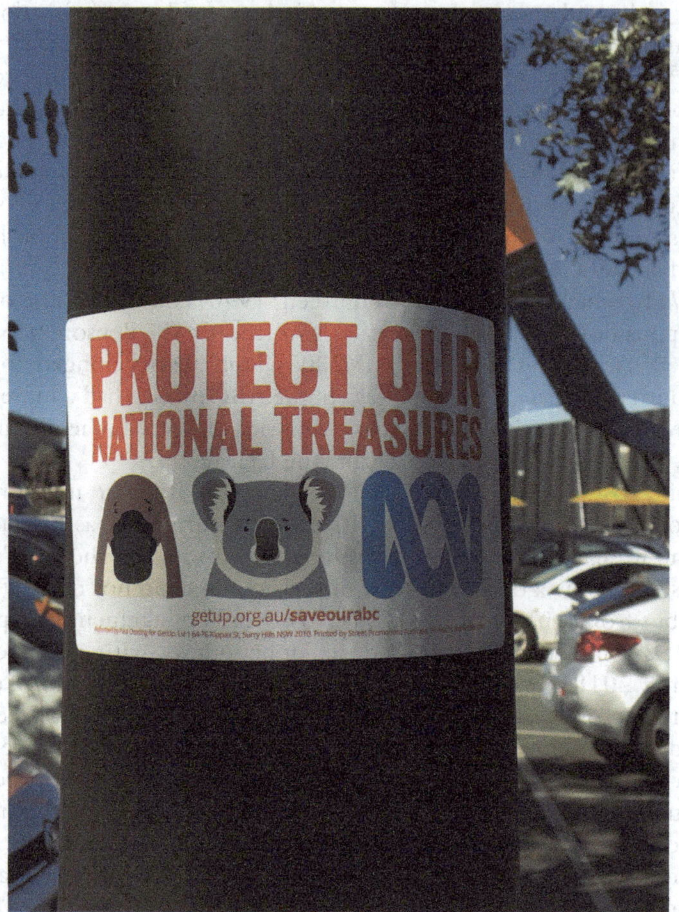

Image 1.2 The ABC Lissajous (far right) in a sticker made by Friends of the ABC on a light pole in a Canberra public carpark. It shows how the ABC has been appropriated as an endangered "animal" (icon), along with the Australian animals the platypus (far left) and koala (middle). All have been anthropomorphised with mournful eyes and the stark dissimilarities between a national institution and national fauna overlooked to press the link between the ABC and Australian identity—the space of shared habitus between the three. Photo: Virginia Small

iconic status (interestingly here with endangered native animals) in the mindset of Australians that the commercial operators could only dream of attaining.

Bourdieu said *habitus* was:

> Structured structures predisposed to function as structuring structures that is as principles which generate and organize 'practice's and representations that can be objectively adapted to their outcomes without presupposing a conscious aiming at ends or an express mastery of the operations necessary in order to attain them. (Bourdieu, 1990)[262]

It was "a system of dispositions common to all products of the same conditionings" (Bourdieu, ibid.).[263]

Diagram 1.1 helped to describe how the ABC has shifted *field*, using Bourdieusian theory and an interpretation of Bourdieu's *field* theory. Part of this drifting of the ABC into the emergent commercial/social media field has been a loss of *capital.* Bourdieu (1986) claimed *economic capital* was "immediately and directly convertible into money and may be institutionalized" and in the case of the ABC this could be represented in the form of ABC funding and Australian citizens interest in funding the ABC. But it also has economic capital in its valuable name (ABC). Hence talk of privatisation pressures points to a loss of *capital*, or at least a commercial monetisation of a national asset. *Cultural capital* was "convertible, on certain conditions, into economic capital and may be institutionalized in the forms of educational qualifications" (ibid.) and this could be applied to the ABC in terms of its reputation for quality, independent, mostly impartial news. While there is also quality news within the commercial *field*, the ABC's shift into social media and citizen journalism means that individuals can control the news agenda rather than the traditional editors and content makers—the ABC gatekeepers—and commercial online activities, including advertising and the commoditisation and parcelling-up of audiences, have infiltrated ABC content, beliefs, plans and without prior planning to retain a point of difference.

In essence, the ABC has exercised forms of *symbolic power* (Bourdieu, 1991)[264]: *economic* and *cultural*, which are "invisible power which can be exercised only with the complicity of those who do not want to know that they are subject to it or even that they themselves exercise it" (ibid.).[265] This power accumulated so that the institution could dominate another class (*symbolic violence*) (ibid.),[266] specifically other media, and influence profoundly Australian cultural life. *Symbolic power* is a mutually agreed system that permits "the power of constructing reality" (ibid.).[267] The ABC had for decades constructed the reality of Australianness and, accordingly, what mattered to Australians, where (to paraphrase Scanlon (1989)) it alerted Australians to moments of Australianness and Australians readily coalesced and fell in behind the lead of the institution. Bourdieu (1991) said that in parliamentary democracies there existed a power struggle between the government and the people with a "struggle for the monopoly of the legitimate use of objectified public resources—the law, the army, police, public finances etc." (ibid.).[268] We can add here public media—the ABC. It then becomes vital that the political powers can control the group, but in addition to this there is the friction from the needs of the people also craving ascendancy (ibid.).[269]

The ABC's symbolic power in Australian society and culture was such that, in Bourdieu's (1991) interpretation of power, it made "people see and believe, of confirming or transferring the vision of the world, and thereby, action on the world and thus the world itself".[270] The ABC once created a worldview of Australians, by Australians, for Australians. There was no serious competition because of its dominance of its own cultural *field*. It had its own sandpit. Then other content—news, current affairs and programs—emerged which harvested this goodwill and credibility and used it as a starting point to build its own status as the premier news provider in Australia. And so it did. The prevailing power and influence of the organisation or government, under which the journalist worked, was identified by Bourdieu (1990) as a locus of activity that involved action and context.[271] According to Bourdieu, the focus on the ***habitus*** of the writer was critical to understand his (sic) position, in that, Bourdieu (1990) said the position taken was an unconscious creation and re-creation of perceptions and *practices*.[272]

Bourdieu (1986) said the various forms of capital had been facilitated by the adoption of economic theory and the necessity of exchanges[273]: "it is not possible to account for the structure and functioning of the social world unless one re-introduced capital in all its forms" (1986).[274] The ABC's ***cultural capital*** was the mindset of the organisation, what it produced and the aspects of the organisation that guaranteed its ***reputational capital*** and ***cultural capital***, such as the ABC brand and its high-profile staff. In Institutional Logics there are similar sites of ontological struggle and contestation for leadership and outcomes within an organisation; and, incorporating Bourdieu into organisational studies research has been undertaken by Mutch (2003), Maclean, Harvey and Chia (2010) and Reed (2012), amongst others.[275]

There has been prior analysis of the cultural production of the ABC using Bourdieu, notably by Johnson (1988)[276] and Jackson (2008)[277] who analysed the interface between culture, institutional policy-making and decision-making. Jackson (ibid.) said, using Bourdieu's theories "provides a more rigorous and systematic approach to understanding the cultural roots of policy formulation and decision-making" (Jackson, 2008)[278] because Bourdieu's theories of *field* and *habitus* "provide a useful way of understanding what culture is and how it shapes social interaction at all levels from individuals, institutions and social groups through to the state" (Jackson, 2008).[279] Jackson (ibid.) said the usefulness of Bourdieu was: "his approach is to focus on the strategies of social actors and to show how these are produced by the interplay of their individual *habitus* and the structures of the particular *field* in which they are acting" (ibid.). The actors, within the institutions and without, make subjective choices that accord with the *field* in which they operate.

The ABC is a major player in the Australian news media and the primacy of its role in the *field* of news and current affairs has grown significantly but was consistently important and durable. It has long ago left behind the role of being Australia's major music outlet with the infiltration of digital music outlets and apps, which means there had to be a shift in priority and the ABC moved to emphasise its role in journalism. An analysis of this will give important insights into understanding the pressures and challenges the ABC has faced. Much of ABC content is now the work of the ABC journalist—the majority of ABC employees now work in News, Analysis and Investigation (32.3%).[280] And in 2019 the ABC described itself as having "news and current affairs coverage that holds power to account and contributes to a healthy democratic process".[281] The organisation said its editorial policies and the ABC Act "ensure that the gathering and presentation of news and information is accurate and impartial according to the recognised standards of objective journalism".[282] Bourdieu (1990) declared that writers create their own "perceptions and practices"[283] and the roles of The Charter, The ABC Act and the journalist are reflexive and normalise ABC *habitus*, but at the same time are in the process of continual re-definition, as this book will analyse.

In placing the ABC within Bourdieu's theoretical *field* framework it should be noted that Bourdieu distinguished between learned journalistic practices (news values) that were acquired, or inculcated, as a result of training (generic skills of asking who, what, when, why and how in order to write and sub-edit a news report) as being separate from the values of the organisation, which, according to Bourdieu (1994), also required conformity: "doing one's duty as a man means conforming to the social order; this is fundamentally a question of respecting rhythms, keeping pace, not falling out of line".[284] ABC journalists, for example, have the skills of the trade acquired at university but also, and according to Bourdieu's theory (1994), must then align themselves with the social order of the organisation; they must work within a staff culture. How topics or issues are represented on the ABC can also be analysed in terms of Bourdieu's understandings of sources of power, or *symbolic power*, which he described as the ability "of making people see and believe, of confirming or transferring the vision of the world, and thereby, action on the world and thus the world itself".[285] The power of the ABC journalist's role in expressing depictions of power is of interest to this research, as is the prevailing power of the institution or government under which the journalist works. Bourdieu (1990) identified this 'practice' as a locus of activity that involved action and context.[286]

Bourdieu's theories of *field* and *capital* can be used to understand how actors "are shaped by, and also shape, the organizational contexts in which they work" (Tomlinson et al., 2013).[287] Bourdieu (1984) said:

> The charismatic leader manages to be for the group what he is for himself, instead of being for himself, like those dominated in the symbolic struggle, what he is for others. He 'makes' the opinion that 'makes' him.[288]

Added to that the words that groups use to describe themselves can endow them with power: "so to mobilize the union that makes them strong, around the unifying power of a word".[289] In this instance, that of the ABC. Bourdieu (2005) explained that an entire organisation could be a *field*:

> Though the surrounding *field* affects its structure, this embedded *field*, as a specific relation of force and area of fee play, defines the very terms and stakes of the struggle, giving a particular cast to the, which often renders them unintelligible, as first sight, from the outside.[290]

1.10 Chapter 7: Future Options—A Fourth Estate in Disarray, Clouds on the Horizon

This chapter discusses the Fourth Estate, its future and as a term used to describe all news media outlets. As a mythical ideal and in its original form, newspapers were the Fourth Estate, and their role was to be a custodian of the principles of a plural society. Its legitimacy has been disputed regularly

(Schultz, 1998)[291] as is its impartiality, yet there is still a distinct commercial advantage of appearing unbiased. This objective role has been used, historically, as a very successful marketing tool in the enticement of advertisers to sell their wares in newspapers. The "objectivity" of the Fourth Estate bestowed veracity to its content and attracted readers and advertisers, especially department stores which were once major clients of newspapers in the 1920s. It was not until after World War I that there was "*an emergence of serious professional distance about objectivity*" (Høyer & Pöttker, 2005).[292] Then again, the idea of the Fourth Estate segues with the belief that the public sphere should be informed because of the public's right to know, a concept first articulated at the turn of the nineteenth century (Stephens, 2007).[293]

It is understood that the public has a right to know in a democracy so that it can make informed decisions, articulate its public voice at times of crisis, change or choice because "a free and informative press is widely agreed to be crucial to the democratic process" (Gentzkow et al., 2006).[294] There is a powerful case for PSM in a democracy. For example, McChesney (2012)[295] warned that journalism in the US was "in freefall collapse"[296] because the internet was destroying the Fourth Estate due to commercial and advertising pressures exacting a toll on news organisations. As a consequence, there was an imperative to shed staff. This had "gutted and trivialized" news to the extent that: "we are now rapidly approaching a point where there is nowhere near sufficient journalism for the constitutional system to succeed" (McChesney, 2012).[297]

Quality newspapers once provided an advocacy role and were supposed to be 'watchdogs' holding the powerful to account. Procedurally, for speedier dissemination, the inverted triangle style of writing was important to newspapers where the most important information was in the first sentence and information included in decreasing order of importance in subsequent sentences. This was a situation said to be predicated by the unreliability of the telegraph line upon which the news was dispersed, so that if the line dropped out, the recipient had the most important information (hopefully the first paragraph) to hand. Newspapers once set the news agenda for the day. Daily printed copies of all major metropolitan and national newspapers delivered to the ABC newsrooms were consumed by its editors. Now, digital news has been overwhelmed by the infiltration of public relations and promotional or opinion material which has been merged with, or is taken, as fact. Depleted staffing means an impoverishment of research and editing time and debilitated capacity to check. This is coupled with an increased pressure to publish first where there is no longer a deadline online. Newsrooms have been riven with unforeseen challenges.

Commercialism has never been estranged from the operations of the Fourth Estate and newspapers began as commercial exercises dependent on advertising to pay for journalists, so commercialism was also a part of newspapers' public contract to invigilate power on behalf of their readers. However, the legitimacy of this relationship between the media and the public has also always been contested (Schultz, 1998)[298]. Then layered upon this have been the manoeuvres, interests and ambitions of media proprietors. So, while newspapers always promoted themselves as neutral, they were in fact fussy gatekeepers always with an eye to the need to acknowledge and draw on the income of advertisements and especially classified advertisements from which profits were once their major income (referred to in the industry as "the rivers of gold"). The cover price of a newspaper was only ever a token towards the true cost of publishing a paper. Advertisers benefited from this aspiration of editorial distance in the limelight of Fourth Estate's honesty and integrity. Being impartial was once highly marketable for newspapers with journalists wedded to their sense of independence.

Further, it would be difficult *not* to find in newspapers' original mission statements words, or synonyms of, veracity and truth. Even the titles of newspapers gave a platform for those aspirations of reliable, contextual, accurate truth: *The Daily Telegraph*, *The Mirror*, *The Sun*, *The Age*, *The Sydney Morning Herald*, *The Mercury*, *The Cairns Post*, *The Herald-Sun* and so on; and although a scandal rag, the ironically named old Sydney tabloid newspaper *The Truth* even tried to get into the '*journalistic field*' with its own interpretation of honesty through scandal. The *Geelong Advertiser*'s Latin motto was "*fortis est veritas*" ("truth is strong") and the *Melbourne Times*[299] published itself under the motto: "The welfare of the people is the first great law" (*Melbourne Times*, 1842).

Originally, shared orally at the village well or at the market spread by couriers and travelling peddlers when populations were largely illiterate, minstrels sang the news in ballads as a kind of performance; they juggled and did stunts, too. Later, town criers read news. These expressions of information later became printed newspapers giving people a sense of what Benedict Anderson (1983)[300] described as "an imagined community", where people could envisage a social construct beyond their immediate community of nationhood which included a perception of the lives and existences of other, different, far away nations. "News" has since undergone a revolution: defined as public events (Frank, 1961)[301] "overwhelmingly" sourced from government figures (DiMaggio, 2009)[302] where news is truth (HØyer & Pöttker, 2005).[303] The rise of social media and public relations news has brought about hyper-commercialised content sharing, curating and overlaying with interpretation, contradictions, feelings and opinion. It is as if the news has gone back in time to its original, colourful, interpretative, performance-based minstrel delivery that took place up to the seventeenth century. It was highly subjective, open to interpretation and entertainment based—the same theatrical approach to news can be found on the internet. The Fourth Estate's news has pivoted the half-circle, backwards to its theatrical days. News, augmented by a vibrant and endlessly remitting social media community alive with pursuivants, is entertainment once more. The intervention and wisdom of a robust, critical, sceptical, research-based ABC within this emergent, disparate, contradictory commercial field were never more needed in Australia.

Notes

1. The semi-publicly funded Special Broadcasting Service (SBS) established in 1978, which was set up to cater for the ethnic minorities of Australia that were considered under-served by the ABC. SBS began to accept paid advertising in 1989 to supplement a decline in Federal Government funding.
2. Milne, J. and Guthrie, M. (2018). *ABC Annual Report.* Welcome. Retrieved from: https://about.abc.net.au/wp-content/uploads/2018/10/AP18_Vol1_FINALnew.pdf.
3. Lallo, M. (2020). ABC workers face anxious wait over job, program cuts. [online]. *The Herald Sun.* 1 March 2020. Retrieved from https://www.heraldsun.com.au/blogs/andrew-bolt/more-abc-staff-less-value/news-story/e6f8bc5271a1f93606b916a39bddd1b8.
4. *ABC Annual Report* 1932–1933, p. 5.
5. Ibid., p. 17.
6. Loc. Cit.
7. *ABC Annual Report* 1939–1940. p. 11.
8. Inglis, K. (2002). The Media - Aunty at seventy: A health report on the ABC. [online]. 27 November 2002. *Analysis and Policy Observatory.* Retrieved 4 March 2020 from https://apo.org.au/node/6627.
9. Kress, G. (1985). Linguistic processes in sociocultural practice. Deakin University Press. Waurn Ponds, Vic. p. 6.

10. Centre for Media Transition. (2020). News in Australia Impartiality and commercial influence. [online]. January 2020. Retrieved from: https://www.acma.gov.au/sites/default/files/2020-01/News%20in%20Australia_Impartiality%20and%20commercial%20influence_Review%20of%20literature%20and%20research.pdf.
11. Mason, M. (2020a). AAP set to close after 85 years. [online]. *The Australian Financial Review.* Retrieved from: https://www.afr.com/companies/media-and-marketing/aap-set-to-close-in-june-20200303-p546fd.
12. Dailey, D. & Starbird, K. (2014). *Journalists as Crowdsourcerers: Responding to Crisis by Reporting with a Crowd Computer Supported Cooperative Work* (CSCW). 23. pp. 445–481. DOI 10.1007/s10606-014-9208-z.
13. Galston, W. (2018). *The Populist Challenge to Liberal Democracy.* [online]. Brookings Institute. 17 April 2018. Retrieved from: https://www.brookings.edu/research/the-populist-challenge-to-liberal-democracy/.
14. Newman, N. with Fletcher, R., Levy, D.A.L. & Kleis Nielsen, R. (2016). Digital News Report. [online]. *Reuters Institute & Oxford University.* Retrieved from: http://media.digitalnewsreport.org/wp-content/uploads/2018/11/Digital-News-Report-2016.pdf?x89475.
15. Rousseau, J.J. (1762 in 2003 Edition & Transl. V. Gourevitch). *The Social Contract and other later political writings.* Cambridge University Press. Cambridge. p. xxii.
16. ABC (2019a). ABC NEWS named Accessible App of the Year. [online]. 19th December 2019. *ABC.* Retrieved from: https://about.abc.net.au/press-releases/abc-news-named-accessible-app-of-the-year/.
17. Inglis, K. (1983). *This is the ABC. The Australian Broadcasting Commission 1932–1983.* Melbourne University Press. p. 8.
18. Bourdieu, P. (1984). *Sociology in Question.* Sage Publications. London and California. p. 20.
19. Dubois, E., Gruzd, A. & Jacobson, J. (2020). Journalists' Use of Social Media to Infer Public Opinion: The Citizens' Perspective. *Social Science Computer Review.* 38:1. pp. 57–74. Retrieved from: https://doi.org/10.1177/0894439318791527.
20. Created by ABC Senior Graphic Designer Bill Kennard in 1965 who won the £25 staff competition prize for a new logo (Hogan, I & Kennard, S. (2001). Auntie's artist who gave us that squiggle. [online]. *The Sydney Morning Herald.* 27 September 2001. Retrieved from: http://www.milesago.com/Obits/kennard-obit.htm. It was named after the French physicist Jules Antoine Lissajous (1822 to 1880) who first observed the figure eight wave of sound produced by tuning forks.

21. Inglis, K. (1983). *This is the ABC: The Australian Broadcasting Commission 1932–1983.* Melbourne University Press. Melbourne. p. 25.
22. Chadwick. P. (2012). Adapting a public broadcaster's self-regulation for the convergence era. [online]. *RIPE@2012 Conference*, Sydney 4–7 September 2012. Retrieved from: http://about.abc.net.au/wp-content/uploads/2012/10/AdaptingAPublicBroadcastersSelfRegulationForTheConvergenceEraRIPE2012.pdf.
23. *Courier Mail, The.* (1938, 8 January). Catering for diverse tastes: ABC policy explained at 4QR opening. [online]. p. 13. Retrieved from Trove.
24. Petersen, N. (1993). *News not Views: The ABC, the Press, & Politics 1932–1947.* Hale & Iremonger. Sydney. p. 19.
25. FarmOnline & AAP (2020). ABC Life becomes ABC Local as national broadcaster restructured. [online]. *FarmOnline.* 24 June 2020. Retrieved from: https://www.farmonline.com.au/story/6804883/regional-focus-boost-for-abc-in-major-restructure/.
26. ABC (2016). ABC submission to the House of Representatives Standing Committee on Communications and the Arts. Inquiry into the importance of public and commercial broadcasting, online content and live production to rural and regional Australia, including the arts, news and other services. [online]. *ABC.* February 2016. Retrieved from: http://d3n8a8pro7vhmx.cloudfront.net/abcfriends/legacy_url/2756/ABC_Submission_Reps_Feb2016_Sub009.pdf?1563515036. p. 1.
27. Duke, J. (2019a). ABC books Bankstown boot camp to reconnect with burbs. [online]. *The Sydney Morning Herald.* 16 September 2019. Retrieved from: https://www.smh.com.au/business/companies/abc-books-bankstown-boot-camp-to-reconnect-with-burbs-20190915-p52rf0.html.
28. *Parliament of Australia* (2019). Amendments to *Australian Broadcasting Corporation Act 1983* to: amend the Australian Broadcasting Corporation (ABC) Charter. [online]. Retrieved from: https://www.aph.gov.au/Parliamentary_Business/Bills_Legislation/Bills_Search_Results/Result?bId=r6382.
29. Spigelman, J. (2013). The ABC and Australia's media landscape. *Media International Australia, Incorporating Culture & Policy.* 146. pp. 12–24. Retrieved from: https://primoa.library.unsw.edu.au/permalink/f/11jha62/TN_informit182288913833846 p. 24.
30. Whitehead, G. (1988). *Inside the ABC: Geoffrey Whitehead's Personal Account.* Penguin Books. Victoria. p. 63.
31. Meade, A. (2018b). 'Unprecedented hostility': Murdoch, the government, and an ABC under attack. [online]. *The Guardian.* 25 July 2018. Retrieved from https://www.theguardian.com/media/2018/jul/25/

unprecedented-hostility-murdoch-the-government-and-an-abc-under-attack.
32. Tracey, M. (1998). *The Decline and Fall of Public Broadcasting.* Oxford University Press. p. 265.
33. Tracey, M. (1998). *The Decline and Fall of Public Broadcasting.* Oxford University Press. p. 265.
34. Tracey, M. (1998). *The Decline and Fall of Public Broadcasting.* Oxford University Press. p. 265.
35. Cunningham, S. (2013). *Hidden Innovation: Policy, Industry and the Creative Sector.* University of Queensland Press. Brisbane.
36. Thornton, P. H., Ocasio, W., & Lounsbury, M. (2012a). *The Emergence and Evolution of field-Level Logics.* DOI:10.1093/acprof:oso/9780199601936.003.0007.
37. Pascoe, M. (2020). Michael Pascoe: More job losses are a safe bet after Network Ten's dark day. *The New Daily.* 12 August 1010. Retrieved from: https://thenewdaily.com.au/finance/finance-news/2020/08/12/network-ten-michael-pascoe/.
38. Mason, M. (2020b). Hundreds more jobs to go at News Corp, ABC. *The Australian Financial Review.* 9 June 2020. Retrieved from: https://www.afr.com/companies/media-and-marketing/hundreds-more-jobs-to-go-at-news-corp-abc-20200609-p550wz.
39. Bourdieu, P. Ibid., p. 53.
40. Bourdieu, P. (1983). "The *field* of Cultural Production, or: The Economic World Reversed". *Poetics.* I2. pp. 311–356.
41. Lincoln, J. R. (1995). Book Review. W. W. Powell & P. DiMaggio (Eds.): The new institutionalism in organizational research. *Social Forces.* 73. pp. 1147–1148. p. 1147.
42. Thornton, P.H., Ocasio, W. and Lounsbury, M. (2012b). *Introduction to the Institutional Logics Perspective: A new approach to culture, structure and processes.* Oxford University Press. Oxford.
43. Thornton, P.H., Ocasio, W. and Lounsbury, M. (2012b). *Introduction to the Institutional Logics Perspective: A new approach to culture, structure and processes.* Oxford University Press. Oxford.
44. Glynn, M. (2000). When Cymbals Become Symbols: Conflict Over Organizational Identity Within a Symphony Orchestra. *Organization Science.* 11:3. Special Issue: Cultural Industries: Learning from Evolving Organizational Practices (May–June 2000). pp. 285–298. https://www.jstor.org/stable/2640262.
45. Glynn, M., & Lounsbury, M. (2005). From the Critics' Corner: Logic Blending, Discursive Change and Authenticity in a Cultural Production System. *The Journal of Management Studies.* 42:5. pp. 1031–1055. https://doi.org/10.1111/j.1467-6486.2005.00531.x.

46. Thornton, P.H., Ocasio, W. and Lounsbury, M. (2012b) *Introduction to the Institutional Logics Perspective: A new approach to culture, structure and processes.* Oxford University Press. Oxford.
47. Jones, P. K., & Pusey, M. (2010). Political communication and 'media system': the Australian canary. *Media, Culture & Society.* 32:3. pp. 451–471. https://doi.org/10.1177/0163443709361172.
48. Media Logic (originally no 's') was developed by Altheide, D.L. & Snow, R.P. (1979) Media Logic. Sage Publications. Beverly Hills.
49. Bourdieu, P. Transl. R. Nice. (1984). *Distinction: A Social Critique Of The Judgement Of Taste.* Harvard University Press. Cambridge, MA.
50. Barley, S. R., & Tolbert, P. S. (1997). Institutionalization and Structuration: Studying the Links between Action and Institution. *Organization Studies.* 18:1. pp. 93–117. https://doi.org/10.1177/017084069701800106.
51. Crisp, L. (2011). The Saddest of Days. The Deal. *The Australian Business Magazine.* October 2011. 4:9. p. 19.
52. Funston, A. The ABC and citizenship [online]. *Overland.* 147. Winter 1997. pp. 59–62. Retrieved from: <https://search-informit-com-au.wwwproxy1.library.unsw.edu.au/documentSummary;dn=971111828;res=IELAPA> p. 59.
53. Thomson, P. (2005). Bringing Bourdieu to policy sociology: codification, misrecognition and exchange value in the UK context. *Journal of Education Policy.* 20:6. pp. 741–758. Retrieved from: https://doi.org/10.1080/02680930500238929. p. 746.
54. Martin, F. (2002). Beyond Public Service Broadcasting? ABC Online and the User/Citizen [online]. *Southern Review: Communication, Politics & Culture.* 35:1. pp. 42–62. Availability: <https://search-informit-com-au.wwwproxy1.library.unsw.edu.au/documentSummary;dn=743199784542203;res=IELAPA> ISSN: 0038-4526.
55. Bourdieu, P. (1991). *Language and Symbolic Power.* Harvard University Press. Cambridge MA. & Bourdieu, P. (1998). *On Television and Journalism.* (P. Parkhurst Ferguson, Transl.) Pluto Press. London.
56. Bourdieu, P. (1996). (Transl. S. Emanuel). *The Rules of Art. Genesis and Structure of the Literary field.* Stanford University Press. Stanford.
57. Matei S.A., Bertino E., Russell M. (2015) Introduction. In: Matei S., Russell M., Bertino E. (eds) Transparency in Social Media. *Computational Social Sciences.* Springer, Cham.
58. Smith M.A., Himelboim I., Rainie L., Shneiderman B. (2015) The Structures of Twitter Crowds and Conversations. In: Matei S., Russell M., Bertino E. (eds) Transparency in Social Media. *Computational Social Sciences.* Springer, Cham.
59. Bourdieu, P. (Transl. R. Nice). (1984). *Distinction: A social critique of the judgement of taste.* Harvard University Press. Cambridge, MA.

60. Thomas, A. (1980). *Broadcast and be damned: The ABC's first two decades.* Globe Press. Fitzroy Victoria. p. 151.
61. Thomas, A. (1980). *Broadcast and be damned: The ABC's first two decades.* Globe Press. Fitzroy Victoria. p. 152.
62. Bourdieu, P. (1986). The forms of capital. In J. Richardson (Ed.) *Handbook of Theory and Research for the Sociology of Education.* Greenwood. New York. pp. 241–258.
63. Bourdieu, P. (Transl. R. Nice). (1984). *Distinction: A social critique of the judgement of taste.* Harvard University Press. Cambridge, MA. p. 18.
64. Ibid.
65. Worthington, B. & Hitch, G. (2020). Up to 250 ABC jobs to go, ABC Life brand scrapped, flagship radio news bulletin dumped to tackle $84 million budget cut. [online]. *ABC News.* 24 June 2020. Retrieved from: https://www.abc.net.au/news/2020-06-24/abc-announces-cuts-to-programming-and-jobs-funding/12384972.
66. Inglis, K. (1983). *This is the ABC: The Australian Broadcasting Commission 1932–1983.* Melbourne University Press. p. 146.
67. Inglis, K. (1983). *This is the ABC: The Australian Broadcasting Commission 1932–1983.* Melbourne University Press. p. 150.
68. Couldry, N. (2004). "Theorising Media as practice." *Social Semiotics.* 14:2. pp. 115–132. doi:10.1080/1035033042000238295. p. 117.
69. Dalzell, S. (2019). There will be job losses': ABC Managing Director confirms staff to go following budget freeze. [online]. *ABC News.* 23 October 2019. Retrieved from: https://www.communications.gov.au/what-we-do/television/national-broadcasters-efficiency-review.
70. Bourdieu, P. (Transl. R. Nice). (1984). *Distinction: A social critique of the judgement of taste.* Harvard University Press. Cambridge, MA. p. 20.
71. Benson, R. & Neveu, E. (2005). *Bourdieu and the Journalistic field.* Polity Press. Cambridge. p. 5.
72. Bourdieu, P. (1998). *On Television.* New Press. New York. p. 70.
73. These are a pinnacle award for an Australian journalist, established in 1956; they are peer-awarded and in various categories recognise excellence in the profession. The ABC has historically won most.
74. Clark, M. (1995, orig. published 1962). *History of Australia.* Melbourne University Press, Melbourne. p. 537.
75. DiMaggio, P. (1987). Managers of the Arts: Careers and opinions of senior administrators of U.S. art museums, symphony orchestras, resident theatres, and local arts agencies. *Research Division Report #20 National Endowment for the Arts.* Seven Locks Press Publishers. Washington, DC.
76. Thomson. P. (2005). Bringing Bourdieu to policy sociology: codification, misrecognition and exchange value in the UK context. *Journal of*

Education Policy. 20:6. pp. 741–758. https://doi.org/10.1080/02680930500238929.

77. Bourdieu, P. (1977). Transl. R. Nice. *Outline of a Theory of Practice*. Cambridge University Press. Cambridge. p. 78.
78. Bourdieu, P. (1990). (Transl. M. Adamson). *In other words: Essays towards a reflexive sociology*. Stanford University Press. Stanford, CA. p. 110.
79. Bourdieu, P. (1984). (Transl. R. Nice). *Distinction: A Social Critique of the Judgement of Taste*. Harvard University Press. Massachusetts.
80. Bourdieu, P. (Transl. R. Nice) (1977). *Outline of a Theory of Practice*. Cambridge University Press. Cambridge. p. 78.
81. Malsch, B., & Gendron, Y. (2013). Re-Theorizing Change: Institutional Experimentation and the Struggle for Domination in the *field* of Public Accounting. *Journal Of Management Studies*. 50:5. pp. 870–899. https://doi.org/10.1111/joms.12006.
82. Hastings, A, & Matthews, P. (2015). Bourdieu and the Big Society: empowering the powerful in public service provision? *Policy & Politics*. 43. pp. 545–560. 10.1332/030557314X14080105693951.
83. Bourdieu, P. & Wacquant, L. (1992). *An Invitation to Reflexive Sociology*. University of Chicago Press, Chicago. p. 23.
84. Bourdieu, P. & Wacquant, L. (1992). *An Invitation to Reflexive Sociology*. University of Chicago Press, Chicago. p. 3.
85. Bourdieu, P. (Ed. R. Johnson). (1993). *The field of Cultural Production: Essays on Art and Literature*. Polity Press, Cambridge. p. 162.
86. Bourdieu, P. (1990). (Trans. M. Adamson). *In other words: Essays towards a reflexive sociology*. Stanford University Press. Stanford CA. p. 61.
87. Bourdieu, P. (1984). *Distinction: A Social Critique of the Judgement of Taste*. Harvard University Press. Cambridge, MA.
88. Bourdieu, P. (1984). *Distinction: A Social Critique of the Judgement of Taste*. Harvard University Press. Cambridge, Massachusetts. p. 55.
89. Bourdieu, P. (1992). *Les Règles de L'art: Genèse et structure du champ littéraire*. Editions du Seuil. Paris. p. 171.
90. Bourdieu, P. (1983). The Forms of Capital. In J. G. Richardson (Ed.), *Handbook of Theory and Research for the Sociology of Education* (pp. 241–258). Greenwood Press. New York. p. 294.
91. Bourdieu, P. & Wacquant, L. (1992). *An Invitation to Reflexive Sociology*. University of Chicago Press. Chicago. p. 101.
92. Lieberman, D. (2007). Murdoch grew up on 'ritual feuding with other media'. [online]. *USA Today*. 6 August 2007. Retrieved from: https://abcnews.go.com/Business/story?id=3434589&page=1.
93. Morton, R. (2020). Exclusive: New govt report targets ABC. [online]. *The Saturday Paper*. 306. 25–26 June 2020. Retrieved from: https://

www.thesaturdaypaper.com.au/news/politics/2020/06/27/exclusive-new-govt-report-targets-abc/159318000010021.

94. Meade, A. (2018a). Australia bushfire coverage: ABC emergency fire broadcasts praised but News Corp goes on attack. [online]. *The Guardian*. 4 January 2020. Retrieved from: https://www.theguardian.com/australia-news/2020/jan/04/australia-bushfire-coverage-abc-emergency-fire-broadcasts-praised-as-news-corp-goes-on-attack.
95. Meade, A. (2018b). 'Unprecedented hostility': Murdoch, the government, and an ABC under attack. [online]. *The Guardian*. 25 July 2018. Retrieved from: https://www.theguardian.com/media/2018/jul/25/unprecedented-hostility-murdoch-the-government-and-an-abc-under-attack.
96. Rudd, K. (2018). 'Culture of fear': Murdoch, the ABC and how to fix a media in crisis. [online]. *The Sydney Morning Herald*. Opinion. 2 October 2018. Retrieved from: https://www.smh.com.au/national/culture-of-fear-murdoch-the-abc-and-how-to-fix-a-media-in-crisis-20181001-p5073f.html.
97. Flanagan, M. (2014). Rupert Murdoch's attack on 'our ABC' like a mediaeval siege. [online]. *The Sydney Morning Herald*. 8 February 2014. Retrieved from: https://www.smh.com.au/opinion/rupert-murdochs-attack-on-our-abc-like-a-mediaeval-siege-20140207-32746.html.
98. Flanagan, M. (2014). Rupert Murdoch's attack on 'our ABC' like a mediaeval siege. [online]. *The Sydney Morning Herald*. 8 February 2014. Retrieved from: https://www.smh.com.au/opinion/rupert-murdochs-attack-on-our-abc-like-a-mediaeval-siege-20140207-32746.html.
99. Chaucer, G. (1476, orig.). The Canterbury Tales: The Knight's Tale. [online]. Retrieved from: http://art3idea.psu.edu/metalepsis/texts/knights_tale.pdf. p. 3.
100. Thornton, P.H., Ocasio, W. and Lounsbury, M. (2012b) *Introduction to the Institutional Logics Perspective: A new approach to culture, structure and processes*. Oxford University Press. Oxford. p. 2.
101. Telegraph, The (Brisbane). Empire Broadcasting: Early Inauguration. [online]. 13 July 1932, p. 10. Retrieved from: https://trove.nla.gov.au/newspaper/article/181268000?searchTerm=abc%20inaugural&searchLimits=exactPhrase|||anyWords|||notWords|||requestHandler|||dateFrom=1932-06-01|||dateTo=1932-07-31|||sortby.
102. The Sydney Morning Herald. (1932). BROADCASTING. Control by Commission. Inaugural Speeches. New Policy Outlined. [online]. 2 July 1932. p. 14. Retrieved from Trove. https://trove.nla.gov.au/newspaper/article/16906832?searchTerm=inaugurated%20Lyons&searchLimits=exactPhrase|||anyWords|||notWords|||requestHandler|||dateFrom=1932-

07-01|||dateTo=1932-07-31||||l-advstate=National||||l-advstate=New+South+Wales||||l-advstate=Victoria|||sortby.
103. Thornton, P. H., & Ocasio, W. (2008). Institutional Logics. In R. Greenwood, C. Oliver, K. Sahlin-Andersson, & R. Suddaby (Eds.). *The Sage Handbook of Organisational Institutionalism*. Sage. Thousand Oaks, CA.
104. Thornton, P. H., Ocasio, W., & Lounsbury, M. (2012b). *The Institutional Logics Perspective: A New Approach To Culture, Structure And Process*. Oxford University Press. Oxford.
105. Paterson, T., Harms, P., & Tuggle, C. (2018). Revisiting the rigor–relevance relationship: An institutional logics perspective. *Human Resource Management*. 57:6. pp. 1371–1383. https://doi.org/10.1002/hrm.21911.
106. Suddaby, R. (2010). Challenges for Institutional Theory. *Journal of Management Inquiry*. 19:1. p. 15.
107. Lincoln, J. R. (1995). Book Review. (Eds. W. W. Powell & P. DiMaggio): The new institutionalism in organizational research. *Social Forces*. 73. pp. 1147–1148. p. 1147.
108. Amans, P., Mazars-Chapelon, A., & Villesèque-Dubus, F. (2015). Budgeting in institutional complexity: The case of performing arts organizations. *Management Accounting Research*. 27. pp. 47–66. https://doi.org/10.1016/j.mar.2015.03.001.
109. Suddaby, R. (2010). Challenges for Institutional Theory. *Journal of Management Inquiry*. 19:1. p. 15.
110. Jensen, A. (2019). Interdisciplinary arts and health practice with an institutional logics perspective. *Arts & Health*. 11:3. pp. 219–231. https://doi.org/10.1080/17533015.2018.1443950.
111. Suddaby, R. (2010). Challenges for Institutional Theory. *Journal of Management Inquiry*. 19:1. pp. 14–20.
112. van Dijk, T. (1992). Discourse and the Denial of Racism. *Discourse & Society*. 3:1. pp. 87–118. https://doi.org/10.1177/0957926592003001005.
113. Houghton, D. (2011). Groupthink. In B. Badie, D. Berg-Schlosser & L. Morlino (Eds.), *International Encyclopedia of Political Science*. pp. 1058–1060). SAGE Publications. Thousand Oaks, CA. doi: 10.4135/9781412959636.n244.
114. Coates, B. (2010). Cracking into the panes of corporate denial. *Business Renaissance Quarterly*. 5:3. pp. 23–46. Retrieved from http://ezproxy.library.usyd.edu.au/login?url=https://search-proquest-com.ezproxy2.library.usyd.edu.au/docview/814814238?accountid=14757.
115. Berger, P. & Luckmann, T. (1967). *The social construction of reality*. Doubleday Anchor. New York. Retrieved from Google Scholar: http://www.perflensburg.se/Berger%20social-construction-of-reality.pdf.

116. (2010, ibid.).
117. Foucault, M. (1983). (Ed. J. Pearson). *Discourse and truth: The problematization of Parrhesia*. Taken from a series of lectures. October-November 1983. University of California. Berkeley. Retrieved from: https://foucault.info/parrhesia/.
118. Friedland, R. (2018). Moving Institutional Logics Forward: Emotion and Meaningful Material Practice. *Organization Studies*. 39:4. pp. 515–542. https://doi.org/10.1177/0170840617709307.
119. Swinehart, K., & Graber, K. (2012). Tongue-tied territories: Languages and publics in stateless nations. *Language and Communication*. 32:2. pp. 95–97. https://doi.org/10.1016/j.langcom.2011.05.007.
120. Suddaby, R. (2010). Challenges for Institutional Theory. Journal of Management Inquiry. 19:1. pp. 14–20 refers to the work of Green, S.E., Babb, M., & Alpaslan, M. (2008). Institutional field dynamics and the competition between institutional logics: The role of rhetoric in the evolving control of the modern corporation. Management Communication Quarterly. 22. Pp. 40–73; Heracleous, L., & Barrett, M. (2001). Organizational change as discourse: Communicative actions and deep structures in the context of IT implementation. *Academy of Management Journal*. 44. pp. 755–778; Suddaby, R., & Greenwood, R. (2005). Rhetorical strategies of legitimacy *Administrative Science Quarterly*. 50. pp. 35–67; Vaara, E., & Tienari, J. (2008). A discursive perspective on legitimation strategies in MNCs. *Academy of Management Review*. 33. pp. 985–993, as being notable in this area.
121. Bourdieu, P. (1991). (Ed. J.B. Thompson). *Language and Symbolic Power*. Harvard University Press. Cambridge, MA. p. 105.
122. Robinson, S. L. (1996). Trust and breach of the psychological contract. *Administrative Science Quarterly*. 41:4. pp. 574–599. https://doi.org/10.2307/2393868 p. 576.
123. Thornton, P. H. (2004). *Markets from culture: Institutional logics and organizational decisions in higher education publishing*. Stanford University Press. Stanford, CA.
124. Ibid.
125. Ibid. and citing Lawrence, T.B., & Suddaby, R. (2006) *Institutions and Institutional work*. In Stewart R. Clegg, Cynthia Hardy, Thomas B. Lawrence & Walter R. Nord (Eds.S) age *Handbook of Organization Studies*. 2nd Edition. pp. 215–254. London: Sage.; and Lawrence, T. B., Suddaby, R., & Leca, B. (2009). *Introduction: Theorizing and studying institutional work*. In T. B. Lawrence, R. Suddaby, & B. Leca (Eds.) *Institutional work: Actors and agency in institutional studies of organizations*. pp. 1–27. Cambridge, UK: Cambridge University Press.
126. Ibid.

127. Corbett, J., Webster, J., & Jenkin, T. (2018). Unmasking Corporate Sustainability at the Project Level: Exploring the Influence of Institutional Logics and Individual Agency. *Journal of Business Ethics.* 147:2. pp. 261–286. https://doi.org/10.1007/s10551-015-2945-1.
128. Holmes, J. (2019). *On Aunty.* Melbourne University Press. Carlton, Victoria.
129. Scannell, P. (1989). Public service broadcasting and modern public life. *Media, Culture & Society.* 11(2). pp. 135–166. https://doi.org/10.1177/016344389011002002.
130. Scannell, P. (1997). "Public Service Broadcasting and Modern Public Life" in T. O'Sullivan and Y. Tewkes (Eds) *The Media Studies Reader.* Arnold. London. pp. 60–71. Originally published in *Media Culture and Society.* (1989) 11. pp. 135–166. p. 62.
131. Scannell, P. (1997). "Public Service Broadcasting and Modern Public Life" in T. O'Sullivan and Y. Tewkes (Eds) *The Media Studies Reader.* Arnold. London. pp. 60–71. Originally published in *Media Culture and Society.* (1989) 11. pp. 135–166. p. 65.
132. Scannell, P. (1997). "Public Service Broadcasting and Modern Public Life" in T. O'Sullivan and Y. Tewkes (Eds) *The Media Studies Reader.* Arnold. London. pp. 60–71. Originally published in *Media Culture and Society.* (1989) 11. pp. 135–166. p. 141.
133. Mellet, K. (2011). Online Marketing. *Communications.* 88:1. pp. 103–111. https://doi.org/10.3917/commu.088.0103.
134. Elliott, G., Sainsbury, M. & Overington, C. (2010). ABC picks sides while the 'editor-in-chief' watches on. [online]. *The Australian.* 24 July 2010. Retrieved from: https://www.theaustralian.com.au/national-affairs/abc-picks-sides-while-the-editor-in-chief-watches-on/news-story/59e747a64f4d496c33e661f4ab25a6e2.
135. Kim, M.N. (2018). The Role of Chief Editor in Managerial System of Editorial Board. *Upravlencheskoe Konsul'tirovanie.* 6. pp. 182–189. https://doaj.org/article/6dc6b7258546412bbececb6622d09299.
136. White, D., & Lynch, J. (2014, November 20). Turnbull takes on ABC, SBS. [online]. *The Australian Financial Review.* http://search.proquest.com/docview/1748835968/.
137. The ABC even had a staff choir of Sydney staff that continues to 2020.
138. Charles Buttrose was the current ABC Chair's late father.
139. Semmler, C. (1981). *The ABC - Aunt Sally and Sacred Cow.* Melbourne University Press. Melbourne. p. 93.
140. Radioinfo.com.au. (2020). RIP ABC 0745 News bulletin. Retrieved from: https://www.radioinfo.com.au/news/rip-abc-0745-news-bulletin.

141. DiMaggio, P. (2018). Our faith-based economy. *Distinktion: Journal of Social Theory.* 19:3. pp. 328–335. DOI: 10.1080/1600910X.2018.1452769. p. 330.
142. MacInnis, F. (2005). Towards a New Definition of Service. *Chief Executive.* Apr 2004. 197. p. 16.
143. Lau, T., Wang, H.C., Chuang, C.C. (2011). A Definition of Service as Base for Developing Service Science. *2011 International Joint Conference on Service Science.* Conference Paper. May 2011. pp. 49–53.
144. Ibid.
145. Fitzsimmons, J.A. and Fitzsimmons, M.J. (2004). *Service Management: Operations, Strategy, and Information Technology.* 4th ed. McGraw-Hill. New York, NY.
146. Bennett, L. (2018). Fairfax calls out ABC for running YouTube ads. *AdNews.* 24 September 2018. Retrieved from: https://www.adnews.com.au/news/fairfax-calls-out-abc-for-running-youtube-ads.
147. Cooper, S. (2009). Murdoch's Boyer Lectures: [Why was Rupert Murdoch chosen to give the 2008 ABC Boyer Lectures?] [online]. *Arena Magazine* (Fitzroy, Vic). 99. Feb-Mar 2009: 5–6. Retrieved from: <https://search-informit-com-au.ezproxy1.library.usyd.edu.au/documentSummary;dn=200903402;res=IELAPA> ISSN: 1039-1010.
148. Harding, R. (1979). *Outside Interference: The Politics of Australian Broadcasting.* Sun Books, South Melbourne.
149. Cai, Z., Parker, S., Chen, Z., & Lam, W. (2019) How does the social context fuel the proactive fire? A multilevel review and theoretical synthesis. *Journal of Organizational Behaviour.* 40:2. February. pp. 209–230. Quoting from pp. 222–223.
150. Manz, C., Skaggs, B., Pearce, C., Wassenaar, C. (2015). Serving one another: Are shared and self-leadership the keys to service sustainability? *Journal of Organizational Behaviour.* 36:4. May. pp. 607–612.
151. *QSRweb.com.* (2015). How customers' expectations defines your brand. [online]. 11 February 2015. Retrieved from: Cengage Learning, Inc. https://www.gale.com or https://www.qsrweb.com/blogs/how-customers-expectations-defines-your-brand/.
152. Swartz, N. P. "'Dumbing down' the CBC news." *Humanist Perspectives.* 183. Winter 2012. p. 18. Retrieved from: http://search.proquest.com/docview/1268836316/.
153. Hanusch, F. (2017). Web analytics and the functional differentiation of journalism cultures: individual, organizational and platform-specific influences on newswork. *Information, Communication & Society.* 20:10, pp. 1571–1586. DOI: 10.1080/1369118X.2016.1241294.
154. Retrieved from: https://downloads.bbc.co.uk/aboutthebbc/policies/pdf/bpv.pdf.

155. Ibid., p. 5
156. Ibid., p. 6.
157. Ibid., p. 7.
158. Spigelman, J. (2012). Public broadcasting, public value. [online]. The Drum. Analysis. *ABC*. 6 September 2012. Retrieved from: https://www.abc.net.au/news/2012-09-05/spigelman-public-broadcasting-public-value/4244468.
159. Wilson, Z. (2019). David Anderson named ABC Managing Director. *Radio Today*. Retrieved from https://www.radiotoday.com.au/david-anderson-named-abc-managing-director/.
160. Rousseau, J.J. (1795). On the Social Compact: Or, The Principles of Political Law. Eaton. London.
161. Doerr, A. D. (2019). *Canadian Encyclopedia*, English ed.; Toronto. Historica Canada. Toronto.
162. Dickinson, H., Needham, C., Mangan, C. & Sullivan, H. Eds. (2019). *Reimagining the Future Public Service Workforce*. Springer Books Singapore.
163. Cola, M. & Prario, B. (2012). New ways of consumption: the audiences of public service media in Italy and Switzerland. *Media, Culture & Society*. March 2012. 34:2. pp.181–194. Retrieved from https://journals-sagepub-com.wwwproxy1.library.unsw.edu.au/doi/pdf/10.1177/0163443711430757.
164. Denhardt, J.V. & Denhardt, R.B. (2007). *The New Public Service: Serving, Not Steering*. M.E. Sharpe. New York, London.
165. Ibid.
166. *Sydney Morning Herald, The*. (1932). BROADCASTING. Control by Commission. INAUGURAL SPEECHES. New Policy Outlined. [online]. 2 July 1932. p. 14. Retrieved from: https://trove.nla.gov.au/newspaper/article/16906832?searchTerm=inaugurated%20Lyons&searchLimits=exactPhrase|||anyWords|||notWords|||requestHandler|||dateFrom=1932-07-01|||dateTo=1932-07-31||||l-advstate=National||||l-advstate=New+South+Wales||||l-advstate=Victoria||sortby.
167. Ibid.
168. Shergold, P. (2017). Re-imagining public service [online]. *The Australian Journal of Social Issues*. 52:1. 2017. pp. 4–12. Retrieved from: <https://search-informit-com-au.wwwproxy1.library.unsw.edu.au/documentSummary;dn=035171807770944;res=IELAPA>.
169. Scott, M. (2016). *A Media Odyssey: Speeches of an ABC Managing Director 2006–2016*. ABC Books, Sydney. p. 92.
170. Jolly, R. (2014). The ABC: an overview (updated). [online]. Parliamentary Library Research Paper. *Parliament of Australia*. 11 August 2014. Retrieved 19/12/19 from: https://parlinfo.aph.gov.au/parlInfo/

download/library/prspub/3346567/upload_binary/3346567.pdf;fileType=application/pdf.

171. Patriarche, G. & Dufrasne, M. (2014). Penser la diversité des pratiques médiatiques: Le réseau comme catégorie conceptuelle pour la recherche sur les audiences et les publics. *Réseaux*. 187:5. pp. 195–232. doi:10.3917/res.187.0195.
172. Patriarche, G. & Dufrasne, M. (2014). Penser la diversité des pratiques médiatiques: Le réseau comme catégorie conceptuelle pour la recherche sur les audiences et les publics. *Réseaux*. 187:5. pp. 195–232. doi:10.3917/res.187.0195. p. 2.
173. Patriarche, G. & Dufrasne, M. (2014). Penser la diversité des pratiques médiatiques: Le réseau comme catégorie conceptuelle pour la recherche sur les audiences et les publics. *Réseaux*. 187:5. pp. 195–232. doi:10.3917/res.187.0195. p. 19.
174. Schulz, A. Levy, D.A.L. and Kleis Nielsen, R. (2019). Old, Educated, and Politically Diverse: The Audience of Public Service News. *Reuters Institute Report*. September 2019. Retrieved from: https://reutersinstitute.politics.ox.ac.uk/sites/default/files/2019-09/The_audience_of_public_service_news_FINAL.pdf p. 20.
175. Schulz, A. Levy, D.A.L. and Kleis Nielsen, R. (2019). Old, Educated, and Politically Diverse: The Audience of Public Service News. *Reuters Institute Report*. September 2019. Retrieved from: https://reutersinstitute.politics.ox.ac.uk/sites/default/files/2019-09/The_audience_of_public_service_news_FINAL.pdf.
176. Ibid., p. 13.
177. Ibid., p. 8.
178. Ibid., p. 14.
179. Ibid., p. 15.
180. Ibid., p. 30.
181. Ibid., p. 608.
182. Bruns, A. (2012). Journalists and Twitter: How Australian News Organisations Adapt to a New Medium. *Media International Australia*. 144. August. p. 99.
183. Schulz, A. Levy, D.A.L. and Kleis Nielsen, R. (2019). Old, Educated, and Politically Diverse: The Audience of Public Service News. *Reuters Institute Report*. September 2019. Retrieved from: https://reutersinstitute.politics.ox.ac.uk/sites/default/files/2019-09/The_audience_of_public_service_news_FINAL.pdf. These authors speak about "reduced or non-profit organisations" in this context. p. 607.
184. Ibid., p. 608.

185. Palfreyman, R. (1993). Palfreyman, Richard. (1993, November). Opening the airwaves: Cultural squeeze for national broadcasting? *Current Affairs Bulletin*. 70:6. pp. 19–25. p. 20.
186. Smith, A. & Anderson, M. (2018). Social Media use in 2018. *Pew Research Center* (2018). Retrieved from https://www.pewresearch.org/internet/2018/03/01/social-media-use-in-2018/.
187. Inglis, K. (2006). *Whose ABC? The Australian Broadcasting Corporation. 1983–2006*. Black Inc. Melbourne. p. 49.
188. Griffith, C. (1996). The ABC and Multimedia: A New Media Form [online]. *Media International Australia*. 81. Aug 1996. pp. 49–53. Retrieved from: <https://search-informit-com-au.wwwproxy1.library.unsw.edu.au/documentSummary;dn=078935934053890;res=IELLCC> ISSN: 1324-5325.
189. Cooke, M. (2007). Our Digital Aunty - the ABC's new Media Future. *Metro Magazine: Media & Education Magazine*. 154. pp. 120–124.
190. Given, J. (1998). *The Death of Broadcasting? Media's Digital Future*. Communications Law Centre. UNSW Press. Kensington, Sydney. ISBN 0868 40449 7.
191. Spigelman, J. (2013). The ABC and Australia's media landscape. *Media International Australia, Incorporating Culture & Policy*. 146. pp. 12–24. https://primoa.library.unsw.edu.au/permalink/f/11jha62/TN_informit182288913833846.
192. *Cambridge Dictionary* (n.d.). Retrieved from: https://dictionary.cambridge.org/dictionary/english/impartial
193. Brown, E. (2010). Digital Media: Knowing Your ABCs [online]. *Inside Film*. 134. Aug 2010. p. 36. Retrieved from: <https://search-informit-com-au.wwwproxy1.library.unsw.edu.au/documentSummary;dn=293302582189347;res=IELLCC> ISSN: 1447–2252.
194. Ulin, J. (2009). *The business of media distribution: monetizing film, TV and video content in an online world*. Focal. Elsevier E-Book. https://primoa.library.unsw.edu.au/permalink/f/jhud33/UNSW_ALMA51181866550001731.
195. Bolter, J.D. (2019). Social Media Are Ruining Political Discourse. *The Atlantic*. 19 May 2019. Retrieved from: https://www.theatlantic.com/technology/archive/2019/05/why-social-media-ruining-political-discourse/589108/.
196. Jones, P. K., & Pusey, M. (2010). Political communication and 'media system': the Australian canary. *Media, Culture & Society*. 32:3. pp. 451–471. https://doi.org/10.1177/0163443709361172.
197. Owen, D. (2018). "The Past Decade and Future of Political Media: The Ascendance of Social Media." In: *Towards a New Enlightenment? A Transcendent Decade*. Madrid: BBVA, 2018. Retrieved from: https://

www.bbvaopenmind.com/en/articles/the-past-decade-and-future-of-political-media-the-ascendance-of-social-media/.

198. Nolan, D. (2006). Media, Citizenship and Governmentality: Defining "The Public" of Public Service Broadcasting. *Social Semiotics.* 16:2. pp. 225–242. Retrieved from: https://doi-org.wwwproxy1.library.unsw.edu.au/10.1080/10350330600667501.
199. Scott, M. (2014). Our ABC, Our Future. A message from Mark Scott. *ABC.* Retrieved from: https://about.abc.net.au/our-abc-our-future/.
200. *Australian Academy of Science.* (1996.). Submission - Mans *field* enquiry into the Australian Broadcasting Corporation (ABC). 22 August 1996. Retrieved from: https://www.science.org.au/supporting-science/science-policy/submissions-government/submission%E2%80%94mans*field*-enquiry-australian.
201. Sheridan, G. (2020). Victoria pays for collapse of democracy. *The Australian.* Commentary. 9 July 2020. Retrieved from: https://www.theaustralian.com.au/commentary/democracy-is-slowly-eclipsed-in-victoria/news-story/d3c7ef0603b1e9c619fc3cee38724247.
202. Meade, A. (2016). Faith leaders petition Michelle Guthrie over ABC religious programming cuts. [online]. *The Guardian.* 10 November 2016. Retrieved from: https://www.theguardian.com/media/2016/nov/10/faith-leaders-meet-with-michelle-guthrie-over-abc-religious-programming-cuts.
203. Ursell, G. (2003). Creating Value and Valuing Creation in Contemporary UK Television: or "dumbing down" the workforce. *Journalism Studies.* 4:1. pp. 31–46. https://doi.org/10.1080/14616700306501.
204. Hyland, A. (2015). Mark Scott's ABC exit interview: 'I had no idea of the scale of the challenge'. *The Australian Financial Review.* 27 November 2015. Retrieved from: https://www.afr.com/life-and-luxury/abcs-mark-scott-on-success-and-his-legacy-20151019-gkcgi8.
205. Santana, A. D., & Hopp, T. (2016). Tapping Into a New Stream of (Personal) Data: Assessing Journalists' Different Use of Social Media. *Journalism & Mass Communication Quarterly.* 93:2. pp. 383–408. https://doi.org/10.1177/1077699016637105.
206. Nah, S., & Chung, D. S. (2012). When citizens meet both professional and citizen journalists: Social trust, media credibility, and perceived journalistic roles among online community news readers. *Journalism.* 13:6. pp. 714–730. https://doi.org/10.1177/1464884911431381.
207. Gibson, C. (2007). The ABC's digital future. *The Australian Library Journal.* 56:2. pp. 114–127.
208. Fardouly, J., & Holland, E. (2018). Social media is not real life: The effect of attaching disclaimer-type labels to idealized social media images

on women's body image and mood. *New Media & Society*, *20*(11), 4311–4328. https://doi.org/10.1177/1461444818771083.

209. Colliander, J. (2019). "This is fake news": Investigating the role of conformity to other users' views when commenting on and spreading disinformation in social media. *Computers in Human Behavior.* 97. pp. 202–215. https://doi.org/10.1016/j.chb.2019.03.032.
210. ABC. (2014). GUIDELINES FOR PERSONAL USE OF SOCIAL MEDIA. [online]. Document: D11/22627. Retrieved from: http://about.abc.net.au/wp-content/uploads/2014/10/PersonalUseOfSocialMediaINS1.pdf. NOTE: now a dead link.
211. Livingston, J., Holland, E., & Fardouly, J. (2020). Exposing digital posing: The effect of social media self-disclaimer captions on women's body dissatisfaction, mood, and impressions of the user. *Body Image.* 32. pp. 150–154. https://doi.org/10.1016/j.bodyim.2019.12.006.
212. Brems, C., Temmerman, M., Graham, T. & Broersma, M. (2017) Personal Branding on Twitter. *Digital Journalism.* 5:4. pp. 443–459. DOI: 10.1080/21670811.2016.1176534.
213. Powers, M., & Vera-Zambrano, S. (2018). How journalists use social media in France and the United States: Analyzing technology use across journalistic *fields*. *New Media & Society.* 20:8. pp. 2728–2744. https://doi.org/10.1177/1461444817731566.
214. Lysak, S., Cremedas, M., & Wolf, J. (2012). Facebook and Twitter in the Newsroom: How and Why Local Television News is Getting Social With Viewers? *Electronic News.* 6:4. pp. 187–207. https://doi.org/10.1177/1931243112466095.
215. Demaria, A. (2015). Employer's Requirement to Post a Social Media Disclaimer Passes NLRB Muster. *Management Report for Nonunion Organizations.* 38:1. pp. 3–4. https://doi.org/10.1002/mare.30020.
216. Lariscy, R., Avery, E., Sweetser, K., & Howes, P. (2009). An examination of the role of online social media in journalists' source mix. *Public Relations Review.* 35:3. pp. 314–316. https://doi.org/10.1016/j.pubrev.2009.05.008.
217. Schifferes, S., Newman, N., Thurman, N., Corney, D., Goker, A. S. and Martin, C. (2014). Identifying and verifying news through social media: Developing a user-centred tool for professional journalists. *Digital Journalism.* 2:3. pp. 406–418. doi: 10.1080/21670811.2014.892747.
218. Mergel, I. & Greeves, B. (2013). *Social Media in the Public Sector field Guide: Designing and Implementing Strategies and Policies.* Jossey-Bass. San Francisco.
219. Lieberman, D. (2007). Murdoch grew up on 'ritual feuding with other media'. *USA Today.* 6 August 2007. Retrieved from https://abcnews.go.com/Business/story?id=3434589&page=1.

220. Smolkin, R. (2006). Adapt or die: as newspaper companies confront a challenging future, they are increasingly viewing their trademark print product as the engine driving a diverse "portfolio" that embraces other "platforms" such as Web sites and niche publications. Is this a strategy for survival? *American Journalism Review*. 28:3. p. 16.
221. Smolkin, R. (2006). Adapt or die: as newspaper companies confront a challenging future, they are increasingly viewing their trademark print product as the engine driving a diverse "portfolio" that embraces other "platforms" such as Web sites and niche publications. Is this a strategy for survival? *American Journalism Review*. 28:3. p. 16.
222. Grossman, L. (2010). Mark Zuckerberg: Person of the Year. [online]. *Time Magazine*. 15 December 2010. Retrieved from http://content.time.com/time/specials/packages/article/0,28804,2036683_2037183_2037185-1,00.html.
223. Letamendia, A. (2017). "Towards the Aestheticisation of the Resistances in the Digital Age? A Critical Approach" (Chapter 9) in *Precarity within the Digital Age Media Change and Social Insecurity*. Springer, Wiesbaden. Retrieved from: https://link-springer-com.wwwproxy1.library.unsw.edu.au/content/pdf/10.1007%2F978-3-658-17678-5.pdf.
224. Tucker, J. A., Theocharis, Y., Roberts, M. E., & Barberá, P. (2017). From Liberation to Turmoil: Social Media and Democracy. *Journal of Democracy*. 28:4. pp. 46–59. https://doi.org/10.1353/jod.2017.0064.
225. Couldry, N. (2003). *Media rituals: A critical approach*. Routledge. London. p. 28.
226. Ibid., p. 30.
227. Ward, T. (2009). 'The heart of what it means to be Australian'. *Soccer & Society*. 10:5. pp. 532–543. DOI: 10.1080/14660970902955463.
228. Couldry, N. (2003). *Media rituals: A critical approach*. Routledge. London. p. 27.
229. Couldry, N. (2003). *Media rituals: A critical approach*. Routledge. London. p. 29.
230. Loc. cit.
231. Loc. cit.
232. Couldry, N. (2003). *Media rituals: A critical approach*. Routledge. London.
233. Bell, C. (1997). *Ritual: Perspectives and Dimensions*. Oxford University Press. New York.
234. Bell, C. (1997). *Ritual: Perspectives and Dimensions*. Oxford University Press. New York. p. 2.
235. Bell, C. (1997). *Ritual: Perspectives and Dimensions*. Oxford University Press. New York. p. 3

236. Bell, C. (1997). *Ritual: Perspectives and Dimensions.* Oxford University Press. New York. p. 251.
237. Bell, C. (1997). *Ritual: Perspectives and Dimensions.* Oxford University Press. New York. p. 78.
238. Couldry, N. (2003). *Media Rituals: A Critical Approach.* Routledge: London and New York.
239. Couldry, N. (2003). *Media Rituals: A Critical Approach.* Routledge: London and New York. p. 2.
240. Bourdieu, P. (1980). (Trans. R. Nice) The aristocracy of culture. *Media, Culture and Society.* 2. pp. 225–254. p. 237.
241. Bourdieu, P. (1980). (Trans. R. Nice). The aristocracy of culture. *Media, Culture and Society.* 2. pp. 225–254. p. 229.
242. Bourdieu, P. (1980). (Trans. R. Nice). The aristocracy of culture. *Media, Culture and Society.* 2. pp. 225–254. p. 231.
243. Bourdieu, P. (1979). (Transl. R. Nice.). Distinction: A Social Critique of the Judgement of Taste. Harvard University Press. Cambridge, MA.
244. Bourdieu, P. & Wacquant, L. (1992). *An Invitation to Reflexive Sociology.* University of Chicago Press. Chicago, Ill. p. 99.
245. Bourdieu, P. & Wacquant, L. (1992). *An Invitation to Reflexive Sociology.* University of Chicago Press. Chicago, Ill. p. 99.
246. Scannell, P. (2019). *Why do people sing? On voice.* Polity Press. Cambridge. p. 2–3.
247. Scannell, P. Ed. (1991). Broadcast Talk. *Introduction: The Relevance of Talk.* (P. Scannell). Sage Publications. London. p. 1.
248. Carr, D., & Bard, M. (2018). Even a Celebrity Journalist Can't Have an Opinion: Post-Millennials' Recognition and Evaluation of Journalists and News Brands on Twitter. *Electronic News.* 12:1. pp. 3–22. https://doi.org/10.1177/1931243117710280.
249. Girard, R., & Grayson, R. (2016). Belonging. *Contagion: Journal of Violence, Mimesis, and Culture.* 23:1. pp. 1–12. doi:10.14321/contagion.23.1.0001.
250. Murphy, J., Link, M. W., Childs, J. H., Tesfaye, C. L., Dean, E., Stern, M., Pasek, J., Cohen, J., Callegaro, M., & Harwood, P. (2014). Social Media in Public Opinion Research. *Public Opinion Quarterly.* 78:4. pp. 788–794. https://doi.org/10.1093/poq/nfu053.
251. Murphy, J., Link, M. W., Childs, J. H., Tesfaye, C. L., Dean, E., Stern, M., Pasek, J., Cohen, J., Callegaro, M., & Harwood, P. (2014). Social Media in Public Opinion Research. *Public Opinion Quarterly.* 78:4. pp. 788–794. https://doi.org/10.1093/poq/nfu053. p. 791.
252. O'Sullivan, P. B. (2005). Masspersonal Communication: An Integrative Model Bridging the Mass-Personal Divide. In *Annual Meeting of the International Communication Association.* New York City, New York.

Retrieved from: *http://ilstu.academia.edu/PatrickBOSullivan/Papers/457584/Masspersonal_communication_Rethinking_the_mass_interpersonal_divide.*
253. Santana, A. D., & Hopp, T. (2016). Tapping Into a New Stream of (Personal) Data: Assessing Journalists' Different Use of Social Media. *Journalism & Mass Communication Quarterly.* 93:2. pp. 383–408. https://doi.org/10.1177/1077699016637105.
254. Lee, J. (2015). The Double-Edged Sword: The Effects of Journalists' Social Media Activities on Audience Perceptions of Journalists and Their News Products. *Journal of Computer-Mediated Communication.* 20:3. pp. 312–329. https://doi.org/10.1111/jcc4.12113.
255. Lee, J. (2015). The Double-Edged Sword: The Effects of Journalists' Social Media Activities on Audience Perceptions of Journalists and Their News Products. *Journal of Computer-Mediated Communication.* 20:3. pp. 312–329. https://doi.org/10.1111/jcc4.12113. p. 313.
256. Bourdieu, P. (1990). *The Logic of Practice.* Stanford University Press. Stanford. p. 67
257. Bourdieu, P. (1990). *The Logic of Practice.* Stanford University Press. Stanford. p. 163.
258. Bourdieu, P. (1990). *The Logic of Practice.* Stanford University Press. Stanford. p. 164.
259. Bourdieu, P. (1990). *The Logic of Practice.* Stanford University Press. Stanford. p. 179.
260. Benson, R., & Neveu, E. (2005). *Bourdieu and the Journalistic field.* Polity Press. Cambridge, U.K. p. 3
261. Watkins, E. (2018). 'Disappointing' internal ABC survey shows staff distrust management. [online]. *Crikey.* 5 March 2018. Retrieved from https://www.crikey.com.au/2018/03/05/disappointing-internal-abc-survey-shows-staff-distrust-management/.
262. Bourdieu, P. (1990). Structures, *habitus*, practice, in The Logic of Practice. Polity. Cambridge. p. 53.
263. Bourdieu, P. (1990). Structures, *habitus*, practice, in The Logic of Practice. Polity. Cambridge. p. 59
264. Bourdieu, P. (1991). (Ed. J. Thompson) (Transl. G. Raymond & M. Adamson) *Language and Symbolic Power.* Harvard University Press. Massachusetts.
265. Bourdieu, P. (1991). (Ed. J. Thompson) (Transl. G. Raymond & M. Adamson) *Language and Symbolic Power.* Harvard University Press. Massachusetts. p. 164.
266. Bourdieu, P. (1991). (Ed. J. Thompson) (Transl. G. Raymond & M. Adamson) *Language and Symbolic Power.* Harvard University Press. Massachusetts. p. 167.

267. Bourdieu, P. (1991). (Ed. J. Thompson) (Transl. G. Raymond & M. Adamson) *Language and Symbolic Power.* Harvard University Press. Massachusetts. p. 166.
268. Bourdieu, P. (1991). (Ed. J. Thompson) (Transl. G. Raymond & M. Adamson) *Language and Symbolic Power.* Harvard University Press. Massachusetts. p. 181.
269. Bourdieu, P. (1991). (Ed. J. Thompson) (Transl. G. Raymond & M. Adamson) *Language and Symbolic Power.* Harvard University Press. Massachusetts. p. 185.
270. Bourdieu, P. (1991) (Ed. J. Thompson) (Transl. G. Raymond & M. Adamson) *Language and Symbolic Power.* Harvard University Press. Cambridge Massachusetts. p. 170.
271. Bourdieu, P. (1990). (Transl. R. Nice). *The Logic of Practice.* Stanford University Press. Stanford, California.
272. Ibid.
273. Bourdieu, P. (1986). Ed. I. Szeman, & T. Kaposy. (2011). The Forms of Capital. Chapter 8. *Cultural Theory: An Anthology.* Wiley-Blackwell. UK. p. 81.
274. Ibid.
275. Mutch, A. (2003). Communities of 'practice' and '*habitus*': A Critique. *Organization Studies.* 24:3. pp. 383–401. Retrieved from: https://journals-sagepub-com.wwwproxy1.library.unsw.edu.au/doi/pdf/10.1177/0170840603024003909; Maclean, M., Harvey, C. & Chia, R. (2010). Dominant Corporate Agents and the Power Elite in France and Britain. *Organization Studies.* 31:3. pp. 327–348. Retrieved from: https://journals-sagepub-com.wwwproxy1.library.unsw.edu.au/doi/pdf/10.1177/0170840609357377; Reed, M. (2012). Masters of the Universe: Power and Elites in Organization Studies. *Organization Studies.* 33:2. pp. 203–221. Retrieved from https://journals-sagepub-com.wwwproxy1.library.unsw.edu.au/doi/pdf/10.1177/0170840611430590.
276. Johnson, L. (1988) *The Unseen Voice: A cultural study of early Australian radio.* (2017 ed.) Vol. 3. Routledge Library Editions. London and New York.
277. Jackson, P. (2008). Pierre Bourdieu, the 'cultural turn' and the 'practice' of international history. *Review of International Studies.* 34. pp. 155–181.
278. Jackson, P. (2008). Pierre Bourdieu, the 'cultural turn' and the 'practice' of international history. *Review of International Studies.* 34. p. 156.
279. Jackson, P. (2008). Pierre Bourdieu, the 'cultural turn' and the 'practice' of international history. *Review of International Studies.* 34. p. 163.

280. *ABC* Annual Report. (2019). Retrieved from: https://about.abc.net.au/wp-content/uploads/2019/10/ABC-Annual-Report-201819v2.pdf. p. 102.
281. Ibid. Chair Ita Buttrose, Letter to Minister, p. iii.
282. Ibid., p. 115.
283. Bourdieu, P. (Transl. R. Nice). (1990). Ibid.
284. Bourdieu, P. (1994). "Structures, '*habitus*', Power: Basis for a theory of Symbolic Power". Chapter 4 in Dirks, N., Eley, G., Ortner, S. *Culture/Power/History: A Reader in Contemporary Social Theory.* Princeton Uni. Press N.J. p. 157.
285. Bourdieu, P. (1991). *Language and Symbolic Power.* Harvard University Press. Cambridge Massachusetts. p. 170.
286. Bourdieu, P. (Transl. R. Nice). (1990). *The Logic of Practice.* Stanford University Press. Stanford, California.
287. Tomlinson, M., O'Reilly, D., Wallace, M., Edwards, G., Elliott, C., Iszatt-White, M., Schedlitzki, D. (2013). Developing Leaders as Symbolic Violence: Reproducing Public Service Leadership through the (misrecognized) Development of Leaders' Capitals. 44:1. *Management Learning.* pp. 81–97. Quoting Golsorkhi et al., 2009; Ozbiglin and Tatli, 2005.
288. Bourdieu, P. (1984). *Distinction: A Social Critique of the Judgement of Taste.* Routledge and Kegan Paul. USA. p. 208.
289. Bourdieu, P. (1984). *Distinction: A Social Critique of the Judgement of Taste.* Routledge and Kegan Paul. USA. p. 481.
290. Bourdieu, P. (2005). (Transl. C. Turner). *The Social Structures of the Economy.* Polity Press. Cambridge. p. 205.
291. Schultz, J. (1998). *Reviving the Fourth Estate: Democracy, Accountability and the Media.* Cambridge: Cambridge University Press.
292. HØyer, S. & Pöttker, H. Eds. (2005). *Diffusion of the News Paradigm.* Nordicom. Göteborg. p. 25.
293. Stephens, M. (2007). *A History of News.* (3rd Ed.) Oxford University Press. New York, Oxford. p. 251.
294. Gentzkow, M., Glaeser, E.L. & Goldin, C. (2006). The Rise of the Fourth Estate. How Newspapers Became Informative and Why It Mattered. (Eds.). E.L. Glaeser & C. Goldin in *Corruption and Reform: Lessons from America's Economic History.* University of Chicago Press. Chicago. p. 188.
295. McChesney, R.W. (2012). Farewell to Journalism? Time for a rethinking. *Journalism Studies.* 13:5–6. pp. 682–694. DOI: 10.1080/1461670X.2012.679868.
296. McChesney, R.W. (2012). Farewell to Journalism? Time for a rethinking. *Journalism Studies.* 13:5–6. pp. 682–694. DOI: 10.1080/1461670X.2012.679868. p. 682.

297. McChesney, R.W. (2012). Farewell to Journalism? Time for a rethinking. *Journalism Studies*. 13:5–6. pp. 682–694. DOI: 10.1080/1461670X.2012.679868. p. 684.
298. Schultz, J. (1998). *Reviving the Fourth Estate: Democracy, Accountability and the Media*. Cambridge University Press. Cambridge.
299. First published 9 April 1842.
300. Anderson, B. (1983). *Imagined Communities*: Reflections on the Origin and Spread of Nationalism. Verso. London.
301. Frank, J. (1961). *The Beginnings of the English Newspaper, 1620–60*. Harvard University Press. Cambridge, Mass. p. 269.
302. DiMaggio, A. 2009. *When Media Goes to War: Hegemonic Discourse, Public opinion and the Limits of Dissent*. Monthly Review Press. New York. p. 14.
303. HØyer, S. & Pöttker, H. Eds. (2005). *Diffusion of the News Paradigm*. Nordicom. Göteborg. p. 112.

References

ABC. (2016, February). *ABC Submission to the House of Representatives Standing Committee on Communications and the Arts*. Inquiry Into the Importance of Public and Commercial Broadcasting, Online Content and Live Production to Rural and Regional Australia, Including the Arts, News and Other Services. [online]. *ABC*. http://d3n8a8pro7vhmx.cloudfront.net/abcfriends/legacy_url/2756/ABC_Submission_Reps_Feb2016_Sub009.pdf?1563515036

ABC. (2014). GUIDELINES FOR PERSONAL USE OF SOCIAL MEDIA. [online]. Document: D11/22627. Retrieved from: http://about.abc.net.au/wpcontent/uploads/2014/10/PersonalUseOfSocialMediaINS1.pdf. NOTE: now a dead link.

ABC. (2020, April). *Interview ABC News24. Strapline: "Pell Released. George Pell Freed from Prison After High Court ruling"*. https://www.youtube.com/watch?v=7x29VznAZOE

Amans, P., Mazars-Chapelon, A., & Villesèque-Dubus, F. (2015). Budgeting in Institutional Complexity: The Case of Performing Arts Organizations. *Management Accounting Research, 27*, 47–66. https://doi.org/10.1016/j.mar.2015.03.001

Anderson, B. (1983). *Imagined Communities: Reflections on the Origin and Spread of Nationalism*. Verso.

Barley, S. R., & Tolbert, P. S. (1997). Institutionalization and Structuration: Studying the Links Between Action and Institution. *Organization Studies, 18*(1), 93–117. https://doi.org/10.1177/017084069701800106

Bell, C. (1997). *Ritual: Perspectives and Dimensions*. Oxford University Press.

Bennett, L. (2018, September 24). Fairfax Calls Out ABC for Running YouTube Ads. *AdNews.* https://www.adnews.com.au/news/fairfax-calls-out-abc-for-running-youtube-ads

Benson, R., & Neveu, E. (2005). *Bourdieu and the Journalistic Field.* Polity Press.

Berger, P., & Luckmann, T. (1967). *The Social Construction of Reality.* Doubleday Anchor. New York. Retrieved from Google Scholar http://www.perflensburg.se/Berger%20social-construction-of-reality.pdf

Bolter, J. D. (2019, May 19). Social Media Are Ruining Political Discourse. *The Atlantic.* https://www.theatlantic.com/technology/archive/2019/05/why-social-media-ruining-political-discourse/589108/

Bolton, G. C. (1967). *Dick Boyer: An Australian Humanist.* Australian National University Press. Canberra.

Bourdieu, P. (1977). *Outline of a Theory of Practice* (R. Nice, Trans.). Cambridge University Press.

Bourdieu, P. (1979). *Distinction: A Social Critique of The Judgement of Taste* (R. Nice (1984), Trans.). Harvard University Press. Preface to the English Language Edition.

Bourdieu, P. (1980). (Trans. R. Nice) The Aristocracy of Culture. *Media, Culture and Society, 2*(3), 225–254. https://doi.org/10.1177/016344378000200303

Bourdieu, P. (1983). The Forms of Capital. In J. G. Richardson (Ed.), *Handbook of Theory and Research for the Sociology of Education* (pp. 241–258). Greenwood Press. New York.

Bourdieu, P. (1984). *Sociology in Question.* Sage Publications.

Bourdieu, P. (1990). *In Other Words: Essays Towards a Reflexive Sociology* (M. Adamson, Trans.). Stanford University Press. Stanford, CA.

Bourdieu, P. (1991). *Language and Symbolic Power* (J. Thompson, Ed., G. Raymond & M. Adamson, Trans.). Harvard University Press.

Bourdieu, P. (1994). Structures, '*Habitus*', Power: Basis for a Theory of Symbolic Power. Chap. 4 in N. Dirks, G. Eley, & S. Ortner (Eds.), *Culture/Power/History: A Reader in Contemporary Social Theory.* Princeton Uni. Press.

Bourdieu, P. (R. Johnson, Ed.). (1993). *The Field of Cultural Production: Essays on Art and Literature.* Polity Press.

Bourdieu, P. (1996).*The Rules of Art. Genesis and Structure of the Literary Field* (S. Emanuel, Trans.). Stanford University Press. Stanford.

Bourdieu, P. (1998). *On Television and Journalism* (P. Parkhurst Ferguson, Trans.). Pluto Press.

Bourdieu, P. (2005). *The Social Structures of the Economy* (C. Turner, Trans.). Polity Press.

Bourdieu, P., & Wacquant, L. (1992). *An Invitation to Reflexive Sociology.* University of Chicago Press.

Brems, C., Temmerman, M., Graham, T., & Broersma, M. (2017). Personal Branding on Twitter. *Digital Journalism, 5*(4), 443–459. https://doi.org/10.1080/21670811.2016.1176534

Bruns, A. (2012). Journalists and Twitter: How Australian News Organisations Adapt to a New Medium. *Media International Australia, Incorporating Culture & Policy, 144*, 97–107. https://primoa.library.unsw.edu.au/permalink/f/11jha62/TN_scopus2-s2.0-84864412059

Buttrose, C. (1984). *Words and Music: Press Barons, Prima Donnas and Coping with the ABC.* Angus and Robertson Publishers.

Cai, Z., Parker, S., Chen, Z., & Lam, W. (2019). How Does the Social Context Fuel the Proactive Fire? A Multilevel Review and Theoretical Synthesis. *Journal of Organizational Behaviour, 40*(2), 209–230.

Carr, D., & Bard, M. (2018). Even a Celebrity Journalist Can't Have an Opinion: Post-Millennials' Recognition and Evaluation of Journalists and News Brands on Twitter. *Electronic News, 12*(1), 3–22. https://doi.org/10.1177/1931243117710280.

Centre for Media Transition. (2020, January). News in Australia Impartiality and Commercial Influence. [online]. https://www.acma.gov.au/sites/default/files/2020-01/News%20in%20Australia_Impartiality%20and%20commercial%20influence_Review%20of%20literature%20and%20research.pdf

Chadwick, P. (2012, September 4–7). Adapting a Public Broadcaster's Self-Regulation for the Convergence Era. [online]. *RIPE@2012 Conference*, Sydney. http://about.abc.net.au/wp-content/uploads/2012/10/AdaptingAPublicBroadcastersSelfRegulationForTheConvergenceEraRIPE2012.pdf

Chaucer, G. (1476, orig.). The Canterbury Tales: The Knight's Tale, p. 3. [online]. http://art3idea.psu.edu/metalepsis/texts/knights_tale.pdf

Clark, M. (1995, orig. published 1962). *History of Australia* (p. 537). Melbourne University Press.

Coates, B. (2010). Cracking Into the Panes of Corporate Denial. *Business Renaissance Quarterly, 5*(3), 23–46. http://ezproxy.library.usyd.edu.au/login?url=https://search-proquest-com.ezproxy2.library.usyd.edu.au/docview/814814238?accountid=14757

Cola, M., & Prario, B. (2012, March). New Ways of Consumption: The Audiences of Public Service Media in Italy and Switzerland. *Media, Culture & Society, 34*(2), 181–194. https://journals-sagepub-com.wwwproxy1.library.unsw.edu.au/doi/pdf/10.1177/0163443711430757

Colliander, J. (2019). "This Is Fake News": Investigating the Role of Conformity to Other Users' Views When Commenting on and Spreading Disinformation in Social Media. *Computers in Human Behavior, 97*, 202–215. https://doi.org/10.1016/j.chb.2019.03.032

Cooper, S. (2009, Feb-Mar). Murdoch's Boyer Lectures: [Why was Rupert Murdoch chosen to give the 2008 ABC Boyer Lectures?] [online]. *Arena Magazine* (Fitzroy, Vic), *99*, 5–6. Retrieved from: ISSN: 1039–1010.

Cooke, M. (2007). Our Digital Aunty—The ABC's New Media Future. *Metro Magazine: Media & Education Magazine, 154*, 120–124. https://search.informit.org/doi/10.3316/INFORMIT.003683049332154

Corbett, J., Webster, J., & Jenkin, T. (2018). Unmasking Corporate Sustainability at the Project Level: Exploring the Influence of Institutional Logics and Individual Agency. *Journal of Business Ethics, 147*(2), 261–286. https://doi.org/10.1007/s10551-015-2945-1.

Couldry, N. (2003). *Media Rituals: A Critical Approach*. Routledge.

Couldry, N. (2004). Theorising Media as Practice. *Social Semiotics, 14*(2), 115–132. https://doi.org/10.1080/1035033042000238295

Courier Mail, The. (1934, July 25). Educational Broadcasts: Policy of the A.B.C, p. 20. https://trove.nla.gov.au/newspaper/article/36733653?searchTerm=Educational%20broadcasts%3A%20Policy%20of%20the%20A.B.C

Crisp, L. (2011). The Saddest of Days. The Deal. *The Australian Business Magazine, 4*, 9.

Cunningham, S. (2013). *Hidden Innovation: Policy, Industry and the Creative Sector*. University of Queensland Press.

Dailey, D., & Starbird, K. (2014). *Journalists as Crowdsourcerers: Responding to Crisis by Reporting with a Crowd Computer Supported Cooperative Work* (CSCW) (Vol. 23, pp. 445–481). https://doi.org/10.1007/s10606-014-9208-z

Dalzell, S. (2019, October 23). 'There Will Be Job Losses': ABC Managing Director Confirms Staff To Go Following Budget Freeze [online]. ABC News. *Australian Broadcasting Corporation*. https://www.abc.net.au/news/2019-10-23/abc-boss-confirms-staff-to-go-following-budget-cuts/11629336

Davis, G. (1988). *Breaking Up the ABC*. Allen and Unwin.

Demaria, A. (2015). Employer's Requirement to Post a Social Media Disclaimer Passes NLRB Muster. *Management Report for Nonunion Organizations, 38*(1), 3–4. https://doi.org/10.1002/mare.30020

Dempster, Q. (2000). *Death Struggle: How Political Malice and Boardroom Powerplays are Killing the ABC*. Allen and Unwin.

Denhardt, J. V., & Denhardt, R. B. (2007). *The New Public Service: Serving, Not Steering*. M.E. Sharpe.

Dickinson, H., Needham, C., Mangan, C., & Sullivan, H. E. (2019). *Reimagining the Future Public Service Workforce*. Springer Books.

DiMaggio, A. (2009). *When Media Goes to War: Hegemonic Discourse, Public opinion and the Limits of Dissent*. Monthly Review Press.

DiMaggio, P. (1987). *Managers of the Arts: Careers and Opinions of Senior Administrators of U.S. Art Museums, Symphony Orchestras, Resident Theaters, and Local Arts Agencies*. Research Division Report #20 National Endowment for the Arts. Seven Locks Press Publishers. Washington, DC.

DiMaggio, P. (2018). Our Faith-Based Economy. *Distinktion: Journal of Social Theory, 19*(3), 328–335. https://doi.org/10.1080/1600910X.2018.1452769

Dixon, F. (1975). *Inside the ABC: A Piece of Australian History*. The Hawthorn Press.

Dubois, E., Gruzd, A., Jacobson, J., Chen, W., & Quan-Haase, A. (2020). Journalists' Use of Social Media to Infer Public Opinion: The Citizens' Perspective. *Social Science Computer Review, 38*(1), 57–74. https://doi.org/10.1177/0894439318791527

Elliott, G., Sainsbury, M., & Overington, C. (2010, July 24). ABC Picks Sides While the 'Editor-in-Chief' Watches On. [online]. *The Australian*. https://www.theaustralian.com.au/national-affairs/abc-picks-sides-while-the-editor-in-chief-watches-on/news-story/59e747a64f4d496c33e661f4ab25a6e2

Fardouly, J., & Holland, E. (2018). Social Media Is Not Real Life: The Effect of Attaching Disclaimer-Type Labels to Idealized Social Media Images on women's Body Image and Mood. *New Media & Society, 20*(11), 4311–4328. https://doi.org/10.1177/1461444818771083

FarmOnline, & AAP. (2020, June 24). ABC Life Becomes ABC Local as National Broadcaster Restructured. [online]. *FarmOnline*. https://www.farmonline.com.au/story/6804883/regional-focus-boost-for-abc-in-major-restructure/

Fitzsimmons, J. A., & Fitzsimmons, M. J. (2004). *Service Management: Operations, Strategy, and Information Technology* (4th ed.). McGraw-Hill.

Flanagan, M. (2014, February 8). Rupert Murdoch's Attack on 'Our ABC' Like a Mediaeval Siege. [online]. *The Sydney Morning Herald, The*. https://www.smh.com.au/opinion/rupert-murdochs-attack-on-our-abc-like-a-mediaeval-siege-20140207-32746.html

Foucault, M. (1983, October–November). *Discourse and Truth: The Problematization of Parrhesia* (J. Pearson, Ed.). Taken from a Series of Lectures. University of California. https://foucault.info/parrhesia/

Frank, J. (1961). *The Beginnings of the English Newspaper, 1620–60*. Harvard University Press.

Friedland, R. (2018). Moving Institutional Logics Forward: Emotion and Meaningful Material Practice. *Organization Studies, 39*(4), 515–542. https://doi.org/10.1177/0170840617709307

Friedland, R., & Alford, R. R. (1991). Bringing Society Back. In W. W. Powell & P. J. DiMaggio (Eds.), *Symbols, Practices and Institutional Contradictions (The New Institutionalism in Organisational Analysis)*. University of Chicago Press. Chicago, IL.

Funston, A. (1997). The ABC and Citizenship [online]. *Overland, 147*(Winter), 59–62. https://search-informit-com-au.wwwproxy1.library.unsw.edu.au/documentSummary;dn=971111828;res=IELAPA

Galston, W. (2018, 17 April). *The Populist Challenge to Liberal Democracy*. [online]. Brookings Institute. https://www.brookings.edu/research/the-populist-challenge-to-liberal-democracy/

Gentzkow, M., Glaeser, E. L., & Goldin, C. (2006). The Rise of the Fourth Estate. How Newspapers Became Informative and Why It Mattered. In E. L. Glaeser & C. Goldin (Eds.), *Corruption and Reform: Lessons from America's Economic History*. University of Chicago Press.

Girard, R., & Grayson, R. (2016). Belonging. *Contagion: Journal of Violence, Mimesis, and Culture, 23*(1), 1–12. https://doi.org/10.14321/contagion.23.1.0001

Given, J. (1998). *The Death of Broadcasting? Media's Digital Future*. Communications Law Centre. UNSW Press.

Glynn, M. (2000, May–June). When Cymbals Become Symbols: Conflict Over Organizational Identity Within a Symphony Orchestra. *Organization Science, 11*(3). Special Issue: Cultural Industries: Learning from Evolving Organizational Practices, pp. 285–298. https://www.jstor.org/stable/2640262

Glynn, M., & Lounsbury, M. (2005). From the Critics' Corner: Logic Blending, Discursive Change and Authenticity in a Cultural Production System. *The Journal of Management Studies., 42*(5), 1031–1055. https://doi.org/10.1111/j.1467-6486.2005.00531.x

Goffman, E. (1961). *Encounters: Two Studies in the Sociology of Interaction*. Bobbs-Merrill. Indianapolis. IN.

Greenwood, R., Oliver, C., Suddaby, R., & Sahlin-Andersson, K. (2012). *The SAGE Handbook of Organizational Institutionalism. SAGE Publications. ProQuest Ebook Central.* https://ebookcentral.proquest.com/lib/unsw/detail.action?docID=1024020

Griffith, C. (1996, August). The ABC and Multimedia: A New Media Form [online]. *Media International Australia,* 81, 49–53. https://search-informit-com-au.wwwproxy1.library.unsw.edu.au/documentSummary;dn=078935934053890;res=IELLCC

Grossman, L. (2010, December 15). Mark Zuckerberg: Person of the Year. [online]. *Time Magazine*. http://content.time.com/time/specials/packages/article/0,28804,2036683_2037183_2037185-1,00.html

Hanusch, F. (2017). Web Analytics and the Functional Differentiation of Journalism Cultures: Individual, Organizational and Platform-Specific Influences on Newswork. *Information, Communication & Society, 20*(10), 1571–1586. https://doi.org/10.1080/1369118X.2016.1241294

Harding, R. (1979). *Outside Interference: The Politics of Australia Broadcasting*. Sun Books.

Harvey, C., & Chia, R. (2010). Dominant Corporate Agents and the Power Elite in France and Britain. *Organization Studies, 31*(3), 327–348. https://journals-sagepub-com.wwwproxy1.library.unsw.edu.au/doi/pdf/10.1177/0170840609357377

Hastings, A., & Matthews, P. (2015). Bourdieu and the Big Society: Empowering the Powerful in Public Service Provision? *Policy & Politics, 43*(4), 545–560. https://doi.org/10.1332/030557314X14080105693951

Holmes, J. (2019). *On Aunty*. Melbourne University Press. Carlton, Victoria.

Houghton, D. (2011). Groupthink. In B. Badie, D. Berg-Schlosser, & L. Morlino (Eds.), *International Encyclopedia of Political Science* (pp. 1058–1060). SAGE Publications. Thousand Oaks, CA. https://doi.org/10.4135/9781412959636.n244.

Høyer, S., & Pöttker, H. (Eds.). (2005). *Diffusion of the News Paradigm.* Nordicam. Göteborg University. https://www.nordicom.gu.se/sv/system/tdf/publikationer-hela-pdf/diffusion_of_the_news_paradigm_1850-2000.pdf?file=1&type=node&id=10239&force=0

Hua, D. (2016). *Harnessing the Opportunities of Digital Disruption: the ABC story. 2nd Annual Digital Disruption X 2016.* Retrieved from: https://www.iqpc.com/media/1002146/55636.pdf

Hyland, A. (2015, November 27). Mark Scott's ABC Exit Interview: 'I Had No Idea of the Scale of the Challenge'. *The Australian Financial Review.* https://www.afr.com/life-and-luxury/abcs-mark-scott-on-success-and-his-legacy-20151019-gkcgi8

Inglis, K. (1983). *The is the ABC: The Australian Broadcasting Commission 1932–1983.* Melbourne University Press.

Inglis, K. (2002, November 27). The Media—Aunty at Seventy: A Health Report on the ABC. [online]. *Analysis and Policy Observatory.* Retrieved March 4, 2020, from https://apo.org.au/node/6627

Inglis, K. (2006). *Whose ABC? The Australian Broadcasting Corporation 1983–2006.* Black Inc.

Jackson, P. (2008). Pierre Bourdieu, the 'Cultural Turn' and the 'Practice' of International History. *Review of International Studies, 34*(1), 155–181. https://doi.org/10.1017/S026021050800795X

Jensen, A. (2019). Interdisciplinary Arts and Health Practice with an Institutional Logics Perspective. *Arts & Health, 11*(3), 219–231. https://doi.org/10.1080/17533015.2018.1443950

Johnson, L. (1988). *The Unseen Voice: A Cultural Study of Early Australian Radio* (Vol. 3, 2017th ed.). Routledge Library Editions.

Jones, P. K., & Pusey, M. (2010). Political Communication and 'Media System': The Australian Canary. *Media, Culture & Society, 32*(3), 451–471. https://doi.org/10.1177/0163443709361172

Kim, M. N. (2018). The Role of Chief Editor in Managerial System of Editorial Board. *Upravlencheskoe Konsul'tirovanie, 6,* 182–189. https://doaj.org/article/6dc6b7258546412bbececb6622d09299

Kress, G. (1985). *Linguistic Processes in Sociocultural Practice.* Deakin University Press.

Lallo, M. (2020, March 1). ABC Workers Face Anxious Wait Over Job, Program Cuts. [online]. *The Herald Sun.* https://www.heraldsun.com.au/blogs/andrew-bolt/more-abc-staff-less-value/news-story/e6f8bc5271a1f93606b916a39bddd1b8

Lariscy, R., Avery, E., Sweetser, K., & Howes, P. (2009). An Examination of the Role of Online Social Media in Journalists' Source Mix. *Public Relations Review, 35*(3), 314–316. https://doi.org/10.1016/j.pubrev.2009.05.008

Lau, T., Wang, H. C., & Chuang, C. C. (2011, May). A Definition of Service as Base for Developing Service Science. *2011 International Joint Conference on Service Science*, 49–53. Conference Paper. https://doi.org/10.1109/IJCSS.2011.18

Letamendia, A. (2017). Towards the Aestheticisation of the Resistances in the Digital Age? A Critical Approach. Chap. 9 in *Precarity within the Digital Age Media Change and Social Insecurity.* Springer. https://link-springer-com.wwwproxy1.library.unsw.edu.au/content/pdf/10.1007%2F978-3-658-17678-5.pdf

Lieberman, D. (2007, August 6). Murdoch Grew Up on 'Ritual Feuding with Other Media'. [online]. *USA Today.* https://abcnews.go.com/Business/story?id=3434589&page=1

Lincoln, J. R. (1995). Book Review. (Eds. W. W. Powell & P. DiMaggio): The New Institutionalism in Organizational Analysis. *Social Forces, 73*(3), 1147–1148. https://doi.org/10.1093/sf/73.3.1147

Littlemore, S. (1996). *The Media and Me.* ABC Books for the Australian Broadcasting Corporation, Sydney.

Livingston, J., Holland, E., & Fardouly, J. (2020). Exposing Digital Posing: The Effect of Social Media Self-Disclaimer Captions on Women's Body Dissatisfaction, Mood, and Impressions of the User. *Body Image, 32*, 150–154. https://doi.org/10.1016/j.bodyim.2019.12.006

Lysak, S., Cremedas, M., & Wolf, J. (2012). Facebook and Twitter in the Newsroom: How and Why Local Television News is Getting Social With Viewers? *Electronic News, 6*(4), 187–207. https://doi.org/10.1177/1931243112466095

MacInnis, F. (2005, April). Towards a New Definition of Service. *Chief Executive, 197.* https://primoa.library.unsw.edu.au/permalink/f/11jha62/TN_cdi_proquest_reports_212103313

Malsch, B., & Gendron, Y. (2013). Re-Theorizing Change: Institutional Experimentation and the Struggle for Domination in the *field* of Public Accounting. *Journal Of Management Studies, 50*(5), 870–899. https://doi.org/10.1111/joms.12006

Manz, C., Skaggs, B., Pearce, C., & Wassenaar, C. (2015). Serving One Another: Are Shared and Self-Leadership the Keys to Service Sustainability? *Journal of Organizational Behaviour, 36*(4), 607–612. https://doi.org/10.1002/job.1991

Martin, F. (2002). Beyond Public Service Broadcasting? ABC Online and the User/Citizen. *Southern Review: Communication, Politics & Culture, 35*(1), 42–62. https://search-informit-com-au.wwwproxy1.library.unsw.edu.au/documentSummary;dn=743199784542203;res=IELAPA

Marquis, C., & Lounsbury, M. (2007). Vive La Resistance: Competing Logics and the Consolidation of US Community Banking. *Academy of Management Journal, 50*(4), 799–820.

Matei, S. A., Bertino, E., & Russell, M. (2015). Introduction. In S. Matei, M. Russell, & E. Bertino (Eds.), *Transparency in Social Media. Computational Social Sciences.* Springer International Publishing AG. https://doi.org/10.1007/978-3-319-18552-1

McChesney, R. W. (2012). Farewell to Journalism? Time for a Rethinking. *Journalism Studies, 13*(5-6), 682–694. https://doi.org/10.1080/1461670X.2012.679868

Mellet, K. (2011). Online Marketing. *Communications, 88*(1), 103–111. https://doi.org/10.3917/commu.088.0103

Mergel, I., & Greeves, B. (2013). *Social Media in the Public Sector Field Guide: Designing and Implementing Strategies and Policies.* Jossey-Bass.

Mintz, A., & Wayne, C. (2016). The Polythink Syndrome and Elite Group Decision-making. *Political Psychology, 37*(S1), 3.

Molomby, T. (1991). *Is There a Moderate on the Roof? ABC Years.* William Heinemann.

Morton, R. (2020, June 25–26). Exclusive: New Govt Report Targets ABC. [online]. *The Saturday Paper, 306.* https://www.thesaturdaypaper.com.au/news/politics/2020/06/27/exclusive-new-govt-report-targets-abc/159318000010021

Murphy, J., Link, M. W., Childs, J. H., Tesfaye, C. L., Dean, E., Stern, M., Pasek, J., Cohen, J., Callegaro, M., & Harwood, P. (2014). Social Media in Public Opinion Research. *Public Opinion Quarterly, 78*(4), 788–794. https://doi.org/10.1093/poq/nfu053

Mutch, A. (2003). Communities of 'Practice' and '*Habitus*': A Critique. *Organization Studies, 24*(3), 383–401. M. Maclean. https://journals-sagepub-com.wwwproxy1.library.unsw.edu.au/doi/pdf/10.1177/0170840603024003909

Nah, S., & Chung, D. S. (2012). When Citizens Meet Both Professional and Citizen Journalists: Social Trust, Media Credibility, and Perceived Journalistic Roles Among Online Community News Readers. *Journalism, 13*(6), 14–730. https://doi.org/10.1177/1464884911431381

Newman, N. with Fletcher, R., Levy, D. A. L., & Kleis Nielsen, R. (2016). Digital News Report. [online]. *Reuters Institute & Oxford University.*http://media.digitalnewsreport.org/wp-content/uploads/2018/11/Digital-News-Report-2016.pdf?x89475

Nolan, D. (2006). Media, Citizenship and Governmentality: Defining "The Public" of Public Service Broadcasting. *Social Semiotics, 16*(2), 225–242. https://doi.org/10.1080/10350330600667501

O'Brien, K. (2018). *Kerry O'Brien: A Memoir.* Allen and Unwin.

O'Sullivan, P. B. (2005). Masspersonal Communication: An Integrative Model Bridging the Mass-Personal Divide. In Annual Meeting of the International Communication Association. New York City, New York. Retrieved from: http://ilstu.academia.edu/PatrickBOSullivan/Papers/457584/Masspersonal_communication_Rethinking_the_mass_interpersonal_divide.

Owen, D. (2018). The Past Decade and Future of Political Media: The Ascendance of Social Media. In *Towards a New Enlightenment? A Transcendent Decade*. Madrid: BBVA. Retrieved from: https://www.bbvaopenmind.com/en/articles/the-past-decade-and-future-of-political-media-the-ascendance-of-social-media/.

Palfreyman, R. (1993, November). Opening the Airwaves: Cultural Squeeze for National Broadcasting? *Current Affairs Bulletin, 70*(6), 19–25. https://hdl.handle.net/10070/89994

Parliament of Australia. (2019). Amendments to *Australian Broadcasting Corporation Act 1983* To: Amend the Australian Broadcasting Corporation (ABC) Charter. [online]. https://www.aph.gov.au/Parliamentary_Business/Bills_Legislation/Bills_Search_Results/Result?bId=r6382

Pascoe, M. (2020, August 12). Michael Pascoe: More Job Losses Are a Safe Bet After Network Ten's Dark Day. *The New Daily*.https://thenewdaily.com.au/finance/finance-news/2020/08/12/network-ten-michael-pascoe/#:~:text=Michael%20Pascoe%3A%20More%20job%20losses,after%20Network%20Ten's%20dark%20day&text=A%20well%2Dknown%20TV%20star,as%20income%20falls%20below%20costs.

Paterson, T., Harms, P., & Tuggle, C. (2018). Revisiting the Rigor–Relevance Relationship: An Institutional Logics Perspective. *Human Resource Management, 57*(6), 1371–1383. https://doi.org/10.1002/hrm.21911

Patriarche, G., & Dufrasne, M. (2014). Penser la diversité des pratiques médiatiques: Le réseau comme catégorie conceptuelle pour la recherche sur les audiences et les publics. *Réseaux, 187*(5), 195–232. https://doi.org/10.3917/res.187.0195

Petersen, N. (1993). *News Not Views: The ABC, the Press, & Politics. 1932–1947*. Hale and Iremonger.

Powers, M., & Vera-Zambrano, S. (2018). How Journalists Use Social Media in France and the United States: Analyzing Technology Use Across Journalistic Fields. *New Media & Society, 20*(8), 2728–2744. https://doi.org/10.1177/1461444817731566

Pullan, R. (1986). *Four Corners: Twenty-Five Years*. ABC Enterprises.

QSRweb.com. (2015, February 11). *How Customers' Expectations Defines Your Brand*. [online]. Cengage Learning, Inc. https://link-gale-com

Radioinfo.com.au. (2020). RIP ABC 0745 News Bulletin. https://www.radioinfo.com.au/news/rip-abc-0745-news-bulletin

Reed, M. (2012). Masters of the Universe: Power and Elites in Organization Studies. *Organization Studies, 33*(2), 203–221. https://journals-sagepub-com.wwwproxy1.library.unsw.edu.au/doi/pdf/10.1177/0170840611430590

Robinson, S. L. (1996). Trust and Breach of the Psychological Contract. *Administrative Science Quarterly, 41*(4), 574–599. https://doi.org/10.2307/2393868

Salter, D. (2007). *The Media We Deserve: Underachievement in The Fourth Estate.* Melbourne University Press.

Samios, Z. (2021). ABC to relocate 300 Ultimo staff to Parramatta. The Sydney Morning Herald. 16 June 2021. Retrieved from: https://www.smh.com.au/politics/federal/abc-to-relocate-300-staff-to-parramatta-20210616-p581eh.html.

Santana, A. D., & Hopp, T. (2016). Tapping Into a New Stream of (Personal) Data: Assessing Journalists' Different Use of Social Media. *Journalism & Mass Communication Quarterly, 93*(2), 383–408. https://doi.org/10.1177/1077699016637105

Scannell, P. (1989). Public Service Broadcasting and Modern Public Life. *Media, Culture & Society, 11*(2), 135–166. https://doi.org/10.1177/016344389011002002

Scannell, P. (1997). Public Service Broadcasting and Modern Public Life. In T. O'Sullivan & Y. Jewkes (Eds.), *The Media Studies Reader.* Arnold.

Scannell, P. (2005). In G. Ferrell Lowe & P. Jauert (Eds.), *The Meaning of Broadcasting in the Digital Era. Cultural Dilemmas in Public Service Broadcasting* (pp. 141–142). Ripe@2005. Nordicom. Göteborg. Retrieved from: https://www.diva-portal.org/smash/get/diva2:1534711/FULLTEXT01.pdf#page=15

Scannell, P. (2019). *Why Do People Sing? On Voice.* Polity Press.

Scannell, P. (Ed.). (1991). Broadcast Talk. In *Introduction: The Relevance of Talk.* Sage Publications.

Schifferes, S., Newman, N., Thurman, N., Corney, D., Goker, A. S., & Martin, C. (2014). Identifying and Verifying News Through Social Media: Developing a User-Centred Tool for Professional Journalists. *Digital Journalism, 2*(3), 406–418. https://doi.org/10.1080/21670811.2014.892747

Schultz, J. (1998). *Reviving the Fourth Estate: Democracy, Accountability and the Media.* Cambridge University Press.

Schulz, A. Levy, D. A. L., & Kleis Nielsen, R. (2019, September). Old, Educated, and Politically Diverse: The Audience of Public Service News. *Reuters Institute Report.* https://reutersinstitute.politics.ox.ac.uk/sites/default/files/2019-09/The_audience_of_public_service_news_FINAL.pdf

Scott, M. (2016). *A Media Odyssey: Speeches of an ABC Managing Director 2006–2016.* ABC Books.

Sehl, A. (2020). Public Service Media in a Digital Media Environment: Performance from an Audience Perspective. *Media and Communication, 8*(3), 359–372. https://doi.org/10.17645/mac.v8i3.3141.

Semmler, C. (1981). *The ABC—Aunt Sally and Sacred Cow.* Melbourne University Press.

Shergold, P. (2017). Re-Imagining Public Service [online]. *The Australian Journal of Social Issues, 52*(1), 4–12. https://search-informit-com-au.wwwproxy1.library.unsw.edu.au/documentSummary;dn=035171807770944;res=IELAPA

Smith, M. A., Himelboim, I., Rainie, L., & Shneiderman, B. (2015). The Structures of Twitter Crowds and Conversations. In S. Matei, M. Russell, & E. Bertino (Eds.), *Transparency in Social Media. Computational Social Sciences*. Springer.

Smolkin, R. (2006). Adapt or Die: As Newspaper Companies Confront a Challenging Future, They Are Increasingly Viewing Their Trademark Print Product as the Engine Driving a Diverse "Portfolio" That Embraces Other "Platforms" Such as Web Sites and Niche Publications. Is This a Strategy for Survival? *American Journalism Review, 28*(3). https://go.gale.com/ps/anonymous?id=GALE%7CA147375836&sid=googleScholar&v=2.1&it=r&linkaccess=abs&issn=10678654&p=AONE&sw=w

Spigelman, J. (2012, September 6). Public Broadcasting, Public Value. [online]. The Drum. Analysis. *ABC*. https://www.abc.net.au/news/2012-09-05/spigelman-public-broadcasting-public-value/4244468

Spigelman, J. (2013). The ABC and Australia's Media Landscape. *Media International Australia, Incorporating Culture & Policy, 146*, 12–24. https://primoa.library.unsw.edu.au/permalink/f/11jha62/TN_informit182288913833846

Stephens, M. (2007). *A History of News* (3rd ed.). Oxford University Press.

Suddaby, R. (2010). Challenges for Institutional Theory. *Journal of Management Inquiry, 19*(1), 14–20. https://doi.org/10.1177/1056492609347564

Swartz, N. P. (2012, Winter). 'Dumbing Down' the CBC News. *Humanist Perspectives, 183*, p. 18. Retrieved from: http://search.proquest.com/docview/1268836316/.

Swinehart, K., & Graber, K. (2012). Tongue-Tied Territories: Languages and Publics in Stateless Nations. *Language and Communication, 32*(2), 95–97. https://doi.org/10.1016/j.langcom.2011.05.007

Telegraph, The (Brisbane). Empire Broadcasting: Early Inauguration. [online]. 13 July 1932, p. 10. Retrieved from: https://trove.nla.gov.au/newspaper/article/181268000?searchTerm=abc%20inaugural&searchLimits=exactPhrase|||anyWords|||notWords|||requestHandler|||dateFrom=1932-06-01|||dateTo=1932-07-31|||sortby.

Thomas, A. (1980). *Broadcast and be Damned: The ABC's First Two Decades*. Melbourne University Press.

Thomson, P. (2005). Bringing Bourdieu to Policy Sociology: Codification, Misrecognition and Exchange Value in the UK Context. *Journal of Education Policy, 20*(6), 741–758. https://doi.org/10.1080/02680930500238929

Thornton, P. H. (2004). *Markets from Culture: Institutional Logics and Organizational Decisions in Higher Education Publishing*. Stanford University Press.

Thornton, P. H. (2001). Personal Versus Market Logics of Control: A Historically Contingent Theory of the Risk of Acquisition. *Organization Science, 12*(3), 294–311.

Thornton, P. (2002). The Rise of the Corporation in a Craft Industry: Conflict and Conformity in Institutional Logics. *Academy of Management Journal, 45*(1), 81–101.

Thornton, P. H., & Ocasio, W. (2008). Institutional Logics. In R. Greenwood, C. Oliver, K. Sahlin-Andersson, & R. Suddaby (Eds.), *The Sage Handbook of Organisational Institutionalism*. Sage.

Thornton, P., & Ocasio, W. (1999). Institutional Logics and the Historical Contingency of Power in Organizations: Executive Succession in the Higher Education Publishing Industry, 1958–1990. *American Journal of Sociology, 105*(3), 801–843. https://doi.org/10.1086/210361

Thornton, P. H., Ocasio, W., & Lounsbury, M. (2012a). *The Emergence and Evolution of Field-Level Logics*. https://doi.org/10.1093/acprof:oso/9780199601936.003.0007.

Thornton, P. H., Ocasio, W., & Lounsbury, M. (2012b). *Introduction to the Institutional Logics Perspective: A New Approach to Culture, Structure and Processes*. Oxford University Press. Oxford.

Tomlinson, M., O'Reilly, D., Wallace, M., Edwards, G., Elliott, C., Iszatt-White, M., & Schedlitzki, D. (2013). Developing Leaders as Symbolic Violence: Reproducing Public Service Leadership Through the (Misrecognized) Development of Leaders' Capitals. *Management Learning, 44*(1), 81–97. https://doi.org/10.1177/1350507612472151

Tracey, M. (1998, reprinted 2002). *The Decline and Fall of Public Service Broadcasting*. Oxford University Press.

Tucker, J. A., Theocharis, Y., Roberts, M. E., & Barberá, P. (2017). From Liberation to Turmoil: Social Media and Democracy. *Journal of Democracy, 28*(4), 46–59. https://doi.org/10.1353/jod.2017.0064

Turner, G. (2020). Dealing with Diversity: Australian Television, Homogeneity and Indigeneity. *Media International Australia, 174*(1), 20–28. DOI: i1.o0r.gl/10 7.171/1737/2193829787X8X1919886699481

Ulin, J. (2009). *The Business of Media Distribution: Monetizing Film, TV and Video Content in an Online World*. Focal. Elsevier E-Book. https://primoa.library.unsw.edu.au/permalink/f/jhud33/UNSW_ALMA51181866550001731

Ursell, G. (2003). Creating Value and Valuing Creation in Contemporary UK Television: or "Dumbing Down" the Workforce. *Journalism Studies., 4*(1), 31–46. https://doi.org/10.1080/14616700306501

Van den Bulck, H., & Moe, H. (2018). Public Service Media, Universality and Personalisation through Algorithms: Mapping Strategies and Exploring Dilemmas. *Media, Culture & Society, 40*(6), 875–892. https://doi.org/10.177/016344371773407

van Dijk, T. (1992). Discourse and the Denial of Racism. *Discourse & Society, 3*(1), 87–118. https://doi.org/10.1177/0957926592003001005

Varpio, L, O'Brien, B., Hu, W., ten Cate, O., Durning, S. J., van der Vleuten, C., Gruppen, L., Irby, D., Humphrey-Murto, S., Hamstra, S. J. (2017). Exploring the Institutional Logics of Health Professions Education Scholarship Units. *Medical Education, 51*(7), 755.

Ward, T. (2009). The Heart of What It Means to Be Australian. *Soccer & Society, 10*(5), 532–543. https://doi.org/10.1080/14660970902955463

White, D., & Lynch, J. (2014, November 20). Turnbull Takes on ABC, SBS. [online]. *The Australian Financial Review*. http://search.proquest.com/docview/1748835968/

Whitehead, G. (1988). *Inside the ABC: Geoffrey Whitehead's Personal Account*. Penguin Books Victoria.

Williams, R. (1996). *Normal Service Won't Be Resumed: The Future of Public Broadcasting*. Allen & Unwin, Sydney.

Wilson, Z. (2019). David Anderson Named ABC Managing Director. *Radio Today*. https://www.radiotoday.com.au/david-anderson-named-abc-managing-director/

Worthington, B., & Hitch, G. (2020, June 24). Up to 250 ABC Jobs to Go, ABC Life Brand Scrapped, Flagship Radio News Bulletin Dumped to Tackle $84 Million Budget Cut. [online]. *ABC News*. https://www.abc.net.au/news/2020-06-24/abc-announces-cuts-to-programming-and-jobs-funding/12384972

CHAPTER 2

Managing the ABC

2.1 Management and Leadership

The purpose of the chapter is to highlight instances where the ABC has acted against the ***cultural capital*** obtained in its élite, privileged ***field*** by merging with the wild west and hyper-creative commercial ***field***. It is not an analysis of the ABC's management since inception, rather it highlights examples of leadership and how it has shaped or detained the organisation. It also avoids an analysis of every manager since the ABC's launch. Rather it makes two leadership-related assertions. First, with the ABC's shift into the digital field, there was no apparent vision for taking its ***cultural capital*** and ***reputational capital*** with it into the emergent commercial ***field*** where, instead, forming alliances with commercial media was prioritised. For example, in 2016 the commercial arm of the ABC—ABC Commercial—announced it was again partnering with the privately owned Singaporean telecommunications company Optus on a resilience app for retail workers. Optus said the ABC partnership involved creating "content that would resonate with not just our retail employees, but a program that will be useful across the retail landscape" (M2 Presswire, 2016).[1] The ABC said it followed a previous Optus partnership called The Happy Body program consisting of "scalable, digital wellbeing programs" (Ibid.).

Second, ABC leaders and managers do not receive consistent support from staff, governments, parliaments and its new commercially-oriented

V. Small, *Strangling Aunty: Perilous Times for the Australian Broadcasting Corporation*,
https://doi.org/10.1007/978-981-16-0776-9_2

audiences to enable them to operate the organisation with a clearly defined vision of independence while upholding the Charter. Institutional leaders tread a tricky path in ameliorating a range of interests, many internal, seeking competing outcomes. In contrast, in 1932, the first ABC Chairman Charles Lloyd-Jones, said in his ABC inauguration speech to all Australians:

> The service now belongs to you we are your trustees. It is a service that is not run for profit but purely in the interests of every section of the community. (*The Sydney Morning Herald*, 1932)[2]

That role of leadership and recruiting the right Managing Director to steer the public media outfit is now problematised. It is challenged to address more severe budget downturns, as well as a range of new ones: value, translate and maintain the ABC's cultural capital, control restive staff, embrace and be innovative in the digital world, survive the heat of technological changes and spot commercial opportunities, as exemplified in the preceding ABC Commercial instance. The board now has to appoint a Managing Director who is adept and capable of accommodating these disparate, competing demands. Former Chairman Justin Milne pointed out how different public service broadcasting management was to other management when he said recruiting the right Managing Director was "a lottery" (Meade, 2018)[3] while in 2002 former Deputy Chair Di Gribble said:

> I think anyone who came into the ABC with the kind of MBA kind of approach to management technique, a kind of manual, a kind of "management" sort of approach, would be absolutely at sea. All of the kind of books that "wannabe" managers would read about managing corporations or whatever, it's very different in public broadcasting. (Wilson et al., 2010)[4]

This chapter will also analyse ABC leadership in the light of Institutional Logics. The ABC is not an organisation, it is an institution, but an institution also has an organisational structure. This book will not be looking at institutions as stereotyped examples, for example, of feminism or intersectionality (Sanchez Perry, 2017),[5] but rather it will examine the ABC as a unique institution charged with representing everyone, an institution that is entrusted to look at and beyond diversity to discern a holistic representation of a democratic society—to quote former Prime Minister Kevin Rudd one that was "above and beyond the reach of frontline culture warriors" (Lewis, 2009, quoting Rudd).[6] A successful institution is regarded as "central to the achievement of economic growth and development" (Shand, 2015 quoting Jütting, 2003, Leftwich & Sen, 2010, Andrews et al., 2012)[7] and is defined as "the rules of the game in a society or, more formally, are the humanly devised constraints that shape human interaction" (North, 1990).[8] An institution will "reduce uncertainty by providing a structure to everyday life" (Ibid.).[9] They not only affect economies they affect how a society performs (Ibid.). Institutional Logics provides a means of analysing how actors function within the institution, in this instance the ABC, and how managers and leaders have been able to operate within the various constraints of initiating change, enacting change or being thwarted by resistance or blow-back to change.

The central construct of neo-institutional theory is the organisational field (Scott, 1991, in Wooten & Hoffman, 2008)[10] and the organisational *field* is a constellation of actors that comprise this central organising unit structured by a network of relationships. Social normative regulative structures are called social facts—and actors consider these social facts when making decisions (Scott, 1991 in M. Wooten & A.J. Hoffman Ibid.). In addition, Wooten and Hoffman (2008) said institutional theory stated that organisations sought survival and legitimacy anyway, rather than efficiency. Lindenberg (1998)[11] said understanding cultural and cognitive processes that guided *field* members' behaviour—what are referred to as symbolic constructions—was *field-level logic* (quoting Friedland & Alford, 1991 in Wooten & Hoffman Ibid.). Institutional Logics helped explain changes in organisations such that institutions were no longer places of isomorphic dialogues (the old way of viewing them) but contested fields of struggle (Bourdieu & Wacquant, 1992).[12] In such an environment, Seo and Creed (2002) said the impetus for change involved resolving contradictory institutional arrangements or incongruous demands (Wooten & Hoffman, 2008).[13] But institutions in this field are also acted upon by other institutions (Scott, 1994),[14] so the ABC cannot exist in a bubble, especially not that it is competing in the commercial field. Institutional Logics also looks at the actions of state and the influence of the legal/regulatory environment on major organisations (Wooten & Hoffman, 2008).[15] It is aimed at developing uniformity but also can create ambiguity in how organisations can be compliant because *fields* then become "relational spaces" (Wooten & Hoffman Ibid.) in this case between the ABC and governments.[16]

The *field* of the ABC is both governed (through legislation and policy) and managed. Governance takes the form of The Australian Broadcasting Corporation Act 1983 and the ABC Charter. It is also governed by Sect. 2.3 of the Broadcasting Services Act 1992 which covers all broadcasting, public and private. Initially, it was managed by people better described as cultural entrepreneurs, such as Charles Moses, his board and his key management appointments who were charged with building Australia's cultural dimensions. Management as leadership is a more contentious issue as, over time, managers, especially ABC Managing Directors, have been troubled increasingly by a strong staff culture, managerialism and tough external political and financial pressures that compromise leadership. Yet, a central aspect of the past and future of the ABC has been leadership, and leadership is a subject that occupies diverse understandings scaffolded by many theories. This section will consider leadership in a general sense, but how it situates in the public service, including the ABC. This then will establish understandings to support the analysis of ABC staff culture and its interface with leadership, in the following chapter, Chap. 3.

Leadership is complex and incorporates many factors over large time frames (Dinh et al., 2014).[17] Leaders have agency in the institution in guiding policy and outcomes which may at times be imaginative and pioneering as in the case of Charles Moses; confrontational involving staff and content cuts as has been the case with many managers since the 1970s–1980s; and, also may rely on the leader's connections with other institutions, such as that of Michelle Guthrie and her past association with the digital media organisation Google. This chapter will examine some of the main types of leadership, generally, and it will commence with a wider analysis of leadership in Australian society, and how it is received and judged. It will also look at the bigger picture of views of leadership in hostile, cynical times. In terms of the workforce in relation to its leaders, the literature said more research was needed to unravel the complexity of the moral motivations of staff and their reactions (Brewster et al., 2018).[18]

Ultimately, the literature said the role of all leaders was to prevent, curtail or manage the challenges and threats that blocked their leadership goals for an organisation (Kacała, 2015),[19] create ethical norms (Dinh et al., 2014),[20] and not only understand the expectations of followers (Magsaysay and Hechanova, 2017)[21] but "have an ethical responsibility to attend to the needs and concerns of followers" (Northouse, 2010).[22] However, the ABC has demonstrated that long-term successful leadership may not be sustainable and there were a range of factors blocking the success of key actors. There is a staff culture hostile to change, staff concerns disquietude for possible excessive workloads, a perceived lack of preparation by management for what staff losses entailed, and uncertainly among stakeholders over how they viewed their role in this changing work situation (Bottery and Herrington, 2016).[23] In the case of the ABC, a Managing Director is required to engage fully with the political climate of the Federal Parliament in Canberra while also managing a national public organisation for the greater good. In addition, a lack of management understanding of the peculiarity of the ABC and the value of its *cultural capital* and how the staff will respond to staffing or policy changes can also hamper successful management. Leadership psychologists argue that one of the threats to world stability is a lack of exemplary "leadership of human institutions" (Bennis, 2007)[24] but that their staff will also have implicit leadership theories (ILTs) or assumptions about what they see as an ideal leader (Epitropaki and Martin, 2004).[25] ABC leaders have to manage and navigate these sometimes conflicting expectations, too.

Since the emergence of Twitter in 2006, leaders have had to contend with a dissenting Twitterverse where "failed leadership" has become amplified as a meme through sharing and liking and media consumers can subscribe to it through the social media hashtag folksonomy #failedleadership. According to Twitter, the use of the "#" before a word can categorise it, make it into a topic and make it easier to follow. It is a form of indexing content and also creates a faux validity of itself as indicative public opinion. Hashtags become a form of sustainability of a topic, attesting to the truth. It becomes a prominent topic when it is a trending topic, and this can increase 'likes', postings and re-postings. The person who posts the comment becomes prominent too (provided it is a public/named real person and not a bot (and that can be hard to discern). The platformed veracity of the claim #failed leadership transforms it into an incontrovertible truth, where a hashtag on Twitter legitimates content and the complaint. This content can then be perverted for abuse and trolling (the most sinister aspects of this will be analysed in Chap. 4).

Respect has been identified as a central aspect of effective leadership in the research literature, whether given or received (Clarke, 2011).[26] Literature said respect for a leader was influenced by the "followers' perceptions of alignment with ideal leader prototype and personal identification with the leader" (Pircher Verdorfer, 2019),[27] especially in the servant leader scenario. Other literature said leaders should promote "a culture of acceptance, dignity, and respect", in addition they needed to work with their staff to build this culture in the organisation (Wallace et al., 2020).[28] Respect in the media field is a more complex concept, especially in the age where abusive comments can be made without consequence in a virtual world where participants are hiding behind highly marketable contributions. The possibility for mis-use is exacerbated by anonymity and has encouraged communication to lapse into assertions of hatred and hostility. The online abuse of women, for example, has received growing attention in feminist research literature which has pointed out that the consequence of the online abuse of women curtailed their engagement in civil society

(Lewis et al., 2017).[29] There was a gap in the literature of accounts from people who have received abuse (Ibid.),[30] but earlier research has shown that internet abuse can cause significant harm to the abused, notably psychological harm (Williams, 2006),[31] and that the clinical separation by perpetrators of harm done online from harm done in the real world both mitigates the online abuse and shifts responsibility away from the abuser (Ibid.)[32] to blaming the reaction of the abused. The literature also pointed out that the internet allows both "normal and pathological" behaviours not evident elsewhere (Morahan-Martin, 2005, p. 46) and, further, that the internet can be used "for reenacting the kinds of difficulties that plagued [them] in real life" (Turkle, 1995, p. 199). In a recent interview, Turkle said (Simon & Sykes Wylie, 2021) "we live in a technological world that's often set up so we treat each other like things" (Ibid.).

This mitigation of consequence means that the offender is free to pursue abuse and humiliation because it is "not real" (Williams, 2006)[33] and, further, the abuser is free to be even more threatening where there is no form of re-dress, legal recourse and inattention to abuse by the platform providers because it is so valuable as content. Language is a highly powerful tool of abuse because language "both constitutes and de-constitutes the victims' identity" (Ibid.).[34] Online texts allow for a physical performance and it "carries a heavier burden in sustaining individual identities" (Ibid.).[35] Academic analysis of virtual (online) rape, for example, explains that the destructiveness of online texts of this nature is not only abusive but a damaging "tool of derision" (Ibid.).[36] The theatrical, performance, participatory strident space of social media actually becomes theatre of the obscure and obscene. Yet, the point here is that these spaces have also become a main source of news, information and journalism activity.

In such an environment, where leadership is held in such low esteem, what is the impact on and consequences for leadership in the Australian public service and the ABC, including any other iterations of government? The literature said, in terms of social psychology, respect has been identified as a chief factor that impacts on group behaviour and how the group interacts with leaders (Clarke, 2011).[37] Harvard Professor Sara Lawrence-Lightfoot (1999) said there were six windows of respect: "empowerment, healing, dialogue, curiosity, self-respect, and attention"[38] where dialogue was essential to fostering this respect. There was a fundamental absence of dialogue in online postings where the target of abuse was dehumanised and as a consequence there was no opportunity, or context, for reasoned debate or discussion.

> Respect often implies required expressions of esteem, approbation, of submission. By contrast, I focus on the way respect creates symmetry, empathy, and connection in all kinds of relationships, even those such as teacher and student, doctor and patient, commonly seen as unequal. (Ibid.)[39]

Somewhat counter-intuitively here, a survey has shown that social media has a positive impact on trust towards institutions when used for civic engagement (Warren et al., 2014)[40] but that while there had been a shift away from trusting institutions generally, there should be more engagement by governments in putting citizens at the centre of power so that they "feel needed and appreciated" (Ibid.).[41] Leadership was also about mundane, un-acknowledged activities:

> What makes business and organizations function is the work that happens in the space between people; the unglamorous processes of coordination, collaboration and communication that knit the various and varied activities of workers together. (Liu, 2020)[42]

2.2 Leadership and Institutional Logics

Across governments, across organisations, across small business, no one organisation, group or person can claim to be *the* definitive leader. Similarly, there is no one style of best leadership. The literature also explained that "as an organization changes over time, strategies of leadership will also change" (Biggart and Hamilton, 1987)[43] and that "(Marshall) McLuhan's understanding of media ecology as a constructive force that shapes our reality has deep implications for leadership" (Gray-Hoehn, 2020).[44] It has also been argued that the various leadership constructs lacked practical applications, were socially constructed and over-burdened with theories (Sanders, 2020).[45] But even though the academic literature on leadership is contested, it is important to provide a working definition of leadership for clarity of analysis. Chemers (2014 in Gray-Hoehn, 2020) said:

> A definition of leadership that would be widely accepted by the majority of theorists and researchers might say that 'leadership is a process of social influence in which one person is able to enlist the aid and support of others in the accomplishment of a common task'.[46]

As leadership comes in many styles, there are many approaches to leadership; even bullying can get mistaken for leadership, because it seems to show apparent assertiveness and control of people, and achieves some sort of results, in the first instance. These results can emerge from intimidation and culling staff and in its nascent stage such a leader can be valued because there may be a high staff turnover which is perceived as "removing dead wood" and "being proactive".

Leadership is also a performance (Fairhurst, 2008).[47] The performance involves enacting and convincing an audience of stakeholders and employees. In terms of Institutional Logics the leader works within a context and manages a role within an "institutional framework of a society" that "encompasses the vital role of regulatory, normative and cognitive pillars that promote successful entrepreneurial activity" (Scott, 2001).[48] Overlaying this is the additional role of public servants, in what Benington (2011) described as having "particular responsibilities as co-creators and guardians of public value" (Ibid.) where short-term political election cycles must be balanced against long-term public need (Loc. Cit., p. 49). In organisational and management literature the phrase "servant leader" has become popular and may have become somewhat faddish and, therefore, misunderstood. It means "the leader's needs are subservient to those of the worker" (Wander, 2013)[49] deriving from a Christian context and the story of Jesus washing the feet of his disciples ahead of his crucifixion. The Head of the Catholic Church, Pope Francis I, said Jesus' gesture was "the service and the gift of life" (Spadaro, 2020)[50] which speaks to the servant leader model (sometimes misconstrued and stereotyped as a voiceless servant who "waits hand and foot" on a master/mistress). The theory said that the gesture invoked the prime example of a model servant leader because Jesus was not only a leader of 12, but he inspired his followers to assume the leadership, subsequent to his death (Wright, 2013).[51]

Servant leadership in its current iterations has its flaws. Critics have said that if the leader becomes the servant, he/she is no longer the leader (Leaderonomics.com, 2018)[52] and that it was a new form of paternalism where staff did not have to think for themselves (McCrimmon, 2010).[53] The origins of the servant leader theory proposed that each person was both a physical and a spiritual being. First theorised by Robert Greenleaf (1977),[54] a Quaker,[55] it had many other iterations from the Bible, for example, when Jesus told his disciples: "If anyone desires to be first, he shall be last of all and servant of all".[56] On the surface, it appears unattainable because it is a paradox, but at a theological level it is a complex ethical and moral mindset of leadership. It does not require a leader to slave, perform the menial tasks and subordinate themselves literally before the staff, rather that the leader looks to the needs of the group instead of the leader's selfish needs (e.g., improving their annual bonus, profits at the expense of staff welfare or raising the limit on the corporate expense account). Ultimately, servant leadership is an enlarged view focusing on the "greater good" of society as a whole (Northouse, 2013).[57]

Servant leaders have the qualities of listening, empathy, healing, awareness, persuasion, conceptualisation, foresight, stewardship, commitment to the growth of people and building community (Northouse, 2013 quoting Spears, 2002[58]) and servant leadership contrasts transactional leadership, which is styled around offering rewards and creating staff that are self-motivated. Servant leader theory is concerned with higher order needs of self-fulfilment and self-actualisation. Servant leader was a personalist theory also developed by Karol Wojtyla (Pope John Paul II) at the heart of which he said lies: "the dignity and value of the human person" (Whetstone, 2002).[59] This perspective is used in many Christian religious leadership contexts, especially schools, where it is believed humanity is made in the image of God and God has instructed and challenged humanity to love both God and their neighbour, as themselves (Ibid.).[60]

The servant leader is supposed to listen to his or her underlings and be inspired by their needs. Whetstone (2002) said: "the advantages of the servant leadership model are its altruism, simplicity, and self-awareness".[61] But servant leadership has also been misunderstood as giving in to staff (Sendjaya, 2010, in van Dierendonck & Patterson, 2010),[62] or that the leader has to be religious (Ibid.). Servant leadership has also been criticised for preventing profit growth by placing workers' needs first (Loc. Cit.). This is not the original intention of the meaning of the theory, and research shows that servant leaders can inspire trust in their employees (Ibid.) but only as a long-term strategy. This places the servant leader at odds with the shareholder who wants short-term profits (Ibid.) and quick results. To situate this in the case of the ABC, a servant leader would be at odds with governments focused on policy shifts, funding cuts, and federal election horizons.

Another style of leadership, transformational, is one of the most important theories of organisational change because it emphasises "intrinsic motivation" and "the positive development of followers" (Barrett and Barrington, 2005).[63] It is focused on the moral order and the greater good, the intangible vision where lives are not only improved now, but for years to come. This type of leadership encourages staff to appreciate and uphold the values and vision of the organisation and achieve desired outcomes and targets. It has been criticised as having a downside where leaders might promote egotistic self-interests and ignore the contributions of subordinates: "the most serious weakness of transformational leadership theory, and the danger of its practice, is that it can be so effectively used for immoral ends" (van Dierendonck and Patterson, 2010).[64] However, research has found transformational leadership improved public service motivation (Wright et al., 2012)[65] and made employees more satisfied. At public service organisations it has been found that employees were more likely to uphold the organisation's values because they coincided with their own values (Ibid.)[66] and, consequently, staff internalised these values as part of their identities (Ibid.).[67] Conflicting research showed public service management struggled to link staff with the values of the organisation (Ibid.)[68] and research on leaders' capacity to inspire and communicate a vision to staff has had limited attention (Ibid.).[69]

Transformational leadership is about the leader, whereas Institutional Logics is about leadership within a constrained context and *field*, such that "organisations have material and symbolic characteristics which interplay in the organisational field" (Pureza & Lee, 2020; quoting Scott, 2000 & Thornton, 2004)[70] with actors, or leaders, "departing from established roles to create a new organisational field condition" (Pureza & Lee, 2020; Friedland & Alford, 1991; Scott, 2008). Further, "Institutional logics constitute the social identities and behavior of actors on the micro-level" (Aagaard, 2016).[71] This has been described as post-transformative leadership (Pureza & Lee Ibid.). It has also been acknowledged in "mixed management" literature that public organisations can have different mixes of leadership and logics and this can be adjusted by the leader (Aagaard, ibid.).[72] Public service leadership is understood within Institutional Logics as being sensitive to changing demands, policy shifts or political pressures (Loc. Cit.) with pressure on public facilities to create "new, cheaper or smarter" means of production (Aagaard, 2016). So, Institutional Logics is limited in describing public service leadership because of a lack of knowledge of the complexities imposed and created on the public institution (Ibid.) and where even the nature of public itself is "a contested space where competing interests conflict" (Bromell, 2019, p. 164).

2.3 Leading the Institution of the ABC

Now is a time of major transformation for the public service, generally, and ABC in particular, because of demands for cost cuts, efficiencies, organisational change and a collapsing market for traditional ABC media programming with technology transforming content creation, delivery and uses of media. The demise of 'appointment', time-bound public service broadcasting and the emergence of public service media have changed everything. Mark Pegg, Former Director of the UK-based Ashridge Public Leadership Centre, said that public service leaders:

> Must be masters of change management, able to motivate their teams to shift from delivering what they think should be offered, to a world shaped by customer requirements, with a focus on innovation and delivery by those best able to satisfy them. They have to be able to work together across government rather than in their silos, to influence change and listen to consumers. (Powe, 2010)[73]

The traditional silo aspects of the ABC, where staff resided in program units or departments which tended to disengage from the organisation in terms of collaboration and did not necessarily (or consistently) identify with the whole, will be examined in the light of this quote. In terms of the ABC "the siloes" once referred to the separation of radio and television, news from current affairs, specialist programming from regional teams and sport and music all on their own. In private industry, managerialism has found silos have destroyed the value chain such as meeting demand and supply (Ireland, 2005)[74] and led to duplication and intransigence towards policy change. Yet, if siloes are to exist it hinges on staff complicity. An ABC manager was quoted in 2017 "if the staff don't support this change it won't happen" (Brook, 2017).[75] Attempts by managers to break down these ABC silos of radio and television, as well as their individual program units by shutting them down, have had a long history at the ABC. In 1997, (the late) Managing Director Brian Johns launched "One ABC". In eulogising Johns just after he died, Managing Director Mark Scott was quoted:

> Almost more than any other media leader in the country he understood the impact that digital technology was going to make on media organisations and he drove the organisation to change to respond to that phenomenon.[76]

Scott also said: "much of the work we still do is a direct result of the innovation he brought to the broadcaster" (Brereton, 2016).[77] According to Inglis (2006) part of the "One ABC" plan was that in-house and outside producers would compete to make programs, that 20% of senior executives would be sacked (60 in number) and that this would amount to AUD27 million savings (Inglis, 2006).[78]

In 2007, the next Managing Director, Mark Scott, dismantled the organisation's Media and Digital Services Division because "new media" was now mainstream. Cooke (2007) said part of this was to also to expand the ABC's "editorial scope and interests".[79] ABC News Online staff were merged with ABC News and Current Affairs. The success of online content was measured by its iterations online. Scott said of a new program on gaming on ABC2 (Australia's first free-to-air digital television channel launched on 7 March 2005): "Already you will find copies of Good Game on YouTube, it has a Wikipedia entry and is getting significant traffic online" (Ibid.). Meanwhile, the Media Entertainment and Arts Alliance cautioned in a submission to the Federal Government's Digital Action Plan: "The ABC must be resourced to take a leading role in digital free-to-air broadcasting. Without new funds it will be unable to do so" (Ibid.). The union's words "leading role" here were cautionary, perspicacious but publicly unremarked by recipients of ABC funding. In 2017, Managing Director Michelle Guthrie announced the creation of three content groups—news, opinions and investigations (Brook, 2017)[80]—by moving 3000 staff members from the former "silos" of radio and television and said that:

> This exercise today is about making sure we work collectively in better and smarter ways to serve our audiences. There is no dumbing down. We will be boosting the capability and output of genre specialist teams. (Brook, 2017)

Guthrie's vision was that staff would "keep faith with our obligation to inform, educate and entertain" and all content made for radio and television should have "equal digital life" (Ibid.). Feedback from staff quoted in the article warned that there would be push-back from staff culture. Former ABC staff member Monica Attard was quoted in the article: "But the question whether it will work is a much bigger one and a lot of that depends on how well the staff take to it and how easy the lines of authority and command are" (Brook Ibid.). In addition, an anonymous ABC staff member was blunt, as quoted previously: "If the staff don't support this change it won't happen" (Loc. Cit.). Peter Fray, Professor of the Practice of Journalism at the University of Technology Sydney and former Editor-in-Chief of *The Sydney Morning Herald* said the Guthrie move would be subject to two tests: "if the content noticeably improves … and … whether the great promises made by the consultants in their shiny report ever come to pass" (Brook, 2017). Nonetheless, the future of the ABC also depends on re-thinking its public role and funding mindful of its historical expectations and future digital opportunities (Martin, 2002).[81]

One example of how staff siloes have operated, somewhat naively, at the ABC was provided by Tim Bowden who in 1965 was Talks Supervisor in Tasmania—radio and television. Bowden said he received a telephone call from the ABC's accountant who told Bowden he had spent the entire year's artists' fees budget in the first three months (Bowden & Borchers,

2006).[82] Bowden replied: "what budget?" (Ibid.). He reflected: "but those days are long gone" (Loc. Cit.).[83] The operation of siloes has proven to be an ongoing distraction, complication and problem for ABC managers, and possibly one that does not have comparison in private commercial media where profit declines can justify (or can be correlated directly with) upheaval and quick action.

Analysis of public service leadership overall is fragmented and convoluted because of the diverse types of studies that have been done (Chapman et al., 2016),[84] lack of sustained consistent methodologies used and difficulties in distinguishing public sector leadership from private sector leadership (Ibid.).[85] Consequently, no comprehensive theoretical understanding or paradigm of public service leadership prevails in the research literature. However, it has been decided that public service managerialism began in the 1970s, occurred in all industrialised Western nations, and was supported by all major political parties (Diefenbach, 2009)[86] with a view to make public service "more 'business-like' and 'market oriented'" (Diefenbach Ibid.). Also, there is a complexity in the exercise of leadership in the public sphere which this book will attempt to analyse in the media field. Jurisdictional boundaries, real or perceived, have also been found to create a barrier for public service leadership (Ibid., quoting Kettl, 2006)[87] and public service leaders may be accountable to a range of actors in an environment where there are limited rewards to motivate staff, imposed quotas and other limitations (Ibid.)[88] which hamper recruitment. In the UK, there has been an emphasis on training public service leaders as transformational leaders to drive necessary change (Tomlinson et al., 2013).[89]

A striking aspect of public service leadership is that it is in a state of change and that it may now need "distributed or dispersed" (Dickinson et al., 2019)[90] leadership that is collaborative and reaches across former boundaries (silos). The role of the public service broadcaster as a leader of opinion and information has changed radically since the ABC's inception. Public broadcasting is in decline. Everywhere. Prominent US communications and media academic and author Professor Robert McChesney (1997) wrote that it was receding in importance because of new technologies delivering more options, resulting in smaller audiences, but most importantly it was diminishing because of the adoption of neo-liberal commercial values as the means of controlling media (Dickinson et al., 2019).[91] This pressure on public services to operate as if they were in a marketplace with all other businesses began to weigh heavily on the ABC in Australia in the 1990s with the Coalition Government insisting the public service manage efficiencies, become performance based, and provide choice for consumers (Edwards et al., 2012).[92] A consequence of this was actually an increase in silos and fragmentation (Ibid.). While this was a focus on the entire Australian federal public service, it also had an impact on the ABC in the form of funding cuts and pressure for efficiencies by shifting senior public servants to individual contracts, for example.

As to the future the report into the Australian Public Service (2012) said:

> increasingly we can expect successful leadership in the public sector to display a capacity to drive complex multi-organisational networks that encourage individual and institutional contributions to shared goals, if not also shared leadership. (Ibid.)[93]

Leadership of any organisation is fundamentally important and Bourdieu (2005) said leaders reproduced and legitimated their élite *fields*. However, the *fields* in which they existed were not stable and are "continually negotiated by disparate, competing social groups, and can themselves be radically restructured, as with the field of public service partnerships" (Tomlinson et al., 2013).[94] Another aspect of leadership was that it could be dysfunctional: "the cancer that eats many organizations" (Dandira, 2012).[95]

The Australian Broadcasting Commission at its inception seemed to have shrugged off its first strangulation point applied by its government supervisor, its first Postmaster-General, Archibald Cameron, to whom the ABC was responsible and who declared:

> I know nothing about broadcasting. I am not interested in it. If I had my way I would stop broadcasting. No time for these mechanical things. Don't know anything about music. As for people who give talks and commentaries on air—I would bring them under the Vermin Act. (*The Sydney Morning Herald*, 1932)[96]

Contrasting this the first ABC Chairman, Charles Lloyd-Jones, said: "The service now belongs to you we are your trustees. It is a service that is not run for profit but purely in the interests of every section of the community" (Letter by Cleary, 1938 in C. Semmler, 2001).[97] Setting aside Cameron's jarring institutional disavowal, the first General Manager of the ABC, Charles Moses, had to rise above government ignorance and was an example of a successful yet challenged leader on an annual salary of £2000 in 1932[98] (Walker, 1973) (today worth AUD197,898 and compared with the current Managing Director's salary of AUD918,924 in 2019). Moses had a reputation described by Professor of Modern History at the University of Western Australia, Geoffrey Bolton, as "fearsome" (Blain, 1977)[99] but in the end Moses was a victim of organisational deficiencies "largely of his own making" (Ibid.)[100] because he was described as unwilling to delegate and shouldered too much. He was animated by the BBC's first Director-General, John Reith, who had "an ethical mission of high moral responsibility ... to enhance the quality of life of all British citizens" (Banerjee & Seneviratne, 2006).[101] In addition, the BBC was established in response to "cultural conservatism" based on fears of the "crass ... US broadcasting system" infiltrating British culture (McChesney & Herman, 1997),[102] and the ABC was party to that opinion too.

The early field of management at the ABC was very much about cultivating the upper echelons of Australian society to divine the cultural needs of the audience. Of relevance to Institutional Logics analysed in this chapter is the role of actor managers, their agency in the field and their capacity to identify and introduce changes. The theory asserts that it operates at a societal level (Thornton et al., 2012)[103] and this research has shown many instances where those who occupied the field worked with each other at a social level for mutual benefit. It is not always about "the common good"; there were individual interests at stake. These actors also exemplified the educated *field*, where people of similar income, aspirations and backgrounds benefit mutually from association. This idea can be tied into Institutional Logics. Glynn (2000)[104] explicated how the construction of core capabilities lay at the intersection of identification and interpretive processes in an organisation:

> It is through their particular identity lens (artistic or utilitarian) that organizational actors, by virtue of their organizational position and/or professional affiliation, craft their particular definitions of institutional resources and core capabilities. (Glynn, Ibid.)[105]

The capabilities of the ABC arose from the intersection of different cultural identities seeking individual benefits. Moses, for example, occupied a similar field of influence with his contacts and connections. He entertained the major international musicians and artists when they visited Australia. Charles Buttrose,[106] then head of the concert department for the ABC, described "through a Moses lunch at Beppis,[107] the Sydney restaurant, I was able to consolidate the good relationship I had with Ančerl"[108][109] (Buttrose, 1984). The Czech Philharmonic Orchestra was the first foreign orchestra to tour Australia, organised by the ABC. This was a substantial flag for the institution to plant in the field of *cultural capital*. It was another marker of how the ABC brought the world to its public.

In a separate recount by Buttrose in 1963 he described how Moses spent the day with the late Australian conductor Charles Mackerras and others over lunch and wine in a Western Australian vineyard (bad weather apparently prevented a game of backyard cricket and a barbecue) (Buttrose, 1984).[110] Buttrose said he was lobbying Moses (on Mackerras' behalf) to be conductor of the Sydney Symphony Orchestra but Moses told Buttrose: "No ... tell him to go away again and prove himself. The Sydney Symphony Orchestra still regards him as a second oboe player".[111] Buttrose (1984) thought differently and expressed remorse that "we will not get ranking conductors like Mackerras to give much time to Australia—or to come here at all—until orchestras improve" (Ibid.).[112] Moses was highly influential in the field of Australian culture.

The role of management in the early days is reflective of what was once described as a "Mandarin class" which is a reference to the tough exams aspiring members of the Chinese Civil Service would have to undergo (prior to 1912 with the overthrow of the emperor). Similarly, "the upper caste in Her Majesty's Civil Service used to be recruited solely from candidates with a non-technical, generalist background"[113] from Oxford or Cambridge Universities since "administrators occupy and operate within a value-saturated universe".[114] According to Marshal McLuhan (1964) the mass media consisted of games being played and that games needed "rules, conventions and spectators"[115] and were contrived for participation on some level. Essential to that functioning, however, was that the rules of the games be observed (Bourdieu, 1986).[116] These are the rules of the *field* that support cultural capital and cultural production, as evidenced by the early understandings of ABC senior managers of their roles and the appointment and recruitment of like-minded. This will be discussed next.

The trend in public service management from the 1980s was towards professionalisation of the role (Voxted, 2017)[117] and managerialism which has meant that managers were looking towards being a "symbol, generating activity" where they motivated, contextualised and co-ordinated "the independent contributions of the employees" (Ibid.).[118] In addition, the advent of the MBA style (Master of Business Administration) of management means a generic style of leading and managing is applied to all organisations across the board and it could be said the ABC, and public service in general, has suffered from this lack of specificity and knowledge of public media management, the uniqueness of public broadcasting and the role of public service. When the primary objective is to serve, profits, shareholder dividends and bonuses for performance are not essentials within the frame of the public good. In tandem with this has been the rising importance of human resource management (from the former days of personnel management) which has direct involvement in the organisation's strategic objectives and business targets (e.g., the use of quotas to ensure there are equal numbers of men and women employed as well as ethnicities, sexes, genders, cultures and nationalities). Workers have been re-named "resources" and the nomenclature around "human resources" has been hugely consequential in de-humanising the workforce as expendable, from once being "personnel"—people—"boots on the ground" and its original military meaning (OED, 2021).[119]

In addition, the ABC has been regularly pressured to commercialise its operations (Brown & Althaus, 2009)[120] and is regularly beset and besieged with government applications of funding cuts, threats of funding cuts, bungling Managing Directors, and then becalmed by visionary Managing Directors. In 1978, internationally famous Australian comedian and satirist Barry Humphries wrote an ironic epigraph in regard to ABC *cultural capital* on behalf of one of his alter egos, the perpetually inebriated Australian cultural attaché Sir Les Patterson: "There's nothing I would rather be /Than Chairman of the ABC. (Sir Les) Patterson's Prayer, 1978" (Humphries, 1991)[121] at a time when ABC staff had declared "no confidence in the then Chairman John Norgard "for his failure to represent the interest of the ABC" (*The Canberra Times*, 1978)[122] in two related accusations: not allowing the creation of a staff-appointed board member role and failing to eliminate institutional political bias (*The Canberra Times*, 1978)[123] towards the (then) Liberal Government.

In addition to funding turmoil and political influence/s are threats of privatisation, untrumpeted self-privatisation, accusations of bias, proof of bias, rejections of bias, government reviews and committees of inquiry, or threats of government reviews and inquiries. Those are the immutable, bankable facts of the daily life of public service media. In fact, in public service organisations, generally, it is now received knowledge in the literature that governments play an increasingly larger role in their running under the guise of "auditing outcomes", "consumer choice" and "decentralisation" (Stacey & Griffin, 2006)[124] in an economic environment where knowledge is a key economic resource. Management has been displaced. Public Service organisations, including the ABC, operate under a governance where perceived "under-performers" are performance managed out of the organisation such that flaws or believed shortcomings in an individual's work performance become the cause of sacking. Yet, contradicting this is the public service originating concept of service which was based on "an ideology of vocation and professional freedom" (Ibid.),[125] and even the role of Western abstract thinking where ABC employees were allowed to "think outside the box" in creating challenging content. The impact of this centralisation of control and scrutiny of the public service—and the crushing outcome for the ABC—means "power is heavily tilted to the scrutinizing bodies of central government and away from the delivering institutions" (Stacey & Griffin, 2006).[126] Aunty's voice is being strangled, remotely.

2.4 Managing the Educated Cultural *Field* of the ABC

The ABC was launched very much at the behest of businessman, pastoralist and benefactor Herbert Brookes, ironically a political conservative but "a powerful figure at the time in both industry and conservative politics who was not afraid of taking on the commercial media establishment" (Australian Rationalist, 2016).[127] Brookes' role merits consideration in the light of this books claim to the diversity and divergence of ongoing support for the ABC support. He was the ABC's first Vice-Chairman and ABC Director Melbourne. He was described as "complex" (Murray, 1994)[128] because he was both a "gentle and cultivated" (Ibid.) philanthropist but also belonged to the far-right who formed the Loyalty League—a secret anti-Catholic, anti-union and anti-Australian Labor Party service (Ibid.). He also helped devise the practice within the ABC of so-called self-censorship (Ibid.) prior to World War II where there was "an acknowledged difference between official ABC policy and unofficial ABC practice" (Ibid.) where it proclaimed independence but supported government policy (Ibid.) and gave the Postmaster-General the right to suppress any ABC broadcast. Brookes helped support a heavily nuanced definition of ABC independence, which the ABC still struggles with today in other iterations. In addition, Brookes was "a powerful figure … in both industry and conservative politics who was not afraid of taking on the commercial media establishment of the time" (Australian Rationalist, 2016).[129] An important part of the power of Brookes and his contribution to the *cultural capital* of the ABC, was his wife, Ivy Brookes, who was the eldest daughter of former conservative Prime Minister Alfred Deakin (Protection Party) and a professional violinist held in high regard in Melbourne classical music circles (Rickard, 2003).[130] The pair was prominent and influential in Australian cultural and intellectual life. They were what would now be described as "a power couple".

Management of the speaking of English on the ABC began controversially yet was another manifestation of the organisation's cultural capital and establishment of its own field. Overlaying a duty to build an Australian culture, the ABC was conceived as an antipodean hybrid of the BBC to the point of encouraging the use of British accents by its presenters on air (The Courier Mail, 1934)[131] and the first "real" Australian accent not heard on the ABC until Talbot Duckmanton in 1939 (*The Canberra Times*, 1995).[132] Duckmanton later became Managing Director, an iteration of style in leadership. The support for the British accent was aided by "distributing the BBC's booklet on pronunciation" (*The Courier Mail*, 1934) to the ABC staff. These competing expectations on the ABC—Australian content with a public-school British accent—forced it into a strangely conflicted identity. The acute emphasis from government policy was to broadcast Australian culture and this was supported by British-born Charles Moses. The quaintly nuanced style of broadcasting and educating in the Australian culture was confirmed in the announcement that the ABC would host the fourth world concert organised by the Radio Union (Geneva) when Moses said the concert would open with "calls by the lyre bird and kookaburra" (The Courier Mail, 1938)[133] followed by "an Australian corroboree" (*The Courier Mail*, ibid.). Moses (knighted in 1961) said a range of other Australian artists would perform including the ABC Radio Chorus and the ABC Orchestra playing "national airs" (Loc. Cit.).

In 1931 the ABC (originally, the Australian Broadcasting Company) was given control of Australian broadcasting under Federal legislation charged with upholding Australian culture, but later became a vital constituent of Australian investigative news media. This was because from the outset, it was not set up to represent the public interest (Petersen, 1993)[134] but, at the behest of the powerful newspaper lobby, ABC management was supposed to be tasked with assisting the Australian people in being "culturally uplifted" (Ibid.).[135] Overlaying the ABC's duties was that it would build an Australian culture, which has been a constant challenge for the organisation with changing historical immigration patterns. The ABC established a national symphony orchestra and choir, a military band and a dance band (*The Canberra Times*, 1936).[136] In addition, it was to run a national music composition competition and bring in performing artists from overseas. In fact, the ABC's vision for itself became one Chairman Charles Lloyd-Jones said aimed "to encourage the creative side of our people in a musical sense" (*The Advertiser*, 1934).[137]

Herein lies the essential point of contention between the ABC and the rest. While the ABC was managed to create citizens, other media existed to create audiences for advertisers. That was then the commercial *field*, their domain, they ruled. Originally, the acceptance of advertising in newspapers gave reporters a buffer from newspaper investors as it was the advertisers' support which sealed the deal on whether the media outfit was a profitable and viable entity. The ABC was the exception to this situation. It had its own public funding which removed it from the pressures faced by commercial media to earn revenue. Historically, news did not become news until the invention of the telegraph in 1844 (Nerone & Barnhurst, 2003)[138]; prior to that people were reliant on the mail being left hanging "on the post" at a "post" office, conveyed by horses, bullock carts, boats, then trains from point to point or personal delivery. Information flowed more slowly then. The commercialisation of the news as a result also gave rise to journalists re-defining themselves as purveyors of impartial news (Shaw, 1959;[139] Lee, 1976;[140] Williams, 2010[141]). Press barons could publish instantaneously and politicians have ever since been aware of this. The development of the inverted pyramid style of news writing with the most important information in the first sentence, all arose from the telegraph and the propensity for the line to drop out—the first sentence had to stand up if there was no subsequent information reported (Stephens, 2007).[142]

At its inception, the ABC was a minor information service. It fulfilled a far more powerful role as an actor in Australian music[143] and its impact was formative and nurturing on Australian music, talent, culture and society. It is not over-stating the point that music in Australia provided a pivotal role in nation-building and morale boosting—especially with the aftermath and consequences of The Great Depression and World War II. There was a "strong community interest in music and concerts during the anxious war years of the early '40s" (Nelson, 2003).[144] ABC managers employed musicians, organised concerts, supervised choirs and orchestras in the six states, as well as dance bands and military bands and ran music competitions because "the ABC's leaders were determined to raise musical standards and to provide the best possible in music for its audience" (Ibid.).[145] Those ABC managers who supported and facilitated this role for the ABC in the educated cultural 'field' were General Manager, Charles Moses; Federal Controller of Music, William James; Musical Advisor, Bernard Heinze and Chairman William Cleary[146] (Fraser, 2014). In addition, were the "power couple" Herbert Brookes and Ivy Brookes who helped establish the ABC's *field* of cultural capital. Music was the key opening the gate to the *field*.

American conductor and composer Howard Shanet wrote in 1975: "orchestras have always played a role as 'cultural mirrors', reflecting 'the social environment, the economic conditions, the ethnic changes, the urban growth, the political events, and the educational state' of their communities" (Fraser, 2014).[147] And the movement away from the popularity of bands and the setting up and special status endowed on orchestras around Australia, was a further claim to the educated field of the ABC. Levine (1988) described this in his text *Highbrow/Lowbrow* (Levine 1988) as a shift from a "rich, shared public culture" towards a "hierarchically organized" and "fragmented" modern culture (Fraser, 2014).[148] The ABC fostered the shift from high culture to reflect a changed, socially modern Australia as "the orchestra became an arm of the élite classes" (Ibid.)[149] Image 2.1 indicates how the ABC sought to build Australian's *cultural capital* by attracting international conductors and musicians to its Australian performance space.

Educating the public and bringing the world to Australia has been an important dimension of the ABC charter. In 1998, ABC Head of National Networks Andy Lloyd James said "education and lifelong learning services would represent an increasingly important part of the ABC's Charter activities in the emerging digital broadcasting environment" (ABC, 1998).[150] The importance of educating the public began in Victorian England (McDowell, 1975)[151] and spread to Australia in the nineteenth century to a variety of institutions, most notably the Schools of Art and Mechanics' Institutes, the buildings of which today are all that remain and used by councils as community centres or for hire. These institutes "were an important part of the rise of popular education" (McDowell, ibid.). Workers were provided with non-secular education on poetry, travel, music, art and science: "the mechanics institutes in Australia, as in England, were the backbone of popular education and the foundation of technical education" (Ibid.).[152] Jeremy Bentham and John Stuart Mill were also supporters of the institute movement (Ibid.).[153] The aim for the Schools of Arts was to give:

> elementary education by classes in arithmetic, geometry, algebra and anything else that might make a working man able to become a freer and more privileged human being, as well as a more efficient worker. (Warburton, 1963)[154]

The initial role of the ABC was to build Australia's culture on the back of this belief—to give privilege to Australians. Inglis (1983)[155] said for the ABC's precursor—the Australian Broadcasting Company—"music remained the staple of broadcasting" (Inglis, ibid.) but that it also aimed for "the highest authority in music, education, sport and feminine

Image 2.1 World renowned conductor, (Charles) Dean Dixon, appointed permanent conductor of the Sydney Symphonic (later Symphony) Orchestra in 1964. Dixon was the third conductor in the history of the orchestra and his engagement with the SSO ended in 1967. Dixon had also conducted the New York Philharmonic. Australian News & Information Bureau. 1963. Courtesy National Archives of Australia. Personalities—The ABC appointed Mr Dean Dixon as the permanent conductor of the Sydney Symphonic Orchestra. Principal Credit: Australian News & Information Bureau. 1963. Series: A1200, L43222. Item ID: 30672627. Canberra

interests" (Loc. Cit.). The government intended that broadcasting be operated by private interests (Brown & Althaus, 2009)[156] and so this original (ABC) company was formed by culturally-connected men: Sir Benjamin Fuller (theatre owner), Stuart Doyle (cinema owner) and Frank Albert (music publisher) (Inglis, 1983). The schools of arts and subsequent efforts by the Australian Broadcasting Company/then Commission were important steps towards creating "a freer and more privileged human being" (Warburton, ibid.) and an informed public capable of contributing to the public sphere, which Jurgen Habermas (1962) first theorised:

> The sphere of private people come together as a public; they soon claimed the public sphere regulated from above against the public authorities themselves, to engage them in a debate over the general rules governing relations in the basically privatized but publicly relevant sphere of commodity exchange and social labor. (Ibid.)[157]

The cultural aspects of the ABC cultivated Australian music tastes and dispersed the surfacing educated Australian accent to the broader public through talks, children's sessions and religious services. The ABC now functions in a media environment that includes everything and operators make money out of niche services, which for the ABC have been criticised as "a self-defeating idea" (Funston, 1997).[158] Public service media is expected to stand as an out-rider, funded by all citizen taxpayers, on the proviso that it is all things to all people, all of the time—universality. The ABC's first Chairman Sir Charles Lloyd-Jones promised at the ABC's inauguration in 1932 "the service now belongs to you" (Inglis, ibid.), but it is doubtful now **all** Australians see themselves as owning, or identify themselves with, this historically universal provider—but in 1932 that was what a public broadcaster not only claimed, it happened. Broadcasting audiences (television and radio) are in decline and the ABC managers have taken up the challenge to create a service that is capable of growing audiences by "driving digital radio behaviours and investing in platforms to enable this, e.g. ABC Listen" (ABC Annual Report, 2019).[159] It sees this as the ultimate pursuit for the organisation to ensure its survival. It needs to work out how to corral the technologically adept and expert digital natives, the hopelessly and embarrassingly incompetent digital immigrants (people born before the 1980s) (Cut, 2017)[160] and the manifestly unpredictable and slippery digital nomads who are nothing better than ubiquitous and ephemeral in their support and media interests and end up reading curated, manipulating content that serves their personal, algorithmed tastes. Media consumption has become faddish; no one buys the afternoon paper to read on the train anymore—and since COVID-19 a sizeable number of workers have been encouraged or forced to work from home anyway. It may prove enticing for businesses to shift away from expensive rents and running costs on an ongoing basis.

2.5 "The cone of silence"[161,162]: ABC Management Culture

There is a belief that Aunty's loss of her cultivated voice amidst the raucousness of the emergent commercial digital space is similar to the international condition of public broadcasting:

> National broadcasters around the democratic world are suffering from the perception that their paternalistic value-setting and educative roles—so valued after the Second World War—are inappropriate in these (post)modern times where difference and pluralism are celebrated and the nation, the public and the citizen are contested notions. (Funston, 1997)[163]

This contestation has been played out in ABC content and programs which have been the site of struggles for management over many years in retaining quality but appealing to ever more diverse audiences. This reference to quality in content and programming was described by Hawkins (1997)[164] as referring to "an authoritarian paternalism" (Hawkins, ibid.). As a consequence, there have been lapses and discrepancies to meet these competing requirements. In 2007, former Managing Director Mark Scott acknowledged that bias in content had to be addressed at the ABC (Scott 2006).[165] Former Director of ABC-TV (2006–2013) Kim Dalton blamed the loss of Aunty's voice on a misalignment at the ABC between policy, strategy and funding[166] where there was policy incoherence, lack of strategic engagement and precarious, erratic and uncommitted funding allocated by the ABC *itself* for its own projects. For example, he said that despite the importance of children's television "ensuring Australian children grew up hearing Australian voices and Australian stories"[167] it was never taken seriously by the ABC due to a lack of commitment by ABC managers. In 2009, a new children's television service (ABC3) was funded by Prime Minister Kevin Rudd's Labor Government (AUD27 million) but "within less than four years the ABC was reallocating these funds"[168] and had undermined that government goodwill gesture to foster the youth of Australia. There is a similar story with documentaries when by 2013 with a budget of AUD2 million and generating AUD10 million in production the ABC decided "documentaries in general, and history documentaries in particular were no longer a priority".[169] Yet, Dalton argued that:

> Television plays an important, arguably central, role in people's sense and understanding of their own history. History should be core to the ABC's remit. (Dalton, 2017)[170]

Dalton (2017) complained that all these decisions were taken without "transparency, public discussion or reference to any policy settings".[171] A decision was taken by the ABC in regard to ending natural history documentaries without public discussion, for example. Similarly, there was a "de-commitment" to ABC Aboriginal and Torres Strait Islander television programming and Dalton said funds for it were "allocated elsewhere" (Ibid.). In 2004, the Howard Liberal Government gave the ABC AUD500,000 to upgrade the ABC at Geelong, a regional city in Victoria, and build a radio station for the city. However, in 2014, Sarah Henderson, Federal Coalition member of parliament and former ABC journalist, learned the money had been "redirected elsewhere within the organisation" (Lynch, 2014)[172] with Geelong to remain serviced by ABC Melbourne (Ibid.). Other grey literature described the role of the Howard Government differently, quoting the former Prime Minister and his chief of staff Grahame Morris as describing the ABC as an organisation as "our enemy talking to our friends" (Seccombe, 2020).[173]

Dalton said there was a similar deprioritising of Australian history, and drama and a new emphasis on children's programming—later depleted by the ABC's failure to "internalise the idea that children's television was important". Dalton (2017) stated that the size of the reduction in funding by ABC senior management to indigenous television was greater than the funding cuts imposed by Prime Minister Tony Abbott's government on the entire ABC "and at least in part it preceded them".[174] In fact, Dalton (2017) argued consistently throughout his essay that there was a lack of management consultation with the public, and the film production industry with regards to all the chopping and changing of government specifically allocated funding at the ABC, with no information of "where the money had gone" (Loc. Cit.) and that management had pursued its own agenda to such an extent that it had isolated the ABC.

Dalton (2017) accused ABC managers of a lack of transparency at the ABC, as is required of public sector organisations, a lack of commitment by the organisation, and no governance or accountability "to sustain the alignment between public policy and ABC strategy".[175] He said the ABC operated in a "cone of silence", cultivated by management, which is accepted by government and its supporters yet "the ABC is not called to account over publicly taking money from government on the promise of

50 per cent Australian content on its children's channel, only to privately decide that 25 per cent is enough".[176] He said the government was caught in a bind, whereby it had no way to measure ABC Australian content because it would be considered to be meddling in the ABC's independence. The ABC has, at worst, a management culture of secrecy or, at best, a lack of consultation with other stakeholders.

In 2009, Prime Minister Kevin Rudd added AUD40 million to the ABC's budget for drama (as well as AUD27 million for a digital children's channel providing education and entertainment for various ages). Yet according to Dalton the money for these projects was siphoned away to other areas of the ABC within a decade because of an absence of ABC policy to build futures for the funding allocations. Rudd also tried to exercise leadership of the ABC from a distance when he announced he would de-politicise it by putting the ABC "above and beyond the reach of front-line culture warriors" (Lewis, 2009, quoting Rudd).[177] The plan, announced when he was Opposition Leader, involved introducing a new format for electing board members using a "merit-based" system overseen by an independent panel. The plan stipulated that the Prime Minister and Federal Communications Minister would have the final agreement on board members and the Prime Minister would nominate the Chairman and have it 'signed off' by the Opposition Leader. Rudd said:

> There has been too much of a culture in the past, from whichever side of politics wins the election, to import its own people into these sorts of positions. ... I believe the ABC is too important and too central an institution in Australian life for that to continue into the future. (Ibid.)

Further he said the ABC was:

> Too important a part of our national life to be captured in any way by either side of politics. ... Whether it is perceptions of political bias to the Left or Right, I don't want to see the ABC in the future subject to those accusations. (Ibid.)

However, this unparalleled attempt to remove political appointments and support the ABC by giving it an opportunity to recruit apolitical or bipartisan leadership was unravelled after Rudd's departure from government (Knott & Hunter, 2014).[178] Rudd had tried to shore up the integrity of the ABC by eliminating one of the three threats to the organisation and its leadership—the other two were funding cuts and privatisation—or as this book argues, its shift to the *field* of commercial media. If this check on ABC leadership, instituted by Rudd, had been sustained it would have given the ABC *cultural capital* in its new commercial *field* as a truly "independent" actor and managed by independent leaders. It would have forced a revaluation of its *cultural capital* and how best to defend and frame it in the commercial *field*.

There have been many reports of instances and insinuations of government interference, or intermittent meddling. Neither the literature, nor the research conducted for this book pointed to that occurring consistently and in large measure. There is manifestly much respect for the ABC from many quarters. Yet this does not fit the narrative of "attack and destroy tactics by ABC enemies" held by those who believe the ABC is under siege. There is even some sorrow that the ABC has found itself being strangled. A notable exception was in the case of Chairman Justin Milne, who resigned because of allegations that he had compromised the independence of the ABC by allegedly telling Managing Director Michelle Guthrie to dismiss Senior Reporter Emma Alberici on behalf of the government because "they hate her" (Meade, 2018)[179] and to "shoot" another senior reporter Andrew Probyn because Prime Minister Malcolm Turnbull "hated him" (Meade, 2018).

Dalton (2017) said while the Liberal Party did not have a large library of policy on the ABC, the Australian Labor Party had been inconsistently interested in the ABC and the late first female Chair of the ABC, Dame Leonie Kramer, confirmed: "there is no reason to doubt that in principle, governments recognise the ABC's right to life" (Kramer, 1983).[180] However, contrary to this, David Gyngell, former Chief Executive of Nine Entertainment Company and current board director, made other intimations when Mark Scott resigned as Managing Director: "running the ABC under a Liberal government is never easy. Mark's managed that fine line very well."[181] Former Managing Director Geoffrey Whitehead said: "governments are able to deny direct involvement in such appointments (referring to appointments of Managing Directors); they do appoint board members and they also create the overall climate in which their boards operate" (Whitehead, 1988).[182] Contradicting all this, in one of the final public exit interviews with former Managing Director Michelle Guthrie, she said: "we are not here to please governments of either side. We hold governments to account: that's what we do" (Cadzow, 2018).[183] Underscoring all this is the strong case for public service leadership to not just have political knowledge but also political skills to quarantine, finesse or neutralise those influences:

> To analyse and interpret political, social, economic trends; to evaluate the consequences of administrative actions; and to persuade and bargain and thereby further their organisation's objectives. Society suffers a great loss when otherwise talented people are so politically inept that they can contribute only a fraction of their talents. (Starling, 2008)[184]

ABC leadership's political engagement also involves talking with politicians so as to divine the future and maintain consistent policies and programming decisions. Institutional Logics research identifies how political influence from organisational actors is dependent on maintaining what was described somewhat oxymoronically as a "coherent past" (Golant et al., 2015)[185] and order in an organisation "serves to reassure external stakeholders of the status of the organization as an accountable and responsible social actor" (Ibid.)[186] in the *field*. Order, also obtained by political engagement, provides legitimacy for management. An institution was first described by Philip Selznick in 1957. He defined it as "an organization infused with value" (Selznick, 1957),[187] as a field in which people interact on the basis of shared meaning and manage behaviour through shared norms and understandings. If Australia's courts, as public institutions, have an important role in not just dispensing of the rule of law but also public confidence in the execution of the justice system (Beazley, 2016),[188] it could be a responsibility of the ABC to have a similar role in Australia's media—upholding objectivity and independence but also providing transparency and accountability. A role model for other serious professional media, too. If judicial independence is a core tenet of the separation of powers, then the ABC can uphold the same commitment as an objective Fourth Estate. The research for this book has shown there is some merit in re-embracing what would now be regarded as "old school" methods of journalism which were included under the Accuracy heading in the ABC's News Editorial Policy 2011:

> The ABC has a statutory duty to ensure that the gathering and presentation of news and information is accurate according to the recognised standards of objective journalism. Credibility depends heavily on factual accuracy. (*Australian Broadcasting Corporation*, 2011)[189]

The organisational changes in the face of digitised media at the ABC have impacted on the shared meaning of ABC content and programming. For example, the ABC's marketing of itself as "yours" and "ours" and "telling stories" and "having conversations" shows the ABC is grappling with its new field by handing over decision-making to the audiences. But in a publicly-funded organisation, such as the ABC, there is a need for clearer criteria of what constitutes these anecdotal stories. For instance, when the ABC ascribes content in its marketing pitch as "yours"—this provokes the questions—if "yours" refers to every taxpayer in Australia, what and who is "ours"? Is there an "ours"? Apart from the literal differences in the two words, there are separate morphologies. Further, whose story has greater value and importance for an audience? Is it "yours" or "ours"? The binarising of these two terms sets them in a power relationship where "yours" takes superiority over "ours" (the ABC). What form of public discussion preceded this policy change? These are pressing questions but their extrapolations are absent from annual reports and policy statements. It is a given that the ABC is under funding pressure, but in the rush to digital media and its abandonment of the authority of a quality field, there were no parameters established of worthy content. This then places the ABC's editorial policies under unequalled pressure. Since its launch, ABC Online has been the most successful news website in Australia. In 2020, it ranked 10th and was the lead Australian website, although it had slipped three places since the previous year (Similar Web, 2020).[190] It was ahead of Netflix and behind Live.com. There is an overwhelming urge to be liked and compete with the big commercial players. But the question remains to be asked, upon what basis is the ABC, in the emergent digital commercial field, to be 'liked'? This is a whole new game, a brutal sand-pit, for a public service institution.

Past annual reports have been more revealing of future objectives than more recent ones. Take for example the ABC's annual report in 1997 which conveyed a serious undertone that the ABC might have to "consider options unpalatable to audiences" if funding cuts were pursued (ABC Annual Report, 1997).[191] It was the year that the ABC walked away from paying for quality music and fostering musicians by jettisoning its respected symphony orchestras. It said: "the ABC has more clearly differentiated its role as a producer and broadcaster from that of operating symphony orchestras" (ABC Annual Report, 1997).[192] It was also the year of the Federal Government's Mansfield Review titled "Review of the Role and Functions of the ABC" and the year when the Federal Government reduced substantially its "financial commitment" to the ABC (Ibid.) involving an AUD11 million cut to base funding plus a AUD55 million per annum cut for the triennium funding from 1997 to 1998. The ABC's digital platform ABC Online was over one year old (launched 14 August 1995) and ABC Radio and Television News and Current Affairs were merged. The arm called ABC Enterprises then had 26 physical ABC Shops and 96 ABC Centres selling ABC-produced books, audios, videos and other licensed products from popular programs (all now gone, but also unprofitable due to the increasing sales of merchandise from other content producers, including the BBC, relative to ABC content).[193] Then there were 17 international bureaux and correspondents (by 2020 there were 11).

In 1997 the Managing Director was Brian Johns, the Chairman was Donald McDonald and the organisation was under enormous challenges, and as stated in the annual report, the re-shaping of the organisation had to be accelerated from a four-year restructure to a 12- to 18-month overhaul (Ibid.). The overhaul was named 'One ABC' and it achieved staff losses through 345 voluntary redundancies. This shedding of personnel was a major initial move towards preparing for the oncoming wave of digital media. The Mansfield Review suggested funding for digital upgrades and that it was "noted that the vast majority of submissions did not mention the issue of perceived bias in the presentation of issues" (Ibid.).

In an interview about his role at the ABC Johns said:

> ABC Staff have always been volatile by nature and quotes a mate, an occasional ABC freelance, who says it's the only organisation where everyone from the messenger boy up knows how to run the place.[194]

Johns pushed back on pressure from the board (Board member Michael Kroger proposed to privatise ABC Online; this will be discussed later in this chapter) and used the revenue to pay for additional ABC content. However, Johns said ABC Online "was not a limb that could be severed".[195] Johns' successor, Jonathan Shier, Managing Director from 2000 to 2001, built on this legacy and tried in vain to encourage a pay-per-view or subscriber basis for some of ABC programming, but succeeded in establishing a production division for "new media" and gained AUD17.8 million additional government funding to allocate multimedia producers to the regional offices in Australia (Goggin, 2004).[196] There were regular tensions between management and staff on funding online activities when it meant other areas had to be cut.

How does the ABC manage its own leadership training and motivation? In 2019 it trained 902 from a total staff of 4649. Intriguingly, one person attended a course "Effective Supervision Skills" while most attended "Managing Performance". In 2018 it launched a program called The ABC Principles. There are five: We are ABC, Straight Talking, People Focused, Accountable, Open and Transparent (ABC Annual Report, 2019).[197] Then there is the role of the ABC Board which is to safeguard the ABC's independence and integrity. Notable was in 1984 when the Board voted:

> The Board of the Australian Broadcasting Corporation believes that one of its fundamental responsibilities is to preserve the independence of the organisation. It believes that independence would be compromised by the ABC yielding, or being seen to yield, to pressure from anyone, whether government or otherwise, concerning the content of its programs. (Molomby, 1991)[198]

Over the years, there have also been many instances of hostility from outside actors, as well as from internal managers and where the Managing Director was not willing to stand up for the independence of ABC journalists.

This Board statement was triggered by the "Nyaro Episode" when ABC *Four Corners* journalist Alan Hogan interviewed a leader of the independence movement in Irian Jaya (OPM), James Nyaro, in Papua New Guinea (PNG). The then PNG Prime Minister, Michael Somare, threatened to close the ABC's Port Moresby office in retaliation for this because it "was in direct conflict with Papua New Guinea's security interests and Papua New Guinea's obligations under international law" (Molomby, 1991).[199] Papua New Guinea was concerned it was being portrayed as assisting the rebels (and anti-Indonesia who controlled the territory) by allowing the interview in Port Moresby, the capital. The program went to air, even though ABC Manager Stuart Revill had told Papua New Guinea the report would not go to air and Managing Director Geoffrey Whitehead had agreed not to screen it. But this was opposed by several board members and Chairman Ken Myers threatened to resign over this. The situation was a catalyst for bad will towards Whitehead and his management style which was taken as interference in editorial content.

Later in 1985, Whitehead committed another public blunder when he described a cohort of 1000 ABC staff revealed in an audit as a "phantom army" (*The Sydney Morning Herald*, 1985)[200]—staff of which the organisation was unaware. These people were "ghosts" because they were employed on a part-time, casual or contract basis to evade the staff ceiling imposed in the 1970s (Molomby, 1991). Whitehead claimed he did not know this "army" existed (*The Sydney Morning Herald*, 1985).[201] The consequence of this startling finding was that management announced that the planned 5% staff cuts (350–400 staff members) would be increased to 600 (*The Sydney Morning Herald*, 1985).[202] Tom Molomby (1991), a former staff-elected board member, said the cost of this "army" was quoted in the Senate Estimates Committee as AUD9 million per annum (for 1248 staff).[203] Privately, Whitehead blamed the Controller of Corporate Relations, Keith Jackson, for the "army". That management unannounced the "phantom army" in a news release was according to Molomby revealing that management was "incompetent … and stupid because they announced it" (Ibid.).[204] Summarily, it drew the organisation into public derision and revealed an inefficient and vague side of management at a time when private corporations were expected to transition to managerialism, targets, efficiency dividends and all the other benchmarks of success. As a public organisation, the ABC was expected to be more accountable than employing 'ghosts', implying people were employed to do nothing. It was also in 1985 that the Federal Government was accused of "stacking the ABC board with intellectuals from right-wing think tanks hostile to government enterprises" (Knight, 2007).[205]

It was a trigger incident that served to erode ongoing confidence in the ***cultural capital*** of the ABC as well as government funding, such that the organisation had lost over AUD350 million a year since 1985 (O'Mallon, 2020).[206]

The report "It's Our ABC" by activist group GetUp! (2020) found that 53% of Australians would now agree to pay AUD6 a year per person to fund public interest journalism (Ibid.).[207] This support for the ABC was corroborated one year earlier in a Roy Morgan survey which found in its *Media Net Trust Survey* that the ABC was the most trusted media outfit in Australia.[208] Nonetheless, the controversial Managing Director Michelle Guthrie noted the historical extent of funding cuts in 2018 and the reality of having to staff a vast and expanding territory: "Thirty years ago, the ABC had five platforms and 6000 people working around the country. Today, Your ABC has two-thirds the number of people operating six times the number of platforms and services with half the real per capita funding" (Grattan, 2018).[209]

Management struggles with funding and reinforcing the ABC as an icon of trust and education was never easy. From its beginnings, one of the most bitter and trenchant opponents of the ABC, Sir Keith Murdoch, was also one of the first to identify its early élitism. He explained the ABC's *field* as: "the present services are a bit academic and lofty in their tone, and I don't think they have wide appeal" (*The Sydney Morning Herald*, 1941).[210] In terms of the methodology of this book, it was an early example of these *field* clashes between the ABC and commercial media. Sir Keith Murdoch spotted the ABC's accretions and potential accretions of *cultural capital* even before the ABC became aware of it and the power they bestowed on the institution. The sub-text was that Murdoch was also keen for the ABC to buy his news. He told a Parliamentary Inquiry into broadcasting that on the ABC "there ought to be more good Australian news, live and interesting news" (Ibid.). He was 'talking his book', and it turned against him when the ABC did create their own news service—but independently. An analysis of archived Australian newspapers revealed they were awash with protests, led mostly by Murdoch and other Australian newspaper proprietors. Their concern was financial, panicked over a loss of market share and advertising revenue. It was feared the ABC would take away audiences and deplete advertiser interest in them when there was a small pool that newspapers relied upon. Seeking to assure Australians of its role, the then ABC Chairman, William Cleary, had already articulated very separate objectives to the market and of what its *field* would consist: "the commission, for its part, will strive to provide for you a banquet of interests, from which we hope you will never turn away unsatisfied" (*The Advertiser*, 1937).[211] Nonetheless, the worries over the ABC taking away a large chunk of the market from newspapers was so real and imminent that newspapers decided to establish their own radio stations and were permitted to own "B" class stations which could accept advertising (*The Advertiser*, 1941).[212]

The creation of extra radio licences in Australian broadcasting also helped segment the ABC from its original role to address 'market failure' and building its *cultural capital*. It could be argued that from that point on, the ABC was a unique presence and given the chance to create its own *field*. It did. Accompanying the launch of the ABC, broadcasting was split into two categories: "A" and "B" licences where "A" or national licences were under the control of the ABC and were run on a non-commercial basis. To support this impartiality, they were funded by licence fees from the listeners, which in 1932 totalled A£403,000 (*The Sydney Morning Herald*, 1932),[213] or AUD806,000 in 2018. The "B" licences were for advertising-funded broadcasting. At the same time, however, the opposition remained spirited and nasty from Keith Murdoch (Ibid.), calling for legislation to prevent ABC's access to and use of radio content sponsored by advertisers (newspapers and "B" class broadcasting stations) while enjoying access to funding from licence fees.

The ABC under Federal legislation was given a mandate over Australian broadcasting in 1931. Its role was prioritised in upholding Australian culture, not news. Addressing the so-called market failure was not meant to be a makeshift or impromptu one, which is what the use of the term implies. While its news gathering service began in 1933 with the proviso that newsreaders read the contents to newspapers to air, not news gathered or sourced independently, in an extraordinary twist the organisation later became a vital force in Australian investigative journalism. Equally surprising—and ironic—however, has been that the credibility it had established was through patriarchal-based ***cultural capital***. The removal of a régime is justified when something better takes its place. But this book argues that the ABC's institutional beginnings as a cultural organisation ensured its survival because the ABC educated its market and inspired confidence in the institution and in Australian identity through credible, privileged content delivered to its audiences. Because it was never consumer, and ratings oriented it eschewed the consumer-led market, until now. Nothing had surpassed the ABC, before it embraced consumer-driven strategies.

Because the ABC was not set up to represent the public interest (Petersen, 1993)[214] as a purveyor of news but, at the behest of the powerful newspaper lobby, was instead to assist the Australian people in being "culturally uplifted" (Ibid.),[215] it was given an even more powerful mandate from the outset to educate. Significantly, it was a largely "white" male cultural institution. It was upon this basis that it later built its credibility as a superior news outlet to one that became universally Australian and universally respected by Australians—of all backgrounds. This point is overlooked or avoided in the analyses of the ABC but it is a very (now) awkward, unacknowledged truth about its origins and the broad success and appeal those origins have had because of those origins. It envisaged a unified, unilateral, cohesive Australian identity and made great achievements in fulfilling this aim with a range of different offerings: national events, reaching out to children, "housewives", regional outposts and foreign bureaux; yet now it surveys a society riven with division and splintered with intersectional feuding and seems to have no choice but to find sides, pick sides and join the fray.

ABC management appointed its first journalist in 1934 and its first Federal News Editor in 1936 (Knight, 2007)[216] but newspaper archive research indicates that it was not until 1946, when it was inaugurated and war censorship was lifted, that the ABC was formally allowed to operate its own independent newsgathering and broadcasting service. In fact, it was reported in federal parliament that year that when the bill for ABC News Services was passed 99% of the organisation's national news services were compiled by ABC employees, 40% state news was collected by its staff and it only needed 19 more journalists to have a completely independent news service (*The Sydney Morning Herald*, 1946).[217] *Cultural capital* was now being appropriated by news bulletins, sourced by Australians with educated Australian accents or faux British accents, with news and programs accompanied by an orchestral anthem that educated audiences in a higher register about themselves, the world—and the ABC. The ABC institutionally located itself with its audience as partners in learning and living Australian culture and by nailing those values that supported and enriched a democracy.

The former ABC Managing Director, Michelle Guthrie, said she was taking the broadcaster into more narrow and specialised areas. This was in pursuit of markets, but flagged from an institutional perspective or understanding, that the ABC had not only moved into the commercial *field* but was going to imitate its content. Discussions she had with ABC staff (personal communication to staff 2018) suggested that ABC Radio News was to have a narrower focus with Generation X in mind (those born between 1966 and 1980). The Australian Bureau of Statistics (2006) had already established that a majority of the 'Xers' were better educated with a greater proportion having higher education than previous generations (Australian Bureau of Statistics, 2006).[218] Publicly, Guthrie said: "as the independent national public broadcaster, our purpose is to provide a balance between broadcasting programs of wide appeal as well as specialised interest" (Grattan Ibid.). It had already begun in 2014 when Managing Director Mark Scott confirmed that the ABC was "repositioning itself" and "management will also be stripped back" (ABC, 2014)[219] and that "the very nature of the media business means that some savings inevitably impact content" (Ibid.). This was to be done in a process of "efficiencies", "savings" and adding value for best practice resource management. When his successor, Michelle Guthrie, was sacked by the ABC Board she said her efforts to support the ABC in its new commercial *field* were carried out by continuing "the transformation of the ABC and to support the great work of ABC's dedicated and passionate employees to ensure our continuing trust, quality and distinctiveness as the source of Australian culture, conversations and stories" (Guardian Staff, 2018).[220] When she was sacked by the ABC Board she said:

> I am devastated by the board's decision to terminate my employment despite no claim of wrongdoing on my part. … At no point have any issues been raised with me about the transformation being undertaken, the Investing in Audiences strategy and my effectiveness in delivering against that strategy. (Koziol, 2018)[221]

Management statements show that it assumed the *cultural capital* nurtured since 1932 would travel with the ABC to the emergent commercial *field* and all the new products it created or mimicked in the commercial *field*.

Overlaying the changes that were envisaged, however, there was the constant pressure of the two most enduring issues that confronted management. These were noted in the 1980s by then Managing Director Geoffrey Whitehead as "politics and money" (Whitehead, 1988)[222] as the big pressure points for ABC management with the board appointed by the Federal Government and one staff-elected representative. The appointments to this board are often accused of being partisan (Manne, 2007).[223] As a sign of these problems, euphemistically addressed as 'challenges' in 2006, the then Managing Director, Russell Balding, resigned saying: "This has been a difficult decision for me as I have found my time with the ABC to be without doubt the most challenging, but most rewarding, of my professional career" (ABC, 2006)[224]; Mark Scott said in 2015: "I have made no secret of the fact that I think 10 years is a long time to run an organisation, particularly in a sector as dynamic and fast-changing as media" (ABC, 2015).[225] Former ABC Chairman Justin Milne said the job of choosing the right ABC Managing Director was "a lottery" (Meade, 2018).[226]

2.6 Managing the *Field*

Management's discernment of its audiences has attempted to be nuanced and 'unbinaried' and former Managing Director Michelle Guthrie pointed this out: "to pigeonhole our audience as being of a particular political bent or social strata" was wrong because: "In the two years since I've been in this role, I have been constantly reminded how wrong that is" (Grattan, 2018).[227] Also, there have been far more serious background issues which do not fit this binaried, generalised and incorrect marketing narrative of audiences corralled into "left" and "right", "young" and "old", "this gender" and "that gender"—as argued previously, quality is immutable and it is strange that there is a perceived need to work out how youth define quality in order to attract that audience, as if there are various standards of quality and when that audience (like the rest) is already pre-occupied with commercial media in the *field* anyway. These matters have created onerous complications for ABC management trying to handle staff concerns about the abandonment of quality in search of new "quality", and the new micro-objective of having "conversations" with all audience members, of all opinions. It is curious that quality has been challenged and that it is seen to be a relative concept for the ABC.

This, in part, is a manifestation of the constant pressure on management within their Institutional Logics *field* to control the language used by themselves and their organisation and manage the coverage of certain content that, from time to time, governments have decided was sensitive. In issues of national security, for example, the ABC has been under increased pressure to control content. At various times ABC staff has felt the scrutiny of Australia's intelligence organisation, Australia Security and Intelligence Organisation (ASIO). ASIO is the Australian equivalent of Britain's MI6 and the US's Federal Bureau of Intelligence (FBI). Pressures on the ABC have peaked at times of war and World War II government censorship on the ABC was an example of this as explained in Chap. 1 and elsewhere in the book. During the Cold War and with the emergence of television in Australia there was a government initiative to "ensure conservatism within public broadcasting" and "an official culture of anti-communism in all public institutions during the Cold War" (McKnight, 1998) because "ASIO was the powerful, sharp sword of Cold War Australia" and in contact with "the highest levels of ABC management" (McKnight, 1998).[228] McKnight's analysis of papers released under the Archives Act up to 1966 showed:

> In order to understand political surveillance of the ABC, it is necessary to construct a broader narrative using a large number of files in combination with broader histories of the ABC, such as Ken Inglis's *This is the ABC*, and with contemporary press coverage.[229]

It was a layered, tricky situation where there was overt government pressure, covert government pressure (ASIO) overlaid with a conservative management and board (McKnight, 1998). In some ways the influence of ASIO on the ABC was not unique because it was required to vet all Commonwealth Government employees (Ibid.). McKnight (1998) said the effect of the presence of ASIO was to "reinforce a politically conservative agenda and to have a chilling effect on cultural and political innovation". It meant that during the 1950s and 1960s staff recruitment and promotion was vetted by the ASIO for security clearance. McKnight (1998) explained that in security parlance the ABC was described as a 'key point', as were a wide range of public and private organisations and assets. Importantly, here, for the purposes of this analysis, McKnight (1998) argued that this surveillance and pressure on management helped fortify the ABC's conservatism not in explicit content but in "setting the boundaries" (McKnight, ibid.) at that time. It developed a conservatism, as a survival mechanism. One could then extrapolate on this that the latter-day shape-shifting of the ABC to embrace more stridency and popular causes is seen as helping it gain a place in the new emergent commercial field.

These reinforced the *cultural capital* in the *field* as a conservative broadcaster, aided by all the other factors which promoted its unique role in its own *field* of the media. McKnight (1998) said the conservatism of the ABC began to fade in the late 1960s and early 1970s, possibly with the emergence of the concept of 'participation' infiltrating Western thinking, generally (Carpentier, 2014).[230] Interestingly, surveillance of the ABC and its actors is so much easier now through their use of internet service providers (ISPs) and social media where personal, political, ideological, private information and personal details are handed over freely to unknown recipients. Individuals can be monitored for security risks by governments as well as reputational risk by their organisations (Uldam, 2016),[231] or what is described as "delegated surveillance" (Uldam, Ibid., quoting DeNardis, 2014) where online visibility bestowed on agency. Also, the ease of the use of the internet for surveillance has left seemingly untroubled individuals exposed to its companion—vulnerability (Ibid.).

2.7 Blowing Up Aunty's Skirt: Upheaval at the ABC

The ABC is legally an authority, which means it can manage public money on its own. As part of its governance, the Federal Government appoints its board to oversee that. Over the decades this has also been a highly politicised and fractious situation, and, as a consequence, the board has caused controversy from time to time. This is no marginal matter for the ABC, because it means the public service organisation is sometimes riven with politics. The 2012 Public Sector Governance in Australia report said in reference to the ABC (but couched in general terms):

> It can only be a matter of time before a political appointment to a high-profile board in Australia backfires enough to severely dent faith in public integrity and confidence in its key institutions.[232]

As mentioned earlier, there had been moves to create order in the Board. The National Broadcasting Legislation Amendment Bill 2010 changed the appointment of board members so that they were "merit based". This step taken by the ALP government in 2007 under Prime Minister Kevin Rudd, which stated it would appoint board members based on "the Nolan Rules". This referenced the steps taken in 1994 by the UK Government's Prime Minister John Major who established a Committee on *Standards* in Public Life, chaired by Lord Michael Nolan, to draw up standards of behaviour for public office. It focused more on leadership in public service, but the list of values—The Seven Principles of Public Life—or "the Nolan Rules" recommended:

1. Selflessness,
2. Integrity,
3. Objectivity,
4. Accountability,
5. Openness,
6. Honesty and
7. Leadership.[233]

These rules had iterations for the BBC in that from then onwards the BBC has had Chairs appointed based on "the Nolan Rules".

The Communication Minister during the Rudd Administration, Stephen Conroy, said: "We are seeking advice as to the best way to implement the Nolan principles in terms of new appointments to the ABC" (Sainsbury, 2007).[234] The aim of the changes was to restore a measure of public faith, independence and transparency in the ABC, to remove it from the challenges created by political appointments to the board. 'Tainted' appointments are seen to have support from and allegiances to the political party and politician who appointed them, rather than remain separate from the executive. It is acknowledged that this should be board members' goal and helps separate the matters of the Board and puts political pressures at arm's length. The 2010 legislation also made provision for an Independent Nomination Panel. However, the research has found that subsequent senior political leaders said the process had not been observed, nor upheld, and political interference in appointments had resumed and undermined the lifeline on probity. This has been confirmed in the academic literature where the ABC (and SBS) legislation has been criticised as allowing gaps and paying:

> Scant attention to the specific role of ministers between the setting of the selection criteria and receiving the short list of recommended candidates from the nomination panel. (Edwards et al., 2012)[235]

Further:

> Without this attention in the Bill, or a separate code of practice, real difficulties can be expected and public confidence undermined for any government that is planning to adopt this approach. (Edwards et al., ibid.)[236]

And that:

> Any reforms will require a civic education component, transparency and independent monitoring processes. (Loc. Cit.)[237]

In 2012, the Public Sector Governance in Australia report by Emeritus Professor Meredith Edwards and her research team said political appointments to the ABC: "have the potential to undermine public confidence in Australia's appointment processes"[238] and "for decades, governments on all sides of politics have been accused of stacking the ABC board with their 'mates' or, as one interviewee called them, 'chums'".[239] However, Inglis (2006) provided other insights when he quoted a former ABC board member: "we leave our guns outside" and board members actually can develop an affection and custodian loyalty for the ABC that overrides any political positioning that may have opened the door on their apportionments.[240] This research has made similar findings to Inglis in interviewing former board members. There is an enduring sense of contributing to something larger than the individual and a great sense of noble purpose bestowed on the ABC because of that aspiration. This research did not find political affiliations that overrode goodwill towards the ABC.

Then in 2018, chaos beset Aunty with the resignation of her Managing Director, Michelle Guthrie, and her Chairman, Justin Milne. The board was mired in controversy and the independence of the ABC severely tested. 2018 proved a tumultuous year for Aunty—she lost her Managing Director, Michelle Guthrie, and her Chairman, Justin Milne. It needs to be said that the ABC is often a fractious beast. There is a substantial history of staff: Dixon (1975), Thomas (1980), Semmler (1981), Buttrose (1984), Whitehead (1988), Molomby (1991), Petersen (1993), Littlemore (1996), Williams (1996), Dempster (2000), Salter (2007), Scott (2016), O'Brien (2018) and Holmes (2019) at the public broadcaster publicly airing their views when management, governments or other staff displeased them. Also, there have been public comments by non-staff about staff, namely Styles (2002).[241] And expurgations do not always satisfy, nor justify, these concerns because they never seem to be resolved, as evidenced by ongoing, repetitive or similar complaints. The attitudes of staff in the organisation as a whole can also impact on the particular success of leadership. For instance, well before the resignation of former Managing Director, Michelle Guthrie, in 2018 the mood at the ABC was described as "funereal" in the words of one senior broadcaster, and "paranoid" in the words of another (Seccombe, 2016).[242]

2.8 Michelle Guthrie and Capture Theory

The management theory of 'capture' describes how actors conform to the desires of subordinates or sub-groups. The academic literature on the metatheory of policy 'capture' says it can also be included as a political and an economic theory and that it originally described how special interests were able to direct government policy-settings, regulations and legislation. Capture theory has an ideological basis (Levine Forrence, 1990)[243] and speaks broadly to political influence (Dal Bo', 2006).[244] In another iteration, regulatory capture "is specifically the process through which regulated monopolies end up manipulating the state agencies that are supposed to control them" (Dal Bo', Ibid.).[245] Capture theory also examines the role of "interest groups" in creating and influencing public policy (Laffont & Tirole, 1991)[246] where they are able to exert power but also "may be hurt by its own power" (Laffont & Tirole, ibid.).[247] The initial analysis of factors that limited actors' agency was named capture theory by Stigler (1971) who scrutinised regulation through economics and identified a view of the political process that "defies rational explanation:

'politics' is an imponderable, a constantly and unpredictably shifting mixture of forces of the most diverse nature" (Stigler, 1971).[248] In his analysis "capture" worked by creating obstacles or opportunities and further that the problem was understanding "when or why an industry (or other group of like-minded people) is able to use the state for its purposes, or is singled-out by the state to be used for alien purposes" (Stigler, ibid.).[249] The literature is agreed and explicit that when organisations are captured by interest groups they are no longer working in the public interest.

Capture can involve politicians, public figures and bureaucrats and exists quite frequently in institutions (Levine & Forrence, 1990). Levine and Forrence (1990) asserted that capture engaged bureaucrats who were motivated by personal gain, such as "personal utility derived from office-holding" (Ibid.).[250] The "capture" theory of political behaviour was first given substance by Downs (1957) and Olson (1965) (cited by Levine & Forrence, 1990)[251] where "public officials will consider the costs and benefits of forming and maintaining the coalitions necessary to maintain them in office or enhance their wealth or power" (Levine & Forrence, ibid.).[252] Further, it describes: "actors in the regulatory process as having narrow, self-interested goals-principally job retention or the pursuit of re-election, self-gratification from the exercise of power, or perhaps post office holding personal wealth"[253] and that "people should be expected to act no less rationally or self-interestedly as politicians or bureaucrats than they do in the course of their private exchanges in markets" (Loc. Cit.).[254]

Capture theory has also been situated in an analysis of special interests (where its opposite is general, public interests). It can be located with the public interest role of the ABC as well as in the contestation of the field of Institutional Logics and Bourdieu's *field* theory. Capture theory can be used to explain how the ABC has developed a self-reinforcing staff culture which has had a strong impact on government policy-making and management policy-making with regard to national broadcasting and the role of the ABC itself. It describes how public interest rhetoric and practices, used by the ABC and actors within the organisation, have supported the broadcaster. The metatheory asserted that it was a self-interested position that dominated "the regulatory process" (Ibid.)[255]:

> Public interests are derived from preferences held by individuals (who may or may not hold public office) about the private or collective behavior or condition of others, including the behavior of the government toward the polity at large or toward some subset of it.[256]

And, as to the leader, Levine and Forrence (1990) argued:

> If her hold on power or position is tenuous, we can predict that she will be very open to capture in order to secure special-interest support, which can be turned into activity that influences the general polity.[257]

The ABC faces strong competition for funds from all other publicly supported organisations and policy programs; it also supports a strong staff culture, analysed in the next chapter, Chap. 3 of this book "The ABC: Service for Funding". The literature described politicians as another group that could be subject to capture—supporting selfish interests to enable re-election and accumulate power (Dal Bo', 2006).[258] The ABC Board is then significant, and possibly distinguishable from this individual model of leadership because its constituents are appointed by the government, the board acts in unison and, therefore, not necessarily beholden to selfish interests. The literature said such a group provided "a main protection against vulnerability" because (and also in the case of the ABC Board) its constituents were accountable to the government, not the dominant groups within the organisation (Dal Bo', ibid.).[259] This, then, also sets the board up for clashes with staff culture—and possibly the Managing Directors, who may be 'captured' by staff but hold a prevailing allegiance to the Board. At best, they can be sometimes "the ham in the sandwich" of organisational policy-making and situations can be very complex for them to manage. There is also limited literature on the impact of consumer pressure (audiences) on the role of capture in an organisation (Dal Bo', Ibid.),[260] although ABC audiences can impact on voting patterns depending on the funding promises of the political candidates but "the empirical evidence on the causes and consequences of regulatory capture is scarce" (Ibid.).[261]

Research into committees has shown that boards needed to be of a substantial size to avoid capture, they should be fully informed and consist of members who are not motivated to be taken capture (Name-Correa & Yildirim, 2018).[262] Name-Correa and Yildirim (2018) also suggested that board members' identities be concealed, although this is not possible with a publicly-funded organisation such as the ABC. Capture theory also means that the industry must be able to gather substantial support to counter those opposed to the organisation's aims and policies. It is important that management is not captured by the staff (Stigler, 1971)[263] if staff culture is strong, because a captured organisation means that it becomes enthralled to the decisions of the special interest groups within the organisation (Potter et al., 2014).[264] The ABC has a large footprint in Australian rural and regional broadcasting; for example, because of such coverage it seeks to create content in the public, national interest and government policy is playing a role in rectifying a market void by encouraging this activity. So, the government has tasked the ABC in what can be described as a "benevolent maximiser of social welfare" (Laffont & Tirole, 1991).[265] Yet, because the ABC is a city-based organisation (Sydney and Melbourne head offices) and has been captured by city-dwelling staff there was concern that city-based matters were preferred over rural or regional interests.

Academic literature said when an organisation had been captured it operated for the "benefit of its regulated community, rather than in the public interest, often presenting a practical dilemma for bureaucrats" (Potter et al., 2014).[266] Selznick (1949) studied how experts in organisations could shape policy-making through the organisational culture and were also able to exclude or suppress other groups in the organisation judged non-specialists or non-expert: "in one respect individual parts of the administration tend to become like private pressure groups in that they have their own particularistic and parochial interests to defend and promote" (in Potter et al., 2014).[267] One example on the public record of how capture theory has worked at the ABC was when former ABC Managing Director, Michelle Guthrie, was interviewed (well before she resigned from her role in 2018). Guthrie told the interviewer she: "had a conversation the other night with Laura Tingle (Chief Political Correspondent for the ABC). … I mean, who gets to do that?" (Cadzow, 2018).[268] Further, she also told the interviewer that she had introduced herself and chatted to another ABC employee, Triple J presenter (and champion Wimbledon athlete) Dylan Alcott, at the airport and that she was left with a spring in her step for the rest of the day: "I sort of skipped through the airport. It was fantastic" (Ibid.).[269]

The academic literature would describe this situation of Guthrie and her engagements with higher profile, more senior staff as providing a challenge for her in that she would have to balance that staff capture with her role leading a body with many thousands of other staff all employed equally to serve the public interest, but which may be challenging especially at times of critical decisions (Potter et al., 2014).[270] This reported insight into Guthrie shows that she may have needed to "critically separate" (Potter, ibid.)[271] herself from her organisation so that she could "deconstruct the values system under which they (she) operate(d)" (Loc.

Cit.)[272] because she ran the risk of "becoming ineffective when they are too reliant on information from their (her) regulated community" (Loc. Cit.).[273] If staff capture is strong, the literature said, it could then lead to regulatory capture which is defined as: "over-reliance on information from the supervised community at the expense of the public interest" (Ibid.).[274] A consequence of this, beyond the input of other staff, is that there is a failure to capture public interest because of narrow or unchanging institutional interests. ABC staff culture has impacted on how the key actors, over time, who lead the organisation have carried out their roles. This has either enabled or limited their capacities to lead. A former senior ABC staff member expressed to this research that Managing Directors have, at times, allowed themselves to be hostage to the ABC staff culture and seduced by key staff actors' 'celebrity' status. This research was also told by other senior figures that managers had been intellectually brow-beaten by what were described as "staff celebrities".

2.9 Management Inaction Versus Active Staff

Being independent wins no friends. The ABC has to maintain independence in the face of substantive political criticism and other criticism from all angles. Yet because of this, this creation of upset amongst everyone for a long time was good circumstance for the public service media outlet. It meant that if everyone was upset, the ABC believed it was doing its job—and doing it well. The research challenges that understanding and suggests that may no longer be the case. This section will explore if staff has the capacity within the ABC to run individual personal issues and whether this, then, incapacitates management agency. Two case studies will be examined.

(a) ABC Managing Director Brian Johns

On 26 February 2001, Wayne Swan, ALP Member for Lilley in the House of Representatives, rose to his feet and spoke. It was a response to an investigation by the Australian Federal Police (AFP) into his conduct during the 1996 Federal election when it was alleged by the ABC's 7.30 current affairs television program that he had paid money to the Australian Democrats Party in his electorate to preference him, a decision, the program alleged, that was made at the national level between the ALP and the Democrats (Sanderson, 2000).[275] The amount of money paid was alleged on the program to be "around AUD1400" (Sanderson, ibid.)[276] and this was disputed by Swan as being a lesser amount of AUD500 and, further, it was paid "to buy election signs" (Swan, 2001).[277] Contextual literature said the election was going to be a difficult one for the ALP to win, and the ALP was then led by Paul Keating. The result on election night was a win for the Liberal National Coalition led by John Howard. At the time these allegations were televised, the ABC's Managing Director was the late Brian Johns (his term finished in March 2000).

What followed was an Australian Electoral Commission examination into the donation and a referral to the Commonwealth Director of Public Prosecutions and the Australian Federal Police, which found no evidence of any breach of law (Karvelas, 2007)[278] in a situation where: "the practice of helping 'rival' campaigns financially dates to at least the 1950s, as evidence of Country Party assistance to the DLP reveals" (Orr, 2010)[279] and where "major parties provide cash and in-kind benefits to minor parties. These are rarely pocketed personally, but enhance the minor candidate's campaign, to the benefit of both sides of the deal" (Ibid.).[280] On 26 February 2001, the AFP investigation cleared Swan of electoral bribery and Swan confirmed he had donated to the other party, but not in return for preferences (Schubert & Canberra Bureau, 2007).[281] [282].

One of the interviewees for the ABC 7.30 program was ALP state organiser Lee Birmingham, who said he conveyed the money to the Democrats in what he described as "an envelope. I had a feeling that it was brown in colour so it was nondescript other than that" (Sanderson, 2000).[283] It evoked the metaphor of the clichéd (and actual) symbol of Australian political corruption "the brown paper bag" but it falsely accused Swan by conflating him within that misconduct narrative. Soon after this Swan stood down in what was labelled by the media as "the Queensland vote-rorting scandal" and "the electoral rorts affair" (Lewis, 2000).[284]

When Swan addressed parliament, now in Hansard, he was scathing of the ABC "fabricating" (Swan, 2001)[285] the scandal:

> The replay of this re-enactment on news broadcasts, the references to and repetition of the image of brown paper envelopes, the government's referral to the Australian Electoral Commission and ultimately to the Australian Federal Police, all called into question my standing in the community. (Ibid.)

He blamed an "unprofessional journalist" who caused a "public humiliation because of a journalist's personal hatred of me" for the false allegations, and that there was no brown paper bag or envelope and that the re-enactment was "an event that never happened" (Ibid.).

Further, he said:

> The re-enactment on the ABC was in breach of the ABC's own editorial policies, the ABC Code of Practice and the journalists' code of ethics. It was irresponsible sensationalism adopting the McCarthyist attitude 'know nothing, suspect everything'. Unsupported and denied allegations should never be put to air, but when they are done in such a way as to create a dramatic image, they leave a lasting impression, long after the real facts have come out. Of critical relevance has been the unethical and unprofessional conduct of the journalist who reported this story.

Swan said: "Mr Sanderson relied upon the evidence of Mr Lee Birmingham, a person with a longstanding personal grudge against me since his sacking from the Labor Party in 1997". In addition, he complained that the ABC journalist who wrote the report had told Senator Bartlett (then an Australian Democrats Senator) "who was also misrepresented in the report" he was "going to get Swan"—"prior to the program going to air".

> Mr Sanderson and the 7.30 Report are in breach of the ABC editorial policy section 4.3, 'Accuracy, impartiality and objectivity', as well as section 4.8, relating to re-enactments. They are also in breach of the ABC Code of Practice sections 4.1(a), 4.1(c), 4.2(a) and 4.2(b). Mr Sanderson has, repeatedly, on ABC radio, denigrated, ridiculed and misrepresented events regarding me. He has a hatred and an obsession with any person seen to have been close to or involved in the Goss government.

Swan also listed to parliament other examples of Sanderson's public abuse of him and false accusations.

> Mr Sanderson is part of a small clique of people pursuing political vendettas against me, and his journalistic conduct has been both unethical and unprofessional. It was this prejudice that led Mr Sanderson to fabricate the image of a secret transfer of money in a brown envelope. He knew this would translate in the wider media into images of the brown paper bags of the Bjelke-Petersen era.
>
> It is a matter of common knowledge in and around the ABC and throughout Brisbane's political circles that Mr Sanderson and his boss Mr Steve Austin[286] regularly joke about getting Swan and other prominent

> Labor identities in Queensland. This is in breach of all of the editorial policies and codes of ethics previously mentioned. But Mr Sanderson in particular is in breach of section 2.4 of the Code of Practice relating to discrimination by the presentation or portrayal of people in a way which is likely to encourage denigration because of their political belief.

These false accusations and attacks on Swan's character had echoes into the future and were sustained purely through reiteration when Treasurer Peter Costello said in parliament in 2007: "The nine words I like are: 'Wayne Swan had money in brown paper bags'" (Schubert & Canberra Bureau, 2007).[287] In 2001, Swan had rebuffed the false accusations using a quote from French newspaper editor and writer Émile Zola who published a famous open letter to the French President in 1898 in defence of Alfred Dreyfus, a French Jewish officer, accused of treason (but also regarded as an anti-Semitic persecution):

> But it is with this poisoned bread that the unclean press has been nourishing our poor people now for months. And it is not surprising if we are witnessing a dangerous crisis, for when folly and lies are thus sown broadcast, you necessarily reap insanity. (Swan, 2001)[288]

Swan called on the ABC to launch an investigation. This research was unable to find evidence of a public apology or publicly released investigation by the ABC into Swan's requests and complaints. The maligning of Swan and the publicly-ignored complaint demonstrated that the ABC staff could operate in self-governed siloes placing it beyond the reach of management. This is not a staff problem, it is a management one. The Managing Director following Johns (from 2000-December 2001) was Jonathan Shier. In 2014 and not in reference to this matter, the then Managing Director Mark Scott said: "we have a detailed upward referral on editorial judgement at the ABC to help guided thinking in complex or contentious matters".[289]

(b) ABC Managing Director Mark Scott

The big challenges faced during the Managing Directorship of Mark Scott were exemplified in Federal Government budget cuts in 2014 of AUD250 million over five years which gave Scott and his team leaders a chance to tackle the staff siloes (pockets of staff culture) and eliminate trouble spots. The then Prime Minister Tony Abbott told Federal

Parliament "the ABC should not be exempted from the kind of measures that are being applied to almost every other part of government" (Kidd et al., 2014).[290] The staff silos had cramped the ABC's ability to pivot in a digital ecology because it was beset regularly with resistance from staff at times of change where previous Managing Directors had tried to institute new (decreased) staffing and re-allocation of resources (BBC, 2020[291]; SBS, 2020[292]) in the staff belief that the budget cuts, in the first instance, were "ideological and vindictive" (Watkins, 2018).[293] Later cuts appeared especially nasty in 2020 and with the AUD41 million funding reduction (Carson, 2020)[294] management was accused of using those reduced funds as an opportunity to cut staff numbers and get rid of unwanted people:

> Senior people are put on rosters that are very, very difficult to work, constantly changing hours and jobs. I think it's being done to put people under pressure to leave the organisation, rather than have payouts. (Seccombe, 2020)[295]

There had already been significant shifts for the ABC during the time of Managing Director Mark Scott who restructured the ABC into a digital networking media organisation, created a new department for regional divisions and merged the news division with television. All received significant staff push-back because of the loss of roles, loss of jobs (Seccombe, 2014 & 2020[296]) and concomitant diminution of staff siloes. When Mark Scott resigned in 2015 he said in a published exit interview "I had no idea of the scale of the challenge" (Hyland, 2015).[297]

After Scott departed the ABC at the expiration of his term, there was praise for his efforts. Professor of Journalism at the University of Canberra, Matthew Ricketson, said: "he's taken most people in the organisation with him, which is not to be taken for granted in an organisation such as the ABC" (Hyland, ibid.) and he had "personality and people skills" compared with his predecessor Jonathan Shier (Hyland, loc. cit.). Dr Fiona Stanley, ABC Board member and professor at the University of Western Australia, said: "It will be the Mark Scott era that they will talk about, even though it's been a tough one". Another ABC board director Simon Mordant said of Scott: "The organisation has had a lot of challenges and he's tried to see them coming and worked to position the organisation for those changes" (Loc. Cit.). Former ABC Board member Steven Skala said he was an "outstanding manager … we needed a chief executive who was sophisticated in editorial content and who also had very strong people management skills" (Hyland, 2015).

Nonetheless, there were accusations of ABC bias during Scott's time which provided concerns over the consequences of the ABC shifting its field to the digital commercial *field* on the assumption that the reputational capital it accrued in its exclusive, privileged, élite *field* had not been packaged for travel and re-purposed for product. The Managing Director is also the Editor-in-Chief and two examples of bias will be analysed here. First, the ABC's comedy television program, *The Hamster Decides*, performed by the ABC's comedy team *The Chaser*, televised a skit depicting The Australian newspaper columnist, Chris Kenny, in a bestial act with a dog with the caption "dog fucker" (ABC, 2013).[298] This triggered a defamation law suit. The ABC's Audience and Consumer Affairs Department launched its own investigation and decided that the segment did not breach its editorial standards. It found that it was offensive, but legitimate satire. Independently, however, the Australian Communications and Media Authority (ACMA) investigated and ruled that the content *was un*acceptable. It found that the ABC did breach ABC Editorial Policy and overruled the ABC decision that it was 'fair'. ACMA said the segment breached the ABC's own "harm and offence" standard 7:1: "content that is likely to cause harm or offence must be justified by the editorial context".[299] It also cautioned the ABC Board that it needed to consider "whether its code of practice is operating effectively when it comes to harm and offence" (Knott, 2014) because "the present standards on harm and offence serve to complicate and obscure rather than simplify or clarify" (Knott, 2014). Mark Scott made a formal apology to Kenny; there was a settlement of AUD35,000 and an on-air apology by the ABC (Knott, 2014). Kenny said the point of the legal action was "to show that the broadcaster should not be able to silence or intimidate its critics" (Knott 2014). The Editor-in-Chief of *The Australian*, Chris Mitchell, said that he contacted Scott to manage the issue in the early stage, leader to leader, "but it went nowhere" (Hyland, 2015):

> [Mark's] set up a large network of bureaucrats around himself who have produced large amounts of paper about any given problem, most of which no daily newspaper editor would do. Daily newspaper editors would simply pick up the phone and fix the problem. (Hyland, 2015)[300]

Mitchell praised Scott for making achievements in multi-platforming the ABC but said "he's done that while abrogating his responsibilities as editor-in-chief" (Hyland, 2015). In regard to the Kenny defamation, media analyst Fusion Strategy's spokesperson Steve Allen said it was "a mark against Scott" (Hyland, 2015) that the ABC had "been extraordinarily reluctant to even admit to their faults and apologise where it's clearly necessary" (Hyland, 2015). Reflecting on assertion, Scott said:

> I should have apologised for the Kenny thing quickly. ... We have a lot of processes here and at times you still have to trust your instinct above and beyond the process. But we threw that into a process and the process took forever. There are times when we just get paralysed by process. (Hyland, 2015)[301]

The second incident involved a 2015 ABC television debate program *Q and A* when a former terrorist suspect and supporter was invited to ask a question of Parliamentary Secretary Steven Ciobo about Australia's terrorism laws. In 2003, Zaky Mallah was convicted of threatening to kill Commonwealth officials and found not guilty of terrorism offences in 2005. Ahead of the program Mallah tweeted that two female News Ltd journalists should be "gang banged"[302] (Robinson, 2015).[303] A Department of Communications report later found that *Q and A*, prior to the program had done checks on Mallah: "It was decided 'he was not dangerous, would not be disruptive and would be a suitable audience member to ask a question'" (ABC, 2015)[304], although program host Tony Jones was reported saying that: "had the program known of Mallah's tweets inciting the gang rape of two News Corp Australia journalists, producers would not have invited him on to the program" (Robinson Ibid.). The report also found that Mallah had been rejected twice before as a program panel member. Managing Director Mark Scott defended the ABC in a newspaper article in response to complaints by then Liberal Prime Minister Tony Abbott who said:

> They've given this disgraceful individual a platform and in so doing I believe the national broadcaster has badly let us down, Abbott said. "I think many millions of Australians would feel betrayed by our national broadcaster right now. I do think the ABC needs to have a long hard look at itself, and answer a question I've posed before: whose side are you on? (Davidson, 2015)[305]

Federal Liberal Communications Minister, Malcolm Turnbull, said: "A person with those opinions, being allowed to express them without any hindrance on live television raises very real concerns" (Ibid.). Scott replied that the ABC was a public broadcaster, not a state broadcaster and that (using the satirical newspaper Charlie Hebdo massacre in Paris as an example[306]): "You have to set the bar very high before you begin to exclude certain views or perspectives" (Scott, 2015)[307] but that:

> Some ABC staff argue that to make any concession in the face of criticism is to buckle. Who say it's a sign of weakness. I disagree. It's not weakness to say you made the wrong call. (Scott, ibid.)

The ABC also had to increase its own security as a result of the program after receiving threatening phone calls (Robertson, 2015).[308] An outlying perspective on this is that the program relies on *Twitter* as a substantial part of its perceived audience engagement. It is therefore curious that a guest who had made violent, degenerate tweets would have gone unnoticed by the program. The feminist literature said that online content can enforce gender-based violence and carries sinister undertones of victim blaming (Barratt, 2018),[309] while the legal literature said the related activity—hate speech—had become a major source of concern for minorities in the US, including African Americans, and that there was a correlation between the rise in hate speech and hate crime (Delgado & Stefancic, 2014).[310] In September of that year, the ratification of the Istanbul Convention by Portugal on sexual verbal abuse decreed "practicing exhibitionist acts, forcing a contact of a sexual nature, or verbalising proposals of sexual nature" (Simões & Silveirinha, 2019)[311] were crimes. Australian research has found that online abuse and harassment had negative consequences on women's livelihoods (Jane, 2018)[312] in many areas including "economic vandalism" (Ibid.).

2.10 The ABC's Institutional Significance

The fundamental identifier of the ABC is the Lissajous—the unending wavelength logo—and it "consistently shows up as one of the best-known brand symbols in Australia" (Simons, 2008).[313] It was designed by a staff member in 1965. Drori et al. (2016)[314] researched universities' institutional narratives and quoted a Director of Business Development of a US University: "'[The logo] represents your mission, who you are. We are not Coca Cola; we are not trying to sell products on a shelf'" (Ibid.).[315] The same concept of vision and mission could be applied to the ABC. Van Der Houwen and Sliedrecht (2016)[316] asserted that formulations of narratives were also crucial to understanding institutions, as well as the construction of their narratives.

While Institutional Logics has applicability to understanding management situations at the ABC, managers can find themselves in situations that are differing, complex and demanding (Tengblad, 2012).[317] They are able to access narratives that legitimise institutions (Loseke, 2007)[318] and cultural narratives which can construct boundaries around actors. Narratives also describe the founding of the organisation, past experiences of the organisation and its struggles (Robbins et al., 2019[319]): "these stories anchor the present in the past and explain and legitimise current practices" (Robbins et al., 2019).[320] In addition, institutions are supported by "causal stories" whereby the problem is identified and the policy response framed (Loseke, ibid.).[321] ABC staff and managers speak to the organisation in terms of upholding the dominant narratives of their role within the organisation because the organisation is privileged over the individual (Ibid.).[322] For example, former Managing Director Mark Scott said in 2014 when he announced major staff cuts: "working together, we can be confident in our ability to see through these changes and to build a stronger ABC" (Kidd et al., 2014).[323]

In 2011 the Australian Public Service said:

> Innovation is at the heart of good public administration. A high-performing public service is relentless in its commitment to continuous improvement. It never assumes that the current policies, processes and services are the best or only solution. (Australian Public Service Commission, 2010)[324]

Creed (2011) asserted that for this to be achieved there had to be an alignment between the implicit culture with the explicit culture of the organisation.[325] Part of the ABC's narrative is its explicit culture, the story of its origins and the factual basis for this tied to the ABC Charter and ABC Act in what could be described as having a "high context culture" where there is implicit communication as well as reliance on the broadcaster's context of power relations (Creed, 2011).[326] Emerging from this, however, at the ABC has been a strong, defensive organisational culture, typified in the literature as one where it is difficult to introduce change and referencing values deriving from founders and perpetuated by managers and staff (Ibid.).[327] To change the culture, the organisational behaviour literature said senior managers had to "model the behaviour they want to see" (Ibid.)[328] and should be "standing up first so that others can follow"

(McGuire et al., 2008).[329] ABC staff culture will be analysed in the following chapter, Chap. 3.

Institutional narratives are an important aspect of not just how the ABC is described by its audiences, but also how it describes itself. They are embedded by formulations (Van Der Houwen & Sliedrecht, 2016)[330] and reiterated by managers. Formulations are defined as occurring in the conversations among staff and managers within an organisation that describe "what we are talking about" and "function as an interactional tool to negotiate knowledge and attain mutual understanding" (Ibid.). Public utterances by ABC managers, therefore, become a guide to its institutional narrative. In addition to responding to these implicit or explicit formulations on the public record, the ABC must translate these into an appealing institutional narrative to its audiences/the public/Australians. We are also living in a "brand society" (Drori et al., quoting Kornberger, 2009)[331] where narrative changes can be substantial or sometimes boil down to creating new commercial emphases by re-branding—down to fonts, colour palettes, livery, letterheads. This then is designed to refocus attention on the product.

In 2014, the ABC re-branded with the hashtag #ourabc "highlighting togetherness and connecting Australians".[332] Another goal was to encourage everyone to contribute their stories—the ABC was no longer the originator, curator or repository of Australian stories—the taxpayers were—and those of the cohort who operated on social media were able to contribute and share. The ABC Television's Head of Marketing and Communications, Diana Costantini, said: "The ABC is for everyone, everywhere, every day and this tagline reflects that perfectly … (Meade, 2014)[333] … This rebrand is about providing a stage and the magic comes from authenticity, diversity and a few damn fine yarns as told by colourful Australian characters" (ABC, 2014).[334] The ABC said: "On air, the ABC 'worm'—one of the most recognisable logos in the country—will represent the channel. We're confident audiences will instantly associate the 'worm' with the ABC and that the 'ABC' typography is no longer needed" (Ibid.)[335] The ABC described the re-branding as "bold, simple, raw and real" (Loc. Cit.).[336] Then in 2017 the Lissajous logo went from a blue colour palette to black and white and the letters ABC were dropped in favour of the logo. There was also a merger of Twitter accounts across all news and current affairs departments to @abcnews (Knox, 2017).[337] Essentially, all news, factual content and comment were merged under the heading "ABC News".

2.11 Digitising the ABC

Evelyn Waugh wrote dismissively about journalism in his satirical novel, *Scoop*: "News is what a chap who doesn't care much about anything wants to read. And it's only news until he's read it. After that it's dead" (Waugh, 1938/1982).[338] The preceding Waugh moment could just as easily have been written to describe news content on the ephemeral internet and social media, just as it applied to newspapers of the English writer and journalist's day. The brevity of news interest has also been subjected to other influences, apart from reader whim. The phenomenon of "churnalism" has also eventuated where news information from other sources takes the place of critically researched news reports. This situation has been caused by fewer reporting staff and "the PR-isation of democracy" (Jackson & Moloney, 2016).[339] Surprisingly, this development has caused consternation among the public relations industry which, when surveyed, said it would actually prefer news be more widely researched and sourced (Ibid.) and stay behind its barricades. Another factor controlling news content is technology which had: "altered the means and methods of international news sourcing, construction, dissemination and, above all, participation" (Clarke & Bromley, 2011).[340]

The ABC has been an industry leader in digitising the way in which it innovated, invented, gathered, stored and disseminated news, information and entertainment. It was the first broadcaster to re-write its editorial policies to incorporate user-generated content and the only broadcaster to offer multi-channel content after launching iView in 2008 (Cunningham & Turner, 2010).[341] In 1995, it had established a multimedia unit to develop online publishing policy and it launched its website late that year (ABC, 2008).[342] It had already invented its own form of radio digital audio—D-Cart—which it sold to other broadcasters overseas (Ibid.). These innovations gave the new ABC Online the opportunity in 1996 to demonstrate its new technological capacities in the coverage of the federal election (Ibid.). In 1997, the ABC trialled audio streaming and began to present news and feature articles online. The 2000s saw the ABC re-fit studios with the digital system—Netia (ABC, 2008).[343] In 1998, the Federal Government gave the ABC an extra AUD20 million for the transition to the first phase of digital transmission (Inglis, 2006).[344]

There were three examples given by Australian academic Stuart Cunningham (2013)[345] of the challenges facing the ABC with its digitisation. For the purposes of this book, they could also be used as examples of the ABC's *field* shift into commercial media and the unforeseen re-adjustments it needed to make. Such was the success of ABC Online that Cunningham (2013) said ABC Board Member Michael Kroger (Cunningham Ibid.) proposed selling it to raise money for two reasons—the potential compromises to the ABC Charter and that the publicly developed technology could be sold to other media as part of its public service (Cunningham, 2013).[346] It is argued that public service providers innovate for the public good and they provide this for the system—the greater good. Cunningham (2013) also quoted another example of the ABC's *field* departure when it launched ABC Open—targeting localised news. This was criticised by regional commercial media as encroaching into their territory. ABC Open closed on 30 June 2019 because it was "built on technology which is no longer supported" (ABC Open, 2020).[347] A substitute ABC My Photo #abcmyphoto (https://www.abc.net.au/news/abcmyphoto/abc-open/) was launched as a replacement that "uses industry standard technology which we hope will enable us to add further features in the future" (ABC Open, 2020). The third example of *field* departure was when the regional newspaper organisation APN told the subscription television outfit ASTRA that commercial regional news outlets should be allowed to distribute ABC content, and, further:

> It should not be the role of the national broadcaster to produce content that is already provided by, and directly competes with, the private sector. (ASTRA submission in response to Interim Report, p. 15) (Cunningham, 2013)

The slow process of managing the ABC's policy changes in switching to digitisation and digital media and the ongoing necessary changes took place under the Managing Directorships of David Hill, then Brian Johns, who was credited with anticipating the digital age (Clark, 2016),[348] Jonathan Shier, Russell Barton, Mark Scott, Michelle Guthrie and David Anderson. As far back as Brian Johns it was noted that he encouraged the board to persist in its lobbying for extra money for the ABC to take a strong part in the new digital ecology (Inglis, 2006).[349] Mark Scott said that the development of ABC multi-channelling of free-to-air and subscription commercial television was "needed to play in the space" (Scott, 2019)[350] if it were "to remain the national news leader" (Ibid.). This was a call to arms that the commercial *field* was entirely winnable if the ABC imbibed the 'doxa' (rules of the game) of its new *field*. However, the encouragement of this "play" or experimentation has also brought the ABC into controversy as not just mimicking commercial content, but a concomitant downgrading, forgetfulness, of its own *cultural capital* and *reputational capital* and, thirdly, compromising its Charter. In Bourdieu's *field* theory, it shifted its *field* but with a naïve understanding, at best, of how life in the commercial *field* would be consequently for the ABC, believing that its quality brand reputation was permanent and immutable.

This *field* shift was exemplified in the 2010 creation of the ABC Television's News 24, a 24-hour television news service to tackle the commercials head-on. Scott observed that the most strident opposition to News 24 came from News Corporation because of its existing subscription news channel Sky News. This is not surprising given the ABC had left its own *field* to compete with the commercial operators on their turf. There was also the issue of anti-siphoning laws which have prevented commercial operators from televising exclusively sports events, although this is being eroded. As Scott said, "sport was important to all Australians" (Ibid.) and free-to-air broadcasting on the ABC seemed the fairest way of sharing sport. Now, however, sport is not a simple, shared, entertaining event, it is a matter of huge sponsorship, gambling, government funding and considerable advertising, product placement and promotional business. Sports content is highly attractive to commercial media operators once they pull it into the commercial *field* where paying audiences are sought and found.

In 2008, Stephen Conroy, Federal Labor Minister for Broadband, Communications and the Digital Economy, launched a discussion paper titled: "ABC and SBS: Towards a digital Future"[351] carrying a warning "with the expected proliferation of internet-based services, traditional broadcasting may not continue to hold the same degree of influence it had in an analogue world" (2008). It also considered that outsourcing of ABC production offered "flexibility", "efficiencies" and supported the "independent production industry" and offered the potential for "production efficiencies" (Ibid.). It suggested that the ABC may consider charging online viewers of content (pay per view). The report drew a similarity where the then ABC Shops already sold ABC content (CDs and DVDs), and that: "the sheer pace of technology change makes it difficult to gauge what the media and broadcasting industry might look like in just over a decade's time" (Ibid.). It concluded: "By 2020, the national broadcasters will probably look quite different. They—and Government—face important choices as they determine their future directions and pursue their mandates across multiple platforms" (Ibid.). In the era of economic efficiencies, cutbacks caused by the economic shock of the coronavirus pandemic, ongoing quests for smaller government (which means less expenditure on public enterprises and activities), deregulation and endless convergence, the ABC is being ladled with challenges that are causing a strangulation to Aunty's voice.

In 2018, as a further reinforcement of the ABC's commercial *field* shift, Chairman Justin Milne was reported calling for "the ABC to ramp up its expansion into the digital realm, against the wishes of its commercial rivals and some critics 'on the political fringe'" (Koziol, 2018).[352] Milne noted that News Corporation and Fairfax Media had challenged that the ABC should receive public money to digitise its news service—when those two organisations had already fulfilled that activity (Ibid.). The ABC had told the Inquiry into the Competitive Neutrality of the National Broadcasters its online news platform "enhances competition and innovation" (Ibid.). Yet, Fairfax Media accused the ABC at the inquiry that it "undermined commercial news media and produced "clickbait" that was "neither high quality nor distinctive"" (Ibid.). The final report of the competitive neutrality inquiry (2018)[353] said:

> Fairfax considers that the ABC has an important role to play in this environment, by giving the commercial sector the space it needs to thrive.

Further, Fairfax said it said that the ABC should confine itself to areas where it was not profitable for commercial media—"in line with the spirit of the Charter" and falling back to the "market failure" argument where the ABC should only operate in areas where it is too expensive for commercial operators. In part, this is suggesting that the ABC create a *field* within the digital field—or transplant its old field into its new territory. What these commercial operators were fundamentally explaining to the inquiry can be transposed into Bourdieusian theory. Fairfax and News Corporation said that the ABC had entered their *field* and offered similar content. In response, the ABC told the inquiry that:

> The ABC maintains that [c]onsistent with its Charter, the ABC's digital news team actively considers what stories they can leave to the commercial networks and what issues the ABC can cover to deliver value to the overall media market.

In essence, the choice of words furnishes further evidence of the ABC's shift to the new *field*, how it has sought to retain its authority and influence by cherry-picking stories, yet it has had to surrender its quality by recontextualising content in an emergent digital commercial field. It was also trying to articulate its intellectual power amassed from its *cultural capital* in its old élite *field*, where it had a prominent and privileged role as a premier Australian news organisation. It asserted a point of difference, it was actually a media binary of "us" and "them". One, that worked for Aunty—once. But the binary has dissolved in the commercial *field*. Possibly, the preceding statement inferred that it dealt with the more high-brow content, but from an 'all to all' universal service operating in the commercial sphere with capricious audiences, where the rules of the game involved competing for "clicks" and eyeballs—that seems unrealistic and unachievable.

The final report of the competitive neutrality inquiry was all about how the ABC functioned in the commercial *field*: "so long as they operate within their statutory Charters they are operating in the public interest" (Australian Government, 2018).[354] However, it found that for the ABC "accountability is difficult, especially as there is no opportunity for Charter complaints to be addressed" and that while the ABC was: "not causing significant competitive distortions beyond the public interest ... some improvements in the way they interact with markets should be contemplated" (Ibid.), also that: "some improvements in competitive neutrality transparency and internal processes are possible and warranted" (Loc. Cit.). The report noted that the strongest competition to Australian media organisations for news, entertainment and advertising was from the media giants—the so-called FAANGs (Facebook, Apple, Amazon, Netflix and Google) (Ibid.)—and that the ABC did not have a competitive neutrality policy and "it is not clear how the ABC considers competitive neutrality in decision-making" (Ibid.). Even though it had shifted into the commercial *field*, this lack of clarity had become a significant issue for ABC managers and policy-makers. The report noted that: "News publishers Fairfax Media and News Corp Australia raise concerns that the free online news services of both the ABC and SBS are competing for the same audiences and therefore undermining the revenue base of commercial news media" (Ibid.) and that the speed of changes in the media market meant that there was growing occurrence of the national broadcasters (the ABC) "'rubbing up' against" (Ibid.) Australia's commercial media. On that count, Aunty seems to find herself in a real complication.

Notes

1. *M2 Presswire.* (2016). Optus partners with ABC Commercial to revolutionise retail employee wellbeing. (2016). Retrieved from: http://search.proquest.com/docview/1815277669/
2. *Sydney Morning Herald, The.* (1932). Broadcasting. Control By Commission. Inaugural Speeches. New Policy Outlined. 2 July 1932. p. 14. Retrieved from https://trove.nla.gov.au/newspaper/article/16906832?searchTerm=address%20Charles%20Lloyd%20Jones%20Earle%20Page&searchLimits=dateFrom=1932-06-29|||dateTo=1932-07-20|||l-state=New+South+Wales#
3. Meade, A. (2018). Michelle Guthrie 'considering legal options' after being sacked by ABC board. *The Guardian.* 24 September 2018. Retrieved from: https://www.theguardian.com/media/2018/sep/24/michelle-guthrie-considering-legal-options-after-being-sacked-by-abc-board
4. Wilson, C., Hutchinson, J., & Shea, P. (2010). Public Service Broadcasting, Creative Industries, and Innovation Infrastructure: The Case of ABC's Pool. *Australian Journal of Communication.* 37:3. Pp. 15–32. http://search.proquest.com/docview/884025623/
5. Sanchez Perry, H. (2017). Intersectionality as an institution: Changing the definition of feminism. *DePaul Journal of Women, Gender and the Law.* 7:1. Pp. 140–174. https://via.library.depaul.edu/jwgl/vol7/iss1/4
6. Lewis, S. (2009). Rudd vows bipartisan ABC board. 17 March 2009. *News.com.au.* Retrieved from https://www.news.com.au/national/rudd-vows-bipartisan-abc-board/news-story/ceac18bd56ef5ff51aed0b9b58140d1b?sv=8d736175966893030944 3ad4dee66a24
7. Shand, W. (2015). *Exploring institutional change: The contribution of co-production to shaping institutions.* International Institute for Environment and Development. Chapter 2. Pp. 6–8. Retrieved from: www.jstor.org/stable/resrep18045.4
8. North, D. (1990). *Institutions, Institutional Change and Economic Perfor*mance (Political Economy of Institutions and Decisions). Cambridge: Cambridge University Press. doi:https://doi.org/10.1017/CBO9780511808678 p. 3
9. North, D. (1990). *Institutions, Institutional Change and Economic Performance (Political Economy of Institutions and Decisions).* Cambridge: Cambridge University Press. doi:https://doi.org/10.1017/CBO9780511808678 Ibid.
10. Wooten, M. & Hoffman, A.J. (2008). Organizational Fields: Past, Present and Future. Ed. R. Greenwood, C. Oliver, R. Suddaby, K. Sahlin-Andersson. *The SAGE Handbook of Organizational Institutionalism.* SAGE Publications. London. Ch. 4. p. 130.

11. Lindenberg, S. (1998). 'The Cognitive Turn in Institutional Analysis: Beyond NIE, and NIS?' *Journal of Institutional and Theoretical Economics.* 154:4. Zeitschrift Für Die Gesamte Staatswissenschaft. Pp. 716–727.
12. Bourdieu, P. & Wacquant, L.J.D. (1992). An Invitation to Reflexive Sociology. University of Chicago Press. Chicago.
13. Wooten, M. & Hoffman, A.J. (2008). Organizational Fields: Past, Present and Future. Ed. R. Greenwood, C. Oliver, R. Suddaby, K. Sahlin-Andersson. *The SAGE Handbook of Organizational Institutionalism.* SAGE Publications. London. Ch. 4. p. 134.
14. Scott, W. R. (1994). 'Conceptualizing Organizational Fields: Linking Organizations and Societal Systems.' *Systems Rationality and Partial Interests.* Eds. H-U. Derlien, U. Gerhardt & F.W. Scharpf. Nomos Verlagsgesselschaft. Baden-Baden, Germany. Pp. 203–221.
15. Wooten, M. & Hoffman, A.J. (2008). Organizational Fields: Past, Present and Future. Ed. R. Greenwood, C. Oliver, R. Suddaby, K. Sahlin-Andersson. *The SAGE Handbook of Organizational Institutionalism.* SAGE Publications. London. Ch. 4. p. 132.
16. Wooten, M. & Hoffman, A.J. (2008). Organizational Fields: Past, Present and Future. Ed. R. Greenwood, C. Oliver, R. Suddaby, K. Sahlin-Andersson. *The SAGE Handbook of Organizational Institutionalism.* SAGE Publications. London. Ch. 4. p. 138.
17. Dinh, J., Lord, R., Gardner, W., Meuser, J., Liden, R. & Hu, J. (2014). Leadership theory and research in the new millennium: Current theoretical trends and changing perspectives. *Leadership Quarterly.* 25:1. Pp. 36–62. https://doi.org/10.1016/j.leaqua.2013.11.005
18. Brewster, Z.W., Brauer, J.R. & Lynn, M. (2018). Morality at Work: Do Employees' Moral Commitments Inhibit Service Disparities and Reactive Workplace Behaviors? *Social Currents.* 5:3. Pp. 244–263. Retrieved from: https://doi.org/10.1177/2329496517725330
19. Kacała, T. (2015). Military Leadership in the Context of Challenges and Threats Existing in Information Environment. *Journal of Corporate Responsibility and Leadership.* 2:1. Pp. 9–21. https://doi.org/10.12775/JCRL.2015.001
20. Dinh, J., Lord, R., Gardner, W., Meuser, J., Liden, R. & Hu, J. (2014). Leadership theory and research in the new millennium: Current theoretical trends and changing perspectives. *Leadership Quarterly.* 25:1. Pp. 36–62. https://doi.org/10.1016/j.leaqua.2013.11.005
21. Magsaysay, J. F., & Hechanova, M. R. M. (2017). Building an implicit change leadership theory. *Leadership & Organization Development Journal.* 38:6. Pp. 834–848. doi: http://dx.doi.org.wwwproxy1.library.unsw.edu.au/10.1108/LODJ-05-2016-0114

22. Northouse, P. G. (2004). *Leadership: Theory and Practice* (3rd Ed.). Sage. Thousand Oaks, Calif.
23. Bottery, M., & Herrington, N. (2016). Not so simple: The threats to leadership sustainability. *Management in Education.* 30:3. Pp. 97–101. https://doi.org/10.1177/0892020616653059
24. Bennis, W. (2007). The challenges of leadership in the modern world: introduction to the special issue. (Author abstract). *The American Psychologist.* 62.1. pp. 2–5. https://doi.org/10.1037/0003-066X.62.1.2
25. Epitropaki, O. & Martin, R. (2004). Implicit Leadership Theories in Applied Settings: Factor Structure, Generalizability, and Stability Over Time. *Journal of Applied Psychology.* 89:2. Pp. 293–310. Retrieved from: http://ovidsp.ovid.com/ovidweb.cgi?T=JS&PAGE=reference&D=ovftg&NEWS=N&AN=00004565-200404000-00008
26. Clarke, N. (2011). An integrated conceptual model of respect in leadership. *The Leadership Quarterly.* 22:2. Pp. 316–327. Retrieved from: https://www-sciencedirect-com.wwwproxy1.library.unsw.edu.au/science/article/pii/S1048984311000208
27. Pircher Verdorfer, A. (2019). The paradox of serving: Can genuine servant leadership gain followers' respect for the leader? Evidence from Germany and Lithuania. *German Journal of Human Resource Management.* 33:2. Pp. 113–136. Retrieved from: https://doi.org/10.1177/2397002218793840
28. Wallace, D.M., Raver Luning, C., Rosenstein, J.E., Ledford, A. & Cyr-Roman, B. (2020). A culture of respect: Leader development and preventing destructive behavior. *Industrial and Organizational Psychology.* 13:2. Pp. 225–229. Retrieved from: https://doi.org/10.1017/iop.2020.46
29. Lewis, R., Rowe, M. & Wiper, C. (2017). 'Online Abuse of Feminists as An Emerging Form of Violence Against Women and Girls'. 57:6. *British Journal of Criminology.* Pp. 1462–1481. Retrieved from https://academic-oup-com.wwwproxy1.library.unsw.edu.au/bjc/article/57/6/1462/2623986
30. Lewis, R, Rowe, M. & Wiper, C. (2017). 'Online Abuse of Feminists as An Emerging Form of Violence Against Women and Girls'. 57:6. *British Journal of Criminology.* Pp. 1462–1481. Retrieved from https://academic-oup-com.wwwproxy1.library.unsw.edu.au/bjc/article/57/6/1462/2623986
31. Williams, M. (2006). *Virtually Criminal: Crime, Deviance and Regulation Online.* Routledge. New York.
32. Williams, M. (2006). *Virtually Criminal: Crime, Deviance and Regulation Online.* Routledge. New York. p. 98.

33. Williams, M. (2006). *Virtually Criminal: Crime, Deviance and Regulation Online*. Routledge. New York. Ibid.
34. Williams, M. (2006). *Virtually Criminal: Crime, Deviance and Regulation Online*. Routledge. New York. p. 99.
35. Williams, M. (2006). *Virtually Criminal: Crime, Deviance and Regulation Online*. Routledge. New York. p. 102.
36. Williams, M. (2006). *Virtually Criminal: Crime, Deviance and Regulation Online*. Routledge. New York. p. 103.
37. Clarke, N. (2011). An integrated conceptual model of respect in leadership. *The Leadership Quarterly*. 22:2. Pp. 316–327. Retrieved from: https://www-sciencedirect-com.wwwproxy1.library.unsw.edu.au/science/article/pii/S1048984311000208
38. Lawrence-Lightfoot, S. (1999). *Respect: An Exploration*. Perseus Books. Reading, MA. p. 13.
39. Lawrence-Lightfoot, S. (1999). *Respect: An Exploration*. Perseus Books. Reading, MA. pp. 9–10.
40. Warren, A.M., Sulaiman, A. & Ismawati Jaafar, N. (2014). Social media effects on fostering online civic engagement and building citizen trust and trust in institutions. *Government Information Quarterly*. 31. Pp. 291–301. Retrieved from www.elsevier.com/locate/govinf
41. Warren, A.M., Sulaiman, A. & Ismawati Jaafar, N. (2014). Social media effects on fostering online civic engagement and building citizen trust and trust in institutions. *Government Information Quarterly*. 31. Pp. 291–301. Retrieved from www.elsevier.com/locate/govinf p. 299.
42. Liu, H. (2020). *Redeeming Leadership. Chapter: Undoing Leadership*. Bristol University Press. Bristol. Retrieved from: https://www.jstor.org/stable/j.ctvtv93zk
43. Biggart, N. W., & Hamilton, G. G. (1987). An Institutional Theory of Leadership. *The Journal of Applied Behavioral Science*. 23:4. Pp. 429–441. https://doi.org/https://doi.org/10.1177/002188638702300401
44. Gray-Hoehn, H. (2020). in Eds. K. Bezio & G. Goethals, G. (2020). *Leadership, Populism, and Resistance*. Edward Elgar Publishing. Northampton. p. 109.
45. Sanders, P. (2020) in Eds. K. Bezio & G. Goethals, G. (2020). *Leadership, Populism, and Resistance*. Edward Elgar Publishing. Northampton. p. 24.
46. Chemers, M. (2014). In H. Gray-Hoehn. (2020). Chapter 6: "Talking the talk: communication as the essential element of leadership". Eds. K.M.S. Bezio & G.R. Goethals. *Leadership, Populism, and Resistance*. Jepson Studies in Leadership series. Monograph Book. Elgar Online. ISBN: 978 1 78897 925 2
47. Fairhurst, G. (2008). Discursive Leadership: A Communication Alternative to Leadership Psychology. *Management Communication*

Quarterly. 21:4. Pp. 510–521. https://doi.org/10.1177/0893318907313714

48. Scott, W. R. (2001). Institutions and Organizations, 2nd ed. Thousand Oaks, CA: Sage. p. 51. In S. Yousafzai, S. Saeed & M. Muffatto. (2015). Institutional Theory and Contextual Embeddedness of Women's Entrepreneurial Leadership: Evidence from 92 Countries. *Journal of Small Business Management.* 53:3. Pp. 587–604. https://doi.org/10.1111/jsbm.12179
49. Wander, F. Ed. (2013). The Servant Leader. Chapter 10. Pp. 123–136. *Transforming IT Culture.* Wiley. Hoboken, New Jersey.
50. Spadaro SJ, A. (2020) Defy the Apocalypse. *La Civiltà Cattolica.* 20 January 2020. Retrieved from: https://www.laciviltacattolica.com/defy-the-apocalypse/
51. Wright, F. (1940). Leadership. *The Phi Delta Kappan.* 23:1. Pp. 3–5. Retrieved from www.jstor.org/stable/20330821
52. Leaderonomics.com (2018). The pitfalls of servant leadership. 29 March 2018. Retrieved from https://leaderonomics.com/leadership/the-pitfalls-of-servant-leadership
53. McCrimmon, M. (2010). Why servant leadership is a bad idea. *Management Issues.* 16 August 2010. Retrieved from https://www.management-issues.com/opinion/6015/why-servant-leadership-is-a-bad-idea/
54. Greenleaf, R. (1977). *Servant Leadership: A journey into the nature of legitimate power and greatness.* Paulist Press. New York.
55. van Dierendonck, D. & Patterson, K. (Eds). (2010). *Servant Leadership: Developments in Theory and Research.* Palgrave Macmillan. UK. p. 31. Quoting p. 101.
56. *The Bible.* Gospel of Mark. 9:35.
57. Northouse, P.G. (2013). *Leadership: Theory and Practice.* (6th Edition). Sage Publications. London, Los Angeles.
58. Spears, L.C. (2002). Tracing the past, present and future of servant leadership. In L.C. Spears & M. Lawrence (Eds.). *Focus on leadership: Servant leadership for the 21st century.* John Wiley & Sons. New York. (Quoting p. 222–223).
59. Whetstone, J.T. (2002). Personalism and moral leadership: the servant leader with a transforming vision. *Business Ethics: A European Review.* October. 11:4. Pp. 385–392. https://doi.org/10.1111/1467-8608.00298
60. Ibid. p. 386.
61. Ibid., p. 389.
62. van Dierendonck, D. & Patterson, K. (Eds). (2010). *Servant Leadership: Developments in Theory and Research.* Palgrave Macmillan. UK.

63. Bass, B. M., & Riggio, R. E. (2005). *Transformational Leadership*. Lawrence Erlbaum Associates. New Jersey. p. xi.
64. Ibid., p. 387.
65. Wright, B.E., Moynihan, D.P, & Pandey, S. J. (2012). Pulling the Levers: Transformational Leadership, Public Service Motivation, and Mission Valence. *Public Administration Review.* 72:2. Pp. 206–215. The American Society for Public Administration. https://doi.org/10.1111/j.1540-6210.2011.02496.x
66. Ibid., p. 207.
67. Ibid.
68. Ibid.
69. Ibid. p. 212.
70. Pureza, A. P., & Lee, K. (2020). Corporate social responsibility leadership for sustainable development: An institutional logics perspective in Brazil. *Corporate Social Responsibility and Environmental Management.* 27:3. Pp. 1410–1424. https://doi.org/10.1002/csr.1894
71. Aagaard, P. (2016). How to Make the Mix Matter: A Case Study of Post-Transformational Leadership in Hybrid Public Management. *International Journal of Public Administration.* 39:14. Pp. 1171–1179. https://doi.org/10.1080/01900692.2015.1072211
72. Aagaard, P. (2016). How to Make the Mix Matter: A Case Study of Post-Transformational Leadership in Hybrid Public Management. *International Journal of Public Administration.* 39:14. Pp. 1171–1179. https://doi.org/10.1080/01900692.2015.1072211
73. Powe, J. (2010). Public service leadership in times of significant change and uncertainty. The International Journal of Leadership in Public Services. 6:4. November 2010. Quoting Pegg, M. (2008). Developing new leaders for the responsive state. 360 Degrees. *The Ashridge Journal.* Autumn. pp. 13–18. Retrieved from https://www-emerald-com.www-proxy1.library.unsw.edu.au/insight/content/doi/10.5042/ijlps.2010.0631/full/pdf?title=when-the-going-gets-tough-public-service-leadership-in-times-of-significant-change-and-uncertainty
74. Ireland, R. (2005). ABC of Collaborative Planning Forecasting and Replenishment. *The Journal of Business Forecasting.* 24:2. Pp. 3–4+. http://search.proquest.com/docview/226915396/
75. Brook, S. (2017). Waste not, want not the message for ABC silos. *The Australian.* 20 November 2017. Retrieved from: https://login.www-proxy1.library.unsw.edu.au/login?qurl=https%3A%2F%2Fsearch.proquest.com%2Fdocview%2F1990857104%3Facco
76. Australian Broadcasting Corporation. (2016). Tributes paid to former ABC Managing Director Brian Johns, who has died aged 79. *ABC.* 1 January 2016. Retrieved from: https://www.abc.net.au/

news/2016-01-01/former-abc-managing-director-brian-johns-dies-aged-79/7062934

77. Brereton, A. (2016). Former ABC Managing Director Brian Johns dies aged 79. *The Guardian.* 1 January 2016. Retrieved from: https://www.theguardian.com/media/2016/jan/01/brian-johns-a-great-australian-who-positioned-the-abc-for-the-digital-age#:~:text=Former%20ABC%20managing%20director%20Brian%20Johns%20has%20died%20of%20cancer,of%20digital%20news%20and%20entertainment.
78. Inglis, K. (2006). *Whose ABC? The Australian Broadcasting Corporation 1983–2006.* Black Inc. Melbourne. p. 391.
79. Cooke, M. (2007). Our Digital Aunty: The ABC's New Media Future. *Metro.* 153. Pp. 142–146.
80. Brook, S. (2017). Waste not, want not the message for ABC silos. *The Australian.* 20 November 2017. Retrieved from https://www.theaustralian.com.au/business/media/abc-reform-waste-not-want-not-is-the-message-for-silos/news-story/bb492ec2c27512645daea3cf8737f9ec
81. Martin, F. (2002). Beyond Public Service Broadcasting? ABC Online and the User/Citizen [online]. *Southern Review: Communication, Politics & Culture.* 35: 1. Pp. 42–62. Availability: <https://search-informit-com-au.wwwproxy1.library.unsw.edu.au/documentSummary;dn=743199784542203;res=IELAPA> ISSN: 0038-4526.
82. Bowden, T. & Borchers, W. (2006). *50 Years Aunty's Jubilee! Celebrating 50 years of ABC-TV.* ABC Books. Sydney. p. 316.
83. Ibid.
84. Chapman, C., Getha-Taylor, H., Holmes, M.H., Jacobson, W.S., Morse, R.S & Sowa, J.E. (2016). How Public Service Leadership Is Studied: An Examination of a Quarter Century of Scholarship. *Public Administration.* March 2016. 94:1. Pp. 111–128. Retrieved from https://onlinelibrary-wiley-com.wwwproxy1.library.unsw.edu.au/doi/pdfdirect/10.1111/padm.12199
85. Ibid.
86. Diefenbach, T. (2009). New Public Management In Public Sector Organizations: The Dark Sides Of Managerialistic 'Enlightenment'. *Public Administration (London).* 87:4. Pp. 892–909. Retrieved from: https://doi.org/10.1111/j.1467-9299.2009.01766.x
87. Ibid. quoting Kettl 2006.
88. Ibid., p. 114.
89. Tomlinson, M., O'Reilly, D., Wallace, M., Edwards, G., Elliott, C., Iszatt-White, M., Schedlitzki, D. (2013). Developing Leaders as Symbolic Violence: Reproducing Public Service Leadership through the (misrecognized) Development of Leaders' Capitals. 44:1. *Management Learning.* Pp. 81–97. https://doi.org/10.1177/1350507612472151

90. Dickinson, H., Needham, C., Mangan, C. & Sullivan, H. Eds. (2019). *Reimagining the Future Public Service Workforce.* Springer Books. Singapore. p. 9.
91. McChesney, R. (1997). *The Mythology of Commercial Broadcasting and the Contemporary Crisis of Public Broadcasting.* University of Wisconsin-Madison. Madison.
92. Edwards, M., Halligan, J, Horrigan, B. & Nicoll, G. (2012). *Public Sector Governance in Australia.* Australian National University EPress. Griffin Press. Canberra. Retrieved from: https://press-files.anu.edu.au/downloads/press/p190701/pdf/book.pdf
93. Edwards, M., Halligan, J, Horrigan, B. & Nicoll, G. (2012). *Public Sector Governance in Australia.* Australian National University EPress. Griffin Press. Canberra. Retrieved from: https://press-files.anu.edu.au/downloads/press/p190701/pdf/book.pdf p. 233
94. Tomlinson, M., O'Reilly, D., Wallace, M., Edwards, G., Elliott, C., Iszatt-White, M., Schedlitzki, D. (2013). Developing Leaders as Symbolic Violence: Reproducing Public Service Leadership through the (misrecognized) Development of Leaders' Capitals. 44:1. *Management Learning.* Pp. 81–97. Quoting McNulty, 2004. https://doi.org/10.1177/1350507612472151
95. Dandira, M. (2012). Dysfunctional leadership: organizational cancer. *Business Strategy Series.* 13:4. Pp. 187–192. https://doi.org/10.1108/17515631211246267
96. *Sydney Morning Herald, The.* (1932). Broadcasting. Control By Commission. Inaugural Speeches. New Policy Outlined. 2 July 1932. p.14. Retrieved from: https://trove.nla.gov.au/newspaper/article/16906832?searchTerm=address%20Charles%20Lloyd%20Jones%20Earle%20Page&searchLimits=dateFrom=1932-06-29|||dateTo=1932-07-20|||l-state=New+South+Wales#
97. Letter by ABC Chairman William Cleary, to ABC Vice-Chairman Herbert Brookes, 15 July 1938. In C. Semmler. (2001). *The ABC—Aunt Sally and Sacred Cow.* Melbourne University Press. Melbourne. p. 27.
98. Walker, R.R. (1973). *The Magic Spark: 50 Years of Radio in Australia.* Hawthorn Press. Melbourne. p. 38.
99. Blain, E. (1977). *Life with Aunty: 40 years with the ABC.* Methuen. Australia. p. 158.
100. Ibid., p. 160.
101. Banerjee, I. & Seneviratne, K. (2006). *Public Service Broadcasting in the Age of Globalization.* Asian Media Information and Communication Centre. Nanyang Technological University. Singapore. p. 2.
102. McChesney, R.W. & Herman, E.D. (1997). *The Global Media: the news missionaries of global capitalism.* Cassell. Washington and London. p. 166.

103. Thornton, P.H., Ocasio, W. & Lounsbury, M. (2012). "The Emergence and Evolution of Field-Level Logics" in *The Institutional Logics Perspective*. eBook. Retrieved from: https://www.researchgate.net/publication/300275744_The_Emergence_and_Evolution_of_Field-Level_Logics
104. Glynn, M. (2002). Chord and discord: Organizational crisis, institutional shifts, and the musical canon of the symphony. *Poetics*. 30:1–2. Pp. 63–85. https://doi.org/10.1016/S0304-422X(02)00004-9
105. Glynn, M. (2002). Chord and discord: Organizational crisis, institutional shifts, and the musical canon of the symphony. *Poetics*. 30:1–2. Pp. 63–85. https://doi.org/10.1016/S0304-422X(02)00004-9 p. 70.
106. Charles Buttrose was the late father of the ABC's current Chair, Ita Buttrose.
107. Beppi's is an Italian restaurant in Sydney that still operates.
108. Karel Ančerl was a famous Czechoslovak conductor who also conducted the Czech Philharmonic Orchestra.
109. Buttrose, C. (1984). *Words and Music: Press barons, prima donnas, coping with the ABC*. Angus and Robertson. Australia. p. 67.
110. Buttrose, C. (1984). *Words and Music: Press barons, prima donnas, coping with the ABC*. Angus and Robertson Publishers. Australia. p. 89.
111. Ibid.
112. Buttrose, C. (1984). *Words and Music: Press barons, prima donnas, coping with the ABC*. Angus and Robertson. Australia. p. 90.
113. Hodgkinson, C. (1975). Philosophy, Politics, and Planning. An Extended Rationale for Synthesis. *Educational Administration Quarterly*. 11:1. Pp. 11–20. https://doi.org/https://doi.org/10.1177/0013161X7501100102 p. 16.
114. Hodgkinson, C. (1975). Philosophy, Politics, and Planning. An Extended Rationale for Synthesis. *Educational Administration Quarterly*. 11:1. Pp. 11–20. https://doi.org/https://doi.org/10.1177/0013161X7501100102 p. 17.
115. McLuhan, M. (1964). *Understanding Media*. Abacus. London. p. 256.
116. Bourdieu, P. (1986). The forms of capital. J. Richardson (Ed.) *Handbook of Theory and Research for the Sociology of Education*. Greenwood. New York. Pp. 241–258.
117. Voxted, S. (2017). 100 years of Henri Fayol. *Management Revue*. 28:2. Pp. 256–274. Retrieved from https://doi.org/10.5771/0935-9915-2017-2-256
118. Voxted, S. (2017). 100 years of Henri Fayol. *Management Revue*. 28:2. Pp. 256–274. Retrieved from https://doi.org/10.5771/0935-9915-2017-2-256

119. Oxford English Dictionary. (2021). Retrieved from: https://www-oed-com.wwwproxy1.library.unsw.edu.au/view/Entry/141512?redirectedFrom=personnel&
120. Brown, A. & Althaus, C. (2009). Public Service Broadcasting in Australia. *The Journal of Media Economics*. 9:1. Pp. 31–46. https://doi.org/info:doi/
121. Humphries, B. (1991). *Selected Poems and Other Creatures*. Angus and Robertson, Pymble, Sydney. p. 70.
122. Canberra Times, The. (1978). ABC Staff Plans Strike Campaign. *The Canberra Times*. 26 October 1978. p. 3. Retrieved from: https://trove.nla.gov.au/newspaper/article/110919174?searchTerm=John%20Norgard%20ABC
123. Canberra Times, The. (1978). ABC Staff Appointee Unnecessary: Chaney. *The Canberra Times*. 26 October 1978. p. 12. Retrieved from: https://trove.nla.gov.au/newspaper/article/110919069?browse=ndp%3Abrowse%2Ftitle%2FC%2Ftitle%2F11%2F1978%2F10%2F26%2Fpage%2F12383855%2Farticle%2F110919069
124. Stacey, R. & Griffin, D. (2006). *Complexity and the Experience of Managing in Public Sector Organizations*. Routledge. London & New York. p. 26.
125. Stacey, R. & Griffin, D. (2006). *Complexity and the Experience of Managing in Public Sector Organizations*. Routledge. London & New York. p. 16.
126. Stacey, R. & Griffin, D. (2006). *Complexity and the Experience of Managing in Public Sector Organizations*. Routledge. London & New York. p. 18.
127. Australian Rationalist (2016). Destroying the ABC.100. Autumn 2016. Pp. 40–41. Retrieved from: <https://search-informit-com-au.www-proxy1.library.unsw.edu.au/fullText;dn=20190613012323;res=AGISPT> ISSN: 1036-8191.
128. Murray, J. (1994). The institutional origins of ABC censorship in the 1930s [online]. *Australian Journalism Review*. 16:2. July-Dec 1994. Pp. 125–131. Retrieved from: <https://search-informit-com-au.www-proxy1.library.unsw.edu.au/documentSummary;dn=960808235;res=IELAPA> ISSN: 0810-2686.
129. *Australian Rationalist*. (2016). Destroying the ABC. 100. Autumn 2016. Pp. 40–41. Availability: <https://search-informit-com-au.www-proxy1.library.unsw.edu.au/fullText;dn=20190613012323;res=AGISPT> ISSN: 1036-8191.
130. Rickard, J. (2003). Symposium: Choral Music in Melbourne—"Messiahs," "Elijahs" and All that Jazz: Melbourne Musical Taste

Between the Wars. *Context.* Pp. 35–39. Retrieved from: http://search.proquest.com/docview/1465088/

131. *Courier Mail, The.* (1934, 25 July). Educational broadcasts: Policy of the A.B.C. p. 20. Retrieved from: https://trove.nla.gov.au/newspaper/article/36733653?searchTerm=Educational%20broadcasts%3A%20Policy%20of%20the%20A.B.C.
132. *Canberra Times, The.* (1995). Born to Head the ABC. Talbot Duckmanton 1921–1995. *The Canberra Times.* 14 June 1995. p. 4. Retrieved from: https://trove.nla.gov.au/newspaper/article/127530651?searchTerm=ABC%20British%20accents
133. *Courier Mail, The.* (1938). Catering for diverse tastes: ABC policy explained at 4QR opening. 8 January 1938. p. 13. Retrieved from: https://trove.nla.gov.au/newspaper/article/39744258?searchTerm=Catering%20for%20diverse%20tastes%3A%20ABC%20policy%20explained%20at%204QR%20opening
134. Petersen, N. (1993). *News not views: The ABC, the Press, and Politics 1932–1947.* Hale and Iremonger. Sydney.
135. Petersen, N. (1993). *News not views: The ABC, the Press, and Politics 1932–1947.* Hale and Iremonger. Sydney. p. 35.
136. *Canberra Times, The.* (1936). A.B.C. ARTISTS. All will visit Canberra. 2 July 1936. p. 2. Retrieved from: https://trove.nla.gov.au/newspaper/article/2420561?searchTerm=A.B.C.%20ARTISTS.%20All%20will%20visit%20Canberra.%20
137. *Advertiser, The.* (1934). POLICY OF A.B.C. REVIEWED "Encouraging Creative Side of our People". 26 June 1934. Retrieved from: https://trove.nla.gov.au/newspaper/article/35116153?searchTerm=to%20encourage%20the%20creative%20side%20of%20our%20people%20in%20a%20musical%20sense
138. Nerone, J. & Barnhurst, K. (2003). US newspaper types, the newsroom, and the division of labor, 1750–2000. *Journalism Studies.* 4:4. Pp. 435–449. https://doi.org/10.1080/1461670032000136541
139. Shaw, S. (1959). Colonial newspaper advertising: A step toward freedom of the press. *Business History Review (pre-1986).* 33:000003. p. 409. http://search.proquest.com/docview/205528871/
140. Lee, A.J. (1976). *The Origins of the Popular Press in England. 1855–1914.* Croom Helm. London.
141. Williams, K. (2010). *Read All About It: A History of the British Newspaper.* Routledge. Oxford & Cambridge.
142. Stephens, M. (2007). *A History of News.* (3rd Ed.). Oxford University Press. New York & Oxford.
143. Nelson, K.E. (2003). The Melbourne Philharmonic Society under Contract to the Australian Broadcasting Commission: Preservation and

Triumph [online]. *Context: Journal of Music Research*. 25. Autumn 2003. Pp. 25–33. Retrieved from: http://search.proquest.com/docview/200101339/

144. Ibid. p. 32.
145. Ibid. p. 26
146. Loc. Cit.
147. Fraser, F. (2014). Orchestrating the Metropolis the Creation of the Sydney Symphony Orchestra as a Modern Cultural Institution. *History Australia*. 11:2. Pp. 196–221, Retrieved from: https://doi.org/10.1080/14490854.2014.11668522 p. 197.
148. Ibid., p. 198 quoting L.W. Levine (1988). *Highbrow/Lowbrow*. Harvard University Press. Cambridge, MA. p. 104.
149. Loc. cit. Quoting P. DiMaggio. (1991). 'Cultural Entrepreneurship in Nineteenth-Century Boston: The Creation of an Organizational Base for High Culture in America', in *Rethinking Popular Culture: Contemporary Perspectives in Cultural Studies*. Eds. C. Mukerji & Schudson, M. University of California Press. Berkeley. p. 374.
150. Australian Broadcasting Corporation (1998). The ABC boosts commitment to education and lifelong learning. (1998, October 21). *M2 Presswire*. Normans Media Ltd. Retrieved from: Gale General OneFile.
151. McDowell, D.H. (1975). *The development and educational role of schools of arts in England: and their influence on the development and educational role of schools of arts in Australia*. Masters thesis. Retrieved from http://handle.unsw.edu.au/1959.4/61038
152. Ibid. p. 126.
153. Loc. cit.
154. Warburton, J.W. (1963). Schools of Arts. *The Australian Quarterly*. 35:4. Dec. 1963. pp. 72–80. Retrieved from https://doi.org/10.2307/20633919
155. Inglis, K. S. (1983). This is the ABC—the Australian Broadcasting Commission: 1932–83. Melbourne University Press. Victoria.
156. Brown, A. & Althaus, C. (2009). Public Service Broadcasting in Australia. *The Journal of Media Economics*. 9:1. Pp. 31–46. https://doi.org/info:doi/
157. Habermas, J. (1989). *The Structural Transformation of the Public Sphere: An Inquiry into a Category of Bourgeois Society*. Transl. T. Burger & F. Lawrence. Polity Press. Cambridge. p. 27
158. Funston, A. (1997). The ABC and citizenship. (Australian Broadcasting Corporation). *Overland, 147*.
159. *Australian Broadcasting Corporation* (2019). Annual Report. Retrieved from https://about.abc.net.au/wp-content/uploads/2019/10/ABC-Annual-Report-201819v2.pdf p. 94.

160. Cut, M. (2017). Digital natives and digital immigrants—how are they different. *Digital Reflections.* Retrieved from https://medium.com/digital-reflections/digital-natives-and-digital-immigrants-how-are-they-different-e849b0a8a1d3
161. Dalton, K. (2017). Missing in Action: The ABC and Australia's screen culture. Platform Papers. *Quarterly Essays on the Performing Arts from Currency House.* 51. May 2017. Currency House. p. 23.
162. "Cone of Silence" was a phrase used in the 1960s US comedy television series, Get Smart, about an incompetent spy, Maxwell Smart, who when he wanted to deliver confidential information to his boss called for the "cone of silence" and two linked Perspex cones would be lowered onto them. It was an ironic gag because it was easy for those outside the cone to hear the conversation, but the two in the cone could not hear each other.
163. Funston, A. (1997). The ABC and citizenship. *Overland.* 147. Winter 1997. Pp. 59–62. ISSN: 0030-7416.
164. Hawkins, G. (1997). "The ABC and the Mystic Writing Pad." *Media international Australia.* 83. p. 11. ISSN: 1324-5325.
165. Scott, M. (2007). The Editorial Values of the ABC. *The Sydney Papers.* 19:1. Pp. 64–77.
166. Dalton, K. (2017). Missing in Action: The ABC and Australia's screen culture. Platform Papers. *Quarterly Essays on the Performing Arts from Currency House.* 51. May 2017. Currency House.
167. Ibid., p. 10–11.
168. Ibid., p. 12.
169. Ibid., p. 14.
170. Dalton, K. (2017). Missing in Action: The ABC and Australia's screen culture. Platform Papers. *Quarterly Essays on the Performing Arts from Currency House.* 51. May 2017. Currency House. p. 14.
171. Ibid., p. 15.
172. Lynch, J. (2014). ABC redirected funds, says Lib MP. *The Australian Financial Review.* 22 November 2014. p. 5.
173. Seccombe, M. (2020). Hundreds facing the sack with ABC cuts. *The Saturday Paper.* 9–15 May 2020. 300. Retrieved from: https://www.thesaturdaypaper.com.au/news/politics/2020/05/09/hundreds-facing-the-sack-with-abc-cuts/15889464009792
174. Ibid., p. 18.
175. Ibid., p. 23.
176. Ibid., p. 24.
177. Lewis, S. (2009). Rudd vows bipartisan ABC board. 17 March 2009. *News.com.au.* Retrieved from https://www.news.com.au/national/rudd-vows-bipartisan-abc-board/news-story/ceac18bd56ef5ff51aed0b9b58140d1b?sv=8d7361759668930309443ad4dee66a24

178. Knott, M. & Hunter, F. (2014). Partisan appointments to ABC, SBS selection panel crushed Rudd's dream. *The Sydney Morning Herald*. 4 July 2014. Retrieved from: https://www.smh.com.au/politics/federal/partisan-appointments-to-abc-sbs-selection-panel-crushes-rudds-dream-20140704-zsvkz.html
179. Meade, A. (2018). Justin Milne resigns and denies government interference in ABC. *The Guardian*. 27 September 2018. Retrieved from: https://www.theguardian.com/media/2018/sep/27/justin-milne-resigns-and-denies-government-interference-in-abc
180. Kramer, L. (1983). This Is the ABC: The Australian Broadcasting Commission, 1932–1983 by Ken S. Inglis. *Australian Book Review*. 56. Melbourne University Press. Melbourne. p. 121.
181. Hyland, A. (2015). Mark Scott's ABC exit interview: 'I had no idea of the scale of the challenge'. *The Australian Financial Review Magazine*. 27 November 2015. Retrieved from https://www.afr.com/life-and-luxury/abcs-mark-scott-on-success-and-his-legacy-20151019-gkcgi8
182. Whitehead, G. (1988). *Inside the ABC: Geoffrey Whitehead's Personal Account*. Penguin Books. Melbourne. Pp. 172–173.
183. Cadzow, J. (2018). Culture Clash. *The Good Weekend Magazine*. 6 October 2018. p. 24.
184. Starling, G. (2008). *Managing the Public Sector*. 8th Edition. Thomson Wadsworth. Boston MA. p. 17.
185. Golant, B.D., Sillince, J.A.A., Hervey, C. Maclean, M. (2015). 'Rhetoric of Stability and Change: The Organizational Identity Work of Institutional Leadership' 68:4. April 2015. *Human Relations*. Pp. 607–631.
186. Ibid. p. 608. (citing Whetten, 2006; Whetten and Mackey, 2002).
187. Selznick, P. (1957). *Leadership in administration*. University of California Press. Berkeley, Calif. p. 17.
188. Beazley, M. J. (2016). Institutional leadership amongst equals. *Judicial Officers Bulletin*. 28:7. August 2016. Pp. 65–69. Retrieved from <https://search-informit-com-au.wwwproxy1.library.unsw.edu.au/documentSummary;dn=268275964401160;res=IELAPA> ISSN: 1036-1294.
189. *Australian Broadcasting Corporation*. (2011). Editorial Policies. Retrieved from http://about.abc.net.au/wp-content/uploads/2012/06/EditorialPOL2011.pdf
190. Similar Web (2020). Top Websites Ranking. Retrieved from: https://www.similarweb.com/top-websites/australia
191. *Australian Broadcasting Corporation*. (1997). Annual Report. Retrieved from: https://about.abc.net.au/wp-content/uploads/2012/06/AnnualReport1996-1997_CompleteReport.pdf

192. *Australian Broadcasting Corporation.* (1997). Annual Report. Retrieved from: https://about.abc.net.au/wp-content/uploads/2012/06/AnnualReport1996-1997_CompleteReport.pdf
193. Of course, with the outsourcing of television production the shops were merely handling revenue for outside parties which became unsustainable in the longer term.
194. Hooks, B. (1995). Johns knows his ABC. *The Canberra Times.* 11 September 1995. p. 29. Retrieved from: https://trove.nla.gov.au/newspaper/article/127280233?searchTerm=ABC%20staff%20culture&searchLimits=
195. Goggin, G. Ed. (2004). *Virtual Nation: The Internet in Australia.* UNSW Press, Kensington, Sydney. p. 198.
196. Goggin, G. Ed. (2004). *Virtual Nation: The Internet in Australia.* UNSW Press, Kensington, Sydney. p. 199.
197. *Australian Broadcasting Corporation* (2019). Annual Report. Retrieved from https://about.abc.net.au/wp-content/uploads/2019/10/ABC-Annual-Report-201819v2.pdf
198. Molomby, T. (1991). *Is there a moderate on the roof? ABC Years.* William Heinemann. Australia.
199. Molomby, T. (1991). *Is there a moderate on the roof? ABC Years.* William Heinemann. Australia. p. 193.
200. *Sydney Morning Herald, The.* (1985). How the ABC's phantom army grew like Topsy. The Sydney Morning Herald. 12 June 1985, p. 1.
201. *Sydney Morning Herald, The.* (1985). Australia. The Sydney Morning Herald. 11 June 1985, p. 23.
202. *Sydney Morning Herald, The.* (1985). ABC's silence may bring even sharper cost cuts. The Sydney Morning Herald. 22 June 1985, p. 10.
203. Molomby, T. (1991). *Is there a moderate on the roof? ABC Years.* William Heinemann. Australia. p. 213–214.
204. Molomby, T. (1991). *Is there a moderate on the roof? ABC Years.* William Heinemann. Australia. p. 215.
205. Knight, A. (2007). Stacking the ABC: Alan Knight investigates the Howard strategy. (Arts and Culture). *Arena Magazine.* 91. Pp. 42–43. https://primoa.library.unsw.edu.au/permalink/f/11jha62/TN_informit_apaft200712551
206. O'Mallon, F. (2020). ABC lost more than $350 m per year: report. *The West Australian.* 4 May 2020. Retrieved from: https://thewest.com.au/politics/abc-lost-more-than-350m-per-year-report-ng-s-2008375
207. The report said its research method was conducted by uComms on the evening of 23 March 2020. "The survey gathered views from a nationally representative sample of 1,286 residents across Australia". Dawson, E. (2020). It's Our ABC: A research report for GetUp! by Per Capita. Per

Capita, GetUp!. May 2020. Retrieved from: http://cdn.getup.org.au/2745-ABC_Report.pdf p. 24.
208. Roy Morgan (2019). ABC still most trusted—Facebook improves. 22 July 2019. Finding 8064. Retrieved from: http://www.roymorgan.com/findings/8064-abc-remains-most-trusted-media-201907220424
209. Grattan, M. (2018). **ABC contributes as much to the economy as it costs the taxpayer: Michelle Guthrie. 19 June 2018. *The Conversation.* Retrieved from:** https://theconversation.com/abc-contributes-as-much-to-the-economy-as-it-costs-the-taxpayer-michelle-guthrie-98553
210. *Courier-Mail, The.* (1941). "Newspaper Radio Most Listeners". The Courier Mail. 21 October 1941. p. 5. Retrieved from: https://trove.nla.gov.au/newspaper/article/41950322?searchTerm=%22The%20present%20services%20are%20a%20bit%20academic%20and%20lofty%20in%20their%20tone%22&searchLimits=
211. *Advertiser, The.* (1937). Vigorous Defence of ABC Policy "We Remain Serene Under Sneers" Not Gods, says Mr Cleary Broadcast at Opening of New Station. The Advertiser, Adelaide. 16 October 1937. p. 26. Retrieved from: https://trove.nla.gov.au/newspaper/article/36379142?searchTerm=%22a%20banquet%20of%20interests%2C%20from%20which%20we%20hope%20you%20will%20never%20turn%20away%20unsatisfied%22&searchLimits=
212. *Advertiser, The.* (1941). Newspapers and Radio: Ownership of Stations Defended. 21 October 1941. p. 8. Retrieved from: https://trove.nla.gov.au/newspaper/article/44962736?searchTerm=Newspapers%20radio%20stations
213. *Sydney Morning Herald, The.* (1932). Broadcasting: The Appointment of Commissioners: Proposed Legislation. 10 March 1932. p. 11. Retrieved from: https://trove.nla.gov.au/newspaper/article/29946918?searchTerm=Broadcasting%3A%20The%20Appointment%20of%20Commissioners%3A%20Proposed%20Legislation.%20
214. Petersen, N. (1993). *News not views: The ABC, the Press, and Politics 1932–1947.* Hale and Iremonger. Sydney. p. 34
215. Petersen, N. (1993). *News not views: The ABC, the Press, and Politics 1932–1947.* Hale and Iremonger. Sydney. p. 35.
216. Knight. A. (2007). Australian based foreign correspondents and their sources. *ejournalism.com.au.* Retrieved from https://ejournalist.com.au/public_html/v1n1/correspondents.pdf
217. *Sydney Morning Herald, The.* (1946). Important Development in News System. 23 December 1946. p. 4. Retrieved from Trove.
218. *Australian Bureau of Statistics.* (2006). A Picture of the Nation: the Statistician's Report on the 2006 Census, 2006. Released 29 January

2009. Retrieved from: https://www.ausstats.abs.gov.au/ausstats/subscriber.nsf/LookupAttach/2070.0Publication29.01.091/$File/2070 0_A_Picture_of_the_Nation.pdf p. 120.

219. *Australian Broadcasting Corporation*. (2014). Our ABC, Our Future. A message from Mark Scott. 24 November 2014. Retrieved from: https://about.abc.net.au/our-abc-our-future/

220. Guardian Staff (2018). ABC in turmoil: who said what on boss Michelle Guthrie's sacking. *The Guardian*.
 24 September 2018. Retrieved from: https://www.theguardian.com/media/2018/sep/24/abc-in-turmoil-who-said-what-on-boss-michelle-guthries-sacking

221. Koziol, M. (2018). 'Devastated': Sacked ABC boss Michelle Guthrie threatens to sue over 'unjustified' termination. *The Sydney Morning Herald*. 24 September 2018. Retrieved from: https://www.smh.com.au/national/devastated-sacked-abc-boss-michelle-guthrie-threatens-to-sue-over-unjustified-termination-20180924-p505mt.html

222. Whitehead, G. (1988). *Inside the ABC: Geoffrey Whitehead's Personal Account*. Penguin Books. Ringwood Victoria. p. 178.

223. Manne, R. (2007). New Teeth for Aunty: Reinvigorating the National Broadcaster. *The Monthly*. December 2007–January 2008. Retrieved from: https://www.themonthly.com.au/monthly-essays-robert-manne-new-teeth-aunty-reinvigorating-national-broadcaster-749#mtr p. 40

224. *Australian Broadcasting Corporation*. (2006). ABC Managing Director to leave the Corporation. 20 January 2006. Retrieved from: https://about.abc.net.au/press-releases/abc-managing-director-to-leave-the-corporation/

225. *Australian Broadcasting Corporation*. (2015). Mark Scott confirms he will step down as ABC Managing Director in 2016. 14 September 2015. Retrieved from https://www.abc.net.au/news/2015-09-14/mark-scott-abc-managing-director-announces-he-will-step-down/6774236

226. Meade, A. (2018). Michelle Guthrie 'considering legal options' after being sacked by ABC board. *The Guardian*. 24 September 2018. Retrieved from; https://www.theguardian.com/media/2018/sep/24/michelle-guthrie-considering-legal-options-after-being-sacked-by-abc-board

227. Grattan, M. (2018). **ABC contributes as much to the economy as it costs the taxpayer: Michelle Guthrie. *The Conversation*. 19 June 2018. Retrieved from:** https://theconversation.com/abc-contributes-as-much-to-the-economy-as-it-costs-the-taxpayer-michelle-guthrie-98553

228. McKnight, D. (1998). Broadcasting and the Enemy within: Political Surveillance and the ABC, 1951–64. *Media International Australia, Incorporating Culture & Policy.* 87. May 1998. Pp. 35–48. Availability: <https://search-informit-com-au.wwwproxy1.library.unsw.edu.au/documentSummary;dn=093749146204159;res=IELLCC> ISSN: 1329-878X. p. 36.
229. McKnight, D. (1998). Broadcasting and the Enemy within: Political Surveillance and the ABC, 1951–64. *Media International Australia, Incorporating Culture & Policy.* 87. May 1998. Pp. 35–48. Availability: <https://search-informit-com-au.wwwproxy1.library.unsw.edu.au/documentSummary;dn=093749146204159;res=IELLCC> ISSN: 1329-878X p. 37.
230. Carpentier, N. (2014). Participation as a Fantasy: A Psychoanalytical Approach to Power-Sharing Fantasies in Eds. L. Kramp, N. Carpentier, A. Hepp, I. Tomanic-Trivundza, H. Nieminen, R. Kunelius, T. Olsson, E. Sundin & R. Kilborn. *Everyday Media Agency in Europe.* Edition Lumière. Section 4:5. pp. 319–330. p. 319.
231. Uldam, J. (2016). Corporate management of visibility and the fantasy of the post-political: Social media and surveillance. *New Media & Society.* 18:2. Pp. 201–219. https://doi.org/10.1177/1461444814541526
232. Edwards, M., Halligan, J., Horrigan, B. & Nicoll, G. (2012). *Public Sector Governance in Australia.* ANU ePress. Retrieved from https://press-files.anu.edu.au/downloads/press/p190701/pdf/book.pdf p. 201.
233. Nolan, M. (1994). *First Report of the Committee on Standards in Public Life.* Retrieved from https://webarchive.nationalarchives.gov.uk/20131205101339/http://www.archive.official-documents.co.uk/document/parlment/nolan/nolan.htm
234. Edwards, M., Halligan, J., Horrigan, B. & Nicoll, G. (2012). *Public Sector Governance in Australia.* ANU ePress. Retrieved from https://press-files.anu.edu.au/downloads/press/p190701/pdf/book.pdf p. 210.
235. Edwards, M., Halligan, J., Horrigan, B. & Nicoll, G. (2012). *Public Sector Governance in Australia.* ANU ePress. Retrieved from https://press-files.anu.edu.au/downloads/press/p190701/pdf/book.pdf p. 215.
236. Loc. cit.
237. Edwards, M., Halligan, J., Horrigan, B. & Nicoll, G. (2012). *Public Sector Governance in Australia.* ANU ePress. Retrieved 10 March 2020 from https://press-files.anu.edu.au/downloads/press/p190701/pdf/book.pdf p. 219.

238. Edwards, M., Halligan, J., Horrigan, B. & Nicoll, G. (2012). *Public Sector Governance in Australia*. ANU ePress. Retrieved 10 March 2020 from https://press-files.anu.edu.au/downloads/press/p190701/pdf/book.pdf
239. Edwards, M., Halligan, J., Horrigan, B. & Nicoll, G. (2012). *Public Sector Governance in Australia*. ANU ePress. Retrieved 10 March 2020 from https://press-files.anu.edu.au/downloads/press/p190701/pdf/book.pdf p. 212.
240. Inglis, K, (2006). *Whose ABC? The Australian Broadcasting Corporation 1983–2006*. Black Inc. Melbourne. p. 33.
241. Styles, J. (2002). The ABC: Unique unto itself. Review. *Institute of Public Affairs*. 54:1. p. 27
242. Seccombe, M. (2016). Senior ABC staff say Michelle Guthrie 'out of her depth'. The Saturday Paper. 3 December 2016. Retrieved from: https://www.thesaturdaypaper.com.au/news/media/2016/12/03/senior-abc-staff-say-michelle-guthrie-out-her-depth/14806836004053
243. Levine, M., & Forrence, J. (1990). Regulatory Capture, Public Interest, and the Public Agenda: Toward a Synthesis. *Journal of Law, Economics, & Organization*. 6. Pp. 167–198. Retrieved from www.jstor.org/stable/764987 p. 172.
244. Dal Bo′, E. (2006) Regulatory Capture: A Review. *Oxford Review of Economic Policy*. 22:2. pp. 203–225. Retrieved from DOI: https://doi.org/10.1093/oxrep/grj013 p. 204.
245. Dal Bo′, E. (2006) Regulatory Capture: A Review. *Oxford Review of Economic Policy*. 22:2. pp. 203–225. Retrieved from DOI: https://doi.org/10.1093/oxrep/grj013
246. Laffont, J-J., & Tirole, J. (1991). The Politics of Government Decision-Making: A Theory of Regulatory Capture. *The Quarterly Journal of Economics*. 106:4. Pp. 1089–1127. Retrieved from www.jstor.org/stable/2937958
247. Laffont, J-J. & Tirole, J. (1991). The Politics of Government Decision-Making: A Theory of Regulatory Capture. *The Quarterly Journal of Economics*. 106:4. Nov. 1991. Pp. 1089–1127. Retrieved from https://www.jstor.org/stable/2937958 p. 1117.
248. Stigler, G.J. (1971). The Theory of Economic Regulation. *The Bell Journal of Economics and Management Science*. 2:1. (Spring, 1971). Pp. 3–21. Retrieved from: https://www.jstor.org/stable/3003160 p. 3.
249. Stigler, G.J. (1971). The Theory of Economic Regulation. *The Bell Journal of Economics and Management Science*. 2:1. (Spring, 1971). Pp. 3–21. Retrieved from: https://www.jstor.org/stable/3003160 p. 4.
250. Levine, M., & Forrence, J. (1990). Regulatory Capture, Public Interest, and the Public Agenda: Toward a Synthesis. *Journal of Law, Economics, &*

Organization. 6. Pp. 167–198. Retrieved from www.jstor.org/stable/764987

251. Ibid., p. 169.
252. Ibid., p. 170.
253. Ibid., p. 169.
254. Ibid., p. 169.
255. Ibid., p. 178.
256. Ibid., p. 175.
257. Ibid., p. 190.
258. Dal Bo′, E. (2006) Regulatory Capture: A Review. *Oxford Review of Economic Policy.* 22:2. pp. 203–225. Retrieved from DOI: https://doi.org/10.1093/oxrep/grj013. p. 205.
259. Dal Bo′, E. (2006) Regulatory Capture: A Review. *Oxford Review of Economic Policy.* 22:2. pp. 203–225. Retrieved from DOI: https://doi.org/10.1093/oxrep/grj013. p. 213.
260. Dal Bo′, E. (2006) Regulatory Capture: A Review. *Oxford Review of Economic Policy.* 22:2. pp. 203–225. Retrieved from DOI: https://doi.org/10.1093/oxrep/grj013. p. 218.
261. Dal Bo′, E. (2006) Regulatory Capture: A Review. *Oxford Review of Economic Policy.* 22:2. pp. 203–225. Retrieved from DOI: https://doi.org/10.1093/oxrep/grj013. p. 220.
262. Name-Correa, A.J. & Yildirim, H. (2018). A capture theory of committees. *Public Choice.* 177:1. Pp. 135–154 https://doi.org/10.1007/s11127-018-0593-6
263. Stigler, G.J. (1971). The Theory of Economic Regulation. *The Bell Journal of Economics and Management Science.* 2:1. (Spring, 1971). pp. 3–21. Retrieved from: https://www.jstor.org/stable/3003160
264. Potter, M.R., Olejarski, A.M. & Pfister, S.M. (2014). Capture Theory and the Public Interest: Balancing Competing Values to Ensure Regulatory Effectiveness. *International Journal of Public Administration.* 37. Pp. 638–645. DOI: https://doi.org/10.1080/01900692.2014.903266. p. 641.
265. Laffont, J-J. & Tirole, J. (1991). The Politics of Government Decision-Making: A Theory of Regulatory Capture. *The Quarterly Journal of Economics.* 106:4 (Nov., 1991). Pp. 1089–1127. Retrieved from https://www.jstor.org/stable/2937958 p. 1089.
266. Potter, M.R., Olejarski, A.M. & Pfister, S.M. (2014). Capture Theory and the Public Interest: Balancing Competing Values to Ensure Regulatory Effectiveness. *International Journal of Public Administration.* 37. Pp. 638–645. DOI: https://doi.org/10.1080/01900692.2014.903266. p. 638.

267. Selznick, P. (1949). *TVA and the grass roots.* Berkeley, CA: University of California Press. p. 146. Quoting V.O. Key. "politics and Administration" in L. D. White (Ed). (1942). *The Future of Government in the United States.* University of Chicago Press. Chicago. p. 151.
268. Cadzow, J. (2018). "Culture Clash". Good Weekend. *The Sydney Morning Herald.* The Culture Issue. 6 October 2018. p. 18.
269. Ibid.
270. Potter, M.R., Olejarski, A.M. & Pfister, S.M. (2014). Capture Theory and the Public Interest: Balancing Competing Values to Ensure Regulatory Effectiveness. *International Journal of Public Administration.* 37. Pp. 638–645. DOI: https://doi.org/10.1080/01900692.2014.903266
271. Ibid., p. 642.
272. Ibid., p. 643
273. Loc. cit.
274. Ibid., p. 639.
275. Sanderson, W. (2000). "Preferential Treatment". 7.30 Program. *ABC Television.* Broadcast 27 November 2000. Retrieved from http://www.abc.net.au/7.30/stories/s217353.htm
276. Ibid.
277. Swan, W. (2001). Grievance Debate. Australian Labor Party: Queensland. *House of Representatives Hansard.* 26 February 2001. p. 24394. Retrieved from https://parlinfo.aph.gov.au/parlInfo/search/display/display.w3p;db=CHAMBER;id=chamber/hansardr/2001-02-26/0129;query=Id:%22chamber/hansardr/2001-02-26/0000%22
278. Karvelas, P. (2007). 'Kick Swan out' for Democrats donation. *The Australian.* 14 August 2007. Retrieved from https://web.archive.org/web/20071203213618/http://www.theaustralian.news.com.au/story/0,25197,22241106-11949,00.html
279. Orr, G.D. (2010). The Australian Experience of Electoral Bribery: Dealing in Electoral Support. *Australian Journal of Politics & History.* June 2010. p. 232. Retrieved from https://www.researchgate.net/publication/47456681
280. Ibid. Pp. 232–233.
281. Schubert, M & Canberra Bureau. (2007). Costello attacks Swan over Democrats money. *The Age.* 14 August 2007. Retrieved from https://www.theage.com.au/national/costello-attacks-swan-over-democrats-money-20070814-ge5kuv.html
282. Swan also lost the seat by 0.73%. Ref: footnotes Orr, G.D. (2010). The Australian Experience of Electoral Bribery: Dealing in Electoral Support. *Australian Journal of Politics & History.* June 2010. p. 231. Retrieved from https://www.researchgate.net/publication/47456681

283. Sanderson, W. Ibid.
284. Lewis, S. (2000). Swan stands aside while Labor Party implodes. *The Australian Financial Review Weekend.* 2 December 2000. Retrieved from https://www.afr.com/politics/swan-stands-aside-while-labor-party-implodes-20001202-jl3ic
285. Swan, W. (2001). Grievance Debate. Australian Labor Party: Queensland. *House of Representatives Hansard.* 26 February 2001. p. 24394. Retrieved from https://parlinfo.aph.gov.au/parlInfo/search/display/display.w3p;db=CHAMBER;id=chamber/hansardr/2001-02-26/0129;query=Id:%22chamber/hansardr/2001-02-26/0000%22
286. At the time, Steve Austin was a senior employee on 7.30. His biography on the ABC Radio webpage said: Steve left high school with a notation on his report card: "Steve has a problem with authority". Ref: ABC Radio. ND. Steve Austin. Retrieved 29 February 2020 from https://www.abc.net.au/radio/people/steve-austin/7951910
287. Schubert, M. & Canberra. Ibid.
288. Swan, W. (2001). Ibid.
289. Jones, S. (2015). ABC Managing Director Mark Scott: we're a public broadcaster not a state broadcaster. *Mumbrella.* 25 June 2015. Retrieved from: http://mumbrella.com.au/abc-managing-director-mark-scott-were-a-public-broadcaster-not-a-state-broadcaster-302022
290. Kidd, J. and staff. (2014). ABC cuts: Managing Director Mark Scott announces more than 400 jobs to go. *ABC News.* 25 November 2014. Retrieved from: https://www.abc.net.au/news/2014-11-24/mark-scott-announces-abc-job-cuts/5913082?nw=0
291. *British Broadcasting Corporation.* (2020). ABC job cuts: Australian pubic broadcaster to shed 250 jobs. 24 June 2020. Retrieved from: https://www.bbc.com/news/world-australia-53160411
292. *Special Broadcasting Service.* (2020). Jobs and content cut in ABC shake-up designed to save $40 million. 24 June 2020. Retrieved from: https://www.sbs.com.au/news/jobs-and-content-cut-in-abc-shake-up-designed-to-save-40-million
293. Watkins, E. (2018). 'Ideological and vindictive': reactions to ABC budgets cuts. *Crikey.com.* 9 May 2018. Retrieved from: https://www.crikey.com.au/2018/05/09/ideological-and-vindictive-reactions-to-abc-budgets-cuts/
294. Carson, A. (2020). Cutting the ABC cuts public trust. 10. June 2020. *La Trobe University.* News Articles. Retrieved from: https://www.latrobe.edu.au/news/articles/2020/opinion/cutting-the-abc-cuts-public-trust
295. Seccombe, M. (2020). Hundreds facing the sack with ABC cuts. *The Saturday Paper.* 300. 9–15 May 2020. Retrieved from: https://www.thesaturdaypaper.com.au/news/politics/2020/05/09/hundreds-facing-the-sack-with-abc-cuts/15889464009792

296. Seccombe, M. (2014). What Mark Scott is really doing with the ABC cuts. *The Saturday Paper.* 40. 29 November–5 December 2014. Retrieved from: https://www.thesaturdaypaper.com.au/news/media/2014/11/29/what-mark-scott-really-doing-with-the-abc-cuts/14171796001308
297. Hyland, A. (2015). Mark Scott's ABC exit interview: 'I had no idea of the scale of the challenge'. *The AFR Magazine.* 27 November 2015. Retrieved from: https://www.afr.com/life-and-luxury/abcs-mark-scott-on-success-and-his-legacy-20151019-gkcgi8
298. Australian Broadcasting Corporation (2013). Media Watch. Australian Broadcasting Corporation. 16 September 2013. Retrieved from: https://www.abc.net.au/mediawatch/episodes/media-watch-doesnt-get-the-joke/9980760
299. Australian Broadcasting Corporation. (2014). Editorial Policies. Harm and Offence. Retrieved from: https://edpols.abc.net.au/guidance/84/
300. Hyland, A. (2015). Mark Scott's ABC exit interview: 'I had no idea of the scale of the challenge'. *The Australian Financial Review Magazine.* 27 November 2015. Retrieved from https://www.afr.com/life-and-luxury/abcs-mark-scott-on-success-and-his-legacy-20151019-gkcgi8
301. Hyland, A. (2015). Mark Scott's ABC exit interview: 'I had no idea of the scale of the challenge'. *The Australian Financial Review Magazine.* 27 November 2015. Retrieved from https://www.afr.com/life-and-luxury/abcs-mark-scott-on-success-and-his-legacy-20151019-gkcgi8
302. "Gang-banged" is slang for gang rape.
303. Robinson, N. (2015). Q&A guest Zaky Mallah hits back with new gang-bang tweets. *The Australian.* 1 July 2015. Retrieved from https://www.theaustralian.com.au/business/media/qa-guest-zaky-mallah-hits-back-with-new-gangbang-tweets/news-story/fe0701f40bc64bc45b2053194949d81c
304. Department of Communications (2015). Context and decisions regarding the appearance of Mr Zaky Mallah on the ABC's Q&A program on 22 June 2015. 1 July 2015. Retrieved from: https://www.abc.net.au/news/2015-07-03/report-finds-q&a-did-investigate-zaky-mallah-before-appearance/6593810
305. Davidson, H. (2015). Abbott asks the ABC 'whose side are you on?' over Zaky Mallah's Q&A appearance. *The Guardian.* 23 June 2015. Retrieved from: https://www.theguardian.com/australia-news/2015/jun/23/abbott-asks-the-abc-whose-side-are-you-on-over-zaky-mallahs-qa-appearance
306. This will be analysed in the next chapter, but in 2015 12 journalists and publishing staff were killed by Al-Qaeda operatives at the magazine in retaliation for publishing mocking cartoons of the Prophet Mohammed.

307. Scott, M. (2015). ABC is a public broadcaster, not a state broadcaster. *The Sydney Morning Herald*. 26 June 2015. Retrieved from https://www.smh.com.au/opinion/abc-is-a-public-broadcaster-not-a-state-broadcaster-20150625-ghxt5m.html
308. Robertson, J. (2015). ABC offices in security lockdown after threats following Q&A Zaky Mallah episode. *The Sydney Morning Herald*. 26 June 2015. Retrieved from: https://www.smh.com.au/politics/federal/abc-offices-in-security-lockdown-after-threats-following-qa-zaky-mallah-episode-20150626-ghy48b.html
309. Barratt, S. (2018). Reinforcing Sexism and Misogyny: Social Media, Symbolic Violence and the Construction of Femininity-as-Fail. *Journal of International Women's Studies*. 19:3. Pp. 16–31. http://search.proquest.com/docview/2057939820/
310. Delgado, R. & Stefancic, J. (2014). Hate speech in cyberspace. *Wake Forest Law Review*. 49:2. Pp. 319–343. https://doi.org/info:doi/
311. Simões, R. B. & Silveirinha, M.J. (2019): Framing street harassment: legal developments and popular misogyny in social media. *Feminist Media Studies*. Pp. 1–17. https://doi.org/10.1080/14680777.2019.1704816
312. Jane, E.A. (2018). Gendered cyberhate as workplace harassment and economic vandalism. *Feminist Media Studies*. 18:4. Pp. 575–591. https://doi.org/10.1080/14680777.2018.1447344
313. Simons, M. (2008). No new logo for the ABC, but rebranding on the cards. *Crikey.com*. 30 January 2008. Retrieved from: https://www.crikey.com.au/2008/01/30/no-new-logo-for-the-abc-but-rebranding-on-the-cards/
314. Drori, G., Delmestri, S., & Oberg, G. (2016). The iconography of universities as institutional narratives. *Higher Education*. 71:2. Pp. 163–180. https://doi.org/10.1007/s10734-015-9894-6
315. Drori, G., Delmestri, S., & Oberg, G. (2016). The iconography of universities as institutional narratives. *Higher Education*. 71:2. Pp. 163–180. https://doi.org/10.1007/s10734-015-9894-6 p. 164.
316. Van Der Houwen, F., & Sliedrecht, K. (2016). The form and function of formulations: Co-constructing narratives in institutional settings. *Journal of Pragmatics. 105*. Retrieved from http://search.proquest.com/docview/2061520159/
317. Tengblad, S. (2012). *The work of managers towards a practice theory of management*. Oxford University Press. Oxford.
318. Loseke, D. R. (2007). The Study of Identity as Cultural, Institutional, Organizational, and Personal Narratives: Theoretical and Empirical Integrations. *The Sociological Quarterly*. 48:4. pp. 661–688. https://doi.org/10.1111/j.1533-8525.2007.00096.x quoting Alexander 1992. p. 662.

319. Robbins, S., Judge, T.A., Edwards, M., Sandiford, P., Fitzgerald, M. & Hunt, J. (2019). *Organisational Behaviour.* 9th Edition. EBook. Pearson Education Australia. Retrieved from: ProQuest Ebook Central, http://ebookcentral.proquest.com/lib/unsw/detail.action?docID=5220538. 9th Ed. Pearson. Australia.
320. Robbins, S., Judge, T.A., Edwards, M., Sandiford, P., Fitzgerald, M. & Hunt, J. (2019). *Organisational Behaviour.* 9th Edition. EBook. Pearson Education Australia. p. 422. Retrieved from: ProQuest Ebook Central, http://ebookcentral.proquest.com/lib/unsw/detail.action?docID=5220538
321. Loseke, D. R. (2007). The Study of Identity as Cultural, Institutional, Organizational, and Personal Narratives: Theoretical and Empirical Integrations. *The Sociological Quarterly.* 48:4. Pp. 661–688. https://doi.org/10.1111/j.1533-8525.2007.00096.x quoting Alexander 1992. Quoting Lamont and Virag, 2002. p. 666–667.
322. Loseke, D. R. (2007). The Study of Identity as Cultural, Institutional, Organizational, and Personal Narratives: Theoretical and Empirical Integrations. *The Sociological Quarterly.* 48:4. Pp. 661–688. https://doi.org/10.1111/j.1533-8525.2007.00096.x quoting Alexander 1992. Quoting Lamont and Virag, 2002. p. 675.
323. Kidd, J. and staff. (2014). ABC cuts: Managing Director Mark Scott announces more than 400 jobs to go. *ABC News.* 25 November 2014. Retrieved from: https://www.abc.net.au/news/2014-11-24/mark-scott-announces-abc-job-cuts/5913082?nw=0
324. Australian Public Service Commission. (2010). Empowering Change: Fostering Innovation in the Australian Public Service—report by the Management Advisory Committee. P. iii. In: Creed, A. (2011). *Organisational Behaviour*, Oxford University Press. ProQuest Ebook Central. http://ebookcentral.proquest.com/lib/unsw/detail.action?docID=1985999.
325. Creed, A. (2011). *Organisational Behaviour*, Oxford University Press. ProQuest Ebook Central. http://ebookcentral.proquest.com/lib/unsw/detail.action?docID=1985999. p. 208.
326. Creed, A. (2011). *Organisational Behaviour*, Oxford University Press. ProQuest Ebook Central. http://ebookcentral.proquest.com/lib/unsw/detail.action?docID=1985999. p. 212.
327. Creed, A. (2011). *Organisational Behaviour*, Oxford University Press. ProQuest Ebook Central. http://ebookcentral.proquest.com/lib/unsw/detail.action?docID=1985999. p. 222.
328. Creed, A. (2011). *Organisational Behaviour*, Oxford University Press. ProQuest Ebook Central. http://ebookcentral.proquest.com/lib/unsw/detail.action?docID=1985999. p. 167.

329. McGuire, J., Rhodes, G. & Palus, C. (2008). Inside out: Transforming your leadership culture. *Leadership in Action.* 27. Pp. 3—7. DOI: https://doi.org/10.1002/lia.1226.
330. Van Der Houwen, F., & Sliedrecht, K. (2016). The form and function of formulations: Co-constructing narratives in institutional settings. *Journal of Pragmatics.* 105. Retrieved from: http://search.proquest.com/docview/2061520159/ p. 55.
331. Drori, G., Delmestri, S., & Oberg, G. (2016). The iconography of universities as institutional narratives. *Higher Education.* 71:2. Pp. 163–180. https://doi.org/10.1007/s10734-015-9894-6
332. Herbison, M. (2014). ABC rebrand takes main TV channel back to its roots. *MarketingMag.* 4 August 2014. Retrieved from https://www.marketingmag.com.au/news-c/abc-rebrand-takes-main-tv-channel-back-to-its-roots/
333. Meade, S, (2014). ABC rebrands its main television channel using social media hashtag. *The Guardian.* 10 July 2014. Retrieved from: https://www.theguardian.com/media/2014/jul/10/abc-rebrands-its-main-television-channel-using-social-media-hashtag
334. *Australian Broadcasting Corporation.* (2014). ABC Television throws its arms around Australians in channel rebrand. 10 July 2014. Retrieved from: https://about.abc.net.au/press-releases/abc-television-throws-its-arms-around-australians-in-channel-rebrand/
335. *Australian Broadcasting Corporation.* (2014). ABC Television throws its arms around Australians in channel rebrand. 10 July 2014. Retrieved from: https://about.abc.net.au/press-releases/abc-television-throws-its-arms-around-australians-in-channel-rebrand/
336. *Australian Broadcasting Corporation.* (2014). ABC Television throws its arms around Australians in channel rebrand. 10 July 2014. Retrieved from: https://about.abc.net.au/press-releases/abc-television-throws-its-arms-around-australians-in-channel-rebrand/
337. Knox, D. (2017). New-look ABC News ditches News 24. 8 April 2017. TV Tonight blog. Retrieved from https://tvtonight.com.au/2017/04/new-look-abc-news-ditches-news-24.html
338. Waugh, E. (1938/1982). *Scoop.* Penguin Books. Harmondsworth, England.
339. Jackson, D. & Moloney, K. (2016). Inside Churnalism. *Journalism Studies.* 17:6. Pp. 763–780. https://doi.org/10.1080/1461670X.2015.1017597 p. 764.
340. Clarke, J. & Bromley, M. (Eds). (2011). *International News in the Digital Age: East-West Perceptions of a New World Order.* Taylor & Francis Group. ProQuest Ebook Central, http://ebookcentral.proquest.com/lib/unsw/detail.action?docID=957408. p. 4–5.

341. Cunningham, S. & Turner, G. Eds. (2010). *The Media and Communications in Australia*. 3rd Edition. Allen and Unwin. Crows Nest, Sydney. p. 47.
342. *Australian Broadcasting Corporation*. (2008). *About the ABC—History of the ABC*. Retrieved from: https://archive.is/20121206003650/http://abc.net.au/corp/history/hist7.htm
343. *Australian Broadcasting Corporation*. (2008). About the ABC—History of the ABC. Retrieved from: https://archive.is/20121206003650/http://abc.net.au/corp/history/hist7.htm
344. Inglis, K. (2006). *Whose ABC? The Australian Broadcasting Corporation 1983–2006*. Black Inc. Melbourne.
345. Cunningham, S. (2013). *Hidden Innovation: Policy, Industry and the Creative Sector*. University of Queensland Press. Brisbane.
346. Cunningham, S. (2013). *Hidden Innovation: Policy, Industry and the Creative Sector*. University of Queensland Press. Brisbane.
347. *Australian Broadcasting Corporation*. (2020). ABC Open closes. Retrieved from: https://www.abc.net.au/news/abcmyphoto/abc-open/
348. Clark, A. (2016, Jan 04). Johns had lasting impact on ABC and SBS: Obituary. *The Australian Financial Review*. Retrieved from http://ezproxy.library.usyd.edu.au/login?url=https://search-proquest-com.ezproxy2.library.usyd.edu.au/docview/1752885352?accountid=14757
349. Inglis, K. (2006). *Whose ABC? The Australian Broadcasting Corporation 1983–2006*. Black Inc. Melbourne. p. 462.
350. Scott, M. (2019). *On Us*. Melbourne University Press. Carlton, Victoria. p. 44.
351. *Australian Government*. (2008). ABC and SBS: Towards a digital future Discussion paper. Department of Broadband, Communications and Digital Economy. Retrieved from: https://www.ames.net.au/-/media/files/policy/7_abc_and_sbs_towards_a_digital_future_low_resolution.pdf
352. Koziol, M. (2018). Invest in the ABC's digital future or it will 'cease to exist', warns chairman. *The Sydney Morning Herald*. 11 July 2018. Retrieved from: https://www.smh.com.au/politics/federal/invest-in-the-abc-s-digital-future-or-it-will-cease-to-exist-warns-chairman-20180711-p4zqsp.html
353. *Australian Government*. (2018). Inquiry into the Competitive Neutrality of the National Broadcasters—report by the Expert Panel. September 2018. Retrieved from: https://www.communications.gov.au/documents/inquiry-competitive-neutrality-national-broadcasters-report-expert-panel

354. *Australian Government.* (2018). Inquiry into the Competitive Neutrality of the National Broadcasters -report by the Expert Panel. September 2018. Retrieved from: https://www.communications.gov.au/documents/inquiry-competitive-neutrality-national-broadcasters-report-expert-panel

References

Aagaard, P. (2016). How to Make the Mix Matter: A Case Study of Post-Transformational Leadership in Hybrid Public Management. *International Journal of Public Administration., 39*(14), 1171–1179. https://doi.org/10.1080/01900692.2015.1072211

ABC. (2013). Guidelines for Personal Use of Social Media. [online]. Document: D11/22627. http://about.abc.net.au/wp-content/uploads/2014/10/PersonalUseOfSocialMediaINS1.pdf

Advertiser, The. (1937, October 16). Vigorous Defence of ABC Policy "We Remain Serene Under Sneers" Not Gods, says Mr Cleary Broadcast at Opening of New Station. *The Advertiser, Adelaide*, p. 26. https://trove.nla.gov.au/newspaper/article/36379142?searchTerm=%22a%20banquet%20of%20interests%2C%20from%20which%20we%20hope%20you%20will%20never%20turn%20away%20unsatisfied%22&searchLimits=

Advertiser, The. (1941, October 21). Newspapers and Radio: Ownership of Stations Defended, p. 8. https://trove.nla.gov.au/newspaper/article/44962736?searchTerm=Newspapers%20radio%20stations

Andrews, R., Boyne, G. A., & Walker, R. M. (2012). Overspending in Public Organizations: Does Strategic Management Matter? *International Public Management Journal, 15*(1), 39–61. https://doi.org/10.1080/10967494.2012.684017

Australian Broadcasting Corporation Annual Report. (2019). *ABC.* https://about.abc.net.au/wp-content/uploads/2019/10/ABC-Annual-Report-201819v2.pdf

Australian Broadcasting Corporation. (2006). ABC Managing Director to leave the Corporation. 20 January 2006. Retrieved from: https://about.abc.net.au/press-releases/abc-managing-director-to-leave-the-corporation/

Australian Broadcasting Corporation. (2015). Mark Scott confirms he will step down as ABC Managing Director in 2016. 14 September 2015. Retrieved from: https://www.abc.net.au/news/2015-09-14/mark-scott-abc-managing-director-announces-he-will-step-down/6774236

Australian Public Service Commission. (2010). Empowering Change: Fostering Innovation in the Australian Public Service—report by the Management Advisory Committee. P. iii. In: Creed, A. (2011). Organisational Behaviour,

Oxford University Press. ProQuest Ebook Central. http://ebookcentral.proquest.com/lib/unsw/detail.action?docID=1985999.

Australian Rationalist. (2016). Destroying the ABC.100. Autumn, pp. 40–41. https://search-informit-com-au.wwwproxy1.library.unsw.edu.au/fullText;dn=20190613012323;res=AGISPT

Banerjee, I., & Seneviratne, K. (2006). *Public Service Broadcasting in the Age of Globalization*. Asian Media Information and Communication Centre. Nanyang Technological University.

Barratt, S. (2018). Reinforcing Sexism and Misogyny: Social Media, Symbolic Violence and the Construction of Femininity-as-Fail. *Journal of International Women's Studies, 19*(3), 16–31. http://search.proquest.com/docview/2057939820/

Barrett, A. W., & Barrington, L. W. (2005). Is a Picture Worth a Thousand Words?: Newspaper Photographs and Voter Evaluations of Political Candidates. *Harvard International Journal of Press/Politics, 10*(4), 98–113. https://doi.org/10.1177/1081180X05281392

Beazley, M. J. (2016, August). Institutional Leadership Amongst Equals. *Judicial Officers Bulletin, 28*(7), 65–69. https://search-informit-com-au.wwwproxy1.library.unsw.edu.au/documentSummary;dn=268275964401160;res=IELAPA

Benington, J. (2011). From private choice to public value? Chapter in J. Benington & M. Moore (Eds.). Public value: Theory and practice (pp. 31–51). Palgrave Macmillan. London.

Bennis, W. (2007). The Challenges of Leadership in the Modern World: Introduction to the Special Issue. (Author Abstract). *The American Psychologist, 62*(1), 2–5. https://doi.org/10.1037/0003-066X.62.1.2

Biggart, N. W., & Hamilton, G. G. (1987). An Institutional Theory of Leadership. *The Journal of Applied Behavioral Science, 23*(4), 429–441. https://doi.org/10.1177/002188638702300401

Blain, E. (1977). *Life with Aunty: 40 Year with the ABC*. Methuen Australia.

Bottery, M., & Herrington, N. (2016). Not so Simple: The Threats to Leadership Sustainability. *Management in Education, 30*(3), 97–101. https://doi.org/10.1177/0892020616653059

Bourdieu, P. (2005). *The Social Structures of the Economy* (C. Turner, Trans.). Polity Press.

Bourdieu, P., & Wacquant, L. (1992). *An Invitation to Reflexive Sociology*. University of Chicago Press.

Bowden, T., & Borchers, W. (2006). *50 Years Aunty's Jubilee! Celebrating 50 Years of ABC-TV*. ABC Books.

Brereton, A. (2016, January 1). Former ABC Managing Director Brian Johns Dies Aged 79. *The Guardian*. https://www.theguardian.com/media/2016/jan/01/brian-johns-a-great-australian-who-positioned-the-abc-for-the-digital-age#:~:text=Former%20ABC%20managing%20director%20Brian%20

Johns%20has%20died%20of%20cancer,of%20digital%20news%20and%20 entertainment

Brewster, Z. W., Brauer, J. R., & Lynn, M. (2018). Morality at Work: Do Employees' Moral Commitments Inhibit Service Disparities and Reactive Workplace Behaviors? *Social Currents, 5*(3), 244–263. https://doi.org/10.1177/2329496517725330

Bromell, D. (2019). Ethical Competencies for Public Leadership: Pluralist Democratic Politics in Practice (1st Ed. 2019.). Springer International Publishing. Cham. Imprint. Springer.

Brook, S. (2017, November 20). Waste Not, Want Not the Message for ABC Silos. *The Australian.* https://login.wwwproxy1.library.unsw.edu.au/login?qurl=https%3A%2F%2Fsearch.proquest.com%2Fdocview%2F1990857104%3Facco

Brown, A., & Althaus, C. (2009). Public Service Broadcasting in Australia. *The Journal of Media Economics, 9*(1), 31–46. https://doi-org.wwwproxy1.library.unsw.edu.au/10.1207/s15327736me0901_4

Buttrose, C. (1984). *Words and Music: Press Barons, Prima Donnas and Coping with the ABC.* Angus and Robertson Publishers.

Cadzow, J. (2018). "Culture Clash". Good Weekend. *The Sydney Morning Herald, 6*(The Culture Issue), 18–24.

Canberra Times, The. (1936, July 2). ABC ARTISTS. All Will Visit Canberra. *The Canberra Times,* p. 2. https://trove.nla.gov.au/newspaper/article/2420561?searchTerm=ABC%20ARTISTS.%20All%20will%20visit%20Canberra

Carpentier, N. (2014). Participation as a Fantasy: A Psychoanalytical Approach to Power-Sharing Fantasies. In L. Kramp, N. Carpentier, A. Hepp, I. Tomanic-Trivundza, H. Nieminen, R. Kunelius, T. Olsson, E. Sundin & R. Kilborn (Eds.), *Everyday Media Agency in Europe, Chapter: Participation as a Fantasy: A Psychoanalytical Approach to Power-Sharing Fantasies* (pp. 319–330). Edition Lumière. Section 4:5. https://www.researchgate.net/publication/268980799_Participation_as_a_Fantasy_A_Psychoanalytical_Approach_to_Power-Sharing_Fantasies

Carson, A. (2020, June 10). Cutting the ABC Cuts Public Trust. *La Trobe University.* News Articles. https://www.latrobe.edu.au/news/articles/2020/opinion/cutting-the-abc-cuts-public-trust

Chapman, C., Getha-Taylor, H., Holmes, M. H., Jacobson, W. S., Morse, R. S., & Sowa, J. E. (2016, March). How Public Service Leadership Is Studied: An Examination of a Quarter Century of Scholarship. *Public Administration, 94*(1), 111–128. https://onlinelibrary-wiley-com.wwwproxy1.library.unsw.edu.au/doi/pdfdirect/10.1111/padm.12199

Chemers, M. (2014). In H. Gray-Hoehn. (2020). Chapter 6: "Talking the Talk: Communication as the Essential Element of Leadership". In K. M. S. Bezio &

G. R. Goethals (Eds.), *Leadership, Populism, and Resistance* (Jepson Studies in Leadership Series). Monograph Book. Elgar Online.

Clark, A. (2016, January 4). Johns Had Lasting Impact on ABC and SBS: Obituary. *The Australian Financial Review*.http://ezproxy.library.usyd.edu.au/login?url=https://search-proquest-com.ezproxy2.library.usyd.edu.au/docview/1752885352?accountid=14757

Clarke, J., & Bromley, M. (Eds.). (2011). *International News in the Digital Age: East-West Perceptions of a New World Order.* Taylor & Francis Group. ProQuest Ebook Central. http://ebookcentral.proquest.com/lib/unsw/detail.action?docID=957408

Clarke, N. (2011). An Integrated Conceptual Model of Respect in Leadership. *The Leadership Quarterly, 22*(2), 316–327. https://www-sciencedirect-com.wwwproxy1.library.unsw.edu.au/science/article/pii/S1048984311000208

Cooke, M. (2007). Our Digital Aunty—The ABC's New Media Future. *Metro Magazine: Media & Education Magazine, 154*, 120–124. https://search.informit.org/doi/10.3316/INFORMIT.003683049332154

Courier Mail, The. (1934, July 25). Educational Broadcasts: Policy of the A.B.C, p. 20. https://trove.nla.gov.au/newspaper/article/36733653?searchTerm=Educational%20broadcasts%3A%20Policy%20of%20the%20A.B.C

Courier Mail, The. (1938, January 8). Catering for Diverse Tastes: ABC Policy Explained at 4QR Opening, p. 13. https://trove.nla.gov.au/newspaper/article/39744258?searchTerm=Catering%20for%20diverse%20tastes%3A%20ABC%20policy%20explained%20at%204QR%20opening

Creed, A. (2011). Organisational Behaviour, Oxford University Press. ProQuest Ebook Central. http://ebookcentral.proquest.com/lib/unsw/detail.action?docID=1985999.

Cunningham, S. (2013). *Hidden Innovation: Policy, Industry and the Creative Sector.* University of Queensland Press.

Cunningham, S. & Turner, G. Eds. (2010). The Media and Communications in Australia. 3rd Edition. Allen and Unwin. Crows Nest, Sydney.

Cut, M. (2017). Digital Natives and Digital Immigrants—How Are They Different. *Digital Reflections.* https://medium.com/digital-reflections/digital-natives-and-digital-immigrants-how-are-they-different-e849b0a8a1d3

Dal Bo', E. (2006). Regulatory Capture: A Review. *Oxford Review of Economic Policy, 22*(2), 203–225. https://doi.org/10.1093/oxrep/grj013

Dalton, K. (2017, May). Missing in Action: The ABC and Australia's Screen Culture. Platform Papers. *Quarterly Essays on the Performing Arts from Currency House, 51.* Currency House.

Dandira, M. (2012). Dysfunctional Leadership: Organizational Cancer. *Business Strategy Series, 13*(4), 187–192. https://doi.org/10.1108/17515631211246267

Davidson, H. (2015, June 23). Abbott Asks the ABC 'Whose Side Are You On?' Over Zaky Mallah's Q&A Appearance. *The Guardian*. https://www.theguardian.com/australia-news/2015/jun/23/abbott-asks-the-abc-whose-side-are-you-on-over-zaky-mallahs-qa-appearance

Delgado, R., & Stefancic, J. (2014). Hate Speech in Cyberspace. *Wake Forest Law Review., 49*(2), 319–343.

Dempster, Q. (2000). *Death Struggle: How Political Malice and Boardroom Powerplays are Killing the ABC*. Allen and Unwin.

DeNardis, L. (2014). The global war for internet governance. Yale University Press. New Haven.

Department of Communications. (2015, July 1). Context and Decisions Regarding the Appearance of Mr Zaky Mallah on the ABC's Q&A Program on 22 June 2015. https://www.abc.net.au/news/2015-07-03/report-finds-q&a-did-investigate-zaky-mallah-before-appearance/6593810

Dickinson, H., Needham, C., Mangan, C., & Sullivan, H. E. (2019). *Reimagining the Future Public Service Workforce*. Springer Books.

Diefenbach, T. (2009). New Public Management in Public Sector Organizations: The Dark Sides of Managerialistic 'Enlightenment'. *Public Administration (London), 87*(4), 892–909. https://doi.org/10.1111/j.1467-9299.2009.01766.x

Dinh, J., Lord, R., Gardner, W., Meuser, J., Liden, R., & Hu, J. (2014). Leadership Theory and Research in the New Millennium: Current Theoretical Trends and Changing Perspectives. *Leadership Quarterly, 25*(1), 36–62. https://doi.org/10.1016/j.leaqua.2013.11.005

Dixon, F. (1975). *Inside the ABC: A Piece of Australian History*. The Hawthorn Press.

Downs, A. (1957). *An economic theory of democracy*. HarperCollins. New York.

Drori, G., Delmestri, S., & Oberg, G. (2016). The Iconography of Universities as Institutional Narratives. *Higher Education, 71*(2), 163–180. https://doi.org/10.1007/s10734-015-9894-6

Edwards, M., Halligan, J, Horrigan, B., & Nicoll, G. (2012). *Public Sector Governance in Australia*. Australian National University EPress. Griffin Press. https://press-files.anu.edu.au/downloads/press/p190701/pdf/book.pdf

Epitropaki, O., & Martin, R. (2004). Implicit Leadership Theories in Applied Settings: Factor Structure, Generalizability, and Stability Over Time. *Journal of Applied Psychology, 89*(2), 293–310. http://ovidsp.ovid.com/ovidweb.cgi?T=JS&PAGE=reference&D=ovftg&NEWS=N&AN=00004565-200404000-00008

Fairhurst, G. (2008). Discursive Leadership: A Communication Alternative to Leadership Psychology. *Management Communication Quarterly, 21*(4), 510–521. https://doi.org/10.1177/0893318907313714

Fraser, F. (2014). Orchestrating the Metropolis the Creation of the Sydney Symphony Orchestra as a Modern Cultural Institution. *History Australia, 11*(2), 196–221. https://doi.org/10.1080/14490854.2014.11668522

Friedland, R., & Alford, R. R. (1991). Bringing Society Back, in: W.W. Powell & P.J. DiMaggio (Eds). Symbols, Practices and Institutional Contradictions. The New Institutionalism in Organizational Analysis. Chicago, IL. University of Chicago Press.

Funston, A. (1997). The ABC and Citizenship [online]. *Overland, 147*(Winter), 59–62. https://search-informit-com-au.wwwproxy1.library.unsw.edu.au/documentSummary;dn=971111828;res=IELAPA

Glynn, M. (2000, May–June). When Cymbals Become Symbols: Conflict Over Organizational Identity Within a Symphony Orchestra. *Organization Science, 11*(3). Special Issue: Cultural Industries: Learning from Evolving Organizational Practices, pp. 285–298. https://www.jstor.org/stable/2640262

Goggin, G. (Ed.). (2004). *Virtual Nation: The Internet in Australia*. UNSW Press.

Golant, B., Sillince, J., Harvey, C., & Maclean, M. (2015). Rhetoric of Stability and Change: The Organizational Identity Work of Institutional Leadership. *Human Relations, 68*(4), 607–631. https://doi.org/10.1177/0018726714532966

Grattan, M. (2018, June 19). ABC Contributes as Much to the Economy as it Costs the Taxpayer: Michelle Guthrie. *The Conversation*.https://theconversation.com/abc-contributes-as-much-to-the-economy-as-it-costs-the-taxpayer-michelle-guthrie-98553

Gray-Hoehn, H. (2020). In K. Bezio & G. Goethals (Eds.), *Leadership, Populism, and Resistance*. Edward Elgar Publishing.

Greenleaf, R. (1977). *Servant Leadership: A Journey Into the Nature of Legitimate Power and Greatness*. Paulist Press.

Guardian Staff. (2018, September 24). ABC in Turmoil: Who Said What on Boss Michelle Guthrie's Sacking. *The Guardian*. https://www.theguardian.com/media/2018/sep/24/abc-in-turmoil-who-said-what-on-boss-michelle-guthries-sacking

Habermas, J. (1962, repr. 1991). *The Structural Transformation of the Public Sphere: An Inquiry Into a Category of Bourgeois Society* (T. Burger, Trans.). MIT Press.

Hawkins, G. (1997). The ABC and the Mystic Writing Pad. *Media International Australia, 83*, 11–17. https://doi.org/10.1177/1329878X9708300104

Humphries, B. (1991). *Selected Poems and Other Creatures*. Angus and Robertson.

Hyland, A. (2015, November 27). Mark Scott's ABC Exit Interview: 'I Had No Idea of the Scale of the Challenge'. *The Australian Financial Review*. https://www.afr.com/life-and-luxury/abcs-mark-scott-on-success-and-his-legacy-20151019-gkcgi8

Inglis, K. (1983). *The is the ABC: The Australian Broadcasting Commission 1932–1983*. Melbourne University Press.

Inglis, K. (2006). *Whose ABC? The Australian Broadcasting Corporation 1983–2006*. Black Inc.

Ireland, R. (2005). ABC of Collaborative Planning Forecasting and Replenishment. *The Journal of Business Forecasting, 24*(2), 3–4. http://search.proquest.com/docview/226915396/

Jackson, D., & Moloney, K. (2016). Inside Churnalism. *Journalism Studies, 17*(6), 763–780. https://doi.org/10.1080/1461670X.2015.1017597

Jane, E. A. (2018). Gendered Cyberhate as Workplace Harassment and Economic Vandalism. *Feminist Media Studies, 18*(4), 575–591. https://doi.org/10.1080/14680777.2018.1447344

Jütting, J. (2003). "Institutions and Development: A Critical Review". OECD Development Centre Working Papers. 210. OECD Publishing. https://doi.org/10.1787/341346131416

Kacała, T. (2015). Military Leadership in the Context of Challenges and Threats Existing in Information Environment. *Journal of Corporate Responsibility and Leadership, 2*(1), 9–21. https://doi.org/10.12775/JCRL.2015.001

Karvelas, P. (2007, August 14). 'Kick Swan Out' for Democrats Donation. *The Australian*. https://web.archive.org/web/20071203213618/http://www.theaustralian.news.com.au/story/0,25197,22241106-11949,00.html

Kidd, J., & Staff. (2014, November 25). ABC Cuts: Managing Director Mark Scott Announces More Than 400 Jobs To Go. *ABC News*. https://www.abc.net.au/news/2014-11-24/mark-scott-announces-abc-job-cuts/5913082?nw=0

Knott, M. (2014, February 5). ABC Admits Errors in Navy Burns Report on Asylum Seeker Claims. *The Sydney Morning Herald*. https://www.smh.com.au/politics/federal/abc-admits-errors-in-navy-burns-report-on-asylum-seeker-claims-20140204-31zft.html

Knott, M., & Hunter, F. (2014, July 4). Partisan Appointments to ABC, SBS Selection Panel Crushed Rudd's Dream. *The Sydney Morning Herald*. https://www.smh.com.au/politics/federal/partisan-appointments-to-abc-sbs-selection-panel-crushes-rudds-dream-20140704-zsvkz.html

Knox, D. (2017, April 8). New-Look ABC News Ditches News 24. *TV Tonight Blog*. https://tvtonight.com.au/2017/04/new-look-abc-news-ditches-news-24.html

Kornberger, M. (2009). *The brand society: How brands transform management and lifestyle*. Cambridge University Press. Cambridge.

Kramer, L. (1983). This Is the ABC: The Australian Broadcasting Commission, 1932–1983 by Ken S. Inglis. *Australian Book Review, 56*. Melbourne University Press.

Laffont, J.-J., & Tirole, J. (1991, November). The Politics of Government Decision-Making: A Theory of Regulatory Capture. *The Quarterly Journal of Economics, 106*(4), 1089–1127. https://www.jstor.org/stable/2937958

Lawrence-Lightfoot, S. (1999). *Respect: An Exploration.* Perseus Books.

Leaderonomics.com. (2018, March 29). The Pitfalls of Servant Leadership. https://leaderonomics.com/leadership/the-pitfalls-of-servant-leadership

Lee, A. J. (1976). *The Origins of the Popular Press in England. 1855–1914.* Croom Helm.

Leftwich, A., & Sen, K. (2010). 'Beyond Institutions: Institutions and Organisations in the Politics and Economics of Poverty Reduction - a Thematic Synthesis of Research Evidence'. IPPG Research Consortium on Improving Institutions for Pro-Poor Growth, University of Manchester. Retrieved from: https://gsdrc.org/document-library/beyond-institutions-institutions-and-organisations-in-the-politics-and-economics-of-poverty-reduction-a-thematic-synthesis-of-research-evidence/

Levine, L. W. (1988). Highbrow/Lowbrow. Harvard University Press. Cambridge Mass.

Levine, M., & Forrence, J. (1990). Regulatory Capture, Public Interest, and the Public Agenda: Toward a Synthesis. *Journal of Law, Economics, & Organization, 6*, 167–198. www.jstor.org/stable/764987

Lewis, R., Rowe, M., & Wiper, C. (2017). Online Abuse of Feminists as An Emerging Form of Violence Against Women and Girls. *British Journal of Criminology, 57*(6), 1462–1481. https://academic-oup-com.wwwproxy1.library.unsw.edu.au/bjc/article/57/6/1462/2623986

Lewis, S. (2000, December 2). Swan Stands Aside While Labor Party Implodes. *The Australian Financial Review Weekend.* https://www.afr.com/politics/swan-stands-aside-while-labor-party-implodes-20001202-jl3ic

Lewis, S. (2009, March 17). Rudd Vows Bipartisan ABC Board. *News.com.au.*https://www.news.com.au/national/rudd-vows-bipartisan-abc-board/news-story/ceac18bd56ef5ff51aed0b9b58140d1b?sv=8d7361759668930309443ad4dee66a24

Lindenberg, S. (1998). The Cognitive Turn in Institutional Analysis: Beyond NIE, and NIS? *Journal of Institutional and Theoretical Economics, 154*(4), 716–727. Zeitschrift Für Die Gesamte Staatswissenschaft. https://primoa.library.unsw.edu.au/permalink/f/11jha62/TN_cdi_webofscience_primary_000165539200010CitationCount

Littlemore, S. (1996). The media and me. ABC Books for the Australian Broadcasting Corporation. Sydney.

Liu, H. (2020). *Redeeming Leadership. Chapter: Undoing Leadership.* Bristol University Press. https://www.jstor.org/stable/j.ctvtv93zk

Loseke, D. R. (2007). The Study of Identity as Cultural, Institutional, Organizational, and Personal Narratives: Theoretical and Empirical Integrations.

The Sociological Quarterly, 48(4), 661–688. https://doi.org/10.1111/j.1533-8525.2007.00096.

Lynch, J. (2014, November 22). ABC Redirected Funds, Says Lib MP. *The Australian Financial Review*, p. 5.

M2 Presswire. (2016). Optus Partners with ABC Commercial to Revolutionise Retail Employee Wellbeing. http://search.proquest.com/docview/1815277669/

Magsaysay, J. F., & Hechanova, M. R. M. (2017). Building an Implicit Change Leadership Theory. *Leadership & Organization Development Journal, 38*(6), 834–848. http://dx.doi.org.wwwproxy1.library.unsw.edu.au/10.1108/LODJ-05-2016-0114

Manne, R. (2007, December–2008, January). New Teeth for Aunty: Reinvigorating the National Broadcaster. *The Monthly*, p. 40. https://www.themonthly.com.au/monthly-essays-robert-manne-new-teeth-aunty-reinvigorating-national-broadcaster-749#mtr

Martin, F. (2002). Beyond Public Service Broadcasting? ABC Online and the User/Citizen. *Southern Review: Communication, Politics & Culture, 35*(1), 42–62. https://search-informit-com-au.wwwproxy1.library.unsw.edu.au/documentSummary;dn=743199784542203;res=IELAPA

McChesney, R. W. (1997). *The Mythology of Commercial Broadcasting and the Contemporary Crisis of Public Broadcasting*. University of Wisconsin-Madison.

McDowell, D. H. (1975). *The Development and Educational Role of Schools of Arts in England: And Their Influence on the Development and Educational Role of Schools of Arts in Australia*. Masters Thesis. http://handle.unsw.edu.au/1959.4/61038

McGuire, J., Rhodes, G., & Palus, C. (2008). Inside Out: Transforming Your Leadership Culture. *Leadership in Action, 27*, 3–7. https://doi.org/10.1002/lia.1226

McKnight, D. (1998, May). Broadcasting and the Enemy Within: Political Surveillance and the ABC, 1951–64. *Media International Australia, Incorporating Culture & Policy, 87*, 35–48. https://search-informit-com-au.wwwproxy1.library.unsw.edu.au/documentSummary;dn=093749146204159;res=IELLCC

Molomby, T. (1991). *Is There a Moderate on the Roof? ABC Years*. William Heinemann.

Morahan-Martin, J. (2005). Internet Abuse. Social Science Computer Review. 23:1. Pp. 39–48. https://doi.org/10.1177/0894439304271533

Murray, J. (1994, July–December). The Institutional Origins of ABC Censorship in the 1930s [online]. *Australian Journalism Review, 16*(2), 125–131. https://search-informit-com-au.wwwproxy1.library.unsw.edu.au/documentSummary;dn=960808235;res=IELAPA

Name-Correa, A. J., & Yildirim, H. (2018). A Capture Theory of Committees. *Public Choice, 177*(1), 135–154. https://doi.org/10.1007/s11127-018-0593-6

Nelson, K. E. (2003). The Melbourne Philharmonic Society Under Contract to the Australian Broadcasting Commission: Preservation and Triumph [online]. *Context: Journal of Music Research, 25*(Autumn), 25–33. http://search.proquest.com/docview/200101339/

Nerone, J., & Barnhurst, K. G. (2003). US Newspaper Types, the Newsroom, and the Division of Labor, 1750-2000. *Journalism Studies, 4*(4), 435–449. https://doi.org/10.1080/1461670032000136541

North, D. (1990). *Institutions, Institutional Change and Economic Performance.* Political Economy of Institutions and Decisions. Cambridge University Press. https://doi.org/10.1017/CBO9780511808678

Northouse, P. G. (2010). *Leadership : Theory and Practice* (5th ed.). Sage Publications. Thousand Oaks.

Northouse, P. G. (2013). *Leadership: Theory and Practice* (6th ed.). Sage Publications.

O'Brien, K. (2018). *Kerry O'Brien: A Memoir.* Allen and Unwin.

Olson, M. (1965). *The Logic of Collective Action: Public Goods and Theory of Groups.* Harvard University Press. Cambridge, Mass.

O'Mallon, F. (2020, May 4). ABC Lost More Than $350m Per Year: Report. *The West Australian.* https://thewest.com.au/politics/abc-lost-more-than-350m-per-year-report-ng-s-2008375

Orr, G. D. (2010, June). The Australian Experience of Electoral Bribery: Dealing in Electoral Support. *Australian Journal of Politics & History*, p. 232. https://www.researchgate.net/publication/47456681

Oxford English Dictionary. (2021). https://www-oed-com.wwwproxy1.library.unsw.edu.au/view/Entry/141512?redirectedFrom=personnel&

Petersen, N. (1993). *News Not Views: The ABC, the Press, & Politics. 1932–1947.* Hale and Iremonger.

Pircher Verdorfer, A. (2019). The Paradox of Serving: Can Genuine Servant Leadership Gain Followers' Respect for the Leader? Evidence from Germany and Lithuania. *German Journal of Human Resource Management, 33*(2), 113–136. https://doi.org/10.1177/2397002218793840

Potter, M. R., Olejarski, A. M., & Pfister, S. M. (2014). Capture Theory and the Public Interest: Balancing Competing Values to Ensure Regulatory Effectiveness. *International Journal of Public Administration, 37*, 638–645. https://doi.org/10.1080/01900692.2014.903266

Powe, J. (2010, November). Public Service Leadership in Times of Significant Change and Uncertainty. *The International Journal of Leadership in Public Services, 6*(4). https://www-emerald-com.wwwproxy1.library.unsw.edu.au/insight/content/doi/10.5042/ijlps.2010.0631/full/pdf?title=when-the-going-gets-tough-public-service-leadership-in-times-of-significant-change-and-uncertainty

Pureza, A. P., & Lee, K. (2020). Corporate Social Responsibility Leadership for Sustainable Development: An Institutional Logics Perspective in Brazil. *Corporate Social Responsibility and Environmental Management, 27*(3), 1410–1424. https://doi.org/10.1002/csr.1894

Rickard, J. (2003). Symposium: Choral Music in Melbourne—"Messiahs," "Elijahs" and All that Jazz: Melbourne Musical Taste Between the Wars. *Context*, 35–39. http://search.proquest.com/docview/1465088/

Robbins, S., Judge, T. A., Edwards, M., Sandiford, P., Fitzgerald, M., & Hunt, J. (2019). *Organisational Behaviour* (9th ed.). EBook. Pearson Education Australia. http://ebookcentral.proquest.com/lib/unsw/detail.action?docID=5220538

Robertson, J. (2015, June 26). ABC Offices in Security Lockdown After Threats Following Q&A Zaky Mallah Episode. *The Sydney Morning Herald*. https://www.smh.com.au/politics/federal/abc-offices-in-security-lockdown-after-threats-following-qa-zaky-mallah-episode-20150626-ghy48b.html

Robinson, N. (2015, July 1). Q&A guest Zaky Mallah Hits Back with New Gang-Bang Tweets. *The Australian*. https://www.theaustralian.com.au/business/media/qa-guest-zaky-mallah-hits-back-with-new-gangbang-tweets/news-story/fe0701f40bc64bc45b2053194949d81c

Roy Morgan. (2019, July 22). ABC Still Most Trusted—Facebook Improves. *Finding 8064*. http://www.roymorgan.com/findings/8064-abc-remains-most-trusted-media-201907220424

Sainsbury, M. (2007). Media. The Australian. 6 December 2007.

Salter, D. (2007). *The Media We Deserve: Underachievement in The Fourth Estate*. Melbourne University Press.

Sanchez Perry, H. (2017). Intersectionality as an Institution: Changing the Definition of Feminism. *DePaul Journal of Women, Gender and the Law,* 7(1), 140–174. https://via.library.depaul.edu/jwgl/vol7/iss1/4

Sanders, P. (2020). In K. Bezio & G. Goethals (Eds.), *Leadership, Populism, and Resistance*. Edward Elgar Publishing.

Sanderson, W. (2000, November 27). "Preferential Treatment". 7.30 Program. *ABC Television*. Broadcast. http://www.abc.net.au/7.30/stories/s217353.htm

Schubert, M., & Canberra Bureau. (2007, August 14). Costello Attacks Swan Over Democrats Money. *The Age*. https://www.theage.com.au/national/costello-attacks-swan-over-democrats-money-20070814-ge5kuv.html

Scott, B. (2000). Consulting on the inside: an internal consultant's guide to living and working inside organizations. Alexandria, VA: American Society for Training & Development.

Scott, W. R. (2008). Institutions and organizations: ideas and interests (3rd ed.). Sage Publications. Thousand Oaks, Calif.

Scott, M. (2015, June 26). ABC Is a Public Broadcaster, Not a State Broadcaster. *The Sydney Morning Herald*. https://www.smh.com.au/opinion/abc-is-a-public-broadcaster-not-a-state-broadcaster-20150625-ghxt5m.html

Scott, M. (2016). *A Media Odyssey: Speeches of an ABC Managing Director 2006–2016*. ABC Books.

Scott, W. R. (1994). Conceptualizing Organizational Fields: Linking Organizations and Societal Systems. In H.-U. Derlien, U. Gerhardt, & F. W. Scharpf (Eds.), *Systems Rationality and Partial Interests* (pp. 203–221). Nomos Verlagsgesselschaft.

Scott, W. R. (2001). *Institutions and Organizations* (2nd ed.). Sage in S. Yousafzai, S.

Seccombe, M. (2014, November 29–December 5). What Mark Scott Is Really Doing with the ABC Cuts. *The Saturday Paper, 40*. https://www.thesaturdaypaper.com.au/news/media/2014/11/29/what-mark-scott-really-doing-with-the-abc-cuts/14171796001308

Seccombe, M. (2016, December 3–9). Senior ABC Staff Say Michelle Guthrie 'Out of Her Depth'. *The Saturday Paper, 137*. https://www.thesaturdaypaper.com.au/news/media/2016/12/03/senior-abc-staff-say-michelle-guthrie-out-her-depth/14806836004053

Seccombe, M. (2020, May 9–15). Hundreds Facing the Sack with ABC Cuts. *The Saturday Paper, 300*. https://www.thesaturdaypaper.com.au/news/politics/2020/05/09/hundreds-facing-the-sack-with-abc-cuts/15889464009792

Selznick, P. (1949). *TVA and the Grass Roots* (p. 146). University of California Press. Quoting Key, V. O. Politics and Administration. In L. D. White (Ed.) (1942), *The Future of Government in the United States*. University of Chicago Press.

Selznick, P. (1957). *Leadership in Administration*. University of California Press.

Semmler, C. (1981). *The ABC—Aunt Sally and Sacred Cow*. Melbourne University Press.

Shand, W. (2015). *Exploring Institutional Change: The Contribution of Co-Production to Shaping Institutions*. International Institute for Environment and Development, Chapter 2, pp. 6–8. www.jstor.org/stable/resrep18045.4

Shaw, S. J. (1959). Colonial Newspaper Advertising: A Step Toward Freedom of the Press. *Business History Review (pre-1986), 33*(000003), p. 409. http://search.proquest.com/docview/205528871/

Similar Web. (2020). Top Websites Ranking. https://www.similarweb.com/top-websites/australia

Simões, R. B., & Silveirinha, M. J. (2019). Framing Street Harassment: Legal Developments and Popular Misogyny in Social Media. *Feminist Media Studies*, 1–17. https://doi.org/10.1080/14680777.2019.1704816

Simons, M. (2008, January 30). No New Logo for the ABC But Rebranding on the Cards. *Crikey.com*. https://www.crikey.com.au/2008/01/30/no-new-logo-for-the-abc-but-rebranding-on-the-cards/

Simon, R. & Sykes Wylie, M. (2021). Comment by S. Turkle. Technology: Tool for Therapeutic Connection, or a Hindrance? Psychotherapy Networker. Posted: 11 Jun 2021. Retrieved from: https://www.psychotherapynetworker.

org/blog/details/521/technology-tool-for-therapeutic-connection-or-a-hindrance?_ga=2.195534188.1776400064.1626134387-711596993.1626134387

Spadaro, S. J. A. (2020, January 20). Defy the Apocalypse. *La Civiltà Cattolica.* https://www.laciviltacattolica.com/defy-the-apocalypse/

Spears, L. C. (2002). Tracing the Past, Present and Future of Servant Leadership. In L. C. Spears & M. Lawrence (Eds.), *Focus on Leadership: Servant Leadership for the 21st Century.* John Wiley & Sons.

Stacey, R., & Griffin, D. (2006). *Complexity and the Experience of Managing in Public Sector Organizations.* Routledge.

Starling, G. (2008). *Managing the Public Sector* (8th ed.). Thomson Wadsworth.

Stephens, M. (2007). *A History of News* (3rd ed.). Oxford University Press.

Stigler, G. J. (1971). The Theory of Economic Regulation. *The Bell Journal of Economics and Management Science, 2*(1, Spring), 3–21. https://www.jstor.org/stable/3003160

Styles, J. (2002, April). *The ABC: Unique Unto Itself. The Institute of Public Affairs Review: A Quarterly Review of Politics and Public Affairs.* Institute of Public Affairs. https://search.informit.org/doi/10.3316/ielapa.200203149

Swan, W. (2001, February 26). Grievance Debate. Australian Labor Party: Queensland. *House of Representatives Hansard*, p. 24394. https://parlinfo.aph.gov.au/parlInfo/search/display/display.w3p;db=CHAMBER;id=chamber/hansardr/2001-02-26/0129;query=Id:%22chamber/hansardr/2001-02-26/0000%22

Tengblad, S. (2012). *The Work of Managers Towards a Practice Theory of Management.* Oxford University Press.

Thomas, A. (1980). *Broadcast and be Damned: The ABC's First Two Decades.* Melbourne University Press.

Thornton, P. H. (2004). *Markets from Culture: Institutional Logics and Organizational Decisions in Higher Education Publishing.* Stanford University Press.

Tomlinson, M., O'Reilly, D., Wallace, M., Edwards, G., Elliott, C., Iszatt-White, M., & Schedlitzki, D. (2013). Developing Leaders as Symbolic Violence: Reproducing Public Service Leadership Through the (Misrecognized) Development of Leaders' Capitals. *Management Learning, 44*(1), 81–97. https://doi.org/10.1177/1350507612472151

Turkle, S. (1995). *Life on the screen: identity in the age of the Internet.* Simon & Schuster. New York.

Uldam, J. (2016). Corporate Management of Visibility and the Fantasy of the Post-Political: Social Media and Surveillance. *New Media & Society, 18*(2), 201–219. https://doi.org/10.1177/1461444814541526

Van Der Houwen, F., & Sliedrecht, K. (2016). The Form and Function of Formulations: Co-Constructing Narratives in Institutional Settings. *Journal of Pragmatics, 105.* http://search.proquest.com/docview/2061520159/

van Dierendonck, D., & Patterson, K. (Eds.). (2010). *Servant Leadership: Developments in Theory and Research.* Palgrave Macmillan.

Voxted, S. (2017). 100 Years of Henri Fayol. *Management Revue, 28*(2), 256–274. https://doi.org/10.5771/0935-9915-2017-2-256

Walker, R. R. (1973). *The Magic Spark: Fifty Years of Radio in Australia.* The Hawthorn Press.

Wallace, D. M., Raver Luning, C., Rosenstein, J. E., Ledford, A., & Cyr-Roman, B. (2020). A Culture of Respect: Leader Development and Preventing Destructive Behavior. *Industrial and Organizational Psychology, 13*(2), 225–229. https://doi.org/10.1017/iop.2020.46

Wander, F. (Ed.). (2013). The Servant Leader. Chap. 10 in *Transforming IT Culture* (pp. 123–136). Wiley.

Warburton, J. W. (1963). Schools of Arts. *The Australian Quarterly, 35*(4), 72–80. https://doi.org/10.2307/20633919

Warren, A. M., Sulaiman, A., & Ismawati Jaafar, N. (2014). Social Media Effects on Fostering Online Civic Engagement and Building Citizen Trust and Trust in Institutions. *Government Information Quarterly, 31*, 291–301. www.elsevier.com/locate/govinf

Whetstone, J. T. (2002). Personalism and Moral Leadership: The Servant Leader with a Transforming Vision. *Business Ethics: A European Review, 11*(4), 385–392. https://doi.org/10.1111/1467-8608.00298

Whitehead, G. (1988). *Inside the ABC: Geoffrey Whitehead's Personal Account.* Penguin Books Victoria.

Williams, R. (1996). Normal Service Won't Be Resumed: The Future of Public Broadcasting. Allen & Unwin. Crows Nest. Sydney.

Williams, K. (2010). *Read All About It: A History of the British Newspaper.* Routledge.

Williams, M. (2006). *Virtually Criminal: Crime, Deviance and Regulation Online.* Routledge.

Wilson, C. K., Hutchinson, J., & Shea, P. (2010). Public Service Broadcasting, Creative Industries, and Innovation Infrastructure: The Case of ABC's Pool. *Australian Journal of Communication, 37*(3), 15–32. https://primoa.library.unsw.edu.au/permalink/f/11jha62/TN_informit_apaft201102742

Wooten, M., & Hoffman, A.J. (2008). Organizational Fields: Past, Present and Future. Chap. 4 in R. Greenwood, C. Oliver, R. Suddaby, & K. Sahlin-Andersson (Eds.), *The SAGE Handbook of Organizational Institutionalism.* SAGE Publications.

Wright, B. E., Moynihan, D. P., & Pandey, S. J. (2012). Pulling the Levers: Transformational Leadership, Public Service Motivation, and Mission Valence. *Public Administration Review, 72*(2), 206–215. The American Society for Public Administration. https://doi.org/10.1111/j.1540-6210.2011.02496.x

CHAPTER 3

The ABC: Service for Funding

3.1 ABC Staff: To Serve through Service

This chapter (and indeed this book) argues that more than ever there is a need for public service media in Australia. But the corollary of this is that it needed to re-invent itself, preserve or reconstitute its values, to provide the much-needed plurality of an increasingly divided, polarised world. Media has provided the platform for serious divisions to emerge and be cultivated, not of itself serious but it has come at the expense of collaboration, considered debate and negotiation which has been drained in favour of clash, hatred and entertainment. It is taking democracy down a slippery slope with extreme and often over-simplifying binarised views gaining ascendancy representative of public views in the belief it is aiding the common good.

This chapter makes the point that public institutions, like the ABC, can be changed and transitioned without destroying them. Public broadcasting institutions could create a neutral space where structured debate is restored augmented by a non-partisan support of accurate information and facts. The ABC could present an adjunct to the strident voices and overwhelmingly introverted, emotion-focus of social media. It can provide a civic forum for the dissemination and appraisal of understandings, an antidote to nugatory disinformation and destructive, at times deliberately humiliating negativity. This chapter argues that the ABC's voice

V. Small, *Strangling Aunty: Perilous Times for the Australian Broadcasting Corporation*,
https://doi.org/10.1007/978-981-16-0776-9_3

could be threatened with strangulation on three fronts: economic, internal staff culture where idiosyncratic and reactive staff culture has caused a management incapacity and assuming the commercial values of digitisation. What seems to have been overlooked in the debate about the future of public media, specifically in the Australian context is not only the lack of gravitas accorded to the work of public servants but also, and critically, ABC staff—who are public servants too. They already have a unique, specialised role, responsibility and mission within the Australian public service. It will be investigated in this chapter.

On 1 July 1932 at the Australian Broadcasting Commission's taking control of Australian broadcasting, Stuart Doyle, co-founder of its predecessor the Australian Broadcasting Company, said presciently "the history of Australian Government enterprises had not been a happy one, but he hoped the new Commission would prove the exception to the rule" (*The Sydney Morning Herald*, 1932).[1] The ABC is definably public service, yet not quite public service because its status is nuanced. The ABC is a corporation and separate from the public service because of its corporation status, having obtained this separation from the Public Service Board in 1983 when it was given a Charter. To add to the complexity, it is "a component of the establishment media. Like the corporate media it privileges official government and corporate news sources" (Bainbridge, 2018)[2] yet ABC employees are public servants, paid by the public to provide it a service. The repetitive, consistent use of the word "service" by ABC management and in utterances around the ABC's original mission demonstrates that there is an awareness of that permanent role. In 2018 the Managing Director David Anderson told the National Press Club: "No matter who you are, where you live, who you vote for, we are here to serve all Australians, now and for generations to come" (ABC, 2018).[3] In ABC leadership itself, familial public service is valued and recurs: the former Managing Director Mark Scott came from "a family tradition of public service" (Murray, 2006b)[4,5] and the current Chair Ita Buttrose's father, Charles Buttrose, was a former ABC Assistant General Manager. There have been many other instances, historically, of members of families employed at the ABC, concurrently and subsequent to each other.

ABC employees are paid wages by the public, as are other Australian public servants yet they are now conflicted and problematised as a result of competing directly with commercial media in their new emergent commercial field. ABC employees now compete with "show biz" but are not "show biz", yet they "tread the boards" on the same stage, although perhaps performing in different sectors of the nine parts of a stage. As academics Richard Harding wrote in 1979 and was reiterated by Glyn Davis (1988) the institution carries out a diverse variety of roles—what Harding (1979) described as "service tasks"[6] which is a very individuating set of expectations. Therefore, this chapter will begin with an examination of the meaning of public servant and what literally and symbolically it means to Australia's democratic nation and commonwealth. It will discuss how public servants serve Australians. Public broadcasting was central to a democratic media because it was best placed to access and discern the values of the citizens in the public sphere because of its universal ownership and concern for all (Curran, 1991).[7]

The ABC has dual roles—as public broadcasting plus public service, or research institution as well as a public role (Nature, 1978).[8] The public role of institutions has a long history and can be represented in other areas of public, civil engagement. A 1753 UK Act of Parliament, for example, instituted a renowned British public facility, the British Museum, stating: "the said Museum or Collection may be preserved and maintained, not only for the Inspection and Entertainment of the learned and the curious, but for the general Use and Benefit of the public" (ibid.).[9] The formation of the British Museum in the eighteenth century spoke to the value of public assets and repositories of knowledge and learning and the service they provided through the work of their public servants. This essential role has not changed, only the technology, work conditions and means of sharing that information and knowledge.

The academic research demonstrated that public servants were mostly a committed and dedicated cohort and the basis of public service ethos suggests that public sector professionals are "motivated to perform helping behaviors due to an intrinsic value system that includes altruistic behavior as well as a belief in a 'public service ethos'" (Audit Commission, 2002; Hebson et al., 2003; Le Grand, 2003; quoted in Rayner et al., 2012).[10] In addition, it has been shown that public servants demonstrate Organizational Citizenship Behaviour (OCB) by working longer hours to complete a task or project (Bolino & Turnley, 2003).[11] This attitude and commitment also help build-up the 'social capital' of the organisation (Bolino et al., 2002)[12] in supporting its reliability and commitment to serve. To serve is to look after the broad public interest through transparent governance aimed at supporting social cohesion, generally. Similarly, the role of the Governor-General of Australia, as a public servant, has a cohesive role in Australian governance. Although the role of Governor-General was disparaged in some recent literature as being too costly. While in 2021 there had been a drop in support (34 per cent) among Australians for the nation to become a republic (the lowest recorded since 1979 by Ipsos and Nielsen polls) (Topsfield, 2021), elsewhere the trend in Head of State appointments was criticised as favouring "old army men" who report to "no one" (Schultz & Napier-Raman, 2020).[13]

In the case of the ABC, its service is to supply all Australians with news, information and entertainment. Many actors in society seek to serve; some are paid, others are unpaid: scientists (Beachy, 2003),[14] community volunteers, religious volunteers, jurors, charity workers, blood donors (unpaid in Australia) and volunteer fire fighters all form this cohort of servers. David Marquand (2004) argued that the public service was created to guard the public good from the marketplace at a time when "citizenship" and "equality" were emerging in the late nineteenth and early twentieth centuries (Marquand, 2004).[15] He asserted that the public service had declined due to the emergence of the New Right in the latter twentieth century and the overlaying of public sector bodies with private sector managerialism and marketisation: efficiencies, targets and outcomes, competitiveness and economies of scale. These were criticised in the literature as "inherently inefficient" (Dorey, 2015)[16] expectations overlaid on the public service. Targets are seen as contradictory to "public service", which can have unquantified reverberations through generations and unseen parties.

Service can be viewed through a religious perspective as well as a secular, ethical prism. Either way, the notion of 'to serve' and 'service' has a very long human history. The origins of 'service' bear analysis because of the strong ethical and moral links it has within Australian society, and, in the context of this analysis, public service and public service broadcasters. The ancient Greek philosopher, Plato, devised an education plan for training guardians—taken from the élite class—to serve, and it began in the womb and continued to age 50 (Arora, 2010)[17]; it involved "physical, intellectual, military, moral and practical education" (ibid.). These guardians, also called 'philosopher kings', were intelligent and educated and constituted the third tier of his proposed ideal city-state (workers first tier and soldiers second). These guardians' roles, atop society, were to make decisions for the betterment of society and to provide a service for the common good. This is somewhat akin to what the public service aspires to do and especially the desire of élite privileged actors in public broadcasting.

In Christian traditions, there is another emphasis on acts of service as being an equality of shared responsibility. St Paul's Letter to the Galatians exhorts the early church to serve and: "serve one another in love".[18] The Gospel of Matthew instructs "whoever wants to become great among you must be your servant, and whoever wants to be first must be your slave—just as the Son of Man did not come to be served, but to serve, and to give his life as a ransom for many".[19] Service has Judeo-Christian-Islamic origins and all the monotheistic faiths understand and acknowledge that service, or serving, is to put the needs of others first and, further, that service is doing the work of the divine. It is not servitude, it is enrichment. The religious context of "service" also touches on many of the institutions that "serve" parliamentary democracies. In a secular context, it means looking to better the situation of others and to pursue and value the positive outcomes that eventuate. This is also known as pro-social activity. The first US President George Washington[20] served as commanding general of the US army without pay, mostly because men who aimed to succeed in business or civic affairs were obliged to serve as military officers first (Hillman, 2009).[21] In the military, 'to serve' also carries a guardianship role where trained, armed people protect the unarmed people (Stiehm, 2002).[22]

In the world of art, service carries a religious meaning. When AMDG (Latin: Ad Majorem Dei Gloriam—or, to the greater glory of God) was added to the corner of a work of art, it was a sign by the great Renaissance painters, for example, that their labours were a form of altruism, to better society rather than line their purses. AMDG on artwork stated that the work was not an outburst of individual ego but an extension of the artist's spirit to create an alignment and understanding with the world of God's creation and intentions. It emphasised that there was a greater good to service, remote from selfish, egotistical interests. Christians believe it furthered what they describe as 'The Kingdom' and God's presence amongst them. When AMDG was first attached to art it was a then-Christian Roman Catholic view of the public service of art, and this is just one area in which the origins of "service" manifested in the entire Christian tradition implying "service to, and for, God". AMDG has a resonant meaning. It asks followers to remember that "man exists 'for the glory of God'. … [To] the greater glory of God' is not a mere label, but the baring of one's soul" (Horski, 1998, quoting W.J. Ong, 1952).[23] The famous Baroque composer Johann Sebastian Bach always included at the end of his musical scores the letters SDG (Latin: *Soli Deo Gloria*—Glory to God Alone) to affirm that his work was to glorify God and this was his testament 'to serve' through his musical compositions.

AMDG was the motto of Spaniard St Ignatius of Loyola, a soldier who became a priest and a saint. The Society of Jesus (Jesuit) order of priests and brothers Ignatius founded in 1540 propounded their mission was

AMDG as well as to "seek God in all things" (Georgetown University, 2018)[24] based on a spirituality "to know, love and serve".[25] Many generations of Roman Catholics educated in Australian Catholic schools were required to write AMDG on the top of each page of their school work to remind them that they did not exist for themselves alone and that they and their work must be alert to the service of others. As an example of how the Jesuits manifest service, amongst a wide remit of their activities, they have an "ecological apostate" furthering their vision for an "ecological conversion" (McCarthy & Karsh, 2007)[26] of people towards restoring and valuing the environment. The order said it had practical aspects that supported education on the environment, sustainable farming and forest conservation (ibid.).[27] In 1897, The Jewish Messenger newspaper was quoted in The New York Times: "the religion which most clearly discerns its real responsibilities and nearer duties is the religion for the times" (Jewish Messenger, 1897)[28] (the contrasting argument was articulated by Richard Dawkins, evolutionary biologist and atheist who said: "living organisms exist for the benefit of DNA" (Stove, 1992)[29]).

If it is believed—irrespective of religious, secular, or non-religious beliefs—that all human actions should, as their first priority, serve the greater good, then these actions should include, logically, defending good. Service involves risk and a tender vulnerability; there is always a risk that service is rejected, mocked or deprecated. Therefore, service—any service—requires courage. The point being made here is that there has been a strong cross-over from religious to secular understandings of service and their contributions to the greater good. Public servants work towards the non-religious and secular, but with similar, ambitions of "service" and the betterment of all. Public service motivation, however, is an understudied area of research (Pandey et al., 2012).[30] Australian barrister and writer Moira Rayner said:

> The public interest and the common good are not protected and promoted unless the values, the institutions and the processes set collective priorities in ways that: ensure that we do not privilege some groups over others; ensure that the processes work fairly—assuming fairness to be a democratic virtue; and ensure that its institutions are accessible. (Rayner, 1997)[31]

Service is enshrined in Australia's Constitution which describes elected representatives as rendering "service" and that the Federal Government provides "services" (Commonwealth of Australia).[32] Australian public servants are employed under the Public Service Act (1999) and the first value of the Australian public service enshrined in this legislation is that they are:

Committed to service

(1) The APS is professional, objective, innovative and efficient, and works collaboratively to achieve the best results for the Australian community and the Government. (10A Public Service Act, 1999)[33]

Five Australian Public Service values have been identified in the Public Sector Governance in Australia report:

1. societal values (e.g. community 'diversity'),
2. democratic values (e.g. 'the effectiveness and cohesion of Australia's democratic system of government'),
3. governmental values (e.g. ministerial responsibility),
4. workplace values (e.g. meritorious, non-discriminatory, and equal opportunity employment),
5. professional values (e.g. an 'apolitical', 'impartial', and 'professional' outlook, for the provision of 'frank, honest, comprehensive, accurate and timely advice' to the government of the day). (Edwards et al., 2012)[34]

Allied with this service is accountability. To serve the public good is a virtue (Northridge, 2009)[35] but answerable to taxpayers and citizens (Reddan, 2017).[36] In France, public service is considered a "noble" value because it has a long-term eye to the betterment of the people (ibid.)[37] but there are many understandings of public service. Ghosn (2015) explained that public service was: "characterized in opposition to the concept of 'private' because it guaranteed a principle of cohesion and unity, contrary to the private *field* which was more defined by the principle of diversification" (Ghosn, ibid.).[38] Public service serves all of society, does not pursue diversified matters, and thereby: "eliminates the risks of arbitrary decision, sovereignty and domination" (Loc. Cit.).[39] In more recent times there has been concern that public service facilities "favoured the upper classes and were unequally distributed" (ibid.).[40] The ABC's shift to the emergent commercial media *field* has therefore attracted criticism of its relevance and whether it was truly public, and really necessary when it has merged its content, originally intended for the cohesion of society, into a field that prioritises and values diversification. On the other hand, criticism of the ABC has been continual. In 1953, it was defended by Chairman Richard Boyer who said: "no other public institution in Australia was so consistently and violently criticised as the Australian Broadcasting Commission" (*The Courier-Mail*, 1953).[41] It has also had to listen to accusations from private media that it was a monopoly because it had privileged, élite, protected access; but it was never a monopoly, it just controlled its own exclusive *field*.

There are various arguments put forward that de-value the role of public service media. One put forward by US Presidential Republican Candidate Mitt Romney in 2012 was that commercial media could provide everything done by public broadcasting. A researcher looking into this called it "the Big Bird effect" (O'Mahen, 2016)[42]—the character from the US children's program Sesame Street created by the US Public Broadcasting Service (PBS). Romney argued that while Big Bird was appealing—commercial media could have created similar content—at no cost to the public. This fails to take into account the experimentalism possible in public media. O'Mahen's (2016) research found benefits of public broadcasting were that it was not beholden to shareholders waiting for profits, so public broadcasters have no pressing need to focus on audience size. It was argued that this, then, enhanced the political knowledge of the people (ibid.)[43] by not chasing consumer-related topics. Research has also found that PSB free-to-air television limits the profitability of pay-television and so commercial operations have to offer free-to-air in order to compete with the PSB (Torii, 2017).[44] Public broadcasters have an advantage where they can analyse, report and provide summative details on the state of the economy without pursuing sectional, financial interests, for example. Earlier, in 1980, the academic literature said: "public television is seen by many as a quality alternative to commercial fare" (Leroy, 1980) but that "however it has been measured, the profile of the audience for public television has turned out to be a well-educated, affluent minority" (ibid.).[45] That very point has been one directed at the ABC—as appealing only to the intelligentsia of Australian society with historic regularity, and this book provides instances where that occurred. Even the ABC's Director of News, Gaven Morris, was reported to have told an October 2020 staff meeting that there was too much ABC focus on the issues of interest to "inner-city left-wing elites" (Koziol, 2020).[46] The report said he told staff it was a concern directed at future funding, but the report later interviewed Morris who said his remarks related to the "public's perception" of the ABC (Koziol, ibid.). This book does not use the word élite as a pejorative and contests its current usage as such, because of its place within the theoretical institutional framework.

It should be noted here that public service broadcasting is not a generic internationally understood concept. The perceptions of an ABC audience member will not accord with those of audience members who consume public broadcasting in China and North Korea, for example, which function as public relations and propaganda bodies working on behalf of the state, as state broadcasters. In Australia and the UK (except the BBC is now a not-for-profit trust and in peril of privatisation), they have been designated as separate from direct government intervention and control, especially content. Locally, this is articulated in the ABC Charter and ABC Act of 1983. However, in spite of this, there has been an undeniable breakdown in the understanding of the public service and those whom the ABC serves through creeping commercialisation and its values, and managerialism. This chapter seeks to examine background to that shift.

The ABC now refers to its Australian citizens/audiences as "customers" (Milne, 2017).[47] This significant shift in nomenclature eliminates the concept of the greater good and places the citizen in the role of consumer who can "shop around", demand better and become commoditised. In that process the ABC has become a disposable commodity in the context of the public service, which was once the exemplar of public good. Now, the ABC has been forced/forced itself to re-define its role in a marketplace, competing with commercial services, using a shared language, marketing strategies and technology. Dawes (2017) said there were two critical factors precipitating this move—the public service had shifted to "market interests in the cultural sector" (quoting D. Hesmondhalgh, 2013) and had re-defined "public information" intended for public good as a "private commodity" (quoting N. Garnham, 1986).[48] This also had the effect of de-humanising people and their status in society because citizens have been stripped of their egalitarian dignity as "citizens". No longer people, they have become monetised objects in the economic system. John Stuart Mills warned in 1859 'On Liberty' (Image 3.1):

> The tendency of all the changes taking place in the world is to strengthen society, and diminish the power of the individual, this encroachment is not one of the evils which tend spontaneously to disappear, but, on the contrary, to grow more and more formidable. (Mills, 1859)[49]

And so, the public is already traumatised because of this erosion of respect, generally. Allied with this is a nostalgic memory of the public service broadcaster's attention to the greater good. The Australian public understands what it should expect from public service in a society based on "deeply held Australian values of democracy, freedom and respect for the

Image 3.1 "The ABC stands corrected." Cartoon by Andrew Dyson, *The Age. Fairfax Photos. Nine.* Published 17 October 2006. Re-printed with permission from the artist. The cartoon was published in the same edition of The Age (Melbourne) in which the then Managing Director, Mark Scott, had written an article: "Stamping out bias at the ABC" on changes that were to be implemented to improve its "editorial health" (ibid.). The characters depicted in the cartoon are the two main characters (B1 and B2) from the popular ABC children's television program "Bananas in Pyjamas"

individual" (Debell, 2015).[50] Alford and O'Flynn (2009) described three aspects to a public service organisation through the scholarship of Harvard Kennedy School's Professor Mark Moore's public value framework (1995) as a "strategic triangle" (ibid.). The organisation must first, create something of public value, second, be legitimate; and, third, attract support from political stakeholders. It also must be "operationally and administratively feasible" (Alford & O'Flynn, 2009).[51] Moore (1995) first described the Public Value of public service outfits. These consisted of: "value-creating enterprise that helps create the conditions for economic prosperity, civility in social relationships, and the advancement of justice"

(Moore & Benington, 2011, p. 257). While arguing for the Public Value of public service bodies, Moore (1995) said there needed to be reform as well as improved management as they coped with ongoing change and cautioned—that institutions' moves to decentralise "often depend crucially on the performance of lower level managers" (1995, p. 4). Complicating these expectations of public institutions further, not only Australian citizens should expect service, advancement and support from its public servants, so should Australian businesses, the other group of citizens in the societal framework (OECD, 2011).[52] In this case, citizens who may not necessarily be members of the ABC audience. Higton (2012) argued that this public mindset should also extend to a university (most of which were still considered public institutions in Australia because they received substantial public funding) and: "needs to be characterized by serious, socially inclusive, secular and religiously plural public arguments about the common good, and to promote such argument in the wider world by being thoroughly entangled in that world's conversational ecology" (ibid.).[53]

Counteracting this, society has been moving in a retrograde direction, infantilised by technology and gadgetry (Gottschalk, 2018)[54] where individuals are treated as ignorants fixated on evolving cultural norms of the media, attendant technology and algorithms curating (and cocooning) the consumer's beliefs and values. As a consequence, Western culture and its proprietors are encouraging a diminution of responsible adult behaviour that demonstrates "service to the common good" in favour of selfishness, insularity and chasing damage and revenge—"what's in it for me?". This retrograding is then impoverished by the snippets and fragments circulating in digital media that substitute for researched, contextualised and backgrounded news and information. Society's capacity to act and respond civilly has been maimed and downtrodden by the cheap and easy content that becomes part of the emergent commercial cycle of news media. Democracies have relied and thrived on its constituents working towards the greater good and being ably informed by a sufficiently robust media. Yet, democracies are suffering from a deficit of civic responsibility with the humble "selfie stick" a reminder of how introverted human needs have become, potentially walking backwards towards danger, yet so utterly and narcissistically self-absorbed. The Federal Government issued a reminder of citizenship to Australians during the novel Coronavirus pandemic: "Together we can help stop the spread and stay healthy".[55] The use of the words "together" and "we" were reminders to citizens of shared citizenship, shared responsibilities and shared duties. It is not a culture that is so tightly wedded to the "together" and "we", so the utterance was a subliminal reminder of that.

The Australian public service is challenged in many other ways, criticised as being "bloated" (Chambers & Brown, 2018)[56] and also wielding too much power over governments and policy. The Australian Government announced in 2019 departments would be reduced from 18 to 14, in favour of larger, fewer departments. Australian Prime Minister, Scott Morrison, said the changes would: "bust bureaucratic congestion and improve decision-making" (Chambers & Brown, 2018).[57] This shake-up was flagged earlier in 2019 when Morrison said: "we don't expect the public service to run the government. That's what we were elected to do" (Chambers & Brown, 2018). However, in announcing the changes later in the year Morrison said it was: "not about finding savings or efficiencies, but rather 'better aligning' the public service" (ibid.), the implication here that the public service had strayed from its mission to serve the public and had become politicised. The outstanding questions are: "if so, how has this happened?" and "who was responsible?".

There have been previous moves by governments to exercise greater control and influence over the workings of the public service, generally. In 2013, it was announced by the then Treasurer, Joe Hockey and then Minister for Finance, Mathias Cormann, there would be a *National Commission of Audit—Towards Responsible Government to review the public service through a Phase* One and a Phase Two Report. The Commission reviewed and reported on the performance, functions and roles of the Commonwealth Government. After it wrapped and reported, in 2014, its executive summary stated:

> Improving the overall efficiency and effectiveness of government will be heavily dependent on the performance of the public service. The *Public Service Act 1999* is the principal Act governing the establishment and operation of the Australian Public Service … does not contain any explicit references to the need to improve productivity in the public sector. However, **it does aim to establish a public service that is efficient and effective** and **requires secretaries of departments to manage 'the affairs of the department efficiently, effectively, economically and ethically'** (National Commission of Audit, 2014)[58] (my emphases)

Following the 2019 announcement of the cuts to departments and loss of department heads, the head of the Department of Communications and the Arts, Mike Mrdak (who later lost his job in the shake-up), expressed surprise at these government decisions but also said: "I will do my best with our SES (executive) team to ensure that there is as much certainty as possible for all of you, and our agencies, and a continuity of services for the community we serve" (Osborne, 2019. Researcher's underlining). Earlier in 2019, Mrdak complained about the jargon used by the Australian Public Service (such as "stakeholder" and "looking at things holistically") that put the public that it served at a distance (Easton, 2019).[59] He said the Australian Public Service (APS) was "uniquely in the people-business. In fact, we are a profession like few others, [in] that we are totally dependent on our personal relationships" (ibid.). Australian High Court Justice, Mary Gaudron, was quoted as having said in a judgement in 1995: "so much was recognised as the duty of kings … no less is required of a government and the courts of a civilised democratic society" (Rayner, 2009).[60]

The ABC is the Federal Government's emergency broadcaster, even though this is not stipulated in its Charter. However, as part of its role as public broadcaster and providing public benefit it is required to give bushfires and floods and any widespread devastation or emergency undivided and prioritised attention by all platforms of the ABC. However, after widespread devastating bushfires around Australia in 2019–2020, the cost of this 'on-call' coverage proved to be costly to the ABC. A statement released by the ABC (Duke, 2020) said:

> The cost of the ABC's emergency broadcasting coverage come out of base funding—there is no specific government funding for this coverage. These costs are growing. We will always prioritise coverage of emergency information and will continue to speak with government to ensure that we are adequately funded to serve the Australian public. (Duke, 2020)[61]

It was also reported that there were 670 emergency broadcasting events for the 2019–2020 financial year (to 3 January 2020) compared to 371 for 2018–2019 (and 256 events in 2017–2018) (ibid.). A representative for the Federal Communications Minister, Paul Fletcher, was quoted in the same article as saying there had been no request by the ABC for additional funding to support its emergency broadcasting but that "should such a request be made, the government will quickly consider it as part of a broader relief package" (ibid.). Like all other public services, the ABC has expectations overlaid to its role and also must make preparations and send signals ahead of budget allocation discussions.

A further conundrum for public servants (and the public broadcaster) is that the appetite for governments to pay for anything public has been waning and the economic consequences of the Coronavirus pandemic can only make it more difficult for public outfits to achieve sustained/increased funding when governments are draining coffers to support locked down workers and business. News reports that describe the ABC Managing Director, David Anderson, earning AUD1.14 million (2018–2019), a termination package of AUD1.35 million paid to former Managing Director Michelle Guthrie, and a total senior ABC management and Board bill of AUD6 million (AUD3.6 million 2017–2018) (Hunter, 2019)[62] are the public's reminder about the cost of the ABC. Yet, these sums are low compared with what their equivalents earn in the private/commercial media. For example, the CEO of Fairfax Media, Greg Hywood, earned AUD7.2 million in 2016 (Robertson & Meade, 2017).[63] At the same time, the ***reputational*** and ***cultural capital*** of the ABC goes unvalued. As a key Australian cultural institution and public service organisation it attracted and employed staff who were usually creative, motivated and willing to receive less pay than their counterparts in privately-owned media, or elsewhere in self-employment. Long-serving former staffer Ellis Blain complained of the long-term deleterious impact of this on staff: "the public service sees people as ciphers … and is fatal to creativity where the ego—for better or worse—is at the core" (Blain, 1977).[64]

Speaking in a broader context, Reserve Bank of Australia governor Philip Lowe was critical of the amount paid to CEOs in Australia:

> As a regular Australian, it disturbs me. Some people who are paid extraordinarily high amounts of money and working Australians have relatively low wages and getting small wage increases, I think it's an issue for the society. (Cranston, 2019)[65]

Lowe made an implicit plea for managers to turn their thoughts to the greater good: "people should be happy to deliver value to a company without $20 million pay" (Cranston, ibid.). Professor Carl Rhodes, deputy dean of the School of Business at the University of Technology Sydney, said the advent of the engorged pay packet for senior managers had its origins in the "heroisation" of a CEO from being "a bland, grey-suited character" (Robertson, 2019)[66] and the emergence of free markets and deregulation in the 1980s (Robertson, ibid.). The highest paid public servant in Australia was former Australia Post's Christine Holgate who earned AUD2.565

million in 2018–2019 (AUD1.646 million the previous year) (McIlroy & Cranston, 2019).[67] Holgate resigned in November 2020 after she had been stood aside two weeks earlier. It was reported to a Senate Estimates Committee hearing she had given four Cartier watches in 2018 to other senior executives as bonuses. This was at a time when mail deliveries were being reduced and the cost of parcel post rising. There were additional concerns raised from a four-week Federal Government investigation into Australia Post's financial management and governance finding that Holgate had spent AUD300,000 on corporate credit cards and chauffeur-driven cars in the 2019/2020 financial year (Visentin, 2020).[68] She is also alleged to have paid a reputation management firm AUD119,000 in the 2020 financial year between June and July (Visentin, ibid.). However, the literature also said that the treatment of her had been unfair because the: "view widely held in the industry is that the bonuses were within the normal operation practices of a commercial enterprise" (Alexander, 2021), and where cash bonuses go unremarked. Holgate's resignation announcement said: "I have made the difficult decision to resign, hoping it will allow the organisation to fully focus on serving our customers" (Clayton, 2020).

As previously discussed, there has been a deterioration in respect for civil engagement and even understandings of a civil society. When citizens have been "consumerised" and re-defined by the public service, it is no wonder that taxpayers are jaded by funding a public service—and then reports of this happen. The distinction has been lost in chasing private sector jargon and their profit-loaded objectives. Since the 1980s governments have been re-designing the public service to be "the primary administrator of social assistance" (Ouellette, 2008).[69] Publics are critical of governments for this shift for three reasons: a loss of the concept of citizenship, a wariness of where governments spend money and thirdly, increasing public incapacity to understand the distinction between the elected government with the public service. The waning of this contradistinction will be analysed later in this book. Also, "for the vast majority, both the sources of identity and the concerns of politics lay increasingly close to home, and are, correspondingly, more removed from national and collective activity (Bennett, 1998)[70]" and the ABC exists in an ecology where there has been: "a proliferation of disconnected public spheres flooded with personal concerns" (ibid.).[71] In other words, the ABC competes in a crowded emergent commercial arts *field* and while content favours individualised concerns, it asks for money to address a generalised Charter. There are implicit tensions between the two. Coupled with that the ABC competes with other publicly-funded activities from the same 'money pot'—ballet, opera, dance, orchestras, theatre, art galleries, libraries.

Further, the ABC vies with an odd assortment in the media *field*—including online retailers—all trying to "sell their wares". News becomes just another commodity jostling around the cyber-spaces and the capacity for audiences to sort the quality from the shabby; a huge task for a public broadcaster to finesse, as audiences are unknowingly being packaged-up and on-sold to other outlets for a price. The sometimes-attendant social media outrage accompanying news reports attracts the reader and so supports a profitable, profit-making, rent-seeking market. It is a situation that does not necessarily give a nuanced, contextual understanding of the activities of governments, their policies, economic strategies, the role of business and public service and their combined impact on the economy. This impoverishment of information results in a jaundiced and generalised view that "the privileged" are overwhelmingly out of control. In this reactive and superficial environment, that favours scandal and group outrage, it has become more difficult for the ABC to educate all Australians in their culture and national wellbeing and supply necessary information for all the electorate to sort, consider, chat about and vote upon. While Australians have been described as "early adopters of technology" (Missingham, 2009, p. 387), allied to this is that "Australia has some way to go before universal access is achieved" (Ibid.) and other research into access to digital Australian health services had found inequity where "access to, and use of, computers, the Internet and mobile phones varied considerably in extent, frequency and quality within and across groups due to differences in abilities, resources and life experience" (Newman et al., 2012, p. 125).

Finally, there exists the issue of a lack of sustained commitment by successive Federal Governments from both sides of politics to the ABC, more recently with serious cuts in 2014 of 2%, and an additional funding cut in 2016 of AUD20 million (based on a triennial funding arrangement of AUD3.1 billion). Historically, money has been a perennial problem for the ABC and shortfalls and compromises are nothing new. In 1946, for example, at a time of post-war austerity and federal budget deficits to pay for a world war the ABC argued for an increase in revenue (from its share of licence fees) because it said it was drawing down on reserves to maintain services and they had not been topped up for six years. Its words were truly prophetic:

> Unless the national broadcasting service can maintain its position in line with the current world standards … it must vacate the *field* (author's emphasis) in favour of a purely commercial system. (The Advertiser, 1946)[72]

The ABC has been situated in an institutional role described variously. Robert Manne (2007) said "there is almost no institution in Australia that is more generally trusted, valued and loved than the ABC" (ibid.).[73] In 2017 it was portrayed by the Federal Department of Communications as: "one of the country's most important cultural institutions".[74] But in 2019 the ABC was condemned by its former Head of Television, Kim Dalton as: "failing viewers and external producers ... while using its statutory independence to deflect valid criticism" (Dalton, 2017). Dalton (2017) added: "In every debate, in every discussion about the ABC's services, its operations, its allocation of resources ... the ABC draws the line, brings down the shutters, circles the wagons, and claims its independence" (ibid.).[75] Dalton (2017) was critical of a shift in institutional language where it resorted to defensive narratives and failed to deal with specific criticism. In addition, as a publicly-funded broadcaster, while independent of the government it was also reliant on it (and the people) for money and needed be alert and probably receptive to blow-back when it upset political or vested interests—it was a form of financial codependency. Nonetheless, bunkered ABC institutional thinking also has shown a lack of capacity to surveil its own performance. The former editor of Melbourne's *The Age* newspaper, Graham Perkin, made a comment about newspapers that could be extrapolated to the ABC. At Australia's 2012 Finkelstein inquiry into media and media regulation Perkin said:

> My great fear is that unless the newspaper industry establishes some form of self-surveillance ... then we will one day, perhaps soon, have surveillance forced upon us by Government. (Finkelstein, 2012)[76]

These words followed recommendations from the 2012 report by the Right Honourable Lord Justice Leveson's Inquiry into the Culture, Practices and Ethics of the Press which advised an independent regulatory body be set up to set standards of journalism and protect the citizens.[77] The inquiry was triggered by public furore over the Rupert Murdoch-owned now closed newspaper, *The News of the World*'s, phone hacking of a murdered teenager but as Lord Justice Leveson pointed out it was the "seventh time in less than 70 years" that the British Government had commissioned a report to investigate press concerns (ibid.).

In terms of any government's capacity to exercise control through manipulating public funding, the Organisation for Economic Cooperation and Development (2011) warned that "civil service cuts can concentrate the mind for necessary change and "doing things differently" (ibid.).[78]

Funding cuts and its capacity to focus mindsets are times of critical recrudescence for the ABC, or as Samuel Johnson (who wrote the first English dictionary in 1755) was said to observe about another terminal situation: "Depend upon it, sir, when a man knows he is to be hanged in a fortnight, it concentrates his mind wonderfully" (Boswell, 1851).[79]

3.2 The ABC as a Public Broadcaster

Public service broadcasting must be situated it in the context of its origins to see where it fits in the media ecology (Tracey, 2002).[80] It was established in Australia in the context of what is described as "unusual and trying circumstances" (Tracey, ibid.)[81] and remote from government, as Prime Minister Joseph Lyons said: "The Government would not agree to any political appointments to this organisation" (The Labor Daily, 1938).[82] Australia faced the arduous economic recovery from World War I: the substantial loss of a generation of 55,000 young Australians (Tibbitts, n.d.),[83] the pandemic Spanish' Flu which killed either around 12,000 Australians (Curson & McCracken, 2014),[84] or as many as 15,000 in a population of 5 million (Smith, 2020) followed by The Great Depression which hit in 1929. It is upon this basis that the beginnings of broadcasting were a moral force for good, to build-up communities and nationhood (as much as a want to control new technology) (Tracey, ibid.).[85] The rise of Nazism and Fascism in Europe were a background concern in growing worries about how other governments used propaganda to mould and manage national thinking. Radio was seen as particularly potent as a force for controlling the national mindset. In 1934, the newly-appointed ABC Chairman, William Cleary, said that the ABC's role was to: "harmonise the tastes of the community and to balance the programme so that consideration may be given to each section of listeners" (Central Queensland Herald, Rockhampton, 1934).[86] It was a very diluted reference to that fear.

In 1935, as newly-appointed ABC Commissioner James Kitto (former Deputy Director of Posts and Telegraphs) reflected on both the good of the public service in general and how it had helped the Australian economy recover from The Great Depression: "the spirit of the Commonwealth Public Service is to an extent responsible for the rehabilitation of this community, and for its emergence from the depths to which It had sunk" (The Sun, 1935).[87] Although described by Inglis (1983) as "a dour sixty-four-year-old former postal official" (ibid.)[88] who "left not much of a mark" on the ABC (Loc. Cit.);[89] Kitto was described by his peers as having been "deeply interested and active in the welfare of the community, particularly in the youth of the nation" (Newcastle Morning Herald & Miners' Advocate, 1935).[90] At his retirement from the ABC and in response to Country Party calls for an inquiry to investigate ABC broadcasting policy servicing rural areas, Kitto said:

> There never has been any failure by the Australian Broadcasting Commission to minister to the needs of country listeners ... and I shall be surprised if the reconstituted Commission will find it possible to give any further country service than there Is now. (The Sun, 1939)[91]

He and other commissioners were retired in favour of younger people (*Queensland Times*, 1937)[92] and new appointments were for one year only, increasing commissioners from five to seven and these positions made full-time. Some commissioners had also meddled with staff appointments and the hiring of artists so there was a perceived need to more clearly define and demarcate the role of the commissioners. Their actual role was to oversee and lay-out policy, while the general manager implemented the policy (*The Sydney Morning Herald*, 1939).[93] Overwhelmingly, however, "not one of them had any practical experience of broadcasting or any first-hand acquaintance with its technical problems before being appointed to the Commission" (*The Sydney Morning Herald*, 1939).[94] This has been a recurrent criticism of ABC board members (and managing directors) throughout the organisation's history (*The Sydney Morning Herald*, 1939[95]; *The Canberra Times*, 1978[96]; *Australian Associated Press*, 2018[97]). This perceived lack of broadcasting knowledge or experience from the board triggered the need for a separation of leadership authority and a strengthening of the powers of the general manager vis-à-vis the board. This tussle between ABC actors has been recurrent, the Managing Director and its board—then as now (Loc. Cit.). According to Bourdieu (1990) in this situation leaders exert *symbolic violence*. *Symbolic violence* is the power differential, the tension, between actors and a group, invisible not physical coercion.[98] Power, domination and social positioning are negotiated by institutional actors, and recipients of *symbolic violence* are compliant, resulting in this symbolic form of control (Tomlinson et al., 2013).[99] Therefore, it would be expected that the senior management team of the ABC would be building its (cultural) *capital* to accentuate its power and also legitimate leadership (ibid.)[100] through *symbolic violence*.[101] *Symbolic violence* can also be exerted by other actors or groups within the organisation, such as staff against management.

The manoeuvring in the public service and its objectives should be directed towards the "accomplishing side of government" (Starling, 2008)[102] where government policies are implemented. It is also the place where resources are "marshalled" and directed at public problems in the community (ibid.).[103] It is one of the "building blocks" of government (Loc. Cit.).[104] The formation of the ABC took place at a time when there was consideration given to offering access amid a scarcity of content and this, in addition to its government mandate, helped shaped the ABC along public service lines as a statutory authority providing a service. By the nature of being a taxpayer funded organisation, it has also been a regular target of attack from diverse interests where there have been accusations of imbalanced, offensive content (to be analysed in Chap. 4), its focus on supporting city-based offices Sydney and Melbourne at the expense of the so-called BAPH states (an ABC acronym for Brisbane, Adelaide, Perth and Hobart), declining regional and rural coverage (Juddery, 1976; Dawson, 1985)[105] and accusations of mis-spending of the public dollar, raised, notably, by the Federal Government's Dix Committee in 1980 (*The Canberra Times*, 1980).[106] Although, as Australian academic Glyn Davis pointed out the Dix Committee report of 1981 (known as the Committee of Review of the Australian Broadcasting Commission) actually showed the ABC placed too much responsibility on too few senior managers (Davis, 1988)[107] which slowed decision-making and created inefficiencies.

Elsewhere, there have been accusations of "board stacking" (Murray, 2006a[108]) where appointments have been derided as politically-motivated rather than in the best interests of the corporation. Former ABC broadcaster, Quentin Dempster, said the ABC board has been subjected to various political taintings since its inception in 1932 (Briggs, 2006).[109] In addition, there are concerns expressed about the outsourcing of ABC programs—but this privatisation by stealth through commercialisation is something that has been happening for decades. There have also been accusations of an expansionist Aunty. In 2007, SBS Managing Director Shaun Brown accused the former ABC Managing Director, Russell Balding, of lobbying the government to take over SBS. Brown said the consequence would have been "commercialisation by stealth of the ABC" (Pearlman, 2007).[110] As well, there are concerns that the ABC outsources content to commercial outfits who can then on-sell the product once their work with the ABC is done: "Increasingly the ABC makes few of the programs it broadcasts; it transmits material made by outside interests rather than produce its own" and "commercial interests ... don't make risky programs or explore unpopular issues" (Collins, 2011).[111] In 2004,

Murdock said public service was over: "public service broadcasting is a project whose time has finally come both philosophically and practically" (Murdock, 2004).[112]

ABC Radio was once a highly successful mass medium at a time of scarcity. Now, the reverse applies because the Australian media and the ABC are immersed in abundance. Content in the emergent digital commercial *field* is bountiful and the ABC is a keen distributor to new digital sources, away from traditional "outlets" of radio and television and favoured by "older" Australians, anyway. This anticipation is in the belief that: "the ABC can't afford to wait until they move to new platforms. It must be there waiting for them" (Simons, 2016).[113] The ABC digitised to become a player in this new online territory, Federal Government funding supported this re-positioning, and it is now platformed and augmented with websites and busy social media accounts. It has relinquished its élite *field* through a frenetic involvement of the ABC in digital commercial media. Yet because of the scale of the activity in the commercial *field* the ABC is convinced that, ipso fact, it is carrying out its Charter obligations by being 'all for all' simply by belonging to this emergent *field*. Planning for a digitising of the ABC began with Managing Director David Hill but was set in motion by Brian Johns who instigated ABC Online and "positioned it for the digital age" (Burrowes, 2016).[114] Yet the literature identified that when public institutions relinquished its ground in favour of private interests it was considered "public failure" (Andrejevic, 2013).[115] The ABC, for example, now competes with the Hydra's heads of social media (Hydra was a monster in Greek mythology with nine heads, lop off one and two will grow in its place) in supplying objective knowledge and impartial information. It is a congested public sphere no longer in an exclusive bond with traditional media outlets and where there is quality confusion—boundless. In addition, Swedish research has found that the decline in legacy media and the rise in "hyperlocal" media (targeted at people in a particular location) has resulted in "news deserts" (Nygren et al., 2018, p. 44) where there are absences of any coverage of people and topics in other communities. This calls into question the ABC's latest quest in 2021 for audiences by relocating a large cohort of staff to a western suburb of Sydney (Parramatta) to boost coverage of that area of Australia. Murdock (2004) argued that more than ever there was a need for public service media but it needed to re-invent itself (Ibid.)[116] rather than collapse itself into the crowd because it "has a pivotal role to play in building this digital commons" (Ibid.).

> In a situation where world views are increasingly polarised and talking across differences on a basis of knowledge and respect is more vital than ever to a working deliberative system, this hollowing out of collective space present a major challenge to democratic culture. (Loc. Cit.)[117]

Australia's public service media increasingly had "hybrid arrangements" (Burns & Hawkins, 2013)[118] which blurred boundaries between commercial and public. In the mix, mega organisations like Google are regarded aberrantly (according to the definition established in this book) and bizarrely as both a public service provider and a public utility (Andrejevic, 2013).[119] In addition, broadcasters have moved away from a "culture in common approach", once designated by editors and program-makers to one that sees culture and history as fluid and constantly being re-shaped by individuals in society (Murdock, 2004).[120] Because of this shift Murdock (2004) said public broadcasters could "counter fragmentation" (ibid.).[121] Further, public broadcasters could work with governments in a non-partisan way to provide accurate information to citizens, thereby upholding the struts of democracy and also providing the vaccine against disinformation that infiltrates Australian media via other nation states. This will be developed in Chap. 4—What Ideas Rule?

The ABC has an opportunity to provide fora dedicated to reasoned debate and discussion: "addressing problems through deliberation rather than force" (Murdock, 2004).[122] In 2018, Head of the ABC branch of the Community and Public Sector Union, Sinddy Ealy, reflected: "the public service ethos is vanishing from the upper echelons of the organisation. Paying it lip service in public forums is very different to imbibing it into the day to day operations of the ABC."[123] The reasons for the devaluing of public service is that it was regarded as a leftover of nineteenth-century Victorian society (Stacey & Griffin, 2006),[124] and therefore no longer tenable in a performance-managed, outcomes, targets-based, efficiencies era where the public service was compared unfavourably with its binaried other—the private sector (ibid.). The rush to meet targets means the private sector has become the apparent role model for the aspirational public service; its "good twin".

The concept of public service dates to the mid-fourteenth century (Cooper, 2014)[125] and strong areas of emphases for the role of public service have been communications and commerce (ibid.)[126] and by the latter part of the seventeenth century, governments began to deal with businesses separately rather than collectively, except those that had a "common" interest for the public (Loc. Cit.).[127] The notion of public good has a long and influential tail; it could not be embodied in a singular gift or moment but was an outcome of public service. The literature quoted an example of a court ruling from 1701 using a blacksmith as an example of public good obligations under common law:

> Whenever any subject takes upon himself a Publick [sic] Trust for the Benefit of the rest of his fellow Subjects, he is ... bound to serve the Subject in all the Things that are within the Reach and Comprehension of such an Office. ... If on the Road a Shoe fall off my Horse, and I come to a Smith to have one put on and the Smith refuse to do it, an Action will lie against him, because he has made Profession of a trade which is for the Publick Good. ... One that has made Profession of a Publick Employment is bound to the utmost Extension of that Employment to serve the Publick. (ibid.)[128]

So, not only organisations, individuals too are held accountable for their contributions to the public good because, for one reason, "the movement of goods and ideas is essential to the success of the capitalist economy and the democratic polity" (ibid.).[129] By the end of the nineteenth century public service obligations had become institutionalised (ibid.).[130] Yet with the spread of obligations and commitments of mass communication and connectivity, the role and viability of public service media has been increasingly under challenge and threat. Media abundance has not provided any security for the ABC as an individual entity, its cherished separateness once a unique quality of public service media.

Former senior Australian public servant, Jane Halton (2004) said: "there is now much greater emphasis on results, and on value-for-money in service provision ... but the

> Public service is not an end in itself. It exists to serve the needs of the Australian community—and the professional ethics that underlie it have not changed, despite the huge changes in the way we work and what we are working on." (Halton, 2004)[131]

Professor John Halligan (2001) identified two major periods of change for the Australian public service—from the 1880s to 1920s, then from the 1980s onwards (Halligan, 2001).[132] After the 1980s the literature identified this as a series of major cutbacks on public service staff numbers with the Federal Liberal Government's (Prime Minister Malcolm Fraser) reductions on expenditures (including the ABC). While ABC depicts government funding cuts as retribution it fails to see them as part of the overall profile of funding cuts to the public domain—many other institutions have suffered too. Following Fraser's cuts were those of the Federal Labor Governments' (Labor Prime Minister Bob Hawke and Prime Minister Paul Keating) then the Federal Liberal Government's reductions in the 1990s on staff numbers (Prime Minister John Howard) (Jones, 2002).[133]

Halligan (2001) said when the public service was formed in Australia it inherited the Westminster system as well as the colonial system: "the common elements included responsible government and an apolitical public service consisting of permanent professionals" (Halligan, 2001)[134] and "the concepts of public service and neutrality were established, as was the clear distinction between the official and political realms" (ibid.).[135] Although colonialism is now used as a pejorative, its iterations included and resulted in giving Australia a neutral ABC. The government had a role as "entrepreneur" from colonial times and hence the formation of the Commonwealth Bank in 1911, for example, and later the ABC in 1932 (Halligan ibid.)[136]; it also gave Australia its international airline Qantas (Queensland and Northern Territory Aerial Service), nationalised in 1947 and privatised in 1993; and a convict was made Australia's first postmaster in 1809 to collect mail from ships and sort it in his home (Australia Post, n.d.). The Postmaster General's Department (PMG) was established in 1902 to look after all of Australia's mail and the telephone (ibid.), with later having oversight of the ABC). Halligan (2001) said the future for the public service in Australia involved being:

> Flexible, pragmatic, innovative, responsive to environmental change and government agendas, performance focused but situated within a framework of accountability and public interest. (Halligan, 2001)[137]

Purging the public service of staff is a long, complicated and recurrent story. But as a 'for instance', in the 1950s Liberal Prime Minister Sir Robert Menzies made a failed attempt to trim the public service by 10,000 where "at base the dominant criterion for retrenchment appears to have been élitism: those in steerage go overboard first" (Jones, 2002).[138] At the time the Postmaster-General's Department (which still supervised the ABC) was asked for cutbacks and said that the department was already short of 5000 people. So, the review into getting rid of the staff was "a fizzer as ministers and departments sought to reclaim their turf" (Jones, 2002)[139] with only several hundred staff removed from the public service.

3.3 Impact of ABC Staff Culture

Q. What do you call a quiet Australian working at the ABC?
A. Lonely.[140]

This section will take an overview of aspects of conflict and division within the ABC in terms of staff culture and public service staff culture described in the academic and grey literature. It will situate understandings of how the public service mission of the ABC has been captured by a staff culture. This section examines the influence and impact of the staff culture on management capacity to bring about change. Firstly, this section will discuss how staff culture forms in general. Everywhere. Staff culture is a bonding social force but it is also a means of determining "who belongs to the group and who does not" (Winslow, 1999)[141]; it is an exclusionary device. Staff culture is a form of collective efficacy. Collective efficacy can have many benefits such as improving security, safety and health (Collins et al., 2014).[142] Further, it has been shown through research that team identity is a fundamental part of bonding social networks (Henttonen et al., 2014)[143] and that there is also competition among individuals for achieving a positive identity for themselves (ibid.)[144] within these networks.

Winslow (1999) said culture was "a social force that controls patterns of organisational behaviour".[145] A consequence of this is bonding, which is based on the theory of social capital. This means a bonded team will perform better and cooperation is enhanced (Henttonen et al., 2014).[146] Staff culture has been described as "relational glue" (Moore et al., 2018)[147] and those wishing to fit-in will adopt the group's norms and values, while the development of social networks helps sustain the team as well (Henttonen et al., 2014)[148]: "acknowledgement among members that they share a common identity minimises the chances of sub-group categorisation and bias in relation to identity and association" (ibid.).[149] Meanwhile, research by Moore et al. (2018) revealed that social bonding in organisations did not, necessarily, achieve positive outcomes (ibid.)[150] and that while trust and reciprocity were important (Loc. Cit.)[151] there were institutional "costs" associated with managing these social networks. So much so that, these strong relational ties between staff may end up being an "impediment" for the organisation especially in complex situations (Moore et al., 2018).[152]

Staff culture is a powerful force in influencing the behaviour of individuals, but it can also deviate from the organisation; norms and values. It can also develop very localised norms that deviate dramatically from the institution's standards and where leadership is unheeding. For example, in 1993, six Canadian soldiers of the Airborne Regiment were court-martialled over war crimes in Somalia during a peace-keeping mission and the unit was disbanded (Winslow, 1999).[153] Then, in 2020 another example of leadership failure came to light after a Four Corners investigation into war crimes alleged to have been committed by élite Australian forces on Afghan civilians in Afghanistan in 2012 and 2013. A subsequent Defence inquiry by Justice Brereton into the Australian Special Forces found "commanders set the conditions in which their units may flourish or wither, including the culture which promotes, permits or prohibits certain behaviours" (IGADF Afghanistan Inquiry Report, 2020).[154] While the ABC and the military are dissimilar, the purpose of these defence force examples serves to furnish how staff culture, when left to its own devices and with absent leadership, can create destructive environments and negative impressions of the entire institution. When there is no firm hand on what was taking place in the group a failure, even abrogation, of leadership resulted.

This section will also situate the analysis of staff culture within the framework of Institutional Logics and Bourdieu's *field*. The ABC's institutional staff culture was described by former Director of ABC-TV Kim Dalton as: "inwardly focused and very white Anglo-Saxon" (Dalton, 2017)[155] consisting of "a lot of 'very, very long ABC stories'" (Simons, 2016).[156] Bourdieu (1985) said groups demonstrated significant symbolic struggle in their *field* over "the very representation of the social world and, in particular, the hierarchy within each of the *fields* and among the different *fields*" (Bourdieu, 1985).[157,158] The strength of ABC staff culture is of such impact that it means the organisational voice could be threatened with strangulation on three fronts: economic, giving away content and copying unsafe digitised collaborations, and internal staff culture. Part of the cultural strangulation comes from its own unique and perplexingly idiosyncratic and reactive staff culture.

In 2002, former ABC Deputy Chair Di Gribble said:

> The role of the employees of the ABC is different from the role of employees in another kind of company. They have, they bring a particular set of skills and there's a tremendous sense of ownership. (Wilson et al., 2010)[159]

Australian sports journalist and author Gideon Haigh (2011) said ABC staff were "purveyors of mediocrity" and "trendy hucksters"[160] (Haigh, 2011).[161] In another light, former ABC cameraman, Ellis Blain (1977) identified a problem with the intransigence among senior ABC staff who had "grown-up" within the organisation, "learn the ABC approach ... and carry it through to the end" (Blain, 1977).[162] But in order to understand fully the complexity of the ABC, as an independent statutory authority, former ABC journalist and staff-elected director, Quentin Dempster (2000) made a salient point that while the ABC noted government policy, this was not prescriptive on how the organisation functioned (Dempster, 2000).[163] There is government policy for the ABC and media—and then there is what the ABC chooses to make of it.

The literature agreed that the role of institutional management was to build team identity and social networks where "performance-management and reward systems could also be used to align the behaviour of team members" (Henttonen et al., 2014).[164] The research literature also drew a distinction between organisational culture and organisational climate, where the culture explained how decisions were made, while the climate was the psychological aspect of how staff functioned and "both culture and climate influences what happens in the workplace" (Spath et al., 2013).[165] It also need to be noted that the ABC as an institution means: "the unfolding outcome of people's and collective actors' continual efforts to maintain, modify, or disturb them" (Reay et al., 2019 quoting Lawrence and Suddaby, 2006). Spath et al. (2013) found that a negative staff culture can be caused by a lack of shared decision-making and communication. Another factor in negative culture is lack of acknowledgement or rewards in workplaces. Workplaces with a passive-defensive culture are the opposite of constructive cultures because they "are associated with dissatisfaction and high stress" (ibid.)[166] and "is approval oriented and conflict avoidant" (Loc. Cit.).[167]

Disengaged employees made up more than half of an organisation's workforce (Swindall, 2011).[168] They are culturally disengaged. But what is culture in the workplace? It was first described by Edward Hall (1959) as "a silent language"[169] and that the culture that exists in public service organisations can be described as bureaucratic (Arunchand & Ramanathan, 2013).[170] Donny Walford, ABC Board Director, told a Senate Estimates Committee in 2019:

> I've taken pride in walking around this organization—regionally, locally and in different states—and none of the journos or even the staff have ever reported to me their concerns about political interference. I think a good measure of culture is that they can talk openly and honestly to this board and board members, but they hadn't raised it and neither had the previous managing director.[171]

In a negative culture staff feel "unloved". Situating this research perspective within the ABC, staff operate in a general media environment where if all their professional practice is devalued it will always be taken personally because so much of it is creative, original and aspires to serve 'the greater good'. A sign of this genuineness is that the majority accept pay that is not at the high end of the media scale (Indeed.com, 2020)[172] earning an average of AUD79,000 (*Payscale.com*)[173] compared with the average annual wage in Australia in 2019 of AUD86,252 (*Australian Bureau of Statistics*, 2019).[174] An average digital media specialist wage is AUD61,369 (*Payscale.com*).[175]

Although there is a paucity of research into public service media staff culture, research on organisational culture has specific application to the ABC. Strong relational ties between staff have proven to be a challenge for successive ABC management when funding cuts have precipitated shedding staff, policy changes or cutting programming. Organisational culture literature said according to Henri Fayol's (1949) 14 principles of management, a key objective should be to build an "esprit de corps" (Fayol, 1949).[176] An attempt at this was made in 2016, when new Managing Director Michelle Guthrie chose to rotate the chair amongst the executive members for the management team's regular meetings, overturning the tradition of the Managing Director being the chair (Simons, 2016).[177] Then in 2018 Guthrie introduced a motivational scheme for all staff as part of an "ABC Recognition Project". Guthrie's email to staff introducing the program said: "The goal is to increase employee engagement, motivate high performance and build a positive work environment" (Meade, 2014).[178]

Guthrie's strategies looked to provide a more unified, positive outlook for all staff as a result of government funding cuts and concomitant staff losses of 1012 people since 2014 (Meade, 2014).[179,180] Guthrie announced a set of "guiding principles" for staff—the ABC Principles. There were three:

1. "We think whole of ABC first";
2. "We work across teams to get the best outcome for the organisation and our audiences"; and,
3. "When we fail, we stop, assess, learn and move on."

However, her complementary strategy, using 'Larry' cards, was seen as unsuccessful. The Larry cards were a group of cards attached to an email sent to all staff. The cards featured a photograph of a fictional man Larry wearing a yellow, ABC logo'd, T-shirt. The point was that the recipient could download the card with message of their choice, write a personal note on it and send it to a colleague or team recognising their skills, or hard work. There were four types of Larry cards to choose from: People Focused, Open & Transparent, Straight Talking and Accountable. Anecdotally, it was understood that news staff derided and parodied the whole exercise. Rewards for those recognised with a Larry card included: the opportunity to attend industry events, be a guest behind-the-scenes of ABC productions, attend a celebratory event in Sydney, "and receive other great products such as Google headphones" (Brook, 2018).[181]

Guthrie announced a second recognition program to reward staff who demonstrated these ABC Principles. The prizes included a set of Google headphones. She then announced a competition to name the new recognition awards with a list of four names to choose from: "Props" (Peer Recognition of Outstanding People), "Aunty Awards", "Kudos" or "The Gunstons" (in honour of ABC fictional comedic television character of the 1970s–1980s Norman Gunston, portrayed by Australian actor Garry McDonald). The secretary of the ABC section of the Community and Public Sector Union, Sinddy Ealy, said the email "had evoked great derision and anger from staff who felt they were being treated like toddlers at a time when morale was already low" (ibid.).[182]

> The last thing they want to see is money being spent on things like this. They want to see more staff employed, more training and better leadership, to be frank. (ibid.)[183]

An anonymous member of ABC staff was quoted in the article:

> It's like The Wiggles for grown-ups. I mean, who the fuck is Larry? I have no idea what they're thinking upstairs. Weirdos. I wonder if this is in lieu of actual pay rises, as there's no money for that. (ibid.)[184]

The Australian newspaper said the project "attracted widespread derision from staff and unions".[185] Quoting an anonymous ABC journalist:

> It is a pathetic, desperate attempt to boost morale when all it's done is the exact opposite. Everyone was laughing about it: how out of touch can an MD be? It probably hasn't lessened morale—nobody has any respect for her or management because they are so out of touch. (Brook, 2018)[186]

The article said staff had come up with an alternative name for the awards: "The Marios" named after a "much-loved facilities staff member who was regarded as the guardian of ABC's Ultimo headquarters"[187] (Brook, 2018) and made redundant around that time.

Perhaps the most rejected attempt to build team identity and networks was through Guthrie's "Larry cards". It demonstrated that management problems may persist after introducing this kind of reward system because it did not achieve the desired outcome and may have encouraged the emergence of any of the three unwanted aspects of staff culture—sycophantism, bullying and cynicism. Staff were encouraged to praise each other, but more importantly be seen to be praising others, while it also allowed staff to potentially ignore or snub staff, who may have been hardworking, and this then appeared as silent condemnation of their dedication. Provoking cynicism can have the result of a lack of cooperation and detracts from a management moves for change (Wanous et al., 2004).[188] Reward systems often do no more than offer staff an opportunity to give problematic responses, or encourage avoidance if the rewards are seen as patronising (Line, 1992).[189] When managers seeking organisational change are confronted with cynicism Wanous et al. (2004) said it was based on two factors: pessimism about change and that those who attempted change before were incompetent (ibid.). This, then, also provokes consideration of the efficaciousness of institutional changes by past ABC managing directors, when staff derision for this was so prompt and volatile.

3.4 Genesis of Staff Culture?

The ABC grew from being "a dumping ground of ex-actors, ex-vaudeville players and ex-musicians" (Semmler, 1981)[190] with few university graduates (Semmler, ibid.) to emerge within seven years (by 1939) united under one cause and driven by a "survival" instinct to become "an institution to be reckoned with" (Semmler, ibid.). In that sense, too, ABC staff culture has always been unique. Emeritus Professor of Politics and Vice-Chancellor's Fellow at La Trobe University, Melbourne, Robert Manne, described ABC staff culture as "idiosyncratic" (Fraser & O'Reilly, 1996).[191] This peculiarity, and its sometimes-consequent assertiveness, has had a long history. In 1946, Maurice James McCarthy, ABC Chief of Staff and Deputy News Editor Sydney was suspended for speaking to the ABC

General Manager, Charles Moses, in Moses' office in "abusive and insulting terms in the hearing of other officers" (The Sun, 1946).[192] In a subsequent inquiry it was learned that McCarthy thumped the table and told Moses:

> You are a lousy pommy—and I'll see that you are sent back to Lancashire where you belong. You're no Australian. This country is too good for lousy scum like you. (The Truth, 1948)[193]

The discriminatory outburst was prompted by Moses' concern that McCarthy had "discussed commission matters" (*The Argus*, 1948)[194] with then Attorney-General and Minister for External Affairs, Dr H. V. Evatt, when McCarthy was alleged to have asked Evatt about McCarthy's superannuation matters (ibid.).[195] Other literature said McCarthy had spoken to Evatt about a news matter (Semmler, 1981),[196] while other literature said McCarthy had complained to Evatt that the ABC's superannuation had not been extended to news staff (Dixon, 1975).[197] McCarthy's former colleague and Former Federal News Editor, Frank Dixon, said not only had McCarthy denied this to him that it took place but that another source corroborated Dixon's denial of the alleged event (ibid.).[198] At the subsequent court case when McCarthy sued the ABC for wrongful dismissal, McCarthy denied, again, having met Dr Evatt. Moses told a subsequent inquiry into McCarthy's sacking: "I read McCarthy an ABC regulation which forbids the staff from seeking outside influence for promotion or other advantages" (*The Argus*, 1948).[199] Dixon said:

> McCarthy had worked hard during the war, coming on duty five mornings a week at 4 o'clock to monitor overseas broadcasts, and I felt that in common gratitude the Commission should not have taken such drastic action against him. (Dixon, 1975)[200]

Frank Dixon was considered by the ABC to be one of the heroes of its independence (ABC, n.d.)[201] in managing its capacity to run a news service in its own right. The titanic struggle to attain this goal was at a time when *The Herald and Weekly Times* (run by Sir Keith Murdoch) wanted to sell its news to the ABC. Although Dixon was described in personal terms by Inglis (1983) as "a priggish old-fashioned man, wearing wing collars, never touching alcohol, a pious old Catholic with a countryman's handshake and a headmaster's voice and gaze" (ibid.).[202] Dixon described himself differently. He said he belonged to “a handful of idealistically-minded journalists” who:

> Were able to convince the government of the day that in the interests of Australian democracy, the national broadcasting instrumentality should have its own news service, free of newspaper, political and advertising ties. (Dixon, 1975)[203]

ABC independence was gained as a result, but he said he suffered “mentally” from this arduous process and resigned in 1950 due to what he described as being subjected to “self-interest, prejudice and misunderstanding … at work both inside and outside the commission” (Dixon, 1975).[204] Or, what would be described today as bullying and marginalisation. He oversaw this “fight” with politicians and newspapers for the ABC news independence from 1936 when the ABC was paying newspapers A£200 a year (around AUD19,525 in 2019, *Reserve Bank of Australia*)[205] for news. This payment continued until 1947 when the ABC was liberated to collect and source news. Dixon justified the fight for the ABC’s news independence because “something vital was at stake” (Dixon, 1975).[206] In an early example of documented political interference, Dixon blamed his semi-forced retirement and victimisation on the election of a Menzies-Fadden Government which created more favourable opportunities for his departure without threat of ministerial interference: “I doubt if it would have had the temerity to do this had Labor remained in power” (ibid.).[207] Dixon provided an interesting insight into political meddling in staffing at the ABC at that time. However, politics (and private media gripes) to one side, one of the main challenges to the ABC in creating its own news service, according to Dixon, was that the ABC “literally shuddered at the cost” (Loc. Cit.).[208]

Another example of the power of staff culture, especially if backed by management, was in 1970, the official newspaper of the Communist Party of Australia, *The Tribune*, said that ABC staff was on the verge of forming a counter-culture. The observation was prompted by ABC staff’ industrial action in response to Federal Government cuts of AUD500,000, half of which were to come from the current affairs budget. This was perceived as censorship (strangling) of Aunty’s independent voice. ABC staff also had the support of ABC Chairman Sir Robert Madgwick on the issue: “the most popular chairman in the ABC’s history” (University of New England, 2020).[209] Inglis (1983) said that during the chairmanship of Madgwick the

ABC budget rose to almost AUD90 million in 1973–74, compared with almost AUD50 million in 1969–70 (ibid. p. 327 and 337). Even though Madgwick was also a practitioner of Management by Walking (Wandering) Around (MBWA) and, although not required, would visit the ABC everyday to make himself available to talk to staff (Inglis 1983, p. 325). MBWA is one management practice, whereby the manager walks around chatting to staff in the hopes of catching up on any staff grievances but also motivating staff (Law, 2009). Even though Postmaster-General, Alan Hulme believed: "there to be bias, not balance, in ABC news and commentary" (Coleman, 2007)[210] he backed down on the current affairs funding cuts. The Tribune observed insightfully that the incident had fortified staff culture and its more appreciative understanding of the role of the ABC: "The ABC employees are already, in essence, embarked on the road towards workers' control and self-management" (Robertson, 1970).[211] Building on this success, in 1976, the ABC Staff Association launched a publicity campaign accusing ABC management of trying to exercise excessive control over program-makers and heads of departments in what they called an attempt to "divide and rule" (*The Canberra Times*, 1976).[212]

Other methods of controlling staff culture have taken a more individual-level approach. It was noted by the former employee Frank Dixon that, in his own words, he was "regressed"[213] as Director of News after a career at the broadcaster from 1936 to 1950. Among his concluding observations in his departure book was: "in the last 7 or 8 years of my time with the ABC the development of cliques among the staff replaced the trust and friendship which had been in the early days".[214] He blamed this for a consequent drop in broadcasting standards (ibid.). Looking even further back, Dixon said the sudden resignation of Chairman William Cleary in 1945 was because of "'inside' influences which he seemed powerless to grapple with" (Dixon, 1975).[215] This was confirmed by Cleary in his farewell speech to staff: "I could no longer command the loyalty of some people I trusted" (*Daily Examiner*, 1945).[216] In his exit speech, it was reported that Cleary had "clashed with the former Prime Minister, Mr Menzies, over the "A.B.C. Weekly" magazine, but had proceeded with the journal (anyway)". The ABC's annual report for the year ended 1944 showed a loss on the ABC Weekly magazine of AU£7553 (compared with a loss of AU£21,108 in 1943). It was not a howling success. In addition, Cleary "sought an interview with the Prime Minister, Mr. Curtin, but was advised that Senator Ashley, then Postmaster-General, would speak with him" and help decide if an interview with the Prime Minister was needed.

No meetings took place (*The Sydney Morning Herald*, 1945b).[217] Then, it was also reported that there was a clash of ideas between Cleary and the General Manager Charles Moses (*The Sydney Morning Herald*, 1945a).[218] Cleary was concerned that Moses was involved in growing his own power at the organisation at the expense of the Chairman in talks Moses was having with key politicians in Canberra (Petersen, 2009).[219]

Staff capacity to procure managing director support and advocacy is important and its absence can be dire for leadership. For example, former Managing director Michelle Guthrie was opposed by her staff because: "she did not fraternise with the staff, and refused to be their spokeswoman" (Westmore, 2018).[220] After Guthrie's sacking, Sydney ABC Television newsreader Juanita Phillips was quoted in a newspaper report that she had said on Twitter Guthrie's replacement would "need a deep understanding of the history, purpose and importance of an independent public broadcaster, and be ready to fight bare-knuckled to protect it" (Brook, 2018),[221] implying Guthrie had not done so. ABC Television *Four Corners* Producer Sally Neighbour was reported in the same news report that she had said on Twitter Guthrie's departure was an "excellent decision" (ibid.)[222] and Melbourne radio broadcaster Jon Faine was also quoted in the article as having said on Twitter that Guthrie's time as managing director had been an "astonishing fail", that she was focused on flow-charts with "no interest in journalism", was not "champion of the organisation" and was "all but invisible" (Loc. Cit.).[223] A freelance ABC journalist, quoted in the same newspaper report was said to have commented: "she has failed to defend the ABC—an organisation crucial to the functioning of Australian democracy—from a hostile Coalition government, and protect specialist and crucial parts of the ABC, like Radio National" (ibid.).[224] The ABC had shifted and shaped content more emphatically to the emergent commercial *field*.

Senior ABC broadcaster, Phillip Adams, was quoted in a newspaper report that she was a "charmless and absent manager who had trashed staff morale and infected the ABC with "managerial nonsense" (Duke et al., 2018)[225]: "she didn't say hello to me for a year. She didn't walk the corridors. She just wasn't around the place" (ibid.).[226] Adams added: "Poor Michelle was charmless, absolutely and utterly charmless, and couldn't seduce the staff at all the way Mark (Scott) did". Her Chairman, Justin Milne said: "she'd lost the faith of the folks" (ABC, 2018).[227] Of her replacement, David Anderson, an unnamed staffer was quoted as saying: "he's the smartest, most respected executive at the ABC. Spent his entire career there and is respected across the production sector. This is the smartest thing they've done in a long time" (Duke et al., 2018).[228] Chairman, Justin Milne, had dismissed Guthrie half-way through her contract for three reasons: "low staff morale, her travel to Singapore (where her husband was based), and poor feedback from executives working for her" (ibid.).[229] In her defence a colleague, ABC Chief Finance and Strategy Officer, Louise Higgins, credited Guthrie with eliminating "a bloated bureaucracy under Mark Scott" (Meade, 2018b).[230] While, an anonymous ABC employee complained about management preference for eliminating legacy knowledge in staff retrenchments where "the contempt of managers for older experienced staff has become a culture which has flowed out into the work floor and there's now a generational divide" (Meade ibid.) and the reductions and losses of its libraries and historic music collection collapsed (ibid.) another example of the constricting of Aunty's voice and loss of a public asset.

The social media melée by ABC staff personalised Guthrie's management and leadership and was described in a report as "kicking her on her way out" (Kenny, 2018),[231] but subsequent to her departure and contradicting the online hostility directed at her, she was also found to "have stood firm for journalists against her chairman and resisted political interference" (ibid.).[232] Ironically, only a few weeks before her sacking and online abuse, she had defended an ABC female presenter who cried in response to an abusive text message from an audience member. Guthrie said prophetically in a newspaper reported staff email: "the line needed to be drawn at threats and harassment". Feedback, debate or dissent should not descend into personal abuse" (Meade, 2018a).[233] The reported avalanche of personal comments reported in newspapers that were made on Twitter about Guthrie after her sacking, were described by Alex Wake, senior media lecturer at RMIT and former ABC reporter as "uncalled for" but that Guthrie let herself down because she: "hasn't understood how to play [the] politics of it" (Chung 2018).[234] Wake also said Mark Scott, her predecessor, "was one of the ABC's best MDs. He had lots of failings but he absolutely had staff behind him" (Meade, ibid.). A prior view expressed by Neil Chenoweth in *The Australian Financial Review* in 2014 on the ABC was that: "there's a view that ABC internal politics are so torrid that anything politicians say about ABC staff is nothing compared with what they say about each other. That's our ABC" (Chenoweth, 2014).[235] Australia's Prime Minister Scott Morrison commented towards the end of the institutional mêlée: "I expect the ABC board to do better. And if they don't, well they can expect a bit more attention from me" (Remeikis, 2018).[236]

Nonetheless, strong staff support, it would even appear affection, is a critical institutional acquisition for the managing director and institutional leadership at the public broadcaster. One contra-voice was ABC journalist Monica Attard who was reported in a newspaper to have posted on Twitter: "Might be nice for people to remember Guthrie is actually a human being. Might be feeling rather low and bruised."[237] In response to this, the Secretary of the ABC section of the Community and Public Sector Union, Sinddy Ealy, was reported by a newspaper to have tweeted: "True but Michelle Guthrie has presided over the sacking of more than 400 staff, then encouraged those left behind to send Larry cards. Her lack of passion for the ABC and her tin ear won't be missed by most."[238] But there had been precedence for this strong invective directed at Guthrie. Jonathan Shier was managing director for only one year—2000-2001 and seemed to have been similarly disliked by staff. In 2019, former ABC journalist and presenter, Kerry O'Brien said at his Induction into the Hall of Fame at the Australian television awards night—called the Logies—"The day Jonathan Shier was appointed to run the ABC in the Howard years was the beginning of a dark time in that place" (Crikey, 2019).[239]

In the past, the dynamic of goodwill generated, historically, by ABC staff culture has also seen magnanimous gestures made for greater good of the community. For example, as far back as 1939 the ABC held a "crazy whist and bridge party"[240] in Melbourne to raise money for knitting wool; and knitting items for Australian troops. During both World War I and World War II the support of Australians was critical in supplying what were called "comforts" to boost morale to Australia's defence forces on active service and the ABC staff was active, busy and supportive of these efforts.

Yet, the overall effect of a powerful staff culture is that there is a watchdog guarding the watchdog. Staff have commented over the years that they had to fight for the ABC's independence at all times and like Bourdieu's metaphor that staff were 'at war'—the ABC has projected this towards an enemy (Rupert Murdoch), even though as a counter-fact there is no public pronouncement by Murdoch or his News Corporation that it is 'at war' with the ABC, and Murdoch does not make public statements about the ABC, rather his media outlets and commentators point out where and when the broadcaster errs or blunders (Kenny, 2020).[241]

To counter this enemy, the ABC staff have developed a defensive culture to alert the public that they are doing their best to fight off Murdoch's "attacks" which forms part of the amorphous "reactionary right-wing media" which, ironically, inhabits the same *field* as the newly-transposed ABC. Former senior journalist, Kerry O'Brien, was also critical of the ABC in reference to climate change reporting because it had "not cut through the fake news effectively, we have not properly held politicians to account" (O'Brien, 2019).[242] Former Chairman James Spigelman (whose office concluded in 2017) identified a key problem at the ABC was that one quarter of "staff think they can do the best job running the national broadcaster" (Varga, 2018).[243] He said there were siloes within the ABC, each looking after themselves and it was this that prevented or hampered change. However, while Guthrie's actions to eliminate staff siloes received the opprobrium of staff, ABC Chairman during part of her tenure, Spigelman, backed Guthrie (Varga, 2018) and said she had the support of the board and had "slashed middle management" in positive moves to eliminate previous platform-based structures (ibid.).[244]

ABC staff have been accused of creating a disconnected "public service culture" (Mitchell, 2019)[245] creating a need to "align ABC news values with community values" (ibid.).[246] Former ABC journalist and now contributor at *The Australian*, Geoffrey Luck, said the ABC had "powerful staff interests" (Luck, 2018)[247] but also struggled with the stereotype under which all public sector workers labour; that they are perceived as not having to work as hard as their private sector counterparts (Willem et al., 2010).[248] It had also suffered the blight of comeuppance from former staff who, once departed the organisation, have continued to prosecute their cases. Geoffrey Luck (2018), wrote:

> Management lost control with the arrival of current affairs. While news was strictly held to editorial standards—and its journalists were actively deterred from broadcasting—ambitious executives recruited young university graduates to launch current affairs programs—*AM* and *PM* on radio, and This Day Tonight on TV. (Luck, 2018)[249]

The situation of staff versus the government was exemplified in 1987 when Labor Prime Minister, Bob Hawke, referred to the ABC Television investigative journalism program *Four Corners* as a "nest of vipers" (Inglis, 1983).[250] By the 1990s the Mansfield Report (1997) "The Challenge of a Better ABC" was actually critical of ABC management as weak when it said the organisation needed "better management" and that there was a "lack of trust" between management and staff which could be overcome by management showing more leadership, rather than being guided by staff (Mansfield, 1997).[251] The report also said that the ABC was burdened by having to be 'all to all' because "it is always under pressure to expand its services and has difficulty defining priorities" (ibid.).[252] In addition, "its major ventures into commercial territory were disastrous" (Burns "From Dix to Mansfield" pp. 62–63, in Martin, 2002)[253] and during the managing directorship of Jonathan Shier, "the pursuit of popularity led ABC TV into the bland, safe terrain of infotainment programming" (ibid.). As Martin (2002)[254] identified the ABC was in pursuit of audiences that had been quantified by government policy but overlaid with commercial definitions of public. This then created a headache for a public media organisation when it had to service narrowly-defined ideas of who belonged to their publics or audiences (and the great definitional shift in nomenclature from serving "publics" now named "audiences" which implies a performative, artistically judgemental role on behalf of the individuals). In shifting *field* and language use, the ABC lost its original public audience.

The ABC's latest strapline "yours" simulates a rough attempt to call out to whomever wants to listen. The trouble with this approach is that instead of attracting a public gathering, the online digital milieu draws highly personal and local responses that may not reflect broader public interest issues. Chasing individual concerns may not address the greater good. When asking for "yours" it is responding to its call to speak to audiences but in so doing is splintering the notion of public good into personal issues, as if personal now represents universal/national. As a consequence of the "yours" campaign, the ABC now has "conversations" to obtain stories from its audiences, as do all emergent commercial media. But in regard to the ABC, it has forsaken an authorial voice, its *cultural capital* of the Australian public interest in favour of private concerns. As Guthrie was reported to have asked her executive staff: "Are we the *home* of Australian stories or the *source* of Australian stories?" (Simons, 2016).[255] The question would imply that the ABC should see itself as a domicile of stories, rather than an originator. Further, it overlooked: how do we shift our *cultural capital* and *reputational capital* into the emergent commercial field? This shift is no marginal matter for a Commonwealth publicly-representative institution. In addition, the use of the word "conversation" as the ABC's new mode of engagement can be described as the organisation's metaphor for establishing a new peer-to-peer relationship with its audiences/citizens, as befits the technology of social media. The literature said this was because "managers try to make sense of organizational realities by invoking varied metaphors" (Vakkayil, 2008)[256] where "the use of metaphors is fundamental to our thinking" (Vakkayil, 2008, quoting G. Lakoff & M. Johnson, 1980). Use of such metaphors can incorporate "multiple perspectives" (ibid.) and conversations can create dialogue and build positive encounters with difference. Alternatively, narrowly-focused conversations can generate sectional, marginal conflict which is extrapolated to represent the whole of society and where attention is no longer observant of the broader interests of society. It is this eventuality that challenges the moral and funding value of public service media. So much so, that it can become distracted by the need for content that attracts 'likes', 'clicks' and 'hearts' and other endearing emojis—a pursuit of so-called impact fetishism (Klikauer, 2018).[257] This point is examined further in Chap. 4.

Academic research of public sector organisations showed they valued fairness and honesty, but these ideals were not expressed in a trusting relationship between the employer and their employees (Martin, 2002).[258] This is also described as the 'psychological contract' between workers and their employers in the literature, but there is not the scope here to develop that point and can be taken up with other research. However, the matter about the ABC and its recurrent staff upsets with its management require further analysis. Media and its support of a democracy through its pursuit of veracity have been examined widely in the academic and grey literature and there is a belief, originating in the US, that the media should belong to a free market because public control of media imperilled freedom of speech (Curran, 2011).[259] In addition, journalists should be encouraged to work within a professional framework to guarantee the media provided a service to the people (ibid.).[260] Yet, a free media did not provide the highest level of journalism because there were temptations to sensationalise and free markets tended to allow monopolists to accumulate power. This then created potential for abuse of power (Loc. Cit.).[261] ABC news staff have always valued their separation from management (and the commerical field) in choosing news they believed was the public's right to know. The recruitment of former journalists to management positions has assisted in developing that understanding and trust. Former ABC Head National Programs, News & Current Affairs, Walter Hamilton, and former ABC journalist wrote in 2013:

> No journalist worth his salt would sit on an important story simply to avoid upsetting the powers that be. … The ABC even does not have an obligation to weigh up what the majority of the public might think to do in such a situation. (Hamilton, 2013)[262]

But former ABC Producer David Salter (2007) said ABC management made a consistent mistake:

> Assuming that staff don't dare to think independently about key issues, or won't take direct action to voice those opinions. … They forget that it is the staff, not management, which holds the most powerful collective memory all the bitter battles fought over the decades to protect the ABC's independence. (Salter, 2007)[263]

William Cleary, the ABC's first Chairman, also had to grapple with fractious and resistant staff. His dream was for "a committed staff, imbued with an institutional ethos working towards a common goal" (Thomas, 1980).[264] However, the reality was that during his chairmanship staff spoke publicly about their disputes with him and his management on their concerns for "ABC policy and purpose" (ibid.).[265] In fact, World War II gave staff the golden opportunity to expand their influence on programming as well as their terms of employment (Loc. Cit.)[266] and increased "militancy" (ibid.)[267] while other staff were serving in the defence forces.

What this analysis and research of ABC staff culture revealed was an underlying disconnect between staff and its management; an uncoupling of staff and institutional authority. Institutional Logics theory frames this tension as the staff and management both competing for the same *field* in trying to control the organisation and its message.[268] Staff is a powerful élite of the ABC competing with the management élite for which there have been historical instances of being cowed, threatened or debilitated by this competition. They both compete for control of Aunty's voice and can strangle it. This form of struggle for domination of an apparent *field* (within the emergent commercial media *field*) makes the ABC distinctive from other media outlets, which do not allow staff the same capacity to express personal views on the organisation and its management. Insubordination is not entertained (for long) in the commercial *field*; another clash for Aunty in her new *field* and another point of contention and difference for the ABC now that it inhabits the emergent commercial *field*. ABC staff have latitude to express personal upsets with management and publicly give specific direction on content, for example, and this ABC staff *symbolic power* expresses itself in these various ways through media leaks and "off the record" comments to other commercial media. A consequence of this is turmoil, upheaval, uncertainty and changes in management, unable to control this insurrection.[269] The contested property in the case of the ABC is the institution itself, a necessary outfit. Legitimacy in the historical literature on power, ultimately, speaks about the subordinated and the dominant and the struggle between them. In this instance management and staff and, in that tussle, one tries to gain the upper hand.

Former deputy General Manager Clement Semmler (1981) observed that many senior staff had also "played politics" and even politicians had insinuated themselves into the offices of ABC managers:

> Prime ministerial and ministerial secretaries and press relations officers—and on occasion the VIPs themselves, have direct access to management, and they do not hesitate to use the facility. ... Power at the executive level, in the ABC or anywhere else, is heady wine. (Semmler, 1981)[270]

However, Semmler (1981) said as a result of the ABC "reaping the dragon's teeth" (attracting the ire of politicians) there had been a tendency for the broadcaster to "play it safe, or to go along as far as possible with the political masters, rather than to oppose them" (ibid.).[271] As an adjunct to this, Dr Denis Muller, Senior Research Fellow, Centre for Advancing Journalism, University of Melbourne, related a personal anecdote to a Senate Estimates Committee hearing on the pressures of staff self-censorship at the ABC:

> In the midst of the Barnaby Joyce and Vikki Campion revelations, the ABC emailed me, inviting me to write a comment piece on Joyce's decision to accept a reported $150,000 for giving Channel Seven an interview about his relationship with Campion. ... Shortly after I filed the piece, I had a further email from the ABC asking if I would agree to having the intro deleted. By way of explanation I was told that 'Things were a bit delicate with the government at the moment'. I refused to have the intro deleted and withdrew the story, sending it instead to The Conversation from which it was picked up by The Age—published by them, as you can see—and later by a magazine that circulates among public servants. It was a sobering experience. It brought home to me just how cowered the ABC has become in the face of the government's relentless attacks.[272]

But it would be aberrant to think of staff as one homogenised mass all vying and lobbying for the same objectives, there are many who choose not to speak publicly about the ABC nor express dissension. Nonetheless, the few are taken to represent the many and they compete within the *field* and must learn Bourdieu's *doxa*—"the rules of the game" in order to survive. Contestation is part of the rules of the game in the *field*. As senior ABC Broadcaster, Phillip Adams, said in a magazine interview (2018): "when people are under pressure, and in competition for diminishing resources, that's going to make them turn on each other to a certain extent" (Cadzow, 2018).[273] Another example of how this internal competition manifests in the *field* was when concerns about the development of warring groups within the ABC were expressed by an unnamed ABC staff member in a newspaper interview[274]:

> If the ABC starts to career around without a clear sense of what it's doing and why, you get various groups turning on each other. You get cabals forming. (Seccombe, 2016)[275]

This segregation of staff into discrete groups was confirmed by former Managing Director, Michelle Guthrie, when she was quoted saying she had difficulty in locating content because of "silos" and "cul-de-sacs" (Seccombe, 2016)[276] at the ABC. Senior broadcaster, Phillip Adams, also commented about a lack of "camaraderie and unity" (Cadzow, 2018)[277] among staff, while an anonymous ABC presenter said that journalists did not just hate management, they also hated each other (Cadzow, 2018). The anonymous presenter said: "you've got all these little empires" (Cadzow, 2018).[278] The genesis of this shift in staff culture was confirmed decades earlier by former ABC senior employee Frank Dixon (1975): "in the last seven or eight years of my time with the ABC the development of cliques among the staff replaced the trust and friendship which had been general in the early days" (Dixon, 1975).[279] Dixon (1975) said the result was that the "standard of broadcasting suffered" blaming it on "political and religious antagonisms" (Ibid.).[280] The year 1975 was also the start of a tranche of major Federal Government funding cuts to the ABC. A 2008 submission by the ABC section of the Community and Public Sector Union said:

> The key to the transition lies in breaking down the ABC culture of working in 'silos' (TV, Radio and News Divisions) and overhauling the commission-

> ing process so that it is genuinely multiplatform in nature. The 'silos' are a major source of inefficiency. They lock up resources and limit the capacity of the organisation to derive benefit from multiplatform production.[281]

Further, the submission said: "The majority of staff believe that the ABC is handicapped by a poorly managed regime that is parochial and risk averse" (ABC Section CPSU 2008)[282] at a time when the Managing Director was Mark Scott.

In 1981, former deputy General Manager, Clement Semmler (1981) expressed concerns that the staff culture was perpetuating a "comfortable and dangerous philosophy" (Semmler, 1981)[283] that justified a narrative that "no large organisation is perfect" and that even with mistakes to "consider all the good things that come out of it" (ibid.). He said the development of this meant that content talked down to the audience and that it "inevitably nourishes the second-rate" where the ABC was then broadcasting to the middle in "broad strokes" "so that the majority, or the majority's presumed taste, dominates the scene" (Loc. Cit.).[284] Semmler (1981) also pointed out that anyone who criticised the ABC, for the commercialisation of the organisation, was running the risk of being accused of "intellectual elitism", or, helping frame a case against the ABC on behalf of the commercial media. Since then, management has faced similar challenges.

Some of the literature tended to agree that leaders were considered a type of hero, hence there were huge, perhaps unrealistic, expectations on their performance (Kurtulmuş, 2019).[285] Askeland et al. (2020) said institutional leadership should be freed from this heroic view because leadership was a "constant dialogue between leaders and followers" (ibid.).[286] Using the Society of Jesus (Jesuit) organisation's vow of poverty as an example, the researchers said, as a model of leadership and responsibility, the vow was not strictly defined, but negotiated. Leadership, ergo, needs to be negotiated, not templated with unrevised institutional and staff expectations.

Values are the struts that support the legitimacy of an institution (Askeland et al., 2020),[287] in fact, they are part of the defining the institution in Institutional Logics[288] (Thornton & Ocasio, 2008). In addition, the actors in charge of an organisation, including those who lead the ABC, exercise their agency in their *field* to effect change and therefore "values are critical in the establishment or implementation of institutionalised practice" (Askeland et al., 2020).[289] 'Values work' is also a significant issue at the ABC. 'Values work' has been defined as "motivational factors and guiding principles in people's lives, which could challenge and change highly resistant institutions" (ibid.).[290] An example of this was articulated by ABC Broadcaster, Geraldine Doogue: "I always think the nearest equivalent to working in the ABC must be living within a political party—with one obvious difference—polling day" (Fraser & O'Reilly, 1996).[291] Doogue's comparison of the ABC with a political party is interesting to analyse within institutional theory where values are seen to accomplish "the desirables" derived from a performative perspective directing right or wrong behaviour (Askeland et al., 2020),[292] in this instance staff perceptions of the need to take/or the even existence of a political line. This suggests a resistance or stance in regard to change in a situation where these political values "can reflect rationalised myths (Meyer & Rowan, 1977)[293]" which, nonetheless, shape the organisation's identity and point to a sense, a desire, of striving for a staff-perceived interpretation of common good:

> Friedland (2013)[294] explains that institutional logics are composed of a multiplicity of 'value spheres'. Confirming the 'validity of such values' is a 'matter of faith', which individuals seek and for "which they claim to be instruments". (Askeland et al., 2020)[295]

Former staff member Ellis Blain (1977) identified the political influences among staff when he described staff-elected ABC Board member Marius Webb:

> Who was not selected by the Staff Association but elected by a free vote of all ABC staff ... holds strong leftist political views and was suspected of unduly influencing the voting at Commission meetings. ... Not surprisingly, he was something of a folk hero in the context of staff distrust of Sir Henry Bland. (Blain, 1977)[296]

So, politics and religious faith are not remote concepts, both founded on firm beliefs, commitments and ideals. They have a reflexive relationship where religion can be politicised and politics can become religious. The internal practice of Institutional Logics in this instance showed that ABC staff culture aimed to legitimise its hold over the journalism *field*.[297] It is this independence of thought, acquired from the journalistic *field*; which had infiltrated much of the staff culture of the ABC as well as the mindset of management. Further, although the ABC produced a wide variety of content—news and current affairs have become the most dominant areas of the institution.

This book's examination of staff culture looks to fill a gap in the literature by examining how ABC staff culture worked in terms of the internal practice of Institutions Logics (Askeland et al., 2020)[298] and the consequent impact upon its public service role. Emeritus Professor of Politics and Vice-Chancellor's Fellow at La Trobe University, Melbourne, Robert Manne (Fraser & O'Reilly, 1996)[299] affirmed this infiltration of the staff culture into the *field* of journalistic power and the manifestation of internal practice of Logics in an essay (in the same book sponsored by the Friends of the ABC) that: "the culture of the ABC was not planned. It grew over time as a consequence of hundreds of separate decisions. What now exists is not amenable to rational justification" (Fraser & O'Reilly, 1996).[300]

Just as politics and religion have interface, so too does management and staff and not all leaders contribute to positive outcomes, work in the best interests of their organisation nor their society at large. Also, their staff can actually contribute to the same problem they seek to resolve. This given has been described by Kurtulmuş (2019) as: "dark leaders with rather a large playing *field* on which to strive for their goals, at the expense of followers and organizations" (ibid.).[301] It can mean leaders' actions may not benefit all stakeholders. Allied to this, institutional frameworks can hamper leaders and they are also not immune from external events about which they have no control. Federal Government funding of the ABC is a prominent example of an external threat. Fundamental, however, is the dyadic relationship between leaders and their workers where the worker may choose to reject the leader (Kurtulmuş, 2019)[302] yet leadership was "one of the most important assets of an organization" (Kurtulmuş, 2019).[303] This means "if the dark side of personality affects leaders, then it can also influence their followers in a similar way—which means followers can also be on the dark side (Clements & Washbush, 1999).[304] As well, both leaders and followers "may be high in Machiavellianism, narcissism or sub-clinical psychopathy".[305] Kurtulmuş (2019) added: "It should be noted, therefore, that destructive organizational outcomes are not only the responsibility of toxic leadership but also that of susceptible followers ... they may also have hidden agendas that are different from the organizational or group goals (citing Clements & Washbush, 1999)" (ibid.).[306]

Added to the pressure on staff and corresponding resistance are the emergence since the 1980s of the ubiquitous key performance indicators (KPIs) used to plan individual careers and project goals—measurables as a way of gauging deliverables. When a situation for a staff member goes awry, instead of counselling, management can activate the process of performance management. There is a growing interest in the values of organisations (Askeland et al., 2020)[307] and performance management was devised to support the improvement of the workforce based on identified core values. But these same core values can also be used as a punitive, insidious form of control, marginalising and encouraging unsuitable (unwanted, unliked) staff to resign. This occurs within a situation where: "the larger your firm, the easier it is to drift from your core values" (Hansen, 1998)[308] anyway and it takes finessed, skilled leadership to avoid that situation arising. Yet institutional research showed that managers only had greater opportunity to change tactics where "the validity of past commitments has been undermined" (Golant et al., 2015).[309] In other words, a resolute staff culture ensured there were limitations on change; and performance management of staff in a public service outfit may indicate more underlying problems than the staff members themselves.

3.5 Management Versus Staff

Politicians and ABC management 'run-ins' have persisted. In 2003, the ABC's Independent Complaints Review Panel (ICRP) upheld 17 of Communications Minister Senator Richard Alston's 68 complaints about the coverage of the Iraqi war on its morning radio current affairs program, *AM*. An initial internal investigation upheld two of the complaints. The findings included 12 complaints that the ABC showed "serious bias" and in another four complaints, journalists had breached the ABC's editorial directive that they refrain from "emotional language or editorialisation" when reporting the war. Another was that sources were not adequately identified in one case (*The Sydney Morning Herald*, 2003).[310] In response Senator Alston was quoted: "This brutal reality check must shake ABC senior management out of its entrenched culture of denial" (ibid.).[311] The ABC Managing Director, was Russell Balding, said he stood "vigorously" by *AM*'s coverage and that: "as is demonstrated by these processes, coverage of a war by a high-profile current affairs program such as *AM*, in a contested and difficult environment, is not a simple matter" (Loc. Cit.).[312]

In Federal Parliament's upper house, the Senate, four days later Senator Santo Santoro (Liberal for Queensland) said that the panel had "set the bar so high that only the most blatant instances of prejudice would be counted as amounting to impropriety" (Santoro, 2013).[313] Further, he wrote to Managing Director Russell Balding and quoted this response: "We prefer to present a range of views in accordance with our published editorial policies and leave it to the audience to make up their own minds about the merits of these different perspectives" (ibid.). Santoro (2013) said: "That is how the system is supposed to work, of course. The problem is that it is not working that way. The problem is that the ABC still does not see that there is a problem" (ibid.).[314] Santoro (2013) added:

> The panel's report, defensive of the ABC as it is, surely made one thing clear. The ABC's much-vaunted complaints review executive is a sham. Even the panel notes that the complaints review executive, when it upheld a complaint, only did so in a grudging way. Obviously. there were many faults that the panel found which the complaints review executive had chosen to ignore. This is obvious. It is incontestable. Yet the corporation treats it as if it had not occurred. Rather than admit there is a problem that needs to be addressed, Mr Balding merely notes the panel's 'taking a different view to the Complaints Review Executive on some issues'. (ibid.)[315]

In addition, a lack of support from management has been a longstanding theme of criticism levelled at the ABC management, even by its own employees and the push, pull and angst between ABC Current Affairs and the ABC has had a long history. In 1976, the then ABC Chairman Sir Henry Bland said: "I could not care less if the ABC had no current affairs programs" (*The Sydney Morning Herald*, 1976).[316] The same great matter (and lack of support) has befuddled other areas of ABC content. In 1984 Charles Buttrose (1984) lamented in his memoirs that when he was head of the ABC Concert Department there was a need to "revive by some means top management interest in and enthusiasm for the work the (ABC) orchestras do" (Buttrose, 1984).[317] Buttrose believed it had waned since the ABC's inception. An earlier book, by a former staffer, Ellis Blain (1977), looked to the next level and expressed concern that there was a lack of understanding of the role of the ABC among politicians. But likewise, he said, the ABC Chairman, Sir Henry Bland, also failed to understand the role of ABC orchestras. Remarks Bland made in *The Sydney Morning Herald* (1976)[318] implied that Australia had more orchestras than it needed (compared with Britain and Japan, both of which had fewer). Bland said that orchestras were not "sacrosanct" and that "nobody can these days put a fence around anything and say that is absolutely taboo" (*The Sydney Morning Herald* ibid.). Blain (1977) explained that there was a logical need for more orchestras because of the comparative vastness of Australia:

> This vastness is the principal factor which has obliged the ABC to depart radically from BBC practice in the several fields, one of the most important of which has been the necessity to first-class orchestral support in every state. (ibid.)[319]

Other literature explained that the growth of ABC orchestras as public performers giving concerts separate to the ABC was not the original plan. They were intended to be for radio broadcast only (Garrett, 2012)[320] then the Melbourne-based Australian conductor Bernard Heinze and Deputy Chairman Herbert Brookes decided that the Melbourne Symphony Orchestra should be the premier orchestra to perform in Australia. However, this temporary ascendancy (known as "the Melbourne Agenda") of the MSO was only due to squabbles over the ABC's music policy (Garrett, 2012). Ultimately, the emergence of six state orchestras meant that the ABC had "a near monopoly of orchestral concert giving in Australia" (Garrett, 2012). This gave the ABC extraordinary ***cultural capital*** and ***reputational capital*** in developing the musical experiences, tastes and knowledge of Australians of the Commonwealth of Australia.

3.6 ABC Staff 'Spooked'

There have been instances where media reports on ABC staff culture have said that there was an atmosphere of fear as to whether content or a presentation would offend political interests or governments. An anonymous presenter was quoted in 2018: "Frankly, we are all spooked by everything in here" (Meade, 2018b).[321] Further, the same report said that: "across news, radio and TV there is a concerted push from managers to find conservative voices to keep the accusation of left-wing bias at bay" (ibid.).[322] Contrary to this, former ABC religion editor, Paul Collins said over two decades earlier that "there is not so much an editorial bias as a lack of editorial direction" and that "important areas of the ABC are influenced by journalists and broadcasters of a progressive stamp" (Fraser & O'Reilly,

1996).[323] Further Collins said: "what is lacking in the ABC is a strong and mature editorial drive to broaden the range of stories and issues that the corporation covers ... there is far too little of this editorial leadership in the contemporary ABC" (ibid.).[324] He identified that the criticism of the ABC becoming "politically correct" was not internally generated but rather imposed by the Federal Labor Government: "it was political correctness imposed on a statutory body from the outside" (Loc. Cit.).[325]

This concern has a long history. As former Deputy General Manager, Clement Semmler (1981), combining the ABC with a religious metaphor that once news and current affairs gained the ascendancy at the ABC, people in power became upset:

> Man is born into trouble as the sparks fly upward, it is recorded in the Book of Job, and certainly whatever tribulations of political and public criticism the ABC had endured previously were like moonlight unto sunshine of what shone upon it after its introduction of regular public affairs programmes.[326]

In 1977, the industrial advocate for the ABC Staff Association, Andrew Watson, said within five years Federal Government interference at the ABC would damage it to the extent that it would be "a debilitated, dispirited, unwholesome, sycophantic ghost of an organisation" (*The Canberra Times*, 1977).[327] The causes of this interference were staff ceilings and funding cuts. In addition, Watson said that "experienced staff were leaving because of the uncertainty surrounding their employment" (ibid.).[328] Haunting by spectres and resisting them has been a recurring trauma for poor Aunty. As a consequence of these staff ceilings and cuts, the ghost metaphor was revived in 1985 when the ABC was found to have created a "phantom army". Newspapers called out the ABC's "phantom army" discovered by ABC management and described as such by the Managing Director Geoffrey Whitehead, when funding cuts necessitated another need to shed personnel. Staff then took offence at having those on contract "who had been employed by the ABC for many years" (*The Canberra Times*, 1985)[329] being described as a "phantom army".

According to former ABC staff-elected board member, Tom Molomby (1991),[330] the existence of around 1000 people employed in part-time, casual or contract roles was to evade a staff ceiling imposed on the ABC in the 1970s. A Senate Estimates Committee had been told the cost of these 1248 staff was AUD9 million (Molomby, ibid.). According to Molomby (1991), the "phantom army" media release was made by Whitehead on the Friday before a long weekend and the board was not notified beforehand, implying it was made in haste and without the counsel of his board. It should also be noted here that there are disagreements in the literature. Whitehead said he did *not* have the full support of all board members, including Molomby who took him to court, and in addition Whitehead said he had been "singled out by the NSW branch of the staff association in a campaign of personal vilification" (Whitehead, 1988).[331] Molomby (1991) said Whitehead blamed the ABC's Controller of Corporate Relations, Keith Jackson, for the use of the word "phantom" (Molomby, 1991).[332] But Whitehead (1988) said he did agree with the "dramatization" of the staffing situation[333]:

> It was contrary to all my previous experience in management but I felt the very high risks would be justified if we pulled it off. We needed to get the numbers down, force a hotter pace for necessary changes, and then go back to government with a stronger case for funds in the second half of the financial year. (Whitehead, 1988)[334]

Molomby (1991) said the news release also implied that ABC management was "incompetent" and "stupid" because of these "phantom" people (Molomby, 1991).[335] Molomby (Loc. Cit.) claimed the incident not only created "extensive and damaging publicity" (ibid.)[336] for the ABC it indicated there was a breakdown between management and the board. Staff also blamed management's remoteness and not representing the ABC's interests (Loc. Cit.).[337] Whitehead resigned half-way through his five-year term.

As part of the accusation against the managing director, the Staff Association printed a newsletter headed: "Geoffrey Whitehead: A Chronology of Failure". Whitehead (1988) said legal advice told him it was defamatory, but he chose not to act, instead writing to staff:

> My argument is not with the vast majority of union members—only with a small group of activists who have for years exercised more influence than they warrant, and are now resorting to personal vilification.[338]

After Whitehead's resignation in 1986, *The Sydney Morning Herald* said: "There should be an acceptance, especially by the ABC unions, that while the public perception remains that the ABC is not giving value for money, the politicians will continue to inflict the death of a thousand budget cuts on it" (ibid.).[339]

Then in 2018 another phantom emerged when ABC staff accused Managing Director Michelle Guthrie of being "an invisible MD" (Meade, 2018b)[340] with staff saying they were "spooked" (ibid.).[341] A news report said that the ABC "fostered a culture of anxiety" for fear of upsetting élites. A broadcaster told a newspaper: "Frankly, we are all spooked by everything in here" (Loc. Cit.). The trepidation originated from senior actors requiring more conservative voices for the ABC, a more conservative tone for Aunty (ibid.).[342] The ghostly metaphor was extended further when staff accused the ABC news director, Gaven Morris, of "jumping at shadows" (ibid.)[343] when he handed over a file of documents to the Department of the Prime Minister and Cabinet that had been sold at an auction of old government furniture in Canberra and passed on to the ABC. The ABC said:

> The Cabinet Files is one of the biggest breaches of cabinet security in Australian history. Thousands of pages of documents, some marked "top secret" and "AUSTEO" (for Australian Eyes Only), were contained in the sold-off filing cabinets. (Clarke, 2018)[344]

3.7 Challenging Times for Any Public Funding

One salient point about the erosion of funding to public broadcasting, around the world, has meant that there has been a loss of "the language" (Tracey, 1998)[345] of public broadcasting in favour of having to count money, monitor performance and accommodate creeping commercialism. Specifically, there has been a loss of the authoritative voice of Australia's Aunty. Narratives about creating content have been subsumed by words, themes and discourses about creating efficiencies and cutting costs. Tracey (1998) said: "one sees a shift from having key decision-makers with a commitment to using broadcasting for some decent social purpose to those who think and act more like accountants" (ibid.).[346] He (1998) also identified that funding contractions had shifted public broadcasters from being broadcaster-producers to broadcaster-publishers which, he said, "triggered a cultural anorexia" (Loc. Cit.)[347] because public broadcasters were no longer able to nurture talent across all genres. In 2013, the licence-funded Greek public broadcaster (ERT) was shut down in the nation's fourth year of recession and harsh austerity because the Economy Ministry denounced its staff as: "unproductive and live at the expense of the rest of society and the state—a clientelistic and nepotistic state parasite" (Fouskas, 2013).[348]

In Australia, the situation has been different. A 2006 leaked KPMG report, commissioned by the Australian Federal Government found:

> The ABC provides a high volume of outputs and quality relative to the level of funding it receives … the ABC appears to be a broadly efficient organisation. (Simons, 2006)[349]

According to Fouskas (2013) the Greek ERT, which eventually re-opened in 2015 after being sustained by staff, was being punished because: "the aim was that ERT would become the government's mouthpiece, but this did not happen" (ibid.). It was re-opened, albeit with limited capacity because of "the contribution by a public broadcaster to informing, educating and entertaining the Greek people and the diaspora" (President of the Council of State, 2013)[350]. Even so, the ABC's funding, programming and staffing shrinkages have led to a divestment of legacy knowledge and institutional memory within the ABC and make it less resilient overall in forgetting its ***cultural capital*** and ***reputational capital***. Research for this book has shown that retaining, restoring, and drawing on legacy knowledge is anathema to an ABC management which is trying to act more pragmatically and be seen to be more agile, recruiting digital natives, in a new ***field*** of digital prospects, commercial collaborations and dwindling resources.

A consequence of the downsizing of the ABC has been a loss of legacy knowledge. Long-time staff can be seen by management as an impediment to change and obsolete, while the literature said legacy staff was an asset to an outfit. Feldman (2014) described it as: "a repository of key organizational routines, which are the product of accumulated knowledge and experiences and thereby guide corporate decision making" (March & Simon, 1958; Cyert & March, 1963; Nelson & Winter, 1982).[351] Datta et al. (2010) said downsizing was "a planned set of organizational policies and practices aimed at workforce reduction with the goal of improving firm performance" (p. 282).[352] Yet there is ongoing conflict where remaining staff may regard themselves as custodians of the old model of public service media and battle in the ***field*** even harder. It is a public media environment described by Quentin Dempster (2000) as one where there were "attempts … by federal governments of all political persuasions to marginalise public broadcasting in our national life" (Dempster, 2000).[353]

ABC staff are, on one hand, in a struggle for survival for their own careers, many developed over decades at the ABC. As well, they want to be politically active in pushing their memories of what a public broadcaster once was (and what they want it to be again/still think it is). This is being pursued, the literature said in tandem with a lack of public will to spend on the arts, an example of which was in the United Kingdom in the 1980s when then British Prime Minister Margaret Thatcher decided that public arts organisations "should become more self-sufficient by seeking alternative sources of operating revenue" (Chong & Bogdan, 2010).[354] However, other research showed that publics in South East Asia and Australia supported more government spending in general terms, than less (Park, 2010).[355] Government spending has increased each year overall with 35% on welfare and social security (Klapdor & Arthur, 2017)[356] but this "blew out" due to the impact of the Coronavirus on the economy of an almost AUD86 billion deficit for 2019–2020 (when an AUD5 billion surplus had been forecast). Confounding the money situation and the future for Australian public spending, there has never been a received definition of 'public interest' in Australia (Simshaw, 2012),[357] which would provide support for public broadcasting's base claims and demands. Research literature from the United Kingdom (Booth, 2020) said that public funding for the BBC had been undermined by technological change, and that in an economics theory—club good (Buchanan, 1965) the BBC had stopped being a public good and become a club good—halfway between a private good and a public good.

Further, Australian society does not value public broadcasting as it once did because it has been swamped with an abundance of the other and government is supportive of private funding for the arts, generally (Tong, 2020); where only those who patronise the arts are more likely to support public funding (Katz-Gerro, 2012). Downsizing can only go so far when money becomes tight, and then comes pressure to privatise, commercialise or take sponsorship—what Dempster (2000) described as being "subverted to the commercial imperative" (ibid.).[358] The ABC takes suggestions of its privatisation as hostile, aggressive and coming from Rupert Murdoch, or "the conservative press": "for "conservative press" read Rupert Murdoch's News Corp and its columnists" (Barry, 2018).[359] Yet, from a raw economic and accounting point of view there is much else that needs to be heard and considered. The ABC has abandoned the élite exclusive *field* it once occupied and must re-establish itself as a sub-*field* within the emergent commercial digital *field*—or risk being drowned-out in the battle that is smothering its voice.

3.8 What Are They Fighting For?

The extant, current and grey literature explained that ABC staff culture has had a powerful impact on the running of the public service media outlet. However, it was a double-edged sword. The role of the ABC Staff Association had played a critical role in establishing fair work standards and equitable remuneration for staff. The formation of the association in 1939 was a watershed and culmination of a *cri du coeur* from staff for regular, reasonable work hours (in 1938 the NSW Manager and his staff were working until 11.30 pm four nights a week, plus most Saturday afternoons, see Thomas, 1980[360]). They wanted their conditions and wages to match those of other government employees. They had to battle to prove that they were public servants, too, and therefore entitled to regulated work conditions. They knew they were public servants and wanted it acknowledged in their pay and conditions. ABC senior executives then worked "ridiculously long hours and had annual leave accumulating in arrears" (ibid.),[361] to the extent that Charles Moses and Chairman William Cleary "worked often to two or three in the morning, refused bonus payments and rarely took a holiday"—"at the heart of Cleary's recruitment philosophies lay a belief that being permitted to work in the ABC was sufficient reward in itself" and "related partly to the Fabian view that what really mattered was 'a life of fascinating interest to the exercise of faculty, and in the consciousness of service rendered'" (Loc. Cit.).[362]

The ABC Staff Association's formation indicated there was "a staff dissatisfaction that existed in almost every section and at almost every level of the ABC" (Blain, 1977)[363] and there was concern that staff positions were filled without a plan (ibid.)[364] and that "to ever reach the top you would have had to begin at least half-way up" (ibid.).[365] The association quickly took root and by the close of 1939 all states had local committees of the staff association and, following that, the first Staff Rules were composed containing rights and conditions—even though they had flimsy legal status and the ABC was not compelled to live up to them (ibid.).[366] Conditions were still rough, nonetheless, by today's industrial standards: the commission could fill jobs without notification, women had to resign upon marriage, married women could not be given a classified position and striking was prohibited. Yet passion for industrial unity grew quickly and by 1944, 72.2% of staff belonged to the association (ibid.).[367] However, it never formed an alliance with the Australian Journalists Association—the AJA—which "opposed house unions" and worked under different conditions with "more generous leave provisions and overtime payments" (Loc. Cit.).[368] It was also important to note that unionism generally was growing in Australia during World War II, workers were more 'put upon' with staff shortages caused by many absent workers serving in the armed forces and ancillary activities and encouragement was also given to the unions by the Australian Labor Party (ibid.).[369] The ABC Staff Association tactics at the time were to be: "a capable spokesman for its members" and "never a hint of strike action" (ibid.).[370] It controlled the contested staff *field* through negotiation with management and occasional votes of 'no confidence' in the commission.

The ABC Staff Association (non-journalists) no longer exists as its own entity and is now part of the Community and Public Sector Union. Prior to this merger there were ongoing concerns that the ABC Staff Association was a "highly centralised bureaucracy" (Thomas, 1980)[371] which successive managers have tried (many unsuccessfully) to change. Former Managing Director Geoffrey Whitehead expressed concerns about the association (and also reflective of the ABC staff culture) that as an in-house union it was: "more likely to become preoccupied with old battles, it is therefore less likely to anticipate changing times" (Whitehead, 1988).[372] There are comments in the historical literature on the role of the ABC Staff Association which was described as "being worthy of a book in itself" (Blain, 1977).[373] Former staffer Ellis Blain (1977) quoted Ian Wynne from the Forbes Street announcing staff "once the most militant groups in the whole ABC" and that the "aggressive policy of the Association" (in the 1970s) dated from the introduction of television in 1956 and the arrival of so-described "pale blue-collar workers" (ibid.).[374]

In addition, a shift in staff culture occurred within the staff association when television was launched in 1956 because there was an influx of technicians and engineers (ibid.).[375] Previously, the association had been inhabited by "white collar workers" and at that time the association was in the dying stages of what Blain referred to as "the old family-style ABC" (ibid.).[376] Yet, this arrival of engineers and technicians changed the staff association "quite radically" (ibid.)[377] such that by 1976 it was "an industrial force to be reckoned with. Its attitude was: 'This is what we want. We're going to get it'" (ibid.).[378]

The literature describes corporate culture as one of the "informal factors" of corporate governance (Kumar & Zattoni, 2018).[379] So, organisational culture was somewhat of a conundrum. It was something which existed, it was abstract and intangible, yet staff imbibed it and it was a lived reality. This lived phenomenon of working in a group cannot be packaged—it is not a "drop it on your foot" commodity. Schein (2010) said organisational cultures were vital, healthy and provided stability. On the other hand, they could negate progress and success by constraining the sorts of leadership that were acceptable to an organisation (Schein, 2010)[380]: "culture creates within us mindsets and frames of reference that Marshak (2006) identified as one of a number of important covert processes" (ibid.)[381] another was interpersonal competition (ibid.).[382] By way of counterpoint, Pope Francis I defined the positive aspects of a healthy, engaged culture as:

> Living culture tends to open up, to integrate, to multiply, to share, to dialogue, to give and receive within a people and with other peoples with whom it enters into relationship. (Spadaro, 2020)[383]

The role of senior leaders in turning around organisations was widely recognised as an important factor in an organisation's success (ibid.)[384] and many ABC managing directors have achieved outstanding results in progressing the organisation, in terms of making it relevant to changing media times. Research done of founder CEOs of other types of organisations has found, for example, that instead of retrenching staff to save short-term costs, successful organisations had looked to strategies that would increase long-term prospects (Abebe & Tangpong, 2017)[385] and that work culture was important to the process and represented much more than how things were done:

> Culture is a critical strategy for large-scale change. It involves the articulation and consistent, long-term promotion of the values, norms, and daily behaviors that allow people, organizations, and communities to align their actions in a disciplined way that contributes to progress. (Celep & Mosher-William, 2016)[386]

Further it was found that cultures which embraced change were: more innovative; more racially inclusive; transparent and collaborative; and, the staff culture was more aligned with the values of the institution (ibid.).[387] There was also evidence that if staff culture held sub-conscious beliefs, such as believing it knew better than management how to run the organisation, then this caused conflict with the institutional objectives overall (Loc. Cit.).[388]

Once staff was enculturated it became a form of "social control" (Schein, 2010).[389] However, embedded staff cultures, such as that at the ABC, were hard to shift because there was "resistance to change" (ibid.).[390] When the staff was delivered "disconfirming" information, such as audience reaction against content for example, it may not point to the exact problem but instead revealed: "that something is wrong somewhere" (Loc. Cit.)[391] this then induced "survival anxiety" (Loc. Cit.)[392] and created a defensive culture. On 24 June 2014, senior ABC broadcaster Quentin Dempster and also former staff-elected board member was reported in a newspaper as having tweeted: "ABC/SBS boards need dynamic, quality directors, not Murdoch-approved party political hacks or ideologues" (Price, 2014).[393] This was in response to the appointments of Janet Albrechtsen a political conservative, and ABC board member appointed by the government of former Prime Minister John Howard, and former deputy Liberal Party leader Neil Brown to a panel to oversee appointments to the ABC and SBS boards. Albrechtsen had been publicly critical of the ABC, which was received with foreboding by ABC staff.

ABC staff culture had become so reactive (as evidenced by staff activity on social media) that instead of creating what Schein (2010) called "psychological safety" the ABC was in state where senior staff, as individual actors, were taking it upon themselves to be reactive to any criticism (notably this played out on Twitter). Individual staff and the organisation had placed themselves under permanent attack by engaging strongly in the cyber-realm where anonymity and abuse also thrived. Organisational management theorists said institutions limited themselves when they were permanently defensive. If this defensiveness were to dissipate, the staff culture would have to move to one where there was a sense of safety. Schein (2010) said: "when an organisation sets out to really transform itself by creating psychological safety, real and significant changes can be achieved" (Schein, 2010).[394] In addition, senior ABC management seemed to be playing no public role in providing steps to create "psychological safety" when managing change.

There have been many colourful episodes where senior managers have sought to contain and placate restive staff. In 1944, General Manager Charles Moses conducted angry exchanges with a staff member over a pay dispute through the newspapers. Moses went straight to the press to speak about the resignation of the conductor of the Melbourne Symphony Orchestra,[395] Haydn Beck, and handed over Beck's resignation letter for publication. Beck then reacted through the press that the ABC had treated him with "almost contempt" (*The Mercury*, 1944)[396] in accepting his resignation without regret or negotiation and publishing his resignation in the press without his knowledge, after ten years conducting for the MSO. He said his attempts at seeking a pay rise were frustrated such that "any attempt to speak with responsible officers was met with rudeness" (*The Argus*, 1944).[397]

Moses riposted (through newspapers, again) that Beck had "virtually held a pistol at the commission's head" (*The Advertiser*, 1944)[398] and that "a very grave scandal could have been caused by the attitude of the former leader of the Melbourne Symphony Orchestra (Mr Haydn Beck) in demanding an increase in salary and allowances as an alternative to his resignation half-way through the Ormandy[399] season", and he revealed that Beck's salary "was practically double what it was when he joined the ABC Orchestra eight years ago" (*The Advertiser* ibid.). Beck then told *The Sydney Morning Herald*: "mine is not an isolated case there is general dissatisfaction among principal musicians regarding the Commission's relationship with them. Leaders of sections of the ABC orchestras are paid an inadequate rate. They are highly skilled few in number and should be given better conditions" (*The Sydney Morning Herald*, 1944).[400]

Blain said in 1975 with the arrival of the Fraser Liberal Government "the ABC faced its first hint of a future all-in fight for economic and political survival" (ibid.).[401] Other literature and research supported this view. It was a watershed year. The ABC ended up with a 15% funding cut for 1976/77. Blain (1977) quoted Ian Wynne from the Staff Association about the large budget cut: "It's like garnisheeing a man's wages and telling him he can have dinner at the Hilton if he wants to" (ibid.).[402] The ABC responded by dismissing short-term contract employees. Wynne also said: "it's no use the ABC screaming in public they are being badly done by. The 85% who don't watch the ABC don't care" (Loc. Cit.).[403] At the time the union passed a vote of no confidence in the ABC's Chairman, Sir Henry Bland. Since 1976 that funding situation has deteriorated for the ABC, or been a battle fought regularly. A significant gain in staff influence in the running of the ABC had been identified as occurring when the first staff-elected representative was allowed to sit on the Board in 1983. This was a decision of the Hawke Labor Government. Originally two staff members were proposed on the board but that was reduced to one. Since then, staff have at times demonstrated and spoken that they know what the ABC should do, the manner in which it should be run and how it can best live up to its Charter obligations.

Also, since the 1970s, ABC Staff tended to operate more strongly in discrete, defensive siloes, which the literature describes as "sub-cultures" and it was these which prevented a future 'whole of organisation' approach. However, it had been found that organisations where there was a culture which promoted staff training and opportunities to move within and around the organisation meant people were more connected with each other and communicating across the organisation (Passmore, 2013),[404] although this varies from industry to industry.

3.9 Alan Ashbolt

As this book is making the case for assessing the ABC in the light of Bourdieu's theories of *field*, *habitus* and *cultural capital*, the case of ABC senior staff member and Director of Radio Special Projects, Alan Ashbolt, illustrates a clear attempt by an ABC staff member to control the *field* through the exercise of their *political capital*. The literature said Ashbolt was a controversial staff member, a "prominent member of the ALP" (Harding, 1979) and "lion of the ABC left" (Edwards, 1974, in Harding, 1979)[405] who held strong political views and was not prepared to compromise them. In 1977 he wrote in the literary journal *Meanjin* (Harding, 1979) that there can be no "even-handedness" in the Australian media because the commercial media supported right-wing views, so the ABC should be redressing that imbalance. He explained the organisation's *field*: "The ABC is the ideological arm of the capitalist state machinery, fulfilling the task of disseminating bourgeois tastes, opinions and attitudes" and that the term "even-handedness" was used as a means of controlling the ABC, "a device for protecting the status quo, for preserving inequality and injustice, while trying to project an image of democratic fairness" (Harding, 1979, quoting Ashbolt, 1977).[406] Ashbolt also wrote that: "no genuinely creative artist or thinker lives in a self-made world of pure abstraction, but is always responding (if sometimes only by withdrawal or rebellion) to social, economic and political conditions" (Ashbolt, 1986).[407]

Ashbolt was a socialist and expressed bitter disappointment at the ALP for failing to further the cause of socialism[408] in Australia. Former Deputy Managing Director, Clement Semmler (1981), said the subject of Ashbolt was featured on most of the Boards' agendas with the recurrent question: "how could they rid themselves of this turbulent priest?" (Semmler, 1981).[409]

Inglis (1983) described several examples where "transgressing" (ibid.) staff were retrieved from dismissal by a vigilant and vocal staff association and one of the more controversial members of staff was Ashbolt: "a long thorn in the side of the ABC establishment" (Loc. Cit.),[410] a broadcaster with radical views as an anti-Vietnam War activist and vocal ALP supporter, who was removed in 1964 as editor and compere of Four Corners for an item that criticised the Returned Servicemen's League (now the Returned Services League or RSL). Ashbolt was described variously as "a very delicate problem" (Bowman, 2005),[411] "an apostle of Marxism" (ibid.)[412] and "cerebral" (ibid.).[413] ABC Journalists, on the other hand, described him as "the Lion of the ABC" (ibid.),[414] and he was quoted having said that Marxism was: "a legitimate tool of social analysis, and a legitimate mode of political action" (ibid.).[415] He also, according to Inglis' (1983) personal description, was a "warm man, good-looking and a solid 188 centimetres tall" (ibid.)[416] and this stature would have helped him accumulate Bourdieusian ***political capital***.[417]

Ashbolt's time at the ABC also demonstrated that the management lacked legitimacy in the eyes of the staff and that Ashbolt had strong staff support to counteract management. Management was able neither to manage, nor remove him, from the organisation.[418]

Bourdieu (1991) said that when such groups had established their ***political capital*** they were more likely to mobilise in a military style and enter into a war situation on whatever was confronting the organisation (ibid.).[419] This was manifested in several ways at the ABC. One of which was that there was an explicit understanding among staff that it knew better how to manage resources. Contained in ABC staff understandings is that they know better than the ABC management, the Managing Director, the Chair, the Board, the Minister for Communications and the Federal Government. This was articulated earlier on by Alan Ashbolt:

> I hoped that the staff union would be used to build up a collective responsibility for standards. … I considered that control over program content should be exercised by producers at the work points, not by administrators and policy-framers. … I was aiming for democratisation. (Bowman, 2005)[420,421]

Semmler (1981), former ABC deputy general manager (1965–1977), related an incident concerning Ashbolt who was at that time the organiser of the ABC Boyer Lectures (a prestigious annual series of talks given by an eminent Australian on a topic of their choice and named after Sir Richard Boyer the ABC Chairman in 1961 when they were launched).[422] In 1976, Professor Manning Clark was the invited speaker. The Head of Radio, Keith Mackriell, requested copies of Professor Clark's scripts for review. Of chief concern was that Clark had already spoken at an anti-Whitlam government dismissal rally and there was existing criticism the ABC wanted to avoid fuelling—accused of bias in condemning the sacking of the Whitlam Labor Government in the 1975 constitutional crisis and deploring the dismissal of that government by Governor-General Sir John Kerr.

However, this request for the scripts triggered belligerence from the ABC Staff Association which released a newsletter to members headed:

"Censorship—Battle lines drawn between ABC Programme makers and their Bureaucrats" (Semmler, 1981).[423] It was seen by staff as an attempt by management to assume censorship and editorial control. But as Semmler said: "a series as important as the Boyer Lectures, editorial control clearly rested much further up the line than at the radio producer level" (ibid.).[424]

Ashbolt responded to Mackriell and the response was leaked to newspapers:

> Again, what can be the purpose of your wanting to see those scripts except to exercise a blatant form of political censorship? Are you insisting that Manning Clark adjust is views on history and historiography according to your political dictates? And do you propose that Boyer Lectures should in future be screened by you for political correctness? (ibid.)[425]

Semmler noted:

> The point is overlooked that at a time when political tensions were at breaking-point, and when the ABC was under fire for alleged partisanship in some of its programmes on this issue. … Mackreill was merely endeavouring to follow the classic precept that 'Caesar's wife must be above suspicion'—a precept, indeed, that the ABC commissioners and senior executives have habitually beaten their breasts about, in public statements down the years. (ibid.)[426]

Semmler (1981) said that it was also an imperative that policy was adhered to through middle and senior management of the ABC, implicitly it was not a staff only responsibility. Semmler also blamed the diversity and lack of knowledge of the board as a problem in trying to obtain unified, coherent decisions and policymaking: "*quot homines, tot sententiae*—there are as many opinions as there are men" (ibid.).[427]

Ashbolt wrote for the *New Statesman* (an English socialist newspaper) critical of the Liberal Party government in Australia (ibid.)[428] and was also a member of the ALP Sub-committee. High-level robust discussions between the government and the ABC ensued with concerns Ashbolt was being paid for these articles. The ABC was questioned if Ashbolt had been given permission from his managers for this freelancing. However, tensions were relieved when there was a change of government and a Whitlam-lead ALP government won office. This seemed to have neutralised any concerns[429] about the staff member. Although, Inglis (1983) said, as a consequence, Ashbolt was then "quarantined at radio" to Special Projects Radio (Inglis, 1983).[430] Inglis (1983) also said that, in general, ABC staff was not completely loyal to the organisation and readily supplied commercial media with leaks "who lived by an ethic in which confidentiality and loyalty to the organisation were not necessarily virtues" (ibid.).[431] One of his sources for his first book on the ABC told him: "put nothing in a memo … unless you want to see it in tomorrow's papers" (ibid.).[432]

3.10 Addressing Accusations of Bias

In order to provide some understanding of how the ABC provides public service for funding, this book will thematically analyse a case study of a significant and controversial matter attracting both national and international media attention. It took place over a period of five years and concerned Australia's highest-ranking Catholic, His Eminence Cardinal George Pell A.C. There was public criticism (Sheridan, 2020[433]; Bolt, 2020a[434]; Donnan, 2020[435]) of the media coverage of his court cases, singling out ABC and Channel Nine journalists, as having been biased against Pell for urging-on his prosecution and reporting in a biased manner. Even the courts themselves expressed concern about a "witch-hunt" (County Court of Victoria at Melbourne Criminal Division, 2019)[436] and that Pell was a "scapegoat" (Victorian Court of Appeal, 2019).[437] In 2019, as the ABC was evaluating the next round of cuts to accommodate reduced funding, the ABC Chair, Ita Buttrose, said that the ABC "might be biased" where "some staff at the broadcaster unconsciously let their biases show through" (Bonyhady, 2019).[438] US sociologist Herbert Gans (2003) situated bias as: "when not telling the whole story is viewed as inaccuracy, the term becomes a synonym for bias" (Gans, 2003).[439] Bias was also a sign that journalists were failing to understand themselves (Gans, 2003) and ultimately, this resulted in a disempowered professional media where audiences can search for information to make up their own minds.

Concerning the Pell case, there was particular criticism of the ABC's investigative news reporting on *730* and *Four Corners* television programs which had both done special episodes on Pell (Henderson, 2020[440]; Sheridan, 2020[441]). The impact of the coverage provoked international attention with Pope Francis 1 calling for Pell to be trialled by the justice system rather than trialled by the media (Enus et al., 2016).[442] Pell asserted that the bias of the ABC accompanied the dissonance of it being "partly funded by Catholic taxes" (Bowling, 2020).[443] Of concern, was criticism that Pell was held accountable for all abuse that has been carried out by all actors within the Catholic Church. He was being punished, in a collective act, for all the abusers and those who chose to facilitate or ignore the abuse and support the abusers, among which there were countless and many deceased. In addition, a report came to light after Pell's release from prison that a former Vatican official paid Australian accusers AUD1.1 million (700,000 Euros) as bribes (West, 2020[444]; Bucci, 2020[445]). The investigation is ongoing at the time of this publication.

The focus of this research point, however, is that perceived, fabricated or background wrongdoings do not form part of a legal prosecution nor defence under Australian law. Australia has adversarial justice, meaning the prosecution has to prove the accused is guilty beyond reasonable doubt. Conversely, the defence does not have to prove its innocence. Consequently, past convictions are not reported before or after charges are laid, nor when a trial is underway. Concerns about media bias were raised by both individuals and the courts in so far as Pell was conflated with all accusations made of him, as well as all abuse by all Church actors and all convicted paedophiles in general. The universalised, received implication was that Pell had either conducted, orchestrated or condoned all abuse—probably all three. The concerning issue here, and the salient point in terms of Australian journalism is a technical one under law: enlarged matters, rumours or hunches, cannot be overlaid on specific charges in a trial. Pell was arraigned, convicted and then granted leave to appeal by the High Court of Australia, and acquitted unanimously with all convictions quashed on five specific charges. Throughout this he had maintained his innocence. However, the media bias surrounding the case threatened to subvert, subsume and marginalise the unique, vital role of all courts and justice in Australia in deciding guilt, innocence and punishment ahead of the trial. This is the central point of the bias criticism made and the prompt for this thematic analysis of ABC coverage of the case.

Horrifying details established by Australia's Royal Commission into Institutional Responses to Child Sexual Abuse (2017) pointed out the prominent role of the Catholic Church in historic sexual abuse of Australian children and this book is not analysing that serious and damning matter and its perpetrators. Nor does it seek to take sides, nor analyse the decades (centuries) of criminal wrongdoing, neglect and suffering where there was an acceptance of depravity and violent abuse meted out by Catholic religious in schools, churches and institutions to the most vulnerable, to children. Court cases, witness statements and inquiries have revealed a normalisation and tacit encouragement of child sexual abuse within, and by, Catholic Church actors.

Rather, this book is seeking to textually analyse the language used in the specialised sub-*field* of court reporting by the ABC using one particular case study where there were accusations of ABC bias, to develop one of the aims of the book—to analyse where Aunty's voice is being strangled. It seeks to identify "choke points" and accusations of bias provide opportunity for analysis. In this instance the court case was time-bound but was also of such national and international significance that ABC coverage became a focal point of how Australians received and understood the case and its outcome. The purpose of this analysis is to identify any evidence of bias in specific online reporting surrounding the case. It looks at the published words only on ABC webpages.[446] The context and content of ABC News reports online and allegations of bias were accused of placing the court cases of Pell within the context of other, but legally irrelevant details and turned the case against Pell into a case against all religious who have abused children (and adults). The consequences of biased or inaccurate media reporting are sub judice contempt of court, disobedience, scandalising the court and perverting the course of justice. If convicted of these, a consequence for journalists could be gaol.

Of larger matter, biased reporting of cases and their outcomes can also undermine public confidence in the judicial process if the desired outcome is not obtained in a verdict or appeal. The ABC, as an independent entity in Australian society, as an institution, is assumed to recognise the independence of another pillar of society, and another institution, the judiciary. Courts are open for scrutiny (subject to the judge's discretion), but not influence. The ABC has been accused in the reporting of the Pell case of including themes that referenced extraneous matters, instead of reporting only what was said by the judge and before a jury and how those specific matters were resolved legally. The Catholic Church resides with the religious right and with the ABC's content shift to the left, it brings the two into a tighter opposition—a binary of which most other religions are also part, although largely left alone. The Catholic Church, as another institution, is also problematised for the media because of its benevolence and social justice advocacy, especially for asylum-seekers, emphasis on welfare, its substantial role in Australian healthcare, aged care, work with indigenous Australian communities, and all levels of education as well as a "realpolitik" role aimed at "protecting and extending" its influence (Chapman, 2009).[447]

In a court of law, the accused only has to respond to the specific charges. After the verdict against Pell was handed down Professor Emeritus at the Crawford School of Public Policy, the *Australian National University*, Ramesh Thakur (2019), said that he found this media contextualising of Pell within the entire framework of abuse "deeply disquieting" because:

> The suspicion persists that the jury was not so much persuaded of Pell's guilt by a careful evaluation of the evidence, as swayed by the nature of the alleged offence amidst a climate of abhorrence at the systemic coverup by the church (in which Pell seems to have played a significant part) of priests' predatory behaviour. Allegations of historical sexual assault are among the easiest to make but the hardest to refute. (Thakur, 2019)[448]

Pell's court cases took place in the foreground of the Pell reports published by the ABC on its current affairs television program *730* "conspiring to pervert the course of justice" (Bourke, 2016[449]) and on its weekly investigative television program *Four Corners* (ABC, 2019a).[450] The ABC reporting of Pell on Four Corners was also criticised by ABC presenter Paul Barry because it: "did not canvass any of Pell's defence from the trial" (Media Watch, 2020).[451] Barry (Media Watch, ibid.) was also critical of other senior ABC staff who publicly doubted Pell's innocence after his successful appeal to the High Court.

Backgrounding this, have been horrifying abuse allegations (and some convictions) perpetrated by religious within the Australian Catholic Church (and within the context of other religious as well as secular institutions) against children, including both abuse and trauma. Australians had been appalled at the allegations and subsequent findings made at the five-year Royal Commission into Institutional Responses to Child Sexual Abuse. Its final report handed down in December 2017 noted it had made 2575 referrals to authorities (including police) (Royal Commission into Institutional Responses to Child Sexual Abuse, 2017).[452] The widespread shock of the scale of the sexual abuse of children, the torture of the innocent, not only damages the abused, but also those who witnessed the abuse. On another level it destroys trust in the institutions and on a wider level damage to society's future. That the Catholic Church carried it out for decades and simply moved abusers on to new parishes and institutions was deeply disturbing and unforgettable to Australian society at large. Redacted parts of the Royal Commission final report (released after the Pell High Court decision) covered by the media alleged Pell was part of this process of moving offenders on (Dunstan et al., 2020).[453] The crime of child sexual abuse both horrifies and traumatises society with many details of the crimes revealed through the judicial process and reported by the media at large.

The abuse by the Catholic Church occurred elsewhere—Canada, Chile, much of Europe (Paulson, 2002),[454] the US (*USA Today*, 2004)[455] and Ireland (*BBC*, 2009)[456] which have given the crimes international prominence and ramifications with early denials of the abuse by the Vatican that it was "a manifestation of cultural depravity and a news media crazed by sex" (Paulson, ibid.) inflaming outrage and perpetuating damage. Backgrounding Australian's perspectives on this further, was the 2009 Cloyne Report in Ireland (the Commission of Investigation, Dublin Archdiocese, Catholic Diocese of Cloyne) which examined allegations of sexual abuse of children in that diocese, perpetrated by members of the Catholic Church in Ireland. It was the fourth report into abuse by the Irish Catholic Church and followed the diocese of Ferns Report in 2005, the 2009 Ryan Report (abuse in residential institutions) and the Dublin Archdiocese Report (also 2009) (*BBC News*, 2011).[457] The then Irish Taoiseach, Enda Kenny, gave a powerful summation of the Cloyne Report and the malice of the Catholic Church and its actors:

> The Cloyne Report excavates the dysfunction, disconnection, elitism, the narcissism that dominate the culture of the Vatican to this day. The rape and torture of children were downplayed or "managed" to uphold, instead, the primacy of the institution, its power, standing and "reputation". (*The Irish Times*, 2011)[458]

The report also shined a light on the role of Gardai (the Irish police) in protecting perpetrators by failing to attend to, or pursue, complaints of sexual, psychological and other physical abuse made against Irish religious. Then Irish Minister for Children, Frances Fitzgerald, said "never again will someone be allowed to place the protection of their institution above the protection of children" (*BBC News*, 2011).[459]

Children are not only heard now, they are listened to with great care, and society is acting on their behalf in many ways (stepping up standards on the Working With Children Check clearance (WWCC) among those who work with children, is just one example); to protect them, prosecute for them and prevent the recurrence of this abuse to them, or adults. The emphasis now is on creating a safe, nurturing environment for children everywhere. These investigations, however, have not only had devastatingly revealing reverberations for the Catholic Church and other institutions where children have been abused, the knowledge of this abuse is now embedded within society's collective memory and understandings of how power and innocence are abused and hidden under the cloak of religion. In the case of the Catholic Church the power coalesced around male leaders, sometimes with the tacit support of female religious or similar abuse by female religious, in a ***field*** of exclusive religious ***cultural capital and reputation capital***. It was a ***field*** of power that was apparently unchallengeable and the frustration this has caused has been devastating.

Table 3.1 Summary corpus of analysis in ABC coverage of Pell case

Date of publication	*Topic*	*Number of reports*
1. 26 July 2017	Pell's Day One Trial (Cathedral case)	2
2. 26 February 2019 (actually handed down 11 December 2018, but suppressed)	Pell's second trail (first mistrial, suppression order) Guilty verdict	4
3. 27 February 2019	Pell's second trail (first mistrial, suppression order) Guilty verdict	4
4. 28 February 2019	Pell's second trail (first mistrial, suppression order) Guilty verdict	4
5. 13 March 2019	Sentencing	5
6. 14 March 2019	Sentencing	2
7. 21 August 2019	Loses appeal	13
8. 22 August 2019	Loses appeal	2
9. 13 November 2019	High Court agrees to hear appeal	1
10. 14 November 2019	High Court agrees to hear appeal	1
11. 11 March 2020	First day of appeal	1
12. 12 March 2020	First day of appeal	1
13. 7 April 2020	High Court quashes convictions	7
14. 8 April 2020	High Court quashes convictions	2
TOTAL REPORTS 49 TOTAL ANALYSED 38		

In 2020, the ABC published a response to accusations of bias in its coverage of the Pell court cases, written by its Editorial Director, four days after the High Court quashed convictions and acquitted verdicts against Pell of all charges (one offence of Sexual Penetration of a Child under 16 years and four offences of committing an Indecent Act with or in the presence of a Child under 16 years) relating to the alleged sexual assault of two 13 year old who were choirboys at St Patrick's Cathedral Melbourne in the 1990s. The ABC gave a detailed defence of its coverage of the Pell case (ABC, 2020).[460] The ABC article rebuffed the use of the word "witch-hunt" to describe ABC reporting of the Pell case was in response to a blog posting by the Melbourne Herald Sun Newspaper (owned by Rupert Murdoch's News Corporation) conservative commentator Andrew Bolt headlined: "High Court: Pell Innocent" (Bolt, 2020b)[461] Bolt (2020b) said:

> Shame on everyone who joined this witch hunt against an innocent man, ruining him and sending him to jail for 405 days for a crime he could not have committed. … Not a single ABC presenter or reporter publicly doubted his farcical and obscene conviction.[462]

The word "witch-hunt" was reprised from that used at Pell's sentencing by County Court Chief Judge, Peter Kidd, who said (researcher has underlined word "witch-hunt"):

> 12. Next, in sentencing you today, Cardinal Pell, I am not sitting in judgment of the Catholic religion or the Catholic Church. It is George Pell who falls to be sentenced.
> 13. Finally, with respect to these preliminary observations, over the last period we have witnessed, outside of this court and within our community, examples of a 'witch-hunt' or 'lynch mob' mentality in relation to Cardinal Pell. I utterly condemn such behaviour. That has nothing to do with justice or a civilized society. The Courts stand as a bulwark against such irresponsible behaviour.
> 14. Cardinal Pell, I want to acknowledge that in sentencing you today, I do so on the basis that you are a member of the community, like any other. Most importantly, while I must punish you for your offending, like anyone who falls to be sentenced by our courts, you are entitled to the balanced and steady hand of justice.[463]

In a Sky television interview after his release from prison, when asked by Bolt if the ABC's role in his "persecution" concerned him, Pell replied:

> Yes, it does. Because I mean, it's partly financed by Catholic taxes. I believe in free speech. I acknowledge the right of those who differ from me to, you know, to just state their views. But in a national broadcaster, to have an overwhelming presentation of one view and only one view, I think that's a betrayal of the national interest. (Smith, 2020a)[464]

Pell also said:

> The culture wars[465] are real. There is a systematic attempt to remove the Judeo-Christian legal foundations, with the examples of marriage, life, gender, sex, and [towards] those who oppose that, unfortunately there's less rational discussion and there's more playing the man. More abuse and intimidation, and that's not good for a democracy. (ABC, 2020)[466]

The High Court decision found: "a significant possibility that an innocent person has been convicted because the evidence did not establish guilt to the requisite standard of proof" (ABC, 2020).[467]

Following the handing down of the High Court decision, there was a tense television interview exchange between an ABC News 24 presenter and the Vice-Chancellor of the Australian Catholic University, Gregory Craven, who accused the ABC of being complicit in Pell's arrest, charging and conviction—"part of the cheer squad that made that happen".[468] The interview commenced with the presenter situating Craven as a "staunch" supporter of Pell and asked if he felt "vindicated". To which Craven replied that it was not a question of being vindicated, rather that the case had "always had a reasonable doubt a mile wide" (ABC ibid.). The interview took two directions with Craven wanting to explain why there was reasonable doubt in the case and the presenter wanting to pursue Craven's interest in supporting Pell. Craven then pointed out: "a large group of the ABC and a group of Nine journalists did everything they could to put as much pressure to drown out any possible contraventions, I think worked closely with police to make sure that there were coincidental leaking of information, references to 'victims' rather than 'complainants'" (Loc. Cit.). He then accused the ABC of "trying to talk up redacted bits of the royal commission, talk up civil cases that haven't even been held, it's extraordinary" (ibid.). Any accusations made by Craven of ABC bias were interrupted or curtailed by the presenter eight times (ibid.). Questioning then focused on whether Craven felt any sympathies for the prosecution witnesses (referred to by the interviewer as the "accuser" and "victims") and damage done to the Catholic Church. Craven's closing remark was: "It was a case where a member of the Catholic Church was found not guilty of something ah that a very wide range of the media had been pushing as far as it could, for as long as it could" (ibid.). Even long after the High Court acquittal of Pell, ABC Television described him as "disgraced", then had to issue a correction and clarification that said the use of that word was "inappropriate in light of his successful appeal and acquittal by the High Court of his previous conviction for child sexual abuse" (ABC 2020). The use of the word "inappropriate" refers to behaviour, but not the rectification of a mistake.

Other criticism of media coverage of the Pell matter challenged a mocking 2016 AAP-supplied news photograph posted by the ABC online to illustrate a report on Pell (prior to Pell being charged) (Margetts et al., 2016).[469] The news report said that Pell was unwell and unable to travel to Australia to give evidence for the Royal Commission into Institutional Responses to Child Sexual Abuse in 2016 (Quadrant, 2016).[470] The news report was neutral-content themed and stated the facts. But the illustrating photograph was at odds with this. It depicted a red toy truck covered in toy rubber spiders with a cardboard cut-out of Pell in the driver's seat. The truck labelled "Pell Trucking Co.", was made presumably by a protester, placed outside the Royal Commission hearing, photographed by someone and picked up by the ABC for its news report. Nearby the truck display toy spiders were positioned as if crawling or hiding under rocks. This depiction of Pell also referenced his comments at a Royal Commission hearing two years previously that "the Catholic Church is no more legally responsible for priests who abuse children than a trucking company that employs a driver who molests women" (Mills, 2014). The ABC labelled the photo: "Protest signage featuring Cardinal George Pell outside the Royal Commission into Institutional Responses to Child Sexual Abuse" (Margetts et al., 2016).[471] Although not sub judice at a royal commission, the placement of the photo on the ABC website was an endorsement of a message and had the impact of projecting a duplicity from the organisation: reporting the event neutrally, then illustrating it with a partial and libellous photograph. Aunty was presenting a complicated opinion to the general public. Andén-Papadopolous (2008) challenged the view that news illustrations were passive: "Images which contradict or disrupt a dominant discursive frame might have a considerable impact" (2008, p. 6) where "visuals have become an important part of the news product" (de Smaele et al., 2017, p. 57) and citizen photojournalism belongs in the same emergent commercial field, supported by social media and commoditisation.

Photography is not benign, nor is it merely decorative. US Research in 2005 (Barrett & Barrington, 2005) found that the use of photographs in elections could shape, significantly, voters' attitudes to candidates and whether they would vote for them, or not, and that candidates favoured by a particular news organisation had more flattering photos published of them (Barrett & Barrington, 2005).[472] Conversely, fewer flattering photos were published by organisations that did not favour an individual political candidate. While this ABC News report with the toy truck illustration was published well prior to charges being laid against Pell it is an indicative sample of the institutional background attitude to him in the ABC *field* and appeared to have supported bias accusations.

Postmodern society is saturated with images where there is:

> relentless traffic in images, often borrowed from diverse times and places, and patched together in ever changing ways. This traffic serves commercial purposes, shapes identities, and increasingly stands in for reality itself. (Werner, 2004)[473]

If it is true that the media image "evinces the power and point of view of the political elite" (Gamson et al., ibid.),[474] then the journalist reflects in their writing their values as well as that of the organisation at which they are employed. Further, consideration must be given to the influence of the organisation, processes and parameters of the environment in which journalists operate (Tuchman, 1978[475]; Weaver, 1998[476]; Tiffen, 1989[477]; Josephi, 2000[478]). The journalist is not separate from the organisation and disclaimers have been discussed elsewhere in this book as not providing the distance from an organisation to which management aspires to place its staff. Staff and their employers are actually integrated when so much of a journalists' career depends on their activities on social media. A US study found that the regard for a news organisation was diminished when one of its journalists tweeted an opinion (Johnson, 2020).[479] This situation means serious news reports posted on social media alongside trivial or entertaining content, comment and opinion blurs the credibility of both journalist and news organisation (Johnson, ibid.).

The power of images and photographs chosen for a particular context serve to provide a perceived bias for the audience to consider. In the Pell toy truck photo there was ample intertextuality with the red colour of the truck (the colour of a cardinal's hat) and the truck itself. A truck is a favoured toy traditionally of little boys. Males formed 73.9% of abuse survivors who reported to Australia's Royal Commission into Institutional Responses to Child Sexual Abuse and carried out by Catholic Church's ordained, religious and their affiliates. These boys were abused at an average age of 10.4 years, in the first instance, and 96.2% of perpetrators were male adults. Overall, 61.8% of cases of abuse reported to the Royal Commission were carried out at religious institutions run by the Catholic

Church (*Royal Commission into Institutional Responses to Child Sexual Abuse*, 2017).[480] The spiders to evoke the term "rock spiders" is a label used in prison to describe paedophiles and the cardboard cut-out of Pell, as the most senior Australia Catholic cleric and once occupier of the third most senior role in the Catholic Church, delegitimised and impugned him in an otherwise neutral news report. As French semiotician Roland Barthes (1977) said that both the "denoted and connoted messages" of a photograph needed to be understood in order to show how a "connoted message … does comprise a plane of expression and a plane of content" (Barthes, 1977).[481]

ABC broadcaster and former Federal Coalition Minister and Senator Amanda Vanstone said: "the media are not outsiders looking in … they're players and equally fallible" (Vanstone, 2019).[482] Equally, the literature said illustrations it uses were powerful and can neither be viewed at arm's length nor irrelevant. By way of backgrounding the climate of abhorrence directed at Pell, the power of images and illustrations can have a deadly and dire impact in other contexts also. For example, the 2015 murder of 12 journalists and publishing staff by Al-Qaeda operatives at the satirical magazine *Charlie Hebdo* in Paris was in retaliation for the publication of cartoons depicting and mocking the Prophet Mohammed (whose depiction is forbidden by Islam): "In single moments as well as over the course of time, media representations can define problems, diagnose causes, make moral judgments, and suggest remedies" (Gustafson & Kenix, 2016).[483] The massacre of the *Charlie Hebdo* staff prompted a *"Je suis Charlie"* (I am Charlie) campaign among journalists around the world and they were photographed in many workplaces holding up sheets of paper with *"Je suis Charlie"* written on them. Journalists who believed they had complete freedom of speech used it as an opportunity to campaign for the value of their work everywhere. *Charlie Hebdo* had earlier been firebombed in 2011 after the publication changed its name for one edition to *Charia (Sharia) Hebdo* and mocked the Prophet Mohammed by saying they would invite him to be "editor in chief".

On a larger scale the *Charlie Hebdo* massacre serves to show that while illustrations and images are used aspirationally to suggest new aspects to news reports, create interest, entertain and provide additional context; they are not discrete, gently distracting nor irrelevant. In this instance, they were blasphemous, sacrilegious and violated the anti-idolatry beliefs of Islam. Ten years earlier staff at a Danish newspaper, *Jyllands-Posten*, received death threats for publishing satirical cartoons of the Prophet

Mohammed. More recently, in 2020 a French history teacher was decapitated in Paris in what French President Emmanuel Macron described as "Islamist terrorist attack" (*Agence France Press* 2020)[484] after the teacher showed his class cartoons of the Prophet Mohammed while giving a lesson in freedom of speech. Images are not impartial—they deliver a point—and news cartoonists are acutely and bravely aware of that when they draw their daily cartoon. Journalists and their editors regard cartoons and illustrations as part of the audience' news consumption and offers a capacity to laugh at, challenge and de-authorise issues or beliefs—but not all audiences share these views. It is also curious circumstance that when the media directs deep, provoking offence at a religion a negative reaction from that religion is always received with shock. Generally speaking, religions do not see themselves as institutions of ridicule, and this book suggests that neither did the media, nor the ABC see itself as an institution to be mocked. A non-religious media has to keep being reminded of this, or so it seems.

At the time of Pell's charging and conviction his 'Melbourne Response' (*Catholic Archdiocese of Melbourne*, n.d.)[485]—a compensation scheme of up to AUD150,000 (it had been doubled in 2016) for abused individuals and counselling established in 1996 to those who made: "complaints of sexual, physical and emotional abuse by clergy, other religious and church personnel of the Catholic Archdiocese of Melbourne"—was rejected as inadequate, even "insulting to victims" (Marr, 2013, quoting a complainant's lawyer).[486] It was also said at the Royal Commission that Pell had been dismissive of others who had lodged complaints of abuse (Toscano & Lee, 2015).[487] In addition to this more general context, Pell has also been a source of frustration to Victorian Police, as David Marr (2013) pointed out when Pell was Archbishop of Melbourne while payments were made to individuals through 'The Melbourne Response', no cases were brought to the Victoria Police to prosecute (ibid.).[488] It gave the appearance that the abused were paid to go away. Marr (2013) said Pell was also seen generally as insensitive and dismissive and "his detachment was astonishing" (ibid.)[489] to the extent of the abuse. When Pell made a statement at a press conference in 2013 after Australia's Royal Commission into Institutional Reponses to Child Sexual Abuse was announced by the Prime Minister, Julia Gillard, Marr said Pell spoke in jarring language from the position of victim because he said the press had waged a "persistent campaign" (Atherton, 2012)[490] against the Catholic Church and that because:

> There is a press campaign focused largely on us, it does not mean that we are largely the principal culprits. We object to [the extent of misdoing] being exaggerated, we object to being described as the only cab on the rank. (Atherton, ibid.)[491]

In another example of reported public incongruence, in 2002, Pell was quoted as having told a World Youth Day gathering in Toronto Canada that "abortion is a worse moral scandal than priests sexually abusing young people" (Toronto Start, 2002)[492] then, in another clashing inconsistency he later told *The Sydney Morning Herald* he was quoted out of context because "abortion destroys innocent life" (ibid.).[493] It was another example of an apparent failure to grasp the breadth, intensity and pervasiveness of child abuse, the extent of the Catholic Church's historic cover-ups and denials, and consequences that not only damaged the individual victims but echoed through generations beyond the lives of the abused.

This section is not an exposition on Cardinal Pell and the Catholic Church. It is not an attempt to justify or defend bias in the court reporting of Pell or the complainant, or any other person before any court in Australia. All citizens should expect equal treatment. Rather this overview serves by way of a contextual understanding of the ABC's new role in the *field* of commercial media, its interface with the Australian public and the consequences of its shift in *field*. *The Australian Financial Review* editorial described the media coverage of the Pell case as "entangled in the broader culture war, whereby the position taken on his case has become virtually a tribal marker of political belonging" (AFR, 2020).[494] Accusations of bias, also directed at the ABC, provided an opportunity to include this content in the book because it was relevant to analysing the role of the ABC and its *field* shift. The case provided an example of where there were specific accusations of bias that could be analysed within a measurable, defined time frame of court cases. The ABC has always had a vital role at divisive, confronting and challenging times in Australian society, such as in wars, political upheaval, bushfires, floods and the pandemic. It has always related the Australian informed élite, privileged perspective, and was respected as such. So, while this analysis looks at the reporting of a significant legal matter in the life of Australian society, the case attracted a large public and international interest in the outcome. The media was in a situation of having to demonstrate restraint and impartiality under pressure from outside actors to do otherwise: As one journalist from *The Guardian* newspaper stated:

> Some other abuse survivors and their advocates would plant themselves among the journalists, seeing them as allies, with at least one whispering their thoughts while witnesses were cross-examined. It put journalists in an awkward position—we were there not to take sides but to record an important trial unfolding. (Davey, 2019)[495]

The revelation was serious because McNair (1994) said that:

> Journalistic output is shaped primarily by a combination of ideological, economic and cultural influences acting on the news organisation from without. ... Journalists ... nevertheless reproduce preferred accounts and interpretations of social reality by internalising the dominant value structure of their society. (ibid.)[496]

As well, there is a pressure and propensity with digitised content to prefer threats—or, as sociologist Stanley Cohen's (1972) "moral panic" theory described:

> A condition, episode, person or group of persons emerges to become defined as a threat to societal values and interests; its nature is presented in a stylized and stereotypical fashion by the mass media. (Cohen, 2002)[497]

Cohen developed this theory by considering how the rise and pervasiveness of information technology had made the spread of moral panic easier and helped construct "ideological panics" (Cohen, 2011)[498] such as "social movements, identity politics and victims" (ibid.).[499] In addition to this, news is located around a set of intellectual constructs where underlying assumptions and embedded narratives are placed within the broader context of discourses and then linked and segued with other news reports. This becomes the framework from which other news reports are developed, themes from news reports are inserted in meta-themes, überthemes are unfurled and the media can then develop a prevailing and premature judgement of the accused, for example, with the use of this process and construction. This has become a greater challenge for journalists' court reporting and the legal demands, restrictions and responsibilities of impartiality and objectivity. Concurrent with this, it could also have become challenging to find individuals to empanel into a jury that had not been educated in the themes and binaried depictions surrounding the reporting of this event: "power", "maleness", "male dominance", "institutions", "religion", "Catholic Church", "abuse", "survivors", "victims" and "activists". All were merged into an über theme of 'masculinised abuse of power'.

Concern about the impact of media portrayals infiltrating public opinion and juries (rather than analysis only of court evidence) was raised by Appellate Judge Roy Ellis of Newcastle District Court in 2018. Ellis quashed, on appeal, the conviction of the late Catholic former Archbishop of Adelaide Philip Wilson (who died suddenly in early 2021) on failing to report child sex allegations about a priest. Ellis said: "large numbers of members of media from all around Australia" were "the elephant in the room" (McCarthy, 2018)[500] in juries reaching guilty verdicts in some cases. He said this:

> May amount to perceived pressure for a court to reach a conclusion which seems to be consistent with the direction of public opinion, rather than being consistent with the rule of law that requires a court to hand down individual justice in its decision-making processes. (ibid.)

At Wilson's funeral the Apostolic Administrator for the Archdiocese of Adelaide, Bishop Greg O'Kelly SJ, said Emeritus Archbishop Wilson had received "disgraceful and insulting treatment" from the media (Tomevska, 2021), bearing in mind this case study is looking only at media bias in court reporting, not analysing innocence or guilt and that the there is no court of public opinion operating as the alternative to the justice system. Other aspects of news reporting that had infiltrated public opinion were demonstrated in what Skidmore (1995) described as the peculiar media tendency of celebrity personalisation of child sexual abuse. Skidmore's analysis (1995) cited the "paramount" role of personalisation in the child sexual abuse allegations against the celebrities Woody Allen and the late Michael Jackson (ibid.).[501] The Hon Justice Michael Kirby AC CMG (2002) warned that "the global dimension of multimedia and information technology has meant that, in large part, we have become a segment of the media of the United States. We should resist this tendency" (Kirby, 2002).[502] In addition, Kirby was critical of Australian media where "court decisions are reported in Australia it is usually in terms of personality and controversy. The issues before the High Court are commonly reduced to such terms" (Kirby, 2002).[503]

Gamson (in A. Drozdek 2015) described the term "celebrity" as meaning "mass-produced distractions" (Gamson, in A. Drozdek, 2015, p. 275) with an "ideological role in promoting consumption, competition, individualism, and the myth of open opportunity" (Ibid.).[504] Rojek (2001,

p. 98) had earlier identified the rise of the celebrity with the need for social acknowledgment, idealised narcissism (accompanied by lack of self-esteem) and the decline of religion in the West.[505] While the main corpus does not analyse images, it is important to note that in the light of the literature (Skidmore, 1995; Gamson in A. Drozdek, 2015), an ABC news report published online on the day of Pell's sentencing by the Victoria County Court was illustrated with a photo of Pell on left and a photo of Michael Jackson on the right, side by side. Both photos were taken of the accused men on their way to their separate court hearings and used widely by media in reports about them, individually. The headline accompanying the photographs was: "The psychological reason why some can't believe the evidence against George Pell and Michael Jackson" (Sharman, 2020).[506] The report, labelled "Opinion", was written by a senior lecturer in psychology who described those who were "unable to accept unpalatable evidence" against Pell as having the psychological impediment of cognitive dissonance in their inability to accept the guilt, and the result was their defence of "powerful individuals" (Sharman, ibid.). The photo descriptor said: "Supporters have had trouble believing the claims against both George Pell and Michael Jackson" (Loc. Cit.). The elevation of Pell to the same celebrity status as Jackson placed them together as symbolic entities of child abuse. Specifically, Pell became a "celebrity paedophile" by linking his sentencing in a report that included information on the previous release of a Jackson video "Finding Neverland". This was supported by the text and two photographs. The article stated that after the release of the movie Jackson fans protested in disbelief at the "child grooming and abuse claims", which also showed their "cognitive dissonance" (ibid.). The subtext of the article was that those who believed Pell innocent, despite the guilty verdict, had a psychological impediment.

Other matters concerning the ABC's service to public opinion was the media's universal incapacity to report proceedings because of court suppression orders made on 25 June 2018 on the reporting of the Pell cases. Nonetheless, there were 36 individuals and media outlets accused of breaking the orders and facing contempt charges in 2020 because the Director of Public Prosecutions said the reports/commentary "had a tendency to interfere with the due administration of justice in the prosecution of Pell" (Percy, 2019)[507] while other reports were accused of "scandalising the court" because they were critical of the court (Percy, ibid.). The ABC was not being prosecuted, although it was mentioned: "The ABC received an initial letter about coverage by RN Breakfast, in a segment about newspaper front pages, but it was not included on the list of those called to the hearing next month" (ibid.). The case was the first in Australian legal history (Younger, 2019)[508] and part of the temptation to publicise the result in Australia was that international news outlets, which fall outside the Victorian Country Court's jurisdiction, published the outcome freely and this was easily retrieved by audiences online.

Moving forward to the next trial, Davey (2019) observed that the number of journalists reporting Pell's second trial dropped to "around eight". This was attributed to stretched newsrooms unable to dedicate resources to the entirety of another five-week trial" (Davey, ibid.).[509] The second trial attracted public interest but did not capture the media as did the first. However, there were also the added comprehensive suppression orders which prevented journalists reporting the trials as they unfolded as there were two against Pell in progress simultaneously: "the cathedral trial" (which ultimately led to Pell's acquittal) and "the swimmers' trial" which collapsed because the judge found the prosecution's evidence was inadmissible and one of the key accusers had died.[510]

3.11 Specialist Court Reporting

Court reporting is a specialised journalism because it is confined to the conventions, law and rules of the courts and the journalist needs to know these before proceeding into the room. The presiding judge is the boss, not the media editor. Unlike other venues and events which are subject to re-interpretation or spin, court expectations and laws cannot be altered or nuanced by the media. Even the ancient Greek philosopher Aristotle (G.A. Kennedy, 2007, active 384–322 BCE) was aware of this when he wrote: "it is wrong to warp the jury by leading them into anger or envy or pity; that is the same as if someone made a straight-edge ruler crooked before using it" (Aristotle, G.A. Kennedy, 2007).[511]

Specifically, journalists have to report courts under the law of sub judice contempt. In Australia, this restricts media outlets from publishing information that would pre-judge a trial, influence the conduct of the court or colour the proceedings. For example, journalists cannot publish details of prior convictions of the accused, nor can they offer their views, or other's views, on the guilt or innocence of the accused. Juries also need to be remote from other information about the accused that could sway their verdicts. Witnesses, the accused and the complainant are all protected by sub judice. This is based on the defendant/accused's right to a presumption of innocence. Presumption of innocence is the cornerstone of Australia's criminal judicial system, which means the onus of proof is on the prosecution, as explained earlier and the accused does not have to prove innocence.

Juries find a defendant 'guilty' or 'not guilty' based on the evidence presented to them and they can only convict when the guilt has been established 'beyond reasonable doubt'. It means that juries assess the evidence as presented to them and then consider the guilt of the accused. If there is any doubt, then the accused must be found 'not guilty'. They are judged within the parameter of reasonable doubt. Australian contempt laws have been criticised as being so strict that "there is ... very little that the media can do to be certain of avoiding liability" (Luzung, 2004)[512] because there is also the public interest to consider as well as freedom of discussion (Luzung, 2004) and debate, and this is blocked by the offence of scandalising the court (Swannie, 2019).[513] Journalists now augment their media coverage with the use of Twitter, tweeting information from the court room in real time, blow by counter-blow. Gleeson (2013/2014)[514] identified four concerns with this use of Twitter as a speedier replacement, or supplement, for court reporting: (1) risk of inaccuracies (2) the inclusion of personal observations (3) material could be published that is actually under a suppression order and (4) Jurors who are permitted to use smart phones in court may be influenced by commentators' tweets when they read them while empanelled. Jurors were allowed to bring in mobile phones and laptops into the court but are told they must be turned off during a sitting (Juries Victoria, 2020).[515] Gleeson (2013/2014) said tweets from journalists may also influence witnesses waiting outside to give evidence when they, too, read these tweets before their appearances. The media was not allowed to use mobile phones or laptops in Pell's High Court case (Eddie, 2020),[516] by way of contrast.

Developing meaning-making in court reporting, Waterhouse-Watson (2016) said, was a situation where: "subtle discursive and narrative strategies privilege either the prosecution or defence's narrative, portraying the defendant or complainant as 'guilty' even without overt sensationalising or vilification".[517] Waterhouse-Watson's (2016) analysis of a high-profile Australian sexual assault trial of a New South Wales footballer asserted that: "current ethical standards can be ethically questionable, including reinforcing myths and stereotypes about rape, and subtly positioning the defendant or complainant as guilty or innocent" and where "even when journalists strive for objectivity, the selection and presentation of events remains subjective" (ibid.).[518] Specifically, Waterhouse-Watson (2016) identified a "guilt narrative" and an "innocence narrative"[519] in court reporting and that these were sustained by developing them as part of overall narrative coherence. Yet, in a conflicted courtroom environment the journalist has to prioritise content to tell stories, as well as report facts so that:

> When an event is removed from the courtroom context and placed in a headline or lead, it alone evokes a Point—that is, in the context of a media narrative, whichever event is highlighted means guilt or innocence, simply because of its position in the article, no matter where it came in the courtroom narrative.[520]

Further: "simply placing an event in an article's opening imbues it with the meaning of guilt or innocence" (Waterhouse-Watson, 2016).[521] She claimed that the way in which a sexual assault was reported by the media affected not just that trial, "but also perceptions of other trials and the public's perception of sexual assault generally" (ibid.).[522] When the ethics of court reporting were discussed by journalists, there also was an assumption they had a knowledge of ethics, although this may not be so (Waterhouse-Watson, 2016). She quoted Gregory (2005) that understandings of ethical reporting were based on the simplistic view of not getting charged with contempt, rather than engaging with a deep understanding of ethics, in and of themselves; and, argued this led to a debased understanding of 'fairness' and 'balance' among journalists.

This aspect of reporting had relevance for questions about media morality, which according to media ethicist Stephen Ward (2014) had been "shattered" by digital media and where ethics were "a faint memory" because media had transitioned from a "tidy" ethical world of professionals to an "untidy world of "everyone" (ibid.).[523] Ward (2014) said two trends were impacting on this radical change in ethics—interactive media and globalisation of news (ibid.).[524] Fragmentation of content meant there was a diversity of journalistic forms (Ward, 2014) and homogeneity had ended. Media ethics has been widely considered by the academy (Kieran, 1998) as in need of redefinition in a digital world, rather than collapsing into the "anything goes approach" (Ward, 2014), which was the trend. The much-celebrated fragmentation that gives audiences abundant choices has been to the detriment of quality, ethically-sound, ethically-bound, legally accurate reporting.

> Journalism ethics should reject the idea that fragmentation is a positive state of affairs or a fait accompli. (Ward Loc. Cit.)[525]

Court reporting is at odds with the permissive commercial media field (of all media, including the professional). Court reporting is intended to be blind-folded from opinion, as the feminised allegorical statue of justice depicts, weighing evidence on scales and with the authority of a sword. New modes of court reporting, however, demonstrate the clash with this and the social sciences which disputes the supremacy of objective truth and the law: your truth is not my truth. In addition, the 'politics of precarity' (Standing, 2011; Hardy, 2017; Masquelier, 2019)[526] had infiltrated media—creating media precarity where fundamental changes in workplaces had also created uncertainty of employment and journalists are pressured to perform. Employers have greater facility to replace staff with ease in an overall employment environment described by Standing (2011) as 'the precariat' (Standing, 2011).[527] In the media work has been widely casualised making the rush to be first with news of the utmost importance coupled with a pressing need for an attendant, supportive following on social media to support career aspirations. The pressures on professional journalists have never been greater. Compounding this was the fact that because journalists' careers were increasingly peripatetic, short-term contracts and "gigs" had become prevalent forms of employment, with journalists moving between employers to sustain livelihoods.

3.12 Thematic Analysis of the ABC Coverage

The tables containing the thematic analysis of the Pell trials are appended at the end of this chapter. As a consequence of criticism of the ABC coverage of the Pell trial and a robust response from the ABC (as described at the start of this sub-chapter), the researcher tested the accusation against a thematic content analysis of 38 news reports. On some days there was more than one report on the day, so covering 14 days. This was an analysis of online written content only, including headline and hyperlink headlines in the side-bar of the report. The analysis captured content in the public domain on ABC News webpages and avoided analysis of Twitter content where the ABC also posted reports because Twitter and social media sites were appended with user comments, which should at least be remarked bias the reading of the content, too. There were photos included in most postings, sometimes videos, but these were not included in the analysis, with the exception of the preceding meme analysed and the Jackson/Pell report, as that incorporated an established understanding of both tacit and explicit media contempt for Pell, prior to his court case(s).

Court reporting could be considered a sub-*field* of the *field* of cultural production.[528] Journalists express Bourdieu's '*cultural capital*' through skills and knowledge of journalism, court procedure and law. For the purposes of the exercise only the written word was selected and analysed because they are symbols used by the ABC to support its unique agency in the *field* of public broadcasting, journalism, with the aim of supporting the public interest online—its new *field*. In addition, words and headlines now hold currency when audiences are scanning for content—they attract and become tracking content for the 'eyeballs', so are valued by all media outlets and a vital part of accumulating audiences for advertisers, and for the ABC in informing the public sphere.

The following Table 3.2 identifies all reports related to coverage of the main Pell trial; however, some were not news reports, rather they were one descriptive summative paragraph with an accompanying video (no longer available for view) and so were not analysed. The corpus shows clusters of interest emerged in the coverage, although it also needs to be re-stated that this coverage was hampered by suppression orders on the reporting of the trials. This meant if journalists attended the first and second trial they could not report on proceedings. Then, when the first verdict from the second trial was handed down it could not be reported immediately as there was a concurrent trial emerging in which Pell was the accused/defendant.

However, the ABC published examples of fragmentation of content repeatedly in the coverage of the trials and appeals, and it was this type of fragmentation that was criticised by Ward (2014) as leading to a weakening of media ethics. There also had to be some latitude in sampling overall because some opinion and analysis reports were posted the day after the event, which are examples of this fragmentation. The random purposive

Table 3.2 ABC News and views reports authorship

News author	*Number of reports*
1. Anonymous[a]	16
2. ABC court reporter	4
3. ABC reporter(s)	14
4. *730* Program	2
5. *PM* Program	1
6. ABC and agencies	2
7. Judge	1
Views author	
1. Opinion	2
2. Analysis—an ABC journalist for all	3
3. Academic	2

[a]"Anonymous" here should not be construed as concealment, deception or a desire to remain anonymous. In rolling news coverage, the journalist's name may simply not be included in the report

sampling was done of ABC News Online content on the coverage of Pell's case from six key events:

1. **Day One in Trial 1 Pell's first court appearance:** 26 July 2017
2. ***(Mis-trial declared: 20 September 2018. Jury failed to reach verdict). Not covered.)***
3. *(Day One in Trial 2: 7 November 2018 Committal hearing. Not covered.)*
4. **The Verdict: 26 February 2019**
5. **Sentencing: 13 March 2019**
6. **Victorian Court of Appeal decision: 21 August 2019, appeal dismissed 2–1**
7. **High Court agrees to agrees to hear appeal: 13 November 2019**
8. **High Court appeal decision:** 7 April 2020 unanimously quashed convictions, allowed appeal.

The purpose of this content analysis was to survey the ABC reports relating to the coverage of the case in the light of criticisms levelled at the ABC that it had been biased in its reporting. This research was not conducted to establish the guilt or innocence of Pell nor the veracity or otherwise of the complainants, nor analyse child abuse and its ramifications. It was not conducted to challenge either the complainant or the accused on the serious child abuse allegations made in courts of law. This research did not analyse the conduct of the courts, its actors or the law itself. The case was prominent, the background on historical child sexual abuse by the Catholic Church publicly well-understood and outlined earlier, therefore interest was piqued on that largely unresolved abuse issue alone. The court matters relating to Cardinal Pell took place over an extended time period. This research is not disputing that the abuses have taken place, it is examining how the ABC reported a specific court case that involved child sexual abuse and a prominent Australian religious figure and whether it displayed bias and impartiality in its reporting, as it was accused.

Purposive random sampling is a form of qualitative research, which is used in social sciences and based on accessing a sample of content based on it being representative of a larger group (Brown, 2010).[529] The corpus of reports was obtained from the ABC website using the search term "Pell" and this resulted in a corpus of 39 news reports in the given time from of day one of the trial to the High Court decision. Qualitative research is useful inductive analysis because like positivist research is works towards an understanding (Merriam, 2010) in this instance because the objective is to discover interpretations of experiences and analyse constructivist reality and to understand:

> How people make sense out of their lives, to delineate the process (rather than the outcome or product) of meaning-making, and to describe how people interpret what they experience. (Merriam, 2010)[530]

Berger (1998) said that humanities research had to also navigate creativity and very often ended up asking more questions than answering them. Berger (1998) said there was also the challenge of generalisability from content analysed, as well as the bias of the researcher who is influenced by their particular society (ibid.).[531]

The content analysis of the corpus categorised words or phrases used in ABC News reporting into four themes. The aim was to discover the recurrence of these themes (and concomitant potential biases) depicted in the text and headlines. Headlines are also not neutral. Dor (2003) said headlines "optimize relevance" of stories, direct readers interpretations and contextual understandings and the way the headline is written shows the news outlet understands their readers' beliefs.[532] In an online world, sometimes only the headline is read because readers are trained to understand it encapsulates the main point (Dor, 2003). Schudson (2008) quoted Harold Evans[533]: "the headline ... is not an act of journalism but an act of marketing" (Schudson, 2008).[534] In addition, the hierarchical use of headlines online, is "motivated by the need to persuade visitors to linger at the site" (Flores, 2002).[535] The role of headlines is to assist news discourses of which intertextuality is a prominent feature (Xie, 2018)[536] in a media environment where context has always been seen as a prominent requisite for news reporting, to aid the reader with more meaning and understanding (Kobre, 1955).[537]

In line with criticisms of ABC coverage, the four prevailing themes designated in this research were divided into three sub-themes each to which content was assigned: positive, neutral or negative:

1. Positive Catholic Church or Religion/Neutral Catholic Church or Religion/Negative Catholic Church or Religion.
2. Positive Male/Neutral Male/Negative Male
3. Positive (Supportive) Accused/Neutral Accused/Negative Accused.
4. Positive (Supportive) Complainant/Neutral Complainant/Negative Complainant.

The themes chosen for analysis of this news coverage focused around fear. Altheide's (2002) research used fear as a "basic unit of analysis" of news reports because fear was a dominant "public perspective" where:

> The fear "market" and appeal has also promoted an extensive cottage industry that promotes new fears, and particularly an expanding array of "victims". It is as though there is a tireless army trying to destroy an expanding source of fear that is producing seemingly endless victims.[538]

And, allied with fear, victimhood has become a significant theme of media coverage, in general and with the spread of social media its depiction is "proliferating" (Munt, 2017).[539] This research avoided using the word "victim" as a thematic analysis because in a court of law the person making the accusation is the 'complainant', they are not a 'victim' until they have proven their case. 'Victim' is an emotive word and in a court of law carries an implication of guilt towards the defendant. It can also accompany what the literature refers to as the vicarious entertainment of "dark tourism" on the internet seeking amusement and enjoyment from someone's pain (Munt, ibid.). Research into cases of police violence against racial and ethnic minorities in the US, for example, show that the type of information media released about a victim and the perpetrator can influence attitudes, trigger stereotyping, apportionment of blame and punishment—which then has ramifications for an equitable political justice system (Dukes & Gaither, 2017).[540]

Sociology Professor Frank Furedi (2006) described the emergence of this fear in the media as belonging to the growth of a 'culture of fear' that had become a "cultural idiom through which we signal a sense of growing unease about our place in the world" (Furedi, ibid.).[541] He said it manifested itself in society's weakened faith in humanity, misanthropy, "intellectual pessimism and cultural disorientation" and "obsession with abuse" (ibid.)[542] such that "the theme of abuse has become one of the most distinct features of contemporary western culture" (ibid.).[543] Further, Furedi (2006) argued the media was counter-intuitive in that it normalised abuse through its many depictions of it in entertainment content (movies, drama, computer games). The inducement of fear and resort to victimhood was heightened in response to that. In addition, Furedi (2006) said there was now an emphasis on believing the accuser and "by stigmatising the refusal to believe, the accuser is accorded monopoly over some transcendental truth … and the *a priori* belief in the prevalence of abuse has led to a standard of evidence which is characteristically flexible" (ibid.).[544]

This level of fear in society has reached the point where "at all levels of society there is a manifest lack of confidence about the working of society" (ibid.)[545] and this included its institutions. There was an increasing sense of powerlessness, isolation and lack of trust in society, accentuated by media which "derides those who have heroic pretensions. The new role models are those who can suffer" (ibid.)[546] and where there is a "mood of low expectations" (ibid.).[547] Furedi (2006) said allied with this had been social disengagement, erosion of civic responsibility and individualism—which have all given rise to activism (ibid.).[548] This was contextualised in other earlier academic literature (Curran & Seaton, 1997) as an overall pluralist position where "the media do not merely 'reflect' social reality; they increasingly help to make it" (Curran & Seaton, 1997)[549] and where "the press and broadcasting function as an ideological marketplace" (ibid.).[550]

The themes that were selected for this content news report analysis were chosen because, as the literature identified, they were identifiable as "the recurring typical themes that run through a lot of the reports" (Altheide & Schneider, 2013).[551] Altheide (1996; Altheide & Schneider, 2013) recommended selecting content from the beginning and conclusion of the "crisis" event as an easier way of sampling (ibid.)[552] and using around 15–20 reports (Altheide, 1996).[553]

This analysis is replicable and did incorporate two examples of repurposed content taken from the ABC's television current affairs program *730*, which had been criticised as biased (Bourke, 2016),[554] as well as repurposed content from the ABC's radio current affairs program *PM*. There was also content that had been supplied from outside media, *The Conversation*, as well as content from news agencies. It was also significant to incorporate themes that included gender (male) because the feminist literature said that media portrayals could perpetuate gender stereotypes (van Acker, 2003[555]; Chakvetadze et al., 2016[556]; Goodall, 2012[557]). US gender theorist, Judith Butler (1990) said there were "limits of gender as an exclusive category of analysis" (ibid.)[558] but that "gender is constructed through relations of power" (ibid.).[559] The theme of 'Catholic Church' and 'religion' were blended as both the particular and general categories of belief have traditionally held strong political and social views. Religions continue to hold strict moral authority in many diverse societies, in addition to those who follow Christianity.

The corpus excluded telecast ABC Television and broadcast ABC Radio news reports as these are different genres and could have skewed the perceived ABC coverage in a particular way because content analysis assumes: "behavioural patterns, values, and attitudes found in this material reflect and affect the behaviors, attitudes, and values of the people who create the material" (Berger, 1998).[560] Verbal delivery analysis also would have had to be incorporated—tone of voice, intonation patterns, pausing and phrasing; while, visual delivery would have had to incorporate footage included with the report. It was, therefore, important to establish and separate categories for this analysis as published words only.

Höijer's (2011) media research on climate change reporting using social representations theory found that ideas were identified and communicated by the media as if common sense, collective thinking, something everyone is agreed upon and that this "naturalises social thinking" (Höijer, 2011).[561] This form of social representation in media also allowed the audience to classify people, explain them and objectify them (Höijer, 2011, quoting Moscovici, 1988). Social representation helped provide the audience with an emotional anchor (Höijer, 2011) and this could also be applied to instances of child abuse (or in the case of Australian bushfire reporting the plight of wounded, or homeless, native animals). Social representations theory also provided a code to understanding the world (Höijer, 2011 quoting Moscovici, 1988). However, these codes were not logical thought patterns and might contain contradictions (Höijer, 2011). Sense-making in the media through social representations was evident in the use of antimonies or thinking in opposites (through the linguistic device of binaries), in this case "victim" versus "guilty"/"perpetrator". Yet this "may become a source of tension, conflict or problem" (Höijer, 2011) when cases are not resolved as depicted,[562] for example, if the "guilty" is found innocent. Analysing antimonies through themes, in the reporting of the Pell case, assisted in identifying underlying sources of conflict and inconsistencies in news coverage.

In this instance, the start and end points of the trial were truncated into the second trial and appeals, so these had to be incorporated in the corpus. There was a first trial (ending in a hung jury and not reported due to suppression orders) so the days identified for the purposes of this research were analysed: the charges laid, the verdict, the sentencing, the High Court decision. However, it must also be noted that this non-probability sampling may not allow for the development of a statistical theory (Brown, 2010).[563]

In addition, the authors of the reports were categorised into 'news' and 'views'. See Table 3.2.

3.13 Research Findings

This research found a divided result. ABC court reporting of the Pell case could not be described as largely biased, nor partial coverage, and to accuse the entire ABC's literal online coverage of being overtly biased as an institutional position was not found in this research. However, it did find biased coverage in terms of legal inaccuracy and insertions of opinion, often due to aspects of creative writing employed in court reporting which then coloured the ABC's coverage and prompted the accusation by the Vice-Chancellor of the Australian Catholic University, Professor Greg Craven, that the ABC was a "cheer squad" for the jailing of Pell (Lackey & *Australian Associated Press*, 2020)[564] (the author also viewed the interview on You Tube).[565] Craven was also referring to television coverage of the Pell cases, and these did not form the corpus of this specific research. This analysis found there had been a departure in strict, formulaic court reporting in an attempt to appeal to different audiences and to create a more entertaining online experience. This is evidenced in the wording of headlines. Court reporting requires that the legal details of a court case that have been heard before a jury, or judge, should be reported accurately and often repetitively. Those facts and the argy-bargy of the courtroom arguments are expected to speak for themselves, and, ironically, when reported accurately and without the backdrop of opinion, they can result in highly readable and "entertaining" reports.

Opinion journalism is not a widely researched topic (Kelling & Thomas, 2018)[566] so it is difficult to measure the impact of opinion journalists relative to the typified reporting of facts and "hard news" and their opinion function in a news context is ill-defined anyway (Kelling & Thomas, 2018).[567] However, this means in an evolving media landscape the job of the professional journalist has been problematised, changed and attenuated because of diverse demands and changed news consumption habits that seek opinion. This incorporation of opinion on news pages was the second main concern identified by this research that could trigger accusations of bias. The need to appeal has gained greater ascendancy in news coverage everywhere. It is also understood that the fragmentation of media has also given journalists opportunities to explore various ways of multiplatforming their content and incorporating a range of techniques, including referential interpretations, creativity and technologies. Where once news was considered neutral and separate from opinion, the use of social media is a key research tool for exchanging information and this has changed the way information is selected, created and curated for audiences. The audience is also responding to content instantly and the feedback can be highly fortifying and satisfying as consumers. Audiences are also now invited to contribute what *they* know to a story. This means that journalists' use of social media has become a form of branding themselves, representing their organisation and gathering their professional lifeblood of information all at once. Lawrence (2012) observed that journalists regarded Twitter as their news wire (ibid.).[568] Journalists are now conflicted by their traditional gate-keeping neutral role and their desire and professional need to contribute opinion and views, capture useful responses, and be 'liked' and re-posted on social media sites. ABC reporting must now take part in this emergent commercial field, as do the professional commercial journalists and their organisations. Vigilant, cynical watchdogs of society (the traditional metaphor for journalists) must now also be 'liked' and fêted in an emergent commercial *field* where emotions are prioritised over due process and restraint. Journalism finds itself in a compromising professional paradox. No wonder Aunty is in such a muddle.

The advent of creative writing as a sub-category of court reporting relies more on manipulating the emotions by developing themes and narratives existing in the zeitgeist that surround the issues, rather than reporting matters being disclosed in the court room and on the public record. It means reporting court cases becomes especially dangerous to the legal process if the zeitgeist had already condemned an individual, and the media and courts were thereafter expected to be working together to prove the accused guilty in line with the opinion at large. Guilt becomes transmogrified into received wisdom. Theme-based creative reporting also conflates the accused with larger issues which are then attributed to the accused. Embellishment with opinion as an adjunct to court reporting could result in sub judice contempt charges, because slanted or coloured reports may impress the jury with a media-induced bias and lead to an unsafe verdict. This becomes an erosion of the judicial process for all when courts no longer stand aloof from media judgement, organisational actors, opinion, audiences' tastes and digital organisations' demands. Courts are a 'theatre' in themselves, but a theatre of fact, evidence and rebuttal, not an entertaining adjunct to the performing and creative arts.

Ultimately, what the Pell matter demonstrated was that the ABC had failed to invest in the human capital it needed to cover courts to a consistently high standard. Designated court reporters, named as such in reports, covered only four of the news reports within this corpus and all supplied neutral, impartial reporting of the case. However, there was also an inconsistency in the use of reporters evidenced by the majority of reports written by anonymous journalists or ABC reporters who were not described as court reporters. The use of wire services—Reuters and Associated Press—although not to a large extent—is another instance of the ABC standards being out-sourced to other media and indicative of staffing shortages which have forced a reliance on outside media reports. Without challenging the probity of wire service news, Aunty's voice is still compromised, stifled or mashed with other voices because it is no longer independent, and that is the point to be made here. In addition, there is the impact of sub-editors on news reports who are traditionally anonymous and, therefore, their role cannot be analysed in this corpus.

There has been a significant loss of many ABC senior reporters (and senior editors) over the years who covered/knew the court rounds (and once there were specialist reporters for a wide range of rounds). It shows the extent of the damage done to the loss of rounds reporting in general in the media where journalists can be parachuted into reporting any matters without necessarily having the years of learning and grounding in the particular regime of court reporting, the strict legalities and the somewhat formulaic nature of court reporting. It is not a creative writing activity. The consequence of this, and other matters, is that the ABC has been accused of bias. The analysis of this corpus show there has been an abandonment of specific training and failure to pass on institutional and legacy knowledge of rounds (courts here, but also police, education, environment, business & economics, health, politics, trade unions). These senior "specialist" reporting roles are no longer regarded as necessary, eroded by the general loss of the profession of journalism across the commercial media with a greater presence and endowment given to online citizen journalists and blogs, for example. Funding cuts have also led to this attrition of specialisation and shows that the stretching of the federal budget allocation has become too thin. Details of court reporting apply to court etiquette, protocol, procedure, what can be expected from a particular sitting, who to talk to for a briefing, as well—and most importantly in this instance—the expectations of public service court reporting that has been valued by Australians for decades. In an interview with the ABC quoted earlier, Craven (Lackey & Australian Associated Press, 2020) called the ABC to account on its values:

> It's astonishing that an organisation like the ABC that places so much emphasis on its trust, is rapidly now trying to divert attention from that fundamental fact that you got it hopeless (interrupted, but in cross talk "hopelessly wrong").[569]

As this book has pointed out there had been almost a covenant between the ABC and its audience that the public service media organisation would always serve the interests of the people, not individuals, groups or interests. It was trusted to be a Fourth Estate to hold the other (somewhat now corroded) pillars of society to account (courts, parliament, the executive—and what was once considered another pillar—the church (where the Church of England was the nation's foundational church). Importantly, it also held the commercial media to account. It was able to do this by virtue of being in its own *field*. Instead of which it now refrains from this duty in its commercial mindset and takes a defensive line when criticised, perpetuating the narrative that the commercial media is out to get it. It should be noted that the ABC also works collaboratively with other news outlets, with all newsrooms challenged to supply adequate staffing for one particular researched story, this then introduces a whole new set of challenges for the institutions about the traditional boundary between public service content and other.

The ABC was never invested with a role to undermine legal and democratic process. If the media were to be submerged in opinion—if the accused in courts were depicted and described as guilty before a verdict was handed down, if simply being in court itself decreed guilt—whose interests would the media then serve? It would be a depiction of mob rule. It would mean the separation of the estates was over. Where does this ABC see itself in this scenario? There is a highly motivated desire to express opinion, especially in this instance of court reporting where "victimhood" is made ascendant, as the academic literature describes. Sufferers are to be respected, supported and heard, but under the present legal process in Australia justice can only take place when matters are heard before a court and evidence interrogated by a judge, or judge and anonymous representative jury, where the "complainant" prosecutes a case versus the "accused" which defends that case. McMurtrie (2020), in explaining ABC reporting of the Pell case, implied that bias was justified because of the external, contextual situation: "in a church already rocked by a staggering number of historic child sexual abuse accusations" (ibid.).[570] However, the bench twice directed the media to desist from this line. The Honourable Victorian Chief Justice, Anne Ferguson of Victoria's Court of Appeal reiterated similar instructions as County Court Chief Judge Peter Kidd. The Victorian Chief Justice Ferguson said in handing down the bench's 2–1 dismissal of Pell's appeal against his convictions, said Pell: "is not to be made a scapegoat" and that his conviction only concerned the cases prosecuted against him (*ABC News*, 2019b).[571]

The ABC is tasked with being Australians' biggest champion of free speech to provide impartial and independent news and information where the audiences are permitted to make their own judgement of content. While news media is now telling as many stories as possible and allowing experiences to infiltrate neutral reporting, the fundamental concept or idea of media freedom and independence from influence and control by governments and ideologies is under attack. Media, too, specifically the ABC has a responsibility to safeguard its independence and not resort to an institutional victim narrative. Elsewhere in the world, for example, during the Novel Coronavirus pandemic, it was asserted by Al Jazeera that India had become one of the "riskiest countries for journalists (Al Jazeera, 2020)[572] "for reporting on COVID-19 or exercising freedom of opinion and expression" on the topic (ibid.). In addition, Filipina executive editor, Maria Ressa, was found guilty and sentenced to jail for 'cyber libel' of a Filipino businessman and criticism of the government of President Roderigo Duterté. There were at least seven other cases that had been filed against Ressa and her website Rappler (Regencia, 2020)[573] for similar charges that have been critical of The Philippines Government. The Foreign Correspondents' Association of The Philippines said the Ressa judgement was "a menacing blow to press freedom" (ibid.). The 2020 World Press Freedom Index had dropped Australia's ranking to 26 from 180 countries (21 in 2019, 19 in 2018) after the Federal police raids in June 2019 on the home of a News Corporation journalist and the ABC offices (Reporters Sans Frontières, 2020).[574]

Australia has implied freedom of the media; it is not legislated in the Constitution. However, it does have the separation of powers: legislative, executive and judiciary enshrined under its Constitution. These mean there is:

1. The supremacy of the law.
2. The supremacy of the Crown.
3. The supremacy of Parliament (Warren, 2005 quoting Sir Owen Dixon).[575]

In 2005, Chief Justice of the Supreme Court of Victoria, Marilyn Warren, quoted High Court Chief Justice Murray Gleeson from 2003:

> It is self-evident that the exercise of [judicial review] will, from time to time, frustrate ambition, curtail power, invalidate legislation, and further adminis-

> trative action. ... This is part of our system of checks and balances. People who exercise political power, and claim to represent the will of the people, do not like being checked or balanced. (Warren, ibid.)

In the Pell matter, both the Victoria Court of Appeal and the County Court cautioned the media that there were defined boundaries for them to observe in reporting court cases. The court was saying that it did not matter if you did not like an accused, approve or believe in a person who had been charged, around which there were other allegations or reports elsewhere, the media should look to the enforcement and upholding of justice, in that particular court, on those particular charges. The courts were reminding the media of due process, the rule of law, burden of proof, the presumption of innocence and trial by jury, from which *all* Australians benefit. The alternative is unthinkable. By way of backgrounding the court's perceptions of media bias, during the court prosecution, it was reported that police command, Detective Superintendent Paul Sheridan, who had lead Operation Sano/Tethering investigation to find unreported crimes allegedly committed by Pell to build a case was asked by Defence Barrister, Robert Richter, whether it was a "get Pell operation". Sheridan replied: "I wouldn't use those words but I guess you could term it the way you did" (Dowsley & Deery, 2020).[576] It should be noted that this response was quoted slightly differently by another newspaper: "I guess you could term it the way you did but I wouldn't term it that way" (Ferguson, 2018).[577] In 2020, however, Chief Commissioner of Victoria Police Graham Ashton denied there was a "get-Pell" agenda in his cross-examination over the police's Operation Tethering (Smith, 2020b).[578]

Creating victims also had serious consequences for complainants. The work by Victoria Police in the case was described by Professor of law at Australian Catholic University, Human Rights Lawyer and Jesuit priest Frank Brennan SJ (Sky, 2020) a "tragedy" and the case should never have been brought to trial, where the complainant had to endure police "stuff ups", four years of additional trauma, and the handling of the case which was:

> Very shoddy ... the supervision of the brief by the Victoria Director of Public Prosecutions was shoddy, the way the Director of Public Prosecutions conducted herself, particularly in the High Court, was appalling. (Sky, 2020)[579]

and that the Victorian Court of Appeal and "the behaviour of the senior judiciary, of the director of public prosecutions and of the deputy police commissioner of Victoria I think it's been absolutely below par" (ibid.).[580] Brennan asserted:

> Sure there's all the ABC commentary about it out there, but if you actually look at the evidence and if you actually look at the conduct of the police, and if you actually look at the conduct of the DPP—those who are serious about the wellbeing of victims and bone fide complainants would be saying 'come on we need better from the Victorian police than this, we need better from the DPP than this and we definitely deserve better from the Chief Justice and the President of the Court of Appeal in Victoria'—otherwise what we get is years of this sort of trauma in the community generally. (Sky, 2020)[581]

Power is fragile and has to be reproduced or lost (Bourdieu, 1983)[582] and while there is power in media independence it has to be re-asserted and demonstrated consistently to continue. Traditionally, the ABC has eschewed and frowned on, a formulaic approach of pushing agendas, as the commercial organisations may have succumbed, where maximising profits can take precedence over coverage. It prized its independence. The ABC has had latitude for creativity, free expression and expectations of attention to detail. But the other side of this free expression is that its information has to have concordance with truth. This is the trust to which Craven[583] was referring in his criticism of ABC coverage of Pell that was conflated with the court coverage. Accusations of bias may also be attributed to the abandonment of specific be-spoke newsroom training, as each organisation used to carry out, to inculcate/indoctrinate each member of staff with the values and expectations of the specific institution. This role has been deferred to universities where more generic training is preferred in the belief that journalists can work anywhere, for anyone, on any platform. Certainly, in a digital age there is a need for diversity in content style and the capacity to pivot, but it should not be at a cost of content accuracy and organisational commitments. News is not a film script, just as fact is not fiction.

This corpus analysis also identified that the ABC had shifted its role to become an actor in the *field* of opinion-making. Ironically, it did not have an enemy so much as it had become its own worst enemy. The ABC's nemesis and reputed foe, Rupert Murdoch, has already been accused of performing this opinion-making activity (King, 2018)[584] and his institutional role has been analysed in the literature as "a king-maker" (Benson, 2012),[585] "sun king"[586] (Hasan, 2011)[587] and "King Murdoch" (ibid.) who was "above the law" (Evans, 2015).[588] Harold Evans (ibid.) said it was with British Prime Minister, Margaret Thatcher's support and "collusion" with Murdoch in the 1980s that lead in the UK to a "press power that became increasingly arrogant and careless of human dignity" (Loc. Cit.). It was this very point about Murdoch's operations in the commercial *field* that had been of regular concern to the ABC, and in the national interest the ABC believed it was important to individuate itself from that commercial *field* and that type of content. Murdoch has been instrumental in several leadership challenges and it has been quoted that the new prime minister of Australia makes one of his/her first visits to see Murdoch. More about the influence of Murdoch will be examined in the next chapter, Chap. 4. Now, however, the ABC—a non-commercial entity operating in the interests of all Australians—is seeking to occupy the same emergent commercial ground as Murdoch (and the multitudinous rest). The ramifications and consequences of this development go uncommented publicly by the ABC.

It is this shift in the *field* that has caused the "culture of journalistic professionalism has been undermined in important ways by the shift to commercialism" (Hallin, in A. Drozdek, 2015).[589] Even though the ABC is only partly commercialised with its outsourcing of television production, for example, it now has to write and publish news that sells in the emergent commercial *field*. All content has to suit that *field*. Internet organisations have set this new criterion for news and information. It has also set this new enfeebling target for the ABC. Accompanying this, Hallin (in A. Drozdek, 2015) identified that there had been cultural shifts in journalism as well "from 'modernism' to 'postmodernism'" (Hallin, in A. Drozdek, 2015) and with that a shift from centralised monopoly media to niche markets (Drozdek, 2015).[590] Aunty has been disoriented by this shift from her own *field* to its new role in the emergent commercial *field* where it is in a fierce competition to cater for and search out hidden niches and fresh opinions.

There has been scant research or analysis into the ABC on this salient point of the significant shift in Australia's public service media. It is a challenge for the ABC because the once privileged aloof ABC has moved herself into a crowded news market where there is fierce competition, a counter-intuitive sameness in content ("churnalism") and copious opinion-based content, or unsourced information. The media is now jumping at shadows. The interplay between social media information and ABC media staff would need to be researched to understand its impact on ABC staff in that new *field*. There is scope for future research into how social media has guided public service journalism by bringing journalists into close personal contact with the three audience areas in the *field*: bona fide audience members engaging in informed debate; comments generated from automated bot farms; and abusive, anonymous strident voices. The pressure on discernment in this *field* is now onerous and for a public service institution where profit has not been the motive, the survival of the ABC's voice has met a formidable threat.

3.14 Analysis: Choice of Words

In court reporting choice of words is critical, words are muscular. It should be noted that reporting analysed in Appendix 3:1 refrained from using the legal terminology 'complainant' or 'accuser', instead preferring to use the nouns 'victim', 'survivor', 'sexual abuse survivor', 'survivor of child sex abuse' and 'choirboy'. While the suppression of reporting made it impossible to identify the complainant; the various use of these substitute words believed to be synonymous with the word 'complainant' was a striking aspect of ABC reporting and opinion writing, manifestly. The corpus showed some examples of the use of the legally-appropriate word 'complainant' (which does not apportion guilt) but analysis of the data showed it was regarded only as a synonym for the preferred 'victim'. This would have given the audience the impression that the ABC had made a judgement in favour of the complainant early and reverted to the use of 'victim' and 'survivor' to show this, once the media had been permitted to report the verdict. In summary, analysis of this ABC content, showed that judgement had already been made by the ABC and only required a court to agree with the institution. Labelling has a very powerful impact on the audience and research has found that intergroup bias is also a factor that manifests where there is a "tendency of group members to display behaviours that favour the ingroup over the outgroup (Brewer, 2007; Tajfel & Turner, 1979, quoted in F. Fasoli et al., 2015).[591] In this case, intergroup bias facilitated an easy binary and then connected Pell with any other victim, found in a court of law or otherwise, of child sexual abuse.

The one case was conflated as if representative of the whole and Pell was the figurehead to be punished for all of these crimes because of media and societal concerns: the Catholic Church's lack of action, Pell's lack of action, and the overall denial of child sexual abuse not just by the Catholic Church but other institutions and groups. It was a powerful subtext and compellingly easy to include. Nonetheless, judges and juries do not assess sub-texts and meta-narratives and this is an important distinction that the ABC needed to adhere to more closely in its coverage. Given Pell's seniority in the Catholic Church and the degree of anger and frustration at the Catholic Church over child sexual abuse and inaction to prosecute or take responsibility both by the institution and any other perpetrators of child sexual abuse, the urge and calls to convict him was emotionally understandable, but not permissible, rational, nor legal, nor just. In reporting matters in a court of law it is understood that one person does not represent an endless log of accusations and allegations against others. They can only be tried on the specific charges and evidence presented within that court and pertaining to those specific charges. Yet, there was an accretion of accusations that related to other convicted paedophile priests and religious who were named in reporting on Pell, as if they were part of the trial, or should have been, supported by an apparent "if not why not?" lynching attitude.

The use of the word 'complainant' was used with particularity by the early reporting on the case by the ABC's Court Reporters (notably Report #2 26 July 2017 and Report #6 26 February 2019). After these two reports on Day One of the second trail, there was no further reporting from by-lined "court reporters" until the verdict when there were two additional reports published by "court reporters". This was a significant change in moving away from constituent specialist reporting for the duration of a trial. There was also an absence of these same court reporters supplying analysis, which was executed by another ABC journalist who had written a book on Pell. In understaffed newsrooms, court reporters have a multiplicity of courts to cover and their workload is formidable, yet when significant cases such as this cannot be resourced by regular attendance from specialist court reporters it leads to a loss of authority. This loss of Aunty's voice of authority was depleted by a merger with bias.

Subsequent reports much later:

Report 26—written by named ABC Journalist,
Report 27—written by anonymous ABC Journalists,
Report 34—opinion article from The Conversation,
Report 39—written by anonymous ABC Journalists,
Report 42—written by named ABC Journalists, and,
Report 43—written by an ABC Journalist

used the word 'complainant' synonymously/interchangeably with 'victim' and 'choirboy'. Reports 32 and 41 were written by anonymous ABC

Journalists who used the word 'complainant' quoting a victims' advocate in the former and 'complainant' in the latter to quote the dissenting appeal court judge. All other reports refrained from using the word 'complainant' to describe the 'complainant', which was as significant omission in court reporting and created another grey area in the overall coverage of the case. This corpus analysis found that the word 'choirboy' was used in lieu of the word 'complainant'. That the complainant was a choirboy is not being disputed here, and the serious nature of the allegations is also not being examined here. The question remains to be answered as to why the media easily collapsed its communication of court reporting into the use of narratives and binaries that help furnished perceptions of bias where the research literature into racism, for example, said labels were known to carry bias (Harsányi & Carbon, 2015[592]). Wood and Schaffer (1985)[593] said labelling expressed power relations and dominance. In other contexts, noun labels stigmatised people with mental ill-health (Howell et al., 2014[594]) and in other reporting created a negative link between Muslims and terrorism (West & Lloyd, 2017[595]), for example. Labels change understandings of individuals and "media bias can strongly impact the individual and public perception of news events" (Hamborg et al., 2019).[596] Labelling "helps us to define the terms on which we relate to 'others'" (Eyben & Moncrieffe)[597] and places exclusionary barriers on what belongs to this label.

There is a large volume of content, interviews and data that analyses and exposes Catholic Church child sexual abuse and that the Church has tacitly supported, perpetuated and condoned, historical criminal activity. However, in this fraught and charged context, the challenge for journalists reporting on this is that those details cannot form the basis of journalists' writing—unless it is raised, verbalised or evidenced in the court. That is the central consideration here. The challenge for ABC journalists, and their Aunty's voice, is that she is funded and supported to maintain standards of due process that form part of a liberal democracy where courts are a strut of that governance. Aunty, herself, is historically well versed in attending to due process. As another key institution, she is part of it.

3.15 Advocacy and Activist Journalism Versus Neutral Reporting

Digital disruption has helped support the rise of activist and advocacy journalists writing in pursuit of causes and in support of victims. Activist journalists have been defined as "typically activists first and journalists second" (Harcup, 2014) while advocacy journalism "eschews a commitment to formal objectivity, impartiality, or giving both sides of a story an equal hearing" (Harcup, 2014).[598] Both are problematised, newly emerging areas of news reporting and challenge established journalistic values of objectivity and neutrality, and therefore, change substantially the work of a journalist (Vine, 2017).[599] But they also signal that professional journalism once secluded is now merging into one multimedia re-interpreted, entertainment format (Ernst, 2010).[600] Yet, the over-arching concern for public broadcasters is that they "have to make a distinction between an interest group and a not-for-profit news provider" (Ernst, 2010).[601] This is because journalists usually do not get involved in issues that have been fully-shaped with an apparent consensus for them (Wade, 2011),[602] they interrogate the consensus. They have at their disposal techniques to manipulate narratives and construct themes to posit the desired consensus, and they can achieve consciousness raising of an issue in the general community (Wade, 2011).[603] Traditionally, it was left for the community/ public to decide and there is an expression in the Australian vernacular "the pub test" that loosely describes that process of public decision-making through exchange and discussion.

Other literature argues that all journalism is advocacy (Fisher, 2016)[604] and the idea of journalistic objectivity was only ever assumed and used as a bulwark against the encroachment and infiltration of public relations into news in the 1920s. Journalistic objectivity was an early strategy adopted by newspapers that were inundated with advertisers (Nerone & Barnhurst, 2003).[605] Neutral news sold newspapers and the valuing of objectivity has permeated other media industry since. That the news media describes itself as the Fourth Estate indicates it has placed itself among other political institutions (Blach-Ørsten & Burkal, 2014)[606] and claims the same seriousness and authority. Yet, as it only clings to ideals of objectivity, the advent of digital disruption means rapid changes in content and presentation make objectivity unviable—even redundant. Nonetheless, as Blach-Ørsten and Burkal (2014) pointed out institutional credibility and reliability were still important. No less so in a publicly-owned institution that has to justify, minute by minute, the expenditure of taxpayer money under an umbrella of expectation that it will provide 'all for all'—universality no longer just in coverage, but general content in a niche world.

In a 2014 study of Danish journalists it was found that there was increasing concern that ethics were being eroded because of pressure from understaffed, overstretched newsrooms (Blach-Ørsten & Burkal, 2014)[607] and that credibility needed to be addressed with as much urgency as the rapid cutbacks in staffing. However, Michael Schudson (2005)[608] identified the shift to what he labelled "interpretative journalism" had occurred as far back as the 1930s when opinions, rather than facts, began to reshape reporting. The digital era and citizen journalism have given it renewed vigour, and persuasion has become a manifest form of communication. It calls into question whether journalists are being conscripted into propaganda and partisanship (Fisher, 2016). For example, ABC staff was criticised in 2019 for acting in contravention of ABC Editorial Policies when it formed a climate change crisis group based on what the group described as "solutions journalism", to advise Aunty on how to report the climate crisis (Shanahan, 2019).[609] ABC Chair, Ita Buttrose, rejected the plan publicly: "it was one of those ideas that is not going to happen … policy is decided by the leadership, not by members of the staff" (Meade, 2019).[610] Nonetheless, putting management censure and control of policy aside, *The Guardian* newspaper said that the group, numbering 77, was going ahead anyway (Meade, 2019).[611]

Another major concern of online journalism is that bias in some opinion and analysis writing appears to the audience as if it is in the institution's opinion and not that of the individual commentator. This creates ambiguity for the ABC in that the organisation appears biased when opinion articles are placed on its news pages. The use of 'loaded' headlines and hyperlink headlines in the Pell case such as "Vile: Pell's police Interview" (26 February 2019) and "Jesus warned against men like Cardinal Pell. His message could save the Church" (27 February 2019) and "Only those in court saw Pell's reaction to his sentence. He was impervious" (13 & 14 March 2019) "The psychological reason why we can't believe the evidence against George Pell and Michael Jackson" (13 March 2019), "George Pell appeal decision means abuse victims will be 'hurt yet again', advocate says" (13 November 2019) and "Vatican 'welcomes' overturning of George Pell's conviction, Pope tweets cryptic message. For the Vatican it's victory" (8 April 2020). While journalists who write the reports do not write headlines, these nonetheless serve to foster the appearance of an opinion-oriented news service and give a de facto colouration to the work of the ABC journalist, in this instance, in the coverage of a prominent court case.

The opinion and analysis reports, one of which was written by an ABC journalist, also problematised the ABC's neutrality by providing examples of bias and, in one instance an opinion writer made a reference to "Mr Jesus Christ" which was deliberately denigrating of Christianity and blasphemous to the faithful. In traditional, organised religions, it is considered insulting to mock the divinity of the leader/founder of the faith, in this instance to reduce their role to "Mr". The Charlie Hedbo attack in Paris, described earlier in this analysis, where the Prophet Mohammed was vilified, was another example of how the media considered religion fair game for ridicule but without acknowledging the serious reaction against deliberately damaging deeply held beliefs. In the background of media reporting is the use of intersectionality where a 'victim' (and use of the word 'victim') identifies a person at the intersection of identified male power. There is now a hefty confrontation between the way the law courts try to uphold society's ideal of "blind-folded" justice, on the one hand, and media encouragement of mob rule to exact revenge on the other.

3.16 Conclusion

In general, specialised court reporting, the ABC tended to a balanced approach providing the audience with neutral information on the proceedings or results, especially that provided by its dedicated court reporters. Notably, there was evidence of the expression of themes supporting the bourgeois *field* of *cultural capital*, and there was also evidence of the use of the themes of 'victimisation'.[612] The expansion of synonyms used for 'victims', in lieu of the words 'complainants', or even 'accusers', was noted in the previous discussion. Allied to this, was counterbalanced by the ABC providing a list of hotline numbers for depression and anxiety support services. The ABC added to its *cultural capital* by publishing opinion and analysis articles written by lawyers, psychologists, an ABC journalist who was a published author on Pell, and an ABC Religion Expert. This was an intentional aid by the institution to the public to help it recognise itself, and what it believed mattered to Australians, in the ABC coverage.[613]

Another possible cause of perceived bias was that of fragmented content. It is a serious issue for news organisations which now curate content from a variety of sources. For the ABC it now musters and endorses multivalenced content under its historically respected imprimatur, its corporate colours and paraphernalia. Accusations of bias are made easily where all content appears to have the seal of the organisation. As with all other media, the incorporation of opinion gives a publication a certain flavour. This opinion-placement amongst court reporting, in this instance, in this case, muddied the serious attempts by journalists to simply report a case from a courtroom, and matters at hand, accurately. Entertaining, biased headlines may work well as click bait and help eyeball tracking but in hindsight are damaging to the reputation of the ABC. The *cultural capital* and *reputational capital* of a public service media outlet is eroded when it places fact beside opinion. They do not blend comfortably in Aunty's house—they have their place, and will continue to have a valued place—but not as merged reading content. This *laissez faire*, promiscuous approach to placing fact with opinion has serious consequences and provoked allegations of bias. It also accentuated how Australia's main public media service had re-positioned itself in an awkward emergent commercial *field* without safeguarding its *reputational capital*.

The ABC has failed to buttress its valued content in the digitisation shift without protecting its independence, neutrality and élite, privileged, hard won *cultural capital*. All content is now placed online together with the use of salacious headlines to grab the audience' attention. This crisis of content has arisen because the ABC has failed to create a stricter delineation of fact and opinion, there is a place for both in a multimedia outfit but merged they are a confusing mix leading the audience to wonder "what does the ABC stand for?" "How is the Australian citizen being served?". It leaves the organisation wide open to criticism of imbalance and bias. It has failed to plan for the sustenance and survival of its most valuable possession—Aunty's heirloom treasure. In the excitement of being 'all to all' in cyber space it has left its audiences confused because it now dabbles in the same contested commercial opinion in the same field as everyone else. Before it had the upper hand in Australian media as controlling the élite privileged *field* by trying as hard as possible to keep the two separate—and be a valued watchdog keeping an eye on commercial media, too. The necessary move to digital media has had repercussions for which current ABC management now has to negotiate, re-negotiate and provide apology. The ABC has by-passed the process of analysing where opinion and fact lay in their online menus and have placed them in a dangerously undifferentiated context. ABC management is now ambushed regularly and its weak public response is taken as inferential validation of bias, or at least an effete capacity to control it. Neither are good for Aunty's voice.

The ABC has shifted to the same *field* as Rupert Murdoch of commercial opinion. Comment by individuals has a place, and indeed can illuminate or give perspective to an issue. But in this drift into the emergent commercial field Aunty is in danger of becoming what she has always hated—and the pressure to be liked has never been greater. Despite the

ABC defence of its own analysis of its coverage of the Pell case as having "presented a wide range of opinions on the case" (ABC, 2020)[614] which "sets a high bar" (ibid.), the content of its webpages analysed in this corpus conveys a confusing message, undermining integrity of the brand in the short-term and in the long-term hindering the institution's funding claims for its service. The ABC said it conducted a "rough breakdown" content analysis of its media output on Pell looking at "broad categories" of those interviewed where "more than 80 different voices/interviews/reactions" (Loc. Cit.)[615] were obtained. However, in media analysis a power relationship exists between the interviewer and in the interviewee and voices recruited for interviews can have different impacts on content. For example, Hartley (1982) said there were two types of interviews "on the spot" and "in the studio" and that "the consequences on the production of meaning … can be decisive" (ibid.)[616] as to whether the information is treated as a fact, or event. To extrapolate on Hartley (1982) in the ABC context, there was some confusion as to whether Pell's trial was fact or event; where facts can range from raw to anodyne—events must always be performative and momentous. Further, the types of questions asked by journalists elicit different responses to support these choices. These selected voices and the questions they answer all contribute to what Hartley (1982) described as "the reality effect"[617]:

> Despite the care with which institutional and accessed voices are marked and separated from each other, there is a higher level of organisation of the material in which they are re-integrated. This is at the level of the news narrative as a whole. At this level, all the voices contribute to the production of the reality effect.[618]

Part of this process Hartley (1982) said meant that voices must be stereotyped "to make them meaningful within the continuation saga of news-discourse" (ibid.).[619] They must contribute to the narrative and personalised contributions "are then exploited to render events 'meaningful'"[620] often through the binaried use of "us and them" (Hartley, 1982).[621] The impact of social media as an adjunct to news media would have an even greater influence on Hartley's "reality effect" where performative, attention-getting content is prioritised over fact. Allied to this is the silent pressure placed on public service ABC actors to compete and boost institutional popularity in a complicated, fierce, emergent commercial digital *field*.

Appendix: Service for Funding

Table 3.3 Corpus analysis

News content		*Prominent themes/choice of words*	
Event *Report date* *Journalist/s* *URL*	*Main headline* *Hyperlink headline*[a]	*Positive Catholic Church and religion/* *Neutral Catholic Church and religion/* *Negative Catholic Church and religion/*	*Positive male/* *Neutral male/* *Negative male*
Day One Trial 1: 1. 26/07/17 *Anonymous* https://www.abc.net.au/news/2017-07-26/pell-faces-massive-media-scrum-at-court-arrival/8744156	*Main Headline:* Pell faces massive media scrum at court arrival		
2. 26/07/17 *ABC Court Reporter* https://www.abc.net.au/news/2017-07-26/george-pell-in-court-for-first-time-over-alleged-sexual-offences/8723576	*Main Headline:* Cardinal George Pell to appear in court for first time over historical sexual offence charges	*Positive Catholic Church and Religion/* Neutral Catholic Church and Religion/ Australia's most senior Catholic *Negative Catholic Church & Religion/*	*Positive Male:* represented by top criminal barrister Robert Richter QC. Neutral Male/ Victoria Police Deputy Commissioner Shane Patton Negative Male/
Mistrial declared 3. 20/09/18	Jury unable to reach verdict (suppression order)[b]	No report	No report
Day 1 Trial 2 4. 7/11/18	Arraignment (suppression order)	No report	No report
Conviction 5. 11/12/18	Jury unanimous verdict of guilty, all five charges (suppression order)	No report	No report

Positive-supportive Accused/ Neutral accused/ Negative accused/	*Positive-supportive complainant/ Neutral complainant/ Negative complainant/*
x Simple description only	
Positive-Supportive Accused: Pell has always maintained his innocence and strenuously denied allegations/victim of "relentless character assassination"/the charges "strengthened his resolve" to clear his name/looking forward to day in court/"I'm innocent of those charges. They are false. The whole idea of sexual abuse is abhorrent to me"/George Pell 'grateful' for public support/spokeswoman for Pell issued statement saying his return should come as no surprise/totally rejected allegations/completely innocent of charges/would return to Australia to vigorously defend himself and clear his name/His return today then should not be a surprise/he is grateful for the numerous messages of support he continues to receive/fights historical sexual offence charges/ *Neutral Accused:* would not receive any special treatment/front a Melbourne court/front a short hearing/"process and procedures" followed same as those applied "in a whole range of historical sex offences, whenever we investigate them"/unable to travel from Rome in 2016 to give evidence in person to the Royal Commission into Institutional Responses to Child Sexual Abuse/commission accepted Pell would be at risk of heart failure if forced to fly to Australia/Pell staggered his journey over "several days" on advice from doctors, to avoid long-haul flights/ *Negative Accused:* No report	*Positive-Supportive Complainant/* Neutral Complainant/ offences involving multiple complainants/ *Negative Complainant/* No report
No report	No report
No report	No report

(*continued*)

Table 3.3 (continued)

News content		*Prominent themes/choice of words*	
Event *Report date* *Journalist/s* *URL*	*Main headline* *Hyperlink headline*[a]	*Positive Catholic Church and religion/* *Neutral Catholic Church and religion/* *Negative Catholic Church and religion/*	*Positive male/* *Neutral male/* *Negative male*
Verdict 6. 26/02/19 *ABC Court Reporter* https://www.abc.net.au/news/2019-02-26/george-pell-guilty-child-sexual-abuse-court-trial/10837564	*Main Headline:* George Pell guilty of sexually abusing choirboys Hyperlink Headline: Pell abused two choirboys. One of them didn't live to see justice (Trigger event: 'Swimmers trial' dropped owing to court finding a lack of evidence, judge ruling evidence inadmissible).	*Positive Catholic Church/Religion:* *Neutral Catholic Church/Religion:* *Negative Catholic Church/Religion:* "Catholic Church grappling (verdict)"/"trying to make sense with the George Pell they know" *Quoting former priest:* "Catholics in Australia are punch-drunk"/ Bishops abject failures (appointed by Pell)/Melbourne Response complainants: lack of independence and inconsistency/ "Australia's most powerful Catholic a convicted child sex offender"/	*Positive Male:* "other witnesses, all men"/ Jesuit priest and human rights lawyer Father Frank Brennan, and former deputy prime minister and ambassador to the Holy See Tim Fischer. *Neutral Male:* quoting the judge "the accused man" *Negative Male:* Would be removed as Cardinal/never return to Vatican/his gold ecclesiastical ring/ ***lightning rod for outrage/ defence:*** dismissive reputation/ dominated Catholic Church
7. 26/02/19 *Anonymous* https://www.abc.net.au/news/2019-02-26/george-pell-child-sex-abuse-guilty-verdict-chrissie-foster/10845500	*Main Headline:* Chrissie Foster calls for George Pell's Melbourne Response to be 'torn down'	*Positive Catholic Church/religion:* Neutral Catholic Church/religion: *Negative Catholic Church/religion:* "I'm just pretty upset. It's a big shock"/"scared clergy"/"should be hunted down"/"As a Catholic myself, I think God, has it come to this?"/"it's like our whole approach to life has been put through the wringer/institution of the church … brought to its knees"/"lost its credibility"/"There's an arrogance that's still there about this, in the institutional player, and until they realise the community has turned their back on them then that institution is doomed"/bishops were "shocked"/mix of emotions/church to be destroyed and for the police to seize all church documents/Paedophile priest Kevin O'Donnell/Controversial Melbourne Response/"trying to shut us down"/"scheme should be closed in the wake of Pell's conviction"/	*Positive male:* *Neutral male:* Negative male: "Pell was one of the architects"/

Positive-supportive Accused/ *Neutral accused/* *Negative accused/*	*Positive-supportive complainant/* *Neutral complainant/* *Negative complainant/*
Positive-Supportive Accused: "first archbishop to deal with sexual abuse"/products of fantasy/ absolute and disgraceful rubbish/Quoting judge: "not a scapegoat for conduct not contained in the charges"/ fundamentally improbable and most certainly false *Pell statement:* "always maintained his innocence" *Defence:* "Only a madman would attempt to rape boys in the priest's sacristy immediately after Sunday solemn Mass"/ commiserate with Pell/a woman kissed his cheek/other people approached to shake his hand/shook Pell's hand *Neutral Accused:* "Accused"/Judge: to give the dock a wide berth. *Negative Accused:* "the eyes of the world"/"the world has ever seen"/ "all over the globe"/ characteristically forceful denials/voice of Pell/"The Cardinal sucked on a lolly as he was shown photos of the choirboys involved"/Pell uncrossed his arms to take notes/ "Combative response" (to Melbourne Response complainants) angrier, challenged/"this is why he was trying to shut us down then"/"parade of witnesses/"	*Positive-Supportive Complainant/* *former choirboy/the choirboy/former choirboys (witnesses)* *victim/a student/* *Long-time advocate/* */victim/* Quoting "victim"—(1) "survivors", (2) "shame, loneliness, depression and struggle", (3) "we trusted someone we should have feared" *Neutral Complainant:* "The guilty verdict made the complainant a victim". *Negative Complainant:*
Positive-Supportive Accused: *Neutral accused:* *Negative accused:* "cheered when I heard that he had been convicted"/"the verdict helped her understand Pell's 'angry' response to her family"/"This is actually someone right at the top, committing these offences"/ Richmond Football Club removing Pell as a vice-patron/	*Positive-Supportive Complainant/* ABC Radio caller: a victim of abuse/"a lot of sadness that has gone on for so long and it's damaged so many people's lives". *Neutral complainant:* *Negative complainant:*

(*continued*)

Table 3.3 (continued)

News content		*Prominent themes/choice of words*	
Event *Report date* *Journalist/s* *URL*	*Main headline* *Hyperlink headline*[a]	*Positive Catholic Church and religion/* *Neutral Catholic Church and religion/* *Negative Catholic Church and religion/*	*Positive male/* *Neutral male/* *Negative male*
8. 26/02/19 *ABC Court Reporter* https://www.abc.net.au/news/2019-02-26/george-pell-trial-why-cardinal-court-case-held-in-secret/10233118	*Main Headline:* George Pell's trial for child sexual abuse was held in secret. This is why	*Positive Catholic Church/religion:* *Neutral Catholic Church/religion:* *Negative Catholic Church/religion:*	Positive male: Neutral male: Negative male:
9. 26/02/19 *ABC Court Reporter* https://www.abc.net.au/news/2019-02-26/cardinal-george-pell-police-interview-rape-claims/10233556	*Main Headline:* George Pell's reaction to the 'vile and disgusting' child abuse claims put to him by police Hyperlink Headline: 'Vile': Pell's police interview	Positive Catholic Church/religion: Neutral Catholic Church/religion: Negative Catholic Church/religion: Pell: Immeasurable damage will be done to me and to the church by the mere laying of charges	Positive male: Neutral male: *Negative male:* *"meteoric rise"*
10. 27/02/19 *Anonymous* https://www.abc.net.au/news/2019-02-26/jon-faine-on-pell-talkback-response/10850254	*Main Headline:* Jon Faine says Pell talkback response overwhelmingly one of disgust One paragraph, opinion based.	*Positive Catholic Church/religion:* *Neutral Catholic Church/religion:* *Negative Catholic Church/religion:* "the Catholic Church had already spent significant resources on the case"	*Positive male:* *Neutral male:* *Negative male:*

Positive-supportive Accused/ *Neutral accused/* *Negative accused/*	*Positive-supportive complainant/* *Neutral complainant/* *Negative complainant/*
Positive-Supportive Accused: *Neutral accused:* Judge: "perfect storm of potential prejudice" against Pell that could damage his right to a "fair trial"/banned reporting of the fact there would be two trials, which would suggest to potential jurors that Pell was facing other serious sexual offences/the suppression order had been breached in the "most egregious way possible"/The Director of Public Prosecutions considering whether other contempt offences had been committed by the media, potentially prejudiced second trial/"rewarding bad behaviour" by lifting the suppression. Negative accused:	*Positive-Supportive Complainant/* *Neutral complainant:* *Negative complainant:*
Positive-Supportive Accused: Pell: "What a load of absolute and disgraceful rubbish"/"What a load of garbage and falsehood and deranged falsehood"/"vague and imprecisely defined circumstances and timeframes" which made it "practically impossible" to prove them to be "false"/"vile and disgusting conduct contrary to everything I hold dear and contrary to the explicit teachings of the church, which I have spent my life representing"/"The allegations are the product of fantasy"/"help heal the wounds"/Most things on … this story are counterfactual and with a bit of luck, I'll be able to demonstrate point by point/ improbabilities/Completely false. Madness/That's completely false/I'm certainly not guilty/ *Neutral accused:* *the accused man* *Negative accused:* "winced"/"disdainfully"/The Cardinal sucked on a lolly as he was shown photos of the choirboys involved/Pell uncrossed his arms to take notes/Pell quipped/	*Positive-Supportive Complainant/* "a former choirboy"x2/ choirboyx16 *Neutral complainant:* *Negative complainant:* Pell: cavorting in the sacristy
Positive-Supportive Accused: *Neutral accused:* *Negative accused:* "disgust"/cast doubt on Cardinal Pell's chances of a successful appeal	*Positive-Supportive Complainant/* *Neutral complainant:* *Negative complainant:*

(*continued*)

Table 3.3 (continued)

News content		*Prominent themes/choice of words*	
Event *Report date* *Journalist/s* *URL*	*Main headline* *Hyperlink headline*[a]	*Positive Catholic Church and religion/* *Neutral Catholic Church and religion/* *Negative Catholic Church and religion/*	*Positive male/* *Neutral male/* *Negative male*
11. 28/02/19 *ABC Reporter* https://www.abc.net.au/news/2019-02-28/vatican-launches-investigation-into-george-pell-sex-abuse/10855782	*Main Headline:* Vatican launches investigation into George Pell's child sexual abuse offences	*Positive Catholic Church/religion:* Neutral Catholic Church/religion: the Congregation for the Doctrine of the Faith (CDF) will now handle the case/Pope historic summit on child sexual abuse/global Catholic Church taking Pell's conviction seriously/removed from the Council of Cardinal Advisers in October/expiration of his five-year term this month/could lead to a canonical trial/would happen in private/defrock the cardinal/Pope Francis is under pressure to deliver decisive action on the clergy abuse crisis/credibility of the church will be destroyed forever Negative Catholic Church/religion:	*Positive male:* *Neutral male:* *Negative male:*
12. 28/02/19 *730 Program Reporter re-purposed for online* https://www.abc.net.au/news/2019-02-27/catholics-call-for-change-after-george-pell-conviction/10854010	*Main Headline:* Grassroots Catholics call for change after George Pell's conviction	*Positive Catholic Church/religion:* opportunity to refashion itself/time for the church to change/look at what a church really is/the people of God, not bishops or priests or cardinals/to make it better for our children/The Catholic Church is probably the safest place for children right now/The church is meant to incarnate Jesus on Earth/ *Neutral Catholic Church/religion:* Negative Catholic Church/religion: a crisis but also a challenge/the church gets a bad rap/a lot to do from the bottom up/a long road for the church to regain the trust it has lost/I don't think it will be easy/I don't think it will be just given back/a challenge to see how more live that role and be a sign to the rest of the world/	*Positive male:* *Neutral male:* *Negative male:* Women are half the church x2—they should have more sayx2/George Pell is a cardinal but he's also a man/hierarchical/they aren't the church/if laity in general and women were involved wouldn't be so much secrecy/things would be more open … more talked about/more honest/

Positive-supportive Accused/ *Neutral accused/* *Negative accused/*	*Positive-supportive complainant/* *Neutral complainant/* *Negative complainant/*
Positive-Supportive Accused: Neutral accused: influential figure in Rome Negative accused: disgraced cardinal George Pell/dismissed from the priesthood/the sooner the church acts the better for the sake of damage limitation	*Positive-Supportive Complainant/* *Neutral complainant:* *Negative complainant:*
Positive-Supportive Accused: *he's a good man* Neutral accused: Negative accused:	*Positive-Supportive Complainant/* prays for the victims of clerical abuse/to call this a crisis is probably not respectful for the victims/ *Neutral complainant:* *Negative complainant:*

(*continued*)

Table 3.3 (continued)

News content		*Prominent themes/choice of words*	
Event *Report date* *Journalist/s* *URL*	*Main headline* *Hyperlink headline*[a]	*Positive Catholic Church and religion/* *Neutral Catholic Church and religion/* *Negative Catholic Church and religion/*	*Positive male/* *Neutral male/* *Negative male*
13. 28/02/19 *Anonymous* https://www.abc.net.au/news/2019-02-27/george-pell-spends-first-night-in-jail-after-bail-revoked/10852940	*Main Headline:* George Pell spends night in Melbourne Assessment Prison after his bail is revoked	*Positive Catholic Church/religion:* *Neutral Catholic Church/religion:* *Negative Catholic Church/religion:* *painful news/shocked many people*	Positive male: Neutral male: Negative male:
14. 27/02/19 *Opinion* *Writer and lawyer* https://www.abc.net.au/news/2019-02-27/george-pells-conviction-opportunity-australian-catholic-church/10852688	*Main Headline*: Jesus warned against men like Cardinal Pell. His message could save the Church	*Positive Catholic Church/religion:* many good and kind people in the church *Neutral Catholic Church/religion:* Negative Catholic Church/religion: Australian church on a Sunday … half-full/cynical and godless age/market just isn't buying what the church is selling/an unattractive message/Christ preached empathy and inclusion. The church has highlighted what separates/must change/yet another failure of the church/terrible outcome for Catholics and priests who have laboured to preserve their faith/failed leadership/opportunity for the Catholic Church in Australia to alter its trajectory and find a better, more Christ-like mission and message/Faith and good deeds were meaningless unless matched the church/One theologian, Mr Jesus Christ/its most visible flag bearer has been revealed as utterly unworthy/must acknowledge the failings of its figurehead/church has opportunity to be something more.	*Positive male:* *Neutral male:* *Negative male:* Pell was the man who established the problematic Melbourne Response … undermining a more generous regime preferred by the Bishops Conference/abuse victim … find a place in this man's organisation?/gay couple welcomed?/arrogance of a man who deemed his views immune from challenge because of doctrinal purity/a cabal of hateful men who choose bigotry in a misguided attempt to be dogmatically constant/

Positive-supportive Accused/ *Neutral accused/* *Negative accused/*	*Positive-supportive complainant/* *Neutral complainant/* *Negative complainant/*
Positive-Supportive Accused: Well, I hope/ Defence: plain vanilla sexual penetration case where the child is not volunteering or actively participating/continued to maintain his innocence/the right to pursue his legal rights/Cardinal Pell maintains his innocence and has the right to defend himself until the last stage of appeal/ Neutral accused: his personal safety. The risk was likely to be high, given his public profile and the nature of the crimes of which he has been convicted/Prisoners are allowed one pair of shoes, one pair of pyjamas, and six pairs of underwear and socks, six books and six magazines, o four tops, four pairs of jeans, trousers or shorts. The suit of clothes George Pell has chosen to wear to court next month for sentencing/nominate people for his visit and telephone call lists and would have been allowed to make one phone call/the Congregation for the Doctrine of the Faith will now handle the case *Negative accused:* "Goodbye you creep",/unprecedented media coverage/Cardinal Pell is prohibited from exercising public ministry and from having any voluntary contact whatsoever with minors/Vatican investigating Pell/could result in his removal from the priesthood/no longer Prefect of the Secretariat for the Economy.	*Positive-Supportive Complainant/* Judge: two vulnerable boys/humiliating and degrading towards each boy and gave rise to distress in each boy/two choirboys *Neutral complainant:* *Negative complainant:*
Positive-Supportive Accused: *Neutral accused:* *Negative accused:* offence reprehensible ... good that justice served/a cold, stony, Easter Island statue of a face/dismissive of their suffering/Pell quoted x4: homosexual activity to be a "much greater health hazard than smoking"/if young kids did not want to be the victims of homophobia, they should not be gay/counselled Catholic politicians that their "place in the life of the church" would be affected if they supported embryonic stem cell research/condoms encouraged promiscuity and spread AIDS/Pell was the archetypal Pharisee/observing and parroting dogmas while luxuriating in his superior sanctity, indifferent to the human toll/the Easter Island statue has cracked and crumbled/exclusionary dogmatism, typified by Pell/leader has fallen.	*Positive-Supportive Complainant/* *the most vulnerable* *Neutral complainant:* *Negative complainant:*

(*continued*)

Table 3.3 (continued)

News content		*Prominent themes/choice of words*	
Event *Report date* *Journalist/s* *URL*	*Main headline* *Hyperlink headline*[a]	*Positive Catholic Church and religion/* *Neutral Catholic Church and religion/* *Negative Catholic Church and religion/*	*Positive male/* *Neutral male/* *Negative male*
15. 27/02/19 *ABC & Associated Press* https://www.abc.net.au/news/2019-02-26/george-pell-sexual-abuse-conviction-reaction-to-guilty-verdict/10851446	*Main Headline:* George Pell's conviction for child sexual abuse reverberates around Australia	*Positive Catholic Church/religion:* *Neutral Catholic Church/religion:* Negative Catholic Church/religion: the everyday Catholic left to grapple with their faith/good "people of faith" had "been betrayed"/I grew up in very strict Catholic family, but I have no faith whatsoever/They've let us all down, and they're still letting us all down/the church had been "brought to its knees"/hard for a lot of Catholics/As a Catholic myself, I think, God, has it come to this?/our whole approach to life has been put through the wringer/church is not the only institution left to wonder/gave Pell a private tour of the school as calls mounted for the prelate to answer questions for the royal commission/It was a great thrill to be able to escort His Eminence around the college grounds and witness the way he interacted with staff and students alike/"reserves the right to revisit" the stripping of Pell's school honours if he successfully appeals the ruling/commitment to our current families, and boys in our care that we will role model behaviours which aspire to the highest possible standards/College put a line through Pell's name on a board listing the school's ordained alumni, something it has done with five other clergymen, including convicted abuser Gerald Ridsdale/strikethroughs "stand both as a symbol for the bravery of victims and survivors of child sexual abuse and their families, and for the college's deep remorse for the pain and suffering caused by the actions of these individuals/Pope Francis told a summit that clergy who preyed on children were the "tools of Satan"/bishops were "shocked" by the guilty verdict.	*Positive male:* *Neutral male:* *Negative male:*

Positive-supportive Accused/ *Neutral accused/* *Negative accused/*	*Positive-supportive complainant/* *Neutral complainant/* *Negative complainant/*
Positive-Supportive Accused: await the outcome of the appeals process/Cardinal Pell maintains his innocence and has the right to defend himself until the last stage of appeal/. Neutral accused: Our hope, at all times, is that through this process, justice will be served/ Negative accused: outrage and disgust reverberating around the world/a convicted paedophile/You're an absolute pig. Burn in hell/a heckler yelled at Pell/deeply shocked at the crimes/a cardinal being convicted, it's more than a person being convicted in a way/At his old school in Ballarat, Pell's name has literally been scratched off the windows of a building/Pell attended prestigious St Patrick's College and had been inducted as a legend of the school—an honour now been stripped/untenable and not appropriate to have our students walk through a building that carries Cardinal Pell's name/scrub his name from the school's honour lists/Richmond AFL club removed Pell as a vice-patron/painful news/Holy Father confirmed precautionary measures imposed on Cardinal George Pell in Australia. Awaiting definitive assessment of the facts Cardinal Pell is prohibited from exercising public ministry and from having any voluntary contact whatsoever with minors/	*Positive-Supportive Complainant/* victims and their families/suffered from sexual abuse by those they should have been able to trust/ prolonged pain and suffering/pray for all abused and their loved ones ... commit ourselves anew to doing everything possible to ensure that the Church is a safe place for all, especially the young and the vulnerable. *Neutral complainant:* I don't think there's any winners in the sexual abuse issue/ Negative complainant:

(*continued*)

Table 3.3 (continued)

News content		*Prominent themes/choice of words*	
Event *Report date* *Journalist/s* *URL*	*Main headline* *Hyperlink headline*[a]	*Positive Catholic Church and religion/* *Neutral Catholic Church and religion/* *Negative Catholic Church and religion/*	*Positive male/* *Neutral male/* *Negative male*
16. 27/02/19 *ABC Reporters* https://www.abc.net.au/news/2019-02-27/george-pell-plaque-to-stay-at-st-marys-cathedral/10852422	*Main Headline:* George Pell plaque to stay at Sydney's St Mary's Cathedral despite child sex offences conviction	*Positive Catholic Church/religion:* praying for truth and justice/my commitment—shared by all at Sydney Catholic schools—to ensuring safety and wellbeing young and vulnerable people in the church Neutral Catholic Church/religion: *Negative Catholic Church/religion:* ***the purification of our church/my shame/ abuses suffered at the hands of church personnel***	*Positive male:* *Neutral male:* *Negative male:*
17. 28/02/19 *ABC Reporters* https://www.abc.net.au/news/2019-02-28/george-pell-lawyer-robert-richter-vanilla-comment-sparks-outrage/10855272	*Main Headline:* Why George Pell's lawyer Robert Richter described his offending as 'plain vanilla'	*Positive Catholic Church/religion:* *Neutral Catholic Church/religion:* *Negative Catholic Church/religion:* How out of touch these people are/	Positive male: *Neutral male:* *Negative male:*

Positive-supportive Accused/ *Neutral accused/* *Negative accused/*	*Positive-supportive complainant/* *Neutral complainant/* *Negative complainant/*
Positive-Supportive Accused: Defended Pell/appeal would find him not guilty/didn't do a thing, nothing to do with it/not that type of person/ Neutral accused: found guilty/conviction/everyone should be equal under the law/ respect the Australian legal system Negative accused: justice came/those who are sinners/shocked many. … Catholic bishops of Australia/conviction was shocking	*Positive-Supportive Complainant/* Choirboys/pray for all those who have been abused and their loved ones/apology to all those affected/ *Neutral complainant:* *Negative complainant:*
Positive-Supportive Accused: no more than a plain vanilla sexual penetration case/ Neutral accused: Convicted/investigating Pell/really serious example of contempt" if anyone was caught assaulting Mr Richter/bog standard plea discussion/rank the crime against every other possible crime/rank in terms of seriousness/the vanilla comment/Mr Richter is not talking to a jury, he is not talking to the media, he is talking to a judge/ Negative accused: a serious example of this kind of offending/normal plea discussions/ outrageous/"dirty money"/he could have chosen a better word.	*Positive-Supportive Complainant/* Two choirboys cold comfort to abuse survivors/advocates/ abused/such rape/insulting/what victims have to put up with/furious/abuse survivors/advocates/ advocacy group/horrified and concerned/child sexual abuse survivors/minimises what has happened to them/nothing much, get over it/ People take that as a slap/lack of understanding about the impacts of child sexual abuse/really telling thing/offensive *Neutral complainant:* *Negative complainant:*

(*continued*)

Table 3.3 (continued)

News content		*Prominent themes/choice of words*	
Event *Report date* *Journalist/s* *URL*	*Main headline* *Hyperlink headline*[a]	*Positive Catholic Church and religion/* *Neutral Catholic Church and religion/* *Negative Catholic Church and religion/*	*Positive male/* *Neutral male/* *Negative male*
Sentencing 18. 13/03/19 *Anonymous* https://www.abc.net.au/news/2019-03-13/george-pell-sentenced-for-sexually-abusing-choirboys/10876012	*Main Headline:* George Pell sentenced to six years' jail for sexually abusing two choirboys Hyperlink Headline: George Pell jailed for 'breathtakingly arrogant' abuse of two choirboys	*Positive Catholic Church/religion:* *Neutral Catholic Church/religion:* Negative Catholic Church/religion: power imbalance between the victims and Pell as a senior church official was "stark"/then-archbishop moved his robes to expose his penis and forced one of the boys' heads down towards it/.	*Positive male:* *Neutral male:* *a high-profile person* *Negative male:* The man once Australia's most powerful Catholic/your sense of authority and power in relation to the victims/ May have thought you could control the situation by reason of your authority, as archbishop/whether or not that belief was well-founded/ extraordinarily arrogant/ breathtakingly arrogant/ some guy's two minutes of pleasure/shouted at Mr Richter

Positive-supportive Accused/ *Neutral accused/* *Negative accused/*	*Positive-supportive complainant/* *Neutral complainant/* *Negative complainant/*
Positive-Supportive Accused: deny he sexually abused the boys/lodged an appeal against his conviction/jury verdict was unreasonable/a "lynch mob" mentality against Pell/sentence not a judgement of Catholic Church/ examples of a witch-hunt [or] lynch mob mentality in relation to you, Cardinal Pell/utterly condemn such behaviour/nothing to do with justice of civilised society. The courts stand as a bulwark against such irresponsible behaviour"/sentence took into account Pell's heart problems and high blood pressure, likely to be aggravated by stress in prison/shorter non-parole period/Pell's "good character and otherwise blameless life"/Pell had maintained his innocence/ Neutral accused: Sentenced/found guilty/sexually abusing/assaulting/without a clerical collar/serve/before eligible for parole/no evidence of remorse or contrition on Pell's part to reduce his sentence/ Negative accused: clear relationship of trust with the victims and you breached that trust/abused your position to facilitate this offending/ Breathtakingly arrogant' offending/brazenness of your conduct/ Pell's abuse/profound impact your offending has had/your offending immediate and significant impact on R/sentence was "insufficient"/hoping for 20 [years] but maybe 10/satisfaction he's going to be on sex offenders register rest of his life/his abuser/ hard to "take comfort" in Pell's sentence, because "overshadowed" by Pell's appeal/a "plain vanilla" case/reject submission the offending was at, or towards lower end of the spectrum of seriousness/Pell registered for life as a sexual offender/Pell abused the choirboys/Pell moved onto the other choirboy. He pushed the boy's head down to his crotch and orally raped him/Pell ordered the boy to remove his pants and then molested him as he masturbated/Pell abused that boy a second time two months later, after another Sunday mass/groped him briefly/.	*Positive-Supportive Complainant:* Two choirboys/choirboysx4/choirboyx2/former choirboys/victim/ these abuses and breaches as grave/victims/ significant and long-lasting impact "on the wellbeing of one of his victims/struggled for many years/issues of trust and anxiety/not possible for me to quantify the harm caused/no doubt it did in some way/court room was packed with abuse survivors, advocates/father of Pell's late victim/he's incarcerated, he can't hurt anybody/good feeling" to know son's abuser in jail/my son's life was wasted. Why was it wasted?/Pell's surviving victim said he appreciated the court had "acknowledged what was inflicted upon me as a child"/justice is done. Neutral complainant: the offending/Judge: "a brazen and forcible sexual attack on the victims"/acts were sexually graphic, both victims were visibly and audibly distressed/the offending/added layer of degradation and humiliation that each of your victims must have felt in knowing that their abuse had been witnessed by the other/R died of a heroin overdose in 2014 and never reported the abuse/survivors of child sexual abuse that the sentence "is not and cannot be a vindication of your trauma"/Cardinal Pell has not been convicted of any wrongs against you. Cardinal Pell does not fall to be punished for any such wrongs/ Negative complainant: you seek justice, but it can only be justice if it is done in accordance to law/"For me to punish Cardinal Pell for the wrongs committed against you would be contrary to the rule of law and it would not be justice at all".

(*continued*)

Table 3.3 (continued)

News content		*Prominent themes/choice of words*	
Event *Report date* *Journalist/s* *URL*	*Main headline* *Hyperlink headline*[a]	*Positive Catholic Church and religion/* *Neutral Catholic Church and religion/* *Negative Catholic Church and religion/*	*Positive male/* *Neutral male/* *Negative male*
19. 13/03/19 *Judge's verbatim statement.* https://www.abc.net.au/news/2019-03-13/george-pells-full-sentencing,-as-issued-by-peter-kidd/10897650	*Main Headline:* George Pell's full sentencing, as issued by Chief Judge Peter Kidd *Hyperlink Headlines to "Related Stories":* George Pell jailed for 'breathtakingly arrogant' abuse of two choirboys Only those in court saw Pell's reaction to his sentence. He was impervious 'It makes me sick': Catholics attend mass at site of Pell's abuse	Chief Judge Peter Kidd Verbatim statement. *Positive Catholic Church/religion:* *Neutral Catholic Church/religion:* *Negative Catholic Church/religion:* *Positive Catholic Church/religion:* *Neutral Catholic Church/religion:* *Negative Catholic Church/religion:* *Positive Catholic Church/religion:* *Neutral Catholic Church/religion:* Negative Catholic Church/religion: 'It makes me sick'/Catholics attend mass at site of Pell's abuse/	Chief Judge Peter Kidd Verbatim statement. *Positive male:* *Neutral male:* *Negative male:* *Positive male:* *Neutral male:* Negative male: He was impervious *Positive male:* *Neutral male:* Negative male:
20. 14 March 2019 *ABC Journalist—authored book The Rise and Fall of George Pell. Analysis* https://www.abc.net.au/news/2019-03-13/george-pell-sentencing-inside-the-court/10896292	*Main Headline:* George Pell looked a changed man as he was sentenced for his crime *Hyperlink Headline:* *Only those in court saw Pell's reaction to his sentence. He was impervious*	Positive Catholic Church/religion: Neutral Catholic Church/religion: Negative Catholic Church/religion: Not a prince of the church, not a cardinal/clerical collar and Order of Australia pin conspicuously absent"/ power imbalance between the victims and senior church leaders or officials, yourself included, was stark"/cast an enormous shadow over the Catholic Church and Australian culture life/The same face that once glided through St Patrick's Cathedral in Melbourne where those two choirboys were abused/supposed to represent all that is good in the world/.	*Positive male:* Neutral male: just an elderly, grey-faced man in the dock/in protective custody/ Negative male: A changed man/man convicted of and sentenced for terrible crimes against children/this man is and remains a lightning rod for discontent in the Australian community/man who once flew first class/a man in a beige jacket and black shirt who seemed to have aged years in a matter of weeks/face was impassive/mouth in a firmly pressed straight line/the man who dined with prime ministers/went into battle in the culture wars/spent his days telling the rest of us how we ought to live our lives/continued to stare ahead, face as impervious as an Easter Island statue/the fall from grace that this represents for a man/marked out for greatness since he was at secondary school/Oxford graduate/Vatican treasurer/ man for all seasons/childhood was ripped from them by this man/

Positive-supportive Accused/ *Neutral accused/* *Negative accused/*	*Positive-supportive complainant/* *Neutral complainant/* *Negative complainant/*
Chief Judge Peter Kidd Verbatim statement. Positive-Supportive Accused: Neutral accused: *Negative accused:* *"breathtakingly arrogant"* Positive-Supportive Accused: Neutral accused: Negative accused: Positive-Supportive Accused: Neutral accused: Negative accused:	Chief Judge Peter Kidd Verbatim statement. *Positive-Supportive Complainant:* *abuse of two choirboys* Neutral complainant: Negative Complainant: Positive-Supportive Complainant: Neutral complainant: Negative Complainant: Positive-Supportive Complainant: Neutral complainant: Negative Complainant:
Positive-Supportive Accused: has lodged an appeal against his conviction and denies the abuse—many times during the sentence/. Neutral accused: this crime/ Negative accused: prisons are full of victims of these crimes/blistering hour or so of Chief Judge Kidd's sentence/crimes were brazen/"breathtakingly arrogant"/scratching out his signature on the sex offender register/could be on that register for life/I craned my neck to look at Pell and saw a millisecond glimmer of recognition in his eyes as he saw me looking/however long Pell languishes in jail, however the cards in relation to his appeal may fall, there will be no rest for this young man/	*Positive-Supportive Complainant:* Victims/the awful abuse of those boys/crying and sobbing/whimpering and whispering/crying/young man who was the victim of this crime/another victim/died of an overdose/mother wept today/surviving victim/inflicted upon me as a child/a tragedy *Neutral complainant:* two 13-year-old choirboys. *Negative complainant:*

(*continued*)

Table 3.3 (continued)

News content		*Prominent themes/choice of words*	
Event *Report date* *Journalist/s* *URL*	*Main headline* *Hyperlink headline*[a]	*Positive Catholic Church and religion/* *Neutral Catholic Church and religion/* *Negative Catholic Church and religion/*	*Positive male/* *Neutral male/* *Negative male*
21. 13/03/19 *ABC Journalists* https://www.abc.net.au/news/2019-03-13/george-pell-sentence-abuse-catholics-divided-survivors/10896802	*Main Headline*: George Pell's sentence divides Catholics at Melbourne's St Patrick's Cathedral *Hyperlink headline:* *'It makes me sick': Catholics attend mass at site of Pell's abuse*	*Positive Catholic Church/religion:* Catholic faithful/Worshipper/did not change his belief in God or the church/our faith is in God's hands/result did not shake his faith in the church/Catholics are getting a bashing and it seems like it's a popular thing to do/commitment to ensure the safety of all children in his diocese/ Neutral Catholic Church/religion: Catholics arrived for afternoon mass/accept the decision/people are fallible, priests are fallible too. Negative Catholic Church/religion: loved ones and survivors of clergy abuse at fence outside St Patrick's Cathedral, tying ribbons to honour the victims/a sad situation for Catholics/really, really sad thing for Catholics like me//Catholic Church is shuffling it under the carpet/makes me sick that I pay school fees to a Catholic system/some of that money goes to the Catholic Church/raped by a Catholic priest/very long road to get justice from the Catholic priesthood/because of his position he should have been sentenced a lot harder/abuse the position he was in/	Positive male: Neutral male: Negative male: an "arrogant" man/found him arrogant then/"breathtakingly arrogant".
22. 13/03/19 *ABC Radio PM Program, re-purposed report.* *ABC journalists* https://www.abc.net.au/news/2019-03-13/george-pell-sentencing-analysis-three-factors/10897388	*Main Headline*: George Pell's sentence was influenced by three things	*Positive Catholic Church/religion:* Neutral Catholic Church/religion: the most high-profile priest to be found guilty of abusing children in the world/"he's spent the last 22 years living a life within the Vatican and within the church". *Negative Catholic Church/religion:*	Positive male: Neutral male: his situation is somewhat unique/ *Negative male:*

Positive-supportive Accused/ *Neutral accused/* *Negative accused/*	*Positive-supportive complainant/* *Neutral complainant/* *Negative complainant/*
Positive-Supportive Accused: not convinced by the guilty verdict/very difficult to perceive/six-year sentence was reasonable. Neutral accused: Abused/assaulted/eligible for parole after three years and eight months/sentencingx2/conviction/wait and see what happens at the appeal/given a sentence, the courts have prevailed/a high-profile individual is not being punished for his perceived role in other broader issues/the sentencex2/juries are generally diligent and responsible/Pell's conviction Negative accused: hoped Pell would never leave prison/it makes me sick/sentences are never long enough/Pell had always seemed untouchable/it's a wonderful thing/no sympathy for Pell/don't have any sympathy for him/	*Positive-Supportive Complainant:* Abuse survivors/pray for the victims/justice had been served/a survivor/victims who haven't survived/victims have been heard/victims/Abuse advocates/sexual abuse survivors/confidence in the legal system/Child sexual abuse survivor/assaulted at a different institution/feel for the victims, I understand the victims/very triggering and very distressing/what they've been through/People/use their voices and speak up and be heard Neutral complainant: abused two choirboys/choirboys/a very considered sentencing/ *Negative complainant:*
Positive-Supportive Accused: pilloried in the media/publicity and stigma Pell will live with/a form of punishment over and above the court/It's something very, very unusual/Judge: did "make allowances for those matters"/media coverage of the conviction was worth considering/considered Pell's age/Pell's age and health "is significant"/ Neutral accused: did not mean the sentence was reduced based on that consideration/a uniqueness to this case/sentencing principles at the time of the offending was possible sentence of only 10 years/parliament of Victoria has recognised that was too lenient and they've changed that/offended now he'd face a sentence of up to 15 years/argument for changing for cases involving historic child sexual abuse/Changes were introduced in New South Wales last year/a real possibility you may not live to be released from prison/found guilty 22 years later/ *Negative accused:*	*Positive-Supportive Complainant:* *child sexual abuse/* *Neutral complainant:* *really important day for Australian justice/can see exactly what a judge is doing/transparency was good for the justice system/understand why decisions were being made/how judges balanced the factors/* *Negative complainant:*

(*continued*)

Table 3.3 (continued)

News content		*Prominent themes/choice of words*	
Event *Report date* *Journalist/s* *URL*	*Main headline* *Hyperlink headline*[a]	*Positive Catholic Church and religion/* *Neutral Catholic Church and religion/* *Negative Catholic Church and religion/*	*Positive male/* *Neutral male/* *Negative male*
23. 13/03/19 *Opinion* *Academic* https://www.abc.net.au/news/2019-03-13/george-pell-michael-jackson-cognitive-dissonance/10892948	*Main Headline:* The psychological reason why some can't believe the evidence against George Pell and Michael Jackson	*Positive Catholic Church/religion:* *Neutral Catholic Church/religion:* *Negative Catholic Church/religion:*	Positive male: Neutral male: well-known people like Pell Negative male: child grooming and abuse claims against Michael Jackson/keeping powerful abusers safe/process can assist paedophiles/rack up victims/If you were so wrong about this person, what does that say about your character assessment of everyone else you know and love?/what if you have genuinely supported this individual through similar allegations, claims, or trials: what does that say about you? If you publicly declare a person is innocent, you are more likely to believe it privately/private belief means you are more likely to support the accused person even more strongly in order to reinforce your own long-held beliefs/conviction of serial killer Ivan Milat/cognitive dissonance/murder of seven backpackers/can't believe Ivan capable of these crimes/emotionally safer to believe the police must have set him up/divisions that follow one member being outed as a perpetrator are alarmingly common/oust a more powerful perpetrator/resources, connections and years of genuinely loving and positive relationships with other family members/powerful individuals defending figures of similar power or status/Those who are unable to accept unpalatable evidence should think twice about declaring their cognitive dissonance publicly/

Positive-supportive Accused/ *Neutral accused/* *Negative accused/*	*Positive-supportive complainant/* *Neutral complainant/* *Negative complainant/*
Positive-Supportive Accused: appealed his conviction and denies that abuse *Neutral accused:* some people refuse to accept the court's conviction of George Pell *Negative accused:*	*Positive-Supportive Complainant:* child sex abuse against two choirboys/rack up victims/Many victims are shocked to discover that when they put forth their allegations/find themselves ostracised from the family/easier to save face by casting the accuser as a liar, insane, or having a hidden agenda/Accusers disclosing their experience will bear the full responsibility for "tearing the family apart"/guilted into silence/ victims as "wicked" or crazed/confused or carrying out some ulterior agenda/the pain they are causing to others/ *Neutral complainant:* *Negative complainant:*

(*continued*)

Table 3.3 (continued)

News content		Prominent themes/choice of words	
Event *Report date* *Journalist/s* *URL*	*Main headline* *Hyperlink headline*[a]	*Positive Catholic Church and religion/* *Neutral Catholic Church and religion/* *Negative Catholic Church and religion/*	*Positive male/* *Neutral male/* *Negative male*
24. 14/03/19 *ABC Journalists* https://www.abc.net.au/news/2019-03-13/-george-pell-being-sentenced/10879958	*Main Headline:* Cardinal Pell being sentenced for sexually abusing two choirboys	*Positive Catholic Church/religion:* Neutral Catholic Church/religion: not sitting in judgement of the Catholic religion or the Catholic Church. Negative Catholic Church/religion: Melbourne Response, a scheme to deal with sexual abuse claims against clergy/	*Positive male:* Neutral male: without a clerical collar/two weeks in custody waiting to be sentenced/ Negative male: The man who was once Australia's most powerful Catholic
Victoria Court of Appeal Judgement 25. 21/08/19 LIVE BLOG *ABC Journalist* https://www.abc.net.au/news/2019-08-21/george-pell-live-appeal-court-judgment-child-sex-abuse/11431738	*Main Headline:* George Pell 'disappointed' by appeal judgement as victim hopes to move on	Positive Catholic Church/religion: *Neutral Catholic Church/religion:* The Catholic Church is also examining his case/the Vatican will wait to see if there's a High Court appeal before possibly expelling Pell from the priesthood. *Negative Catholic Church/religion:* the case was separate to the broader issue of child sex abuse in the church/George Pell's seniority and his involvement in designing and administering the church's response to the issue/many have already renewed calls for change/the ramifications of this case will continue to reverberate around the world.	*Positive male:* Prime Minister Scott Morrison says he understands Pell will be stripped of his Order of Australia honour/, *Neutral male:* the 78-year-old will continue to serve his time in prison/. *Negative male:*

Positive-supportive Accused/ *Neutral accused/* *Negative accused/*	*Positive-supportive complainant/* *Neutral complainant/* *Negative complainant/*
Positive-Supportive Accused: Judge condemns 'witch hunt' mentality/you are not to be made a scapegoat for any failings or perceived failings of the Catholic Church/ Nor are you being sentenced for any failure to prevent or report child sexual abuse by other clergy within the Catholic Church/condemned a "lynch mob" mentality against Pell/examples of a witch hunt [or] lynch mob mentality in relation to you, Cardinal Pell/utterly condemn such behaviour, that has nothing to do with justice of civilised society/ Pell continues to deny he sexually abused the boys/ *Neutral accused:* Sentenced/sentencing you within a unique context/You have not been charged with or convicted of any such failings/courts stand as a bulwark against such irresponsible behaviour/other victims of clerical or institutional sexual abuse this sentence is not and cannot be a vindication of your trauma/Cardinal Pell has not been convicted of any wrongs convicted against you. Cardinal Pell does not fall to be punished for any such wrongs/can only be justice if done in accordance to law/punish Cardinal Pell for the wrongs committed against you would be contrary to the rule of law and it would not be justice at all/found guilty/The trial had been suppressed to avoid potentially influencing jurors/The then-archbishop/abusex2/appealing against his conviction/ *Negative accused:* profound impact your offending has had on J's life/ your offending must have had an immediate and significant impact on R/Pell abused the choirboys/brazen and forcible sexual attack on the victims/orally raped him ordered the boy to remove his pants molested him/pushed him up against the wall/groped him briefly/ sexually graphic, both victims were visibly and audibly distressed during the offending,	*Positive-Supportive Complainant:* abuse victims/advocates/first attack/Pell's abuse had had a "significant and long lasting impact" on the wellbeing of one of his victims/range of negative emotions/struggled to deal with for many years since this offending/difficult because of issues of trust and anxiety/not possible for me to quantify the harm caused/no doubt that it did in some way/ victimsx4/added layer of degradation and humiliation that each of your victims must have felt/their abuse had been witnessed by the other/ Pell's surviving victim said he had experienced shame, loneliness and depression/survivors/years to understand the impact on my life/we trusted someone we should have feared/we fear those genuine relationships that we should trust/two choirboys/the choirboys/former choirboys/ choirboys/choirboyx2/ *Neutral complainant:* sexually abusing/sexually abusing/then assaulting one/ *Negative complainant:* did not have the benefit of a victim impact statement from his other victim, referred to as R, who died of a heroin overdose in 2014 and never reported the abuse/
Positive-Supportive Accused: *Neutral accused:* Pell appeal dismissed/Two of the three judges agreed the jury's guilty verdict was reasonable/Pell will continue to serve his six-year sentence/legal team is examining judgement to seek appeal in the High Court/child sex abuse convictions/dismissed the cardinal's appeal on all three grounds/George Pell's defence team is now going over the decision *Negative accused:* If he fails to win a final appeal in the High Court, he'll likely be stripped of his Order of Australia.	*Positive-Supportive Complainant:* Pell's surviving victim welcomed dismissal of appeal/A journalist who covered the trial extensively says not surprised Pell's appeal failed/ *Neutral complainant:* unlikely this will be the end of the matter/ *Negative complainant:*

(*continued*)

Table 3.3 (continued)

News content		*Prominent themes/choice of words*	
Event *Report date* *Journalist/s* *URL*	*Main headline* *Hyperlink headline*[a]	*Positive Catholic Church and religion/* *Neutral Catholic Church and religion/* *Negative Catholic Church and religion/*	*Positive male/* *Neutral male/* *Negative male*
26. 21/08/19 *ABC Journalist—author The Rise and Fall of George Pell* *Analysis* https://www.abc.net.au/news/2019-08-21/george-pell-appeal-failure-no-surprise/11435046	*Main Headline:* As a witness at George Pell's trial, I saw first-hand the strength of his victim Hyperlink Headline: As a witness at George Pell's trial, I saw first-hand the strength of his victim	*Positive Catholic Church/religion:* Neutral Catholic Church/religion: the third most senior person in the worldwide Catholic Church/The world's third most senior Catholic will return to prison/nor different strands of Catholicism, *Negative Catholic Church/religion:* Imagine taking on Cardinal George Pell/survived industrial-scale abuse by Catholic clergy in this country/a leftist conspiracy against a conservative Catholic/the then-Archbishop lifted his famed robes to sexually assault me/pundits shouting at whoever will listen/pundits who adopted this case as the latest episode in their culture war/	*Positive male:* *Neutral male:* *Negative male:* a man who was supposed to represent all that was good in the world/he has had the best legal representation that money can buy/for years cultivated and supported by the powerful/A man supported by two former prime ministers who didn't spend a minute in court, didn't hear or read a word of your evidence and yet nonetheless, by implication, branded you a liar/Pell's combative QC, Robert Richter/who was also abused by a powerful man the day I was raped/This isn't about a culture war/who espoused a muscular conception of the faith/The culture war will inevitably roll on/nor a man who was a lightning rod for dissent in his Church/

Positive-supportive Accused/ *Neutral accused/* *Negative accused/*	*Positive-supportive complainant/* *Neutral complainant/* *Negative complainant/*
Positive-Supportive Accused: Neutral accused: the then-Archbishop of Melbourne/Cardinal George Pell's appeal was dismissed/the criminal process had afforded Pell "every opportunity to challenge the charges and every opportunity to be heard"/There are lots of checks and balances in the criminal justice system"/this case is not about ideology/, *Negative accused:* what George Pell did to them/other complainants against George Pell/The Rise and Fall of George Pell/a well-resourced defendant/acceptance that justice, of some sort, has been served/They will be comforted by the dissenting opinion of Justice Mark Weinberg/claims that George Pell had betrayed the trust of children/As is his legal right, the Cardinal will undoubtedly appeal to the High Court—although he has limited grounds for doing so and may not be granted leave by their Honours/	*Positive-Supportive Complainant:* two little boys/from humble backgrounds/they could sing their little hearts out/whose childhoods, a court has again found, were stolen from them/One succumbed in 2014 to the heroin addiction that overwhelmed him from the age of 14/changed their lives/this young man was a truth-teller/Someone who was telling the truthx2/Judge: He did not seek to embellish his evidence or tailor it in a manner favourable to the prosecution/fiercely private/finding is not a surprise to me/I have never had any reason to believe that J is not telling the truth/I would defy anyone who had met him to find any reason why this young man would invent this story and to go through what has been a four-year ordeal/"The journey has taken me to places that, in my darkest moments, I feared I would not return from",/"the justice machine/forgetting about the people at the heart of the matter"./characteristically measured statement, too/trauma can't be underestimated/the ultimate David and Goliath tale/a young man who never sought fame, just wanted justice/trauma and anxiety for all involved/the entire community of people (abused)/cannot be underestimated/process is brutal and one you would be mad to seek out for any other reason than that you spoke the truth/a child rape survivor/grieving a friend/falsely accused of trying to do this for my own personal gain/Nothing further from the truth/claims he was somehow after compensation/risked my privacy, my health, my wellbeing and my family/not instructed to a claim for compensation/not about money and it never has been/gaping hole left by abuse/father, who wept tears of relief/mother is making peace with it all/Mother's intuition had twice prompted her to ask her son if he had been "interfered with", but the boy said no/not a surprise/his addiction took him from his mum's life/left with the gaping hole in her heart/This isn't about a culture war/as the latest episode in their culture war/I cannot begin to imagine how difficult it is to recall the finer details of an episode that happened when I was just 13 years old/child protection x2 *Neutral complainant:* Two 13-year-old choristers/Two boys/chorister/only 31 when he died/other choirboy remained silent/private and resolute determination, he told his truth/several blocks away from where the boy was orally raped/R's father … is taking civil action/The Royal Commission into Institutional Responses to Child Sexual Abuse found it took victims of Catholic clergy an average of 33.3 years to come forward/ *Negative complainant:*

(*continued*)

Table 3.3 (continued)

News content		*Prominent themes/choice of words*	
Event *Report date* *Journalist/s* *URL*	*Main headline* *Hyperlink headline*[a]	*Positive Catholic Church and religion/* *Neutral Catholic Church and religion/* *Negative Catholic Church and religion/*	*Positive male/* *Neutral male/* *Negative male*
27. 21/08/19 *Anonymous* https://www.abc.net.au/news/2019-08-21/cardinal-george-pell-child-sex-abuse-convictions-appeal-decision/11432066	*Main Headline:* George Pell loses appeal against child sex abuse convictions, may lose Order of Australia honour Hyperlink headline: Governor-General won't revoke honours before Pell's legal bids 'run their course'	*Positive Catholic Church/religion:* the Catholic Church remained committed to pursuing members of the clergy who commit abuse/together with the Church in Australia, the Holy See confirms its closeness to the victims of sexual abuse/commitment to pursue, through competent ecclesiastical authorities members of clergy who commit such abuse/ *Neutral Catholic Church/religion:* a spokesperson for Pell at the Catholic Archdiocese of Sydney/The Vatican issued a statement/statement by the Holy See on the Vatican News website said the Church acknowledged the court's decision *Negative Catholic Church/religion:* Cardinal George Pell will be stripped of his Order of Australia honour/daughters raped by Melbourne priest Kevin O'Donnell/	Positive male: Neutral male: Negative male:

Positive-supportive Accused/ *Neutral accused/* *Negative accused/*	*Positive-supportive complainant/* *Neutral complainant/* *Negative complainant/*
Positive-Supportive Accused: *his team would* "thoroughly examine" the judgement in order to determine a special leave application to the High Court/Cardinal Pell maintains his innocence/thank his many supporters/Pell had always maintained his innocence throughout the judicial process and that it was his right to appeal to the High Court/Pell holds onto Order of Australia honour/Pell a Companion of the Order of Australia in 2005 contribution to the Catholic Church/Pell's legal team had argued 13 reasons why offending was "impossible", but Justice Ferguson and Justice Maxwell rejected all 13/Pell's robes were too heavy to be moved aside to commit the sexual acts convicted of/stressed the conviction only concerned five offences Pell was convicted of/ vigorous and sometimes emotional criticism of the Cardinal, and he has been publicly vilified in some sections of the community/also been strong support for the Cardinal by others. *Neutral accused:* Pell plans to take rejected appeal against his child sex abuse convictions to High Court/turned down Pell's primary ground of appeal, that the jury's verdict was unreasonable/judges unanimously dismissed two other grounds of appeal/Pell sentenced to a six-year jail term/found guilty by a jury of five offences including sexual penetration of a child/minimum jail term of three years and eight months/dismissed the appeal on the ground of an unreasonable jury verdict/Justice Mark Weinberg upheld appeal ground/open to the jury to be satisfied beyond reasonable doubt Cardinal Pell was guilty as charged/Cardinal Pell is obviously disappointed/noting the 2–1 split decision/courts have done job, rendered verdict/the system of justice must be respected/ Governor-General no action until appeal to the High Court decided/ Council for the Order of Australia may make a recommendation/appeal on the unreasonableness ground has been dismissed because two of us took a different view of the facts/agreed with County Court Chief Judge ruling not to admit defence's animation/Cardinal Pell's conviction and appeal attracted widespread attention, in Australia and beyond/senior figure in the Catholic Church and internationally well-known/this case has divided the community/Cardinal Pell's conviction only concerns the five offences alleged to have been committed by him/Pell's legal team to seek leave to appeal to the High Court/lots of legal minds poring over that decision/ *Negative accused:* Pell likely to lose his Order of Australia honour/result in stripping of honours decided externally to the Government/of course will now follow/termination for conviction for a crime or offence under a law of the Commonwealth, State or Territory/Robes "were not so heavy or so immoveable as … had been suggested/a "distorted picture" of events at the cathedral/unanimous ruling to dismiss appeal on third ground—Pell should have been arraigned in front of jury/no matter how high you are, or how old you are, or what your job is/	*Positive-Supportive Complainant:* Mr Morrison said his sympathies were with victims/ Pell's surviving victim/very relieved" by outcome/ very long journey for him/very private person and very family-oriented/very much focused on doing his best to look after his family and get on with his life/anti-abuse advocate/"joyous moment"/so glad that it was not overturned after everything/sends a message that they will be believed/other victims of institutional abuse/a wonderful, wonderful day for survivors, for victims/sends a message that justice will be served/This is a crime, against children … innocence taken and destroyed. [Abuse] ruins people's lives/a good day, a good counter for that/ *Neutral complainant:* *Negative complainant:* Justice Weinberg, who dissented found the complainant's evidence had discrepancies/his evidence contained discrepancies, displayed inadequacies and lacked a probity of value so as to cause him to have a doubt as to the applicant's guilt/other evidence made the complainant's account "impossible to accept"/

(*continued*)

Table 3.3 (continued)

News content		*Prominent themes/choice of words*	
Event *Report date* *Journalist/s* *URL*	*Main headline* *Hyperlink headline*[a]	*Positive Catholic Church and religion/* *Neutral Catholic Church and religion/* *Negative Catholic Church and religion/*	*Positive male/* *Neutral male/* *Negative male*
28. 21/08/19 *ABC Journalist* https://www.abc.net.au/news/2019-08-21/inside-the-courtroom-where-george-pells-appeal-was-rejected/11434166	*Main Headline:* What happened inside the courtroom when Cardinal Pell learned he had lost his appeal Hyperlink Headline: Confusion, then an audible gasp—what happened inside the courtroom when Pell learned his fate	*Positive Catholic Church/religion:* *Neutral Catholic Church/religion:* Negative Catholic Church/religion: save for the clerical collar/	*Positive male:* Neutral male: moved carefully and slowly, holding onto the clerk's bench for support/eased his giant, stooped frame down to the dock/bowed slightly to the judges and took his seat/sat stock-still with his hands resting on the bench in front of him, staring directly at Chief Justice/waited to hear if his 175 days of confinement were about to come to an end/ *Negative male:*
29. 21/08/19 *730 Television Program* *Re-purposed content* *ABC Journalist* https://www.abc.net.au/news/2019-08-21/george-pell-decision-should-be-accepted-by-church-priest-says/11434786	*Main Headline:* Catholic priest says church should accept George Pell decision and be accountable for abuse	Positive Catholic Church/religion: urged Catholics in Australia to "keep calm, and carry on praying"/all Christians believe there's an ultimate tribunal anyway, in the next world, in eternity/urged his parishioners to keep up their support of Pell/Keep praying for him … keep calm and carry on praying/optimistic about the future of the church/church moved beyond status quo defending, and looking for change, looking for healing for poor people/The church has been a great light in the world for a lot of our history, so we can be again, it's just working through the darkness that we brought on ourselves/ Neutral Catholic Church/religion: We need to be held accountable x2/ *Negative Catholic Church/religion:* *Catholic priest called on* church to accept verdict on George Pell/Today is another dark day/church's reputation is in tatters … has been since I was a child/I don't know that we can sink any lower in terms of reputation in the community, in the country/People are really angry with us, angry with the church/time for the church to also accept the court's ruling/people around the country, they had the church on trial here/there will be some satisfaction for some people that someone in leadership is being severely punished today and for some years/only way things would change for church was if accepted responsibility/It's hurtful. It's embarrassing/Each time we have a convicted priest in the media, more ribbons go on the fence at my place/this has been appalling/if it remembers what its purpose is/	*Positive male:* Bishop Elliott studied with Pell at Oxford more than 50 years ago/ *Neutral male:* *Negative male:*

Positive-supportive Accused/ *Neutral accused/* *Negative accused/*	*Positive-supportive complainant/* *Neutral complainant/* *Negative complainant/*
Positive-Supportive Accused: friends and family of Cardinal George Pell/Jaws dropped/someone hyperventilating came from the back of the gallery/ *Neutral accused:* international significance of the decision/Pell waited to be called/ Pell was brought in, flanked by four guards/clad entirely in black/ Pell, did not move and did not take eyes off the judges/took a long drink of water/Pell did not take notes/Occasionally bowed his head, or rested chin in hand/showed no emotion or acknowledgement/looked at his legal team, but gave nothing away/neither celebration, nor grief/Cardinal George Pell—the most senior Catholic cleric to be convicted of child sexual abuse/ rose slowly from seat, bowed to bench, walked door at back of the court to return to his cell/Pell would not be going home. *Negative accused:*	*Positive-Supportive Complainant:* survivors of sexual abuse by other members of the clergy/. *Neutral complainant:* *Negative complainant:*
Positive-Supportive Accused: Bishop Peter Elliot backing Pell/'Keep calm and carry on praying' for Pell/refuses to accept the guilt of his long-time friend/don't accept this outcome because I hope it is appealed to a higher court/ *Neutral accused:* Pell lost appeal against conviction of sexual abuse against two boys while Archbishop of Melbourne/Father Hayes' would have accepted whatever decision the court handed down on Wednesday/ Our justice system is very, very good in Australia and it serves us well/if Cardinal Pell is guilty, then I'll accept that he's guilty. And if was free and let go, I'd have accepted that/ *Negative accused:* I wasn't surprised	*Positive-Supportive Complainant:* hopeful today brings some peace, some healing for people/hope brings more resolution for the fellow who was accuser, and his mate and their families/ hope that this brings another step to closure for them/I believe George Pell totally incapable of what he's been accused of, and what he's been convicted for. Totally incapable/If brings some peace for people, if brings some accountability, then that's OK, that's good/ *Neutral complainant:* *Negative complainant:*

(*continued*)

Table 3.3 (continued)

News content		*Prominent themes/choice of words*	
Event *Report date* *Journalist/s* *URL*	*Main headline* *Hyperlink headline*[a]	*Positive Catholic Church and religion/* *Neutral Catholic Church and religion/* *Negative Catholic Church and religion/*	*Positive male/* *Neutral male/* *Negative male*
30. 21/08/19 *ABC Journalist* https://www.abc.net.au/news/2019-08-21/george-pell-likely-jail-hopkins-correctional-centre-ararat/11435466	*Main Headline:* George Pell likely to be jailed with former friend, notorious paedophile priest Gerald Ridsdale	*Positive Catholic Church/religion:* *Neutral Catholic Church/religion:* *Negative Catholic Church/religion:*	*Positive male:* Neutral male: most "at-risk" prisoners at Hopkins and the prison population consists largely of convicted sex offenders and criminals requiring "special needs"/ often refers to high-profile criminals or convicted police officers who fear for their safety in jail/"aged" criminals/ *Negative male:* Prison population consists largely of convicted sex offenders/
31. 21/08/19 *Anonymous* https://www.abc.net.au/news/2019-08-21/lawyer-representing-complainant-in-pell-case-reads/11434582	*Main Headline:* Lawyer Vivian Waller reads a statement on behalf of George Pell's surviving victim	Simple descriptive paragraph	Simple descriptive paragraph

Positive-supportive Accused/ *Neutral accused/* *Negative accused/*	*Positive-supportive complainant/* *Neutral complainant/* *Negative complainant/*
Positive-Supportive Accused: the old age and medical requirements of his client/ *Neutral accused:* Cardinal George Pell/high-profile cleric/Cardinal almost six months in solitary confinement at Melbourne Remand Centre let out of his cell for an hour a day/Pell lost appeal against conviction over sexual offences against two choirboys in Melbourne in the 1990s/Pell highest-ranking Catholic convicted of sexual offence/ His fame and nature of his offending ... consider prisons that protect him from other inmates who may regard him as a target/"[Pell] is a high-profile prisoner, who has been given protection status, where there are significant security concerns"/ later served as a priest/priority to ensure prisoner safety/ ensure their placement is safe and secure/Prisoner placements are regularly monitored and reviewed/Pell not eligible for parole until 2022/ *Negative accused:* likely to be housed in same prison as former friend and notorious paedophile priest Gerald Ridsdale/Hopkins Correctional Centre in Ararat, 200 kilometres west of Melbourne, to be the most appropriate place/Ridsdale, former housemate of Pell, is serving a 29-year sentence after being convicted of 45 counts of child sex abuse spanning several decades/Pell ardent supporter of Ridsdale/ often stressed no knowledge of Ridsdale's abuse/If Pell sent there, may be required to work full time on tasks including building wooden products, screen printing, welding, cooking or laundry cleaning/ Simple descriptive paragraph	*Positive-Supportive Complainant:* Choirboys *Neutral complainant:* *Negative complainant:* Simple descriptive paragraph

(*continued*)

Table 3.3 (continued)

News content		*Prominent themes/choice of words*	
Event *Report date* *Journalist/s* *URL*	*Main headline* *Hyperlink headline*[a]	*Positive Catholic Church and religion/* *Neutral Catholic Church and religion/* *Negative Catholic Church and religion/*	*Positive male/* *Neutral male/* *Negative male*
32. 21/08/19 *Anonymous* https://www.abc.net.au/news/2019-08-21/george-pells-surviving-victim-reacts-to-appeal-dismissal/11434894	*Main Headline:* George Pell's surviving victim reacts to the cardinal's appeal being dismissed	*Positive Catholic Church/religion:* recommitted himself and the Archdiocese of Sydney to "ensure past crimes are never repeated"/ *Neutral Catholic Church/religion:* Pell attended the prestigious St Patrick's College and spent much of his time as a priest/Catholic Archbishop of Melbourne "respectfully" received the court's decision and encouraged everyone to do the same/complexity of the search for the truth has tested many, and may very well continue to do so/Archbishop of Sydney, said the prospect of a High Court appeal meant "limited" in his ability to comment/Pell's status within the Church only determined by the Vatican and Holy See "may well wait until the appeal process has been exhausted"/ *Negative Catholic Church/religion:* deep impact decision on Melbourne diocese/ Archbishop of Ballarat, "troubling time" for Catholic community/	*Positive male:* *Neutral male:* Negative male: the big arrogant man that he is, and he certainly was the big arrogant man in Rome/ now actually back in his place where he belongs because of what he's done, it's all caught up with him/

Positive-supportive Accused/ *Neutral accused/* *Negative accused/*	*Positive-supportive complainant/* *Neutral complainant/* *Negative complainant/*
Positive-Supportive Accused: Cardinal Pell provided pastoral and spiritual support while he serves sentence/indicating continue to visit Pell in prison/Cardinal strenuously maintained innocence … continues to do so notwithstanding decision/ *Neutral accused:* Cardinal George Pell/Two of three judges turned down Pell's primary ground of appeal, that the jury's verdict was unreasonable/ judges unanimously dismissed two other grounds of appeal/Pell returned to prison … serving six-year prison sentence for abusing two choirboys when archbishop of Melbourne in 1990s/Pell's convictions could not be vindication of the trauma suffered by other victims of sexual abuse/ *Negative accused:* Pell's name was scratched off windows of a building named in his honour at the school/known Pell since the 1970s and was glad to see the courts deliver justice/.	*Positive-Supportive Complainant:* welcomed the dismissal of Pell's appeal, saying hopes "it is all over now"/One of victims died of a heroin overdose/never lived to report the abuse or see justice/the surviving victim/hit back at commentators who questioned his motives/not an advocate or champion for cause of sexual abuse survivors/risked his privacy, his health, his wellbeing and his family/journey has not been easy/more stressful because high-profile figure/hope all over now/Father of Pell's late victim 'tears in his eyes'/ second choirboy/"a tear or two" in his eyes/relief of the stress/wasn't expecting for that to be dismissed/pressure off shoulders, melted away/my son and the other young fellow/brave enough to come out and make complaint/brave fellow/heart goes out to him and his family/victims are heard/ survivors of other institutional abuse and victims' advocates celebrated/hope that this shows that no-one is above the law/victims advocate/not always faith in the justice system but that changed/ greeted with nods and words of encouragement/ other victims' advocates/thanked the complainant in Pell's case for his courage/a "true hero"/"brave, brave man"/stronger voice to survivors/survivors believed now/for decades not believed/now we are believed and that is wonderful/Anti-abuse advocate/joyous moment/Survivors/sexually abused as a student/opportunity to "put a full stop on it"/opportunity to reset/get back to real issues surrounding this whole quagmire of problems that have happened over a number of decades/child sexual abuse survivor/thoughts and prayers are with the man who brought this matter before the courts/offered support to the complainant and survivors of child sexual abuse/prayed for and supported survivors of child sexual abuse/hope and pray finalisation of legal processes bring some sense of resolution to all those affected by proceedings/ surviving victim's statement/ *Neutral complainant:* Former choirboy sexually abused by Cardinal George Pell *Negative complainant:*

(*continued*)

Table 3.3 (continued)

News content		*Prominent themes/choice of words*	
Event *Report date* *Journalist/s* *URL*	*Main headline* *Hyperlink headline*[a]	*Positive Catholic Church and religion/* *Neutral Catholic Church and religion/* *Negative Catholic Church and religion/*	*Positive male/* *Neutral male/* *Negative male*
33. 21/08/19 *Anonymous* https://www.abc.net.au/news/2019-08-21/george-pell-appeal-judgment-summary-transcript/11434304	*Main Headline:* George Pell Victorian Court of Appeal judgement summary transcript	*x*	*x*
34. 21/08/19 *Article from outside media:* *The Conversation.* *Academic* https://www.abc.net.au/news/2019-08-21/george-pell-has-lost-his-appeal-what-happens-next/11434216	*Main Headline:* George Pell has lost his appeal. What did the court decide and what happens now?	*Positive Catholic Church and Religion:* *Neutral Catholic Church and Religion:* Save for a successful appeal in the High Court, Pope Francis will likely expel Cardinal Pell from the priesthood. Negative Catholic Church and Religion:	*Positive Male:* *Neutral Male:* Seniority Catholic Church/ former Vatican Treasurer *Negative Male:*
35. 21/08/19 *Moderated by ABC Journalists* https://www.abc.net.au/news/2019-08-21/george-pell-live-appeal-court-judgment-child-sex-abuse/11431738	*Main Headline:* George Pell 'disappointed' by appeal judgement as victim hopes to move on Hyperlink Headline: How George Pell's judgement day unfolded	Blog and summary	Blog and summary
36. 21/08/19 *Anonymous* https://www.abc.net.au/news/2019-08-21/pell-appeal-judgement-is-read-in-court/11434714	*Main Headline:* The justices from Victoria's Court of Appeal read their finding on Cardinal Pell's appeal	Bench reading decision (video).	Bench reading decision (video).
37. 21/08/19 *Anonymous* https://www.abc.net.au/news/2019-08-21/cardinal-george-pell-loses-appeal/11434044	*Main Headline:* Cardinal George Pell loses appeal against historical child abuse convictions	Bench reading decision (video)	Bench reading decision (video).

Positive-supportive Accused/ *Neutral accused/* *Negative accused/*	*Positive-supportive complainant/* *Neutral complainant/* *Negative complainant/*
x	*x*
Positive-Supportive Accused: Can seek leave to appeal to High Court *Neutral Accused:* unanimously found Pell guilty/Pell argued appeal/ technicalities of 'unreasonable' verdict/Pell remain in jail/ Negative Accused: exceptionally difficult for survivors of child sexual abuse to bring successful criminal complaints, especially against powerful offenders.	*Positive-Supportive Complainant:* Both victims were choirboys/recipients of choral scholarships/at elite school/ complainant compelling/not liar or fantasist/family of second survivor suing Pell or Church for civil damages/judgement may encourage other courageous survivors to make complaints/ *Neutral Complainant:* two 13-year-old boys/the boys/normal for survivors of sexual abuse to delay disclosure/juries judge complainants account/ reforms still required to better facilitate prosecutions of child sexual offences. *Negative Complainant:*
Blog and summary	Blog and summary
Bench reading decision (video).	Bench reading decision (video).
Bench reading decision (video).	Bench reading decision (video).

(*continued*)

Table 3.3 (continued)

News content		*Prominent themes/choice of words*	
Event *Report date* *Journalist/s* *URL*	*Main headline* *Hyperlink headline*[a]	*Positive Catholic Church and religion/* *Neutral Catholic Church and religion/* *Negative Catholic Church and religion/*	*Positive male/* *Neutral male/* *Negative male*
38. 22/08/19 *Analysis* *ABC Journalist* *Co-authored book with mother of child abuse victims* https://www.abc.net.au/news/2019-08-22/george-pell-appeal-catholic-church-next-step/11435338	*Main Headline:* With George Pell back in jail, now we wait for the Catholic Church's next move	*Positive Catholic Church/religion:* *Neutral Catholic Church/religion:* *Negative Catholic Church/religion:* His defenders, including a few media headline hawkers/"Melbourne Response" an attempt to treat survivors with compassion/repeatedly discredited by formal inquiries/Vatican has stood by it/still in place/despite heavy criticisms/How do politicians and church leaders view this scheme now/Archbishop of Melbourne said rather go to jail than report child abuse revealed to him in confessional/accepted rule of law in this case/Archbishop Comensoli deal with the legacy of his friend/Royal Commission into Institutional Responses to Child Sexual Abuse asked Vatican to hand over files/allegations of clergy sexual abuse in Australia/church said "neither possible nor appropriate"/Australia Catholic Bishops' Conference said nothing about Pell's crimes/only awaiting appeal/statement still does not condemn high-ranking colleague/message from the pulpit this Sunday?/hopefully community leaders remember to quote court, which found victim "not a liar"/	Positive male: Neutral male: Negative male:

Positive-supportive Accused/ *Neutral accused/* *Negative accused/*	*Positive-supportive complainant/* *Neutral complainant/* *Negative complainant/*
Positive-Supportive Accused: *Neutral accused:* judges dismissed Cardinal George Pell's appeal against his convictions over sexual offences against two choirboys in Melbourne in the 1990s/rendered their verdict, and that's system of justice in this country and must be respected/respectfully receive the court's decision/encourage everyone to do the same/Cardinal Pell's legal team has said will examine judgement to determine special leave application to High Court/his criminal conviction. *Negative accused:* Pell now likely to be stripped of Order of Australia/Pell leading figure in the Roman Catholic Church's harmful response to child abuse in this country/set up in the 1990s, around the time Pell was abusing children/Pell told commissioners their request was "unreasonable"/should now be viewed in the context of his criminal conviction/	*Positive-Supportive Complainant:* Events like this bring it all back/urge Australians reliving these experiences to reach out to those around them, to the services there for them/victims were not believed and children not protected/worn down by the institutions that enabled their abuse/ Bishops realise this has been and remains a most difficult time for survivors of child sexual abuse and those who support them/ *Neutral complainant:* *Negative complainant:*

(*continued*)

Table 3.3 (continued)

News content		*Prominent themes/choice of words*	
Event *Report date* *Journalist/s* *URL*	*Main headline* *Hyperlink headline*[a]	*Positive Catholic Church and religion/* *Neutral Catholic Church and religion/* *Negative Catholic Church and religion/*	*Positive male/* *Neutral male/* *Negative male*
39. 22/08/19 *ABC Journalists* https://www.abc.net.au/news/2019-08-22/george-pell-failed-appeal-is-test-for-vatican-and-pope-francis/11436654	*Main Headline:* George Pell's failed appeal is now a monumental test for Pope Francis and the Vatican	*Positive church and religion:* committed to "pursue" clergy who commit sexual abuse/Vatican does not take lightly sentences or rulings of Australian courts/Pope Francis called summit on abuse of children by priests around the world/we have seen under this Pope more transparency and more updates/ Neutral Catholic Church/religion: stunned and divided the Catholic Church hierarchy at the Vatican/Australia's most senior Catholic once wielded enormous power/shaken an institution/Holy See announced internal inquiry into Pell, run by Congregation for the Doctrine of Faith/not clear focus of Vatican's investigation/likely comprehensive inquiry/wait until Pell exhausted every avenue for appeal/ investigative work not yet begun/ acknowledged court's decision/The Congregation for the Doctrine of the Faith awaiting outcome of ongoing proceedings/Vatican "prudent" delaying investigation/Catholic Church hierarchy split on how to handle case/very challenging, delicate case/Important test for Pope Francis/Pell's case uncharted territory for Vatican/ Negative Catholic Church/religion: Vatican's "treasurer" working within imposing centuries-old apostolic palace/ tone deaf to pain of victims/line in the sand for the Vatican/calls into question seriousness church taking abuse/still "denial" in some parts of church/ misunderstanding of process in Australia/ view there's lots of different goes at getting the verdict that they might want/ lot of pressure on the Vatican to take action against the Cardinal/American cardinal Theodore McCarrick defrocked after church found he abused seminarians/McCarrick's case not subject of a trial/decision on Pell's fate within church one of most important tests for action and accountability Pope has faced/ If church to make progress has to believe and listen to victims of abuse/	Positive male: Neutral male: Negative male:

Positive-supportive Accused/ *Neutral accused/* *Negative accused/*	*Positive-supportive complainant/* *Neutral complainant/* *Negative complainant/*
Positive-Supportive Accused: cases where innocent people accused and won their appeals/Some feel no proof to demonstrate he committed these acts/Vatican noted Pell always maintained innocence/his right to appeal to High Court/ *Neutral accused:* convicted of abuse as member College of Cardinals/remains member College of Cardinals/still has power to vote to elect new pope/Pell most senior Catholic convicted of child sex offences/Pell had been removed from public ministry/Pell promoted by Pope Francis in 2014/an influential figure in Rome/ *Negative accused:* Vatican probe could lead to 'defrocking'/Pope may decide to laicise, or "defrock"/expects Pell will be removed from priesthood/	*Positive-Supportive Complainant:* victims' groups want immediate and decisive action from Pope/promising to listen to victims of clergy abuse/tested by courts and found to convince juries *Neutral complainant:* *Negative complainant:*

(*continued*)

Table 3.3 (continued)

News content		*Prominent themes/choice of words*	
Event *Report date* *Journalist/s* *URL*	*Main headline* *Hyperlink headline*[a]	*Positive Catholic Church and religion/* *Neutral Catholic Church and religion/* *Negative Catholic Church and religion/*	*Positive male/* *Neutral male/* *Negative male*
High Court agrees to allow appeal 40. 13/11/2019 *Anonymous* https://www.abc.net.au/news/2019-11-13/george-pells-child-sex-abuse-appeal-bid-high-court-ruling/11695564	*Main Headline:* George Pell's appeal against child sex abuse convictions to be heard by High Court Hyperlink Headline: George Pell appeal decision means abuse victims will be 'hurt yet again', advocate says	*Positive Catholic Church/religion:* *Neutral Catholic Church/religion:* Negative Catholic Church/religion: why Catholic Church continued to insist on celibacy for priests/As Catholic felt betrayed by church/his abuse at hands of three priests/	Positive male: Neutral male: Negative male:

Positive-supportive Accused/ *Neutral accused/* *Negative accused/*	*Positive-supportive complainant/* *Neutral complainant/* *Negative complainant/*
Positive-Supportive Accused: is in poor health/likely to die in jail/submission to the High Court argued Court of Appeal's ruling was wrong/suggested court required Pell to prove the offending was impossible, rather than placing the onus of proof on prosecutors/ *Neutral accused:* final chance to fight his convictions for child sex abuse offences/ High Court agreed to hear his appeal/Pell serving a six-year jail sentence/jury unanimously found he had sexually assaulted two choirboys while he was the Archbishop of Melbourne in the mid-1990s/referred the case to the full bench of seven justices/ Australia's highest-ranking Catholic/must serve minimum three years and eight months/former adviser to Pope/on hold the release of never-before-seen findings of the Royal Commission into Institutional Responses to Child Sexual Abuse/final report heavily redacted after Pell charged with child sex abuse offences/ *Negative accused:* George Pell responsible for son's downhill spiral and fatal heroin overdose/wants to see Pell behind bars/no contact with innocent children/man written to Pope demanding to know why Pell kept his title Cardinal/Why not defrocked him and stripped him of his status within the church/father asked for update on Holy See's investigation into Pell/convicted of assaulting the boys at St Patrick's Cathedral in the mid-1990s after celebrating one of his first Sunday masses as Archbishop/convicted of abusing one of the boys a second time, two months later/pulled one of the boys aside and pushed his head down to his exposed penis/forced the other choirboy to perform oral sex on him before fondling him as he masturbated/molested him in a brief incident/	*Positive-Supportive Complainant:* decision has "gutted" the father of one of Pell's victims/two choirboys/Pell's late victim/sad day for her client/hopeful that it would all be over/ re-traumatised by unending legal action/pain and suffering raw and unresolved/hurt never goes away and I cry a lot over the loss of my son/will always miss the innocent little choirboy that was my son/ tragic waste of beautiful boy/life became nightmare for himself and those around him/shocked and upset when told his son had been named a victim/ as parent felt like a failure/found complainant truthful/victims' advocate/High Court decision "very disappointing"/Victims of abuse/feel very disappointed that this permission has been granted and it's going to continue/hoping it would go the way that the DPP asked or recommended/just so hard to hold onto a conviction and make it stick/ abuse survivor/High Court's decision would cause more pain to survivors/so many survivors who are on the edge/going to hurt yet again/evidence of abuse came from just one of the choirboys/other victim died in 2014 and never made a complaint/ surviving victim's evidence/former choirboy/ Evidence from one choirboy/choirboys/died of heroin overdose 2014/ *Neutral complainant:* taskforce investigating child sexual abuse/sexually assaulting the two 13-year-old/ *Negative complainant:* dissenting judge believed his account was "impossible to accept"/"contained discrepancies displayed inadequacies"/

(*continued*)

Table 3.3 (continued)

News content		*Prominent themes/choice of words*	
Event *Report date* *Journalist/s* *URL*	*Main headline* *Hyperlink headline*[a]	*Positive Catholic Church and religion/* *Neutral Catholic Church and religion/* *Negative Catholic Church and religion/*	*Positive male/* *Neutral male/* *Negative male*
41. 14/11/19 *Anonymous* https://www.abc.net.au/news/2019-11-13/george-pell-appeal-in-high-court-what-happens-next/11700954	*Main Headline:* George Pell's fight against his convictions will be heard by the High Court. Here's what happens next	*Positive Catholic Church/religion:* Neutral Catholic Church/religion: leaving the Vatican in uncharted waters/ Holy See's Congregation for the Doctrine of the Faith investigating Pell/ common for the Catholic Church to wait for criminal proceedings to be over/ Vatican unwilling to discuss what action would take against Pell/Only one other cardinal in history—Theodore McCarrick—laicised but no criminal proceedings/ *Negative Catholic Church/religion:* church's investigations often viewed as 'clandestine'/all done behind closed doors/even priests defrocked by the church remain priests, according to the Catholic belief/	Positive male: Neutral male: Negative male:

Positive-supportive Accused/ *Neutral accused/* *Negative accused/*	*Positive-supportive complainant/* *Neutral complainant/* *Negative complainant/*
Positive-Supportive Accused: best argument is he's an old man, potentially in poor health/in danger in the prison or has to be subject to really strict regimes to keep him safe and only a few years left before parole/ *Neutral accused:* child sex abuse convictions/High Court agreed to refer his appeal to full bench/former adviser to Pope/did not formally grant Pell special leave to appeal against conviction/agreed to hear arguments for and against conviction/requires all parties to prepare and argue cases before seven judges/why his conviction should be overturned/rule on whether Pell has right to appeal at same time as decision on whether or not appeal successful/most likely case will decide one way or the other/possible court could reach decision at end first hearing/originally found guilty by a jury in the Victorian Supreme Court/took the matter to state's Court of Appeal/he lost again/Two judges/found jury's verdicts convicting Pell of the five charges against the two choirboys were reasonable/only avenue of appeal left High Court/whether Court of Appeal made right decision when it upheld convictions/High Court will ... decide which of them got it right/they could decide neither of them got it quite right and come up with a judgement of their own/issue has moved on to not 'did the jury do its job properly' but 'did the Court of Appeal do its job properly'/Pell's final chance to be freed from prison and clear his name/If succeeds he will walk free no longer a convicted child sex abuser/if dismiss appeal stays in prison until at least 80/will live and die a convicted sex offender/the stakes/most senior member of Catholic Church convicted of child sexual abuse/George Pell will have to rely on his lawyers/High Court doesn't often do things in rush, but when it acts its decisions are clear and final/ *Negative accused:* only a partial win/possible court could disallow appeal partway through hearings/might decide 'we've heard enough, we don't need to hear anymore, we're not going to hear your case/may have to wait some time to know fate/High Court unlikely to run any hearing until well into next year/more likely they'll say 'we're going to think about this' and they'll reach a decision in the middle of next year/Why is Pell still a Cardinal?/process could lead to him laicised, more commonly referred to as defrocked/	*Positive-Supportive Complainant:* the two choirboys/ *Neutral complainant:* defence will have to mount case in support of the Victorian Court of Appeal's/dissenting ruling/ *Negative complainant:* third judge, disagreed/found discrepancies in the evidence of the complainant, which left him with a doubt about Pell's guilt/

(*continued*)

Table 3.3 (continued)

News content		*Prominent themes/choice of words*	
Event *Report date* *Journalist/s* *URL*	*Main headline* *Hyperlink headline*[a]	*Positive Catholic Church and religion/* *Neutral Catholic Church and religion/* *Negative Catholic Church and religion/*	*Positive male/* *Neutral male/* *Negative male*
High Court first day of appeal 42. 11/03/20 *ABC Journalists* https://www.abc.net.au/news/2020-03-11/pell-appeal-makes-it-to-the-high-court-of-australia/12041226	*Main Headline:* George Pell's appeal makes it to the High Court of Australia—and the world is awaiting its decision	*Positive Catholic Church/religion:* *Neutral Catholic Church/religion:* *Negative Catholic Church/religion:* sexual offences against two choirboys	*Positive male:* *Neutral male:* *Negative male:* standard historical sexual abuse case based on the word of a victim against that of a person of authority, years after the events/Pell's lawyer Robert Richter said he was so "angry and upset" by the result he could not go on/

Positive-supportive Accused/ Neutral accused/ Negative accused/	*Positive-supportive complainant/ Neutral complainant/ Negative complainant/*
Positive-Supportive Accused: Justice Virginia Bell questioned why the full bench had not been invited to watch the same evidence/Why are we being taken to selected portions of the transcript?/"why aren't we getting the whole transcript?"/Pell's lawyers make 'reasonable doubt' argument/hoping to convince the High Court the jury made a mistake and his conviction should be quashed/argued prosecution did not reach the bar of proving "reasonable doubt"/Pell could never have committed the abuse in the midst of a "hive of activity"/not deserted premises, not areas where nothing is going on/"sheer unlikelihood" events aligned to ensure five minute hiatus of activity for Pell to have been alone with the choirboys/judges who believed victim's evidence as truthful not properly consider testimony by other witnesses that suggested it "unlikely" if not "improbable" Pell was alone with him and his friend/ High Court looking at the evidence as a whole, and looking at specific legal points in terms of the appeal/Witnesses involved in church activities at time gave evidence that raised series of questions about whether crime was possible, and whether Pell had opportunity to commit the offences/evidence ranged from centuries-old tradition of never leaving an Archbishop alone while robed; whether Pell could have committed the offences while robed; and whether the scene of the crime, the Priest's Sacristy, would have been vacant for the five or six minutes the offending was said to have taken place/practices and routines at Cathedral effectively provided Pell with an alibi, and showed lack of opportunity/Pell's lawyers argue that Court of Appeal did not apply M Test correctly treating each issue in isolation/the majority did not independently weigh the combined effect of the evidence/dissenting opinion of Justice Mark Weinberg, found compounding improbabilities established by evidence/Onus of proof reversed, Pell's lawyers argue/appeal ruling reversed onus of proof and required Pell to establish actual innocence/accused the appeal judges of basing their decision on belief in 'A' alone/remains very hopeful and confident the High Court will agree with the Court of Appeal majority and the convictions against George Pell will be upheld/ *Neutral accused:* George Pell/High Court decides future of former advisor to Pope and most senior Catholic convicted of child sex offences/serving maximum six years in jail after jury found him guilty of sexual offences against two choirboys in the late 1990s when he was Archbishop of Melbourne/Pell's case is extraordinary because of who is involved and what is at stake/jury convicted Pell of five charges in 2018/Victorian Court of Appeal, found 'A' was a witness of truth and it was open to the jury to find Pell guilty beyond reasonable doubt/ *Negative accused:* Pell's case "weak" and glosses over evidence that supports the victim known as 'A'/A great deal was also made of how Pell would spend time on the church steps after mass, talking to worshipers/ two of the judges on appeal, disagreed, saying they were not convinced/No witness could say with certainty that these routines and practices were never departed from/	*Positive-Supportive Complainant:* two choirboys/the choirboys/victim's/two choirboys/reasonable doubt can co-exist with belief in the victim's testimony/victim known as 'A'/ Pell's accuser/"The majority did not reason on the basis of 'belief' in A/"Rather they 'reviewed the whole of the evidence' and made assessment of A's credibility and reliability"/account by 'A' was supported by evidence, including his account of the offence happening in the priest's sacristy/sacristy being renovated at the time—a detail not many other witnesses could recall/feeling apprehensive about the day's challenge/understandably quite anxious and unsettled by this/ *Neutral complainant:* Belief in complainant does not eliminate possibility of co-existent reasonable doubt as to guilt/five to six minute window in which the abuse said to have occurred/father of one of victims, who has since died/second boy had died before the matter was reported to police 2015/Victorian Court of Appeal did not stick to the transcripts/watched videos of the victim and several other witnesses giving their evidence, in the same way jury would have/also visited cathedral/ *Negative complainant:* "people we believe may be wrong—either lying … or simply wrong"/when asked in 2001 by his mother, he had denied ever suffering abuse.

(*continued*)

Table 3.3 (continued)

News content		*Prominent themes/choice of words*	
Event *Report date* *Journalist/s* *URL*	*Main headline* *Hyperlink headline*[a]	*Positive Catholic Church and religion/* *Neutral Catholic Church and religion/* *Negative Catholic Church and religion/*	*Positive male/* *Neutral male/* *Negative male*
43. 12/03/20 *ABC Journalist* https://www.abc.net.au/news/2020-03-10/george-pells-high-court-appeal-final-bid-for-freedom/12039628	*Main Headline:* George Pell's Appeal went before the High Court on Tuesday. Here's what might happen	*Positive Catholic Church/religion:* *Neutral Catholic Church/religion:* *Negative Catholic Church/religion:*	*Positive male:* Bret Walker SC, probably Australia's top lawyer/ *Neutral male:* *Negative male:*

Positive-supportive Accused/ *Neutral accused/* *Negative accused/*	*Positive-supportive complainant/* *Neutral complainant/* *Negative complainant/*
Positive-Supportive Accused: many of his supporters hopeful convictions would be overturned on appeal/evidence at the trial means that even if you accept the complainant's testimony as seemingly credible, not enough to convict Pell because other evidence creates too much doubt/still technically possible for Pell to have convictions overturned/only exception is if fresh and compelling evidence of his innocence emerges down the track/Melbourne man Faruk Orman had murder conviction quashed despite earlier having his application for leave to appeal rejected by the High Court/Orman was freed by Victorian Court of Appeal after it emerged his lawyer Nicola Gobbo (aka Lawyer X) was a police informer and had helped coach the main witness/Lindy Chamberlain-Creighton was also eventually freed despite losing at the High Court/ *Neutral accused:* George Pell/final bid for freedom/one of the most high-profile and contentious High Court cases in recent memory—up there with Lindy Chamberlain/jury found Pell guilty of sexually abusing two choirboys/Pell to continue serving a six-year jail term/Pell's lawyers argue the Victorian Court of Appeal should have ruled that the guilty verdict handed down by the jury was unsafe/Court of Appeal majority left without doubt that Pell was guilty./If leave is not granted, appeal fails, and Pell must serve his time/five possible outcomes from Pell's High Court application/more likely the court would reserve a decision/typically takes a few months to make a decision and write a judgement/Pell at Barwon Prison while case heard/ *Negative accused:* If you have time for the long version, Pell's legal team sets out its case/Has the High Court agreed to hear the appeal?/Funnily enough the answer is no, or at least, not yet/possible the court could decide to throw out Pell's appeal after his lawyers put their case forward/"could wait until Pell's counsel finished and say, we have heard enough, he can't win, and they could dismiss his appeal then and there or deny special leave."/Is this Pell's last chance to beat his convictions?/Pretty much/c/f Faruk Orman and Lindy Chamberlain.	*Positive-Supportive Complainant:* two choirboys/former choirboys/ *Neutral complainant:* the other died of a drug overdose in 2014/ *Negative complainant:*

(*continued*)

Table 3.3 (continued)

News content		*Prominent themes/choice of words*	
Event *Report date* *Journalist/s* *URL*	*Main headline* *Hyperlink headline*[a]	*Positive Catholic Church and religion/* *Neutral Catholic Church and religion/* *Negative Catholic Church and religion/*	*Positive male/* *Neutral male/* *Negative male*
High Court Decision 44. 8/4/20 *ABC Journalist* https://www.abc.net.au/news/2020-04-08/vatican-welcomes-overturning-of-george-pell-conviction/12131042	*Main Headline:* Vatican 'welcomes' overturning of George Pell's conviction, Pope tweets cryptic message. For the Vatican it's a victory.	*Positive Catholic Church/religion:* An Australian judicial system it says it has always had faith in/unanimous decision to free one of its most senior clerics/Holy See reaffirmed "its commitment to preventing and pursuing all cases of abuse against minors/Pope Francis has really made it a priority of his papacy/Catholic Archbishop of Melbourne said reaction of relief for the Cardinal/Pope recalled persecutions suffered by Jesus and prayed for those who had suffered unjust sentences/like to pray today for all those people who suffer unjust sentences resulting from intransigence/tweeted about Jesus "judged ferociously, even though innocent"/ *Neutral Catholic Church/religion:* For the Vatican it's a victory/no reference to the Church's own inquiry into Cardinal Pell that had been on hold/Vatican announced doctrinal congregation would be pursuing a case/later said that case was on hold/there may not be much evidence to go on/many in Vatican did have concerns and doubts over the case against Cardinal Pell/many people in the Vatican will be quite relieved by this news/"case bring some relief to the Catholic Church/now that conviction is overturned/that's an enormous deal for the Vatican."/a very difficult case *Negative Catholic Church/religion:* Pope tweets cryptic message/wait now on for some sort clarifying statement from the Congregation for the Doctrine of the Faith/We don't know where the case was before it was put on hold/probably not very far along/international interest in case will mean Vatican will follow through with investigation in some way/high-profile nature of case going to be pressure on Vatican to conduct robust investigation/Pope tweets cryptic message/Not a moment for triumphalism'/scrutiny over its handling of sexual abuse will remain/The church globally has been under a lot of pressure in terms of clergy sexual abuse/one of his major advisors—one of the most important Cardinals in the Catholic Church—convicted of historic sexual offences/not a moment for triumphalism by anyone in the church/	*Positive male:* past year and a half he's been incredibly strong/I had my own understanding of the man and my knowledge of him so when he said he was innocent, I accepted that *Neutral male:* *Negative male:*

Positive-supportive Accused/ *Neutral accused/* *Negative accused/*	*Positive-supportive complainant/* *Neutral complainant/* *Negative complainant/*
Positive-Supportive Accused: praised George Pell having "waited for truth to be ascertained"/ Entrusting his case to the court's justice/Cardinal Pell has always maintained his innocence, and has waited for the truth to be ascertained/Pope loyal to Cardinal Pell—despite theological differences/Pope Francis has always stood by Cardinal Pell/Pell's supporters welcome ruling/Archbishop Comensoli said always believed in Cardinal Pell's innocence/Archbishop of Sydney Anthony Fisher said the result should invite a reflection on Australia's justice system and the community's commitment to the presumption of innocence/pleased that the Cardinal will now be released and I ask that the pursuit of him that brought us to this point now cease/Former prime minister Tony Abbott, who supported Cardinal Pell throughout the legal process including visiting him in prison/ *Neutral accused:* clears path for public release of until-now unpublished findings from the Royal Commission into Institutional Responses to Child Sexual Abuse/Cardinal voluntarily gave evidence from Rome/ *Negative accused:* have to be a preliminary investigation but it will look at the wider scope of the allegations made against the Cardinal over the years/ unlikely that he will return to the Vatican in any formal capacity/ previous role as chief financier filled late last year/60 pages detailing the commission's findings regarding Cardinal Pell and his evidence were heavily redacted/What he may have known about paedophile priest Gerald Ridsdale and other priests' offending was scrutinised by the commission/Cardinal Pell questioned about knowledge of crimes committed by Monsignor John Day, former Christian Brother Ted Dowlan, and priest Peter Searson—died in 2009 without facing charges/Cardinal Pell also questioned about Catholic Church's hard-line approach to sexual abuse cases, during his time as Archbishop of Sydney/	*Positive-Supportive Complainant:* abuse victim/ruling has brought feelings of confusion among those who suffered clerical abuse/ important case and conviction for survivors/people are really—survivors are really stunned by this/ abuse victim/They're really traumatised by this/ really confused/a lot of confusion about how this decision was made/Catholic Archbishop of Melbourne said … immediate concern for J [the complainant who gave evidence], because he has gone through this journey offering his story and wanting to be able to be heard/particularly mindful of those who are struggling with the experience of being abused and wanting to find pathways to healing and justice/My mind has been particularly with J and how this will be affecting him in this time/Prime Minister Scott Morrison extended his sympathies to abuse survivors who found coverage of case upsetting/Abuse survivors struggling with decision/Victorian Premier Daniel Andrews said … a message for every single victim and survivor of child sex abuse: I see you. I hear you. I believe you/ Former prime minister Julia Gillard, encouraged those struggling with today's news to seek support/ helpline inundated by survivors experiencing, rage, fury, disgust, distress/completely overwhelmed with incredibly strong emotions and not knowing what to do/particularly important that abuse survivors remained as connected as possible/very important people can speak to someone so they'll be seen, heard, listened to and believed, because validation is absolutely bottom line/People want answers *Neutral complainant:* Blue Knot Foundation, runs helpline for adult survivors of childhood trauma, reported influx in calls since the High Court's decision/service put on extra staff to handle increase/ *Negative complainant:*

(*continued*)

Table 3.3 (continued)

News content		*Prominent themes/choice of words*	
Event *Report date* *Journalist/s* *URL*	*Main headline* *Hyperlink headline*[a]	*Positive Catholic Church and religion/* *Neutral Catholic Church and religion/* *Negative Catholic Church and religion/*	*Positive male/* *Neutral male/* *Negative male*
45. 7/4/20 *ABC Journalists and Reuters* https://www.abc.net.au/news/2020-04-07/george-pell-wins-high-court-appeal-child-sex-abuse-convictions/12048726	*Main Headline:* George Pell freed from prison after High Court quashes child sex abuse convictions	*Positive Catholic Church/religion:* Pope Francis invited the congregation to pray for "all those people who suffer unjust sentences resulting from intransigence [against them]"/recent weeks Pope's intentions largely focused on coronavirus pandemic. *Neutral Catholic Church/religion:* Each morning at the Mass Pope chooses an intention for the service, such as remembering the poor, homeless or sick/ *Negative Catholic Church/religion:* raped as a nine year-old by Gerald Ridsdale/Ridsdale parish priest at St Colman's Parish in Mortlake in 1982/awarded a settlement of more than $1 million in a landmark legal case last year, after he sued Ballarat's Catholic diocese for breaching its duty of care/diocese well aware of Ridsdale's record of offending against children, years before he was posted to Mortlake/.	Positive male: Neutral male: Negative male:

Positive-supportive Accused/ *Neutral accused/* *Negative accused/*	*Positive-supportive complainant/* *Neutral complainant/* *Negative complainant/*
Positive-Supportive Accused: nun greeted him at the door and helped him inside/consistently maintained his innocence/his lawyers went to the High Court, arguing the appeal court failed to take proper account of evidence that cast doubt on his guilt/the Catholic Church's leader drew a comparison between those suffering unjust persecution and Jesus on social media/Cardinal Pell says 'only basis for justice is truth'/ High Court stated Victorian Court of Appeal judges "failed to engage with the question of whether there remained a reasonable possibility that the offending had not taken place"/jury, acting rationally on the whole of the evidence, ought to have entertained a doubt as to the applicant's guilt/possibility an innocent person convicted "because the evidence did not establish guilt to the requisite standard of proof"/ *Neutral accused:* Cardinal George Pell/highest court quashed his child sexual abuse convictions/unanimous decision handed down less than a month after the High Court of Australia heard two days of intense legal arguments/serving a six-year jail sentence after he was convicted in 2018 of abusing two choirboys in the 1990s, while he was the archbishop of Melbourne/accused of committing the crimes/jury convicted him … a decision that the Victorian Court of Appeal upheld in a two-to-one decision/Cardinal Pell's application for special leave and unanimously acquitting him/George Pell, then the archbishop of Melbourne, would greet parishioners on the cathedral steps, for up to 15 minutes after mass/Cardinal Pell was accused of abusing died in 2014 *Negative accused:* no longer has faith in our country's criminal justice system/ struggling to comprehend decision by High Court of Australia/let down by legal process forced him to relive his pain and trauma for no benefit/much of detail around the decision-making of its leadership has been blacked out so as not to prejudice Cardinal Pell's legal proceedings.	*Positive-Supportive Complainant:* Cardinal Pell said he held "no ill will" towards his accuser/ Family of former choirboy 'heartbroken'/former choirboys/father of the late former choirboy was "in shock"/heartbroken for the surviving victim/ stuck his neck out by coming forward to tell his story/Victoria Police would continue to provide support to the complainants/Victoria Police committed to investigating sexual assault offences/ providing justice for victims no matter how many years have passed/"thorough work on this case by Taskforce Sano investigators over many years."/ People want answers/they want reasons and they want to know why/like putting massive jigsaw puzzle together/a lot of us still working on it/you think it's finished, it doesn't go away/increasingly urgent for survivors of child sexual abuse/People dying and taking their own lives/every day that that report remains redacted is a day that someone will potentially continue to suffer unnecessarily/ *Neutral complainant:* *Negative complainant:* other witnesses' evidence was "inconsistent with the complainant's account"/

(*continued*)

Table 3.3 (continued)

News content		*Prominent themes/choice of words*	
Event *Report date* *Journalist/s* *URL*	*Main headline* *Hyperlink headline*[a]	*Positive Catholic Church and religion/* *Neutral Catholic Church and religion/* *Negative Catholic Church and religion/*	*Positive male/* *Neutral male/* *Negative male*
46. 7/4/20 *ABC Journalists* https://www.abc.net.au/news/2020-04-07/george-pell-wins-high-court-appeal-what-happens-next/12126266	*Main Headline:* George Pell's child sex abuse convictions have been quashed by the High Court. So what happens now?	*Positive Catholic Church/religion:* *Neutral Catholic Church/religion:* former Catholic priest and historian/if Vatican wanted to conduct investigation into allegations of sexual abuse, canon law stated it would need to be proved "beyond reasonable doubt"/Catholic Church stating it would "remain on church grounds" until the end of the legal case/ *Negative Catholic Church/religion:* a saga/at the hands of other priests/vowed to pursue the Catholic Church and Cardinal Pell for damages/man abused by Dowlan at Cathedral College in East Melbourne/not all institutions were as quick to act following Cardinal Pell's convictions in 2018/Australian Catholic University said the name of the Pell Centre at its Ballarat Campus would not be changed until all legal avenues were exhausted/gold-coloured plaque still exists at St Mary's College in Sydney/	Positive male: Neutral male: Negative male:

Positive-supportive Accused/ *Neutral accused/* *Negative accused/*	*Positive-supportive complainant/* *Neutral complainant/* *Negative complainant/*
Positive-Supportive Accused: five-year legal battle to an end/always maintained his innocence/ Vatican vowed to wait until all legal avenues exhausted before any internal investigation/could now be lifted with the High Court's findings/it's likely they will now close the investigation/Cardinal has always vehemently denied all allegations/Cardinal Pell denies allegations/Cardinal Pell now a free man—unlikely he will be stripped of the distinction/ *Neutral accused:* Cardinal George Pell/High Court overturned his convictions for child sexual abuse/which saw the former advisor to the Pope become the highest-ranking Catholic official to be convicted of child sexual abuse/ he's beyond the retirement age of people working within the Vatican … don't think he'll be going back there/when he turns 80, Cardinal Pell no longer allowed a vote in the election of any new pope/ Vatican's Congregation for the Doctrine of the Faith placed its own investigation on hold until legal process over/clearing way for public release of until-now unpublished findings from the Royal Commission into Institutional Responses to Child Sexual Abuse/College will review the findings and determine what, if any, steps to take with respect to naming honours previously bestowed upon Cardinal Pell/ Pell also has an Order of Australia in recognition of his contribution to the Catholic Church/Governor-General—who the decision rests with—said he would wait until Cardinal Pell's legal case was over/ *Negative accused:* Holy See ban on Cardinal Pell exercising the ministry or having contact with minors/Pope Francis removed him from his inner council of advisers in December 2018/unclear whether he will return to the inner sanctum of the hierarchy of the Catholic Church/Pope had already appointed someone else to fill Cardinal Pell's former role/ don't know where he will go/may want to return to Rome although wouldn't be a good prospect with the state of Italy/Holy See did open investigation into allegations levelled against George Pell, and technically could still hold a canonical trial in Rome/findings regarding George Pell and his evidence were heavily redacted/What Pell may have known about paedophile priest Gerald Ridsdale and offending of other priests scrutinised/Cardinal voluntarily giving evidence from Rome/Cardinal Pell questioned about knowledge of crimes committed by Monsignor John Day, former Christian Brother Ted Dowlan and priest Peter Searson—died in 2009 without facing charges/Pell also scrutinised about the Catholic Church's hard-line approach to sexual abuse cases, during his time as archbishop of Sydney/number of civil cases set to be launched against Cardinal Pell, either by people who allege abused by him or allege he did nothing to prevent their abuse/Cardinal Pell's alleged crimes/Cardinal Pell also being sued in Victorian Supreme Court by man abused by paedophile Christian Brother Edward "Ted" Dowlan/Cardinal Pell knew Dowlan was abusing children and was involved in moving him from school to school, allowing the abuse to continue/immediate action taken by some organisations to distance themselves from him/St Patrick's College in Ballarat immediately renamed wing of classrooms named in his honour, struck his name from honour board and revoked status as an inducted "legend of the school"/Prime Minister Scott Morrison said likely Pell would be stripped of his Order of Australia/	*Positive-Supportive Complainant:* Civil cases … claims focusing on compensation/ threshold for a civil case is "on the balance of probabilities"/father of one of the boys who Cardinal Pell was originally convicted of abusing/ former choirboy/father claims his son had post-traumatic stress disorder/ *Neutral complainant:* died from a drug overdose in 2014/ *Negative complainant:*

(*continued*)

Table 3.3 (continued)

News content		*Prominent themes/choice of words*	
Event *Report date* *Journalist/s* *URL*	*Main headline* *Hyperlink headline*[a]	*Positive Catholic Church and religion/* *Neutral Catholic Church and religion/* *Negative Catholic Church and religion/*	*Positive male/* *Neutral male/* *Negative male*
47. 07/04/20 *Anonymous* https://www.abc.net.au/news/2020-04-07/george-pell-high-court-of-australia-full-judgment-summary/12128468	*Main Headline:* Read the full judgement summary from George Pell's successful High Court of Australia appeal	High Court summary	High Court summary
48. 7/4/20 *Analysis* *ABC Religion Expert* https://www.abc.net.au/news/2020-04-07/george-pell-appeal-vatican-christian-response/12130182	*Main Headline:* George Pell's successful appeal was a clear result in a case that cut the nation to the core	*Positive Catholic Church/religion:* *Neutral Catholic Church/religion:* The Vatican said it would wait until the legal processes had concluded before it would consider its next move/ *Negative Catholic Church/religion:* lives had been destroyed by clerical sexual abuse and cover-up/	Positive male: Neutral male: Negative male:

Positive-supportive Accused/ Neutral accused/ Negative accused/	*Positive-supportive complainant/ Neutral complainant/ Negative complainant/*
High Court summary	High Court summary
Positive-Supportive Accused: What of the prisoner?/High Court quashed the verdict/very clear result/public lightning rod/"transference". It is a process where a person redirects some of their feelings or desires for another person to an entirely different person/elements of transference in the public discussion around Cardinal Pell and this case/a lightning rod for the deep hurt and anger surrounding clerical sexual abuse/ shock and anguish among those who believed in his innocence/ Tears shed/people were accused of being unable to admit the facts/They went quiet for the most part—telling me they were afraid of the public mood/may also be invited to take on other roles within the Church of Rome, or elsewhere/Repairing reputational damage he suffered will be hard, but he has never been one to shy away from challenge/significant parts of the media appeared to be prosecuting a case against the Cardinal/Other parts of media stridently defended his innocence, but minority voices/ debate over innocent or guilty was dismissed as an extension of the culture wars. Turns out it wasn't/Palm Sunday story cautions Christians about how behaviour in groups of people can change—suddenly and threateningly/taken as a warning about how we ourselves can behave/a warning about impartiality/And justice/ *Neutral accused:* Highest court in the land has quashed his conviction/Pell matter/ someone would be anxious and hurt/Pell case a focus for the suffering of so many people who identify their own personal experiences and feelings with the Cardinal and his public role/ Whatever you may think of him/the cardinal/Australia's most powerful Catholic cleric/responsibility for dealing with sexual abuse/Court says he is acquitted of these charges/George Pell remained a Cardinal elector/has the right to elect the next pope/ Should a papal election be needed before his birthday, he will have right to vote/ *Negative accused:* social media have exploded with outrage at the verdict/anger about the Vatican not "defrocking" the Cardinal/People were angry he had not been laicised/	*Positive-Supportive Complainant:* I hold no ill will toward my accuser, I do not want my acquittal to add to the hurt and bitterness so many feel; there is certainly hurt and bitterness enough/Words touching upon a world of pain reaching across generations of Australians/lives forever changed/Aware of lives damaged/What of the alleged victim who told his story?/a genuine need to listen to victims and to hear their stories/ *Neutral complainant:* one of the hardest things has been any attempt to remain impartial, and to listen simply to evidence/ *Negative complainant:*

(*continued*)

Table 3.3 (continued)

News content		*Prominent themes/choice of words*	
Event *Report date* *Journalist/s* *URL*	*Main headline* *Hyperlink headline*[a]	*Positive Catholic Church and religion/* *Neutral Catholic Church and religion/* *Negative Catholic Church and religion/*	*Positive male/* *Neutral male/* *Negative male*
49. 7/4/20 *From outside media: The Conversation* *Opinion* *Academic* https://www.abc.net.au/news/2020-04-07/george-pell-appeal-jury-system/12129940	*Main Headline:* Why was George Pell's appeal successful when our justice system values jury verdicts?	*Positive Catholic Church/religion:* *Neutral Catholic Church/religion:* *Negative Catholic Church/religion:*	*Positive male:* *Neutral male:* *Negative male:*
50. 07/04/20 *Anonymous* https://www.abc.net.au/news/2020-04-07/george-pell-released-from-barwon-prison/12128922	*Main Headline:* George Pell released from Barwon Prison	Descriptive only	Descriptive only
51. 07/04/20 *Anonymous* https://www.abc.net.au/news/2020-04-07/george-pell-arrives-at-melbourne-monastery/12129232	Main Headline: George Pell arrives at a church property in Melbourne	Descriptive only	Descriptive only

[a]Hyperlink headline only included in analysis if located on the web-page of main story analysed

[b]A suppression order prevented journalists from reporting what was known as the "Cathedral Trial" owing to an upcoming "Swimmers Trial", for which Pell was also on trial and due in April 2019. Swimmers trial dropped after judge ruled 'tendency evidence' inadmissible)

Positive-supportive Accused/ *Neutral accused/* *Negative accused/*	*Positive-supportive complainant/* *Neutral complainant/* *Negative complainant/*
Positive-Supportive Accused: defence counsel, argued before the High Court convictions were unsound because it was not open to the jury to find Pell guilty beyond reasonable doubt/"sheer unlikelihood" of events and times aligning in the way that had been put forth/But one victim of this appeal result may be a loss of public confidence in the jury system/ *Neutral accused:* Quashed conviction of Cardinal George Pell/originally found guilty on number of charges by a jury of 12 people/jury of a dozen men and women deliberated for almost five days before returning their verdicts of guilty on all five charges/jury decision is safe decision that has not been infected with the hue and cry or matters outside the evidence that was put to them/ Whatever one may think of the Pell decision/for all the store we place on juries in determining issues of guilt and innocence, their role can be dispensed with so easily/ *Negative accused:*	*Positive-Supportive Complainant:* others may lose confidence in the justice system/ *Neutral complainant:* *Negative complainant:* argued story of the complainant could not be credible/
Descriptive only	Descriptive only
Descriptive only	Descriptive only

Notes

1. *Sydney Morning Herald, The*. (1932). Broadcasting. Control by Commission. To take effect today. 1 July 1932. p. 9. Retrieved from: https://trove.nla.gov.au/newspaper/article/16915407?searchTerm=ABC%20to%20serve%20Lloyd%20JOnes
2. Bainbridge, A. (2018). ABC crisis shows need for independent and democratised public broadcaster [online]. *Green Left Weekly*. 1198. 9 Oct 2018. p. 10. Retrieved from: https://search-informit-com-au.ezproxy1.library.usyd.edu.au/documentSummary;dn=935516978501507;res=IELHSS ISSN: 1036-126X.
3. *Australian Broadcasting Corporation*. (2020). Connecting and Uniting All Australians: National Press Club address. 8 July 2020. Retrieved from: https://about.abc.net.au/speeches/connecting-and-uniting-all-australians-national-press-club-address/
4. Murray, L. (2006). Scott of the ABC: a family affair of service. *The Sydney Morning Herald*. 23 May 2006. Retrieved from: https://www.smh.com.au/national/scott-of-the-abc-a-family-affair-of-service-20060523-gdnlkg.html
5. Scott's grandfather Walter Scott was Chairman of the Decimal Currency Board which introduced decimal currency in 1966, his father Brian Scott reviewed the NSW Department of Education in the 1980s (Murray 2006).
6. Harding, R. (1979). *Outside Interference: The Politics of Australian Broadcasting*. Sun Books. Melbourne. p. 123.
7. Curran, J. (1991). *Mass Media and Democracy: A Reappraisal. Mass Media and Society*. Eds. J. Curran and M. Gurevitch. pp. 82–117. Edward Arnold. London.
8. *Nature*. (1978). The public's right to know. 26 October, 1978. 275, p. 682. https://doi-org.wwwproxy1.library.unsw.edu.au/10.1038/275682a0
9. Ibid. (1978).
10. Rayner, J., Lawton, A. & Williams, H. (2012). Organizational Citizenship Behavior and the Public Service Ethos: Whither the Organization? *Journal of Business Ethics*. 106. pp. 117–130. Retrieved from https://link-springer-com.wwwproxy1.library.unsw.edu.au/content/pdf/10.1007/s10551-011-0991-x.pdf pp. 117–118.
11. Bolino, M. C., & Turnley, W. H. (2003). Going the extra mile: Cultivating and managing employee citizenship behavior. *Academy of Management Executive*. 17:3. pp. 60–71.
12. Bolino, M. C., Turnley, W. H., & Bloodgood, J. M. (2002). Citizenship behavior and the creation of social capital in organizations. *Academy of Management Review*. 27. pp. 505–522.

13. Schultz, A. & Napier-Raman, K. (2020). What does the governor-general do—and how much does it cost the country? *The Mandarin and Crikey.* 16 July 2020. Retrieved from: https://www.themandarin.com.au/136189-what-does-the-governor-general-do-and-how-much-does-it-cost-the-country/?utm_source=TheJuice&utm_medium=email&utm_source=newsletterandcrikey.com.au
14. Beachy, R.N. (2003). IP Policies and Serving the Public. Editorial. Science. 24 January 2003. 299:5606. pp. 473. Retrieved from https://libkey.io/libraries/757/articles/13426582/full-text-file?utm_source=api_231
15. Marquand, D. (2004). *Decline of the Public: the hollowing out of citizenship.* Polity Press. Oxford.
16. Dorey, P. (2015).The Legacy of Thatcherism—Public Sector Reform. *Observatoire de la société britannique* [En ligne]. 17. Retrieved from: https://doi.org/10.4000/osb.1759
17. Arora, N.D. (2010). Political Science for Civil Services Main Examination. McGraw Hill. New Delhi.
18. *Bible, The.* The Letter of St Paul to the Galatians. 5:13.
19. *Bible, The.* The Gospel of Matthew. 20:26–28.
20. Also considered a model servant leader. van Dierendonck, D. & Patterson, K. (Eds). (2010). *Servant Leadership: Developments in Theory and Research.* Palgrave Macmillan, UK.
21. Hillman, E.L. (2009). Heller, citizenship, and the right to serve in the military. *Hastings Law Journal.* June 2009. 60:6. pp. 1269–1283. p. 1273.
22. Stiehm, J.H., (2002). *U.S. Army War College: Military Education in a Democracy.* Temple University Press. Philadelphia. p. 1.
23. Horski, E. (1998). "Grounded in Love: An Investigation of the Fundamental Ignatian Teaching on Discernment within the Tradition of Askesis". *School of Theology and Seminary Graduate Papers/Theses.* 1173. https://digitalcommons.csbsju.edu/sot_papers/1173
24. Georgetown University. (2018). What is a Jesuit? Retrieved from: https://www.georgetown.edu/news/the-jesuit-mission-seeking-god-in-all-things/#:~:text=What%20is%20a%20Jesuit%3F,seek%20God%20in%20all%20things
25. Australian Province of the Society of Jesus (Jesuits). (2020). "To Know, Love and Serve." Retrieved from: https://jesuit.org.au/vocations/know-love-serve/
26. McCarthy, J.W. & Karsh, M. (2007). Jesuits and ecology—For the Greater Glory of God! *Forestry Chronicle.* March. 83:2. pp. 162–163. Retrieved from https://pubs.cif-ifc.org/doi/pdf/10.5558/tfc83159-2
27. Ibid.

28. *Jewish Messenger, The*. Quoted in *The New York Times* (1897). Good-will to men. *The New York Times*. 2 January 1897. p. 3.
29. Stove, D. (1992). A New Religion. *Philosophy*. 67:260. pp. 233–240. p. 234. Retrieved from: www.jstor.org/stable/3751453
30. Pandey, S.K., Wright, B.E. & Moynihan, D.P. (2012). Pulling the Levers: Transformational Leadership, Public Service Motivation, and Mission Valence. *Public Administration Review, American Society for Public Administration*. 72:2 (March/April). pp. 206–215. Retrieved from: https://www.jstor.org/stable/41433294
31. Rayner, M. (1997). Democracy and the good life. *Leading and Managing*. 3:4. pp. 237–244. Summer. Retrieved from: https://search-informit-com-au.wwwproxy1.library.unsw.edu.au/fullText;dn=89267;res=AEIPT ISSN: 1329-4539. p. 238.
32. *Australian Government* (2020). Commonwealth of Australia Constitution Act. (The Constitution). Retrieved from: https://www.legislation.gov.au/Details/C2013Q00005
33. *Australian Government* (1999). The Public Service Act #147. 10A APS Employment Principles. Retrieved from: https://www.legislation.gov.au/Details/C2019C00057
34. Edwards, M., Halligan, J, Horrigan, B. & Nicoll, G. (2012). *Public Sector Governance in Australia*. Australian National University EPress. Griffin Press. Canberra. Retrieved from: https://press-files.anu.edu.au/downloads/press/p190701/pdf/book.pdf p. 25.
35. Northridge, M. (2009). Serving the Public Good. *American Journal of Public Health*. 99:3. p. 393. Retrieved from: https://search-proquest-com.wwwproxy1.library.unsw.edu.au/docview/215089511?rfr_id=info%3Axri%2Fsid%3Aprimo
36. Reddan, F. (2017). Serving the public good. *Accountancy Ireland*. 49:2. (April). pp. 20–22.
37. Ghosn, N. (2015). The Decline of Public Broadcasting in France. *E-journal of Intermedia*. Spring. 2:1. pp. 143–157. Retrieved from: https://search-proquest-com.wwwproxy1.library.unsw.edu.au/docview/1810112560?rfr_id=info%3Axri%2Fsid%3Aprimo
38. Ibid., p. 144.
39. Loc. cit.
40. Ibid.
41. *Courier-Mail, The*. (1953). "Serve the democratic processes. "ABC IS CONSISTENTLY, VIOLENTLY CRITICISED"." *The Courier-Mail, Brisbane*. 29 June 1953. p. 5. Retrieved from: https://trove.nla.gov.au/newspaper/article/50541530?searchTerm=ABC%20serve
42. O'Mahen, P. (2016). A Big Bird effect? The interaction among public broadcasting, public subsidies, and political knowledge. *European*

Political Science Review. 8:2. pp. 311–332. Retrieved from https://www-cambridge-org.wwwproxy1.library.unsw.edu.au/core/services/aop-cambridge-core/content/view/8EC8052F26A223A76ED7D07A386E10D5/S175577391500003Xa.pdf/big_bird_effect_the_interaction_among_public_broadcasting_public_subsidies_and_political_knowledge.pdf

43. Ibid.
44. Torii, A. (2017). Effects of public broadcasting on the competition among private broadcasters and the total surplus. *Journal of Media Business Studies*. 14:2. pp. 116–145. Retrieved from: https://www-tandfonline-com.wwwproxy1.library.unsw.edu.au/doi/pdf/10.1080/16522354.2017.1290023?needAccess=true
45. Leroy, D. (1980). Public Broadcasting. *Journal of Communication*. June 1980. 30:3. p. 2159. Retrieved from: https://onlinelibrary-wiley-com.wwwproxy1.library.unsw.edu.au/doi/epdf/10.1111/j.1460-2466.1980.tb02002.x
46. Koziol, M. (2020). ABC news boss warns staff against focus on 'inner city left-wing elites'. The Sydney Morning Herald. 25 October 2020. Retrieved from: https://www.smh.com.au/national/abc-news-boss-warns-staff-against-focus-on-inner-city-left-wing-elites-20201023-p56849.html
47. Milne, J. (2017). Hector Crawford Oration 2017: ABC Chairman Justin Milne. *Australian Broadcasting Corporation*. 15 November 2017. Retrieved from: https://about.abc.net.au/speeches/hector-crawford-oration-2017/
48. Dawes, S. (2017). *British Broadcasting and the Public-Private Dichotomy : Neoliberalism, Citizenship and the Public Sphere*. Springer International Publishing.
49. Mill, J.S. (2009, orig. 1859). *On Liberty*. Cosimo Classics. New York. p. 18.
50. Debell, G. (2015). Malcolm Fraser: realist to radical and the great Asia project. *Australian Journal of International Affairs*. 69:6. pp. 625–636. Retrieved from: https://doi.org/10.1080/10357718.2015.1081147 p. 632.
51. Alford, J. and O'Flynn, J. (2009). Making Sense of Public Value: Concepts, Critiques and Emergent Meanings. *International Journal of Public Administration*. 32. pp. 171–191. citing p. 173.
52. *OECD* (2011), Regulatory Policy and Governance: Supporting Economic Growth and Serving the Public Interest, OECD Publishing. Retrieved from: https://doi.org/10.1787/9789264116573-en
53. Higton, M. (2012). *A theology of Higher Education*. Oxford Scholarship Online. Chap. 8. Retrieved from: https://www-oxfordscholarship-com.wwwproxy1.library.unsw.edu.au/view/10.1093/acprof:oso/9780199643929.001.0001/acprof-9780199643929-chapter-9?rskey=MxVQlf&result=5

54. Gottschalk, S. (2018). The infantilization of Western culture. *The Conversation*. Retrieved from: https://theconversation.com/the-infantilization-of-western-culture-99556
55. Australian Government (2020) https://www.health.gov.au/sites/default/files/documents/2020/03/coronavirus-covid-19-print-ads-simple-steps-to-stop-the-spread-coronavirus-covid-19-print-ads-simple-steps-to-stop-the-spread.pdf
56. Chamber, G. & Brown G. (2018). Former premiers take aim at bloated public sector. *The Australian*. 29 January 2018. Retrieved from: https://www.theaustralian.com.au/nation/politics/former-premiers-take-aim-at-bloated-public-sector/news-story/4798c1ce6d315bcb77296b9f1303ef73
57. Ibid.
58. *National Commission of Audit*. (2014). Executive Summary. Second Phase Report. Retrieved from: https://www.ncoa.gov.au/report/phase-two/executive-summary
59. Easton, S. (2019). Mike Mrdak: public servants must ditch the business jargon, stop being scared of citizens. *The Mandarin*. 8 May 2019. Retrieved from: https://www.themandarin.com.au/108114-mike-mrdak-public-servants-must-ditch-the-business-jargon-stop-being-scared-of-citizens/
60. Rayner, M. (2009). Democracy and the good life. *Leading and Managing*. 3:4. pp. 237–244. Summer. Retrieved from: https://search-informit-com-au.wwwproxy1.library.unsw.edu.au/fullText;dn=89267;res=AEIPT ISSN: 1329-4539.
61. Duke, J. (2020). ABC under 'growing' cost pressure as bushfire emergency broadcasts surge. *The Sydney Morning Herald*. 3 January 2020. Retrieved from: https://www.smh.com.au/business/companies/abc-under-growing-cost-pressure-as-bushfire-emergency-broadcasts-surge-20200103-p53ohp.html
62. Hunter, F. (2019). ABC boss' pay passes $1 million for first time. *The Sydney Morning Herald*. 21 October 2019. Retrieved from: https://www.smh.com.au/politics/federal/abc-boss-pay-passes-1-million-for-first-time-20191021-p532o3.html
63. Robertson, J. & Meade, A. (2017). Fairfax boss Greg Hywood was paid as much as $7.2 m in 2016. *The Guardian*. 9 May 2017. Retrieved from: https://www.theguardian.com/media/2017/may/09/fairfax-boss-greg-hywood-paid-more-2016
64. Blain, E. (1977). *Life with Aunty: 40 years with the ABC*. Methuen. Australia. p. 158.
65. Cranston, M. (2019). 'It disturbs me': RBA boss hits out at CEO salaries. *The Australian Financial Review*. 25 September 2019. Retrieved from:

https://www.afr.com/policy/economy/it-disturbs-me-rba-boss-hits-out-at-ceo-salaries-20190924-p52ul7

66. Robertson, A. (2019). How did CEO pay get to 500 times the wages of ordinary workers? Analysis. *Australian Broadcasting Corporation*. 28 September 2019. Retrieved from: https://www.abc.net.au/news/2019-09-28/how-did-ceo-pay-get-to-500-times-the-wages-of-ordinary-workers/11556394
67. McIlroy, T. & Cranston, M. (2019). Australia's best paid bureaucrat rakes in $2.5 m. *The Australian Financial Review*. 18 October 2019. Retrieved from: https://www.afr.com/politics/federal/australia-s-best-paid-bureaucrat-rakes-in-2-5m-20191017-p531hy
68. Visentin, L. (2020). 'Deep regret': Christine Holgate to forgo payout as Australia Post chief. The Sydney Morning Herald. 2 November 2020. Retrieved from: https://www.smh.com.au/politics/federal/christine-holgate-to-resign-as-australia-post-chief-20201102-p56ask.html
69. Ouellette, L. (2008). Makeover television, governmentality and the good citizen. *Continuum*. 22:4. pp. 471–484. Retrieved from: https://doi.org/info:doi/
70. Bennett, W. (1998). 1998 Ithiel De Sola Pool Lecture: The UnCivic Culture: Communication, Identity, and the Rise of Lifestyle Politics. *PS: Political Science and Politics*. 31:4. pp. 741–761. Retrieved from: https://doi.org/10.2307/420711 p. 758.
71. Bennett, W. (1998). 1998 Ithiel De Sola Pool Lecture: The UnCivic Culture: Communication, Identity, and the Rise of Lifestyle Politics. *PS: Political Science and Politics*. 31:4. pp. 741–761. https://doi.org/10.2307/420711 p. 758.
72. *Advertiser, The*. (1946). ABC Service. *The Advertiser, Adelaide*. 19 June 1946. p. 8. Retrieved from: https://trove.nla.gov.au/newspaper/article/35700411?searchTerm=ABC%20service
73. Manne (2007). New Teeth for Aunty: Reinvigorating the national broadcaster. *The Monthly*. Essays. December 2007–January 2008. p. 34.
74. *Australian Government*. (2017). Australian Broadcasting Corporation Entity: Resources and Planned Performance. Department of Infrastructure, Transport, Regional Development and Communications. Retrieved from https://www.communications.gov.au/file/17236/download?token=atNjL8Za
75. Dalton, K. (2017). *Missing in Action: The ABC and Australia's Screen Culture*. May. Platform Papers: Currency House.
76. Finkelstein, R. (2012). Report of The Independent Inquiry into The Media and Media Regulation. *Australian Government*. 28 February 2012. Retrieved from: http://www.abc.net.au/mediawatch/transcripts/1205_finkelstein.pdf

77. Leveson, B.H., Sir. (2012). An Inquiry into the Culture, Practices and Ethics of the Press Executive Summary and Recommendations (aka the Leveson Inquiry). The Right Honourable Lord Justice Leveson. Retrieved from: https://assets.documentcloud.org/documents/526073/leveson-summary.txt
78. *OECD* (2011), Regulatory Policy and Governance: Supporting Economic Growth and Serving the Public Interest. OECD Publishing. Retrieved from: https://doi.org/10.1787/9789264116573-en
79. Boswell, J. (1851). *Life of Johnson, Volume 31776–1780.* T. Nelson & Sons. London.
80. Tracey, M. (2002, 1998). *The Decline and Fall of Public Service Broadcasting.* Oxford University Press. Oxford.
81. Tracey, M. (2002, 1998). *The Decline and Fall of Public Service Broadcasting.* Oxford University Press. Oxford. p. 19.
82. *Labor Daily, The.* (1938). Clean Sweep for ABC. *The Labor Daily.* 15 June 1938, p. 5. Retrieved from: https://trove.nla.gov.au/newspaper/article/236409865?searchTerm=ABC%20commissioner%20kitto&searchLimits=
83. Tibbitts, C. (ND). Casualties of war. *The Australian War Memorial.* Retrieved from: https://www.awm.gov.au/wartime/article2
84. Curson, P. & McCracken, K. (2014). An Australian Perspective of the 1918–1919. Influenza Pandemic. *NSW Public Health Bulletin.* 17:7–8. pp. 103–107. Retrieved from: https://www.phrp.com.au/wp-content/uploads/2014/10/NB06025.pdf
85. Tracey, M. (2002, 1998). *The Decline and Fall of Public Service Broadcasting.* Oxford University Press. Oxford.
86. *Central Queensland Herald* (Rockhampton). (1934). Sydney Letter: Obligations of Broadcasting. Pronouncement by New ABC Chairman. 9 August 1934. p. 8. Retrieved from: https://trove.nla.gov.au/newspaper/article/70566782?searchTerm=ABC%20board%20members&searchLimits=exactPhrase|||anyWords|||notWords|||requestHandler|||dateFrom=1932-01-01|||dateTo=1935-12-31|||sortby
87. Sun, The. (1935). Kitto's Praise for Public Service. *The Sun.* 17 June 1935, p. 9. Retrieved from: https://trove.nla.gov.au/newspaper/article/230251698?searchTerm=ABC%20commissioner%20kitto&searchLimits=
88. Inglis, K. S. (1983). *This is the ABC: The Australian Broadcasting Commission. 1932–1983.* Melbourne University Press. Melbourne. p. 41.
89. Inglis, K. S. (1983). *This is the ABC: The Australian Broadcasting Commission. 1932–1983.* Melbourne University Press. Melbourne. p. 41.
90. Newcastle Morning Herald and Miners' Advocate. (1935). ABC Appointment: Professor Wallace Retires. *Newcastle Morning Herald and*

Miners' Advocate. 6 June 1935. p. 7. Retrieved from: https://trove.nla.gov.au/newspaper/article/139259689?searchTerm=ABC%20commissioner%20kitto&searchLimits=

91. Sun, The. (1939). New ABC Critics Answered. *The Sun*. 30 December. p. 3. Retrieved from: https://trove.nla.gov.au/newspaper/article/231500394?searchTerm=ABC%20commissioner%20kitto&searchLimits=
92. Queensland Times. (1937). ABC Changes? Younger Commissioners Likely. *Queensland Times*. 9 February. p. 6. Retrieved from https://trove.nla.gov.au/newspaper/article/117630789?searchTerm=ABC%20commissioner%20kitto&searchLimits=
93. Sydney Morning Herald, The. (1939). Anomalies in Structure. Commissioners' Powers. *The Sydney Morning Herald*. 25 March. p. 10. Retrieved from: https://trove.nla.gov.au/newspaper/article/17570409?searchTerm=ABC%20commissioner%20kitto&searchLimits=
94. Sydney Morning Herald, The. (1939). Anomalies in Structure. Commissioners' Powers. *The Sydney Morning Herald*. 25 March. p. 10. Retrieved from: https://trove.nla.gov.au/newspaper/article/17570409?searchTerm=ABC%20commissioner%20kitto&searchLimits=
95. Sydney Morning Herald, The. (1939). REFORMING THE A.B.C: ANOMALIES IN STRUCTURE. Commissioners' Powers. By a Special Correspondent. *The Sydney Morning Herald*. 25 March. p. 10. Retrieved from: https://trove.nla.gov.au/newspaper/article/17570409?searchTerm=ABC%20commissioners%20experience
96. Canberra Times, The. (1978). Opposition Seeks ABC Inquiry. 1 June. p. 13. Retrieved from: https://trove.nla.gov.au/newspaper/article/131856355?searchTerm=ABC%20commissioners%20experience
97. Australian Associated Press. (2018). ABC board lacks media experience: analyst. *The Newcastle Herald*. 2 October. Retrieved from: https://www.newcastleherald.com.au/story/5678912/abc-board-lacks-media-experience-analyst/send-us-your-news/
98. symbolic violence, gentle, invisible violence, unrecognized as such, chosen as much as undergone, that of trust, obligation, personal loyalty, hospitality, gifts, debts, piety, in a word, all of the virtues honoured by the ethic of honour (Bourdieu, 1990).
99. Tomlinson, M., O'Reilly, D., Wallace, M., Edwards, G., Elliott, C., Iszatt-White, M., Schedlitzki, D. (2013). Developing Leaders as Symbolic Violence: Reproducing Public Service Leadership through the (misrecognized) Development of Leaders' Capitals. 44:1. Retrieved from: *Management Learning*. p. 83. https://doi.org/10.1177/1350507612472151
100. Ibid. p. 85.

101. Bourdieu's theory of '*cultural capital*' and power is a twist on Max Weber's sociological definition of the form of state power—legitimate physical violence. Bourdieu's legitimate 'symbolic violence' is a tacit form of control manifested in a public servant's claim to exercise authority because of their position (Bourdieu 2005).
102. Starling, G. (2008). *Managing the Public Sector.* 8th Edition. Thomson Wadsworth. Boston MA. p. 1.
103. Starling, G. (2008). *Managing the Public Sector.* 8th Edition. Thomson Wadsworth. Boston MA. p. 2.
104. Starling, G. (2008). *Managing the Public Sector.* 8th Edition. Thomson Wadsworth. Boston MA. p. 7.
105. Juddery, B. (1976). Disquiet and despondency in the ABC. *The Canberra Times.* 3 December. p. 2. Retrieved from: https://trove.nla.gov.au/newspaper/article/131798978?searchTerm=ABC%20BAPH
106. Canberra Times, The. (1980). ABC's structure, waste studied. *The Canberra Times.* 17 April. p. 3. Retrieved from: https://trove.nla.gov.au/newspaper/article/110591023?searchTerm=ABC%20waste
107. Davis, G. (1990). "Federalism Versus Centralisation: Organizational Design and Public Broadcasting in America and Australia". *Journal of Public Policy.* 10:2. Cambridge University Press. April. 1990. pp. 195–219. Retrieved from: https://doi.org/10.1017/S0143814X00004815
108. Murray, A. (2006). Australia: Australian Broadcasting Corporation Board Must Be Appointed on Merit. *US Fed News Service* Including *US State News, HT Digital Streams Limited.* 24 March 2006. Retrieved from: http://search.proquest.com/docview/470140665/
109. Briggs, G. (2006). Right angles [The ABC Board and the appointment of Keith Windschuttle]. *Big Issue Australia.* 258. 17 July-1 Aug 2006. pp. 12–15. Retrieved from: https://search-informit-com-au.www-proxy1.library.unsw.edu.au/documentSummary;dn=200609050;res=IELAPA
110. Pearlman, J. (2007). SBS not dumbing down, says boss. *The Sydney Morning Herald.* 30 August. Retrieved from: https://www.smh.com.au/entertainment/sbs-not-dumbing-down-says-boss-20070830-gdqzj9.html
111. Collins, P. (2011). The Commercialisation of the ABC. *Eureka Street.* 21:15. August 2011. pp. 27–28. Retrieved from: https://search-informit-com-au.wwwproxy1.library.unsw.edu.au/documentSummary;dn=380461935545072;res=IELAPA ISSN: 1036-1758.
112. Murdock, G. (2004). Building the Digital Commons: Public Broadcasting in the Age of The Internet. University of Montreal. *The 2004 Spry Memorial Lecture Vancouver.* 18 November 2004/ Montreal, 22 November 2004. Retrieved from: http://citeseerx.ist.psu.edu/viewdoc/download?doi=10.1.1.627.2917&rep=rep1&type=pdf

113. Simons, M. (2016). Is Michelle Guthrie tuned in to the ABC? *The Monthly*. September 2016. Retrieved from: https://www.themonthly.com.au/issue/2016/september/1472652000/margaret-simons/michelle-guthrie-tuned-abc#mtr
114. Burrowes, T. (2016). Former ABC managing director Brian Johns was 'a man ahead of his time'. *Mumbrella*. 1 January 2016. Retrieved from: https://mumbrella.com.au/former-abc-boss-brian-johns-was-a-man-ahead-of-his-time-337460
115. Andrejevic, M. (2013). Public Service Media Utilities: Rethinking Search Engines and Social Networking as Public Goods. *Media International Australia, Incorporating Culture & Policy*. 146. pp. 123–132. Retrieved from: http://web.a.ebscohost.com.wwwproxy1.library.unsw.edu.au/ehost/pdfviewer/pdfviewer?vid=2&sid=68647279-624f-4ba5-9fda-d25caae82e74%40sdc-v-sessmgr02 p. 124.
116. Murdock, G. (2004). Building the Digital Commons: Public Broadcasting in the Age of The Internet. The 2004 Spry Memorial Lecture Vancouver. 18–22 November 2004. University of Montreal. Vancouver. Retrieved from: http://citeseerx.ist.psu.edu/viewdoc/download?doi=10.1.1.627.2917&rep=rep1&type=pdf
117. Murdock, G. (2004). Building the Digital Commons: Public Broadcasting in the Age of The Internet. The 2004 Spry Memorial Lecture Vancouver. 18–22 November 2004. *University of Montreal. Vancouver*. Retrieved from: http://citeseerx.ist.psu.edu/viewdoc/download?doi=10.1.1.627.2917&rep=rep1&type=pdf
118. Burns, M. & Hawkins, G. (2013). Investigating Public Service Media as Hybrid Arrangements. *Media International Australia*. 146. February 2013. Retrieved from: http://web.b.ebscohost.com.wwwproxy1.library.unsw.edu.au/ehost/pdfviewer/pdfviewer?vid=2&sid=14b54c95-45ab-4a7e-938c-82fd0668a7dc%40sessionmgr101 p. 79.
119. Andrejevic, M. (2013). Public Service Media Utilities: Rethinking Search Engines and Social Networking as Public Goods. *Media International Australia, Incorporating Culture & Policy*. 146. pp. 123–132. Retrieved from: http://web.a.ebscohost.com.wwwproxy1.library.unsw.edu.au/ehost/pdfviewer/pdfviewer?vid=2&sid=68647279-624f-4ba5-9fda-d25caae82e74%40sdc-v-sessmgr02 p. 124.
120. Murdock, G. (2004). Building the Digital Commons: Public Broadcasting in the Age of The Internet. The 2004 Spry Memorial Lecture Vancouver. 18–22 November 2004. *University of Montreal. Vancouver*. Retrieved from: http://citeseerx.ist.psu.edu/viewdoc/download?doi=10.1.1.627.2917&rep=rep1&type=pdf
121. Murdock, G. (2004). Building the Digital Commons: Public Broadcasting in the Age of The Internet. The 2004 Spry Memorial Lecture Vancouver.

18–22 November 2004. University of Montreal. Vancouver. Retrieved from: http://citeseerx.ist.psu.edu/viewdoc/download?doi=10.1.1.627.2917&rep=rep1&type=pdf

122. Murdock, G. (2004). Building the Digital Commons: Public Broadcasting in the Age of The Internet. The 2004 Spry Memorial Lecture Vancouver. 18–22 November 2004. University of Montreal. Vancouver. Retrieved from: http://citeseerx.ist.psu.edu/viewdoc/download?doi=10.1.1.627.2917&rep=rep1&type=pdf
123. Meade, A. (2018). The ABC in turmoil: 'Frankly, we are all spooked about everything in here.' *The Guardian*. 1 August 2018. Retrieved from https://www.theguardian.com/media/2018/aug/01/the-abc-in-turmoil-frankly-we-are-all-spooked-about-everything-in-here
124. Stacey, R. & Griffin, D. (2006). *Complexity and the Experience of Managing in Public Sector Organizations*. Routledge. London & New York. p. 17.
125. Cooper, M. (2014). The long history and increasing importance of public-service principles for 21st century public digital communications networks. *Journal on Telecommunications & High Technology Law*. Spring. 12:1. pp. 1–54. p. 3. Retrieved from: https://primoa.library.unsw.edu.au/primo-explore/fulldisplay?docid=TN_gale_legal388675657&context=PC&vid=UNSWS&lang=en_US&search_scope=SarchFirst&adaptor=primo_central_multiple_fe&tab=default_tab&query=any,contains,history%20public%20service&offset=0
126. Cooper, M. (2014). The long history and increasing importance of public-service principles for 21st century public digital communications networks. *Journal on Telecommunications & High Technology Law*. Spring. 12:1. pp. 1–54. p. 3. Retrieved from: https://primoa.library.unsw.edu.au/primo-explore/fulldisplay?docid=TN_gale_legal388675657&context=PC&vid=UNSWS&lang=en_US&search_scope=SearchFirst&adaptor=primo_central_multiple_fe&tab=default_tab&query=any,contains,history%20public%20service&offset=0
127. Cooper, M. (2014). The long history and increasing importance of public-service principles for 21st century public digital communications networks. *Journal on Telecommunications & High Technology Law*. Spring. 12:1. pp. 1–54. p. 4. Retrieved from: https://primoa.library.unsw.edu.au/primo-explore/fulldisplay?docid=TN_gale_legal388675657&context=PC&vid=UNSWS&lang=en_US&search_scope=SearchFirst&adaptor=primo_central_multiple_fe&tab=default_tab&query=any,contains,history%20public%20service&offset=0
128. Cooper, M. (2014). The long history and increasing importance of public-service principles for 21st century public digital communications networks. *Journal on Telecommunications & High Technology Law*. Spring.

12:1. pp. 1–54. p. 4. Retrieved from: https://primoa.library.unsw.edu.au/primo-explore/fulldisplay?docid=TN_gale_legal388675657&context=PC&vid=UNSWS&lang=en_US&search_scope=SearchFirst&adaptor=primo_central_multiple_fe&tab=default_tab&query=any,contains,history%20public%20service&offset=0 quoting Lane v. Cotton, 12 Mod. 472, 484 (1701), cited in A. Stone, Public Service Liberalism: Telecommunications And Transitions In Public Policy 29 (1991).

129. Cooper, M. (2014). The long history and increasing importance of public-service principles for 21st century public digital communications networks. *Journal on Telecommunications & High Technology Law*. Spring. 12:1. pp. 1–54. p. 6. Retrieved from: https://primoa.library.unsw.edu.au/primo-explore/fulldisplay?docid=TN_gale_legal388675657&context=PC&vid=UNSWS&lang=en_US&search_scope=SearchFirst&adaptor=primo_central_multiple_fe&tab=default_tab&query=any,contains,history%20public%20service&offset=0
130. Cooper, M. (2014). The long history and increasing importance of public-service principles for 21st century public digital communications networks. *Journal on Telecommunications & High Technology Law*. Spring. 12:1. pp. 1–54. p. 8. Retrieved from: https://primoa.library.unsw.edu.au/primo-explore/fulldisplay?docid=TN_gale_legal388675657&context=PC&vid=UNSWS&lang=en_US&search_scope=SearchFirst&adaptor=primo_central_multiple_fe&tab=default_tab&query=any,contains,history%20public%20service&offset=0
131. Halton, J. (2004). A Healthy Public Sector—Vital to Australia's Health? Peter Wilenski Memorial Lecture, 20 February 2004. *Australian Quarterly*. 76:2. (Mar-Apr., 2004). pp. 19–24. Retrieved from: https://www-jstor-org.wwwproxy1.library.unsw.edu.au/stable/pdf/20638245.pdf?refreqid=excelsior%3Ab09ce3da49e5285ebaec51142ff95634
132. Halligan, J. (2001). Contribution of the Australian Public Service to public administration and management [Edited version of a paper presented to The Australian Public Service: 100 Years of Change, the Centenary Conference of the Institute of Public Administration (ACT Division), Rydges Lakeside (2001: Canberra).] [online]. *Canberra Bulletin of Public Administration*. 101. Sept 2001. pp. 20–25. Retrieved from: https://search-informit-com-au.wwwproxy1.library.unsw.edu.au/documentSummary;dn=200116077;res=IELAPA
133. Jones, E. (2002). Menzies' razor gang: public service retrenchment in 1951 [online]. *CANBERRA BULLETIN OF PUBLIC ADMINISTRATION*. 104. June 2002. pp. 33–36. Retrieved from: https://search-informit-com-au.wwwproxy1.library.unsw.edu.au/fullText;dn=20023710;res=AGISPT

134. Halligan, J. (2001). Contribution of the Australian Public Service to public administration and management [Edited version of a paper presented to The Australian Public Service: 100 Years of Change, the Centenary Conference of the Institute of Public Administration (ACT Division), Rydges Lakeside (2001: Canberra).] [online]. *Canberra Bulletin of Public Administration.* 101. Sept 2001. pp. 20–25. Retrieved from: https://search-informit-com-au.wwwproxy1.library.unsw.edu.au/documentSummary;dn=200116077;res=IELAPA. p. 21.
135. Halligan, J. (2001). Contribution of the Australian Public Service to public administration and management [Edited version of a paper presented to The Australian Public Service: 100 Years of Change, the Centenary Conference of the Institute of Public Administration (ACT Division), Rydges Lakeside (2001: Canberra).] [online]. *Canberra Bulletin of Public Administration.* 101. Sept 2001. pp. 20–25. Retrieved from: https://search-informit-com-au.wwwproxy1.library.unsw.edu.au/documentSummary;dn=200116077;res=IELAPA ISSN: 0811-6318. p. 21.
136. Halligan, J. (2001). Contribution of the Australian Public Service to public administration and management [Edited version of a paper presented to The Australian Public Service: 100 Years of Change, the Centenary Conference of the Institute of Public Administration (ACT Division), Rydges Lakeside (2001: Canberra).] [online]. *Canberra Bulletin of Public Administration.* 101. Sept 2001. pp. 20–25. Retrieved from: https://search-informit-com-au.wwwproxy1.library.unsw.edu.au/documentSummary;dn=200116077;res=IELAPA ISSN: 0811-6318. p. 22.
137. Halligan, J. (2001). Contribution of the Australian Public Service to public administration and management [Edited version of a paper presented to The Australian Public Service: 100 Years of Change, the Centenary Conference of the Institute of Public Administration (ACT Division), Rydges Lakeside (2001: Canberra).] [online]. *Canberra Bulletin of Public Administration.* 101. Sept 2001. pp. 20–25. Retrieved from: https://search-informit-com-au.wwwproxy1.library.unsw.edu.au/documentSummary;dn=200116077;res=IELAPA ISSN: 0811-6318. p. 24.
138. Jones, E. (2002). Menzies' razor gang: public service retrenchment in 1951 [online]. *Canberra Bulletin of Public Administration.* 104. June 2002. pp. 33–36. Retrieved from: https://search-informit-com-au.wwwproxy1.library.unsw.edu.au/fullText;dn=20023710;res=AGISPT
139. Jones, E. (2002). Menzies' razor gang: public service retrenchment in 1951 [online]. *Canberra Bulletin of Public Administration.* 104. June 2002. pp. 33–36. Retrieved from: https://search-informit-com-au.wwwproxy1.library.unsw.edu.au/fullText;dn=20023710;res=AGISPT p. 35.
140. A riddle doing the rounds.

141. Winslow, D. (1999). Rites of Passage and Group Bonding in the Canadian Airborne. *Armed Forces & Society*. 25. p. 429. Retrieved from: http://afs.sagepub.com/content/25/3/429
142. Collins, C., Neal, J. & Neal, Z. (2014). Transforming Individual Civic Engagement into Community Collective Efficacy: The Role of Bonding Social Capital. *American Journal of Community Psychology*. 54. pp. 328–336. https://doi.org/10.1007/s10464-014-9675-x
143. Henttonen, K., Johanson, J., & Janhonen, M. (2014). Work-team bonding and bridging social networks, team identity and performance effectiveness. *Personnel Review*. 43:3. pp. 330–349. Retrieved from: http://dx.doi.org.wwwproxy1.library.unsw.edu.au/10.1108/PR-12-2011-0187
144. Henttonen, K., Johanson, J., & Janhonen, M. (2014). Work-team bonding and bridging social networks, team identity and performance effectiveness. *Personnel Review*. 43:3. pp. 330–349. Retrieved from: http://dx.doi.org.wwwproxy1.library.unsw.edu.au/10.1108/PR-12-2011-0187
145. Winslow, D. (1999). Rites of Passage and Group Bonding in the Canadian Airborne. Armed Forces & Society. 25. Retrieved from: https://doi.org/10.1177/0095327X9902500305 p. 429.
146. Henttonen, K., Johanson, J., & Janhonen, M. (2014). Work-team bonding and bridging social networks, team identity and performance effectiveness. *Personnel Review*. 43:3. pp. 330–349. Retrieved from: http://dx.doi.org.wwwproxy1.library.unsw.edu.au/10.1108/PR-12-2011-0187
147. Moore, C.B., Payne, G. T., Autry, C.W. & Griffis, S.E. (2018). 'Project Complexity and Bonding Social Capital in Network Organizations'. 43:6. *Group & Organization Management*. pp. 936–970. Retrieved from: https://doi.org/10.1177/1059601116650556
148. Henttonen, K., Johanson, J., & Janhonen, M. (2014). Work-team bonding and bridging social networks, team identity and performance effectiveness. *Personnel Review*. 43:3. pp. 330–349. Retrieved from: http://dx.doi.org.wwwproxy1.library.unsw.edu.au/10.1108/PR-12-2011-0187
149. Henttonen, K., Johanson, J., & Janhonen, M. (2014). Work-team bonding and bridging social networks, team identity and performance effectiveness. *Personnel Review*. 43:3. pp. 330–349. Retrieved from: http://dx.doi.org.wwwproxy1.library.unsw.edu.au/10.1108/PR-12-2011-0187
150. Moore, C.B., Payne, G. T., Autry, C.W. & Griffis, S.E. (2018). 'Project Complexity and Bonding Social Capital in Network Organizations'. 43:6. *Group & Organization Management* pp. 936–970. Retrieved from: https://doi.org/10.1177/1059601116650556

151. Moore, C.B., Payne, G. T., Autry, C.W. & Griffis, S.E. (2018). 'Project Complexity and Bonding Social Capital in Network Organizations'. 43:6. *Group & Organization Management* pp. 936–970. p. 961. Retrieved from: https://doi.org/10.1177/1059601116650556
152. Moore, C.B., Payne, G. T., Autry, C.W. & Griffis, S.E. (2018). 'Project Complexity and Bonding Social Capital in Network Organizations'. 43:6. *Group & Organization Management* pp. 936–970. p. 961. Retrieved from: https://doi.org/10.1177/1059601116650556
153. Winslow, D. (1999). Rites of Passage and Group Bonding in the Canadian Airborne. *Armed Forces & Society.* 25. p. 429. Retrieved from: http://afs.sagepub.com/content/25/3/429
154. IGADF Afghanistan Inquiry Report (2020). Inspector-General of the Australian Defence Force Afghanistan Inquiry Report. *Australian Government.* 10 November 2020. Retrieved from: https://afghanistan-inquiry.defence.gov.au/sites/default/files/2020-11/IGADF-Afghanistan-Inquiry-Public-Release-Version.pdf
155. Dalton, K. (2017). Missing in Action: The ABC and Australia's screen culture. Platform Papers. *Quarterly Essays on the Performing Arts from Currency House.* 51. May 2017. Currency House. p. 15.
156. Simons, M. (2016). Is Michelle Guthrie tuned in to the ABC? *The Monthly.* September 2016. Retrieved from: https://www.themonthly.com.au/issue/2016/september/1472652000/margaret-simons/michelle-guthrie-tuned-abc#mtr
157. Bourdieu, P. (1985). The Social Space and the Genesis of Groups. *Theory and Society.*
    14:6. (Nov., 1985). pp. 723–744. Retrieved from: https://link-springer-com.wwwproxy1.library.unsw.edu.au/content/pdf/10.1007/BF00174048.pdf
158. Bourdieu (1991) also acknowledged that "there is no political enterprise which, however, monolithic it may appear, is not the site of confrontation between divergent tendencies and interests" (Bourdieu 1991).
159. Wilson, C., Hutchinson, J., & Shea, P. (2010). Public Service Broadcasting, Creative Industries, and Innovation Infrastructure: The Case of ABC's Pool. *Australian Journal of Communication.* 37:3. pp. 15–32. http://search.proquest.com/docview/884025623/
160. In 1985 authors Patrick White, Tom Kenneally, Frank Moorehouse and artist Lloyd Rees denounced ABC content on this basis.
161. Haigh, G. (2011). Why, Oh Why, Must They Be Such Tightwads? *The Australian Rationalist.* No. 87. Summer 2011. pp. 5–8. Retrieved from: https://primoa.library.unsw.edu.au/permalink/f/11jha62/TN_informit_apaft201103405

162. Blain, E. (1977). *Life with Aunty: Forty Years with the ABC.* Methuen of Australia. Sydney. p. 200.
163. Dempster, Q. (2000). *Death Struggle: How political malice and boardroom powerplays are killing the ABC.* Allen and Unwin. Crows Nest. p. 224.
164. Henttonen, K., Johanson, J., & Janhonen, M. (2014). Work-team bonding and bridging social networks, team identity and performance effectiveness. *Personnel Review.* 43:3. pp. 330–349. Retrieved from: http://dx.doi.org.wwwproxy1.library.unsw.edu.au/10.1108/PR-12-2011-0187
165. Spath, R., Strand, V., & Bosco-Ruggiero, S. (2013). What Child Welfare Staff Say about Organizational Culture. *Child Welfare.* 92:*1*1. pp. 9–31. Retrieved from: http://search.proquest.com/docview/1509394964/
166. Spath, R., Strand, V., & Bosco-Ruggiero, S. (2013). What Child Welfare Staff Say about Organizational Culture. *Child Welfare.* 92:11. pp. 9–31. Retrieved from: http://search.proquest.com/docview/1509394964/
167. Spath, R., Strand, V., & Bosco-Ruggiero, S. (2013). What Child Welfare Staff Say about Organizational Culture. *Child Welfare.* 92:11. pp. 9–31. Retrieved from: http://search.proquest.com/docview/1509394964/
168. Swindall, C. (2011). Engaged Leadership: Building a Culture to Overcome Employee Disengagement. 2nd Edition. John Wiley and Sons, New Jersey.
169. Hall, E.T. (1959) (republished 1980). The Silent Language. Anchor Books, New York.
170. Arunchand, C.H., Ramanathan, H. N. (2013). Organizational Culture and Employee Morale: A Public Sector Enterprise Experience. *Journal of Strategic Human Resource Management.* New Delhi. Vol. 2:1. pp. 1–8. Retrieved from: http://search.proquest.com/docview/1478029898/
171. Commonwealth of Australia, The. (2019). Senate Estimates Committee. Australian Broadcasting Corporation, Committee Hansard. *The Commonwealth of Australia.* Sydney, 5 March 2019. Retrieved from: https://www.aph.gov.au/Parliamentary_Business/Hansard/Estimates_Transcript_Schedule. p. 22.
172. Indeed.com. (2020). Australian Broadcasting Corporation (ABC) Salaries in Australia. *Indeed.com.* July 2020. Retrieved from: https://au.indeed.com/cmp/Australian-Broadcasting-Corporation-%28abc%29/salaries
173. Payscale.com (2020). Average Salary for ABC Corp. Employees in Australia AU$79 k. *Payscale.com.* Retrieved from: https://www.payscale.com/research/AU/Employer=Abc_Corp./Salary
174. Australian Bureau of Statistics. (2019). Average Weekly Earnings, Australia November 2019. 6302.0. *Australian Bureau of Statistics.*

Released 20 February 2020. Retrieved from: https://www.abs.gov.au/ausstats/abs@.nsf/mf/6302.0?opendocument&ref=HPKI
175. Payscale (2020). Average Digital Media Specialist Salary in Australia. *Payscale*. Retrieved from: https://www.payscale.com/research/AU/Job=Digital_Media_Specialist/Salary
176. Fayol, H. (1949). *General and Industrial Management*. Pitman. London. Quoted in Maughan, M. (2014). *Organisational behaviour*. Houndsmills. Basingstoke, Hampshire. New York, NY: Palgrave Macmillan. p. 11.
177. Simons, M. (2016). Is Michelle Guthrie tuned in to the ABC? *The Monthly*. September 2016. Retrieved from: https://www.themonthly.com.au/issue/2016/september/1472652000/margaret-simons/michelle-guthrie-tuned-abc#mtr
178. Meade, A. (2018). 'The Wiggles for grown-ups': ABC staff bemused by Utopia-like 'Larry cards'. *The Guardian*. 5 September 2018. Retrieved from: https://www.theguardian.com/media/2018/sep/05/the-wiggles-for-grown-ups-abc-staff-bemused-by-utopia-like-larry-cards?CMP=Share_iOSApp_Other
179. Meade, A. (2018). ABC has shed 1,012 jobs since 2014, Senate estimates told. *The Guardian*. 24 May 2018. Retrieved from: https://www.theguardian.com/media/2018/may/24/abc-has-shed-1012-jobs-since-2014-senate-estimates-told
180. Confirmed by ABC finance executive Louise Higgins at a Senate Estimates Committee hearing in May 2018. (Ibid.).
181. Meade, A. (2018). 'The Wiggles for grown-ups': ABC staff bemused by Utopia-like 'Larry cards'. *The Guardian*. 5 September 2018. Retrieved from: https://www.theguardian.com/media/2018/sep/05/the-wiggles-for-grown-ups-abc-staff-bemused-by-utopia-like-larry-cards?CMP=Share_iOSApp_Other
182. Meade, A. (2018). 'The Wiggles for grown-ups': ABC staff bemused by Utopia-like 'Larry cards'. *The Guardian*. 5 September 2018. Retrieved from: https://www.theguardian.com/media/2018/sep/05/the-wiggles-for-grown-ups-abc-staff-bemused-by-utopia-like-larry-cards
183. Meade, A. (2018). 'The Wiggles for grown-ups': ABC staff bemused by Utopia-like 'Larry cards'. *The Guardian*. 5 September 2018. Retrieved from: https://www.theguardian.com/media/2018/sep/05/the-wiggles-for-grown-ups-abc-staff-bemused-by-utopia-like-larry-cards
184. Meade, A. (2018). 'The Wiggles for grown-ups': ABC staff bemused by Utopia-like 'Larry cards'. *The Guardian*. 5 September 2018. Retrieved from: https://www.theguardian.com/media/2018/sep/05/the-wiggles-for-grown-ups-abc-staff-bemused-by-utopia-like-larry-cards
185. Brook, S. (2018). ABC staffers not happy as Larry. The Diary. *The Australian*. 10 September 2018. Retrieved from: https://www.theaus-

tralian.com.au/business/media/abc-staffers-not-happy-as-larry/news-story/3bfc71c86335c675005f72b2c6cf385d

186. Brook, S. (2018). ABC staffers not happy as Larry. The Diary. *The Australian.* 10 September 2018. Retrieved from: https://www.theaustralian.com.au/business/media/abc-staffers-not-happy-as-larry/news-story/3bfc71c86335c675005f72b2c6cf385d
187. Brook, S. (2018). ABC staffers not happy as Larry. The Diary. *The Australian.* 10 September 2018. Retrieved from: https://www.theaustralian.com.au/business/media/abc-staffers-not-happy-as-larry/news-story/3bfc71c86335c675005f72b2c6cf385d
188. Wanous, J. P., Reichers, A. E., & Austin, J. T. (2004). Cynicism about Organizational Change: An Attribution Process Perspective. *Psychological Reports.* 94 (3. Suppl.). pp. 1421–1434. Retrieved from: https://doi.org/10.2466/pr0.94.3c. 1421–1434.
189. Line, M. B. (1992). How to demotivate staff: A brief guide. *Library Management.* 13:1. p. 4. Retrieved from: http://dx.doi.org.wwwproxy1.library.unsw.edu.au/10.1108/01435129210009832
190. Semmler, C. (1981) *The ABC: Aunt Sally or Sacred Cow?* Melbourne University Press. Melbourne. p. 18.
191. Fraser, M. & O'Reilly, J. Eds. (1996). *Save our ABC: The case for maintaining Australia's national broadcaster.* Hyland House. South Melbourne. p. 56.
192. *Sun, The.* (1946). Suspension of ABC Staff Chief. 16 October 1946. p. 5. Retrieved from: https://trove.nla.gov.au/newspaper/article/229551981?searchTerm=ABC%20staff&searchLimits=
193. Truth, The. (1948). Tale Of Table-Thumping In A.B.C. Chief's Office. *The Truth.* 13 June 1948. p. 8. Retrieved from https://trove.nla.gov.au/newspaper/article/169378780?searchTerm=ABC%20staff%20McCarthy&searchLimits=
194. Argus, The. (1948). ABC head denies accusations. *The Argus.* 12 June 1948. p. 3. Retrieved from: https://trove.nla.gov.au/newspaper/article/22548011?searchTerm=ABC%20staff%20McCarthy&searchLimits=
195. Argus, The. (1948). Former ABC man in damages suit. *The Argus.* 11 June, 1948. p. 5. Retrieved from https://trove.nla.gov.au/newspaper/article/22541049?searchTerm=ABC%20staff%20McCarthy&searchLimits=
196. Semmler, C. (1981). *The ABC—Aunt Sally and Sacred Cow.* Melbourne University Press. Melbourne. p. 87.
197. Dixon. F. (1975). *Inside the ABC: A Piece of Australian History.* Hawthorn Press. Melbourne. p. 164.
198. Dixon. F. (1975). *Inside the ABC: A Piece of Australian History.* Hawthorn Press. Melbourne. p. 164.

199. *Argus, The.* (1948). ABC head denies accusations. *The Argus.* 12 June 1948. p. 3. Retrieved from https://trove.nla.gov.au/newspaper/article/22548011?searchTerm=ABC%20staff%20McCarthy&searchLimits=
200. Dixon. F. (1975). *Inside the ABC: A Piece of Australian History.* Hawthorn Press. Melbourne. p. 164.
201. ABC. (n.d.). Frank Dixon. 1 June 2017. Australian Broadcasting Corporation. Retrieved from: https://www.abc.net.au/news/2017-06-01/frank-dixon/8576568
202. Inglis, K. (1983). *This is the ABC. The Australian Broadcasting Commission, 1932–1983.* Melbourne University Press. Melbourne. p. 65.
203. Dixon. F. (1975). *Inside the ABC: A Piece of Australian History.* Hawthorn Press. Melbourne. p. 1.
204. Dixon. F. (1975). *Inside the ABC: A Piece of Australian History.* Hawthorn Press. Melbourne. p. 1.
205. Reserve Bank of Australia. (2020). Pre-Decimal Inflation Calculator. *Reserve Bank of Australia.* Retrieved from: https://www.rba.gov.au/calculator/annualPreDecimal.html
206. Dixon. F. (1975). *Inside the ABC: A Piece of Australian History.* Hawthorn Press. Melbourne. p. 3.
207. Dixon. F. (1975). *Inside the ABC: A Piece of Australian History.* Hawthorn Press. Melbourne. p. 7.
208. Dixon. F. (1975). *Inside the ABC: A Piece of Australian History.* Hawthorn Press. Melbourne. p. 9.
209. University of New England. (2020). Sir Robert Madgwick and his Legacy. Our Values and Culture. *University of New England.* Retrieved from: https://www.une.edu.au/about-une/our-values-and-culture/sir-robert-madgwick
210. Coleman, P. (2007). Hulme, Sir Alan Shallcross (1907–1989). *Australian Dictionary of Biography.* National Centre of Biography. Australian National University. Retrieved from: http://adb.anu.edu.au/biography/hulme-sir-alan-shallcross-12666/text22827
211. Robertson, A. (1970). ABC censorship move stirs new staff challenge. *The Tribune.* 3 June 1970, p. 4. Retrieved from: https://trove.nla.gov.au/newspaper/article/237505888?searchTerm=ABC%20staff%20culture&searchLimits=
212. *Canberra Times, The.* (1976). 'Support' for ABC staff campaign. 8 October 1976, p. 3. Retrieved from: https://trove.nla.gov.au/newspaper/article/110829449?searchTerm=ABC%20staff&searchLimits=
213. Dixon, F. (1975). *Inside the ABC: A Piece of Australian History.* The Hawthorn Press. Melbourne. p. 211.
214. Dixon, F. (1975). *Inside the ABC: A Piece of Australian History.* The Hawthorn Press. Melbourne.

215. Dixon, F. (1975). *Inside the ABC: A Piece of Australian History*. The Hawthorn Press. Melbourne. p. 210.
216. Daily Examiner, The (1945). Reason for Resignation of ABC Chairman. *Daily Examiner, Grafton*. 30 March 1945, p. 3. Retrieved from: https://trove.nla.gov.au/newspaper/article/193817668?searchTerm=chairman%20ABC&searchLimits=exactPhrase|||anyWords|||notWords|||requestHandler|||dateFrom=1944-01-01|||dateTo=1946-12-31|||l-advstate=National|||l-advstate=ACT|||l-advstate=New+South+Wales|||sortby
217. Sydney Morning Herald, The. (1945). Mr Cleary Talks of Clashes. 30 March 1945. p. 4. *The Sydney Morning Herald*. Retrieved from: https://trove.nla.gov.au/newspaper/article/17937290?searchTerm=chairman%20ABC&searchLimits=exactPhrase|||anyWords|||notWords|||requestHandler|||dateFrom=1945-01-31|||dateTo=1945-04-30|||l-advstate=National|||l-advstate=ACT|||l-advstate=New+South+Wales|||sortby
218. Sydney Morning Herald, The. (1945). How much freedom for the ABC? 17 April 1945, p. 2. *The Sydney Morning Herald*. Retrieved from: https://trove.nla.gov.au/newspaper/article/27932662?searchTerm=chairman%20ABC&searchLimits=exactPhrase|||anyWords|||notWords|||requestHandler|||dateFrom=1944-01-01|||dateTo=1946-12-31|||l-advstate=National|||l-advstate=ACT|||l-advstate=New+South+Wales|||sortby
219. Petersen, N. (2009). "A Biography of Sir Charles Moses". *Global Media Journal*. 3(1). Retrieved from: https://www.hca.westernsydney.edu.au/gmjau/archive/v3_2009_1/3vi1_neville_petersen.html
220. Westmore, P. (2018). Media: Internal strife at Fortress ABC [online]. *News Weekly*. 3031. 20 Oct 2018. p. 13. Retrieved from: https://search.informit.com.au/documentSummary;dn=988136489334664;res=IELAPA
221. Brook, B. (2018). The mistakes Michelle Guthrie made that led to her sacking from $891 k managing director role: FORMER ABC staffers have revealed their views about why ABC chief Michelle Guthrie had to go—and what her fatal errors were. *News.com.au*. 25 September 2018. Retrieved from: https://www.news.com.au/finance/business/media/the-mistakes-michelle-guthrie-made-that-led-to-her-sacking-from-891k-managing-director-role/news-story/fc9ef1c147df93253bd30b22de8f84b7
222. Ibid.
223. Ibid.
224. Ibid.
225. Duke, J., Carmody, B., & Koziol, M. (2018). Michelle Guthrie: The inside story behind her sacking. *The Sydney Morning Herald*. 24 September 2018. Retrieved from: https://www.smh.com.au/business/companies/michelle-guthrie-the-inside-story-behind-her-sacking-20180924-p505ok.html

226. Ibid.
227. Australian Broadcasting Corporation. (2018). 730 Program. Justin Milne Interview. *Australian Broadcasting Corporation.* 27 September 2018. Retrieved from: https://www.abc.net.au/news/2018-12-19/justin-milne-announces-his-resignation-as-abc/10627896?nw=0
228. Duke, J. Carmody, B. & Koziol, M. (2018). Michelle Guthrie: The inside story behind the ABC boss' sacking. *The Sydney Morning Herald.* 24 September 2018. Retrieved from: https://www.smh.com.au/business/companies/michelle-guthrie-the-inside-story-behind-her-sacking-20180924-p505ok.html
229. Ibid.
230. Meade, A. (2018). The ABC in turmoil: 'Frankly, we are all spooked about everything in here'. *The Guardian.* 1 August 2018. Retrieved from: https://www.theguardian.com/media/2018/aug/01/the-abc-in-turmoil-frankly-we-are-all-spooked-about-everything-in-here
231. Kenny, C. (2018). ABC Chairman Justin Milne has to go over push to sack Emma Alberici. *The Australian.* Retrieved from: https://www.theaustralian.com.au/business/media/abc-chairman-justin-milne-has-to-go-over-push-to-sack-emma-alberici/news-story/e326ac54ba0a027e70231f3edc3152b3
232. Ibid.
233. Meade, A. (2018). Michelle Guthrie says abuse of ABC staff unacceptable after presenter cries on air. *The Guardian.* 21 August 2018. Retrieved from: https://www.theguardian.com/media/2018/aug/21/michelle-guthrie-says-abuse-of-abc-staff-unacceptable-after-presenter-cries-on-air
234. Chung, L. (2018). Michelle Guthrie sacked: Why more trouble lies ahead for ABC. *Nine.com.au.* 24 September 2018. Retrieved from: https://finance.nine.com.au/business-news/why-more-trouble-lies-ahead-for-abc/846781d2-7df0-46fd-808d-0a8818bff342
235. Chenoweth, N. (2014). Aunty faces cuts, job losses and old scores: Media. *The Australian Financial Review.* 1 February 2014. p. 21. Retrieved from: https://search-proquest-com.wwwproxy1.library.unsw.edu.au/docview/1753219424?rfr_id=info%3Axri%2Fsid%3Aprimo
236. Remeikis, A. (2018). ABC board must get back to work and 'do better', Scott Morrison says". *The Guardian.* 30 September 2018. Retrieved from: https://www.theguardian.com/media/2018/sep/30/abc-board-must-get-back-to-work-and-do-better-scott-morrison-says
237. Retrieved 19 March 2020 from: https://twitter.com/AttardMon/status/1044037566993846272

238. Retrieved 20 March 2020 from https://twitter.com/sinddyealy/status/1044063333635112960
239. O'Brien, K. (2019). 'Don't ever again allow politicians to diminish the public broadcaster'. Logies Speech. Induction into the Hall of Fame. 1 July 2019. *Crikey.com*. Retrieved from: https://www.crikey.com.au/2019/07/01/kerry-obrien-logies-speech/
240. Age, The. (1939). ABC Staff Party. *The Age*. 24 October, 1939. p. 3. Retrieved from: https://trove.nla.gov.au/newspaper/article/206338437?searchTerm=ABC%20staff&searchLimits=
241. Kenny, C. (2020). Cue the violins: ABC needs to put its trivial troubles into perspective. *The Australian*. 29 June 2020. Retrieved from: https://www.theaustralian.com.au/business/media/abc-crybabies-need-to-put-their-trivial-troubles-into-perspective/news-story/af90438cc7f3d09c5767c8004da51170
242. O'Brien, K. (2019). 'Don't ever again allow politicians to diminish the public broadcaster'. *Crikey.com*. 1 July 2019. Retrieved from: https://www.crikey.com.au/2019/07/01/kerry-obrien-logies-speech/
243. Varga, R. (2018). Spigelman hits out over Guthrie sacking. *The Australian*. 26 September, 2018. Retrieved from: https://www.theaustralian.com.au/business/media/abc-former-chairman-james-spigelman-hits-out-over-guthrie-sacking/news-story/9951e4c9f27ef10813f0ecd1abca7e3a
244. Ibid.
245. Mitchell, C. (2019). ABC gave us groupthink on steroids. *The Australian*. 27 May 2019. Retrieved from: https://www.theaustralian.com.au/commentary/abc-gave-us-groupthink-on-steroids/news-story/da95e8a9d851509bf8538df28c630c15
246. Mitchell, C. (2019). ABC gave us groupthink on steroids. *The Australian*. 27 May 2019. Retrieved from: https://www.theaustralian.com.au/commentary/abc-gave-us-groupthink-on-steroids/news-story/da95e8a9d851509bf8538df28c630c15
247. Luck, G. (2018). The rot set in with current affairs, and ABC news has since lost its bearings. 30 June 2018. *The Australian*. Retrieved from https://www.theaustralian.com.au/news/inquirer/the-rot-set-in-with-current-affairs-and-abc-news-has-since-lost-its-bearings/news-story/06202187428fc0e6b2a14b60f940c8de
248. Willem, A., De Vos, A. & Buelens, M. (2010). Comparing Private and Public Sector Employees' Psychological Contracts Do they attach equal importance to generic work aspects? *Public Management Review*. 12:2. pp. 275–302. Retrieved from https://www-tandfonline-com.www-proxy1.library.unsw.edu.au/doi/pdf/10.1080/14719031003620323?needAccess=true

249. Luck, G. (2018). Ibid.
250. Inglis, K. (2006). *Whose ABC?: The Australian Broadcasting Corporation, 1983–2006.* Black Inc. Melbourne. p. 155.
251. Mansfield, B. (1997). The challenge of a better ABC: The review of the role and functions of the ABC. *Australian Government Publishing Service.* Canberra.
252. Mansfield, B. (1997). The challenge of a better ABC: The review of the role and functions of the ABC. Vol. 1. *Australian Government Publishing Service.* Canberra.
253. Martin, F. (2002). Beyond Public Service Broadcasting? ABC Online and the User/Citizen. *Southern Review: Communication, Politics & Culture.* 35:1. pp. 42–62. Retrieved from: https://search-informit-com-au.www-proxy1.library.unsw.edu.au/documentSummary;dn=743199784542203;res=IELAPA ISSN: 0038-4526.
254. Martin, F. (2002). Beyond Public Service Broadcasting? ABC Online and the User/Citizen. *Southern Review: Communication, Politics & Culture.* 35:1. pp. 42–62. Retrieved from: https://search-informit-com-au.www-proxy1.library.unsw.edu.au/documentSummary;dn=743199784542203;res=IELAPA ISSN: 0038-4526.
255. Simons, M. (2016). Is Michelle Guthrie tuned in to the ABC? *The Monthly.* September 2016. Retrieved from: https://www.themonthly.com.au/issue/2016/september/1472652000/margaret-simons/michelle-guthrie-tuned-abc#mtr
256. Vakkayil, J. (2008). Learning and organizations: towards cross-metaphor conversations. *Learning Inquiry.* 2:1. pp. 13–27. https://doi.org/10.1007/s11519-008-0025-5
257. Klikauer, T. (2018). Media and Capitalism [Review of *Media and Capitalism*]. *Critical Sociology.* 44:6. pp. 969–981. SAGE Publications. Retrieved from: https://doi.org/10.1177/0896920518774091
258. Martin, F. (2002). Beyond Public Service Broadcasting? ABC Online and the User/Citizen [online]. *Southern Review: Communication, Politics & Culture.* 35:1. pp. 42–62. Retrieved from: https://search-informit-com-au.wwwproxy1.library.unsw.edu.au/documentSummary;dn=743199784542203;res=IELAPA ISSN: 0038-4526. Quoting Perry and Wise research, 1990.
259. Curran, J. (2011). *Media and Democracy.* Routledge. London & New York.
260. Ibid.
261. Ibid.
262. Hamilton, W. (2013). Rights and wrongs of ABC spy reports. *Eureka Street.* 23:23. Nov 2013. pp. 4–6. Retrieved from: https://search.informit.com.au/documentSummary;dn=730862220180851;res=IELAPA

263. Salter, D. (2007). *The Media We Deserve.* Melbourne University Press. Melbourne. p. 77.
264. Thomas, A. (1980). *Broadcast and be damned. The ABC's first two decades.* Melbourne University Press. Melbourne. p. 141.
265. Ibid.
266. Loc. cit.
267. Ibid., p. 145.
268. ABC staff exercise what Bourdieu (1991) described as 'symbolic power' which was "invisible" but embedded such that it was "misrecognised" by those who were beholden to it (management, in this instance) and "which can be exercised only with the complicity of those who do not want to know that they are subject to it or even that they themselves exercise it (Bourdieu 1991).
269. Bourdieu (1991) drew on his analysis of power from Karl Marx and his depiction of class and élitism as deriving from property ownership (capital) and Max Weber's definitions of the representations that legitimise and uphold power. Bourdieu adopted Marx's capital to create the theory of '*cultural capital*' and the symbols of power.
270. Semmler, C. (1981) *The ABC—Aunt Sally and Sacred Cow.* Melbourne University Press. Melbourne. p. 32.
271. Ibid., p. 32.
272. Commonwealth of Australia, The. (2019). Senate Estimates Committee. Australian Broadcasting Corporation, Committee Hansard. Sydney, 6 March 2019. Retrieved from: https://www.aph.gov.au/Parliamentary_Business/Hansard/Estimates_Transcript_Schedule. p. 18.
273. Cadzow, J. (2018). "Culture Clash". The Good Weekend Magazine. *The Sydney Morning Herald.* The Culture Issue. 6 October 2018. p. 20.
274. Bourdieu's (1986) theory described such struggles as examples of how '*fields*', or sub-*fields* in this case, become contested when resources and status were disputed, and where the struggle between the dominant and dominated was "the most fundamental" struggle (Bourdieu 1986).
275. Seccombe, M. (2016). Senior ABC staff say Michelle Guthrie 'out of her depth'. *The Saturday Paper. 137.* 3–9 December, 2016. Retrieved from: https://www.thesaturdaypaper.com.au/news/media/2016/12/03/senior-abc-staff-say-michelle-guthrie-out-her-depth/14806836004053
276. Seccombe, M. (2016). Senior ABC staff say Michelle Guthrie 'out of her depth'. *The Saturday Paper. 137.* December 3–9, 2016. Retrieved from: https://www.thesaturdaypaper.com.au/news/media/2016/12/03/senior-abc-staff-say-michelle-guthrie-out-her-depth/14806836004053
277. Cadzow, J. (2018). "Culture Clash". The Good Weekend Magazine. *The Sydney Morning Herald.* The Culture Issue. 6 October 2018. p. 14.
278. Cadzow, J. (2018). "Culture Clash". The Good Weekend Magazine. *The Sydney Morning Herald.* The Culture Issue. 6 October 2018. p. 14.

279. Dixon, F. (1975). *Inside the ABC: A Piece of Australian History*. The Hawthorn Press. Melbourne. p. 211.
280. Ibid.
281. *ABC Section of the Community and Public Sector Union*. (2008). Towards a Digital Future. December 2008. Retrieved from: https://iloveabc.org.au/wp-content/uploads/2018/11/Towards-a-Digital-Future-2008-1.pdf. p. 12.
282. Ibid., p. 13.
283. Semmler, C. (1981). *The ABC—Aunt Sally and Sacred Cow*. Melbourne University Press. Melbourne. p. 185.
284. Ibid., p. 185.
285. Kurtulmuş, B. E. (2019). *The Dark Side of Leadership*. iBooks. Springer. Retrieved from: https://doi.org/10.1007/978-3-030-02038-5_1
286. Askeland, H., Espedal, G., Jelstad Løvaas, B. & Sirris, S. Eds. (2020). *Understanding Values Work: Institutional Perspectives in Organizations and Leadership*. eBook. Springer International. Retrieved from https://primoa.library.unsw.edu.au/primo-explore/fulldisplay?docid=UNSW_ALMA51279111340001731&context=L&vid=UNSWS&lang=en_US&search_scope=SearchFirst&adaptor=Local%20Search%20Engine&tab=default_tab&query=any,contains,institutional%20leadership&offset=0 pp. 30–31.
287. Ibid.
288. Thornton, P. H., & Ocasio, W. (2008). Institutional Logics. In R. Greenwood, C. Oliver, R. Suddaby, & K. Sahlin (Eds.). *The Sage Handbook of Organizational Institutionalism*. 840. pp. 99–128. Sage. London.
289. Askeland, H., Espedal, G., Jelstad Løvaas, B. & Sirris, S. Eds. Ibid. p. 63.
290. Ibid., p. 104.
291. Fraser, M. & O'Reilly, J. Eds. (1996). *Save our ABC: The case for maintaining Australia's national broadcaster*. Hyland House. South Melbourne. p. 61.
292. Askeland, H., Espedal, G., Jelstad Løvaas, B. & Sirris, S. Eds. Ibid. p. 104.
293. Askeland, H., Espedal, G., Jelstad Løvaas, B. & Sirris, S. Eds. Ibid. p. 107.
294. Friedland, R. (2013b). The gods of institutional life: Weber's value spheres and the practice of polytheism. *Critical Research on Religion*. 1:1. pp. 15–24. Retrieved from: https://doi.org/10.1177/2050303213476104
295. Askeland, H., Espedal, G., Jelstad Løvaas, B. & Sirris, S. Eds. Ibid. pp. 114–115.
296. Blain. Ibid., p. 206.
297. In what Bourdieu (1984) described as an area that is contested and constrained as a field of cultural production within a '*habitus*' of a "structuring structure, which organizes practices, and the perception of practices"

(Bourdieu 1984). The journalistic field is a field of power that belongs to the larger field of cultural production (Benson & Neveu 2005) and according to Bourdieu (1993) obeyed "its own laws, its own nomos" (ibid.).

298. Askeland, H., Espedal, G., Jelstad Løvaas, B. & Sirris, S. (Eds.). Ibid. p. 116.
299. Fraser, M. & O'Reilly, J. Eds. (1996). *Save our ABC: The case for maintaining Australia's national broadcaster.* Hyland House. South Melbourne. p. 56.
300. Fraser, M. & O'Reilly, J. Eds. (1996). *Save our ABC: The case for maintaining Australia's national broadcaster.* Hyland House. South Melbourne. p. 56.
301. Kurtulmuş. p. 10.
302. Kurtulmuş. p. 16.
303. Kurtulmuş. p. 26.
304. Kurtulmuş. p. 42.
305. Ibid.
306. Ibid., p. 43.
307. Askeland, H., Espedal, G., Jelstad Løvaas, B. & Sirris, S. (2020). *Understanding Values Work: Institutional Perspectives in Organizations and Leadership.* eBook. Springer International. Retrieved from: https://primoa.library.unsw.edu.au/primo-explore/fulldisplay?docid=UNSW_ALMA51279111340001731&context=L&vid=UNSWS&lang=en_US&search_scope=SearchFirst&adaptor=Local%20Search%20Engine&tab=default_tab&query=any,contains,institutional%20leadership&offset=0
308. Hansen, H. (1998). Core values key to attracting and retaining the most qualified staff. *Bowman's Accounting Report.* 12(12). pp. 12–15. Retrieved from: http://search.proquest.com/docview/206573843/
309. Golant, B., Sillince, J., Harvey, C., & Maclean, M. (2015). Rhetoric of stability and change: The organizational identity work of institutional leadership. *Human Relations.* 68:4. pp. 607–631. Retrieved from: https://doi.org/10.1177/0018726714532966 p. 608.
310. Sydney Morning Herald, The. (2003). ABC loses points in Alston's 'bias' plea. *The Sydney Morning Herald.* 11 October 2003. Retrieved from https://www.smh.com.au/national/abc-loses-points-in-alstons-bias-plea-20031011-gdhkgd.html
311. Ibid.
312. Ibid.
313. Santoro, S. (2013). Senate. Official Hansard. Parliamentary Debates. *Commonwealth of Australia.* 13:2003, 15 October 2003. Fortieth Parliament First Session—Sixth Period. Retrieved from: https://parlinfo.

aph.gov.au/parlInfo/download/chamber/hansards/2003-10-15/toc_pdf/2939-2.pdf;fileType=application%2Fpdf#search=%22chamber/hansards/2003-10-15/0000%22
314. Ibid.
315. Ibid.
316. Sydney Morning Herald, The. (1976). Sir Henry spells out views on ABC. *The Sydney Morning Herald*. 9 December 1976. p. 10. Retrieved from: https://trove.nla.gov.au/newspaper/article/131800175?searchTerm=henry%20bland%20ABC%20orchestras
317. Buttrose, C. (1984). *Words and Music: Press barons, prima donnas, coping with the ABC*... Angus and Robertson. Australia. p. 90.
318. Sydney Morning Herald, The. (1976). Sir Henry spells out views on ABC. *The Sydney Morning Herald*. 9 December 1976. p. 10. Retrieved from: https://trove.nla.gov.au/newspaper/article/131800175?searchTerm=henry%20bland%20ABC%20orchestras
319. Blain, E. (1977). *Life with Aunty: 40 Years with the ABC*. Methuen. Australia. p. 207.
320. Garrett, D. (2012). The accidental entrepreneur—how ABC music became more than broadcasting. Doctor of Philosophy thesis. Faculty of Creative Arts. *University of Wollongong*. 2012. https://ro.uow.edu.au/theses/3680
321. Meade, A. (2018). The ABC in turmoil: 'Frankly, we are all spooked about everything in here'. *The Guardian*. 1 August 2018. Retrieved from https://www.theguardian.com/media/2018/aug/01/the-abc-in-turmoil-frankly-we-are-all-spooked-about-everything-in-here
322. Ibid.
323. Fraser, M. & O'Reilly, J. (1996). *Save Our ABC: Maintaining Australia's National Broadcaster*. Hyland House. South Melbourne. pp. 89–90.
324. Ibid., p. 90.
325. Ibid., p. 90
326. Semmler, C. (1981). *The ABC—Aunt Sally and Sacred Cow*. Melbourne University Press. Melbourne. p. 100.
327. *Canberra Times, The*. (1977). 'Interference' to ABC 'insidious'. *The Canberra Times*. 24 October 1977. p. 7. Retrieved from: https://trove.nla.gov.au/newspaper/article/110874090?searchTerm=ABC%20ghost&searchLimits=
328. Canberra Times, The. (1977). 'Interference' to ABC 'insidious'. *The Canberra Times*. 24 October 1977. p. 7. Retrieved from: https://trove.nla.gov.au/newspaper/article/110874090?searchTerm=ABC%20ghost&searchLimits=
329. Canberra Times, The. (1985). 'Phantom army' found in ABC. *The Canberra Times*. 11 June 1985. p. 7. Retrieved from: https://trove.nla.

gov.au/newspaper/article/122515191?searchTerm=ABC%20phantom%20army&searchLimits=

330. Molomby, T. (1991). *Is There a Moderate on the Roof? ABC Years.* William Heinemann. Australia. pp. 213–214.
331. Whitehead, G. (1988). *Inside the ABC: Geoffrey Whitehead's Personal Account.* Penguin Books. Victoria. p. 110.
332. Molomby, T. (1991). *Is There a Moderate on the Roof? ABC Years.* William Heinemann. Australia. pp. 213–215.
333. Whitehead, G. (1988). *Inside the ABC: Geoffrey Whitehead's Personal Account.* Penguin Books. Victoria. p. 113.
334. Whitehead, G. (1988). *Inside the ABC: Geoffrey Whitehead's Personal Account.* Penguin Books Victoria. p. 114.
335. Molomby, T. (1991). *Is There a Moderate on the Roof? ABC Years.* William Heinemann. Australia. pp. 213–215.
336. Molomby, T. (1991). *Is There a Moderate on the Roof? ABC Years.* William Heinemann, Australia. pp. 213–216.
337. Molomby, T. (1991). *Is There a Moderate on the Roof? ABC Years.* William Heinemann. Australia. pp. 213–220.
338. Whitehead, G. (1988). *Inside the ABC: Geoffrey Whitehead's Personal Account.* Penguin Books. Victoria. p. 116.
339. *Sydney Morning Herald, The.* (1986). THE ABC AFTER WHITEHEAD. Editorial. 26 September 1986. p. 12.
340. Meade, A. (2018). The ABC in turmoil: 'Frankly, we are all spooked about everything in here.' *The Guardian.* 1 August 2018. Retrieved from: https://www.theguardian.com/media/2018/aug/01/the-abc-in-turmoil-frankly-we-are-all-spooked-about-everything-in-here
341. Meade, A. (2018). The ABC in turmoil: 'Frankly, we are all spooked about everything in here.' *The Guardian.* 1 August 2018. Retrieved from: https://www.theguardian.com/media/2018/aug/01/the-abc-in-turmoil-frankly-we-are-all-spooked-about-everything-in-here
342. Meade, A. (2018). The ABC in turmoil: 'Frankly, we are all spooked about everything in here.' *The Guardian.* 1 August 2018. Retrieved from: https://www.theguardian.com/media/2018/aug/01/the-abc-in-turmoil-frankly-we-are-all-spooked-about-everything-in-here
343. Meade, A. (2018). The ABC in turmoil: 'Frankly, we are all spooked about everything in here.' *The Guardian.* 1 August 2018. Retrieved from: https://www.theguardian.com/media/2018/aug/01/the-abc-in-turmoil-frankly-we-are-all-spooked-about-everything-in-here
344. Clarke, M. (2018). ASIO takes custody of secret cabinet documents, obtained by the ABC. *ABC Online.* 2 February 2018. Retrieved from: https://www.abc.net.au/news/2018-02-01/asio-takes-custody-of-cabinet-documents/9386328

345. Tracey, M. (1998). *The Decline and Fall of Public Broadcasting*. Oxford University Press. Oxford. p. 266.
346. Tracey, M. (1998). *The Decline and Fall of Public Broadcasting*. Oxford University Press. Oxford. p. 266.
347. Tracey, M. (1998). *The Decline and Fall of Public Broadcasting*. Oxford University Press. Oxford. p. 266.
348. Fouskas, V. K. (2013). Athens has No Voice: On the closure of Greece's Public Broadcasting Corporation (ERT). *Debatte: Journal of Contemporary Central and Eastern Europe*. 21:1. pp. 107–111. Retrieved from: https://doi.org/10.1080/0965156X.2013.836858
349. Simons, M. (2006). 'Leaked KPMG Report: ABC Efficient but Underfunded.' *Crikey*. 21 November, 2016. Retrieved from: https://www.crikey.com.au/2006/11/21/leaked-kpmg-report-abc-efficient-but-underfunded/
350. *President of the Council of State* (2013). Temporary Injunction. President of the Council of State 17 June 2013. Archived 5 September 2013. Retrieved from: http://www.ste.gr/portal/page/portal/StE/Prosfates Apofaseis
351. Feldman, E. (2014). Legacy Divestitures: Motives and Implications. *Organization Science*. 25:3. pp. 815–832. Retrieved from: https://doi.org/10.1287/orsc.2013.0873
352. Datta, D. K., Guthrie, J. P., Basuil, D., & Pandey, A. (2010). Causes and effects of employment downsizing: A review and synthesis. *Journal of Management*. 36. pp. 281–348. Retrieved from: https://doi.org/10.1177/0149206309346735
353. Dempster, Q. (2000). *Death Struggle: How political malice and boardroom powerplays are killing the ABC*. Allen and Unwin. Crows Nest. p. xiii.
354. Chong, D., & Bogdan, E. (2010). Plural public funding and Canada's contemporary art market system. *Cultural Trends: Centre/Periphery: Devolution/Federalism: New Trends In Cultural Policy*. 19:1–2. pp. 93–107. Retrieved from: https://doi.org/10.1080/09548961003696096
355. Park, C.-M. (2010). Public Attitudes toward Government Spending in the Asia-Pacific Region. *Japanese Journal of Political Science*. 11:1. pp. 77–97. Retrieved from: https://doi.org/10.1017/S1468109909990144
356. Klapdor, M. & Arthur, D. (2017). Welfare—what does it cost? *Parliament of Australia*. Retrieved from: https://www.aph.gov.au/About_Parliament/Parliamentary_Departments/Parliamentary_Library/pubs/BriefingBook45p/WelfareCost
357. Simshaw, D. (2012). "Survival of the standard: today's public interest requirement in television broadcasting and the return to regulation."

Federal Communications Law Journal. 64:2. March 2012. p. 401. Retrieved from: https://link-gale-com.wwwproxy1.library.unsw.edu.au/apps/doc/A287390717/LT?u=unsw&sid=LT&xid=8c9308f1
358. Dempster, Q. (2000). *Death Struggle: How Political Malice And Boardroom Powerplays Are Killing The ABC.* Allen and Unwin. Crows Nest. p. xiii.
359. Barry, P. (2018). MediaWatch. *Australian Broadcasting Corporation.* 25 June 2018. Retrieved from: https://www.abc.net.au/mediawatch/episodes/privatising-the-abc/9972184
360. Thomas, A. (1980). *Broadcast and be damned. The ABC's first two decades.* Melbourne University Press. Melbourne. p. 59.
361. Thomas, A. (1980). *Broadcast and be damned. The ABC's first two decades.* Melbourne University Press. Melbourne. p. 60.
362. Thomas, A. (1980). Ibid. Quoting *The Sydney Morning Herald* 2 May, 1945.
363. Blain, E. (1977). *Life with Aunty: 40 years with the ABC.* Methuen. Australia.
364. Ibid. p. 156.
365. Ibid., p. 157.
366. Ibid., p. 60.
367. Ibid., p. 134.
368. Loc. cit.
369. Ibid., p. 135.
370. Ibid., p. 138.
371. Thomas, A. (1980). *Broadcast and be damned. The ABC's first two decades.* Melbourne University Press. Melbourne. p. 147.
372. Whitehead, G. (1988). *Inside the ABC: Geoffrey Whitehead's Personal Account.* Penguin Books. Melbourne. p. 177.
373. Blain, E. (1976). *Life with Aunty. 40 Years with the ABC.* Methuen. Australia. p. 160.
374. Ibid.
375. Ibid., p. 160.
376. Ibid., p. 161.
377. Ibid.
378. Ibid., p. 161.
379. Kumar, P., & Zattoni, A. (2018). Internal culture and outside influence in corporate governance. *Corporate Governance: An International Review.* January 2018. 26:1. pp. 2–3. Retrieved from: https://primoa.library.unsw.edu.au/primo-explore/search?query=any,contains,internal%20culture&tab=default_tab&search_scope=SearchFirst&vid=UNSWS&offset=0

380. Schein, E. H. (2010). *Organizational Culture and Leadership*. 4th Edition. The Jossey-Bass Business & Management Series. 2:4. Wiley. San Francisco.
381. Ibid.
382. Ibid. p. 206.
383. Spadaro, S. J. A. (2020) Defy the Apocalypse. *La Civiltà Cattolica*. 20 January 2020. Retrieved from: https://www.laciviltacattolica.com/defy-the-apocalypse/
384. Ibid.
385. Abebe, M. & Tangpong, C. (2017). Founder-CEOs and Corporate Turnaround among Declining Firms: Founder CEOs and Turnaround. *Corporate Governance an International Review*. 26:3. August 2017. Retrieved from: https://doi.org/10.1111/corg.12216
386. Celep, A. & Mosher-William, R. (2016). Internal Culture, External Impact: How a Change-Making Culture Positions Foundations to Achieve Transformational Change. *The Foundation Review*. 8:1. pp. 116–129. Retrieved from: https://doi.org/10.9707/1944-5660.1288
387. Ibid.
388. Loc. Cit.
389. Ibid., p. 19.
390. Ibid., p. 301.
391. Loc. Cit.
392. Loc. Cit.
393. Price, S. (2014). Public broadcasting under threat. *Green Left Weekly*. 1015, 9 July 2014. 3. Retrieved from: https://primoa.library.unsw.edu.au/permalink/f/11jha62/TN_informit441816198109046
394. Schein, E. H. (2010). *Organizational Culture and Leadership*. 4th Edition. The Jossey-Bass Business & Management Series. 2:4. Wiley. San Francisco. p. 307.
395. Then under the control and management of the ABC.
396. *Mercury, The*. (1944). Haydn Beck resigns ABC post. *The Mercury*. 7 September 1944, p. 14. Retrieved from: https://trove.nla.gov.au/newspaper/article/26036060?searchTerm=haydn%20beck%20ABC&searchLimits=exactPhrase|||anyWords|||notWords|||requestHandler|||dateFrom=1940-01-01|||dateTo=1945-12-31|||sortby
397. *Argus, The*. (1944). Resignation of Mr Haydn Beck: ABC methods criticised. *The Argus*. 7 September 1944, p. 7. Retrieved from: https://trove.nla.gov.au/newspaper/article/11360062?searchTerm=haydn%20beck%20ABC&searchLimits=exactPhrase|||anyWords|||notWords|||requestHandler|||dateFrom=1940-01-01|||dateTo=1945-12-31|||sortby

398. *Advertiser, The.* (Adelaide). (1944). Haydn Beck's resignation: ABC Manager's explanation. *The Advertiser.* 11 September 1944. p. 6. Retrieved from: https://trove.nla.gov.au/newspaper/article/43219618?searchTerm=haydn%20beck%20ABC&searchLimits=exactPhrase|||anyWords|||notWords|||requestHandler|||dateFrom=1940-01-01|||dateTo=1945-12-31|||sortby
399. The Ormandy season refers to the first season of the orchestras after recommendations of visiting conductor Eugene Ormandy were implemented which built the state symphony orchestra to full symphonic strength.
400. *Sydney Morning Herald, The.* (1944). "Mr Moses most unfair" Haydn Beck's reply. *The Sydney Morning Herald.* 12 September 1944, p. 4. Retrieved from: https://trove.nla.gov.au/newspaper/article/17920452?searchTerm=haydn%20beck%20ABC&searchLimits=exactPhrase|||anyWords|||notWords|||requestHandler|||dateFrom=1940-01-01|||dateTo=1945-12-31|||sortby
401. Ibid., p. 162.
402. Ibid., p. 163.
403. Loc. cit.
404. Passmore, A. (2013). The other culture shock: The internal culture at CUs. *Credit Union Journal.* 17:22. 3 June 2013. 16. Retrieved from: https://search-proquest-com.wwwproxy1.library.unsw.edu.au/docview/1362107663?rfr_id=info%3Axri%2Fsid%3Aprimo
405. Harding, R. (1979). *Outside Interference: The Politics of Australian Broadcasting.* Sun Books. Melbourne. p. 14.
406. Harding, R. (1979). *Outside Interference: The Politics of Australian Broadcasting.* Sun Books. Melbourne. p. 14. Quoting A. Ashbolt. (1977). Meanjin. Issue 2.
407. Ashbolt, A. (1986). Keynote 4: The Age of Cultural Confusion [online]. In: W. Bourne. (Editor). Proceedings: *Sixth National Conference of the Australian Society for Music Education.* Australia Makes Music; Action for a Changing Society. Adelaide, SA: Australian Society for Music Education. pp. 38–43. Retrieved from: https://primoa.library.unsw.edu.au/permalink/f/11jha62/TN_informit444911808726330
408. Ashbolt, A. (2010). The vision of socialism. *Australian Socialist.* 19:1. Spring 2010. pp. 14–21. Retrieved from: https://search-informit-com-au.wwwproxy1.library.unsw.edu.au/documentSummary;dn=497288127945562;res=IELAPA
409. Semmler, C. (1981). *The ABC—Aunt Sally and Sacred Cow.* Melbourne University Press. Melbourne. p. 36.
410. Semmler, C. (1981). *The ABC—Aunt Sally and Sacred Cow.* Melbourne University Press. Melbourne. p. 36.

411. Bowman, D. (2005). Ibid.
412. Ibid.
413. Ibid.
414. Ibid.
415. Ibid.
416. Ibid.
417. A form of Bourdieu's (1991) *symbolic power*, within the organisation and he was able to exercise this through his own ***cultural capital.***

   Bourdieu (1991) said political power only existed "in and through representation, in and through trust, belief and obedience" (Bourdieu 1991). The politically powerful person, said Bourdieu, needed people to believe in him, and he "lavishes benefits on those who support him" (ibid.). Bourdieu (1991) said: Credo ... is literally "to place one's cred", that is "magical powers", in a person from whom one expects protection thanks to "believing" in him. "The kred, the credit, the charisma, the 'je ne sais quoi' with which one keeps hold over those from whom one holds it, is this product of the credo, of belief, of obedience, which seems to produce the credo, the belief, the obedience" (ibid.). ***Political capital*** could also be described as political clout and Bourdieu, quoting Marxist philosopher Antonio Gramsci, said trade union officials manifested this control as: "a banker of men in a monopoly system" (ibid.).
418. Ibid., p. 202.
419. Bowman, D. (2005). Radical giant of Australian broadcasting. *The Sydney Morning Herald*. 15 June 2005. Retrieved from: https://www.smh.com.au/national/radical-giant-of-australian-broadcasting-20050615-gdliic.html
420. Bourdieu (1991) said the man with ***political capital***: "is a champion, united by a magical relation of identification with those who, as the saying goes, 'pin their hopes on him'" (ibid.). Ashbolt, as a broadcaster acquired Bourdieu's professional capital and personal capital. Bourdieu (1991) said this was formed in a crisis situation and supported by the language of mobilisation (war). Over time, Bourdieu said while the personal capital passes away, it gets transferred or delegated as symbolic capital through "recognition and loyalties" (ibid.), and staff culture accrues.
421. The BBC has a similar series of talks called the Reith Lectures and the Canadian Broadcasting Corporation has the Massey Lectures.
422. Semmler, C. (1981). *The ABC—Aunt Sally and Sacred Cow*. Melbourne University Press. Melbourne. p. 46.
423. Ibid., p. 46.
424. Ibid., p. 47.
425. Loc. Cit.
426. Ibid., p. 49.

427. Loc. Cit.
428. Ibid.
429. Inglis, K. (1983). *This is the ABC. The Australian Broadcasting Commission 1932–1983.* Melbourne University Press. Melbourne. p. 313.
430. Inglis, K. (1983). *This is the ABC. The Australian Broadcasting Commission 1932–1983.* Melbourne University Press. Melbourne. p. 334.
431. Loc. Cit.
432. Sheridan, G. (2020). ABC's groupthink on George Pell a sin against journalism. *The Australian.* 16 April 2020. Retrieved from: https://www.theaustralian.com.au/commentary/abcs-groupthink-on-george-pell-a-sin-against-journalism/news-story/ba3a43fe6ca1d4625a3857884dfaad2c
433. Bolt, A. (2020). Andrew Bolt George Pell Blog. *The Daily Telegraph.* Retrieved from: https://www.dailytelegraph.com.au/blogs/andrew-bolt/George%20Pell
434. Donnan, P. (2020). Pell-mell and reform paths in Catholic media. *John Menadue Pearls and Irritations.* Public Policy Journal. 4 May 2020. Retrieved from: https://johnmenadue.com/peter-donnan-pell-mell-and-reform-paths-in-catholic-media/
435. *County Court of Victoria at Melbourne Criminal Division.* (2019). DPP v Pell (Sentence). His Honour Chief Judge Kidd. 13 March 2019. Retrieved from: https://content.countycourt.vic.gov.au/sites/default/files/documents/2019-03/dpp-v-pell-sentence-2019-vcc-260.pdf
436. Supreme Court of Victoria. (2019). George Pell V. The Queen. *Supreme Court of Victoria.* Retrieved from: https://www.supremecourt.vic.gov.au/case-summaries/court-of-appeal-proceedings/george-pell-v-the-queen
437. Bonyhady, N. (2019). 'We might be biased': More diverse views needed at ABC, says Buttrose. *The Sydney Morning Herald.* 29 May 2019. Retrieved from: https://www.smh.com.au/entertainment/tv-and-radio/we-might-be-bi...e-diverse-views-needed-at-abc-says-buttrose-20190529-p51sj2.html
438. Gans, H. J. (2003). *Democracy and the News.* Oxford University Press. Oxford. p. 33.
439. Henderson, G. (2020). George Pell: Fairness trampled by social media mob. *The Australian.* 11 April 2020. Retrieved from: https://www.theaustralian.com.au/inquirer/george-pell-fairness-trampled-by-social-media-mob/news-story/187e8e447ea804fa35748de1d58e452c
440. Sheridan, G. (2020). ABC's groupthink on George Pell a sin against journalism. *The Australian.* 16 April 2020. Retrieved from: https://www.theaustralian.com.au/commentary/abcs-groupthink-on-george-pell-a-sin-against-journalism/news-story/ba3a43fe6ca1d4625a3857884dfaad2c

441. Enus, A., Petersen, J., Abo, S., Brennan, F., Pope Francis & Levey, P. (2016). The Pope says Cardinal George Pell should not face a trial by media, following allegations against him, aired on Australian television. In World News Australia. *RMIT Publishing*. Melbourne (Vic.). Retrieved from: https://primoa.library.unsw.edu.au/permalink/f/11jha62/TN_informit_tvnewsTSM201608010257
442. Bowling, M. (2020). Cardinal Pell describes reaction to prosecutors, reporters and police in first television interview. *The Catholic Leader*. 15 April 2020. Retrieved from: https://catholicleader.com.au/news/cardinal-pell-describes-reaction-to-prosecutors-reporters-and-police-in-first-television-interview
443. West, A. (2020). Did a former Vatican official pay a bribe to tilt the George Pell trial? ABC. The Religion and Ethics Report. Retrieved from: https://www.abc.net.au/radionational/programs/religionandethicsreport/could-former-vatican-staffer-have-bribed-to-tilt-the-pell-case/12738792
444. Bucci, N. (2020). George Pell's lawyer calls for investigation into claim bribes paid to influence sexual assault case. The Guardian. Retrieved from: https://www.theguardian.com/australia-news/2020/oct/05/george-pells-lawyer-calls-for-investigation-into-claim-bribes-paid-to-influence-sexual-assault-case
445. As representing Bourdieu's theory of '*cultural capital*' that caters to what Bourdieu (1986) described as "bourgeois" intellectual taste, the ABC's field.
446. Chapman, R. (Ed.) (2009) *Culture Wars: An Encyclopedia of Issues, Viewpoints, and Voices (Two-Volume Set)*. M. E. Sharpe Incorporated. ProQuest Ebook Central. Retrieved from: ISBN 978 0 7656 1761.
447. Thakur, R. (2019). Cardinal Pell's guilty verdict is deeply troubling. *John Menadue: Pearls and Irritations*. 2 September 2019. Retrieved from: https://johnmenadue.com/ramesh-thakur-cardinal-pells-guilty-verdict-is-deeply-troubling/
448. Bourke, L. (2016). Furious George Pell demands Victoria Police investigation as ABC airs abuse claims. *The Sydney Morning Herald*. 28 July 2016. Retrieved from: https://www.smh.com.au/national/furious-george-pell-demands-victoria-police-investigation-as-abc-airs-abuse-claims-20160728-gqfb41.html
449. Australian Broadcasting Corporation. (2019). Guilty: The conviction of Cardinal Pell. Four Corners. *Australian Broadcasting Corporation*. 4 March 2019. Retrieved from: https://www.abc.net.au/4corners/guilty:-the-conviction-of-cardinal-pell/10869116
450. MediaWatch. (2020). Pell—The final verdict. *Australian Broadcasting Corporation*. 20 April 2020. Retrieved from: https://www.abc.net.au/mediawatch/episodes/pell/12166274

451. *Royal Commission into Institutional Responses to Child Sexual Abuse.* (2017). Final Report. Royal Commission into Institutional Responses to Child Sexual Abuse. Retrieved from: https://www.childabuseroyalcommission.gov.au/
452. Dunstan, J., Longbottom, J., Farnsworth, S., King, C. (2020). George Pell 'surprised' by royal commission finding he was told of Ridsdale abuse. *ABC News.* 7 May 2020. Retrieved from: https://www.abc.net.au/news/2020-05-07/royal-commission-findings-on-cardinal-george-pell-released/12217362
453. Paulson. M. (2002). World doesn't share US view of scandal: clergy sexual abuse reaches far, receives an uneven focus. *The Boston Globe.* 8 April 2002. Retrieved from: http://archive.boston.com/globe/spotlight/abuse/print/040802_world.htm
454. USA Today. (2004). Religion. USW Today. 19 June 20014. Retrieved from: https://usatoday30.usatoday.com/news/religion/2004-06-19-church-abuse_x.htm
455. British Broadcasting Corporation. (2009). Police Examine Sex Abuse Report. *British Broadcasting Corporation.* 25 May 2009. Retrieved from: http://news.bbc.co.uk/2/hi/uk_news/northern_ireland/8066994.stm
456. *BBC News.* (2011). The Cloyne Report: A detailed guide. 13 July 2011. Retrieved from: https://www.bbc.com/news/uk-northern-ireland-14143822
457. *Irish Times, The* (2011). Taoiseach's speech on Cloyne motion. 20 July 2011. Retrieved from: https://www.irishtimes.com/news/taoiseach-s-speech-on-cloyne-motion-1.880466
458. *BBC News.* (2011). The Cloyne Report: A detailed guide. 13 July 2011. Retrieved from: https://www.bbc.com/news/uk-northern-ireland-14143822
459. https://about.abc.net.au/statements/the-abcs-reporting-on-cardinal-george-pell/
460. Bolt, A. (2020). High Court: Pell Innocent. Andrew Bolt Blog Posts. *The Herald Sun.* 7 April 2020. Retrieved from: https://www.heraldsun.com.au/blogs/andrew-bolt/high-court-pell-innocent/news-story/655c1462896c6ac287391203137d7d8b
461. Bolt, A. (2020). High Court: Pell Innocent. Andrew Bolt Blog Posts. *Herald Sun.* 7 April 2020. Retrieved from: https://www.heraldsun.com.au/blogs/andrew-bolt/high-court-pell-innocent/news-story/655c1462896c6ac287391203137d7d8b
462. *County Court of Victoria at Melbourne Criminal Division.* (2019). DPP v Pell (Sentence). His Honour Chief Judge Kidd. 13 March 2019.

Retrieved from: https://content.countycourt.vic.gov.au/sites/default/files/documents/2019-03/dpp-v-pell-sentence-2019-vcc-260.pdf

463. Smith, Z. (2020). 'Unjust' to take accusations as gospel. *The Herald-Sun*. 14 April 2020. Retrieved from: https://www.pressreader.com/australia/herald-sun/20200414/281547998017480
464. "Culture Wars" was a term first used by campaigning US Republican Catholic conservative presidential nominee, Patrick Buchanan, in 1992. He believed the polarising of beliefs in the "culture wars" had taken the place of the Cold War (Rust, M. (1993). An old soldier fights a new war. *Insight on the News*, *9*(29), 6. http://search.proquest.com/docview/205873827/). It was borrowed from the German *kulturkampf*, used in the 1870s by German Chancellor von Bismarck in his rejection of Roman Catholic Church influence.
465. Australian Broadcasting Corporation. (2020). George Pell says 'culture wars' contributed to him being wrongfully jailed for child sexual abuse. *Australian Broadcasting Corporation*. 14 April 2020. Retrieved from: https://www.abc.net.au/news/2020-04-14/cardinal-george-pell-andrew-bolt-sky-news-interview/12146594
466. Australian Broadcasting Corporation. (2020). Read the full judgement summary from George Pell's successful High Court of Australia appeal. *Australian Broadcasting Corporation*. 7 April 2020 Retrieved from: https://www.abc.net.au/news/2020-04-07/george-pell-high-court-of-australia-full-judgment-summary/12128468
467. ABC. (2020). Interview ABC News24. Strapline: "Pell released. George Pell freed from prison after High Court ruling." April 2020. Retrieved from: https://www.youtube.com/watch?v=7x29VznAZOE Dur: 7′09″.
468. Margetts, J., Brown, M., staff (2016). Cardinal George Pell 'too ill' to travel from Rome for child sex abuse inquiry. *Australian Broadcasting Corporation*. 5 February 2016. Retrieved from https://www.abc.net.au/news/2016-02-05/cardinal-george-pell-too-ill-to-child-sex-abuse-inquiry-lawyers/7140584
469. Quadrant. (2016). The ABC's cardinal sins. *Quadrant*. 6 February 2016. Retrieved from: https://quadrant.org.au/abcs-cardinal-sins/
470. Margetts, J., Brown, M., staff (2016). Cardinal George Pell 'too ill' to travel from Rome for child sex abuse inquiry. *Australian Broadcasting Corporation*. 5 February 2016. Retrieved from: https://www.abc.net.au/news/2016-02-05/cardinal-george-pell-too-ill-to-child-sex-abuse-inquiry-lawyers/7140584
471. Barrett, A. W., & Barrington, L. W. (2005). Is a Picture Worth a Thousand Words?: Newspaper Photographs and Voter Evaluations of Political Candidates. *Harvard International Journal of Press/Politics*.

10:4. pp. 98–113. Retrieved from: https://doi.org/10.1177/1081180X05281392

472. Werner, W. (2004). "What Does This Picture Say?" Reading the Intertextuality of Visual Images. *International Journal of Social Education*. 19. Retrieved from: https://eric.ed.gov/?id=EJ718728
473. Gamson, W., Croteau, D., Hoynes, W., Sasson, T. 1992 "Media Images and the Social Construction of Reality". *Annual Review of Sociology*. 18. pp. 373–393. Retrieved from: http://search.proquest.com/docview/199734271/
474. Tuchman, G. (1978). Making News: A Study in the Construction of Reality. *Social Forces*. 59:4. January 1978 Retrieved from: https://doi.org/10.2307/2578016
475. Weaver, D. (Ed.) (1998). *The Global Journalist: News People Around the World*. Hampton Press. Creskill, NJ.
476. Tiffen, R. (1989). *News and Power*. Allen & Unwin. Sydney.
477. Josephi, B. 2000 "Newsroom research: its importance for journalism studies". *Australian Journalism Review*. 22:2. pp. 75–87. Retrieved from: https://primoa.library.unsw.edu.au/permalink/f/11jha62/TN_informit_apaft200204995
478. Johnson, K. A. (2020). I Got a New Puppy! The Impact of Personal, Opinion, and Objective Tweets on a Journalist's and a News Organization's Perceived Credibility. *Journalism Practice*. 14:1. pp. 48–66. Retrieved from: https://doi.org/10.1080/17512786.2019.1597637
479. *Royal Commission into Institutional Responses to Child Sexual Abuse*. (2017). Final Report. Royal Commission into Institutional Responses to Child Sexual Abuse. Retrieved from: https://www.childabuseroyalcommission.gov.au/
480. Barthes, R. (1977). Image Music Text. (transl. S. Heath). Fontana Books. Hammersmith London. p. 20.
481. Vanstone, A. (2019). Media members have lead roles, too. 28 October 2019. *The Sydney Morning Herald*.
482. Gustafson, K.L. & Kenix, L.J. (2016) Visually Framing Press Freedom and Responsibility of a Massacre: Photographic and Graphic Images in Charlie Hebdo's Newspaper Front Pages Around the World. *Visual Communication Quarterly*. 23:3. pp. 147–160. https://doi.org/10.1080/15551393.2016.1190623
483. AFP. (2020). History teacher decapitated in France after showing Mohammed cartoons. 17 October 2020. *The Australian*. Retrieved from: https://www.theaustralian.com.au/world/history-teacher-decapitated-in-france-after-showing-mohammed-cartoons/news-story/9df25c93d927f22a26a381d2ea6446a7

484. Catholic Archdiocese of Melbourne. (N.D.) Melbourne Response. *Catholic Archdiocese of Melbourne*. Retrieved from: https://www.cam.org.au/en-us/Safeguarding-Children-Young-People-and-Vulnerable-Persons/Melbourne-Response
485. Marr, D. (2013). *The Prince: Faith, Abuse, George Pell*. Quarterly Essay 51. Black Inc. Melbourne.
486. Toscano, N. & Lee, J. (2015). Cardinal George Pell denies allegations of involvement in abuse cover-up. *The Sydney Morning Herald*. 21 May 2015. Retrieved from: https://www.smh.com.au/national/cardinal-george-pell-denies-allegations-of-involvement-in-abuse-coverup-20150520-gh67ml.html
487. Marr, D. (2013). *The Prince: Faith, Abuse, George Pell*. Quarterly Essay 51. Black Inc. Melbourne. p. 6.
488. Marr, D. (2013). *The Prince: Faith, Abuse, George Pell*. Quarterly Essay 51. Black Inc. Melbourne. p. 8.
489. Atherton, B. (2012). Pell accuses press of exaggerating Catholic abuse. *ABC*. 13 November 2012. Retrieved from: https://www.abc.net.au/news/2012-11-13/pell-accuses-press-of-exaggerating-catholic-abuse/4369214
490. Atherton, B. (2012). Pell accuses press of exaggerating Catholic abuse. *ABC*. 13 November 2012. Retrieved from: https://www.abc.net.au/news/2012-11-13/pell-accuses-press-of-exaggerating-catholic-abuse/4369214
491. Toronto Star. (2002). Australian Archbishop accused of child abuse. *Toronto Star*. 21 August 2002. p. 3. Retrieved from: https://search-proquest-com.wwwproxy1.library.unsw.edu.au/docview/438492151?rfr_id=info%3Axri%2Fsid%3Aprimo
492. Toronto Star. (2002). Australian Archbishop accused of child abuse. *Toronto Star*. 21 August 2002. p. 3. Retrieved from: https://search-proquest-com.wwwproxy1.library.unsw.edu.au/docview/438492151?rfr_id=info%3Axri%2Fsid%3Aprimo
493. *Australian Financial Review, The*. (2020). Pell's acquittal is justice served. The Australian Financial Review. 8 April 2020. Retrieved from https://www.afr.com/politics/federal/pell-s-acquittal-is-justice-served-20200407-p54hzs
494. Davey, M. (2019). Inside the Pell trial: we sat in court for months, forbidden from reporting a word. *The Guardian*. 27 February 2019. Retrieved from: https://www.theguardian.com/australia-news/2019/feb/27/inside-the-pell-trial-we-sat-in-court-for-months-forbidden-from-reporting-a-word
495. McNair, B. (1994). *News and Journalism in the UK*. Routledge. London & New York. p. 48.

496. Cohen, S. (2002). *Folk Devils and Moral Panics*. 3rd Edition. First published 1972. Routledge. London & New York. p. 1.
497. Cohen, S. (2011). Whose side were we on? The undeclared politics of moral panic theory. *Crime Media Culture*. 7:3. pp. 237–243. Retrieved from: https://doi.org/10.1177/1741659011417603
498. Cohen, S. (2011). Whose side were we on? The undeclared politics of moral panic theory. *Crime Media Culture*. 7:3. pp. 237–243. Retrieved from: https://doi.org/10.1177/1741659011417603. p. 241.
499. McCarthy, J. (2018). 'Catholic Church has a lot to answer for': Philip Wilson's conviction overturned. *The Sydney Morning Herald*. 6 December 2018. Retrieved from: https://www.smh.com.au/national/nsw/catholic-church-has-a-lot-to-answer-for-philip-wilson-s-conviction-overturned-20181206-p50kqg.html
500. Skidmore, P. (1995). "Telling tales: Media power, Ideology and the Reporting of Child Sexual Abuse in Britain. In *Crime and the Media: A Post-modern Spectacle*. Ed. D. Kidd-Hewitt & R. Osborne. Pluto Press. London & East Haven CT.
501. Kirby, M. (2002). Law and media: adversaries or allies in safeguarding freedom? *Southern Cross University Law Review*. 6. 2002. pp. 1–7. Retrieved from: https://primoa.library.unsw.edu.au/permalink/f/11jha62/TN_informit_agis20033704
502. Kirby, M. (2002). Law and media : adversaries or allies in safeguarding freedom? *Southern Cross University Law Review*. 6. 2002. pp. 1–7. Retrieved from: https://primoa.library.unsw.edu.au/permalink/f/11jha62/TN_informit_agis20033704
503. Drozdek, A. (2015). Media Ethics. In *International Encyclopedia of the Social & Behavioral Sciences: Second Edition* (pp. 42–47). Elsevier Inc. Retrieved from: https://doi.org/10.1016/B978-0-08-097086-8.11017-7
504. Drozdek, A. (2015). Media Ethics. In *International Encyclopedia of the Social & Behavioral Sciences: Second Edition* (pp. 42–47). Elsevier Inc. in J. Gamson. Celebrity. pp. 274–278. Citing Rojek, 2001, p. 90. Retrieved from: https://doi.org/10.1016/B978-0-08-097086-8.11017-7
505. Sharman, R. (2019). The psychological reason why some can't believe the evidence against George Pell and Michael Jackson. *Australian Broadcasting Corporation*. 13 March 2019. Retrieved from: https://www.abc.net.au/news/2019-03-13/george-pell-michael-jackson-cognitive-dissonance/10892948
506. Percy, K. (2019). George Pell trial suppression orders breached by news organisations, Victorian prosecutor alleges. *Australian Broadcasting Corporation*. 26 March 2019. Retrieved from: https://www.abc.net.au/news/2019-03-26/journalists-accused-of-breaking-george-pell-suppression-order/10939980

507. Younger, E. (2019). George Pell media contempt case could have 'chilling effect' on open justice, court hears. *Australian Broadcasting Corporation*. 15 April 2019. Retrieved from: https://www.abc.net.au/news/2019-04-15/george-pell-guilty-verdict-coverage-media-contempt-case/11002760
508. Davey, M. (2019). Inside the Pell trial: we sat in court for months, forbidden from reporting a word. *The Guardian*. 27 February 2019. Retrieved from: https://www.theguardian.com/australia-news/2019/feb/27/inside-the-pell-trial-we-sat-in-court-for-months-forbidden-from-reporting-a-word
509. Davey, M. (2019). Inside the Pell trial: we sat in court for months, forbidden from reporting a word. *The Guardian*. 27 February 2019. Retrieved from: https://www.theguardian.com/australia-news/2019/feb/27/inside-the-pell-trial-we-sat-in-court-for-months-forbidden-from-reporting-a-word
510. Aristotle. (2007) Transl. G.A. Kennedy. *On Rhetoric*. Book 1. Chap. 1. pp. 31–32. 2nd Edition. Oxford University Press. New York, Oxford.
511. Luzung, A. (2004). Contempt by publication: improving the law on court reporting by the media [online]. *Reform*. 85. Summer 2004/2005. pp. 27–30. 59. Retrieved from: https://search-informit-com-au.www-proxy1.library.unsw.edu.au/fullText;dn=20051670;res=AGISPT ISSN: 0313-153X.
512. Swannie, B.J. (2019). In Australia, criticising a judge can land you in jail. This is a danger for democracy. *The Conversation*. 4 July 2019. Retrieved from: https://theconversation.com/in-australia-criticising-a-judge-can-land-you-in-jail-this-is-a-danger-for-democracy-119296
513. Gleeson, C. (2013/14). Social media and the courts [online]. *Bar News: The Journal of the NSW Bar Association*. Summer 2013–2014. pp. 54–59. Retrieved from: https://search-informit-com-au.wwwproxy1.library.unsw.edu.au/documentSummary;dn=125912803397523;res=IELHSS ISSN: 0817-0002.
514. Juries Victoria (2020). Attending for Jury Service. *Juries Victoria*. 6 April 2020. https://www.juriesvictoria.vic.gov.au/individuals/attending-for-jury-service
515. Eddie, R. (2020). High Court sets the date for George Pall's final appeal. *The Sydney Morning Herald*. 14 February 2020. Retrieved from: https://www.smh.com.au/national/high-court-sets-the-date-for-george-pell-s-final-appeal-20200214-p540ub.html
516. Waterhouse-Watson, D. (2016). News media on trial: towards a feminist ethics of reporting footballer sexual assault trials. *Feminist Media Studies*. 16:6. pp. 952–967. Retrieved from: https://doi.org/10.1080/14680777.2016.1162827

517. Waterhouse-Watson, D. (2016). News media on trial: towards a feminist ethics of reporting footballer sexual assault trials. *Feminist Media Studies* 16:6. pp. 952–967. Retrieved from: https://doi.org/10.1080/14680777.2016.1162827. p. 952.
518. Waterhouse-Watson, D. (2016). News media on trial: towards a feminist ethics of reporting footballer sexual assault trials. *Feminist Media Studies* 16:6. pp. 952–967. Retrieved from: https://doi.org/10.1080/14680777.2016.1162827. p. 955.
519. Waterhouse-Watson, D. (2016). News media on trial: towards a feminist ethics of reporting footballer sexual assault trials. *Feminist Media Studies* 16:6. pp. 952–967. Retrieved from: https://doi.org/10.1080/14680777.2016.1162827. p. 956.
520. Waterhouse-Watson, D. (2016). News media on trial: towards a feminist ethics of reporting footballer sexual assault trials. *Feminist Media Studies* 16:6. pp. 952–967. Retrieved from: https://doi.org/10.1080/14680777.2016.1162827. p. 956.
521. Waterhouse-Watson, D. (2016). News media on trial: towards a feminist ethics of reporting footballer sexual assault trials. *Feminist Media Studies* 16:6. pp. 952–967. Retrieved from: https://doi.org/10.1080/14680777.2016.1162827. p. 956.
522. Ward, S.J.A. (2014). Radical Media Ethics: Ethics for a global digital world. *Digital Journalism*. 2:4. pp. 455–471. Retrieved from: https://doi.org/10.1080/21670811.2014.952985
523. Ward, S.J.A. (2014). Radical Media Ethics: Ethics for a global digital world. *Digital Journalism*. 2:4. pp. 455–471. Retrieved from: https://doi.org/10.1080/21670811.2014.952985. p. 457.
524. Ward, S.J.A. (2014). Radical Media Ethics: Ethics for a global digital world. *Digital Journalism*. 2:4. pp. 455–471. Retrieved from: https://doi.org/10.1080/21670811.2014.952985. p. 468.
525. Masquelier, C. (2019) Bourdieu, Foucault and the politics of precarity. *Distinktion: Journal of Social Theory*. 20:2. pp. 135–155. Retrieved from: https://doi.org/10.1080/1600910X.2018.1549999
526. Standing, G. (2011). *The Precariat: The New Dangerous Class*. Bloomsbury Academic. London. Retrieved from: https://doi.org/10.5040/9781849664554
527. Bourdieu's (1977) theoretical model described a symbolic role of activities that identified power relations and supported a designated field, which in this instance the journalist has legitimate domination of the field of journalism built up by his/her own cultural practices, or '*habitus*', in addition they know the rules of that field (*doxa*) in Bourdieu's (1985) 'sub-*field*'; and, in this instance (Table 3.1).

528. Brown, R.S. (2010). Sampling. (Eds. P. Peterson, E. Baker & B. McGaw). *International Encyclopedia of Education* (Third Edition). Elsevier. pp. 142–146. Elsevier Ltd. Retrieved from: https://doi.org/10.1016/B978-0-08-044894-7.00294-3
529. Merriam, S.B. (2010). Qualitative Case Studies. Eds.: P. Peterson, E. Baker & B. McGaw. *International Encyclopedia of Education* (Third Edition). Elsevier. pp. 456–462. Retrieved from: https://doi.org/10.1016/B978-0-08-044894-7.01532-3. p. 457
530. Berger, A. A. (1998). *Media Research Techniques.* (2nd ed.). Sage Publications: Thousand Oaks.
531. Dor, D. (2003). On newspaper headlines as relevance optimizers. *Journal of Pragmatics.* 35:5. pp. 695–721. Retrieved from: https://doi.org/10.1016/S0378-2166(02)00134-0
532. Former editor of *The Sunday Times* (1967–1981) and *The Times* (1981–1982) newspapers, London.
533. Schudson, M. (2008). *Why Democracies Need an Unlovable Press.* Polity Press. Cambridge. p. 45.
534. Flores, R. (2002). Press Headlines on the Internet: An Aspectual Analysis. *Signos Literarios y Linguisticos.* 4:1. pp. 45–57. Retrieved from: http://search.proquest.com/docview/85615892/
535. Xie, Q. (2018). Analysis of Intertextuality in English News Headlines. (Report). *Theory and Practice in Language Studies.* 8:8. pp. 1010–1014. Retrieved from: https://doi.org/10.17507/tpls.0808.13
536. Kobre, S. (1955). *News behind the headlines: background reporting of significant social problems* (p. iv+204). University of California. Berkeley. Retrieved from: http://hdl.handle.net/2027/uc1.b3552959
537. Altheide, D. & Schneider, C. (2013). Process of qualitative document analysis. In Altheide, D., & Schneider, C. *Qualitative Media Analysis* (pp. 38–74). SAGE Publications. London. Retrieved from: https://doi.org/10.4135/9781452270043 Quoting D. Altheide (2002) p. 4.
538. Munt, S. R. (2017). Argumentum ad misericordiam: the cultural politics of victim media. *Feminist Media Studies.* 17:5. pp. 866–883. Retrieved from: https://doi.org/10.1080/14680777.2016.1259176
539. Dukes, K. N., & Gaither, S. E. (2017). Black Racial Stereotypes and Victim Blaming: Implications for Media Coverage and Criminal Proceedings in Cases of Police Violence against Racial and Ethnic Minorities. *Journal Of Social Issues.* 73:4. pp. 789–807. Retrieved from: https://doi.org/10.1111/josi.12248
540. Furedi, F. (2006). *Culture of Fear Revisited: Risk-taking and the Morality of Low Expectation.* 4th Edition. Continuum. London & New York. p. vii.

541. Furedi, F. (2006). *Culture of Fear Revisited: Risk-taking and the Morality of Low Expectation*. 4th Edition. Continuum. London & New York. p. xvi–xvii.
542. Furedi, F. (2006). *Culture of Fear Revisited: Risk-taking and the Morality of Low Expectation*. 4th Edition. Continuum. London & New York. p. 82.
543. Furedi, F. (2006). *Culture of Fear Revisited: Risk-taking and the Morality of Low Expectation*. 4th Edition. Continuum. London & New York. p. 85.
544. Furedi, F. (2006). *Culture of Fear Revisited: Risk-taking and the Morality of Low Expectation*. 4th Edition. Continuum. London & New York. p. 150.
545. Furedi, F. (2006). *Culture of Fear Revisited: Risk-taking and the Morality of Low Expectation*. 4th Edition. Continuum. London & New York. p. 178.
546. Furedi, F. (2006). *Culture of Fear Revisited: Risk-taking and the Morality of Low Expectation*. 4th Edition. Continuum. London & New York. p. 178.
547. Furedi, F. (2006). *Culture of Fear Revisited: Risk-taking and the Morality of Low Expectation*. 4th Edition. Continuum. London & New York. p. 191.
548. Curran, J. & Seaton, J. (1997). *Power without Responsibility: The Press and Broadcasting in Britain*. 5th Edition. Routledge. London & New York. p. 285.
549. Curran, J. & Seaton, J. (1997). *Power without Responsibility: The Press and Broadcasting in Britain*. 5th Edition. Routledge. London & New York. p. 285.
550. Altheide, D.L. & Schneider, C. (2013). Process of qualitative document analysis. In Altheide, D., & Schneider, C. *Qualitative Media Analysis* (pp. 38–74). SAGE Publications. London. Retrieved from: https://doi.org/10.4135/9781452270043
551. Altheide, D.L. & Schneider, C. (2013). Process of qualitative document analysis. In Altheide, D., & Schneider, C. *Qualitative Media Analysis* (pp. 38–74). SAGE Publications. London. Retrieved from: https://doi.org/10.4135/9781452270043
552. Altheide, D.L. (1996). *Qualitative Media Analysis (Qualitative Research Methods. 38)*. Sage Publications. Thousand Oaks, California.
553. Bourke, L. (2016). Furious George Pell demands Victoria Police investigation as ABC airs abuse claims. *The Sydney Morning Herald*. 28 July 2016. Retrieved from: https://www.smh.com.au/national/furious-george-pell-demands-victoria-police-investigation-as-abc-airs-abuse-claims-20160728-gqfb41.html
554. van Acker, E. (2003). Media Representations of Women Politicians in Australia and New Zealand: High Expectations, Hostility or Stardom. *Policy and Society*. 22:1. pp. 116–136. https://doi.org/10.1016/S1449-4035(03)70016-2
555. Chakvetadze, L., Dautova, R., & Shakurova, A. (2016). Gender Stereotypes, Mass Media and Migrants. *Journal of Organizational*

Culture, Communications and Conflict. 20. pp. 39–45. Retrieved from: http://search.proquest.com/docview/1827843344/

556. Goodall, H. (2012). Media's Influence on Gender Stereotypes. *Media Asia*. 39:3. pp. 160–163. Retrieved from: https://doi.org/10.1080/01296612.2012.11689932
557. Butler, J. (1990). *Gender Trouble: Feminism and the Subversion of Identity*. Routledge. New York & London.
558. Butler, J. (1993). *Bodies that Matter: On the Discursive Limits of "sex"*. Routledge. New York & London. p. x.
559. Berger, A. A. (1998). *Media Research Techniques*. SAGE Publications. ProQuest Ebook Central. Retrieved from: http://ebookcentral.proquest.com/lib/unsw/detail.action?docID=997016
560. Höijer, B. (2011). Social representations theory: A new theory for media research. *Nordicom Review*. 32:2. pp. 3–16. Retrieved from: https://doi.org/10.1515/nor-2017-0109
561. Höijer, B. (2011). Social representations theory: A new theory for media research. *Nordicom Review*. 32:2. pp. 3–16. Retrieved from: https://doi.org/10.1515/nor-2017-0109. p. 10.
562. Brown, R.S. (2010). Sampling. Eds. P. Peterson, E. Baker & B. McGaw. *International Encyclopedia of Education* (Third Edition). Elsevier. pp. 142–146. Elsevier Ltd. Retrieved from: https://doi.org/10.1016/B978-0-08-044894-7.00294-3
563. Lackey, D. & AAP (2020). High-profile George Pell supporter accuses the ABC of acting as a 'cheer squad' to have the cardinal jailed in a VERY fiery interview on the public broadcaster. *The Daily Mail*. 7 April 2020. Retrieved from: https://www.dailymail.co.uk/news/article-8195489/George-Pell-supporter-accuses-ABC-acting-cheer-squad-cardinal-jailed.html
564. ABC. (2020). Interview ABC News24. Strapline: "Pell released. George Pell freed from prison after High Court ruling." April 2020. Retrieved from: https://www.youtube.com/watch?v=7x29VznAZOE
    Dur: 7′09″.
565. Kelling, K., & Thomas, R. J. (2018). The roles and functions of opinion journalists. *Newspaper Research Journal*. 39:4. pp. 398–419. Retrieved from: https://doi.org/10.1177/0739532918806899
566. Kelling, K., & Thomas, R. J. (2018). The roles and functions of opinion journalists. *Newspaper Research Journal*. 39:4. pp. 398–419. Retrieved from: https://doi.org/10.1177/0739532918806899
567. Lawrence, R.G. (2012). "Campaign News in the Time of Twitter: An Observational Study". Prepared for presentation at the annual meeting of the *American Political Science Association*. New Orleans. August 30–September 2, 2012.

568. ABC. (2020). Interview ABC News24. Strapline: "Pell released. George Pell freed from prison after High Court ruling." April 2020. Retrieved from: https://www.youtube.com/watch?v=7x29VznAZOE
Dur: 7′09″.
569. McMurtrie, C. (2020). Why the ABC's reporting of the George Pell case wasn't a witch-hunt. *Australian Broadcasting Corporation*. 11 April 2020. Retrieved from: https://www.abc.net.au/news/about/backstory/news-coverage/2020-04-11/why-the-abc-reporting-of-the-pell-case-was-not-a-witch-hunt/12137620
570. Australian Broadcasting Corporation. (2019). Victorian Chief Justice says Pell "is not to be made a scapegoat". *Australian Broadcasting Corporation*. 21 August 2019. Retrieved from: https://www.abc.net.au/news/2019-08-21/judge-says-pell-isnt-to-be-made-scapegoat/11434086
571. Al Jazeera. (2020). 'Decisive measures' in Beijing as coronavirus cases spike: Live blog. *Al Jazeera*. 15 June 2020. Retrieved from: https://www.aljazeera.com/news/2020/06/measures-beijing-coronavirus-cases-spike-live-200614233622226.html
572. Regencia, T. (2020). Maria Ressa found guilty in blow to Philippines' press freedom. *Al Jazeera*. 15 June 2020. Retrieved from: https://www.aljazeera.com/news/2020/06/philippine-court-rappler-maria-ressa-guilty-cyberlibel-200614210221502.html
573. *Reporters Sans Frontières*. (2020). 2020 World Press Freedom Index. Reporters Sans Frontières. Retrieved from: https://rsf.org/en/ranking
574. Warren, M. (2005). What separation of powers? (Australia). *Monash University Law Review*. 31:1. Retrieved from: ISSN: 0311-3140.
575. Dowsley, A. & Deery, A. (2020). Freed George Pell faces new abuse claims. *The Herald Sun*. 13 April 2020. Retrieved from: https://global-factiva-com.ezproxy2.library.usyd.edu.au/ha/default.aspx#./!?&_suid=158683457315200967428676337888l
576. Ferguson, J. (2018). George Pell committal: extraordinary scenes inside court 22. *The Australian*. 30 March 2018. Retrieved from: https://www.theaustralian.com.au/nation/inquirer/george-pell-committal-extraordinary-scenes-inside-court-22/news-story/bf3e7f5bafed31e451d3b1680a1776fb
577. Smith, Z. (2020). Pell attacks system. *The Herald Sun*. 14 April 2020. Retrieved from: https://global-factiva-com.ezproxy2.library.usyd.edu.au/ha/default.aspx#./!?&_suid=1586834573152009674286763378881
578. *Sky News*. (2020). Rule of law 'was not extended' to George Pell. Interview with Frank Brennan SJ. *Sky News*. 8 April 2020. Retrieved from: https://www.skynews.com.au/details/_6147968194001

579. *Sky News.* (2020). Rule of law 'was not extended' to George Pell. Interview with Frank Brennan SJ. *Sky News.* 8 April 2020. Retrieved from: https://www.skynews.com.au/details/_6147968194001
580. Sky News (2020). Rule of law 'was not extended' to George Pell. Interview with Frank Brennan SJ. 8 April 2020. Retrieved from: https://www.skynews.com.au/details/_6147968194001
581. Bourdieu (1983) said "the accumulation has to be reproduced with every generation or it is lost".
582. ABC. (2020). Interview ABC News24. Strapline: "Pell released. George Pell freed from prison after High Court ruling." April 2020. Retrieved from: https://www.youtube.com/watch?v=7x29VznAZOE
Dur: 7'09".
583. King, L. (2018). Rupert Murdoch, Mischief-Maker on a Global Scale. *Inside Sources.* 20 July 2018. Retrieved from: https://www.insidesources.com/rupert-murdoch-mischief-maker-global-scale/
584. Benson, R. (2012). Murdoch in the United States: Kingmaker or Ringmaster? *Global Media and Communication.* 8:1. pp. 4–7. Retrieved from: https://www.researchgate.net/publication/330508663_Murdoch_in_the_United_States_Kingmaker_or_Ringmaster_Global_Media_and_Communication_8_1_2012_4-7/citation/download
585. A reference to the French King Louis XIV, who centralised power and about whom all power revolved, hence "sun". He built the Versailles Palace as his court and reigned for 72 years.
586. Hasan, M. (2011). Is there a more sickening sight than leaders sucking up to the sun king? *New Statesman.* 11 July. 140:23. Retrieved from: http://ezproxy.library.usyd.edu.au/login?url=https://search-proquest-com.ezproxy1.library.usyd.edu.au/docview/876179782?accountid=14757
587. Evans, H. (2015). How Thatcher and Murdoch made their secret deal. *The Guardian.* 28 April 2015. Retrieved from: https://www.theguardian.com/uk-news/2015/apr/28/how-margaret-thatcher-and-rupert-murdoch-made-secret-deal
588. Hallin, D.C. in A. Drozdek. (2015). Media Ethics. In *International Encyclopedia of the Social & Behavioral Sciences: Second Edition* (pp. 42–47). Journalism. pp. 851–856. Elsevier Inc. Retrieved from: https://doi.org/10.1016/B978-0-08-097086-8.11017-7
589. Hallin, D.C. in A. Drozdek. (2015). Media Ethics. In *International Encyclopedia of the Social & Behavioral Sciences: Second Edition* (pp. 42–47). Journalism. p. 855. Elsevier Inc. Retrieved from: https://doi.org/10.1016/B978-0-08-097086-8.11017-7
590. Fasoli, F., Maass, A., & Carnaghi, A. (2015). Labelling and discrimination: do homophobic epithets undermine fair distribution of resources?

The British Journal of Social Psychology. 54:2. pp. 383–393. Retrieved from: https://doi.org/10.1111/bjso.12090

591. Harsányi, G. & Carbon, C. (2015). How Perception Affects Racial Categorization: On the Influence of Initial Visual Exposure on Labelling People as Diverse Individuals or Racial Subjects. *Perception*. 44:1. pp. 100–102. Retrieved from: https://doi.org/10.1068/p7854
592. Wood, G., & Schaffer, B. (1985). *Labelling in Development Policy: Essays in Honour of Bernard Schaffer*. Sage Publications. New York.
593. Howell, A., Ulan, J., & Powell, R. (2014). Essentialist beliefs, stigmatizing attitudes, and low empathy predict greater endorsement of noun labels applied to people with mental disorders. *Personality and Individual Differences*. 66. Retrieved from: https://doi.org/10.1016/j.paid.2014.03.008
594. West, K. & Lloyd, J. (2017). The Role of Labelling and Bias in the Portrayals of Acts of "Terrorism": Media Representations of Muslims vs. Non-Muslims. *Journal of Muslim Minority Affairs*. 37:2. pp. 211–222. Retrieved from: https://doi.org/10.1080/13602004.2017.1345103
595. Hamborg, F., Zhukova, A. & Gipp, B. (2019). "Automated Identification of Media Bias by Word Choice and Labelling in News Articles," *2019 ACM/IEEE Joint Conference on Digital Libraries (JCDL)*. Champaign, Il. pp. 196–205. Retrieved from: https://doi.org/10.1109/JCDL.2019.00036
596. Eyben, R. & Moncrieffe, J. Eds. (2007). *The Power of Labelling: How People Are Categorized and Why It Matters*. Earthscan London and Sterling VA. p. 7.
597. Harcup, T. (2014). *A Dictionary of Journalism*. Oxford University Press. Retrieved from: https://www-oxfordreference-com.ezproxy1.library.usyd.edu.au/view/10.1093/acref/9780199646241.001.0001/acref-9780199646241
598. Vine, P. (2017). When is a journalist not a journalist? Negotiating a new form of advocacy journalism within the environmental movement [online]. *Pacific Journalism Review*. 23:1. Jul 2017. pp. 43–54. Retrieved from: https://doi.org/10.24135/pjr.v23i1.212
599. Ernst, H. (2010). Whither Advocacy Journalism? *World Future Review*. 2:6. pp. 43–46. Retrieved from: https://doi.org/10.1177/194675671000200606
600. Ernst, H. (2010). Whither Advocacy Journalism? *World Future Review*. 2:6. pp. 43–46. Retrieved from: https://doi.org/10.1177/194675671000200606 p. 45.
601. Wade, L. (2011). Journalism, advocacy and the social construction of consensus. *Media, Culture & Society*. 33:8. pp. 1166–1184. Retrieved from: https://doi.org/10.1177/0163443711418273

602. Wade, L. (2011). Journalism, advocacy and the social construction of consensus. *Media, Culture & Society. 33:*8). pp. 1166–1184. Retrieved from: https://doi.org/10.1177/0163443711418273
603. Fisher, C. (2016). The advocacy continuum: Towards a theory of advocacy in journalism. *Journalism.* 17:6. pp. 711–726. Retrieved from: https://doi.org/10.1177/1464884915582311
604. Nerone, J., & Barnhurst, K. G. (2003). US newspaper types, the newsroom, and the division of labor, 1750–2000. *Journalism Studies.* 4:4. pp. 435–449. Retrieved from: https://doi.org/10.1080/1461670032000136541
605. Blach-Ørsten, M. and Burkal, R. (2014). Credibility and the Media as a Political Institution. *Nordicom Review.* 35. pp. 67–79. Retrieved from: https://primoa.library.unsw.edu.au/permalink/f/11jha62/TN_scopus2-s2.0-84907170653
606. Blach-Ørsten, M. and Burkal, R. (2014). Credibility and the Media as a Political Institution. *Nordicom Review.* 35. pp. 67–79. Retrieved from: https://primoa.library.unsw.edu.au/permalink/f/11jha62/TN_scopus2-s2.0-84907170653
607. Schudson, M. (2005). "The Virtues of an Unlovable Press." Intro. *Political Quarterly.* Supp. 1:76. 2 August. pp. 23–32. Retrieved from: https://doi.org/10.1111/j.1467-923X.2006.00745.x
608. Shanahan, L. (2019). ABC Staff Push for Climate Group. *The Australian.* 17 November 2019. Retrieved from: https://www.theaustralian.com.au/business/media/abc-staff-propose-climate-group/news-story/50af6696dbff695d103f9fba77f1ed05
609. Meade, A. (2019). ABC journalists' climate crisis group survives political heat. *The Guardian.* 22 November 2019. Retrieved from: https://www.theguardian.com/media/2019/nov/22/abc-journalists-climate-crisis-group-survives-political-heat
610. Meade, A. (2019). ABC journalists' climate crisis group survives political heat. *The Guardian.* 22 November 2019. Retrieved from: https://www.theguardian.com/media/2019/nov/22/abc-journalists-climate-crisis-group-survives-political-heat
611. Bourdieu (1986) described: "the anti-bourgeois pessimism of people with problems" (ibid.)—what he described as *la vie en noir* (dark thoughts—the opposite of *la vie en rose*, literally 'life in pink' or in the English equivalent 'rose-coloured glasses'). Bourdieu described this as: "anti-bourgeois pessimism with problems" (ibid.).
612. Bourdieu also explained that prevailing over the expression of *cultural capital* in the *field* of journalism—was that the bourgeois must also recognise "himself" in the art (writing) (Bourdieu 1986). Bourdieu (1986) said intellectuals and artists "owe their quasi-automatic perfection to the

fact that" they "make a virtue of necessity in order to discredit as arbitrary the 'virtues' corresponding to other necessities" (ibid.) and where religion was concerned there was: "the immanence of struggles of interest" (Loc. Cit.). This was evidenced in the corpus of this study.

613. *Australian Broadcasting Corporation.* (2020). The ABC's reporting on Cardinal George Pell. Australian Broadcasting Corporation. 20 April, 2020. Retrieved from: https://about.abc.net.au/statements/the-abcs-reporting-on-cardinal-george-pell/
614. *Australian Broadcasting Corporation.* (2020). The ABC's reporting on Cardinal George Pell. Australian Broadcasting Corporation. 20 April, 2020. Retrieved from: https://about.abc.net.au/statements/the-abcs-reporting-on-cardinal-george-pell/
615. Hartley, J. (1982). *Understanding News.* Methuen. London and New York. p. 112.
616. Hartley, J. (1982). *Understanding News.* Methuen. London and New York. p. 114.
617. Hartley, J. (1982). *Understanding News.* Methuen. London and New York. p. 114.
618. Hartley, J. (1982). *Understanding News.* Methuen. London and New York. p. 115.
619. Hartley, J. (1982). *Understanding News.* Methuen. London and New York. p. 115.
620. Hartley, J. (1982). *Understanding News.* Methuen. London and New York. pp. 116–117.

References

ABC. (2018, June). *The Cost of Being the ABC: Delivering the Best and Most Efficient Public Broadcasting.* http://www.abc.net.au/cm/lb/9944818/data/the-cost-of-being-the-abc-data.pdf

ABC. (2020, April). *Interview ABC News24. Strapline: "Pell Released. George Pell Freed from Prison After High Court ruling".* https://www.youtube.com/watch?v=7x29VznAZOE

ABC. (n.d., June 1). *Frank Dixon.* Australian Broadcasting Corporation. https://www.abc.net.au/news/2017-06-01/frank-dixon/8576568

Abebe, M., & Tangpong, C. (2017). Founder-CEOs and Corporate Turnaround Among Declining Firms: Founder CEOs and Turnaround. *Corporate Governance an International Review, 26*(3). https://doi.org/10.1111/corg.12216

Advertiser, The. (1946, 19 June). ABC Service. *The Advertiser, Adelaide,* p. 8. https://trove.nla.gov.au/newspaper/article/35700411?searchTerm=ABC%20service

Advertiser, The. (Adelaide). (1944, September 11). Haydn Beck's Resignation: ABC Manager's Explanation. *The Advertiser*, p. 6. https://trove.nla.gov.au/newspaper/article/43219618?searchTerm=Haydn%20Beck%E2%80%99s%20resignation

Al Jazeera. (2020, June 15). 'Decisive Measures' in Beijing as Coronavirus Cases Spike: Live Blog. *Al Jazeera*. https://www.aljazeera.com/news/2020/06/measures-beijing-coronavirus-cases-spike-live-200614233622226.html

Alexander, P. (2021). Australia Post's worst nightmare: Christine Holgate to head delivery rival Global Express. *The Conversation*. 10 May 2021. Retrieved from: https://theconversation.com/australia-posts-worst-nightmare-christine-holgate-to-head-delivery-rival-global-express-160606

Alford, J., & O'Flynn, J. (2009). Making Sense of Public Value: Concepts, Critiques and Emergent Meanings. *International Journal of Public Administration, 32*, 171–191.

Altheide, D., & Schneider, C. (2013). Process of Qualitative Document Analysis. In D. Altheide & C. Schneider (Eds.), *Qualitative Media Analysis* (pp. 38–74). SAGE Publications. https://doi.org/10.4135/9781452270043

Altheide, D. L. (1996). *Qualitative Media Analysis (Qualitative Research Methods. 38)*. Sage Publications.

Altheide, D. L. (2002). *Creating Fear: News and the Construction of Crisis*. Aldine de Gruyter. New York.

Andén-Papadopoulos, K. (2008). The Abu Ghraib Torture Photographs: News Frames, Visual Culture, and the Power of Images. *Journalism, 9*(1), 5–30. https://doi.org/10.1177/1464884907084337

Andrejevic, M. (2013). Public Service Media Utilities: Rethinking Search Engines and Social Networking as Public Goods. *Media International Australia, Incorporating Culture & Policy, 146*, 123–132. http://web.a.ebscohost.com.wwwproxy1.library.unsw.edu.au/ehost/pdfviewer/pdfviewer?vid=2&sid=68647279-624f-4ba5-9fda-d25caae82e74%40sdc-v-sessmgr02

Argus, The. (1944, September 7). Resignation of Mr Haydn Beck: ABC Methods Criticised. *The Argus*, p. 7. https://trove.nla.gov.au/newspaper/article/11360062?searchTerm=haydn%20beck%20ABC&searchLimits=exactPhrase|||anyWords|||notWords|||requestHandler|||dateFrom=1940-01-01|||dateTo=1945-12-31|||sortby

Aristotle. (2007). *On Rhetoric* (G. A. Kennedy, Trans.). Book 1. Chapter 1, pp. 31–32, 2nd ed. Oxford University Press.

Arora, N. D. (2010). *Political Science for Civil Services Main Examination*. McGraw Hill.

Arunchand, C. H., & Ramanathan, H. N. (2013). Organizational Culture and Employee Morale: A Public Sector Enterprise Experience. *Journal of Strategic Human Resource Management, 2*(1), 1–8. http://search.proquest.com/docview/1478029898/

Ashbolt, A. (1986). Keynote 4: The Age of Cultural Confusion [online]. In W. Bourne, (Ed.), *Proceedings: Sixth National Conference of the Australian Society for Music Education. Australia Makes Music; Action for a Changing Society* (pp. 38–43). Australian Society for Music Education. https://primoa.library.unsw.edu.au/permalink/f/11jha62/TN_informit444911808726330

Askeland, H., Espedal, G., Jelstad Løvaas, B., & Sirris, S. (Eds.). (2020). *Understanding Values Work: Institutional Perspectives in Organizations and Leadership*. eBook. Springer International. https://primoa.library.unsw.edu.au/primo-explore/fulldisplay?docid=UNSW_ALMA51279111340001731&context=L&vid=UNSWS&lang=en_US&search_scope=SearchFirst&adaptor=Local%20Search%20Engine&tab=default_tab&query=any,contains,institutional%20leadership&offset=0

Atherton, B. (2012, November 13). Pell Accuses Press of Exaggerating Catholic Abuse. *ABC*. https://www.abc.net.au/news/2012-11-13/pell-accuses-press-of-exaggerating-catholic-abuse/4369214

Australia Post. (n.d.). Heritage Strategy Australia Post Heritage Places. *Corporate Infrastructure Services Division – CRE*. Retrieved from: https://auspost.com.au/content/dam/auspost_corp/media/documents/heritage-strategy.pdf

Australian Associated Press. (2018, October 2). ABC Board Lacks Media Experience: Analyst. *The Newcastle Herald*. https://www.newcastleherald.com.au/story/5678912/abc-board-lacks-media-experience-analyst/send-us-your-news/

Australian Broadcasting Corporation. (2019a, March 4). Guilty: The Conviction of Cardinal Pell. Four Corners. *Australian Broadcasting Corporation*. https://www.abc.net.au/4corners/guilty:-the-conviction-of-cardinal-pell/10869116

Australian Broadcasting Corporation. (2019b, August 21). Victorian Chief Justice Says Pell "Is Not to Be Made a Scapegoat". *Australian Broadcasting Corporation*. https://www.abc.net.au/news/2019-08-21/judge-says-pell-isnt-to-be-made-scapegoat/11434086

Australian Broadcasting Corporation. (2020). Cardinal Pell. *Corrections and Clarifications*. 2 November 2020. Retrieved from: https://www.abc.net.au/news/corrections/2020-11-02/cardinal-pell/12839220

Australian Bureau of Statistics. (2019, November). Average Weekly Earnings, Australia. 6302.0.

Australian Financial Review, The. (2020, April 8). Pell's Acquittal Is Justice Served. *The Australian Financial Review*.https://www.afr.com/politics/federal/pell-s-acquittal-is-justice-served-20200407-p54hzs

Bainbridge, A. (2018, October 9). ABC Crisis Shows Need for Independent and Democratised Public Broadcaster [online]. *Green Left Weekly*. 1198, p. 10. https://search-informit-com-au.ezproxy1.library.usyd.edu.au/documentSummary;dn=935516978501507;res=IELHSS

Barrett, A. W., & Barrington, L. W. (2005). Is a Picture Worth a Thousand Words?: Newspaper Photographs and Voter Evaluations of Political Candidates. *Harvard International Journal of Press/Politics, 10*(4), 98–113. https://doi.org/10.1177/1081180X05281392

Barry, P. (2018, June 25). MediaWatch. *Australian Broadcasting Corporation.* https://www.abc.net.au/mediawatch/episodes/privatising-the-abc/9972184

Barthes, R. (1977). *Image Music Text* (S. Heath, Trans.). Fontana Books.

Beachy, R. N. (2003, January 24). IP Policies and Serving the Public. *Editorial. Science, 299*(5606), 473. https://libkey.io/libraries/757/articles/13426582/full-text-file?utm_source=api_231

Bennett, W. (1998). 1998 Ithiel De Sola Pool Lecture: The UnCivic Culture: Communication, Identity, and the Rise of Lifestyle Politics. *PS: Political Science and Politics, 31*(4), 741–761. https://doi.org/10.2307/420711

Benson, R. (2012). Murdoch in the United States: Kingmaker or Ringmaster? *Global Media and Communication, 8*(1), 4–7. https://www.researchgate.net/publication/330508663_Murdoch_in_the_United_States_Kingmaker_or_Ringmaster_Global_Media_and_Communication_8_1_2012_4-7/citation/download

Benson, R., & Neveu, E. (2005). *Bourdieu and the Journalistic Field.* Polity Press.

Berger, A. A. (1998). *Media Research Techniques* (2nd ed.). Sage Publications. http://ebookcentral.proquest.com/lib/unsw/detail.action?docID=997016

Blach-Ørsten, M., & Burkal, R. (2014). Credibility and the Media as a Political Institution. *Nordicom Review, 35.* Special Issue. https://content.sciendo.com/view/journals/nor/35/s1/nor.35.issue-s1.xml

Blain, E. (1977). *Life with Aunty: 40 Year with the ABC.* Methuen Australia.

Bolino, M. C., & Turnley, W. H. (2003). Going the Extra Mile: Cultivating and Managing Employee Citizenship Behavior. *Academy of Management Executive, 17*(3), 60–73. https://doi.org/10.5465/AME.2003.10954754

Bolino, M. C., Turnley, W. H., & Bloodgood, J. M. (2002). Citizenship Behavior and the Creation of Social Capital in Organizations. *Academy of Management Review, 27,* 505–522.

Bolt, A. (2020a). Andrew Bolt George Pell Blog. *The Daily Telegraph.*https://www.dailytelegraph.com.au/blogs/andrew-bolt/George%20Pell

Bolt, A. (2020b, April 7). High Court: Pell Innocent. Andrew Bolt Blog Posts. *Herald Sun.* https://www.heraldsun.com.au/blogs/andrew-bolt/high-court-pell-innocent/news-story/655c1462896c6ac287391203137d7d8b

Bonyhady, N. (2019, May 29). 'We Might be Biased': More Diverse Views Needed at ABC, Says Buttrose. *The Sydney Morning Herald.* https://www.smh.com.au/entertainment/tv-and-radio/we-might-be-bi...e-diverse-views-needed-at-abc-says-buttrose-20190529-p51sj2.html

Booth, P. (2020). The Future of Public Service Broadcasting and the Funding and Ownership of the BBC. *Economic Affairs (Harlow), 40*(3), 324–343. https://doi.org/10.1111/ecaf.12419

Boswell, J. (1851). *Life of Johnson, Volume 3 1776–1780*. T. Nelson & Sons.

Bourdieu, P. (1977). *Outline of a Theory of Practice* (R. Nice, Trans.). Cambridge University Press.

Bourdieu, P. (1984). *Sociology in Question*. Sage Publications.

Bourdieu, P. (1985). The Social Space and the Genesis of Groups. *Theory and Society, 14*(6), 723–744. Elsevier, Amsterdam. https://doi.org/10.1007/BF00174048

Bourdieu, P. (1990). *The Logic of Practice* (R. Nice, Trans.). Stanford University Press. Stanford.

Bourdieu, P. (1991). *Language and Symbolic Power* (J. Thompson, Ed., G. Raymond & M. Adamson, Trans.). Harvard University Press.

Bourdieu, P. (1993). *The Field of Cultural Production: Essays on Art and Literature*. Columbia University Press. New York.

Bourdieu, P. (2005). *The Social Structures of the Economy* (C. Turner, Trans.). Polity Press.

Bourke, L. (2016, July 28). Furious George Pell Demands Victoria Police Investigation as ABC Airs Abuse Claims. *The Sydney Morning Herald*. https://www.smh.com.au/national/furious-george-pell-demands-victoria-police-investigation-as-abc-airs-abuse-claims-20160728-gqfb41.html

Bowling, M. (2020, April 15). Cardinal Pell Describes Reaction to Prosecutors, Reporters and Police in First Television Interview. *The Catholic Leader*. https://catholicleader.com.au/news/cardinal-pell-describes-reaction-to-prosecutors-reporters-and-police-in-first-television-interview

Bowman, D. (2005, June 15). Radical Giant of Australian Broadcasting. *The Sydney Morning Herald*. https://www.smh.com.au/national/radical-giant-of-australian-broadcasting-20050615-gdliic.html

Briggs, G. (2006, July 17–Aug 1). Right Angles [The ABC Board and the Appointment of Keith Windschuttle]. *Big Issue Australia, 258*, 12–15. https://search-informit-com-au.wwwproxy1.library.unsw.edu.au/documentSummary;dn=200609050;res=IELAPA

British Broadcasting Corporation. (2009, May 25). Police Examine Sex Abuse Report. *British Broadcasting Corporation*. http://news.bbc.co.uk/2/hi/uk_news/northern_ireland/8066994.stm

British Broadcasting Corporation. News. (2011, July 13). The Cloyne Report: A Detailed Guide. https://www.bbc.com/news/uk-northern-ireland-14143822

Brown, R. S. (2010). Sampling. In P. Peterson, E. Baker, & B. McGaw (Eds.), *International Encyclopedia of Education* (pp. 142–146, 3rd ed.). Elsevier. https://doi.org/10.1016/B978-0-08-044894-7.00294-3.

Bucci, N. (2020). George Pell's Lawyer Calls for Investigation Into Claim Bribes Paid to Influence Sexual Assault Case. *The Guardian*. https://www.theguardian.com/australia-news/2020/oct/05/george-pells-lawyer-calls-for-investigation-into-claim-bribes-paid-to-influence-sexual-assault-case

Buchanan, J. (1965). An Economic Theory of Clubs. *Economica, 32*, 125. New series, 1–14. https://doi.org/10.2307/2552442

Burns, M., & Hawkins, G. (2013). Investigating Public Service Media as Hybrid Arrangements. *Media International Australia, 146*(1), 79–81. https://doi.org/10.1177/1329878X1314600111

Burrowes, T. (2016, January 1). Former ABC Managing Director Brian Johns was 'a Man Ahead of His Time'. *Mumbrella*. https://mumbrella.com.au/former-abc-boss-brian-johns-was-a-man-ahead-of-his-time-337460

Butler, J. (1990). *Gender Trouble: Feminism and the Subversion of Identity*. Routledge.

Buttrose, C. (1984). *Words and Music: Press Barons, Prima Donnas and Coping with the ABC*. Angus and Robertson Publishers.

Cadzow, J. (2018). "Culture Clash". Good Weekend. *The Sydney Morning Herald, 6*(The Culture Issue), 18–24.

Canberra Times, The. (1976, October 8). 'Support' for ABC Staff Campaign, p. 3. https://trove.nla.gov.au/newspaper/article/110829449?searchTerm=ABC%20staff&searchLimits=

Canberra Times, The. (1977, October 24). 'Interference' to ABC 'Insidious'. *The Canberra Times*, p. 7. https://trove.nla.gov.au/newspaper/article/110874090?searchTerm=ABC%20ghost&searchLimits=

Canberra Times, The. (1980, April 17). ABC's Structure, Waste Studied. *The Canberra Times*, p. 3. https://trove.nla.gov.au/newspaper/article/110591023?searchTerm=ABC%20waste

Canberra Times, The. (1985, June 11). 'Phantom Army' Found in ABC. *The Canberra Times*, p. 7. https://trove.nla.gov.au/newspaper/article/122515191?searchTerm=ABC%20phantom%20army&searchLimits=

Catholic Archdiocese of Melbourne. (n.d.) Melbourne Response. *Catholic Archdiocese of Melbourne*.https://www.cam.org.au/en-us/Safeguarding-Children-Young-People-and-Vulnerable-Persons/Melbourne-Response

Celep, A., & Mosher-William, R. (2016). Internal Culture, External Impact: How a Change-Making Culture Positions Foundations to Achieve Transformational Change. *The Foundation Review, 8*(1), 116–129. https://doi.org/10.9707/1944-5660.1288

Central Queensland Herald (Rockhampton). (1934, August 9). Sydney Letter: Obligations of Broadcasting. Pronouncement by New ABC Chairman, p. 8. https://trove.nla.gov.au/newspaper/article/70566782?searchTerm=ABC%20board%20members&searchLimits=exactPhrase|||anyWords|||notWords|||requestHandler|||dateFrom=1932-01-01|||dateTo=1935-12-31|||sortby

Chakvetadze, L., Dautova, R., & Shakurova, A. (2016). Gender Stereotypes, Mass Media and Migrants *Journal of Organizational Culture, Communications and Conflict, 20*, 39–45. http://search.proquest.com/docview/1827843344/

Chambers, G., & Brown G. (2018). Former Premiers Take Aim at Bloated Public Sector. *The Australian*. 29 January, 2018. Retrieved from https://www.theaustralian.com.au/nation/politics/former-premiers-take-aim-at-bloated-public-sector/news-story/4798c1ce6d315bcb77296b9f1303ef73

Chapman, R. (Ed.). (2009) *Culture Wars: An Encyclopedia of Issues, Viewpoints, and Voices (Two-Volume Set)*. M. E. Sharpe Incorporated. ProQuest Ebook Central.

Chenoweth, N. (2014). Aunty Faces Cuts, Job Losses and Old Scores: Media. *The Australian Financial Review*. 1 February 2014. p. 21. Retrieved from: https://search-proquest-com.wwwproxy1.library.unsw.edu.au/docview/1753219424?rfr_id=info%3Axri%2Fsid%3Aprimo

Chong, D., & Bogdan, E. (2010). Plural Public Funding and Canada's Contemporary Art Market System. *Cultural Trends: Centre/Periphery: Devolution/Federalism: New Trends in Cultural Policy, 19*(1-2), 93–107. https://doi.org/10.1080/09548961003696096

Chung, L. (2018, September 24). Michelle Guthrie Sacked: Why More Trouble Lies Ahead for ABC. *Nine.com.au*. https://finance.nine.com.au/business-news/why-more-trouble-lies-ahead-for-abc/846781d2-7df0-46fd-808d-0a8818bff342

Clarke, M. (2018, February 2). ASIO Takes Custody of Secret Cabinet Documents, Obtained by the ABC. *ABC Online*. https://www.abc.net.au/news/2018-02-01/asio-takes-custody-of-cabinet-documents/9386328

Clayton, R. (2020). Australia Post chief executive Christine Holgate resigns 'with immediate effect'. *ABC News*. 2 November 2020. Retrieved from: https://www.abc.net.au/news/2020-11-02/australia-post-ceo-christine-holgate-resigns/12839502

Clements, C., & Washbush, J. B. (1999). The Two Faces of Leadership: Considering the Dark Side of Leader-Follower Dynamics. *The Journal of Workplace Learning, 11*(5), 170–176. https://doi.org/10.1108/13665629910279509

Cohen, S. (2002). *Folk Devils and Moral Panics* (3rd ed.). First published 1972. Routledge: London & New York.

Cohen, S. (2011). Whose Side Were We On? The Undeclared Politics of Moral Panic Theory. *Crime Media Culture, 7*(3), 237–243. https://doi.org/10.1177/1741659011417603

Coleman, P. (2007). Hulme, Sir Alan Shallcross (1907–1989). *Australian Dictionary of Biography*. National Centre of Biography. Australian National University. http://adb.anu.edu.au/biography/hulme-sir-alan-shallcross-12666/text22827

Collins, C., Neal, J., & Neal, Z. (2014). Transforming Individual Civic Engagement into Community Collective Efficacy: The Role of Bonding Social Capital. *American Journal of Community Psychology, 54*, 328–336. https://doi.org/10.1007/s10464-014-9675-x

Collins, P. (2011, August). The Commercialisation of the ABC. *Eureka Street, 21*(15), 27–28. https://search-informit-com-au.wwwproxy1.library.unsw.edu.au/documentSummary;dn=380461935545072;res=IELAPA

Cooper, M. (2014). The Long History and Increasing Importance of Public-Service Principles for 21st Century Public Digital Communications Networks. *Journal on Telecommunications & High Technology Law, 12*(1, Spring), 1–54. https://primoa.library.unsw.edu.au/primo-explore/fulldisplay?docid=TN_gale_legal388675657&context=PC&vid=UNSWS&lang=en_US&search_scope=SearchFirst&adaptor=primo_central_multiple_fe&tab=default_tab&query=any,contains,history%20public%20service&offset=0

County Court of Victoria at Melbourne Criminal Division. (2019, March 13). DPP v Pell (Sentence). His Honour Chief Judge Kidd. https://content.county-court.vic.gov.au/sites/default/files/documents/2019-03/dpp-v-pell-sentence-2019-vcc-260.pdf

Courier Mail, The. (1953, June 29). Serve the Democratic Processes. "ABC Is Consistently, Violently Criticised". *The Courier-Mail, Brisbane*, p. 5. https://trove.nla.gov.au/newspaper/article/50541530?searchTerm=ABC%20serve

Cranston, M. (2019, September 25). 'It Disturbs Me': RBA Boss Hits Out at CEO Salaries. *The Australian Financial Review*. https://www.afr.com/policy/economy/it-disturbs-me-rba-boss-hits-out-at-ceo-salaries-20190924-p52ul7

Crikey. (2019, May 30). Ita Buttrose Picks a Side—And It Isn't the ABC's. Tips and Rumours. *Crikey.com*. https://www.crikey.com.au/2019/05/30/tips-ita-buttrose-abc/

Curran, J. (1991). *Mass Media and Democracy: A Reappraisal. Mass Media and Society* (J. Curran & M. Gurevitch, Eds.) (pp. 82–117). Edward Arnold.

Curran, J. (2011). *Media and Democracy*. Routledge.

Curran, J., & Seaton, J. (1997). *Power Without Responsibility: The Press and Broadcasting in Britain* (5th ed.). Routledge.

Curson, P., & McCracken, K. (2014). An Australian Perspective of the 1918–1919. Influenza Pandemic. *NSW Public Health Bulletin, 17*(7–8), 103–107. https://www.phrp.com.au/wp-content/uploads/2014/10/NB06025.pdf

Cyert, R. M., & J. G. March. (1963). *A Behavioral Theory of the Firm*. Prentice Hall. Englewood Cliffs, NJ.

Daily Examiner, The. (1945, March 30). Reason for Resignation of ABC Chairman. *Daily Examiner, Grafton*, p. 3. https://trove.nla.gov.au/newspaper/article/193817668?searchTerm=chairman%20ABC&searchLimits=exactPhrase|||anyWords|||notWords|||requestHandler|||dateFrom=1944-01-01|||dateTo=1946-12-31|||l-advstate=National|||l-advstate=ACT|||l-advstate=New+South+Wales|||sortby

Dalton, K. (2017, May). Missing in Action: The ABC and Australia's Screen Culture. Platform Papers. *Quarterly Essays on the Performing Arts from Currency House, 51*. Currency House.

Datta, D. K., Guthrie, J. P., Basuil, D., & Pandey, A. (2010). Causes and Effects of Employment Downsizing: A Review and Synthesis. *Journal of Management, 36*, 281–348. https://doi.org/10.1177/0149206309346735

Davey, M. (2019, February 27). Inside the Pell Trial: We Sat in Court for Months, Forbidden from Reporting a Word. *The Guardian*. https://www.theguardian.com/australia-news/2019/feb/27/inside-the-pell-trial-we-sat-in-court-for-months-forbidden-from-reporting-a-word

Davis, G. (1988). *Breaking Up the ABC*. Allen and Unwin.

Dawson, J. (1985). The ABC Pseudo-Crisis. 1 May 1985. *P. 4. Filmnews*. Sydney. Retrieved from: https://trove.nla.gov.au/newspaper/article/213877547?searchTerm=ABC

de Smaele, H., Geenen, E., & De Cock, R. (2017). Visual Gatekeeping – Selection of News Photographs at a Flemish Newspaper. *Nordicom Review, 38*(2), 57–70. https://doi.org/10.1515/nor-2017-0414

Debell, G. (2015). Malcolm Fraser: Realist to Radical and the Great Asia Project. *Australian Journal of International Affairs, 69*(6), 625–636. https://doi.org/10.1080/10357718.2015.1081147

Dempster, Q. (2000). *Death Struggle: How Political Malice and Boardroom Powerplays are Killing the ABC*. Allen and Unwin.

Dixon, F. (1975). *Inside the ABC: A Piece of Australian History*. The Hawthorn Press.

Donnan, P. (2020, May 4). Pell-Mell and Reform Paths in Catholic Media. *John Menadue Pearls and Irritations*. Public Policy Journal. https://johnmenadue.com/peter-donnan-pell-mell-and-reform-paths-in-catholic-media/

Dor, D. (2003). On Newspaper Headlines as Relevance Optimizers. *Journal of Pragmatics, 35*(5), 695–721. https://doi.org/10.1016/S0378-2166(02)00134-0

Dorey, P. (2015). The Legacy of Thatcherism—Public Sector Reform. *Observatoire de la société britannique* [En ligne]. 17. https://doi.org/10.4000/osb.1759

Dowsley, A., & Deery, A. (2020, April 13). Freed George Pell Faces New Abuse Claims. *The Herald Sun*. https://global-factiva-com.ezproxy2.library.usyd.edu.au/ha/default.aspx#./!?&_suid=1586834573152009674286763378881

Drozdek, A. (2015). Media Ethics. In *International Encyclopedia of the Social & Behavioral Sciences: Second Edition* (pp. 42–47). Elsevier Inc. https://doi.org/10.1016/B978-0-08-097086-8.11017-7

Duke, J. (2020, January 3). ABC Under 'Growing' Cost Pressure as Bushfire Emergency Broadcasts Surge. *The Sydney Morning Herald*. https://www.smh.com.au/business/companies/abc-under-growing-cost-pressure-as-bushfire-emergency-broadcasts-surge-20200103-p53ohp.html

Duke, J., Carmody, B., & Koziol, M. (2018, September 24). Michelle Guthrie: The Inside Story Behind Her Sacking. *The Sydney Morning Herald*. https://www.smh.com.au/business/companies/michelle-guthrie-the-inside-story-behind-her-sacking-20180924-p505ok.html

Dukes, K. N., & Gaither, S. E. (2017). Black Racial Stereotypes and Victim Blaming: Implications for Media Coverage and Criminal Proceedings in Cases of Police Violence against Racial and Ethnic Minorities. *Journal of Social Issues, 73*(4), 789–807. https://doi.org/10.1111/josi.12248

Dunstan, J., Longbottom, J., Farnsworth, S., & King, C. (2020, May 7). George Pell 'Surprised' by Royal Commission Finding He Was Told of Ridsdale Abuse. *ABC News*. https://www.abc.net.au/news/2020-05-07/royal-commission-findings-on-cardinal-george-pell-released/12217362Dur:7'09"

Easton, S. (2019, May 8). Mike Mrdak: Public Servants Must Ditch the Business Jargon, Stop Being Scared of Citizens. *The Mandarin*. https://www.themandarin.com.au/108114-mike-mrdak-public-servants-must-ditch-the-business-jargon-stop-being-scared-of-citizens/

Eddie, R. (2020, February 14). High Court Sets the Date for George Pall's Final Appeal. *The Sydney Morning Herald*. https://www.smh.com.au/national/high-court-sets-the-date-for-george-pell-s-final-appeal-20200214-p540ub.html

Edwards, M., Halligan, J, Horrigan, B., & Nicoll, G. (2012). *Public Sector Governance in Australia*. Australian National University EPress. Griffin Press. https://press-files.anu.edu.au/downloads/press/p190701/pdf/book.pdf

Enus, A., Petersen, J., Abo, S., Brennan, F., Francis, P., & Levey, P. (2016). The Pope Says Cardinal George Pell Should Not Face a Trial by Media, Following Allegations Against Him, Aired on Australian Television. In *World News Australia*. RMIT Publishing. https://primoa.library.unsw.edu.au/permalink/f/11jha62/TN_informit_tvnewsTSM201608010257

Ernst, H. (2010). Whither Advocacy Journalism? *World Future Review, 2*(6), 43–46. https://doi.org/10.1177/194675671000200606

Evans, H. (2015, April 28). How Thatcher and Murdoch Made Their Secret Deal. *The Guardian*. https://www.theguardian.com/uk-news/2015/apr/28/how-margaret-thatcher-and-rupert-murdoch-made-secret-deal

Fasoli, F., Maass, A., & Carnaghi, A. (2015). Labelling and Discrimination: Do Homophobic Epithets Undermine Fair Distribution of Resources? *The British Journal of Social Psychology, 54*(2), 383–393. https://doi.org/10.1111/bjso.12090

Fayol, H. (1949). *General and Industrial Management*. Pitman. Quoted in Maughan, M. (2014). *Organisational Behaviour*. Palgrave Macmillan.

Feldman, E. (2014). Legacy Divestitures: Motives and Implications. *Organization Science, 25*(3), 815–832. https://doi.org/10.1287/orsc.2013.0873

Ferguson, J. (2018, March 30). George Pell Committal: Extraordinary Scenes Inside Court 22. *The Australian*. https://www.theaustralian.com.au/nation/inquirer/george-pell-committal-extraordinary-scenes-inside-court-22/news-story/bf3e7f5bafed31e451d3b1680a1776fb

Finkelstein, R. (2012, February 28). Report of The Independent Inquiry Into The Media and Media Regulation. Report to the Minister for Broadband, Communications and the Digital Economy. *Australian Government*. http://www.abc.net.au/mediawatch/transcripts/1205_finkelstein.pdf

Fisher, C. (2016). The Advocacy Continuum: Towards a Theory of Advocacy in Journalism. *Journalism, 17*(6), 711–726. https://doi.org/10.1177/1464884915582311

Flores, R. (2002). Press Headlines on the Internet: An Aspectual Analysis. *Signos Literarios y Linguisticos,* 4(1), 45–57. http://search.proquest.com/docview/85615892/

Fouskas, V. K. (2013). Athens Has No Voice: On the Closure of Greece's Public Broadcasting Corporation (ERT). *Debatte: Journal of Contemporary Central and Eastern Europe, 21*(1), 107–111. https://doi.org/10.1080/0965156X.2013.836858

Fraser, M., & O'Reilly, J. (Eds.). (1996). *Save Our ABC: The Case for Maintaining Australia's National Broadcaster*. Hyland House.

Friedland, R. (2013). The Gods of Institutional Life: Weber's Value Spheres and the Practice of Polytheism. *Critical Research on Religion, 1*(1), 15–24. https://doi.org/10.1177/2050303213476104

Furedi, F. (2006). *Culture of Fear Revisited: Risk-Taking and the Morality of Low Expectation* (4th ed.). Continuum.

Gamson, J. (2015). Celebrity. In A. Drozdek. (2015). Media Ethics. *In International Encyclopedia of the Social & Behavioral Sciences, 15*, 42–47.

Gans, H. J. (2003). *Democracy and the News*. Oxford University Press.

Garnham, P. (1986). 'The media and the public sphere'. In P. Golding, G. Murdock & P. Schiesinger (Eds.), *Communicating Politics: Mass Communication and the Political Process*. Leicester University Press. Leicester.

Garrett, D. (2012). The Accidental Entrepreneur—How ABC Music Became More Than Broadcasting. Doctor of Philosophy thesis. Faculty of Creative Arts. *University of Wollongong*. https://ro.uow.edu.au/theses/3680

Georgetown University. (2018). What is a Jesuit? Retrieved from: https://www.georgetown.edu/news/the-jesuit-mission-seeking-god-in-all-things/#:~:text=What%20is%20a%20Jesuit%3F,seek%20God%20in%20all%20things

Ghosn, N. (2015). The Decline of Public Broadcasting in France. *E-journal of Intermedia, 2*(1, Spring), 143–157. https://search-proquest-com.www-proxy1.library.unsw.edu.au/docview/1810112560?rfr_id=info%3Axri%2Fsid%3Aprimo

Gleeson, C. (2013/14). Social Media and the Courts [online]. *Bar News: The Journal of the NSW Bar Association* (Summer), 54–59. https://search-informit-com-au.wwwproxy1.library.unsw.edu.au/documentSummary;dn=125912803397523;res=IELHSS

Golant, B., Sillince, J., Harvey, C., & Maclean, M. (2015). Rhetoric of Stability and Change: The Organizational Identity Work of Institutional Leadership. *Human Relations, 68*(4), 607–631. https://doi.org/10.1177/0018726714532966

Goodall, H. (2012). Media's Influence on Gender Stereotypes. *Media Asia, 39*(3), 160–163. https://doi.org/10.1080/01296612.2012.11689932

Gottschalk, S. (2018). The Infantilization of Western Culture. *The Conversation*. https://theconversation.com/the-infantilization-of-western-culture-99556

Gregory, P. J. (2005). *Court Reporting in Australia*. Cambridge University Press. Cambridge; New York.

Gustafson, K. L., & Kenix, L. J. (2016). Visually Framing Press Freedom and Responsibility of a Massacre: Photographic and Graphic Images in Charlie Hebdo"s Newspaper Front Pages Around the World. *Visual Communication Quarterly, 23*(3), 147–160. https://doi.org/10.1080/15551393.2016.1190623

Haigh, G. (2011). Why, Oh Why, Must They Be Such Tightwads? *The Australian Rationalist, 87*(Summer), 5–8. https://primoa.library.unsw.edu.au/permalink/f/11jha62/TN_informit_apaft201103405

Hall, E.T. (1959, republished 1980). *The Silent Language*. Anchor Books.

Halligan, J. (2001, September). *Contribution of the Australian Public Service to Public Administration and Management*. Edited version of a paper Presented to The Australian Public Service: 100 Years of Change, the Centenary Conference of the Institute of Public Administration (ACT Division), Rydges Lakeside (2001: Canberra). [online]. *Canberra Bulletin of Public Administration, 101*, 20–25. https://search-informit-com-au.wwwproxy1.library.unsw.edu.au/documentSummary;dn=200116077;res=IELAPA

Halton, J. (2004, March–April). A Healthy Public Sector—Vital to Australia's Health? Peter Wilenski Memorial Lecture, 20 February 2004. *Australian Quarterly, 76*(2), 19–24. https://www-jstor-org.wwwproxy1.library.unsw.edu.au/stable/pdf/20638245.pdf?refreqid=excelsior%3Ab09ce3da49e5285ebaec51142ff95634

Hamilton, W. (2013, November). Rights and Wrongs of ABC Spy Reports. *Eureka Street, 23*(23), 4–6. https://search.informit.com.au/documentSummary;dn=730862220180851;res=IELAPA

Hansen, H. (1998). Core Values Key to Attracting and Retaining the Most Qualified Staff. *Bowman's Accounting Report, 12*(12), 12–15. http://search.proquest.com/docview/206573843/

Harcup, T. (2014). *A Dictionary of Journalism*. Oxford University Press. https://www-oxfordreference-com.ezproxy1.library.usyd.edu.au/view/10.1093/acref/9780199646241.001.0001/acref-9780199646241.

Harding, R. (1979). *Outside Interference: The Politics of Australia Broadcasting*. Sun Books.

Hardy, J. A. (2017). Re-conceptualising Precarity: Institutions, Structure and Agency. *Employee Relations, 39*(3), 263–273. https://doi.org/10.1108/ER-06-2016-0111

Harsányi, G., & Carbon, C. (2015). How Perception Affects Racial Categorization: On the Influence of Initial Visual Exposure on Labelling People as Diverse Individuals or Racial Subjects. *Perception, 44*(1), 100–102. https://doi.org/10.1068/p7854

Hartley, J. (1982). *Understanding News*. Methuen.

Hasan, M. (2011, July 11). Is There a More Sickening Sight Than Leaders Sucking Up to the Sun King? *New Statesman, 140*(23). http://ezproxy.library.usyd.edu.au/login?url=https://search-proquest-com.ezproxy1.library.usyd.edu.au/docview/876179782?accountid=14757

Henderson, G. (2020, April 11). George Pell: Fairness Trampled by Social Media Mob. *The Australian*. https://www.theaustralian.com.au/inquirer/george-pell-fairness-trampled-by-social-media-mob/news-story/187e8e447ea804fa35748de1d58e452c

Henttonen, K., Johanson, J., & Janhonen, M. (2014). Work-Team Bonding and Bridging Social Networks, Team Identity and Performance Effectiveness. *Personnel Review, 43*(3), 330–349. http://dx.doi.org.wwwproxy1.library.unsw.edu.au/10.1108/PR-12-2011-0187

Hesmondhalgh, D. (2013). *The Cultural Industries*. 3rd Edition. SAGE. London.

Higton, M. (2012). *A theology of Higher Education*. Oxford Scholarship Online. Chapter 8. https://www-oxfordscholarship-com.wwwproxy1.library.unsw.edu.au/view/10.1093/acprof:oso/9780199643929.001.0001/acprof-9780199643929-chapter-9?rskey=MxVQlf&result=5

Hillman, E. L. (2009, June). Heller, Citizenship, and the Right to Serve in the Military. *Hastings Law Journal, 60*(6), 1269–1283. https://heinonline-org.wwwproxy1.library.unsw.edu.au/HOL/P?h=hein.journals/hastlj60&i=1309.

Höijer, B. (2011). Social Representations Theory: A New Theory for Media Research. *Nordicom Review, 32*(2), 3–16. https://doi.org/10.1515/nor-2017-0109

Horski, E. (1998). Grounded in Love: An Investigation of the Fundamental Ignatian Teaching on Discernment Within the Tradition of Askesis. *School of Theology and Seminary Graduate Papers/Theses, 1173*. https://digitalcommons.csbsju.edu/sot_papers/1173

Howell, A., Ulan, J., & Powell, R. (2014). Essentialist Beliefs, Stigmatizing Attitudes, and Low Empathy Predict Greater Endorsement of Noun Labels

Applied to People with Mental Disorders. *Personality and Individual Differences, 66*. https://doi.org/10.1016/j.paid.2014.03.008

Hunter, F. (2019, October 21). ABC Boss' Pay Passes $1 Million for First Time. *The Sydney Morning Herald*. https://www.smh.com.au/politics/federal/abc-boss-pay-passes-1-million-for-first-time-20191021-p532o3.html

IGADF Afghanistan Inquiry Report. (2020, November 10). Inspector General of the Australian Defence Force Afghanistan Inquiry Report. *Australian Government*. https://afghanistaninquiry.defence.gov.au/sites/default/files/2020-11/IGADF-Afghanistan-Inquiry-Public-Release-Version.pdf

Indeed.com. (2020, July). Australian Broadcasting Corporation (ABC) Salaries in Australia. *Indeed.com*. https://au.indeed.com/cmp/Australian-Broadcasting-Corporation-%28abc%29/salaries

Inglis, K. S. (1983). *The is the ABC: The Australian Broadcasting Commission 1932–1983*. Melbourne University Press. Melbourne.

Irish Times, The. (2011, July 20). Taoiseach's Speech on Cloyne Motion. https://www.irishtimes.com/news/taoiseach-s-speech-on-cloyne-motion-1.880466

Jewish Messenger, The. (1897, January 2). Quoted in *The New York Times*. Good-Will to Men. *The New York Times*, p. 3.

Johnson, K. A. (2020). I Got a New Puppy! The Impact of Personal, Opinion, and Objective Tweets on a Journalist's and a News Organization's Perceived Credibility. *Journalism Practice, 14*(1), 48–66. https://doi.org/10.1080/17512786.2019.1597637

Jones, E. (2002, June). Menzies' Razor Gang: Public Service Retrenchment in 1951 [online]. *Canberra Bulletin of Public Administration, 104*, 33–36. https://search-informit-com-au.wwwproxy1.library.unsw.edu.au/fullText;dn=20023710;res=AGISPT

Josephi, B. (2000). Newsroom Research: Its Importance for Journalism Studies. *Australian Journalism Review, 22*(2), 75–87. https://primoa.library.unsw.edu.au/permalink/f/11jha62/TN_informit_apaft200204995

Juddery, B. (1976, December 3). Disquiet and Despondency in the ABC. *The Canberra Times*, p. 2. https://trove.nla.gov.au/newspaper/article/131798978?searchTerm=ABC%20BAPH

Juries Victoria. (2020, April 6). Attending for Jury Service. *Juries Victoria*. https://www.juriesvictoria.vic.gov.au/individuals/attending-for-jury-service

Katz-Gerro, T. (2012). Do Individuals Who Attend the Arts Support Public Funding of the Arts? Evidence from England and the USA. *Journal of Policy Research in Tourism, Leisure and Events, 4*(1), 1–27. https://doi.org/10.1080/19407963.2011.597507

Kelling, K., & Thomas, R. J. (2018). The Roles and Functions of Opinion Journalists. *Newspaper Research Journal, 39*(4), 398–419. https://doi.org/10.1177/0739532918806899

Kenny, C. (2018). ABC Chairman Justin Milne Has to Go Over Push to sack Emma Alberici. *The Australian*.https://www.theaustralian.com.au/business/media/abc-chairman-justin-milne-has-to-go-over-push-to-sack-emma-alberici/news-story/e326ac54ba0a027e70231f3edc3152b3

Kenny, C. (2020, June 29). Cue the Violins: ABC Needs to Put Its Trivial Troubles Into Perspective. *The Australian*. https://www.theaustralian.com.au/business/media/abc-crybabies-need-to-put-their-trivial-troubles-into-perspective/news-story/af90438cc7f3d09c5767c8004da51170

Kieran, M. (1998). *Media Ethics*. Routledge. London.

King, L. (2018, July 20). Rupert Murdoch, Mischief-Maker on a Global Scale. *Inside Sources*. https://www.insidesources.com/rupert-murdoch-mischief-maker-global-scale/

Kirby, M. (2002). Law and Media: Adversaries or Allies in Safeguarding Freedom? *Southern Cross University Law Review, 6*, 1–7. https://primoa.library.unsw.edu.au/permalink/f/11jha62/TN_informit_agis20033704

Klapdor, M., & Arthur, D. (2017). Welfare—What Does It Cost? *Parliament of Australia*. https://www.aph.gov.au/About_Parliament/Parliamentary_Departments/Parliamentary_Library/pubs/BriefingBook45p/WelfareCost

Klikauer, T. (2018). Media and Capitalism [Review of *Media and Capitalism*]. *Critical Sociology, 44*(6), 969–981. SAGE Publications. https://doi.org/10.1177/0896920518774091

Kobre, S. (1955). *News Behind the Headlines: Background Reporting of Significant Social Problems* (p. iv+204). University of California. http://hdl.handle.net/2027/uc1.b3552959

Koziol, M. (2020). ABC News Boss Warns Staff Against Focus on 'Inner City Left-Wing Elites'. *The Sydney Morning Herald*. 25 October 2020. Retrieved from: https://www.smh.com.au/national/abc-news-boss-warns-staff-against-focus-on-inner-city-left-wing-elites-20201023-p56849.html

Kumar, P., & Zattoni, A. (2018, January). Internal Culture and Outside Influence in Corporate Governance. *Corporate Governance: An International Review, 26*(1), 2–3. https://primoa.library.unsw.edu.au/primo-explore/search?query=any,contains,internal%20culture&tab=default_tab&search_scope=SearchFirst&vid=UNSWS&offset=0

Kurtulmuş, B. E. (2019). *The Dark Side of Leadership*. iBooks. Springer. https://doi.org/10.1007/978-3-030-02038-5_1

Labor Daily, The. (1938). Clean Sweep for ABC. *The Labor Daily*, 5. 15 June, 1938. Retrieved from: https://trove.nla.gov.au/newspaper/article/236409865?searchTerm=ABC%20commissioner%20kitto&searchLimits=

Lackey, D., & AAP. (2020, April 7). High-Profile George Pell Supporter Accuses the ABC of Acting as a 'Cheer Squad' to Have the Cardinal Jailed in a VERY Fiery Interview on the Public Broadcaster. *The Daily Mail*. https://www.dailymail.co.uk/news/article-8195489/George-Pell-supporter-accuses-ABC-acting-cheer-squad-cardinal-jailed.html

Law, J. (2009). MBWA. In: *A Dictionary of Business and Management* (5th Ed.). Oxford University Press. Oxford.

Lawrence, R. G., & Schafer, M. L. (2012). Debunking Sarah Palin: Mainstream News Coverage of 'Death Panels'. *Journalism, 13*(6), 766–782. https://doi.org/10.1177/1464884911431389

Lawrence, T. B., & Suddaby, R. (2006). Institutions and Institutional Work. In S. R. Clegg, C. Hardy, W. R. Nord, & T. Lawrence (Eds.), *Handbook of Organization Studies.* Sage. Thousand Oaks, CA.

Leroy, D. (1980, June). Public Broadcasting. *Journal of Communication, 30*(3), 2159. https://onlinelibrary-wiley-com.wwwproxy1.library.unsw.edu.au/doi/epdf/10.1111/j.1460-2466.1980.tb02002.x

Line, M. B. (1992). How to Demotivate Staff: A Brief Guide. *Library Management, 13*(1), 4. http://dx.doi.org.wwwproxy1.library.unsw.edu.au/10.1108/01435129210009832

Luck, G. (2018, June 30). The Rot Set in with Current Affairs, and ABC News Has Since Lost Its Bearings. *The Australian.* https://www.theaustralian.com.au/news/inquirer/the-rot-set-in-with-current-affairs-and-abc-news-has-since-lost-its-bearings/news-story/06202187428fc0e6b2a14b60f940c8de

Luzung, A. (2004/2005). Contempt by Publication: Improving the Law on Court Reporting by the Media [online]. *Reform,* 85(Summer), 27–30, 59. https://search-informit-com-au.wwwproxy1.library.unsw.edu.au/fullText;dn=20051670;res=AGISPT

Manne, R. (2007, December–2008, January). New Teeth for Aunty: Reinvigorating the National Broadcaster. *The Monthly,* p. 40. https://www.themonthly.com.au/monthly-essays-robert-manne-new-teeth-aunty-reinvigorating-national-broadcaster-749#mtr

Mansfield, B. (1997). *The Challenge of a Better ABC: The Review of the Role and Functions of the ABC.* Australian Government Publishing Service.

March, J. C., & Simon, H. A. (1958). *Organizations.* Wiley. New York.

Margetts, J., Brown, M., & Staff. (2016, February 5). Cardinal George Pell 'Too Ill' to Travel from Rome for Child Sex Abuse Inquiry. *Australian Broadcasting Corporation.* https://www.abc.net.au/news/2016-02-05/cardinal-george-pell-too-ill-to-child-sex-abuse-inquiry-lawyers/7140584

Marquand, D. (2004). *Decline of the Public: The Hollowing Out of Citizenship.* Polity Press.

Marr, D. (2013). *The Prince: Faith, Abuse, George Pell.* Quarterly Essay 51. Black Inc.

Marshak, R. J. (2006). *Covert Processes at Work: Managing the Five Hidden Dimensions of Organizational Change.* Berrett-Koehler Publishers. San Francisco, CA.

Martin, F. (2002). Beyond Public Service Broadcasting? ABC Online and the User/Citizen. *Southern Review: Communication, Politics & Culture, 35*(1),

42–62. https://search-informit-com-au.wwwproxy1.library.unsw.edu.au/documentSummary;dn=743199784542203;res=IELAPA

Masquelier, C. (2019). Bourdieu, Foucault and the Politics of Precarity. *Distinktion: Journal of Social Theory, 20*(2), 135–155. https://doi.org/10.1080/1600910X.2018.1549999

McCarthy, J. (2018, December 6). 'Catholic Church Has a Lot to Answer For': Philip Wilson's Conviction Overturned. *The Sydney Morning Herald*. https://www.smh.com.au/national/nsw/catholic-church-has-a-lot-to-answer-for-philip-wilson-s-conviction-overturned-20181206-p50kqg.html

McCarthy, J. W., & Karsh, M. (2007, March). Jesuits and Ecology—For the Greater Glory of God! *Forestry Chronicle, 83*(2), 162–163. https://pubs.cif-ifc.org/doi/pdf/10.5558/tfc83159-2

McIlroy, T., & Cranston, M. (2019, October 18). Australia's Best Paid Bureaucrat Rakes in $2.5m. *The Australian Financial Review*. https://www.afr.com/politics/federal/australia-s-best-paid-bureaucrat-rakes-in-2-5m-20191017-p531hy

McMurtrie, C. (2020, April 11). Why the ABC's Reporting of the George Pell Case Wasn't a Witch-Hunt. *Australian Broadcasting Corporation*. https://www.abc.net.au/news/about/backstory/news-coverage/2020-04-11/why-the-abc-reporting-of-the-pell-case-was-not-a-witch-hunt/12137620

McNair, B. (1994). *News and Journalism in the UK*. Routledge.

Meade, A. (2018a, August 21). Michelle Guthrie Says Abuse of ABC Staff Unacceptable After Presenter Cries on Air. *The Guardian*. https://www.theguardian.com/media/2018/aug/21/michelle-guthrie-says-abuse-of-abc-staff-unacceptable-after-presenter-cries-on-air

Meade, A. (2018b, August 1). The ABC in Turmoil: 'Frankly, We Are All Spooked About Everything in Here.' *The Guardian*. https://www.theguardian.com/media/2018/aug/01/the-abc-in-turmoil-frankly-we-are-all-spooked-about-everything-in-here

MediaWatch. (2020, April 20). Pell—The final verdict. *Australian Broadcasting Corporation*. https://www.abc.net.au/mediawatch/episodes/pell/12166274

Mercury, The. (1944, September 7). Haydn Beck Resigns ABC Post. *The Mercury*, p. 14. https://trove.nla.gov.au/newspaper/article/26036060?searchTerm=haydn%20beck%20ABC&searchLimits=exactPhrase|||anyWords|||notWords|||requestHandler|||dateFrom=1940-01-01|||dateTo=1945-12-31|||sortby

Merriam, S. B. (2010). Qualitative Case Studies. In P. Peterson, E. Baker, & B. McGaw (Eds.), *International Encyclopedia of Education* (3rd ed., pp. 457, 456–462). Elsevier. https://doi.org/10.1016/B978-0-08-044894-7.01532-3

Meyer, J. W., & Rowan, B. (1977). Institutionalized Organizations: Formal Structure as Myth and Ceremony. *American Journal of Sociology, 83*(2), 340–363. https://doi.org/10.1086/226550

Mill, J. S. (1859). *On Liberty*. The Walter Scott Publishing Co., Ltd. http://www.gutenberg.org/files/34901/34901-h/34901-h.htm

Mills, T. (2014). George Pell's Truck Driver Analogy Veers into Hostile Territory. *The Age*. 22 August 2014. Retrieved from: https://www.theage.com.au/national/victoria/george-pells-truck-driver-analogy-veers-into-hostile-territory-20140822-1076i4.html

Milne, J. (2017, November 15). Hector Crawford Oration 2017: ABC Chairman Justin Milne. *Australian Broadcasting Corporation*. https://about.abc.net.au/speeches/hector-crawford-oration-2017/

Missingham, R. (2009). Encouraging the Digital Economy and Digital Citizenship. *The Australian Library Journal, 58*(4), 386–399. https://doi.org/10.1080/00049670.2009.10735927

Mitchell, C. (2019, May 27). ABC Gave Us Groupthink on Steroids. *The Australian*. https://www.theaustralian.com.au/commentary/abc-gave-us-groupthink-on-steroids/news-story/da95e8a9d851509bf8538df28c630c15

Molomby, T. (1991). *Is There a Moderate on the Roof? ABC Years*. William Heinemann.

Moore, C. B., Payne, G. T., Autry, C. W., & Griffis, S. E. (2018). Project Complexity and Bonding Social Capital in Network Organizations. *Group & Organization Management, 43*(6), 936–970. https://doi.org/10.1177/1059601116650556

Moore, M. H. (1995). *Creating Public Value*. Harvard University Press. Cambridge. Mass.

Moore, M. H. & Benington, J. (2011). Conclusions: Looking Ahead. In M. H. Moore & J. Benington (Eds.), *Public Value: Theory and Practice*, (pp. 256–274). Palgrave Macmillan. London.

Munt, S. R. (2017). Argumentum Ad Misericordiam: The Cultural Politics of Victim Media. *Feminist Media Studies, 17*(5), 866–883. https://doi.org/10.1080/14680777.2016.1259176

Murdock, G. (2004, November). Building the Digital Commons: Public Broadcasting in the Age of the Internet. University of Montreal. *The 2004 Spry Memorial Lecture*. https://www.researchgate.net/publication/254750526_BUILDING_THE_DIGITAL_COMMONS_PUBLIC_BROADCASTING_IN_THE_AGE_OF_THE_INTERNET

Murray, A. (2006a, March 24). Australia: Australian Broadcasting Corporation Board Must be Appointed on Merit. *US Fed News Service* Including *US State News, HT Digital Streams Limited*. http://search.proquest.com/docview/470140665/.

Murray, L. (2006b, May 23). Scott of the ABC: A Family Affair of Service. *The Sydney Morning Herald*. https://www.smh.com.au/national/scott-of-the-abc-a-family-affair-of-service-20060523-gdnlkg.html

National Commission of Audit. (2014). Executive Summary. Second Phase Report. https://www.ncoa.gov.au/report/phase-two/executive-summary

Nature. (1978, October 26). The Public's Right to Know, *275*, 682. https://doi-org.wwwproxy1.library.unsw.edu.au/10.1038/275682a0

Nelson, R. R., & Winter, S. G. (1982). *An Evolutionary Theory of Economic Change*. Belknap Press of Harvard University Press. Cambridge, Mass.

Nerone, J., & Barnhurst, K. G. (2003). US Newspaper Types, the Newsroom, and the Division of Labor, 1750-2000. *Journalism Studies, 4*(4), 435–449. https://doi.org/10.1080/1461670032000136541

Newcastle Morning Herald and Miners' Advocate, The. (1935, June 6). ABC Appointment: Professor Wallace Retires. *Newcastle Morning Herald and Miners' Advocate*, p. 7. https://trove.nla.gov.au/newspaper/article/139259689?searchTerm=ABC%20commissioner%20kitto&searchLimits=

Newman, L., Biedrzycki, K., & Baum, F. (2012). Digital Technology Use among Disadvantaged Australians: Implications for Equitable Consumer Participation in Digitally-Mediated Communication and Information Exchange with Health Services. *Australian Health Review, 36*(2), 125–129. https://doi.org/10.1071/AH11042

Northridge, M. (2009). Serving the Public Good. *American Journal of Public Health, 99*(3), 393. https://search-proquest-com.wwwproxy1.library.unsw.edu.au/docview/215089511?rfr_id=info%3Axri%2Fsid%3Aprimo

Nygren, G., Leckner, S., & Tenor, C. (2018). Hyperlocals and Legacy Media: Media Ecologies in Transition. *Nordicom Review, 39*(1), 33–49. https://doi.org/10.1515/nor-2017-0419

O'Brien, K. (2019, July 1). 'Don't Ever Again Allow Politicians to Diminish the Public Broadcaster'. Logies Speech. Induction into the Hall of Fame. *Crikey.com*.https://www.crikey.com.au/2019/07/01/kerry-obrien-logies-speech/

O'Mahen, P. (2016). A Big Bird Effect? The Interaction Among Public Broadcasting, Public Subsidies, and Political Knowledge. *European Political Science Review,* 8(2), 311–332. https://www-cambridge-org.wwwproxy1.library.unsw.edu.au/core/services/aop-cambridge-core/content/view/8EC8052F26A223A76ED7D07A386E10D5/S175577391500003Xa.pdf/big_bird_effect_the_interaction_among_public_broadcasting_public_subsidies_and_political_knowledge.pdf

OECD. (2011). *Regulatory Policy and Governance: Supporting Economic Growth and Serving the Public Interest*. OECD Publishing. https://doi.org/10.1787/9789264116573-en

Osborne, P. (2019). Department Boss Blindsided by Morrison Axe. Australian Associated Press. *The Canberra Times*. 5 December, 2019. Retrieved from: https://www.canberratimes.com.au/story/6527946/department-boss-blindsided-by-morrison-axe/

Ouellette, L. (2008). Makeover Television, Governmentality and the Good Citizen. *Continuum, 22*(4), 471–484.

Pandey, S. K., Wright, B. E., & Moynihan, D. P. (2012, March/April). Pulling the Levers: Transformational Leadership, Public Service Motivation, and Mission Valence. *Public Administration Review, American Society for Public Administration, 72*(2), 206–215. https://www.jstor.org/stable/41433294

Park, C. M. (2010). Public Attitudes toward Government Spending in the Asia-Pacific Region. *Japanese Journal of Political Science, 11*(1), 77–97. https://doi.org/10.1017/S1468109909990144

Passmore, A. (2013, June 3). The Other Culture Shock: The Internal Culture at CUs. *Credit Union Journal, 17*(22), 16. https://search-proquest-com.www-proxy1.library.unsw.edu.au/docview/1362107663?rfr_id=info%3Axri%2Fsid%3Aprimo

Paulson, M. (2002, April 8). World Doesn't Share US View of Scandal: Clergy Sexual Abuse Reaches Far, Receives an Uneven Focus. *The Boston Globe.* http://archive.boston.com/globe/spotlight/abuse/print/040802_world.htm

Pearlman, J. (2007, August 30). SBS Not Dumbing Down, Says Boss. *The Sydney Morning Herald.* https://www.smh.com.au/entertainment/sbs-not-dumbing-down-says-boss-20070830-gdqzj9.html

Percy, K. (2019, March 26). George Pell Trial Suppression Orders Breached by News Organisations, Victorian Prosecutor Alleges. *Australian Broadcasting Corporation.* https://www.abc.net.au/news/2019-03-26/journalists-accused-of-breaking-george-pell-suppression-order/10939980

Petersen, N. (2009). A Biography of Sir Charles Moses. *Global Media Journal, 3*(1). https://www.hca.westernsydney.edu.au/gmjau/archive/v3_2009_1/3vi1_neville_petersen.html

President of the Council of State. (2013, September 5). Temporary Injunction. President of the Council of State 17 June 2013. http://www.ste.gr/portal/page/portal/StE/ProsfatesApofaseis

Price, S. (2014, July 9). Public Broadcasting Under Threat. *Green Left Weekly, 1015*(3). https://primoa.library.unsw.edu.au/permalink/f/11jha62/TN_informit441816198109046

Quadrant. (2016, February 6). The ABC's Cardinal Sins. *Quadrant.* https://quadrant.org.au/abcs-cardinal-sins/

Queensland Times. (1937, February 9). ABC Changes? Younger Commissioners Likely. *Queensland Times*, p. 6. https://trove.nla.gov.au/newspaper/article/117630789?searchTerm=ABC%20commissioner%20kitto&searchLimits=

Rayner, J., Lawton, A., & Williams, H. (2012). Organizational Citizenship Behavior and the Public Service Ethos: Whither the Organization? *Journal of Business Ethics, 106*, 117–130. https://link-springer-com.wwwproxy1.library.unsw.edu.au/content/pdf/10.1007/s10551-011-0991-x.pdf

Rayner, M. (1997). Democracy and the Good Life. *Leading and Managing, 3*(4, Summer), 237–244. https://search-informit-com-au.wwwproxy1.library.unsw.edu.au/fullText;dn=89267;res=AEIPT

Reay, T., Zilber, T. B., Langley, A., & Tsoukas, H. (2019). *Institutions and Organizations*. Oxford University Press. Oxford. https://doi.org/10.1093/oso/9780198843818.001.0001

Reddan, F. (2017, April). Serving the Public Good. *Accountancy Ireland, 49*(2), 21–22. https://www.charteredaccountants.ie/docs/default-source/Publishing/accountancy-ireland-archive/accountancy-ireland-april-2017.pdf?sfvrsn=4

Regencia, T. (2020, June 15). Maria Ressa Found Guilty in Blow to Philippines' Press Freedom. *Al Jazeera*. https://www.aljazeera.com/news/2020/06/philippine-court-rappler-maria-ressa-guilty-cyberlibel-200614210221502.html

Remeikis, A. (2018, September 30). ABC Board Must Get Back to Work and 'Do Better', Scott Morrison Says. *The Guardian*. https://www.theguardian.com/media/2018/sep/30/abc-board-must-get-back-to-work-and-do-better-scott-morrison-says

Reporters Sans Frontières. (2020). 2020 World Press Freedom Index. Reporters Sans Frontières. https://rsf.org/en/ranking

Robertson, A. (1970, June 3). ABC Censorship Move Stirs New Staff Challenge. *The Tribune*, p. 4. https://trove.nla.gov.au/newspaper/article/237505888?searchTerm=ABC%20staff%20culture&searchLimits=

Robertson, A. (2019, September 28). How Did CEO Pay Get to 500 Times the Wages of Ordinary Workers? Analysis. *Australian Broadcasting Corporation*. https://www.abc.net.au/news/2019-09-28/how-did-ceo-pay-get-to-500-times-the-wages-of-ordinary-workers/11556394

Robertson, J., & Meade, A. (2017, May 9). Fairfax Boss Greg Hywood was Paid as Much as $7.2m in 2016. *The Guardian*. https://www.theguardian.com/media/2017/may/09/fairfax-boss-greg-hywood-paid-more-2016

Rojek, C. (2012). Demand Side Factors. Ch. 7. In *Fame Attack: The Inflation of Celebrity and Its Consequences* (pp. 98–122). Bloomsbury Academic. London. http://dx.doi.org/10.5040/9781849661386.ch-007

Royal Commission into Institutional Responses to Child Sexual Abuse. (2017). Final Report. Royal Commission into Institutional Responses to Child Sexual Abuse. https://www.childabuseroyalcommission.gov.au/

Salter, D. (2007). *The Media We Deserve: Underachievement in The Fourth Estate*. Melbourne University Press.

Santoro, S. (2013). Senate. Official Hansard. Parliamentary Debates. *Commonwealth of Australia*.

Schein, E. H. (2010). *Organizational Culture and Leadership* (4th Ed.). The Jossey-Bass Business & Management Series, 2(4). Wiley.

Schudson. (2005). "The Virtues of an Unlovable Press" Intro. *Political Quarterly, 1*(76), 23–32. https://doi.org/10.1111/j.1467-923X.2006.00745.x

Schudson, M. (2008). *Why Democracies Need an Unlovable Press.* Polity Press.

Schultz, A., & Napier-Raman, K. (2020, July 16). What Does the Governor-General Do—And How Much Does It Cost the Country? *The Mandarin and Crikey.* https://www.themandarin.com.au/136189-what-does-the-governor-general-do-and-how-much-does-it-cost-the-country/?utm_source=TheJuice&utm_medium=email&utm_source=newsletter; crikey.com.au

Seccombe, M. (2016, December 3–9). Senior ABC Staff Say Michelle Guthrie 'Out of Her Depth'. *The Saturday Paper, 137.* https://www.thesaturdaypaper.com.au/news/media/2016/12/03/senior-abc-staff-say-michelle-guthrie-out-her-depth/14806836004053

Semmler, C. (1981). *The ABC—Aunt Sally and Sacred Cow.* Melbourne University Press.

Shanahan, L. (2019, November 17). ABC Staff Push for Climate Group. *The Australian.* https://www.theaustralian.com.au/business/media/abc-staff-propose-climate-group/news-story/50af6696dbff695d103f9fba77f1ed05

Sharman, R. (2019). The Psychological Reason Why Some Can't Believe the Evidence Against George Pell and Michael Jackson. *Australian Broadcasting Corporation.* 13 March, 2019. Retrieved from: https://www.abc.net.au/news/2019-03-13/george-pell-michael-jackson-cognitive-dissonance/10892948

Sheridan, G. (2020, April 16). ABC's Groupthink on George Pell a Sin Against Journalism. *The Australian.* https://www.theaustralian.com.au/commentary/abcs-groupthink-on-george-pell-a-sin-against-journalism/news-story/ba3a43fe6ca1d4625a3857884dfaad2c

Simons, M. (2006). 'Leaked KPMG Report: ABC Efficient but Underfunded.' *Crikey.* 21 November, 2016. Retrieved from: https://www.crikey.com.au/2006/11/21/leaked-kpmg-report-abc-efficient-but-underfunded/

Simons, M. (2016, September). Is Michelle Guthrie Tuned in to the ABC? *The Monthly.* https://www.themonthly.com.au/issue/2016/september/1472652000/margaret-simons/michelle-guthrie-tuned-abc#mtr

Skidmore, P. (1995). Telling Tales: Media Power, Ideology and the Reporting of Child Sexual Abuse in Britain. In D. Kidd-Hewitt & R. Osborne (Eds.), *Crime and the Media: A Post-modern Spectacle.* Pluto Press.

Smith, L. (2020). 2020 versus 1919: Is COVID-19 as bad as the 'Spanish' Flu? Analysis. The University of Sydney. *News and Opinion.* 27 May 2020. Retrieved from: https://www.sydney.edu.au/news-opinion/news/2020/05/27/2020-versus-1919--is-covid-19-as-bad-as-the--spanish--flu-.html

Smith, Z. (2020a, April 14). 'Unjust' to Take Accusations as Gospel. *The Herald-Sun.* https://www.pressreader.com/australia/herald-sun/20200414/281547998017480

Smith, Z. (2020b, April 14). Pell Attacks System. *The Herald Sun*. https://global-factiva-com.ezproxy2.library.usyd.edu.au/ha/default.aspx#./!?&_suid=15868345731520096742867633788 81

Spadaro, S. J. A. (2020, January 20). Defy the Apocalypse. *La Civiltà Cattolica*. https://www.laciviltacattolica.com/defy-the-apocalypse/

Spath, R., Strand, V., & Bosco-Ruggiero, S. (2013). What Child Welfare Staff Say about Organizational Culture. *Child Welfare, 92*(11), 9–31. http://search.proquest.com/docview/1509394964/

Stacey, R., & Griffin, D. (2006). *Complexity and the Experience of Managing in Public Sector Organizations*. Routledge.

Standing, G. (2011). *The Precariat: The New Dangerous Class*. Bloomsbury Academic. https://doi.org/10.5040/9781849664554

Starling, G. (2008). *Managing the Public Sector* (8th ed.). Thomson Wadsworth.

Stiehm, J. H. (2002). *U.S. Army War College: Military Education in a Democracy*. Temple University Press.

Stove, D. (1992). A New Religion. *Philosophy, 67*(260), 233–240, 234. www.jstor.org/stable/3751453

Sun, The. (1935, June 17). Kitto's Praise for Public Service. *The Sun*, p. 9. https://trove.nla.gov.au/newspaper/article/230251698?searchTerm=ABC%20commissioner%20kitto&searchLimits=

Sun, The. (1939, December 30). New ABC Critics Answered. *The Sun*, p. 3. https://trove.nla.gov.au/newspaper/article/231500394?searchTerm=ABC%20commissioner%20kitto&searchLimits=

Sun, The. (1946, October 16). Suspension of ABC Staff Chief. *The Sun*, p. 5. https://trove.nla.gov.au/newspaper/article/229551981?searchTerm=ABC%20staff&searchLimits=

Supreme Court of Victoria. (2019). George Pell V. The Queen. *Supreme Court of Victoria*.https://www.supremecourt.vic.gov.au/case-summaries/court-of-appeal-proceedings/george-pell-v-the-queen

Swannie, B. J. (2019, July 4). In Australia, Criticising a Judge Can Land You in Jail. This Is a Danger for Democracy. *The Conversation*. https://theconversation.com/in-australia-criticising-a-judge-can-land-you-in-jail-this-is-a-danger-for-democracy-119296

Swindall, C. (2011). *Engaged Leadership: Building a Culture to Overcome Employee Disengagement* (2nd ed.). John Wiley and Sons.

Sydney Morning Herald, The. (1932, March 10). Broadcasting: The Appointment of Commissioners: Proposed Legislation, p. 11. https://trove.nla.gov.au/newspaper/article/29946918?searchTerm=Broadcasting%3A%20The%20Appointment%20of%20Commissioners%3A%20Proposed%20Legislation.%20

Sydney Morning Herald, The. (1944, September 12). "Mr Moses Most Unfair" Haydn Beck's Reply. *The Sydney Morning Herald*, p. 4. https://trove.nla.gov.au/newspaper/article/17920452?searchTerm=haydn%20beck%20ABC&searchLimits=exactPhrase|||anyWords|||notWords|||requestHandler|||dateFrom=1940-01-01|||dateTo=1945-12-31|||sortby

Sydney Morning Herald, The. (1945a, April 17). How Much Freedom for the ABC?, p. 2. *The Sydney Morning Herald*.https://trove.nla.gov.au/newspaper/article/27932662?searchTerm=chairman%20ABC&searchLimits=exactPhrase|||anyWords|||notWords|||requestHandler|||dateFrom=1944-01-01|||dateTo=1946-12-31|||l-advstate=National|||l-advstate=ACT|||l-advstate=New+South+Wales|||sortby

Sydney Morning Herald, The. (1945b, March 30). Mr Cleary Talks of Clashes, p. 4. *The Sydney Morning Herald*.https://trove.nla.gov.au/newspaper/article/17937290?searchTerm=chairman%20ABC&searchLimits=exactPhrase|||anyWords|||notWords|||requestHandler|||dateFrom=1945-01-31|||dateTo=1945-04-30|||l-advstate=National|||l-advstate=ACT|||l-advstate=New+South+Wales|||sortby

Sydney Morning Herald, The. (1976, December 9). Sir Henry Spells Out Views on ABC. *The Sydney Morning Herald*, p. 10. https://trove.nla.gov.au/newspaper/article/131800175?searchTerm=henry%20bland%20ABC%20orchestras

Sydney Morning Herald, The. (2003, October 11). ABC Loses Points in Alston's 'Bias' Plea. *The Sydney Morning Herald*. https://www.smh.com.au/national/abc-loses-points-in-alstons-bias-plea-20031011-gdhkgd.html

Thakur, R. (2019, September 2). Cardinal Pell's Guilty Verdict Is Deeply Troubling. *John Menadue: Pearls and Irritations*. https://johnmenadue.com/ramesh-thakur-cardinal-pells-guilty-verdict-is-deeply-troubling/

Thomas, A. (1980). *Broadcast and be Damned: The ABC's First Two Decades*. Melbourne University Press.

Thornton, P. H., & Ocasio, W. (2008). Institutional Logics. In R. Greenwood, C. Oliver, K. Sahlin-Andersson, & R. Suddaby (Eds.), *The Sage Handbook of Organisational Institutionalism*. Sage.

Tibbitts, C. (n.d.). Casualties of War. *The Australian War Memorial*.https://www.awm.gov.au/wartime/article2

Tiffen, R. (1989). *News and Power*. Allen & Unwin.

Tomevska, S. (2021). Philip Wilson, former Catholic Archbishop of Adelaide, farewelled at St Francis Xavier's Cathedral. *ABC News*. 3 February 2021. Retrieved from: https://www.abc.net.au/news/2021-02-03/former-adelaide-catholic-archbishop-philip-wilson-funeral-held/13116352

Tomlinson, M., O'Reilly, D., Wallace, M., Edwards, G., Elliott, C., Iszatt-White, M., & Schedlitzki, D. (2013). Developing Leaders as Symbolic Violence: Reproducing Public Service Leadership Through the (Misrecognized) Development of Leaders' Capitals. *Management Learning*, *44*(1), 81–97. https://doi.org/10.1177/1350507612472151

Tong, K. (2020). Funding for Small-to-Medium Art Music Organisations in Brisbane (Queensland, Australia): A Case Study. *Music Education Research, 22*(5), 495–504. https://doi.org/10.1080/14613808.2020.1840538

Topsfield, J. (2021).'No sense of momentum': Poll finds drop in support for Australia becoming a republic. *The Sydney Morning Herald*. 25 January 2021. Retrieved from: https://www.smh.com.au/national/no-sense-of-momentum-poll-finds-drop-in-support-for-australia-becoming-a-republic-20210125-p56wpe.html

Torii, A. (2017). Effects of Public Broadcasting on the Competition Among Private Broadcasters and the Total Surplus. *Journal of Media Business Studies, 14*(2), 116–145. https://www-tandfonline-com.wwwproxy1.library.unsw.edu.au/doi/pdf/10.1080/16522354.2017.1290023?needAccess=true

Toronto Star. (2002, August 21). Australian Archbishop Accused of Child Abuse. *Toronto Star*, p. 3. https://search-proquest-com.wwwproxy1.library.unsw.edu.au/docview/438492151?rfr_id=info%3Axri%2Fsid%3Aprimo

Toscano, N., & Lee, J. (2015, May 21). Cardinal George Pell Denies Allegations of Involvement in Abuse Cover-Up. *The Sydney Morning Herald*. https://www.smh.com.au/national/cardinal-george-pell-denies-allegations-of-involvement-in-abuse-coverup-20150520-gh67ml.html

Tracey, M. (1998, reprinted 2002). *The Decline and Fall of Public Service Broadcasting*. Oxford University Press.

Truth, The. (1948, June 13). Tale of Table-Thumping in A.B.C. Chief's Office. *The Truth*, p. 8. https://trove.nla.gov.au/newspaper/article/169378780?searchTerm=ABC%20staff%20McCarthy&searchLimits=

Tuchman, G. (1978, January). Making News: A Study in the Construction of Reality. *Social Forces, 59*(4). https://doi.org/10.2307/2578016

University of New England. (2020). Sir Robert Madgwick and His Legacy. Our Values and Culture. *University of New England*.https://www.une.edu.au/about-une/our-values-and-culture/sir-robert-madgwick

USA Today. (2004, June 19). Religion. *USW Today*. https://usatoday30.usatoday.com/news/religion/2004-06-19-church-abuse_x.htm

Vakkayil, J. (2008). Learning and Organizations: Towards Cross-Metaphor Conversations. *Learning Inquiry, 2*(1), 13–27. https://doi.org/10.1007/s11519-008-0025-5

van Acker, E. (2003). Media Representations of Women Politicians in Australia and New Zealand: High Expectations, Hostility or Stardom. *Policy and Society, 22*(1), 116–136. https://doi.org/10.1016/S1449-4035(03)70016-2

Vanstone, A. (2019, October 28). Media Members Have Lead Roles, Too. *The Sydney Morning Herald*, p. 21. Dow Jones Global Factiva.

Varga, R. (2018, September 26). Spigelman Hits Out Over Guthrie Sacking. *The Australian*. https://www.theaustralian.com.au/business/media/abc-former-chairman-james-spigelman-hits-out-over-guthrie-sacking/news-story/9951e4c9f27ef10813f0ecd1abca7e3a

Vine, P. (2017). When Is a Journalist Not a Journalist? Negotiating a New Form of Advocacy Journalism Within the Environmental Movement [online]. *Pacific Journalism Review,* 23(1), 43-54. https://doi.org/10.24135/pjr.v23i1.212

Visentin, L. (2020, November 2). 'Deep Regret': Christine Holgate to Forgo Payout as Australia Post Chief. *The Sydney Morning Herald*. https://www.smh.com.au/politics/federal/christine-holgate-to-resign-as-australia-post-chief-20201102-p56ask.html

Wade, L. (2011). Journalism, Advocacy and the Social Construction of Consensus. *Media, Culture & Society, 33*(8), 1166–1184. https://doi.org/10.1177/0163443711418273

Wanous, J. P., Reichers, A. E., & Austin, J. T. (2004). Cynicism about Organizational Change: An Attribution Process Perspective. *Psychological Reports, 94*(3, Suppl), 1421–1434. https://doi.org/10.2466/pr0.94.3c.1421-1434

Ward, S. J. A. (2014). Radical Media Ethics: Ethics for a Global Digital World. *Digital Journalism, 2*(4), 455–471. https://doi.org/10.1080/21670811.2014.952985

Warren, M. (2005). What Separation of Powers? (Australia). *Monash University Law Review, 31*(1). (Contribution posted 2019). https://doi.org/10.26180/5db7f780d5393

Waterhouse-Watson, D. (2016). News Media on Trial: Towards a Feminist Ethics of Reporting Footballer Sexual Assault Trials. *Feminist Media Studies, 16*(6), 952–967. https://doi.org/10.1080/14680777.2016.1162827

Weaver, D. (Ed.). (1998). *The Global Journalist: News People Around the World.* Hampton Press.

Werner, W. (2004). "What Does This Picture Say?" Reading the Intertextuality of Visual Images. *International Journal of Social Education, 19.* https://eric.ed.gov/?id=EJ718728

West, A. (2020). Did a Former Vatican Official Pay a Bribe to Tilt the George Pell Trial? *ABC.* The Religion and Ethics Report. https://www.abc.net.au/radionational/programs/religionandethicsreport/could-former-vatican-staffer-have-bribed-to-tilt-the-pell-case/12738792

West, K., & Lloyd, J. (2017). The Role of Labelling and Bias in the Portrayals of Acts of "Terrorism": Media Representations of Muslims vs. *Non-Muslims. Journal of Muslim Minority Affairs, 37*(2), 211–222. https://doi.org/10.1080/13602004.2017.1345103

Westmore, P. (2018, October 20). Media: Internal Strife at Fortress ABC [online]. *News Weekly.* 3031, p. 13. https://search.informit.com.au/documentSummary;dn=988136489334664;res=IELAPA

Whitehead, G. (1988). *Inside the ABC: Geoffrey Whitehead's Personal Account.* Penguin Books Victoria.

Willem, A., De Vos, A., & Buelens, M. (2010). Comparing Private and Public Sector Employees' Psychological Contracts Do They Attach Equal Importance to Generic Work Aspects? *Public Management Review, 12*(2), 275-302. https://www-tandfonline-com.wwwproxy1.library.unsw.edu.au/doi/pdf/10.1080/14719031003620323?needAccess=true

Wilson, C. K., Hutchinson, J., & Shea, P. (2010). Public Service Broadcasting, Creative Industries, and Innovation Infrastructure: The Case of ABC's Pool. *Australian Journal of Communication, 37*(3), 15–32. https://primoa.library.unsw.edu.au/permalink/f/11jha62/TN_informit_apaft201102742

Winslow, D. (1999). Rites of Passage and Group Bonding in the Canadian Airborne. *Armed Forces & Society, 25.* http://afs.sagepub.com/content/25/3/429

Wood, G., & Schaffer, B. (1985). *Labelling in Development Policy: Essays in Honour of Bernard Schaffer.* Sage Publications.

Xie, Q. (2018). Analysis of Intertextuality in English News Headlines. (Report). *Theory and Practice in Language Studies., 8*(8), 1010–1014. https://doi.org/10.17507/tpls.0808.13

Younger, E. (2019, April 15). George Pell Media Contempt Case Could Have 'Chilling Effect' on Open Justice, Court Hears. *Australian Broadcasting Corporation.* https://www.abc.net.au/news/2019-04-15/george-pell-guilty-verdict-coverage-media-contempt-case/11002760

CHAPTER 4

What Ideas Rule? A Decline Towards "pop and pap" or a "duty to serve"?

4.1 A Confused World Seeking a Truth

In 2018, the Secretary General of the United Nations, António Guterres, warned that the world had "a bad case of trust deficit disorder" because "democratic principles are under siege, and the rule of law is being undermined" (Guterres, 2018).[1] Professor Ian Goldin, from Oxford University in the UK said: "We've seen that time and again around the world. That's what populism and nationalism are based on, the illegitimacy of many decisions" (Funnell, 2020).[2] Goldin gave as an example US President Donald Trump, who did not support the international order (as past incumbents) and had a narrower framing of US interests. Populist politics have emerged around the world and are now having a serious impact on the functioning of democracies. For instance, it has been described as the "demented twin—political + populism" (Beaglehole, 2018).[3] Communication becomes limited because it can only happen when there is "shared cultural meaning, the essence of communication" (Castells, 2008).[4]

Çıdam (2016) said in terms of social riots there is much to be lost when matters degenerate into a violent collective outburst because it indicates confusion and lack of capacity to state a common, organised purpose (ibid.).[5] The same sorts of chaos could be ascribed to social media which encourages agitprop (political propaganda) and all views are platformed equally. Social media also has the capacity to erase acknowledgement of

V. Small, *Strangling Aunty: Perilous Times for the Australian Broadcasting Corporation*,
https://doi.org/10.1007/978-981-16-0776-9_4

how resistance measures of the past were successful (Loc. Cit.).[6] Post-Marxist political intellectual Ernesto Laclau (1990)[7] said there was a need for hegemonic alliances in the struggle for equality. This view stands in stark contrast to the divisions among groups in society and inchoate voices on social media that, bewilderingly, all claim similar objectives—yet represent separate factions (Devenney et al., 2016).[8] Accetti et al. (2016) contended that democracy's central claim was to freedom of opinion, yet this had been distorted when it was re-defined as "will and opinion" (ibid.) and that these then by-passed representative democracy in favour of "reducing politics to a zero-sum struggle between the 'people' and its 'other' in which pluralism and individual rights are ultimately under threat" (Accetti et al., 2016).[9] Cultural relativism also plays a part in challenging the people's voice in a democracy (Macmullan, 2005)[10] where no single view is representative of the common good.

Waisbord (2018) argued the rise of populist politics was a consequence of "post truth communication" because of the decline in the traditions of mass media information gathering and dissemination and a rise in populism that pursues, in its stead, an inverted Manicheism where the material world becomes good and the spiritual world becomes evil. At odds with this is the collectivist approach that reaches a consensus of reality and assertions (Ibid.).[11] SØren Kierkegaard (1941) identified a performative element of truth and that this truth was created by a chain of performances (ibid.).[12] This same performative truth supports the strident voices of social media. Looking even further back, the fourth President of the US, James Madison (also known as the father of the US Constitution), said that ultimately: "all governments rest on opinion, it is no less true that the strength of opinion in each individual, and its practical influence on his conduct, depend much on the number which he supposes to have entertained the same opinion" (Madison, 1788).[13]

As a dominant mindset it means individuals and state actors will look inwards and split the world and issues into simplistic binaries of good and evil, powerful and oppressed, black and white, left and right, with no tolerance of the nuanced 'grey' areas of discussions. In 1859, British political philosopher and classical liberalist John Stuart Mill (1859) wrote in his profoundly influential essay "On Liberty" that: "there is no such thing as absolute certainty" and that its danger is that it assumes the truth and denies judgement. He gave as an example, "the most intolerant of churches, the Roman Catholic Church, even at the canonisation of a saint, admits, and listens patiently to, a "devil's advocate""(ibid.).[14][15] Francis Fukuyama (2018) has described the current times as a "democratic recession"[16] (quoting democracy scholar Larry Diamond) which was triggered by the deleterious effect on the individual of unemployment and money worries in the 2008 US sub-prime market collapse, as well was the threat to the European Union (EU) because of Greece's insolvency. As a consequence, Russia and China became "much more self-confident and assertive" (Fukuyama, ibid.).[17] Further examples of this, he said, was the election of US President Donald Trump and the British vote to leave the EU both because of workers' concerns about job losses: due to mass immigration to the UK and loss of industry to other countries and similar concerns about fewer industries in the US.

There have been large-scale negative consequences from the rush to embrace globalisation. This has given rise to what Fukuyama's defined as the "politics of resentment" (2018)[18] and "resentment at indignities" (ibid.)[19] where actors mobilised groups of people to support a belief when they felt insulted and outraged by political developments. He said new groups had emerged because they believed their identities were not taken seriously—hence the rise of identity politics based on "nation, religion, ethnicity, sexual orientation, sex, or gender".[20] Fukuyama (2018) said that while humans have always had individual identities the view had taken hold that "the authentic inner self is intrinsically valuable, and the outer society systematically is wrong and unfair in its valuation" (Loc. Cit.)[21] of the individual's identity. The individual no longer has to fit into society, society has to fit-in with the individual and these feelings of the individual (of being ignored or abused) are far stronger than economic and political complaints.

Many populist narratives blame power élites, ruling élites and privileged people (of any grouping) for problems and crises and much of media discourse involves struggles over meaning (Gamson et al., 1992[22]) for these groupings. Labels are common when actors are perceived as traitors; such as "Crooked Hilary",[23] a term used by US President Donald Trump to describe Hilary Clinton in the 2016 Presidential election. Academics Mudde and Kaltwasser (2013) described populism as not only being a binaried battle between good and evil but also a belief in popular sovereignty "at all cost" (ibid.).[24] However, this can have consequences for democracy in that populism forces the conviction that it is asserting the will of the people, but often fakes a consensus. This can lead to authoritarianism—where attacks on actors who do not agree with populist views are de-legitimated (Loc. Cit.),[25] de-platformed and denigrated. Academic research has found that people with populist views are heavy Facebook users (Fletcher, 2018).[26]

In Australia, trust in governments is declining as it is around the world, and backlash against social change has triggered support for minor political parties (Wood et al., 2018).[27] There was also a "coarseness" emerging in Australia's public debates that promoted violence (Soutphommasane, 2018)[28] and the level of engagement of Australians in the public sphere and on social media had reached abusive and destructive levels. Jürgen Habermas (1962)[29] theorised that the public sphere was the formative place for democracy where there was a free engagement with representative ideas resulting in the formation of public opinion. When conceived, the theory envisaged that mass communication, in its idealised form, guaranteed access and universality. It was this ideal that had sustained the ABC, originally as a broadcaster to the masses. The literature said that there had been a change in the media long ago towards serving the interests of the individual reader (Eisenstein, 1979)[30] rather than the public interest. Social media had accentuated this shift. The ABC no longer spoke to one public—it catered for multiple "publics" (dispersed individuals) who could be anywhere, anytime, anyone and anything (an internet robot). Since the departure from a vision and mandate that supported, informed and inspired a common, universal, public good; it had handed control of the Australian imagination to its 2.0 audiences. It had drifted from its historic assertion "this is who you are—I see you" to asking an unresolvable: "what do you think?".

U.S. political scientist, Lance Bennet, said in his 1998 lecture "uncivic culture" that "coherent societies and effective governments" were confronting "the breakdown of broadly shared social and political experience, and the rise of personalized realities" (ibid.).[31] This had been caused by the advance of individualism and personal communication technologies. Fewer people join groups, yet ironically more people display social trust in online tribes with people they do not know and these tribes develop their own momentum to become a bandwagon with the capacity to gerrymander and manipulate opinions. Concomitant with that has been a decline in trust in leaders and leadership and a growth in public cynicism (ibid.).[32] A consequence of this, is that it is increasingly problematic for governments, and the ABC, to represent the interests of 'the public' because it has ruptured into disparate groups constantly shifting and changing (Loc. Cit.).[33] There is no money anymore in representing the public view, rather it is hoped the goal to hunt down the latest tribe in the zeitgeist will bear fruit. Allied to this, consumerism has created a greater value placed on acquisition, yet set in an environment of precarious employment pressuring individuals into performing multiple paid jobs to create a single "living wage". Bennett (1998) said the fragmenting of society along these lines, and in-built uncertainty, may be a hidden trigger of anger and belligerence, or what he termed "anger politics" (ibid.).[34]

Outbursts could be considered an individual's expression of their own identity politics and personal identity, where both have replaced collective identity. It was on this level of anger that people now engaged with politics and political actors (Bennett, 1998)[35]—and they expressed themselves in a similar way online. In addition, the professional media, as part of this larger process of media, has encouraged participants to treat politics as a game—winners, losers, rules, point scoring, cutting people off, rough treatment, speaking to them as if they were players (Bennett ibid.).[36] The has meant the contested media 'field' is a 'field' of war—one where the media has, unfortunately, presided over a decline in standards of trust, civility and erosion of respect—everyone is a player/combatant aiming to get the advantage/humiliate and win. Interviews with politicians now take this format and audiences are disadvantaged as the engagement is turned into another form of combat sport which the journalist aims to win. The more battered and bruised the politicians, the more successful, knowledgeable and meritorious is considered the journalist. In the absence of researched and specifically backgrounded questions, the use of "gotcha" moments[37] helps enliven the scoreboard and shared snippets of these interviews ("grabs") then set social media alight with support and disparagement of the politician.

The consequence of these "journalism sports" is that they often leave fragmented audiences even more confused and poorly informed. Aunty is in a dither over this. In an intense online media field of war it was claimed in 2020 that the ABC was paying Google AUD500,000 to boost its television audiences through buying 1289 keyword search terms, including misspellings, to direct traffic to its online television content advertisements (Tabakoff, 2020).[38] This was not new to the commercial 'field' where it is done as a matter of course to herd and corral audiences. In 2018 the ABC spent AUD2 million per annum promoting ABC content on Google and Facebook (McCauley, 2018).[39] In a Senate Estimates Committee hearing ABC Chief Financial Officer, Louise Higgins, said around AUD1.4 million would be spent on Facebook advertising and AUD500,000 on Google AdWords. The committee was told this was around half the ABC's AUD4 million annual marketing budget (ibid.). In an interesting exchange, Higgins told the committee it was "not a competition":

> Our job is not just making great distinctive Australian content and ensuring it's distributed on the platforms that Australians want to consume it. ... It's also about them being aware of the content that's available to them. (McCauley, ibid.)

However, two contentious challenges from commercial media competing in the same 'field' were that:

(1) The ABC had emerged from public broadcasting to become a commercial publisher; and,
(2) It was spending public money to compete with the private sector by driving traffic in the emergent commercial field.

Three additional accusations were made by Fairfax Media in 2017. Former Chief Executive Officer Fairfax Media (now Nine Entertainment), Greg Hywood, said the ABC was disadvantaging commercial outfits, paying taxpayer money to Google—a firm that pays minimal tax itself—for its search engine marketing and, ultimately, these disadvantage "traditional media companies" by furthering the digital duopoly of Facebook and Google (Bingemann, 2017).[40] It is good business practice for commercial media outlets to try to drive "eyeballs" to their content by buying up search terms on Google and advertising on Facebook. But the literature argued that in an era of information abundance, the role of the public broadcaster had to change from its model of information scarcity (Andrejevic, 2013)[41] but that chasing and poaching the major media monopolies' (Nine Entertainment and News Corporation) audiences may not be the best priority in re-casting its operating model without first defining and defending its individuating qualities.

The situation also provoked the discussion of whether internet service providers were "essential facilities" or "natural monopolies" that required regulation (Thierer, 2013)[42] and further: "marketplace experimentation in search of sustainable business models should not be made illegal" (ibid.).[43] The reliance by public corporations (e.g., the ABC) on online media corporations (e.g., Google) has been described as a "public failure" (Vaidhyanathan, 2011 in Andrejevic, 2013). Andrejevic (2013) said given the Google has made a business model that relies on monitoring its users browsing habits and tracking consumption, this presented a challenge for public service media which was supposed to hold a non-discriminatory stance of 'all to all' an allowing its audience freedom to pursue content without being monetised. Google is being used by the ABC and commercial media competitors, where Google is a public information provider and top search engine on the internet (@Alexa 2020).[44] As a public information provider, it surveils activities and behaviours. It plys its trade in what is described as the attention economy. There are concerns that the internet in Western societies focuses on entertainment and commerce (Lee, 2010).[45] In addition to this, the ABC copes with additional attendant expectations and requirements from its funders (the people and their governments) of impartiality and views not limited and defined by financial opportunity. That the ABC has segued to a reliance on Google, means there is an overlap of the accountable with the unaccountable, and ABC audiences are now the prey of Google and its accompanying business, marketing and contractual arrangements elsewhere.

In the ABC's shift to the crowded commercial 'field', not the ABC, but the public, has been privatised. Graeme Murdock (2004) (quoted in the previous chapter) said: "public service broadcasting is a project whose time has finally come both philosophically and practically".[46] He also said commercial arguments dispute public service media's role, serve to nobble the capacity of public service media as well as "jettison" the public service role of commercial media. He said where once the state sought to shore-up for its citizens: "information rights", "knowledge rights", "deliberative rights" (viewing, listening to, or contributing to debates), "representation rights" and "participation rights"; public service media should now look to lead and be the heart of a "digital commons" where they linked with other public and civil organisations to become: "defined by its shared refusal of commercial enclosure and its commitment to free and universal access, reciprocity, and collaborative activity" (Murdock, ibid.).[47] He said PSM had the capacity to counter the fragmentation of the internet caused by the binaries of "them" and "us" by providing this central hub where ideas can be debated in safety, thereby reclaiming, shoring-up public trust (ibid.) in PSM.

4.2 "Getting down" with Social Media

Social media refers to "an activity, a software tool or a platform" (Hermida, 2012)[48] and one of the main tools used in social media is Twitter, requiring the user to confine comments to no more than 140 characters and encourages users to label their messages with a #hashtag—a topic—which aids in grouping comments. It is a marketing tool that aggregates users on the same topic. Described in the literature as "ambient journalism" (ibid.)[49] or to the other extreme by sociologist Stanley Cohen (2011) as "sporadic, mindless and staccato yelps",[50] Twitter brought together journalists with everyone else in a very hectic environment where "everyone is a publisher" and "powerful corporations and advertisers ... can easily do "brand journalism"" (Ward, 2014) where journalists can also be employed to tell stories about products (influencers) and editorial integrity for professional journalists is compromised (Ward ibid.).[51] All this content resides in the context where reporting can mean anything. It is an ideal environment for journalists to inhabit because news moves swiftly through the cyber-sphere environment seething with "networks of outrage and hope" (Castells, 2012).[52] Backgrounding this is media ethics, the chief concerns of which were: "truth … freedom and responsibility … privacy … and the quality of media content" (Drozdek, 2015).[53]

Schneider (Altheide & Schneider, 2013) said research on the uses of social media showed how elements of culture and digital communication have changed social action and broadened meanings of social control and social interaction (Ibid.).[54] US academic and journalist, Allissa Richardson (2017), said the rise of digital technology had brought about "impromptu acts of journalism" (ibid.)[55] and posed the question whether "counter publics" were now setting the agenda for the professional media through social media, or whether journalists were still able to do so because they were believed to be more astute to their voices (Richardson ibid.).[56] Social media is an indispensable research tool for ABC journalists, as well as all others, which means professional communicators must be networked. The rise of 'mobile journalism' means reporters can use their personal devices and take full responsibility for every aspect of the content of their news reports, including the production and editing of photography and videos.

US Research showed that mobile journalists had less expertise and specialist knowledge (Blankenship, 2016), burdened by having to do everything. CNN Pentagon correspondent, Jamie McIntyre said in 2008: "When you're a TV reporter and you're doing everything yourself, it changes the way you tell a story" (Blankenship, ibid.).[57] There is also a perceived lack of need to train journalists in the finer skills of using the new technologies because of their relative ease of use and certain belief that everyone has a mobile phone and uses it with extreme competence and optimal expertise. Yet, studies have also raised concern that the new "multi-skilled" journalist may be forced to compromise standards because of the need for speed. In 2011, former ABC senior investigative journalist Chris Masters wrote positively about the ABC: "I don't know if that happens often enough in journalism, where we can arrive at a workplace and be allowed to do our duty as good journalists and responsible citizens" (Masters, quoted in Higgins, 2011).[58] Perhaps, in the devolution of newsrooms and febrile multi-tasking now demanded, that—and the enjoyment of doing one's duty—may be becoming a memory?

Everyone wants to be first. Of course. Most especially in the media. But the trends towards bias and partiality "deprofessionalise" journalism and means reporters are becoming less professional, ethically, as has been found in other areas of employment that now also favoured the 'multi-task', flexible approach to jobs (Blankenship, 2016) and in a society known to be in "an era of moral chaos" (Kamto, 1997). Gone are the days when journalists from rival news organisations would run into each other and ask "what do you know?" and the standard guarded, elusive reply would always be "not much". Backpack journalism and activity on social media give a lot away—work, interests and opinions—and journalists follow and praise each other online, anyway. Journalists' online activity also gives the policing, security and foreign agencies abundant information to reap on what they know. Individuals leave detectable and, usually, permanent footprints. Sloan and Warner (2016)[59] said privacy was being violated by both governments and business where "the governmental threat is serious and increasingly worrisome" (ibid.) although concerns have been articulated and better understood—those less discussed were privacy incursions on the individual by business which "now have the technological means to merge your online and offline footprints into profiles of surprising intrusiveness and accuracy" (Loc. Cit.). Data mining and databases are extraordinarily valuable, and to track and trace the ABC audience offers a whole new market to be pursued and watched. Social media might also provide a wealth of understandings for foreign actors, for example, in understandings the private views of citizens of Central Asian nations restricted by governments (Imamova, 2015).[60] Mindful of this, journalists had resorted to encryption and security technologies to exchange secure information with a heightened awareness of the dangers involved online (Waters, 2018).[61]

Journalists had another form of intelligence and information gathering; that supplied by their publics—what Steve Mann (2004)[62] first described as "sousveillance" or the opposite of surveillance. 'Sousveillance' ('*sous*' from the French 'under') means the people are watching the government, while surveillance implies that "Big Brother" is watching the people ('*sur*' from the French 'above'). Mann's (2004) description signalled a significant shift in watching and witnessing when the use of portable devices made sousveillance (watching underneath) by the public so easy and ubiquitous. It now provides the raw material for professional news organisations and augmented gig journalism (casual reporters, contract reporters).

It has seen the demise of professional camera operators and omniaudient sound recorders because everyone had the technology in their hands to bear witness and capture news and it had been seen as an easy (if not unfortunate and lamented) means of cutting costs in newsrooms. The managerialists' belief in their apparent irrelevance has aided the rise of a multi-tasked, can do anything, digital workforce. Quality is not essential, in fact professional expertise, 'polish' and the professional 'eye' are seen to detract from authenticity and the 'real', especially in authentic media depictions, where the authentic is regarded in the literature as culturally constructed, anyway (Jones, 2010; Banet-Weiser, 2012). Nevertheless, there was a counter-cultural emphasis on raw footage as being truly representative of rough and ready verisimilitude. Skilfully shot, lit and edited content supported by clear and deft audio from a pre-emptive sound engineer does not seem to suffice.

This then underscores two larger points that emerge from this compulsory, manifest digital networking in that the professional status of journalists, photographers, camera operators, sound recorders has also been eroded because of the rapid rise of citizen reporters who claim jurisdiction over topics through strident opinions and have footage to back them up through 'sousveillance'—"I'm on it", "I'm across this", "I saw it first". The journalist is no longer the font of information. And, secondly, Twitter was now used by political actors to release and manage breaking news, create reactions and build public support for their political ambitions. Journalists and editors are by-passed and their gate-keeping role redundant. There had been a relocation, or at least a co-location of truth because of the shift away from "the notion of the journalist as the verifier of news and information" (Mann, 2004)[63] which had been "at the core of journalism as a system of knowledge production" (Mann, ibid.). Their by-passing had permitted the undermining of truth with opinion and beliefs. This had been a fundamental shift in media and a major loss for democracy. Once professional journalists sought facts. Negative opinions or personal dislikes for individuals being reported in the news were generally confined to the tea room because journalists intuitively knew they did not constitute truth and the publication of them was not only potentially libellous, it compromised their ethical standing. The facts spoke for themselves; let the public decide. Now journalists had to acknowledge, and incorporate, the voices of their multitudinous, attentive social media audiences as valid, if not more valid because they were 'followers' and provided professional endorsement; thereby confusing truth, or de-prioritising the impartial view, at least.

Research conducted in 2013 (Hanusch, 2013)[64] in Australia of journalism students at universities found that while they saw themselves as the adversarial Fourth Estate they also had a consumer view of the audience, instead of a citizen view and "only a small minority favoured a loyal approach in supporting official policies on national development or conveying a positive image of business or political leadership".[65] Just over half surveyed thought it important to be a detached observer and that the role of watchdog was important. Fewer than half were interested in being a watchdog of business (Hanusch ibid.). Student journalists strongly supported a role as advocates of social change but with less interest in providing citizens with the information they needed to make an informed decision.[66] A large number "supported the use of hidden microphones or cameras" (Hanusch, 2013)[67] as a means of obtaining information. This amounts to an ethical and legal flip that confronts the integrity, and even the role of journalism.

The ABC had a staff social media policy that permitted and encouraged staff to have social media accounts but: "Personal and professional use of social media by ABC staff and contractors must not bring the ABC into disrepute, compromise effectiveness at work, imply ABC endorsement of personal views or disclose, without authorisation, confidential information" (ABC, 2017).[68] The policy, last updated in March 2021, made interesting revisions to the 2017 policy that the ABC was then: "Encouraging staff and contractors to actively engage with social media while being clear who is responsible for personal and professional uses" (ibid). Adding complexity to this policy, it stated (2017): "Interactive services, which include social media like Facebook, YouTube and Twitter, are part of the ABC's future as a public broadcaster and increasingly part of the work and private lives of workers" (ibid.). The revised policy (2021) drew a clear distinction between private social media accounts and ABC ones, meaning staff were at liberty to express personal opinion online because "the ABC distinguishes between its official social media accounts and workers' personal accounts... personal social media activity is not ABC content" (ABC, 2021). This permits ABC journalists to have at least two distinct identities, delineated and dissociative. The BBC begs to differ that this is possible or permissible. It updated its staff social media policy in October 2020 to a much stricter level of accountability for staff's use of social media. Both 'private' or BBC accounts were viewed the same and, therefore, staff could not: "express a personal opinion on matters of public policy, politics, or controversial subjects" (BBC, 2020). Further the BBC said: "If your work requires you to maintain your impartiality, don't express a personal opinion on matters of public policy, politics, or 'controversial subjects'" and, to underline accountability, staff members must "disclose their earnings outside of the corporation on a public database" (BBC, 2020).

Convoluting the ABC's position: "official ABC accounts may be listed and cross-promoted on ABC platforms. Personal accounts may not be listed or cross-promoted on ABC platforms unless editorially justified." The meaning of editorial justification was implied but not defined. The revised ABC social media policy set five standards (adding one to the 2020/2017 four standards below). The additional fifth standard was: "Do not damage the ABC's reputation for impartiality and independence", the others remain the same, although re-ordered. The new standard begged the questions: what did the institution quantify as "damage"? What have been instances in the past of "damage" to provide direction on this point? And, was social media activity a possible area of "damage"?

1. Do not mix the professional and the personal in ways likely to bring the ABC into disrepute.
2. Do not undermine your effectiveness at work.
3. Do not imply ABC endorsement of your personal views.
4. Do not disclose confidential information obtained through work.

ABC journalists and presenters are users of Twitter and some regularly post their opinions on current issues. Twitter account augment their roles. Most have disclaimers that their views are not that of the institution. In 2019 the ABC's Managing Director, David Anderson, was quoted in Australian newspapers saying there was "no evidence of systemic bias at the broadcaster" but "the make-up of the broadcaster's panel shows—which also include weekday current affairs discussion program *The Drum*—could negatively affect public perception" (Duke 2019).[69] Anderson was quoted in the article saying: "the perspective of views that we represent is something that we could improve on" (Duke ibid.). His comments were also posted on the ABC Television News Channel's News Breakfast program Twitter feed during an interview at that time (Meade 2019).[70] Table 4.1 Australian Broadcasting Corporation. (2020). ABC Staff Policy on social media. Retrieved from http://about.abc.net.au/wp-content/uploads/2016/11/2016FederalElectionECRCRPT.pdf ABC social media policy Use of social media. Use of personal social media

Table 4.1 Australian Broadcasting Corporation Editorial Policies. (2014). 7 HARM AND OFFENCE. 9 October 2014. *ABC*. Retrieved from Https://Edpols.Abc.Net.Au/Policies/7-Harm-And-Offence/

Standards
7.1 Content that is likely to cause harm or offence must be justified by the editorial context.
7.2 Where content is likely to cause harm or offence, having regard to the context, make reasonable efforts to provide information about the nature of the content through the use of classification labels or other warnings or advice.
7.3 Ensure all domestic television programs—with the exception of news, current affairs and sporting events—are classified and scheduled for broadcast in accordance with the ABC's Associated Standard on Television Program Classification.
7.4 If inadvertent or unexpected actions, audio or images in live content are likely to cause harm or offence, take appropriate steps to mitigate.
7.5 The reporting or depiction of violence, tragedy or trauma must be handled with extreme sensitivity. Avoid causing undue distress to victims, witnesses or bereaved relatives. Be sensitive to significant cultural practices when depicting or reporting on recently deceased persons.
7.6 Where there is editorial justification for content which may lead to dangerous imitation or exacerbate serious threats to individual or public health, safety or welfare, take appropriate steps to mitigate those risks, particularly by taking care with how content is expressed or presented.
7.7 Avoid the unjustified use of stereotypes or discriminatory content that could reasonably be interpreted as condoning or encouraging prejudice.

accounts during the election period means there can be particular scrutiny of the ABC and the way it upholds its standards. ABC staff and contractors are reminded of the ABC's Use of Social Media Policy and the four standards set out in that policy: 1. Do not mix the professional and the personal in ways likely to bring the ABC into disrepute. 2. Do not undermine your effectiveness at work. 3. Do not imply ABC endorsement of your personal views. 4. Do not disclose confidential information obtained through work. As always, take care not to make comments or post content on official or personal accounts that might compromise the ABC's impartiality or bring the ABC into disrepute. Editorial staff should avoid advocating for a group or cause, or expressing a partisan view on political or controversial issues, where this is likely to create a reasonable perception of bias that may compromise their ability/credibility to report or cover these issues for the ABC.

4.3 Challengers to Anzac Day and Yassmin Abdel-Magied

In a liberal democracy ideas must be constantly tested and debated as the mark of a healthy representative government. In June 2016, Yassmin Abdel-Magied, a Sudanese Australian Muslim Engineer, Young Queenslander of the year in 2010 and Queensland's Young Australian of the Year in 2015, then one of the presenters of the ABC television program, Australia Wide,[71] spoke in support of Sharia Law on an ABC television program *The Drum* saying that Sharia Law "allows for multiple interpretations ... it's about mercy, it's about kindness" (Hall, 2016).[72] The following year, on 13 February 2017, Abdel-Magied had a heated exchange with Independent Senator, Jacqui Lambie, over Sharia Law on ABC Televisions' debate panel *Q and A* program (ABC, 2017).[73] Lambie said supporters of Sharia Law should be deported from Australia. In response, Abdel-Magied said: "Islam to me is the most feminist religion. We got equal rights well before the Europeans. We don't take our husbands' last names because we ain't their property"[74] (ABC, ibid.). Lambie responded: "The fact is we have one law in this country and it is the Australian law—not Sharia Law, not in this country, not in my day" (Loc. Cit.).[75]

Then it was reported by the BBC in 2017, that Abdel-Magied had posted on her Facebook page on Anzac Day a message that denigrated the day. It is a significant public holiday for Australia to commemorate the deaths and service of all Australians who fought or served in wars on behalf of the nation, and the British Empire (especially the Boer War and World War I). While it commemorates the specific day of the landing of Australian and New Zealand (ANZAC) forces at Gallipoli on 25 April 1915 during World War I, the day has become amplified as one that represents Australian values of mateship, endurance and resourcefulness. Abdel-Magied's post referenced Australia's offshore detention centres which held people seeking asylum in Australia, as well as ongoing conflicts in the Middle East, and the Australian Government's support of Israel, described by the Australia department of Foreign Affairs and Trade as "a warm and close relationship with Israel ... supported strongly by Australia's active Jewish community" (Australian Government, n.d.).[76] The BBC said the post was condemned by the Prime Minister, Malcolm Turnbull and senior government ministers (BBC, 2017),[77] while former Federal Labor Government Minister for Transport and Communications, Graham Richardson, was quoted that it "demonstrates what is wrong with the ABC" (Grattan, 2017).[78]

Abdel-Magied's post prompted a furore on social media such that it was reported she deleted the comment and posted a response. The ABC reported that she acknowledged the post was disrespectful and apologised unreservedly (ABC, 2017).[79] Adelaide's Imam Sheikh Mohammad Tawhidi called for her to be sacked and that the ABC should distance itself from the presenter (*The Guardian,* 2017).[80] In addition, a right-wing group named Alt-Con gathered more than 15 000 signatures in a petition on Change.org calling for her to be sacked (ibid.).[81] The group accused Abdel-Magied of "blatantly lying to the public about the merits of Sharia Law and the oppressive impact it has on non-Muslim groups, homosexuals and women". The then (and current) Deputy Prime Minister Barnaby Joyce said: "It starts to become a sense that the culture of the ABC is in some instances at odds with the culture of Australia" (ABC, ibid.). The ABC absolved itself of any consequences of the comments, consistent with its social media policy for staff that: "Ms Abdel-Magied is also engaged in a range of other activities and work that is not related to the ABC. Her views and opinions in that capacity are her own and do not represent those of the ABC" (Loc. Cit.). Former federal Liberal minister (now ABC Radio presenter), Amanda Vanstone, said Abdel-Magied's Facebook post "was inevitably going to cause offence and controversy. ... Many find it difficult to accept that she didn't understand that at the time" (Ibid.).[82]

Further, the ABC confirmed Abdel-Magied had not violated ABC policies and that "Yassmin was aware the program was under review and we are discussing with her future opportunities at the ABC" (Meade, 2017).[83] Abdel-Magied had to move to another home and change her telephone number (Marks, 2017)[84] because media reports said she had received death and sexual assault threats. Such violent hostility emerged that one Sydney radio commentator said she would be "tempted to run over Yassmin Abdel-Magied" (Zhou, 2017).[85] Then in November 2017, on Remembrance Day (the cessation of hostilities in Europe ending World War I) Abdel-Magied was reported to have posted on Facebook a revived recontextualisation of her offending Anzac Day tweet. This time linking Remembrance Day (11 November) with Australia's use of offshore detention centres (Wilkie, 2017).[86] Abdel-Magied then moved to London saying she was "the most publicly hated Muslim in Australia" (Abdel-Magied, 2017)[87] and "betrayed by my own country" (ibid.).[88] She told a news outlet her crime was to "imagine I was Australian enough to be able to criticise Australia or contribute to public discussion on my own terms" (Loc. Cit.).[89] There was support for Abdel-Magied in the belief she had been subjected to racism.

Anzac Day, and the mythology and history surrounding it, were firmly entrenched in Australian's understandings of themselves. Public broadcasters were inevitably part of upholding that narrative of nationhood and there were expectations created, chiefly from its own past policy and programming efforts, for example the live coverage of the Anzac Day Dawn Services and marches in capital cities, in tandem with government policy, that it should be upheld and respected—universally. This analysis showed one of the ways in which the ABC had abandoned Bourdieu's field of intellectual and cultural debate by encouraging its actors to have direct contact with audiences through social media, while also not having the capacity to deflect accusations of bias or controversy when opinions offended. This strategy of direct contact aimed at endearing staff to audiences was a high risk institutional strategy that could also backfire, leaving Aunty voiceless—and that disclaimers, ultimately only served a thin legal purpose (possibly) and are neither shields to hide behind nor successful devices to de-couple the employer from the employee. It effectively meant that each staff member was a spokesperson for the ABC. The corporate literature cautioned that only trained spokespeople should speak on behalf of an organisation and be limited to speaking notes—otherwise the message was unclear (Bonk, 2008). While some outfits used spokespeople to "humanise their brands" (Fleck et al. 2014), the advertising literature warned that brand spokespeople could "depict too much reality, ... and the result may be scepticism, doubting, and perhaps even a backlash on the part of the intended audience". The literature said that Twitter users regarded any activity on Twitter by any broadcasters as showing they were active participants (Drauker, 2015 in Dynel et al., 2015).[90]

4.4 Q&A and Feminists

When UNSW Professor of Law and Social Theory, Martin Krygier, presented an ABC Boyer lecture on ABC Radio in 1997 on The Uses of Civility (Krygier, 1997) he observed that: "not only is civility better than incivility, when non-intimates meet, but it is immensely productive" (Krygier, ibid.). This section will analyse another example of the ABC's *field* drift to the commercial *field* in terms of how it now conducted public television debates on significant topics. This section will examine disagreements surrounding the content and execution of a specific episode of the ABC's television forum program *Q and A*. The ABC has regularly looked to keep pace with perceived shifts in Australian values, and part of this expression manifested in the founding of the annual radio Boyer Lectures which began in 1959 on ABC Radio. At first named the ABC Lectures, they were renamed the Boyer Lectures in 1959 after Chairman Richard Boyer who first suggested the lectures. They consisted of a series of talks each year by a prominent Australian and covered all areas of intellectual life and learning in Australia.[91] It had been a consistent presentation of Australian views; the sub-text was that it asked Australian audiences to listen carefully and consider their place in the world.

Another form of citizen engagement offered by the ABC was that of ABC Television's Q and A program where current major topics were debated by a panel with an ABC moderator. In 2015, Senator James McGrath told a Senate Estimates Committee about concerns with the ABC Television debate program *Q and A* that "there was a widespread view within the Coalition that the program is biased against the conservative side of politics" (Knott, 2015).[92] The Managing Director, Mark Scott, told McGrath at the hearing: "It is not the first time I've heard that depiction". Scott said in the program's defence it: "regularly features one politician from the left and one from the right" (Ibid.).[93]

However, a controversial turn of events occurred on 4 November 2019 that challenged the belief that the ABC program upheld institutionally a balance of ideologies, sparked questions of relevance and even raised ethical considerations related to the ABC's Charter. It confronted the ABC's capacity to hold a debate—a formal, mediated discussion. In 2019, *Q and A* televised a program titled "Broadside" named after the feminist festival in Melbourne at that time. In summary, the program televised views that exhorted Australians to carry out extrajudicial killings and arson and *The Sydney Morning Herald* reported: "The word "f---", or various iterations of it, were used at least 10 times during the broadcast" (Carmody, 2019).[94] Egyptian-American author and feminist, Mona Eltahawy, declared on the television program: "How long must we wait for men and boys to stop murdering us, to stop beating us and to stop raping us. How many rapists must we kill … until men stop raping us (ABC, 2019).[95] In the program, Aboriginal and Torres Strait Islander screenwriter, Nayuka Gorrie, said violence was "okay" in the context of reacting against the oppression of Aboriginal people and referred to that as a tipping point where she looked forward to the time when "people start burning stuff" (ABC, 2019).[96]

The program, which consisted of five panellists, was taken down from the ABC's catch-up television service iView four days later and there was a neutral response from the ABC with an implied acceptance that women were allowed to incite violence publicly. The Managing Director, David Anderson, said there would be an investigation into the program but that:

> The intention of the program was to present challenging ideas from high-profile feminists whose expertise ranges across ageism, disability, Indigenous and domestic violence issues. The ABC acknowledges that the program was provocative in regard to the language used and some of the views presented. (ABC, 2019)[97]

ABC Chair, Ita Buttrose said: “I agree with David’s statement, which I’ve discussed with him … we can’t do much more than issue the statement that we have, and we won’t be repeating the program. The plan is to take it off” (ABC, ibid.).[98] The Federal Communications Minister, Paul Fletcher, said: “while the ABC had editorial independence, he believed the investigation was “appropriate”, given the “significant community concern” generated” (Loc. Cit.).[99] The Australian Communications and Media Authority received 53 complaints (Denholm ibid.)[100] but a subsequent ACMA investigation found that the ABC did not breach its Code of Practice (ACMA, 2020).[101] The ABC was reported to have taken 235 complaints (Carmody, 2019).[102] A subsequent ABC investigation found that it had taken appropriate and “sufficient” (Carmody, ibid.) action by removing the program from digital platforms.

There is a widely shared view in the literature, however, that violence is a negative act (Fishman & Marvin, 2003)[103] and language promoting it detrimental to society because “too many morbid, violent, and negative media stories may overpower the human capacity for optimism” (Edwards & Fuller, 2020). Further, there were laws and policies in place which created deterrence and punishment for violence—violent crimes. The program was another example of how the ABC had abandoned Bourdieu’s *field* of intellectual and cultural debate in favour of a performative ruckus and confronting theatre. It also showed how the drift from the intellectual *field* of debate meant that the ABC had become engaged in a cultural battle over narratives of sexuality, culture, appropriate levels of violence (in this instance) and the destruction of authority, but not in aid of determining civil engagement and justice. In effect, the ABC had taken on the *field* of commercial media—redolent with ad hoc reality entertainment and the multi-faceted content of digitisation—but the commensurate loss meant the ABC was in a new realm where:

> The web flattens hierarchies, exposes content sources, and deforms journalistic authority by disarticulating the audience. (Nerone & Barnhurst, 2001)[104]

Federal Liberal Senator Eric Abetz said the *Q and A* program showed a "cultural problem with the ABC" and that "the average Australian would be horrified at the suggestion that violence might be an appropriate course of action in relation to political matters, yet not one of the chosen panel were of that (anti-violence) view" (Denholm, 2019).[105] In 1997, Professor Gay Hawkins, had decided there were cultural problems at the ABC, one of which was:

> "Logistics and economics of a national broadcasting service place difficult constraints on how difference can be recognized and serviced ..." there is "a deep contradiction within the current practices of the ABC between an audience imagined as heterogeneous and a schedule that grows more and more homogenized by the day". (Hawkins, 1997)[106]

And that from Hawkins' research project it was found that while ABC Television aspired to be representative of Australian society, it had come at the cost of "difference and diversity in programming" (Hawkins, ibid.).

The ABC had moved from its civic and representative duty towards what Federal Communications Minister, Paul Fletcher, described as "offensive language" and "endorsement of violence" (Blackiston, 2019).[107] There was a subsequent blaze of reaction on social media with positive and supportive Twitter comments for *Q and A* quoted by The Guardian newspaper (Henriques-Gomez, 2019).[108] Some of these included praise and relief that the ABC was keeping politicians and those who support politicians out of the program (Coë & Moore, 2019).[109] The program also sparked a furore on social media "shocked by such brazen support for violence" (Coë & Moore, ibid.). It was reported by London's The Daily Mail that Tweets covered topics such as removing ABC funding, accusations of partisan broadcasting and veiled concerns that the ABC was repeatedly promoting violence (Loc. Cit.). Further, these Twitter activities were not only instances which challenged the authorial 'field' of journalism as the voice of authority, but it also showed how panellists had subverted the "top down approach of traditional journalism" (Hermida, 2012).[110] The use of expletives, even though the moderator of the panel Fran Kelly, cautioned that "We are trying to keep the language under control. If you're offended by the profanity, maybe leave now" (Henriques-Gomez, 2019)[111] was aimed at an imagined, homogeneous Australian audience that would be watching and would find this style of communication engaging and entertaining. The program signalled that the ABC had merged into the commercial field of sensation genre through offensive language, advocating violence, extrajudicial killings and arson. It was reality television without attendant commercial worries about offending advertisers and driving away audiences, but it had also lost sight of its general ABC audience that included all tastes, and not one necessarily in pursuit of wrangles that failed to achieve a conciliated outcome as a priority.

Social psychology academic Leary (1995) said "people regularly tailor their self-presentations to the target's values" and that "people tend to present themselves in a self-enhancing way" because they had already assumed the attitude of the audience and how they would impress them with their particular image (Leary, 1995).[112] Institutional analysis literature said the ABC consisted of: "interpretive mechanisms that filter, decode and translate the semiotics of broader social systems" (Rao & Giorgi, 2006).[113] As such, Suddaby (2010) said researchers should look at the processes rather than the products. So, for example, this controversial episode of *Q and A* provided a good example of how the ABC operated in its emergent commercial ***field*** and the move away from its ***habitus***. As such Suddaby (2010) said institutions should be regarded as "engage(d) in structured patterns of collective *interpretation* which involves the attachment of meaning to events and the infusion of value into organizational processes and outcomes" (ibid).[114] Institutions, according to Suddaby (2010), needed to be viewed as "sophisticated managers of symbolic resources".[115] This program also showed the ABC was fully engaged in the commercial sphere where sensational conflict and destructive comment was valued and marketable. After the program, it was reported that *Q and A* tweeted an ameliorative comment from Mona Eltahawy in her calls for extrajudicial killings that softened her calls for violence (Truu, 2019)[116] and situated violence as a daily reality for women. It is mandated that programming on all broadcast media is that if a program contains language that may offend there is a warning issued at the start of the program. The ABC has rules for strong language requiring that programs announce up front if "strong" language was being used. Following are the ABC Editorial Policies relating to Harm and Offence (Table 4.1):

In addition, in the preamble to the ABC's Editorial Policies on Hate Speech, Terrorism & Mass Killings it states:

> The media, public officials, politicians, commentators and the general public can all fuel extremism and division—sometimes deliberately and sometimes inadvertently ...
>
> Inappropriate media coverage can encourage copy-cat behaviour and propagate ideas that can cause significant harm and offence.
>
> It can also increase prejudice and stigmatisation of vulnerable communities and individuals.
>
> The ABC, along with other mass media, plays an important role shaping community debate as well as the critical role of informing the public.
>
> This document seeks to provide assistance to content makers looking to find a balance between the often-competing demands of the ABC's commitment to freedom of speech, impartiality and the public's right to be informed against the potential harm this content may cause.[117]

An article critical of ABC content offerings for 2020 by culture writer for *The Sydney Morning Herald* and *The Age*, Karl Quinn, quoted by *The Australian* columnist Gerard Henderson said:

> The ABC's war with conservative commentators and politicians looks likely to continue with the national broadcaster unveiling on Thursday a 2020 TV programming slate almost guaranteed to fire up the national broadcaster's critics. Indigenous issues, climate change and clerical abuse spearhead a line-up of original Australian content that Michael Carrington, ABC's director of entertainment and specialist programming, promised "will speak to and for all Australians, firing their imagination through bold content and creativity. (Henderson, 2019)[118]

Further, the article quoted ABC Director of Entertainment and Specialist programming, Michael Carrington: "We would be letting them down if we chose our content based on the views of a relatively small number of critics" (Henderson ibid.). On the subject of ABC relevance, former ABC Chairman, James Spigelman, was quoted in 2013 alighted upon a point of difference between the ABC and its general audience: "the ABC invariably forgets that some people are more interested in electricity prices than same-sex marriage".[119] Crikey journalist, Stephen Brook, who attended the 2020 ABC program launch was quoted:

> The ABC laid it on thick, with commitments to First Australians, diversity and inclusion mentioned continually. In fact, the only place where this commitment to diversity evaporates is at the top of the ABC. The board and executive team are whiter than a loaf of Tip-Top Sunblest. It is easy to chide

the ABC for wokeness, and I made passing reference to this to an ABC staffer on the way out, who smiled and said "well this is the national broadcaster". (Henderson, 2019)[120]

4.5 Manifest Offence

In 2020 reference to the same editorial policies on harm and offence saw the ABC disown its previously commissioned and screened top-rating comedy productions made by Australian comedian Chris Lilley, after they were reconsidered as offensive some decades post-screening. Lilley portrayed a Tongan boy painted with a "brown face" and the reaction against this became pronounced in response to the deleting of the comedian's work from leading online entertainment providers Netflix and Stan. The trigger event was the Black Lives Matter protests around Australia in response to the sadistic killing of an unarmed black American by US police in 2020 and consequent calls for racial justice. Chris Lilley was once described by *The Guardian* newspaper as: "a homegrown critical and audience success story for the ABC" (Meade, 2015) was no longer so, for re-framed cultural reasons. In 2011 *The Sydney Morning Herald* described Lilley as a "comic chameleon" (O'Dwyer, 2011).[121] His other comedy *Angry Boys* had also been screened by BBC3 although it was not a ratings success and unrelated to this matter. The four series mockumentaries: *We Can Be Heroes (2005)*, *Summer Heights High (2007)*, Angry Boys *(2011)* and *Jonah from Tonga (2014)* had been co-productions by the ABC where the comedian Lilley parodied various demographics and cultural figures from Australian society. His series, *We Can Be Heroes*, in which Lilley portrayed a Chinese doctoral student, won a Logie for *Best New Talent and in 2014 Lilley won a Logie for "Most Popular Actor" for Ja'mie: Private School Girl (2013).*

His more recent series on Netflix *Lunatics (2019)* was also been criticised as "brown face" for portraying a South African woman with thick, curly hair. However, Lilley's producer, Laura Waters, was quoted in the media as having tweeted a rebuttal against accusations of "brown face" that in fact Lilley was portraying a white woman with 1970s curly hair (Boseley, 2020).[122] Prior to the controversy, Lilley was quoted by Gizmodo as having posted on Twitter his congratulations to Netflix for the success of Lunatics as a high-rating program (Jones, 2020).[123] Lilley had been compared to Peter Sellers and Spencer Tracy; and former ABC satirist John Clarke said he was "gifted", Barry Humphries said Lilley was "an absolute unique genius", while Australian comedian Michael Vietch said: "You can't see the craft, all you can see is him" (O'Dwyer, 2011).

Subsequent to the Netflix banning, the ABC released a statement:

> We are reviewing our content to ensure it meets current community standards and reflects our editorial policies on harm and offence. ... Community attitudes change across time and context, and we recognise that the ways in which some characters have been depicted in the past might be considered deeply objectionable or offensive today. (Flint, 2020)[124]

Prior to this in 2014 the ABC director of television, Richard Finlayson, was far more positive about Lilley's work when he said of the screening of series *Angry Boys* over a weekend:

> ABC TV is committed to innovation in new platforms to connect audiences with our incredible Australian-made shows. ... The Jonah preview binge rewrites the traditional TV rulebook. ... Big congratulations go to Chris Lilley and Laura Waters from Princess Pictures, who had the guts and foresight to support this initiative in advance of the series launch on ABC1 and BBC Three this week. (Meade, 2014)[125]

In 2013, Lilley said:

> I don't think there should be any rules. Things seem to be a little more relaxed in Australia with that kind of thing. But I think it's all about the context. The stuff I did in *Angry Boys*, it was designed to be confronting and challenging to watch. It's all about that context. If I just dressed up like a Japanese woman and started doing stupid voices, I don't know. ... I'd still find that funny. My line is a little further out than everyone else. (Spitznagel, 2013)[126]

In 2011, he said:

> I think people who take things out of context might think that it crosses the line. ... Most people who see it get it and, once you're there in that world, it makes sense. (O'Dwyer ibid.)

Aunty in her efforts to be innovative sometimes had to choke her creative voice, retrospectively.

4.6 What Remains of Aunty's Voice?

Federal Government policy decides ultimately, the fate, existence and role of the ABC, and the ABC has played a vital role as a strut of Australia's democracy, culture and values. Australians have held the ABC in sacred trust such that if Australia were under threat in any way, the ABC would broadcast and post online the salient details and pertinent facts to enable citizens to form an informed opinion. The ABC has shaped Australian citizenry and told Australians who they were. Yet, the ABC is also a site of struggles, highly sensitive and vulnerable to shifts in political ideas and expectations. In fact, it has presented "an image of permanent trauma" since the 1970s (Davis, 1988).[127] Part of this trauma continues with the 2019 ABC Annual Report putting as its first priority of infrastructure and operation: "Meeting audiences on their terms" (ABC, 2019).[128] In what it referred to as a 'dual track' basis it said it would aim to "deliver digital growth and engagement while maintaining broadcast transmission to service loyal audiences" (Ibid.). It identified this as one of its challenges. Its audiences are facing other matters. One of the biggest questions for audiences everywhere is finding the answer to "what exactly is news?". It now includes advertising, public relations, End of Financial Year car sales and infotainment in a profit-maximising strategy that drives everyone to the one place. Rumours and news have merged into one highly saleable product. It calls to mind the old journalists' sarcastic adage: "never let the facts interfere with a good story"—except now it is actually the reality because of this online cacophony of voices herding consumers in various directions. The truth is that facts do not interfere with a story anymore—and this is an almighty challenge for serious news outlets in not just competing with this junk, fake food of information, but also reminding its reporters to resist the temptation of becoming immersed in expressing personal views as they pursue what seem to be hot leads and in giving their audiences what they appear to want, without actually understanding the consequences of "the want".

We live in an age of 'post-truth', the international word of the year according to the Oxford Dictionary in 2016; and, fact-checking has become the new vogue in journalism, described by the ABC as "a global phenomenon. It is still in its relative infancy, although as a form of journalism it is growing rapidly" (Gordon, 2018).[129] The whole concept of journalistic objectivity did not emerge as an active quality of newspaper writing until the 1920s when public relations emerged and journalists and their newspaper proprietors decided they wanted separation from "spin". To deal with the travels of media to the digital space, it has invested in fact-checking because objectivity is no longer enough and audiences are lost in the 'spin' cycle. Lazer et al. (2018)[130] said that deciding if a news report was fake should focus on the publisher, so it then becomes an issue for the news organisation to establish and arbitrate that truth. The dictionary defined 'fake news' as: "relating to or denoting circumstances in which objective facts are less influential in shaping public opinion than appeals to emotion and personal belief" (Oxford University Press, 2016).[131] The ABC responded to the post-truth era by setting up a Fact Checking unit in 2003 after received AUD60 million funding over three years from Labor Prime Minister, Kevin Rudd's government to be spent on the News Division (Meade, 2017),[132] implying that people needed educating and the ABC's mandate needed support. The perceived need for the renaissance of facts could signify something more like "a new iteration of ideological struggle under capitalist hegemony" (Jaques et al., 2019).[133] As well, media organisations are manifestly concerned about the use of false information circulated on Facebook and Google (Krause et al., 2019).[134] Academics say the concern is that users of social media lack the skills to spot fake news, hampered by an unwillingness to engage with other media that could potentially provide different or conflicting information (Krause et al., ibid.).

Online social media were often imbued with the pursuit of values, ideas and feelings and these are gaining the ascendancy in society's thinking. The ABC validated this shift in its 2018 Annual Report: "values matter because they anchor communities in times of disruption. They provide security, stability and dependability" (Milne & Guthrie, 2018).[135] After the ABC set up the fact-checking unit in 2013, Prime Minister Tony Abbott questioned the need, because the corporation should "focus on straight news gathering and reporting" (Bourke, 2014).[136,137] While there are no limits to citizen and crowd-sourced journalism, there have been constraints on professional journalism. As former ABC foreign correspondent, Peter George, wrote in 1996:

> I have always belonged to the old school for journalism that believes the reporter should be little more than a grey-faced presence, whose role is to try to tell the story in quiet, authoritative tones, restraining a natural tendency to jump in to the middle of things and shout, 'Hey look at me, I'm here! Isn't this amazing?' (George, 1996)[138]

Social media encouraged the "look at me" approach, professional journalism had encouraged the "look at this" approach; and the two are not the same.

Thus, the ABC is problematised. While it is at the forefront in depicting power struggles of the post-truth era in its public role "to serve" and provide balanced information and views to the Australian populace, in also had to provide a platform for post-truth and then engaged with and supplied opinion. The ABC now has a "blended approach" (Posetti & Ping, 2012)[139] to its traditional media and social media: "in emergency situations we have core responsibilities that have long been built up on the key, robust platforms of radio, online and television. We now have those same responsibilities with social media, and it is up to us to embrace them as a standalone resource, not simply as an adjunct" (Posetti & Ping ibid.).[140]

Its reporters posted their own news report on their social media accounts—which many subsequently then commented on and drew comments and criticism from their followers. It is one way the ABC was being accused of being partisan, or confusing everyone, because in trying to be 'all to all', it appeared as 'all for some'. This competition within the commercial 'field' is an attempt to accumulate cultural capital. Individuals seek "material, cultural or symbolic rewards"[141] and lobby for *field* positions. This could include recognition of their role at the ABC and their status. In the past staff were prevented from publishing personal views, even if framed and disclaimed as they are today. For example, in 1955 when former deputy General Manager, Clement Semmler, wanted to publish a book on broadcasting in Australia through Oxford University Press, it was blocked by General Manager Charles Moses who wrote:

> The Commission, after examining your manuscript, regrets it must withdraw the permission to publish this book given at its meeting in September last. … The Commission feels that many of the views expressed in your manuscript would be damaging to our good relations with other organisations, including Government departments, and that these criticisms would inevitably be regarded as the ABC's views.[142]

This had resonance into the future when in October 2009 the senior editor of *The Washington Post* issued this edict to reporters:

> When using social networking tools for reporting or for our personal lives, we must remember that Washington Post journalists are always Washington Post journalists. (Milton Coleman 2009 in Grensing-Pophal, 2010)[143]

This came ten years prior to the current stance of the BBC. The capacity and enthusiasm of journalists to communicate with a vast international audience now meant their activities online could have a far reach of contacts and information unobtainable by previous generations of journalists. The old contact book was passé, a mere artefact of the past. But this new kind of circulation of views also holds a dark side in that journalists "views, privacy of themselves and their contacts and personal advocacy for issues" is "much more transparent and pervasive than ever before" (Grensing-Pophal, 2010).[144] It also bears noting here that not every journalist and every potential contact and every audience member is on social media at all times. It is not universal access to everyone, it is fragmented and personalised. Newsmakers, especially, can be hamstrung by a variety of matters ranging from connectivity to censorship—and even technology and access fails. However, the consequences of the global networks do effect everyone (Castells, 2008),[145] whether online or not. See the following table (Table 4.2).

Journalists activity and engagement on multimedia platforms and social media means news has evolved from being an isolated report to embracing a range and variety of inputs (Aufderheide et al., 2013).[146] The role of the expert has been shared, for example, and now consists of a diverse platform of views. Then there's the challenge of copyright and plagiarism—with everyone posting and sharing under their own accounts, the ownership of news and reports becomes muddied at best, absent at worst. Where does "fair use" reside in a sharing, uploading, liking, posting and downloading in the interconnected media world? In addition, as the ABC

Table 4.2 *Exalted Digital.* (2019). Social media statistics. World + Australia. Retrieved from: https://www.exalteddigital.com/social-media-statistics-world-australia/

Social media usage (Exalted Digital, 2018 research) *Australian users of social media—Australia's population 25.3*[a]	
Facebook	15 million active users
Twitter	4.6 million users
Instagram	9 million active users
Pinterest	300,000 active users
LinkedIn	4.5 million active users
YouTube	15 million active users

[a]Estimate. Australian Bureau of Statistics. Retrieved 6 January 2020 from https://www.abs.gov.au/AUSSTATS/abs@.nsf/mf/3101.0

Section of the Community Public Sector Union pointed out in 2008, cuts to journalist numbers in ABC newsrooms meant that journalists were tied up with production and not spending enough time on research: "this encourages lazy journalism … journalism that relies on the reformatting of press releases and from rehashing stories already published/broadcast by other news providers" (Ibid.).[147] The union's submission included a perspicacious comment by *The Australian* journalist Mark Day:

> Some proponents of blogging, principally in the US, have declared that credible stories can be written only with input from bloggers, people with intimate knowledge of the situations in question. That presupposes people in the know will openly come forward with confidential information, a proposition that, in my experience, is far from the truth. Mark Day Blog, September 2008. (ABC Section Community and Public Sector Union 2008)[148]

It is also known that social media causes a complex contagion of information (Mønsted et al., 2017)[149] where algorithms sort news feeds and create social uncertainty and emotional upheaval through filter bubbles and echo chambers. It also encouraged homophily where people will be congregated with like-minded others and everyone is angry together. People who would not normally have a platform for their views—can make one and furthermore, find a crowd that supports them. The "disruptor" now has legitimacy because they can gather fellow activists, promote boycotts and protests and run abuse, trolling and humiliation campaigns. Yet, "social media are neither inherently democratic nor inherently undemocratic … they "constitute a space in which political interests battle for influence, and not all these interests are liberal or democratic" (Tucker et al., 2017).[150] Psychological research has shown that individuals use social media because of a deep need to belong (Nadkarni & Hofmann, 2012)[151] .

4.7 What Exactly Do Journalists Now Do?

Where once objectivity was the sacred role of the journalist, this has shifted. There is nothing sacred about objectivity anymore, because it simply has become de-valued. This has come about because of what former senior policy advisor to the US Democrat President Bill Clinton, George Stephanopoulos, described as "the obsession on the part of the press with process—with who makes the decisions—rather than the outcome of policies—who is affected" as well as "the fascination with celebrity and the cult of personality" (Gardels, 1995).[152] Journalists convey culture through language and stories and this can help create, shape or reinforce meanings in public discourse as well as inform understandings or misunderstandings. They provide an analysis of issues; they influence and inform debate within the public sphere. Journalist's participation in social media can even undermine the quality of news and information they post because of the generated level and tone of discussion which can become malevolent and malicious. People quickly herd themselves into hostile online partisan groups taking sides with views that can (ultimately) be manipulative and damaging, psychologically. Yet social media also impacts on discourses away from the internet,[153] for example in political discourses and expectations. Psychologists have described the "hostile media effect" (Vallone et al., 1985)[154] where opposing groups can accuse identical media content of being biased against one side or the other and this is due to the role that values and interpretations play when audiences "read" media. Reading the media relies on cognitive processes and groups will identify themselves as the "ingroup" or "outgroup".

Australian journalists are considered to work within a code of ethics[155] (there is also an International Federation of Journalists code of ethics). Other factors need consideration such as the influence of the organisation and the processes and parameters of the environment in which journalists work (Tuchman, 1978; Weaver, 1998; Tiffen, 1989; Josephi, 2000). Journalists are sources of power, or *symbolic power*, which could also be described as the ability "of making people see and believe, of confirming or transferring the vision of the world, and thereby, action on the world and thus the world itself" (Bourdieu, 1991).[156,157] It is also understood that texts are a social process (Schirato & Yell, 1997)[158] which encode "power relations, specify what relations are possible and valued in specific contexts" (Schirato & Yell, ibid).[159] The contra view is posited by Facebook's mission: "the more we connect, the better it gets".[160]

In 2018, a series of news reports written by the then ABC's chief economics correspondent, Emma Alberici, was critical of the Federal Government's proposed company tax cuts and cast doubt on predicted AUD65 billion cuts. The cuts favoured Australia's largest companies (NSW Nurses and Midwives' Association, 2018).[161] Alberici's report stated that one in five of Australia's biggest companies paid no tax for the previous three financial years. Her argument was that there was no justification for tax cuts for these businesses because they had paid no tax. Alberici said the case was so strong against tax cuts because they would:

> blow a massive hole in the government's revenues and push the budget and national debt further into the red. … It's been 10 years since the Australian budget was last in surplus. With a debt of more than $600 billion, many are questioning the merits of prioritising a $65 billion giveaway to big business in the form of a tax cut. (Ibid.)[162]

The ABC received complaints about the reports from the Prime Minister Malcolm Turnbull, Communications Minister Mitch Fifield, then Treasurer Scott Morrison, Finance Minister, Mathias Cormann, Qantas Chief Executive Alan Joyce and the Business Council of Australia Chief Executive Jennifer Westacott. Fifield wrote to Managing Director, Michelle Guthrie that the reports were: "neither fair, balanced, accurate nor impartial. It fails to present a balance of views on the corporate tax policy." Joyce said in a letter to Guthrie the ABC had "slanted analysis" and "poor reporting":

> Any reasonable person consuming the ABC's coverage would incorrectly be led to believe that Qantas (along with other large corporations) was in some way shirking its tax responsibilities and not contributing to the Australian economy. This could not be further from the truth. (Meade, 2018)[163]

Westacott wrote to Guthrie:

> Emma Alberici's story—'Tax-free billions: Australia's largest companies haven't paid corporate tax in 10 years'—is not only grossly inaccurate and unbalanced, it implies these reputable Australian companies have broken the law.
>
> The leading companies under attack in Ms Alberici's report employ thousands of Australian workers, pay taxes, pay dividends, make other contributions, and invest heavily in the Australian economy.
>
> "Equally, Business Council member companies provided material information to Ms Alberici but it was not included in the story. (Meade, 2018)[164]

In parliament, the Prime Minister Malcolm Turnbull described the news article as: "one of the most confused and poorly researched articles I've seen on this topic on the ABC's website. … The ABC has the same understanding of the commercial world as does the opposition" (Meade, ibid.).[165]

The Guardian newspaper said:

> One error was that it was "not clear what the author means by 'generous tax concessions' in relation to Qantas. Depreciation, amortisation and operating losses are not tax concessions".
>
> Another said "Etihad, Emirates and Qatar are not Australian airlines" in relation to a line in the story that called them "Australia's biggest airlines". However, the sub-editor introduced this mistake not Alberici. (Meade, 2018)[166]

The ABC removed the reports because they "did not meet editorial standards" (NSW Nurses and Midwives' Association, 2018).[167] The report about corporate tax avoidance was amended and re-posted (Alberici, 2018)[168169] while the analysis article was removed. An ABC investigation into the reporting found that "the original news story headline and 'teasers' … were materially inaccurate". *The Sydney Morning Herald* reported that "the ABC told a Senate Estimates Committee the tax stories contained nine errors or omissions of fact and that a number of elements were misleading (Koziol, 2018).[170] ABC Managing Director, Michelle Guthrie, said that the ABC "clearly failed" in the publication of the articles (Koziol ibid.). *The Sydney Morning Herald* said that at the Senate Estimates Committee Guthrie "failed to express confidence in Alberici, saying only that she would continue in her role as Chief Economics Correspondent. … "I do not think at all that we have hung Ms Alberici out to dry."[171] ABC's Head of Editorial Alan Sunderland told the committee: "We thought some things could be better expressed and more clearly contextualised. The story should have been perfect when it was published—it wasn't."[172] The ABC has admitted mistakes were made in the editorial process allowing them to be published:

> The ABC agreed that the original news story headline and 'teasers' for both stories written by the ABC's business desk were materially inaccurate. … The ABC acknowledged that at times the analysis article read as opinion content … the piece did not meet ABC editorial standards for impartiality. (Koziol, 2018)[173]

The news report and analysis were re-published with major revisions: "Critics said the pieces confused revenue with profit and unfairly targeted Qantas for a failure to pay tax when the company had in fact carried over a series of large losses" (Koziol, 2018).[174] Guthrie told the Senate Estimates Committee:

> While both pieces went through the online sub-editing process, they were not upwardly referred to more senior editors prior to publication. This was a lapse and one ABC News and Editorial Policies have taken steps to avoid in the future. (Patrick, 2018)[175]

The ABC internal reviews also found that the report:

> Didn't mention that all the largest five and most of the top-ten companies by value pay corporate tax; that depreciation, amortisation and operating losses are not tax concessions, which was implied by the article; and that the suggestion that JP Morgan was writing off a US fine against its Australian income was highly implausible. (Meade, 2018)[176]
>
> Other problems included describing Etihad, Emirates and Qatar as Australian airlines; accusing companies of lending money to Australian operations at inflated prices to reduce tax; implying Babcock & Brown shifted profits overseas to avoid tax; failing to mention that property trusts are not liable for corporate tax; not realising CSR had sold its sugar business; and describing MYOB as a corporate adviser instead of a software company. (Patrick, 2018)[177]

Alberici said that according to the company's (MYOB) website it said it did offer an advisory service (Koziol, 2018).[178]

Anonymous ABC staff interviewed by *The Sydney Morning Herald* said that the incident revealed that ABC Management was "out of touch" (ABC *Media Watch*, 2018),[179] while there were complaints on social media that it was an example of sexism, and suggested that Alberici had been silenced after she posted a cartoon on her Twitter account suggesting this. Former ABC broadcaster Quentin Dempster was quoted by the ABC television media analysis program MediaWatch as having posted a tweet criticising the ABC for its censorship of Alberici and alluding to pressure being applied from outside the ABC (ABC Media Watch, ibid.)[180] while the ABC's *Media Watch* program concluded Alberici's analysis "blurred the line with commentary but argued the ABC's guidelines for its writers were too strict to be practical" (ABC Media Watch, 2018).[181] Further, the program said: "we believe it needed to be—to clear up the confusion between income and profit, to moderate the tone, and to get rid of gratuitous swipes like this depiction of Goldman Sachs as: ... the great vampire squid wrapped around the face of humanity, relentlessly jamming its blood funnel into anything that smells like money—ABC News, 14 February, 2018" (ABC Media Watch, 2018).[182] Goldman Sachs is Jewish firm and such lurid, evocative imagery could be taken as anti-Semitic and placed in the context of historical anti-Jewish vilification.

In 2010 The Simon Wiesenthal Centre reported an online surge of anti-Semitism after an investigation into Goldman Sachs was announced. Founder and Dean of the Center Rabbi Marvin Hier said: "irrespective of legitimate grievances that people may have, we are shocked at the level of anti-Semitism and hatred spewed on the Internet against Judaism and the Jewish people".[183] While the ABC comment in the analysis article was not intended as explicitly racist, in an era of intersectionality where marginalised groups are fighting back, it is a striking description to attach to the Jewish-owned organisation when the ABC itself is so aware, and promotes, supporting the disparate cultural and religious groupings in multicultural, multi-faith Australian society (and the diaspora).

In 2019, the Executive Council of Australian Jewry (which represents Australia's Jews) released a "Report on Antisemitism in Australia 2019" (Nathan, 2019).[184] The report said that there had been a 30% rise from the previous year on reported "verbal abuse, harassment and intimidation" (Nathan, 2019), which the report said indicated anti-Semites "felt increasingly emboldened" (ibid.)[185] and that "there is an increasing evidence that those who wish harm to Jews are being inspired and their views reinforced online" (Loc. Cit.).[186] The report also said that the growing need for tight security at both Jewish and Muslim buildings was "a telling sign of a fraying of the social fabric—a deterioration in the strength and cohesiveness of Australian society" (Nathan ibid.).[187]

The report on antisemitism in Australia criticised mainstream media for perpetuating racist feedback online that is attached to online newspaper reports but also subsequent comments when the report is posted on Facebook. The report provided evidence that inflammatory, racist or violence-invoking speech had been used by members of all Australian political parties. Then, once it reached social media it became normalised, partly due to social media's lack of any specific contextualisation and the easy approach of the big narratives that perpetuate the binaries of love-hate, peace-war, black-white, Jewish-everyone else, a religion-everyone else. The content becomes acceptable and gains veracity merely by virtue of being "published" and it becomes a rallying point for the disaffected and, further, it becomes fuel for additional inchoate abuse. The report also criticised the ABC for a 2018 opinion piece (Walker, 2018)[188] published during the last Federal Election in which the first paragraph revived the demonising story that Jews betrayed Jesus for 30 pieces of silver. The news report began: "In the Gospel of Matthew 26:15, it took 30 pieces of silver for Judas Iscariot to betray Jesus. In modern Australian politics it has taken the prospect of a loss of a by-election for a political leader to opportunistically up-end longstanding policy" (Nathan, 2019).[189] The offence taken here is that the constituents of Wentworth, a Federal electorate of Sydney, with a sizeable Jewish community, were likened to '30 pieces of silver' and insinuated all the legacy blame that Jews have had directed at them over the centuries in relation to this Bible story of Judas, the paid betrayer of Jesus who has been co-opted here into an embodiment of anti-Semitism. Nathan's report said even invoking the story itself was offensive. There is a malignant subtlety to racism that can infiltrate so-called received narratives about a group and begins with the defences: "it was just a joke, where's your sense of humour?", or delegitimising the person: "you're just touchy" and even abdicating blame: "that's what everyone thinks anyway, I'm just repeating it".

Alberici disputed there were inaccuracies in her reports and was quoted on the ABC's Media Watch program:

> I set about testing the claim that tax cuts for big companies are necessarily linked to wages growth. As the ABC's chief economics correspondent, with 25 years' experience in the 'field' of business and finance reporting, I would be expected to do that—Emma Alberici, Chief economics correspondent, ABC News, 18 February, 2018. (ABC *Media Watch*, 2018)[190]

It was reported by *The Guardian* newspaper that in her defence, Alberici had also tweeted that she had been a Walkley Award finalist in 2001 for a report on tax minimisation (Meade, 2018).[191]

Following this complaint, Prime Minister Malcolm Turnbull made a second series of complaints over Alberici's reporting on innovation tax credits (nine.com.au, 2018).[192] Turnbull sent 11 complaints to the ABC, one of which was that "Alberici had wrongly described UTS Professor, Roy Green, as an advisor to the Coalition government when he had reviewed policy for a Labor-dominated Senate committee" (ibid.).[193] In addition, he complained a story "had asserted a company called Carbon

Revolution deserved government support—but failed to mention two grants it received from the Turnbull government" (Loc. Cit.).[194] The ABC issued a correction acknowledging the Professor Green error. The ABC statement said:

> The report focused on concerns and criticisms raised by experts regarding the approach taken to innovation by Australian business, and to some degree the government
>
> The ABC's independent complaints review department has investigated the complaint. Apart from one clarification, which was promptly acknowledged—that Dr Roy Green is not currently an advisor to the government—all aspects of the complaint were rejected.
>
> The review concluded that the story was accurate, newsworthy, in the public interest and presented in context. (ABC, 2018)[195]

More than 2000 years ago, Cicero complained that news was "tittle tattle" consisting of nothing more than "reports of the gladiatorial pairs, the adjournment of trials and burglary" (Stephens, 2007).[196] Accelerating time, the "mediaeval view was that knowledge was a gift from God not to be sold" (Stephens, ibid.).[197] While the media world is now enervated by the capacity to publish quickly, sell and disseminate large amounts of information instantly, more than ever there is a pressure for accuracy (Pearlman, 2008)[198] but also corral and engage fickle, flighty, fragmented audiences. There has also been an emergence of what is referred to as "wisdom journalism" (Stephens, 2009)[199] where investigative or exclusive reporting provides detailed analysis and insight and that there is now pressure on media organisations to provide "wisdom journalism", yet when this type of content is supplied it attracts accusations of bias (Stephens, ibid.).[200] Media operates in an environment where "form has superseded content" (Lewis, 2006).[201] However, the literature said that the most common aim of journalism was still accuracy (Shapiro et al., 2013)[202] because journalism was a "discipline of verification" (Lippmann 1920/1995, in Shapiro, et al., 2013)[203]; Shapiro et al., 2013). Yet Australian social researcher, Hugh Mackay (2002), said it had always been compromised:

> The underlying point here is that even when the media are at their most overtly persuasive, they are mainly reinforcing what people already think, feel or want. (Mackay, 2002)[204]

The idea of a free and accurate press was associated, ultimately, with "a fairer society" (Chalaby, 1998).[205] Sir Arthur fforde,[206] former BBC Chairman (and prior to that a Headmaster of Rugby and a solicitor) wrote in 1963, the year prior to his retirement: "by its nature broadcasting must be in a constant and sensitive relationship with the moral condition of society" (fforde in M. Tracey, 2002)[207] in tandem with this thought former BBC Director, Ian Jacob, wrote in an internal document in 1958 that public service broadcasting was one where "the attitude of mind was an intelligent one capable of attracting to the service the highest quality of character and intellect" (in Tracey, 2002).[208] The over-riding value of public service broadcasting, both in Australia and Britain, was a commitment to ethical and moral standards many of which were inspired and forged by the First Director General of the BBC, John Reith (Tracey, 2002).[209] There is still a role for such high standards in public media in a society where all media remains highly influential. Yet the ABC functions in an environment, as so other public broadcasters, where there is no legal definition that explicates for them broadcasting in "the public interest" (Berg & Davidson, 2018),[210] the aspirational standard to which they must operate.

In return for servicing the public interest, public broadcasters have had free access to the spectrum of radio and television as well as the internet. Enshrined in this non-existent definition of public interest the ABC took upon itself the duties to provide the public with access to the workings of parliament, policy and politicians, as well as educate children and provide religious services, orchestras, choirs and bands, educate and entertain housewives (Inglis, 1983),[211] for example. In US legislation there was a loose contextualisation of the 'public interest' in the Radio Act of 1927 where: "broadcasters were required to operate in the "public convenience, interest, or necessity" (Simshaw, 2012).[212] But, in many ways, the public interest became a creative exercise for the pioneers of the ABC, as discussed with various examples in this chapter. That pioneering spirit of creativity remains with content such as the controversial episode of *Q and A* analysed previously, although at odds with the role of a public broadcaster to uphold a civil society through nuanced discussion.

4.8 iWar on the Internet: And What Should Keep Australians up at Night

Australia is at war. On 19 June 2020, Australia's Prime Minister, Scott Morrison, announced that Australia was under cyber-attack by "a sophisticated state-based cyber actor" (Hurst, 2020).[213] The attacks were against all levels of governments and critical infrastructure and the ABC said: "Government sources have told the ABC that China is likely behind the sustained cyber-attack" (Bogle, 2020).[214] Reasons for such attacks were described as intellectual property theft and large-scale intelligence gathering, especially information on a possible Novel Coronavirus vaccine (Bogle ibid.) while Associate Professor and Associate Dean of Computing and Security at Edith Cowan University, Paul Haskell-Dowland, said: "You could certainly imagine a situation where an aggression level between countries has escalated to the point where they want to set an example, but they don't want to take that in a military form" (Loc. Cit.).

It is called the iWar and this is more pernicious and invasive than the nation's most recent major world war, World War II. In 1939, Prime Minister Robert Menzies broadcast on the ABC and commercial radio simultaneously: "it is my melancholy duty to inform you ...",[215] Australians have not yet had that call to arms. The reason is that this is not an armed, hot war, mobilising our army, navy, air force and reserves, nor do we fight specific geographic battles in defined theatres and fields. However, our defence forces are already engaged at the front. Australia's frontline forces are named Information Warfare. However, getting the public's attention focused on the seriousness of the situation has proven challenging. The battle is no longer a physical wrestle for territory and objects as much as it is for control of minds, economies, societies as well as personal identity and privacy.

From the off, the internet promised interconnectivity and e-democracy through e-participation as society transitioned from "old" media to "new" media. Everyone would have a voice at any time believing "the logic of networks, openness and connection are political acts that realise democracy" (Bollmer, 2016).[216] However, this was not to be. The internet is not a substitute democracy (Massaka, 2017)[217] because, as Manuel Castells (2008) explained, the internet is the antithesis of a civil society where consumerism is prioritised and "anything that does not add value to the network is excluded" (ibid.).[218] In addition there are the new gatekeepers—search engines—that have superceded the journalists and the encyclopaedias (Schroeder, 2018). Literature warns that since the promise of e-democracy, social media has become "a tool of outside actors who want to attack democracies" (Tucker et al., 2017).[219] For example there were reports of Russian-connected Twitter bots (automated accounts impersonating humans also used on Facebook trolling) supporting Donald Trump's run for president in the 2016 election campaign (Tucker at al. ibid.),[220] for which the Chief Executive of Facebook, Mark Zuckerberg, claimed some responsibility (Egan, 2019).[221] Ironically, the liberating online systems that promised freedom have the power to shut-down, congregate marginalise. Democracies are being infected with autocratic tools of control and "the complexity of the network that produces and re-transmits fake news often makes it hard to pinpoint the source of a false claim" (Persily, 2017).[222] Facebook would be the biggest religion in the world—if it were one—because it has 2.4 billion users (Egan ibid.)[223] and the "religion" is owned by one man making it "the world's most powerful gatekeeper of information" (Loc. Cit.).[224] Egan (2019) declared:

> Facebook is one of the main reasons democracy is in such peril. The company's algorithms favor the echo chamber, backing a user's bias. That black hole is so full of fantasies and half-truths that it's impossible for millions of people to have a basic grasp of the facts needed to make informed decisions.

However, these filtering and echoing spaces are also domains to the journalist looking for news and expressing their opinions. Yet, research shows that journalist's professional reputations and the regard or esteem held by the public for their media organisations are negatively impacted upon by journalists' online interactions (Lee, 2015).[225] They are seen to be passing on the fake news, hysteria or abuse and in that process preferencing partiality.

The professional media has a significant role to play. The ABC has a substantial role to play in Australia. Hampering this proactive necessity was the departure of media as a pillar institution, the weakening of the watchdog. The consequence for Australian society is:

> the past platforms of discourse and debate that served as a foundation for civil society have deteriorated into a primordial chaos of survival of the fittest. Decorum and civility have been abandoned along the way. (Erbschloe, 2017)[226]

But a lack of funding of research into the use of social media in iWar (Erbschloe ibid.)[227] means information, as well as attention, is only developing on the topic. The US Center for Strategic and International Studies said:

> Russian disinformation is hidden beneath the surface of the vast sea of social media content. It deploys social media trolls and bots to spread online content that undermines faith in democracies and their institutions. (Spaulding et al., 2020)[228]

The non-partisan Australian Strategic Policy Institute (2020) said "a range of actors are manipulating the information environment to exploit the COVID-19 crisis for strategic gain" by spreading reports on social media that is designed to spread: "disinformation, propaganda, extremist narratives and conspiracy theories" and exemplifies this with ten reports that include instances from You Tube, Twitter and Facebook. ASPI (2020) added: "In times of crisis, these digital structures—the online communities, the content, the shaping of recommendation algorithms—serve to channel anxious, uncertain individuals towards conspiratorial beliefs." In 2019, Major General Marcus Thompson, Head of Australia's Information Warfare, Joint Capabilities Group asked an iWar conference rhetorically: "How do we have a meaningful conversation with the public about a contested environment they may know very little about?" (Thompson, 2019).[229] He told the gathering Australia was so imperilled by this iWar that: "the seams of our democratic system are vulnerable to exploitation" (Thompson ibid.) and that there was a compelling need for a shared understanding of the situation between the Australian Defence Forces and the public. Thompson (2019) cited a Lowy Institute Poll (2019) that showed Australians were sensing an increased insecurity from cyber-attacks and foreign interference in Australian politics (49%, up from 41% in 2018). Thompson (2019) said: "outgoing Director General of ASIO, our domestic intelligence agency ..., described foreign interference as an "existential threat" to the nation" (ibid.).[230] He said actors' motives for these cyber-attacks on Australian democracy were to "erode trust ... in our institutions, our values, each other" (ibid.). Ultimately these damaged national interests, sovereignty and the foundations of Australian society. He said:

> misinformation ripples across social networks at a pace that outstrips truth … a recent study at MIT found that disinformation travels six times faster than the truth across Twitter. (Loc. Cit.)

and that 1/5 of the population was using Twitter. The three pillars of this iWar are individualisation, identity and information (Voelz, 2015)[231] and the actors who fought this war were "dispersed and highly adaptive" (Voelz ibid.)[232] "nations, organisations and persons" (Loc. Cit.).[233] These actors, according to Bennett and Livingston (2018), were nationalist (primarily radical right) and foreign (commonly Russian) undermining the legitimacy of democratic institutions, democratically elected governments, democratically elected leaders, destabilising centre parties and causing upheaval at elections (ibid.).[234]

There was an insistent need for a culture of truth and evidence in news and information. In the report for the Council of Europe "Information Disorder" (Wardle & Derakhshan, 2017)[235] said as well as truth there was an urgent need for media literacy education and changes in media ownership models:

> Government, academia, and civil society need to lead the conversation on how to address the problem of the millions of lies and propaganda mentions that can spread so quickly on social media. (Wardle & Derakhshan, ibid.)[236]

Thompson (2019) said: "To extrapolate that out, one fifth of the population can be reached, targeted and potentially influenced by a malign actor. But that's just one slice of the population, and it's just one social media platform" (ibid.).[237] He cited research that showed manipulating search engine rankings could move the voting preferences of undecided voters. Director of the UK's Government Communications Headquarters has described Twitter, Facebook, and WhatsApp as the "command-and-control networks of choice for terrorists and criminals" (Voelz, 2015).[238] As a relatively new arrival and participant in the commercial 'field' of commercial media, the ABC is well-placed to reclaim its 'cultural capital' as a guiding light in a situation easily exploited by other state actors in defending the public interest in the public sphere in a democratic society. Democracy is not a vague concept. Jacques Derrida (2005) said "[if] we did not have some idea of democracy, we … would never seek to elucidate its meaning or, indeed call for its advent" (Derrida, ibid.).[239]

Social media creates a "fantasy of participation" (Carpentier, 2014)[240] yet the reality is that full and equal, participation and democracy itself can never be achieved and every site is one of struggles trying to prove a fantasy is real. However, once the participant enters this fantasy world "we lose access to the Real" (Carpentier ibid.) and as a consequence "this fantasy may result in the exclusion of what (or who) is defined as outside" (Ibid.) which means the agency invested in participation may be also a fantasy (Ibid.). This is especially so when inauthentic information is consumed and welcomed so readily. This desire to be a part of something bigger than the individual, encourages others to exploit others by controlling individuals, as well as societies. This freeing up of individual inhibition in that process provides unprecedented access to individuals' personal preferences, politics, private details of income and home location, as well as friends and networks. Once infiltrated they provide a wealth of knowledge. As a consequence of all this networking by individuals who give freely of their personal lives, expose their "friends" and their personal views, it lends more credence to these inauthentic messages (from "friends" and "friends of friends") than from online government institutions, for example, which ironically, are regarded as intrusive or sinister, as discussed earlier.

Content offered up freely for anyone also provides rich pickings for state actors to destabilise a society, because living online is viewed by many citizens as a form of emancipation and ultimate assertion of rights with the cri de coeur—"I've got nothing to hide" and where "the veracity of a post is judged more on the number of followers and 'likes' than it is on the content and credibility of the source" (Thompson, 2019).[241] It allows room for any actors to supply disinformation or propaganda which is given authenticity by virtue of being passed among associates on social media. Research shows that half of social media users are addicted to it (Voelz, 2015)[242] and it is a highly effective tool to radicalise and recruit people for social change movements connecting the "disillusioned and persecuted" (Thompson, 2011).[243] Karinthy's (1929) idea developed in his popular short story "Chains" where everyone was linked to each other by six steps or fewer had become was passé … "social media provides one degree of separation between people" (Thompson, ibid.)[244] and as much intimate knowledge as can be supplied. The Chinese military strategist, Sun Tzu, advised sagely on spying several centuries BCE:

Whenever you want to attack an army, besiege a city, or kill a person, first you must know the identities of their defending generals, their associates, their visitors, their gatekeepers, their chamberlains.[245]

Concerns in the academy over the access of organisations and actors to personal data allowing manipulation and influence were voiced by, Columbia University Law Professor, Tim Wu, who said "Facebook should become a non-profit or public benefit corporation", while "Columbia University professor Joseph Stiglitz argues that Facebook is similar to a public utility and should be strongly regulated" (Schiffrin, 2017).[246] The internet has been used by authoritarian governments such as China, Iran, Russia, Turkey some Gulf states and the Philippines to shore up their rule through heavy surveillance, strict censorship and harsh, fatal consequences for transgressors. Research in the US shows that anonymous trolls in Russia were posting news reports to Facebook and Twitter and adding tens of thousands of comments each day in support of the Kremlin, for example (Voelz, 2015).[247]

China has gone so far as to introduce a system of social credits (Zhou & Xiao, 2020)[248] whereby citizens are given points based on all their online behaviour and personal information so as to assess their loyalty and worthiness as citizens. While these countries were building their own powerbases and controlling their own people they were also attacking democratic countries (Voelz, 2015)[249] where "disinformation campaigns weaponize digital platforms, whose algorithms seem to reward outrage because that is what keeps users engaged" (Kornbluh, 2018)[250] and "YouTube's recommendation algorithm steers viewers toward increasingly radical and extremist videos" (Ibid.).[251] For example, Cambridge Analytics, the consulting firm harvested the personal information of 87 million Facebook users. This was used in political campaigns in the US and elsewhere (Ibid.).[252] China paid:

two million persons … a modest amount to post comments on social media. Collectively, approximately 448 million phony comments are posted … each year. (Bennett & Livingston, 2018)[253]

Russia has one troll factory that employed about 600 people:

expected to post on news articles 50 times a day. Others had to maintain six Facebook accounts and publish at least three posts daily. Twitter trolls were required to have at least 10 accounts and tweet at least 50 times daily on each. (Bennett & Livingston, ibid.)[254]

Scientific American Journal has concluded that the willingness to share information gives state actors opportunities to exploit the situation and spread disinformation creating "New World Disorder" (Wardle, 2019).[255] This disorder can take the form of impersonated accounts, manipulation of true content and fabricated events or videos, on one hand, and wholesale harvesting of government business and private enterprise business on the other. The faintly novel alliterative nomenclature of 'digital disruption' implies a minor inconvenience, like a delay in the travel timetable. It is more aptly named 'digital disorder', 'digital discord' or even 'digital disaster' when consequences are accounted. The concept of digital disruption, a general term (Skog et al., 2018), was met with excitement because it was the way forward for organisations, such as universities, to innovate education and be successful (Thomas, 2016).[256] 'Needs must', media organisations rushed headlong into this cyberworld. But it has had a deleterious impact, too. It means valuable content can be infiltrated with red herring fallacies, or straightforward untruths. I also means valuable content and information can be high-jacked and acquired into a business model that pays minimal overheads, no superannuation to staff, avoids taxes and prices it may pay for content do not bear the market cost.

Allied with this 'digital disorder', Wardle (ibid.) said in regard to the avidity with which audiences share personal data: "state and non-state actors are becoming increasingly adept at exploiting these behaviours to spread propaganda, deliver cognitive effects, and mobilise behavioural change". These groups included "authoritarian regimes, revisionist powers, extremist groups" (Wardle Loc. Cit.).[257] There is now a heightened level of false information in democratic nations circulating through social media that have the appearance of journalism (Bennett & Livingston, 2018).[258] While digital media is described as the great disruptor of media, the information iWar has far greater significance in that it is destabilising democracies and has caused: "declining citizen confidence in institutions undermines the credibility of official information in the news and opens publics to alternative information sources" (Bennett & Livingston, ibid.).[259]

Skimming over the top of this, commercial businesses making money out of clicks, shares and 'likes' (cohort approvals) and perpetuating disinformation becomes an important part of their income streams (Bennett & Livingston ibid.).[260] The scholars also cautioned against the use of the term "fake news" as it isolated the news incident. They preferred the term disinformation because there was a more systematic interference in information (ibid.). They also cautioned that fact-checking alone was not enough and that there needed to be more fundamental attention paid to "repairing political institutions and democratic values" (Bennett & Livingston, 2018).[261] Consequently, journalism had become a grey area and the public sphere was no longer a place of free exchange of information. The public is less trusting of *all* institutions which face now a "legitimacy crisis" (Ibid.).[262] The "radical right movement's" (Loc. Cit.)[263] and radical left's rejection of democratic institutions and their leaders have created a growing demand for alternatives. These strident judgemental voices and de-humanising abuse can be easily observed on Twitter following the trending hashtag #failedleadership, for example. Three questions arise from these demands: what specific leadership failure has the leader demonstrated in this instance, once the ridicule subsides? What is the public sphere's definition and model of successful leadership (to what does the new public sphere of social media aspire)? And, how is it that leaders are now accused of consistently, and abjectly failing?

The era has been described in the literature as one of post-truth plus post-democracy (Bennett & Livingston, 2018)[264]—also defined as democracy in "poor health" with minimal capacity, institutions nobbled and a society ruled by a new "élite" (Ibid.).[265] The re-establishment of credibility amongst Australian democratic institutions is an area where the ABC could assist; by arresting the decline of Australia's democratic institutions, of which it is one, by promoting free and fair debate and wresting a professional control of the political discourse, ideologies and institutional narratives from social media dictates. Its policies need to match its content. It can hold everyone to account, including citizen journalists, by seeking their constructive solutions to solving their assertions of government policy failings. It needs to allow the 'grey' voices to be heard. Media has become overwhelmed with narratives of intersectionality and theoretical frameworks of analysing power that emanate from liberal arts courses at Australian universities. Intersectionality is "rooted in Black feminism and Critical Race Theory" (Carbado et al., 2013)[266] and it had helped describe the problems of domestic violence and the inequality experienced by women, as two examples.

The theory of intersectionality was first proposed by academic activist Kimberlé Crenshaw (1989) who explained how "gender and race intersected with each other to multiply the negative effects of systems of power on women of color" (Goldman, 2019).[267] Since then, Crenshaw's theory has been appropriated into "queer theory, feminist legal theories, and theories on sexuality, race, and gender, the focus morphed from her agenda of empowerment to an emphasis on the import and individuality of identity" (ibid.).[268] As a consequence, social justice activists have used intersectionality to bring together all the various and disunited groups into a single narrative of victimisation—"the identity of shared victimhood" (Goldman, ibid.).[269] Goldman (2019) criticised victimhood as defining groups in depleted terms rather than claiming and articulating their empowerment. Victimhood as a narrative, resorts to abuse, vilification and calls for violence as an attempt to over-turn power structures without offering an alternative legislative, policy, ethical framework, for example to support a positive outcome for the common good—'all for all'.

Marxist-Feminist theoretical frameworks analyse power in terms of binaries and critique discrimination based on race, gender and class. Intersectionality is now used to describe all perceived inequalities of gender, sexuality and race. Jewish American Scholar, Sharon Goldman, however, cautioned against Jews embracing intersectionality and victimhood because Israel was one of "the greatest progressive societies" (Ibid.)[270] and Jews no longer saw themselves as "victims" in that nation-state context. Philosophers also examined intersections, but in terms of where ideas overlapped in determining logical thinking. Cultural studies subjects looked at intersections to create new identities and stereotypes although there was a lack of applicability, or shared negative connotation, for example powerful white men would have no exact equivalence in the governing and running of China, or African nations. Would anyone even dare to provide a stereotypically dominant moral equivalence of a powerful, oppressive male leader in China, for example? There is a dearth of literature and research into male privilege and its attendant oppressive, patriarchal institutions in non-Western cultures, particularly in countries such as China and African countries. However, the research literature pointed to a nuanced cultural/social situation where:

> the male-privilege-female-disadvantage argument overlooks the fact that men's attempt to sustain male privileges through the provider role is confounded with their desire to be adequate breadwinners (Crowley, 1998) ... women may actually have a stake in shying away from the provider role. (Potuchek, 1997) (Zuo, 2003)[271]

There is also a lack of research into Russian society of powerful men. However, there has been research into Kenyan male élite power which showed it led to the rise of corruption, polarisation and ethnic militias, causing a loss of belief in democratic institutions (Branch & Cheeseman, 2008).[272] Ultimately, however, a breakdown in this power structure in Kenya occurred when it was taken over by armed mob rule and the élites were fragmented (Ibid.). Once institutions had been nobbled, decisions were made on the street (Loc. Cit.)—mob rule. Ultimately, this resulted in a humanitarian crisis of 2000 deaths and 300 000 people fleeing their homes (Kagwanja & Southall, 2009).[273] Conclusively, it showed that privileged Kenyan males' "élite interest in political stability prevented the country falling apart" (Ibid.). Nature abhors a vacuum (this has contested attribution: Aristotle, or Philo of Byzantium in the thirteenth century—Grant, 1973).[274]

4.9 The ABC's Regional Footprint

The previous discussion analyses the impact of social media in putting Australia on an iWar footing. It also examined, on a broad scale the influences on the ABC through social media and the complications it faces in ABC representing all Australians as one group of citizens. To cope with this it has drifted into the emergent commercial field and now seeks to represent segments of Australians and snippets of opinions, rather than those held manifestly, or generally. It has run the risk of incoherence as it races around tending to divergent views and even reinterprets its Code of Practice in these decisions. While the ABC has long held a gaze towards the rest of the world on behalf of Australians' held views, the internet encourages splintering and, in that sense, works against the concept of nationhood and forming citizenry. In terms of coverage of overseas events, the internet has created much ease and facility for that to occur. But the ABC was also tasked with attending to the needs of Australia's near neighbours, and this remains a complex situation because of the remoteness from digital technology of some communities, for example, but many with ready access to the "old" media of radio.

The growth of the internet coincided with Australian governments and the ABC winding back the role of the ABC in the South East Asia and South Pacific regions—a form of soft diplomacy can assert democratic values to economically vulnerable and developing nations of the South Pacific. A Lowy Institute report in 2019 called Australia's withdrawal from

Pacific broadcasting by the ABC as "a missed opportunity" (O'Keeffe & Greene, 2019).[275] The report was damning:

> The Australian government has been silent on the role of international public broadcasting in supporting Australia's brand and reputation overseas, particularly in the Pacific. This has impaired the projection of Australia's soft power and ignores the ABC's long and distinguished history of broadcasting into a region which the government now identifies as a principle geo-strategic priority. (Ibid.)[276]

Further:

> Australia's international public broadcasting has been diminished through a combination of government inconsistency and neglect, ideology-driven decisions, budget cuts and apparent ABC management indifference. (Loc. Cit.)[277]

Adding:

> The Australian Government and the ABC have each withdrawn significant resources from Australia's international broadcasting in an unfocused, piecemeal and unstrategic manner, leaving Australia's international media reputation much diminished, particularly across the Pacific.

The report says "China is energetically attempting to influence countries across the Indo-Pacific region to support and advance its own ambitions" (ibid.). And yet with the abundance of media that has proliferated and the pressure on PSMs to differentiate themselves:

> Fragmentation of audiences accelerated with the increasing ability of media consumers to deal with the over-abundance of choice by filtering what they accessed: a paradoxical process that has resulted in many people narrowing their range of information sources. (Ibid.)

Counter-intuitively, the Australian government recognises that the Indo-Pacific region is one of major geo-strategic priority and that China "is a large aid donor and lender to the region", "the region's seas and airspace are becoming more contested" and "economic power is also being used for strategic ends".[278]

In 2017 a Foreign Policy White Paper said "five objectives of fundamental importance to Australia's security and prosperity" were:

- Promotion of an "open, inclusive and prosperous Indo-Pacific region";
- Delivering more opportunities for Australian businesses;
- Ensuring Australians remain safe;
- Promoting and protecting the international rules that support stability and prosperity; and
- Stepping up support for "a more resilient Pacific and Timor-Leste. (Australian Government, 2017)[279]

As the key cultural and educational institution in Australian public life, the ABC is well placed to manage the disinformation and disruption with probity and vigour. The media once had an important role in the public sphere as did "libraries, schools, churches, trade unions" (McChesney & Herman, 1997).[280] Ironically, the ABC was also established by powerful white men and they, together with the one woman on the board, Dame Elizabeth Couchman, never envisaged in their public statements they had created an exclusive male domain for the exclusive betterment of male Australian society. In all the literature, the organisation spoke at all times for the good of all Australians, without exception. However, while the whole concept of the ABC serving the Australian public sphere has changed fundamentally from 1932, the ABC is well placed to meet this shift, especially in being a watchdog safeguarding Australia's democracy and security as well as the needs of the collective society.

There have been some public steps made by the organisation in this direction. In its annual report 2019 the ABC described a Media Literacy Week site it had created as well as the placement of resources by ABC Education for schools online: "to better distinguish between legitimate and illegitimate ('real' and 'fake') news sources" (ABC, 2019)[281] as well as provide guidance on "cryptology, big data, tracking and cookies" (Ibid.).[282] In 2019, the ABC held a conference: "Navigating the News" with "media organisations, academics and educators together to discuss how to build trust in public-interest journalism and advance community media literacy" (Loc. Cit.).[283] There is huge potential for the corporation to defend its citizens and the health of its civil society. The ABC is well placed to work with Defence, for example, and re-visit those early goals of upholding the public's right to know with vigour and independence in courter-acting online chaos caused by state actors. It would appear an over-reliance on looking at herself in social media has distracted Aunty, and this narcissism is strangling Aunty's important, outward-looking, candid voice. She is ideally placed to focus her binoculars on the horizon to protect Australia's sovereign interests and democracy.

4.10 Digital Disruptors and Activist Publicists

The loss of the authority of Australia's institutions and the decline in respect and trust in them and the media at large means the ABC resides within a diverse cohort of the perfidious and the principled in the emergent commercial *field*. The field struggles for respect. It has less authority over the information it once handled because alternative news/views sites are becoming popular and accusations of bias are biting more deeply into the ABC as a participant in this *field* where its management shows an apparent public lack of concern for the public consequence of bias. Innovation has become synonymous with destruction—although offering no constructive replacement. The ABC was once a revered gatekeeper of constructive information for Australians and it was able to gatekeep and supervise the flow of ideas, somewhat influentially too. Without any mawkish idealising of the institution, it once strived to be a citadel of democracy in Australia.

Now there are counter-cultural ideas that oppose the key values of democracy, tolerance, support for rational reasoned debate, respect for individuals and individual views and evidence-based opinion; even basic civility has diminished in the quest for the new. The internet has become weaponised with key actors potentially represented by fake news and social media bots (automated media accounts) who represent no-one. Social media organisations operate under what the business literature described as a clever predatory model. They could plunder news for free already paid for by news organisations and hard-working journalists. These same news organisations have already met the costs of training staff and meeting regulatory requirements, so like other predatory models, the social media organisations could skim off reputations of established businesses. They then published without accountability. The ABC is in the middle of a tug-of-war with these powerful forces and ponders the length of the accountability tail.

With this highly successful social media model in place and the ongoing iWar it seems logical that mainstream media, as well as political parties, have lost their power around the world (Persily, 2017)[284] and that there was "dissatisfaction with legacy institutions both inside and outside politics" (ibid.).[285] Ironically, The ABC is a legacy institution, yet contributed to the undermining of fellow institutions. Social media has become an easy and profitable facility for abuse, vilification, violence and invective. Social media liberates individuals into a space where they are free to abuse without recourse (although there have been some exceptions to this with social media platforms deleting content and suspending accounts after complaints were made and deemed fit). For example, Twitter "permanently suspended" outgoing US President Donald Trump's Twitter account (Collins & Zadrozny, 2021)[286] accusing him of inciting violence that occurred after people challenging the validity of the election stormed the Capitol building in Washington DC. The previous year Twitter closed his account because it said he violated "Twitter Rules" and was "glorifying violence" (BBC, 2020)[287] in his tweets which blamed the riots in response to the killing of African American man by police, George Floyd, on a lack of leadership from the Minneapolis mayor. Trump's tweet was in response to violent civil disturbances around the US in response to the police killing of Floyd (asphyxiated while his neck was crushed by the knee of a police officer and his back crushed by two other officers). The shocking video showing the brutality of his arrest and death sparked protests and riots across the US.

One compelling comment about these instances was raised when the Financial Time pointed out these internet social media companies were: "a powerful group of tech executives, who all run American companies but whose decisions have global implications" (Waters & Murphy, 2021).[288] The second troubling aspect of these protests was that professional journalists were also attacked by police. The BBC (2020) said reporters and camera people from the BBC, Reuters, Deutsche Welle, Vice News, two from Channel 7 Australia and two local US radio reporters (in Kentucky and California) had been attacked or had rubber bullets fired at them. In addition, one CNN reporter was arrested, a freelance journalist permanently blinded by a police projectile and a crew from Fox News chased by a mob of protesters and attacked (BBC, 2020).[289] The conflation of mainstream journalism with social media and the turbulence created by "digital disruption" has had the tragic consequence of blurring or eroding the separation that helped provide some ramparts, or eyries, for a professional, impartial, journalist.

Journalists who now position themselves as online activist journalists or advocate journalists mean they have taken sides and are all being treated as one group. Journalists are now fair game for both the police and the activists. Coupled with this anyone can be a journalist yet planning for this calamitous professional merger of citizen journalists with professional journalists was not planned by any news organisations in Australia in the rush to take the digital leap. In addition, news tweets are snatched up by activists and re-posted, this brings them closer to journalists and, while flattering, may also have undesirable repercussions. Louisville police said: "Targeting the media is not our intention" (BBC 2020),[290] although there was no redress in this comment for the consequences of doing so in a confused, rapidly changing situation. Truth has never been more in peril. It means that Western journalists are under attack, literally. A "press" labelled flak jacket is meaningless anywhere and is now decoded as "activist publicist". The erosion of respect for aloof journalism has never been more concerning. This is another ugly consequence of social media and mainstream news media merging with not "setting up of boundaries". The Australian Opposition Leader and Labor Party Leader, Anthony Albanese, said: "in a democratic society, the role of the media is crucial. It's important that the media is able to report on crises, like the one in the United States, free of harassment" (Ferguson & Vitorovich, 2020).[291] Yet, that is precisely the problem, "the media" is one big, indistinguishable, amorphous group. Traditional news has collapsed in favour of being with the rest. News and information has become integrated with activism, advocacy and peace journalism.

In 2007, Andrew Keen's book "The Cult of the Amateur, declared: "this undermining of truth is threatening the quality of civil public discourse, encouraging plagiarism, and intellectual property theft, and stifling creativity" (Keen, 2007).[292] The internet has unleashed mediocrity. Keen said: "Web 2.0 ... delivers ... more dubious content from anonymous sources, hijacking our time and playing to our gullibility" (Loc. Cit.).[293] As discussed, in an earlier chapter, the near closure of Australian Associated Press' newswire in June 2020, was blamed on a significant loss of subscribers, and was a prime example of how the impact of the Web 2.0 and the internet technology companies, especially Google and Facebook, their anti-competitive nature and 'digital disruption' through their dominance, have changed the way news is created and shared. The struggling news organisations erect paywalls (pay for access) around their content in an effort to preserve their businesses. The near loss of AAP to Australian democracy forms part of this concern. Established by Rupert Murdoch's father Keith Murdoch on 1 July 1935 as a central intake point for overseas news as a not for profit co-operative for newspapers, AAP was not made an independent association until 1936. Sir Keith Murdoch was joint managing director of AAP until 1944. AAP expanded over the years to also provide local news, so its loss would have been a significant blow to Australia's flow of factual, unbiased information locally and from overseas.

At the time of its near closure in 2020, AAP had four owners, none with majority shareholding—Nine Entertainment Company, News Corporation each had 47.4% with remainder owned by The West Australian. It was rescued by philanthropists and several other organisations. The chair of AAP rotated through shareholders. AAP was in operation for 85 years and about 180 journalists in Australia, foreign correspondents and a New Zealand offshoot would have been retrenched (Vitorovitch & Shanahan, 2020).[294] The AAP website said: "our news service sets the standard for accuracy, reliability and impartiality".[295] The ABC is well-positioned as a national media outfit to support this need by reclaiming its own élite, privileged 'field'. No other organisation is placed to grab such an opportunity. The public had seen this role for the ABC as vital for Australia for decades and respected it for its accrued 'cultural capital'.

AAP originated news reports, videos and photos, it also fed news from the major wire services overseas to Australian media, including the ABC, from major wire services such as: Reuters, Associated Press, Press Association and so on, based on subscription fees paid by media outlets. When Keith Murdoch established AAP, he organised 13 Australian newspapers to share the costs of news. At that time the expense of overseas cable news was so high it was agreed to share it among the newspapers (and later radio). The Chairman of AAP, Campbell Reid, said when the prospect of terminating the organisation seemed imminent "the AAP decision is a wake-up call for Australia that the detrimental impact the digital platforms are having on media companies is very real and has now reached a tipping point" (Dudley-Nicholson, 2020).[296] The reality is that the giant technology companies that operate online want—and are getting—their content free, they will not pay. Reid warned:

> Until the platforms start paying publishers for their journalism instead of distributing it for free for their own profit, then we are going to, sadly, see a lot more bad news in the media sector. (ibid.)[297]

This book argues that the ABC, as a separate media institution, achieved its own legitimacy and authority in spite of resistance from the commercial media by cultivating its own, unique *cultural capital*. It operated tangentially to commercial media and this was its "safe space". The leaders who were first charged with its establishment and development oversaw the acquisition of a *habitus* in this *field* which became élite and privileged because of its uniqueness in Australian society and became treasured by all its Australian owners—all.

In 2019, the Australian Competition & Consumer Commission recommended a new code of conduct requiring online businesses share revenue for their use of news stories written by Australian media organisations. Reid said: "it is a great loss that professional and researched information provided by AAP is being substituted by with the unresearched and often inaccurate information that masquerades as real news on digital platforms" (Vitorovitch & Shanahan, 2020)[298] "the elephant in the room in these conversations is never in the room, which is Google and Facebook" (ibid.).[299] An editorial in *The Australian* on AAP's possible demise quoted the Australian Competition & Consumer Commission chairman Rod Sims: "Google and Facebook have grown to have almost unfettered market power" (*The Australian*, 2020).[300] The Australian Competition & Consumer Commission Chairman, Rod Sims, said on the then believed closure of AAP "I don't want to signal anything in particular, but it is a big development, and a very sad development—not just for the people involved but for journalism generally" (Vitorovitch & Swan, 2020).[301]

Thompson said "the informational element of Australia's statecraft needs a focus, a champion" to counter act "these actors all want us to understand their disregard for the rule of law and the international rules-based order". He said "Australia's focus on the Pacific step-up requires us to project a clear vision for the region and our role in it. We need to assert our values as strengths—democratic values and transparency, an independent and high-quality media (Thompson, 2019).[302] The term to describe this warfare was coined "netwar" in the mid-1990s by US international relations scholar John Arquilla (Foreign Policy editorial, 2010).[303] Thompson (2019) said warfare was now working to "find new ways to impose political will on individuals, groups and societies using technology's now alarming reach into our everyday lives" (ibid.)[304] and there was a case for focusing on the common good: "Government, industry, and our civilian population" (Loc. Cit.).[305] Extrapolating from Thompson (2019) the ABC was well placed to help champion the information needed for Australia's statecraft.

Clause *13 of AAP's Code of Conduct, for example, on social media stated*: "13.1 *AAP* journalists may not use personal blogs or social networking sites like Twitter and Facebook to post AAP-generated material or links to such material, or to make comments relating to their work, other *AAP* employees or to *AAP* and its policies and practices" (*AAP*, 2020).[306] This is a higher standard of restraint than that required of ABC journalists. Keen (2007) was scathing about the insidious role of the Internet in undermining credible authoritative journalism and the integrity and standards of the Fourth Estate. He quoted Habermas (2006) on the threat of "Web 2.0" which gave rise to the new media phenomenon of the media "prosumer" (the term describes the person who is both a producer and consumer of media content):

> The price we pay for the growth in egalitarianism offered by the Internet is the decentralized access to unedited stories. In this medium, contributions by intellectuals lose their power to create a focus.[307]

In fact, the word "prosumer" was created to acknowledge this change in the audience (Toffler, 1984)[308] and the value-add of audiences. Media consumption has changed such that the reader of a newspaper could also be a content creator—"prosumers" produce and consume media content in participatory digital media and use social media for peer-to-peer sharing and blogging to augment debates and discussions. A key aspect of Keen's (2007) concern was that there was fiction, anonymity, opinion and irresponsibility embedded and even celebrated in the creativity of Web 2.0:

> The owners of traditional newspapers and news networks were held legally accountable for the statements of their reporters, anchors, and columnists, encouraging them, to uphold a certain standard of truth in the content they allowed their paper to publish or distribute through the internet. Web site owners, on the other hand, were not liable for what was posted by a third party. (Keen, 2007)[309]

Australian media academic Margaret Simons observed in 2011 the ABC was now not only giving away content free but also "becoming more of an organizer, commissioner and enabler of content than a broadcasting institution" (Simons, 2011).[310]

Such creativity yet lack of control of outcome, according to Keen (2007), was at odds with political scientist Benedict Anderson's theory of Imagined Communities (1983) where nation states were believed to have been formed on the basis of shared and understood narratives and discourses represented in the first newspapers. Anderson's notion of the "Imagined Community" (Anderson, 1983)[311] was based on the spread of "print capitalism" as having given rise to: "the nation: it is an imagined community—and imagined as both inherently limited and sovereign" (Anderson, ibid.). The press' role as watchdog of (a democratic) society and guardianship of the public's right to know was fortified by the upheaval of the French Revolution. Even then, it took almost a century for it to be realised more fully. So, apart from laying claim to being key constituents and founding members of the Fourth Estate, the press attracts and demands scrutiny in that it has been a unifying and informing force in building nationhood and there is, or should be, reflexivity and accountability in this process. Although it is also known that "advertising has traditionally been an important source of revenue for the British press since the 18th Century" (Harris & Lee 1986, in Chalaby, 1997)[312] yet "only through the development of profitable advertising that editors in England and the United States were finally able to free themselves from the subsidy and control of governors and political parties" (Shaw, 1959).[313]

Letters to the Editor pages and talkback radio ("old" media) are appealing to older demographics as their participatory media. Journalists rely on "Twitter" to keep up with developments in a news report (Persily, 2017),[314] to network with colleagues and contacts or gather fresh intelligence ("leads"). Online citizen journalism feeds the Fourth Estate with snippets (Wilson, 2008).[315] Of course, advertising also plays a ubiquitous and opportunistic role in every aspect of the Fourth Estate's functioning with the advent of instant and multi-platformed communication. Commercial media have been quick to seize upon this by augmenting their content on paying websites, but limiting free content with firewalls so as to encourage the purchase of news and support advertisers. In the spirit of "never say die", Melbourne was supplied with a free daily News Corporation afternoon entertainment newspaper in 2001, mX and Sydney was supplied with the free daily afternoon from 2005. They closed in 2015. They were an attempt to support, or inspire a newspaper reading habit in younger commuters. This was the demographic that had most abandoned newspapers in favour of the Internet. Their habits and practices of news consumption had seen then abandon print media in favour of digital information that could be consumed in their own time, and in their own way.

On the Internet, deadlines are now simply that—dead. They no longer exist because news had to be constantly updated. The definition of the role of the journalist had come under reappraisal from another quarter with

Julian Assange's *Wikileaks* and the publishing of confidential unedited content to a website. Here, the journalist had become the conduit, no longer the interpreter, filterer or prioritiser. It is a war between state actors and their institutions and the publisher/journalist. The public then became the editor sorting through what they wanted to know, what they believed mattered; and, how they would find out what they needed to know. This turned the profession of journalism and the definition of news as a created product on their heads and inside out. Assange had brought himself into direct conflict with state actors and he faced their ire once authorities extracted him after six years at the Ecuador Embassy in London. The US sought extradition of him on 17 charges after his website published large quantities of classified documents from 2010 to 2011 (Quinn, 2020).[316] The US Government would be appealing against a British court ruling that found that Assange should not be extradited on mental health grounds (ABC, 2021).[317] As he described himself as a "journalist" (Ignatius, 2019),[318] and is defended by other journalists as a member of the Australian Journalists section of the Media Entertainment and Arts Alliance (MEAA, 2020),[319] the argument of who is journalist and who enabler is passé.

As author Peter Singer and Emerson Brooking (2018)[320] said in *Likewar: The Weaponization of Social Media* people now experienced news together through social media, which had an original benign purpose of linking people but which were "on platforms designed to be addictive" (ibid.). We have quickly ended up with such a combative situation that it has become "war" (ibid.). In addition, the language used has power to harm and kill. Singer and Brooking (2018) quoted a former US gang member who told them that in regard to US gang activity that had gone global with social media: "is the faceless enemy …, the old adage 'sticks and stones may break my bones but words do not hurt me', I believe is no longer true. I believe words are causing people to die" (ibid.).[321] There is a reason to this in that people can post insults and then wait for their followers to join in so that it becomes a form of entertainment—online theatre. They also have the "safety" of not speaking the insult to the person. There is no chance of tone of voice or body language being shared with the other—they can be anonymous. The response of the recipient is also not considered part of the communication activity, so the person who is insulted is objectified, and de-personalised. It allows for more a forceful anger to be projected. It is aimed carefully at attacking the victim's "centre of gravity". This was a significant place to attack according to the famous military theorist, General Carl Von Clausewitz's (1874).[322] Von Clausewitz was referring to attacking armies' locus of power in the battle. Singer and Brooking (2018) advanced this expression to apply to social media as useful in describing attacks on "the spirit of the people" where social media was a weapon to fight personal, national and international battles through online abuse, stalking and where even its information content "is weaponised" (Ibid).[323] Social media warfare preys on online chatter that depicts "a growing distrust in politics globally, fuelled by disengagement" (Roe, 2020).[324]

The internet not only allowed authoritarian governments the capacity and ease of intercepting, influencing and persecuting people, they were aided by algorithms and bots that are programmed to stalk, pry and churn out abuse, adding to what's called colloquially in Australia a "pile on". Humans are "dopamined" through their biology to enjoy 'likes' and 'loves' to posts. When a human gets a "like" they feel good and certain—like being in love. Social media companies already know this. In Western democracies, this realignment of who is in charge of ideas signals a shift in power from democratically elected governments—to social media companies. The emergence of social media, such as Twitter, Facebook and Instagram have led to anomie. It is a space where anonymity is powerful, common and anything can be said, provided the social media platform (the arbiter of important content for society) considers it publishable. The ABC, immersed in social media, has struggled at times with this quandary. Concerns were raised in US print media research when it revealed that journalists received no organisational support for this activity in terms of valuing it as part of an already truncated workload, nor providing resources to assist (Lee, 2015).[325] Hence, interaction with social media was done 'on the fly'. There was also a lack of understanding given to journalists as to what their audiences wanted (Ibid.). This may help explain the nimble resort to opinion by ABC journalists active on social media and blogging, as well as mis-steps and exposing a 'false-positive' bias in the organisation through expressions of personal views and personal interpretations of the news.

4.11 ABC New Years' Coverage

The ABC's New Year's coverage on television is relevant for analysis because not only has it been a focal point for the organisation in terms of its content, but in 2018–2019 it was the network's top-rating program for

ABC television for that year attracting 1.8 million viewers and reached 3.8 million people when ABC, ABC ME and ABC NEWS are combined (ABC, 2019).[326] The ABC said this result was an increase on the previous year's New Year coverage (2017–2018, 3.7 million). It was one justification of continued funding when many Australians could be identified as having watched the open air, live events from the Sydney Opera House forecourt in celebrating beginning a calendar day/year's end. It is an indicator from the broadcaster that it considered the staging of such an event was of relevance to all Australians. The ABC also stages a New Year's Eve concert in the capital city of Victoria, Melbourne. Yet, the question of how the public service media creates and discerns relevance in a digital world where content is abundant overshadowed public media outfits. Whether European public broadcasters should be funded in a digitised media age was debated for many years but resolved that it was an important "tool of expression of fundamental European values" (Brevini, 2013)[327] with Spain's PSB and the BBC re-writing their Charters to suit the digital media world (Brevini, ibid.) framed by the "market failure" argument which has gained more traction.

The ABC suffers from the same criticism—along the lines of its model the BBC that it was "unnecessary, élitist and anti-competitive" (Born & Prosser, 2001) and, like the BBC, the ABC runs the risk of criticism if all they do is 'plug the gaps' left by the commercial media, or, if they try to compete with commercial content (Born & Prosser ibid.).[328] Damned either way. All public broadcasters in Europe have been constructed from "an ethic of comprehensiveness" (Open Society Institute 2003, quoting J. G. Blumler)[329] yet were being "dumbed down" (Ibid.). Born and Prosser (ibid.) said the observance of what the BBC was required to do as a public service media outlet was between itself and the government and fell into the category of 'soft' rather than 'hard' law or any specific view of its citizenship responsibilities. This can help explain the ABC's tendency to be experimental and provocative. The whole definition of public broadcasting is now uncertain with the shift of the ABC into the emergent commercial 'field' and its online presence in a wide-ranging cyber media marketplace. Public broadcasting (here, the concepts of 'public good' and 'citizenship responsibilities') in Australia is a shared, vague understanding rather than constitutionally enshrined, as it is in France and Italy, for example.

New Years' Eve 2017–2018

The 'soft law' disposition of the ABC was evident in New Years' presentations of the annual fireworks and concerts. ABC presenter Charlie Pickering counting down to 2018 at the live broadcast of the ABC's New Year's Eve coverage said to the large crowd and on national television:

> And I want to give a round of applause to the Australian taxpayer, without whom this concert would not be happening, those fireworks would not be happening, none of this would be possible without you ladies and gentlemen. We're getting ready to count it down to the magical moment, the only time it's OK to kill a police officer … to, kiss a police officer without asking? (Burrowes, 2018)[330]

After this exhortation, just before midnight, for Australians to kill (or kiss) a police officer, it was reported by Mumbrella that Pickering posted after midnight a thanks to the audience for watching, apologised for his error and praised the police officers working that night (Burrowes, 2018).[331] Many responses on social media, however, took umbrage with the gaffe (Burrowes ibid.). News.com website published several Twitter responses including one that said families of police killed in the line of duty would not find the mistake funny (News.com.au, 2018)[332] others said that killing police was not a topic for jokes. It was described by one media outlet as "either a slip of the tongue or a misreading of his autocue" (Burrowes, 2018).[333]

The ABC has sometimes attracted other controversy because of its experimental, public broadcasting "soft law" (Born & Prosser, 2001) disposition. The cost of the harbour fireworks display that year was reported to be AUD5.8 million (*The Australian Financial Review*, 2019).[334] Organisers quoted in the news article said the display was worth an: "estimated AUD133 million to the local economy and is seen by an estimated one billion audience across the globe" (ibid.).[335] In 2015 there was an online petition to the then Prime Minister Malcolm Turnbull for the government to donate the equivalent amount to farmers suffering drought. In 2019, the ABC reported on social media other smaller fireworks displays in Sydney have been called "hypocritical" with the state of NSW in the midst of widespread, catastrophic bushfires and total fire bans (*ABC*, 2019).[336]

New Year's Eve 2019–2020

Another furore erupted the next year, when at the ABC Television 2019 New Year's Eve concert televised live from the Sydney Opera House on Sydney Harbour a singer raised the middle finger on his left hand in the direction of the Prime Minister's official residence at Kirribilli (on the opposite shore) saying at the same time "this one's for the Prime Minister" and said he was dedicating his next song to "Scott Morrison" (the Prime Minister). The song was "The Honeymoon is Over" (Ross, 2020a).[337] Former ABC Chairman, Maurice Newman, said this obscene gesture and reference required the ABC to apologise to the Prime Minister and that the incident was a breach of the ABC Charter (Ross, 2020b)[338]: "if that is what is considered to be upholding Australian values, which is one of the tenets of the Charter of the Act that brought the ABC into being, it seems to me that it is past redemption" (ibid.).[339] Former ABC journalist Quentin Dempster said the performer, Tex Perkins, "will have to be held to account for his actions for sure" (Loc. Cit.).[340] Another ABC source interviewed for the news report was quoted as saying that the ABC had "not received any complaints via our switchboard for what was clearly his personal opinion and not that of the ABC" (Ross, ibid.).[341] Federal Liberal Senator, Eric Abetz, said the incident showed that the ABC was: "out of touch with the sentiment of the vast bulk of Australians, who are the ones that fund the ABC" (Ibid.). The incident satirised by The Australian cartoonist, Johannes Leak, (see following Image 4:1) also provided an enlarged and serious consideration on the state of ABC content, as an institutional entity.[342]

Responsibility for the content of this event was side-stepped by ABC management. But there is consistency in this stance on Perkins with, for example, its policy on social media use which permits staff freedom to use social media without (public) consequence. It was not the only controversial event from the ABC that evening with political editor of the ABC's 7.30 current affairs television program reported by environmental activist website The Fifth Estate as having tweeted an expletive in response to another Twitter user who complained about unbalanced ABC coverage of devastating bushfires burning around Australia at the time (The Fifth Estate, 2021).[343] This exchange raised several contentious aspects of the role of journalists at the ABC, the role of social media within news and the institutional expectations on actors in the digital field. It raised the vexed tripartite question of: how representative the institutions' actors (journalists and guests) were in a public capacity? Did the institution see its actors

Image 4.1 "Tex arcana: The man in black and the ring of fire." Cartoon by Johannes Leak, *The Australian*. Published 3 January 2020. Reprinted with permission from the artist. This cartoon referred to the ABC's 2019-2020 New Year's Eve concert in Sydney

as belonging and therefore responsible contributors to the institution, or were they outriders? Or, was it management by denial and confusion? Lastly, in terms of institutional capacity, should staff be tasked with addressing and managing complaints when ABC management demonstrated avoidance? There has been increasing interest among various stakeholders in the phenomenon of online abusive behaviour because it has "social, political and also economic relevance" (Bourgonje et al., 2018, in Rehm & Declerck, 2018).[344] Second, almost half of the world's population accesses the Internet "most of whom also use the WorldWideWeb and one or more of the big social networks" (Bourgonje et al., ibid.), and it ceases to be a niche activity when social media moments are elevated to the status of professional news. Second, and allied with this, "the internet has become mainstream and acts like an amplifier, maybe also as an enabler, of social trends" and social media is an easy form of communication with "the lack of any immediate negative repercussions" (Ibid.). And third, according to researchers (Loc. Cit.), analysis of public utterances by an identifiable individual matter because the person is using language which represents engagement with "symbolic systems that are the property of everyone" (Ibid.). According to the established branch of effects research, the media is highly influential anyway (Sparks, 2013).[345]

Perplexing this position, is that journalists themselves are subjected to regular online abuse and research into its impact on journalists' behaviour showed "women were more likely than men to report often receiving insults or threats, and had stronger emotional reactions to abuse" (Binns, 2017). Journalists had a tough role to maintain in the robustness of the media jungle, while their organisations encouraged them to do so as a career and content promotion priority. They should be online and active. The dark side of this expectation is that they are highly exposed to abuse, and therefore vulnerable to angry outbursts. Social media has lifted the veil on once private exchanges and created a public forum for humiliation, from which internet companies re-circulate and profit. Internet companies have transformed abuse into theatre containing the most savage voyeurism and vilifying attacks, including threats of harm to an individual. This happenstance, therefore, places the Australian public broadcaster with its aim of 'all for all' and its actors in an awkward, and possibly invidious, position. Journalists have been directed to promote 'the business' while also weathering the storm of random attacks. What was ultimately, the most testing was that, in a virtual space, journalists might be under attack, or their information infiltrated from automated bots designed to provoke discord. This lightly acknowledged topic has serious consequences for democratic debate, and the impact is just as disruptive as if from a real person. It is another example of where the exciting promise of "digital disruption" regresses into digital disturbance—digital disorder.

It, then, needs to be determined where institutional responsibility lies when staff is encouraged to engage in a combative highly environment. Consequently, it further queries whether the ABC's move into the emergent commercial digital field was planned carefully enough to manage accusations, evidence of bias and individual staff responses. A hostile reaction by a high-profile staff member to complaints of bias (and other complaints) is nothing new in the history of the ABC. However, on the other hand, the absence of a solid institutional reaction to public exchanges where the employee takes responsibility for redressing accusations, has to imply the ABC tacitly supports this engagement, or regarded it as so trivial as to be unruffled. Either is disturbing. This development has signalled a lack of nuanced institutional and legal understandings of managing such exchanges in a public forum, a lack of strategy to protect the ABC's *reputational capital*, and ultimately an avoidance in managing and supporting staff in the emergent commercial digital field. It suggested that some of the ABC's complaints handling procedures were being left for frontline staff to manage. The academic literature on complaints handling said it needed to be impartial and procedural yet could often be "complex and technical" (Nicholson, 2016).[346] So, while staff was already placed in an ambiguous (yet onerous) situation of 'representing the ABC/not representing the ABC' by virtue of their social media disclaimers and ABC "hands off" social media policy, it is damned either way and abandoned in that process. In addition, with a strong staff culture and the cost of pursuing complaints, the institution may see it as an appropriate and convenient adjunct to allow staff to manage as best they can with their audiences. Ultimately, it challenged the institution's accountability and policy planning for such contingencies. But the ABC is not perplexed alone: "many institutions have not taken planning seriously because the perception is that strategic plans have rarely worked to move them forward" (Fleuriet & Lee Williams, 2015).

The institution may have made plans for the way in which Web 1.0 (websites) curated and presented content, but Web 2.0 (unmediated exchanges) were treated as more laissez faire. The institution may have made plans for the former, but not so well the latter. In simple terms, it is a comparison of top down (Web 1.0) and bottom up (Web 2.0) (Ceron, 2015). Ceron (2015) said news organisations tended to publish news which was written from an official government perspective. The content on ABC platforms had become disputed in two key areas: when contributions were prioritised from audiences and designated or self-appointed experts, and journalists expressed personal opinions on news reports on their social media accounts—both areas defined as 'out of bounds' of ABC management control. The confused general public was then led to question all content from the organisation—a difficulty for the institution to unravel. The ABC platforms journalists' opinion aside professional news. The result may be accusations of bias where the two 'bleed into each other' by association under the one umbrella (the ABC). It leads to a possible interpretation of content that: "this may be what we say, but this is what we *really* think". Audiences could be fortified by hearing alternative views (Ceron, 2015)[347] although research has also found that: "the negative relation between social media and trust (in institutions) can be damaging for the democratic political system" (Ceron, 2015) (Image 4.1).[348]

4.12 The ABC's Role in Social Media

Journalism is going through "troubled times" (Alvarez et al., 2012)[349]; no longer the mediators and curators of news and information journalists work in a period of "disintermediation" (ibid.) with competition from Twitter, Google, Yahoo, YouTube and so on. They compete with an online bloggers. It means that newsrooms are gutted of editorial staff and in a world where "no one reads newspapers anymore". Online advertising is all about aggregating content for advertisers and marketing campaigns. Newspapers are in a declining market for their advertising and face stiff competition when trying to sell their news reports with attendant advertising content because news (any news) is now so manifestly reported and shared online—to put it simply, no one buys their widgets through newspapers, they shop for them online. Nothing happens in isolation. Journalists are part of an enlarged, all-inclusive emergent commercial ecosystem where institutions and actors are either vying for attention, or running from attention, and both sell.

The academic literature observed that there was a phenomenon of "emotional contagion" in online engagement (Kušen et al., 2019)[350] where strong emotions triggered a strong reaction. Other manifold uses of social media have also emerged that showed that it had led to "e-democracy" (Ceron, 2015)[351] where controversial and provocative ideas could be expressed through "the democratization of interests and ideas" (Auger, 2013),[352] but there were divided views on whether the internet created shared opinion (Ceron, 2015). The internet had a plethora of uses, some positive and some negative but often it seemed the good aspects of the internet, the ease and facility of communication, maintaining relationships and managing personal life administration far outweighed the downside. The internet had also become a magnet for hate speech, 'othering' (and an over-simplified, binaried rendition of the world and all its issues), racism, extremism, radicalisation (Lumsden & Harmer, 2019)[353] and a platform for grooming (the process of an adult preparing a child for sexual abuse) leading to either virtual child sexual abuse online or that which occurred in an actual physical capacity. Digital communication developed a darker side during the Covid-19 pandemic where research (including studies from Australia) found addictive internet behaviours had increased in "online gaming disorder, online gambling disorder, pornography use, and smart-phone use disorder... due to financial hardships, isolation, problematic substance use, and mental health issues such as depression, anxiety, and stress" (Masaeli & Farhadi, 2021).

Aside from the preceding research that called for interventions and guidelines and warned of the "considerable" impact Covid-19 had had on mental health (Masaeli & Farhadi, ibid.), there were negative consequences, generally, for bio-psycho-social wellbeing because of online augmentation, victimisation and cyber-bullying (Machimbarrena et al., 2018)[354] which could lead to IAD (Internet Addiction Disorder) where individuals might develop anxiety and depression through spending long hours on the internet without forming relationships with real people in a real context (Tonioni et al., 2012).[355] Negativities and illegalities withstanding there is also the counterbalancing argument of freedom of expression where the law is tasked with treading the line between free speech and allowing individuals and communities to damage themselves and each other. Free speech absolutists argue that the dark side of free speech is worth the cost when weighed with freedom of all speech (Weinert, 2019). But Weinert (2019) problematised the notion of free speech in arguing that: "speech is produced for a reason: in order to advance an agenda or urge action" (Ibid.).[356] Yet, the purpose of speech is a prior constraint, anyway, where the individual self-censors for a reason.

The Twitter incidents described earlier raise the question of whether the ABC policy had become both wedded and victim to social media in its shift from a top-down to a bottom-up approach—from 'one to all' transmission, to 'all to one' networking had not proved a smooth, consistent transition in terms of its content. Former Managing Director Mark Scott said: "what you see in your feed becomes your news and your version of truth … you trust them and your confidence in them washes over into the other things coming into your feed" (Scott, 2018).[357] Rather than using social media as a professional means of engagement in upholding its Fourth Estate role, journalists now succumb to popularity and respond to the rapid pace of social media. 'Likes' and 're-tweets' have become a prevailing value in the *habitus* of professional media actors in terms of their success as communicators and their professional prominence. Making no reference to the controversy of its 2019 New Year's Eve televised concert, on Friday 3 January, 2020 the ABC's Managing Director David Anderson was quoted as having issued an email of praise to staff saying "the New Year's Eve coverage had reached 3.5 million people and raised $2.8 million for the Red Cross" (Duke, 2020),[358] and no mention of the other issues that backgrounded/foregrounded coverage that evening's performance, instead a deflection. Anderson was quoted as saying in the staff email that the national bushfire emergency had been a "whole-of-ABC effort" (ibid.). Three days after this, Director of ABC Regional and Local, Judith Whelan, released a statement:

> Thanks, too, to the ABC broadcasters, reporters, presenters, producers, staff and crew who continue to deliver emergency broadcasting services to communities under threat. People turn to the ABC at such times and we are proud of our role in helping to keep them informed and safe. (ABC, 2019)[359]

4.13 Impact of Social Media and How It Shapes Knowledge

Social media has become a convenient form of trading anger and outrage. Even the co-Founder of Twitter, Evan Williams, was bereft of what his creation had become: "I think the internet is broken … and it's a lot more obvious to a lot of people that it's broken" (Streitfeld, 2017).[360] Williams was referring to the use of Twitter for abuse, trolling and sledging as well the use of Facebook to show suicides and murders—in real time (referencing the New Zealand Christchurch Shootings in 2019, killing 51 people, where the murderer was able to live-stream his killings and attacks via his Facebook page). The question lingers about how society manages and draws meaning, as a form of civil engagement and democratic enlightenment, from this online chaos, internet homicide, tragedy and markedly inconsistent approach to content. Paul Monk (2016)[361] pointed out that there was an even more important role now for critical reasoning and rationalism in Western society given the complexities and challenges confronting humanity. Twitter abuse had failed to nuance debate and forge understandings, because critical reasoning and integrity was not valued universally in the emergent commercial *field*. Another deleterious consequence of this was that social media was so highly influential that leaders and politicians responded and altered government policy in a knee-jerk manner if there was an outbreak of abuse, threats and vilification against them, fearful of nasty electoral consequences. *The Australian's* columnist, and former editor in chief, Chris Mitchell, observed "modern media needs to return to conventional market research rather than treating social media as a compass because that is only driving scepticism about journalism" (Mitchell, 2019).[362]

Appeasing the strident voices results in policy incoherence and general uncertainty. Many who may not be aware of the invective happening on social media platforms would fail to understand why governments can be so skittish on policy. This sort of 'quick change/nothing to see here' politics then provides momentum for claims of the social media hashtag #failedleadership. It has become a situation where governments are led by pressure from social media activism, such that the underpinnings of a democratically-elected government are eroded to appease this artful anger. It becomes inchoate, emotional and chaotic for citizens when opinions and feelings are more important than facts, and facts are disputed and dismissed as "just your facts, not my facts" (or "alternative facts") and it becomes urgent that selected institutions must be destroyed because they represent selected aspects of unacceptable power, identified through the use of simplified, generalising binaries. The ABC, too, is an institution. Former US President Barak Obama warned about this use of binaries: "we are operating in completely different information universes" (Stuever, 2018).[363]

The lines are now dangerously blurred in a world where people are increasingly isolated and fearful of existential threats fed to them on the social media. Political theorist Hannah Arendt (1968) said in analysing an earlier time: "totalitarianism appeals to the very dangerous emotional needs of people who live in complete isolation and in fear of one another" (ibid.).[364] Many years earlier, she observed presciently: "the ideal subject of totalitarian rule is not the convinced Nazi or the convinced Communist, but people for whom the distinction between fact and fiction (i.e., the reality of experience) and the distinction between true and false (i.e., the standards of thought) no longer exist" (Arendt, 1968).[365] The popular quote wrongly-attributed to Josef Goebbels (Adolf Hitler's propagandist) "if you lie make it big and keep repeating it" is actually true of social media (except Goebbels was not talking about his own style, he was condemning how he believed the British had lied (Goebbels, 1941)). Michiko Kakutani (2018) quoted Arendt at the start of her book The Death of Truth (2018)[366] in which Kakutani said "relativism has been on the ascendant since the culture wars began in the 1960s" (ibid.) at a time when the New Left promoted perceived biases in Western, liberal, male-dominated culture and postmodernists argued there was 'no truth', rather there were perspectives of truth and identity became the defining quality and dominant truth in describing people, over-riding institutional concerns. People were assigned groups according to labels that battled for ascendancy of sexuality, gender, race, ethnicity, religion, creationists, evolutionists, climate change activists, climate change deniers, et cetera. Cicero argued in 52 BCE *silent enim leges inter arma*—in time of war, the law falls silent (Cicero, 52BCE).[367]

We now have decisions made according to 'the wisdom of the crowd' or what could also be described as mob or lynch mob rule. The positive aspects of crowd-sourced support had iterations in the "phone a friend" for old television quiz shows where contestants could speak with a "smart" person they knew to provide the answer to a question, or when stumped at a trivia night (someone, somewhere must have been tempted at some time). It should not be confused with crowd-sourcing which is a term used in business and marketing to describe the sharing of information and expertise (Guillot, 2013).[368] 'The wisdom of the crowd' is also prevailed upon when people are crowd-funding money online for perceived worthy causes. It had appealing collaborative dimensions for individuals to add 'their bit' towards a cooperative outcome for a civic society. However, Kakutani (Ibid.) warned 'the wisdom of the crowd' had now taken the place of expertise and research. This displacement of proficiency and mastery in favour of a media-assigned commentator or expert is explored further in the next chapter, Chap. 5: 'Losing the Brand in the Australian Media Landscape'.

The appealing reason for using social media, broadly speaking, is that it appeared enticing in offering easy and quick ways to satisfy the upper layers of Maslow's Hierarchy of Needs: love, belonging, esteem and self-actualisation (Shah, 2017)[369]. It also helped people: "stay within their own comfort zones in regard to information seeking and information sharing, rather than venture into zones that involve a lot of sense-making" (Shah, 2017, quoting B. Narayan 2013). English Victorian author Charles Dickens once wrote satirically that when random voices sang together "the chorus was the essence of the song; and, as each gentleman sang it to the tune he knew best, the effect was very striking indeed" (Dickens, 1836).[370] The same could be said of social media where a range of voices believed they sang the same song but added their own bits and chunks of knowledge and ideas, ending up with discordance and incoherence, like the inharmonious chorus Dickens once described ironically.

The Victorian novel became an important platform for social change with warnings of upheaval and dislocation and Dicken's poignant depictions of abused children raised consciousness in his society about the need to protect, love and educate children, amongst other issues. Society no longer had a Dickens (who also controversially damned his society), instead there was Twitter and Facebook[371] to build consciousness, but in many instances instead of imparting a deeper enrichment and knowledge, they creating disharmony, fragmentation and vilification. Victorian novelists, like London-based Dickens and the lesser known Manchester author Elizabeth Gaskell, warned of the damaging isolation of the individual brought by economic and social forces at that time. Those warnings have re-emerged in an unexpected way through social media which when coupled with the power of advertising revenue, means the audience may no longer engage with content to be enlightened but because social media platforms have converted sentient beings into algorithms and commodities.

Social media makes business sense and helps advertisers profile and target potential consumers. There is a multiplicity of choices, but it also had a deleterious impact on the way it changed and fragmented styles of communication and content. US business reporter Ken Auletta (2009)[372] said that Google "took much of the guessing out of advertising" (ibid.) with precise algorithms tracking people, the sites they visited, their locations and their choices of products and news. He said the predatory role of Google had caused major upheaval for traditional media and warned that Google was the new "Evil Empire" (Ibid.):[373]

> Google's way of building business—make it free and attract users before figuring out a way to make money—became the template for Web start-ups from Facebook to You Tube to Twitter to Ning. (Auletta ibid.)[374]

Google had also precipitated the loss of appetite for costly investigative journalism. Australian author and former News Corporation journalist, Scott Monk, said that old media had shifted its interests and was attracted to opinion, rather than hard news because: "they want you permanently angry, fearful and ready to get onto social media to vent and bring in more clicks for them ... Turn on Sky News, the ABC or the afternoon news and you'll see a swag of journalists pontificating" on what Monk described as "pandering to the élites and their current social justice agendas" (Monk, 2019).[375]

The ABC had abandoned its generalised élite public field to attend to its new pockets of élites. Australians belonged to a representative culture, where the media showed the nation (and the world) mediated, personalised representations of reality. Marshall McLuhan's (1964) "the medium is the message"[376] still holds true because media impacts on how we perceive, interpret and think of an event, person or thing. As if to presage social media, McLuhan also said:

> Any medium has the power of imposing its own assumption on the unwary. Prediction and control consist in avoiding this subliminal state of Narcissus trance. But the greatest aid to this end is simply in knowing that the spell can occur immediately upon contact, as in the first bars of a melody (Ibid.).[377]

And he sounded the alarm:

> The American stake in literacy as a technology or uniformity applied to every level of education, government, industry, and social life is totally threatened by the electric technology. The threat of Stalin or Hitler was external. The electric technology is within the gates, and we are numb, deaf, blind, and mute about its encounter with the Gutenberg technology, on and through which the American way of life was formed. (Ibid.)[378]

The uses of language and images are powerful and formative in social media's claim to represent public opinion, but in this distortion, it polarises debate, curates anger and outrage and is ultimately destructive of civil and representative society. It leads to commentators being "de-platformed" (having their speaking engagements suddenly removed or planned interviews terminated) if their views were not compatible with these strident voices. French philosopher and sociologist Jacques Derrida (1992)[379] said the loudest voices, or "lethal power", held sway in the rise of Nazism (but this could also apply to other uses and manipulations of language to gain power and control):

> Evil, that is to say lethal power, comes to language by way of, precisely, *representation,* in other words, by that dimension of language as means of communication that is re-presentative, mediating, thus technical, utilitarian, semiotic, informational—all of those powers that uproot language and cause it to decline, to fall far from or outside of its originary destination which was appellation, nomination, the giving or the appeal or presence in the name. (Derrida, 1992)[380]

4.14 The Contribution of ABC Journalists to the New *Field*

The contribution of the ABC to Australians' news diet has been historically substantial and the way the ABC preferred to measure that was through reach. Reach measured the percentage of Australians who used ABC content over a given time-frame. The reach was substantial when one considers 71% of Australians watch, read or listened to the ABC each week (ABC Annual Report, 2018)[381] and that in 2018 "ABC news and current affairs online reached an average 4.8 million Australian users each month, close to one in four (24%) of the active online Australian population" (ibid.). In 2019, the audience reach had declined to 68.3% with 30% digital reach.[382] The 2019 report also showed declines in broadcast audiences but increases in online audiences. The organisation was trusted in 2019 by 81% of those surveyed (82% previous year) and was valued by 49% Australian adults (this was a new performance measure with a target of 40%) (ibid.). The organisation said it experienced a downturn in how Australians valued the ABC because it "has been impacted (sic) by declining reach and share across traditional platforms, which have not been entirely offset by digital growth" (ibid.). Such is the unbounded vastness of its emergent commercial 'field'.

Journalists' writing within the *field* then becomes complicated when overlaid by social media. Social media was once, briefly, "outside the closed worlds of journalism and the media" (Bromley & Neal, 2009),[383] but no longer. Now the aim of the ABC is "meeting audiences on their terms" (ABC Annual Report, 2019)[384] through "core digital products such as iView and the ABC News app the team aims to deliver digital growth and engagement while maintaining broadcast transmission to service loyal audiences" (Ibid.) because "audiences are at the heart of everything the ABC does" (Ibid.).[385]

Journalists were once not at the heart of audiences, and further they eschewed and were quite "sniffy" about such proximity. They were on the sidelines. Watching. Schudson (2008) said journalists' impartiality, driven by a desire to distance themselves from emerging public relations at the turn of the last century, was exemplified in the early 1920s when the American Society of Newspaper Editors declared "news reports should be free from opinion on bias of any kind" (Ibid.).[386] Can the same be said now of the news report that a journalist sources, writes, posts and re-posts on Twitter, or Facebook? Schudson (2008) argued that journalists were merely marketing themselves and with no desire to resolve conflict anyway (Schudson, 2008). What has the professional media become? Its employers were reading its postings and 'likes' also, including those employees who posted and tweeted regularly and engaged in abuse and vilification. Humans have developed a human disconnect between the real world and fantasy of social media—a dual personality of the individual's real life versus "the best version of ourselves". Taken further, it had also seen the dignity of the individual violated with intrusiveness; and the increase in the cybercrimes of harassment and menace “capable of inflicting tremendous, ongoing harm” (Bandler & Merzon, 2020).

It has become almost as a side issue now, but the contribution made by journalists is vital for a democracy (Schudson, 2005)[387] with the tabloidization of the news media (Conboy, 2013) and shift of news values towards sensational tabloid newspapers which had addressed parochial markets (city based or nation based), emphasised controversy, sensation and “shock—horror” and in the more “seamy” press facts were given scant regard or exaggerated for the sake of the story. Social media had helped facilitate the professional media to ‘cross the Rubicon’ and to further the Julius Caeser idiom “the die is cast”. Former Editor of London’s *The Sunday Times*, Sir Harold Evans said:

> We see this new invention called ‘fake news’. It is an attempt to remove one of the barriers protecting the freedom and dignity of individuals, and any of those individuals so credulous to believe it are actually betraying themselves. (Cannane, 2017)[388]

Evans blamed this on the rise of relativism, where ‘your truth is not my truth’ because we have different values and feelings. He sheeted home responsibility for this to the French sociologists: Emile Durkheim, Jacques Derrida and French anthropologist Lucien Lévy-Bruhl. (Baghramian & Carter, 2015)[389] said these people theorised that truth was relative and objectivity was, therefore, not possible because of various contexts and perceptions. Evans told the ABC’s Europe Correspondent Stephen Cannane (Cannane ibid.) of challenges during the UK’s Brexit referendum:

> During the referendum campaign, key Brexiteer and Conservative minister Michael Gove attacked economists and others who questioned the benefits of leaving the EU, by saying, “people in this country have had enough of experts”. (Ibid.)

He said the comments were “appalling” (Ibid.):

> I’d like to say to them, next time you’re having an operation, I’m going to send my carpenter in to do the surgery. He’s not an expert, you understand, so I think he will be perfectly acceptable to you. … Those morons are trying to deny centuries of advancement in education, science, research and inde-

> pendence, nibbling away at civilised standards. They are the real enemies of the people. (Ibid.)

John Ralston Saul (1993)[390] said that the English language no longer distinguished between meritocracy and expertise and as a result confounded both. It resulted in journalists and political actors appointing people as experts who may or may not have specialisation in the area on which they claim authority.

> The underlying assumptions of meritocracy are open-ended and embracing … they presume generosity … if … often betrayed. The underlying assumptions of expertise and specialist knowledge are … elitist … presume superiority and privileged possession of answers … promote both social barriers and political exclusion. (Saul, ibid.)

Residing with this clash of commentary is that journalism had always had a "recurrent anarchic quality" (Schudson, 2008)[391] anyway because "almost all journalists relish conflict" (ibid.). Schudson (2008) said this conflict was necessary and unavoidable because of what he described about the US press as "a morbid sports-minded fascination with gladiatorial combat" (ibid.). He said news events presented journalists with "anarchy" (or to quote Schudson, 2005: "shit happens"[392]). Schwartz (2008) said that politics had become a "blood sport": "Australians love their sport and the media feed them ongoing stories of victories, defeats, dramas, leaders, and strategies" (ibid.).[393] This sense of anarchy played well on social media and had become a natural attraction to journalists engaging with this conflict, anarchy and juxtaposition because "newspapers [the media] … have no ambition that they make sense together" (Schudson, 2008).[394]

Journalism was a research practice at university level (Nash, 2013)[395] and it concurrently dovetailed into the university training for public relations and marketing (Carey, 1996).[396] Critics said its cultural studies subjects had been "educationally corrupting and professionally embarrassing for journalism education" (Windschuttle, 2000)[397] and that "its success derives from academic fashions and politics rather than logic and scholarship" (ibid.).[398] Cunningham and Turner (2010) drew a substantive difference between cultural studies and media studies. Media studies had: "'real world' orientation... as well... rigorous collection and evaluation of empirical evidence, and... development of appropriate methodologies for doing this" (Ibid.). Journalism education had been described as "a struggle between interest groups, ... a tale about the journalistic trade gradually losing control over its education" (Gardeström, 2017). Research by Cunningham and Bridgstock (2012)[399] said journalism studies provided graduates with generic skills that helped them transition into the Australian workplace. While, Cokley and Ranke (in Franklin & Mensing, 2010) found that university-trained journalists (2006–2008) were more likely to work *outside* media organisations after graduation. Part of the reason was that they were graduated into a world where editorial jobs were shrinking and newsrooms being obliterated. In a declining employment market, it was not the best time to aspire to be a journalist, nor study for a journalism degree. The established newsrooms had been gutted along with the expertise and legacy knowledge they carried about historical context, political frameworks, institutions and the background facts and circumstance on issues, court cases and people. Media ethicist Stephen Ward (2014) had been critical of university education of journalists because it trained only in objectivity and writing skills, but failed to develop courses in data journalism. Ward (2014) said journalists needed to have a wider knowledge of global issues to use technology to educate audiences, and be equipped with a greater capacity for evaluating opinion (ibid.).[400]

There had always been tensions between cultural studies and journalism and media studies (Turner, 2000). Cultural studies included media theory, gender studies, queer theory and literary theory. Historian James Carey (1996)[401] said these frameworks for analysis had motivated journalists to split the "body politic" into the "used and using" (ibid.).[402] A reliance on the resources of social media, "there is also a tendency in journalistic writing to place people, events and topics into binaries" (Derrida, 1992).[403] The loss in understanding complexities of situations, or the substantial grey of inconsistencies, had resulted in a polarisation of events and matters. Orientalism was a pronounced theory studied by many Australian student journalists and it was expounded by post-colonialist Edward Said in his landmark text Orientalism (1978). The theory described how from a Western perspective the East was cast as "the other", exotic, child-like, primitive, female, inferior and therefore to be conquered and subjugated. Orientalism, it was explained, was the power motivating colonialism, slavery and racism. Older media depictions of race and culture were said to perpetuate these.

The theory of binaries analysed how meanings were defined by two opposing binaries. Binaries according to Jacques Derrida were not neutral, but hierarchical: "never the face-to-face of two terms, but a hierarchy and an order of subordination" (Derrida, in Anderson & Schlunke, 2008).[404] Binaries worked in opposition so that meaning was influenced by one set of values that got to determine reality and shape how humans understood the world: "the deconstruction of oppositions reveals that there is a limit or boundary between the two terms in an opposition and, at the same time, that each term always already 'haunts' or informs the other and vice versa. This haunting was a consequence of what Derrida called "*différance*" (Anderson & Schlunke, 2008).[405] Derrida argued that binaries were arbitrary and unstable. A favourite theme of binaries was the dominated versus the dominant, so in news reporting binaries were about power and relations. When the media evoked a sense of fear it did so by creating a sense there was a threat to the powerful. Derrida's semiotic analysis described an example of a binary pair as nature and culture (Derrida, 1998),[406] for instance.

Arbitrary, over-simplified binaries meant the world was divided into good versus evil, black versus white, climate change scientist versus climate change denier, woman versus man, man versus everyone else, left-right, up-down and so on. The point here is that there was ongoing power struggles for supremacy within these binaries, and a human has to essentially belong to one, or the other. Both poles of the binary cannot be correct—or have elements of truth each—one is totally wrong, the other incontrovertibly correct, moral or justified. Journalists' use of these oppositional relationships between binaries results in meanings being influenced by one set of values that determine reality and shape how audiences understand the world. The concern with this, apart from the obvious elimination of debate and diversity, is instead of resorting first to facts for the audience to analyse, it is instead presented with this over-simplified view of the world. Then, if topics (humans) do not fit into this binary, they are potentially avoided. The overall narrative, then, becomes an 'all or nothing' fait accompli. Binaries are a shorthand, convenient and lazy way of looking at and understanding what could be highly complex and nuanced world: "journalism should, however, foster greater awareness by backgrounding and questioning and shedding light on complex and contested subjects" (Dodd et al., 2017).[407] It, therefore, must be questioned whether placing groups, issues or humans into oppositional camps and providing unequal and/or generalised representation for both halves aids in a clear and accurate understanding of serious issues confronting a democracy and gives an adequate opportunity for policy discussion. Instead of facilitating an enlarged knowledge promoting harmony, clarity and mutual benefit—dissonance, lack of understanding and conflict is furthered. At the heart of it, it meant people and issues were shuffled into binaries whether they are happy and comfortable to be there, or not.

Complementing and supporting Orientalism, there were discourse inversions taking place where institutions of the West were described and depicted as inferior, abusive and primitive using phrases: "toxic masculinity", "toxic older white men", "white male patriarchy", "toxic patriarchy", "toxic power", "colonial oppression", "oppressive male institutions", for example. Analyses of hegemonic patriarchal discourses have served society well in delegitimising male-only interpretations of sexual abuse of women, for example, by prioritising female voices. It has ensured that domestic and family violence has shifted from the private sphere ("what happens in the home stays in the home") to the public sphere, where it can be identified as criminal, legally prosecuted and anti-violence education programs rolled-out.

On another level, however, there has been a loss to journalism and its public obligation to nuance and finesse the spoken and written word, with skilled interviewing and wordsmithing to explain and describe experiences and cultural understandings in communication contexts. Compounding that, there was a lack of knowledge (or care) for correct spelling, grammar, punctuation and paragraphing—lending support to a more free-form and personal presentation style, yet this approach also tended to invalidate the impact and reduce the heft of the communication. In accuracies indicate lack of preparation and, worse, reduced authority. Newspaper reports and television "supers" (superimposed headlines or descriptors) give ample evidence of this decline and de-emphasis on correct spelling and grammar. Or maybe it is better to take George Orwell's view: "any struggle against the abuse of language is a sentimental archaism, like preferring candles to electric light" (Orwell, 1946)? Newsrooms used to be inhabited by the best-read people in society with a fine knowledge of history, politics, literature, language and its uses (and abuses) and a probable knowledge of a wide range of other matters purely through being well-read—and were intensely curious about the written word. The 'profession' of journalism was treated as one of the professions by universities in their elevation of "journalism training", yet journalism never been acknowledged as a profession by having its own professional body so as to preserve and uphold standards and set university education requirements. This was not the case with law, medicine, engineering and psychology—which were regulated and standardised by their respective professions. The loss of bodies such as the Australian Journalists' Association, although a trade union and not one that accredited journalists—was part of a decline, or disaggregation in the profession.

Carey (in Stryker-Munson & Warren, 1997) considered robust journalism vital for a democracy, but now riven with conflicting allegiances and expectations and inspired by what's happening on social media.

Professional journalists aim to uphold values of objectivity, accuracy and fairness but are conflicted because their product can be:

1. Hostage to advertisers *or* hostage to government policy favour/disfavour
2. Hostage to business considerations and the pressing need for their proprietors to make profits *or* hostage to meeting efficiency targets with few staff and dwindling resources
3. Propelled by an overwhelming psychological compulsion to be 'liked', followed and popular in a digital media world to advance careers, and compete in a shrinking market for their professional news.

Ultimately, and most worryingly, what all this has signalled is a loss of respect for journalists. Their rush to embrace digital opinion and be part of the noisy throng had only exacerbated this situation. In 2008, *objectivity* was defined in the ABC Editorial Policies as: "an attitude that":

(1) Values evidence and weighs it carefully. It puts what the evidence indicates above what one may want or hope to be the case.
(2) Cares deeply about the truth. It doesn't just accept what truths are presented, but seeks truth out with a critical mind, rejecting impostors to the truth.
(3) Is concerned to avoid error. This concern naturally complements the desire for truth, but also acts as a brake on the enthusiasm accompanying that desire.
(4) Cultivates the virtues of honesty and accuracy, both of which promote the achievement of truth.
(5) Is open to learning from others, especially from disagreement, divergent viewpoints and unpalatable insights. (Coady, 2008)[408]

The ABC had always been considered a prestigious place to work for journalists (Cokley & Ranke, in Franklin & Mensing 2011).[409] Paletz and Entman (1981)[410] argued that "by granting élites substantial control over the content, emphases, and flow of public opinion, media practices diminish the public's power" (Ibid.). Therefore, "the mass media are often the unwitting handmaidens of the powerful" (Ibid.).[411] Organisations, including the ABC, use social media as a way of promoting news reports, events, staff members' careers and in turn individual actors use social media to promote their own news reports as well as their opinions and successes on their social media feeds. It also served to promote their writing to their followers and the amount of Twitter followers; retweets and tweets they receive then become a focal point in assessing career success and KPIs. Social media forms an important role in the development of online promotion because it: "provides the overwhelming majority of ordinary men and women with access to intimations of elevated existence" (Rojek, 2012). Rojek (2012) attributed the rise of the celebrity as proportional to the decline in organised religion and "celebrity culture provides a desacralized highway to transcendence" (Rojek, ibid.). The ground between the individual and the institution was contested hotly. Social media actors also had to 'stand for something', otherwise they created no attention, so they had become partisan in politicising not just themselves, but also the institutions—the ABC—they represented. Popular social media operatives formed the new élite, displacing the institution and its vision. The academic literature stated long ago that "little actual or objective information is disseminated to or processed by the mass public; instead, élites shape opinion by spinning or framing the facts and interpreting events (Druckman, 2004; Kahneman & Tversky, 1979)" in Entman, 2004.[412]

The way in which social media functioned, in lock step with professional media, as firmly part of the emergent commercial field (and Fourth Estate), signalled a dramatic change in journalism. Research showed that there was a lot of fakery and falsity on social media by virtue that people could hide behind an assumed moniker -r create automated bots to do the hard work; that emotion and outrage were stoked by trolls and, even more concerning, a major study showed false news travelled faster and more invasively online than facts (Vosoughi et al., 2018)[413] because "false stories inspired fear, disgust, and surprise" (Ibid.).[414] Coupled with this the strident voices of social media that were promulgated by bots, or even public relations firms recruited for the purposes of providing anger and 'push-back', were "masquerading as humans routinely insert inflammatory remarks into public discussion" (ibid.) and that "emotionally charged Twitter messages tend to be re-tweeted more often and more quickly compared to neutral ones" (Stieglitz & Dang-Xuan, 2013).[415]

In addition, there were individuals or influencers who were "paid to post", duplicate accounts and make fake accounts (Murphy et al., 2014).[416] Lazer et al. (2018) said that the whole process of liking, searching and sharing triggered social bots to spread and amplify content (Lazer et al., 2018).[417] Identities online could be anonymous, ambiguous or real and the capacity of online social media citizen users to discern between those is fraught. Researchers estimated that "between 9 and 15% of active Twitter accounts are bots ... Facebook estimated that as many as 60 million bots may be infesting its platform" (ibid.). George Orwell (1949) had never been more resonant: "Big Brother is watching you" (Orwell, 1949)[418] and he described presciently the curating capacity of online media, shepherding of information as facts and fact-checking: "who controls the past controls the future: who controls the present controls the past" (ibid.). It is estimated that 99% of online data may never be analysed, but it is out there (Shah, 2017).[419] Psychologists and psychiatrists have a new expression to describe the cases for a growing number of children who are online for protracted periods: 'Facebook depression' (Blease, 2015[420]) although the extent of this had been contested in prior research (Jelenchick et al., 2012).[421] Overall, the sharing of information meant the altering and re-contextualising of information, and this book argues that the ABC failed to plan and is yet to grapple with how it manages this as a focal, vital member of Australia's Fourth Estate—but also a needed public service.

The debate whether the ABC was remaining relevant to all Australians was ongoing. The organisation's Managing Director, Michelle Guthrie, when she was a few days new to the role told staff via an email that:

> We must extend our reach and our relevance into areas where we are under-represented. That means more diversity in both our staff and our content. We must collaborate more, with a clear focus on *serving the audience*, regardless of platform or device. (Guthrie, staff email, 2 May 2016) (author's emphasis)

It is part of an ongoing discernment of relevance by public broadcasters which Miragliotta and Errington (2012)[422] have described as "power centres in their own right" (ibid.). The arrival of digital technology had made the ABC responsible for a wider menu of new, information and entertainment options. *The Canberra Times* (2016) newspaper pointed out in an editorial the: "broadly worded public charter is open to nit-picking by those with ideological wheelbarrows to push". Watson (2014) described the conservative criticism of the ABC was as if it were describing "an irrelevant item of mega fauna" (ibid.)[423] faced with lower audiences and concomitant accusations of irrelevance. Yet, more significantly, these concerns about relevance were being watered down with new understandings of how the ABC hybridised itself (Burns & Hawkins, 2013)[424] to meet changing niche markets through its activities in digital media. Freed from commercial pressures to attract advertisers and make profits, it could experiment and inhabit digital media in innovative ways. Miragliotta and Errington (2012) argued that "classical market failure arguments that formerly sustained the sector have been substantially weakened" (Ibid.) and that public broadcasters were in fact "more nimble than their neo-liberal critics had imagined" (2012).[425] This book argues that this "nimbleness" had been sustained mostly because of the ABC's 'cultural capital' and early educative role, now shifted online. However, this 'cultural capital' was challenged through its lack of preservation, a lack of content planning and preparedness for its new commercial 'field' gaps in policy making that left management ineffectual, the shoddy aspects of commercial digitisation and fierce competition in areas of opinion-making and audience chasing. Drifting to the emergent commercial *field* had required the ABC to alter its editorial content and be bolder, and it had done that with gusto, but examples analysed in this chapter pointed to how this broad-brush approach had also been to the detriment and damage of its élite and privileged reputation and *capital*. Aunty—and governments—needed to first put a value on this priceless, incomparable capital, as they it have on its tangible assets.

4.15 Moving Along and Digitising the ABC

In 2016 the ABC spent AUD1.5 million on search engine marketing and social media marketing which was 0.14% of its budget (Radio Info, 2016).[426] The Senate Estimates Committee (2017) was also told that in 2016 there were 198 full-time employees of online content based on a budget of AUD37.8 million (ibid.).[427] Social media was identified as a key asset for the ABC to develop and exploit, and rightly so. But how do journalism ethics map into a forum where opinion is not only expected, it is encouraged and ABC journalists will offer opinions on the news on Twitter, for example? How are journalism ethics charted on social media? The answers are not simple. There has been an overall push in journalism to move from the uncontested truth-telling of the "old fashion" journalist towards a collaborative and collective approach to truth (Hermida, 2012).[428] In an effort to aggregate and connect with social media as a content priority, the ABC appointed its first Political and Social Media Reporter in December 2010 (Australian Broadcasting Corporation Media Centre, 2010). The new role was explained by the broadcaster as:

> Social media is a rapidly expanding area of communication, and is playing a growing role in the reporting of politics. As well as acting as a source of instant breaking news, social media platforms provide new ways to communicate with new audiences and link to the rest of the ABC's political reporting. (Australian Broadcasting Corporation Media Centre, 2010)

ABC News Director, Kate Torney said in the release:

> I am delighted to welcome Latika to our Canberra team. The ABC has a strong tradition of embracing and exploring new ways of communicating with our audience across a range of new and emerging platforms. This latest appointment continues that tradition. (Ibid.)[429]

However, there were two sides of keeping abreast of social media. There was the reporting/observing of it—and deciding the relevance of it, which the ABC had covered off. But the greater conundrum for an impartial public broadcaster representing the nation's interests occurred when their journalists become personal contributors, to Twitter for example. While the ABC publicly saw no problem with this, other professional media outlets and the academic research literature would beg to differ. Content could be exposed to risk of compromise when:

> News stories encountered by readers because they were shared on Twitter by a specific journalist may no longer be understood by readers as bearing the imprint of a trusted news organisation, but the by-line or personal endorsement of that journalist. (Bruns, 2012)[430]

Journalists, at best, had always presented a mediated truth. What then becomes of that mediation when that mediation was re-mediated repeatedly with opinions? Regrettably, they risked becoming paired with the influence-makers that permeated online where in the US the literature had observed: "bad faith actors in American politics and media continue to actively use both misinformation and accusations of fake news to destabilize the institutions of liberal democracy, usually at the behest of a murkier agenda" (Bennett & Livingston, 2018).[431,432] The ABC journalist walked into an online political struggle where the journalistic *field* had become part of an emergent commercial *field* where there is also a preferencing reaction over research. Rogstad (2014) said:

> Many journalists today use social media to show off their personalities through humour and personal updates (Holton & Lewis, 2011), and strategically to present themselves to the public and build celebrity status (Sanderson, 2008; Marwick & Boyd, 2011; Hedman & Djerf-Pierre, 2013). In fact, social media's efficiency as marketing tools has been used to explain their overall popularity among journalists. (Lasorsa et al., 2011) (Rogstad, 2014)[433]

We live in a mediated world and the role of the journalist as a neutral mediator was being challenged by journalists' enthusiasm for publishing opinions (Ibid.),[434] especially their own. However, with the growing market value of opinion and surge in self-promotion and career expansion through social media, journalists at the ABC and in their shared *field* with emergent commercial media had adopted the same willingness to express personal views on news, issues and government policies. The public broadcaster had embraced that shift towards journalists and presenters offering opinions and promoting political causes. This drift to opinion appeared to put the public institution into conflict with itself, being played out as cognitive dissonance—and Aunty did not know what to do with herself. If we were to re-visit the ABC Charter, here, there is clear conflict. While there has not been substantial academic research on journalists' use of social media, a random sampling of ABC journalists' and presenters' Twitter postings showed a shift towards opinion, some of it personalised. Rogstad (2014) quoted a study of journalist "tweeters" in 2011 that showed:

> Journalists working for élite media (meaning larger, well-known news media) were less inclined to violate traditional journalistic norms … might have more vested in existing norms and have been more strongly socialised to accept them, while journalists working for less élite media perhaps feel the need to work harder to get the attention of others and thus engage more in the characteristic features of Twitter. (Rogstad, 2014)[435]

However, an organisation, under duress of funding cuts and staff cuts, and on a quest for relevance in the emergent commercial *field* could place its journalists and presenters under greater pressure to prove themselves, to be 'liked'. Perhaps the ABC is not "less élite" (Rogstad, 2014) but certainly it is under pressure to perform, and investing in the dissemination of opinion may be part of that eagerness to please in a crowded marketplace, overwhelmed with content, but much of which was of compromised, uncertain quality. Elsewhere, "a novel study comparing British, German, Swedish, and Finnish journalists' social media practices" (Gulyas, 2013) showed "a majority of the journalists agreed that it was important to separate their professional and private social media use" (Rogstad, 2014)[436]. China had drawn a much clearer line in the sand and demoted the 'social' from social media in favour of it being used as "a public space for releasing investigative reporting" responsible for "empowering and engaging the public" (Bixiao He, 2021).[436]

4.16 Pressure to Grow Audiences

The original pressure to grow audiences when the ABC had its own élite *field* was just as great, but it played out very differently. The ABC children's television program *Play School*, launched in 1964, was Australia's longest running children's program and educated through fun, music, listening, participation and mimicry. Bourdieu (1984) theorised that education in cultural capital began in childhood. If so, then the ABC has had access to a longitudinal cohort of Australians to inculcate it in the ways of the ABC and Australian society through *Play School.* The youth radio network, Triple J, aimed at 18–24-year-olds was another example of how the ABC managed to corral demographic groups and taught them Australian culture by sponsoring "gigs" as well as through its Unearthed program where it scouted for talented rock bands at Australian high schools. The re-launch of the Double J (the ABC's former AM radio youth network) occurred "amid unprecedented levels of audience input" (*ABC*, 2014).[437] This capacity to grow support of itself through other cultural resources that it had created was what Bourdieu would call "objectified aestheticism" (Bourdieu, 1984),[438] evidenced in Triple J and the reprise of Double J. It did not survive by "explicitly demanding" (Bourdieu ibid.)[439] attention but by giving access to informed social positions (Loc. Cit.) and encouraging participation, thereby sustaining its relevance and ensuring its survival. Former ABC Managing Director, Mark Scott, described the organisation in similar participatory terms:

> All those Australians who have grown up with the ABC, who love it. Those who understand that in a vast continent like Australia, it is a commons, a shared space. That the ABC is a shared reference point within Australian life, a cultural experience we all have in common, at a time when common cultural experiences are becoming harder to come by. (Scott, 2009)[440]

The repeated use of the word "commons" and "common" was significant here in that it indicated a vision for the broadcaster after its drift into the emergent digital commercial field. It also situated the ABC in an historical place, but long ago and far away. Once the (British) commons were fields where the "commoners" could farm and forage freely. The enclosure laws brought that to an end in fencing these spaces into private property. This process began in the thirteenth century in Britain but reached its peak in the eighteenth century (Wallach, 2005).[441] It then became a pattern of how European countries colonised new lands. In Britain, the ending of the commons meant farmers had to rent land from the owner. The quote previously described an incongruity for the ABC whereby an implicit free-roaming hunter-gatherer that had drifted into the enclosed lands of commercial media and its accompanying rent-seekers, still believed itself fully capable of being true to itself while playing but in the aggressively competitive emergent commercial field. This helped illuminate another clash between commercial media and the ABC competing for the same turf; Aunty's naivete versus seasoned commercial outfits. The ABC's exclusive *field* was a unique commons—but the commercial *field* was not—it had never been so. Greer (2012) said while "the commons" today covered air, oceans and the internet but the commons was not a synonym for "open-access resources". He said the commons were "jointly owned and, in most cases, collectively managed; the latter are portions of the environment that are not property" (Ibid.).[442]

To carve out a space within this commons, social media had encouraged journalists and presenters to become a "brand". They included a photo, personal (often witty or even self-deprecating details) about themselves. ABC journalists could self-promote as personalities, thereby avoiding any need for ABC publicity to promote their careers. This was cost effective. However, not all journalists opined and revelled in their celebrity and there would appear to be a significant number of journalists and presenters absent from Twitter in the regular argy-bargy of daily events. Impartiality would appear, in this instance, to be valued above career development. Nonetheless, even with the absence of a large cohort of journalists and presenters from social media news commentary, those who did express and promote views created, inevitably, an impression or 'flavour' of the organisation. Individuals created an impression of the entire staff and institution, representative or not, and this was as true of public broadcasting as of life itself. Rogstad's (2014) study of the Norwegian Parliamentary Press Gallery's attitude to social media found that very *few* were comfortable sharing opinions on social media. Then, there is Twitter with its own promotional advice encouraging journalists in their use of Twitter:[443]

> Reporters can do more than just Tweet out links. Interact with your readers to get the most out of your time spent on Twitter.
>
> Journalists can make the most out of Twitter by engaging with their audiences to grow their followers.
>
> Twitter is a window into what's happening in the world, which is why some of the most active Twitter accounts belong to journalists. News often breaks first on Twitter, and everyone from national media outlets to reporters on the ground often use Twitter to update the public on developing stories.
>
> Unlike with a traditional TV broadcast or newspaper article, however, the public can take an active role in a story by replying directly to journalists on Twitter. People are more likely to reply to journalists who are willing to engage with them by replying, Retweeting, answering questions, or soliciting news tips. That, in turn, increases a reporter's followers and drives more interest and trust in the journalist's work. (ibid.)

Robinson (2016)[444] said journalists were now part of a "content mill" (Robinson ibid.)[445] describing Twitter as "a god-send to journalists ... offers a sprawling bank of quotable sources" with the use of hashtags offering further capacity for media outlets to commoditise their product. It meant intellectual property was re-used as part of this echo-chamber effect. Robinson (2016) likened Twitter to a "Petri dish forgotten in a warm, moist cabinet, it has developed some truly curious cultures", explaining the facility of anonymity allowed activists for social justice and the environment to express views freely amongst the rest of the group which could include irony tweeters, and even ISIS tweeters (Loc. Cit.)[446] to jostle around together, all as one. The popularity of certain hashtags gave the impression that it was the major topic being considered by everyone that day—although it was only popular among Twitter users who used or followed it. Abusive tweets, by both anonymous sources and identified journalists, of US President Donald Trump, British Prime Minister Boris Johnson and Australia's Prime Minister Scott Morrison, for example, showed how debates on government policy and matters of national and international significance were easily degenerated into individualised remarks—and over-simplified into a hashtag or 140 characters (280 characters for CJK languages Chinese, Japanese, Korean) into personalised 'like the look of them/hate the look of them binaries' where the individual was attacked and the policy ignored. One example, in the environmental literature, noted the powerful impact of Twitter in undermining Australian government policy and trade in 2012 (Miller, 2012). The then Labor Environment Minister, Tony Burke, complained that Australia's fisheries management was damaged by a "massive public focus" (Miller, 2012) from a Twitter campaign. As a consequence, Burke stopped a Dutch fishing trawler from catching in Australian waters and other trawlers were banned for two years, even though the catch had been approved by an independent regulator based on internationally recognised scientific sustainability and conservative estimates (Miller, 2012).

The professional media's reliance on Twitter and Twitter campaigns as news events, was such that Twitter had served to create a detachment by journalists from the public in that journalists were speaking to their followers on Twitter and groups of interest, rather than serving their citizen publics. There may be overlap, but they are not the same cohort and it is certainly not the public as defined in the ABC Charter. Twitter is very supportive of mutually-serving activity generating anger and outrage but failed to engage with the majority of Australians who were not using Twitter all day, every day—and who were not angry. But that is not Twitter's role, it is not a public service. The creator of the open-source website Twitter, Jack Dorsey, sent the first tweet in 2006. Since then, over 8700 tweets (December 2019) have been sent on Twitter each second (Internet Live Stats).[447] In 2015, Kamps showed that 25% of US Twitter users were journalists or media employed (Ibid.).[448] In 2019, a New York Times Columnist warned journalists to "disengage" from Twitter because it is "the world's most damaging social network" and "encourages a mind-set antithetical to journalistic inquiry: It prizes image over substance" (Manjoo, ibid.).[449]

Yet, at the same time, Twitter had become an essential component in the journalists' toolkit. At the ABC it was a place for breaking news, which also created complications for journalists placing content online where there was an overwhelming need to check whether it represented the organisation's best interests and how it would be contextualised. It should not be considered coincidental, therefore, that at the same time Twitter rose to prominence for journalists, the ABC set up a "Fact Checking" Unit. The reliance on social media had set up conundrums about accuracy, the role/relevance of journalists as primary researchers, the "arm's length" from opinions and the general distance, or overview that journalists should provide. On Twitter, journalists could drive the story, rather than observe, relate and reflect. They were no longer the traditional recorders of news; they had become actual participants in news. In democratic societies, the commercial media had also held governments and powerful organisations to account; it had been either non-aligned, or partisan with vested interests. The significance of the drift that had occurred meant when ABC journalists/broadcasters were expressing opinions, they became news and institutional actors, not impartial or neutral observers. This was a hugely consequential, but lightly considered, repositioning of the institution. Journalism loses its robustness and the ABC its impartiality. Office banter could be elevated to public knowledge.

Fact-checking, or what Bill Adair (2013) described "reported conclusion" journalism (Gillin, 2013),[450,451] had revolutionised the way journalists conducted their trade. Where once journalists quoted their sources as accurately as possible—preferably verbatim—and left the audiences/publics to make up their minds as to the veracity of the statement, or published fact, now, the journalist could be observed to give a judgement on their own reported source. Decision made. For the ABC it had placed itself in an adversarial role in that it was no longer a conduit for news and information, it was a refiner and assessor of the fact—even its own facts. Yet, there was the argument in favour of this where the institution must please its piper who calls the tune on budget allocations and the ABC had always been suffering from that underlying nervous anxiety. In more recent times, it had disturbed its situation further by calling politicians, controllers of its breadbasket, to account under its re-definition of probity developed in the emergent commercial field—opinion merged with facts. The emergent commercial media field, to which the ABC now belonged, meant while government actors had power in their institutional *field* it could be flipped quickly into negative coverage or even ridicule (Nyhan & Reifler, 2015).

Fact-checking organisations had almost tripled since 2014 (Rashkin et al., 2018)[452] but US research had found that they were not effective in preventing public misperceptions of issues and instead might be advantageous to the political élites and their reputations (Nyhan & Reifler, 2015)[453] by improving their political discourse and getting through a clearer message to their electorates. Fact-checking had been described as naïve epistemology (Uscinski & Butler, 2013)[454] because of "the tacit presupposition that there cannot be genuine political debate about facts, because facts are unambiguous and not subject to interpretation" (Ibid.). Therefore, any deviation or reapplication of facts was dismissed as lies. Fact-checking was also time consuming and intellectually demanding so there was a time delay between the claim and the check (Hassan et al., 2015)[455] and news organisations content management systems might be dated in handling the sheer quantity of work (ibid.) and in its research capacity.

In terms of engagement, 2015 US media research showed that journalists were likely to tweet their own content from their own organisation than from other organisations (Russell et al., 2015)[456] and, interestingly, were more likely to interact with other journalists than members of the public (ibid.).[457] This then sets up an echo chamber—voices are listening to those that affirm the others. The proliferation of mobile phones, now vital for human life with organisations pushing back administration to the client/consumer, means journalists were photographers and filmmakers. This thereby deleted the need for photographers, camera people and sound people in newsrooms. The removal of these trained positions was incorporated as necessary change due to funding cuts, but the devaluing of those skills had impacted upon the veracity of ABC News when the trained 'camera-eye' and trained 'sound ear' was no longer regarded as needed. The ubiquitous mobile phone and the internet had become the main sources of content capture and retrieval in newsrooms everywhere and this had diminished attendant costs. This evolved/devolved newsroom situation conflicts and challenged the ABC's role "to serve" through "public service" when one member of staff was stretched to do everything and there was a manifest belief that "everything is on the 'net".

The ABC was set up as a symbolic defender of a Western liberal democracy, taking care of Western values within a liberal society. Digitisation had seen an unravelling of trust in the ABC as a defender of free speech and egalitarianism. For example, the ABC's Chas Licciardello told a Sky News program *Outsiders* that: "I do think the ABC is a left-wing network. I do think that. Especially, a left-wing sort of upper-middle class kind of sensibility. I do think that's the case" (Bolt, 2018).[458] Licciardello added: "I think you should have more conservative views on the ABC, personally, as a taxpayer's network and I think there are ways to do that. I think selling it is not the way to do it."[459] On the same day, *The Australian* reported that ABC presenter Julia Baird had tweeted that there were many conservative members of staff and interviewees at the ABC, and further, that presenters were apolitical. (Henderson, 2018).[460]

Swirling around the ABC at this time were calls to privatise the ABC after a vote to do so by the Liberal Party's Federal Council in June 2018. In response, the then Prime Minister, Malcolm Turnbull, said on 25 June: "The ABC will never be sold. That is my commitment. It is a public broadcaster" (Calcutt, 2018).[461] Former Prime Minister, John Howard, said on 10 July 2018: "I think the ABC needs greater balance, but I don't think the solution is to abolish or to privatise the ABC"[462] (Ibid.). This was not the first time privatisation of the ABC was placed onto the Liberal Party agenda. In 1998, the Victorian Liberal Party State Council called for the selling of the ABC and SBS (Inglis, 2006)[463] and in 2013 *The Sydney Morning Herald* reported that the then Leader of the Liberal Opposition, Tony Abbott, was facing pressure to privatise the ABC and SBS should his party win the upcoming election (Gordon, 2013).[464] In 2018 the annual Liberal Party Federal Council called for "full privatisation of the Australian Broadcasting Corporation, except for services into regional areas" (Norman, 2018).[465] Then in October 2018 amid all the tumult and turbulence of the resignations of the ABC Chairman and Managing Director the Tasmanian Liberal state council called for the ABC to be "tendered out" (*SBS*, 2018).[466]

Another way of gauging ABC success in its new commercial space was by reviewing the ratings. Commercial ratings were converted into advertisers and revenue, the higher the better, but in the public domain of the ABC ratings were a measure of relevance. The ABC's audience share for 2019 was 16.8% down from 17% the previous year, which was down 0.1% on 2017 (Lallo, 2018, 2019).[467][468] The top-rating channel in 2019 was Channel 9 on 29.4% and in 2018 it was Channel 7 with 30.5% (Lallo, 2019).[469] Sociologist and social researcher, Hugh Mackay (2010), said one of his professional mentors was Dr Peter Kenny, the ABC's Head of Audience Research in the 1960s. Mackay said Dr Kenny had upset senior management when he told them: "our policy is what we do" (Mackay ibid.)[470] meaning that there was no need for more policy, only engagement with audiences. Mackay added: "audiences ... will draw their own conclusions from their direct experience of how the organisation actually treats them" (Loc. Cit.).[471]

The role of social media as a complement to audience engagement was somewhat capricious and deceptive; an important source for journalists to obtain information, yet this makes them vulnerable, as well. It had long been argued by academic researchers that social media was a relational agenda-setting device (Johnson Ed., 2013;[472] Yang et al., 2016[473]) between the audience and the journalists, in addition to websites. But research had found that: "the openness of participation for user-generated content online also increases the likelihood of poor-quality messages, anecdotes, and misinformation" (Lin et al., 2016).[474] It had brought about "bottom-up news "produsage" (Bruns, 2008 in Pentina & Tarafdar, 2014[475]) "where consumers collaboratively create and curate news stories, offer a novel socially-negotiated informational product that heavily relies on opinions, and substitutes the journalistic ideal of objectivity with that of balance (or 'multi-perspectivality')" (Gans 1980, in Pentina & Tarafdar, 2014).

In 2012, the Pew Research Centre[476] published a warning that "technology intermediaries now control the future of news" (Pew Research Center, 2012)[477] and "a year ago, we wrote here: "The news industry, late to adapt and culturally more tied to content creation than engineering, finds itself more a follower than leader shaping its business. In 2012, that phenomenon has grown" (ibid.).[478] The report described how in the future it was conceivable that Facebook could buy *The Washington Post* (it already has partnerships with that newspaper, as well as *The Wall Street Journal* and *The Guardian*. It purchased *New Republic* magazine in 2012). The report cautioned that with the decline in newspapers and the vanishment of: "the primary source people turn to for news about government and civic affairs. If these operations continue to shrivel or disappear, it is unclear where, or whether, that information would be reported" (Ibid.).[479]

4.17 ABC Election Reporting

The ABC had an Election Coverage Review Committee and re-constituted itself with ABC staff members for each federal, state and territory election. It was formed in 1984 (Inglis, 2006).[480] It served to allocate free time to political parties as well as monitor election coverage. It provided guidelines and guidance and published a report on each federal election (ABC, 2020).[481] In 1998, then ABC Managing Director, Brian Johns, said:

> I have full confidence that we are meeting our stringent guidelines for fairness and balance in reporting. I also have full confidence in our monitoring of that performance through the ABC's Election Review Committee. This committee operates during the period of an election campaign to formally assess the achievement of balance in the ABC's coverage through monitoring of complaints, as well as air-time given to all parties in the election. (ABC, 1998)[482]

During the ABC's 2016 election television coverage, the ABC's senior journalists were observed to be morose and downcast and described by journalist Hamish McDonald, now an ABC employee, as bantering and sounding "delirious" (Styles, 2016).[483] It was decoded from this behaviour that the ABC was upset by a possible Liberal Party and National Party Coalition victory in the federal election—and maybe subliminal fears of deeper funding cuts. There were several more tweets by McDonald with defensive responses from current ABC staff supporting the coverage. ABC Director of News, Gaven Morris, was quoted in the same news report: "One thing I don't get in the habit of doing is commenting on one person's commentary on Twitter, it's not a particularly representative voice out there" (Ibid.). Yet this comment contradicted the managing director, David Anderson's stated faith in social media as being representative not just of Australians but the world where the ABC looked to its development so as to "reach millions of people through social media" (Anderson, 2019).[484] Another example of the ABC's discrepant and inconsistent views (and policies) on its role in social media and its failure to interpret its place in the emergent commercial *field*. The literature stated that political parties were reaching out to voters during election campaigns via Twitter and other social media (Carson et al., 2020).[485] They took social media very seriously and had considered understandings.

The findings of a review by the ABC into its 2016 election coverage were that it provided: "unparalleled coverage of the election campaign" (Sunderland, 2016)[486] and "dominated the ratings across all platforms", that "The Coalition had the highest share of voice across all platforms, and the ALP had the second- highest share of voice" (Ibid.).[487] The organisation's policy on election coverage was:

> The ABC supports fundamental democratic principles, among them parliamentary democracy. Since its inception in 1932, the national public broadcaster has facilitated the democratic process by making broadcast time

> available to registered political parties so that they may have an opportunity to explain directly to the electorate the policies for which they are seeking voters' support. (Loc. Cit.)[488]

It reported that:

> During the election period, the ABC recorded a total of 1189 written audience complaints relating to the Federal Election. This was almost 20% more than during the 2013 Federal Election, but it should be remembered that the 2016 campaign was significantly longer. In 2010, there had been 1447 written complaints. Allegations of bias formed the category with the largest number of complaints (669). Of these, 63% alleged that coverage favoured the Government, while 24% alleged that it favoured the Opposition. (Ibid.)

Concerns about the ABC's 2016 election coverage included complaints about the new style of graphics used as well as slow updates (Styles, 2016).[489]

In 2019, *The Canberra Times* News Director identified a pro-Australian Labor Party bias in the ABC's coverage (Lawson, 2019)[490] owing to an expectation (hope?) that the ALP would win the election. The ABC's election analyst, Antony Green, said the reason for the surprising result was: "a bit of a spectacular failure of opinion polling" (Prosser Scully, 2019)[491] with the analyst revealing a personal bias: "There's a swing against us. Oh. I mean against the Labor Party, of between 4 and 5 percent" (Jo Nova, 2019).[492] Former ABC broadcaster Kerry O'Brien had said on a previous election night's coverage in regard to the ALP winning a seat: "Well, we won that one" (Ibid.).[493] In 1993, former Fairfax editor Max Suich criticised that the ABC's coverage of the election was "influenced by fear of a Coalition victory". Inglis (2006) quoted Suich (1995):

> Senior broadcasters made no secret of their belief that the Labor government had to be re-elected to save the ABC from savage financial pruning. He said the bias was confirmed in casual conversations with ABC journalists. (Inglis, 2006)[494]

The ABC's 2019 election coverage proved controversial in another way. While it was a ratings success for the organisation with 1.336 million television viewers nationally (Burrowes, 2019)[495] there were observations from National Party Deputy Prime Minister, John Anderson, that the ABC lacked the economic coverage to analyse Labor's policies: "Where is the ABC's economic unit analysing this? Where are they? Where's their work?" (Visontay, 2019).[496] Other disputed matters surrounding the ABC's 2019 election coverage and accusations of de facto bias occurred when former ABC broadcaster, Quentin Dempster, voiced a political announcement video, also screened on television, for the activist group "Get Up" in which he said: "This election, vote for a strong ABC. Don't vote Liberal" (Benns, 2019; Meade, 2019).[497] Dempster was reported to have responded that "he considered his journalism was separate from his advocacy on behalf of the public broadcaster" (Benns, ibid.). An ABC representative was quoted: "The ABC didn't authorise this advertisement, or have any prior knowledge of it, and we don't consider it to be proper use of ABC content" (Meade, 2019). Gideon Rozner, policy director of the right-wing Institute of Public Affairs developed this point: "many media outlets have some kind of bias. The problem is that each and every Australian subsidises the ABC, no matter how much or how little they agree with its editorial position" (Benns, ibid.). In the background of this was a statement by the ABC's Managing Director that there would be large cuts to staff and content if the Federal Coalition's AUD84 million indexation freeze was implemented on 1 July 2019. The ALP had already promised to reverse these cuts. Former ABC Chairman Maurice Newman responded in the media that "It's very clear: what he's saying is that if you care about the ABC vote Labor or anything other than the Coalition" (Ibid.).[498] In the comments section appended to a Mumbrella news report on media bias, it said the ABC branch of the Community and Public Sector Union had emailed ABC staff to vote Labor in the election (Muller, 2019).[499]

Dempster was interviewed on Sky News about the perceived ALP bias of the ABC on election night (and disappointment at the party's failure to capture government) "few others saw the result coming and ABC political reporters were basing their views on published polling that showed Labor likely to win" (Mitchell, 2019).[500] Other media commented on the ABC's "maudlin performance of its election-night hosts … as they realised Labor was losing" (Ibid.).[501] Another source of this bias accusation was enunciated by former ABC presenter Jonathan Holmes who said: "I think the sort of person that most ABC people think about when they make their programs are the sort of people (who) think roughly the same as they do and I think that's somebody a bit left of centre. They are talking to people like me and they are not talking to people who think differently to me" (Mitchell, 2019).[502]

Then in late May 2019 the ABC's newly appointed chair Ita Buttrose said the organisation "might be biased" (Crikey, 2019)[503] in its reporting regarding the election and that some staff could be unconsciously showing bias and that the organisation "could do with more diversity of views":

> I haven't got a problem with anybody's view but I think we need to make sure ours is as diverse as it can be. … The more diverse views we can represent, the better it will be for us. (Ibid.)[504]

The ABC's election coverage was also an upset for some former ABC staff. The Chaser political comedy program, which had usually covered election campaigns since 2001, had been cancelled prior to the election and therefore not part of the ABC's 2019 election coverage. The exchange between the program and the ABC's then Executive Producer of Comedy and Drama, Que Ming Luu, on Twitter was reported by news website News Mail in 2018 which re-published a series of tweets that were later deleted (*News Mail*, 2018).[505] In essence, the exchange started with The Chaser complaining on Twitter that its election show had been cancelled. It was responded to by Luu that their response was obnoxious, and subsequently referred to their white male, middle class, privilege as a reason that they were not so funny anymore and insinuating the reason for ending their program (*News Mail*, 2018). News Mail (2018) explained that the cast of The Chaser consisted of Charles Firth, Dominic Knight, Julian Morrow, Craig Reucassel, Chas Licciardello, Chris Taylor and Andrew Hanson (Ibid.). When News Mail reached out to the ABC for a comment on the exchange, Luu said : "Oh thank you for checking in but goodness no. I'm no one worth seeking public comment from, in fact in this context I'm just a dickhead mouthing off on the internet" (Zineldin & Hytter, 2012). It was another example of how the ABC had no misgivings about drawing a clear border in social media—when staff was free to discuss programming decisions through their personal accounts, and on the other side when the institution was promoting itself and assembling an audience.

The literature on leadership said that research into a leader's negative emotions was relatively unexplored; however, it had been identified there was a definite need for strong inter-personal relations between management and staff and that job satisfaction resulted from good inter-personal relations, which then had a big impact on the health and wellbeing of workers (Zineldin & Hytter, ibid.).[506] In addition, research has found there was a need for loyalty between workers and leaders in organisations so that these relationships could function at a mutually beneficial level (ibid.).[507] From the content of the previous re-published exchange on social media, it would appear that the leader felt under attack and was bolstering her position by using rhetoric to humiliate the former colleague as a means of inducing compliance and limiting her own reputational harm—although, it should also be noted that the comments were reported to have been removed from Twitter. However, there had been little research into management vulnerability to social influence (Shani & Westphal, 2016),[508] as this example might enlighten. Other research has found, however, that this form of "social distancing ... can occur at the ego-network level" (Ibid.).[509] A study of Chief Executive Officers (CEOs) found that they were: "socially and psychologically connected in determining the impact of negative forms of social influence in relations between leaders and constituents" (Loc. Cit.).[510]

It is true that in Institutional Logics, leaders are contesting the field in which they operated and that then is dictated by their choice of management style in maintaining respect and loyalty from staff to hold that *field* and leading with vision and support. Similarly, leaders in a large organisation would identify with each other as part of the organisation's élite (Shani & Westphal, ibid.)[511] from whence they derived their mutual support. However, there was an assumption in this exchange by the leader that she had what is referred to in leadership and management theory as "bounded solidarity" (Ibid.),[512] meaning she had an understanding that other leaders within the organisation would have reacted to this Twitter post by The Chaser staff member in the same manner. According to the literature, this manager was defending her reputation and social standing as a focal actor (George et al., 2016).[513] Elsewhere, the psychology literature would describe this as abusive behaviour (Johnson et al., 2012)[514] while in terms of the leadership literature it was described as "coercive power" (Yukl, 2010).[515] Yet abuse should be used advisedly in institutions because "coercion often arouses anger or resentment, and it may result in retaliation" and was "not likely to result in commitment" (Ibid.).[516] Leadership literature identified successful leaders as motivating their staff and getting them to follow—that leaders should "guide, structure, and facilitate activities and relationships" (Loc. Cit.)[517] and actually poor communication had been cited as "a sign of dysfunctional leadership" (Dandira, 2012).[518]

4.18 Conclusion

This chapter explored the key theses of the impact of digital media and its interface with the ABC now in the emergent commercial field. It examined some of the consequences of this in regard to ideas, values, understandings, policy and ultimately how the institution perceived itself. It explored instances where the public broadcaster came up short on policy in regard to social media, embracing staff use of it on one hand but backing away when comments were made that created controversy—thereby creating a push and pull effect on Aunty. It has discovered that there have been instances a lack of synergy between management expectations and staff actions and a lack. There is even confusion and avoidance within the institution about upholding public values; and this deprives people of access to "public deliberation into government decisions making" (Jacobs, 2014) and where "fostering wider public debate may create openings for improving the conditions for vibrant public life" (Jacobs, ibid.). Public values were: "an informed citizenry's values and public policy and government operations that engage citizens and generate the conditions for vibrant communities" (Loc. Cit.). Part of this institutional distraction from public values can also be demonstrated in the evident pressure for staff to be active online. The boundaries in which they operate in this space were movable and reliant on the good judgement of the account holder, beyond the reach of institutional borders and removed from the public value. The next chapter will analyse how the ABC has shifted focus from public values and its primary stakeholders (the Australian taxpayer) to secondary stakeholders (activist causes) and how it responds, institutionally, to the derogatory treatment given to it by other media—other players in the emergent commercial field where they all now reside. The ABC struggles in a field where news can be sourced and shared online.

The ABC accounted for (June 2019) "14.6 million international followers across ABC Facebook accounts (63% of global total), and 375,000 international followers across ABC Instagram accounts (23% of global total) … 245.3 million views of ABC YouTube channels from international audiences, equating to 72% of global views" and reached into China's social media with "16,000 followers on WeChat and 166,000 on Weibo" (Anderson, 2019).[519] It counts social media amongst its stakeholders (ibid.)[520] with style guides created for social media producers. The ABC's annual report states and celebrates that it believed these online groups and spaces as representative of its new communities. Also, the fact that ABC staff respond defensively to negative tweets about fellow staff members or the institution shows that it relies on opinions of it in its emergent commercial *field* and was aware of the need to maintain a 'good' image with its (fragmented) audiences and communities. [521]

The next chapter will discuss other examples of how the ABC's public broadcasting has been challenged in its role as definer and defender of truth in the public interest promoting public values and motivated for the public good.

Notes

1. Guterres, A. (2018). Secretary-General's Address to the General Assembly. *UN Secretary General.* 23 September 2018. Retrieved from: https://www.un.org/sg/en/content/sg/statement/2018-09-25/secretary-generals-address-general-assembly-delivered-trilingual
2. Funnell, A. (2020). Is this the end of the liberal international order? And what might take its place? ABC Radio National. Future Tense. ABC Radio Online. 31 January 2020. Retrieved from: https://www.abc.net.au/news/2020-01-31/liberal-international-order-under-threat-china-us/11905652
3. Beaglehole, P. (2018). What Matters?: Talking Value in Australian Culture. *Transnational Literature.* 11:1. Retrieved from: http://search.proquest.com/docview/2164085415/
4. Castells, M. (2008). The New Public Sphere: Global Civil Society, Communication Networks, and Global Governance. *The Annals of the American Academy of Political and Social Science.* 616. pp. 78–93. Retrieved from: www.jstor.org/stable/25097995
5. Çıdam, Ç. (2016). Public space, material worlds, and democratic aspirations. *Contemporary Political Theory.* 15:4. pp. 417–426. Retrieved from: https://doi.org/10.1057/s41296-016-0011-0
6. Çıdam, Ç. (2016). Public space, material worlds, and democratic aspirations. *Contemporary Political Theory.* 15:4. pp. 417–426. Retrieved from: https://doi.org/10.1057/s41296-016-0011-0
7. Laclau, E. (1990). *New Reflections on the Revolution of Our Time.* Verso. London, New York.
8. Devenney, M., Howarth, D., Norval, A. J., Stavrakakis, Y., Marchart, O., Biglieri, P., & Perelló, G. (2016). Ernesto Laclau. *Contemporary Political Theory.* 15:3. pp. 304–335. Retrieved from: https://doi.org/10.1057/cpt.2016.8
9. Accetti, C. I., Mulieri, A., Buchstein, H., Castiglione, D., Disch, L., Frank, J. &. Urbinati, N. (2016). Debating representative democracy. *Contemporary Political Theory.* 15:2. pp. 205–242. Retrieved from: https://doi.org/10.1057/cpt.2015.57

10. Macmullan, T. (2005). Challenges to Cultural Diversity: Absolutism, Democracy, and Alain Locke's Value Relativism. *The Journal of Speculative Philosophy*. 19:2. pp. 129–139. Retrieved from: https://doi.org/10.1353/jsp.2005.0013
11. Waisbord, S. (2018). The elective affinity between post-truth communication and populist politics. *Communication Research and Practice: Special Issue: ANZCA 2017—Communication Worlds: Access, Voice, Diversity, Engagement*. Guest Editor: F. Martin. 4:1. pp. 17–34. Retrieved from: https://doi.org/10.1080/22041451.2018.1428928
12. Kierkegaard, S. (1941). Transl. W. Lowrie & J. Campbell. *Concluding Unscientific Postscript*. Princeton Legacy Library. Princeton.
13. Madison, J, (1788). *Popular Basis of Political Authority. The Founders' Constitution*. 1:2. Document 19. The University of Chicago Press. Retrieved from: http://press-pubs.uchicago.edu/founders/documents/v1ch2s19.html
14. Mill, J.S. (1859). *On Liberty*. The Walter Scott Publishing Co., Ltd. London and Felling-on-Tyne, New York and Melbourne. Retrieved from: http://www.gutenberg.org/files/34901/34901-h/34901-h.htm, p. 39.
15. Deceased Catholic men and women considered to have led virtuous and holy lives not only require two miracles to occur after their deaths for them to be canonised (made into a saint), the proposition also had to be tested by an *advocatus diaboli* (devil's advocate) in the church. This person's role was to find out what the devil would say about the candidate—their transgressions, omissions, commissions and any other deed or oversight that would prevent them from being considered holy. The role was diminished in 1983 by Pope John Paul II.
16. Fukuyama, F. (2018). *Identity: The Demand for Dignity and the Politics of Resentment*. Farrar, Straus & Giroux. New York. p. 5.
17. Fukuyama, F. (2018). *Identity: The Demand for Dignity and the Politics of Resentment*. Farrar, Straus & Giroux. New York. Loc. Cit.
18. Fukuyama, F. (2018). *Identity: The Demand for Dignity and the Politics of Resentment*. Farrar, Straus & Giroux. New York. p. 7.
19. Fukuyama, F. (2018). *Identity: The Demand for Dignity and the Politics of Resentment*. Farrar, Straus & Giroux. New York. p. 8.
20. Fukuyama, F. (2018). *Identity: The Demand for Dignity and the Politics of Resentment*. Farrar, Straus & Giroux. New York. p. 9.
21. Fukuyama, F. (2018). *Identity: The Demand for Dignity and the Politics of Resentment*. Farrar, Straus & Giroux. New York. p. 10.
22. Gamson, W., Croteau, D., Hoynes, W., Sasson, T. 1992 "Media Images and the Social Construction of Reality". *Annual Review of Sociology*. 18. pp. 373–393. Retrieved from: http://search.proquest.com/docview/199734271/

23. Lavelle, D. (2018) From 'Slimeball Comey' to 'Crooked Hillary', why Trump loves to brand his enemies. *The Guardian*. 17 April 2018. Retrieved from: https://www.theguardian.com/us-news/shortcuts/2018/apr/17/presidents-nicknames-slimeball-comey-former-fbi-director
24. Mudde, C. & Kaltwasser, C. R. Eds. M. Freeden & M. Stears. (2013). Populism. *The Oxford Handbook of Political Ideologies*. Retrieved from: https://www-oxfordhandbooks-com.wwwproxy1.library.unsw.edu.au/view/10.1093/oxfordhb/9780199585977.001.0001/oxfordhb-9780199585977-e-026
25. Ibid.
26. Fletcher, R, (2018). The Rise of Populism and the Consequences for News and Media Use. *Digital News Report*. Reuters Institute & University of Oxford. Retrieved from: http://www.digitalnewsreport.org/survey/2019/the-rise-of-populism-and-the-consequences-for-news-and-media-use/
27. Wood, D., Daley J. & Chivers, C. (2018). Policy Forum: Economics and Populism Australia Demonstrates the Rise of Populism is About More than Economics. *The Australian Economic Review*. 51:3. pp. 399–410. Retrieved from: https://doi.org/10.1111/1467-8462.12294.
28. Soutphommasane, T. (2018). Cultural backlash and the rise of populism. Speech to *Sydney Ideas*, The University of Sydney. 19 July 2018. Retrieved from: https://www.humanrights.gov.au/about/news/speeches/cultural-backlash-and-rise-populism
29. Habermas, J. (1962, repr. 1991). Transl. T. Burger. *The Structural Transformation of the Public Sphere: An inquiry into a category of Bourgeois Society*. MIT Press. Cambridge, MA.
30. Eisenstein, E. (1979). *The Printing Press as an agent of change: Communications and Cultural Transformations in early Modern Europe*. 1. Cambridge University Press. Cambridge.
31. Bennett, W. (1998). 1998 Ithiel De Sola Pool Lecture: The UnCivic Culture: Communication, Identity, and the Rise of Lifestyle Politics. *PS: Political Science and Politics*. 31:4. pp. 741–761. Retrieved from: https://doi.org/10.2307/420711
32. Bennett, W. (1998). 1998 Ithiel De Sola Pool Lecture: The UnCivic Culture: Communication, Identity, and the Rise of Lifestyle Politics. *PS: Political Science and Politics*, 31:4. pp. 741–761. Retrieved from: https://doi.org/10.2307/420711, p. 742.
33. Bennett, W. (1998). 1998 Ithiel De Sola Pool Lecture: The UnCivic Culture: Communication, Identity, and the Rise of Lifestyle Politics. *PS: Political Science and Politics*, 31:4. pp. 741–761. Retrieved from: https://doi.org/10.2307/420711, p. 745.

34. Bennett, W. (1998). 1998 Ithiel De Sola Pool Lecture: The UnCivic Culture: Communication, Identity, and the Rise of Lifestyle Politics. *PS: Political Science and Politics,* 31:4. pp. 741–761. Retrieved from: https://doi.org/10.2307/420711, p. 755.
35. Bennett, W. (1998). 1998 Ithiel De Sola Pool Lecture: The UnCivic Culture: Communication, Identity, and the Rise of Lifestyle Politics. *PS: Political Science and Politics,* 31:4. pp. 741–761. Retrieved from: https://doi.org/10.2307/420711, p. 755.
36. Bennett, W. (1998). 1998 Ithiel De Sola Pool Lecture: The UnCivic Culture: Communication, Identity, and the Rise of Lifestyle Politics. *PS: Political Science and Politics,* 31:4. pp. 741–761. Retrieved from: https://doi.org/10.2307/420711, p. 755.
37. A moment of entrapment, damage or compromise of the person being interviewed.
38. Tabakoff, N. (2020). Google-boosting ABC accused of 'cutting the grass' of TV rivals. The Australian. 8 June 2020. Retrieved from: https://www.theaustralian.com.au/business/media/googleboosting-abc-accused-of-cutting-the-grass-of-tv-rivals/news-story/02b0a37ab0e022bb36daa36116a3fe68?from=htc_rss
39. McCauley, D. (2018). ABC spends up on Google, Facebook ads. *The Australian.* 25 May 2018. Retrieved from: https://www.theaustralian.com.au/business/media/abc-spends-up-on-google-facebook-ads/news-story/5e6a36fcf3463cb5522fec4a5bcf0918
40. Bingemann, M. (2017). ABC part of our problem, says Fairfax boss Greg Hywood. *The Australian.* 18 May 2017. Retrieved from: https://www.theaustralian.com.au/business/media/print/abc-part-of-our-problem-says-fairfax-boss-greg-hywood/news-story/ecb28edeb8303c10a28b1816ecce41a7
41. Andrejevic, M. (2013). Public service media utilities: Rethinking search engines and social networking as public gods. *Media International Australia, Incorporating Culture & Policy.* 146. pp.123–132. Retrieved from: https://primoa.library.unsw.edu.au/permalink/f/11jha62/TN_informit182810637029076
42. Thierer, A. (2013). The perils of classifying social media platforms as public utilities. *CommLaw Conspectus.* 21:2. pp. 297–297. Retrieved from: https://primoa.library.unsw.edu.au/permalink/f/11jha62/TN_gale_legal401032615
43. Thierer, A. (2013). The perils of classifying social media platforms as public utilities. *CommLaw Conspectus.* 21:2. p. 251. Retrieved from: https://primoa.library.unsw.edu.au/permalink/f/11jha62/TN_gale_legal401032615

44. @Alexa (2020). The top 500 sites on the web. Retrieved from: https://internetworldstats.com/stats.htm#google_vignette Website updated 12 November 2020.
45. Lee, M. (2010). "Revisiting the 'Google in China' Question from a Political Economic Perspective." *China Media Research*. 6:2. Retrieved from: https://primoa.library.unsw.edu.au/permalink/f/11jha62/TN_cdi_gale_infotracacademiconefile_A226568448, pp. 15–24.
46. Murdock, G. (2004). Building the Digital Commons: Public Broadcasting in the Age of the Internet. University of Montreal. *The 2004 Spry Memorial Lecture*. November 2004. Vancouver. Retrieved from: https://www.researchgate.net/publication/254750526_BUILDING_THE_DIGITAL_COMMONS_PUBLIC_BROADCASTING_IN_THE_AGE_OF_THE_INTERNET
47. Murdock, G. (2004). Building the Digital Commons: Public Broadcasting in the Age of the Internet. University of Montreal. *The 2004 Spry Memorial Lecture*. November 2004. Vancouver. Retrieved from: https://www.researchgate.net/publication/254750526_BUILDING_THE_DIGITAL_COMMONS_PUBLIC_BROADCASTING_IN_THE_AGE_OF_THE_INTERNET p. 18.
48. Hermida, A. (2012). Tweets and Truth: Journalism as a discipline of collaborative verification. March 2012. *Journalism Practice*. pp. 1–10. Retrieved from: https://doi.org/10.1080/17512786.2012.667269
49. Ibid., p. 2.
50. Cohen, S. (2011). Whose side were we on? The undeclared politics of moral panic theory. *Crime Media Culture*. 7:3. pp. 237–243. Retrieved from: https://doi.org/10.1177/1741659011417603, p. 240.
51. Ward, S.J.A. (2014). Radical Media Ethics. *Digital Journalism*. 2:4. pp. 455–471. Retrieved from: https://doi.org/10.1080/21670811.2014.952985 and https://doi.org/10.1080/21670811.2014.95, pp. 466–467.
52. Castells, M. (2012). *Networks of Outrage and Hope: Social Movements in the Internet Age*. Polity Press. Cambridge, MA.
53. Drozdek, A. (2015). Media Ethics. *International Encyclopedia of the Social & Behavioral Sciences (Second Edition)*. pp. 42–47. Retrieved from: https://doi.org/10.1016/B978-0-08-097086-8.11017-7
54. Altheide, D. & Schneider, C. (2013). Process of qualitative document analysis. In D. Altheide & C. Schneider. Qualitative Media Analysis. Pp. 38–74. SAGE Publications. London. Retrieved from: https://doi.org/10.4135/9781452270043, p. 41.
55. Richardson, A. (2017). Bearing Witness While Black: Theorizing African American mobile journalism after Ferguson. *Digital Journalism*. 5:6. Pp. 673–698. Retrieved from: https://doi.org/10.1080/21670811.2016.1193818

56. Richardson, A. (2017). Bearing Witness While Black: Theorizing African American mobile journalism after Ferguson. *Digital Journalism*. *5*:6. Pp. 673–698. Retrieved from: https://doi.org/10.1080/21670811.2016.1193818, p. 692.
57. Blankenship, J.C. (2016) LOSING THEIR "MOJO"? Mobile journalism and the deprofessionalization of television news work. *Journalism Practice*. 10:8. pp. 1055–1071. Retrieved from: https://doi.org/10.1080/17512786.2015.1063080
58. Higgins, K. (2011). "A fresh page in news evolution". NIE Supplement for Schools. *The Sunday Telegraph*. 28 August, 2011. pp. 114–115.
59. Sloan, R. & Warner, R. (2016). Unauthorized Access : The Crisis in Online Privacy and Security (Edition 1). In *Unauthorized Access : The Crisis in <b>Online</b> Privacy and <b>Security</b> (Edition 1)* (1st ed.). CRC Press. https://doi.org/10.1201/b15148
60. Imamova, N. (2015). Social Media and Online Public Debate In Central Asia: A Journalist's Perspective. *Demokratizatsiya*. 23:3. pp. 359–376. Retrieved from: http://search.proquest.com/docview/1699511722/
61. Waters, S. (2018). The Effects of Mass Surveillance on Journalists' Relations with Confidential Sources: A constant comparative study. *Digital Journalism*. 6:10. pp. 1294–1313. Retrieved from: https://doi.org/10.1080/21670811.2017.1365616
62. Mann, S. (2004). "Sousveillance"—Inverse surveillance in multimedia imaging. *ACM Multimedia 2004—Proceedings of the 12th ACM International Conference on Multimedia*. pp. 620–627. Retrieved from: https://primoa.library.unsw.edu.au/permalink/f/11jha62/TN_scopus2-s2.0-13444291148
63. Ibid., p. 3.
64. Hanusch, F. (2013). Moulding Industry's Image: Journalism Education's Impact on Students' Professional Views. *Media International Australia (8/1/07-Current)*. 146. pp. 48–59. Retrieved from: https://doi-org.wwwproxy1.library.unsw.edu.au/10.1177/1329878X1314600108
65. Hanusch, F. (2013). Moulding Industry's Image: Journalism Education's Impact on Students' Professional Views. *Media International Australia (8/1/07-Current)*. 146. pp. 48–59. Retrieved from: https://doi-org.wwwproxy1.library.unsw.edu.au/10.1177/1329878X1314600108
66. Hanusch, F. (2013). Moulding Industry's Image: Journalism Education's Impact on Students' Professional Views. *Media International Australia (8/1/07-Current)*. 146. pp. 48–59. Retrieved from: https://doi-org.wwwproxy1.library.unsw.edu.au/10.1177/1329878X1314600108
67. Hanusch, F. (2013). Moulding Industry's Image: Journalism Education's Impact on Students' Professional Views. *Media International Australia (8/1/07-Current)*. 146. pp. 48–59. Retrieved

from: https://doi-org.wwwproxy1.library.unsw.edu.au/10.1177/1329878X1314600108, p. 54.
68. Australian Broadcasting Corporation (nd). *ABC Social Media Policy.* Retrieved from: https://about.abc.net.au/wp-content/uploads/2017/05/SocialMediaPOL.pdf
69. Duke, J. (2019). ABC boss to push for more diversity of views among panel-show guests. *The Age*. 17 June 2019. Retrieved from: https://www.theage.com.au/business/companies/abc-boss-to-push-for-more-diversity-of-views-among-panel-show-guests-20190616-p51y7k.html
70. Meade, A. (2019). ABC managing director rejects accusations he is making funding an election issue. The Guardian. 8 May 2019. Retrieved from: https://www.theguardian.com/media/2019/may/08/abc-managing-director-rejects-accusations-he-is-making-funding-an-election-issue
71. The program was ended after this incident. It has since been revived as a radio program but with a different content focus.
72. Hall, E. (15 June 2016). "The Drum Wednesday June 15". *The Drum*. Retrieved via Wikipedia 15 February 2017. Link removed.
73. Australian Broadcasting Corporation. (2017). Q&A: Jacqui Lambie and Yassmin Abdel-Magied exchange barbs over sharia law. 14 February 2017. *ABC News Online*. Retrieved from: https://www.abc.net.au/news/2017-02-13/jacqui-lambie-and-yassmin-abdel-magied%2D%2Din-fiery-qanda-debate/8267212
74. Australian Broadcasting Corporation News. (2017). Q&A: Jacqui Lambie and Yassmin Abdel-Magied exchange barbs over sharia law. 14 February 2017. *ABC News Online*. Retrieved from: https://www.abc.net.au/news/2017-02-13/jacqui-lambie-and-yassmin-abdel-magied%2D%2Din-fiery-qanda-debate/8267212
75. Ibid.
76. Australian Government. (n.d.). Israel country brief. Retrieved from: https://www.dfat.gov.au/geo/israel/Pages/israel-country-brief
77. British Broadcasting Corporation. (2017). The Anzac post, outrage and a debate about race. 10 August 2017. Retrieved from: https://www.bbc.com/news/world-australia-40712832
78. Grattan, M. (2017). Abdel-Magied **Anzac row is a storm over not much. The Conversation. 26 April 2017. Retrieved from:** https://theconversation.com/abdel-magied-anzac-row-is-a-storm-over-not-much-76708
79. Australian Broadcasting Corporation. (2017). Yassmin Abdel-Magied: ABC can't sweep presenter's Anzac Day controversy under the carpet, Joyce says. *ABC News*. 26 April 2017. Retrieved from: https://www.abc.net.au/news/2017-04-26/yassmin-abdel-magied-under-fire-for-anzac-post/8472414

80. Yahoo News Australia. (2017). Muslim sheikh says ABC should sack Yassmin Abdel-Magied after 'disrespectful' Anzac Day remarks. *Yahoo News Australia*. 26 April 2017. Retrieved from: https://au.news.yahoo.com/muslim-sheikh-imam-shaikh-mohammad-tawhidi-says-abc-should-sack-yassmin-abdel-magied-35165509.html#page1
81. Palin, M. (2017). Thousands call for ABC to sack TV host over 'pro sharia law' comments. *News.com.au*. 21 February 2017. Retrieved from: https://www.news.com.au/entertainment/tv/current-affairs/tens-of-thousands-call-for-abc-to-sack-tv-host-over-pro-sharia-law-comments/news-story/0736c6f509b84c30e1e13d365020d8c6
82. Australian Broadcasting Corporation. (2017). Yassmin Abdel-Magied: ABC can't sweep presenter's Anzac Day controversy under the carpet, Joyce says. *ABC News*. 26 April 2017. Retrieved from: https://www.abc.net.au/news/2017-04-26/yassmin-abdel-magied-under-fire-for-anzac-post/8472414
83. Meade, A. (2017). Yassmin Abdel-Magied program's end unrelated to Anzac Day post, ABC says, 24 May 2017. *The Guardian*. Retrieved from: https://www.theguardian.com/australia-news/2017/may/24/yassmin-abdel-magied-programs-end-not-due-to-anzac-day-post-abc-says
84. Marks, K, (2017). The Anzac post, outrage and a debate about race. *BBC News*. 10 August 2017. Retrieved from: https://www.bbc.com/news/world-australia-40712832
85. Zhou, N. (2017). I'd be tempted to run over Yassmin Abdel-Magied, commentator says: Radio 2GB defends Prue MacSween's comments as 'light hearted' and 'nonliteral' after she says Abdel-Magied was right not to feel safe in Australia. 12 July 2017. *The Guardian*. Retrieved from: https://www.theguardian.com/australia-news/2017/jul/12/conservative-commentator-run-over-yassmin-abdel-magied
86. Wilkie, K. (2017). Controversial Muslim activist Yassmin Abdel-Magied is now flogging products and companies on Instagram as a paid social media 'influencer'. *The Daily Mail*. 15 January 2020. Retrieved from: https://www.dailymail.co.uk/news/article-7887389/Yassmin-Abdel-Magied-flogging-companies-Instagram-paid-social-media-influencer.html
87. Abdel-Magied, Y. (2017). What are they so afraid of? I'm just a young brown Muslim woman speaking my mind. *The Guardian*. 6 July 2017. Retrieved from: https://www.theguardian.com/australia-news/2017/jul/06/what-are-they-so-afraid-of-im-just-a-young-brown-muslim-woman-speaking-my-mind
88. Ibid.
89. Ibid.

90. Dynel, M., Chovanec, M., & Chovanec, Jan. (2015). *Participation in public and social media interactions.* John Benjamins Publishing Company. p. 49. Retrieved from: https://primoa.library.unsw.edu.au/permalink/f/jhud33/UNSW_ALMA51236854060001731
91. In 2008, Rupert Murdoch was invited to present a series of lectures. His theme was: The Gold Age of Freedom.
92. Knott, M. (2015). Everyone from Coalition thinks ABC's Q&A is biased to the left, says LNP senator James McGrath. *The Age*. 28 May 2015. Retrieved from: https://www.theage.com.au/politics/federal/everyone-from-coalition…ed-to-the-left-says-lnp-senator-james-mcgrath-20150527-ghatyw.html
93. Ibid.
94. Carmody, B. (2019). 'Let them be scared': Q&A panellist stands by comments after complaints. *The Sydney Morning Herald*. 8 November 2019. Retrieved from: https://www.smh.com.au/culture/tv-and-radio/let-them-be-scared-q-and-a-panellist-stands-by-comments-after-complaints-20191108-p538qs.html
95. Australian Broadcasting Corporation. (2019). Q and A Broadside. *ABC Online*. 4 November 2019. Retrieved from: https://www.abc.net.au/qanda/2019-04-11/11646878
96. Australian Broadcasting Corporation. (2019). Q and A Broadside. 4 November 2019. *ABC Online*. Retrieved from: https://www.abc.net.au/qanda/2019-04-11/11646878
97. Australian Broadcasting Corporation. (2017). ABC Managing Director statement on Q&A episode of 4 November. *ABC*. 7 November 2019. Retrieved from: https://about.abc.net.au/statements/abc-managing-director-statement-on-qa-episode-of-4-november/
98. Denholm, M. (2019). Ita Buttrose pulls ABC's Q&A show over 'call to violence'. *The Australian*. 8 November 2019. Retrieved from: https://www.theaustralian.com.au/business/media/abc-to-investigate-if-qa-panels-call-to-violence-breached-editorial-standards/news-story/b8c3fd2b5a292bf99eedc0fea1cf9d66
99. Denholm, M. (2019). Ita Buttrose pulls ABC's Q&A show over 'call to violence'. *The Australian*. 8 November 2019. Retrieved from: https://www.theaustralian.com.au/business/media/abc-to-investigate-if-qa-panels-call-to-violence-breached-editorial-standards/news-story/b8c3fd2b5a292bf99eedc0fea1cf9d66
100. Denholm, M. (2019). Ita Buttrose pulls ABC's Q&A show over 'call to violence'. *The Australian*. 8 November 2019. Retrieved from: https://www.theaustralian.com.au/business/media/abc-to-investigate-if-qa-panels-call-to-violence-breached-editorial-standards/news-story/b8c3fd2b5a292bf99eedc0fea1cf9d66

101. Australian Communications and Media Authority. (2020). 2019 Investigations. Retrieved from: https://www.acma.gov.au/investigations-tv-broadcasters#outcome-of-our-2019-investigations
102. Carmody, B. (2019). ABC finalises Q&A investigation over 'radical views' complaints. *The Sydney Morning Herald*. 11 December 2019. Retrieved from: https://www.smh.com.au/culture/tv-and-radio/abc-finalises-q-and-a-investigation-over-radical-views-complaints-20191211-p53iyg.html
103. Fishman, J. M., & Marvin, C. (2003). Portrayals of Violence and Group Difference in Newspaper Photographs: Nationalism and Media. *Journal of Communication*. 53:1. pp. 32–44. Retrieved from: https://doi.org/10.1111/j.1460-2466.2003.tb03003.x
104. Nerone, J., & Barnhurst, K. (2001). Beyond Modernism: Digital Design, Americanization and the Future of Newspaper Form. *New Media & Society*, *3*(4), 467–482. Retrieved from: https://doi.org/10.1177/146144401222226191
105. Denholm, M. (2019). Ita Buttrose pulls ABC's Q&A show over 'call to violence'. 18 November 2019. *The Australian*. Retrieved from: https://www.theaustralian.com.au/business/media/abc-to-investigat...d-editorial-standards/news-story/b8c3fd2b5a292bf99eedc0fea1cf9d66
106. Hawkins, G. (1997). The ABC and the Mystic Writing Pad. *Media International Australia*, *83*, 11–17.
107. Blackiston, H. (2019). Q&A after 'openly feminist' Broadside episode. Mumbrella. 8 November 2019. Retrieved from: https://mumbrella.com.au/abc-launches-investigation-into-qa-after-openly-feminist-broadside-episode-605744
108. Henriques-Gomez, L. (2019). "Let's Burn Stuff: Q&A panellists debate violence and shattering the status quo". *The Guardian*. 5 November 2019. Retrieved from: https://www.theguardian.com/australia-news/2019/nov/05/lets-burn-stuff-qa-panellists-debate-violence-and-shattering-the-status-quo
109. Coë, C. & Moore, H. (2019). ABC finds they were right to pull a controversial Q&A from iView where a radical feminist called for the killing of male rapists—but the writer isn't happy. 11 December 2019. Retrieved from: https://www.dailymail.co.uk/news/article-7779533/ABC-finishes-investigation-radical-female-Q-panel-advocated-killing-rapists.html
110. Hermida, A. (2012). Tweets and Truth: Journalism as a discipline of collaborative verification. March 2012. *Journalism Practice*. pp. 1–10. Retrieved from: https://doi.org/10.1080/17512786.2012.667269
111. Henriques-Gomez, L. (2019). "Let's Burn Stuff: Q&A panellists debate violence and shattering the status quo". *The Guardian*. 5 November 2019. Retrieved from: https://www.theguardian.com/australia-

news/2019/nov/05/lets-burn-stuff-qa-panellists-debate-violence-and-shattering-the-status-quo

112. Leary, M. R. (1995). *Self-presentation: Impression management and interpersonal behavior.* Brown & Benchmark. Madison, WI.
113. Rao, H. & Giorgi, S. (2006). Code Breaking: How Entrepreneurs Exploit Cultural Logics to Generate Institutional Change. Research in Organizational Behavior. 27. Pp. 269-304. https://doi.org/10.1016/S0191-3085(06)27007-2.
114. Suddaby R. (2010). Challenges for Institutional Theory. Journal of Management Inquiry. 19:1. Pp.14-20. https://doi.org/10.1177/1056492609347564
115. Ibid.
116. Truu, M. (2019). Minister for Communications Paul Fletcher said the decision to investigate Monday night's Q&A program was "appropriate". SBS News. 8 November 2019. Retrieved from: https://www.sbs.com.au/news/abc-announces-probe-into-feminist-q-a-episode-after-audience-complaints
117. Australian Broadcasting Corporation Editorial Policies. (2019). Hate Speech, Terrorism & Mass Killings. *ABC.* 26 November 2019. Retrieved from: Https://Edpols.Abc.Net.Au/Guidance/Hate-Speech-Terrorism-Mass-Killings/
118. Henderson, G. (2019). ABC delays and bungles handling of Q&A 'call to violence' episode. *The Australian.* 8 November 2019. Retrieved from: https://www.theaustralian.com.au/commentary/abc-delays-and-bungles-handling-of-qa-call-to-violence-episode/news-story/b11bb0bc356b056297d2a0ffb922a290
119. Henderson, G. (2019). ABC delays and bungles handling of Q&A 'call to violence' episode. *The Australian.* 8 November 2019. Retrieved from: https://www.theaustralian.com.au/commentary/abc-delays-and-bungles-handling-of-qa-call-to-violence-episode/news-story/b11bb0bc356b056297d2a0ffb922a290
120. Henderson, G. (2019). ABC delays and bungles handling of Q&A 'call to violence' episode. *The Australian.* 8 November 2019. Retrieved from: https://www.theaustralian.com.au/commentary/abc-delays-and-bungles-handling-of-qa-call-to-violence-episode/news-story/b11bb0bc356b056297d2a0ffb922a290
121. O'Dwyer, E. (2011). A bit weird and getting paid for it. *The Sydney Morning Herald.* 14 May 2011. Retrieved from: https://www.smh.com.au/entertainment/tv-and-radio/a-bit-weird-and-getting-paid-for-it-20110514-1en2c.html
122. Boseley, M. (2020). Four Chris Lilley shows removed from Netflix Australia library. *The Guardian.* 11 June 2020. Retrieved from: https://www.theguardian.com/tv-and-radio/2020/jun/11/four-chris-lilley-shows-removed-from-netflix-australia-library

123. Jones, T. (2020). Netflix Removes Most of Chris Lilley's Shows. *Gizmodo*. 11 June 2020. Retrieved from: https://www.gizmodo.com.au/2020/06/chris-lilley-netflix-blackface/
124. Flint, J. (2020). Race protests: Gone with The Wind, Little Britain and comedies by Chris Lilley pulled by streaming services. *The Australian*. 11 June 2020. Retrieved from: https://www.theaustralian.com.au/business/the-wall-street-journal/rhett-forced-to-give-a-damn-about-race-as-gone-with-the-wind-pulled/news-story/10dac76431771e180aa627 54329f9db4
125. Meade, A. (2014). Chris Lilley tastes ratings disaster as just 287,000 viewers tune in. *The Guardian*. 15 May 2014. Retrieved from: https://www.theguardian.com/media/2014/may/15/chris-lilley-tastes-ratings-disaster-as-just-287000-viewers-tune-in#:~:text=Chris%20Lilley%2C%20once%20a%20homegrown,441%2C000%20viewers%20to%20just%20287%2C000.
126. Spitznagel, E. (2013). Q&A: Chris Lilley on Drag, Blackface, Teenage Girls & Confrontational Comedy. *Esquire*. 14 November 2013. Retrieved from: https://www.esquire.com/entertainment/interviews/a25930/chris-lilley-interview/
127. Davis, G. (1988). *Breaking Up the ABC*. Allen and Unwin. Sydney. p. 3.
128. Australian Broadcasting Corporation Annual Report (2019). *ABC*. Retrieved from: https://about.abc.net.au/wp-content/uploads/2019/10/ABC-Annual-Report-201819v2.pdf, p. 118.
129. Gordon, J. (2018). Australians are losing their trust in 'the media', but not in journalism. RMIT. *ABC Fact Check*. Retrieved from: https://www.abc.net.au/news/2018-09-10/fact-checking-the-new-workplace-skill/10209210
130. Lazer, D.M.J., Baum, M.A., Benkler, Y., Berinsky, A.J., Greenhill, K. M., Menczer, F., Metzger, M., Nyhan, B., Pennycook, G., Rothschild, D., Schudson, M., Sloman, S.A., Sunstein, C.R., Thorson E.A.,Watts, D.J., Zittrain, J.L. (2018). The science of fake news. *Science* 359:6380. pp. 1094–1096. Citing p. 1095. Retrieved from: https://doi.org/10.1126/science.aao2998
131. *Oxford University Press* (2016). Word of the Year 2016. Retrieved from: https://languages.oup.com/word-of-the-year/2016/
132. Meade, A. (2017). ABC's Fact Check unit relaunched in partnership with RMIT. *The Guardian*. 14 February 2017. Retrieved from: https://www.theguardian.com/media/2017/feb/14/abcs-fact-check-unit-relaunched-in-partnership-with-rmit
133. Jaques, C., Islar, M., & Lord, G. (2019). Post-Truth: Hegemony on Social Media and Implications for Sustainability Communication. *Sustainability*. 11. Retrieved from: https://doi.org/10.3390/su11072120

134. Krause, N.M., Wirz., Scheufele, D.A. and Xenos, M.A. (2019). Fake News A New Obsession with an Old Phenomenon? In J.E. Katz & K.K. Mays. (2019). *Journalism and Truth in an Age of Social Media.* Oxford Scholarship Online: August 2019. Retrieved from: https://doi.org/10.1093/oso/9780190900250.001.0001
135. Milne, J. & Guthrie, M. (2018) ABC Annual Report. *ABC.* Welcome. Retrieved from: https://about.abc.net.au/wp-content/uploads/2018/10/AP18_Vol1_FINALnew.pdf, p. 3.
136. Bourke, L. (2014). Prime Minister Tony Abbott says ABC not on Australia's side in interview with 2GB. *ABC News Online.* 4 February 2014. Retrieved from: https://www.abc.net.au/news/2014-01-29/tony-abbott-steps-up-criticism-of-abc/5224676
137. The ABC axed the unit in 2016 due to funding cuts, but it re-emerged that year when it combined with RMIT, which provides joint funding.
138. George, P. (1989). *Behind the lines: The personal story of an ABC foreign correspondent.* ABC Books. Sydney. p. viii.
139. Posetti, J. & Ping, L. (2012). The Twitterisation of ABC's emergency and disaster communication. *The Australian Journal of Emergency Management.* 27:1. pp. 34–39. Retrieved from: https://search-informit-com-au.wwwproxy1.library.unsw.edu.au/documentSummary;dn=046926063833158;res=IELAPA
140. Ibid.
141. Tomlinson, M., O'Reilly, D., Wallace, M., Edwards, G., Elliott, C., Iszatt-White, M., Schedlitzki, D. (2013). Developing Leaders as Symbolic Violence: Reproducing Public Service Leadership through the (misrecognized) Development of Leaders' Capitals. 44:1. *Management Learning.* pp. 81–97. Quoting DiMaggio & Powell, 1983. Retrieved from: https://doi.org/10.1177/1350507612472151
142. Semmler, C. (1981). *The ABC—Aunt Sally and Sacred Cow.* Melbourne University Press. Melbourne. p. 68.
143. Grensing-Pophal, L. (2010). Social Media: Journalism's friend or foe? January-February, 2010. *Econtentmag.com.* Retrieved from: http://www.econtentmag.com/Articles/Editorial/Feature/Social-Media-Journalisms-Friend-or-Foe-61147.htm
144. Grensing-Pophal, L. (2010). Social Media: Journalism's friend or foe? January-February, 2010. *Econtentmag.com.* Retrieved from: http://www.econtentmag.com/Articles/Editorial/Feature/Social-Media-Journalisms-Friend-or-Foe-61147.htm, p. 25.
145. Castells, M. (2008). The New Public Sphere: Global Civil Society, Communication Networks, and Global Governance. *The Annals of the American Academy of Political and Social Science.* 616. pp. 78–93. Retrieved from: www.jstor.org/stable/25097995

146. Aufderheide, P., Boyles, J.L., & Bieze, K. (2013) Copyright, Free Speech, and The Public's Right to Know. *Journalism Studies*. 14:6, pp. 875–890. Retrieved from: https://doi.org/10.1080/1461670X.2012.739320
147. ABC Section Community and Public Sector Union (2008). Towards a Digital Future. Submission to Review of ABC and SBS. *iloveabc.org*. Retrieved from: https://iloveabc.org.au/wp-content/uploads/2018/11/Towards-a-Digital-Future-2008-1.pdf, p. 25.
148. Ibid., p. 25.
149. Mønsted, B., Sapieżyński, P., Ferrara, E., Lehmann, S. (2017). Evidence of complex contagion of information in social media: An experiment using Twitter bots. *Plos One*. Retrieved from: https://journals.plos.org/plosone/article/file?id=10.1371/journal.pone.0184148&type=printable
150. Tucker, J.A., Theocharis, Y., Roberts, M.E., Barberá, P. (2017). From Liberation to Turmoil: Social Media and Democracy. *Journal of Democracy*. 28:4, October 2017. pp. 46–59. Retrieved from: https://muse-jhu-edu.wwwproxy1.library.unsw.edu.au/article/671987/pdf. Citing p. 48.
151. Nadkarni, A., & Hofmann, S. G. (2012). Why do people use Facebook? *Personality and Individual Differences*. 52. pp. 243–249. Retrieved from: https://psycnet.apa.org/doi/10.1016/j.paid.2011.11.007
152. Gardels, N. (1995). Is there a liberal bias in the media? *New Perspectives Quarterly*. 12:2. Retrieved from: http://search.proquest.com/docview/196967275/, p. 23.
153. Ferrara, E. & Yang, Z. (2015). Measuring Emotional Contagion in Social Media. *PLoS ONE*. 10:11. Retrieved from: https://journals.plos.org/plosone/article/file?id=10.1371/journal.pone.0142390&type=printable
154. Vallone, R., Ross, L. & Lepper, M.R. (1985). The hostile media phenomenon: Biased perception and perceptions of media bias in coverage of the Beirut massacre. *Journal of Personality and Social Psychology* 49:3 (September). pp. 577–585. Retrieved from: https://doi.org/10.1037/0022-3514.49.3.577
155. The Australian Journalists Association (MEAA) Code of Ethics.
156. Bourdieu, P. (1991). *Language and Symbolic Power*. Harvard University Press. Cambridge MA. p. 170.
157. Another significant area of Bourdieu's (1990) analysis concerned the need to focus on the 'habitus' of the writer to understand his position, in that the position taken was an unconscious creation and recreation of perceptions and practices: "Doing one's duty as a man means conforming to the social order; this is fundamentally a question of respecting rhythms, keeping pace, not falling out of line (Bourdieu 1994)".

158. Schirato, T. & Yell, S. (1997). *Communication and Cultural Literacy: an introduction*. Allen and Unwin. St Leonards NSW.
159. Schirato, T. & Yell, S. (1997). *Communication and Cultural Literacy: an introduction*. Allen and Unwin. St Leonards NSW. p. 103.
160. *Facebook*. (2020). Our Mission. Retrieved from: https://info.internet.org/en/mission/
161. NSW Nurses and Midwives' Association (2018). Turnbull pressures ABC on tax coverage. Tax Justice. *The Lamp*. 5 March 2018. p. 20. Retrieved from: https://thelamp.com.au/workplace-issues/unions/turnbull-pressures-abc-on-tax-coverage/
162. NSW Nurses and Midwives' Association (2018). Turnbull pressures ABC on tax coverage. Tax Justice. *The Lamp*. 5 March 2018. p. 20. Retrieved from: https://thelamp.com.au/workplace-issues/unions/turnbull-pressures-abc-on-tax-coverage/
163. Meade, A. (2018). Qantas boss accuses ABC of anti-business bias over Emma Alberici tax stories. *The Guardian*. 10 April 2018. Retrieved from: https://www.theguardian.com/media/2018/apr/10/qantas-boss-accuses-abc-of-anti-business-bias-over-emma-alberici-tax-stories
164. Meade, A. (2018). Qantas boss accuses ABC of anti-business bias over Emma Alberici tax stories. *The Guardian*. 10 April 2018. Retrieved from: https://www.theguardian.com/media/2018/apr/10/qantas-boss-accuses-abc-of-anti-business-bias-over-emma-alberici-tax-stories
165. Meade, A. (2018). Qantas boss accuses ABC of anti-business bias over Emma Alberici tax stories. *The Guardian*. 10 April 2018. Retrieved from: https://www.theguardian.com/media/2018/apr/10/qantas-boss-accuses-abc-of-anti-business-bias-over-emma-alberici-tax-stories
166. Meade, A. (2018). Qantas boss accuses ABC of anti-business bias over Emma Alberici tax stories. *The Guardian*. 10 April 2018. Retrieved from: https://www.theguardian.com/media/2018/apr/10/qantas-boss-accuses-abc-of-anti-business-bias-over-emma-alberici-tax-stories
167. NSW Nurses and Midwives' Association (2018). (2018). Turnbull pressures ABC on tax coverage. Tax Justice. *The Lamp*. March 2018. p. 20. Retrieved from: https://thelamp.com.au/workplace-issues/unions/turnbull-pressures-abc-on-tax-coverage/
168. Alberici, E. (2018). Why many big companies don't pay corporate tax. *Australian Broadcasting Corporation*. Posted 14 February 2018, updated 16 February 2018. Retrieved from: https://www.abc.net.au/news/2018-02-14/why-many-big-companies-dont-pay-corporate-tax/9443840
169. https://www.abc.net.au/news/2018-02-14/why-many-big-companies-dont-pay-corporate-tax/9443840

170. Carmody, B. (2018). Emma Alberici's controversial tax story contained nine errors. *The Sydney Morning Herald*. 10 April 2018. Retrieved from: https://www.smh.com.au/entertainment/tv-and-radio/emma-alberici-s-controversial-tax-story-contained-nine-errors-20180410-p4z8qm.html
171. Koziol, M. (2018). ABC boss Michelle Guthrie says broadcaster 'clearly failed' in Emma Alberici controversy. *The Sydney Morning Herald*. 29 February 2018. Retrieved from: https://www.smh.com.au/politics/federal/abc-boss-michelle-guthrie-says-broadcaster-clearly-failed-in-emma-alberici-controversy-20180227-p4z21j.html
172. Koziol, M. (2018). ABC boss Michelle Guthrie says broadcaster 'clearly failed' in Emma Alberici controversy. 29 February 2018. Retrieved from: https://www.smh.com.au/politics/federal/abc-boss-michelle-guthrie-says-broadcaster-clearly-failed-in-emma-alberici-controversy-20180227-p4z21j.html
173. Australian Broadcasting Corporation. (2018). Restating the facts on Emma Alberici's corporate tax stories. *The Sydney Morning Herald*. 30 September 2018. Retrieved from: https://about.abc.net.au/correcting-the-record/restating-the-facts-on-emma-albericis-corporate-tax-stories/
174. Koziol, M. (2018). ABC boss Michelle Guthrie says broadcaster 'clearly failed' in Emma Alberici controversy. *The Sydney Morning Herald*. 29 February 2018. Retrieved from: https://www.smh.com.au/politics/federal/abc-boss-michelle-guthrie-says-broadcaster-clearly-failed-in-emma-alberici-controversy-20180227-p4z21j.html
175. Koziol, M. (2018). ABC boss Michelle Guthrie says broadcaster 'clearly failed' in Emma Alberici controversy. *The Sydney Morning Herald*. 29 February 2018. Retrieved from: https://www.smh.com.au/politics/federal/abc-boss-michelle-guthrie-says-broadcaster-clearly-failed-in-emma-alberici-controversy-20180227-p4z21j.html
176. Patrick, A. (2018). Emma Alberici anti-tax cut article contained nine errors. *The Australian Financial Review*. 10 April 2018. Retrieved from: https://www.afr.com/policy/tax-and-super/emma-alberici-antitax-cut-article-contained-nine-errors-20180410-h0ykfs
177. Patrick, A. (2018). Emma Alberici anti-tax cut article contained nine errors. *The Australian Financial Review*. 10 April 2018. Retrieved from: https://www.afr.com/policy/tax-and-super/emma-alberici-antitax-cut-article-contained-nine-errors-20180410-h0ykfs
178. Meade, A. (2018). Qantas boss accuses ABC of anti-business bias over Emma Alberici tax stories. *The Guardian*. 10 April 2018. Retrieved from: https://www.theguardian.com/media/2018/apr/10/qantas-boss-accuses-abc-of-anti-business-bias-over-emma-alberici-tax-stories
179. Koziol, M. (2018). ABC boss Michelle Guthrie says broadcaster 'clearly failed' in Emma Alberici controversy. *The Sydney Morning Herald*. 29

February 2018. Retrieved from: https://www.smh.com.au/politics/federal/abc-boss-michelle-guthrie-says-broadcaster-clearly-failed-in-emma-alberici-controversy-20180227-p4z21j.html

180. ABC MediaWatch. (2018). Taxing Times. *ABC*. 19 February 2018. Retrieved from: https://www.abc.net.au/mediawatch/episodes/taxing-times-at-the-abc/9972348
181. Koziol, M. & Duke, J. (2018). ABC admits mistakes over Cabinet Files, Emma Alberici controversies. *The Sydney Morning Herald*. 27 February 2018. Retrieved from: https://www.smh.com.au/politics/federal/abc-admits-mistakes-over-cabinet-files-emma-alberici-controversies-20180227-p4z20t.html
182. ABC MediaWatch. (2018). Taxing Times. *ABC*. 19 February 2018. Retrieved from: https://www.abc.net.au/mediawatch/episodes/taxing-times-at-the-abc/9972348
183. *Simon Wiesenthal Center*. (2010). Wiesenthal Center Disgusted by Surge of Online Anti-Semitism Triggered By Goldman Sachs Case. 27 April 2010. Retrieved from: http://www.wiesenthal.com/about/news/wiesenthal-center-disgusted.html
184. Nathan, J. (2019). *Report on Antisemitism in Australia 2019*. Executive Council of Australian Jewry. Retrieved from: https://sydney.edu.au/content/dam/corporate/documents/sydney-law-school/research/centres-institutes/antisemitism-report-2019.pdf
185. Ibid., p. 7.
186. Ibid., p. 8.
187. Ibid., p. 9.
188. Walker, T. (2018). Shifting the Australian embassy in Israel to Jerusalem would be a big, cynical mistake. *ABC News Online*. 17 October 2018. Retrieved from: https://www.abc.net.au/news/2018-10-17/australian-embassy-jerusalem-big-cynical-mistake/10388108
189. Nathan, J. (2019). Quoting Walker. p. 73.
190. ABC MediaWatch. (2018). Taxing Times. *ABC*. 19 February 2018. Retrieved from: https://www.abc.net.au/mediawatch/episodes/taxing-times-at-the-abc/9972348
191. Meade, A. (2018). Qantas boss accuses ABC of anti-business bias over Emma Alberici tax stories. *The Guardian*. 10 April 2018. Retrieved from: https://www.theguardian.com/media/2018/apr/10/qantas-boss-accuses-abc-of-anti-business-bias-over-emma-alberici-tax-stories
192. *Nine.com.au* (2018). Emma Alberici under fire again as PM files complaints to the ABC. 23 May 2018. Retrieved from: https://finance.nine.com.au/business-news/emma-alberici-abc-complaints-prime-minister-malcolm-turnbull/4dc648ae-6f69-4f2b-b5fd-8d655c9d84f2

193. *Nine.com.au* (2018). Emma Alberici under fire again as PM files complaints to the ABC. 23 May 2018. Retrieved from: https://finance.nine.com.au/business-news/emma-alberici-abc-complaints-prime-minister-malcolm-turnbull/4dc648ae-6f69-4f2b-b5fd-8d655c9d84f2
194. *Nine.com.au* (2018). Emma Alberici under fire again as PM files complaints to the ABC. 23 May 2018. Retrieved from: https://finance.nine.com.au/business-news/emma-alberici-abc-complaints-prime-minister-malcolm-turnbull/4dc648ae-6f69-4f2b-b5fd-8d655c9d84f2
195. *Nine.com.au* (2018). Emma Alberici under fire again as PM files complaints to the ABC. 23 May 2018. Retrieved from: https://finance.nine.com.au/business-news/emma-alberici-abc-complaints-prime-minister-malcolm-turnbull/4dc648ae-6f69-4f2b-b5fd-8d655c9d84f2
196. Stephens, M. (2007). *A History of News.* 3rd Edition. Oxford University Press. New York and Oxford. p. 55.
197. Stephens, M. (2007). *A History of News.* 3rd Edition. Oxford University Press. New York and Oxford. pp. 28–29.
198. Pearlman, A. (2008). Ethics in Journalism—Accuracy, Honesty, and Credibility. *Journal of the American Society of Echocardiography.* 21:5. pp. 507–508. Retrieved from: https://doi.org/10.1016/j.echo.2008.03.008
199. Stephens, M. (2009), "Beyond News: The Case for Wisdom Journalism," Joan Shorenstein Center on the Press, Politics and Public Policy, *DP Series.* D-53. June. Harvard Kennedy School. Retrieved from: https://shorensteincenter.org/beyond-news-the-case-for-wisdom-journalism-mitchell-stephens/
200. Stephens, M. (2009), "Beyond News: The Case for Wisdom Journalism," Joan Shorenstein Center on the Press, Politics and Public Policy, *DP Series* D-53. June. Harvard Kennedy School. Retrieved from: https://shorensteincenter.org/beyond-news-the-case-for-wisdom-journalism-mitchell-stephens/
201. Lewis, J. (2006). News and the Empowerment of Citizens. *European Journal of Cultural Studies.* 9:3. pp. 303–319. p. 311. Retrieved from: https://doi.org/10.1177/1367549406066075
202. Shapiro, I., Brin, C., Bédard-Brûlé, I., & Mychajlowycz, K. (2013). Verification as a Strategic Ritual: How journalists retrospectively describe processes for ensuring accuracy. *Journalism Practice.* 7:6. pp. 657–673. Retrieved from: https://doi.org/10.1080/17512786.2013.765638
203. Shapiro, I., Brin, C., Bédard-Brûlé, I., & Mychajlowycz, K. (2013). Verification as a Strategic Ritual: How journalists retrospectively describe processes for ensuring accuracy. *Journalism Practice.* 7:6. pp. 657–673. Retrieved from: https://doi.org/10.1080/17512786.2013.765638,

Quoting W. Lippmann [1920] 1995. *Liberty and the News.* New Brunswick, NJ: Transaction Publishers.
204. Mackay, H. (2002). *Media Mania: Why our fear of modern media is misplaced.* UNSW Press. Sydney. p. 31.
205. Chalaby, J.K. (1998). *The Invention of Journalism.* Macmillan Press. UK. p. 22.
206. Correct spelling, no capital letter for the family name.
207. fforde, A. (1963). What is Broadcasting About. Private printing. Quoted in M. Tracey (2002). *The Decline and Fall of Public Service Broadcasting.* Oxford University Press. Oxford.
208. Tracey, M. (2002). *The Decline and Fall of Public Service Broadcasting.* Oxford University Press. Oxford. p. 20.
209. Berg, C. & Davidson, S. (2018). *Against Public Broadcasting: Why we should privatise the ABC and how to do it.* Connor Court Publishing. Brisbane.
210. Simshaw, D. (2012). Survival of the standard: today's public interest requirement in television broadcasting and the return to regulation. *Federal Communications Law Journal.* 64:2. March. P. 401. Retrieved from: http://search.proquest.com/docview/1151042593/
211. Inglis, K. (1983). *The is the ABC: The Australian Broadcasting Commission 1932–1983.* Melbourne University Press. Melbourne. p. 14.
212. Simshaw, D. (2012). Survival of the standard: today's public interest requirement in television broadcasting and the return to regulation. *Federal Communications Law Journal.* 64:2. March. p. 401. Retrieved from: http://search.proquest.com/docview/1151042593/.
213. Hurst, D. (2020). Cyber-attack Australia: sophisticated attacks from 'state-based actor', PM says. *The Guardian.* 19 June 2020. Retrieved from: https://www.theguardian.com/australia-news/2020/jun/19/australia-cyber-attack-attacks-hack-state-based-actor-says-australian-prime-minister-scott-morrison
214. Bogle. A. (2020). Why China is being blamed for cyber attacks on Australia, and what its hackers might be looking for. *ABC News Online.* 19 June 2020. Retrieved from: https://www.abc.net.au/news/2020-06-19/why-would-china-launch-cyber-attack-against-australia/12374990
215. *Australian War Memorial.* (nd). Prime Minister Robert G. Menzies: wartime broadcast. Retrieved from: https://www.awm.gov.au/articles/encyclopedia/prime_ministers/menzies
216. Bollmer, G. (2016). Inhuman Networks: Social Media and the Archaeology of Connection, Bloomsbury Academic & Professional, 2016. ProQuest Ebook Central. Retrieved from: https://ebookcentral.proquest.com/lib/unsw/detail.action?docID=4542880

217. Massaka, I. (2017). Selected Issues of E-Democracy and Political E-Participation. *Historia i Polityka*. 18: 25. pp. 9–18. Retrieved from: https://doi.org/10.12775/HiP.2016.028
218. Castells, M. (2008). The New Public Sphere: Global Civil Society, Communication Networks, and Global Governance. *The Annals of the American Academy of Political and Social Science*. 616. pp. 78–93. Retrieved from: www.jstor.org/stable/25097995
219. Tucker, J.A., Theocharis, Y., Roberts, M.E., Barberá, P. (2017). From Liberation to Turmoil: Social Media and Democracy. *Journal of Democracy*. 28:4. October 2017. pp. 46–59. Retrieved from: https://muse-jhu-edu.wwwproxy1.library.unsw.edu.au/article/671987/pdf
220. Ibid.
221. Egan, T. (2019). Why Doesn't Mark Zuckerberg Get It? The Facebook co-founder's speech at Georgetown was a profile in cowardice. Opinion. *The New York Times*. 25 October 2019. Retrieved from: https://www.nytimes.com/2019/10/25/opinion/facebook-mark-zuckerberg.html?action=click&module=Opinion&pgtype=Homepage
222. Persily, N. (2017). The 2016 U.S. Election: Can Democracy Survive the Internet? *Journal of Democracy*. 28:2, April 2017. pp. 63–76. Retrieved from: https://muse.jhu.edu/article/653377
223. Egan, T. (2019). Why Doesn't Mark Zuckerberg Get It? The Facebook co-founder's speech at Georgetown was a profile in cowardice. Opinion. *The New York Times*. 25 October 2019. Retrieved from: https://www.nytimes.com/2019/10/25/opinion/facebook-mark-zuckerberg.html?action=click&module=Opinion&pgtype=Homepage
224. Ibid.
225. Lee, J. (2015). The Double-Edged Sword: The Effects of Journalists' Social Media Activities on Audience Perceptions of Journalists and Their News Products. Journal of Computer-Mediated Communication. 20 (2015) pp. 312–329. Retrieved from: https://watermark.silverchair.com/jjcmcom0312.pdf
226. Erbschloe, M. (2017). *Social media warfare: equal weapons for all*. Taylor & Francis, Boca Raton, FL. E-book. Retrieved from: https://ebookcentral.proquest.com/lib/unsw/reader.action?docID=4856182 p. 4.
227. Ibid.
228. Spaulding, S., Nair, D., & Nelson, A. (2020). *Russia's attacks on democratic justice systems*. Center for Strategic and International Studies. Retrieved from: https://www.csis.org/features/russias-attacks-democratic-justice-systems
229. Thompson, M. (2019). Speech to "The Missing 'I' In Dime iWar Conference 29 October 2019 Canberra, Australia. *Department of Defence*. Retrieved from: https://www.defence.gov.au/jcg/Docs/191029-Speech-iWar-Forum-Keynote-HIW-Transcript.pdf

230. Ibid.
231. Voelz, G.J. (2015). (Rep.) *The Rise of iWar: Identity, Information, and the Individualization of Modern Warfare.* Strategic Studies Institute, US Army War College. Retrieved from: www.jstor.org/stable/resrep11804
232. Ibid.
233. Ibid., p. 9.
234. Ibid.
235. Wardle, C. & Derakhshan, H. (2017). "Information Disorder: Toward an Interdisciplinary Framework for Research and Policy Making". *Council of Europe, Strasbourg, France.* Retrieved from: https://rm.coe.int/information-disorder-toward-an-interdisciplinary-framework-for-researc/168076277c
236. Ibid.
237. Thompson, M. (2019). Speech to "The Missing 'I' In Dime iWar Conference 29 October 2019 Canberra, Australia. *Department of Defence.* Retrieved from: https://www.defence.gov.au/jcg/Docs/191029-Speech-iWar-Forum-Keynote-HIW-Transcript.pdf
238. Voelz, G.J. (2015). (Rep.) The Rise of iWar: Identity, Information, and the Individualization of Modern Warfare. *Strategic Studies Institute, US Army War College.* Retrieved from: www.jstor.org/stable/resrep11804, p. 73. Quoting M. Chertoff and T. Simon, "The Impact of the Dark Web on Internet Governance and Cyber Security: Global Commission on Internet Governance Paper Series No. 6," Waterloo, Ontario, Canada: *Centre for International Governance Innovation and the Royal Institute for International Affairs.* February 2015. p. 1.
239. Derrida, J. (2005). *Rogues.* Stanford, CA: Stanford University Press. p. 18.
240. Carpentier, N. (2014). Participation as a Fantasy: A Psychoanalytical Approach to Power-Sharing Fantasies in Eds. L. Kramp, N. Carpentier, A. Hepp, I. Tomanic-Trivundza, H. Nieminen, R. Kunelius, T. Olsson, E. Sundin & R. Kilborn, *Everyday Media Agency in Europe, Chapter: Participation as a Fantasy: A Psychoanalytical Approach to Power-Sharing Fantasies.* Edition Lumière. Section 4:5. pp. 319–330. Retrieved from: https://www.researchgate.net/publication/268980799_Participation_as_a_Fantasy_A_Psychoanalytical_Approach_to_Power-Sharing_Fantasies
241. Thompson, M. (2019). Speech to "The Missing 'I' In Dime iWar Conference 29 October 2019 Canberra, Australia. *Department of Defence.* Retrieved from: https://www.defence.gov.au/jcg/Docs/191029-Speech-iWar-Forum-Keynote-HIW-Transcript.pdf
242. Voelz, G.J. (2015). (Rep.) The Rise of iWar: Identity, Information, and the Individualization of Modern Warfare. *Strategic Studies Institute, US Army War College.* Retrieved from: www.jstor.org/stable/resrep11804, p. 73. Quoting M. Chertoff and T. Simon, "The Impact of the Dark Web

on Internet Governance and Cyber Security: Global Commission on Internet Governance Paper Series No. 6," Waterloo, Ontario, Canada. *Centre for International Governance Innovation and the Royal Institute for International Affairs*. February 2015. p. 1.

243. Thompson. R. (2011). Radicalization and the Use of Social Media. *Journal of Strategic Security*. 4:4. pp. 167–190. Retrieved from: https://doi.org/10.5038/1944-0472.4.4.8
244. Thompson. R. (2011). Radicalization and the Use of Social Media. *Journal of Strategic Security*. 4:4. pp. 167–190. Retrieved from: https://doi.org/10.5038/1944-0472.4.4.8, p. 170.
245. Tzu, S. (2005, reprint). *The Art of War. On the Use of Spies*. Shambhala Publications. Boulder, Colorado. pp. 178–179.
246. Schiffrin, A. (2017). Disinformation and Democracy: The Internet Transformed Protest but Did Not Improve Democracy. *Journal of International Affairs*. 71:1. Fall 2016–Winter 2017. Pp. 117–125. Retrieved from: http://search.proquest.com/docview/2054916939/
247. Voelz, G.J. (2015). (Rep.) The Rise of iWar: Identity, Information, and the Individualization of Modern Warfare. *Strategic Studies Institute, US Army War College*. Retrieved from: www.jstor.org/stable/resrep11804
248. Zhou, C. & Xiao, B. (2020). China's Social Credit System is pegged to be fully operational by 2020—but what will it look like? *Australian Broadcasting Corporation*. 2 January 2020. Retrieved from: https://www.abc.net.au/news/2020-01-02/china-social-credit-system-operational-by-2020/11764740
249. Kornbluh, K. (2018). The Internet's Lost Promise: And How America Can Restore It. *Foreign Affairs*. New York. 97:5. Sept/Oct 2018. pp. 33–38. Retrieved from: http://search.proquest.com/docview/2094371395/
250. Ibid.
251. Ibid.
252. Ibid.
253. Bennett, W L., & Livingston, S. (2018). 'The Disinformation Order: Disruptive Communication and the Decline of Democratic Institutions' 33:2. *European Journal of Communication*. pp. 122–139. Retrieved from: https://doi.org/10.1177/0267323118760317, p. 132.
254. Ibid.
255. Wardle, C. (2019). Misinformation Has Created a New World Disorder. *Scientific American*. 1 September 2019. Retrieved from: https://www.scientificamerican.com/article/misinformation-has-created-a-new-world-disorder/

256. Thomas D.R. (2017). Digital Disruption: A Transformation in Graduate Management Online Education. In: Khare A., Stewart B., Schatz R. (eds) *Phantom Ex Machina*. Springer. Cham.
257. Ibid.
258. Bennett, W L., & Livingston, S. (2018). 'The Disinformation Order: Disruptive Communication and the Decline of Democratic Institutions' 33:2. *European Journal of Communication*. pp. 122–139. Retrieved from: https://doi.org/10.1177/0267323118760317
259. Ibid.
260. Ibid., pp. 127–128.
261. Ibid. p. 124.
262. Ibid., p. 127.
263. Ibid., p. 128.
264. Ibid.
265. Ibid.
266. Carbado, D., Crenshaw, K., Mays, V., & Tomlinson, B. (2013). *INTERSECTIONALITY:* Mapping the Movements of a Theory. *Du Bois Review: Social Science Research on Race*. 10:2. pp. 303–312. Retrieved from: https://doi.org/10.1017/S1742058X13000349. Citing p. 303.
267. Goldman, S. (2019, 03). Jews must not embrace powerlessness. *Commentary*. 147. pp. 37–39. Retrieved from: https://www.commentarymagazine.com/articles/sharon-goldman/jews-must-not-embrace-powerlessness/
268. Goldman, S. (2019, 03). Jews must not embrace powerlessness. *Commentary*. 147. pp. 37–39. Retrieved from: https://www.commentarymagazine.com/articles/sharon-goldman/jews-must-not-embrace-powerlessness/
269. Goldman, S. (2019, 03). Jews must not embrace powerlessness. *Commentary*. 147. pp. 37–39. Retrieved from: https://www.commentarymagazine.com/articles/sharon-goldman/jews-must-not-embrace-powerlessness/
270. Goldman, S. (2019, 03). Jews must not embrace powerlessness. *Commentary*. 147. pp. 37–39. Retrieved from: https://www.commentarymagazine.com/articles/sharon-goldman/jews-must-not-embrace-powerlessness/
271. Zuo, J. (2003). From Revolutionary Comrades to Gendered Partners: Marital Construction of Breadwinning in Post-Mao Urban China. *Journal of Family Issues*. *24*:3. pp. 314–337. Retrieved from: https://doi.org/10.1177/0192513X02250888

272. Branch, D. & Cheeseman, N. (2008). Democratization, Sequencing, And State Failure in Africa: Lessons from Kenya. African Affairs. 108:430. pp. 1–26. Retrieved from: https://doi.org/10.1093/afraf/adn065
273. Kagwanjaa, P. & Southall, R. (2009). Introduction: Kenya: A democracy in retreat? Journal of Contemporary African Studies. 27:3. July 2009. pp. 259–277. Retrieved from: https://doi.org/10.1080/02589000903216930
274. Grant, E. (1973). Medieval Explanations and Interpretations of the Dictum that 'Nature Abhors a Vacuum'. *Traditio. 29.* pp. 327–355. https://doi.org/10.1017/S0362152900009004
275. O'Keeffe, A. & Greene, C. (2019). International Public Broadcasting: A Missed Opportunity for Projecting Australia's Soft Power. *Lowy Institute.* 11 December 2019. Retrieved from: https://www.lowyinstitute.org/publications/international-public-broadcasting-missed-opportunity-projecting-australia-s-soft-power
276. Ibid.
277. Ibid.
278. *Australian Government. (2017) Foreign Policy White Paper. 2017 "Opportunity, Security, Strength."* Canberra. 2017. *Australian Government.* Retrieved from: https://www.fpwhitepaper.gov.au/foreign-policy-white-paper/chapter-two-contested-world/power-shifts-indo-pacific
279. *Australian Government. (2017).* Ibid.
280. McChesney, R.W., Herman, E.S. (1997). *The Global Media: the news missionaries of global capitalism.* Cassell. Washington & London. Citing p. 3.
281. Australian Broadcasting Corporation (2019). ABC Annual Report 2019. *ABC.* Retrieved from: https://about.abc.net.au/wp-content/uploads/2019/10/ABC-Annual-Report-201819v2.pdf
282. Australian Broadcasting Corporation (2019). ABC Annual Report 2019. *ABC.* Retrieved from: https://about.abc.net.au/wp-content/uploads/2019/10/ABC-Annual-Report-201819v2.pdf
283. Australian Broadcasting Corporation (2019). ABC Annual Report 2019. *ABC.* Retrieved from: https://about.abc.net.au/wp-content/uploads/2019/10/ABC-Annual-Report-201819v2.pdf
284. Persily, N. (2017). The 2016 U.S. Election: Can Democracy Survive the Internet? *Journal of Democracy.* 28:2. April 2017. pp. 63–76. Retrieved from: https://muse.jhu.edu/article/653377
285. Ibid.
286. Collins, B. & Zadrozny, B. (2021). Twitter permanently suspends Donald Trump. NBC News. 9 January 2021. Retrieved from: https://www.nbcnews.com/tech/tech-news/twitter-permanently-bans-president-donald-trump-n1253588

287. *BBC.* (2020). Twitter hides Trump tweet for 'glorifying violence'. 29 May 2020. Retrieved from: https://www.bbc.com/news/technology-52846679
288. Waters, R. & Murphy, H. (2021). Donald Trump, Twitter and the messy fight over free speech. *The Financial Times.* The Big Read. Social Media. 16 January 2021. Retrieved from: https://www.ft.com/content/78a3ed8c-d930-4bf5-9f6e-1b6b4751090f
289. BBC. (2020). George Floyd: 'Unacceptable' attacks on reporters at protests. *BBC.* 1 June 2020. Retrieved from: https://www.bbc.com/news/world-us-canada-52880970
290. BBC. (2020). George Floyd: 'Unacceptable' attacks on reporters at protests. *BBC.* 1 June 2020. Retrieved from: https://www.bbc.com/news/world-us-canada-52880970
291. Ferguson, R. & Vitorovich, L. (2020). US protests: Police attack Channel 7 news team as Donald Trump walks from White House. *The Australian.* 2 June 2020. Retrieved from: https://www.theaustralian.com.au/business/media/us-protests-police-attack-channel-7-news-team-as-donald-trump-walks-from-white-house/news-story/e326fa536c5b2d15ccca4659ca9ec917
292. Keen, A. (2007). *The Cult of the Amateur.* Doubleday Currency. New York. p. 17.
293. Loc. cit.
294. Vitorovitch, L. & Shanahan. L. (2020). AAP's newswire to close in June. *The Australian.* 3 March 2020. Retrieved from: https://www.theaustralian.com.au/business/media/aaps-newswire-to-close-in-june/news-story/91ae9b35935ced854f8dddadd0616f84
295. *Australian Associated Press.* (2020). About. Retrieved from: https://www.aap.com.au/about-us/#item-1
296. Dudley-Nicholson, J. (2020). AAP demise a 'wake-up call' over tech giants. *The Australian.* 5 March, 2020. Retrieved from: https://www.theaustralian.com.au/business/media/aap-demise-a-wakeup-call-over-tech-giants/news-story/380efd106480aa0eaa5e3b871e2f5bfa
297. Ibid.
298. Vitorovitch, L. & Shanahan. L. (2020). AAP's newswire to close in June. *The Australian.* 3 March 2020. Retrieved from: https://www.theaustralian.com.au/business/media/aaps-newswire-to-close-in-june/news-story/91ae9b35935ced854f8dddadd0616f84
299. Vitorovitch, L. & Swan, D. (2020). Guardian hypocrisy over AAP shutdown. *The Australian.* 5 March 2020. Retrieved from: https://www.theaustralian.com.au/business/media/accc-reviewing-aap-demise-says-rod-sims/news-story/78a2380813fc8574680b81e5ec570ec3

300. Editorial, The. (2020). Time to end free lunch for Google and Facebook. *The Australian*. 11 February 2020. Retrieved from: https://www.theaustralian.com.au/commentary/editorials/time-to-end-free-lunch-for-google-and-facebook/news-story/f84c88b4dd86f54b5cc4397ba07d9cc7
301. Vitorovitch, L. & Swan, D. (2020). Guardian hypocrisy over AAP shutdown. *The Australian*. 5 March 2020. Retrieved from: https://www.theaustralian.com.au/business/media/accc-reviewing-aap-demise-says-rod-sims/news-story/78a2380813fc8574680b81e5ec570ec3
302. Thompson, M. (2019). Speech to "The Missing 'I' In Dime iWar Conference 29 October 2019 Canberra, Australia. *Department of Defence*. Retrieved from: https://www.defence.gov.au/jcg/Docs/191029-Speech-iWar-Forum-Keynote-HIW-Transcript.pdf
303. Foreign Policy editorial. (2010). iWar. *Foreign Policy*. 178:1. March/April 2020. Retrieved from: https://www-jstor-org.wwwproxy1.library.unsw.edu.au/stable/20684986?seq=1#metadata_info_tab_contents, p. 1.
304. Thompson, M. (2019). "We live in an age of political war". Military Communications and Informations Systems (Milcis) Conference. *Department of Defence*. 13 November 2019 Canberra, Australia, Speech. Retrieved from: https://www.defence.gov.au/jcg/Docs/191101-Speech-MILCIS-Conference-HIW-Transcript.pdf
305. Ibid.
306. *Australian Associated Press*. (2020). Code of Practice. Retrieved from: https://www.aap.com.au/about-us/#item-3
307. Habermas, J. (2006). Acceptance speech for the Bruno Kreisky Prize for the Advancement of Human Rights, 9 March, 2006. In A. Keen. (2007). *The Cult of the Amateur: how today's internet is killing our culture*. New York. Doubleday/Currency. p. 55.
308. Toffler, A. (1984). Future Shock. Bantam Books. New York.
309. Keen, A. (2007). *The Cult of the Amateur*. Doubleday Currency. New York. p. 74.
310. Simons, M. (2011, February). Crises of Faith: The Future of Fairfax. *The Monthly*. 64. pp. 30–39. Retrieved from: https://www.themonthly.com.au/issue/2011/january/1298525748/margaret-simons/crises-faith
311. Anderson, B. (1983). *Imagined Communities: Reflections on the Origins and Spread of Nationalism*. Verso. London and New York. p. 5.
312. Harris & Lee 1986, in Chalaby, J. K. (1997). No ordinary press owner: Press barons as a Weberian ideal type. *Media, Culture and Society*. 19:4. pp. 621–641. Retrieved from: https://doi.org/10.1177/016344397019004007. Citing p. 631, referencing Harris & Lee 1986, pp. 19–20.

313. Shaw, S. J. (1959), Shaw, S.J., (1959). Colonial Newspaper Advertising: A Step toward Freedom of the Press. *Business History Review*. 33. Retrieved from: http://search.proquest.com/docview/205528871/. p. 409.
314. A platform heavily used by US President Donald Trump both during the 2016 presidential election campaign and ongoing: "the power of Trump's social-media account owed as much to its prominence in legacy media as it did to its propensity to 'go viral' online". Persily, N. (2017). The 2016 U.S. Election: Can Democracy Survive the Internet? Journal of Democracy, Volume 28, Number 2, April 2017, pp. 63–76. Retrieved from https://muse.jhu.edu/article/653377
315. Wilson. J. (2008). "Will Newspapers Be First Against the Wall?" 13 May, 2008. Retrieved from *New Matilda* http://newmatilda.com/2008/05/13/when-revolution-comes
316. Quinn, B. (2020). Assange misses court hearing amid calls in Australia for his release. *The Guardian*. 1 June 2020. Retrieved from: https://www.theguardian.com/media/2020/jun/01/julian-assange-misses-court-hearing-amid-calls-in-australia-for-his-release
317. Australian Broadcasting Corporation. (2021). Julian Assange's extradition to the US rejected by UK court over mental health fears. 4 January 2021. Retrieved from: https://www.abc.net.au/news/2021-01-04/julian-assange-wont-be-extradited-to-the-us-uk-court-rules/13030240
318. Ignatius, D. (2019). Is Julian Assange a journalist, or is he just an accused thief? 12 April 2019. The Washington Post. Retrieved from: https://www.washingtonpost.com/opinions/is-julian-assange-a-journalist-or-is-he-just-an-accused-thief/2019/04/11/38afac3c-5c9c-11e9-9625-01d48d50ef75_story.html
319. Media Entertainment and Arts Alliance. (2020). Assange case 'an attack on truth': WikiLeaks editor. *Media Entertainment and Arts Alliance*. 24 February 2020. Retrieved from: https://www.meaa.org/news/assange-case-an-attack-on-truth-wikileaks-editor/
320. Singer, P. W., & Brooking, E.T. (2018). *Likewar: The Weaponization of Social Media*. Houghton, Miffler, Harcourt. Boston, NY. p. 3.
321. Singer, P. W., & Brooking, E.T. (2018). *Likewar: The Weaponization of Social Media*. Houghton, Miffler, Harcourt. Boston, NY. p. 14.
322. Von Clausewitz, C. (transl. J.J. Graham) (1874). *On War*. The Project Gutenberg EBook. Retrieved from: http://www.gutenberg.org/files/1946/1946-h/1946-h.htm
323. Von Clausewitz, C. (transl. J.J. Graham) (1874). *On War*. The Project Gutenberg EBook. Retrieved from: http://www.gutenberg.org/files/1946/1946-h/1946-h.htm p. 19.

324. Roe, I. (2020). Distrust, transparency issues blamed for democracy disengagement. PM. *ABC*. 7 February 2020. Retrieved from: https://www.abc.net.au/radio-australia/programs/pm/distrust,-transparency-issues-blamed-for-democracy-disengagement/11945204
325. Lee, A. M. (2015). Social Media and Speed-Driven Journalism: Expectations and Practices. *International Journal on Media Management: Social Media, the Digital Revolution, and the Business of Media*. 17(4). pp. 217–239. Retrieved from: https://doi.org/10.1080/14241277.2015.1107566
326. Australian Broadcasting Corporation. (2019). Reach and Share. ABC Annual Report 2018–2019. *Australian Broadcasting Corporation*. Retrieved from: https://www.transparency.gov.au/annual-reports/australian-broadcasting-corporation/reporting-year/2018-2019-30
327. Brevini, B. (2013). *Public Service Broadcasting Online: A Comparative European Policy Study of PSB 2.0*. Palgrave Macmillan. UK. p. 8.
328. Born, G. & Prosser, T. (2001). Culture and Consumerism: Citizenship, Public Service Broadcasting and the BBC's Fair Trading Obligations. *The Modern Law Review*. 64:5. September 2001. Retrieved from: https://onlinelibrary-wiley-com.wwwproxy1.library.unsw.edu.au/doi/pdfdirect/10.1111/1468-2230.00345 p. 658.
329. Open Society Institute. (2005). Television across Europe: regulation, policy and independence. 2. Monitoring Reports. Open Society Institute. Hungary & New York. Retrieved from: https://www.opensocietyfoundations.org/uploads/c2f2d8d6-3c2c-459a-b2b7-e397987d9236/voltwo_20051011_0.pdf quoting Blumler (2003) "The British approach to public service broadcasting", in Avery R. K. (Ed.) (1993). p. 3.
330. Burrowes, T. (2018). Charlie Pickering apologises for ABC New Year countdown 'kill a police officer' autocue blunder. *Mumbrella*. 1 January 2018. Retrieved 3 January 2020 from: https://mumbrella.com.au/presenter-charlie-pickering-apologises-kill-police-officer-autocue-blunder-491598
331. Burrowes, T. (2018). Charlie Pickering apologises for ABC New Year countdown 'kill a police officer' autocue blunder. *Mumbrella*. 1 January 2018. Retrieved from: https://mumbrella.com.au/presenter-charlie-pickering-apologises-kill-police-officer-autocue-blunder-491598
332. *News.com.au* (2018). Charlie Pickering says sorry for 'kill a police officer' gaffe. 1 January 2018. Retrieved 3 January 2020 from https://www.news.com.au/entertainment/tv/charlie-pickering-says-sorry-for-kill-a-police-officer-gaffe/news-story/a3415b2110377584ca71e9a083ba3829
333. Burrowes, T. (2018). Charlie Pickering apologises for ABC New Year countdown 'kill a police officer' autocue blunder. *Mumbrella*. 1 January 2018, Retrieved 3 January 2020 from: https://mumbrella.com.au/presenter-charlie-pickering-apologises-kill-police-officer-autocue-blunder-491598

334. *The Australian Financial Review.* (2019). Sydney's record-breaking $5.8 million fireworks display welcomes 2019. 1 January 2019. Retrieved from: https://www.afr.com/politics/sydneys-recordbreaking-58-million-fireworks-display-welcomes-2019-20190101-h19l95
335. Ibid.
336. Australian Broadcasting Corporation (2019). Sydney news: 'Hypocritical' Sydney fireworks condemned, plus Police Minister's traffic altercation review and the rise of the bin chicken. *ABC.* 14 November 2019. Retrieved from: https://www.abc.net.au/news/2019-11-14/sydney-fireworks-condemned-on-social-media/11702438
337. Ross, D. (2020a). Tex Perkins upsets viewers of ABC New Year's Eve performance. *The Australian.* 1 January 2020. Retrieved 2 January 2020 from: https://www.theaustralian.com.au/business/media/tex-perkins-upsets-viewers-of-abc-new-years-eve/news-story/4931060d16f89e4d805001eefa3b967b
338. Ross, D. (2020b). Maurice Newman demands ABC apologise over Tex Perkins obscene gesture at NY Eve performance. *The Australian.* 2 January 2020. Retrieved from: https://www.theaustralian.com.au/business/media/tex-perkins-upsets-viewers-of-abc-new-years-eve/news-story/4931060d16f89e4d805001eefa3b967b?fbclid=IwAR1VwTKDvN3FGbGzJVjUzUxgWBtF4ktC5cznayJisQAtXylsxAmo1Qhbo5Y
339. Ross, D. (2020b). Maurice Newman demands ABC apologise over Tex Perkins obscene gesture at NY Eve performance. *The Australian.* 2 January 2020. Retrieved from: https://www.theaustralian.com.au/business/media/tex-perkins-upsets-viewers-of-abc-new-years-eve/news-story/4931060d16f89e4d805001eefa3b967b?fbclid=IwAR1VwTKDvN3FGbGzJVjUzUxgWBtF4ktC5cznayJisQAtXylsxAmo1Qhbo5Y
340. Ross, D. (2020b). Maurice Newman demands ABC apologise over Tex Perkins obscene gesture at NY Eve performance. *The Australian.* 2 January 2020. Retrieved from: https://www.theaustralian.com.au/business/media/tex-perkins-upsets-viewers-of-abc-new-years-eve/news-story/4931060d16f89e4d805001eefa3b967b?fbclid=IwAR1VwTKDvN3FGbGzJVjUzUxgWBtF4ktC5cznayJisQAtXylsxAmo1Qhbo5Y
341. Ross, D. (2020b). Maurice Newman demands ABC apologise over Tex Perkins obscene gesture at NY Eve performance. *The Australian.* 2 January 2020. Retrieved from: https://www.theaustralian.com.au/business/media/tex-perkins-upsets-viewers-of-abc-new-years-eve/news-story/4931060d16f89e4d805001eefa3b967b?fbclid=IwAR1VwTKDvN3FGbGzJVjUzUxgWBtF4ktC5cznayJisQAtXylsxAmo1Qhbo5Y
342. Ross, D. (2020b). Maurice Newman demands ABC apologise over Tex Perkins obscene gesture at NY Eve performance. *The Australian.* 2 January 2020. Retrieved from: https://www.theaustralian.com.au/business/media/tex-perkins-upsets-viewers-of-abc-new-years-eve/news-story/4931060d16f89e4d805001eefa3b967b?fbclid=IwAR1VwTKDvN3FGbGzJVjUzUxgWBtF4ktC5cznayJisQAtXylsxAmo1Qhbo5Y

343. Fifth Estate, The. (2021). On the Australia Fires and what comes next. Environment. Our View. 16 January 2020. Retrieved from: https://www.thefifthestate.com.au/urbanism/environment/on-the-australia-fires-and-what-comes-next/
344. Bourgonje, P., Moreno-Schneider, J., Srivastava, A., & Rehm, B. G. (2018). Automatic Classification of Abusive Language and Personal Attacks in Various Forms of Online Communication. In (Eds.) G. Rehm and T. Declerck: Language Technology Lab. Berlin, Germany. Retrieved from: https://doi.org/10.1007/978-3-319-73706-5_15, pp. 180–191.
345. Sparks, G.G. (2013). *Media Effects Research: A Basic Overview*. 4th Edition. Wadsworth. Cengage Learning. Boston, MA.
346. Nicholson, P. (2016). Balance in redress: too slow? Too rule-bound? Too confusing to the public? The Scottish Legal Complaints Commission is consulting on whether to seek radical changes to its complaint handling procedures. *The Journal of the Law Society of Scotland*. 61:2. Retrieved from: https://primoa.library.unsw.edu.au/permalink/f/11jha62/TN_gale_legal446198366
347. Ceron, A. (2015). Internet, News, and Political Trust: The Difference Between Social Media and Online Media Outlets. *Journal of Computer-Mediated Communication*. 20:5. pp. 487–503. Retrieved from: https://doi.org/10.1111/jcc4.12129
348. Ceron, A. (2015). Internet, News, and Political Trust: The Difference Between Social Media and Online Media Outlets. *Journal of Computer-Mediated Communication*. 20:5. pp. 487–503. Retrieved from: https://doi.org/10.1111/jcc4.12129, p. 496.
349. Alvarez, P.C, Andujar, C.SdeB, Curiel, E.H, Serrano, N.L. (2012). Journalism and Social Media: How Spanish Journalists are Using Twitter. *Estudios Sobre el Mensaje Periodistico*. Madrid. 18:1. pp. 31–53. Retrieved from: https://doi.org/10.5209/revULESMP.2012.v18.n1.39353.
350. Kušen, E., Strembeck, M. & Conti, M. (2019). *Influence and Behavior Analysis in Social Networks and Social Media*. Eds. M. Kaya & R. Alhajj. Springer, 2019. ProQuest Ebook Central. Retrieved from: http://ebookcentral.proquest.com/lib/unsw/detail.action?docID=5613405.
351. Ceron, A. (2015). Internet, News, and Political Trust: The Difference Between Social Media and Online Media Outlets. *Journal of Computer-Mediated Communication*. 20:5. pp. 487–503. Retrieved from: https://doi.org/10.1111/jcc4.12129 Quoting Hilbert (2009).
352. Auger, G. (2013). Fostering democracy through social media: Evaluating diametrically opposed nonprofit advocacy organizations' use of Facebook, Twitter, and YouTube. *Public Relations Review*. 39. pp. 369–376. Retrieved from: https://doi.org/10.1016/j.pubrev.2013.07.013, p. 369.

353. Lumsden, K., & Harmer, E. (2019). *Online Othering: Exploring Digital Violence and Discrimination on the Web.* Cham: Springer International Publishing: Imprint: Palgrave Macmillan. Retrieved from: https://doi.org/10.1007/978-3-030-12633-9.
354. Machimbarrena, J. M., Calvete, E., Fernández-González, L., Álvarez-Bardón, A., Álvarez-Fernández, L., & González-Cabrera, J. (2018). Internet Risks: An Overview of Victimization in Cyberbullying, Cyber Dating Abuse, Sexting, Online Grooming and Problematic Internet Use. *International Journal of Environmental Research and Public Health.* 15:11. Retrieved from: https://doi.org/10.3390/ijerph15112471
355. Tonioni, F., D'Alessandris, L., Lai, C., Martinelli, D., Corvino, S., Vasale, M., Bria, P. (2012). Internet addiction: hours spent online, behaviors and psychological symptoms. *General Hospital Psychiatry.* 34:1. pp. 80–87. Retrieved from: https://doi.org/10.1016/j.genhosppsych.2011.09.013
356. Weinert, E. (2019). Host of Internet Forum Not Liable for Abuse Online—Status Quo But for How Much Longer? *Entertainment Law Review.* 30:5. pp. 162–163. Retrieved from: https://primoa.library.unsw.edu.au/permalink/f/11jha62/TN_gale_legal592533264
357. Scott, M. (2018). *On Us.* Melbourne University Press. Carlton, Victoria. p. 77.
358. Duke, J. (2020). ABC under 'growing' cost pressure as bushfire emergency broadcasts surge. *The Sydney Morning Herald.* 3 January 2020. Retrieved from: https://www.smh.com.au/business/companies/abc-under-growing-cost-pressure-as-bushfire-emergency-broadcasts-surge-20200103-p53ohp.html
359. Australian Broadcasting Corporation (2020). Millions of Australians welcome the new year on the ABC and donate to the Red Cross. *ABC.* 1 January 2020. Retrieved from: https://about.abc.net.au/press-releases/millions-of-australias-welcome-the-new-year-on-the-abc-and-support-bushfire-affected-communities/
360. Streitfeld, D. (2017). 'The Internet Is Broken': @ev Is Trying to Salvage It. *The New York Times.* 20 May 2017. Retrieved from: https://www.nytimes.com/2017/05/20/technology/evan-williams-medium-twitter-internet.html
361. Monk, P. (2016). Reason in Western civilisation. *Australian Rationalist.* 100. Autumn 2016: pp. 5–6. Retrieved from: https://primoa.library.unsw.edu.au/permalink/f/11jha62/TN_informit_agis20190613012326
362. Mitchell, C. (2019). Why our ABC should ignore Twitter. *The Australian.* Retrieved from: https://www.theaustralian.com.au/business/media/take-social-feed-with-pinch-of-salt/news-story/df00b4382e5e8192382d9778df8a2fc7

363. Stuever, H. (2018). Letterman sits down with Obama, but both men seem rusty and off their game. *The Washington Post.* 12 January 2018. Retrieved from: https://www.washingtonpost.com/entertainment/tv/letterman-sits-down-with-obama-but-both-men-seem-rusty-and-off-their-game/2018/01/11/2b6dc8c0-f70c-11e7-a9e3-ab18ce41436a_story.html
364. Arendt, H. (1978). Hannah Arendt: From an Interview. *The New York Review of Books.* 26 October, 1978. Retrieved from: https://www.nybooks.com/articles/1978/10/26/hannah-arendt-from-an-interview/
365. Arendt, H, (1968) *The Origins of Totalitarianism.* Harvest Book. Orlando. Citing, Ch. 13.
366. Kakutani, M. (2018). *The Death of Truth.* William Collins. London.
367. Cicero, M. T. (52BC). (Revised J. W. Parker 1847). *Pro Tito Annio Milone ad iudicem oratio* (*Pro Milone*). Speech on behalf of Titus Annius Milo. Retrieved from: https://babel.hathitrust.org/cgi/pt?id=hvd.hn632b&view=1up&seq=12
368. Guillot, C. (2013). The Wisdom of the Crowd. *Internal Auditor.* 1 October 2013. Retrieved from: http://search.proquest.com/docview/1464388029/
369. Shah, C. (2017). Social Information Seeking Leveraging the Wisdom of the Crowd. *The Information Retrieval Series.* 38. Springer, Cham, Switzerland. Retrieved from: https://primoa.library.unsw.edu.au/permalink/f/jhud33/UNSW_ALMA51227992500001731
370. Dickens, C. (1836). *Pickwick Papers.* The Project Gutenberg EBook 2016. Retrieved from: https://www.gutenberg.org/files/580/580-h/580-h.htm#link2HCH0032 Citing Ch. XXXII
371. Facebook is the biggest online social media platform. As of September 2016, the online social networking application Facebook registered more than 1.18 billion daily active users on average and 1.09 billion daily active users access the site via mobile devices, while 1.79 billion users access the site monthly and 1.66 billion users access the site monthly via mobile. Facebook reports that approximately 84.9% of daily active users are outside the US or Canada (Facebook Inc.: Company info: Facebook newsroom 2016).
372. Auletta, K. (2009). *Googled: The End of the World As We Know It.* Virgin Books, London. Citing p. 7.
373. Auletta, K. (2009). *Googled: The End of the World As We Know It.* Virgin Books, London. Citing p. xii.
374. Auletta, K. (2009). *Googled: The End of the World As We Know It.* Virgin Books, London. Citing p. 282.

375. Monk, S. (2019). Truth v. Fake News. *Southern Cross*. December 2019. Citing p. 20.
376. McLuhan, M. (1964). *Understanding Media: The Extension of Man*. Sphere Books, London. Citing p. 7.
377. McLuhan, M. (1964). *Understanding Media: The Extension of Man*. Sphere Books, London. Citing p. 6.
378. McLuhan, M. (1964). *Understanding Media: The Extension of Man*. Sphere Books, London. Citing p. 8.
379. Derrida, J. Ed. D. Cornell, M. Rosenfeld and Gray Carlson, D. (1992). *Deconstruction and the Possibility of Justice*. Derrida essay: "Mystical Foundation of Authority". Routledge. New York. Citing p. 64.
380. Derrida, J. Ed. D. Cornell, M. Rosenfeld and Gray Carlson, D. (1992). Deconstruction and the Possibility of Justice. Derrida essay: "Mystical Foundation of Authority". Routledge. New York. p. 64.
381. Australian Broadcasting Corporation Annual Report (2018). *ABC*. Retrieved from: https://about.abc.net.au/reports-publications/2017-18-annual-report/, p. 22.
382. Australian Broadcasting Corporation Annual Report (2019). *ABC*. Retrieved from: https://about.abc.net.au/wp-content/uploads/2019/10/ABC-Annual-Report-201819v2.pdf
383. Bromley, M. & Neal, R. (2009). "Farewell old friend or bye-bye bully boy? The closure of 'mediation' and challenging the 'free press' paradigm." *Media International Australia*. August 132. Retrieved from: https://www.researchgate.net/deref/http%3A%2F%2Fdx.doi.org%2F10.1177%2F1329878X0913200105, p. 29.
384. Australian Broadcasting Corporation Annual Report (2019). *ABC*. Retrieved from: https://about.abc.net.au/wp-content/uploads/2019/10/ABC-Annual-Report-201819v2.pdf, p. 118.
385. Australian Broadcasting Corporation Annual Report (2019). *ABC*. Retrieved from: https://about.abc.net.au/wp-content/uploads/2019/10/ABC-Annual-Report-201819v2.pdf, p. 123.
386. Schudson, M. (2008). *Why democracies need an unlovable press*. Polity Press. New York. Citing p. 45.
387. Schudson (2005). The Virtues of an Unlovable Press Intro. *Political Quarterly*. 2 August 2005. Supplement 1. Vol. 76. pp. 23–32. Retrieved from: https://doi.org/10.1111/j.1467-923X.2006.00745.x. Citing p. 23.
388. Cannane, S. (2017). After over 70 years in journalism and publishing, Sir Harry Evans is still irked by bad writing. Correspondents Report. 28 October 2017. *ABC News Online*. Retrieved from: https://www.abc.net.au/news/2017-10-28/does-writing-still-matter-in-the-digital-age/9091716

389. Baghramian, M. & Carter, J. A. (2015). Relativism. September 2015. *Stanford Encyclopedia of Philosophy.* Retrieved from: https://plato.stanford.edu/entries/relativism/
390. Saul, J.R. (1993). Voltaire's bastards: The Dictatorship of Reason in the West. Penguin Books. Camberwell, Victoria. p. 243.
391. Schudson, M. (2008). *Why democracies need an unlovable press.* Polity Press. New York. Citing p. 56, 57, 62.
392. Schudson (2005). The Virtues of an Unlovable Press" Intro. *Political Quarterly.* 2 August 2005. Supplement 1. Vol. 76. pp. 23–32. Retrieved from: https://doi.org/10.1111/j.1467-923X.2006.00745.x
393. Schwartz, J. (2008). The choice between Tweedledum and Tweedledee: Australian Media Coverage of The 2007 Federal Election Campaign. *Metro: Media & Education Magazine.* pp. 110–121. Retrieved from: https://search-informit-com-au.wwwproxy1.library.unsw.edu.au/documentSummary;dn=516965508581790;res=IELLCC
394. Schudson, M. (2008). *Why democracies need an unlovable press.* Polity Press. New York. Citing p. 41.
395. Nash, C. (2013). Journalism as a research discipline. *Pacific Journalism Review.* October 2013. 19:2. pp. 123–135. Retrieved from: https://primoa.library.unsw.edu.au/permalink/f/11jha62/TN_informit605741818647699
396. James Carey (1996) made a controversial speech in 1996 entitled: Where journalism education went wrong. Conference presentation Middle Tennessee State University. With responses by Jay Rosen, Linda Steiner and Ellen Wartella, [online] Retrieved from: https://lindadaniele.wordpress.com/2010/08/11/carey-where-journalism-education-went-wrong/ See later 'Some personal notes on US journalism education', 2000.
397. Windschuttle, K. (2000). The Poverty of Cultural Studies. *Journalism Studies.* 1:1. pp. 145–159. Retrieved from: https://doi.org/10.1080/146167000361221
398. Windschuttle, K. (2000). The Poverty of Cultural Studies. *Journalism Studies.* 1:1. pp. 145–159. Retrieved from: https://doi.org/10.1080/146167000361221, Citing p. 146.
399. Cunningham, S. & Bridgstock, R. (2012). Say Goodbye to the Fries: Graduate Careers in Media, Cultural and Communication Studies. *Media International Australia*, November 2012. 145:1. pp. 6–17. Retrieved from: https://primoa.library.unsw.edu.au/permalink/f/11jha62/TN_wos000312972100002
400. Ward, S. J. A. (2014). Radical Media Ethics: Ethics for a global digital world. *Digital Journalism. 2*:4. pp. 455–471. Retrieved from: https://doi.org/10.1080/21670811.2014.952985 Citing p. 469.
401. Stryker-Munson, E. & Warren, C. (1997). *James Carey: A Critical Reader.* University of Minnesota Press, Minneapolis.

402. Stryker-Munson, E. & Warren, C. (1997). *James Carey: A Critical Reader*. University of Minnesota Press, Minneapolis. p. 122.
403. Derrida, J. (1992). *Positions*. University of Chicago Press. Chicago. Citing p. 41
404. Anderson, N. & Schlunke, K. Eds. (2008). *Cultural Theory in Everyday Practice*. Oxford University Press. South Melbourne. Citing p. 55.
405. Anderson, N. & Schlunke, K. Eds. (2008). *Cultural Theory in Everyday Practice*. Oxford University Press. South Melbourne. Citing p. 55.
406. Derrida, J. (1998) *Of Grammatology*. (Trans. Spivak, G. C. First published 1967). John Hopkins University Press. Baltimore.
407. Dodd, A., Pasandaran, C.C., Green, S., Octavianto, A.W. & Mardjianto F.X.L.D. Proyek Sepaham. (2017). An Experiment in Crosscultural and Collaborative Journalism Education. *Asia Pacific Media Educator*. 27:1. pp. 67–84. Retrieved from: https://doi.org/10.1177/1326365X17701790. Citing p. 68.
408. Coady, C.A.J. (2008). *ABC Editorial Policies: Short looks at some big concepts that govern the ABC*. Australian Broadcasting Corporation. March 2008. p. 2. Retrieved from: http://about.abc.net.au/wp-content/uploads/2012/06/KeyWordsMarch2008.pdf
409. Cokley, J. & Ranke, A. (2011) "There's a 'long tail' in Journalism Education, too." *Journalism Education, Training and Employment*. B. Franklin & Mensing, D. Routledge. New York.
410. Paletz, D.L. & Entman, R.M. (1981). *Media Power Politics*. Free Press. New York. Citing p. 184.
411. Paletz, D.L. & Entman, R.M. (1981). *Media Power Politics*. Free Press. New York. Citing p. 194.
412. Entman, R. M. (2004). *Projections of power: Framing news, public opinion, and U.S. foreign policy*. University of Chicago Press. Chicago. p. 838–839.
413. Vosoughi, S., Roy, D. & Aral, S. (2018). The spread of true and false news online. *Science*. 359:6380. pp. 1446–1151. Retrieved from: https://doi.org/10.1126/science.aap9559
414. Vosoughi, S., Roy, D. & Aral, S. (2018). The spread of true and false news online. *Science*. 359:6380. pp. 1446–1151. Retrieved from: https://doi.org/10.1126/science.aap9559, p. 1146.
415. Stieglitz, S. & Dang-Xuan, L. (2013). Emotions and Information Diffusion in Social Media—Sentiment of Microblogs and Sharing Behavior. *Journal of Management Information Systems*. 29:4. pp. 217–248. Retrieved from: https://doi.org/10.2753/MIS0742-1222290408
416. Murphy, J., Link, M. W., Childs, J. H., Tesfaye, C. L., Dean, E., Stern, M., Pasek, J., Cohen, J., Callegaro, M., & Harwood, P. (2014). Social Media in Public Opinion Research. *Public Opinion Quarterly*. 78:4. pp. 788–794. Retrieved from: https://doi.org/10.1093/poq/nfu053

417. Lazer, D.M.J., Baum, M.A., Benkler, Y., Berinsky, A.J., Greenhill, K. M., Menczer, F., Metzger, M., Nyhan, B., Pennycook, G., Rothschild, D., Schudson, M., Sloman, S.A., Sunstein, C.R., Thorson E.A., Watts, D.J., Zittrain, J.L. (2018). The science of fake news. *Science*. 359:6380. pp. 1094–1096. Retrieved from: https://doi.org/10.1126/science.aao2998
418. Orwell, G. (1949). *1984*. Secker & Warburg. London.
419. Shah, C. (2017). Social Information Seeking Leveraging the Wisdom of the Crowd. *The Information Retrieval Series*. 38. Springer, Cham, Switzerland. Retrieved from: https://primoa.library.unsw.edu.au/permalink/f/jhud33/UNSW_ALMA51227992500001731
420. Blease, C. (2015). Too Many 'Friends,' Too Few 'Likes'? Evolutionary Psychology and 'Facebook Depression'. *Review of General Psychology*. 19. pp. 1–13. Retrieved from: https://doi.org/10.1037/gpr0000030
421. Jelenchick, L. A., Eickhoff, J. C., & Moreno, M. A. (2013). "Facebook depression?" social networking site use and depression in older adolescents. *The Journal of Adolescent Health : Official Publication of the Society for Adolescent Medicine*. 52:1. pp. 128–130. Retrieved from: https://doi.org/10.1016/j.jadohealth.2012.05.008
422. Miragliotta N., Errington W. (2012). The Rise and Fall and Rise Again of Public Broadcasting? The Case of the Australian Broadcasting Corporation. *Australian Journal of Public Administration*. 71:1. pp. 55–64. Retrieved from: https://doi.org/10.1111/j.1467-8500.2012.00755.x. Citing p. 59.
423. Watson, D. (2014). The conservative crusade against the *ABC*. *The Monthly*. March 2014. Retrieved from: https://www.themonthly.com.au/issue/2014/march/1393592400/don-watson/conservative-crusade-against-abc#mtr
424. Burns, M., & Hawkins, G. (2013). Investigating Public Service Media as Hybrid Arrangements. *Media International Australia*. 146:1. pp. 79–81. Retrieved from: https://doi.org/10.1177/1329878X1314600111
425. Miragliotta N., Errington W. (2012). The Rise and Fall and Rise Again of Public Broadcasting? The Case of the Australian Broadcasting Corporation. *Australian Journal of Public Administration*. 71:1. pp. 55–64. p. 59. Retrieved from: https://doi.org/10.1111/j.1467-8500.2012.00755.x Citing p. 56 & 60.
426. *Radio Info*. (2016). Top 20 percent of ABC staff paid $124 million: *Senate Estimates*. 22 July 2017. Retrieved from: https://www.radioinfo.com.au/news/top-20-percent-abc-staff-paid-124-million-senate-estimates
427. *Radio Info*. (2016). Top 20 percent of ABC staff paid $124 million: Senate Estimates. 22 July 2017. Retrieved from: https://www.radioinfo.com.au/news/top-20-percent-abc-staff-paid-124-million-senate-estimates

428. Hermida, A. (2012). Tweets and Truth: Journalism as a discipline of Collaborative verification. *Journalism Practice.* 6:5–6. pp. 659–668. Retrieved from: https://doi.org/10.1080/17512786.2012.667269
429. Australian Broadcasting Corporation Media Centre. (2010). New Social Media Reporter for ABC News In Canberra. 13 December 2010. Retrieved from: http://about.abc.net.au/press-releases/new-social-media-reporter-for-abc-news-in-canberra/
430. Bruns, A. (2012). Journalists and twitter: How Australian news organisations adapt to a new medium. *Media International Australia, Incorporating Culture & Policy.* 144. pp. 97–107. Retrieved from: https://primoa.library.unsw.edu.au/permalink/f/11jha62/TN_scopus2-s2.0-84864412059, Citing p. 100.
431. Bennet and Livingston, in Creech, B. & Roessner, A. (2018). Declaring the Value of Truth. *Journalism Practice.* pp. 263–279. Retrieved from: https://doi.org/10.1080/17512786.2018.1472526, Citing p. 276.
432. Bourdieu (2003) said: "the researcher, artist or writer ... becomes an intellectual, that is, someone who engages his specific authority and the values associated with the exercise and his or her craft, such as the values of disinterestedness and truth, in a political struggle—in other words someone who enters the terrain of politics but without forsaking her exigencies and competencies as a researcher" (Ibid.).
433. Rogstad, I. D. (2014). Political News Journalists in Social Media: Transforming political reporters into political pundits? *Journalism Practice.* Vol. 8:6. Pages 688–703. Retrieved from: https://doi.org/10.1080/17512786.2013.865965 Citing p. 689.
434. Ibid., p. 689.
435. Rogstad, I. D. (2014). Political News Journalists in Social Media: Transforming political reporters into political pundits? *Journalism Practice.* Vol. 8:6. Pages 688–703. Retrieved from: https://doi.org/10.1080/17512786.2013.865965. Citing p. 691.
436. Ibid., Citing, p. 692.
437. Australian Broadcasting Corporation. (2014). Dawn of Double J. 30 April 2014. Retrieved from: http://about.abc.net.au/2014/04/dawn-of-double-j/
438. Bourdieu, P. (1984). *Distinction: A Social Critique of the Judgement of Taste.* Transl. R. Nice. Harvard University Press, Cambridge Massachusetts. Citing p. 22.
439. Bourdieu, P. (1984). *Distinction: A Social Critique of the Judgement of Taste.* Transl. R. Nice. Harvard University Press, Cambridge Massachusetts. Citing. p. 18
440. Scott, M. (2009). Commonwealth Broadcasting Association Lecture 2009. 9 September 2009. In M. Scott. *A Media Odyssey: Speeches of an ABC Managing Director 2006–2016.* (2016). ABC. Sydney. Citing p. 153.

441. Wallach, B. (2005). *Understanding the Cultural Landscape.* The Guilford Press. New York, London. Citing p. 121.
442. Greer, A. (2012). Commons and Enclosure in the Colonization of North America. *The American Historical Review.* 117:2. pp. 365–386. Retrieved from: https://doi.org/10.1086/ahr.117.2.365. Citing p. 368.
443. Retrieved from: https://media.twitter.com/en_us/articles/best-practice/2018/how-journalists-can-best-engage-with-their-audience.html
444. Robinson, E. (2016). Why journalists love Twitter—Tweets make lazy political journalism easier than ever. *Current Affairs.* 30 December 2016. Retrieved from: https://www.currentaffairs.org/2016/11/why-journalists-love-twitter
445. Ibid.
446. Ibid.
447. Retrieved from: https://www.internetlivestats.com/twitter-statistics/#rate
448. Kamps, H.J. (2015). Who Are Twitter's Verified Users? *Medium.* Retrieved from: https://medium.com/@Haje/who-are-twitter-s-verified-users-af976fc1b032
449. Manjoo, F. (2019). Never tweet. 23 January 2019. *The New York Times.* Retrieved from: https://www.nytimes.com/2019/01/23/opinion/covington-twitter.html
450. Gillin, J. (2013). Bill Adair: Fact-checking 'is a good investment'. 8 April, 2013. *The Poynter Institute.* Retrieved from: https://www.poynter.org/reporting-editing/2013/bill-adair-fact-checking-is-a-good-investment/
451. Adair described this as: "We are doing thorough reporting and then drawing a conclusion on whether something is true, false or somewhere between" Gillin, J. (2013). Bill Adair: Fact-checking 'is a good investment'. 8 April, 2013. Retrieved 2 February 2020 from https://www.poynter.org/reporting-editing/2013/bill-adair-fact-checking-is-a-good-investment/
452. Rashkin, H., Choi, E., Jang, J.Y., Volkova, S., Choi, Y. (2017). Truth of Varying Shades: Analyzing Language in Fake News and Political Fact-Checking. Proceedings of the 2017 Conference on Empirical Methods in Natural Language Processing. Pp. 2931–2937. Copenhagen, Denmark, September 7–11, 2017. Retrieved from: https://www.aclweb.org/anthology/D17-1317/
453. Nyhan, B., Reifler, J. (2015). The Effect of Fact-Checking on Elites: A 'field' Experiment on U.S. State Legislators. *American Journal of Political Science.* 59:3. July 2015. pp. 628–640. Retrieved from: https://ore.exeter.ac.uk/repository/bitstream/handle/10871/21568/Nyhan%20Reifler%20AJPS.pdf?sequence=1

454. Uscinski, J.E. & Butler, R.W. (2013). The Epistemology of Fact Checking. *Critical Review—A Journal of Politics and Society.* 25:2. pp. 162–180. Retrieved from: https://www.tandfonline.com/doi/abs/10.1080/08913811.2013.843872
455. Hassan, N., Adair, B., Hamilton, J. T., Li, C., Tremayne, M., Yang, J., & Yu, C. (2015, July). The quest to automate fact-checking. In Proceedings of the 2015 *Computation + Journalism Symposium.* Retrieved from: http://ranger.uta.edu/~cli/pubs/2015/claimbuster-cj15-hassan.pdf
456. Russell, F.M., Hendricks, M.A., Choi, H., Stephens, E.C. (2015). Who Sets the News Agenda on Twitter? Journalists' posts during the 2013 US government shutdown. *Digital Journalism.* 3:6. pp. 925–943. Retrieved from: https://doi.org/10.1080/21670811.2014.995918.
457. Ibid.
458. Bolt, A. (2018). "I Agree': Paul Barry Admits the ABC Is Biased. Quoting Chas Licciardello, *Outsiders, Sky News.* 18 June, 2018. Retrieved from: https://www.heraldsun.com.au/blogs/andrew-bolt/i-agree-paul-barry-admits-the-abc-is-biased/news-story/7afa1bfe14cb3b119891d7b02aed0b46
459. Ibid.
460. Henderson, G. (2018). Michelle Guthrie needs a fact checker; Barrie Cassidy's mea culpa. *The Australian.* 6 August 2018. Retrieved from: https://www.theaustralian.com.au/business/media/michelle-guthrie-needs-a-fact-checker-barrie-cassidys-mea-cuple/news-story/a5d429bb48fd7b4380baa2e442732fcc
461. Calcutt, L. (2018). ABC will never be sold. *Ninenews.com.* 18 June 2018. Retrieved from: https://www.9news.com.au/national/malcolm-turnbull-rules-out-privatising-abc-after-liberal-conference-vote/7220faa9-ebf1-4961-be43-e0ddd32a0afb
462. Ibid.
463. Inglis, K.S. (2006). *Whose ABC? The Australian Broadcasting Corporation 1983–2006.* Black Inc. Melbourne. Citing p. 434.
464. Gordon, J, (2013). State Liberals propose privatising ABC, SBS. *The Sydney Morning Herald.* 22 May 2013. Retrieved from: https://www.smh.com.au/politics/federal/state-liberals-propose-privatising-abc-sbs-20130521-2jz5d.html
465. Norman, J. (2018). Liberal Party members vote to privatise ABC and move Australia's Israel embassy to Jerusalem. *ABC Online.* 16 Jun 2018. Retrieved from: https://www.abc.net.au/news/2018-06-16/liberal-members-vote-to-privatise-abc-move-embassy-to-jerusalem/9877524
466. Special Broadcasting Service. (2018). Liberals to again debate selling the ABC. SBS. 4 October 2018. Retrieved from: https://www.sbs.com.au/news/liberals-to-again-debate-selling-the-abc

467. Lallo, M. (2019). Nine Network tops 2019 ratings ending Seven's 12-year winning streak. *The Sydney Morning Herald*. 1 December 2019. Retrieved from: https://www.smh.com.au/culture/tv-and-radio/nine-network-tops-2019-ratings-ending-seven-s-12-year-winning-streak-20191129-p53fd3.html
468. Lallo, M. (2018). Most-watched programs of 2018 revealed. *The Sydney Morning Herald*. 2 December 2018. Retrieved from: https://www.smh.com.au/entertainment/tv-and-radio/most-watched-programs-of-2018-revealed-20181130-p50jdk.html
469. Lallo, M. (2019). Ibid.
470. Mackay, H. (2010). *What Makes Us Tick? The Ten Desires That Drive Us*. Hachette. Sydney. pp. 247–248.
471. Ibid., p. 248
472. Johnson, T. J. Ed. (2014). *Agenda Setting in a 2.0 World: New Agendas in Communication*. Routledge. New York and London.
473. Yang, X., Chen, B.-C., Maity, M., & Ferrara, E. (2016). Social Politics: Agenda Setting and Political Communication on Social Media. *arXiv.org*. 10046. pp. 330–344. Retrieved from: https://doi.org/10.1007/978-3-319-47880-7_20
474. Lin, X., Spence, P. & Lachlan, K. (2016). Social media and credibility indicators: The effect of influence cues. *Computers in Human Behavior*. 63. pp. 264–271. Retrieved from: https://doi.org/10.1016/j.chb.2016.05.002 Citing: p. 265.
475. Pentina, I. & Tarafdar, M. (2014). From "information" to "knowing": Exploring the role of social media in contemporary news consumption. *Computers in Human Behavior*. 35. pp. 221–223. Retrieved from: https://doi.org/10.1016/j.chb.2014.02.045
476. *Pew Research Centre*. (2012). Millennials Confident. Connected. Open to Change. Retrieved from: https://www.pewresearch.org/wp-content/uploads/sites/3/2010/10/millennials-confident-connected-open-to-change.pdf
477. *Pew Research Center's Project for Excellence in Journalism*. (2012). The State of the New Media 2012: An Annual Report on American Journalism. Retrieved from: https://www.pewresearch.org/wp-content/uploads/sites/8/2017/05/State-of-the-News-Media-Report-2012-FINAL.pdf
478. Ibid.
479. Ibid.
480. Inglis, K. (2006). *Whose ABC? The Australian Broadcasting Corporation 1983–2006*. Black Inc. Melbourne. p. 295.
481. Australian Broadcasting Corporation. (2020). *Election Coverage Review Committee (ECRC)*. Retrieved from: https://about.abc.net.au/how-the-abc-is-run/what-guides-us/election-coverage-review-committee-ecrc/

482. Australian Broadcasting Corporation (1998, 16 September): MD expresses full confidence in fair and reliable coverage. (1998, 16 September). *M2 Presswire.* Retrieved from: http://www.m2.com/m2/web/publication.php/nbr
483. Styles, A. (2016). Federal election 2016: ABC wins election night coverage despite Leigh Sales' 'delirium'. *The Sydney Morning Herald.* 3 July 2016. Retrieved from: https://www.smh.com.au/entertainment/tv-and-radio/federal-election-2016-abc-wins-election-night-coverage-despite-leigh-sales-delirium-20160703-gpxlti.html
484. Anderson, D. (2019). ABC Annual Report 2019. *ABC.* Retrieved from: https://about.abc.net.au/wp-content/uploads/2019/10/ABC-Annual-Report-201819v2.pdf
485. Carson, A., Martin, A.J. & Ratcliff, S. (2020). Negative campaigning, issue salience and vote choice: assessing the effects of the Australian Labor party's 2016 "Mediscare" campaign. *Journal of Elections, Public Opinion and Parties.* 30:1. pp. 83–104. Retrieved from: https://doi.org/10.1080/17457289.2018.1563093
486. Sunderland, A. (2016). 2016 ABC Federal Election Report of the Chairman, Election Coverage Review Committee. *ABC.* 14 July 2016. Retrieved from: http://about.abc.net.au/wp-content/uploads/2016/11/2016FederalElectionECRCRPT.pdf
487. Sunderland, A. (2016). 2016 ABC Federal Election. Report of the Chairman, Election Coverage Review Committee. *ABC.* 14 July 2016. Retrieved from: http://about.abc.net.au/wp-content/uploads/2016/11/2016FederalElectionECRCRPT.pdf
488. Sunderland, A. (2016). 2016 ABC Federal Election. Report of the Chairman, Election Coverage Review Committee. *ABC.* 14 July 2016. Retrieved from: http://about.abc.net.au/wp-content/uploads/2016/11/2016FederalElectionECRCRPT.pdf
489. Styles, A. (2016). Federal election 2016: ABC wins election night coverage despite Leigh Sales' 'delirium'. *The Sydney Morning Herald.* 3 July 2016. Retrieved from: https://www.smh.com.au/entertainment/tv-and-radio/federal-election-2016-abc-wins-election-night-coverage-despite-leigh-sales-delirium-20160703-gpxlti.html
490. Lawson, K. (2019). Election 2019: why the opinion polls were always wrong. *The Canberra Times.* 20 May 2019, 2019. Retrieved from: https://www.canberratimes.com.au/story/6132185/why-the-opinion-polls-were-always-wrong-and-how-we-should-have-spotted-it/
491. Prosser Scully, R. (2019). How did pollsters get the Australian election result so wrong? *New Scientist.* 20 May 2019. Retrieved from: https://www.newscientist.com/article/2203837-how-did-pollsters-get-the-australian-election-result-so-wrong/#ixzz6IKLZ24Mq

492. Jo Nova. (2019). Australia votes 2019: Shock! Climate action bombs. Pollsters crash. Skeptics Win. *Joanne Nova*. Blog. Retrieved from: http://joannenova.com.au/2019/05/it-was-a-climate-election-and-the-skeptics-won-australia-2019/
493. Jo Nova. (2019). Australia votes 2019: Shock! Climate action bombs. Pollsters crash. Skeptics Win. Blog. *Joanne Nova*. Retrieved from: http://joannenova.com.au/2019/05/it-was-a-climate-election-and-the-skeptics-won-australia-2019/
494. Inglis, K. (2006). *Whose ABC? The Australian Broadcasting Corporation 1983–2006*. Black Inc. Melbourne. Citing p. 294.
495. Burrowes, T. (2019). ABC wins the election ratings while Ten slumps to 3.6%. *Mumbrella*. 19 May 2019. Retrieved from: https://mumbrella.com.au/abc-wins-the-election-ratings-while-ten-slumps-to-3-6-580222
496. Visontay, E. (2019). 'Where's their work?' *The Australian*. 15 May 2019. Retrieved from: https://www.theaustralian.com.au/nation/politics/federal-election-2019-campaign-day-35-scott-morrison-bill-shorten-hunt-for-votes/news-story/f0e7301ad5f058fec20a72fd6d9d1264
497. Also reported by Meade, A. (2019). ABC managing director rejects accusations he is making funding an election issue. *The Guardian*. 8 May 2019. Retrieved from: https://www.theguardian.com/media/2019/may/08/abc-managing-director-rejects-accusations-he-is-making-funding-an-election-issue
498. Meade, A. (2019). ABC managing director rejects accusations he is making funding an election issue. *The Guardian*. 8 May 2019. Retrieved 1 April 2020 from: https://www.theguardian.com/media/2019/may/08/abc-managing-director-rejects-accusations-he-is-making-funding-an-election-issue
499. Muller, D. (2019). Outrage, polls and bias: 2019 federal election showed Australian media need better regulation. Opinion. *Mumbrella*. 22 May 2019. Retrieved from: https://mumbrella.com.au/outrage-polls-and-bias-2019-federal-election-showed-australian-media-need-better-regulation-580713 Comment by Jennifer 27 May 19.
500. Mitchell, C. (2019). ABC gave us groupthink on steroids. *The Australian*. 27 May 2019. Retrieved from: https://www.theaustralian.com.au/commentary/abc-gave-us-groupthink-on-steroids/news-story/da95e8a9d851509bf8538df28c630c15
501. Mitchell, C. (2019). ABC gave us groupthink on steroids. *The Australian*. 27 May 2019. Retrieved from: https://www.theaustralian.com.au/commentary/abc-gave-us-groupthink-on-steroids/news-story/da95e8a9d851509bf8538df28c630c15
502. Mitchell, C. (2019). ABC gave us groupthink on steroids. *The Australian*. 27 May 2019. Retrieved from: https://www.theaustralian.com.au/commentary/abc-gave-us-groupthink-on-steroids/news-story/da95e8a9d851509bf8538df28c630c15

503. Crikey. (2019). Ita Buttrose picks a side—and it isn't the ABC's. Tips and Rumours. *Crikey.com.* 30 May 2019. Retrieved from: https://www.crikey.com.au/2019/05/30/tips-ita-buttrose-abc/
504. Crikey. (2019). Ita Buttrose picks a side—and it isn't the ABC's. Tips and Rumours. *Crikey.com.* 30 May 2019. Retrieved from: https://www.crikey.com.au/2019/05/30/tips-ita-buttrose-abc/
505. NewsMail (2018). ABC goes to war with The Chaser boys. 24 November 2018. *News Mail.* Retrieved from: https://www.news-mail.com.au/news/abc-executive-criticises-chaser-after-satirists-co/3584319/
506. Zineldin, M. & Hytter, A. (2012). Leaders' negative emotions and leadership styles influencing subordinates' well-being, *The International Journal of Human Resource Management.* 23:4. pp. 748–758. Retrieved from: https://doi.org/10.1080/09585192.2011.606114
507. Zineldin, M. & Hytter, A. (2012). Leaders' negative emotions and leadership styles influencing subordinates' well-being. *The International Journal of Human Resource Management.* 23:4. pp. 748–758. Retrieved from: https://doi.org/10.1080/09585192.2011.606114
508. Shani, G. & Westphal, J.D. (2016). Persona Non Grata? Determinants and Consequences of Social Distancing From Journalists Who Engage in Negative Coverage of Firm Leadership. *Academy of Management Journal.* 2016. 59:1. pp. 302–329. Retrieved from: https://doi.org/10.5465/amj.2013.1162
509. Shani, G. & Westphal, J.D. (2016). Persona Non Grata? Determinants and Consequences of Social Distancing From Journalists Who Engage in Negative Coverage of Firm Leadership. *Academy of Management Journal.* 2016. 59:1. pp. 302–329. Retrieved from: https://doi.org/10.5465/amj.2013.1162
510. Shani, G. & Westphal, J.D. (2016). Persona Non Grata? Determinants and Consequences of Social Distancing From Journalists Who Engage in Negative Coverage of Firm Leadership. *Academy of Management Journal* 2016. 59:1. pp. 302–329. Retrieved from: https://doi.org/10.5465/amj.2013.1162
511. Shani, G. & Westphal, J.D. (2016). Persona Non Grata? Determinants and Consequences of Social Distancing From Journalists Who Engage in Negative Coverage of Firm Leadership. *Academy of Management Journal* 2016. 59:1. pp. 302–329. Retrieved from: https://doi.org/10.5465/amj.2013.1162
512. Shani, G. & Westphal, J.D. (2016). Persona Non Grata? Determinants and Consequences of Social Distancing From Journalists Who Engage in Negative Coverage of Firm Leadership. *Academy of Management Journal* 2016. 59:1. pp. 302–329. Retrieved from: https://doi.org/10.5465/amj.2013.1162, pp. 318–319.

513. George, G., Dahlander, L., Graffin, S., & Sim, S. (2016). Reputation and Status: Expanding the Role of Social Evaluations in Management Research. *Academy of Management Journal. 59*:1. pp. 1–13. Retrieved from: https://doi.org/10.5465/amj.2016.4001
514. Johnson,R.,Venus,M.,Lanaj,K.,Mao,C.,Chang,C.,&Johnson,R.(2012). Leader identity as an antecedent of the frequency and consistency of transformational, consideration, and abusive leadership behaviors. *The Journal of Applied Psychology.* 97:6. pp. 1262–1272. Retrieved from: https://doi.org/10.1037/a0029043
515. Yukl, G. (2010, republished). *Leadership in Organisations.* 7th Edition. Pearson, US. Citing p. 205.
516. Yukl, G. (2010, republished). *Leadership in Organisations.* 7th Edition. Pearson, US. Citing p. 21.
517. Yukl, G. (2010, republished). *Leadership in Organisations.* 7th Edition. Pearson, US. Citing p. 206.
518. Dandira, M. (2012). Dysfunctional leadership: organizational cancer. *Business Strategy Series.* 13:4. pp. 187–192. Retrieved from: https://doi.org/10.1108/17515631211246267
519. Anderson, D. (2019). ABC Annual Report 2019. *ABC.* Retrieved from: https://about.abc.net.au/wp-content/uploads/2019/10/ABC-Annual-Report-201819v2.pdf
520. Anderson, D. (2019). ABC Annual Report 2019. *ABC.* Retrieved from: https://about.abc.net.au/wp-content/uploads/2019/10/ABC-Annual-Report-201819v2.pdf
521. McMahon, N. (2016). Federal election 2016: 'Suck on that Kerry O'Brien': Leigh Sales' joke caps off a bizarre night of election TV. *The Sydney Morning Herald.* 3 July 2016. Retrieved from: https://www.smh.com.au/politics/federal/suck-on-that-kerry-obrien-leigh-sales-joke-caps-off-a-bizarre-night-of-election-tv-20160703-gpx91t.html

References

ABC. (2018, June). *The Cost of Being the ABC: Delivering the Best and Most Efficient Public Broadcasting.* http://www.abc.net.au/cm/lb/9944818/data/the-cost-of-being-the-abc-data.pdf

ABC. (2020, April). *Interview ABC News24. Strapline: "Pell Released. George Pell Freed from Prison After High Court ruling".* https://www.youtube.com/watch?v=7x29VznAZOE

ABC MediaWatch. (2018, February 19). Taxing Times. *ABC.* https://www.abc.net.au/mediawatch/episodes/taxing-times-at-the-abc/9972348

Abdel-Magied, Y. (2017). What are they so afraid of? I'm just a young brown Muslim woman speaking my mind. The Guardian. 6 July 2017. Retrieved from:

https://www.theguardian.com/australia-news/2017/jul/06/what-are-they-so-afraid-of-im-just-a-young-brown-muslim-woman-speaking-my-mind

Accetti, C. I., Mulieri, A., Buchstein, H., Castiglione, D., Disch, L., Frank, J., & Urbinati, N. (2016). Debating Representative Democracy. *Contemporary Political Theory, 15*(2), 205–242. https://doi.org/10.1057/cpt.2015.57

Alberici, E. (2018). Why Many Big Companies Don't Pay Corporate Tax. *Australian Broadcasting Corporation.* Posted 14 February 2018. Retrieved February 16, 2018, from https://www.abc.net.au/news/2018-02-14/why-many-big-companies-dont-pay-corporate-tax/9443840

Altheide, D. & Schneider, C. (2013). Process of qualitative document analysis. In D. Altheide & C. Schneider. Qualitative Media Analysis. Pp. 38–74. SAGE Publications. London. Retrieved from: https://doi.org/10.4135/9781452270043, p. 41.

Alvarez, P. C., Andujar, C. S. D. B., Curiel, E. H., & Serrano, N. L. (2012). Journalism and Social Media: How Spanish Journalists are Using Twitter. *Estudios Sobre el Mensaje Periodistico, 18*(1), 31–53. https://doi.org/10.5209/revULESMP.2012.v18.n1.39353

Anderson, B. (1983). *Imagined Communities: Reflections on the Origin and Spread of Nationalism.* Verso.

Anderson, D. (2019). ABC Annual Report 2019. *ABC.*https://about.abc.net.au/wp-content/uploads/2019/10/ABC-Annual-Report-201819v2.pdf

Anderson, N., & Schlunke, K. E. (2008). *Cultural Theory in Everyday Practice.* Oxford University Press.

Andrejevic, M. (2013). Public Service Media Utilities: Rethinking Search Engines and Social Networking as Public Goods. *Media International Australia, Incorporating Culture & Policy, 146*, 123–132. http://web.a.ebscohost.com.wwwproxy1.library.unsw.edu.au/ehost/pdfviewer/pdfviewer?vid=2&sid=68647279-624f-4ba5-9fda-d25caae82e74%40sdc-v-sessmgr02

Arendt, H. (1968). *The Origins of Totalitarianism.* Harvest Book.

Aufderheide, P., Boyles, J. L., & Bieze, K. (2013). Copyright, Free Speech, and The Public's Right to Know. *Journalism Studies, 14*(6), 875–890. https://doi.org/10.1080/1461670X.2012.739320

Auger, G. (2013). Fostering Democracy Through Social Media: Evaluating Diametrically Opposed Nonprofit Advocacy Organizations' Use of Facebook, Twitter, and YouTube. *Public Relations Review, 39*, 369–376. https://doi.org/10.1016/j.pubrev.2013.07.013

Auletta, K. (2009). *Googled: The End of the World As We Know It.* Virgin Books.

Australian Broadcasting Corporation. (2021, January 4). Julian Assange's Extradition to the US Rejected by UK Court Over Mental Health Fears. https://www.abc.net.au/news/2021-01-04/julian-assange-wont-be-extradited-to-the-us-uk-court-rules/13030240

Australian Broadcasting Corporation Annual Report. (2018). *ABC.* https://about.abc.net.au/reports-publications/2017-18-annual-report/

Australian Broadcasting Corporation Annual Report. (2019). *ABC.* https://about.abc.net.au/wp-content/uploads/2019/10/ABC-Annual-Report-201819v2.pdf

Australian Communications and Media Authority. (2020). 2019 Investigations. https://www.acma.gov.au/investigations-tv-broadcasters#outcome-of-our-2019-investigations

Australian Financial Review, The. (2019, January 1). Sydney's Record-Breaking $5.8 Million Fireworks Display Welcomes 2019. https://www.afr.com/politics/sydneys-recordbreaking-58-million-fireworks-display-welcomes-2019-20190101-h19l95

Australian, The. (2020, February 11). Editorial. Time to End Free Lunch for Google and Facebook. *The Australian.* https://www.theaustralian.com.au/commentary/editorials/time-to-end-free-lunch-for-google-and-facebook/news-story/f84c88b4dd86f54b5cc4397ba07d9cc7

Australian Broadcasting Corporation. (2021). Personal Use of Social Media Guidelines. ABC People and Culture. March 2021. Retrieved from: https://about.abc.net.au/wp-content/uploads/2021/03/Final-Personal-use-social-media-guidelines.pdf

Australian Broadcasting Corporation. (2017). ABC Social Media Policy. Retrieved from: https://about.abc.net.au/wp-content/uploads/2017/05/SocialMedia POL.pdf Note: now a dead link.

Australian Strategic Policy Institute (2020). Covid-19 Disinformation & Social Media Manipulation. 27 October 2020. Retrieved from: https://www.aspi.org.au/report/covid-19-disinformation

Australian Broadcasting Corporation Media Centre. (2010). New Social Media Reporter for ABC News In Canberra. 13 December 2010. Retrieved from: http://about.abc.net.au/press-releases/new-social-media-reporter-for-abc-news-in-canberra/ Please note: Link removed.

Baghramian, M., & Carter, J. A. (2015. September). Relativism. *Stanford Encyclopedia of Philosophy.* https://plato.stanford.edu/entries/relativism/

Bandler, J., & Merzon, A. (2020). Cybercrime investigations: the comprehensive resource for everyone (1st ed.). CRC Press. Taylor and Francis Group. Boca Raton, FL.

Banet-Weiser, S. (2012). Authentic(tm): The Politics of Ambivalence in a Brand Culture, New York University Press. ProQuest Ebook Central. https://ebookcentral.proquest.com/lib/unsw/detail.action?docID=865546.

Beaglehole, P. (2018). What Matters?: Talking Value in Australian Culture. *Transnational Literature, 11*(1). http://search.proquest.com/docview/2164085415/

Benns, M. (2019b). GetUp told to pull advert defending ABC — by ABC. The Daily Telegraph. Online. 8 May 2019. Retrieved from Factiva.

Benns, M. (2019a). GetUp told not to help ABC — by ABC. The Daily Telegraph. Online. 8 May 2019. Retrieved from: Factiva.

Bennett, W. (1998). 1998 Ithiel De Sola Pool Lecture: The UnCivic Culture: Communication, Identity, and the Rise of Lifestyle Politics. *PS: Political Science and Politics, 31*(4), 741–761. https://doi.org/10.2307/420711

Bennett, W. L., & Livingston, S. (2018). The Disinformation Order: Disruptive Communication and the Decline of Democratic Institutions. *European Journal of Communication, 33*(2), 122–139. https://doi.org/10.1177/0267323118760317

Berg, C., & Davidson, S. (2018). *Against Public Broadcasting: Why We Should Privatise the ABC and How to Do It.* Connor Court Publishing. West End.

Bingemann, M. (2017, May 18). ABC Part of Our Problem, Says Fairfax Boss Greg Hywood. *The Australian.* https://www.theaustralian.com.au/business/media/print/abc-part-of-our-problem-says-fairfax-boss-greg-hywood/news-story/ecb28edeb8303c10a28b1816ecce41a7

Binns, A. (2017). Fair game? Journalists' experiences of abuse online. *Journal of Applied Journalism & Media Studies.* 6. pp. 183–206. https://doi.org/10.1386/ajms.6.2.183_1.

Bixiao He (2021). Haunted by the State. Media History. 27:2. pp. 224–236. https://doi.org/10.1080/13688804.2020.1717939

Blackiston, H. (2019, November 8). *Q&A After 'Openly Feminist' Broadside Episode.* Mumbrella. https://mumbrella.com.au/abc-launches-investigation-into-qa-after-openly-feminist-broadside-episode-605744

Blankenship, J. C. (2016). LOSING THEIR "MOJO"? Mobile Journalism and the Deprofessionalization of Television News Work. *Journalism Practice, 10*(8), 1055–1071. https://doi.org/10.1080/17512786.2015.1063080

Blease, C. (2015). Too Many 'Friends,' Too Few 'Likes'? Evolutionary Psychology and 'Facebook Depression'. *Review of General Psychology, 19,* 1–13. https://doi.org/10.1037/gpr0000030

Bogle, A. (2020, June 19). Why China Is Being Blamed for Cyber Attacks on Australia, and What Its Hackers Might be Looking For. *ABC News Online.* https://www.abc.net.au/news/2020-06-19/why-would-china-launch-cyber-attack-against-australia/12374990

Bollmer, G. (2016). *Inhuman Networks: Social Media and the Archaeology of Connection, Bloomsbury Academic & Professional.* ProQuest Ebook Central. https://ebookcentral.proquest.com/lib/unsw/detail.action?docID=4542880

Bolt, A. (2018, June 18). "*I Agree': Paul Barry Admits the ABC Is Biased. Quoting Chas Licciardello, Outsiders, Sky News.* https://www.heraldsun.com.au/blogs/andrew-bolt/i-agree-paul-barry-admits-the-abc-is-biased/news-story/7afa1bfe14cb3b119891d7b02aed0b46

Bonk, K. (2008). Strategic communications for nonprofits: a step-by-step guide to working with the media (2nd Ed.). Jossey-Bass. San Francisco.

Born, G. & Prosser, T. (2001). Culture and Consumerism: Citizenship, Public Service Broadcasting and the BBC's Fair Trading Obligations. The Modern Law Review. 64:5. September 2001. Retrieved from: https://onlinelibrary-wiley-com.wwwproxy1.library.unsw.edu.au/doi/pdfdirect/10.1111/1468-2230.00345

Boseley, M. (2020, June 11). Four Chris Lilley Shows Removed from Netflix Australia Library. *The Guardian*. https://www.theguardian.com/tv-and-radio/2020/jun/11/four-chris-lilley-shows-removed-from-netflix-australia-library

Bourdieu, P. (1984). *Sociology in Question*. Sage Publications.

Bourdieu, P. (1991). *Language and Symbolic Power* (J. Thompson, Ed., G. Raymond & M. Adamson, Trans.). Harvard University Press.

Bourdieu, P. (1994). Structures, '*Habitus*', Power: Basis for a Theory of Symbolic Power. Chap. 4 in N. Dirks, G. Eley, & S. Ortner (Eds.), *Culture/Power/History: A Reader in Contemporary Social Theory.* Princeton Uni. Press.

Bourgonje, P., Moreno-Schneider, J., Srivastava, A., & Rehm, B. G. (2018). Automatic Classification of Abusive Language and Personal Attacks in Various Forms of Online Communication. pp. 180–191. In (Eds.) G. Rehm and T. Declerck: Language Technology Lab. Berlin, Germany. Retrieved from: https://doi.org/10.1007/978-3-319-73706-5_15.

Bourke, L. (2014, February 4). Prime Minister Tony Abbott Says ABC Not on Australia's Side in Interview with 2GB. *ABC News Online*. https://www.abc.net.au/news/2014-01-29/tony-abbott-steps-up-criticism-of-abc/5224676

Branch, D., & Cheeseman, N. (2008). Democratization, Sequencing, And State Failure in Africa: Lessons from Kenya. *African Affairs, 108*(430), 1–26. https://doi.org/10.1093/afraf/adn065

Brevini, B. (2013). *Public Service Broadcasting Online: A Comparative European Policy Study of PSB 2.0.* Palgrave Macmillan.

British Broadcasting Corporation. (2017, August 10). The Anzac Post, Outrage and a Debate About Race. https://www.bbc.com/news/world-australia-40712832

British Broadcasting Corporation. (2020). BBC issues staff with new social media guidance. 29 October 2020. Retrieved from: https://www.bbc.com/news/entertainment-arts-54723282

Bromley, M. & Neal, R. (2009). "Farewell old friend or bye-bye bully boy? The closure of 'mediation' and challenging the 'free press' paradigm." Media International Australia. August 132. Retrieved from: https://www.researchgate.net/deref/http%3A%2F%2Fdx.doi.org%2F10.1177%2F1329878X0913200105

Bruns, A. (2012). Journalists and Twitter: How Australian News Organisations Adapt to a New Medium. *Media International Australia, Incorporating Culture & Policy, 144*, 97–107. https://primoa.library.unsw.edu.au/permalink/f/11jha62/TN_scopus2-s2.0-84864412059

Burns, M., & Hawkins, G. (2013). Investigating Public Service Media as Hybrid Arrangements. *Media International Australia, 146*(1), 79–81. https://doi.org/10.1177/1329878X1314600111

Burrowes, T. (2018, January 1). Charlie Pickering Apologises for ABC New Year Countdown 'Kill a Police Officer' Autocue Blunder. *Mumbrella*. Retrieved January 3, 2020, from https://mumbrella.com.au/presenter-charlie-pickering-apologises-kill-police-officer-autocue-blunder-491598

Burrowes, T. (2019, May 19). ABC Wins the Election Ratings While Ten Slumps to 3.6%. *Mumbrella*. https://mumbrella.com.au/abc-wins-the-election-ratings-while-ten-slumps-to-3-6-580222

Calcutt, L. (2018, June 18). ABC Will Never Be Sold. *Ninenews.com*. https://www.9news.com.au/national/malcolm-turnbull-rules-out-privatising-abc-after-liberal-conference-vote/7220faa9-ebf1-4961-be43-e0ddd32a0afb

Cannane, S. (2017, October 28). *After Over 70 Years in Journalism and Publishing, Sir Harry Evans Is Still Irked by Bad Writing*. Correspondents Report. *ABC News Online*. https://www.abc.net.au/news/2017-10-28/does-writing-still-matter-in-the-digital-age/9091716

Carbado, D., Crenshaw, K., Mays, V., & Tomlinson, B. (2013). *Intersectionality:* Mapping the Movements of a Theory. *Du Bois Review: Social Science Research on Race, 10*(2), 303–312. https://doi.org/10.1017/S1742058X13000349

Carpentier, N. (2014). Participation as a Fantasy: A Psychoanalytical Approach to Power-Sharing Fantasies. In L. Kramp, N. Carpentier, A. Hepp, I. Tomanic-Trivundza, H. Nieminen, R. Kunelius, T. Olsson, E. Sundin & R. Kilborn (Eds.). *Everyday Media Agency in Europe, Chapter: Participation as a Fantasy: A Psychoanalytical Approach to Power-Sharing Fantasies*. Pp. 319–330. Edition Lumière. 4:5. https://www.researchgate.net/publication/268980799_Participation_as_a_Fantasy_A_Psychoanalytical_Approach_to_Power-Sharing_Fantasies

Carson, A., Martin, A. J., & Ratcliff, S. (2020). Negative Campaigning, Issue Salience and Vote Choice: Assessing the Effects of the Australian Labor Party's 2016 "Mediscare" Campaign. *Journal of Elections, Public Opinion and Parties, 30*(1), 83–104. https://doi.org/10.1080/17457289.2018.1563093

Castells, M. (2008). The New Public Sphere: Global Civil Society, Communication Networks, and Global Governance. *The Annals of the American Academy of Political and Social Science, 616*, 78–93. www.jstor.org/stable/25097995

Castells, M. (2012). *Networks of Outrage and Hope: Social Movements in the Internet Age*. Polity Press.

Ceron, A. (2015). Internet, News, and Political Trust: The Difference Between Social Media and Online Media Outlets. *Journal of Computer-Mediated Communication, 20*(5), 487–503. https://doi.org/10.1111/jcc4.12129\

Chalaby, J. K. (1998). *The Invention of Journalism*. Macmillan Press.

Coady, C. A. J. (2008, March). *ABC Editorial Policies: Short Looks at Some Big Concepts That Govern the ABC*. Australian Broadcasting Corporation, p. 2.

http://about.abc.net.au/wp-content/uploads/2012/06/KeyWordsMarch2008.pdf

Coë, C., & Moore, H. (2019, December 11). ABC Finds They Were Right to Pull a Controversial Q&A from iView Where a Radical Feminist Called for the Killing of Male Rapists—But the Writer Isn't Happy. https://www.dailymail.co.uk/news/article-7779533/ABC-finishes-investigation-radical-female-Q-panel-advocated-killing-rapists.html

Cohen, S. (2011). Whose Side Were We On? The Undeclared Politics of Moral Panic Theory. *Crime Media Culture, 7*(3), 237–243. https://doi.org/10.1177/1741659011417603

Collins, B., & Zadrozny, B. (2021, 9 January). Twitter Permanently Suspends Donald Trump. *NBC News.* https://www.nbcnews.com/tech/tech-news/twitter-permanently-bans-president-donald-trump-n1253588

Conboy, M. (2013). *Journalism Studies: The Basics.* Routledge.

Cunningham, S., & Bridgstock, R. (2012, November). Say Goodbye to the Fries: Graduate Careers in Media, Cultural and Communication Studies. *Media International Australia, 145*(1), 6–17. https://primoa.library.unsw.edu.au/permalink/f/11jha62/TN_wos000312972100002

Cokley, J. & Ranke, A. (2010). There's a "Long Tail" in Journalism Education, Too. In B. Franklin & D. Mensing. (2010). *Journalism Education, Training and Employment.* 1st Ed. Routledge. New York.

Cunningham, S. & Turner, G. (2010). The Media and Communications in Australia. 3rd Ed. Allen & Unwin. Crows News, Sydney.

Crenshaw, K. W. (1989). "Demarginalizing the Intersection of Race and Sex: A Black Feminist Critique of Antidiscrimination Doctrine, Feminist Theory and Antiracist Politics." University of Chicago Legal Forum 1989. 139–67. Retrieved from: https://heinonline.org

Chalaby, J. K. (1997). No ordinary press owner: Press barons as a Weberian ideal type. Media, Culture and Society. 19:4. Pp. 621–641. Retrieved from: https://doi.org/10.1177/016344397019004007.

Carey, J. (1996). Where journalism education went wrong. Conference presentation Middle Tennessee State University. Retrieved from: https://lindadaniele.wordpress.com/2010/08/11/carey-where-journalism-education-went-wrong/

Çıdam, Ç. (2016). Public Space, Material Worlds, and Democratic Aspirations. *Contemporary Political Theory, 15*(4), 417–426. https://doi.org/10.1057/s41296-016-0011-0

Dandira, M. (2012). Dysfunctional Leadership: Organizational Cancer. *Business Strategy Series, 13*(4), 187–192. https://doi.org/10.1108/17515631211246267

Davis, G. (1988). *Breaking Up the ABC.* Allen and Unwin.

Derrida, J. (1992). *Positions.* University of Chicago Press.

Derrida, J. (1998). *Of Grammatology* (G. C. Spivak, Trans., First published 1967). John Hopkins University Press.

Derrida, J. (2005). *Rogues*. Stanford University Press.

Devenney, M., Howarth, D., Norval, A. J., Stavrakakis, Y., Marchart, O., Biglieri, P., & Perelló, G. (2016). Ernesto Laclau. *Contemporary Political Theory, 15*(3), 304–335. https://doi.org/10.1057/cpt.2016.8

Dickens, C. (1836). *Pickwick Papers*. The Project Gutenberg EBook 2016. https://www.gutenberg.org/files/580/580-h/580-h.htm#link2HCH0032

DiMaggio, P. J., & Powell, W. W. (1983). The Iron Cage Revisited: Institutional Isomorphism and Collective Rationality in Organizational Fields. *American Sociological Review, 48*(2), 147–160. https://doi.org/10.2307/2095101

Drozdek, A. (2015). Media Ethics. In I*nternational Encyclopedia of the Social & Behavioral Sciences*. 2nd Ed. Pp. 42–47). Elsevier Inc. Retrieved from: https://doi.org/10.1016/B978-0-08-097086-8.11017-7

Dudley-Nicholson, J. (2020, March 5). AAP Demise a 'Wake-Up Call' Over Tech Giants. *The Australian*. https://www.theaustralian.com.au/business/media/aap-demise-a-wakeup-call-over-tech-giants/news-story/380efd106480aa0eaa5e3b871e2f5bfa

Duke, J. (2020, January 3). ABC Under 'Growing' Cost Pressure as Bushfire Emergency Broadcasts Surge. *The Sydney Morning Herald*. https://www.smh.com.au/business/companies/abc-under-growing-cost-pressure-as-bushfire-emergency-broadcasts-surge-20200103-p53ohp.html

Dynel, M., Chovanec, M., & Chovanec, J. (2015). *Participation in Public and Social Media Interactions* (p. 49). John Benjamins Publishing Company. https://primoa.library.unsw.edu.au/permalink/f/jhud33/UNSW_ALMA51236854060001731

Dodd, A., Pasandaran, C.C., Green, S., Octavianto, A.W. & Mardjianto F.X.L.D. Proyek Sepaham. (2017). An Experiment in Crosscultural and Collaborative Journalism Education. Asia Pacific Media Educator. 27:1. Pp. 67–84. Retrieved from: https://doi.org/10.1177/1326365X17701790.

Egan, T. (2019, October 25). Why Doesn't Mark Zuckerberg Get It? The Facebook Co-Founder's Speech at Georgetown Was a Profile in Cowardice. Opinion. *The New York Times*. https://www.nytimes.com/2019/10/25/opinion/facebook-mark-zuckerberg.html?action=click&module=Opinion&pgtype=Homepage

Eisenstein, E. (1979). *The Printing Press as an Agent of Change: Communications and Cultural Transformations in Early Modern Europe*. 1. Cambridge University Press.

Entman, R. M. (2004). *Projections of Power: Framing News, Public Opinion, and U.S. Foreign Policy*. University of Chicago Press.

Erbschloe, M. (2017). *Social Media Warfare: Equal Weapons for All*. Taylor & Francis. E-book. https://ebookcentral.proquest.com/lib/unsw/reader.action?docID=4856182

Edwards, E. D., & Fuller, T. (2020). Graphic violence: illustrated theories about violence, popular media, and our social lives (First edition.). Routledge. New York.

Ferguson, R., & Vitorovich, L. (2020, June 2). US Protests: Police Attack Channel 7 News Team as Donald Trump Walks from White House. *The Australian*. https://www.theaustralian.com.au/business/media/us-protests-police-attack-channel-7-news-team-as-donald-trump-walks-from-white-house/news-story/e326fa536c5b2d15ccca4659ca9ec917

Fifth Estate, The. (2021, January 16). On the Australia Fires and What Comes Next. Environment. Our View. https://www.thefifthestate.com.au/urbanism/environment/on-the-australia-fires-and-what-comes-next/

Fishman, J. M., & Marvin, C. (2003). Portrayals of Violence and Group Difference in Newspaper Photographs: Nationalism and Media. *Journal of Communication, 53*(1), 32–44. https://doi.org/10.1111/j.1460-2466.2003.tb03003.x

Fletcher, R, (2018). *The Rise of Populism and the Consequences for News and Media Use*. Digital News Report. Reuters Institute & University of Oxford. http://www.digitalnewsreport.org/survey/2019/the-rise-of-populism-and-the-consequences-for-news-and-media-use/

Flint, J. (2020, June 11). Race Protests: Gone with The Wind, Little Britain and Comedies by Chris Lilley Pulled by Streaming Services. *The Australian*. https://www.theaustralian.com.au/business/the-wall-street-journal/rhett-forced-to-give-a-damn-about-race-as-gone-with-the-wind-pulled/news-story/10dac76431771e180aa62754329f9db4

Foreign Policy. Editorial. (2010, March/April). iWar. *Foreign Policy, 178*(1). https://www-jstor-org.wwwproxy1.library.unsw.edu.au/stable/20684986?seq=1#metadata_info_tab_contents

Fukuyama, F. (2018). *Identity: The Demand for Dignity and the Politics of Resentment*. Farrar, Straus & Giroux.

Funnell, A. (2020, January 31). Is This the End of the Liberal International Order? And What Might Take Its Place? ABC Radio National. Future Tense. ABC Radio Online. https://www.abc.net.au/news/2020-01-31/liberal-international-order-under-threat-china-us/11905652

Fleuriet, C.A., & Lee Williams, M. (2015). Improving Institutional Credibility: Communication as the Centerpiece of Planning in the Age of Accountability. 22:1. P. 67. Educational Planning. Buffalo, N.Y. ISSN: 1537-873X

Franklin, B. & Mensing, D. (2010). Journalism Education, Training and Employment. 1st Ed. Routledge. New York.

Fleck, N., Michel, G. & Zeitoun, V. (2014). Brand Personification through the Use of Spokespeople: An Exploratory Study of Ordinary Employees, CEOs, and Celebrities Featured in Advertising. Psychology & Marketing. 31:1. Pp. 84–92. https://doi.org/10.1002/mar.20677

Gamson, W., Croteau, D., Hoynes, W., & Sasson, T. (1992). Media Images and the Social Construction of Reality. *Annual Review of Sociology, 18*, 373–393. http://search.proquest.com/docview/199734271/

Gardels, N. (1995). Is There a Liberal Bias in the Media? *New Perspectives Quarterly, 12*(2). http://search.proquest.com/docview/196967275/

Gillin, J. (2013, April 8). Bill Adair: Fact-Checking 'Is a Good Investment'. *The Poynter Institute*. https://www.poynter.org/reporting-editing/2013/bill-adair-fact-checking-is-a-good-investment/

Goldman, S. (2019, 03). Jews Must Not Embrace Powerlessness. *Commentary, 147*, 37–39. https://www.commentarymagazine.com/articles/sharon-goldman/jews-must-not-embrace-powerlessness/

Gordon, J. (2013, May 22). State Liberals Propose Privatising ABC, SBS. *The Sydney Morning Herald*. https://www.smh.com.au/politics/federal/state-liberals-propose-privatising-abc-sbs-20130521-2jz5d.html

Gordon, J. (2018, November 19). Australians Are Losing Their Trust in 'The Media', But Not in Journalism. RMIT. ABC Fact Check. *Australian Broadcasting Corporation*. https://www.abc.net.au/news/2018-09-10/fact-checking-the-new-workplace-skill/10209210

Grant, E. (1973). Medieval Explanations and Interpretations of the Dictum that 'Nature Abhors a Vacuum'. Traditiom, *29*, 327–355. https://doi.org/10.1017/S0362152900009004

Grattan, M. (2017, April 26). Abdel-Magied Anzac Row Is a Storm Over Not Much. *The Conversation*. https://theconversation.com/abdel-magied-anzac-row-is-a-storm-over-not-much-76708

Greer, A. (2012). Commons and Enclosure in the Colonization of North America. *The American Historical Review, 117*(2), 365–386. https://doi.org/10.1086/ahr.117.2.365

Grensing-Pophal, L. (2010, January–February). Social Media: Journalism's Friend or Foe?. *Econtentmag.com*. http://www.econtentmag.com/Articles/Editorial/Feature/Social-Media-Journalisms-Friend-or-Foe-61147.htm

Guillot, C. (2013, October 1). The Wisdom of the Crowd. *Internal Auditor, 70*(5), 44. http://search.proquest.com/docview/1464388029/

Gulyas, A. (2013). The Influence of Professional Variables On Journalists' Uses And Views Of Social Media: *A Comparative Study of Finland, Germany, Sweden and the United Kingdom. Digital Journalism, 1*(2). https://doi.org/10.1080/21670811.2012.744559

Guterres, A. (2018, September 23). Secretary-General's Address to the General Assembly. *UN Secretary General*. https://www.un.org/sg/en/content/sg/statement/2018-09-25/secretary-generals-address-general-assembly-delivered-trilingual

Goebbels, J. (1941). "Churchill's Lie Factory," (12 January, 1941). Original: "Aus Churchills Lügenfabrik," Die Zeit ohne Beispiel. Zentralverlag der NSDAP. Munich. Pp. 364–369. Jewish Virtual Library. Joseph Goebbels: On the "Big Lie". Retrieved from: https://www.jewishvirtuallibrary.org/joseph-goebbels-on-the-quot-big-lie-quot

Gardeström, E. (2017). Losing Control. Journalism Studies. 18:4. Pp. 511–524. https://doi.org/10.1080/1461670X.2015.1073117

George, P. (1989). Behind the lines: The personal story of an ABC foreign correspondent. ABC Books. Sydney.

George, G., Dahlander, L., Graffin, S., & Sim, S. (2016). Reputation and Status: Expanding the Role of Social Evaluations in Management Research. Academy of Management Journal. 59:1. Pp. 1–13. Retrieved from: https://doi.org/10.5465/amj.2016.4001

Habermas, J. (1962, repr. 1991). *The Structural Transformation of the Public Sphere: An Inquiry Into a Category of Bourgeois Society* (T. Burger, Trans.). MIT Press.

Habermas, J. (2006, March 9). Acceptance Speech for the Bruno Kreisky Prize for the Advancement of Human Rights. In A. Keen. (2007) (Ed.), *The Cult of the Amateur: How Today's Internet Is Killing Our Culture*. Doubleday/Currency.

Hanusch, F. (2013). Moulding Industry's Image: Journalism Education's Impact on Students' Professional Views. *Media International Australia (8/1/07-Current)*, *146*, 48–59. https://doi-org.wwwproxy1.library.unsw.edu.au/10.1177/1329878X1314600108

Hassan, N., Adair, B., Hamilton, J. T., Li, C., Tremayne, M., Yang, J., & Yu, C. (2015, July). The Quest to Automate Fact-Checking. In *Proceedings of the 2015 Computation+ Journalism Symposium*. http://ranger.uta.edu/~cli/pubs/2015/claimbuster-cj15-hassan.pdf

Hawkins, G. (1997). The ABC and the Mystic Writing Pad. *Media International Australia*, *83*, 11–17. https://doi.org/10.1177/1329878X9708300104

Henderson, G. (2018, August 6). Michelle Guthrie Needs a Fact Checker; Barrie Cassidy's Mea Culpa. *The Australian*. https://www.theaustralian.com.au/business/media/michelle-guthrie-needs-a-fact-checker-barrie-cassidys-mea-cuple/news-story/a5d429bb48fd7b4380baa2e442732fcc

Henderson, G. (2019, November 8). ABC Delays and Bungles Handling of Q&A 'Call to Violence' Episode. *The Australian*. https://www.theaustralian.com.au/commentary/abc-delays-and-bungles-handling-of-qa-call-to-violence-episode/news-story/b11bb0bc356b056297d2a0ffb922a290

Henriques-Gomez, L. (2019, November 5). Let's Burn Stuff: Q&A Panellists Debate Violence and Shattering the Status Quo. *The Guardian*. https://www.theguardian.com/australia-news/2019/nov/05/lets-burn-stuff-qa-panellists-debate-violence-and-shattering-the-status-quo

Hermida, A. (2012, March). Tweets And Truth: Journalism as a Discipline of Collaborative Verification. *Journalism Practice*, 1–10. https://doi.org/10.1080/17512786.2012.667269

Hurst, D. (2020, June 19). Cyber-Attack Australia: Sophisticated Attacks from 'State-Based Actor', PM Says. *The Guardian*. https://www.theguardian.com/australia-news/2020/jun/19/australia-cyber-attack-attacks-hack-state-based-actor-says-australian-prime-minister-scott-morrison

Higgins, K. (2011). "A fresh page in news evolution". NIE Supplement for Schools. The Sunday Telegraph. 28 August, 2011. Pp. 114–115.

Hall, E. (2016, 15 June). "The Drum Wednesday June 15". The Drum. Retrieved via Wikipedia 15 February 2017. Link removed.

Ignatius, D. (2019, April 12). Is Julian Assange a Journalist, or Is He Just an Accused Thief? *The Washington Post*. https://www.washingtonpost.com/opinions/is-julian-assange-a-journalist-or-is-he-just-an-accused-thief/2019/04/11/38afac3c-5c9c-11e9-9625-01d48d50ef75_story.html

Imamova, N. (2015). Social Media and Online Public Debate In Central Asia: A Journalist's Perspective. *Demokratizatsiya, 23*(3), 359–376. http://search.proquest.com/docview/1699511722/

Inglis, K. (1983). *The is the ABC: The Australian Broadcasting Commission 1932–1983*. Melbourne University Press.

Inglis, K. (2006). *Whose ABC? The Australian Broadcasting Corporation 1983–2006*. Black Inc.

Jaques, C., Islar, M., & Lord, G. (2019). Post-Truth: Hegemony on Social Media and Implications for Sustainability Communication. *Sustainability, 11*(7), 2120. https://doi.org/10.3390/su11072120

Jo Nova. (2019). Australia Votes 2019: Shock! Climate Action Bombs. Pollsters Crash. Skeptics Win. *Joanne Nova*. Blog. http://joannenova.com.au/2019/05/it-was-a-climate-election-and-the-skeptics-won-australia-2019/

Johnson, C. (2013). From Brand Congruence to the 'Virtuous Circle': Branding and the Commercialization of Public Service Broadcasting. *Media Culture and Society*. http://journals.sagepub.com/doi/full/10.1177/0163443712472088

Johnson, R., Venus, M., Lanaj, K., Mao, C., Chang, C., & Johnson, R. (2012). Leader Identity as an Antecedent of the Frequency and Consistency of Transformational, Consideration, and Abusive Leadership Behaviors. *The Journal of Applied Psychology, 97*(6), 1262–1272. https://doi.org/10.1037/a0029043

Jones, S. (2010). Negotiating Authentic Objects and Authentic Selves. *Journal of Material Culture, 15*(2), 181–203. https://doi.org/10.1177/1359183510364074

Jones, T. (2020, June 11). Netflix Removes Most of Chris Lilley's Shows. *Gizmodo*. https://www.gizmodo.com.au/2020/06/chris-lilley-netflix-blackface/

Josephi, B. (2000). Newsroom Research: Its Importance for Journalism Studies. *Australian Journalism Review, 22*(2), 75–87. https://primoa.library.unsw.edu.au/permalink/f/11jha62/TN_informit_apaft200204995

Jelenchick, L. A., Eickhoff, J. C., & Moreno, M. A. (2013). "Facebook depression?" social networking site use and depression in older adolescents. The Journal of Adolescent Health: Official Publication of the Society for Adolescent Medicine. 52:1. Pp. 128–130. Retrieved from: https://doi.org/10.1016/j.jadohealth.2012.05.008

Kagwanja, P., & Southall, R. (2009). Introduction: Kenya—A Democracy in Retreat? *Journal of Contemporary African Studies: Kenya's Uncertain Democracy: The Electoral Crisis of 2008, 27*(3), 259–277. https://doi.org/10.1080/02589000903216930

Kakutani, M. (2018). *The Death of Truth*. William Collins.

Keen, A. (2007). *The Cult of the Amateur*. Doubleday Currency.

Kierkegaard, S. (1941). *Concluding Unscientific Postscript* (W. Lowrie & J. Campbell, Trans.). Princeton Legacy Library.

Knott, M. (2015, May 28). Everyone from Coalition Thinks ABC's Q&A Is Biased to the Left, Says LNP Senator James McGrath. *The Age*. https://www.theage.com.au/politics/federal/everyone-from-coalition...ed-to-the-left-says-lnp-senator-james-mcgrath-20150527-ghatyw.html

Kornbluh, K. (2018, September/October). The Internet's Lost Promise: And How America Can Restore It. *Foreign Affairs, 97*(5), 33–38. New York. http://search.proquest.com/docview/2094371395/

Krause, N. M., Wirz, C. D., Scheufele, D. A., & Xenos, M. A. (2019, August). Fake News A New Obsession with an Old Phenomenon? In J. E. Katz & K. K. Mays (Eds.), *Journalism and Truth in an Age of Social Media*. Oxford Scholarship Online. https://doi.org/10.1093/oso/9780190900250.001.0001

Kušen, E., Strembeck, M., & Conti, M. (2019). *Influence and Behavior Analysis in Social Networks and Social Media* (M. Kaya & R. Alhajj, Eds.). Springer. ProQuest Ebook Central. http://ebookcentral.proquest.com/lib/unsw/detail.action?docID=5613405

Karinthy, F. (1929). Chain (short story). In: Everything is Different. Budapest. Cited in: F. Karinthy. (2011). Chain-links. In The Structure and Dynamics of Networks. Vol. 9781400841356. Pp. 21–26.

Kamto, M. (1997). Reaffirming Public-Service Values and Professionalism. *International Review of Administrative Sciences, 63*(3), 295–308. https://doi.org/10.1177/002085239706300302

Krygier, M. (1997). The Uses of Civility. ABC Boyer Lecture, 23 November 1997. Retrieved from: https://www.abc.net.au/radionational/programs/boyerlectures/lecture-3-the-uses-of-civility/3460218

Laclau, E. (1990). *New Reflections on the Revolution of Our Time*. Verso.

Lallo, M. (2018, December 2). Most-Watched Programs of 2018 Revealed. *The Sydney Morning Herald*. https://www.smh.com.au/entertainment/tv-and-radio/most-watched-programs-of-2018-revealed-20181130-p50jdk.html

Lallo, M. (2019, December 1). Nine Network Tops 2019 Ratings Ending Seven's 12-Year Winning Streak. *The Sydney Morning Herald*. https://www.smh.com.au/culture/tv-and-radio/nine-network-tops-2019-ratings-ending-seven-s-12-year-winning-streak-20191129-p53fd3.html

Lawson, K. (2019, May 20). Election 2019: Why the Opinion Polls Were Always Wrong. *The Canberra Times.* https://www.canberratimes.com.au/story/6132185/why-the-opinion-polls-were-always-wrong-and-how-we-should-have-spotted-it/

Lazer, D. M. J., Baum, M. A., Benkler, Y., Berinsky, A. J., Greenhill, K. M., Menczer, F., Metzger, M., Nyhan, B., Pennycook, G., Rothschild, D., Schudson, M., Sloman, S. A., Sunstein, C. R., Thorson, E. A., Watts, D. J., & Zittrain, J. L. (2018). The Science of Fake News. *Science, 359*(6380), 1094–1096. https://doi.org/10.1126/science.aao2998

Leary, M. R. (1995). *Self-Presentation: Impression Management and Interpersonal Behavior*. Brown & Benchmark.

Lewis, J. (2006). News and the Empowerment of Citizens. *European Journal of Cultural Studies, 9*(3), 303–319. https://doi.org/10.1177/1367549406066075

Lin, X., Spence, P., & Lachlan, K. (2016). Social Media and Credibility Indicators: The Effect of Influence Cues. *Computers in Human Behavior, 63*, 264–271. https://doi.org/10.1016/j.chb.2016.05.002

Lumsden, K., & Harmer, E. (2019). *Online Othering: Exploring Digital Violence and Discrimination on the Web.* Cham: Springer International Publishing: Imprint: Palgrave Macmillan. https://doi.org/10.1007/978-3-030-12633-9

Machimbarrena, J. M., Calvete, E., Fernández-González, L., Álvarez-Bardón, A., Álvarez-Fernández, L., & González-Cabrera, J. (2018). Internet Risks: An Overview of Victimization in Cyberbullying, Cyber Dating Abuse, Sexting, Online Grooming and Problematic Internet Use. *International Journal of Environmental Research and Public Health, 15*(11). https://doi.org/10.3390/ijerph15112471

Mackay, H. (2002). *Media Mania: Why Our Fear of Modern Media Is Misplaced.* UNSW Press.

Mackay, H. (2010). *What Makes Us Tick? The Ten Desires That Drive Us.* Hachette.

Macmullan, T. (2005). Challenges to Cultural Diversity: Absolutism, Democracy, and Alain Locke's Value Relativism. *The Journal of Speculative Philosophy, 19*(2), 129–139. https://doi.org/10.1353/jsp.2005.0013

Madison, J, (1788). *Popular Basis of Political Authority. The Founders' Constitution, 1*(2). Document 19. The University of Chicago Press. http://press-pubs.uchicago.edu/founders/documents/v1ch2s19.html

Mann, S. (2004). "Sousveillance"—Inverse Surveillance in Multimedia Imaging. *ACM Multimedia 2004—Proceedings of the 12th ACM International Conference on Multimedia*. Pp. 620–627. Retrieved from: https://primoa.library.unsw.edu.au/permalink/f/11jha62/TN_scopus2-s2.0-13444291148

Marks, K. (2017, August 10). The Anzac Post, Outrage and a Debate About Race. *BBC News.* https://www.bbc.com/news/world-australia-40712832

Massaka, I. (2017). Selected Issues of E-Democracy and Political E-Participation. *Historia i Polityka.*, *18*(25), 9–18. https://doi.org/10.12775/HiP.2016.028

McCauley, D. (2018, May 25). ABC Spends Up on Google, Facebook Ads. *The Australian*. https://www.theaustralian.com.au/business/media/abc-spends-up-on-google-facebook-ads/news-story/5e6a36fcf3463cb5522fec4a5bcf0918

Meade, A. (2015, July 23). ABC Shops to Close with Loss of 300 Jobs, Mark Scott Says. *The Guardian*. https://www.theguardian.com/media/2015/jul/23/abc-shops-to-close-with-loss-of-300-jobs-mark-scott-says?CMP=share_btn_link

Media Entertainment and Arts Alliance. (2020, February 24). Assange Case 'An Attack on Truth': WikiLeaks Editor. *Media Entertainment and Arts Alliance*. https://www.meaa.org/news/assange-case-an-attack-on-truth-wikileaks-editor/

Mill, J. S. (1859). *On Liberty*. The Walter Scott Publishing Co., Ltd. http://www.gutenberg.org/files/34901/34901-h/34901-h.htm

Milne, J., & Guthrie, M. (2018). ABC Annual Report. Welcome. *Australian Broadcasting Corporation*. https://about.abc.net.au/wp-content/uploads/2018/10/AP18_Vol1_FINALnew.pdf

Miragliotta, N., & Errington, W. (2012). The Rise and Fall and Rise Again of Public Broadcasting? The Case of the Australian Broadcasting Corporation. *Australian Journal of Public Administration, 71*(1), 55–64. https://doi.org/10.1111/j.1467-8500.2012.00755.x

Monk, P. (2016). Reason in Western Civilisation. *Australian Rationalist, 100*(Autumn), 5–6. https://primoa.library.unsw.edu.au/permalink/f/11jha62/TN_informit_agis20190613012326

Monk, S. (2019, December). Truth v. Fake News. In *Southern Cross*. pp. 17–19. Anglican Media Sydney.

Mønsted, B., Sapieżyński, P., Ferrara, E., & Lehmann, S. (2017). Evidence of Complex Contagion of Information in Social Media: An Experiment Using Twitter Bots. *PloS One*. https://journals.plos.org/plosone/article/file?id=10.1371/journal.pone.0184148&type=printable

Murdock, G. (2004, November). Building the Digital Commons: Public Broadcasting in the Age of the Internet. University of Montreal. *The 2004 Spry Memorial Lecture*. https://www.researchgate.net/publication/254750526_BUILDING_THE_DIGITAL_COMMONS_PUBLIC_BROADCASTING_IN_THE_AGE_OF_THE_INTERNET

Murphy, J., Link, M. W., Childs, J. H., Tesfaye, C. L., Dean, E., Stern, M., Pasek, J., Cohen, J., Callegaro, M., & Harwood, P. (2014). Social Media in Public Opinion Research. *Public Opinion Quarterly, 78*(4), 788–794. https://doi.org/10.1093/poq/nfu053

Masaeli, N. & Farhadi, H. (2021). Prevalence of Internet-based addictive behaviors during COVID-19 pandemic: a systematic review. *Journal of Addictive Diseases*. 1–27. https://doi.org/10.1080/10550887.2021.1895962

Miller, C. (2012). Twitter trumps science in trawler ban. Frontiers in Ecology and the Environment. 10:9. Ecological Society of America. Wiley. Pp. 460-460. https://www.jstor.org/stable/41811850

Meade, A. (2019). ABC managing director rejects accusations he is making funding an election issue. The Guardian. 8 May 2019. Retrieved from: https://www.theguardian.com/media/2019/may/08/abc-managing-director-rejects-accusations-he-is-making-funding-an-election-issue

Muller, D. (2019). Outrage, polls and bias: 2019 federal election showed Australian media need better regulation. Opinion. Mumbrella. 22 May 2019. Retrieved from: https://mumbrella.com.au/outrage-polls-and-bias-2019-federal-election-showed-australian-media-need-better-regulation-580713 Comment by Jennifer 27 May 19.

Mudde, C. & Kaltwasser, C. R. in M. Freeden & M. Stears. Eds. (2013). Populism. The Oxford Handbook of Political Ideologies. Retrieved from: https://www-oxfordhandbooks-com.wwwproxy1.library.unsw.edu.au/view/10.1093/oxfordhb/9780199585977.001.0001/oxfordhb-9780199585977-e-026

Nadkarni, A., & Hofmann, S. G. (2012). Why Do People Use Facebook? *Personality and Individual Differences, 52*, 243–249. https://psycnet.apa.org/doi/10.1016/j.paid.2011.11.007

Nash, C. (2013, October). Journalism as a Research Discipline. *Pacific Journalism Review, 19*(2), 123–135. https://primoa.library.unsw.edu.au/permalink/f/11jha62/TN_informit605741818647699

Nathan, J. (2019). *Report on Antisemitism in Australia 2019*. Executive Council of Australian Jewry. https://sydney.edu.au/content/dam/corporate/documents/sydney-law-school/research/centres-institutes/antisemitism-report-2019.pdf

Nerone, J., & Barnhurst, K. G. (2001). Beyond Modernism: Digital Design, Americanization and the Future of Newspaper Form. *New Media & Society, 3*(4), 467–482. https://doi.org/10.1177/14614440122226191

News.com.au. (2018, January 1). Charlie Pickering Says Sorry for 'Kill a Police Officer' Gaffe. *News.com.au*. https://www.news.com.au/entertainment/tv/charlie-pickering-says-sorry-for-kill-a-police-officer-gaffe/news-story/a3415b2110377584ca71e9a083ba3829

NewsMail. (2018, November 24). ABC Goes to War with The Chaser Boys. *News Mail*. https://www.news-mail.com.au/news/abc-executive-criticises-chaser-after-satirists-co/3584319/

Nicholson, P. (2016). Balance in Redress: Too Slow? Too Rule-Bound? Too Confusing to the Public? The Scottish Legal Complaints Commission Is Consulting on Whether to Seek Radical Changes to Its Complaint Handling

Procedures. *The Journal of the Law Society of Scotland, 61*(2). https://primoa.library.unsw.edu.au/permalink/f/11jha62/TN_gale_legal446198366

Nine.com.au. (2018, May 23). Emma Alberici Under Fire Again as PM Files Complaints to the ABC. https://finance.nine.com.au/business-news/emma-alberici-abc-complaints-prime-minister-malcolm-turnbull/4dc648ae-6f69-4f2b-b5fd-8d655c9d84f2

Norman, J. (2018, June 16). Liberal Party Members Vote to Privatise ABC and Move Australia's Israel Embassy to Jerusalem. *ABC Online.* https://www.abc.net.au/news/2018-06-16/liberal-members-vote-to-privatise-abc-move-embassy-to-jerusalem/9877524

NSW Nurses and Midwives' Association. (2018, March 5). Turnbull Pressures ABC on Tax Coverage. Tax Justice. *The Lamp*, p. 20. https://thelamp.com.au/workplace-issues/unions/turnbull-pressures-abc-on-tax-coverage/

Nyhan, B., & Reifler, J. (2015, July). The Effect of Fact-Checking on Elites: A 'Field' Experiment on U.S. State Legislators. *American Journal of Political Science, 59*(3), 628–640. https://ore.exeter.ac.uk/repository/bitstream/handle/10871/21568/Nyhan%20Reifler%20AJPS.pdf?sequence=1

O'Dwyer, E. (2011, May 14). A Bit Weird and Getting Paid for It. *The Sydney Morning Herald.* https://www.smh.com.au/entertainment/tv-and-radio/a-bit-weird-and-getting-paid-for-it-20110514-1en2c.html

O'Keeffe, A., & Greene, C. (2019, December 11). International Public Broadcasting: A Missed Opportunity for Projecting Australia's Soft Power. *Lowy Institute.* https://www.lowyinstitute.org/publications/international-public-broadcasting-missed-opportunity-projecting-australia-s-soft-power

Orwell, G. (1949). *1984.* Secker & Warburg.

Oxford University Press. (2016). Word of the Year 2016. https://languages.oup.com/word-of-the-year/2016/

Orwell, G. (1946) (2021). Politics and the English Language. Renard Pess. London.

Paletz, D. L., & Entman, R. M. (1981). *Media Power Politics.* Free Press.

Patrick, A. (2018, April 10). Emma Alberici Anti-Tax Cut Article Contained Nine Errors. *The Australian Financial Review.* https://www.afr.com/policy/tax-and-super/emma-alberici-antitax-cut-article-contained-nine-errors-20180410-h0ykfs

Pearlman, A. (2008). Ethics in Journalism—Accuracy, Honesty, and Credibility. *Journal of the American Society of Echocardiography, 21*(5), 507–508. https://doi.org/10.1016/j.echo.2008.03.008

Pentina, I., & Tarafdar, M. (2014). From "Information" to "Knowing": Exploring the Role of Social Media in Contemporary News Consumption. *Computers in Human Behavior, 35*, 221–223. https://doi.org/10.1016/j.chb.2014.02.045

Persily, N. (2017, April). The 2016 U.S. Election: Can Democracy Survive the Internet? *Journal of Democracy, 28*(2), 63–76. https://muse.jhu.edu/article/653377

Pew Research Centre. (2012). Millennials Confident. Connected. Open to Change. https://www.pewresearch.org/wp-content/uploads/sites/3/2010/10/millennials-confident-connected-open-to-change.pdf

Posetti, J., & Ping, L. (2012). The Twitterisation of ABC's Emergency and Disaster Communication. *The Australian Journal of Emergency Management, 27*(1), 34–39. https://search-informit-com-au.wwwproxy1.library.unsw.edu.au/documentSummary;dn=046926063833158;res=IELAPA

Prosser Scully, R. (2019, May 20). How Did Pollsters Get the Australian Election Result So Wrong? *New Scientist*. https://www.newscientist.com/article/2203837-how-did-pollsters-get-the-australian-election-result-so-wrong/#ixzz6IKLZ24Mq

Potuchek, J. L. (1997). Who supports the family?: gender and breadwinning in dual-earner marriages. Stanford University Press, Stanford CA.

Quinn, B. (2020, June 1). Assange Misses Court Hearing Amid Calls in Australia for His Release. *The Guardian*. https://www.theguardian.com/media/2020/jun/01/julian-assange-misses-court-hearing-amid-calls-in-australia-for-his-release

Radio Info. (2016, July 22). Top 20 Percent of ABC Staff Paid $124 Million: *Senate Estimates*. https://www.radioinfo.com.au/news/top-20-percent-abc-staff-paid-124-million-senate-estimates

Robinson, E. (2016, December 30). Why Journalists Love Twitter—Tweets Make Lazy Political Journalism Easier Than Ever. *Current Affairs*. https://www.currentaffairs.org/2016/11/why-journalists-love-twitter

Roe, I. (2020, February 7). Distrust, Transparency Issues Blamed for Democracy Disengagement. PM. *ABC*. https://www.abc.net.au/radio-australia/programs/pm/distrust,-transparency-issues-blamed-for-democracy-disengagement/11945204

Rogstad, I. D. (2014). Political News Journalists in Social Media: Transforming Political Reporters Into Political Pundits? *Journalism Practice, 8*(6), 688–703. https://doi.org/10.1080/17512786.2013.865965

Ross, D. (2020a, January 1). Tex Perkins Upsets Viewers of ABC New Year's Eve Performance. *The Australian*. https://www.theaustralian.com.au/business/media/tex-perkins-upsets-viewers-of-abc-new-years-eve/news-story/4931060d16f89e4d805001eefa3b967b

Ross, D. (2020b, January 2). Maurice Newman Demands ABC Apologise Over Tex Perkins Obscene Gesture at NY Eve Performance. *The Australian*. https://www.theaustralian.com.au/business/media/tex-perkins-upsets-viewers-of-abc-new-years-eve/news-story/4931060d16f89e4d805001eefa3b967b?fbclid=IwAR1VwTKDvN3FGbGzJVjUzUxgWBtF4ktC5cznayJisQAtXylsxAmo1Qhbo5Y

Russell, F. M., Hendricks, M. A., Choi, H., & Stephens, E. C. (2015). Who Sets the News Agenda on Twitter? *Digital Journalism, 3*(6), 925–943. https://doi.org/10.1080/21670811.2014.995918

Rojek, C. (2012). Fame Attack: The Inflation of Celebrity and Its Consequences. Bloomsbury Academic. London. https://doi.org/10.5040/9781849661386

Richardson, A. (2017). Bearing Witness While Black: Theorizing African American mobile journalism after Ferguson. Digital Journalism. 5:6. Pp. 673–698. Retrieved from: https://doi.org/10.1080/21670811.2016.1193818

Rao, H. & Giorgi, S. (2006). Code Breaking: How Entrepreneurs Exploit Cultural Logics to Generate Institutional Change. Research in Organizational Behavior. 27. Pp. 269-304. https://doi.org/10.1016/S0191-3085(06)27007-2.

Rashkin, H., Choi, E., Jang, J.Y., Volkova, S., Choi, Y. (2017). Truth of Varying Shades: Analyzing Language in Fake News and Political Fact-Checking. Proceedings of the 2017 Conference on Empirical Methods in Natural Language Processing. Pp. 2931–2937. Copenhagen, Denmark, September 7–11, 2017. Retrieved from: https://www.aclweb.org/anthology/D17-1317/

Saul, J. R. (1993). *Voltaire's Bastards: The Dictatorship of Reason in the West.* Penguin Books.

Schirato, T., & Yell, S. (1997). *Communication and Cultural Literacy: An Introduction.* Allen and Unwin.

Schudson. (2005). "The Virtues of an Unlovable Press" Intro. *Political Quarterly, 1*(76), 23–32. https://doi.org/10.1111/j.1467-923X.2006.00745.x

Schudson, M. (2008). *Why Democracies Need an Unlovable Press.* Polity Press.

Schwartz, J. (2008). The Choice Between Tweedledum and Tweedledee: Australian Media Coverage of the 2007 Federal Election Campaign. *Metro: Media & Education Magazine.* Pp. 110–121. Retrieved from: https://search-informit-com-au.wwwproxy1.library.unsw.edu.au/documentSummary;dn=516965508581790;res=IELLCC

Scott, M. (2009, September 9). Commonwealth Broadcasting Association Lecture 2009. *ABC Speeches.* https://about.abc.net.au/speeches/association-lecture-2009/

Scott, M. (2018). *On Us.* Melbourne University Press.

Shah, C. (2017). Social Information Seeking Leveraging the Wisdom of the Crowd. In *The Information Retrieval Series* (Vol. 38). Springer. https://primoa.library.unsw.edu.au/permalink/f/jhud33/UNSW_ALMA51227992500001731

Shani, G., & Westphal, J. D. (2016). Persona Non Grata? Determinants and Consequences of Social Distancing From Journalists Who Engage in Negative Coverage of Firm Leadership. *Academy of Management Journal, 59*(1), 302–329. https://doi.org/10.5465/amj.2013.1162

Shapiro, I., Brin, C., Bédard-Brûlé, I., & Mychajlowycz, K. (2013). Verification as a Strategic Ritual: How Journalists Retrospectively Describe Processes for

Ensuring Accuracy. *Journalism Practice. 7*:6. Pp. 657–673. https://doi.org/10.1080/17512786.2013.765638

Shaw, S. J. (1959). Colonial Newspaper Advertising: A Step Toward Freedom of the Press. *Business History Review (pre-1986), 33*(000003), p. 409. http://search.proquest.com/docview/205528871/

Singer, P. W., & Brooking, E. T. (2018). *Likewar: The Weaponization of Social Media*. Houghton, Miffler, Harcourt.

Sloan, R., & Warner, R. (2016). Unauthorized Access: The Crisis in Online Privacy and Security (Edition 1). In *Unauthorized Access: The Crisis in <b>Online</b> Privacy and <b>Security</b> (Edition 1)* (1st ed.). CRC Press. https://doi.org/10.1201/b15148

Soutphommasane, T. (2018, July 19). Cultural Backlash and the Rise of Populism. Speech to *Sydney Ideas*, The University of Sydney. https://www.humanrights.gov.au/about/news/speeches/cultural-backlash-and-rise-populism

Spaulding, S., Nair, D., & Nelson, A. (2020). *Russia's Attacks on Democratic Justice Systems*. Center for Strategic and International Studies. https://www.csis.org/features/russias-attacks-democratic-justice-systems

Special Broadcasting Service. (2018, October 4). Liberals to Again Debate Selling the ABC. *SBS*. https://www.sbs.com.au/news/liberals-to-again-debate-selling-the-abc

Spitznagel, E. (2013, November 14). Q&A: Chris Lilley on Drag, Blackface, Teenage Girls & Confrontational Comedy. *Esquire*. https://www.esquire.com/entertainment/interviews/a25930/chris-lilley-interview/

Stephens, M. (2007). *A History of News* (3rd ed.). Oxford University Press.

Stephens, M. (2009, June). *Beyond News: The Case for Wisdom Journalism*. Joan Shorenstein Center on the Press, Politics and Public Policy, *DP Series*. D-53. Harvard Kennedy School. https://shorensteincenter.org/beyond-news-the-case-for-wisdom-journalism-mitchell-stephens/

Stieglitz, S., & Dang-Xuan, L. (2013). Emotions and Information Diffusion in Social Media—Sentiment of Microblogs and Sharing Behavior. *Journal of Management Information Systems, 29*(4), 217–248. https://doi.org/10.2753/MIS0742-1222290408

Streitfeld, D. (2017, May 20). 'The Internet Is Broken': @ev Is Trying to Salvage It. *The New York Times*. https://www.nytimes.com/2017/05/20/technology/evan-williams-medium-twitter-internet.html

Stuever, H. (2018, January 12). Letterman Sits Down with Obama, But Both Men Seem Rusty and Off Their Game. *The Washington Post*. https://www.washingtonpost.com/entertainment/tv/letterman-sits-down-with-obama-but-both-men-seem-rusty-and-off-their-game/2018/01/11/2b6dc8c0-f70c-11e7-a9e3-ab18ce41436a_story.html

Styles, A. (2016, July 3). Federal Election 2016: ABC Wins Election Night Coverage Despite Leigh Sales' 'Delirium'. *The Sydney Morning Herald*.

https://www.smh.com.au/entertainment/tv-and-radio/federal-election-2016-abc-wins-election-night-coverage-despite-leigh-sales-delirium-20160703-gpxlti.html

Sunderland, A. (2016, July 14). 2016 ABC Federal Election Report of the Chairman, Election Coverage Review Committee. *ABC*. http://about.abc.net.au/wp-content/uploads/2016/11/2016FederalElectionECRCRPT.pdf

Schroeder, R. (2018). Social Theory after the Internet: Media, Technology, and Globalization. UCL Press. London. https://doi.org/10.14324/111.9781787351226

Suddaby R. (2010). Challenges for Institutional Theory. Journal of Management Inquiry. 19:1. Pp.14–20. https://doi.org/10.1177/1056492609347564

Shapiro, I., Brin, C., Bédard-Brûlé, I., & Mychajlowycz, K. (2013). Verification as a Strategic Ritual: How journalists retrospectively describe processes for ensuring accuracy. Journalism Practice. 7:6. Pp. 657–673. Retrieved from: https://doi.org/10.1080/17512786.2013.765638, Quoting W. Lippmann [1920] 1995. Liberty and the News. New Brunswick, NJ: Transaction Publishers.

Schiffrin, A. (2017). Disinformation and Democracy: The Internet Transformed Protest but Did Not Improve Democracy. *Journal of International Affairs*. 71:1. Fall 2016–Winter 2017. Pp. 117–125. Retrieved from: http://search.proquest.com/docview/2054916939/

Skog, D.A., Wimelius, H., & Sandberg, J. (2018). Digital Disruption. Business & Information Systems Engineering. 60:5. Pp. 431–437. https://doi.org/10.1007/s12599-018-0550-4

Sparks, G.G. (2013). Media Effects Research: A Basic Overview. 4th Edition. Wadsworth. Cengage Learning. Boston, MA.

Thierer, A. (2013). The Perils of Classifying Social Media Platforms as Public Utilities. *CommLaw Conspectus, 21*(2), 297–297. https://primoa.library.unsw.edu.au/permalink/f/11jha62/TN_gale_legal401032615

Thomas, D. R. (2016). Digital Disruption: A Transformation in Graduate Management Online Education. In A. Khare, B. Stewart, & R. Schatz (Eds.), *Phantom Ex Machina*. Pp. 223–233. Springer. Retrieved from: https://doi.org/10.1007/978-3-319-44468-0_15

Thompson, R. (2011). Radicalization and the Use of Social Media. *Journal of Strategic Security, 4*(4), 167–190. https://doi.org/10.5038/1944-0472.4.4.8

Tiffen, R. (1989). *News and Power*. Allen & Unwin.

Toffler, A. (1984). *Future Shock*. Bantam Books.

Tonioni, F., D'Alessandris, L., Lai, C., Martinelli, D., Corvino, S., Vasale, M., & Bria, P. (2012). Internet Addiction: Hours Spent Online, Behaviors and Psychological Symptoms. *General Hospital Psychiatry, 34*(1), 80–87. https://doi.org/10.1016/j.genhosppsych.2011.09.013

Truu, M. (2019, November 8). Minister for Communications Paul Fletcher Said the Decision to Investigate Monday Night's Q&A Program Was "Appropriate". *SBS News.* https://www.sbs.com.au/news/abc-announces-probe-into-feminist-q-a-episode-after-audience-complaints

Tuchman, G. (1978, January). Making News: A Study in the Construction of Reality. *Social Forces, 59*(4). https://doi.org/10.2307/2578016

Tucker, J. A., Theocharis, Y., Roberts, M. E., & Barberá, P. (2017). From Liberation to Turmoil: Social Media and Democracy. *Journal of Democracy, 28*(4), 46–59. https://doi.org/10.1353/jod.2017.0064

Tracey, M. (2002). The Decline and Fall of Public Service Broadcasting. Oxford University Press. Oxford.

Turner, G. (2000). 'Media Wars' Journalism, cultural and media studies in Australia. *Journalism, 1*(3), 353–365. https://doi.org/10.1177/146488490000100305

Uscinski, J. E., & Butler, R. W. (2013). The Epistemology of Fact Checking. *Critical Review—A Journal of Politics and Society, 25*(2), 162–180. https://www.tandfonline.com/doi/abs/10.1080/08913811.2013.843872

Vallone, R., Ross, L., & Lepper, M. R. (1985). The Hostile Media Phenomenon: Biased Perception and Perceptions of Media Bias in Coverage of the Beirut Massacre. *Journal of Personality and Social Psychology, 49*(3), 577–585. https://doi.org/10.1037/0022-3514.49.3.577

Visontay, E. (2019, May 15). Where's Their Work? *The Australian.* https://www.theaustralian.com.au/nation/politics/federal-election-2019-campaign-day-35-scott-morrison-bill-shorten-hunt-for-votes/news-story/f0e7301ad5f058fec20a72fd6d9d1264

Vitorovitch, L., & Shanahan. L. (2020, March 3). AAP's Newswire to Close in June. *The Australian.* https://www.theaustralian.com.au/business/media/aaps-newswire-to-close-in-june/news-story/91ae9b35935ced854f8dddadd0616f84

Vitorovitch, L., & Swan, D. (2020, March 5). Guardian Hypocrisy Over AAP Shutdown. *The Australian.* https://www.theaustralian.com.au/business/media/accc-reviewing-aap-demise-says-rod-sims/news-story/78a2380813fc8574680b81e5ec570ec3

Voelz, G. J. (2015). (Rep.) *The Rise of iWar: Identity, Information, and the Individualization of Modern Warfare.* Strategic Studies Institute, US Army War College. www.jstor.org/stable/resrep11804

Von Clausewitz, C. (J. J. Graham, Trans.). (1874). *On War.* The Project Gutenberg EBook. http://www.gutenberg.org/files/1946/1946-h/1946-h.htm

Vosoughi, S., Roy, D., & Aral, S. (2018). The Spread of True and False News Online. *Science, 359*(6380), 1446–1151. https://doi.org/10.1126/science.aap9559

Waisbord, S. (2018). The Elective Affinity Between Post-Truth Communication and Populist Politics. *Communication Research and Practice: Special Issue: ANZCA 2017—Communication Worlds: Access, Voice, Diversity. Engagement, 4*(1), 17–34. https://doi.org/10.1080/22041451.2018.1428928. Guest Editor: F. Martin.

Walker, T. (2018, October 17). Shifting the Australian Embassy in Israel to Jerusalem Would Be a Big, Cynical Mistake. *ABC News Online*. https://www.abc.net.au/news/2018-10-17/australian-embassy-jerusalem-big-cynical-mistake/10388108

Wallach, B. (2005). *Understanding the Cultural Landscape*. The Guilford Press.

Ward, S. J. A. (2014). Radical Media Ethics: Ethics for a Global Digital World. *Digital Journalism, 2*(4), 455–471. https://doi.org/10.1080/21670811.2014.952985

Wardle, C. (2019, September 1). Misinformation Has Created a New World Disorder. *Scientific American*. https://www.scientificamerican.com/article/misinformation-has-created-a-new-world-disorder/

Wardle, C., & Derakhshan, H. (2017). *Information Disorder: Toward an Interdisciplinary Framework for Research and Policy Making*. Council of Europe. https://rm.coe.int/information-disorder-toward-an-interdisciplinary-framework-for-researc/168076277c

Waters, R., & Murphy, H. (2021, January 16). Donald Trump, Twitter and the Messy Fight Over Free Speech. *The Financial Times*. The Big Read. Social Media. https://www.ft.com/content/78a3ed8c-d930-4bf5-9f6e-1b6b4751090f

Waters, S. (2018). The Effects of Mass Surveillance on Journalists' Relations with Confidential Sources: A Constant Comparative Study. *Digital Journalism, 6*(10), 1294–1313. https://doi.org/10.1080/21670811.2017.1365616

Watson, D. (2014, March). The Conservative Crusade Against the *ABC*. *The Monthly*. https://www.themonthly.com.au/issue/2014/march/1393592400/don-watson/conservative-crusade-against-abc#mtr

Weaver, D. (Ed.). (1998). *The Global Journalist: News People Around the World*. Hampton Press.

Weinert, E. (2019). Host of Internet Forum Not Liable for Abuse Online—Status Quo But for How Much Longer? *Entertainment Law Review, 30*(5), 162–163. https://primoa.library.unsw.edu.au/permalink/f/11jha62/TN_gale_legal592533264

Wilkie, K. (2017, January 15). Controversial Muslim Activist Yassmin Abdel-Magied is Now Flogging Products and Companies on Instagram as a Paid Social Media 'Influencer'. *The Daily Mail*. https://www.dailymail.co.uk/news/article-7887389/Yassmin-Abdel-Magied-flogging-companies-Instagram-paid-social-media-influencer.html

Wilson. J. (2008, May 13). Will Newspapers Be First Against the Wall? *New Matilda*. http://newmatilda.com/2008/05/13/when-revolution-comes

Windschuttle, K. (2000). The Poverty of Cultural Studies. *Journalism Studies, 1*(1), 145–159. https://doi.org/10.1080/146167000361221

Wood, D., Daley, J., & Chivers, C. (2018). Policy Forum: Economics and Populism Australia Demonstrates the Rise of Populism Is About More than Economics. *The Australian Economic Review, 51*(3), 399–410. https://doi.org/10.1111/1467-8462.12294

Yang, X., Chen, B. C., Maity, M., & Ferrara, E. (2016). Social Politics: Agenda Setting and Political Communication on Social Media. *arXiv.org, 10046*, 330–344. https://doi.org/10.1007/978-3-319-47880-7_20

Yukl, G. (2010, republished). *Leadership in Organisations* (7th ed.). Pearson.

Zhou, N. (2017, July 12). I'd Be Tempted to Run Over Yassmin Abdel-Magied, Commentator Says: Radio 2GB Defends Prue MacSween's Comments as 'Light Hearted' and 'Nonliteral' After She Says Abdel-Magied Was Right Not to Feel Safe in Australia. *The Guardian*. https://www.theguardian.com/australia-news/2017/jul/12/conservative-commentator-run-over-yassmin-abdel-magied

Zineldin, M., & Hytter, A. (2012). Leaders' Negative Emotions and Leadership Styles Influencing Subordinates' Well-being. *The International Journal of Human Resource Management, 23*(4), 748–758. https://doi.org/10.1080/09585192.2011.606114

Zuo, J. (2003). From Revolutionary Comrades to Gendered Partners: Marital Construction of Breadwinning in Post-Mao Urban China. *Journal of Family Issues, 24*(3), 314–337. https://doi.org/10.1177/0192513X02250888

Zhou, C. & Xiao, B. (2020). China's Social Credit System is pegged to be fully operational by 2020—but what will it look like? Australian Broadcasting Corporation. 2 January 2020. Retrieved from: https://www.abc.net.au/news/2020-01-02/china-social-credit-system-operational-by-2020/11764740

CHAPTER 5

Losing the Brand in the Australian Media Landscape

5.1 Discerning the best pronouns to describe ABC ownership

> One of the great lies put about by purveyors of mediocrity is that the ABC should become "relevant" by abandoning the transmission of cultural excellence and devoting itself to pop culture, but this is anti-democratic.[1]
>
> Justice Elizabeth Evatt, Patrick White, Thomas Keneally, Frank Moorehouse, Nancy Keesing, Chris Koch, Lloyd Rees, Pat Lovell, Les Murray, Edmund Campion, Nigel Butterley, Mr Justice James McClelland, Mr Justice Michael Kirby (1985)

The preceding collective quote of 12 eminent Australians from diverse walks of life actually warns about the shift of the ABC from its *field*. The 12 eminent Australians accused ABC upper and middle management of failure to preserve the ABC's content quality: "because it persists in a clownish quest for popular "relevance", thus bringing the ABC into competition with the commercial stations—a competition it is failing dismally" (*The Canberra Times*, 1985).[2] The Managing Director was then Geoffrey Whitehead who replied that the ABC was in the process of responding to and implementing recommendations from the Dix Report. Subsequent moves by the ABC further into the emergent commercial *field* has seen erosion of the ABC's *cultural capital*. To put this is wider context (and this has been raised elsewhere in this book) in 1938, ABC Board Member

V. Small, *Strangling Aunty: Perilous Times for the Australian Broadcasting Corporation*,
https://doi.org/10.1007/978-981-16-0776-9_5

James Kitto, responding to criticism of ABC programming, said "no matter what it (the ABC) does to meet its critics, it will always be criticised" (The Newcastle Sun, 1938).[3,4] It has been ever thus, even now when it describes itself in promotional advertising with the pronoun "yours".

However, the surfacing problem is that the move has not made it more relevant because in abandoning its *field*, it assumed that its *cultural capital* would follow in the mistaken belief it was embedded in the institution. However, as the literature states, institutions change. Broadcasters, as regulated media providers, were initiated by a proactive government in the early twentieth century, but media now functions in a largely deregulated internet environment where governments react to the rapidly evolving dictates of the digital *field* (Varona, 2009).[5] Professor of Cultural Science at Western Australia's Curtin University, John Hartley, identified a "value chain of meaning" (Ibid., 2008)[6] that existed in the media; where, once the consumer was the passive recipient, now the individual was in "partnership" with producers. "Value chain of meaning" was borrowed from the old business manufacturing model of the "value chain" which described increasing income and cutting costs along the production line. Hartley (2008) re-positioned this process within the context of cultural production where the "value chain" now focused on the consumer's experience. The audience did not bring along old expectations but looked for the new and novel and were more "powerful" and "demanding" (Martinoli, 2016)[7] as a consequence of this power shift. Where once media hankered after advertisers (*ergo,* the audience would follow), it now has also pander to audience power more than ever. In addition, although the role of ABC journalists was under-researched, there is evidence that they are using social media as a powerful platform to project their own opinions and thereby conflicting the ABC as an institution, as analysed in the previous chapter.

Singapore media research found that audiences there expected journalists to serve "the public, the nation and the government—and in that order" (Tandoc & Duffy, 2016),[8] conversely US research found that there was an overriding expectation of all journalists to engage with social media audiences as a normative practice and that this was an important measure for news outlets to measure their impact. Other research in Germany and the UK augmenting this belief, pointing out that audiences' views were still assumed as—"the implied audience" (Das & Graefer, 2017 quoting Lunt & Livingstone, 2012).[9] As a consequence, understandings of truth and reality had changed dramatically, accentuated by the use of online and social media where "truth" has become a collective activity (Floyd, 2019)[10] but accompanied by a "lack of respect for the consequences of words"

(Ibid.). There had been a dramatic change in the way language was used and received compared with centuries ago, or even in the lifetime of the older demographic of the ABC's citizens.

Hartley (2008) said in pre-modern times, for example, meaning was located within texts, literally within "the word"—especially the Bible where the use of "the word" means the precept or command is directly reiterated and spoken from the divine. The Bible (and in other traditional religious scriptures such as the Talmud and Koran) were all "words" from the divine. They were unquestioned. But this shifted in later times when literacy advanced, publishing expanded and the search for meaning moved to one where it was located within the commodity of "the printed word"—the commodity meant what it said, and it said what it meant, and it was on the "public record".[11] It was in "black and white", which was a printing derivation of that expression. The veracity was in the printing. Then, context overwhelmed the invested value and primacy of "the word" when the publisher charged the written word with additional meaning. Publishers then controlled the word further by managing context. Now, "the source of meaning has drifted to the other end of the value chain" (Hartley, 2008)[12] in that the audience and its individual constituents give the text/word meaning. A text means what we say it means—we apply meaning depending on how we experience it, our values and how it dovetails with our beliefs. No longer do we dive into the text to seek meaning constituted in the text—to situate within the author's milieu and beliefs—we look to our own reactions and values, polling, surveys and social media responses for that.

But these transitions have not been smooth and automatic and Hartley (2008) argued we were still at loggerheads with each other about these shifts—manifesting in the culture wars (Hartley, 2008).[13] Redaction, where existing texts are changed to get new meanings and memes (elements of shared culture and parody, first identified as such by Dawkins (1976)), is part of this shift where the individuals now "edit people's choices" (Hartley, Ibid.).[14] Curation of texts by media providers was another means of giving new meaning to texts by placing them in different contexts. For example, when a serious news story is posted on Twitter it can then became torn to shreds by the strident voices who are contesting the authority of the person quoted (as well as the media outlet who placed credence in quoting this figure as a news source in the first place). The considerable damage to the authority of the original text—and the role of the journalist—goes only lightly remarked and researched.

More damage occurs when journalists give opinions based on their own (objective) news reports and the audience can read between the lines of those comments. It can suggest that the authority figure quoted in the report was not to be believed. Journalists have sought popularity and career propulsion by getting published online—and on as many platforms as possible. Lead stories were always the cornerstone of a successful and awarded career. To be well and widely read and respected as an objective reporter was all. Now, when news reporters upload content or personal comment on Twitter or Facebook, they do so in the belief their credibility is boosted. But it comes at a price. Journalists can become compromised because serious journalism and serious journalists have been forced into an "awkward arranged marriage" with Twitter—almost a co-dependence—where a powerful internet company has the capacity to control, censor and hijack content and its Twittering contributors, but they both need each other. The literature said these were "new fangled toxicities in the media ecology we inhabit" (Floyd, 2019) with the undesirable consequence that audiences would increasingly avoid traditional media and gather their news from less authoritative sources (Soysal, 2019).[15]

Hartley (2008) identified post-broadcast media as consisting of "read and write" literacy[16] and originally, (e.g., when the ABC was formed) the consumer was a participant but could change the content in only subtle ways (telephone feedback, talkback, competitions, letters, personal engagement in live performances). Since then, there has been a radical shift. The audience controls all the meaning. In fact, the reader ***is*** the meaning. To illustrate how this shift worked, the ABC promoting itself in 2020 as "Yours" indicated it had correctly identified this power shift in favour of its audience. As discussed in an earlier chapter, the ABC Television network had re-launched itself in 2018 as ABC, "Yours",[17] then in 2019 it changed its tag-line to "ours", reverting to a 2018 view of the audience. Content is unequivocally now "yours" obtained through conversations with "yours"—the ABC says to its vast public "it's all about yours/it's all about you". These are consumer-oriented, commoditised re-positionings of the public broadcaster. The choice of #ourabc (the precursor to #yours) was one way that showed the ABC identified "branding is invaluable in developing and maintaining public support and loyalty for public service broadcasting" (Johnson, 2013).[18] Johnson (2013) argued public broadcasters relied on public loyalty for their survival and both the latest and previous ABC choice of taglines have endeavoured to reinforce the common ownership and familiarity of the organisation (Johnson, Ibid.).

In a much broader information context, "Yours" is also a trigger reminder that news and ideas may no longer even be generated by actual journalists, but "real people". But this is aberrant thinking when automated bots can also churn out stories, as discussed in Chap. 4. Who exactly is "yours", is it a real person, or a concocted bot? This problematises the whole concept and authenticity of news even further. Once audiences were worried about individual traditional media proprietors massaging and directing content to further their agendas, and audiences were able to direct their scorn in the direction of bias and at a specific proprietor based in direct line of sight. Now there is no straight path between two points and these concerns are passé when algorithm driven bits and bytes created by persons and nation states unknown can now motivate, drive and craft the news agenda—for all audiences and with phenomenal reach and impact. They can instantaneously and potentially direct national thinking and government policy in ways that were once inconceivable and unimaginable. 'Fake news' is a somewhat benign cliché and belies its impact.

When in 2018, the ABC launched "ABC, yours" it added a supporting statement to this: "The ABC is Australia's most trusted, valued and distinctive media organisation. In the media world alleged to be perpetuating fake news, this has never been more important, with 82% of Australians saying they trust the information provided by the ABC" (ABC, n.d.).[19] The "#yours" re-branding signalled that the ABC was prepared to communicate with a fragmented, dispersed and personalised audiences, that it no longer spoke to its public or publics, it spoke to a consumer-based audience. Sunstein (2009)[20] said this was problematic because citizens "might want to make choices that diverge from those that they make in their capacity as private consumers" because the role of citizen is at odds with the role of consumer (Ibid.). Good public policy is not a matter of "wants"—it is a matter of "needs"; and, this has implications for democracy where "the choices people make as political participants seem systematically different from those they make as consumers" (Sunstein, Ibid.). The ABC's shift and drift seemed, however, to redress Fiske's (1989) complaint that broadcast media had prevented "grassroots participation" in an environment where its audience was a "fiction" (Ibid.)[21] anyway and aimed at serving the role of the broadcaster rather than the needs of the populace. In terms of a Bourdieusian (1984) analysis, the ABC's "#yours" was also a sign of its displacement from its participation in the public sphere. It was no longer 'all to all' anymore, and it flagged that it was overwhelmed as a public broadcaster and had reached its objective limit.[22] The barriers to participation in public debate were once set high by the *cultural capital* of the ABC but this is no longer the case for the institution. The necessary digital shift required careful, finessed reflection, policy and planning—by governments, the ABC board and ABC management.

These preparations were needed to presage and prepare the organisation to weather more funding cuts and prepare for combat in the commercial *field* in its digital transitions.

The ABC's ***cultural capital*** had been enriched with 'symbolic resources' that have created a cultural expectation in the Australian public's mind. These resources are like first impressions—they can be long-lasting and powerful. The iconic role of the ABC in Australian society provides rich opportunities for analysis of a range of symbols including the three letters of the organisation "ABC"; the ABC logo which is called the Lissajous (i.e. an image of an unending wavelength); the Majestic Anthem theme[23] played at the beginning of major radio news bulletins; the simple, catchy theme music of *Play School* the quinquagenarian-plus pre-school program (1966–current): "There's a bear in there, … and a chair as well"; and the now departed, lunar-dwelling, pencil-nosed artist *Mr Squiggle* (1959–1999): "Here's Mr Squiggle, with lots of fun for everyone, here's Mr Squiggle, sing a happy tune" and his impatient Blackboard intoning slowly "hur-ry uup".

The ABC's embedding of songs and tunes into the national Australian spirit is not a minor consideration. It is something marketing companies can only dream about. Amongst these enduring and treasured icons that were formative of Australianness, should also be included the famous ABC television newsreader, James Dibble. Dibble read the first ABC Television news bulletin in 1956 and retired from the role in 1983. In delivering Dibble's eulogy in 2010, the then Managing Director Mark Scott said Dibble was "for generations of Australians … the face and the voice of the ABC".[24] That is a powerful image for Australians to uphold and respect—yet considering Dibble also formed part of the 'older male whiteness' of the organisation, his very role and presence now would be of deep concern. Yet, the ***cultural capital*** accrued by the dignity and accomplished craft of Dibble for the ABC, radiated over all its actors and journalists. It was ***cultural capital*** that was considerable, formidable and enduring.

Aunty's political capital was once based on being a uniquely reliable and reputable voice of news and investigative reporting. Its investigative journalism (Four Corners program) became the role model for Australian investigative journalism—it was an enduring exemplar. This was gained through its investment in training and development of its journalists, voice coaching for broadcasters, the pursuit of substantive investigative journalism (which consists of long-term projects lasting at least six weeks and therefore hard for commercial operators to afford), an emphasis on sourcing authoritative information where nothing "gets a run" (is published) without credible sources, solid tip-offs, legal compliance, principled, ethical accuracy and an elegant distance from other commercial news media—in fact, a general non-reliance on "the commercials" (as they were referred to at the ABC). There was even a snooty disdain of them. The ABC boasted: absence of opinion in factual issues, disparagement of emotive and personalised language over-loaded with adjectives and adverbs, quality specific writing that communicated clearly to the general public. Its goal was to communicate information that was needed by the general public. Paradoxically, this privileged, élite style and approach aimed to serve all Australians—'all to all'. Now the ABC is caught, as an institution. While it has a corporate reputation and Charter to uphold; existential fears and budgetary erosions have accompanied a substantial decline in its content. In the rush digitisation there was a lack of planning from all quarters and its invaluable *cultural capital* was not monetised. Image 5.1 (following) depicts an early interview style of the prominent ABC investigative news program, Four Corners. The early high esteem for the program was due to the skills and popularity of its inaugural presenter, Michael Charlton, who won a Logie (an Australian television award) the year of this photo for 'Most Popular Personality on Australian Television'. He was also identified as having "an English accent" (Musgrove, 1961)—although born and educated in Australia. Charlton was identified as a presenter who was "one of Australia's best-informed commentators" (Musgrove, Ibid.) giving presentations that were: "notable for their suitability, smoothness, and the facts" (Ibid.).

The institutional literature said when there was a serious threat to primary stakeholder relationships (in this case the ABC's audiences, the publics it serves and governments) and pressure from its secondary stakeholder relationships (for the ABC that means a squeeze from activists to take up causes, "influencers", micro-celebrities and denigration by other media) it signalled this "is a threat to the reputation" (Coombs, 2012) of outfits—in this case the ABC (Ibid.).[25] Action on social media can bring about change for good and raise awareness and consciousness of need and crisis. For example, Cunningham and Craig (2018)[26] said in China LGBTIQ+ content was banned from mainstream media, but awareness had been raised to some extent on (an albeit heavily surveilled and curtailed) social media. The challenges to the ABC of talking to people, however, means it has become highly reactive to social media in driving program content. The previous filters of topics have been removed. Concurrently, emotional voices online can amplify a position into a crisis, forcing institutions into a rapid response (Vignal Lambret & Barki, 2018)[27] in an environment where social media is a vital tool for activists (Youmans & York, 2012).[28] Where once news media shaped serious issues for the general public to

Image 5.1 Four Corners' Michael Charlton interviews Sir Douglas Copland, a delegate of the 1963 Australian Citizenship Convention from 4–7 June 1963, in Canberra. Courtesy of the National Archives of Australia. Immigration—Citizenship Convention. Almost 300 delegates attended the 1963 Australian Citizenship Convention from 4–7 June in Canberra. The Convention was officially opened by the Prime Minister, Sir Robert Menzies, and the Minister for Immigration, Alexander Downer, gave a report to delegates on Immigration developments and trends during 1962–1963. The Australian Broadcasting Commission gave a comprehensive coverage of the Convention of the television program "Four Corners", presented nationally on ABC television. Here the compere, Michael Charlton, interviews Sir Douglas Copland, one of the Convention Delegates. 1963. Series: A12111, 1/1963/11/15. Item ID: 8278160. Canberra

consider through private research and individual contacts, it is now caught in a system of chasing dispersed online views and special interest topics aided by social media organisations which help shape the issue (Youmans & York, Ibid.) through their capacity to "shape interactions within activists' collective action spaces" (Ibid.).[29] This was once the role of the traditional news media. However, it also needs to be acknowledged here that traditional commercial media proprietors and journalists belonged to a disparate *field* consisting of strict, ethical professionals, sensationalists, powerbrokers and fabricators. Journalists' old, cynical maxim "never let the facts interfere with a good story" has antecedents.

This shift in the ABC's *field* also showed it was alert to the challenge of trying to adapt to dramatic changes in "the deliberation, interest formation, and decision-making requirements of societies" (Bennett, 1998).[30] Yet, the ABC has moved to a *field* where information is now trafficked, fractured, monetised/demonetised, commoditised, pranked, algorithmically-architectured, truncated, recontextualised, 'memed' and dislocated. All media outlets and journalists now aim to be shared, 'liked', trending, commented upon, re-tweeted and re-posted in what had proven itself to be an unreliable, unstable new *field*. In many ways this is not dissimilar to the old newspaper competition where every journalist wanted their report to "get a run" on the first page, except now every post is a first page and the trending hashtag is the headline. What seems to have been forgotten in the rush to merge with social media, however, is that social media giants are profit-making businesses—and there is nothing intrinsically wrong with that—but the point this research makes is that internet media corporations are not a social service, they are not a public service—they are not public service media outlets directed to serve the greater good for no profit. There has been much apparent confusion on this point. At the same time, social media has given "rise to both challenge and opportunity" (Artwick, 2013 quoting Braun & Gillespie, 2011),[31] especially in terms of live streaming events and crises, for example, provides outstanding means of content distribution. This book is also not disputing that social media can "enhance the management of public service delivery, to enable online citizen-government interaction and participatory democracy, and to promote accountability" (Reddick & Aikins, 2012).[32] It does challenge that its utilisation by public service media has been benign because immersion in social media has curtailed its capacity to quarantine ("lockdown") fact from opinion and thereby provide impartial news.

Part of microblogging Twitter's revenue stream is fees from organisations paying to link their company to popular search terms and hashtags (Baumann, 2010)[33] while Facebook mines data and networks on individuals and groups and tracks online purchasing, which is hugely valuable knowledge for companies engaged in marketing and reputation management (Liao et al., 2014)[34] which means "Facebook is more than a communicative medium. It closes the missing links between the corporation and its potential clients, so that the most loyal clients could be nurtured" (Liao et al., Ibid.).[35] Jarringly, the ABC operates as a public service in this commercial environment. It has tried to adjust to this *field* shift by re-describing its role as bringing stories together—an umbrella approach to content curation. This re-branding, re-designing has covered all its content and it now competes with the digital sphere with its multi-media offerings, at large and within niches. A criticism of the BBC by British Conservative Prime Minister, Boris Johnson, could apply similarly to the ABC's activities in the emergent commercial field: "they will instinctively gravitate to what they think is the most civilised and liberal option, irrespective of the merits of the case" (Johnson, 2005).

When the digitally-evolving institution began as a discrete radio broadcaster in 1932 (as a result of failure of the Federal Government to provide enough radio licences, according to Semmler, 1981[36]) its original mission was animated by the perceived need for an unbiased source of information "improved and freed from all the evils, real or imaginary, of private enterprise" (The Sydney Morning Herald, 1931).[37] It has taken this thought to the new *field* but in its Institutional Logics there has been a shift in language that acts counter to it. The personalised and anthropomorphised ABC, as an octogenarian Australian who is everybody's, no longer distinguishes itself from private media, as it did originally when it was tasked to: "provide programmes suitable for every section of the community" (*The Sydney Morning Herald*, Ibid.). Ironically, it has joined the "evils … of private enterprise" (Ibid., 1931) and become what it hated. The necessary, inevitable shift into digitisation has also seen it embrace the immersive, contrived and intrusive world of all digital media. It is a dalliance with content Aunty once eschewed.

In the expansive, yet personal marketing gesture of telling Australian it was "yours", it still attends to diverse modes, platforms, programming, content and presenters reiterating the important role the broadcaster has occupied in sharing, educating and reflecting Australia and culture, overseen by ABC policies describing the broadcaster as an all-encompassing quintessentially Australian entity and talking to *all* Australians. Its Charter stipulates this embrace is demonstrated through choice of content. Its role is fortified in digital format with a vast range of participatory programs on radio, television and online—as well as social media sites. All channels are now live-streamed. Immediacy is uppermost. For example, a gate-kept Twitter "ticker" on screen streams audience responses during the panel current affairs television program *Q and A*. In 2018, the ABC iView on-demand internet television portal carried the slogan "Never miss a moment". Even with the intimacy implied by #yours, in 2019 it promoted its news and current affairs online via its meta-description on the iView URL as "Australia's Most Trusted News and Analysis".[38]

The ABC launched its online news website in 1996 and Alysen (2012) said the ABC was the first Australian broadcaster that addressed the issues of repurposing radio and television scripts as online news reports (Alysen, Ibid.).[39] Its founding online news editor, Bob Johnson, said: "Attention to detail is now fundamentally important"[40] (Ibid.). ABC Reporter, Mark Tobin was quoted: "there's a lot more scope to go into detail which is one of the advantages of having that dual capacity to file for different forms of media"[41] (Loc. Cit.). But it also means that there are no deadlines online and there are now vast expanses of cyber pages and spots waiting to be filled, updated and replenished. Where once journalists and editors targeted hourly (half-hourly) deadlines, now too much content is barely enough. As to editorial policy, former ABC Victoria News Editor, Marco Bass, said: "local is not always king, sensational is not always king. The philosophy 'if it bleeds it leads' does not come into ABC news judgement" (Alysen, Ibid.).[42] Yet, all the while ABC content is exposed to the commercial market now and is competing in that *field* for marketing success and audiences. Fiske (1982) said the range of content will decline as market forces exclude "all but the commercially successful" (Fiske, Ibid.)[43] and warned that "the voices which survive will largely belong to those least likely to criticise the prevailing distribution of wealth and power" (Loc. Cit.).[44] The ABC has undertaken a major shift in communicating to an undifferentiated audience, bespoke as a #yours audience, animated by the lifeblood of social media content. This book questions whether that is indicative of general public opinion and whether the ABC can provide robust analysis of policy when helping individuals tell stories is the stated objective. It places itself in the unfeasible position of leading national and geo-political debate in the national interest, for the commonwealth good, while catering for fractured audiences.

In the process of paying more attention to the individual needs of the audience' long-held beliefs within the institution—those established in 1932—on having an authorial and authoritative voice on what the public wanted to hear, see and read had to be abandoned too. Aunty's voice is confused, disoriented—and diminished. She has moved far away from 1932 when the then Prime Minister Joseph Lyons told the fledgling ABC audience at the launch of the Canberra regional station 2CY: "wireless has brought us all much closer to one another in Australia and it has brought us into intimate contact with countries overseas" (*The Canberra Times*, 1938).[45]

> It is not an easy task to try to satisfy millions of Australians in different states and in all walks of life. That the Australian Broadcasting Commission has succeeded so well in its task is a matter for congratulation. (Ibid.)[46]

The voice of 1932 values has gone, and the 1932 audience and its expectations may have also gone, as expected generationally—but especially the entire definition of 'public' has been changed and this situation requires revision for a public institution. The 1932 Australian 'public' expected the ABC to "open" for the day, "close" and have "intermissions" in its broadcast timetable. There was a cinematic, timed, linear physicality in the expectations of the institution vis-à-vis the daily lives of its public. Now, the concept of public itself has been shifted for a range of reasons due to: "state and corporatist strategies" (Low & Smith, 2013)[47] and a creeping privatisation of "the commons" and that there is no one public now anyway (Low & Smith, Ibid.); it is the era of the multiple publics. The use of the word 'public' invokes its alternative 'private' and the concept of ownership in law and deed—and as a political term. Perry and Rainey (1988) said public derives from the "the Latin word for people, and define it as referring to matters pertaining to the people of a community, nation, or state. Private derives from the Latin for deprived or set apart, as in being deprived of public office or set apart from government as a personal matter" (Ibid., p. 183).[48] Latterly, there has been a merger of public with private, or exposure of private, where personal matters are now considered of public interest. Individuals' personal details are tracked, traced and stolen online. In a situation of 'what they don't know, they won't miss' all operators in the emergent commercial field must now play by these lawless understandings in gathering up audiences.

Public is no longer a generic group, it is an oxymoronic vast mass of small groups or disparate tribes, with special interests helpfully cultivated, divided, individuated and identified on digital media where people give their personal details and opinions freely. There is no one, monolithic public. When one recalls the late Prime Minister Gough Whitlam's famous and culturally-reprised memorable opening line of his 1972 election address ABC broadcast[49]: "Men and women of Australia!" (Whitlam, 1972)[50] the greeting (Liberal Prime Minister Robert Menzies in 1942[51] first used "men and women", then in 1943 Labor Prime Minister John Curtin[52] "men and women of Australia") is now hopelessly inadequate at best and exclusionary at worst, and judged to be loaded with bias—in the era of intersectionality. John Hartley (2008) said another part of this shift in publics had been diverted by concerns about media ownership which distracted attention from the main issue—that consumers now had choice, they had the control (Ibid.)[53] and that they had become a powerful "collective intelligence" (Loc. Cit.)[54] and media businesses profited only by "attracting and aggregating attention" (Ibid.).[55] In addition, the Federal Government has identified that:

> Australia has one of the highest concentrations of commercial media ownership in the world and it has been argued that this has led to a dearth of sources of opinion from which people can glean information and make informed decisions about politics and social issues. The existence of public service broadcasters has helped to counter a lack of media diversity. (Jolly, 2014)[56]

Social media is an excellent postmodern marketing tool and all media—and most especially public relations and advertisers—had embraced and actively involved themselves in it. Rightly so. It is a highly effective peer-to-peer sharing and exchange model which freely shares creativity as public goods and chattels and where the audience decides their value or import to society. Attenuating itself to this, marketing on social media is either free or cheap, and Facebook was the most popular social media tool followed by Instagram, which was capturing younger consumers (Krstić & Đurđević, 2017).[57] Riding on this success was the phenomenon of celebrities becoming their own brands (Centeno, 2018),[58] while others were paid as "influencers" to sell products or services by their own personal, day to day, use of the commodities. The message of "influencers" was clear, if the celebrity used social media every day, then it must be a perfect means of communication for each individual. The definition of influencer had also undergone a revolution. Influencers used to be significant, known people in a person's life who provided wise and loving guidance and support, or a politician or civic leader who inspired—such figures as the Enlightenment philosopher John Locke who inspired US independence and the end of slavery in the US (Morgan, 2018),[59] for example.

Now "influencers" are personally unknown celebrities who the individual knows only aspirationally: "who stimulates you to buy something" (Morgan, Ibid.)[60] and contributes to the profits of an enterprise and enriches the social capital and enrichment of the individual merely because they are seen to buy or endorse the product or service. SMIs (Social Media Influencers) are also journalists who "provide orientation in a highly fragmented media landscape, where countless information channels and media outlets compete for the attention of consumers" (Sinnig, 2020)[61] and there were many collaborative platforms where they could manifest and gather their tribes of followers. There are even the "self-exposers" who "engage in deeply personal self-portrayal of their daily lives" (Sinnig, Ibid.).[62] Consequently, social media has had "a permanent and irreversible impact on consumer behavior" (Loc. Cit.).[63] The ABC, as part of the social media realm, is susceptible and captured by all that happens on social media. The consequence for public broadcasters is that they are trusting their content and paying for content aggregation in a commercial environment where market research has found SMIs "lack transparency, if they are documented at all" (Sinnig, Ibid.)[64] and research methods they used do not conform to academic standards. Coupled with that, and confounding for the ABC, is a jaundiced view among citizens that public organisations no longer serve the public and so are no longer supportive of them (Bennett, 1998).[65]

Another key aspect of social media was that the model had harvested the paid hard work and reputations of respected, traditional media in creating and implying trust and insinuating that all information shared had credence. However, one of the ways trust had been eroded had been caused by the very promise and exercise of internet liberty—the emergence of freedom to express any opinion on anything, anytime, anywhere with utmost authority. Authorial authority has been re-defined. All media—the "traditional" and the "new"—operate in the emergent commercial digital *field*. All had fallen foul of this trust erosion with a manifest failure on the part of "serious" organisations to plan. The eager resort to chasing opinion and commentators has taken standards of probity and accuracy downhill. The ABC—a stand out as a fully publicly funded media organisation—has suffered in the wake of this eventuality.

Fake news has always been around, though. The 1920s 'yellow journalism' was a good example of that—so called because the worst US scandal rags were published on yellow newspaper—and content (stuff) was literally made up. The lines have now blurred between fact and fake because of media activities, including those that promote advertorials—where the news organisation promotes a product in the guise of a news report or seizes upon an "expert" interview as the epitome of truth, where the expert may be paid to speak to the good of a product or service. In a funds-starved commercial news media world, the temptation to succumb must be enormous. The literature also pointed out that there was now an emerged 'commons knowledge' where laypeople shared information online "as an alternative to authoritative, institutional forms of knowledge" (Dorsman et al., 2015, citing Burrows et al., 2000).[66] This means compiled knowledge and ideas are in virulent contest with facts. This will be discussed in other contexts in Sect. 5.2 of this chapter.

While research on trust in social media marketing was still in its beginning phase it showed trust was built on recommendations from other consumers (Bhat & Datta in Bikramjit & Bandyopadhyay, 2018).[67] The point is that quite suddenly, there has become a confusion in the consumer's mind and a difficultly in discerning fact, from '*spin*',[68] marketing from reality, opinion from truth and information from disinformation and misinformation. Another major recontextualisation of the news media in "the information age" has happened because of *churnalism*—a term created to describe how news stories have manifest iterations, postings and re-postings on various online platforms. The consequence of this for journalism was that it had created a reliance by news organisations on news sharing analytics, to tell them how many people have read news reports, which headlines attracted more attention, where the media was read (on what device) and details on the reader's profile. The social media tracking company, NewsWhip, for example, counts among its clients: "*BBC*, *BuzzFeed*, *The Guardian*, *CBS*, and *ESPN*" (Sawers, 2015).[69] Allied with this has been the revolution in the way people access news, and it is now mostly through social media (Dwyer & Martin, 2017).[70] Newsrooms now employ analytic groups "to inform editorial process" (Ibid.)[71] and guide the writing of headlines and use of news content towards attracting a larger audience. It means everything read online is tracked and traced and then the news consumer becomes on-sold according to tastes and preferences (academic journal articles online, too, provide statistics on views and citations).

This has impacted on how the news organisation produced and packaged its news. In effect, the audience shaped what it wanted to know, rather than the authority residing in the editor who once had that 'call'. There was no more editorial gatekeeping on content—users dictate content creation and newsrooms chase the spikes in popularity. Once, it was widely accepted that the smartest person in the newsroom was the senior editor. Now the smartest 'person' in the newsroom is the algorithm mining the reaction of the consumer where the consumer has become a commodity represented by a chain of algorithms. Diakopoulos (2019)[72] said:

> Algorithms and automation are suffusing the entire news production chain, whether enhancing investigative journalism with machine- learning and data- mining methods, creating new interactive media such as newsbots that converse with audiences, or optimizing content for various media platforms using data-driven headline testing.

Research has shown that political and public affairs-based news was more shared than other, lesser 'serious' content (Martin & Dwyer, 2019).[73] The point of contention is how to define exactly what is "serious" content now when newsrooms feed off social media and engage with online banter and speculation about issues of national significance. Even more concerning is that politicians and public servants track, stress about and give knee-jerk policy responses to this online chatter which often is not a robust representation of entire populations (Murphy et al., 2014[74]; Michael & Agur, 2018[75]; Dubois et al., 2020[76]) yet these outbursts can disrupt severely a government's policy agenda, even in regard to the food security of another nation (Small & Warn, 2020).[77] It is a fraught situation where even the definition of public opinion is not concrete (Anstead & O'Loughlin, 2015),[78] yet politicians take social media as representative of the view of the public and its public good.

5.2 The COVID-19 Pandemic

Social media was acknowledged in the literature as a very effective form of communication during a health crisis especially because of its speed and ease of communication (Strekalova, 2017)[79]; however, it was also acknowledged in the literature that governments could face chaotic situations when this information was re-interpreted on social media (Strekalova, Ibid.).[80] Research found if health authorities over-informed the public it could lead to a rise in anxiety (Loc. Cit.)[81] because of the lack of homogeneity and deeply fragmented online audiences (Ibid.).[82] Once news (or any content) was appropriated into a social media context it became recontextualised and over-laid with opinion. This phenomenon of 'context collapse' was positive for journalists who can engage with multiple audiences and share their reports.

Prominent Australians, politicians, news organisations and journalists post or share news reports on Twitter to communicate with an unspecific audience, uncertain of potential responses. In an evolving crisis it can be beneficial. On the other hand, it can also cause confusion. At the time of writing, Australia (the world) was in the midst of a pandemic of a novel Coronavirus—COVID-19—a respiratory illness caused by a new virus. Such was concern over the spread of 'wrong' facts, the Prime Minister, Scott Morrison, on several television networks asked citizens to avoid reading social media posts in pursuit of factual information. He said: "There's all sorts of rubbish flying around out there ... the important thing is to go to the right source for information" (nine.com.au, 2020).[83]

Public vitriol on social media towards the government and its instrumentalities was so savage that the names of members of the Federal Government's Infectious Diseases Committee had to be suppressed to protect them from "death threats and abuse" (Patrick, 2020).[84] The level of community hysteria was such that there were viral videos on social media showing Australians fighting each other in the aisles of supermarkets over temporarily diminishing supplies of toilet paper, for example. The government had already decided that it should treat the biological contagion that was "first reported in December 2019 in Wuhan City in China" (Australian Government, 2020),[85] a pandemic (prior to the official declaration by the World Health Organisation on 12 March) after the novel virus had spread to many other countries, including Australia. The Department of Health (and state health departments) had set up a special web-page to provide regular updates (Loc. Cit.).[86]

In an unfolding crisis governments and leaders require sustained messaging. The situation was uncertain, and leaders had to gain legitimacy and authority in the institutional *field* in order for their decisions to gain manifest support and understanding. They also required trust and support for the major policy changes being made to be effective and have efficacy. In the background of this had been a dramatic decline in trust in institutions in democracies (Marozzi, 2015)[87] due to loss of confidence and jaundiced belief in competence and research showed that a loss of trust was more likely in countries where there were higher incomes and higher levels of education (Wang & Gordon, 2011).[88]

It is recognised in the literature that in crisis communication public actors have the task of communicating risk and saving lives while "newspaper journalists have the job of selling newspapers and are not charged with the job of saving lives" (Turner et al., 2013).[89] Yet, news media has a significant role in communicating health risks and can create the public perception of the crisis event where government actors aim for high efficacy so there is "a positive relationship between threat and outcomes (Turner et al., Ibid.). The ABC occupies the role in the middle, as a publicly-owned organisation, as a mediator of government information with no precondition that it must sell news to make profits and can act as an effective conduit between government and publics as the emergency broadcaster. However, in terms of a health crisis, the academic literature also asserted that "the news media is not considered a public health educator" (Loc. Cit.).

The cyber-world creates confusion as the messaging becomes a social experiment as to which information or opinion becomes the most believable, most popular, most sensational. There is contestation among commentators and journalists who leverage their popularity for controlling how the message is framed and to make demands on what they think the government should be doing. Added to this turmoil, analogue communication and broadcasting no longer existed as discrete entities (Gasher & McIntosh, 2019),[90] convergence meant new information consumption behaviours had proven that there was a new era of boutique, curated communication with "open-ended migration of communicative practices across diverse material technologies and social institutions" (Jensen, 2010)[91] where celebrity had ascendancy (Marwick, 2013)[92] to create what psychologists described as "the bandwagon effect" (Colman, 2006).[93] Placing news and information on social media means it is undifferentiated from disinformation, even hysteria. News media had an inherent capacity to calm panic in a crisis (Van der Meer & Verhoeven, 2013)[94] where their role perception may depend on the platform on which they publish (Kelling & Thomas, 2018)[95] causing fragmentation of professional practice (Gulyas, 2013)[96] and where news articles were rated as the most trustworthy compared with radio, television and social media (Hamborg et al., 2019).[97]

It is a given that all messages on social media are equal, on the one platform, yet the promised democracy (rule of the people) and self-determination of the internet has created a robust platform for attacking and delegitimising government messages—a site for mob rule. The time of the novel Coronavirus was one when government leaders were all under pressure from media. But news is a problematised commodity. According to Kuypers (2002) the public looked to the authoritative figures for opinions on controversial issues, usually the messenger is the media whose job it is to mediate the news through values (cultural, personal and professional) (Kuypers, Ibid.).[98] The ABC's role is complicated because unlike its kin traditional newspapers, in the past it never published a daily "ABC editorial" and opinion-editorial (op-ed) pieces by ABC journalists had been limited to senior reporters and placed within their observations and unique experience, such as foreign correspondents for example, who analyse events from an Australian impact/relevance perspective.

However, in this mediation process there is inevitable bias of media choice, in selecting which issues to report, what illustrative content to select, and which interviewees to choose. Bias is exacerbated by the journalists' belief they are acting in the best interests of society coupled with a possible mistaken or misplaced trust by the public in believing that the way information is presented to them should be an impartial account of the situation. Kuypers (2002) said "instead of presenting a representative picture of the public's opinion, the press presents its own partisan views as the prevailing point of view" (Ibid.),[99] as discussed in the previous chapter. Changes in journalism training have also seen a trend towards peace journalism "a journalism of attachment" (Galtung, 1998 in Hanitzsch, 2004)[100] where journalists take a moral position in their reporting, as opposed to the impartial approach advocated in journalism ethics. Peace journalism was originally proposed as a role for media in reporting war and as an antidote to conflict reporting. McGoldrick (2000) said it was a new form of journalism "concerning how journalists could be part of the solution rather than part of the problem" (McGoldrick, Ibid.)[101] in an environment where journalists were no longer functioning within the paradigm of "observer" of the "observed" but as "participant observers" (Lynch, 2002).[102,103]

Leadership literature described leading as a collaborative and negotiated role. In addition, the academic literature said that a crisis response was actually the result of "a network" (Boin et al., 2010)[104] and that "delegation of decision-making authority ... usually enhances resilience rather than detracts from it" (Boin, Ibid.).[105] During the Coronavirus pandemic, the Federal Government delegated message communication through various ministers and public servants contributing information and pursuing policy changes, specifically the Prime Minister, Treasurer, Health Minister and the Chief Medical Officer. At the time, the media was co-incidentally criticising what was considered a dated view of leadership—that the leader was an heroic, mythical crisis leader who made all the major decisions alone based on the flawed belief that the leader's role was to change behaviours (Sinclair, 2007).[106] There was consequently "crisis in political leadership" (Hewett, 2020)[107] where in Victoria the Premier, Daniel Andrews, with the Coronavirus getting out of control in that state forced a hard lockdown on its citizens. Similar actions in other states, as the crisis emerged, prompted street protests against the decisions of leaders. The literature said that responsible leadership takes counsel, delegates and consults, there are several voices, and the aim is to mobilise people (Sinclair, Ibid.) and that there was a myth that everyone can be a leader (Dugan, 2011).[108] There has been a shift in leadership literature from the authoritarian heroic leader to the post-heroic leader who encourages participation and facilitates groups (McCrimmon, 2010).[109]

The ABC Chair Ita Buttrose criticised State and Federal Governments during the national health crisis for confusing Australians with "a barrage of messages" (Pitt, 2020)[110]and that "one or two authoritative ones all singing from the same song sheet would deliver a better, more consistent, public health message" (Pitt, Ibid.).[111] The implicit intent of the ABC Chair was to urge and support a more legitimate voice than those supplied by the government, possibly one that the ABC could offer, because Buttrose did not specify an authorised government medical expert as an "authoritative" singer (Loc. Cit.). Buttrose also asserted here that the role of the leader in a crisis was a 'one-stop shop person' to provide all information.

Buttrose cited her own previous work, as an example of a successful public health campaign. She outlined that when she was Chairperson of the National Advisory Committee on Auto-Immune Deficiency (NACAIDS) from 1984 until 1988 her committee developed and implemented the national HIV/AIDS (Human Immuno-Virus/Acquired Immuno-Deficiency Syndrome) education campaign. She said one of the campaign's features was a controversial "Grim Reaper" television advertisement which warned that all Australians were vulnerable to succumb to the virus. The AUD3 million (Lupton, 1992)[112] three-week national campaign was designed to shock the Australian populace into believing that each person was at risk of contracting the Acquired Immune Deficiency Syndrome (AIDS). The medical literature said: "the commercial … has become one of the most controversial and well-remembered advertisements ever shown on Australian television" (Lupton, Ibid.).[113]

However, the medical literature differed with Buttrose in their assessment of the success of the campaign. Its research findings were that the campaign was not a success. Quite the opposite. In fact, the literature said the campaign induced panic in the community and the media (Ibid.).[114] At the time of the release of the "Grim Reaper" advertisement in 1987 Buttrose told newspapers: "the nation faces a major heterosexual epidemic of AIDS unless Australians radically change their sexual behaviour … the disease is spreading much faster and wider than previously predicted" (Mannix, 1987).[115] This statement and the television advertisement were both criticised heavily in the Australian medical research literature as not effective because they created general anxiety among the population. It was accused of creating panic by exaggerating the threat, where AIDS was "restricted to the established high-risk groups" (Holman et al., 1987).[116]

Medical complaints against the AIDS campaign were that it was too generalised and not targeting the necessary groups (Dwyer et al., 1988)[117] by encouraging a surge of low-risk people to be tested for the Human Immuno-Virus (HIV), instead of the high-risk groups. At that time, the medical research literature identified the most at-risk groups in Australia were "homosexual and bisexual men, intravenous drug abusers and blood-transfusion recipients" (Morlet et al., 1988).[118] Doctors from the Department of Virology at Westmead Public Hospital in Sydney said in a letter to The Medical Journal of Australia that the campaign: "demonstrates how media publicity can dramatically and sometimes unexpectedly increase the workload of a diagnostic laboratory" (Dwyer, Ibid.)[119] with people in low-risk categories rushing for testing. Further the campaign was criticised as not encouraging people to find out more about the virus to prevent transmission (Morlet, Ibid.).[120]

The theatricality of the television campaign advertisement was also criticised as politically appealing but not in the long-term interests of changing Australians behaviours. One positive side of the campaign was reported in research from Sydney Sexually Transmitted Diseases Clinic at Sydney Hospital which found that sex workers who attended their clinic were made more aware of the transmission of the virus as a result of the campaign, as were their "brothel managers" (Harcourt et al., 1988).[121] Overall, however, the academic medical literature cautioned that: "Health educators should be aware that press coverage can support public health information campaigns, as well as undermine them" (Lupton, 1992).[122] The literature also warned that when a campaign was taken to an extreme, such as the "Grim Reaper" campaign, the public would also weary of the message because of its intense dramatisation.

The ABC challenged the authority of state government during the novel Coronavirus Pandemic was when ABC Radio National's Health Report presenter, Dr Norman Swan, a medically-qualified broadcaster, said it was his belief that Australia's state governments were "dicking around" in response to the outbreak (Swan, 2020).[123] Swan (2020) was then the ABC appointed expert on the novel Coronavirus and the ABC set up a daily podcast called Coronacast.[124] The Prime Minister Scott Morrison warned on 16 March 2020 that up to 150,000 Australians could die (McCauley et al., 2020).[125]

There was an avalanche of abusive and negative comments about the Australia's Chief Medical Officer, Professor Brendan Murphy, who was the government's chief adviser on the Novel Coronavirus. Murphy was also Professorial Associate at the University of Melbourne, Adjunct Professor at Monash University, Fellow of the Australian Academy of Health and Medical Sciences, Fellow of the Royal Australian College of Physicians and Australian Institute of Company Directors—and a public servant. *The Sydney Morning Herald* reported that: "some health commentators on social media have said they consider Dr Swan more credible than the Chief Medical Officer" (Topsfield, 2020).[126] The Professor of

Infectious Diseases at Sydney Children's Hospital, David Isaacs, spoke in support of Murphy:

> The people advising Brendan Murphy are the best people in the country. They are the ones I would go to for advice. I think we should trust them. Doctors who should know better are giving advice. I think if Brendan Murphy really needed their advice he would have asked them to be on the advisory committee. (Patrick, 2020)[127]

Swan was described by The Australian Financial Review (2020) as: "one of the main critics of the government's gradual response to the pandemic, turning him into an anti-establishment hero for some, and an example of the broadcaster's policy overreach for others" (Patrick, 2020).[128] The undermining of the government response caused confusion in the public (Razavi, 2020)[129] at apparent government inadequacy, yet the government's responses consisted of an Office of Health Protection's response team with units focusing on epidemiology, logistics, procurement and liaisons with the Department of Foreign Affairs and Trade and "the bulk of the department's resources had been reoriented to the pandemic" accessing Australian and international data at daily briefings (Razavi, 2020). Razavi (2020) quoted Deputy Chief Medical Officer, Dr Nick Coatsworth: "in Australia, this has been a social media pandemic, as much as an infectious one" (Razavi, Ibid.). Coatsworth said: "at every step, the approach has been proportional and scalable, in line with public-health principles, and the Australian Health Protection Principle Committee" (Loc. Cit.).

To complicate the ABC's response to COVID-19 further, it then had to defend Swan after the publication of a news report that Swan, who was critical of the government's education campaign on the novel Coronavirus, was found to be a minority shareholder and director of a company, Tonic Health Media, tendering for a Federal Government contract to educate general practitioners on COVID-19 (Norington, 2020).[130] The ABC responded:

> His contract allows him to undertake external work. All such external work is subject to approval to ensure it does not create any conflicts with the individual's work for the ABC . … Any accusation of a conflict of interest between Dr Swan's contribution to the community about COVID-19 as a journalist and the work of Tonic Health Media is unfounded. Dr Swan is a valued member of the ABC Science Unit. Rightly, he is highly regarded and respected for his commitment to independence and integrity. (Jackson, 2020)[131]

Journalism is now complicated. Journalists see themselves as educators and readily adopt the role of raising awareness of issues (Statham, 2007) yet operated in an environment where there were declining numbers of reporters reliant on a growing use of public relations firms as their suppliers of news (Davies, 2009).[132] There is also the ancillary energy from a brutal and rampant quest for various truths, this derives from journalists' attempts to push-back from the pressure to recirculate public relations and government briefings, but also accommodate the opinions on social media. Added to this maelstrom for professional journalists is the role of participatory journalism where anyone can be a journalist (or photographer, or videographer) and where audiences shape the inconstant and mercurial "conversation" adding personal interpretations and sharing ideas as incontrovertible fact.

The move by the ABC to create its own experts, in many areas, has been an outcome of a manifest trend in the media generally. This has become a situation where "the role of experts in media coverage has become increasingly common in the world of alternative versions of objective reality" (Venger & Matthews, 2019).[133] The use of experts increases an institutions' legitimacy and accredits their experts with the jurisdiction of being seen as knowledge leaders (Venger & Matthews, 2019 quoting Schlesinger & Tumber, 1994; Sigal, 1973).[134] The use of experts was a "mainstay feature of news reporting" (Venger & Matthews, 2019) but the literature also identified that there was also concern that the more prominent use of experts actually exacerbated the knowledge gap between those of high and low socio-economic status (Jerit, 2009).[135]

Journalists are required to somehow manage the endless supply of online opinions while operating in a professional, neutral framework. To enable them to maintain their authority, they recruit expert voices to direct the discussion in this boisterous, crowded, participatory, ersatz democracy e-environment. Ultimately, it means that newsroom culture has been remade. Journalism has undergone revisionism. It once had privileged élite access to the newsmakers and gate-kept content that it believed was 'the public's right to know'. The *field* was staffed by actors who were trained to sort the 'furphy'[136] from the fact. It operated on exclusive networks of dissemination and sources (informants) who were cultivated and held close and confidential by the journalist. Now the public tell the journalists what they want to know and who to speak with, and the media responds by finding and promoting experts to shore-up its credibility in "the conversation", whatever the conversation happens to be and whatever the "journey" people are on—another challenging metaphor for journalists to grapple with that carries political overtones where the actor can manipulate and enlist audiences (Dávid & Furkó, 2015).[137] It is professional one-upmanship where the audiences and internet companies will always win because they cultivate an ideas culture as a marketing imperative, and commercial news outlets collapse their models into this new, more lucrative genre.

In terms of covering health matters, the psychiatric literature (Friedman, 2009) said that most people find out about mental health from the media but that there were concerns that the media tended to favour the format of "if it bleeds it leads", so only extreme psychiatric conditions were of interest. Friedman (2009) said there needed to be a distinction between literature written for the research community where speculation and debate about research and therapies is accepted and understood; and, literature written for the general public, which is a more vulnerable group and susceptible to influence because it is seeking answers and is not equipped for robust scientific debate. The literature said the general public was not educated to dispute science with robustness and provide researched contradictory evidence. Added to this is a cyber-environment the internet has blurred "the distinction between information and expertise" (Friedman, 2009).[138] The ABC's assumption of the need for a medical authority coincided with what was seen as early unclear directives provided by the Federal Government and state governments, a few of whom were then choosing to act alone out of step with the Federal Government. This prompted the perceived need for what the environmental science literature described as "advocacy science" (Javeline et al., 2013. Quoting McGarity & Wagner, 2008; Michaels, 2009; Oreskes & Conway, 2010).[139] However, Ward (2005) warned:

> At a time when health and safety is suffering under the risk-averse glare of public opinion and the vitriolic outpourings of media commentators it is more important than ever for practitioners to defend their profession and make the case for sensible risk management. (Ibid.)[140]

The emergence of the audience interest in the media expert is also allied with a development identified in the medical literature where citizens are refusing to take advice and diagnosis from healthcare professionals and seek it online. This "expert" is referred to disparagingly as "Dr Google". There was an emerging belief that personal physicians, or health providers, knew less than opinions sourced on the internet, the media, family and friends (Keshet & Popper-Giveon, 2018).[141] Medical practitioners are now confronting the growing numbers of patients who self-diagnose from the internet (Kuehn, 2013)[142] and self-treat (D'Ambrosia, 2009).[143] Patients base their diagnosis on a "Googling" of their symptoms and online recommendations from random websites of suitable medications.

So, a doctor's visit is not to seek diagnosis, merely to have the prescriptions filled, as recommended by "Dr Google". Apart from the rejection of personal, targeted professional advice, medical research has found that Google was reducing visibility of health and information websites that were not meeting its high-ranking criteria (Strzelecki, 2020).[144] Google now ranks its main topics into five categories that it calls "Your Money or Your Life" (YMYL) one of which were health pages and those that had the most 'hits' were deemed the better, because they were the most lucrative in attracting advertising. Research has found that Google said it was attempting to be more scrutinising of health websites it recommended, but researchers also found Google was only manually checking health websites and of the health websites the research surveyed:

> Most of them offer pseudo therapies or health tips not sustained by scientific evidence, and even cooperate to provide a platform for distributing fake health tips. (Strzelecki, Ibid.)[145]

A 2005 letter in *The New England Journal of Medicine*[146] *from* a New York rheumatologist "described a scene at rounds where a professor asked the presenting fellow to explain how he arrived at his diagnosis". The reply came: "I entered the salient features into Google, and [the diagnosis] popped right up". It is a situation where: "'do no evil' is a far cry from 'do what's best for humanity'" (Guistini, 2005).[147]

Media outlets now search for opportunities for their own experts because, quite rightly, they too must compete in this 'hydras heads' environment of proliferating medical information online—and also that some audiences were aware that health websites may be unhelpful, or even injurious, so they take recourse to the media to provide experts. Further, the ABC as a national broadcaster, as the national *emergency* broadcaster, has legitimacy as a source of national information because it references a value system that places it as holding the national interest and implementation of government policy at the heart of its operations. It was therefore expected to respond to a public health emergency and, therefore, required to inform the public on this unfolding novel Coronavirus health and economic crisis. But the consequences of the actions taken by the ABC in these instances could also serve to confuse or obfuscate rather than instruct, especially when its health advice was at odds, or undermining that communicated to citizens by the government and government-appointed and accredited medical experts.

The literature explained this backlash against official information as the rise in "the undisciplined patient" (Keshet & Popper-Giveon, 2018)[148] which was a "social phenomenon characteristic of Western neoliberal societies" (Ibid.).[149] The medical literature described "the undisciplined patient" as push-back on credentialed advice (Loc. Cit.)[150] by those who resisted authority, defied recommendations, took health risks, "Googled" their illnesses and refused to conform to medical or health requests from physicians, specialists—and authorities. They attributed this re-orientation by individuals to pursue their own medical diagnosis as a consequence of public organisations' resistance to take responsibility for individual's health. Citizens are now directed to manage and control their own health risks (Keshet & Popper-Giveon, Ibid.)[151] and lives. Allied with this information shift of focus the ABC now competes in the same *field* as emergent commercial media, online citizen journalists and commentators all offering expert opinions on health.

The rise of "the undisciplined patient" has created citizens who are "expert" in their own best health treatments and outcomes. The ease and facility of online information appears to provide them with all the facts they believe they need to make informed and correct decisions on their health, over and above that of health authorities and trained, credentialed, research-active professionals. For example, this "undisciplined patient" behaviour could take the form of non-vaccinators in Australia who refuse to have their children vaccinated against childhood diseases. This meant Australian children were dying from vaccine-preventable diseases. Élite Australian footballers were also refusing to have influenza vaccinations during the novel Coronavirus pandemic, because they disputed the safety of the 'flu vaccines, objected for religious or conscientious grounds; or, believed the vaccine could impact on their health or threaten their families (AAP, 2020).[152] The influenza vaccine was recommended by Federal and State Health authorities for everyone in order to reduce compromised immune systems should individuals also contract the novel Coronavirus at the same time and for which there was no vaccine at that time (early, 2020). Further, those who worked at, or visited, health facilities were required to provide proof of having had the 'flu vaccine.

Swan also called on 14 March for "a severe shut down" (ABC Online, 2020)[153] of all schools to combat the spread of the novel Coronavirus. The report was posted on You Tube (ABC News, 2020)[154] and then another on the ABC News' website[155] the next day (15 March). This was in spite of the official Federal Government position at the time that Australian schools remain open because children were at low risk, their grandparents were at high risk and 30% of the health workforce would disappear if schools closed. *The Sydney Morning Herald* published a critical editorial on 20 March 2020 that said contradicting the government was causing anxiety and confusion: "a group of well-meaning doctors, such as the ABC's Norman Swan, who have, for better or worse, given advice that has at times conflicted with official recommendations" (The Sydney Morning Herald, 2020).[156] Then on 20 March 2020 Swan on his ABC "Coronacast" podcast reversed his advice: "If I had kids at school age ... I would be sending them to school because the risk is actually fairly low at school" (ABC Online, 2020).[157]

Despite all of this, and government health orders, individuals of the public did as they wanted. For instance, although the Federal Government banned large outdoor gatherings to no more than 500, tens of thousands of people congregated tightly on Bondi Beach on Friday 20 March and Saturday 21 March 2020 to swim and sunbath in close proximity (Dumas, 2020).[158] As well, there were protest marches in the streets of Sydney and Melbourne in June when tens of thousands gathered in close proximity to support a "Black Lives Matter" campaign following the murder of an African American man by Atlanta police in the US. The sustained medical advice was that all Australians maintain safe, personal, social distancing to avoid sharing, or catching, the highly communicable virus where a study by the University of Massachusetts Amherst found one person could infect 400 people (Guler, 2020).[159] As a result of the initial en masse, close activity at Bondi Beach the government introduced harsher measures to maintain social distancing including the closure of clubs, places of worship, gyms, as well as all non-essential travel. The Prime Minister, Scott Morrison said: "What happened at Bondi Beach yesterday was not OK. And served as a message to federal and state leaders that too many Australians are not taking these issues seriously enough" (Sky News, 2020).[160] The internet caters for "the undisciplined patient" by creating options of information and options of behavioural responses for the audiences to choose, and the preferenced pursuit of the individual want in lieu of the greater need guided by official directions. Allied to this is the complicating phenomenon, where people are forced into more 'self-administration' as organisations cut back customer service. The outcome is that "citizens are also called upon to play an active role in caring for and governing themselves through a burgeoning culture of entrepreneurship" (Ouellette, 2008).[161]

Furthering the dialectic about the novel Coronavirus, on 16 March 2020 the ABC Television panel debate program *Q and A* held a debate about the pandemic which was televised and platformed. The Federal Minister for Aged Care, Senator Richard Colbeck, representing the Federal Government, was abused by Adjunct Professor Bill Bowtell, who called out loudly the word "rubbish" several times when the Senator said the government had "taken actions to try and slow down the growth of the virus" (ABC, 2020).[162] The exchange between the two on *Q and A* reached a crescendo when Bowtell ordered the Senator off the program: "Well, on behalf of the Australian people, I think you ought to, because you should not be here (*ABC* Q&A, 2020).[163] Apart from attempting to de-platform a Federal Government Minister from the Federal Government broadcaster, Bowtell also abused Colbeck for what he described as state governments' failures to sanitise and disinfect public transport (Zaczek, 2020),[164] except the Federal Government has no jurisdiction over state public transport. Bowtell accused the Federal Government of creating mass panic: "The panic is there because the lies and the misinformation have been circulating in the Australian community for weeks and weeks and weeks" (Zakzek, Ibid.).

Q and A had undergone a change over the years to a more free-form style presentation, as discussed in Chap. 4 about another *Q and A* program—whereby the presenter was no longer moderating the tone and tenor of the debate nor observing traditional rules of engagement in a debate and expectations that there should be lines of arguments, but rather permitting panellists to speak in a 'free for all' approach.[165] Format, timing and rules play crucial roles in the success of a television debate (Work & Boileau, 1985)[166] in a situation where non-verbal communication is more formative of audience opinion than verbal (Maurer et al., 2016)[167] and televised debates "enhances civic engagement" (Lee & Lee, 2017)[168] but where the mediated public act is highly performative (Craig, 2016)[169] and understandings of civil and uncivil behaviour are largely under-researched (Braunstein, 2018).[170] It has been identified that actors engage in "boundary work" to control or delegitimise contrary views (Braunstein, Ibid.) and support political inequality. For example, in the *Q and A* program cited, there was no intervention by the moderator during the hostile attack, yet the exchange had clearly degenerated into personalised language. This is in the context of an environment where social media is toxic for female Australian politicians (Mao, 2019)[171] for example, and the most abused Australian politicians on social media in 2016 were "overwhelmingly" from the Coalition (Hunt & Evershed, 2016).[172]

Q and A described itself on its micro-blogger, Twitter profile as:

> #QandA is a chance to ask questions, challenge power and share your views. We tweet other people's opinions to inspire questions, not express our own views. (ABC Q&A, 2020)[173]

While stating that it was not presenting the program's views in practice it had appeared to abandon the conventions of robust, civil debate and the rules of engagement. Philosopher, John Stuart Mill, said this form of angry suppression of alternative views means "the peculiar evil of silencing the expression of an opinion is, that it is robbing the human race; posterity as well as the existing generations" (Mill, 1863).[174]

Abuse as authentic entertainment, and as a substitute for reasoning and debate, was predicted by US futurist Alvin Toffler who wrote about the consequence of what happens to a society "overwhelmed by change" (Toffler, 1984)[175] and where the audience was in control of the content "the more we move towards advanced manufacturing, and we de-massify and individualize the production, the greater the participation of the client in the production process must necessarily be" (Ibid.).[176] The popularity of reality television and its 'ambush' and 'humiliation' styled content was also influential in supporting the new manner of media conversations. *Q and A* is now very much a "client" playground with gate-kept Twitter feeds "tickered" across the screen as the panellists speak—mocking or supportive. As to this decline in debate and respect for the role, dignity and authority of the individual, the ancient Greek philosopher, Plato, who was a foundational contributor to Western thought, predicted this type of tyranny in his dialogue *The Republic*, where a society would disintegrate into anarchy when citizens rejected government and its decisions:

> The citizens become so sensitive that they cannot endure the yoke of laws, written or unwritten; they would have no man call himself their master. Such is the glorious beginning of things out of which tyranny springs. (Plato 375 BCE, revised, 2002)[177]

The Platonic referential view was that tyranny came from democracy, as democracy came from oligarchy.[178] Plato had a name for strident, destructive voices: "drones". He described the threat to ancient Greek democratic society was from this class of "drones":

> They are more numerous and more dangerous than in the oligarchy; there they are inert and unpractised, here they are full of life and animation; and the keener sort speak and act, while the others buzz about the bema and prevent their opponents from being heard. (Plato, Ibid.)[179]

5.3 Reporting on Crisis Leadership

In crisis management, the institutional leadership literature said the leader's need for a consistent message in the public arena was tough because leaders often had to make quick and consequential decisions with limited information (Boin et al., 2010).[180] It also meant they were subject to complaints from their followers/constituents (audiences). In addition, "core values or vital systems of a community come under threat" (Boin et al., Ibid.)[181] while experts and activists "push their concerns up the political agenda" (Loc. Cit.).[182] The leadership literature said experts and stakeholders would always tend to disagree, anyway. The threat of time pressure was increased on leaders when they were subjected to intense media criticisms (Boin et al., Ibid.)[183] such that: "no set of events or developments is likely to be perceived fully uniformly by members of a community" (Ibid.)[184] and the consequence was that "order-inducing institutions cease to function, appear deficient, and/or are widely called into question" (Ibid.).[185]

An acknowledged aspect of crisis leadership was that there was a need to make urgent decisions as well as "balancing centralization with delegation" (Deitchman, 2013).[186] The academic literature agreed that public leaders "must routinely defend themselves against seemingly incontrovertible evidence of their incompetence, ignorance, or insensitivity" (Boin et al., 2010).[187] The Federal Government's leadership response to the novel Coronavirus was to form a National Security Committee composed of all state premiers and territory chief ministers in regular meetings and empowering them to respond, in accordance with overall Federal Government policy. The Federal Government also formed a National Coronavirus Commission to organise logistics, staffing and supply during the crisis. It also made a series of staged, costly, large-scale financial contributions to the economy in an attempt to sustain losses of incomes and industry.

Crisis leadership was at odds with democratic leadership, which tended to weigh up other options and seek wide support (Weber, 2010).[188] It is understood in the military, for example, that in extremis leadership (where there is an immediate risk of injury or death) must involve mutual trust and loyalty, but this of course is not the case in a democratic civil society.

This would be another factor why public push-back has been exacerbated in the case of the novel Coronavirus in Australia where definite decisions were made by the government, mandated by pre-existing or revised public health laws in regards, for example, to punishment if a person suspected they may be unwell but refrained from practicing "social distancing", or who violated "restrictions on the movement of people and goods between specified places and evacuations" (McPhee, 2020).[189]

The Australia Department of Defence had established a taskforce, to manage the military's response to the Coronavirus, led by a three-star general (Heanue, 2020)[190,191] with the Army Reserve also deployed. The government called out a group of defence personnel under the Defence Assistance to the Civil Community (DACC) rules to help Australian production of personal protective equipment (masks, gowns, goggles and sanitiser) (Burgess, 2020)[192] as well as supervise checkpoints and undertake surveillance. In NSW this 'defence to the civil power' provided by the military to the state police forces was believed to be crucial in managing, in the early stages, containment of those who required a mandatory 14-day isolation in designated hotels after returning from overseas, for example. In addition, a human biosecurity emergency was declared by the National Security Committee and enacted by the Governor-General, David Hurley (McPhee, 2020)[193] under the Biosecurity Act 2015. Yet, the emerging crisis leadership in Australia had also encouraged the media to step away from their objective roles and assume a new "privileged position to point blame toward those with legitimate authority" (Littlefield & Quenette, 2007).[194]

Research into this type of media reaction was studied by US academics who analysed the language used by the media depicting authority figures in the crisis after Hurricane Katrina in the US in 2005.[195] The media's response was based on the premise that media had authority to speak, but the US research found the media was also quick to look for a scapegoat. The researchers warned that: "the association of negative terms with those in authority may result in the premature placement of blame by the public and the effectiveness of those in authority may be compromised" (Littlefield & Quenette, Ibid.).[196] The loss of respect for leaders can be exemplified in very simple ways. The nomenclature used by the *ABC* and *The Australian* newspaper[197] of the Prime Minister for example included naming him simply "Scott Morrison" (Worthington & Snape, 2020),[198] and instances of him being addressed as "Scott Morrison" in interviews instead of using his title, or honorific. This use of first names only or absence of titles and honorifics delegitimises leaders (following Bourdieu, 1984).[199] Bourdieu (1986) would have also described this as a delegitimisation of the prime minister's *cultural capital* and the undermining of the most important aspect of *cultural capital*—what Bourdieu described as—its 'inheritability' (Bourdieu, 1998, 2017)[200]—which meant the role of prime minister was inherited, the incumbent was only elected to the role.[201]

In addition, news conferences were "pseudo-events" (not a spontaneous event) (Boorstin, 1987 in Cotter, 2010) "to what in more recent times has become known as 'info-tainment' and 'spin'" (Cotter, 2010). As a pseudo-event it therefore followed that "pseudo-relationships" (Ibid.) developed between the interviewer and their audience (and possibly with the interviewee) which was aided with a breakdown in formality, across the board. Further, in terms of the media's delegitimising of the titles or nomenclature of leaders is was evidence of the challenges of change, in society generally. But it can also be viewed another way. In the case of the ABC, the structural changes forced by funding cuts and the inherent vulnerabilities that characterised this situation meant that the ABC had become, in Bourdieu's (1984) theoretical framework, in contestation with the state's authority where the "group's presence or absence in the official classification depends on its capacity to get itself recognized, to get itself noticed and admitted, and so to win a place in the social order" (Ibid.).[202] De-funding of the ABC meant the organisation was in a struggle with Federal Governments placing the ABC in the extraordinary situation of what Bourdieu called "the symbolic struggle of all against all" (Bourdieu, 1991).[203]

Morrison was described elsewhere by an ABC journalist as delivering a "folksy address to the nation" on the crisis in the initial days (Tingle, 2020)[204] but the government overall was assessed as having improved its communication since the crisis was elevated higher on the national agenda six days previously (Ibid.).[205] The prime minister was in the foreground of pre-existing negative rhetoric surrounding his contentious lack of response to the Australian bushfire crisis by being on holidays in Hawaii at the start of the national bushfire crisis in late 2019. Mocking and memes of the prime minister wearing an Hawaiian shirt, also challenged his perceived lack of response to global climate change by failing to change Australia's economy where metaphors are a powerful tool to shape and re-direct thinking (Lakoff, 2008),[206] in this instance the Hawaiian shirt, a metaphor for absent leadership, possibly déclassé and evoking derision. This then formed an enlarged background message to the Coronavirus that described the prime minister as incompetent and unfit for leadership, in any crisis, which coupled with his Christian religious beliefs (The Guardian, 2019; Karp, 2020),[207] were used as a metaphor for distractedness and neurosis, and this fed depictions of the prime minister on social media. The blended metaphor of the Hawaiian shirt and religious beliefs had been augmented to "an existence independent of people and contexts" (Lakoff, ibid.).[208]

For female politicians this media disrespect was also challenging, but different. Australia's first female Prime Minister, Julia Gillard, and Labor Party leader was depicted variously in "a newspaper photo that 'caught' her in her house with an empty fruit bowl, and her alleged inability to manage her hair or clothing style effectively" (Hall & Donaghue, 2013). It could be argued that the empty fruit bowl had similar potency to the Hawaiian shirt meme in attempting to negate the competence of both prime ministers. Gillard was even depicted by the ABC in a sex scene under the Australian flag in the prime minister's office in a comedy series that satirised her personality and her life ("At Home with Julia"). There was upset from "Coalition" politicians describing it as "sick" and "tasteless" (ABC, 2011) while the ABC replied it was a: "very gentle, tender scene. If it's OK for others to drape themselves in our flag for all manner of occasions, I really don't see why it can't be draped over our prime minister as a symbol of love" (ABC, ibid.). The response smacks of the tawdry intimidation: "I was only having fun, where's your sense of humour?". Such was the fallibility of Australia's first female prime minister, of national leadership and a woman's role in leadership—from the ABC's perspective. In healthcare leadership, the literature differed on this assumption that flaws were impediments to leadership: "a role model's fallibility could positively influence leadership learnings" (Nicol & Gordon, 2018) by adjusting unrealistic expectations (Ibid.). During the Coronavirus pandemic, the capacity of Chief Medical Officer Brendan Murphy's expertise was questioned in an ABC report: "the chief medical officer is not infallible" (Speers, 2020)[209] but without any supplied evidence of mistakes. Here the journalist was contesting the contentious *field* of the expert. Then, quoting Adjunct Professor Bill Bowtell, the report said the Prime Minister Scott Morrison and Chief Medical Officer Professor Brendan Murphy: "have made a dangerously bad call" in announcing the ban in outdoors gatherings too late and that the Prime Minister and other ministers who came into contact with the Minister for Home Affairs (Peter Dutton, who contracted COVID 19) who had become infected with the virus "should be in isolation" (Speers, 2020).[210] The article also stated that "Professor Bowtell is not infallible" but went on to explain that the panic buying of food in supermarkets meant there needed to be more caution. Again, the journalist was contesting the expert *field* of public health.

This was an example of what the crisis leadership academic literature described when journalists "stepped outside their role of objective observer to assume a privileged position of pointing blame toward legitimate authorities" (Littlefield & Quenette, 2007)[211] and where a crisis situation that is exacerbated by social media (Gruber et al., 2015)[212] where microblogging had "real time power" (Ibid.). This situation helped reshape the public's understanding of the role of authorities in responding to the novel Coronavirus pandemic. Reports like this told the public that the government did not know what it was doing and needed advice. The media used its privileged position to panic an already disoriented and alarmed populace by suggesting ineptitude without solutions and when the media resorts to a "blame game" culprits are sought in politicians or leaders on behalf of a frightened population (Boin et al., 2010)[213] where blame is more powerful than praise because it establishes an undesirable negativity bias (James et al., 2016)[214] that overwhelms positive efforts. Researchers have found when the media apportioned blame it also had the capacity to direct public thinking about a figure in authority (Littlefield & Quenette, 2007)[215] and that "media function as a tool for the construction of blame" (Littlefield & Quenette, Ibid.).[216]

Another important aspect of crisis leadership was that leaders needed extra time to formulate responses to media criticisms. For example, it was not a situation where there was the normal parry and thrust of political debate (as in parliamentary debate) and quarrelling with journalists where responses could be composed, deferred or ignored hurriedly. Yet, if leadership responses in a crisis were judged as 'too slow' by the media, then the media labelled the political leader, or public servant leader, as deficient or incompetent in leadership. The literature said this rush to judgement by the media could compromise the flow of information that may actually be deliberately staged, or staggered, by the government because in an unfolding situation new data continued to emerge requiring re-consideration, re-strategy, change of direction in policy, or accommodation. British Nobel Peace Prize winner, lecturer and Labour Party Member of the UK Parliament, Sir Norman Angell said: "it is true that opinion is created by the way in which the press, plays upon and exploits certain tendencies and instincts" (Angell, 1922).[217]

In analysing this case of the strident voices of the internet undermining public authority, there were four noteworthy parts of this abuse[218]:

(a) Confusing politicians with public servants.

The first was that the Chief Medical Officer of the Commonwealth of Australia, Professor Brendan Murphy, was being confused by Twitter contributors as a member of the Federal Government. That he was a public servant was not understood. This confusion may have arisen because Murphy had appeared on the podium beside the Prime Minister when major televised/videoed announcements and updates were made as the novel Coronavirus crisis unfolded. The understandings of the role of a public servant were analysed in Chap. 1 of this book where the public servant and politician were analysed as quite separate roles. This separation is one of the struts of Australia's democracy but it is clearly now under threat. Murphy's real purpose in being present with the Prime Minister was to legitimate the message given in regard to changes of policy and the urgency of the health situation. His credentials were there to validate the seriousness of the public health crisis and give the content being televised/ reported veracity. But, instead, it was taken as if Murphy were politically partisan with the Liberal-National Party Coalition government and his presence was (apparently) seen as endorsing the Prime Minister, politically and personally. Therefore, Murphy's role was re-purposed by audiences into an elected member of the Federal Government, a politician. And, as a corollary of that confusion, Murphy could then be censured, rejected, libelled, ridiculed and abused, just like Australia's politicians.

(b) Failure to understand the role of public service.

Further to (1), was that the vilification of Murphy showed a deep ignorance as to the role of the public service because the defamation and lampooning of him either stated, or implied, that all public servants were part of the cheer squad of governments. What actually occurred was that Murphy's role was to give non-political, public servant support based on his independent, expert medical advice, assembled clinical advice, the latest research and data which nation states shared peer-to peer, strategies, programs and risk management, with the Prime Minister and government(s). Murphy also maintained pivotal relationships with key stakeholders within the government. Yet, it was distorted into a reason to delegitimise and de-platform him. This lack of understanding of the role of the public service pointed out key aspects of how unexpected events, in this case a misinterpretation of the role of a public servant, could lead to savaging of an individual and create another crisis for leadership (in this case completely unforeseen and maybe "unprecedented") of the Australian

Government, in this instance a public servant having to prove they were serving the public. Moving forward, there may be a lesson in this for the ABC. Influential German philosopher, Jürgen Habermas, said that "the state is the public authority. It owes this attribute to its task of promoting the public or common welfare of its rightful members" (Habermas, 1961, 1989).[219] The Chief Medical Officer of the Commonwealth of Australia, and his expert team, as public authorities, were readily mocked and their best scientific advice rejected as a phony or inadequate by journalists, commentators and strident voices who were not privy to all the information. Demand media means consequences are rarely considered, in favour of instant gratification and unbounded rage.

(c) The ABC is staffed by public servants.

The third revealing point about this abuse matter—and perhaps one of the most contrarian observations to be made in this book—was that the ABC is also staffed by public servants. ABC staff work for a public service enterprise conducted for the people, for the public and funded by the public. The organisation is explicit about this in the opening line of its Editorial Policies:

> The ABC belongs to the Australian people.
>
> Earning and retaining their trust is essential to fulfilling the ABC's charter and its responsibilities under the ABC Act to provide innovative and comprehensive services of a high standard to Australian and international audiences. (my underlining)[220]

ABC journalists were public servants, equally with the Chief Medical Officer. The incident serves to tease out the hypothesis that Aunty's voice is being strangled, in this instance by organisational and staff role confusion about public service. This predicament raised four questions (with some sub-questions):

(1) Are ABC journalists, as public servants, fully accepting and tolerant of ridicule, abuse and damage to their integrity when the online opinion tide turns against them in their public capacity? Should management permit that occurrence?
(2) Where does this locate the ABC as a public service if it is not willing to take down abuse of fellow public servants linked to its Twitter postings and feeds?

(3) Do ABC staff still identify with, or feel camaraderie as, public servants? While the ABC should scrutinise all extensions of power in society, there seemed to be a lack of clarity in its coverage of the Chief Medical Officer and his apolitical role. The ABC is also apolitical and rejects publicly any suggestion that it is biased or partisan, both in policy and in its defence.

(4) Should the ABC no longer identify itself as a public service organisation, what is to be its future in the digital environment? How can it engage in knowledgeable, organised debate in a social media sphere that champions the rejection of authority and fact? The authorial Aunty voice may be strangled in this process, too. Worse, the organisation may be strangling itself with an ongoing failure of staff culture. As a consequence of the Coronavirus Pandemic, the ABC Board took a 10% pay cut for six months (Murphy, 2020)[221] and with the prospect of 250 job losses pending. The impact was savage in the commercial media; staff of Seven West Media, had either lost their jobs, while others had to take a 20% cut in pay and there was the closure of its sales department (Mason, 2020); while, News Corporation Australia and Nine Entertainment cut costs by ordering staff to take leave, or dismissing them (Jackson & Vitorovich, 2020)[222] because of the savage downturn in advertising. News Corporation also announced that it was shutting down newspapers, or ending printing of 60 local newspapers in four states. Executive chairman of News Corp Australasia, Michael Miller said: "COVID-19 did not create this crisis but it brought it to a head … decimated by the sudden collapse of retail, real estate, clubs, restaurant and event advertising" (Miller, 2019).[223]

To support the Australian economy at the time of the pandemic the Federal Government was spending hundreds of billions of dollars to support lost jobs and wages, industry, health and medical needs. Where does this leave the ABC in the future when tough decisions will have to be made about future ABC budget allocations in the face of huge deficits? It would appear that the ABC has not positioned and cemented itself as the indispensable defender of civil society in the public sphere to endure that crisis. In addition, Australian activist group GetUp! launched a report and campaign "It's Our ABC" in May 2020 to seek more funding for the public service media outlet because of the opportunity presented by the delayed Federal Budget (moved from May to October 2020). *The Australian* newspaper obtained a comment from Federal Communications

Minister, Paul Fletcher, that said the ABC had "a level of security that private sector (media) businesses and employees can only dream about" (Tabakoff, 2020).[224] While the campaign could reveal a lack of organisational foresight on the consequences of the savage diminishment of public money generally, looking ahead it meant Aunty's voice could be strangled sooner.

Further, Miller (2019) said the nub of the problem facing all broadcasters, publishers and filmmakers was that:

> The unfairness of the digital playing *field*, along with Australia's draconian tangle of legislation and regulation, means local companies can't compete with international platforms. (Ibid.)[225]

Specifically, platforms such as Google:

> Have no commitment to local communities. They employ no journalists, create no content, face almost no regulation and pay virtually no tax while they make unheard-of profits by taking other people's content. (Loc. Cit.)[226]

Pitching a challenge in the direction of the ABC, Miller asked: "Why, for example, are Australian broadcasters still forced to spend millions of dollars creating children's content that Australian children don't watch?" (Ibid.).[227] Successive governments have presided over the erosion of funding to the broadcaster while also insisting on greater efficiencies and an expansion of services. Ultimately, it means that the marauding pirate behaviour of the major digital companies have built "an internet privatised by tech giants that have created an unfair, toxic trading environment" (Miller, Ibid.).[228] The near loss of AAP, discussed in the previous chapter, is part of this detrimental downturn in quality journalism aided by the plundering of content, for free. This has consequences for Australia's democracy. Concerns over the consequences should the independent news service AAP have collapsed accentuated that never before had Australia needed a robust public broadcaster. Now, more than ever, is the time for the ABC to be strong.

(d) The ABC suffers role confusion.

The fourth point illustrated by this matter was that the ABC was described as "an independent national broadcasting service" in the ABC

Charter (ABC, n.d.),[229] yet this independence was manifesting, in this instance, in promulgating the delegitimisation of fellow public servants, based on personalised opinions rather than substantial, arresting fact. The independence of the ABC was created so that it should be free from political partisanship, aloof from political pressure and entrusted with the broad public interest. It was invested with the capacity and distance to have an overview, just like the role of the public service. Yet, there is also the background challenge where there is a manifest lack of definition of "public Interest" (Simshaw, 2012)[230] and this adds to the complexity of the issue. As part of this book's research, one former board member expressed sorrow that ABC staff had developed a misconstrued, or re-defined, version of the true meaning of 'public interest' and the ABC's independence.

Tracey (1998) said this view typified the public broadcast sector, generally, due to "the fragmentation of social order" (Ibid.),[231] the reliance on social media in the news media ecology and the major social, economic and structural changes public service media have had to navigate and survive. They have scrambled to find a purpose as the struts were removed from them (Tracey, Ibid.).[232] In addition, the ABC was in a similar situation with its model the BBC (and now facing the prospect of subscription only funding) where the first Chairman John Reith "was anxious to avoid having the content of broadcasting politically manipulated ... and the government, anxious to avoid responsibility for trivia, the BBC was left with no effective accountability" (Curran & Seaton, 2018).[233] The BBC has been described as an uneasy compromise made into an ideal (Ibid.).[234] Much the same could be said of the ABC. The literature supported the argument by prominent media history scholars, David Cardiff and Paddy Scannell (1991)[235] that the BBC legitimised itself:

> Not by the huge audience good the service soon attracted but by reference to the élite of the great and the good who trooped into studios to educate and inform on every subject from unemployment to the Origin of the Species. (Ibid.)[236]

The *field* of broadcasting was controlled by a middle-class élite of "reforming intelligentsia" (Curran & Seaton, 2018)[237] and economic theorist John Maynard Keynes argued that "public affairs should and could be managed by an élite of clever and disinterested public servants" (in Curran & Seaton, 2018 quote taken from Encounter April 1979).[238] The ABC once occupied this *field* but with its immersion in digital and social media and absence of policy planning it has had to play by new rules and forego its ***cultural capital*** and its deeply ingrained ***habitus*** to play by the new ***doxa*** of the commercial arena. The ABC's newly developed catering to niche audiences and discrete online, commercially inspired activities and causes was never going to be suitable for the ABC and its mission of 'all to all'. Now there are simply too many fragments of the 'all' manifesting as "all against all" (Bourdieu, 1991). The ABC's post-broadcast role or "second shift" (Rutherford & Brown, 2013)[239] where it has been required by government policy to adopt a "participatory digital media strategy" means its multiple platforms demand that it offers quality (Rutherford & Brown, Ibid.) with diminishing resources.

5.4 ABC Independence

As the research interviews conducted for this book were drawn into views on whether or not the ABC had upheld its independence, it bears some analysis. The feedback was that, yes, it seemed to want to uphold its independence. Some said its responses to, and changes in, the ***field*** had eroded that competency and drawn it into quasi-commercial opinion-demanding activities where 'group think' prevailed. This then left it open to attacks from commercial operators as a coddled, outdated and no longer distinctively independent organisation. The ABC's creation of online platforms with blogs and role in social media—areas where opinion has primacy has seen the de-platforming of individuals. This deteriorates the ABC's claims of independence and impartiality. It is as if sagacious, astucious, reserved Aunty has moved into the same house as her recalcitrant nieces and nephews and she is quietly agreeing with them, while also straining to wear the same disinterested, disciplined poker face.

The BBC model of its independence was "founded on the twin professional ethics of impartiality and objectivity" (Born, 2005),[240] yet the BBC's concept of impartiality "was its own special invention" (Born, Ibid.).[241] There is scant academic literature that analyses the independence of the ABC although there are personal insights provided in *Save our ABC* (Fraser & O'Reilly, 1996)[242] and some historical context in former ABC staff member Neville Petersen's (1993) *News Not Views*[243] but under the heading of impartiality, which is not the same. However, Petersen (1993) pointed out that one of the early successes of the institution in obtaining independence was to extricate itself from having to re-use news from newspapers, striking out from the newspapers led by Sir Keith Murdoch, and thereby enabling itself to research and write its own news. It meant that ABC journalists determined the institution's definition of "impartiality". This then enabled the ABC to accrue its own political power by distinguishing itself from the press, where journalists had allegiances with Labor powerbrokers (Petersen, Ibid.)[244] and that news had become (from 1941) a form of "political communication" (Loc. Cit.).[245]

From then onwards journalists were in charge of news policy (Ibid.).[246] Born (2005) described the journalists' goals of objectivity and impartiality as "performative fictions", "strategic rituals" (Born, Ibid.)[247] as a means of sustaining and enabling legitimacy and authority. There is no fixed definition of media credibility (Blach-Ørsten & Burkal, 2014).[248] But a survey of Danish journalists in 2014 found that a lack of press ethics identified was a growing problem, due to increased pressure in the newsroom—including having to write more news reports with fewer sources upon which to base these stories (Blach-Ørsten & Burkal, Ibid.).[249] Yet, this occurs in an environment where there may be guidelines on ethics upholding impartiality but "without official mechanisms for enforcement" (Meyer, 2011).[250]

The late British philosopher and Professor of Logic at the University of Leeds, Peter Geach, defined impartiality as "an eye of God which looks upon all space impartially" (Sanford, 1983).[251] Impartiality was also described as something "we should consider perceiving from all possible points of view rather than from no point of view" (Sanford, Ibid.).[252] Impartiality also implied a presumption of free speech (Bailey, 2018).[253] However, with the shift of journalism towards being more "oppositional and opinionated" (Bailey, Ibid.)[254] impartiality and free speech had become compromised. The British independent communications regulator *Ofcom* (Office of Communications) 2017 stated "all output must be duly impartial in 'matters of political or industrial controversy and matters relating to current public policy'" (Bailey, Ibid.).[255] The Shakespearean scholar Stanley Greene wrote that the meaning of "impartial" was derived from "the inexorability of fate" (Wells, 1959)[256] and destiny—both impossible to avoid—and that one of the first recorded uses of the word 'impartial' was in Shakespeare's Richard II (Shakespeare 1593) (Ibid.).[257]

The academic literature said it was impossible for news media to be impartial because of a wide range of reasons: it had an ideological role (Curran, 1978),[258] it structured reality (Boyce et al., 1978),[259] it was conflict-oriented (Schudson, 2005),[260] engaged in circumlocution (Ibid.)[261] and had "a morbid fascination with gladiatorial combat"

(Schudson, 2008)[262] where international conflict was linked to security (Conboy, 2013)[263] and journalism a formulaic reproduction of the world (Høyer & Pöttker, 2005).[264] Facts were "consensually validated" (Schudson, 1978)[265] and journalists could be "dangerous and morally reprehensible" in that process (Vulliamy, 1999).[266] News media was highly mediated and culturally selective (Beharrell et al., 1976),[267] and objectivity was at best only ever: "a kind of industrial discipline" (Høyer & Pöttker, Ibid.)[268] where creating conflict for the audience was entertaining (Zaller, 1999)[269] because there was a need to insert "the values of entertainment in the news" (Schultz, 1998).[270] This meant that all sides cannot be represented (Shiffrin, 1994).[271] Cultural Studies scholar Stuart Hall (1973) said the rules of the way news was written was in itself an ideological structure and this had "operationalised the ideology of news".[272]

The BBC's web site was "one of the most trusted and widely used Internet sites in Europe" (Murdock, 2004).[273] Yet, there had also been a significant unravelling in the public sphere, defined by Jürgen Habermas (1989, 1961)[274] as the place where people come together to exchange views freely in a "public sphere in the political realm" (Habermas, Ibid.)[275] which originated in Britain at the turn of the late seventeenth and early eighteenth centuries (Loc. Cit.)[276] and was strengthened by the rise of capitalism in what was called "the golden age" (Sommerville, 1996)[277] of the English coffee house from which the public sphere probably had its origins. It was the time of the formation of the Fourth Estate. But Habermas observed that more recently the public sphere was "in a process of decomposition" (Habermas, Ibid.).[278] The cause was globalisation where there were "all kinds of currents, contradictions, disillusions, reactions, disintegrations" (Tracey, 1998).[279]

The literature blamed complicit audiences in the unravelling of loss of independence of public broadcasters because of: "dumbing down … linguistic poverty and therefore a mental and moral poverty" (Tracey, Ibid.)[280] spurred on by "a broadband culture" that supported the development of unlinked tribal communities and limitless entertainment (Loc. Cit.).[281] The independence of the ABC—and indeed all public broadcasters—is now challenged as to whether they will be "highbrow", "low brow", "universalistic", "particularistic", "upstream", "mainstream, "downstream" "popular", or "élite" (Ibid.).[282] This uncertainty meant the ABC had abandoned Bourdieu's élite *field* that it once occupied and "owned" in Australian media and its pursuit of digital online popularity had taken itself further downmarket into a highly competitive *field* where much of the other media, commercial media, reside and jostle each other for prominence. Aunty is in peril of becoming just another voice in an over-crowded *field*. In such a dire situation Aunty is still supposed to please everyone, but is that even possible now?

5.5 Losing Sport

An English football club vice-president visiting Australia in 1924 remarked "Australians are sport mad" (Goulburn Evening Penny Post, 1924), then the ABC was created and rose to meet the needs of its citizens. Its Chairman Richard Boyer proclaimed in 1948: "The Commission gives great service to the sporting public and to sporting bodies" (The Daily Telegraph, 1948). It had covered the Olympic and Commonwealth Games (British Empire Games) since the institution's inception. In March 2020, the Tokyo Olympic Games for 2020 had been postponed to 2021 because of the novel Coronavirus. So, the ABC's decision in November 2019 not to cover the 2020 Olympics seemed to show that management had the endowment of extraordinary premonition. When the Chair of the ABC, Ita Buttrose, announced that the organisation would not be sending a team to report on the 2020 Tokyo Olympics, it signified a significant shift away from its traditional sports reporting and an acknowledgement of the highly competitive digital world in which it was still trying to carve out a niche, but at a compromised and decreasing level. Firstly, Buttrose blamed the ending of the ABC's 67-year tradition of public coverage of the Olympics on funding cuts, and re-allocation of money is a familiar issue for ABC managers in times of cutbacks. Coverage would have cost AUD1 million. Former senior managers told this research it should not have been hard to find that money. There have been budget struggles for the ABC for many years in providing coverage of major events to all Australians. In 1983, for example, the then Federal Treasurer, Paul Keating, announced in his Budget Speech 1983–1984: "an amount of AUD4.1 million was provided to the ABC in 1982–83 in connection with its role as Host Broadcaster at the 1982 Commonwealth Games in Brisbane, bringing the total funds provided to the ABC for that activity since 1979–80 to AUD18.9 million" (ABC Archives, n.d.).[283]

Funding possibilities aside, it was the second half of Buttrose's media statement that was of greater significance. She said Australians could access Olympic Games coverage in many other ways (ABC, 2019)[284]—meaning the ABC was no longer a broadcaster of any unique significance in

Australia. It disclosed that the disruption of online media had irrevocably taken hold of all news and information, specifically that the ABC's unique voice of sports reporting had been strangled. It had lost its sports brand. Even though the ABC's local radio network reached about 99% of Australians, an ABC article on the subject said: "the golden days of traditional radio commentary, sadly, seem to be gone. Radio needs to add value, not just replicate an increasingly segmented digitally-driven market" (Holmes, 2019).[285] ABC Senior Sports reporter and ABC Radio cricket commentator, Jim Maxwell, said the decision to end Olympics coverage was less to do with money and more to do with "its wavering commitment to sport" (Le Grand, 2019).[286] A report quoted an anonymous ABC employee: "the anti-sport forces within the ABC have always been incredibly powerful, ... what has changed is the advocates for sport are fewer in number and carry less weight" (Le Grand, Ibid.).[287] ABC ratings for the Rio Olympics in 2016 were not impressive and it had been argued that as the commercial networks covered the Olympics, the ABC was not needed anymore. However, Maxwell pointed out an ominous inconsistency with this line of argument, one that threatened to strangle Aunty's entire voice: "if you are saying it is adequately covered elsewhere, so is news and current affairs and a lot of other things the ABC does" (Ibid.).[288] Another anonymous ABC senior manager said the decision to abandon the Olympic Games coverage was more pragmatic: "the $1 million forecast reduction in costs ... didn't require one staff member to be sacked, therefore the internal wheel wasn't going to squeak very much" (Loc. Cit.).[289]

Maxwell said the ABC's sports coverage "barely exists" and is "shown up" by SBS (Ritchie, 2019).[290] He was reported to have communicated this on Twitter in response to a comment by former ABC sports journalist Peter Wilkins. Maxwell was also reported to have tweeted criticism of the ABC decision not to cover the 2020 Olympics in Tokyo with live radio: "ABC credibility not helped by decision NOT to cover the Olympics with live radio coverage. No one else will" (Ibid.). Former ABC journalist John Simpson later said the ABC has lapsed generally in its capacity to cover other areas including "politics, business, finance and crime" (Ibid.).[291] Simpson (2020) said "declining audiences, incessant promotion (and cross-promotion) of so-called celebrity presenters and 'their' shows, woeful summer programming and public criticism by its own staff are just some of the issues it is facing" (Ibid.). He said it struggled in governance, efficiency and prudence. He posed the point: "In an age when commercial television news and current affairs are just about unwatchable, the runway ought to be open to the ABC to excel" (Ibid.). He said reasons for the ABC's situation were doing too much for too many, and conundrums over its role in the digital media, for example there was no more breaking business or finance news.

It should be noted that the ABC Charter does not state that the organisation had to cover sport. Yet, there have been good reasons for covering it because, historically, the ABC has had policies supporting the coverage of sport (The News, 1954)[292] and, as a consequence, has also long complained about being under-resourced to cover all national sports (The Canberra Times, 1981).[293] Australia is internationally successful at sport and Australia has "an effective national sports system" (Sotiriadou & Brouwers, 2012)[294] encouraging both amateurs and élite sports people. Historically, sport has been entrenched in Australian culture for tens of thousands of years. Aboriginal and Torres Strait Islander communities used it as another expression of their culture and community (Blood & May, 2018),[295] the arrival of the convicts added their passion for sport (and then gambling on sport) to compete with their British jailers (Phillips & Magdalinski, 2008)[296] and subsequent waves of migration have added their own sports cultures to enliven the mix, encouraging communities and improved health.

Government involvement in Australian sport has been boosted by perceived political and electoral opportunities to gain votes enhanced by the influence of what is referred to as the "media sports cultural complex" (Phillips & Magdalinski, Ibid.)[297] with the rise of the commercialism of sports following the arrival of television in Australia in 1956 and resultant coverage of sports by media. Sport has been a critical part of the way Australia developed its "nationalist spirit" (Ibid.).[298] In fact, the ABC's first General Manager, Charles Moses started at the ABC as a sports commentator and it was his sporting prowess: rugby union, discus, heavyweight boxing, soccer, cricket and hockey (Petersen, 2012)[299] and broadcasting skills that actually fortified and enlarged support for his appointment in the first place (The Daily Telegraph, 1935).[300] In 1938, Moses even proposed one dedicated sports radio station (which failed to eventuate). The ABC, tasked originally with growing Australian culture, identified sport as a significant way of uniting Australians, promoting Australian nationalism and growing the ABC's privileged *cultural capital*. Those days, that voice and that agenda, are gone.

5.6 Mourning Those Lost Argonauts

Before the sun and night and the blue sea, I vow,
To stand faithfully by all that is brave and beautiful;
To seek adventure and having discovered aught of wonder, or delight, of merriment or loveliness,
To share it freely with my comrades, the Band of Happy Rowers.[301]

This pledge sent to each member of the Argonauts to sign and validate provided Australians with a sense of an "imagined community" (Anderson, 1983)[302] of Australia—"the band of happy rowers". Australians will never meet every other Australian, but they were given a sense of that shared identity, nationalism and place through the ABC—and children's radio program The Argonauts. Part of growing that sense of oneness had been the ABC's pursuit of audiences to support the formation of an Australian culture. In the early days of the ABC the radio series *Blue Hills* had so much credibility, authority and verisimilitude that when a character in the play had a baby, audience devotees would knit and send in baby clothes to that character believing, in a very touching sense, the show was real (Crocker, 1989).[303] ABC administration staff would forward these gifts to charities (Ibid.). No good gestures were wasted. In terms of creating a dedicated audience it was successful, effective and affective—with even charities benefitting from audience' sincere benevolence and faith in an "honest" ABC radio fiction. Now that is but a dream, not just for the ABC but for all media outlets questing for their elusive, disunited, tribalised, "loyal" media consumers. Loyalty has been re-defined from time-consuming knitted booties to quick "likes" and emojis.

However, there was one ABC radio program that literally cultivated a generation of loyal ABC supporters from cradle to grave by inspiring, exciting and educating them, at once. The ABC captured and grew its young Australians who became dedicated adult ABC listeners (and viewers) because of *The Argonauts*. It was one of the most popular, endearing and enduring children's radio programs in Australia. It was only matched for competition in the *field* of ABC children's programming by ABC Televisions' *Play School* in capturing an audience while it was young with Play Schoolers inculcated with the opening tune "There's a bear in there, and a chair as well". The success of this program was due to several factors, including that "children's programming has long been considered one of the pillars of public service broadcasting" (Rutherford & Brown, 2013)[304] and the ABC had little competition in "distinctive" children's programming (Rutherford & Brown, Ibid.). Many former Australian leaders, politicians and ABC staff, interviewed for this research spoke highly of how *The Argonauts* engaged and encouraged them with the written and spoken word and also left them with a lifelong love of literature, music and affection for the broadcaster. That sort of *cultural capital*, that sort of control of the *field* of children's entertainment and education, and the resulting dedication to the brand was extraordinary and of lasting impact. *The Argonauts* made a significant educational contribution to the literacy as well as the musical appreciation and knowledge of a generation. Such education was a massive gift to the future of the nation.

But before the program's enduring legacy, there was a choppy start. In 1931, ABC journalist, Nina Murdoch, proposed the concept of the show to the Australian Broadcasting Company's[305] Victorian Manager, Thomas Bearup. Murdoch's idea was that this program would be based on the classical myth of the search for the golden fleece where Jason would be the main character and listeners would be 'rowers' assigned to his Argonaut's fleet (Semmler, 1981).[306] These 'rowers' (listeners)—aged 7 to 17—would send in their best poetry, creative writing or music compositions based on "their everyday problems" (Ibid.)[307] and the best would be given awards and the accumulation of awards would qualify them for 'The Golden Fleece'. The children were allocated to a ship named after a Greek hero and they were allocated a number as their rowing position in the ship. These 'rowers' had anonymity which gave their creativity wings (Loc. Cit.).[308] The program had been poo-poohed until Bearup became Acting General Manager in 1941 (while Charles Moses was away from his office performing active duty in the war) (Ibid.)[309] and Bearup's efforts were "abetted" by his former colleague Frank Clellow, the ABC's Federal Controller of Productions. This is however, disputed by Inglis (1983) who said that the initiative for The Argonauts in 1941 came from Frank Clellow, who Inglis (1983) described as "white-haired and florid" and an "old actor" (Loc. Cit.).[310] According to Inglis (1983), the program had run for a year in Melbourne on 3LO from 1933 to 1934. Semmler (1981), however, said the program was withdrawn in 1934 because the Australian Broadcasting Company's General Manager, Walter Condor (known as "the Major" because of his rank in the Australian Imperial Forces during World War I) was dismissive of *The Argonauts* idea, saying: "all that children want is Punch and Judy shows" (Ibid.).[311]

Nonetheless, *The Argonauts* re-emerged as a national program. The famous Australian poet, A.D. Hope—with the nom de plume "Anthony Inkwell"—judged the written content and Lindley Evans "The Melody Man" assessed the children's music. Australian author Ruth Park contributed stories and Wilfrid Thomas gave talks on travel (Semmler, 1981).[312] Albert Collins assessed artworks (Inglis, 1983)[313] and the (later) famous Australian conductor Richard Bonynge would come into the studio to play the children's compositions (Ibid.)[314] live to air on the piano and for assessment. Talbot Duckmanton, then an ABC presenter, (later General Manager), would give children a sports presentation each week. By the end of 1945 there were 32,000 Argonauts and within a year of that 150,000. Ellis Blain (1977) said "there has been no children's programme in Australian radio or television which has even remotely approached the success of The Argonaut's Club in its heyday" (Ibid.).[315] Blain (1977) reflected: "children in isolated outback remote areas found *The Argonauts* a lifeline against isolation and their literary contributions were outstanding" (Loc. Cit.).[316] Former Australian entertainer and convicted paedophile Rolf Harris was said to be among the famous Argonaut alumni (Blain, Ibid.).[317]

The Argonauts faded in 1971. Semmler (1981) said ABC management had "stigmatised" the program by the late 1960s as "old fashioned" and in "a chimerical quest for ratings"[318] tinkered with the program because the ABC believed children were now watching television instead, and the program was redundant. In terms of the Bourdieusian educational *field*, the program had succeeded in gaining *cultural capital* because of the high level of audience participation it encouraged and achieved, it was enhanced by the exceptional expertise and quality of the assessors who judged and presented the children's work. The program was a "free" Master Class in the arts for all Australian children. That generalist model of media content directed at children for enlightenment and culture would never be re-visited. The original statement on the role of the ABC from its first annual report in 1932 said the organisation aimed to achieve: "apart from what the child learns of nature or music or history, he may, under the guidance of the teacher develop his powers of concentration and selection when listening to the spoken word" (ABC Annual Report, 1932–1933).[319]

The Argonauts would later support this goal with unforeseen impact and potency. It encouraged the children to care for others. For instance, during World War II and the London blitz,[320] the program asked the Argonauts to raise money so that the ABC could buy, on their behalf, a mobile canteen in London to feed children whose lives had been disrupted by the London Blitz. The Argonauts Club members raised money by "selling vegetables", "coming top of the class", "collecting snails for Dad" and "having five teeth out" (Thomas, 1980).[321] The late Alastair Hetherington, former Controller of BBC Scotland and Editor of The Guardian wrote in 1985 that "no newspaper or broadcast unit can succeed unless it strikes a chord with its audience and keep in tune with them" (Hetherington, 1985).[322] *The Argonauts* had for over 30 years struck the right chord and sustained the notes in developing an Australian culture and culturally-educated children who sang as one.

5.7 Where Are Those Old Argonauts?

In 2019, News Corporation offered its Melbourne *Herald Sun* newspaper journalists a reported bonus of AUD10–50 for encouraging digital subscriptions by driving traffic through their own news reports—that is, if a reader found their story online and wanted to click on the headline and read more by subscribing to access that full story, the journalist was rewarded financially (Meade, 2019).[323] The traffic was being analysed by the analytics group Verity (Ibid.).[324] The use of data analytics in newsrooms is manifest but this instance does raise concerns about the worthiness and probity of news, when it is acknowledged in the literature that formulaic, sensational news gets read/seen first (Langer, 1998[325]; Fitzpatrick, 2000[326]). In addition, journalists are being financially encouraged to make their stories into commodities, which could compete with providing information to their public based on its 'right to know'. The report said journalists were told to think about "selling" their news reports to readers "and being more "proactive" across the website and social media" (Meade, Ibid.).[327] Only three weeks prior to this News Corporation dismissed 55 journalists who Executive Chairman, Michael Miller said were "long-term employees who lack digital skills".[328] Miller said, "journalists needed to be multi-skilled to be valuable to the company" and that "as we get more data, we probably need some new skills journalistically into the business and we're increasingly bringing in audio, video, social" (Loc. Cit.).[329]

For experienced journalists with their legacy knowledge of contacts, news, political and social history, media law, house-style, grammar, spelling and succinct, effective *en pointe* media writing—time was up. Legacy knowledge is a maligning term, implying age, intractability and redundancy because it is used in a binary with 'competence'. Yet cognitive ageing research indicates that prior knowledge can make older employees more valuable than other staff because of their learning and past solutions-oriented experience (Paas et al., 2008 in L. Kester et al., 2008).[330] Legacy knowledge can also form part of knowledge and information management. The literature recommended that to avoid the loss of legacy knowledge there should be cross-training, mentoring and contract employment (Dubie, 2003).[331] In the process of creating so-called sunset (Halverstadt & Kerman, 2017)[332] employees the media (in this instance) fails to engage with gathering and sharing their knowledge as part of the investment it has already made in their institutional memory (Ibid.). The ultimate irony is how quickly the legacy media runs away from its legacy staff in a technology revolution described in the literature as "the great fragmentation" (Sammartino, 2014).[333] The economics of staffing are also an issue where it was reported that at the ABC "experienced staff are an endangered species—not because they rock the boat but because they are a cost burden" (Hardaker, 2020).[334]

The academic literature sees legacy knowledge as "collective knowledge" and in engineering companies loss of legacy knowledge is frowned upon because it leads to duplication or waste (Thilmany, 2004).[335] In organisations, such as the ABC there has been much pioneering work done in creating bespoke technological solutions. Elsewhere, legacy knowledge is vital to scientific discovery—the creating of a new vaccine is only possible through previous discovery and processes. The investment in legacy knowledge and its ally creativity, is inherently valuable. In addition, economists of the industrial era (1890s) identified that knowledge was a basis for sustained economic growth and competitiveness (Meusburger et al., 2013).[336] Current economic theory describes knowledge as something tradable and "amendable to valuation" and has been reduced to information (Meusburger et al., Ibid.).[337] Herein lies the current binary of knowledge and information (or legacy knowledge and competence), where knowledge is devalued because it is embedded and based on experience while information is the hero because it is measurable and more easily replicable in staff—it can be contained in a test. Classifying employees within this apparent binary has been described as "naïve" because it exaggerates the role of the producer at the expense of the receiver (Meusburger et al. Loc. Cit.).

Where does this leave the non-commercial/commercial ABC cutting back jobs of experienced staff yet struggling to uphold its legacy Charter of being 'all to all'? Similar concerns about the need for multi-skilled, 'agile' media operators plagued the ABC in late 2019 when staff cuts were forecast. Managing Director David Anderson said it was due to "a disrupted media landscape" where the ABC had to be "more efficient and focused on distinctive programming" (Duke, 2019).[338] Anderson told a Senate Estimates Committee in 2019: "one of our priorities for the future is certainly to remain as local as possible ... our role is to reflect the culture and community of the country back to itself ... you struggle to do that unless you are local" (Dalzell, 2019).[339] The literature said that the internet was a "political *field* in which a struggle over meaning-making is continuously taking place" (Larsson, 2014, quoting Laclau & Mouffe, 1985)[340] and the ABC is shifting engagement with these citizen opinion-makers at a local level. It is an attempt to re-build its reputation by inspiring confidence amongst small communities and the individuals and organisations inhabiting those spaces.

It is a trend amongst public broadcasters to shift to "local" so as to give voice to the "plurality of voices" (Calvet et al., 2013)[341] and as a way of making their audiences more involved in content (Ibid.) and interacting with each other. Yet, online involvement of audiences: "can improve the public debate if it manages to ensure more balanced citizen participation" (Ibid.). Calvet et al. (2013), citing Bardoel, in Bardoel & Lowe, 2007) argued PSMs are often only pushing existing content instead of actually providing a new facility for target groups. The technological changes actually require an entire re-writing of ABC policies in explaining and delineating exactly what is meant by "local" and how its public funding will serve all Australians and its 'right to know'. Serving special interest groups and their discrete participation is not a representative sample of the entire population, which may or may not engage with the ABC, but would nonetheless benefit from nuanced and informed debate and discussion in support of democratic governance: "participation is a concept with a heavy ideological weight and major political implications" (Calvet et al., Ibid.).[342] The ABC is losing the brand by not articulating how serving the particular local groups serves the whole. The research had found PSMs in Europe have had greater success, compared with commercial providers, in integrating content relevant to migrants (Rogers et al., 2014),[343] for example. Australia's SBS is its multicultural PSM and its success in achieving contact with Australia's diverse communities may be another area of research, but beyond the scope of this book.

In 2018, staff-elected ABC Board member, Dr Jane Connors, said "the pressure to predict where audiences will go and how to move the organisation towards them is profound" (Connors, 2018).[344] Areas of conflict around this point are yet to be resolved by the organisation. The ABC's 1997 annual report said "regional services embodies the ABC's commitment to localism and to providing services which respond to the needs of the diverse State regional and rural audiences throughout Australia"; however, in 2020 it became conflicted about supporting regional Australians, especially those who live in mining communities. For example, a report on the Country Hour for Western Australia called for mining companies to have a "social licence" which was clarified to mean having a mind to "environmental stewardship and carbon emissions" (Daly, 2020)[345] because of the increasing shift to "rare earth minerals", which will displace the use of coal, which emits carbon dioxide when burned. Many Australians, and those on working visas who aspire to Australian citizenship, are employed in mining and related or linked industries. Social licence, itself, is yet to be defined in law (McHugh, 2014)[346] and can be interpreted variously.

The ABC is not chasing audience for profits—rather relevance, but because it now functions in the profit-based world of the internet it finds itself competing in the same commercial *field* as the rest and chasing the same people. These are challenging times. To meet this demand there is a now a pursuit of soft news stories where staff are asked to tell more stories about individuals on their journeys. Hard news also draws the ABC into controversy and political conflict and requires staff numbers with time and ability to pursue contacts and rigorous research. Soft news and "your stories" are cheaper and easier to create. But to counteract this and underline the need for the ABC in providing hard news: "individuals who watch public television in countries that subsidize their public broadcasters have significantly higher levels of political knowledge than both those citizens who watch commercial television and those who watch unsubsidized public broadcasters" (O'Mahen, 2016).[347]

The ABC has described to the government that it is succeeding in attracting younger audiences. Gaven Morris, Director of News told a Select Committee on the Future of Public Interest Journalism (*Commonwealth of Australia*, 2018)[348] there had been a noticeable shift in the audience requirement for "verified information, for trusted content and for explanation of context" (Ibid.). The organisation had found success with that approach: "a lot more than any other strategy to produce popular content or anything else" (Loc. Cit). Morris (*Commonwealth of*

Australia, 2018) said when he was a young journalist the culture of the ABC was aware that audiences were aged in their 50s and young people were not part of the main audience. He said that had all changed. Once mobile phones arrived, younger audiences started accessing ABC content and the "audience profile for ABC news … is that two-thirds of our audience on mobile are under 40 and they're mostly consuming the sorts of stories that we've always pursued" (*Commonwealth of Australia*, Ibid.). Morris said for the first time in the ABC's history there were two audiences, one big audience for radio and television, plus an under-40s audience engaged with the ABC on its social media and mobile platforms.

It presents the ABC with a content quandary and a confusing dual personality to manage the traditionally passive news recipients with the innovative, participant conversationalists. In many ways they are mutually exclusive where social media is based on reaction, reinterpretations and opinions and traditional, serious media was premised on neutral information, distant from opinion source being mulled over by a largely passive audience. Thrown into this mix is the ABC Fact Check Unit, a third branch of journalism, which requires the journalist to become an academic research authority figure.

The old Fourth Estate value of distance and objectivity is redundant where journalists have to give an opinion on the validity of their own news report. In the digital media age where so much content is splintered and catering to specific groups and interests, it is making the job of public interest journalism extremely fraught. The BBC's Reality Check Unit (established 2017) aims further in its role to reach out and "fact check the most popular outliers on Facebook, Instagram and other social media … where we see deliberately misleading stories masquerading as news, we'll publish a Reality Check that says so" (Jackson, 2017).[349] "Facebook has been singled out as the platform that has enabled false stories to spread most widely" (Jackson, Ibid.). The BBC is distracting itself by checking the veracity of social media content—rather than keeping a separation between their verifiable facts, back in their *field*, and those getting traction on social media. Journalism has lost its bravery and splendid isolation.

In effect, the ABC Fact-checking unit is a substitute for the dramatic loss of skilled sub-editors at the ABC who routinely knew facts, or knew when to question them, had an astute knowledge of context and even a good grasp of the law. Funding cuts have removed the jobs of many knowledgeable sub-editors and their premature terminations have been a substantial blow for public journalism. Yet, fact-checking staff was also vulnerable. Professor Angela Romano, the Vice President Networks, Journalism Education and Research Association of Australia (JERAA), said in a statement to the Select Committee on the Future of Public Interest Journalism (*Commonwealth of Australia*, 2018)[350] because they did not have a public profile sub-editors and fact-checkers "are often given the axe quite early in the piece" (Ibid.).[351] Other statements from the ABC's fact-checking partner, RMIT University, said fact-checking was a form of "public interest journalism" and it "deserves public support" (Ibid.). The select committee recommended: "that the ABC and SBS be funded adequately, so that they can deliver on their Charter obligations, support rural and regional service provision and have a strong fact checking capacity" (Ibid.).

The ABC is challenged by two views raised to the committee. First, Christopher Berg, Senior Fellow, Institute of Public Affairs (IPA), said the ABC should be privatised because the ABC was created at a time when there was media scarcity and now there is abundant media (Ibid.). Second, Greg Hywood, former Chief Executive Officer and Managing Director, Fairfax Media, also expressed concern about the ABC's activities where publicly funded internet advertising may impinge on commercial interests (Ibid.). Hywood said that the ABC used taxpayers' money to drive their traffic—taking "eyeballs" and website usage away from the commercial media outlets who relied on site traffic for their income—to sell advertising. He cautioned about:

> Aspects of the new world of media where we have to be careful that the decisions that government institutions make do not impinge upon the diversity and the commercial environment that I think we all value. (Ibid.)[352]

The ABC has no paywalls[353] while commercial media needs them to survive. The media business models have collapsed, newspapers no longer can rely on their "rivers of gold" in classified advertising sustaining them in revenue, and advertisers have to be chased in new ways offering them compelling, creative, retailed options.

5.8 The ABC Fights for Survival

It was widely contended in the literature that since 1975 the ABC has been engaged in a fight for survival (Blain, 1977)[354] because of funding cuts and a neo-liberal emphasis on corporate efficiencies and management performance—coupled with waxing and waning enthusiasm or indifference from most incumbent governments for the ABC's sustenance. Both factors have been debilitating for the ABC. Ewart Chapple, former Manager ABC Victoria was quoted as saying "beware of the clerks, my boy: beware of the clerks. They will bugger the ABC" (Buttrose, 1984).[355] That fear evolved into other forms of internal control. Ken Inglis (1983) quoted a poster on the walls of youth radio station JJ during the mid-1970s "paranoia is true perception"[356] printed in response to funding cuts. At the same time, public support groups were launched including Sydney's Friends of the ABC, and in Melbourne Aunty's Nephews and Nieces (later merged with Friends of the ABC). In January 1976 the ABC's budget was "cut by 15% of committed revenue for the remaining six months of the financial year" which resulted in drastic retrenchments (Blain, 1977)[357] at a time of fiscal crises around the developed world (Andrews et al., 2012 citing Poterba & Von Hagen, 1999).[358] *The Australian* newspaper reported in March 1977 about a forthcoming Federal Government survey: "people are to be asked if they think the ABC should be abolished" (Blain, 1977).[359] The article quoted a spokesman for the Minister for Post and Telecommunications as not being aware of the survey. It was another example of what Blain (1977) described as a stoking of the furnace of fear since the 1970s that the ABC was to be abolished, putting the ABC in "permanent trauma" (Davis, 1988)[360] ever since, or at least suppressed trepidation. Funding fears have known no quiescence.

The literature also noted that there were contradictions to these prevailing fears because "moves to enhance public participation in broadcasting policy in Australia were in fact stronger under the conservative government led by Malcolm Fraser" (Flew, 2006),[361] in particular the establishment of the Australian Broadcasting Tribunal, replacing the Australian Broadcasting Control Board (Ibid.).[362] The Fraser Government also helped establish Australia's public multicultural broadcaster, Special Broadcasting Service (SBS). However, contradicting these positives, there were three reviews of the ABC in the 1980s–1990s critical of a narrowness of the ABC's representations of Australian national identity and calling for more diversity in ABC programs. The Dix Inquiry (known as the Committee of Review of the Australian Broadcasting Commission, 1981) was initiated by the Prime Minister Malcolm Fraser's Coalition Government and the National Advisory Council on Multiculturalism (Varatharajan, 2017),[363] following that was the 1987 review of the ABC review, and the Mansfield (in 1997). The recurrence of reviews and inquiries are of regular disquietude and distress at the ABC and another source of insecurity (and JJ's "paranoia" poster). Nonetheless, the loss of funding, or lack of excitement, for the ABC from political actors has diminished the broadcaster and at a time where immigration is so critical to economic growth. The ABC as a powerful nation-forming organisation could unify Australians and inspire others to become Australians. It could develop the region with a strong sense of Australia's nationhood, freedoms and inclusiveness.

Other, more literal, signs the ABC was losing the brand occurred in 2015 when ABC Shops closed after 35 years operations, with the removal of 300 staff and closure of 50 shops and 78 ABC centres in retail outlets. The ongoing issue exposed the shops were losing profitability because most of the programs on the ABC were not made in-house anymore. The ABC's outsourcing of programs to production companies meant it was those firms which made profits from DVDs and other merchandise, not the ABC which was providing an outlet at ABC cost. The Community and Public Sector Union (CPSU) ABC section secretary, Sinddy Ealy, said: "The ABC has been outsourcing their internal production for the last decade and now there are more job losses on the table because of that" (Meade, 2015).[364] In June 2020, the ABC announced it was closing its portal ABC Life where content focused on lifestyle, health and recipes to be re-branded ABC Local with the sacking of half of its staff and "with a broader editorial direction" (Anderson, 2020).[365] Mostly, the reason for ending ABC Life was that it was involved in the same activities as commercial operators and the push-back from them was ferocious. The ABC was dabbling in another *field* demarcated as belonging to commercial providers. Its place in the commercial *field* was justified in a binaried description of Australians by a former ABC Life staff member:

> As being completely in line with the ABC's charter (young Indian-Australian couples in Parramatta pay tax and deserve relevant ABC content as much as white retirees in Balmain). (Faruqi, 2020)[366]

The ABC was no longer 'all for all' binding Australians culturally, instead it sought to find the divisions, niche hunting, which was a worthwhile exercise but a complicated and weighty one. It required finesse and care, because these niches had to be described to others (education) and then welcomed into the whole. In 1993, the Canadian Broadcasting Corporation (CBC) was accused of "selling its soul" in pursuit of niche markets (Enchin, 1993).[367] Yet, CBC president, Gerard Veilleux, said: "If we don't use the instruments of public broadcasting to define ourselves, to give ourselves our own identity, then somebody else will define us" (Enchin, Ibid.). Social Anthropologist Georgina Born (2005) in her extraordinary in-depth BBC analysis over many years said that public broadcaster "which of necessity must follow as well as court public tastes, has been impelled to join the rush downmarket"[368] while also, counter-intuitively, "it remains the model for public broadcasters on every continent".[369] Born (2005) said the BBC was in crisis because "the world's most famous cultural institution"[370] needed re-invention. Research of European public broadcasters (2013) found that while they encouraged online participation, they were still peripheral and complementary in the media (Calvet et al., 2013).[371] PSBs/PSMs struggled with their desire to gather participation because they were not using the tools they had, effectively, to support democratic values and build a public sphere for all voices encouraging debate and engagement. They were not using their means of engagement in effectively underpinning the traditional role of a public broadcaster (Calvet et al., Ibid.). This is a significant issue that threatens to strangle the voice of Aunty.

Glyn Davis (1988) did a roughly similar study of the ABC as Born's (2005) but not as long term. Davis (1988) said he observed erratic leadership and funding cuts and quoted Managing Director David Hill who warned that the ABC would not exist in ten years (by 1998) if it did not change (Davis, Ibid.). It has been in a state of constant change since then and yet to settle. At that time, Labor Prime Minister, Paul Keating, said the ABC would not get "one zac more out of us. It's the most self-indulgent, self-interested outfit in the country" (Davis, Ibid.). Davis said the ABC was in the dilemma of being "in the cultural arena with no special claim on the public purse" (Ibid.)[372] yet its role should be to provide a "counterbalance to the values and interests of the commercial media" (Ibid.). It is not a comfortable fit in the commercial *field* for the ABC in a situation where "legislation has never created a public and private role for media in Australia" (Davis, Ibid.).[373] It is no longer disinterested—it chases popularity by repeating content already covered by the commercial operators and defines its audiences through intersectionality. This mindset has become an encumbrance for the organisation in a world where its short-term performance and resonance is difficult to quantify unless through the commercial ratings, hits and algorithms system. Its move into the commercial *field* was also criticised by former ABC broadcaster Huw

Evans (1986)[374] who said it was imitating commercial media, was poorly led, and the organisation had become bulky with redundancies:

> It's not that long ago—I can certainly recall it—in times of crisis, Australians would for preference turn to the ABC to see and hear that version of events which could most be trusted to be fair and true. That is no longer the case. (Evans, Ibid.)

The Bourdieusian *field* and doxa were part of the ABC's initial institutional leadership, inspired by the BBC's Edwardian paternalistic management (Nicholls, 2011)[375] which segued at the ABC to a Georgian paternalistic tradition (King George V gave the first Royal Christmas radio broadcast and this is carried on today by his grand-daughter Her Majesty Queen Elizabeth II). This influenced management style. It was said that the ABC's first and second general managers (Charles Moses and his successor, Talbot Duckmanton) believed in "a hierarchical authority" (Inglis, 1983).[376] This approach to style, content and leadership had positive consequences for the ABC in establishing it in Australian nationhood and public life. Nicholls (2011) argued that the advent of public broadcasting in the UK brought manifest and unforeseen social benefits such as contributing to a stable environment of industrial relations with concomitant public expectations of secure employment. The ABC's situation was different; launched as Australia was struggling to emerge from The Great Depression following the Stockmarket Crash of 1929 when unemployment has been quoted widely as reaching 30% in 1932, although has been disputed as being closer to just under 20% (Gruen & Clark, 2010)[377] because according to later statistical analysis there had been "profound changes in collection methodology, including definitions of unemployment" (Gruen & Clark, Ibid.)[378] since the 1920s and 1930s. Nonetheless, Australia had "one of the highest rates of unemployment in the world during the Great Depression" (Ibid.).[379]

Even though this book is considering Australian media within its remit, this ABC analysis of leadership and contesting the *field* is not sufficient without also including the founding principles of the BBC, upon which the ABC was modelled. The origins of public broadcasting in Britain and under the 1927 Royal Charter were that it was "acting in the national interest … as a means of education and entertainment" (BBC Royal Charter, 1927).[380] The literature said it was not until 1939 that there were moves to make ABC news bulletin independent and impartial and "sensational, inconsequential stories were no longer generally included" (Thomas, 1980)[381] and "head office saw that bulletins were constructed in a factual, objective manner" (Ibid.)[382] even though it was still partly dependent on newspapers for news and there were moves towards an "ABC style" that supported this objective: "Sunday-evening bulletins, for example, ran less that their allocated five minutes if nothing more than weekend human-interest stories came to hand" (Loc. Cit.).[383] Given that every program on the ABC had to 'run to time', no exceptions, the decision in the 1930s to simply end when there was nothing more to say was endearingly honest and showed that the time the listener gave to radio was to be valued and bounded.

However, in 1938, the then general manager, Charles Moses, decided there needed to be more focus on the need and interests of the listener and he revealed (The Barrier Miner, Broken Hill, 1938)[384] that the ABC was able to ascertain the views of Australians to ABC content by selecting a panel of 100 listeners "in all parts of the Commonwealth to criticise plays" (Ibid.). Moses said this number was considered representative of Australian public opinion. By 1939, the ABC was starting to find its own voice, not #yours, not ours—its own. In terms of establishing its voice this was a powerful foundation in not just claiming the *field* but establishing the doxa. That year it appointed its first correspondent in Canberra: "a Federal roundsman" (*ABC Annual Report*, 1939–1940)[385] with newspapers supplying most of the news broadcast: "now re-written in suitable broadcast form" (Ibid.). In April, 1940 the ABC bought the right to broadcast BBC News from Australian Associated Press for AU£3000 per annum (Ibid.), half of this amount was being paid by the Australian Federation of Commercial Broadcasting stations so that they could rebroadcast BBC bulletins (Ibid.).

Part of its participatory basis came from an élitist bias that ensured it would acquire and accumulate *cultural capital*. So, cultivated voices were recruited by the radio broadcaster to staff intellectually challenging programming on outlets such as 2FC (later Radio National).

This was supported by its establishment of a national symphony orchestra and choir, a military band and a dance band (The Canberra Times, 1936)[386] the ABC also ran a national music composition contests and brought accomplished performing artists from overseas. In fact, the ABC's establishing vision for itself became one that was participatory "to encourage the creative side of our people in a musical sense" (*The Advertiser*, 1934).[387] Further, the duties of the public broadcaster as a cultural bastion were articulated by the ABC Chairman William Cleary: "Listeners do not want to be patronised by being played down to, or being treated as though they were incapable of intellectual or artistic development" (The Western Argus, 1937).[388] The sincere ambitions for the 'Australianness' of the organisation were clear from the outset when it hosted the fourth world concert in 1938 organised by the Radio Union (Geneva). The ABC General Manager, Charles Moses, said the concert would open with "calls by the lyre bird and kookaburra" (*The Courier Mail*, 1938).[389] This was followed by "an Australian corroboree" (Ibid.) then a range of other Australian artists would perform including the ABC Radio Chorus and the ABC Orchestra playing "national airs" (Ibid.).

In terms of gaining the brand, in 1931 the Australian Broadcasting Company (the Australian Broadcasting Commission in 1932) was given control of Australian broadcasting under Federal legislation but it was actually a minor miracle that the organisation became such a vital constituent of Australian media. This was because from the outset, it was not set up to represent the public interest (Petersen, 1993)[390] but, at the behest of the powerful newspaper lobby, was charged with assisting the Australian people in being "culturally uplifted" (Petersen, Ibid.).[391] The ABC was to support Australian culture by establishing a national symphony orchestra and choir, a military band and a dance band (The Canberra Times, 1936).[392] The financial business of the ABC was overseen by the Postmaster-General from the outset so there was very much a view that the new medium of radio had as its emphasis on the communication of culture, information (allied with the post and telegrams delivered by the post office) and education (The Courier Mail, 1934).[393] It was to emphasise the building of the Australian culture.

This diminishment in national focus has been blamed on funding cuts, political interference and powerful commercial operators, discussed throughout this book. However, of equal significance has been the unacknowledged institutional shift in its perceived role, causing 'role confusion'. This has been precipitated by its activities in the digital space as a quasi-commercial operator, as well as ideological influences which now see 'Australianness' as imposing an undesired culture, and nationhood decoded as bigotry, and therefore impositional and abusive. The past monolithic view of Australia was able to "provide different privileged groups with a sense of shared culture and identity of legitimacy and exclusivity" (Petersen, 1993 quoting Johnson, 1988).[394] Conversely, Paletz and Entman (1981) have argued that this formative public posturing was a means by which "granting élites substantial control over the content, emphases, and flow of public opinion, media practices diminish the public's power" (Paletz & Entman, 1981).[395]

5.9 Losing the Brand

The gradual or dramatic waning of funding and support for the public service media outlet has meant that it has had to cut local production, outsource content and purchase overseas made content—much of it from the BBC. Although the BBC is not anathema to the Australian cultural and information diet, it became another way that Aunty's voice was being strangled by being replaced with British culture. In response to complaints in 1988, the then Managing Director of the ABC David Hill, said: "The ABC must become more Australian in its programs, making less use of imported material" (Vine, 1988).[396] This cause was not pursued with sufficient vigour because it was temptingly cheaper than local production. As a counter to this management is scrutinised and costs are queried all around. For example, ABC management was criticised for spending AUD19.6 million on business class airfares in 2019, yet business class travel is a standard entitlement for senior federal public servants of the Commonwealth of Australia. The Community and Public Sector Union, that deals with the ABC, asked the ABC Managing Director, David Anderson, to investigate what was described as an apparent overuse of domestic flights by some ABC managers. The union said: "the ABC managing director has a responsibility to staff and Australians to make sure he reins in excessive interstate travel of some ABC managers" (Tabakoff, 2019).[397] Sinddy Ealy, CPSU ABC section secretary was reported to have said:

> At a time when staff are anxiously awaiting over 200 job cuts and are dealing with smaller budgets, to see some management spend so much on unnecessary travel is beyond the pale" (Tabakoff, Ibid.). … This does nothing to enhance public empathy when it comes to questions of budgeting for the corporation. (Simpson, Ibid.)

An exception to the business class travel choice of the Board has been the staff-elected board member, Dr Jane Connors, who chooses to travel economy class on local flights. Federal Communications Minister, Paul Fletcher, also chooses economy class on domestic flights. (Ibid.).

As a publicly-funded entity, it is mandatory that the ABC must be held to account by shareholders (taxpayers) and efficient corporate governance is required for efficient management of a public resource. The ABC Board has a role to play in overseeing the appropriate spending of money. This criticism comes after some consideration in the developed world has been given to all publicly funded institutions and the arrival of "cutback management" (Andrews et al., 2012).[398] However, the ABC as a national organisation has diverse divisions and audiences, so the need for travel would be considered important, in lieu of the shortcomings of teleconferencing and cyber-meetings. The literature described a management focus on the role of 'stakeholder participation' where in order to provide a "democratic" environment for voices and interests (Greer & Hoggett, 2000) management reached out to employees in both time, space and visits. Knowledge-sharing and efficient resource management also required managers to assess workplaces in person and speak with staff. Since the 1970s public organisation management has moved attention towards service delivery and strategic management (Andrews et al., 2012 quoting Greer & Hoggett, 1999; Boyne & Walker, 2004; Bozeman & Straussman, 1990; Bryson, 1995).

Miles et al. (1978) said it was normal for institutions to re-evaluate and re-consider their purposes (Ibid.)[399] while efficient organisations can re-set their function if they "establish mechanisms that complement their market strategy" (Loc. Cit.), inefficient institutions flounder with the process because they are unable to manage the complexities. Miles et al. (1978) designed a strategic typology—describing three types of organisations: Defenders (stable), Analysers (minimises risk with a firm base and maximises opportunity), Prospectors (entrepreneurs) and the "failure" group Reactors (inconsistent, unstable) (Ibid.) which consists of: "responding inappropriately to environmental change and uncertainty, performing poorly as a result, and then being reluctant to act aggressively in the future" (Loc. Cit.). The ABC, as a primary Australian institution, strangles its voice when it responds to budget cuts by sacking staff, usually through voluntary redundancy, meaning the highly-trained staff will leave first, the removal of established content areas; and, how to re-build staff morale for the remainers (Thornhill & Gibbons, 1995)[400] where the literature stated "redundancy is a particularly damaging form of organizational change" (Worrall, 2000).[401] The ABC as a Reactor organisation means that:

> Unless an organization exists in a "protected" environment such as a monopolistic or highly-regulated industry, it cannot continue to behave as a Reactor indefinitely. (Miles et al., Ibid.)

The theory argued that it would have to become either a defender, analyser or prospector to survive. Meanwhile, research into public service redundancies showed: "managers need to be better trained to implement change without destroying their colleagues' morale, motivation, loyalty or sense of job security" (Worrall et al., 2000).[402]

Internationally, the voice of Aunty is also being strangled and at a geopolitical time when, arguably, it was never needed more to assert Australia's regional interests, public debate, government policy nuances and national security. The choking of Radio Australia has been significant and deliberate—yet hugely consequential for the loss of Australian interests in the region. The Lowy Institute released a report complaining about the ABC's "neglect of international public broadcasting" (Packham, 2019)[403] while at the same time China has spent AUD6 billion on buying Asia Pacific's media outlets. The report said it was apparent that Australia no longer valued public broadcasting as a tool of what is called soft diplomacy—or international influence. It said the ABC was spending AUD433 million ten years ago on ABC Australia and ABC Radio Australia but now only spends AUD11 million and that this has "created a void which China stands poised to fill" (Ibid.). The report: *International Public Broadcasting: A Missed Opportunity for Projecting Australia's Soft Power* described a lack of strategic vision from both the ABC and the Federal Government and called for "a rejuvenated broadcaster" with a "new institutional basis within the Department of Foreign Affairs and Trade's remit" (O'Keeffe & Greene, 2019).[404] Radio Australia, servicing over 30 countries in the Asia Pacific, shut short wave transmissions 31 January 2017.

The group ABC Alumni mourned: "Australia's voice to our region has been reduced to a whisper" (ABC Alumni, n.d.).[405] In its place the Federal Government has provided AUD17.1 million to Australian commercial networks to provide television content to Pacific nations (Meade, 2019).[406] Curiously, the commercial industry said it was not something they had sought (Meade, Ibid.). It also seemed to contradict the wishes of the South Pacific leaders who made submissions to the government asking for review of Australian broadcasting services in the Asia Pacific and a continuation of public broadcasting from the ABC (Loc. Cit.). As a strongly Christian region, it was understood that the ABC content was more appealing to their local communities. The Lowy report identified the three key drivers of the future of broadcasting in the region and where the ABC's voice is being strangled: "geostrategic factors, the competitive environment and technology" (Ibid.).

5.10 Murdoch: Beware the Bogey Man

In 1946, Arthur Calwell, Federal Minister for Information was quoted: "a public utility should not be debauched by Hendersons and Murdochs who since 1944 had set out to get control of ABC news services".[407] ABC staff dislike for the Murdoch family has only increased since. It could be described as 'ancient hatred'—ancient in that it goes back to the founding of the ABC. But hatred has to be distinguished from prejudice by Plato who described Aristotle's understanding of hatred as not necessarily irrational and could be a reasonable response to hatred of evil (Brudholm quoted in Brudholm & Johansen, 2018),[408] yet generalising 'the hated' into a binary can also be self-serving in liberal democracies (Thorup quoted in Brudholm & Johansen, 2018). The dread and fear of the future has dragged the ABC into an unknown, at times incoherent, Manichean, all-encompassing argument that Rupert Murdoch was standing outside ABC headquarters with a bludgeon and would be the destruction of every staff member of the ABC. There may be little to fear, there may be much to fear—such is Aunty's delicate state of paranoia. The late Professor of Government, The University of Sydney, Henry Mayer, quoted Rupert Murdoch as having said in 1961 (before his newspaper *The Australian* was launched in 1964):

> Unless we can return to the principles of public service we will lose our claim to be the Fourth Estate. What right have we to speak in the public interests when, too often, we are motivated by personal gain?[409]

On the other hand, there is good reason for this fear where McChesney and Herman (1997) said:

> News Corporation has devoted its greatest energy to dominating global sport; here the goal is not merely to have one of the leading channels or services, but to overwhelm the other media giants. (Ibid.)[410]

Although somewhat dated in defining the sports ambitions of News Corporation, it does speak to the wider implications of the power of the media conglomerate, its reach, its vision, its impact and its role as an unelected state actor. In 2020 News Corporation was accused of creating misinformation on both climate change and the novel Coronavirus through its chief news outlets including Fox News, Sky News and its Australian newspaper *The Australian* (Gizbert, 2020).[411] News Corporation and Fox Corporation have their biggest interests in the US and Australia. Its US reporting has been "politically partisan, inaccurate to the point of being a legitimate danger to the health of its viewers" (Gizbert, Ibid.) and *The Australian* "uses a similar formula as Fox" (Loc. Cit.) where right-wing commentators are said to dismiss scientific evidence or research (Ibid.). In 2020 it was also announced that Murdoch's younger son, James Murdoch, had resigned from the board of News Corporation "due to disagreements over certain editorial content published by the company's news outlets and certain other strategic decisions" (news.sky.com, 2020), in other media previously James Murdoch had spoken about how he had disagreed with the editorial line of News Corporation in promoting climate change denialism (Knott & Samios, 2020).[412] Other issues of concern to him were adequate public health care and income inequality. He was reported to have said: "There are views I really disagree with on Fox" (Lutz, 2019).

Rupert Murdoch's media activities have been described as 'the reactionary press' and criticism of his media enterprises has been ongoing for decades. Rupert Murdoch's father Sir Keith Murdoch had nurtured his newspaper empire in Australia, building circulation after taking advice from Lord Northcliffe, the British newspaper magnate, on choosing stories to grow readership (Younger, 2003).[413] Then along came radio and although Murdoch (senior) was supportive of the new technology he was not going to give ground to this "new" media especially when it also offered news reports that threatened to take away his readers, his market, his advertisers and intrude on his *field*. The ABC became a concern to Murdoch in 1935 when it threatened to set up its own news service after previously paying newspapers for its news. The situation was described by Australian tabloid Smith's Weekly[414] as "Sir Keith Murdoch's Little War" (1935).[415] The fear and threat of the Murdochs has never dissipated in the minds of the ABC staff and transitioned from the father Keith to the son Rupert—and to his children, because former senior employees of the ABC observed that one of the major concerns during the time when Mark Scott was Managing Director, was the constant barrage of attacks by the Murdoch-owned media in Australia. Yet, what went unremarked was that by this point, the ABC had well and truly invaded the commercial digital *field* to compete with yet try to assimilate with the assorted gathering.

A crisis situation for the world, on so many fronts due to Coronavirus, provides the perfect "push-back" time for the ABC, re-asserting its independence with impartial information. In a monopolised media environment where *The Australian* is the only national daily newspaper, this actually fortifies the role of Australia's Goliath[416]—the only national entirely public-funded broadcaster—the ABC. Rather than speak of being overwhelmed by actors such as Murdoch and other élite media proprietors, the ABC needs to reacquire and reaffirm the capital of its élite *field* where over the decades so many of its staff have striven for unbiased, non-sectarian information to serve and honour the general Australian public. This has been the real and valued divide between commercial media and the ABC. That is now blurring.

The ABC has for many years been tormented by the threat, or anticipation, of funding cuts and government reviews and whenever a News Corporation media outlet has criticised the ABC there was a sense that this would be used by the government as an excuse for funding cuts or, worse. It was believed that Murdoch held the government's pen when writing the cheque for ABC funding. It was also assumed that attacks by a News Corporation outlet on the ABC was merely voicing government opinion and vice versa (Morton, 2020)[417] and that Murdoch's mighty News Corporation was another arm of the apparatus of the Australian Government. These scenarios have been taken to heart by ABC actors as a future fear for eliminating the ABC but instead of pushing-back by re-asserting itself as a quality provider, the ABC has retreated, curiously, into its shell and become hostile and defensive. Consequently, staff culture has been resistant to change, management and leadership, bolstered by these convinced worries of Murdoch's imminent destruction of the ABC. Such has been the extent of paranoia; any internal organisational modification was also seen as coming from this external threat led by Murdoch. These fears need to be analysed rationally and this research has shown there was no single, umbrella, all-encompassing "bogey man" Murdoch challenge to the ABC—rather there was a constellation of several and different threats creating Aunty's perilous times and strangling her voice. The densely populated commercial media means that Murdoch is only one of the many because of the enlarged digital space, which has a diverse cohort of operators, including overseas businesses. The two biggest operators in the Australian commercial *field*—Murdoch and Nine

Entertainment—should provide the opportunity for the public goliath, the ABC, to contest through contrast—not compete with sameness. Aunty is funded to do just that, she accrued ***cultural capital*** because of that, it needed to be wrapped up in policy and taken with care and prudence to the digital commercial *field*. The sobering (possibly hackneyed) vernacular expression "you had one job" comes to mind when Aunty has outbursts of anguished derangement over Murdoch and distracts herself with proclamations of victimhood. Instead should be reasserting her (historic) reputational capital—and preserving her point of difference.

5.11 Sir Keith Murdoch: Ancient Hatreds

It was not the intention for this research to analyse the role of News Corporation and its proprietor American, Australian-born Rupert Keith Murdoch in Australia, son of the late Australian media baron Sir Keith Murdoch. There is already so much extant academic literature, grey literature and academic expertise on the Murdoch empire including, but not limited to: Chenoweth (2001)[418], Williamson (2013)[419], Guthrie (2010)[420], McKnight (2012)[421], Watson and Hickman (2012)[422], Manne (2012)[423], Barry (2013)[424], Lisners (2013)[425], Tiffen (2014)[426], Davies (2014)[427], and Stelzer (2018).[428] So, at the outset, it seemed irrelevant and impertinent to try to compare and contrast the two—ABC and News Corporation. So much had already been said. However, it quickly became unavoidable to develop this topic in the light of the ABC because at many interviews that formed the corpus of this research, News Corporation or Rupert Murdoch were mentioned. These acknowledgements could be placed into four categories: dread and fear; incidental, contextual references; or, dismissive of fear and suspicions.

During and after the ABC's inception, there were tensions and flare-ups between Keith Murdoch and the ABC. It is an extraordinary irony of Australian media that the ABC, a unique communication organisation that covers news and information collection and dissemination in Australia, was established remote from any commercial pressures to sell content yet, was originally shackled by heavy conditions and controls laid out by the Australian commercial media—especially that of newspaper baron, Keith Murdoch. Ironically, ABC News (Television and Radio) developed aloof from those bias pressures, yet now confront them in the commercial digital *field*. At the time of the ABC's launch, Keith Murdoch was Chairman of the Australian Newspapers' Conference that led the Australian newspaper industry and the other commercial media. His meddling in the creation and disruption to the early years of the ABC was aimed at supporting the primacy of newspapers (and commercial radio stations) in the roles of newsgatherers and disseminators but was also aimed at protecting advertising profits and recouping outlay.

Newspapers were spending large sums installing printing equipment and the cost of newsprint was increasing. For example, Murdoch said (The Argus, 1937)[429] the price of newsprint was expected to rise from AU£9/10 (AUD892) a ton in 1937 to AU£16 (AUD1429) a ton in 1939. He said this would form part of an overall cost increase to the newspaper industry of AU£850,000 (AUD1.7 million) to AUD76 million in 1939 (Ibid.). In the history of Australian media, the cost of collecting and producing news was high for newspapers. In country New South Wales in 1929, there was such concern among newspaper proprietors belonging to the Australian Provincial Press Association about the free distribution of country news to the city that a central agency was formed to sell news to city newspapers (rather than supply it free).

In terms of Keith Murdoch's career in newspapers, as a reporter at Gallipoli in 1915 during World War I he was said to provide the first alert to Australian Prime Minister, Andrew Fisher, personally in a cabled letter of a staggeringly high number of Australian soldiers killed at Gallipoli. There was one account that Fisher sent Murdoch because he was concerned that he may not have been informed accurately from his military's dispatches, the newspapers were overwhelmed in printing the number of deaths and wounded, the press was heavily censored and he wanted another observer to report back (Murdoch Intro. McKernan, 2010).[430] Another account was that Murdoch "wangled for himself four days on the bloody peninsula, betrayed the pledge of confidence he had given to the authorities, and carried back to London tales about the mismanagement of the campaign" (Ryan, 1986).[431] Fisher ended Australia's involvement in the Dardanelles campaign and the letter had a positive impact on the journalist's career. Murdoch soon became the Australian head of United Cable Service in London and built an empire that ultimately was named: "Lord Southcliffe's newspaper empire",[432] after that he was given a knighthood in 1933 supported by the administration of Prime Minister Joseph Lyons for his services to journalism. Yet, Murdoch admitted 20 years later that his correspondence from Gallipoli was "exaggerated to the verge of untruth" (Ryan, 1986): "Yet somehow, through his lifetime, the legend flourished of an Australian patriot whose intervention had helped materially to shorten the suffering on Gallipoli" (Ryan, Ibid.). But Murdoch had a view to the bigger picture because in 1910, he had already founded the trade union, the Australian Journalists' Association (AJA) (Ibid.)[433] (now merged with the Media, Entertainment and Arts Alliance—MEAA).

Creating an enemy is part of the narrative of "war" and while the ABC staff culture has been at war with the Murdoch family since the ABC's inception, it should also be remembered that the ABC was not just at war with Sir Keith Murdoch but also at war with a "hostile daily press" in Australia, generally (Smith's Weekly, 1935).[434] In the early days there was good reason for the ABC to fear the Murdoch empire because of the influence of Keith Murdoch in government and business circles, and his aim to provide the ABC with *his* news content as well as access to the not-for-profit Australian Associated Press (AAP). The ABC had other ideas wanting independence and when Murdoch insisted it take his news offerings he was accused of "bullying and baiting" the ABC (Ibid.)[435] and prodding the ABC into "strong resentment and retaliatory measures" (Loc. Cit.)[436] because "Sir Keith Murdoch has always viewed broadcasting with a jealous suspicion and distrust" (Ibid.).[437] In his biography, Keith Murdoch was described as having written to Prime Minister Joseph Lyons expressing outrage at the newly created ABC for its "intention to use the facilities of newspapers (in news gathering) without paying fairly for these services" (Younger, 2003).[438]

News had commercial value back then, as it does today, which is why newsrooms are struggling to pay for and originate news copy because of fewer staff and the broadband consumer concept encouraged by internet operatives that everything on the internet should be free, yet monetised. At the inception of the ABC, Murdoch was "the most powerful newspaper owner in Australia" (Petersen, 1993)[439] who had a dramatic capacity to influence the government (Ibid.),[440] was seen as someone trying to determine public policy (Loc. Cit.)[441] and had been quoted by a biographer that British newspaper baron Lord Northcliffe was the biggest influence in his life (Ibid.).[442] Davies (2009) quoted the twentieth-century newspaper baron, Lord Beaverbrook: "I run the paper for the purpose of making propaganda and with no other motive" (Davies, Ibid.).[443] As a consequence of this association, Murdoch was known as Lord Southcliffe (in regard to his business empire being in the southern hemisphere). Northcliffe was problematised in his role, however, because he created a paradox of the Fourth Estate:

> The only truly independent newspaperman of the day—Lord Northcliffe—was also regarded as the man most likely to damage the reputation of the British press. (Boyce et al., 1978)[444]

Thus, the ABC sought independence from this partisanship. The early ABC wanted to write its own news. ABC historian, Alan Thomas, said that while Sir Keith, among others, had given initial agreement at the start of World War II that the ABC be given support to broadcast BBC news as well as cabled Australian Associated Press and Consolidated Press 200 words of overseas news per day and broadcast its own bulletin at 7.00 pm (Thomas, 1980)[445]—Murdoch abandoned this agreement when he became Director-General of Information in July 1940 (Ibid.)[446] transferring the evening news bulletin to the Department of Information and employing "newspaper men" to compile bulletins (Loc. Cit.)[447]: "public outcry plus continued representations from Cleary (ABC Chairman) finally resulted in the transfer of news production back to the ABC" (Loc. Cit.).[448] In 1941 it was revealed that the ABC paid Associated Press for 600 words of overseas news daily at a cost of A£2500 per annum, but with the war crisis it had been increased to 1200 words a day (Newcastle Morning Miners Advocate, 1941).[449] The Chairman of the Australian Broadcasting Commission, William Cleary, told a parliamentary inquiry into broadcasting the "outbreak of war the Australian public became news conscious overnight. Never before had there been such a demand for news" (Ibid.).[450]

While the impact and interference of Australian newspapers in the ABC, led by Keith Murdoch, was substantial he denied it: "The newspapers rejected as unjustified any suggestion that their attitude was monopolistic" (The Examiner, 1941).[451] Yet, his influence was profound and resonant until his death, ultimately, Murdoch's fears of loss of newspaper control over the print advertising market with the advent of the ABC were both unfounded and unrealised. The contrary and non-commercial argument about Keith Murdoch's distaste for the ABC was his concern for its élite, privileged status. This was because, ultimately:

> He rejected the ABC as a cultural body because it stood for art and not a technocratic science, the traditions of intellectuals, artists and musicians and not practical common sense, for British/Australian ways and not American/ Australian ways, for cultural heritage and not modern individualism. Thus the ABC was unable to pursue a cultural stance that would have legitimacy among all sections of the powerful, while it was without authority among those who talked power. (Johnson, 1988)[452]

Another aspect to the ancient hatred was that while ABC news services were eventually established to be neutral they have been accused regularly of bias. 'The Troubles' with its foundation as an unbiased entity were conflicted by the powerful newspaper industry, insistent that the ABC buy its news from newspapers, of which Murdoch was a substantial and influential owner. Keith Murdoch told *The West Australian* in an interview:

> We have no right to any monopolistic control over news distribution. All we ask is that the national stations take our news instead of collecting it themselves and observe conditions which, as well as giving the public what it requires, will cause the minimum of interference to the newspapers. (The West Australian, 1936)[453]

The central plank of his argument was that newspapers were traditionally and historically charged with the duty of supplying news and that broadcasters had no role in this. Murdoch said:

> The complete supremacy of newspapers as an advertising medium was unchallenged and was candidly admitted by all leading advertisers throughout the country. (The Argus, 1937)[454]

Further, his justification for an Australian newspaper monopoly of news was likened to news being a staple of a stable community: "Just as essential to the community as its bread or its transport" (Ibid.) and that newspapers needed to work "hand in hand" (Ibid.) with broadcasting: "each helping the other in the task of interesting, enlightening, and informing the public" (Ibid.).

By 1939 the ABC was allowed to re-broadcast BBC News, the copyright of which was owned by Australian Associated Press (AAP) and of which Sir Keith was Chairman. AAP said initially it would not charge the ABC for this news supply, yet the by 1941 the ABC Chairman was reported in The Sydney Morning Herald (1941)[455] that the commission was paying A£3000 a year (offset by a rebate of A£1500 from commercial radio stations by passing on the transmission). The ABC did, however, pay Australian newspapers an annual fee of A£200 for local news (*The Sydney Morning Herald*, Ibid.) and this was supplemented with ABC correspondents' reports from London and news from British Official Wireless (*The Cairns Post*, 1939).[456] Not only was the ABC chafing under these high fees for AAP news, regional newspapers were also facing the same high costs for access to the service (*The Morning Bulletin*, 1939).[457]

At the start of World War II, the ABC had to operate under a strict news regimen controlled by Australian newspapers designed to preserve their commercial interests and control of news creation and flow. Aunty paid for BBC content through Murdoch's organised news channels prior to the war; however, the commission was given free access during the war. Censorship was also overriding content. Newspapers also permitted the ABC to read news bulletins more frequently and at additional times than those previously stipulated by newspapers. However, even with that, the situation could still be described as restrictive[458]:

> The Commission may broadcast up to a maximum of 15 news flashes weekly—not more than three in any one day-such, flashes to be limited to 35 words each. Acknowledgments necessary to inform the public of the sources of their broadcast news and to preserve the copyright interests to the newspaper are to be reduced to two daily. (*The Mercury*, 1939)[459]

However, once the war was underway, Australian newspapers objected to the re-broadcast of BBC News on the ABC when they learned that the BBC was incorporating Reuters news content as part of its service. Murdoch was quoted in *The Courier Mail* (1941)[460] that Australian newspapers paid Reuters A£12,000 a year for the service and that the ABC should not have de facto access to Reuters. He also accused the ABC of bias using BBC bulletins:

> The only difficulty is whether there is too much news on the air in Australia of a slightly propagandist tinge, added Sir Keith Murdoch ... because the BBC had an "essential flavour of success". (Ibid.)

It was not long after this that Murdoch became the Director-General of Information for the Federal Government in 1940 and then immediately set about giving himself virtually unfettered powers to control the media. But this upset other newspaper proprietors as well as the ABC and his position became untenable. His demands that newspapers and radio publish all government statements were described by *The Canberra Times* as: "an extraordinary blunder was made in the blunderbuss regulations for the control of the Press" (1942).[461] Allied with this was simmering newspaper antagonism over the role of radio as a news source and the industry's perception that the ABC, in particular, was a puppet to the government:

> Radio service to the government therefore tends to resemble that of a gramophone record. This is precisely what the Press should and must avoid. (Ibid.)

Newspapers were also ferociously anti-government. In fact, such was the criticism of the Curtin Labor Government during World War II that the Minister for Trade and Customs, Senator Keane, suggested that newspapers controlled by Murdoch should be run by the government to ensure impartiality:

> I am now more inclined to believe that control of such newspapers should be vested in a non-political commission, similar to the Australian Broadcasting Commission, which would ensure that news of national interest is impartially presented. (The Herald, 1943)[462]

Even though the ABC appointed its first journalist in 1934 and its first Federal News Editor in 1936 (Knight, 2007)[463] newspaper archive research indicates that it was not until 1946 that the ABC was formally allowed to operate its own independent news gathering and broadcasting service when it was inaugurated. In fact, it was reported in Federal Parliament that year when the "Bill for A.B.C. News Services" was passed requiring that the 99% of the organisation's national news services be compiled by ABC employees, 40% state news was collected by its staff and only needed 19 more journalists to have a completely independent news service (*The Sydney Morning Herald*, 1946).[464]

However, there was a general weariness among Australians of a war bias in newspapers and as Petersen (1993)[465] summarised: "the perception was that all news bore the indelible imprint of the proprietor" (Ibid.).

The independence of the ABC came under threat again in 1950 when the conservative government threatened to change the legislation and give the ABC's news service (which by then was employing 100 journalists) to Keith Murdoch (Northern Standard, 1950).[466] This proved to be a hollow threat and never eventuated. Murdoch succumbed to illness soon after this and he died in 1952.

5.12 Rupert Murdoch Versus The ABC

Rupert Murdoch began his news business when he inherited the running of *The News* in Adelaide from his late father, who had bought it from the Bonython family of Adelaide for A£1 million (along with two other owners: Theodore Fink and William Baillieu). This was a small beginning for a corporation that was eventually to be enlarged, digitised and globalised with the power to control, terminate, support or at least manage governments (Greenwald, 2004).[467,468] Much later Murdoch established his own newspaper, *The Australian*, on 15 July 1964, at a price of A6d (five cents),[469] originally based in Canberra but later moved to Sydney, it was Murdoch's first morning metropolitan newspaper. It remains the only Australian national general newspaper. The paper's launch described it role: "this paper is tied to no party, to no state, and has no chains of any kind … vigor, truth and information without dullness will be found day by day in these columns"[470] (ibid.). It is published 6 days a week. Now, "media analysts estimate that *The Australian* loses AUD3 million a month".[471] McKnight said Murdoch established the newspaper "to win the respect and influence that his tabloid newspapers could never deliver".[472] Unlike other broadsheet newspapers which have reduced their size to 'compacts' (or 'broadloids', as they are referred to pejoratively combining the words broadsheet with tabloid). Traditionally, broadsheet newspapers were considered more serious and considered publications while tabloid size newspapers have been more sensational, easier to read and printed for 'the man on the tram'. Broadsheets were for 'the man in the office' at a desk. Tabloids were published with the working man to read on public transport, hence the abbreviated ease of size.

Then there is the famous derogatory quote from the Head of the New York department store, Bloomingdales, which was reputed to have rejected Murdoch after he asked the store to advertise with his newly-acquired *New York Post* newspaper in 1976: "The problem, Mr Murdoch, is that your readers are our shoplifters".[473,474] Then, there's the witty line by Mike Royko, the late Chicago newspaper columnist and Pulitzer Prize winner: "No self-respecting fish would want to be wrapped in a Murdoch paper".[475] Lord Conrad Black, Canadian publisher, convicted of fraud, and one-time controller of the Australian Fairfax media organisation after he acquired a majority stake in the 1990s,[476] has said:

> Murdoch is a great white shark who mumbles and furrows his brow compulsively (with) orange-dyed hair … a man who is airtight in his ruthlessness, unlimited in his ambition, with the iron nerves to have bet the company again and again.[477]

Chris Mullins, a member of the UK Blair government who chaired the Home Affairs Committee and was parliamentary under-secretary told ABC Radio: "these institutions, these papers, these media empires are so big now that successive politicians became afraid of them".[478]

Now many ABC staff speak of Rupert Murdoch as if living in fear of him. Fear has evolved as a convenient default, umbrella denial of the other factors strangling Aunty's voice. The creation of a sinister arch-enemy has become easier and less complicated than confronting all the other challenges including a failure to have consistent, and consistently support, ABC leadership; and the need to plan for (the inevitability of) dramatic change at the ABC. It also required deft policy and implementation. It has been shown in the organisational literature that staff 'fear of the unknown' was personalised as threats to an individual's status in the organisation, fear of incompetence, loss of identity and even alienation from the group (Boin et al.).[479] In the organisational literature, this staff fear-based resistance took the form of three stages according to Organisational Management scholar and former professor at the MIT Sloan School of Management, Edgar Schein: denial, scapegoating and manoeuvring.[480] In the ABC's case there has been a strong sense that Rupert Murdoch's News Corporation was the scapegoat in the decline of the ABC, when in fact the failure of the ABC's staff culture, which has never been addressed, was another part of the numerous factors strangling Aunty's voice.

In addition, it is unacknowledged that the ABC has left its élite *field* and moved into the commercial *field*, heavily influenced by Murdoch, a place where "the borders between broadcasting and other communications have become increasingly blurred" (Drozdek, 2015)[481] with convergence and globalisation forcing the voice of public broadcasters into competition on new platforms and in previously undeveloped, unknown ways speaking to niche audiences they never knew. The quaint old fashion model of audiences, the ABC and their special *field* have long gone. In order to retain these "old" audiences the ABC has opted for a mixed model using old technology (radio and television linear narratives) plus streaming, on-demand, applications (apps), the incorporation of opinion and analysis as news content and a more liberal, less prescriptive approach to media and audiences. In addition, there has been the shift from 'professionally managed' media to 'everyone managed' media—citizen journalism.

It would also seem that News Corporation has been pointing out the flaws in the organisation that were visible to outsiders—but, of course, making good mileage out of them all the while. ABC staff have always reacted to these criticisms angrily and blamed Rupert Murdoch personally (also variously referred to as "News Corp" or "the reactionary media") for attacking the organisation. The response to this has been the development of a defensive staff culture, manifesting itself by congratulating each other on Twitter for each other's work, for example. Once public praise was considered anathema to ABC staff because the organisation operated in its own *field* and the privilege of working for the organisation and contributing to the wider knowledge of the public sphere was the reward. Once being in that exclusive *field* itself was the accolade.

Murdoch media's frequent condemnation of ABC content has pointed out disequilibrium in the organisation, or, in Schein's words: "that something is wrong somewhere" (Schein, 2010).[482] The ABC have invented a complicated, destructive narrative around Murdoch in order to avoid any self-analysis. On the other hand, calls for simply privatising the ABC or creating licence fees as a way of funding the organisation do not deliver a fitting response or outcome to a once-revered, unique and centrally important public Australian cultural institution. Flippant threats of licence fees do not trigger an analysis of what went wrong and investigation into solving these challenges. Defensive responses to criticism do not promote the longevity of a needed public service media organisation. Nor do they address why and how the ABC has arrived in a depleted, reduced state of relevance where it clutches at, or contributes to, the next idea on social media as a means of being relevant to its algorithmed publics. That it is so readily attacked does not point to the enemy, but rather problems within. Yet, the ABC has failed to identify specific flaws that need address, or correction. Its drift in content *field* is the topic about which precious little is written or discussed. Management literature referred to this avoidance and censuring of organisational problems as "the organisational elephant". Professionals Australia, a professional body which represents Australia's Federal public servants said "the elephants" survived in organisations where:

> Everyone tiptoes around them and avoids even mentioning their presence. Organisational elephants feed on gossip, mediocrity and dysfunctional politics. "Their effect is often demoralising for the people around them and always productivity-sapping for the organisation as a whole …" but like "wild elephants can live long lives and so can their organisational counterparts". (Fitzell, 1970)[483]

Any analysis or critique of the ABC is taken as abuse and dismissed immediately. It is unfortunate that the ABC has cast itself as a victim here, just at the time it needed to be proactive. In addition, and importantly, News Corporation tends to only challenge or deride the ABC on its news content, because that is the area in which the two are in direct conflict. The media has become increasingly commercialised (Hallin in Drozdek, 2015)[484] and the *field* is crowded and noisy. The ABC has moved itself into the 24-hour news *field* once occupied by News Corporation's Sky News. This then makes ABC News and Current Affairs a direct competitor with Sky News. It is not unusual in businesses for attacks on other businesses when they are trying to control the same *field*. To explicate this point further, there are no regular criticisms by News Corporation media outlets of the choice of music or presenters' comments about composers on the ABC's Classic-FM, for example. There is no criticism by News Corporation outlets of ABC breakfast radio program presenters, for example. They do not compete in those *fields*.

In academic analysis, in order for an enemy to be created, the enemy has to be de-humanised or an abstraction of evil so the battle can be reduced to a simple binary of good and evil (Creed, 2013).[485] Invoking emotions towards the enemy was significant because: "one actor is the aggrieved victim and the other the blameworthy perpetrator; thus, identities and positions within a local moral order are established" (Ibid.)[486]: "thus, emotions entail a point of view, often so much so that the audience emphatically shares the emotion" (Loc. Cit.).[487] As the ancient Greek philosopher Aristotle said: "an emotional speaker always makes his audience feel with him, even when there is nothing in his arguments" (Creed, Ibid.).[488] There is a weaving of myth and narrative in creating an enemy and, as in war, creating an enemy restores a sense of honour (Ibid.).[489] In 2018, Former Labor Prime Minister, Kevin Rudd, described Rupert Murdoch as "the greatest cancer on the Australian democracy" (Rudd, 2018)[490] because Murdoch operated: "as a political party, acting in pursuit of clearly defined commercial interests, in addition to his far-right ideological world view" (Ibid.).[491] Rudd accused Murdoch of running "targeted jihad against those who defy the ideological mood of their master" (Loc. Cit.).[492] Earlier, former ABC journalist, Quentin Dempster said: "I blame Keating[493] (a Labor Prime Minister) for the distorting power of Rupert Murdoch in Australia … [his] dance with … Murdoch … has left this country with an inbuilt imbalance" (Parker, 2014).[494]

There is abundant literature that describes Murdoch as a "king-maker" or meddler and power broker in government affairs (e.g. Evans, 1984; McChesney & Herman, 1997; Inglis, 2006; Watson & Hickman, 2012; Lisners, 2012; McKnight, 2012; Barry, 2013;[495] O'Brien, 2018). Former Prime Minister Malcolm Turnbull (in Whitlam, 2020) provided a quote in his memoirs attributed to Murdoch during the final stage of his government in August 2018: "We have to get rid of Malcolm … he can't win, he can't beat Shorten" (quoted in Whitlam, 2020)[496] and that as a consequence of upheaval in the Liberal Party Murdoch was quoted: "three years of Labor wouldn't be too bad" (Crowe, 2020).[497] *The Sydney Morning Herald* (Crowe, 2020) said that Murdoch's son and co-chairman, Lachlan Murdoch, insisted his father did not make those remarks but Mr Turnbull dismissed that denial (Crowe, 2020). Also, in rebuttal, former News Corp chief executive and former ABC senior executive, Kim Williams, said Turnbull overstated the Murdoch press influence in Australian elections "because News Corp is "old media" with dwindling power"[498] (Meade, 2020). Williams said the reaction from the Australian electorate to News Corporation newspapers' advice on how to vote at election times was "root your boot"[499] (Meade, 2020).

So, there are a range of factors troubling the ABC which form part of the bigger narrative around Murdoch and form an amalgam with—"ongoing funding cuts, complaints of bias, government reviews, Murdoch media antagonism, internal instability" (Meade, 2018)[500] managerial failure and the emergence of federal politicians from time to time who are perceived to have "negative attitudes towards the national broadcaster" (Meade, 2018).[501] On a business level, Rudd said Murdoch saw the government's National Broadband Network, fibre to the household as a threat to his Foxtel cable entertainment empire, which was "his cash cow cross-subsidising his loss-making print mastheads" (Rudd, 2018).[502] He said Murdoch feared NBN would make Netflix a serious Foxtel competitor and, in the light of this, there was a need for a royal commission into Australia's public and private media, to examine abuse of media power for personal benefit but also to preserve democracy. Murdoch was known for his political interests. For example, McChesney and Herman (1997) said:

> Murdoch's power and bias is so great that Labour party candidate Tony Blair travelled to a Murdoch meeting in Australia in 1995 to assure the mogul of his moderation and express hopes of a friendlier electoral treatment. (Ibid.)[503]

As a business, News Corporation looks to thrive by minimising its competitors. It once functioned in a newspaper world where, as the late James Fairfax (1992), former chairman of publisher John Fairfax Limited, quoted retired Fairfax journalist Gavin Souter:

> Australia's principal newspapers had been herded by instincts of attack and defence. An attack by A upon B could lead to defensive action by C, which might consider itself threatened by any change in the balance of power; in these circumstances, defence might well resemble attack. (Fairfax, 1992)[504]

The point to be made here is that attacks by Murdoch on the ABC may not be a specific action of one man or one organisation on a vendetta, the counter-fact is that this is how business operates. Many businesses seek to better their competitors, minimise, or remove them, so that profits are maximised. In addition, the ABC has shifted to the commercial arena. So, where once the ABC and commercial media seemed to happily coincide and 'jolly along' on their separate but similar paths, digitalisation and the abundance of media have shifted the arena and have, incongruously, merged them all into the bottle neck of online information and opinion. The ABC is now competing in that same digital 'free for all' space with the commercials. It is now supplying online opinion and analysis—once the purview of commercial media—except it offers it up paid for by the public. As a public service it is now chasing popularism as a measure of its relevance to its public. But it is a dangerous and unsafe place for the ABC to be—it is strangling its unique voice by hunting down fragmented audiences and forgetting to protect and parcel-up its *reputational capital* earned in its own *field*. While its current Charter asks it to be generalist in its audience approach it is actually: "addressing younger, female, suburban and culturally diverse audiences" through "conversations" and "stories" while also forming "new relationships with people who haven't traditionally grown up with the ABC" (ABC, 2020).[505] In so doing, it has brought itself directly into competition with commercial media—and News Corporation—with these 'conversations' and *field* excursions that compete with commercial media.

Distinguished Emeritus Professor John Curtin University Western Australia, John Hartley (2008), said worries about media ownership and powerful media barons were passé anyway. He asserted that these fears were a "parallax error" (Hartley, 2008),[506] meaning that "the object of analysis is in a different position from the point of observation" (Ibid.).[507]

Hartley (2008) said of greater concern was how the consumer, as the news interpreter and creator, would change the way the world is understood. Hartley (2008) said the focus should be on: "how, for good or ill, the consumer paradigm will turn out, and whether its positive potential will counter-balance its well-documented (but less well-understood) down sides" (Loc. Cit.).[508] The ABC was never designed to compete in the commercial *field*, nor was public broadcasting. It was created for limited, scarce bandwidth not the multiplicity of the internet. For this reason, identical problems of funding scarcity and withering audiences manifest at the BBC, Canadian Broadcasting Corporation (CBC) and the US Public Broadcasting Service (PBS), and so on. Some market analysis has found that diversity in media provided by public broadcasters could be of benefit to the public in increasing choice (Alcock & Docwra, 2005).[509] In terms of neoclassical microeconomics, markets should be free, not publicly-determined. The ABC, therefore, had an unfair advantage. However, research has also shown that in commercial television markets there can be duplication and pursuit of mass audiences (Ibid.)[510] and so the minorities are ignored. Minorities are "discriminated against" (Loc. Cit.).[511] It has been found that if the ABC were to be privatised it would "result in reduced diversity and choice for the viewers and in decreased revenues for the initial market players" (Ibid.).[512]

We are now living in a consumer-based "navigator/aggregator" (Alcock & Docwra, 2005)[513] world. News organisations are no longer the source of information, of knowledge, of truth—they have lost their claim to veracity. News organisations are now just part of the throng trying to engage the mosh-pit and stir up the strident voices and the outrecuidance[514] of the tribes. Social media has changed everything—but without any time to trial or measure potential impacts and consequences, especially on news media. Marshall McLuhan (1973)[515] stated presciently of media (likening it to Plato's ideal training school in Athens): "the greatest school had been put out for human use before it has been thought out" (Ibid.). News organisations were based on old business models of news—they were not designed for massive digital disruption and a de-professionalisation of information. Media consumption is now on a heartbeat by heartbeat basis, with little time for reflection and appropriate contextualisation and perspective. News exists in the same "high frequency" circulation (Hartley, 2008)[516] as other digital media ("churnalism", as discussed earlier). But how do serious news organisations compete in this open *field*? The ABC has entered a digital commercial *field* where profit motives drive selective participation, and rather than an urge for enhanced democracy, providing a sense of participation—the actual result is compromised journalism (Vujnovic et al., 2010).[517]

Murdoch said in 2005: "I didn't do as much as I should have after all the excitement of the late 1990's. I suspect many of you in this room did the same, quietly hoping that this thing called the digital revolution would just limp along" (Murdoch in Kaye & Quinn, 2005).[518] A report by media consultant firm, Merrill-Brown, that had been released that year cautioned: "Instant news on the Internet, other new technologies, and the increasingly held view that news needs to be a two-way process is changing the entire way news is consumed" (Merrill-Brown, 2005).[519] Australia's democracy is in serious danger if it lost the voice of the ABC—initially charged with being an impartial guardian of Australia's public interest. The University of Oxford's Reuters Institute said in 2016 that "Australia has a high concentration of traditional media ownership dominated by News Corporation and Fairfax Media (now dominated by Nine Entertainment) who together own the majority of national and capital city newspapers" (University of Oxford/Reuters Institute for the Study of Journalism, 2016).[520] Academics Flew and Goldsmith (2013) said:

> In 2011 News Corp Australia accounted for 23% of the newspaper titles in Australia. ... News Corp Australia titles account for 59% of the sales of all daily newspapers, ... making it Australia's most influential newspaper publisher by a considerable margin. (Ibid.)[521]

The Finkelstein Inquiry (2012) into Australia's media noted that: "Australia's newspaper industry is among the most concentrated in the developed world" (Ibid.).[522] Prior to this, The Centre for Policy Development said in 2011 that Australian TV and radio ownership was increasingly concentrated and incremental changes to media laws have permitted this accretion of power to fewer owners (Rowland, 2016).[523] Other extant literature spoke of the dangers where: "monopoly control of the media and the means to deliver information are serious threats to democracy" (Barsamian, 2001).[524] Former ABC Producer David Salter (2007) pointed out three "essential truths" to this digital shift:

> "Issues of nationality or geography have no meaning whatsoever once material carries a 'www' prefix ..., our traditional framework of copyright law is dying fast" and third, "the traditional media world of discrete forms and technologically separate services is also coming to an end". (Salter, 2007)[525]

However, as discussed in Chap. 4, those serious threats also take the shape of an information war led by nation state actors destabilising or shouting louder than what is taken as public opinion. Their negative influence on the health and coherence of parliamentary democracies and policy in undermining their stability and cohesion has become even bigger than the now relatively benign impact of the media barons and "the destabilising effect of social media must be acknowledged in the long-run if democracy is to be defended" (Hardinge, 2020).[526]

On another front, concerns about Australia's stability expressed to this researcher by a former political leader who said that Australia was in a "perilous" situation with the control of News Corporation over Australia's media industry saying it was a serious threat to Australia's democracy. Another former ABC leader expressed deep concern about the relentless attacks that have been waged on the ABC by News Corporation-owned media outlets. Similar concerns were also expressed publicly by former Labor Prime Minister Kevin Rudd (2018).[527] It was of some concern to a former senior Australian politician that the ABC never "fights back" against the attacks by News Corporation, which implied that the ABC agreed with the attacks and negativity towards the public broadcaster, or was being cowered. Former ABC senior presenter, Quentin Dempster, defended the ABC with another view of Murdoch in 2012: "the digital revolution is changing everything … to jeopardise the ABC effort now at the vituperative and vengeful urgings of Rupert Murdoch and News Ltd. would be an act of vandalism" (Chenoweth, 2012).[528] A former journalist at News Corporation-owned *The Australian* newspaper for 30 years, Tony Koch, said biased political coverage at that newspaper meant that: "if it is not anti-Labor it is anti-Green or, quite ridiculously, anti-ABC. Anything except a story negative to the Liberal or National parties" (Koch, 2019).[529]

In quantifying the influence of the proprietor, Murdoch, in his own enterprises the literature said Murdoch had had "a hands-on role" (Cryle, 2008)[530] at *The Australian* "from the outset" (Ibid.). John Menadue, former General Manager at News Limited and former head of the Department of Prime Minister and Cabinet from 1974 to 1976 said News Corporation had "become the voice in Australia of the extreme right wing" (ABC, 2010).[531] In regard to Murdoch's influence on his news outlets and operations Koch (2019) wrote that it was more that editors were second-guessing Murdoch rather than taking direct orders: "gone is the requirement for balance" (Ibid.).[532] Another former employee, Bruce Guthrie, who was sacked as Editor-in-Chief of Murdoch's Melbourne's

Herald Sun newspaper said: "most senior executives don't do anything without first asking themselves: "What would Rupert think about this?" (Guthrie, 2010).[533] Andrew Neil, a Britain and former Editor of News Corporation's *The Sunday Times* confirmed this: "Murdoch has a knack of picking people who know how to second guess him" (Neil, 1996).[534] Former UK *The Sun* editor David Yelland, told the *Leveson Inquiry into the Culture, Practices and Ethics of the British Press* prompted by the News International phone-hacking scandal, that editors of Murdoch newspapers "look at the world through Rupert's eyes" (McNally, 2012)[535] "all Murdoch editors, what they do is this: they go on a journey where they end up agreeing with everything Rupert says" (Ibid.).[536] The Leveson Inquiry concluded that politicians had developed "too close a relationship with the press in a way which has not been in the public interest" (BBC, 2012),[537] especially in regard to the impact of News Corporation media where there was:

> At *The News of the World*, quite apart from phone hacking ... a failure of systems of management and compliance. There was a general lack of respect for individual privacy and dignity at the paper. (Ibid.)

The Leveson Inquiry decided that News Corporation had not been particularly ethical nor was it obviously wedded to the public interest. "Hackgate" (as it was known) "reveals the mechanisms of a system based on the corruption of power" (Fenton, 2014)[538]:

> The problem is much broader and deeper than any slippage in ethical practice would seem to suggest and rests not with the individual journalists but with the system of news production they were part of. (Ibid.)

The late James Fairfax (1992) in his autobiography called for a need for diversity and competition in Australian media and that even as far back as the late 1970s he believed "gross imbalances ... would result from a Murdoch takeover" of *The Herald and Weekly Times* (Fairfax, 1991).[539] This takeover came to pass a decade later in 1987. Yet, Fairfax also had prevailing commercial concerns. Fairfax said he was pleased to prevent Murdoch taking control of NSW regional newspapers as it "stopped (News Corporation) from obtaining total country coverage throughout Australia" (Ibid.).[540] But there was a pragmatic business side to this view—Fairfax said Murdoch could have then applied "'across-the board'" advertising discounts in both metropolitan and country areas "which would have been very difficult for us to compete against" (Ibid.).[541] In this instance, Fairfax said his family had been friends with former Liberal Party National Party Coalition Prime Minister Malcolm Fraser's family "for many years and over several generations" (Ibid.).[542] Fraser was the 22nd Prime Minister in 1975 until 1983, and leader of the Liberal Party of Australia. Institutional Logics occupy material practices but also manifest in symbolic constructions, such as these longstanding associations between politicians and media proprietors: "that guide the production and reproduction of institutional practices" (Thornton et al., 2012).[543] The same constructions would apply to Murdoch's relations with politicians in Australia, the UK and the US, in particular.

Australian newspapers no longer exist in quarantined silos. Digitisation and computerisation of content means their impact now ranges globally and instantly. Murdoch is described or understood by the academic academy (as well as the media) as the most powerful media proprietor in the world but in his national broadsheet newspaper, *The Australian* (2003), he was said to be unhappy with a label which confers such unbridled power:

> Murdoch would dismiss the idea that he is anything like a media baron or that the holdings of the company of which he is chairman and chief executive, Australia's biggest media group News Corporation (parent company of News Limited, publisher of *The Weekend Australian*), constitute an empire—a term he dislikes. (Fallows, 2003)[544]

In 2010 his older son, Lachlan Murdoch, was described by a media analyst in *The Sun-Herald* as having "local power and influence (to) rival that of his father, Rupert" (Lee, 2010).[545]

Murdoch's longstanding allegiance to newspapers was most clearly identified by Australian media historian Bridget Griffen-Foley (2001) when she described News Limited, the company created by Keith Murdoch in 1922, as "the bedrock of Rupert Murdoch's global communications and entertainment empire, News Corporation" (Griffen-Foley, 2001).[546] In order to own American television, Rupert Murdoch became an American citizen in 1985, as well, he controlled manifestly the Australian newspaper market by 70–75%. On the 2019 Forbes 400 list, Mr Murdoch and his family were ranked number 24.[547] On the 2018 Forbes most powerful people, Mr Murdoch ranked #39,[548] just below former Japanese Prime Minister Shinzo Abe. Power in and of itself should not be a negative measure of an institution and it is not within the purview of this research and methodology to measure power and the impact of that between competing media groups. However, the extent of that power was waning in 2020 when Roy Morgan Research said News Corporation had a significant drop in revenue (Myer, 2020).[549] Its Sydney tabloid newspaper, *The Daily Telegraph*, lost 15.5% readership and overall, the organisation's Australian mastheads lost 9% in revenue (Myer, 2020). Company Chief Executive Officer, Robert Thomson said: "The results were affected by a sluggish Australian economy, uncharacteristic softness in book publishing, and foreign exchange fluctuations" (Ibid.). News Corporation now shares printing facilities with Fairfax Media (now Nine Entertainment) to reduce costs.

News Corporation is a prominent global organisation and has been found by independent inquiries to have displayed flagrant abuses of power (The Leveson Inquiry, 2012).[550] However, much of the extant literature on News Corporation and Rupert Murdoch is not out of step with the views expressed anonymously to this researcher. Elsewhere, on the public record, former senior ABC presenter and journalist, Kerry O'Brien, has stated:

> The bottom line of it for me is that regardless of who the proprietor is, to have the ownership of more than 70% of Australia's newspapers in the hands of one person is fundamentally unhealthy for democracy. When that proprietor seeks to impose his own extreme ideology on the content of those newspapers—some of which enjoy a monopoly in their capital city or even state—and the influence of those publications the permeates through the rest of the media churn, as it inevitably does, it becomes even more problematic. (O'Brien, 2018)[551]

He asserted: "The capacity for News Corp to skew or, worse, shut down important policy debates shouldn't be underestimated—particularly if the governments don't want to risk crossing The Man". Former Australian Labor Prime Minister, Kevin Rudd, said:

> The cold hard truth is that Murdoch has become a cancer on the Australian, American and British democracies. Murdoch's print media have overwhelmingly backed conservative political parties in all three countries, and conservative policy causes, to the virtual exclusion of all other political voices. Murdoch is free to express his editorial opinion. But long ago this con-

> verged with his "news" coverage so that the two have now become indistinguishable. (Rudd, 2019)[552]

Rudd said that the reasons for this ideological control of the news agenda was that the global reach of the organisation gave it the capacity to influence politics and business, implicit in this accusation was that those influences favoured the proprietor's business interests, rather than the national interest, or the public interest and greater good (Ibid.).[553] *The New York Times Magazine* described Murdoch's control agenda in a headline for an online interactive feature in shouting capital letters: MURDOCH AND HIS CHILDREN HAVE TOPPLED GOVERNMENTS ON TWO CONTINENTS AND DESTABILIZED THE MOST IMPORTANT DEMOCRACY ON EARTH. WHAT DO THEY WANT? (Mahler & Rutenberg, 2019).[554] The article said:

> His newspapers and television networks had been instrumental in amplifying the nativist revolt that was reshaping governments not just in the United States but also across the planet. … In Australia, where Murdoch's power is most undiluted, his outlets had led an effort to repeal the country's carbon tax—a first for any nation—and pushed out a series of prime ministers whose agenda didn't comport with his own. (Ibid.)[555]

Born (2005) observed that the attacks by Murdoch on the BBC were a: "cleverness of the campaign waged by the likes of Murdoch and his political allies is to exploit the BBC's cultural-democratic weaknesses to denounce its very existence" (Born, Ibid.).[556] Born (2005) said there had also been political interference in the UK where British Prime Minister Margaret Thatcher manipulated the BBC with the selection of governors (equivalent to the ABC Board). Born (Ibid.) said previous UK governments had made successive attempts to prevent Murdoch from owning television, in addition to his newspaper interests, but not Thatcher. Much later, Murdoch's planned takeover of BSkyB was scuppered by the 2011 phone-hacking scandal at *The News of the World* which had erupted at that time of the proposed takeover. News Corporation sold its 39% shareholding in BSkyB in 2018.

Murdoch told the Leveson Committee when he was called to answer allegations of illegal telephone-hacking and unethical behaviour by his UK weekly tabloid newspaper *The News of the World*: "This is the most humble day of my life" (Rogers et al., 2011).[557] The motto of the newspaper launched in 1843 was "Our motto is the truth; our practice is the fearless advocacy of the truth" (Burden, 2008)[558] yet as *The Guardian* newspaper observed upon *TNOW*'s demise it had a "total preoccupation with sex" (Jenkins, 2011).[559] Burden (2008) said that Murdoch had mortgaged his Australian newspaper business to buy *The News of the World* in 1969 (Burden, Ibid.)[560] as his first foray into the British newspaper market. As a consequence, of revelations of impropriety, illegality and a slump in advertisers Murdoch announced on 7 July 2011 the closure of the newspaper.

The scandal Hackgate (as it was known) (Fenton, 2014)[561]: involved hacking phones of celebrities, royalty and citizens but the revelation that his newspaper was complicit in ruining a police investigation in a young girl's murder seemed to be the fatal blow to the paper that shocked the most and resulted in advertisers withdrawing their support from the newspaper, which is an important consideration in the viability of commercial media. The Leveson Inquiry found that on 4 July 2011 was that, nearly a decade earlier, a private investigator hired by *The News of the World* had intercepted the voicemails of missing British teenager Milly Dowler (later found murdered) (Leveson, 2012).[562] Her family and police had been led to believe that the girl was alive and receiving their messages because they were deleted after being played.

The impact from the criminal hacking (Burns, 2012)[563] of telephone messages of private individuals, overly close relationships with politicians and police at the highest levels in the UK, and the concomitant ethical violations, resonated world-wide. Eight people received criminal charges including two senior executives, five senior editors and reporters and a private investigator (Burns, Ibid.). In addition, several members of staff were charged with conspiracy to pervert the course of justice as well as illegal phone-hacking and some were jailed in a situation described by Murdoch as "deplorable and unacceptable" (CNN Editorial Research, 2020).[564] It was reported that more than 4000 people had their phones hacked by *The News of the World* (BBC, 2012)[565] and private investigator Glenn Mulcaire was paid an annual retainer of £105,000 (O'Carroll, 2014)[566] to undertake the task. News Corporation set aside £20 million to pay compensation to a long list of celebrities, including members of the Royal Family, the Duchess of York Sarah Ferguson (Evening Standard, 2013),[567] Their Royal Highnesses the Princes William and Harry and the then Catherine Middleton (later the Duchess of Cambridge). Murdoch paid GBP2 million (AUD3.8 million) compensation to the Dowler family and GBP1 million (AUD1.9 million) to the Dowler family's chosen charities (ABC, 2011).[568] A former Murdoch senior executive and aide said: "the hacking at *News of the World* was done on an industrial scale" (Bernstein, 2011).[569]

The closure of *TNOW* (a.k.a. "The News of the Screws"[570]) with its last publication on Sunday 10 July 2011 after 168 years cast a dark shadow over News Corporation and was a grave and resonant example of the consequences when the professional media flouted and abandoned its ethical covenant with the people it attested to serve—and, more importantly on a commercial level, horrified and alienated its lifeblood—its advertisers. On a relatively minor level, it was the end of a profitable newspaper, the "highest selling UK newspaper—3.0 million copies a week" (*The Sydney Morning Herald*, 2011)[571] and was "read by more people than any other English language newspaper" (Washbrook, 2011).[572]

The collapse of the newspaper provoked discussion about the activities of all tabloid newspapers which pursued sales at the expense of right judgement, public good and the law. The ethics of sting journalism were questioned as a legitimate and worthy pastime for the Fourth Estate and indeed for Rupert Murdoch's publications that formed a large part of the global news fraternity. It challenged the commercial view that sting journalism fulfilled and satiated the public's 'right to know' in revealing tawdry salaciousness as well as violations of individual's privacy and civil liberties. It gave substance to the understanding that Murdoch's primary motive was to profit from advertisers where the watchdog role of the newspaper journalists was changed into lapdogs of commerce. *TNOW* may be more aptly described as an extreme tabloid which had created products out of celebrities by becoming a product itself. The financial significance of the loss of *The News of the World* to News Corporation was explained by media analyst, Douglas McCabe:

> 40% of total revenue for the News of the World and its daily sister paper, The Sun, comes from advertising, putting its value at about £260 million ($418 million) a year. (Smith-Spark, 2011)[573]

However, the BBC pointed out that News Corporation's newspapers were a small section of the organisation's investments and were regarded as "loss-making" (Knight, 2011)[574] "many argue that the newspapers are more useful to Rupert Murdoch as a source of political influence than as a profit centre" (Ibid.).[575] Even Murdoch indicated at the public hearing into the phone-hacking scandal the small size of TNOW relative to the entire organisation: "The News of the World is less than one per cent of our company" (Rogers et al., 2011).[576] Murdoch's power manifests itself, ultimately and consummately, in "control over multiple connecting points" (Arsenault & Castells, 2008).[577] He has been quoted as saying: "content is not just king. It is the emperor of all things electronic. We are on the cusp of a digital dynasty in which our company and our shareholders will profit greatly" (Chessell, 2010)[578] and when he bought the Wall Street Journal in 2010 said: "We're going to build a fucking great paper and I do not give a fuck what New York or the media has to say about it! We'll build the world's best paper!" (Ellison, 2010).[579] Murdoch's financial success has been attributed to the belief that he:

> Was more interested in cash than in confrontation, in profits than in political positions. He wanted editors who were safe rather than scintillating, whom he could rely on however far away he might be. (Shawcross, 1997)[580]

Murdoch is still nominal head of News Corporation but in three key ways his control is unique among other media organisations (Arsenault & Castells, 2008).[581] First, he has been at the head of the organisation "throughout its 52-year expansion" (Ibid.)[582] and, second, its impact is global:

> The NewsCorp media empire spans five continents, reaches approximately 75% of the world's population, and has approximately USD68 billion in total assets and USD28 billion in annual revenue. (Loc. Cit.)[583]

Third, is Murdoch's "vertical control"—which is "integral to the overall financial success of the company" (Loc. Cit.)[584] and manifests itself in his maintaining direct contact with his staff when he seeks the answer to a question (Ibid.)[585] and as a consequence "many employees think that Rupert is their boss" (Anand & Attea, 2003 in Monaghan & Prideaux, 2016).[586] Brady (2006) quoting *New York Times* columnist, Anne Kornblutt, that Murdoch had a "tendency to prize political power over ideology" (Brady, 2006).[587] Brady backed up this position by quoting his own exchange with Murdoch in 1974 when he worked for him as editor of the tabloid *National Star*. Brady asked Murdoch how close he was to the Prime Minister of Australia. Murdoch told him: "He comes to dinner at the house" (Brady, ibid.). At that time the Prime Minister of Australia was the Liberal-Coalitions' John Howard. As a sign of a symbiotic relationship between UK politicians and media proprietors, "when David Cameron became UK prime minister in 2010, one of the first visitors to 10 Downing Street was the chairman of News Corporation".[588]

Murdoch's political influence in Britain was clearly articulated in 1992 with the famous headline of his British newspaper, *The Sun*: "It's The Sun Wot Won It" on 11 April 1992. It was a public pronouncement of Murdoch's support for the Conservative Party in its election victory which had installed Conservative John Major as UK Prime Minister. The newspaper, purchased by Murdoch in 1969 as a broadsheet, was converted upon his arrival to a tabloid and rescued from financial collapse. To bolster circulation, for example, by 1972 all page three bikini girls were topless.[589] It should also be noted here that Murdoch later balanced this by buying into the upper echelons of newspapers when he purchased the then respected *The Times* and *The Sunday Times* in 1981 when Conservative Margaret Thatcher was British Prime Minister and the takeovers went through unimpeded by any referral to the Monopolies and Mergers Commission.[590]

5.13 Strangling the Voice of the Public Interest

The preceding discussion flags a concern for Aunty and the strangling of her voice. Concerns abide over powerful, influential people who re-create the public sphere for their own commercial interests. This discussion also must include owners of the world's major internet technology companies: US-based Amazon, Google and Facebook, Chinese-owned JD.com, Ali Baba and Tencent and Swedish-based Spotify. Commercial operators have a primary business principle to grow media businesses, on the other hand, it challenges the operation of democracy when voices are limited and constrained. It is further problematised when organisations become more powerful than governments, yet those few voices can influence government policy and appointments. This is a rational concern. The irrational side of the argument are the ABC's arguments denigrating Murdoch in an over-simplified (but all-encompassing) battle where Murdoch is 'bad' and the ABC 'good'. A personalisation of Murdoch as the existential threat is easily binaried into good and evil, left and right. Murdoch does not see himself as evil; as naïve as that seems to the ABC counter-argument. As operators in the digital commercial field, the ABC needs to take a more nuanced view of the commercial exigencies and priorities to which Murdoch attends, into account. In a seemingly binaried world, challenging this degree of power requires the advancement of reasoned, rationale arguments and cases. Ad hominem attacks do not suffice in arguing cogent cases and only serve to achieve "gotcha" moments at best—and at worst create perpetual, shrill, reactive irrelevance. It has not served the best interests of the Australian citizen and has caused a lack of direction at the ABC.

A healthy democracy serviced by an agile media was described by the late Australian academic and intellectual Donald Horne who said that the media could resemble one of the highest democratic ideals—an "Athenian assembly ... if they are good enough" (Horne, 2001).[591] He said citizens should feel they are capable of taking part in a media discussion, even though they may not be able: "a lively polity needs more than a few media celebrities. It needs a lot of independent intellectual chattering, including the ABC" (Ibid.).[592] Horne asserted:

> Maintaining intellectual reserves in a liberal-democratic society ... requires an enormous superstructure of libraries, universities, museums; specialist books, magazines and journals; quality print and broadcasting media (especially Radio National); research institutes, scholarly websites, discussion platforms, learned societies. (Loc Cit.)[593]

The context of the media environment has changed with the collapse of newsrooms and newspapers. Local newspapers have folded—once the lifeblood of their regional and rural communities. Simons (2017) said the loss in the employment of rounds people—courts, parliaments, local government, has been detrimental to the role of Australia's Fourth Estate due to a "hollowing out of its ... 'journal of record' functions" (Simons, Ibid.).[594] There is an ongoing tension between commercial exigency of selling news with the public's right to know. They are not necessarily compatible. The international news agency, Reuters (n.d.),[595] states that its first rule of journalism is: Always hold accuracy sacrosanct.[596] The adjective Sacrosanct is a religious word, deriving from the Latin "sacro"—a sacred right and "sancto"—meaning to render holy or inviolable. The word is defined in the Oxford English Dictionary as "of persons and things, especially obligations, laws, etc. Secured by a religious sanction from violation, infringement, or encroachment; inviolable, sacred" (Oxford English Dictionary).[597]

Public knowledge is a sacred trust the journalists and their organisation share with their audience—and the audience knows it has a right to knowledge. Journalists must decide where the legitimate public interest lies. At its highest level, journalism and news are mediated to "influence the quality of our lives, our thoughts, and our culture" (Kovach & Rosenstiel, 2007).[598] News is agenda-setting (Semetko & Valkenburg, 2000)[599] impacting on public perceptions of an issue where "media do not tell the audience what to think but, rather, what to think *about*" (Cohen, 1963).[600] The media is a reflexive conduit for authority figures to provide the public with "opinions on controversial issues" and these figures use the media to see how they "look" (Kuypers, 2002).[601]

This mediated role of journalists can be argued to both distance the reader from the event and also objectify the issues or people in the report. It can also be contended that commercial pressures influence the writing-up of an event in that there is considerable pressure on the journalist to "sell" the story to the editor for publication (in the commercial media the editor then has a role to "sell" the publication or platform. For example in 2008 Murdoch told a New Corporation Earnings Conference: "Our newspapers should be seen as services to their publics and their communities, but will be available in every—in every way" (Event Brief of Q4 2008 News Corporation Earnings Conference Call, 2008). Murdoch said the purchase of Dow Jones "an information service, not a newspaper" (Ibid.) for US $5.6 billion was at the forefront of the digital revolution. Davies (2009) said Murdoch, "uses his media outlets as tools to secure political favours" (Ibid.)[602] this then helped to "advance his business" (Ibid.). In the light of ramifications of The News of the World 2011 "phone hacking" scandal, Davies (2009) said presciently:

> Murdoch will turn a blind eye while his newspapers boost their circulation by embarrassing his political allies—unless the threat becomes too great. (Davies, 2009)[603]

The literature agreed that media freedom (as well as democracy) were two key tools in the fight against political corruption (Bhattacharyya & Hodler, 2015)[604] and maintaining a vigilant watch on power and, according to McChesney (2008) "journalism in any meaningful sense cannot survive without a viable democracy" (Ibid.).[605] However, the media reaction that there was a dichotomy between authoritarianism and media freedom was over-simplified and misleading (Fenton, 2014)[606] because the media was dominated by powerful élite and privileged voice, including remaining ***cultural capital*** of the ABC and this is under constant contestation because democracy and the media are: "subject to social forces and indeed social movements that may challenge established and vested interests" (Fenton, Ibid.)[607] where "much news is about the violation of values" (Gans, 2004)[608] anyway and where "government is the primary source of pressure" (Ibid.).[609] The type of stories reported by the ABC in the case of "The Afghan Files" represented what Gans (2004) described as "moral disorder news" where the publication of these reports was aimed at punishing those who deviated from societal values (Loc. Cit.).[610] While "the assumptions and routines of what is known as 'objective journalism', made it exceedingly easy for officials to manipulate day to day news content" (Hallin, 1989)[611] (as was the case in the Vietnam War). It was only those times when media stepped out of familiar rubrics into accessing unnamed sources and publishing secret information that it had fallen foul of government control and hence subjected to harsh legal censure.

Aunty's nervous system is hyper-reactive with anxiety about Rupert Murdoch, but this analysis of the major actor in the commercial digital *field* has only served to individuate the ABC further as a unique and needed public institution. Also, as an independent public service operator she has had much more to be proud of than she now gives herself credit, but there have also been areas of weakness. Within the methodological analysis of this book, using Institutional Logics and Bourdieu, there have been failures: of boards to craft policy to protect specifically ("future proof") the ABC's precious *cultural capital* that would seek to translate the ABC's *habitus* into the commercial digital *field*, and some of these boards were not politically cohesive; of managers who collapsed the execution of policy changes into staff expectations and demands, and in so doing lost valuable staff resources when major sackings occurred; and, of governments which have failed to give forward-looking feedback on the organisation's activities in the digital space and failed to develop policy that would promote the intrinsic and extrinsic value of Australia's national communication treasure. The ABC's *cultural capital* was envied by other actors, now forgotten in the distractions of the rough, tumble and extremes of emergent commercialised digital media.

Notes

1. *Canberra Times, The*. (1985). Top Australians Condemn ABC: Call for government inquiry. Public letter by 13 Australians to the ABC: Justice Elizabeth Evatt, Patrick White, Thomas Keneally, Frank Moorehouse, Nancy Keesing, Chris Koch, Lloyd Rees, Pat Lovell, Les Murray, Edmund Campion, Nigel Butterley, Mr. Justice James McClelland, Mr. Justice

Michael Kirby. *The Canberra Times*. 12 August 1985, p. 3. Retrieved from https://trove.nla.gov.au/newspaper/article/122521924?searchTerm=patrick%20white%20ABC&searchLimits=

2. *Canberra Times, The*. (1985). Top Australians Condemn ABC: Call for government inquiry. Public letter by 13 Australians to the ABC: Justice Elizabeth Evatt, Patrick White, Thomas Keneally, Frank Moorehouse, Nancy Keesing, Chris Koch, Lloyd Rees, Pat Lovell, Les Murray, Edmund Campion, Nigel Butterley, Mr. Justice James McClelland, Mr. Justice Michael Kirby. *The Canberra Times*. 12 August 1985, p. 3. Retrieved from https://trove.nla.gov.au/newspaper/article/122521924?searchTerm=patrick%20white%20ABC&searchLimits=
3. *The Newcastle Sun*. (1938). ABC Ideals. *The Newcastle Sun*. 28 May 1938, p. 4. Retrieved from https://trove.nla.gov.au/newspaper/article/166711374?searchTerm=ABC%20privilege&searchLimits=
4. The quote goes on to say about the ABC: "It is in the position of the Athenian sculptor who set a statue up in a public place and invited the people of Athens to mark in chalk any part of it which displeased them. By the end of the day the statue was covered with marks of disapproval. Next day he rubbed out the marks and invited the public to mark in chalk that portion of the sculpture of which they approved—and at the end of the day, the statue was again covered in chalk" (Newcastle Times, Ibid.).
5. Varona, Anthony E. (2009). Toward a broadband public interest standard. *Administrative Law Review*. 61:1. Pp. 1–135. https://primoa.library.unsw.edu.au/permalink/f/11jha62/TN_gale_legal197493069
6. Hartley, J. (2008). *Television Truths*. Blackwell Publishing. Malden, Massachusetts. p. 19.
7. Martinoli, A. (2016). Digital Media Audience—New Expectations, New Habits. In Medias Res. 5:8. Pp. 1269–1284. Retrieved from: https://doaj.org/article/c7caa3920f984aceb4e9c611dbae7c9c
8. Tandoc, E. C. & Duffy, A. (2016). Keeping Up with the Audiences: Journalistic Role Expectations in Singapore. *International Journal Of Communication*. 10. Pp. 3338–3358. Retrieved from: https://primoa.library.unsw.edu.au/permalink/f/11jha62/TN_wos000390936900001
9. Das, R. & Graefer, A. (2017). Regulatory Expectations of Offended Audiences: The Citizen Interest in Audience Discourse. *Communication, Culture & Critique*. 10:4. Pp. 626–640. Retrieved from: https://doi.org/10.1111/cccr.12179
10. Floyd, J. ""The True" in Journalism" in J. Katz, J. E., & Mays, K. K. (2019). *Journalism and truth in an age of social media*. Oxford University Press. Retrieved from: DOI:https://doi.org/10.1093/oso/9780190900250.001.0001

11. Hartley, J. (2008). *Television Truths.* Blackwell Publishing. Malden, Massachusetts. p. 22.
12. Ibid. p. 21.
13. Ibid. p. 22.
14. Ibid. p. 26.
15. Soysal, Z. (2019). "Truth in Journalism" in J. Katz, J. E., & Mays, K. K. (2019). *Journalism and truth in an age of social media.* Oxford University Press. Retrieved from: DOI:https://doi.org/10.1093/oso/9780190900250.001.0001
16. Ibid. p. 33.
17. ABC. (2019). ABC, "Yours". Media Release. Retrieved from: http://about.abc.net.au/press-releases/abc-yours/
18. Johnson, C. (2013). From brand congruence to the 'virtuous circle': branding and the commercialization of public service broadcasting. *Media Culture and Society.* Retrieved from: http://journals.sagepub.com/doi/full/10.1177/0163443712472088
19. http://about.abc.net.au/press-releases/abc-yours/
20. Sunstein, C. R. (2009). *Republic.com 2.0.* Princeton University Press. Princeton. EBook. Retrieved from: http://ebookcentral.proquest.com/lib/unsw/detail.action?docID=581662 p. 74.
21. Fiske (1989) Moments of television: Neither the text nor the audience. In: E. Seiter, H. Borchers, G. Kreutzner, E-M Warth (eds). *Remote Control: Television Audiences and Cultural Power.* Routledge. London.
22. "A sense of one's place which leads one to exclude oneself from places from which one is excluded' (Bourdieu, 1984). Bourdieu's analysis applied to the working class that did not feel at home in élite establishments, while the ABC recognised it did not fit into the commercial *field* of digital media without shedding its élite status.
23. The theme was played originally at the commencement of the broadcasts of Federal Parliament.
24. Australian Broadcasting Corporation. (2010). Farewell, James Dibble. *Australian Broadcasting Corporation Television.* 20 December 2010. Retrieved from: http://www.abctvgorehill.com.au/assets/press/james_dibble_eulogy.htm
25. Coombs, W.T. (2012). *Ongoing Crisis Communication: Planning, Managing, and Responding.* Sage Publications. Thousand Oaks, Calif. p. 37.
26. Cunningham, S. & Craig, D. (2018). We must not punish content creators in our rush to regulate social platforms. *The Conversation.* 9 May 2018. Retrieved from: https://theconversation.com/we-must-not-punish-content-creators-in-our-rush-to-regulate-social-platforms-96270

27. Vignal Lambret, C., & Barki, E. (2018). Social media crisis management: Aligning corporate response strategies with stakeholders' emotions online. *Journal of Contingencies and Crisis Management*. 26:2. Pp. 295–305. Retrieved from: https://doi.org/10.1111/1468-5973.12198
28. Youmans, W. L., & York, J. C. (2012). Social Media and the Activist Toolkit: User Agreements, Corporate Interests, and the Information Infrastructure of Modern Social Movements. *Journal of Communication*. 62:2. Pp. 315–329. Retrieved from: https://doi.org/10.1111/j.1460-2466.2012.01636.x
29. Youmans, W. L., & York, J. C. (2012). Social Media and the Activist Toolkit: User Agreements, Corporate Interests, and the Information Infrastructure of Modern Social Movements. *Journal of Communication*. 62:2. Pp. 315–329. Retrieved from: https://doi.org/10.1111/j.1460-2466.2012.01636.x p. 317.
30. Bennett, W. (1998). 1998 Ithiel De Sola Pool Lecture: The UnCivic Culture: Communication, Identity, and the Rise of Lifestyle Politics. *PS: Political Science and Politics*. 31:4. Pp. 741–761. Retrieved from: doi:https://doi.org/10.2307/420711 p. 758.
31. Artwick, C. (2013). Reporters On Twitter. *Digital Journalism*. 1:2. Pp. 212–228. Retrieved from: https://doi.org/10.1080/21670811.2012.744555
32. Reddick C.G., Aikins S.K. (2012) Web 2.0 Technologies and Democratic Governance. In: Reddick C., Aikins S. (eds) Web 2.0 Technologies and Democratic Governance. Public Administration and Information Technology, vol 1. Springer, New York, NY. Retrieved from: https://doi-org.wwwproxy1.library.unsw.edu.au/10.1007/978-1-4614-1448-3_1 p.
33. Baumann, M. (2010). @twitter Discloses Business Model #promotedtweets RT. *Information Today*. 27:6. Pp. 1–46. http://search.proquest.com/docview/357026026/
34. Liao, S. H., Hsian, P. Y., & Wu, G. L. (2014). Mining User Knowledge for Investigating the Facebook Business Model: The Case of Taiwan Users. *Applied Artificial Intelligence*. 28:7. Pp. 712–736. Retrieved from: https://doi.org/10.1080/08839514.2014.927695
35. Liao, S. H., Hsian, P. Y., & Wu, G. L. (2014). Mining User Knowledge for Investigating the Facebook Business Model: The Case of Taiwan Users. *Applied Artificial Intelligence*. 28:7. Pp. 712–736. Retrieved from: https://doi.org/10.1080/08839514.2014.927695 p. 734.
36. Semmler, C. (1981). *The ABC: Aunt Sally and Sacred Cow*. Melbourne University Press. Melbourne.
37. *Sydney Morning Herald, The*. (1931). Broadcasting. *The Sydney Morning Herald*. 16 November, 1931. p. 8. Retrieved from: https://trove.nla.

gov.au/newspaper/article/16823317?searchTerm=%22improved%20and%20freed%20from%20all%20the%20evils%2C%20real%20or%20imaginary%2C%20of%20private%20enterprise%22

38. https://iview.abc.net.au ‘ category ‘ news.
39. Alysen, B. (2012). *The Electronic Reporter: Broadcast Journalism in Australia*. UNSW Press. Kensington. p. 120.
40. Alysen, B. (2012). *The Electronic Reporter: Broadcast Journalism in Australia*. UNSW Press. Kensington. p. 120.
41. Alysen, B. (2012). *The Electronic Reporter: Broadcast Journalism in Australia*. UNSW Press. Kensington. p. 129.
42. Alysen, B. (2012). *The Electronic Reporter: Broadcast Journalism in Australia*. UNSW Press. Kensington. p. 207.
43. Fiske, J. (1982). *Studies in Communication*. Metheun. London & New York. p. 133.
44. Fiske, J. (1982). *Studies in Communication*. Methuen. London & New York. p. 133.
45. *Canberra Times, The*. (1938). 2CY Calling. Official Opening. ABC Chairman Invites Critics. *The Canberra Times*. The 24 December 1938. p. 1. Retrieved from: https://trove.nla.gov.au/newspaper/article/2481506?browse=ndp%3Abrowse%2Ftitle%2FC%2Ftitle%2F11%2F1938%2F12%2F24%2Fpage%2F663796%2Farticle%2F2481506
46. *Canberra Times, The*. (1938). 2CY Calling. Official Opening. ABC Chairman Invites Critics. *The Canberra Times*. 24 December 1938. p. 1. Retrieved from: https://trove.nla.gov.au/newspaper/article/2481506?browse=ndp%3Abrowse%2Ftitle%2FC%2Ftitle%2F11%2F1938%2F12%2F24%2Fpage%2F663796%2Farticle%2F2481506
47. Low, S., & Smith, N. (2013). *The Politics of Public Space*. Taylor and Francis. Retrieved from: https://primoa.library.unsw.edu.au/permalink/f/jhud33/UNSW_ALMA51175562100001731
48. Perry, J.L. & Rainey, H.G. (1988). The Public-Private Distinction in Organization Theory: A Critique and Research Strategy Author(s): Source: The Academy of Management Review. 13:2. pp. 182–201. Published by: Academy of Management Retrieved from: http://www.jstor.org/stable/258571
49. *Australian Broadcasting Corporation*. (1972). Gough Whitlam's, 1972 ‘It's Time’ speech. *Australian Broadcasting Corporation*. Retrieved from: https://www.abc.net.au/news/2019-05-16/gough-whitlam-its-time/11118720?nw=0
50. Whitlam, E.G. (1972). Australian Federal Election Speeches. Gough Whitlam. Australian Labor Party. *Museum of Democracy Old Parliament House*. Delivered 13 November, 1972. Blacktown. Retrieved from: https://electionspeeches.moadoph.gov.au/speeches/1972-gough-whitlam

51. Menzies, R. (1942). The Forgotten People. *Liberals.net*. 22 May 1942. Retrieved from: http://www.liberals.net/theforgottenpeople.htm
52. Curtin, J.J.A. (1943). Election speech. Australian Labor Party. *Museum of Democracy Old Parliament House*. 26 July 1943. Retrieved from: https://electionspeeches.moadoph.gov.au/speeches/1943-john-curtin
53. Hartley, J. Ibid., p. 33–34.
54. Ibid.., p. 34.
55. Ibid., p. 34.
56. Jolly, R. (2014). Media of the people: broadcasting community media in Australia. *Commonwealth of Australia*. Retrieved from: https://www.aph.gov.au/About_Parliament/Parliamentary_Departments/Parliamentary_Library/pubs/rp/rp1314/Media
57. Krstić, A. & Đurđević, B. (2017). Social media marketing. Marketing (Beograd. 1991). 48:4. Pp. 254–260. Retrieved from: https://doaj.org/article/9fdc5a48a7a945fdb1de61e44404bd8c
58. Centeno, D. (2018). In R. Bikramjit & S. Bandyopadhyay. *Contemporary Issues in Social Media Marketing*. Routledge. London, New York.
59. Morgan, S. (2018). Influencers. *The Missouri Review*. 41:4. Pp. 5–10. Retrieved from: https://doi.org/10.1353/mis.2018.0040
60. Morgan, S. (2018). Influencers. *The Missouri Review*. 41:4. Pp. 5–10. Retrieved from: https://doi.org/10.1353/mis.2018.0040
61. Sinnig, J. (2020). *The Role of Origin of Fame in Influencer Branding: A Comparative Analysis of German and Russian Consumers* (1st ed. 2020.). Springer Fachmedien Wiesbaden. Wiesbaden. Imprint: Springer Gabler. p. 3.
62. Sinnig, J. (2020). *The Role of Origin of Fame in Influencer Branding: A Comparative Analysis of German and Russian Consumers*. (1st ed. 2020.). Springer Fachmedien Wiesbaden. Wiesbaden. Imprint: Springer Gabler. p. 3.
63. Sinnig, J. (2020). *The Role of Origin of Fame in Influencer Branding: A Comparative Analysis of German and Russian Consumers*. (1st ed. 2020.). Springer Fachmedien Wiesbaden. Wiesbaden. Imprint: Springer Gabler. p. 1.
64. Sinnig, J. (2020). The Role of Origin of Fame in Influencer Branding: A Comparative Analysis of German and Russian Consumers. (1st ed. 2020.). Springer Fachmedien Wiesbaden. Wiesbaden. Imprint: Springer Gabler. p.
65. Bennett, W. (1998). 1998 Ithiel De Sola Pool Lecture: The UnCivic Culture: Communication, Identity, and the Rise of Lifestyle Politics. *PS: Political Science and Politics*. 31:4. Pp. 741–761. Retrieved from: doi:https://doi.org/10.2307/420711 p. 758.

66. Dorsman, S.J., Bekkers, V.J.J.M. & Edwards, A.R. (2015). 'Trust the experts!' Risk definitions in Dutch online forums about the 'swine flu' *Information, Communication & Society.* 18:10. Pp. 1217–1237. Retrieved from: https://doi.org/10.1080/1369118X.2015.1036767
67. Bikramjit, R. & Bandyopadhyay, S. (2018). *Contemporary Issues in Social Media Marketing.* Routledge. London, New York.
68. Spin is slang to describe media that is biased or promoting a particular line or opinion.
69. Sawers, P. (2015). How NewsWhip helps newsrooms track the web's top-trending stories. 7 February 2015. Retrieved from: https://venturebeat.com/2015/02/07/how-newswhip-helps-newsrooms-track-the-webs-top-trending-stories/
70. Dwyer, T. & Martin, F. (2017). Sharing News Online. *Digital Journalism.* 5:8. pp. 1080–1100. Retrieved from: DOI: https://doi.org/10.1080/21670811.2017.1338527. Quoting CNNIC 2016; Newman et al. 2016; Pew Research Center 2016.
71. Ibid. p. 1081.
72. Diakopoulos, N. (2019). *Automating the News: How Algorithms Are Rewriting the Media.* Harvard University Press. Harvard MA. ProQuest Ebook Central. Retrieved from: http://ebookcentral.proquest.com/lib/unsw/detail.action?docID=5761259
73. Martin, F. & Dwyer, T. (2019). *Sharing News Online. Commendary Cultures and Social Media News Ecologies.* Palgrave Macmillan. Chap. 5. p. 130.
74. Murphy, J., Link, M. W., Childs, J. H., Tesfaye, C. L., Dean, E., Stern, M., Pasek, J., Cohen, J., Callegaro, M., & Harwood, P. (2014). Social Media in Public Opinion Research. *Public Opinion Quarterly.* 78:4. Pp. 788–794. Retrieved from: https://doi.org/10.1093/poq/nfu053
75. Michael, G., & Agur, C. (2018). The Bully Pulpit, Social Media, and Public Opinion: A Big Data Approach. *Journal of Information Technology & Politics.* 15:3. Pp. 262–277. Retrieved from: https://doi.org/10.1080/19331681.2018.1485604
76. Dubois, E., Gruzd, A., Jacobson, J., Chen, W., & Quan-Haase, A. (2020). Journalists' Use of Social Media to Infer Public Opinion: The Citizens' Perspective. *Social Science Computer Review.* 38:1. Pp. 57–74. Retrieved from: https://doi.org/10.1177/0894439318791527
77. Small, V. & Warn, J. (2020). "Impacts on food policy from traditional and social media framing of moral outrage and cultural stereotypes". *Agriculture and Human Values.* Springer. The Agriculture, Food, & Human Values Society (AFHVS). 37:2. June. Pp. 295–309, June. https://doi.org/10.1007/s10460-019-09983-6

78. Anstead, N., & O'Loughlin, B. (2015). Social Media Analysis and Public Opinion: The 2010 UK General Election. *Journal of Computer-Mediated Communication*. 20:2. Pp. 204–220. Retrieved from: https://doi.org/10.1111/jcc4.12102
79. Strekalova, Y.A. (2017). Health Risk Information Engagement and Amplification on Social Media: News About an Emerging Pandemic on Facebook. *Health Education & Behavior*. 44:2. Pp. 332–339. Retrieved from: https://journals-sagepub-com.wwwproxy1.library.unsw.edu.au/doi/pdf/10.1177/1090198116660310
80. Strekalova, Y.A. (2017). Health Risk Information Engagement and Amplification on Social Media: News About an Emerging Pandemic on Facebook. *Health Education & Behavior*. 44:2. Pp. 332–339. Retrieved from: https://journals-sagepub-com.wwwproxy1.library.unsw.edu.au/doi/pdf/10.1177/1090198116660310
81. Strekalova, Y.A. (2017). Health Risk Information Engagement and Amplification on Social Media: News About an Emerging Pandemic on Facebook. *Health Education & Behavior*. 44:2. Pp. 332–339. Retrieved from: https://journals-sagepub-com.wwwproxy1.library.unsw.edu.au/doi/pdf/10.1177/1090198116660310
82. Ibid.
83. Nine.com.au (2020). Coronavirus: PM says aged care facilities may be put in 'lock down' if COVID-19 outbreak worsens. A Current Affair. *Channel 9*. Retrieved from: https://9now.nine.com.au/a-current-affair/coronavirus-update-prime-minister-scott-morrison-says-covid19-outbreak-may-lead-to-aged-care-facilities-in-lock-down/2b70072b-758b-4e5e-8144-7f2c9241b8f1
84. Patrick, A. (2020). 'I'm Worried About the Panic Out There' David Isaacs: Germ Expert. *The Australian Financial Review*. 4 April 2020. Retrieved from: https://www.afr.com/policy/health-and-education/the-time-has-come-to-end-the-coronavirus-panic-20200402-p54gap
85. Australian Government. (2020). Coronavirus (COVID-19). Department of Health. Retrieved from: https://www.health.gov.au/health-topics/novel-coronavirus-2019-ncov
86. Loc. Cit.
87. Marozzi, M. (2015). Measuring Trust in European Public Institutions. *Social Indicators Research*. 123:3. Pp. 879–895. Retrieved from: https://doi.org/10.1007/s11205-014-0765-9
88. Wang, L., & Gordon, P. (2011). Trust and institutions: A multilevel analysis. *Journal of Socio—Economics*. 40:5. Pp. 583–593. Retrieved from: https://doi.org/10.1016/j.socec.2011.04.015
89. Turner, M. M., Boudewyns, V., Kirby-straker, R., & Telfer, J. (2013). A double dose of fear: A theory-based content analysis of news articles sur-

rounding the 2006 cough syrup contamination crisis in panama. *Risk Management.* 15:2. Pp. 79–99. Retrieved from: https://doi.org/10.1057/rm.2012.13

90. Gasher, M. & McIntosh, A. (2019). *Media convergence* (English ed.). *Historica Canada.* Toronto. Retrieved from: http://search.proquest.com/docview/2315251385/
91. Jensen, K. B. (2010). *Media Convergence: The Three Degrees of Network, Mass and Interpersonal Communication*, Taylor & Francis Group, 2010. ProQuest Ebook Central. Retrieved from: http://ebookcentral.proquest.com/lib/unsw/detail.action?docID=481099
92. Marwick, A. E. (2013). *Status update: celebrity, publicity, and branding in the social media age.* Yale University Press. Retrieved from: https://primoa.library.unsw.edu.au/permalink/f/1gq3lal/UNSW_ALMA51219826020001731
93. Colman, A. (2006). A Dictionary of Psychology. Oxford University Press. Oxford. Retrieved from: https://archive.org/details/dictionaryofpsyc00colm_0/page/77/mode/2up
94. Van der Meer, T., & Verhoeven, P. (2013). Public framing organizational crisis situations: Social media versus news media. *Public Relations Review*, *39*(3), 229–231. https://doi.org/10.1016/j.pubrev.2012.12.001
95. Kelling, K., & Thomas, R. J. (2018). The roles and functions of opinion journalists. *Newspaper Research Journal*, *39*(4), 398–419. https://doi.org/10.1177/0739532918806899
96. Gulyas, A. (2013). The Influence of Professional Variables On Journalists' Uses And Views Of Social Media: *A comparative study of Finland, Germany, Sweden and the United Kingdom. Digital Journalism. 1:2. Retrieved from:* https://doi.org/10.1080/21670811.2012.744559
97. Hamborg, F., Donnay, K. & Gipp, B. (2019). Automated identification of media bias in news articles: an interdisciplinary literature review. *Int. J. Digit. Libr.* 20. Pp. 391–415. Retrieved from: https://doi.org/10.1007/s00799-018-0261-y
98. Kuypers, J.A. (2002). *Press Bias and Politics: How the Media Frame Controversial Issues.* Praeger. Westport CT & London. p. 1.
99. Kuypers, J.A. (2002). Press Bias and Politics: How the Media Frame Controversial Issues. Praeger. Westport CT & London. p. 238.
100. Hanitzsch, T. (2004). "Journalists as Peacekeeping Force? Peace Journalism and Mass Communication theory". *Journalism Studies.* 5:4. (Quoting Galtung, 1998, p. 8.). Retrieved from: https://doi.org/10.1080/14616700412331296419 p. 486.
101. Hanitzsch, T. (2004). "Journalists as Peacekeeping Force? Peace Journalism and Mass Communication theory". *Journalism Studies.* 5:4. (Quoting McGoldrick, 2000, p. 19–20). Retrieved from: https://doi.org/10.1080/14616700412331296419 p. 484.

102. Lynch, J. (2002). "Impunity in Journalism". *Media Development*. Xlix:2. Pp. 30–32. Retrieved from: http://waccglobal.org/en/20022Gimpunit yGandGtheGmedia/693GImpunityGinG journalism.html
103. Bourdieu (1979) said that "every exercise of power is accompanied by a discourse aimed at legitimising the power of the group that exercises it"
104. Boin, A., McConnell, A. & Hart, P. (2010). Crisis leadership. In R. A. Couto. *Political and civic leadership: A reference handbook* (pp. 229–238). Thousand Oaks, CA: SAGE Publications, Inc. Retrieved from: doi: https://doi.org/10.4135/9781412979337.n27
105. Boin, A., McConnell, A. & Hart, P. (2010). Crisis leadership. In R. A. Couto. *Political and civic leadership: A reference handbook* (pp. 229–238). Thousand Oaks, CA: SAGE Publications, Inc. Retrieved from: doi: https://doi.org/10.4135/9781412979337.n27
106. Sinclair, A. (2007). *Leadership for the disillusioned : moving beyond myths and heroes to leading that liberates*. Allen and Unwin. Crows Nest, Sydney.
107. Hewett, J. (2020). Losing friends and influencing people. *The Australian Financial Review*. 30 July 2020. p. 2. Retrieved from: https://global-factiva-com.wwwproxy1.library.unsw.edu.au/redir/default.aspx?P=sa&an=AFNR000020200801eg7u0000e&cat=a&ep=ASE
108. Dugan, J. P. (2011). Pervasive myths in leadership development: Unpacking constraints on leadership learning. *Journal of Leadership Studies*. 5:2. Pp. 79–84. Retrieved from: https://doi.org/10.1002/jls.20223
109. McCrimmon, M. (2010). Is Heroic Leadership All Bad? *Ivey Business Journal (Online)*. Jan–Feb 2010. Retrieved from: http://search.proquest.com/docview/216176400/
110. Pitt, H. (2020). 'It made a powerful impact': ABC chair says AIDS campaign worked. *The Sydney Morning Herald*. 17 March 2020. Retrieved from: https://www.smh.com.au/national/it-made-a-powerful-impact-abc-chair-says-aids-campaign-worked-20200316-p54an2.html
111. Pitt, H. (2020). 'It made a powerful impact': ABC chair says AIDS campaign worked. *The Sydney Morning Herald*. 17 March 2020. Retrieved from: https://www.smh.com.au/national/it-made-a-powerful-impact-abc-chair-says-aids-campaign-worked-20200316-p54an2.html
112. Lupton, D.A. (1992). 'From Complacency to Panic: AIDS and Heterosexuals in the Australian Press July 1986 to June 1988'. 7:1. *Health Education Research* pp.9–20. Retrieved from: https://academic-oup-com.wwwproxy1.library.unsw.edu.au/her/article/7/1/9/687273
113. Lupton, D.A. (1992). 'From Complacency to Panic: AIDS and Heterosexuals in the Australian Press July 1986 to June 1988'. 7:1. *Health Education Research* pp. 9–20. Retrieved from: https://academic-oup-com.wwwproxy1.library.unsw.edu.au/her/article/7/1/9/687273

114. Lupton, D.A. (1992). 'From Complacency to Panic: AIDS and Heterosexuals in the Australian Press July 1986 to June 1988'. 7:1. *Health Education Research* pp. 9–20. Retrieved from: https://academic-oup-com.wwwproxy1.library.unsw.edu.au/her/article/7/1/9/687273
115. Mannix, T. (1987). Two million Australians risk AIDS. 6 April 1987. *The Canberra Times*. p. 1. Retrieved from: https://trove.nla.gov.au/newspaper/article/118183464?searchTerm=grim%20reaper%20buttrose&searchLimits=
116. Holman C.D.J., Bucens M.R. & Sesnan, T.M.K. (1987). AIDS and the Grim Reaper campaign. *The Medical Journal of Australia*. 147:6. Pp. 306–306. Retrieved from: https://doi.org/info:doi/
117. Dwyer, D. E., Howard, R., Downie, J. & Cunningham, A.L. (1988). The "Grim Reaper" campaign. The Medical Journal of Australia. July 1988. 149:1. Pp. 49–50. Retrieved from: https://onlinelibrary-wiley-com.wwwproxy1.library.unsw.edu.au/doi/abs/10.5694/j.1326-5377.1988.tb120487.x
118. Morlet, A., Guinan, J.J., Diefenthaler, I., Gold, J. (1988). The impact of the "Grim Reaper" national AIDS educational campaign on the Albion Street (AIDS) Centre and the AIDS Hotline. *The Medical Journal of Australia*. March 1988. 148:6. Pp. 282–287. Retrieved from: https://onlinelibrary-wiley-com.wwwproxy1.library.unsw.edu.au/doi/abs/10.5694/j.1326-5377.1988.tb117836.x
119. Dwyer, D. E., Howard, R., Downie, J. & Cunningham, A.L. (1988). The "Grim Reaper" campaign. *The Medical Journal of Australia*. July 1988. 149:1. Pp. 49–50. Retrieved from: https://onlinelibrary-wiley-com.wwwproxy1.library.unsw.edu.au/doi/abs/10.5694/j.1326-5377.1988.tb120487.x
120. Morlet, A., Guinan, J.J., Diefenthaler, I., Gold, J. (1988). The impact of the "Grim Reaper" national AIDS educational campaign on the Albion Street (AIDS) Centre and the AIDS Hotline. *The Medical Journal of Australia*. March 1988. 148:6. Pp. 282–287. Retrieved from: https://onlinelibrary-wiley-com.wwwproxy1.library.unsw.edu.au/doi/abs/10.5694/j.1326-5377.1988.tb117836.x
121. Harcourt, C., Edwards, J. & Philpot, R. (1988). On the "Grim Reaper" campaign. *The Medical Journal of Australia*. 1 August 1988, 149:3. pp.162, 164. Retrieved from: https://onlinelibrary-wiley-com.wwwproxy1.library.unsw.edu.au/doi/epdf/10.5694/j.1326-5377.1988.tb120551.x
122. Lupton, D.A. (1992). 'From Complacency to Panic: AIDS and Heterosexuals in the Australian Press July 1986 to June 1988'. *Health Education Research*. 7:1. pp. 9–20. Retrieved from: https://academic-oup-com.wwwproxy1.library.unsw.edu.au/her/article/7/1/9/687273

123. Swan, N. (2020). Norman Swan answers your coronavirus questions on pregnancy, asthma, pools and schools. ABC News Breakfast Program and ABC News 24. *Australian Broadcasting Corporation*. Televised, broadcast and online 16 March, 2020. Retrieved from: https://www.abc.net.au/news/2020-03-16/coronavirus-questions-on-pregnancy-asthma-pools-and-schools/12058926
124. https://www.abc.net.au/radio/programs/coronacast/
125. McCauley, D., Bagshaw, E. & Harris, R. (2020). Australia prepares for 50,000 to 150,000 coronavirus deaths. *The Sydney Morning Herald*. 16 March 2020. Retrieved from: https://www.smh.com.au/politics/federal/australia-prepares-for-50-000-to-150-000-coronavirus-deaths-20200316-p54amn.html
126. Topsfield, J. (2020). Brendan Murphy: the public face of Australia's fight against COVID-19. *The Sydney Morning Herald*. 20 March 2020. Retrieved from: https://www.smh.com.au/national/brendan-murphy-the-public-face-of-australia-s-fight-against-covid-19-20200320-p54c87.html
127. Patrick, A. (2020). I'm Worried About the Panic Out There: David Isaacs, Germ Expert. *The Australian Financial Review*. 4 April 2020. Retrieved from: https://global-factiva-com.ezproxy2.library.usyd.edu.au/ha/default.aspx#./!?&_suid=158630818658503136619040135381
128. Patrick, A. (2020). I'm Worried About the Panic Out There: David Isaacs, Germ Expert. *The Australian Financial Review*. 4 April 2020. Retrieved from: https://global-factiva-com.ezproxy2.library.usyd.edu.au/ha/default.aspx#./!?&_suid=158630818658503136619040135381
129. Razavi, H. (2020). Notes on a pandemic: How society has responded to Covid-19. *Australian Book Review Magazine*. 421. 20 May 2020. Retrieved from: https://www.australianbookreview.com.au/abr-online/current-issue/788-commentary/6441-notes-on-a-pandemic-how-society-has-responded-to-covid-19-by-hessom-razavi
130. Norington, B. (2020). Cash for coronavirus: ABC 'guru' Norman Swan after money to turn spin doctor. *The Australian*. 18 April 2020. Retrieved from: https://www.theaustralian.com.au/business/media/cash-for-coronavirus-abc-guru-norman-swan-after-money-to-turn-spin-doctor/news-story/804333e72f653d5891e3706035a50563
131. Jackson, S. (2020). ABC statement on Dr. Norman Swan. *Australian Broadcasting Corporation*. 20 April 2020. Retrieved from: https://about.abc.net.au/correcting-the-record/abc-statement-on-dr-norman-swan/
132. Davies, N. (2009). *Flat Earth News*. Vintage Books. London. pp. 96–98.
133. Venger, O., & Matthews, J. (2019). The use of experts in journalistic accounts of media events: A comparative study of the 2005 London

Bombings in British, American, and Russian newspapers. *Journalism*. 20:10. Pp. 1343–1359. Retrieved from: https://doi.org/10.1177/1464884919830479

134. Venger, O., & Matthews, J. (2019). The use of experts in journalistic accounts of media events: A comparative study of the 2005 London Bombings in British, American, and Russian newspapers. *Journalism*. 20:10. Pp. 1343–1359. Retrieved from: https://doi.org/10.1177/1464884919830479
135. Jerit, J. (2009). Understanding the Knowledge Gap: The Role of Experts and Journalists. *The Journal of Politics*. 71:2. Pp. 442–456. Retrieved from: https://doi.org/10.1017/S0022381609090380
136. A 'furphy' is an Australianism originating from World War I soldiers. They gathered around the water carts branded J Furphy and Sons, Shepparton, Victoria for refreshment and exchange of gossip. Hence the use of 'furphy' in parlance means passing on rumours or untruths.
137. Dávid, G., & Furkó, B. (2015). The Journey Metaphor in Mediatized Political Discourse, *Acta Universitatis Sapientiae, Philologica*. *7*:2. Pp. 7–20. Retrieved from: doi: https://doi.org/10.1515/ausp-2015-0043
138. Friedman, R. A. (2009). The role of psychiatrists who write for popular media: experts, commentators, or educators? *The American Journal of Psychiatry*. 166:7. Pp. 757–759. Retrieved from: https://doi.org/10.1176/appi.ajp.2009.08121847
139. Javeline, D., Hellmann, J.J., Castro Cornejo, R. & Shufeldt, G. (2013). Expert Opinion on Climate Change and Threats to Biodiversity. (2013). *BioScience*. 63:8. Pp. 666–673. Retrieved from: https://doi.org/10.1525/bio.2013.63.8.9
140. Ward, L. (2005, September). Stand up for who you are: at a time when health and safety is suffering under the risk-averse glare of public opinion and the vitriolic outpourings of media commentators it is more important than ever for practitioners to defend their profession and make the case for sensible risk management. Louise Ward issues the call to arms. *The Safety & Health Practitioner*. 23:9. p. 37. Retrieved from: http://search.proquest.com/docview/200971662/
141. Keshet, Y., & Popper-Giveon, A. (2018). The undisciplined patient in neoliberal society: conscious, informed and intuitive health behaviours. *Health, Risk & Society*. 20:3–4. Pp. 182–199. Retrieved from: https://doi.org/10.1080/13698575.2018.1432757
142. Kuehn BM. (2013). More Than One-Third of US Individuals Use the Internet to Self-diagnose. *JAMA*. 309:8. Pp. 756–757. Retrieved from: doi:https://doi.org/10.1001/jama.2013.629
143. D'Ambrosia, R.D. (2009). Treating the Internet-informed Patient. *Orthopedics*. Thorofare. 32:1. Jan. p. 13. Retrieved from: https://search.

proquest.com/docview/220412297?pq-origsite=gscholar&fromopenview=true

144. Strzelecki, A. (2020). Google medical update: Why is the search engine decreasing visibility of health and medical information websites? *International Journal of Environmental Research and Public Health.* 17:4. Retrieved from: https://doi.org/10.3390/ijerph17041160
145. Strzelecki, A. (2020). Google medical update: Why is the search engine decreasing visibility of health and medical information websites? *International Journal of Environmental Research and Public Health.* 17:4. Retrieved from: https://doi.org/10.3390/ijerph17041160 p. 8.
146. Giustini, D. (2005). How Google is changing medicine. *British Medical Journal.* 331:7531. Pp. 1487–1488. Retrieved from: https://doi.org/10.1136/bmj.331.7531.1487. Quoting R. Greenwald. (2005). ... And a diagnostic test was performed. N Engl J Med. 353. 208,990.
147. Giustini, D. (2005). How Google is changing medicine. *British Medical Journal.* 331:7531. Pp. 1487–1488. Retrieved from: https://doi.org/10.1136/bmj.331.7531.1487
148. Keshet, Y. & Popper-Giveon, A. (2018) The undisciplined patient in neoliberal society: conscious, informed and intuitive health behaviours. *Health, Risk & Society.* 20:3–4. Pp. 182–199. Retrieved from: DOI: 10.1080/13698575.2018.1432757.
149. Keshet, Y. & Popper-Giveon, A. (2018) The undisciplined patient in neoliberal society: conscious, informed and intuitive health behaviours. *Health, Risk & Society.* 20:3–4. Pp. 182–199. Retrieved from: DOI: 10.1080/13698575.2018.1432757 p. 182.
150. Keshet, Y. & Popper-Giveon, A. (2018) The undisciplined patient in neoliberal society: conscious, informed and intuitive health behaviours. *Health, Risk & Society.* 20:3–4. Pp. 182–199. Retrieved from: DOI: 10.1080/13698575.2018.1432757 p. 182.
151. Keshet, Y. & Popper-Giveon, A. (2018) The undisciplined patient in neoliberal society: conscious, informed and intuitive health behaviours. *Health, Risk & Society.* 20:3–4. Pp. 182–199. Retrieved from: DOI: 10.1080/13698575.2018.1432757 p. 182.
152. Australian Associated Press. (2020). NRL players excused from flu shot after league amends waiver. *The Guardian.* 7 May 2020. Retrieved from: https://www.theguardian.com/sport/2020/may/07/i-wont-be-bullied-bryce-cartwright-refuses-nrl-flu-shot-but-denies-anti-vaxxer-label
153. ABC Online. (2020). Dr. Norman Swan recommends 'severe' shutdowns. *Australian Broadcasting Corporation.* 15 March 2020. Retrieved from: https://www.abc.net.au/news/2020-03-15/dr-norman-swan-recommends-proactive-national-lockdown/12057956

154. Australian Broadcasting Corporation News. (2020). Coronavirus: Dr. Norman Swan recommends proactive national lockdown. *Australian Broadcasting Corporation. You Tube.* 14 March 2020. Retrieved from: https://www.youtube.com/watch?v=znJ9RD8gYsQ
155. Australian Broadcasting Corporation. (2020). Dr. Norman Swan recommends 'severe' shutdowns. *Australian Broadcasting Corporation.* 15 March 2020. Retrieved from: https://www.abc.net.au/news/2020-03-15/dr-norman-swan-recommends-proactive-national-lockdown/12057956
156. *Sydney Morning Herald,* The. Editorial "The Herald's View". The Sydney Morning Herald. 20 March 2020. Retrieved from: https://www.smh.com.au/national/nsw-must-start-preparing-now-for-school-closures-20200320-p54cb5.html
157. Australian Broadcasting Corporation. (2020) Coronacast. Should you just pull your kid out of school? *Australian Broadcasting Corporation.* 20 March 2020. Retrieved from: https://www.abc.net.au/radio/programs/coronacast/should-you-just-pull-your-kid-out-of-school/12072842
158. Dumas, D. (2020). Bondi Beach: how the Australian icon became a coronavirus hotspot. *The Guardian.* 5 April 2020. Retrieved from: https://www.theguardian.com/australia-news/2020/apr/05/bondi-beach-how-the-australian-icon-became-a-coronavirus-hotspot
159. Guler, A.Y. (2020). 'One coronavirus patient can infect up to 400'. *Anadolu Agency.* 14 April 2020. Retrieved from: https://www.aa.com.tr/en/latest-on-coronavirus-outbreak/one-coronavirus-patient-can-infect-up-to-400/1804349
160. Sky News (2020). What happened at Bondi beach was 'not okay': Govt to crackdown on crowds to stop coronavirus spread. *Sky News.* 22 March 2020. Retrieved from: https://www.skynews.com.au/details/_6143724163001
161. Ouellette, L. (2008). Makeover television, governmentality and the good citizen. *Continuum.* 22:4. Pp. 471–484. Retrieved from: https://doi.org/info:doi/
162. Australian Broadcasting Corporation. (2020). Q and A. Transcript. *Australian Broadcasting Corporation.* 16 March 2020. Retrieved from: https://www.abc.net.au/qanda/2020-16-03/12040520
163. Australian Broadcasting Corporation. (2020). Q and A. Transcript. *Australian Broadcasting Corporation.* 16 March 2020. Retrieved from: https://www.abc.net.au/qanda/2020-16-03/12040520
164. Zaczek, Z. (2020). 'We had PLENTY of warning': Infection expert unloads on Scott Morrison and his government for not closing Australia's borders MONTHS ago to stop the spread of the coronavirus. *The Daily*

Mail Australia. 17 March 2020. Retrieved from: https://www.dailymail.co.uk/news/article-8116681/Coronavirus-Bill-Bowtell-unloads-Scott-Morrison-government-COVID-19-response.html

165. Furthering the discussion about Q and A, Bourdieu (2010) can be referenced as having asserted that journalists are so afraid of being "boring" that they "opt for confrontations over debates, prefer polemics over rigorous argument, and in general do whatever they can to promote conflict" (Bourdieu Ibid.). He said journalists prefer to confront politicians instead of arguments, and are interested in political tactics rather than substance, which means they ask cynical questions (Loc. Cit.) talking down to politicians because they have already decided they were just "hyperambitious" (Ibid.). Ultimately, Bourdieu (2010) argued this caused a split between the journalist and their public because the journalist was focused on micro matters while the public was concerned about the big picture impact of policies.

166. Work, W., & Boileau, D. M. (1985). Television debates. *Communication Education*. 34:4. Pp. 369–375. Retrieved from: https://doi.org/10.1080/03634528509378631
167. Maurer, M., Dumitrescu, D., & Bucy, E. P. (2016). Nonverbal Influence During Televised Debates: Integrating CRM in Experimental Channel Studies. *American Behavioral Scientist*. 60:14. Pp. 1799–1815. Retrieved from: https://doi.org/10.1177/0002764216676250
168. Lee, Hansoo, & Lee, Jae-Mook. (2017). Viewing presidential televised debates and civic engagement in Korea. *International Area Studies Review*. 20:4. Pp. 334–348. Retrieved from: https://doi.org/10.1177/2233865917726438
169. Craig, G. (2016). *Performing politics: media interviews, debates and press conferences*. Polity Press. Cambridge UK & Malden MA.
170. Braunstein, R. (2018). Boundary-work and the demarcation of civil from uncivil protest in the United States: control, legitimacy, and political inequality. *Theory and Society*. 47:5. Pp. 603–633. Retrieved from: https://doi.org/10.1007/s11186-018-9329-3
171. Mao, F. (2019). 2019 election: why politics is toxic for Australia's women. *British Broadcasting Corporation*. 16 May 2019. Retrieved from: https://www.bbc.com/news/world-australia-48197145
172. Hunt, E. & Evershed, N. (2016). George Christensen the most abused MP on Twitter, election analysis shows. *The Guardian*. 1 July 2016. Retrieved from: https://www.theguardian.com/australia-news/2016/jul/01/australian-election-2016-turnbull-shorten-coalition-greens-labor-politics-live
173. ABC Q and A. (2020). Twitter profile. Retrieved from: https://twitter.com/QandA

174. Mill, J.S. (1863). *On Liberty.* 2nd Edition. Tickner and Fields. Boston. p. 35.
175. Toffler, A. (1984). *Future Shock.* Bantam Books. New York. p. 1.
176. Toffler, A. (1981). *The Third Wave: The Classic Study of Tomorrow.* Bantam Books. New York. p. 269.
177. Plato. (375 BC, revised Ed. 2002). *The Republic.* Retrieved from: http://www.idph.net
178. Rule by a small group.
179. Plato. (375 BC, revised Ed. 2002). *The Republic.* Retrieved from: http://www.idph.net
180. Boin, A., McConnell, A. & Hart, P. (2010). Crisis leadership. In R. A. Couto *Political and civic leadership: A reference handbook* (pp. 229–238). SAGE Publications, Inc. Thousand Oaks, CA. Retrieved from: doi: https://doi.org/10.4135/9781412979337.n27
181. Boin, A., McConnell, A. & Hart, P. (2010). Crisis leadership. In R. A. Couto *Political and civic leadership: A reference handbook* (pp. 229–238). SAGE Publications, Inc. Thousand Oaks, CA. Retrieved from: doi: https://doi.org/10.4135/9781412979337.n27
182. Boin, A., McConnell, A. & Hart, P. (2010). Crisis leadership. In R. A. Couto *Political and civic leadership: A reference handbook* (pp. 229–238). SAGE Publications, Inc. Thousand Oaks, CA. Retrieved from: doi: https://doi.org/10.4135/9781412979337.n27
183. Boin, A., McConnell, A. & Hart, P. (2010). Crisis leadership. In R. A. Couto *Political and civic leadership: A reference handbook* (pp. 229–238). SAGE Publications, Inc. Thousand Oaks, CA. Retrieved from: doi: https://doi.org/10.4135/9781412979337.n27
184. Boin, A., McConnell, A. & Hart, P. (2010). Crisis leadership. In R. A. Couto *Political and civic leadership: A reference handbook* (pp. 229–238). SAGE Publications, Inc. Thousand Oaks, CA. Retrieved from: doi: https://doi.org/10.4135/9781412979337.n27
185. Boin, A., McConnell, A. & Hart, P. (2010). Crisis leadership. In R. A. Couto *Political and civic leadership: A reference handbook* (pp. 229–238). SAGE Publications, Inc. Thousand Oaks, CA. Retrieved from: doi: https://doi.org/10.4135/9781412979337.n27
186. Deitchman, S. (2013). Enhancing crisis leadership in public health emergencies. Disaster Medicine and Public Health Preparedness. 7:5. Pp. 534–540. Retrieved from: https://doi.org/10.1017/dmp.2013.81
187. Boin, A., McConnell, A. & Hart, P. (2010). Crisis leadership. In R. A. Couto *Political and civic leadership: A reference handbook* (pp. 229–238). SAGE Publications, Inc. Thousand Oaks, CA. Retrieved from: doi: https://doi.org/10.4135/9781412979337.n27

188. Weber, E. (2010). Democratic political leadership. In R. A. Couto *Political and civic leadership: A reference handbook* (pp. 105–110). SAGE Publications, Inc. Thousand Oaks, CA. Retrieved from: doi: https://doi.org/10.4135/9781412979337.n13
189. McPhee, S. (2020). Coronavirus Australia: Human biosecurity emergency declared. *News.com.au.* Retrieved from: https://www.news.com.au/national/politics/coronavirus-australia-human-biosecurity-emergency-declared/news-story/cd7fbff78297c076c8bb774595459c59
190. Lieutenant-General John Frewen.
191. Heanue, S. (2020). Top Australian Army general to head military taskforce to manage coronavirus outbreak. 13 March 2020. *Australian Broadcasting Corporation.* Retrieved from: https://www.abc.net.au/news/2020-03-13/coronavirus-military-taskforce/12051722
192. Burgess, K, (2020). Coronavirus: The Australian army is being subbed in to help make face masks. *The Sydney Morning Herald.* 17 March 2020. Retrieved from: https://www.canberratimes.com.au/story/6684074/the-australian-army-is-being-subbed-in-to-help-make-face-masks/
193. McPhee, S. (2020). Coronavirus Australia: Human biosecurity emergency declared. *News.com.au.* Retrieved from: https://www.news.com.au/national/politics/coronavirus-australia-human-biosecurity-emergency-declared/news-story/cd7fbff78297c076c8bb774595459c59
194. Littlefield, R. S. & Quenette, A.M. (2007). Crisis Leadership and Hurricane Katrina: The Portrayal of Authority by the Media in Natural Disasters. *Journal of Applied Communication Research.* 35:1. Pp. 26–47. Retrieved from: DOI: https://doi.org/10.1080/00909880601065664
195. This hurricane destroyed coastal areas in the US states of Louisiana and Mississippi and resulted in 1200 deaths.
196. Littlefield, R. S. & Quenette, A.M. (2007). Crisis Leadership and Hurricane Katrina: The Portrayal of Authority by the Media in Natural Disasters. *Journal of Applied Communication Research.* 35:1. Pp. 26–47. Retrieved from: https://doi.org/10.1080/00909880601065664 p. 43.
197. Ferguson, R., Bashan, Y., Hannan, E. & Moffet-Gray, L. (2020). Coronavirus Australia live updates: Scott Morrison bans non-citizens from entering Australia. *The Australian.* 19 March 2020. Retrieved from: https://www.theaustralian.com.au/nation/coronavirus-australia-live-updates-donald-trump-closes-uscanada-border/news-story/b60e78b69cb446d3e1a14df02ee8c9de?type=curated&position=1&overallPos=1&utm_source=TheAustralian&utm_medium=email&utm_campaign=editorial&utm_content=TABreakingNews&utm_source=&utm_medium=&utm_campaign=&utm_content=

198. Worthington, B. & Snape, J. (2020). Large indoor gatherings banned, schools to stay open, Scott Morrison tells Australians not to leave the country in face of coronavirus pandemic. *Australian Broadcasting Corporation*. 18 March 2020. Retrieved from: https://www.abc.net.au/news/2020-03-18/coronavirus-australia-live-updates-covid19-latest-news-anzac-day/12064922
199. Bourdieu (1984) identified a struggle over names because: "the imposition of a recognised name is an act of recognition of the full social existence which transmutes the thing names. It no longer exists merely de facto, as a tolerate, illegal, a mission, a task, a role" (Bourdieu, 1984). Bourdieu (1984) said writers (journalists) were amongst a group empowered to name people because they were the "holder of the monopoly of official naming" (Bourdieu, 1991) and that this then "legitimates the vision of the world" (Bourdieu Ibid.). The audience sees and esteems a person as the media describes them.
200. Bourdieu, P. (2017, Orig. 1998). Ed. J.G. Richardson. *The Forms of Capital. Handbook of Theory and Research for the Sociology of Education*. Greenwood Press. West Susses, UK. Pp. 241–258.
201. Bourdieu (1986) described instances of such arbitrariness of name and title usage as an "institutionalised, theatrical version of the incessant struggles over the classifications which help to produce the classes" (Ibid.).

     Bourdieu (1991) said this had inherent risks where the person (media) chose to either insult ("*idios logos*") the other person in order "to impose his point of view" (Ibid.) or "*official naming*" them which had "on its side all the strength of the collective … of common sense" (Loc. Cit.).
202. Bourdieu, P. (1984) [orig. publ. 1979]. Trans. R. Nice. *Distinction: A Social Critique of the Judgement of Taste*. Harvard University Press. Cambridge, MA. Pp. 480–481.
203. Bourdieu, P. (1991). Trans. G. Raymond and M. Adamson. *Language and Symbolic Power*. Harvard University Press. Cambridge, MA. p. 240.
204. Tingle, L. (2020). Coronavirus messaging from political leaders making a much-needed improvement. Analysis. *Australian Broadcasting Corporation*. 18 March 2020. Retrieved from: https://www.abc.net.au/news/2020-03-18/coronavirus-messaging-from-political-leaders-making-improvement/12067290
205. Tingle, L. (2020). Coronavirus messaging from political leaders making a much-needed improvement. ABC News. Analysis. *Australian Broadcasting Corporation*. 18 March 2020. Retrieved from: https://www.abc.net.au/news/2020-03-18/coronavirus-messaging-from-political-leaders-making-improvement/12067290

206. Lakoff, G. (2008). *The Political Mind: Why You Can't Understand twenty-first Century American Politics with an eighteenth Century Brain.* Viking. New York.
207. Guardian, The. (2019). Scott Morrison prays at Hillsong conference—video. *The Guardian.* 10 July 2019. Retrieved from: https://www.theguardian.com/australia-news/video/2019/jul/10/scott-morrison-discusses-freedom-of-religion-during-hillsong-conference-video & Karp, P. (2020). Scott Morrison prays for Australia and commits nation to God amid coronavirus crisis. *The Guardian.* 1 April 2020. Retrieved from: https://www.theguardian.com/australia-news/2020/apr/01/scott-morrison-prays-for-australia-and-commits-nation-to-god-amid-coronavirus-crisis
208. Lakoff, G. & Johnson, M. (1980). *Metaphors We Live By.* University of Chicago Press. Chicago & London. p. 11.
209. Speers, D. (2020). Scott Morrison's 'f-word' misread the public mood on the coronavirus pandemic. ABC News Online. Analysis. *Australian Broadcasting Corporation.* 15 March 2020. Retrieved from: https://www.abc.net.au/news/2020-03-15/coronavirus-scott-morrison-footy-next-information-campaign/12054174
210. Speers, D. (2020). Scott Morrison's 'f-word' misread the public mood on the coronavirus pandemic. ABC News Online. Analysis. *Australian Broadcasting Corporation.* 15 March 2020. Retrieved from: https://www.abc.net.au/news/2020-03-15/coronavirus-scott-morrison-footy-next-information-campaign/12054174
211. Littlefield, R. S. & Quenette, A.M. (2007). Crisis Leadership and Hurricane Katrina: The Portrayal of Authority by the Media in Natural Disasters. *Journal of Applied Communication Research.* 35:1. Pp. 26–47. Retrieved from: DOI: https://doi.org/10.1080/00909880601065664 pp. 27–28.
212. Gruber, D., Smerek, R., Thomas-Hunt, M., & James, E. (2015). The real-time power of Twitter: Crisis management and leadership in an age of social media. *Business Horizons.* 58:2. Pp. 163–172. Retrieved from: https://doi.org/10.1016/j.bushor.2014.10.006
213. Boin, A., Hart, P.T., McConnell, A., & Preston, T. (2010). Leadership Style, Crisis Response and Blame Management: The Case of Hurricane Katrina. *Public Administration.* 88:3. Pp. 706–723. Retrieved from: https://doi.org/10.1111/j.1467-9299.2010.01836.x
214. James, O., Jilke, S., Petersen, C., & Van de Walle, S. (2016). Citizens' Blame of Politicians for Public Service Failure: Experimental Evidence about Blame Reduction through Delegation and Contracting. *Public*

Administration Review. 76:1. Pp. 83–93. Retrieved from: https://doi.org/10.1111/puar.12471

215. Littlefield, R. S. & Quenette, A.M. (2007). Crisis Leadership and Hurricane Katrina: The Portrayal of Authority by the Media in Natural Disasters. *Journal of Applied Communication Research.* 35:1. Pp. 26–47. Retrieved from: DOI: https://doi.org/10.1080/00909880601065664 p. 44.
216. Littlefield, R. S. & Quenette, A.M. (2007). Crisis Leadership and Hurricane Katrina: The Portrayal of Authority by the Media in Natural Disasters. *Journal of Applied Communication Research.* 35:1. Pp. 26–47. Retrieved from: DOI: https://doi.org/10.1080/00909880601065664 p. Ibid.
217. Angell, N. (1922). *The Press and the Organisation of Society.* The Labour Publishing Company Limited. London. p. 21.
218. Abuse analysis can be useful in this academic context as it signals changes in Bourdieu's doxa—the rules of the game.
219. Habermas, J. (1989, origin. publ. 1961). (Transl. T. Burger). *The Structural Transformation of the Public Sphere.* Polity Press. Great Britain. p. 1.
220. *Australian Broadcasting Corporation.* (2014). Editorial Policies. Preamble. *Australian Broadcasting Corporation.* Retrieved from: https://edpols.abc.net.au/home/preamble/
221. Murphy, K. (2020). ABC board elects to take 10% pay cut amid coronavirus economic slump. *The Guardian.* 23 June 2020. Retrieved from: https://www.theguardian.com/media/2020/jun/23/abc-board-elects-to-take-10-pay-cut-amid-coronavirus-economic-slump
222. Jackson, S. & Vitorovich, L. (2020). Seven looks to cut pay,jobs to survive crisis. *The Australian.* 1 April 2020. Retrieved from: https://www.theaustralian.com.au/business/media/seven-looks-to-cut-pay-jobs-to-survive-crisis/news-story/2c57ae3d681c821ed258549c0b95746a
223. Miller, M. (2020). Heavy hearts as the printing presses stop running. *The Australian.* 2 April 2020. Retrieved from: https://www.theaustralian.com.au/commentary/heavy-hearts-as-the-printing-presses-stop-running/news-story/0dad850f021a215cc3d132821d86ab2a
224. Tabakoff, N. (2020). GetUp chases cash via the ABC. The Diary. Media. *The Australian.* 11 May 2020. p. 20
225. Miller, M. (2019). Heavy hearts as the printing presses stop running. *The Australian.* 2 April 2020. Retrieved from: https://www.theaustralian.com.au/commentary/heavy-hearts-as-the-printing-presses-stop-running/news-story/0dad850f021a215cc3d132821d86ab2a
226. Miller, M. (2019). Heavy hearts as the printing presses stop running. *The Australian.* 2 April 2020. Retrieved from: https://www.theaustralian.

com.au/commentary/heavy-hearts-as-the-printing-presses-stop-running/news-story/0dad850f021a215cc3d132821d86ab2a
227. Miller, M. (2019). Heavy hearts as the printing presses stop running. *The Australian*. 2 April 2020. Retrieved from: https://www.theaustralian.com.au/commentary/heavy-hearts-as-the-printing-presses-stop-running/news-story/0dad850f021a215cc3d132821d86ab2a
228. Miller, M. (2019). Heavy hearts as the printing presses stop running. *The Australian*. 2 April 2020. Retrieved from: https://www.theaustralian.com.au/commentary/heavy-hearts-as-the-printing-presses-stop-running/news-story/0dad850f021a215cc3d132821d86ab2a
229. Australian Broadcasting Corporation. (ND). Legislative Framework. *Australian Broadcasting Corporation*. Retrieved from: https://about.abc.net.au/how-the-abc-is-run/what-guides-us/legislative-framework/
230. Simshaw, D. (2012). Survival of the standard: today's public interest requirement in television broadcasting and the return to regulation. *Federal Communications Law Journal*. 64:2. The George Washington University Law School. p. 401. Retrieved from: Gale OneFile. LegalTrac. https://link-gale-com.wwwproxy1.library.unsw.edu.au/apps/doc/A287390717/LT?u=unsw&sid=LT&xid=8c9308f1
231. Tracey, M. (1998). *The Decline and Fall of Public Service Broadcasting*. Oxford University Press. Oxford. p. 262.
232. Tracey, M. (1998). *The Decline and Fall of Public Service Broadcasting*. Oxford University Press. Oxford. p. 262.
233. Curran, J. & Seaton, J. (2018). *Power without Responsibility: press, Broadcasting and the Internet in Britain*. 8th Ed. Routledge. London, New York. p. 205.
234. Curran, J. & Seaton, J. (2018). *Power without Responsibility: press, Broadcasting and the Internet in Britain*. 8th Ed. Routledge. London, New York. p. 205.
235. Scannell, P. & Cardiff, D. (1991). *A Social History of Broadcasting: Volume 1. 1922–1939*. Blackwell. Oxford.
236. Curran, J. & Seaton, J. (2018). *Power without Responsibility: press, Broadcasting and the Internet in Britain*. 8th Ed. Routledge. London, New York. p. 203.
237. Curran, J. & Seaton, J. (2018). *Power without Responsibility: press, Broadcasting and the Internet in Britain*. 8th Ed. Routledge. London, New York. p. 203.
238. Curran, J. & Seaton, J. (2018). *Power without Responsibility: press, Broadcasting and the Internet in Britain*. 8th Ed. Routledge. London, New York. p. 203.

239. Rutherford, L., & Brown, A. (2013). The Australian Broadcasting Corporation's multiplatform projects: Industrial logics of children's content provision in the digital television era. *Convergence*. 19:2. Pp. 201–221. Retrieved from: https://doi.org/10.1177/1354856512457749
240. Born, G. (2005). *Uncertain Vision: Birt, Dyke and the Re-invention of the BBC*. Vintage. London. p. 381.
241. Born, G. (2005). *Uncertain Vision: Birt, Dyke and the Re-invention of the BBC*. Vintage. London. p. 382.
242. Fraser, M. & O'Reilly, J. (Eds.). (1996). *Save our ABC: The Case for Maintaining Australia's National Broadcaster*. Hyland House. Melbourne.
243. Petersen, N. (1993). *News Not Views: The ABC, the Press, & Politics. 1932–1947*. Hale and Iremonger. Marrickville.
244. Petersen, N. (1993). *News Not Views: The ABC, the Press, & Politics. 1932–1947*. Hale and Iremonger. Marrickville. p. 201.
245. Petersen, N. (1993). *News Not Views: The ABC, the Press, & Politics. 1932–1947*. Hale and Iremonger. Marrickville. p. 201.
246. Petersen, N. (1993). *News Not Views: The ABC, the Press, & Politics. 1932–1947*. Hale and Iremonger. Marrickville. p. 201.
247. Born, G. (2005). *Uncertain Vision: Birt, Dyke and the Re-invention of the BBC*. Vintage. London, p. 382.
248. Blach-Ørsten, M. & Burkal, R. (2014). Credibility and the Media as a Political Institution. *Nordicom Review*. 35 (2014) Special Issue. Retrieved from: https://content.sciendo.com/view/journals/nor/35/s1/nor.35.issue-s1.xml
249. Blach-Ørsten, M. & Burkal, R. (2014). Credibility and the Media as a Political Institution. *Nordicom Review*. 35 (2014) Special Issue. Retrieved from: https://content.sciendo.com/view/journals/nor/35/s1/nor.35.issue-s1.xml
250. Meyer, E. L. (2011). Media Codes of Ethics: The Difficulty of Defining Standards. A Report to the *Center for International Media Assistance*. 3 November 2011. Retrieved from: https://new.waccglobal.org/wp-content/uploads/2020/05/10-Media-Codes-of-Ethics-CIMA2011.pdf
251. Sanford, D. (1983). Impartial Perception. *Philosophy*. 58:225. Pp. 392–395. Retrieved from: www.jstor.org/stable/3750775 p. 392.
252. Sanford, D. (1983). Impartial Perception. *Philosophy*. 58:225. Pp. 392–395. Retrieved from: www.jstor.org/stable/3750775
253. Bailey, R. (2018). When journalism and satire merge: The implications for impartiality, engagement and 'post-truth' politics—A UK perspective on the serious side of US TV comedy. *European Journal of Communication*.

33:2. Pp. 200–213. Retrieved from: https://doi.org/10.1177/0267323118760322

254. Bailey, R. (2018). When journalism and satire merge: The implications for impartiality, engagement and 'post-truth' politics—A UK perspective on the serious side of US TV comedy. *European Journal of Communication.* 33:2. Pp. 200–213. Retrieved from: https://doi.org/10.1177/0267323118760322 p. 201.
255. Bailey, R. (2018). When journalism and satire merge: The implications for impartiality, engagement and 'post-truth' politics—A UK perspective on the serious side of US TV comedy. *European Journal of Communication.* 33:2. Pp. 200–213. Retrieved from: https://doi.org/10.1177/0267323118760322 p. 206.
256. Wells, S. W. W. (1959). Impartial. *Notes and Queries.* 6:9. Pp. 353–354. Retrieved from: https://doi.org/10.1093/nq/6.9.353 p. 353.
257. Wells, S. W. W. (1959). Impartial. *Notes and Queries.* 6:9. Pp. 353–354. Retrieved from: https://doi.org/10.1093/nq/6.9.353 p. 353.
258. Curran, J. (Ed.). (1978). *The British Press: A Manifesto.* Acton Society Press Group. The Macmillan Press Ltd. London.
259. Boyce, G., Curran, J. & Wingate, P. (1978). *Newspaper History: from the seventeenth century to the present day.* Constable. London/Sage Publications. Beverly Hills, Calif. p. 168.
260. Schudson, M. (2005). The Virtues of an Unlovable Press. Intro. *Political Quarterly.* 2 August 2005. Supplement 1:76. Pp. 23–32. Retrieved from: https://doi.org/10.1111/j.1467-923X.2006.00745.x
261. Schudson, M. (2008). *Why Democracies Need and Unlovable Press.* Polity Press. New York.
262. Schudson, M. (2008). *Why Democracies Need and Unlovable Press.* Polity Press. New York. p. 62.
263. Conboy, M. (2013). *Journalism Studies: The Basics.* Routledge. London, New York.
264. Høyer, S. & Pöttker, H. (Ed.). (2005). *Diffusion of the News Paradigm.* Nordicam. Göteborg University. Göteborg. Retrieved from: https://www.nordicom.gu.se/sv/system/tdf/publikationer-hela-pdf/diffusion_of_the_news_paradigm_1850-2000.pdf?file=1&type=node&id=10239&force=0 p. 234.
265. Schudson, M. (1978). *Discovering the News: A Social History of American Newspapers.* Basic Books Inc. New York. p. 7.
266. Vulliamy, E. (1999). "Neutrality" and the absence of reckoning: A journalist's account. *Journal of International Affairs.* 1 March 1999. 52:2. p. 604. Retrieved from: https://primoa.library.unsw.edu.au/permalink/f/11jha62/TN_jstor_archive_1424358055

267. Beharrell, P., Davis, H., Eldridge, J, Hewitt, J., Oddie, J. & Philo, G. (1976). Bad News. *Theory and Society*. Glasgow University Media Group. 3:3. Routledge & Kegan Paul. London. p. 339 & p. 346.
268. Høyer, S. & Pöttker, H. (Ed.). (2005). *Diffusion of the News Paradigm*. Nordicam. Göteborg University. Göteborg. Retrieved from: https://www.nordicom.gu.se/sv/system/tdf/publikationer-hela-pdf/diffusion_of_the_news_paradigm_1850-2000.pdf?file=1&type=node&id=10239&force=0 p. 29.
269. Zaller, J. (1999). *A Theory of Media Politics: How the interests of politicians, journalists, and citizens shape the news*. University of Chicago Press. Chicago.
270. Schultz, J. (1998). *Reviving the Fourth Estate: Democracy, Accountability and the Media*. Cambridge University Press. Cambridge. p. 4.
271. Shiffrin, S. (1994). "The Politics of The Mass Media and Free Speech Principle. *Indiana Law Journal*. Law Library. Indiana University. 69:3. Article 2. Pp. 689–721. Retrieved from: https://primoa.library.unsw.edu.au/permalink/f/11jha62/TN_gale_legal15296131
272. Hall, S. (1973). *Encoding and decoding in the television discourse*. Birmingham [West Midlands]: Centre for Contemporary Cultural Studies, University of Birmingham.
273. Murdock, G. (2004). Building the Digital Commons: Public Broadcasting in the Age of The Internet. University of Montreal. *The 2004 Spry Memorial Lecture Vancouver*. 18 November 2004. Montreal, 22 November 2004. Retrieved from: http://citeseerx.ist.psu.edu/viewdoc/download?doi=10.1.1.627.2917&rep=rep1&type=pdf
274. Habermas, J. (1989, origin. publ. 1961). (Transl. T. Burger). *The Structural Transformation of the Public Sphere*. Polity Press. Great Britain. p. 1.
275. Habermas, J. (1989, origin. publ. 1961). (Transl. T. Burger). *The Structural Transformation of the Public Sphere*. Polity Press. Great Britain. p. 56.
276. Habermas, J. (1989, origin. publ. 1961). (Transl. T. Burger). *The Structural Transformation of the Public Sphere*. Polity Press. Great Britain. p. 57.
277. Sommerville, C.J. (1996). *The News Revolution in England: Cultural Dynamics of Daily Information*. Oxford University Press. New York & Oxford. p. 76.
278. Habermas, J. (1989, origin. publ. 1961). (Transl. T. Burger). *The Structural Transformation of the Public Sphere*. Polity Press. Great Britain. p. 3.
279. Tracey, M. (1998). *The Decline and Fall of Public Service Broadcasting*. Oxford University Press. Oxford. p. 262.

280. Tracey, M. (1998). *The Decline and Fall of Public Service Broadcasting*. Oxford University Press. Oxford. p. 264.
281. Tracey, M. (1998). *The Decline and Fall of Public Service Broadcasting*. Oxford University Press. Oxford. p. 264.
282. Tracey, M. (1998). *The Decline and Fall of Public Service Broadcasting*. Oxford University Press. Oxford. p. 265.
283. https://archive.budget.gov.au/1983-84/downloads/Budget_1983-84.pdf
284. Australian Broadcasting Corporation. (2019). ABC Radio will not cover the 2020 Tokyo Olympics. *Australian Broadcasting Corporation*. 13 November 2019. Retrieved from: https://www.radioinfo.com.au/news/abc-radio-will-not-cover-2020-tokyo-olympics
285. Holmes, T. (2019). Is the Olympic Games still relevant to Australians? Analysis. 17 November 2019. *Australian Broadcasting Corporation*. Retrieved from: https://www.abc.net.au/news/2019-11-17/is-the-olympic-games-still-relevant-to-the-abcs-radio-audience/11704654
286. Le Grand, C. (2019). 'Down the gurgler': ABC doyen blasts Olympic boycott, questions commitment to sport. *The Sydney Morning Herald*. 28 November 2019. Retrieved from: https://www.smh.com.au/sport/down-the-gurgler-abc-doyen-blasts-olympic-boycott-questions-commitment-to-sport-20191128-p53f68.html
287. Le Grand, C. (2019). 'Down the gurgler': ABC doyen blasts Olympic boycott, questions commitment to sport. *The Sydney Morning Herald*. 28 November 2019. Retrieved from: https://www.smh.com.au/sport/down-the-gurgler-abc-doyen-blasts-olympic-boycott-questions-commitment-to-sport-20191128-p53f68.html
288. Le Grand, C. (2019). 'Down the gurgler': ABC doyen blasts Olympic boycott, questions commitment to sport. *The Sydney Morning Herald*. 28 November 2019. Retrieved from: https://www.smh.com.au/sport/down-the-gurgler-abc-doyen-blasts-olympic-boycott-questions-commitment-to-sport-20191128-p53f68.html
289. Le Grand, C. (2019). 'Down the gurgler': ABC doyen blasts Olympic boycott, questions commitment to sport. *The Sydney Morning Herald*. 28 November 2019. Retrieved from: https://www.smh.com.au/sport/down-the-gurgler-abc-doyen-blasts-olympic-boycott-questions-commitment-to-sport-20191128-p53f68.html
290. Ritchie, E. (2019). ABC's own calls out drop in news, sport coverage. *The Australian*. 30 December 2019. Retrieved from: https://www.theaustralian.com.au/nation/abcs-own-call-out-drop-in-news-sport-coverage/news-story/590d680302572167e1c3991432144398

291. Simpson, J. (2020). Aunty's radio rules the waves, but ABC TV is listing badly. *The Australian*. 3 January 2020. Retrieved from: https://www.theaustralian.com.au/commentary/auntys-radio-rules-the-waves-but-abc-tv-is-listing-badly/news-story/a0d3ecd28922d461b984cb7ccfe073cc
292. News, The (Adelaide). (1954). ABC sport policy examined. *The News*. 14 September 1954. p. 36. Retrieved from: https://trove.nla.gov.au/newspaper/article/130986285?searchTerm=ABC%20sport&searchLimits=
293. Canberra Times, The. (1981). ABC National Sports Coverage Lacks Resources. *The Canberra Times*. 28 May, 1981. p. 28. Retrieved from: https://trove.nla.gov.au/newspaper/result?q=ABC+sport&s=20
294. Sotiriadou, P. & Brouwers, J. (2012). A critical analysis of the impact of the Beijing Olympic Games on Australia's sport policy direction. *International Journal of Sport Policy and Politics: Olympic and Paralympic Policy*. 4:3. Pp. 321–341. Retrieved from: https://doi.org/10.1080/19406940.2012.656687 p. 321.
295. Blood, G. & May, C. (2018). Australian Sport History. 17 January 2018. *Clearinghouse for Sport and Physical Activity*. Retrieved from: https://www.clearinghouseforsport.gov.au/knowledge_base/organised_sport/value_of_sport/australian_sport_history
296. Phillips, M. & Magdalinski, T. (2008). Sport in Australia. *Sport and Society: A Student Introduction*. Ed. B. Houlihan. Sage Publications. London.
297. Phillips, M. & Magdalinski, T. (2008). Sport in Australia. *Sport and Society: A Student Introduction*. Ed. B. Houlihan. Sage Publications. London.
298. Phillips, M. & Magdalinski, T. (2008). Sport in Australia. *Sport and Society: A Student Introduction*. Ed. B. Houlihan. Sage Publications. London.
299. Petersen, N. (2012). Moses, Sir Charles Joseph (1900–1988). *Australian Dictionary of Biography*. 18. Melbourne University Press. Melbourne. Retrieved from: http://adb.anu.edu.au/biography/moses-sir-charles-joseph-15044
300. *Daily Telegraph, The*. (1935). Announcer may be ABC Head: Moses likely appointee. *The Daily Telegraph*. 9 October, 1935. p. 1. Retrieved from: https://trove.nla.gov.au/newspaper/article/246584742?searchTerm=ABC%20sport%20Moses&searchLimits=
301. Pledge sent to each member of the Argonauts to sign (along with an enamelled badge of an Argonaut boat). Inglis, K. (1983). This is the ABC. Melbourne University Press. Melbourne. p. 91.
302. Anderson, B. (1983). *Imagined Communities: Reflections on the Origin and Spread of Nationalism*. Verso. London.

303. Crocker, P. (1989). *Radio Days: A personal view of Australia's radio heyday.* Simon and Schuster. Brookvale, Sydney. p. 75.
304. Rutherford, L., & Brown, A. (2013). The Australian Broadcasting Corporation's multiplatform projects: Industrial logics of children's content provision in the digital television era. *Convergence.* 19:2. Pp. 201–221. Retrieved from: https://doi.org/10.1177/1354856512457749
305. It became the Australian Broadcasting Commission in 1932.
306. Semmler, C. (1981). *The ABC—Aunt Sally and Sacred Cow.* Melbourne University Press. Melbourne. p. 171.
307. Ibid.
308. Ibid.
309. Ibid.
310. Inglis, K. (1983). *This is the ABC: The Australian Broadcasting Commission 1932–1983.* Melbourne University Press. Melbourne. p. 87 and 90.
311. Semmler, C. (1981). (Ibid.). p. 172.
312. Ibid., p. 173
313. Inglis, K. (1983). p. 91.
314. Ibid.
315. Ibid., p. 174.
316. Blain, E. (1977). *Life with Aunty. 40 Years with the ABC.* Methuen Australia. p. 54
317. Ibid., p. 167.
318. Semmler, C. (1981). *The ABC—Aunt Sally and Sacred Cow.* Melbourne University Press. Melbourne. p. 174.
319. ABC Annual Report (1932–33) Ibid.
320. The bombing of London by the German Luftwaffe (Airforce) was not exclusive and included other British cities.
321. Thomas, A. (1980). *Broadcast and be Damned: The ABC's First Two decades.* Melbourne University Press. Melbourne. p. 97.
322. Hetherington, A. (1985). *News, Newspapers and Television.* The Macmillan Press. Houndmills & London. p. 21.
323. Meade, A. (2019). News Corp tabloid the Herald Sun offers journalists cash bonuses for clicks. *The Guardian.* 24 June 2019. Retrieved from: https://www.theguardian.com/media/2019/jun/24/news-corp-tabloid-the-herald-sun-offers-journalists-cash-bonuses-for-clicks
324. Meade, A. (2019). News Corp tabloid the Herald Sun offers journalists cash bonuses for clicks. *The Guardian.* 24 June 2019. Retrieved from: https://www.theguardian.com/media/2019/jun/24/news-corp-tabloid-the-herald-sun-offers-journalists-cash-bonuses-for-clicks

325. Langer, J. (1998). *Tabloid Television: Popular Journalism and the 'Other News'*. Taylor & Francis Group. ProQuest Ebook Central. Retrieved from: https://ebookcentral.proquest.com/lib/unsw/detail.action?docID=165718
326. Fitzpatrick, S. M. (2000). Sensational news. *Forum for Applied Research and Public Policy.* 15:3. Pp. 95–96. Retrieved from: http://search.proquest.com/docview/235135227/
327. Meade, A. (2019). News Corp tabloid the Herald Sun offers journalists cash bonuses for clicks. *The Guardian.* 24 June 2019. Retrieved from: https://www.theguardian.com/media/2019/jun/24/news-corp-tabloid-the-herald-sun-offers-journalists-cash-bonuses-for-clicks
328. Meade, A. (2019). News Corp Australia plans to axe journalists who lack digital skills. The Guardian. 4 June 2019. Retrieved from: https://www.theguardian.com/media/2019/jun/04/news-corp-australia-plans-to-axe-journalists-without-digital-skills
329. Meade, A. (2019). News Corp Australia plans to axe journalists who lack digital skills. *The Guardian.* 4 June 2019. Retrieved from: https://www.theguardian.com/media/2019/jun/04/news-corp-australia-plans-to-axe-journalists-without-digital-skills
330. Kester, L., Schwartz, N., Seufert, T., & Zumbach, J. (2008). *Beyond Knowledge: The Legacy of Competence: Meaningful Computer-based Learning Environments* (1. ed.). Springer Netherlands.
Chapter 1:1 Interdisciplinary Perspectives on Cognitive Load Research as a Key to Tackle Challenges of Contemporary Education. Retrieved from: https://primoa.library.unsw.edu.au/permalink/f/jhud33/UNSW_ALMA51206795190001731
331. Dubie, D. (2003). Retaining crucial skills. *Network World.* 20:15. p. 43. Retrieved from: http://search.proquest.com/docview/215974301/
332. Halverstadt, A., & Kerman, B. (2017). End-Game Evaluation: Building a Legacy of Learning In a Limited-Life Foundation. *The Foundation Review.* 9:1. Pp. 78–91, 109. Retrieved from: https://doi.org/10.9707/1944-5660.1352
333. Sammartino, S. (2014). *The great fragmentation: and why the future of all business is small* (1st ed.). John Wiley & Sons. Milton, Queensland.
334. Hardaker, R. (2020). Ita and the ABC: out with the old and in with the new. *Crikey.com.* 8 September 2020. Retrieved from: https://www.crikey.com.au/2020/09/08/ita-buttrose-abc-new-staff-hires/
335. Thilmany, J. (2004). Better Housekeeping of Legacy Knowledge. *Mechanical Engineering.* 126:10. p. 22. Retrieved from: http://search.proquest.com/docview/230173378/
336. Meusburger, P., Glückler, J., el Meskioui, M. (2013). *Knowledge and the Economy.* Dordrecht: Springer Netherlands : Imprint: Springer. Retrieved

from: https://primoa.library.unsw.edu.au/permalink/f/jhud33/UNSW_ALMA51206680440001731

337. Meusburger, P., Glückler, J., el Meskioui, M. (2013). *Knowledge and the Economy.* Dordrecht: Springer Netherlands : Imprint: Springer. Retrieved from: https://primoa.library.unsw.edu.au/permalink/f/jhud33/UNSW_ALMA51206680440001731 p. 5.
338. Duke, J., (2019). ABC to grapple with budget freeze, 200 redundancies expected. *The Sydney Morning Herald.* 9 December, 2019. Retrieved from: https://www.smh.com.au/business/companies/abc-to-grapple-with-budget-freeze-200-redundancies-expected-20191206-p53hnr.html
339. Dalzell, S. (2019). 'There will be job losses': ABC managing director confirms staff to go following budget freeze. *Australian Broadcasting Corporation.* 23 October 2019. Retrieved from: https://www.abc.net.au/news/2019-10-23/abc-boss-confirms-staff-to-go-following-budget-cuts/11629336
340. Larsson, S. (2014). Battling mainstream media, commentators and organized debaters: experiences from citizens' online opinion writing in Sweden. *NORDICOM Review: Nordic Research on Media and Communication*, 35(2), 77+. Retrieved from https://link-gale-com.ezproxy2.library.usyd.edu.au/apps/doc/A396138825/AONE?u=usyd&sid=AONE&xid=f8ac48fc
341. Calvet, R.F., Montoya, M.I.V. & García, I.B. (2014). Public Service Broadcasting's Participation in the Reconfiguration of Online News Content. *Journal of Computer-Mediated Communication.* 18. Pp. 378–397. Retrieved from: doi:https://doi.org/10.1111/jcc4.12014
342. Calvet, R.F., Montoya, M.I.V. & García, I.B. (2014). Public Service Broadcasting's Participation in the Reconfiguration of Online News Content. *Journal of Computer-Mediated Communication.* 18. Pp. 378–397. Retrieved from: doi:https://doi.org/10.1111/jcc4.12014 p. 381.
343. Rogers, J., O'Boyle, N., Preston, P., & Fehr, F. (2014). The significance of small differences: Cultural diversity and broadcasting in Ireland. *European Journal of Communication.* 29:4. Pp. 399–415. Retrieved from: https://doi.org/10.1177/0267323114530367
344. Connors, J. (2018). Opening statement (public hearing, Canberra, 30 November 2018). *Inquiry into Allegations of Political Interference in the ABC.* Tabled by: Dr. Jane Connors. 30 November 2018. Retrieved from: https://www.aph.gov.au/Parliamentary_Business/Committees/Senate/Environment_and_Communications/ABCInterferenceAllegations/Additional_Documents?docType=Tabled%20Documents

345. Daly, J. (2020). How social licence and clean energy will change the mining industry by 2030. WA Country Hour. *Australian Broadcasting Corporation*. 6 January 2020. Retrieved from: https://www.abc.net.au/news/rural/2020-01-06/how-social-license-and-clean-energy-change-mining-2030/11839044
346. McHugh, B. (2014). The term 'social licence to operate' brought into question by report. *Australian Broadcasting Corporation*. 17 February 2014. Retrieved from: https://www.abc.net.au/news/rural/2014-02-17/social-licence-to-operate-a-poorly-defined-concept/5264162
347. O'Mahen, P. (2016). A Big Bird effect? The interaction among public broadcasting, public subsidies, and political knowledge. *European Political Science Review*. 8:2. Pp. 311–332. Retrieved from: https://www-cambridge-org.wwwproxy1.library.unsw.edu.au/core/services/aop-cambridge-core/content/view/8EC8052F26A223A76ED7D07A386E10D5/S175577391500003Xa.pdf/big_bird_effect_the_interaction_among_public_broadcasting_public_subsidies_and_political_knowledge.pdf
348. Commonwealth of Australia. (2018). Select Committee on the Future of Public Interest Journalism Report. *Commonwealth of Australia*. February 2018. Retrieved from: https://www.aph.gov.au/Parliamentary_Business/Committees/Senate/Future_of_Public_Interest_Journalism/PublicInterestJournalism/~/media/Committees/journalism_ctte/Report/c06.pdf
349. Jackson, J, (2017). BBC sets up team to debunk fake news. BBC News. 13 January 2017. Retrieved from: https://www.theguardian.com/media/2017/jan/12/bbc-sets-up-team-to-debunk-fake-news
350. Commonwealth of Australia. (2018a). *Select Committee on the Future* of *Public Interest Journalism. The Senate. Commonwealth of Australia*. Retrieved from: https://www.aph.gov.au/Parliamentary_Business/Committees/Senate/Future_of_Public_Interest_Journalism/PublicInterestJournalism/~/media/Committees/journalism_ctte/Report/report.pdf
351. Commonwealth of Australia. (2018b). *Select Committee on the Future* of *Public Interest Journalism. The Senate. Commonwealth of Australia*. Retrieved from: https://www.aph.gov.au/Parliamentary_Business/Committees/Senate/Future_of_Public_Interest_Journalism/PublicInterestJournalism/~/media/Committees/journalism_ctte/Report/report.pdf p. 97.
352. Hywood, G. (2018). *Select Committee on the Future* of *Public Interest Journalism. The Senate. Commonwealth of Australia*. Retrieved from: https://www.aph.gov.au/Parliamentary_Business/Committees/Senate/Future_of_Public_Interest_Journalism/Public

InterestJournalism/~/media/Committees/journalism_ctte/Report/report.pdf p. 101.

353. 'Paywalls' restrict access to online content by asking for a subscription or credit card payments.
354. Blain, E. (1977). *Life with Aunty. 40 Years with the ABC.* Methuen Australia. p. 162, Inglis, K. (1983). *This is the ABC. The Australian Broadcasting Commission. 1932–1983.* Melbourne University Press. Melbourne. p. 389.
355. Buttrose, C. (1984). *Words and Music: Press barons, prima donnas and coping with the ABC.* Angus and Robertson Publishers. Sydney. p. 93. Quoting Ewart Chapple during his final days as ABC Manager Victoria.
356. Inglis, K. (1983). *This is the ABC. The Australian Broadcasting Commission. 1932–1983.* Melbourne University Press. Melbourne. p. 390.
357. Blain, E. (1977). *Life with Aunty: Forty years with the ABC.* Methuen. Australia. p. 2.
358. Andrews, R., Boyne, G. A., & Walker, R. M. (2012). Overspending in Public Organizations: Does Strategic Management Matter? *International Public Management Journal.* 15:1. Pp. 39–61. Retrieved from: https://doi.org/10.1080/10967494.2012.684017
359. Meade, A. (2018). 'Unprecedented hostility': Murdoch, the government, and an ABC under attack. *The Guardian.* 25 July 2018. Retrieved from: https://www.theguardian.com/media/2018/jul/25/unprecedented-hostility-murdoch-the-government-and-an-abc-under-attack
360. Davis, G. (1988). *Breaking up the ABC.* Allen and Unwin. Crows Nest, Sydney. p. 3.
361. Flew, T. (2006). The Social Contract and Beyond in Broadcast Media Policy. *Television & New Media.* 7:3. August. Pp. 282–305. Retrieved from: DOI: https://doi.org/10.1177/1527476404270606 p. 291.
362. Ibid.
363. Varatharajan, P. (2017). A political radio poetics: Ouyang yu's poetry and its adaptation on ABC radio national's poetica. *Cultural Studies Review.* 23:2. pp. 18–34. Retrieved from: doi: http://dx.doi.org.wwwproxy1.library.unsw.edu.au/10.5130/csr.v23i2.5050
364. Meade, A. (2015). ABC shops to close with loss of 300 jobs, Mark Scott says. *The Guardian.* 23 July, 2015. Retrieved from: https://www.theguardian.com/media/2015/jul/23/abc-shops-to-close-with-loss-of-300-jobs-mark-scott-says?CMP=share_btn_link
365. Anderson, D. (2020). ABC Life is getting a rebrand as ABC Local, with up to half its staff set to lose their jobs. *Australian Broadcasting Corporation.* 25 June 2020. Retrieved from: https://www.abc.net.au/news/2020-06-24/abc-life-abc-local-rebrand-job-losses-reduncancies/12388386

366. Faruqi, O. (2020). Closing ABC Life is more about politics and appeasement than good outcomes. *The Guardian*. 25 June 2020. Retrieved from: https://www.theguardian.com/commentisfree/2020/jun/25/closing-abc-life-is-more-about-politics-and-appeasement-than-good-outcomes
367. Enchin, H. (1993). CBC seeks niche in new TV markets: network stresses role as public broadcaster. *The Globe and Mail*. 12 April 1993. Retrieved from: http://search.proquest.com/docview/346810951/
368. Born, G. (2005). *Uncertain Vision: Birt, Dyke and the Re-invention of the BBC*. Vintage. London. p. 11.
369. Ibid., p. 5.
370. Op. Cit.
371. Calvet, R., Montoya, M. I., Garcia, I., Franquet I Calvet, R., Villa Montoya, M., & Bergillos Garcia, I. (2013). Public Service Broadcasting's Participation in the Reconfiguration of Online News Content. *Journal of Computer-Mediated Communication*. 18:3. Pp. 378–397. Retrieved from: https://doi.org/10.1111/jcc4.12014
372. Davis, G. (1988). *Breaking up the ABC*. Allen and Unwin. Crows Nest, Sydney. p. 10.
373. Davis, G. (1988). *Breaking up the ABC*. Allen and Unwin. Crows Nest, Sydney. p. 13.
374. Evans, H. (1986). How the ABC lost the public. *Quadrant*. 30:3. Mar 1986. Pp. 28–29, 31–32. Retrieved from: <https://search-informit-com-au.wwwproxy1.library.unsw.edu.au/documentSummary;dn=329495072963761;res=IELLCC>
375. Nicholls, P. (2011). *A Business and Labour History of Britain Case Studies of Britain in the Nineteenth and Twentieth Centuries*. Eds: M. Richardson & P. Nicholls. Palgrave Macmillan. New York. p. 130.
376. Inglis, K.S. (1983). *This is the ABC: The Australian Broadcasting Commission 1932–1983*. Melbourne University Press. Melbourne. p. 256.
377. Gruen, D & Clark, C. (2010). Nineteenth Colin Clark Lecture: November 2009 What Have We Learnt? The Great Depression in Australia from the Perspective of Today. *Economic Analysis & Policy*. 40:1. March 2010. Retrieved from: https://doi.org/10.1016/S0313-5926(10)50001-8
378. Gruen, D & Clark, C. (2010). Nineteenth Colin Clark Lecture: November 2009 What Have We Learnt? The Great Depression in Australia from the Perspective of Today. *Economic Analysis & Policy*. 40:1. March 2010. Retrieved from: https://doi.org/10.1016/S0313-5926(10)50001-8 p. 5.
379. Gruen, D & Clark, C. (2010). Nineteenth Colin Clark Lecture: November 2009 What Have We Learnt? The Great Depression in

Australia from the Perspective of Today. *Economic Analysis & Policy.* 40:1. March 2010. Retrieved from: https://doi.org/10.1016/S0313-5926(10)50001-8
380. BBC Royal Charter. (1927). History of the BBC. *British Broadcasting Corporation.* Retrieved from: https://web.archive.org/web/20170622230610/http://downloads.bbc.co.uk/bbctrust/assets/files/pdf/regulatory_framework/charter_agreement/archive/1927.pdf
381. Thomas, A. (1980). *Broadcast and be Damned: The ABC's first two decades.* Melbourne University Press. Melbourne. p. 66.
382. Ibid.
383. Ibid.
384. Barrier Miner, Broken Hill. (1938). How ABC learns of public opinion. *The Barrier Miner.* 5 July 1938. p. 4. Retrieved from: https://trove.nla.gov.au/newspaper/article/47976010?searchTerm=How%20ABC%20learns%20of%20public%20opinion
385. Australian Broadcasting Corporation. ABC Annual Report (1939–1940). *Australian Broadcasting Corporation.* ABC Archives. p. 12.
386. Canberra Times, The. (1936). ABC ARTISTS. All will visit Canberra. *The Canberra Times.* 2 July 1936. p. 2. Retrieved from: https://trove.nla.gov.au/newspaper/article/2420561?searchTerm=ABC%20ARTISTS.%20All%20will%20visit%20Canberra
387. Advertiser, The. (1934). POLICY OF ABC Encouraging Creative Side of Our People. *The Advertiser.* 27 June 1934. p. 18. Retrieved from: https://trove.nla.gov.au/newspaper/article/35116153?searchTerm=POLICY%20OF%20ABC%20Encouraging%20Creative%20Side%20Of%20Our%20People
388. Western Argus, The. (1937). ABC POLICY DEFENDED BY CHAIRMAN. Listeners Do Not Want To Be Patronised. *The Western Argus.* 19 October 1937. p. 17. Retrieved from: https://trove.nla.gov.au/newspaper/article/34959094?searchTerm=ABC%20POLICY%20DEFENDED%20BY%20CHAIRMAN.%20Listeners%20Do%20Not%20Want%20To%20Be%20Patronised
389. Courier Mail, The. (1938). Catering for diverse tastes: ABC policy explained at
4QR opening. *The Courier Mail.* 8 January 1938. p. 13. Retrieved from: https://trove.nla.gov.au/newspaper/article/39744258?searchTerm=Catering%20for%20diverse%20tastes%3A%20ABC%20policy%20explained%20at%204QR%20opening
390. Petersen, N. (1993). *News Not Views: The ABC, the Press, & Politics. 1932–1947.* Hale and Iremonger. Marrickville. p. 34.
391. Petersen, N. (1993). *News Not Views: The ABC, the Press, & Politics. 1932–1947.* Hale and Iremonger. Marrickville. p. 35.

392. Canberra Times, The. (1936). ABC ARTISTS. All will visit Canberra. *The Canberra Times.* 2 July 1936. p. 2. Retrieved from: https://trove.nla.gov.au/newspaper/article/2420561?searchTerm=ABC%20ARTISTS.%20All%20will%20visit%20Canberra
393. Courier-Mail, The. (1934). Educational broadcasts: Policy of the ABC. *The Courier-Mail.* 25 July 1934. p. 20. Retrieved from: https://trove.nla.gov.au/newspaper/article/36733653?searchTerm=Educational%20broadcasts%3A%20Policy%20of%20the%20ABC
394. Petersen, N. (1993). *News Not Views: The ABC, the Press, & Politics. 1932–1947.* Hale and Iremonger. Marrickville. p. 31.
395. Paletz D. & Entman R. (1981). *Media Power and Politics. Free Press.* New York, London. p. 184.
396. Vine, D. (1988). "Parochialism or patriotism?" *The Canberra Times.* 11 July 1988, p. 26. Retrieved from: https://trove.nla.gov.au/newspaper/article/102031858?searchTerm=ABC%20patriotism&searchLimits=
397. Tabakoff, N. (2019). ABC executives, staff spend $20 m on travel as axe hovers. *The Australian.* 27 December 2019. Retrieved from: https://www.theaustralian.com.au/business/media/abc-executives-staff-spend-20m-on-travel-as-axe-hovers/news-story/0083a476a9c38ca2f4dfccc6a4c5ffa3
398. Andrews, R., Boyne, G. A., & Walker, R. M. (2012). Overspending in Public Organizations: Does Strategic Management Matter? *International Public Management Journal.* 15:1. Pp. 39–61. Retrieved from: https://doi.org/10.1080/10967494.2012.684017
399. Miles, R., Snow, C., Meyer, A., & Coleman, H. (1978). Organizational Strategy, Structure, and Process. *The Academy of Management Review.* 3:3. Pp. 546–562. Retrieved from: www.jstor.org/stable/257544
400. Thornhill, A., & Gibbons, A. (1995). The positive management of redundancy survivors: issues and lessons. *Employee Counselling Today.* 7:3. Pp. 5–12. Retrieved from: https://doi.org/10.1108/13665629510091060
401. Worrall, L. (2000). Surviving redundancy: The perceptions of UK managers. *Journal of Managerial Psychology.* 15:5–6. Pp. 460–472. Retrieved from: https://doi.org/info:doi/
402. Worrall, L., Cooper, C. L., & Campbell-Jamison, F. (2000). The impact of organizational change on the work experiences and perceptions of public sector managers. *Personnel Review.* 29:5. Pp. 613–636. Retrieved from: doi: http://dx.doi.org.wwwproxy1.library.unsw.edu.au/10.1108/00483480010296429
403. Packham, B. (2019). Lowy Institute slams loss of soft power airwaves in Pacific. *The Australian.* 11 December 2019. Retrieved from: https://www.theaustralian.com.au/nation/politics/lowy-institute-slams-loss-of-

soft-power-airwaves-in-pacific/news-story/518c5a6072055012c9728 28724e104a7

404. O'Keeffe, A. & Greene, C. (2019). International Public Broadcasting: A Missed Opportunity for Projecting Australia's Soft Power. *Lowy Institute.* 11 December 2019. Retrieved from: https://www.lowyinstitute.org/publications/international-public-broadcasting-missed-opportunity-projecting-australia-s-soft-power
405. ABC Alumni. (ND). New Campaign Underway To Rebuild ABC International Service. *ABC Alumni.* Retrieved from: https://www.abcalumni.net/news-and-views/our-voice-to-the-world
406. Meade, A. (2019). Coalition's $17.1 m Pacific broadcasting plan was not 'sought out' by commercial networks. *The Guardian.* 23 January 2019. Retrieved from: https://www.theguardian.com/media/2019/jan/23/coalitions-171m-pacific-broadcasting-plan-was-not-sought-out-by-commercial-networks
407. *The Sydney Morning Herald.* 1946. "Bill For A.B.C. News Services Passed. All-Night Debate In House". 10 August 1946. p. 4.
408. Brudholm, T., & Johansen, B. S. (2018). *Hate, politics, law: critical perspectives on combating hate.* Oxford University Press. Oxford.
409. Mayer, H. (1964). *The Press in Australia.* Lansdowne Press. Hong Kong. p. 51. Quoting R. Murdoch in The Sunday Mirror (1961). 19 March.
410. McChesney, E.S. & and Herman, R.W. (1997). *The Global Media: The new missionaries of corporate capitalism.* Continuum. London, New York. p. 75.
411. Gizbert, R. (2020). Murdoch's misinformation: COVID-19, China and climate change. The Listening Post. *Al Jazeera.* 8 August 2020. Retrieved from: https://www.aljazeera.com/programmes/listeningpost/2020/08/murdoch-misinformation-covid-19-china-climate-change-200808072643503.html (now a dead link)
412. Knott, M. & Samios, Z. (2020). James Murdoch breaks ranks over 'climate change denial'. *The Sydney Morning Herald.* 15 January 2020. Retrieved from: https://www.smh.com.au/national/james-murdoch-breaks-ranks-over-climate-change-denial-20200115-p53rie.html
413. Younger, R.M. (2003). *Keith Murdoch: Founder of a Media Empire.* Harper Collins, Australia.
414. A newspaper was co-founded by the journalist Clyde Packer, father of Sir Frank Packer and grandfather of the late Australian media proprietor Kerry Packer. The Packers were to become a rival media dynasty to that of the Murdochs.
415. Smith's Weekly. (1935). Sir Keith Murdoch's Little War. *Smith's Weekly.* 21 December 1935, p. 4. Retrieved from: https://trove.nla.gov.au/newspaper/article/234617298?searchTerm=ABC%20Keith%20Murdoch&searchLimits=

416. In the Bible Goliath was immensely strong, but vulnerable to David's slingshot. Samuel 17:48–51.
417. Morton, R, (2020). Exclusive: New govt report targets ABC. *The Saturday Paper.* 27 June—3 July 2020. Retrieved from: https://www.thesaturdaypaper.com.au/news/politics/2020/06/27/exclusive-new-govt-report-targets-abc/159318000010021
418. Chenoweth, N. (2001). *Virtual Murdoch : reality wars on the information highway.* Secker & Warburg. London.
419. Williamson, D. (2013). *Rupert.* Currency Press. Sydney.
420. Guthrie, B. (2010). *Man Bites Murdoch: Four Decades in Print, Six Days in Court.* Melbourne University Press. Melbourne.
421. McKnight, D. (2012). Murdoch: An Investigation of Political Power. Allen and Unwin. Sydney.
422. Watson, T. & Hickman, M. (2012). *Dial M for Murdoch: News Corporation and the Corruption of Britain.* Allen Lane. London.
423. Manne, R. (2012). Murdoch and Company. *The Monthly.* June 2012. Retrieved from: https://www.themonthly.com.au/issue/2012/june/1338434837/robert-manne/murdoch-company
424. Barry, P. (2013). *Breaking news : sex, lies & the Murdoch succession.* Allen & Unwin. Sydney.
425. Lisners, J. (2013). *The Rise and Fall of the Murdoch Empire.* John Blake. London.
426. Tiffen, R. (2014). *Rupert Murdoch: A Reassessment.* NewSouth Publishing. Sydney.
427. Davies, N. (2014). *Hack attack: how the truth caught up with Rupert Murdoch.* Chatto & Windus. London.
428. Stelzer, I. (2018). *The Murdoch Method. Notes on Running an Empire.* Atlantic Books. Great Britain.
429. Argus, The (1937). HIGHER COSTS EXPECTED. Newspaper Industry. PRESIDENT'S REVIEW. Future of Paper Making. *The Argus, Melbourne.* 15 April 1937. p. 12. Retrieved from: https://trove.nla.gov.au/newspaper/article/11056793?searchTerm=The%20complete%20supremacy%20of%20newspapers%20as%20an%20advertising%20medium%20was%20unchallenged%20and%20was%20candidly%20admitted%20by%20all%20leading%20advertisers%20throughout%20the%20country
430. Murdoch, K. (Intro. M. McKernan) (2010). *The Gallipoli Letter.* Allen and Unwin. Sydney.
431. Ryan, P. (1986, 6 December). How Sir Keith built, and lost, a newspaper. *The Sydney Morning Herald.* p. 11. Retrieved from: https://global-factiva-com.wwwproxy1.library.unsw.edu.au/ha/default.aspx#./!?&_suid=159677667635208788332424849641

432. Murdoch's mentor was British media baron Lord Northcliffe. Geographically, Murdoch rule his media empire from Melbourne (in the Southern Hemisphere) while Lord Northcliffe was a British newspaper baron (northern hemisphere).
433. Ibid.
434. Smith's Weekly. (1935). Sir Keith Murdoch's Little War. A Fight Between Broadcasting Commission and Daily Press. ABC plans comprehensive news service. *Smith's Weekly.* 21 December 1935. Retrieved from: https://trove.nla.gov.au/newspaper/article/234617298?searchTerm=Keith%20Murdoch%20ABC&searchLimits=
435. Smith's Weekly. (1935). Sir Keith Murdoch's Little War. A Fight Between Broadcasting Commission and Daily Press. ABC plans comprehensive news service. *Smith's Weekly.* 21 December 1935. Retrieved from: https://trove.nla.gov.au/newspaper/article/234617298?searchTerm=Keith%20Murdoch%20ABC&searchLimits=
436. Smith's Weekly. (1935). Sir Keith Murdoch's Little War. A Fight Between Broadcasting Commission and Daily Press. ABC plans comprehensive news service. 21 December 1935. *Smith's Weekly.* Retrieved from: https://trove.nla.gov.au/newspaper/article/234617298?searchTerm=Keith%20Murdoch%20ABC&searchLimits=
437. Smith's Weekly. (1935). Sir Keith Murdoch's Little War. A Fight Between Broadcasting Commission and Daily Press. ABC plans comprehensive news service. 21 December 1935. *Smith's Weekly.* Retrieved from: https://trove.nla.gov.au/newspaper/article/234617298?searchTerm=Keith%20Murdoch%20ABC&searchLimits=
438. Younger, R. M. (2003). *Keith Murdoch: Founder of a Media Empire.* Harper Collins. Sydney. p. 191.
439. Petersen, N. (1993). *News not Views: The ABC, the Press, & Politics 1932–1947.* Hale & Iremonger. Sydney. p. 54.
440. Petersen, N. (1993). *News not Views: The ABC, the Press, & Politics 1932–1947.* Hale & Iremonger. Sydney. p. 80.
441. Petersen, N. (1993). *News not Views: The ABC, the Press, & Politics 1932–1947.* Hale & Iremonger. Sydney. p. 55.
442. Petersen, N. (1993). *News not Views: The ABC, the Press, & Politics 1932–1947.* Hale & Iremonger. Sydney. p. 55.
443. Davies, N. (2009). *Flat Earth News.* Vintage Books. London. p. 16
444. Boyce, G., Curran, J. & Wingate, P. (1978). Newspaper History: from the seventeenth century to the present day. G. Boyce. *The Fourth Estate: The Reappraisal of the Concept.* Communication and Society Series. Constable. London. Sage Publications. Beverly Hills. p. 31.
445. Thomas, A. (1980). *Broadcast and be Damned: the ABC's first two decades.* Melbourne University Press. Melbourne. p. 102.

446. Loc. cit.
447. Loc. cit.
448. Loc. cit.
449. Newcastle Morning Herald and Miners Advocate, The. (1941). "NEWS-CONSCIOUS PUBLIC" A.B.C. Chairman Gives Broadcast Costs. *The Newcastle Morning Herald and Miners Advocate.* 11 July 1941. p. 7. Retrieved from: https://trove.nla.gov.au/newspaper/article/139410923?searchTerm=ABC%20Associated%20Press
450. Ibid.
451. Examiner, The. (1941). BROADCAST OF NEWS: Newspapers' Attitude. *The Examiner.* p. 5. Retrieved from: https://trove.nla.gov.au/newspaper/article/25898225?searchTerm=The%20newspapers%20rejected%20as%20unjustified%20any%20suggestion%20that%20their%20attitude%20was%20monopolistic
452. Johnson, L. (1988) *The Unseen Voice: A cultural study of early Australian radio.* (2017 ed.) Vol. 3. Routledge Library Editions. London and New York.
453. West Australian, The (1936). NEWSPRINT INDUSTRY. AN AUSTRALIAN PROJECT. Sir Keith Murdoch Interviewed. 26 February 1936. *The West Australian.* Retrieved from: https://trove.nla.gov.au/newspaper/article/32978504?searchTerm=keith%20murdoch p. 15.
454. Argus, The (1937). HIGHER COSTS EXPECTED. Newspaper Industry. PRESIDENT'S REVIEW. Future of Paper Making. *The Argus, Melbourne.* 15 April 1937. p. 12. Retrieved from: https://trove.nla.gov.au/newspaper/article/11056793?searchTerm=The%20complete%20supremacy%20of%20newspapers%20as%20an%20advertising%20medium%20was%20unchallenged%20and%20was%20candidly%20admitted%20by%20all%20leading%20advertisers%20throughout%20the%20country
455. Sydney Morning Herald, The. (1941). Broadcasting of news: views of ABC Chairman. *The Sydney Morning Herald.* 11 July 1941. p. 4. Retrieved from: https://trove.nla.gov.au/newspaper/article/17752645?searchTerm=Broadcasting%20of%20news%3A%20views%20of%20ABC%20Chairman
456. Cairns Post, The. (1939). GIVING THE NEWS. BROADCASTING AND NEWS. PAPERS. *The Cairns Post.* 27 September 1939. p. 5. Retrieved from: https://trove.nla.gov.au/newspaper/article/42203333?searchTerm=A.B.C.%20British%20Official%20Wireless
457. Morning Bulletin, The (1939). Newspapers Permit Broadcast of Copyright News. Free Use Allowed of B.B.C. Bulletins. *The Morning Bulletin.* 21 September 1939. p. 7 Retrieved from: https://trove.nla.gov.au/newspaper/article/56046160?searchTerm=A.A.P.%20country%20newspapers

458. At this stage (1939) newspapers had a monopoly on news. They also controlled news supply to ""B" class radio stations, the Postmaster-General's Department and the Intelligence Branch of the Defence Department" (Cairns *Post*, 1939, p. 5).
459. Mercury, The. (1939). News Broadcasts. Free Use of B.B.C. Bulletins To Be Continued. *The Mercury.* 21 September 1939. p. 11. Retrieved from: https://trove.nla.gov.au/newspaper/article/25773673?searchTerm=The%20Commission%20may%20broadcast%20up%20to%20a%20maximum%20of%2015%20news%20flashes%20weekly%20
460. Courier Mail, The. (1941). "NEWSPAPER RADIO MOST LISTENERS". *The Courier Mail.* 21 October 1941. p. 5. Retrieved from: https://trove.nla.gov.au/newspaper/article/41950322?searchTerm=Keith%20Murdoch%20slightly%20propagandist%20tinge
461. Canberra Times, The. (1942). The Department of Information. Editorial. *The Canberra Times.* 19 January, 1942. p. 2. Retrieved from: https://trove.nla.gov.au/newspaper/article/2575300?searchTerm=Keith%20Murdoch%20extraordinary%20blunder%20was%20made%20in%20the%20blunderbuss%20
462. Herald, The. (1943). Senator Keane and the Newspapers. *The Herald.* 16 August 1943. p. 7. Retrieved from: https://trove.nla.gov.au/newspaper/article/246273154?searchTerm=Keane%20ensure%20that%20news%20of%20national%20interest%20is%20impartially%20presented
463. Knight. A. (2007). Australian based foreign correspondents and their sources.
   ejournalism.com.au. Retrieved from: http://ejournalist.com.au/v1n1/correspondents.pdf
464. Sydney Morning Herald, The. (1946). Bill for ABC News Service Passed. All-night Debate in House. *The Sydney Morning Herald.* 10 August 1946. p. 4. Retrieved from: https://trove.nla.gov.au/newspaper/article/17988112?searchTerm=Bill%20for%20A.B.C.%20News%20Services
465. Petersen, N. (1993). *News Not Views: The ABC, the Press, & Politics. 1932–1947.* Hale and Iremonger. Marrickville. p. 61.
466. Northern Standard, The. (1950). Will be Scrapped. *The Northern Standard.* 31 March 1950. p. 6. Retrieved from: https://trove.nla.gov.au/newspaper/article/49475143?searchTerm=ABC%20news%20service
467. Greenwald, R. (2004). *Outfoxed: Rupert Murdoch's War on Journalism.* Brave New Films.
468. The documentary "Outfoxed" provides numerous examples of how Murdoch's US-based Fox News channel provided questionable support for US President George W. Bush's administration. Specifically, the video said Fox News presented biased news, or opinion presented as fact, to support the administration's military ambitions in Iraq and Afghanistan.

The documentary's strongest critique was that the slogan of Fox News "Fair and Balanced" was not an accurate description of the unfair content and unbalanced presenters' views.

469. Decimal currency was introduced in Australia on 14 February 1966.
470. Australian, The. (1964). Launch article. First Edition. *The Australian*. 15 July 1964, p. 1.
471. Ferguson, A. (2013). "Williams walks the News plank". *The Sydney Morning Herald*. 10 August 2013. Retrieved from: http://m.smh.com/business/williams-walks-the-news-plank-20130809-2rngo.html
472. McKnight, D. (2012). *Rupert Murdoch: An Investigation of Political Power.* Allen and Unwin. Sydney. p. 56.
473. Connolly, J. (1999). *Every Dead Thing*. London. Hodder and Stoughton.
474. Quote from text: "I remembered a story I heard about the media tycoon Rupert Murdoch and how he approached Bloomingdale's in the hope of getting its management to advertise in the Post* after he took it over in the 1980s. In response, the head of Bloomingdale's had an arched eyebrow and told him: "The problem, Mr. Murdoch, is that your readers are our shoplifters." * New York Post. Reputed comment by the head of Bloomingdales.
475. Marin, C. 2011. "Voldemort (Murdoch) was here." The *Chicago Sun-Times.* Retrieved from: http://www.suntimes.com/news/marin/6521130-452/voldemort-murdoch-was-here.html
476. The Canadian, Conrad Black, owned Fairfax newspapers from 1994 to 1996. Lord Black was freed from a US prison on bail in 2010 after serving part of this six-year sentence for fraud for stealing US $6.1 million from the Chicago newspaper publisher Hollinger. Ref: Bloomberg. (2010). "Black appeal verdicts". World in Brief. *The Sun-Herald*, 31/10/10. p. 41. Black also owned *The Daily Telegraph* newspaper in London as well as *The Chicago Sun-Times* and *The Jerusalem Post.* Ref: *Daily Mail Online* "Shamed media tycoon Conrad Black has two fraud convictions overturned (but two other charges are upheld)". Retrieved 7 November 2010 from http://www.dailymail.co.uk/news/article-1325059/Conrad-Black-fraud-convictions-overturned.html
477. Greenslade, R. (2010). "Black on Murdoch: a monosyllabic, mumbling, nondescript, coarse great white shark with orange-dyed hair." Greenslade Blog. *The Guardian.* Retrieved from: http://www.guardian.co.uk/media/greenslade/2010/oct/21/conradblack-newspapers. Also posted by Roy Greenslade Thursday 21 October 2010.
478. Colvin, M. 2011. "Former Blair insider speaks of culture of fear of Murdoch." P.M. Radio interview. *Australian Broadcasting Corporation.* 8 September 2011. Retrieved from: http://proquest.umi.com/pqdlink?Ver=1&Exp=09-25-2016&FMT=7&DID=2445713511&RQT=309&cfc=1

479. Boin, A., McConnell, A. & Hart, P. (2010). Crisis leadership. In R. A. Couto *Political and civic leadership: A reference handbook* (pp. 229–238). SAGE Publications. Thousand Oaks, CA. Retrieved from: doi: https://doi.org/10.4135/9781412979337.n27
480. Schein, E. H. (2010). *Organizational culture and leadership* (4th ed.). Jossey-Bass. San Francisco. p. 304–305.
481. Drozdek, A. (2015). Media Ethics. In *International Encyclopedia of the Social & Behavioral Sciences: Second Edition* (pp. 42–47). Elsevier Inc. Retrieved from: https://doi.org/10.1016/B978-0-08-097086-8.11017-7
482. Schein, E. H. (2010). *Organizational culture and leadership* (4th ed.). Jossey-Bass. San Francisco. p. 301.
483. Fitzell, J. (1970). Dealing with the elephant in the room. Career Insights: Management Insights. *Professionals Australia*. Retrieved from: http://www.professionalsaustralia.org.au/australian-government/blog/dealing-with-the-elephant-in-the-room/
484. Drozdek, A. (2015). Media Ethics. In *International Encyclopedia of the Social & Behavioral Sciences: Second Edition* (pp. 42–47). Elsevier Inc. D.C. Hallin. Journalism. Retrieved from: https://doi.org/10.1016/B978-0-08-097086-8.11017-7
485. Creed, P. (2013). *Ethics, Norms and the Narratives of War: Creating and Encountering the Enemy Other*. Taylor and Francis. Abingdon, Oxon.
486. Creed, P. (2013). *Ethics, Norms and the Narratives of War: Creating and Encountering the Enemy Other*. Taylor and Francis. Abingdon, Oxon. p. 26.
487. Creed, P. (2013). *Ethics, Norms and the Narratives of War: Creating and Encountering the Enemy Other*. Taylor and Francis. Abingdon, Oxon. p. 27.
488. Creed, P. (2013). *Ethics, Norms and the Narratives of War: Creating and Encountering the Enemy Other*. Taylor and Francis. Abingdon, Oxon. pp. 26–27.
489. Creed, P. (2013). *Ethics, Norms and the Narratives of War: Creating and Encountering the Enemy Other*. Taylor and Francis. Abingdon, Oxon. p. 92.
490. Rudd, K. (2018). Cancer eating the heart of Australian democracy. Opinion. *The Sydney Morning Herald*. 27 August 2018. Retrieved from: https://www.smh.com.au/politics/federal/cancer-eating-the-heart-of-australian-democracy-20180826-p4zzum.html
491. Rudd, K. (2018). Cancer eating the heart of Australian democracy. Opinion. *The Sydney Morning Herald*. 27 August 2018. Retrieved from: https://www.smh.com.au/politics/federal/cancer-eating-the-heart-of-australian-democracy-20180826-p4zzum.html

492. Rudd, K. (2018). Cancer eating the heart of Australian democracy. Opinion. *The Sydney Morning Herald*. 27 August 2018. Retrieved from: https://www.smh.com.au/politics/federal/cancer-eating-the-heart-of-australian-democracy-20180826-p4zzum.html
493. Labor Prime Minister Paul Keating held the office from 1991–1996.
494. Parker, S. (2014). Quentin Dempster's parting shot at commercialisation of the ABC. 29 November 2014. *The Sydney Morning Herald*. Retrieved from: https://www.smh.com.au/politics/federal/quentin-dempsters-parting-shot-at-commercialisation-of-the-abc-20141129-11wk7z.html
495. Barry, P. (2013). *Breaking news: sex, lies and the Murdoch succession. Allen and Unwin. Crows Nest.*
496. Whitlam, N. (2020). Downfall not for reasons he thinks. *The Australian*. Inquirer. 25–26 April 2020. p. 16.
497. Crowe, D. (2020). Murdoch wanted him out because he was 'his own man', Turnbull claims. *The Sydney Morning Herald*. 16 April 2020. Retrieved from: https://www.smh.com.au/politics/federal/murdoch-wanted-him-out-because-he-was-his-own-man-turnbull-claims-20200416-p54kbc.html
498. Meade, A. (2020). Former News Corp chief says Turnbull overstates role of Murdoch media in political downfall. *The Guardian*. 22 April 2020. Retrieved from: https://www.theguardian.com/media/2020/apr/22/former-news-corp-says-turnbull-overstates-role-of-murdoch-media-in-political-downfall
499. "Go root your boot" is an Australian and New Zealand slang expression of extreme exasperation at someone.
500. Meade, A. (2018). 'Unprecedented hostility': Murdoch, the government, and an ABC under attack. *The Guardian*. 25 July 2018. Retrieved from: https://www.theguardian.com/media/2018/jul/25/unprecedented-hostility-murdoch-the-government-and-an-abc-under-attack
501. Meade, A. (2018). 'Unprecedented hostility': Murdoch, the government, and an ABC under attack. *The Guardian*. 25 July 2018. Retrieved from: https://www.theguardian.com/media/2018/jul/25/unprecedented-hostility-murdoch-the-government-and-an-abc-under-attack
502. Rudd, K. (2018). Cancer eating the heart of Australian democracy. Opinion. *The Sydney Morning Herald*. 27 August 2018. Retrieved from: https://www.smh.com.au/politics/federal/cancer-eating-the-heart-of-australian-democracy-20180826-p4zzum.html
503. McChesney, R.W. & Herman, E.S. (1997). *The Global Media: The News Missionaries of Global Capitalism*. Cassell. Washington and London. p. 169.

504. Fairfax, J. (1992). *My Regards to Broadway.* Angus and Robertson. Pymble. p. 118. Quoting G. Souter. (1981). *Company of Heralds.* University of Melbourne Press. Melbourne. p. 571.
505. Australian Broadcasting Corporation. (2020). Content Plan 2020–2022. *Australian Broadcasting Corporation.* Retrieved from: https://about.abc.net.au/wp-content/uploads/2019/12/ABCContentPlan2020-22.pdf pp. 26 and 8.
506. Hartley, J. (2008). *Television Truths.* Blackwell. Malden, Massachusetts. p. 35.
507. Ibid., p. 33.
508. Ibid., p. 35.
509. Alcock, J. & Docwra, G. (2005). A simulation analysis of the market effect of the Australian Broadcasting Corporation. *Information Economics and Policy.* 17:4. October 2005. Pp. 407–427. Retrieved from: https://www-sciencedirect-com.ezproxy1.library.usyd.edu.au/science/article/pii/S0167624505000193
510. Ibid.
511. Ibid., p. 410.
512. Ibid., p. 423.
513. Loc. Cit.
514. Outrecuidance is originally a French word meaning excessive self-confidence or conceit (Collins English Dictionary, retrieved from: https://www.collinsdictionary.com/dictionary/english/outrecuidance
515. McLuhan, M. (1973) (1964). *Understanding Media.* Abacus. London. p. 59.
516. Hartley, J. Ibid., p. 41.
517. Vujnovic, M., Singer, J. B., Paulussen, S., Heinonen, A., Reich, Z., Quandt, T., Hermida, A., & Domingo, D. (2010). Exploring the Political-Economic Factors of Participatory Journalism: Views of online journalists in 10 countries. *Journalism Practice: The Future of Journalism.* 4:3. Pp. 285–296. Retrieved from: https://doi.org/10.1080/17512781003640588
518. Murdoch, R. in J. Kaye & S. Quinn (2005). *Funding Journalism in the Digital Age: Business Models, Strategies, Issues and Trends.* Peter Lang. New York, Washington. p. 32.
519. Merrill-Brown. (2005). Carnegie Corporation Report Tracks Changes in Media Consumption by 18–34-Year-Olds; Report Survey Data Reveal That Young Adults Surf the Internet for News, Abandoning Newspapers and Traditional Media. *Business Wire.* Retrieved from: https://www.businesswire.com/news/home/20050504005525/en/Carnegie-Corporation-Report-Tracks-Media-Consumption-18-34-Year-Olds

520. University of Oxford/Reuters Institute for the Study of Journalism (2016). Digital News Report. Australia. *University of Oxford/Reuters Institute for the Study of Journalism*. Retrieved from: http://www.digitalnewsreport.org/survey/2016/australia-2016/
521. Flew, T. & Goldsmith, B. (2013). Fact Check: does Murdoch own 70% of newspapers in Australia? *The Conversation*. 8 August 2013. Retrieved from: https://theconversation.com/factcheck-does-murdoch-own-70-of-newspapers-in-australia-16812
522. Finkelstein, R. (2012). Report Of The Independent Inquiry Into The Media And Media Regulation. Report to the Minister For Broadband, Communications and the Digital Economy. *Australian Government*. 28 February, 2012. Retrieved from: http://www.abc.net.au/mediawatch/transcripts/1205_finkelstein.pdf
523. Rowland, M. (2016). Media concentration and public concern in Australia. ABC Fact Check. *Australian Broadcasting Corporation*. Retrieved from: https://cdn.theconversation.com/static_files/files/22/68437-2016-11-22-media-concentration-and-public-concern-in-australia-Research_-_Media_concentration_and_public_concern_in_Australia.pdf?1518059940 Information supplied to the ABC Fact Check Unit from Federal ALP shadow minister for communications, Michelle Rowland.
524. Barsamian, D. (2001). *The Decline and Fall of Public Broadcasting*. 2nd Edition. Southend Press. Cambridge Massachusetts.
525. Salter, D. (2007). *The Media We Deserve: Underachievement in The Fourth Estate*. Melbourne University Press. Melbourne. p. 72–73.
526. Hardinge, B. (2020). The cost of misinformation: social media in a pandemic and representative democracy. Asia and the Pacific Policy Society. *Policy Forum*. 2 April 2020. Retrieved from: https://www.policyforum.net/the-cost-of-misinformation/
527. Rudd, K. (2018). Culture of Fear: Murdoch, the *ABC* and how to fix a media in crisis. 2 October 2018. Retrieved from: https://www.smh.com.au/national/culture-of-fear-murdoch-the-abc-and-how-to-fix-a-media-in-crisis-20181001-p5073f.html
528. Chenoweth, N. (2012). Aunty faces cuts, job losses and old scores: Media. *The Australian Financial Review*. Melbourne 1 February, 2014. p. 21. Retrieved from: https://search-proquest-com.wwwproxy1.library.unsw.edu.au/docview/1753219424?rfr_id=info%3Axri%2Fsid%3Aprimo
529. Koch, T. (2019). For 30 years I worked for News Corp papers. Now all I see is shameful bias. 9 May 2019. *The Guardian*. Retrieved from: https://www.theguardian.com/commentisfree/2019/may/09/for-30-years-i-worked-for-news-corp-papers-now-all-i-see-is-shameful-bias

530. Cryle, D. (2008). *Murdoch's Flagship: 25 Years of The Australian Newspaper.* Melbourne University Press. Melbourne. p. 14.
531. ABC. (2010). Interview with John Menadue on the role of The Australian in the Federal election campaign. Radio 2BL Sydney. *Australian Broadcasting Corporation.* Broadcast 15 September, 2010.
532. Koch, T. (2019). For 30 years I worked for News Corp papers. Now all I see is shameful bias. 9 May 2019. *The Guardian.* Retrieved from: https://www.theguardian.com/commentisfree/2019/may/09/for-30-years-i-worked-for-news-corp-papers-now-all-i-see-is-shameful-bias
533. Guthrie, B. (2010). *Man Bites Murdoch.* Melbourne University Press. Melbourne. p. 18.
534. Neil, A. (1996). *Full Disclosure.* Macmillan. London. p. 160
535. McNally, P. (2012). Murdoch: 'Nonsense' that editors 'agree with everything' I say. 26 April 2012. *The Guardian.* Retrieved from: https://www.journalism.co.uk/news/murdoch-nonsense-that-editors-agree-with-everything-i-say/s2/a548964/
536. McNally, P. (2012). Murdoch: 'Nonsense' that editors 'agree with everything' I say. 26 April 2012. *The Guardian.* Retrieved from: https://www.journalism.co.uk/news/murdoch-nonsense-that-editors-agree-with-everything-i-say/s2/a548964/
537. BBC (2012). Leveson Report at a Glance. *British Broadcasting Corporation.* 29 November 2012. Retrieved from: https://www.bbc.com/news/uk-20543133
538. Fenton, N. (2014). Defending whose democracy? media freedom and media power. *Nordicom Review.* 35. Pp. 31–44. Retrieved from: https://www.nordicom.gu.se/sites/default/files/kapitel-pdf/fenton.pdf p. 34.
539. Fairfax, J. (1991). *My Regards to Broadway.* Angus and Robertson. Pymble, Sydney. p. 118.
540. Fairfax, J. (1991). *My Regards to Broadway.* Angus and Robertson. Pymble, Sydney. p. 118.
541. Ibid., p. 208.
542. Ibid. p. 154.
543. Thornton, P.H., Ocasio, W. & Lounsbury, M. (2012). *The Institutional Logics Perspective: A new approach to culture, structure, and process.* Oxford University Press. Oxford.
544. Fallows, J. (2003). The Age of Murdoch. *The Weekend Australian.* 30 August 2003. p. 24.
545. Lee, J. (2010). Media mogul's quiet life keeps him busy. *The Sun Herald.* 7 November 2010. p. 9.
546. Griffen-Foley, B. (2001). The Battle of Melbourne: The rise and fall of the Star. *Journal of Australian Studies.* 25: 69. Retrieved from: https://doi.org/10.1080/14443050109387690 p. 90.

547. https://www.forbes.com/profile/rupert-murdoch/#50364cc7b1af
548. https://www.forbes.com/powerful-people/list/#tab:overall
549. Myer, R. (2020). News Corp in 'dangerous times' as audience and revenues drop in print and digital. *The New Daily.* 7 February 2020. Retrieved from: https://thenewdaily.com.au/finance/finance-news/2020/02/07/news-corp-rupert-murdoch/
550. Leveson, B. Lord Justice. (2012). Report into the culture, practices and ethics of the press. 29 November 2012. UK Government. Retrieved from: https://www.gov.uk/government/publications/leveson-inquiry-report-into-the-culture-practices-and-ethics-of-the-press
551. O'Brien, K. (2018). *Kerry O'Brien: A Memoir.* Allen and Unwin. Crows Nest Sydney. p. 830.
552. Rudd, K. (2019). The Complacent Country. 4 February 2019. Posting. *Kevinrudd.com.* Retrieved from: http://kevinrudd.com/2019/02/04/the-complacent-country/
553. Ibid.
554. Mahler, J. & Rutenberg, J. (2019). How Rupert Murdoch's Empire of Influence Remade the World. *The New York Times Magazine.* 3 April 2019. Retrieved from: https://www.nytimes.com/interactive/2019/04/03/magazine/rupert-murdoch-fox-news-trump.html
555. Ibid.
556. Born, G. (2005). *Uncertain Vision: Birt, Dyke and the Reinvention of the BBC.* Vintage, London.
557. T. Rogers, S., Sedghi, A. & Evans, L. (2011, 19 July). "James and Rupert Murdoch at the Culture, Media and Sport Select Committee—live transcript". Retrieved from: http://www.guardian.co.uk/news/datablog/2011/jul/19/james-rupert-murdoch-live-transcript
558. Burden, P. (2008). *News of the World? Fake sheikhs and royal trappings.* Eye Books. London. p. 50.
559. Jenkins, S. (July, 82,011). News of the World was not such a steal for Murdoch. *The Guardian.* Retrieved from: http://www.guardian.co.uk/commentisfree/2011/jul/08/news-of-the-world-rupert-murdoch?intcmp=239
560. Burden, P. (2008). *News of the World? Fake sheikhs and royal trappings.* Eye Books. London. p. 55.
561. Fenton, N. (2014). Defending whose democracy? media freedom and media power. *Nordicom Review.* 35. Pp. 31–44. Retrieved from: https://www.nordicom.gu.se/sites/default/files/kapitel-pdf/fenton.pdf p. 34.
562. Leveson, B. Lord Justice. (2012). Report into the culture, practices and ethics of the press. 29 November 2012. UK Government. 1:4.10:14. Retrieved from: https://assets.publishing.service.gov.uk/government/uploads/system/uploads/attachment_data/file/270939/0780_i.pdf p. 411.

563. Burns, J.F. (2012). Phone-Hacking Charges Seen as Chill on British Journalism. *The New York Times.* 24 July 2012. Retrieved from: https://www.nytimes.com/2012/07/25/world/europe/two-ex-editors-for-murdoch-to-be-charged-for-phone-hacking.html
564. CNN Editorial Research (2020). UK Phone Hacking Scandal Fast Facts. *CNN.* Updated 26 April 2020. Retrieved from: https://edition.cnn.com/2013/10/24/world/europe/uk-phone-hacking-scandal-fast-facts/index.html
565. British Broadcasting Corporation. (2012). Q&A: News of the World phone-hacking scandal. *British Broadcasting Corporation.* 4 August 2012. Retrieved from: https://www.bbc.com/news/uk-11195407
566. O'Carroll, L. (2014). Phone hacker Glenn Mulcaire bankrupt over tax on News of the World earnings. The Guardian. 30 June 2014. Retrieved from: https://www.theguardian.com/uk-news/2014/jun/30/phone-hacker-glenn-mulcaire-bankrupt-news-world
567. Evening Standard. (2013). Duchess of York and 16 other phone-hack victims get apologies. *Evening Standard.* 8 February 2013. Retrieved from: https://www.standard.co.uk/news/uk/duchess-of-york-and-16-other-phone-hack-victims-get-apologies-8487104.html
568. Australian Broadcasting Corporation. (2011). Phone hacking: Dowler family to get $4.6 m payout. *Australian Broadcasting Corporation. 20 September 2011. Retrieved from:* https://www.abc.net.au/news/2011-09-20/murdered-girl27s-family-gets-phone-hacking-payout/2907122
569. Bernstein, C. (2011). Is Phone-Hacking Scandal Murdoch's Watergate? *Newsweek.* 7 September 2012. Retrieved from: https://www.newsweek.com/carl-bernstein-phone-hacking-scandal-murdochs-watergate-68411
570. As described by the British satirical magazine *Private Eye* (BBC 2011).
571. Sydney Morning Herald, The. (2011). News of the World to close after hacking scandal. *The Sydney Morning Herald.* 8 July, 2011. Retrieved from: http://m.smh.com.au/business/media-and-marketing/news-of-the-world-to-close-after-hacking-scandal-20110708-1h55o.html?page=2
572. Washbrook, C. (2011). James Murdoch's statement on the closure of the News of the World. *Media Spy.* 8 July 2011. Retrieved from: http://www.mediaspy.org/report/2011/07/08/james-murdochs-statement-on-the-closure-of-the-news-of-the-world/
573. Smith-Spark, L. (2011). Firms reconsider ad deals over newspaper phone hacking scandal. *CNN.* 7 July 2011. Retrieved from: http://edition.cnn.com/2011/BUSINESS/07/06/uk.phonehacking.ads/index.html
574. Knight, L. (2011). News of the World: Counting the cost. BBC News. 7 July 2011. Retrieved from: http://www.bbc.co.uk/news/business-14044052

575. Ibid.
576. Rogers, S., Sedghi, A. & Evans, L. (2011). James and Rupert Murdoch at the Culture, Media and Sport Select Committee—live transcript. 19 July 2011. Retrieved from: http://www.guardian.co.uk/news/datablog/2011/jul/19/james-rupert-murdoch-live-transcript
577. Arsenault, A. & Castells, M. (2008). Switching Power: Rupert Murdoch and the Global Business of Media Politics: A Sociological Analysis. *International Sociology.* 23:4. pp. 488–513. Retrieved from: https://doi.org/10.1177/0268580908090725
578. Chessell, J. (2010). "News Corporation on 'cusp of digital dynasty': Murdoch. *The Australian.* 4 February 2010. Retrieved from: http://www.theaustralian.com.au/business/news-corporation-on-the-cusp-of-digital-dynasty-murdoch/story-e6frg8zx-1225826521766 also p. 12, front page Business section *The Australian.*
579. Murdoch on his purchase of the Wall Street Journal and Dow Jones quoted from Ellison, S. (2010) *War at The Wall Street Journal: How Rupert Murdoch bought an American icon.* Text Publishing. Melbourne. Then quoted in "How Murdoch won a newspaper", *The Sydney Morning Herald*, 1–2 May, 2010. p. 5.
580. Shawcross, W. (1997). *Murdoch: The making of a media empire.* New York: Touchstone. p. 51
581. Arsenault, A. & Castells, M. (2008). Switching Power: Rupert Murdoch and the Global Business of Media Politics: A Sociological Analysis. *International Sociology.* 23:4. pp. 488–513. Retrieved from: https://doi.org/10.1177/0268580908090725
582. Ibid., p. 491.
583. Loc. Cit..
584. Loc. Cit.
585. Ibid., p. 493.
586. Anand, B. & Attea, K. (2003). in M. Monaghan & S. Prideaux (2016). *State Crime and Immorality: The Corrupting Influence of the Powerful.* Polity Press. Bristol & Chicago. p. 140.
587. Brady, J. (2006). 'Red Rupert', The Pragmatist. Brady on Media. *Forbes Magazine.* 18 May 2006. Retrieved from: http://www.forbes.com/2006/05/17/brady-on-media-cx_jb_0518rupert.html
588. Public Broadcasting Service. (2012). Murdoch's Scandal. Frontline. *Public Broadcasting Service.* 27 March, 2012. Retrieved from: https://www.pbs.org/wgbh/frontline/film/murdochs-scandal/transcript/
589. Douglas, T. (2004). "Forty years of The Sun". *British Broadcasting Corporation.* 14 September, 2004. Retrieved from: http://news.bbc.co.uk/2/hi/uk_news/magazine/3654446.stm
590. Ibid.

591. Horne, D. (2001). *Looking for Leadership: Australia in the Howard Years.* Viking. Ringwood, Victoria.
592. Ibid.
593. Ibid., p. 134.
594. Simons, M. (2017). Trump, fake news, and shrinking newsrooms: does journalism still matter in 2017? *The Guardian.* 29 May 2017. Retrieved from: https://www.theguardian.com/media/2017/may/29/trump-fake-news-and-shrinking-newsrooms-does-journalism-still-matter-in-2017
595. Reuter's Telegram Company began in 1851 in England but was not launched in Australia until after the establishment of the telegraph almost twenty years later. In 1872 with the arrival of a direct daily telegram of news via telegraph from Reuters in London, the first official representatives of the Australian news media were two key Australian newspapers—*The Sydney Morning Herald* and *The Argus*, Melbourne. At the same time the Associated Press Agency was operating to circulate news, including local news and Reuter's between newspapers within Australia. They named themselves Australian Associated Press Telegrams, were headquartered in Melbourne and traded news. However, in a letter quoted in *The Sydney Morning Herald* it stated that it was not a profit-making association: "each journal being only required to pay a fair rate" (The Sydney Morning Herald. 1872. "The Australian Associated Press". 25 June, 1872. p. 5.) and news would be dispersed so that no single newspaper would be advantaged over another. It was the beginnings of what would later become the foundation stone for Australian Associated Press-Reuter's (A.A.P.-Reuter's).
596. Reuters. (n.d.). Handbook of Journalism. Standards and Values. *Reuters.* Retrieved from: http://handbook.reuters.com/index.php?title=Standards_and_Values
597. Oxford English Dictionary. (1989). Retrieved from: https://www-oed-com.wwwproxy1.library.unsw.edu.au/view/Entry/169604?redirectedFrom=sacrosanct#eid
598. Kovach, B., and Rosenstiel, T. (2007). *The Elements of Journalism: What Newspeople Should Know and the Public Should Expect.* 1st Rev.Ed. Three Rivers Press. New York. p. 2.
599. Semetko, H. & Valkenburg, P. (2000). Framing European Politics: A Content Analysis of Press and Television News. *Journal of Communication.* Spring. 50:2. Pp. 93–109. Retrieved from: https://doi.org/10.1111/j.1460-2466.2000.tb02843.x p. 93.
600. Cohen, B.C. (1963). *The press and foreign policy.* Princeton University Press. Princeton, N.J. p. 205.

601. Kuypers, J.A. (2002). *Press Bias and Politics: How Media Frame Controversial Issues*. Praegar Publishers. Westport, C.T. p. 1.
602. Davies, N. (2009). *Flat Earth News*. Vintage Books. London. p. 18.
603. Davies, N. (2009). *Flat Earth News*. Vintage Books. London. p. 21.
604. Bhattacharyya, S., & Hodler, R. (2015). Media freedom and democracy in the fight against corruption. *European Journal Of Political Economy*. 39C. Pp. 13–24. Retrieved from: https://doi.org/10.1016/j.ejpoleco.2015.03.004
605. McChesney, R.M. (2008). The Political Economy of Media: Enduring Dilemmas. *Monthly Review Press*. New York. p. 34.
606. Fenton, N. (2014). Defending whose democracy? media freedom and media power. *Nordicom Review*. 35. Pp. 31–44. Retrieved from: https://www.nordicom.gu.se/sites/default/files/kapitel-pdf/fenton.pdf
607. Fenton, N. (2014). Defending whose democracy? media freedom and media power. *Nordicom Review*. 35. Pp. 31–44. Retrieved from: https://www.nordicom.gu.se/sites/default/files/kapitel-pdf/fenton.pdf p. 33.
608. Gans, H.J. (2004). *Deciding What's News: A Study of CBS Evening News, NBC Nightly News, Newsweek and Time*. 25th Anniversary Edition. Northwestern University Press. Evanston, Illinios. p. 40.
609. Gans, H.J. (2004). *Deciding What's News: A Study of CBS Evening News, NBC Nightly News, Newsweek and Time*. 25th Anniversary Edition. Northwestern University Press. Evanston, Illinios. p. 270.
610. Gans, H.J. (2004). *Deciding What's News: A Study of CBS Evening News, NBC Nightly News, Newsweek and Time*. 25th Anniversary Edition. Northwestern University Press. Evanston, Illinios. p. 293.
611. Hallin, D.C. (1989). *The "Uncensored War": The Media and Vietnam*. University of California Press. Berkeley. p. 25.

References

ABC. (2010, September 15). *Interview with John Menadue on the Role of The Australian in the Federal Election Campaign*. Radio 2BL Sydney, Australian Broadcasting Corporation, Broadcast.

ABC. (2020, April). *Interview ABC News24. Strapline: "Pell Released. George Pell Freed from Prison After High Court ruling"*. https://www.youtube.com/watch?v=7x29VznAZOE

ABC. (n.d., June 1). *Frank Dixon*. Australian Broadcasting Corporation. https://www.abc.net.au/news/2017-06-01/frank-dixon/8576568

ABC Alumni. (n.d.). New Campaign Underway to Rebuild ABC International Service. *ABC Alumni*.https://www.abcalumni.net/news-and-views/our-voice-to-the-world

ABC Online. (2020, March 15). Dr Norman Swan Recommends 'Severe' Shutdowns. *Australian Broadcasting Corporation.*https://www.abc.net.au/news/2020-03-15/dr-norman-swan-recommends-proactive-national-lockdown/12057956

Alcock, J., & Docwra, G. (2005, October). A Simulation Analysis of the Market Effect of the Australian Broadcasting Corporation. *Information Economics and Policy, 17*(4), 407–427. https://www-sciencedirect-com.ezproxy1.library.usyd.edu.au/science/article/pii/S0167624505000193

Alysen, B. (2012). *The Electronic Reporter: Broadcast Journalism in Australia.* UNSW Press.

Anand, B., & Attea, K. (2003). In M. Monaghan & S. Prideaux (Eds.) (2016), *State Crime and Immorality: The Corrupting Influence of the Powerful* (p. 140). Polity Press.

Anderson, B. (1983). *Imagined Communities: Reflections on the Origin and Spread of Nationalism.* Verso.

Andrews, R., Boyne, G. A., & Walker, R. M. (2012). Overspending in Public Organizations: Does Strategic Management Matter? *International Public Management Journal, 15*(1), 39–61. https://doi.org/10.1080/10967494.2012.684017

Angell, N. (1922). *The Press and the Organisation of Society.* The Labour Publishing Company Limited.

Anstead, N., & O'Loughlin, B. (2015). Social Media Analysis and Public Opinion: The 2010 UK General Election. *Journal of Computer-Mediated Communication, 20*(2), 204–220. https://doi.org/10.1111/jcc4.12102

Argus, The. (1937, April 15). Higher Costs Expected. Newspaper Industry. President's Review. Future of Paper Making. *The Argus, Melbourne*, p. 12. https://trove.nla.gov.au/newspaper/article/11056793?searchTerm=The%20complete%20supremacy%20of%20newspapers%20as%20an%20advertising%20medium%20was%20unchallenged%20and%20was%20candidly%20admitted%20by%20all%20leading%20advertisers%20throughout%20the%20country

Arsenault, A., & Castells, M. (2008). Switching Power: Rupert Murdoch and the Global Business of Media Politics: A Sociological Analysis. *International Sociology, 23*(4), 488–513. https://doi.org/10.1177/0268580908090725

Artwick, C. (2013). Reporters on Twitter. *Digital Journalism, 1*(2), 212–228. https://doi.org/10.1080/21670811.2012.744555

Australian Broadcasting Commission. Annual Report. (1932–33). ABC Research Archives. *Australian Broadcasting Commission.*

Australian Broadcasting Commission. Annual Report. (1939–1940). ABC Research Archives. *Australian Broadcasting Commission.*

Australian Broadcasting Corporation. (2011, September 20). *MPs Angered over Gillard Satire Sex Scene.* https://www.abc.net.au/news/2011-09-20/mps-angered-over-gillard-satire-sex-scene/2908158

Australian Broadcasting Corporation. (2020, March 16). Q and A. Transcript. Australian Broadcasting Corporation. https://www.abc.net.au/qanda/2020-16-03/12040520

Australian Broadcasting Corporation News. (2020, March 14). Coronavirus: Dr. Norman Swan recommends proactive national lockdown. *Australian Broadcasting Corporation. You Tube.* https://www.youtube.com/watch?v=znJ9RD8gYsQ

AUSTRALIAN PARLIAMENT. (2003, October 15). *Fortieth Parliament First Session—Sixth Period.* https://parlinfo.aph.gov.au/parlInfo/download/chamber/hansards/2003-10-15/toc_pdf/2939-2.pdf;fileType=application%2Fpdf#search=%22chamber/hansards/2003-10-15/0000%22

Bailey, R. (2018). When Journalism and Satire Merge: The Implications for Impartiality, Engagement and 'Post-Truth' Politics—A UK Perspective on the Serious Side of US TV Comedy. *European Journal of Communication, 33*(2), 200–213. https://doi.org/10.1177/0267323118760322

Bardoel, J. (2007) in J. Bardoel & G. F. Lowe (2007). From Public Service Broadcasting to Public Service Media: The Core Challenge. *From Public Service Broadcasting to Public Service Media*, 9–26. Nordicom. Göteburg.

Barrier Miner, Broken Hill. (1938, July 5). How ABC learns of Public Opinion. *The Barrier Miner*, p. 4. https://trove.nla.gov.au/newspaper/article/47976010?searchTerm=How%20ABC%20learns%20of%20public%20opinion

Barry, P. (2013). *Breaking News: Sex, Lies and the Murdoch Succession.* Allen and Unwin.

Barsamian, D. (2001). *The Decline and Fall of Public Broadcasting* (2nd ed.). Southend Press.

Baumann, M. (2010). @twitter Discloses Business Model #promotedtweets RT. *Information Today, 27*(6), 1–46. http://search.proquest.com/docview/357026026/

Beharrell, P., Davis, H., Eldridge, J, Hewitt, J., Oddie, J., & Philo, G. (1976). Bad News. In *Theory and Society* (vol. 3, p. 3). Glasgow University Media Group. Routledge & Kegan Paul.

Bennett, W. (1998). 1998 Ithiel De Sola Pool Lecture: The UnCivic Culture: Communication, Identity, and the Rise of Lifestyle Politics. *PS: Political Science and Politics, 31*(4), 741–761. https://doi.org/10.2307/420711

Bernstein, C. (2011, September 7). Is Phone-Hacking Scandal Murdoch's Watergate? *Newsweek.* https://www.newsweek.com/carl-bernstein-phone-hacking-scandal-murdochs-watergate-68411

Bhattacharyya, S., & Hodler, R. (2015). Media Freedom and Democracy in the Fight Against Corruption. *European Journal of Political Economy, 39*(C), 13–24. https://doi.org/10.1016/j.ejpoleco.2015.03.004

Bikramjit, R., & Bandyopadhyay, S. (2018). *Contemporary Issues in Social Media Marketing.* Routledge.

Blach-Ørsten, M., & Burkal, R. (2014). Credibility and the Media as a Political Institution. *Nordicom Review, 35*. Special Issue. https://content.sciendo.com/view/journals/nor/35/s1/nor.35.issue-s1.xml

Blain, E. (1977). *Life with Aunty: 40 Year with the ABC*. Methuen Australia.

Blood, G., & May, C. (2018, January 17). Australian Sport History. *Clearinghouse for Sport and Physical Activity*.https://www.clearinghouseforsport.gov.au/knowledge_base/organised_sport/value_of_sport/australian_sport_history

Boorstin, D. J. (1987) (orig. pub. 1961). *The Image: A Guide to Pseudo-Events in America*. Atheneum. New York.

Born, G. (2005). *Uncertain Vision: Birt, Dyke and the Re-invention of the BBC*. Vintage.

Bourdieu, P. (1979). *Distinction: A Social Critique of The Judgement of Taste* (R. Nice (1984), Trans.). Harvard University Press. Preface to the English Language Edition.

Bourdieu, P. (1984). *Sociology in Question*. Sage Publications.

Bourdieu, P. (1991). *Language and Symbolic Power* (J. Thompson, Ed., G. Raymond & M. Adamson, Trans.). Harvard University Press.

Bourdieu, P. (1998). *On Television and Journalism* (P. Parkhurst Ferguson, Trans.). Pluto Press.

Bourdieu, P. (2010). Ed. G. Sapiro. *Sociology is a Martial Art: Political Writings of Pierre Bourdieu*. The New Press. New York & London.

Bourdieu, P. (2017, Orig. 1998). *The Forms of Capital. Handbook of Theory and Research for the Sociology of Education* (J. G. Richardson, Ed.). Greenwood Press.

Boyce, G., Curran, J., & Wingate, P. (1978). Newspaper History: From the 17th Century to the Present Day. In G. Boyce (Ed.), *The Fourth Estate: The Reappraisal of the Concept*. Constable and Sage Publications.

Boyne, G. A., & Walker, R. M. (2004). Strategy Content and Public Service Organizations. *Journal of Public Administration Research and Theory, 14*(2), 231–252. https://doi.org/10.1093/jopart/muh015

Bozeman, B., & Straussman, J. D. (1990). *Public Management Strategies: Guidelines for Managerial Effectiveness*. Jossey-Bass, Inc. San Francisco, CA.

Brady, J. (2006, May 18). 'Red Rupert', The Pragmatist. Brady on Media. *Forbes Magazine*. http://www.forbes.com/2006/05/17/brady-on-media-cx_jb_0518rupert.html

Braun, J., & Gillespie, T. (2011). Hosting The Public Discourse, Hosting The Public. *Journalism Practice, 5*(4), 383–398. https://doi.org/10.1080/17512786.2011.557560

Braunstein, R. (2018). Boundary-Work and the Demarcation of Civil from Uncivil Protest in the United States: Control, Legitimacy, and Political Inequality. *Theory and Society, 47*(5), 603–633. https://doi.org/10.1007/s11186-018-9329-3

British Broadcasting Corporation. Royal Charter. (1927). History of the BBC. *British Broadcasting Corporation*. https://web.archive.org/web/20170622230610/http://downloads.bbc.co.uk/bbctrust/assets/files/pdf/regulatory_framework/charter_agreement/archive/1927.pdf

Brudholm, T., & Johansen, B. S. (2018). *Hate, Politics, Law: Critical Perspectives on Combating Hate*. Oxford University Press.

Bryson, J. M. (1995). *Strategic planning for public and nonprofit organizations: a guide to strengthening and sustaining organizational achievement* (Rev. ed.). Jossey-Bass Publishers. San Francisco, CA.

Burden, P. (2008). *News of the World? Fake Sheikhs and Royal Trappings*. Eye Books.

Burgess, K, (2020, March 17). Coronavirus: The Australian Army is Being Subbed in to Help Make Face Masks. *The Sydney Morning Herald*. https://www.canberratimes.com.au/story/6684074/the-australian-army-is-being-subbed-in-to-help-make-face-masks/

Burns, J. F. (2012, July 24). Phone-Hacking Charges Seen as Chill on British Journalism. *The New York Times*. https://www.nytimes.com/2012/07/25/world/europe/two-ex-editors-for-murdoch-to-be-charged-for-phone-hacking.html

Burrows, R., Nettleton, S., Pleace, N., Loader, B., & Muncer, S. (2000). Virtual Community Care? Social Policy and the Emergence of Computer Mediated Social Support. *Information, Communication & Society, 3*, 95–121. https://doi.org/10.1080/136911800359446

Buttrose, C. (1984). *Words and Music: Press Barons, Prima Donnas and Coping with the ABC*. Angus and Robertson Publishers.

Cairns Post, The. (1939, September 27). Giving the News. Broadcasting and News. Papers. *The Cairns Post*, p. 5. https://trove.nla.gov.au/newspaper/article/42203333?searchTerm=A.B.C.%20British%20Official%20Wireless

Calvet, R., Montoya, M. I., Garcia, I., Franquet, I., Calvet, R., Villa Montoya, M., & Bergillos Garcia, I. (2013). Public Service Broadcasting's Participation in the Reconfiguration of Online News Content. *Journal of Computer-Mediated Communication, 18*(3), 378–397. https://doi.org/10.1111/jcc4.12014

Canberra Times, The. (1936, July 2). ABC ARTISTS. All Will Visit Canberra. *The Canberra Times*, p. 2. https://trove.nla.gov.au/newspaper/article/2420561?searchTerm=ABC%20ARTISTS.%20All%20will%20visit%20Canberra

Canberra Times, The. (1942, January 19). The Department of Information. Editorial. *The Canberra Times*, p. 2. https://trove.nla.gov.au/newspaper/article/2575300?searchTerm=Keith%20Murdoch%20extraordinary%20blunder%20was%20made%20in%20the%20blunderbuss%20

Canberra Times, The. (1981, May 28). ABC National Sports Coverage Lacks Resources. *The Canberra Times*, p. 28. https://trove.nla.gov.au/newspaper/result?q=ABC+sport&s=20

Canberra Times, The. (1979, November 8). Sport Call to ABC. Parliament. *The Canberra Times*, p. 12. https://trove.nla.gov.au/newspaper/article/110966616?searchTerm=ABC%20sport%20station&searchLimits=
Centeno, D. (2018). Social Media Stakeholder Co-creation of Celebrities as Human Brands. Chap. 5. in B. Rishi & S. Bandyopadhyay (Eds.), *Contemporary Issues in Social Media Marketing*. Routledge.
Chenoweth, N. (2001). *Virtual Murdoch: Reality Wars on the Information Highway*. Secker & Warburg.
Chenoweth, N. (2012, February 1). Aunty Faces Cuts, Job Losses and Old Scores: Media. *The Australian Financial Review*. Melbourne, p. 21. https://search-proquest-com.wwwproxy1.library.unsw.edu.au/docview/1753219424?rfr_id=info%3Axri%2Fsid%3Aprimo
Chessell, J. (2010, February 4). "News Corporation on 'Cusp of Digital Dynasty': Murdoch. *The Australian*.http://www.theaustralian.com.au/business/news-corporation-on-the-cusp-of-digital-dynasty-murdoch/story-e6frg8zx-1225826521766
CNN Editorial Research. (2020, April 26). UK Phone Hacking Scandal Fast Facts. *CNN*. https://edition.cnn.com/2013/10/24/world/europe/uk-phone-hacking-scandal-fast-facts/index.html
Cohen, B. C. (1963). *The Press and Foreign Policy*. Princeton University Press.
Colman, A. (2006). *A Dictionary of Psychology*. Oxford University Press. https://archive.org/details/dictionaryofpsyc00colm_0/page/77/mode/2up
Committee of Review of the Australian Broadcasting Commission. (1981, May 30). *The ABC in Review: National Broadcasting in the 1980s*. https://apo.org.au/node/41206
Commonwealth of Australia. (2018, February). Select Committee on the Future of Public Interest Journalism Report. *Commonwealth of Australia*. https://www.aph.gov.au/Parliamentary_Business/Committees/Senate/Future_of_Public_Interest_Journalism/PublicInterestJournalism/Report
Commonwealth of Australia. (2018, February). Select Committee on the Future of Public Interest Journalism Report. *Commonwealth of Australia*. https://www.aph.gov.au/Parliamentary_Business/Committees/Senate/Future_of_Public_Interest_Journalism/PublicInterestJournalism/~/media/Committees/journalism_ctte/Report/c06.pdf
Commonwealth of Australia. (2018). Select Committee on the Future of Public Interest Journalism. The Senate. *Commonwealth of Australia*. https://www.aph.gov.au/Parliamentary_Business/Committees/Senate/Future_of_Public_Interest_Journalism/PublicInterestJournalism/~/media/Committees/journalism_ctte/Report/report.pdf
Conboy, M. (2013). *Journalism Studies: The Basics*. Routledge.
Connors, J. (2018, November 30). Opening statement (public hearing, Canberra, 30 November 2018). *Inquiry into Allegations of Political Interference in the ABC*. Tabled by: Dr. Jane Connors. https://www.aph.gov.au/Parliamentary_

Business/Committees/Senate/Environment_and_Communications/ABCInterferenceAllegations/Additional_Documents?docType=Tabled%20 Documents

Coombs, W. T. (2012). *Ongoing Crisis Communication: Planning, Managing, and Responding* (p. 37). Sage Publications.

Cotter, C. (2010). *News Talk*. Cambridge University Press. Cambridge. https://doi.org/10.1017/CBO9780511811975

Courier Mail, The. (1934, July 25). Educational Broadcasts: Policy of the A.B.C, p. 20. https://trove.nla.gov.au/newspaper/article/36733653?searchTerm=Educational%20broadcasts%3A%20Policy%20of%20the%20A.B.C

Craig, G. (2016). *Performing Politics: Media Interviews, Debates and Press Conferences*. Polity Press.

Creed, P. (2013). *Ethics, Norms and the Narratives of War: Creating and Encountering the Enemy Other*. Taylor and Francis.

Crocker, P. (1989). *Radio Days: A Personal View of Australia's Radio Heyday* (p. 75). Simon and Schuster. Brookvale.

Crowe, D. (2020, April 16). Murdoch Wanted Him Out Because He Was 'His Own Man', Turnbull Claims. *The Sydney Morning Herald*. https://www.smh.com.au/politics/federal/murdoch-wanted-him-out-because-he-was-his-own-man-turnbull-claims-20200416-p54kbc.html

Cryle, D. (2008). *Murdoch's Flagship: 25 Years of The Australian Newspaper*. Melbourne University Press.

Cunningham, S., & Craig, D. (2018, May 9). We Must Not Punish Content Creators in Our Rush to Regulate Social Platforms. *The Conversation*. https://theconversation.com/we-must-not-punish-content-creators-in-our-rush-to-regulate-social-platforms-96270

Curran, J., & Seaton, J. (2018). *Power Without Responsibility: Press, Broadcasting and the Internet in Britain* (8th ed.). Routledge.

Curran, J. (Ed.). (1978). *The British Press: A Manifesto*. Acton Society Press Group. The Macmillan Press Ltd.

D'Ambrosia, R. D. (2009, January). Treating the Internet-Informed Patient. *Orthopedics. Thorofare, 32*(1). https://search.proquest.com/docview/220412297?pq-origsite=gscholar&fromopenview=true

Daily Telegraph, The. (1935, October 9). Announcer May Be ABC Head: Moses Likely Appointee. *The Daily Telegraph*, p. 1. https://trove.nla.gov.au/newspaper/article/246584742?searchTerm=ABC%20sport%20Moses&searchLimits=

Daily Telegraph, The. (1948, December 4). *A.B.C. WON'T PAY FOR SPORT*, p. 5. https://trove.nla.gov.au/newspaper/article/248351380?searchTerm=ABC%20sport

Daly, J. (2020, January 6). How Social Licence and Clean Energy Will Change the Mining Industry by 2030. WA Country Hour. *Australian Broadcasting Corporation*. https://www.abc.net.au/news/rural/2020-01-06/how-social-license-and-clean-energy-change-mining-2030/11839044

Dalzell, S. (2019, October 23). 'There Will Be Job Losses': ABC Managing Director Confirms Staff To Go Following Budget Freeze [online]. ABC News. *Australian Broadcasting Corporation.* https://www.abc.net.au/news/2019-10-23/abc-boss-confirms-staff-to-go-following-budget-cuts/11629336

Das, R., & Graefer, A. (2017). Regulatory Expectations of Offended Audiences: The Citizen Interest in Audience Discourse. *Communication, Culture & Critique, 10*(4), 626–640. https://doi.org/10.1111/cccr.12179

Dávid, G., & Furkó, B. (2015). The Journey Metaphor in Mediatized Political Discourse. *Acta Universitatis Sapientiae, Philologica, 7*(2), 7–20. https://doi.org/10.1515/ausp-2015-0043

Davies, N. (2009). *Flat Earth News.* Vintage Books.

Davies, N. (2014). *Hack Attack: How the Truth Caught Up With Rupert Murdoch.* Chatto & Windus.

Davis, G. (1988). *Breaking Up the ABC.* Allen and Unwin.

Dawkins, R. (1976). *The Selfish Gene.* Oxford University Press. Oxford.

Deitchman, S. (2013). Enhancing Crisis Leadership in Public Health Emergencies. *Disaster Medicine and Public Health Preparedness, 7*(5), 534–540. https://doi.org/10.1017/dmp.2013.81

Diakopoulos, N. (2019). *Automating the News: How Algorithms Are Rewriting the Media.* Harvard University Press. ProQuest Ebook Central. http://ebookcentral.proquest.com/lib/unsw/detail.action?docID=5761259

Dorsman, S. J., Bekkers, V. J. J. M., & Edwards, A. R. (2015). Trust the Experts!' Risk Definitions in Dutch Online Forums About the 'Swine Flu'. *Information, Communication & Society, 18*(10), 1217–1237. https://doi.org/10.1080/1369118X.2015.1036767

Drozdek, A. (2015). Media Ethics. In *International Encyclopedia of the Social & Behavioral Sciences: Second Edition* (pp. 42–47). Elsevier Inc. https://doi.org/10.1016/B978-0-08-097086-8.11017-7

Dubie, D. (2003). Retaining Crucial Skills. *Network World, 20*(15), 43. http://search.proquest.com/docview/215974301/

Dubois, E., Gruzd, A., Jacobson, J., Chen, W., & Quan-Haase, A. (2020). Journalists' Use of Social Media to Infer Public Opinion: The Citizens' Perspective. *Social Science Computer Review, 38*(1), 57–74. https://doi.org/10.1177/0894439318791527

Dugan, J. P. (2011). Pervasive Myths in Leadership Development: Unpacking Constraints on Leadership Learning. *Journal of Leadership Studies, 5*(2), 79–84. https://doi.org/10.1002/jls.20223

Dumas, D. (2020, April 5). Bondi Beach: How the Australian Icon Became a Coronavirus Hotspot. *The Guardian.* https://www.theguardian.com/australia-news/2020/apr/05/bondi-beach-how-the-australian-icon-became-a-coronavirus-hotspot

Dwyer, D. E., Howard, R., Downie, J., & Cunningham, A. L. (1988, July). The "Grim Reaper" Campaign. *The Medical Journal of Australia, 149*(1), 49–50. https://onlinelibrary-wiley-com.wwwproxy1.library.unsw.edu.au/doi/abs/10.5694/j.1326-5377.1988.tb120487.x

Dwyer, T., & Martin, F. (2017). Sharing News Online. *Digital Journalism, 5*(8), 1080–1100. https://doi.org/10.1080/21670811.2017.1338527. Quoting CNNIC 2016; Newman et al. 2016; Pew Research Center 2016.

Ellison, S. (2010). *War at The Wall Street Journal: How Rupert Murdoch bought an American icon*. Text Publishing. Melbourne.

Enchin, H. (1993, April 12). CBC Seeks Niche in New TV Markets: Network Stresses Role as Public Broadcaster. *The Globe and Mail*. http://search.proquest.com/docview/346810951/

Evans, H. (1984). *Good Times, Bad Times. Hodder and Stoughton*. London.

Evans, H. (1986, March). How the ABC Lost the Public. *Quadrant, 30*(3), 28–29, 31–32. https://search-informit-com-au.wwwproxy1.library.unsw.edu.au/documentSummary;dn=329495072963761;res=IELLCC

Evening Standard. (2013, February 8). Duchess of York and 16 Other Phone-Hack Victims Get Apologies. *Evening Standard*. https://www.standard.co.uk/news/uk/duchess-of-york-and-16-other-phone-hack-victims-get-apologies-8487104.html

Event Brief of Q4 2008 News Corporation Earnings Conference Call - Final. (2008, Aug 05). *Fair Disclosure Wire*. Retrieved from: https://www.proquest.com/wire-feeds/event-brief-q4-2008-news-corporation-earnings/docview/466169731/se-2?accountid=8194

Examiner, The. (1941). Broadcast of News: Newspapers' Attitude. *The Examiner*, p. 5. https://trove.nla.gov.au/newspaper/article/25898225?searchTerm=The%20newspapers%20rejected%20as%20unjustified%20any%20suggestion%20that%20their%20attitude%20was%20monopolistic

Fairfax, J. (1991). *My Regards to Broadway*. Angus and Robertson.

Fairfax, J. (1992). *My Regards to Broadway*. Angus and Robertson. Pymble.

Fallows, J. (2003, August 30, September). The Age of Murdoch. *The Weekend Australian*. Also in *The Atlantic*. https://www.theatlantic.com/magazine/archive/2003/09/the-age-of-murdoch/302777/

Faruqi, O. (2020, June 25). Closing ABC Life Is More About Politics and Appeasement Than Good Outcomes. *The Guardian*. https://www.theguardian.com/commentisfree/2020/jun/25/closing-abc-life-is-more-about-politics-and-appeasement-than-good-outcomes

Fenton, N. (2014). Defending Whose Democracy? Media Freedom and Media Power. *Nordicom Review, 35*, 31–44. https://www.nordicom.gu.se/sites/default/files/kapitel-pdf/fenton.pdf

Finkelstein, R. (2012, February 28). Report of The Independent Inquiry Into The Media and Media Regulation. Report to the Minister for Broadband,

Communications and the Digital Economy. *Australian Government*. http://www.abc.net.au/mediawatch/transcripts/1205_finkelstein.pdf

Fiske, J. (1982). *Studies in Communication*. Methuen.

Fiske, J. (1989). Moments of Television: Neither the Text Nor the Audience. In E. Seiter, H. Borchers, G. Kreutzner, & E.-M. Warth (Eds.), *Remote Control: Television Audiences and Cultural Power*. Routledge.

Fitzell, J. (1970). Dealing with the Elephant in the Room. Career Insights: Management Insights. *Professionals Australia*.http://www.professionalsaustralia.org.au/australian-government/blog/dealing-with-the-elephant-in-the-room/

Fitzpatrick, S. M. (2000). Sensational News. *Forum for Applied Research and Public Policy, 15*(3), 95–96. http://search.proquest.com/docview/235135227/

Flew, T. (2006). The Social Contract and Beyond in Broadcast Media Policy. *Television & New Media, 7*(3), 282–305. https://doi.org/10.1177/1527476404270606

Flew, T., & Goldsmith, B. (2013, August 8). Fact Check: Does Murdoch Own 70% of Newspapers in Australia? *The Conversation*. https://theconversation.com/factcheck-does-murdoch-own-70-of-newspapers-in-australia-16812

Floyd, J. ""The True" in Journalism" in J. Katz, J. E. & Mays, K. K. (2019). *Journalism and Truth in an Age of Social Media*. Oxford University Press. https://doi.org/10.1093/oso/9780190900250.001.0001

Fraser, M., & O'Reilly, J. (Eds.). (1996). *Save Our ABC: The Case for Maintaining Australia's National Broadcaster*. Hyland House.

Friedman, R. A. (2009). The Role of Psychiatrists Who Write for Popular Media: Experts, Commentators, or Educators? *The American Journal of Psychiatry, 166*(7), 757–759. https://doi.org/10.1176/appi.ajp.2009.08121847

Friends of the ABC (Vic). (2008, December). *Submission: ABC and SBS: Towards a Digital Future*. https://me.abcfriendsvic.org.au/wp-content/uploads/2016/03/abc_review-fabc_submapp08.pdf

Galtung, J. (1998). The Peace Movement: An Exercise in Micro-Macro Linkages. *International Social Science Journal, 50*(157), 401–405. https://doi.org/10.1111/1468-2451.00153

Gans, H. J. (2004). *Deciding What's News: A Study of CBS Evening News, NBC Nightly News, Newsweek and Time*. 25th Anniversary Edition. Northwestern University Press.

Gasher, M., & McIntosh, A. (2019). *Media convergence* (English ed.). *Historica Canada*. http://search.proquest.com/docview/2315251385/

Giustini, D. (2005). How Google is Changing Medicine. *British Medical Journal, 331*(7531), 1487–1488. https://doi.org/10.1136/bmj.331.7531.1487

Gizbert, R. (2020, August 8). Murdoch's Misinformation: COVID-19, China and Climate Change. *The Listening Post. Al Jazeera*. https://www.aljazeera.com/programmes/listeningpost/2020/08/murdoch-misinformation-covid-19-china-climate-change-200808072643503.html (now a dead link)

Goulburn Evening Penny Post. (1924, July 17). "AUSTRALIANS SPORTS MAD". English Visitor's Opinion. *We Don't Walk Enough*, p. 2. https://trove.nla.gov.au/newspaper/article/99288972?searchTerm=australians%20sports%20mad

Greer, A., & Hoggett, P. (1999). Public Policies, Private Strategies and Local Public Spending Bodies. *Public Administration, 77*(2), 235–256. https://doi.org/10.1111/1467-9299.00152

Greer, A., & Hoggett, P. (2000). Contemporary Governance and Local Public Spending Bodies. *Public Administration, 78*(3), 513–529. https://doi.org/10.1111/1467-9299.00216

Greenwald, R. (2004). *Outfoxed: Rupert Murdoch's War on Journalism*. Brave New Films.

Griffen-Foley, B. (2001). The Battle of Melbourne: The rise and fall of the Star. *Journal of Australian Studies, 25*, 69. Retrieved from: https://doi.org/10.1080/14443050109387690

Gruber, D., Smerek, R., Thomas-Hunt, M., & James, E. (2015). The Real-Time Power of Twitter: Crisis Management and Leadership in an Age of Social Media. *Business Horizons, 58*(2), 163–172. https://doi.org/10.1016/j.bushor.2014.10.006

Gruen, D., & Clark, C. (2010). Nineteenth Colin Clark Lecture: November 2009 What Have We Learnt? The Great Depression in Australia from the Perspective of Today. *Economic Analysis & Policy, 40*(1). https://doi.org/10.1016/S0313-5926(10)50001-8

Guardian, The. (2019, July 10). Scott Morrison Prays at Hillsong Conference—Video. *The Guardian*. https://www.theguardian.com/australia-news/video/2019/jul/10/scott-morrison-discusses-freedom-of-religion-during-hillsong-conference-video

Guler, A.Y. (2020, April 14). One Coronavirus Patient Can Infect Up to 400. *Anadolu Agency*. https://www.aa.com.tr/en/latest-on-coronavirus-outbreak/one-coronavirus-patient-can-infect-up-to-400/1804349

Gulyas, A. (2013). The Influence of Professional Variables On Journalists' Uses And Views Of Social Media: *A Comparative Study of Finland, Germany, Sweden and the United Kingdom. Digital Journalism, 1*(2). https://doi.org/10.1080/21670811.2012.744559

Guthrie, B. (2010). *Man Bites Murdoch: Four Decades in Print, Six Days in Court*. Melbourne University Press.

Habermas, J. (1989, origin. publ. 1961). (Trans. T. Burger). *The Structural Transformation of the Public Sphere*. Polity Press. Great Britain.

Hall, S. (1973). *Encoding and Decoding in the Television Discourse*. Centre for Contemporary Cultural Studies, University of Birmingham.

Hall, L. J., & Donaghue, N. (2013). 'Nice girls don't carry knives': Constructions of ambition in media coverage of Australia's first female prime minister. *British Journal of Social Psychology, 52*(4), 631–647. https://doi.org/10.1111/j.2044-8309.2012.02114.x

Halverstadt, A., & Kerman, B. (2017). End-Game Evaluation: Building a Legacy of Learning in a Limited-Life Foundation. *The Foundation Review, 9*(1), 78–91, 109. https://doi.org/10.9707/1944-5660.1352

Hanitzsch, T. (2004). Journalists as Peacekeeping Force? Peace Journalism and Mass Communication Theory. *Journalism Studies, 5*(4), (Quoting Galtung 1998, p. 8.). https://doi.org/10.1080/14616700412331296419

Harcourt, C., Edwards, J., & Philpot, R. (1988, August 1). On the "Grim Reaper" Campaign. *The Medical Journal of Australia, 149*(3), 162, 164. https://onlinelibrary-wiley-com.wwwproxy1.library.unsw.edu.au/doi/epdf/10.5694/j.1326-5377.1988.tb120551.x

Hardaker, R. (2020, September 8). Ita and the ABC: Out with the Old and in with the New. *Crikey.com*. https://www.crikey.com.au/2020/09/08/ita-buttrose-abc-new-staff-hires/

Hardinge, B. (2020, April 2). The Cost of Misinformation: Social Media in a Pandemic and Representative Democracy. Asia and the Pacific Policy Society. *Policy Forum*. https://www.policyforum.net/the-cost-of-misinformation/

Hartley, J. (2008). *Television Truths*. Blackwell Publishing.

Heanue, S. (2020, March 13). Top Australian Army General to Head Military Taskforce to Manage Coronavirus Outbreak. *Australian Broadcasting Corporation*. https://www.abc.net.au/news/2020-03-13/coronavirus-military-taskforce/12051722

Herald, The. (1943, August 16). Senator Keane and the Newspapers. *The Herald*, p. 7. https://trove.nla.gov.au/newspaper/article/246273154?searchTerm=Keane%20ensure%20that%20news%20of%20national%20interest%20is%20impartially%20presented

Hetherington, A. (1985). *News, Newspapers and Television*. The Macmillan Press.

Hewett, J. (2020, July 30). Losing Friends and Influencing People. *The Australian Financial Review*. https://global-factiva-com.wwwproxy1.library.unsw.edu.au/redir/default.aspx?P=sa&an=AFNR000020200801eg7u0000e&cat=a&ep=ASE

Holman, C. D. J., Bucens, M. R., & Sesnan, T. M. K. (1987). AIDS and the Grim Reaper Campaign. *The Medical Journal of Australia, 147*(6), 306–306.

Horne, D. (2001). *Looking for Leadership: Australia in the Howard Years*. Viking.

Høyer, S., & Pöttker, H. (Eds.). (2005). *Diffusion of the News Paradigm*. Nordicam. Göteborg University. https://www.nordicom.gu.se/sv/system/tdf/publikationer-hela-pdf/diffusion_of_the_news_paradigm_1850-2000.pdf?file=1&type=node&id=10239&force=0

Hunt, E. (2016, August 19). Julia Gillard attacks ABC's decision to finance sitcom At Home with Julia. *The Guardian*. https://www.theguardian.com/world/2016/aug/19/julia-gillard-attacks-abcs-decision-to-finance-sitcom-at-home-with-julia

Hunt, E., & Evershed, N. (2016, July 1). George Christensen the Most Abused MP on Twitter, Election Analysis Shows. *The Guardian*. https://www.theguardian.com/australia-news/2016/jul/01/australian-election-2016-turnbull-shorten-coalition-greens-labor-politics-live

Inglis, K. (1983). *The is the ABC: The Australian Broadcasting Commission 1932–1983*. Melbourne University Press.

Inglis, K. (2006). *Whose ABC? The Australian Broadcasting Corporation 1983–2006*. Black Inc.

Jackson, J. (2017, January 13). BBC Sets Up Team to Debunk Fake News. *BBC News*. https://www.theguardian.com/media/2017/jan/12/bbc-sets-up-team-to-debunk-fake-news

Jackson, S. (2020, April 20). ABC Statement on Dr Norman Swan. *Australian Broadcasting Corporation*. https://about.abc.net.au/correcting-the-record/abc-statement-on-dr-norman-swan/

Jackson, S., & Vitorovich, L. (2020, April 1). Seven Looks to Cut Pay,Jobs to Survive Crisis. *The Australian*. https://www.theaustralian.com.au/business/media/seven-looks-to-cut-pay-jobs-to-survive-crisis/news-story/2c57ae3d681c821ed258549c0b95746a

James, O., Jilke, S., Petersen, C., & Van de Walle, S. (2016). Citizens' Blame of Politicians for Public Service Failure: Experimental Evidence About Blame Reduction through Delegation and Contracting. *Public Administration Review, 76*(1), 83–93. https://doi.org/10.1111/puar.12471

Javeline, D., Hellmann, J. J., Castro Cornejo, R., & Shufeldt, G. (2013). Expert Opinion on Climate Change and Threats to Biodiversity. *BioScience, 63*(8), 666–673. https://doi.org/10.1525/bio.2013.63.8.9

Jenkins, S. (2011, July 8). News of the World Was Not Such a Steal for Murdoch. *The Guardian*.http://www.guardian.co.uk/commentisfree/2011/jul/08/news-of-the-world-rupert-murdoch?intcmp=239

Jensen, K. B. (2010). *Media Convergence: The Three Degrees of Network, Mass and Interpersonal Communication*. Taylor & Francis Group. ProQuest Ebook Central. http://ebookcentral.proquest.com/lib/unsw/detail.action?docID=481099.

Jerit, J. (2009). Understanding the Knowledge Gap: The Role of Experts and Journalists. *The Journal of Politics, 71*(2), 442–456. https://doi.org/10.1017/S0022381609090380

Johnson, B. (2005, May 26). I Won't Pay to be Abused by the BBC. Comment. *The Telegraph*. https://www.telegraph.co.uk/comment/personal-view/3617184/I-wont-pay-to-be-abused-by-the-BBC.html

Johnson, C. (2013). From Brand Congruence to the 'Virtuous Circle': Branding and the Commercialization of Public Service Broadcasting. *Media Culture and Society*.http://journals.sagepub.com/doi/full/10.1177/0163443712472088

Johnson, L. (1988). *The Unseen Voice: A Cultural Study of Early Australian Radio* (Vol. 3, 2017th ed.). Routledge Library Editions.

Jolly, R. (2014, August 11). *The ABC: An Overview*. https://www.aph.gov.au/About_Parliament/Parliamentary_Departments/Parliamentary_Library/pubs/rp/rp1415/ABCoverview

Karp, P. (2020, April 1). Scott Morrison Prays for Australia and Commits Nation to God Amid Coronavirus Crisis. *The Guardian*. https://www.theguardian.com/australia-news/2020/apr/01/scott-morrison-prays-for-australia-and-commits-nation-to-god-amid-coronavirus-crisis

Kelling, K., & Thomas, R. J. (2018). The Roles and Functions of Opinion Journalists. *Newspaper Research Journal, 39*(4), 398–419. https://doi.org/10.1177/0739532918806899

Keshet, Y., & Popper-Giveon, A. (2018). The Undisciplined Patient in Neoliberal Society: Conscious, Informed and Intuitive Health Behaviours. *Health, Risk & Society, 20*(3-4), 182–199. https://doi.org/10.1080/13698575.2018.1432757

Kester, L., Schwartz, N., Seufert, T., & Zumbach, J. (2008). *Beyond Knowledge: The Legacy of Competence: Meaningful Computer-Based Learning Environments* (1st ed.). Springer.

Knight, L. (2011, July 7). News of the World: Counting the cost. *BBC News*. http://www.bbc.co.uk/news/business-14044052

Knott, M., & Samios, Z. (2020, January 15). James Murdoch Breaks Ranks Over 'Climate Change Denial'. *The Sydney Morning Herald*.https://www.smh.com.au/national/james-murdoch-breaks-ranks-over-climate-change-denial-20200115-p53rie.html

Kovach, B., & Rosenstiel, T. (2007). *The Elements of Journalism: What Newspeople Should Know and the Public Should Expect* (1st Rev. Ed.). Three Rivers Press.

Krstić, A., & Đurđević, B. (2017). Social Media Marketing. *Marketing (Beograd. 1991), 48*(4), 254–260. https://doaj.org/article/9fdc5a48a7a945fdb1de61e44404bd8c

Kuehn, B. M. (2013). More Than One-Third of US Individuals Use the Internet to Self-Diagnose. *JAMA, 309*(8), 756–757. https://doi.org/10.1001/jama.2013.629

Kuypers, J. A. (2002). *Press Bias and Politics: How Media Frame Controversial Issues*. Praegar Publishers.

Laclau, E., & Mouffe, C. (1985). *Hegemony and Socialist Strategy: Towards a Radical Democratic Politics*. Verso. London.

Lakoff, G. (2008). *The Political Mind: Why You Can't Understand 21st Century American Politics with an 18th Century Brain*. Viking.

Langer, J. (1998). *Tabloid Television: Popular Journalism and the 'Other News'*. Taylor & Francis Group. ProQuest Ebook Central. https://ebookcentral.proquest.com/lib/unsw/detail.action?docID=165718.

Larsson, S. (2014). Battling Mainstream Media, Commentators and Organized Debaters: Experiences from Citizens' Online Opinion Writing in Sweden. *NORDICOM Review: Nordic Research on Media and Communication, 35*(2), 77+. https://link-gale-com.ezproxy2.library.usyd.edu.au/apps/doc/A396138825/AONE?u=usyd&sid=AONE&xid=f8ac48fc

Le Grand, C. (2019, November 28). 'Down the Gurgler': ABC Doyen Blasts Olympic Boycott, Questions Commitment to Sport. *The Sydney Morning Herald*. https://www.smh.com.au/sport/down-the-gurgler-abc-doyen-blasts-olympic-boycott-questions-commitment-to-sport-20191128-p53f68.html

Lee, H., & Lee, J.-M. (2017). Viewing Presidential Televised Debates and Civic Engagement in Korea. *International Area Studies Review, 20*(4), 334–348. https://doi.org/10.1177/2233865917726438

Leveson, B. H., Sir. (2012). *An Inquiry Into the Culture, Practices and Ethics of the Press Executive Summary and Recommendations (aka the Leveson Inquiry)*. The Right Honourable Lord Justice Leveson. https://assets.documentcloud.org/documents/526073/leveson-summary.txt

Liao, S. H., Hsian, P. Y., & Wu, G. L. (2014). Mining User Knowledge for Investigating the Facebook Business Model: The Case of Taiwan Users. *Applied Artificial Intelligence, 28*(7), 712–736. https://doi.org/10.1080/08839514.2014.927695

Lisners, J. (2012). *The Rise and Fall of the Murdoch Empire*. Blake Publishing. London.

Lisners, J. (2013). *The Rise and Fall of the Murdoch Empire*. John Blake.

Littlefield, R. S., & Quenette, A. M. (2007). Crisis Leadership and Hurricane Katrina: The Portrayal of Authority by the Media in Natural Disasters. *Journal of Applied Communication Research, 35*(1), 26–47. https://doi.org/10.1080/00909880601065664

Low, S., & Smith, N. (2013). *The Politics of Public Space*. Taylor and Francis. https://primoa.library.unsw.edu.au/permalink/f/jhud33/UNSW_ALMA51175562100001731

Lunt, P., & Livingstone, S. (2012). *Media Regulation. Governance and the Interest of Citizens and Consumers*. Sage Publications Ltd. London.

Lupton, D. A. (1992). From Complacency to Panic: AIDS and Heterosexuals in the Australian Press July 1986 to June 1988. *Health Education Research, 7*(1), 9–20. https://academic-oup-com.wwwproxy1.library.unsw.edu.au/her/article/7/1/9/687273

Lutz, E. (2019, September 16). James Murdoch Suggests His Dad's Empire Is Ruining America. *Vanity Fair*. https://www.vanityfair.com/news/2019/09/james-murdoch-fox-news-empire

Lynch, J. (2002). Impunity in Journalism. *Media Development, Xlix*(2), 30–32. http://waccglobal.org/en/20022GimpunityGandGtheGmedia/693GImpunityGinG journalism.html

Mahler, J., & Rutenberg, J. (2019, April 3). How Rupert Murdoch's Empire of Influence Remade the World. *The New York Times Magazine*. https://www.nytimes.com/interactive/2019/04/03/magazine/rupert-murdoch-fox-news-trump.html

Manne, R. (2012, June). Murdoch and Company. *The Monthly*. https://www.themonthly.com.au/issue/2012/june/1338434837/robert-manne/murdoch-company

Mannix, T. (1987, April 6). Two Million Australians risk AIDS. *The Canberra Times*, p. 1. https://trove.nla.gov.au/newspaper/article/118183464?searchTerm=grim%20reaper%20buttrose&searchLimits=

Mansfield, B. (1997). *The Challenge of a Better ABC: The Review of the Role and Functions of the ABC*. Australian Government Publishing Service.

Mao, F. (2019, May 16). 2019 Election: Why Politics Is Toxic for Australia's Women. *British Broadcasting Corporation*. https://www.bbc.com/news/world-australia-48197145

Marozzi, M. (2015). Measuring Trust in European Public Institutions. *Social Indicators Research, 123*(3), 879–895. https://doi.org/10.1007/s11205-014-0765-9

Martin, F., & Dwyer, T. (2019). *Sharing News Online. Commendary Cultures and Social Media News Ecologies*. Chapter 5. Palgrave Macmillan.

Martinoli, A. (2016). Digital Media Audience—New Expectations, New Habits. *In Medias Res, 5*(8), 1269–1284. https://doaj.org/article/c7caa3920f984aceb4e9c611dbae7c9c

Marwick, A. E. (2013). *Status Update: Celebrity, Publicity, and Branding in the Social Media Age*. Yale University Press. https://primoa.library.unsw.edu.au/permalink/f/1gq3lal/UNSW_ALMA51219826020001731

Massola, J. (2015, June 23). 'Whose side are you on?' Tony Abbott lashes ABC's Q&A program. *The Sydney Morning Herald*. https://www.smh.com.au/politics/federal/whose-side-are-you-on-tony-abbott-lashes-abcs-qa-program-20150623-ghvd0l.html

Mason, M. (2020, May 7). Seven Axes 50 Sales Staff in Cost Cutting Effort. *The Australian Financial Review*. https://www.afr.com/companies/media-and-marketing/seven-axes-50-sales-staff-in-cost-cutting-effort-20200507-p54qoq

Maurer, M., Dumitrescu, D., & Bucy, E. P. (2016). Nonverbal Influence During Televised Debates: Integrating CRM in Experimental Channel Studies. *American Behavioral Scientist, 60*(14), 1799–1815. https://doi.org/10.1177/0002764216676250

McCauley, D., Bagshaw, E., & Harris, R. (2020, March 16). Australia Prepares for 50,000 to 150,000 Coronavirus Deaths. *The Sydney Morning Herald*. https://www.smh.com.au/politics/federal/australia-prepares-for-50-000-to-150-000-coronavirus-deaths-20200316-p54amn.html

McChesney, R. W. (2008). *The Political Economy of Media: Enduring Issues, Emerging Dilemmas*. Monthly Review Press.

McGarity, T. O., & Wagner, W. E. (2008). Bending Science: How Special Interests Corrupt Public Health Research. *Environmental Health Perspectives, 116*(11), A500–A500. First Harvard University Press. Cambridge. Mass.

McGoldrick, A. (2000). Peace Journalism—an Introduction. In Friedrich-Ebert-Stiftung (Ed.), *Medien im Konflikt—Mittäter oder Mediatoren? The Media in Conflicts—Accomplices or Mediators?* (pp. 95–100). FES. Bonn.

McHugh, B. (2014, February 17). The Term 'Social Licence to Operate' Brought Into Question by Report. *Australian Broadcasting Corporation*. https://www.abc.net.au/news/rural/2014-02-17/social-licence-to-operate-a-poorly-defined-concept/5264162

McKnight, D. (2012). *Rupert Murdoch: An Investigation of Political Power*. Allen and Unwin.

McLuhan, M. (1973) (1964). *Understanding Media*. Abacus. London.

McNally, P. (2012, April 26). Murdoch: 'Nonsense' That Editors 'Agree with Everything' I Say. *The Guardian*.https://www.journalism.co.uk/news/murdoch-nonsense-that-editors-agree-with-everything-i-say/s2/a548964/

McPhee, S. (2020). Coronavirus Australia: Human Biosecurity Emergency Declared. *News.com.au*. https://www.news.com.au/national/politics/coronavirus-australia-human-biosecurity-emergency-declared/news-story/cd7fbff7829 7c076c8bb774595459c59

Meade, A. (2015, July 23). ABC Shops to Close with Loss of 300 Jobs, Mark Scott Says. *The Guardian*. https://www.theguardian.com/media/2015/jul/23/abc-shops-to-close-with-loss-of-300-jobs-mark-scott-says?CMP=share_btn_link

Mercury, The. (1939, September 21). News Broadcasts. Free Use of B.B.C. Bulletins To Be Continued. *The Mercury*, p. 11. https://trove.nla.gov.au/newspaper/article/25773673?searchTerm=The%20Commission%20may%20broad-cast%20up%20to%20a%20maximum%20of%2015%20news%20flashes%20weekly%20

Merrill-Brown. (2005). Carnegie Corporation Report Tracks Changes in Media Consumption by 18-34-Year-Olds; Report Survey Data Reveal That Young Adults Surf the Internet for News, Abandoning Newspapers and Traditional Media. *Business Wire*. https://www.businesswire.com/news/home/20050504005525/en/Carnegie-Corporation-Report-Tracks-Media-Consumption-18-34-Year-Olds

Meusburger, P., Glückler, J., & el Meskioui, M. (2013). *Knowledge and the Economy*. Imprint. Springer. https://primoa.library.unsw.edu.au/permalink/f/jhud33/UNSW_ALMA51206680440001731

Meyer, E. L. (2011, November 3). Media Codes of Ethics: The Difficulty of Defining Standards. A Report to the *Center for International Media Assistance*. https://new.waccglobal.org/wp-content/uploads/2020/05/10-Media-Codes-of-Ethics-CIMA2011.pdf

Michaels, S. (2009). Matching Knowledge Brokering Strategies to Environmental Policy Problems and Settings. *Environmental Science & Policy*. https://doi.org/10.1016/j.envsci.2009.05.002

Michael, G., & Agur, C. (2018). The Bully Pulpit, Social Media, and Public Opinion: A Big Data Approach. *Journal of Information Technology & Politics, 15*(3), 262–277. https://doi.org/10.1080/19331681.2018.1485604

Miles, R., Snow, C., Meyer, A., & Coleman, H. (1978). Organizational Strategy, Structure, and Process. *The Academy of Management Review, 3*(3), 546–562. www.jstor.org/stable/257544

Mill, J. S. (1863). *On Liberty* (2nd ed.). Tickner and Fields.

Miller, M. (2019, April 2). Heavy Hearts as the Printing Presses Stop Running. *The Australian*. https://www.theaustralian.com.au/commentary/heavy-hearts-as-the-printing-presses-stop-running/news-story/0dad850f021a215cc3d132821d86ab2a

Monaghan, M. & Prideaux, S. (2016). *State Crime and Immorality: The Corrupting Influence of the Powerful*. Polity Press. Bristol & Chicago.

Morgan, S. (2018). Influencers. *The Missouri Review, 41*(4), 5–10. https://doi.org/10.1353/mis.2018.0040

Morlet, A., Guinan, J. J., Diefenthaler, I., & Gold, J. (1988, March). The Impact of the "Grim Reaper" National AIDS Educational Campaign on the Albion Street (AIDS) Centre and the AIDS Hotline. *The Medical Journal of Australia, 148*(6), 282–287. https://onlinelibrary-wiley-com.wwwproxy1.library.unsw.edu.au/doi/abs/10.5694/j.1326-5377.1988.tb117836.x

Morning Bulletin, The. (1939, September 21). Newspapers Permit Broadcast of Copyright News. Free Use Allowed of B.B.C. Bulletins. *The Morning Bulletin*, p. 7 https://trove.nla.gov.au/newspaper/article/56046160?searchTerm=A.A.P.%20country%20newspapers

Morton, R. (2020, June 25–26). Exclusive: New Govt Report Targets ABC. [online]. *The Saturday Paper, 306*. https://www.thesaturdaypaper.com.au/news/politics/2020/06/27/exclusive-new-govt-report-targets-abc/159318000010021

Murdoch, K. (Intro. M. McKernan). (2010). *The Gallipoli Letter*. Allen and Unwin.

Murdoch, R. In J. Kaye & S. Quinn. (2005). *Funding Journalism in the Digital Age: Business Models, Strategies, Issues and Trends*. Peter Lang.

Murdock, G. (2004, November). Building the Digital Commons: Public Broadcasting in the Age of the Internet. University of Montreal. *The 2004 Spry Memorial Lecture*. https://www.researchgate.net/publication/254750526_BUILDING_THE_DIGITAL_COMMONS_PUBLIC_BROADCASTING_IN_THE_AGE_OF_THE_INTERNET

Murphy, J., Link, M. W., Childs, J. H., Tesfaye, C. L., Dean, E., Stern, M., Pasek, J., Cohen, J., Callegaro, M., & Harwood, P. (2014). Social Media in Public Opinion Research. *Public Opinion Quarterly, 78*(4), 788–794. https://doi.org/10.1093/poq/nfu053

Murphy, K. (2020, June 23). ABC Board Elects to Take 10% Pay Cut Amid Coronavirus Economic Slump. *The Guardian*. https://www.theguardian.com/media/2020/jun/23/abc-board-elects-to-take-10-pay-cut-amid-coronavirus-economic-slump

Musgrove, N. (1961, April 19). Accent on Michael Charlton. *The Australian Women's Weekly*, p. 53. https://trove.nla.gov.au/newspaper/article/55473519?searchTerm=Michael%20Charlton%20ABC

Myer, R. (2020, February 7). News Corp in 'Dangerous Times' as Audience and Revenues Drop in Print and Digital. *The New Daily*. https://thenewdaily.com.au/finance/finance-news/2020/02/07/news-corp-rupert-murdoch/

Neil, A. (1996). *Full Disclosure*. Macmillan.

News, The (Adelaide). (1954, September 14). ABC Sport Policy Examined. *The News*, p. 36. https://trove.nla.gov.au/newspaper/article/130986285?searchTerm=ABC%20sport&searchLimits=

news.sky.com. (2020, August 1). Rupert Murdoch's Son James Quits News Corporation Board after 'Disagreements over Editorial Content'. *Sky News*. https://news.sky.com/story/rupert-murdochs-son-james-quits-news-corporation-board-after-disagreements-over-editorial-content-12040255

Nicol, J. W., & Gordon, L. J. (2018). Preparing for Leadership in General Practice: A Qualitative Exploration of How GP Trainees Learn about Leadership. *Education for Primary Care, 29*(6), 327–335. https://doi.org/10.1080/14739879.2018.1528896

Nicholls, P. (2011). *A Business and Labour History of Britain Case Studies of Britain in the Nineteenth and Twentieth Centuries* (M. Richardson & P. Nicholls, Eds.). Palgrave Macmillan.

Nine.com.au. (2020). Coronavirus: PM Says Aged Care Facilities May Be Put in 'Lock Down' If COVID-19 Outbreak Worsens. A Current Affair. *Channel 9*. https://9now.nine.com.au/a-current-affair/coronavirus-update-prime-minister-scott-morrison-says-covid19-outbreak-may-lead-to-aged-care-facilities-in-lock-down/2b70072b-758b-4e5e-8144-7f2c9241b8f1

Norington, B. (2020, April 18). Cash for Coronavirus: ABC 'Guru' Norman Swan After Money to Turn Spin Doctor. *The Australian*. https://www.theaustralian.com.au/business/media/cash-for-coronavirus-abc-guru-norman-swan-after-money-to-turn-spin-doctor/news-story/804333e72f653d5891e3706035a50563

Northern Standard, The. (1950, March 31). Will be Scrapped. *The Northern Standard*, p. 6. https://trove.nla.gov.au/newspaper/article/49475143?searchTerm=ABC%20news%20service

O'Brien, K. (2018). *Kerry O'Brien: A Memoir*. Allen and Unwin.

O'Carroll, L. (2014, June 30). Phone Hacker Glenn Mulcaire Bankrupt Over Tax on News of the World Earnings. *The Guardian*. https://www.theguardian.com/uk-news/2014/jun/30/phone-hacker-glenn-mulcaire-bankrupt-news-world

O'Keeffe, A., & Greene, C. (2019, December 11). International Public Broadcasting: A Missed Opportunity for Projecting Australia's Soft Power. *Lowy Institute*. https://www.lowyinstitute.org/publications/international-public-broadcasting-missed-opportunity-projecting-australia-s-soft-power

O'Mahen, P. (2016). A Big Bird Effect? The Interaction Among Public Broadcasting, Public Subsidies, and Political Knowledge. *European Political Science Review,* 8(2), 311–332. https://www-cambridge-org.wwwproxy1.library.unsw.edu.au/core/services/aop-cambridge-core/content/view/8EC8052F26A223A76ED7D07A386E10D5/S175577391500003Xa.pdf/big_bird_effect_the_interaction_among_public_broadcasting_public_subsidies_and_political_knowledge.pdf

Oreskes, N., & Conway, E. (2010). Defeating the Merchants of Doubt. *Nature, 465*, 686–687. https://doi.org/10.1038/465686a

Ouellette, L. (2008). Makeover Television, Governmentality and the Good Citizen. *Continuum, 22*(4), 471–484.

Paas F., van Gog T., Kirschner F., Marcus N., Ayres P., & Sweller J. (2008). Interdisciplinary Perspectives on Cognitive Load Research as a Key to Tackle Challenges of Contemporary Education. In J. Zumbach, N. Schwartz, T. Seufert, & L. Kester (Eds.), *Beyond Knowledge: The Legacy of Competence.* Springer. Dordrecht. https://doi-org.wwwproxy1.library.unsw.edu.au/10.1007/978-1-4020-8827-8_2

Packham, B. (2019, December 11). Lowy Institute Slams Loss of Soft Power Airwaves in Pacific. *The Australian.* https://www.theaustralian.com.au/nation/politics/lowy-institute-slams-loss-of-soft-power-airwaves-in-pacific/news-story/518c5a6072055012c972828724e104a7

Paletz, D. L., & Entman, R. M. (1981). *Media Power Politics.* Free Press.

Parker, S. (2014, November 29). Quentin Dempster's Parting Shot at Commercialisation of the ABC. *The Sydney Morning Herald.* https://www.smh.com.au/politics/federal/quentin-dempsters-parting-shot-at-commercialisation-of-the-abc-20141129-11wk7z.html

Patrick, A. (2020, April 4). I'm Worried About the Panic Out There: David Isaacs, Germ Expert. *The Australian Financial Review.* https://global-factiva-com.ezproxy2.library.usyd.edu.au/ha/default.aspx#./!?&_suid=158630818658503136619040135381

Perry, J. L., & Rainey, H. G. (1988). The Public-Private Distinction in Organization Theory: A Critique and Research Strategy. *The Academy of Management Review, 13*(2), 182–201. Published by: Academy of Management. http://www.jstor.org/stable/258571

Petersen, N. (1993). *News Not Views: The ABC, the Press, & Politics. 1932–1947.* Hale and Iremonger.

Petersen, N. (2012). Moses, Sir Charles Joseph (1900–1988). *Australian Dictionary of Biography, 18.* Melbourne University Press. http://adb.anu.edu.au/biography/moses-sir-charles-joseph-15044

Phillips, M., & Magdalinski, T. (2008). Sport in Australia. In B. Houlihan (Ed.), *Sport and Society: A Student Introduction.* Sage Publications.

Pitt, H. (2020, March 17). 'It Made a Powerful Impact': ABC Chair Says AIDS Campaign Worked. *The Sydney Morning Herald.* https://www.smh.com.au/national/it-made-a-powerful-impact-abc-chair-says-aids-campaign-worked-20200316-p54an2.html

Plato. (375BC, revised Ed. 2002). *The Republic*. http://www.idph.net

Poterba, J. M., & von Hagen, J. (1999). Introduction to "Fiscal Institutions and Fiscal Performance". In *Fiscal Institutions and Fiscal Performance*, pp. 1–12. University of Chicago Press. Chicago.

Razavi, H. (2020, May 20). Notes on a Pandemic: How Society Has Responded to Covid-19. *Australian Book Review Magazine, 421*. https://www.australianbookreview.com.au/abr-online/current-issue/788-commentary/6441-notes-on-a-pandemic-how-society-has-responded-to-covid-19-by-hessom-razavi

Reddick, C. G., & Aikins, S. K. (2012). Web 2.0 Technologies and Democratic Governance. In C. Reddick & S. Aikins (Eds.), *Web 2.0 Technologies and Democratic Governance. Public Administration and Information Technology* (Vol. 1). Springer. https://doi-org.wwwproxy1.library.unsw.edu.au/10.1007/978-1-4614-1448-3_1

Reuters. (n.d.). Handbook of Journalism. Standards and Values. *Reuters*. http://handbook.reuters.com/index.php?title=Standards_and_Values

Ritchie, E. (2019, December 30). ABC's Own Calls Out Drop in News, Sport Coverage. *The Australian*. https://www.theaustralian.com.au/nation/abcs-own-call-out-drop-in-news-sport-coverage/news-story/590d680302572167e1c3991432144398

Rogers, J., O'Boyle, N., Preston, P., & Fehr, F. (2014). The Significance of Small Differences: Cultural Diversity and Broadcasting in Ireland. *European Journal of Communication, 29*(4), 399–415. https://doi.org/10.1177/0267323114530367

Rogers, S., Sedghi, A., & Evans, L. (2011, July 19). James and Rupert Murdoch at the Culture, Media and Sport Select Committee—Live Transcript. http://www.guardian.co.uk/news/datablog/2011/jul/19/james-rupert-murdoch-live-transcript

Rowland, M. (2016). Media Concentration and Public Concern in Australia. ABC Fact Check. *Australian Broadcasting Corporation*.https://cdn.theconversation.com/static_files/files/22/68437-2016-11-22-media-concentration-and-public-concern-in-australia-Research_-_Media_concentration_and_public_concern_in_Australia.pdf?1518059940

Rudd, K. (20yp://kevinrudd.com/2019/02/04/the-complacent-country/

Rutherford, L., & Brown, A. (2013). The Australian Broadcasting Corporation's Multiplatform Projects: Industrial Logics of Children's Content Provision in the Digital Television Era. *Convergence, 19*(2), 201–221. https://doi.org/10.1177/1354856512457749

Ryan, P. (1986, December 6). How Sir Keith Built, and Lost, a Newspaper. *The Sydney Morning Herald*, p. 11. https://global-factiva-com.wwwproxy1.library.unsw.edu.au/ha/default.aspx#./!?&_suid=159677667635208788332424849641

Salter, D. (2007). *The Media We Deserve: Underachievement in The Fourth Estate*. Melbourne University Press.

Sammartino, S. (2014). *The Great Fragmentation: And Why the Future of All Business Is Small* (1st ed.). John Wiley & Sons.

Sanford, D. (1983). Impartial Perception. *Philosophy, 58*(225), 392–395. www.jstor.org/stable/3750775

Sawers, P. (2015, February 7). How NewsWhip Helps Newsrooms Track the Web's Top-Trending Stories. https://venturebeat.com/2015/02/07/how-newswhip-helps-newsrooms-track-the-webs-top-trending-stories/

Scannell, P. (Ed.). (1991). Broadcast Talk. In *Introduction: The Relevance of Talk*. Sage Publications.

Schein, E. H. (2010). *Organizational Culture and Leadership* (4th Ed.). The Jossey-Bass Business & Management Series, 2(4). Wiley.

Schlesinger, P., & Tumber, H. (1994). *Reporting Crime: The Media Politics of Criminal Justice*. Clarendon Press. New York. Oxford University Press. Oxford.

Schudson. (2005). "The Virtues of an Unlovable Press" Intro. *Political Quarterly, 1*(76), 23–32. https://doi.org/10.1111/j.1467-923X.2006.00745.x

Schudson, M. (1978). *Discovering the News: A social History of American Newspapers*. Basic Books Inc.

Schudson, M. (2008). *Why Democracies Need an Unlovable Press*. Polity Press.

Schultz, J. (1998). *Reviving the Fourth Estate: Democracy, Accountability and the Media*. Cambridge University Press.

Semetko, H., & Valkenburg, P. (2000). Framing European Politics: A Content Analysis of Press and Television News. *Journal of Communication, 50*(2, Spring), 93–109. https://doi.org/10.1111/j.1460-2466.2000.tb02843.x

Semmler, C. (1981). *The ABC—Aunt Sally and Sacred Cow*. Melbourne University Press.

Shawcross, W. (1997). *Murdoch: The Making of a Media Empire*. Touchstone.

Shiffrin, S. (1994). The Politics of The Mass Media and Free Speech Principle. *Indiana Law Journal, 69*(3, Article 2), 689–721. Law Library. Indiana University. https://primoa.library.unsw.edu.au/permalink/f/11jha62/TN_gale_legal15296131

Sigal, L. V. (1973). *Reporters and Officials: The Organization and Politics of News-making*. D. C. Heath. Lexington, Mass.

Simons, M. (2017, May 29). Trump, Fake News, and Shrinking Newsrooms: Does Journalism Still Matter in 2017? *The Guardian*. https://www.theguardian.com/media/2017/may/29/trump-fake-news-and-shrinking-newsrooms-does-journalism-still-matter-in-2017

Simpson, J. (2020, January 3). Aunty's Radio Rules the Waves, But ABC TV Is Listing Badly. *The Australian*. https://www.theaustralian.com.au/commentary/auntys-radio-rules-the-waves-but-abc-tv-is-listing-badly/news-story/a0d3ecd28922d461b984cb7ccfe073cc

Sinclair, A. (2007). *Leadership for the Disillusioned: Moving Beyond Myths and Heroes to Leading That Liberates*. Allen and Unwin.

Sinnig, J. (2020). *The Role of Origin of Fame in Influencer Branding: A Comparative Analysis of German and Russian Consumers* (1st ed.). Springer Fachmedien Wiesbaden. Imprint: Springer Gabler.

Small, V., & Warn, J. (2020, June). Impacts on Food Policy from Traditional and Social Media Framing of Moral Outrage and Cultural Stereotypes. *Agriculture and Human Values, 37*(2), 295–309. Springer. The Agriculture, Food, & Human Values Society (AFHVS). https://doi.org/10.1007/s10460-019-09983-6

Smith-Spark, L. (2011, July 7). Firms Reconsider ad Deals Over Newspaper Phone Hacking Scandal. *CNN*. http://edition.cnn.com/2011/BUSINESS/07/06/uk.phonehacking.ads/index.html

Smith's Weekly. (1935, December 21). Sir Keith Murdoch's Little War. A Fight Between Broadcasting Commission and Daily Press. ABC Plans Comprehensive News Service. *Smith's Weekly*, p. 4. https://trove.nla.gov.au/newspaper/article/234617298?searchTerm=Keith%20Murdoch%20ABC&searchLimits=

Sommerville, C. J. (1996). *The News Revolution in England: Cultural Dynamics of Daily Information*. Oxford University Press.

Sotiriadou, P., & Brouwers, J. (2012). A Critical Analysis of the Impact of the Beijing Olympic Games on Australia's Sport Policy Direction. *International Journal of Sport Policy and Politics: Olympic and Paralympic Policy, 4*(3), 321–341. https://doi.org/10.1080/19406940.2012.656687

Soysal, Z. (2019). Truth in Journalism. In J. E. Katz & K. K. Mays (Eds.), *Journalism and Truth in an Age of Social Media*. Oxford University Press. https://doi.org/10.1093/oso/9780190900250.001.0001

Speers, D. (2020, March 15). Scott Morrison's 'F-Word' Misread the Public Mood on the Coronavirus Pandemic. ABC News Online. Analysis. *Australian Broadcasting Corporation*. https://www.abc.net.au/news/2020-03-15/coronavirus-scott-morrison-footy-next-information-campaign/12054174

Statham, P. (2007). Journalists as Commentators on European Politics. *European Journal of Communication, 22*(4), 461–477. London. https://doi.org/10.1177/0267323107083063

Stelzer, I. (2018). *The Murdoch Method. Notes on Running an Empire*. Atlantic Books.

Strekalova, Y. A. (2017). Health Risk Information Engagement and Amplification on Social Media: News About an Emerging Pandemic on Facebook. *Health Education & Behavior, 44*(2), 332–339. https://journals-sagepub-com.www-proxy1.library.unsw.edu.au/doi/pdf/10.1177/1090198116660310

Strzelecki, A. (2020). Google Medical Update: Why Is the Search Engine Decreasing Visibility of Health and Medical Information Websites? *International Journal of Environmental Research and Public Health,* 17(4). https://doi.org/10.3390/ijerph17041160

Sunstein, C. R. (2009). *Republic.com 2.0.* Princeton University Press. *Princeton. EBook.* http://ebookcentral.proquest.com/lib/unsw/detail.action?docID=581662

Swan, N. (2020, March 16). Norman Swan Answers Your Coronavirus Questions on Pregnancy, Asthma, Pools and Schools. ABC News Breakfast Program and ABC News 24. *Australian Broadcasting Corporation.* Televised, Broadcast and Online. https://www.abc.net.au/news/2020-03-16/coronavirus-questions-on-pregnancy-asthma-pools-and-schools/12058926

Switzer, T. (2013, May). 'Why the ABC should be privatised'. *Quadrant.* https://quadrant.org.au/magazine/2013/05/why-the-abc-should-be-privatised/

Sydney Morning Herald, The. (1931, November 16). Broadcasting. *The Sydney Morning Herald*, p. 8. https://trove.nla.gov.au/newspaper/article/16823317?searchTerm=%22improved%20and%20freed%20from%20all%20the%20evils%2C%20real%20or%20imaginary%2C%20of%20private%20enterprise%22

Sydney Morning Herald, The. (1941, July 11). Broadcasting of News: Views of ABC Chairman. *The Sydney Morning Herald*, p. 4. https://trove.nla.gov.au/newspaper/article/17752645?searchTerm=Broadcasting%20of%20news%3A%20views%20of%20ABC%20Chairman

Sydney Morning Herald, The. (2020, March 20). Editorial "The Herald's View". *The Sydney Morning Herald.* https://www.smh.com.au/national/nsw-must-start-preparing-now-for-school-closures-20200320-p54cb5.html

Tabakoff, N. (2019, December 27). ABC Executives, Staff Spend $20m on Travel as Axe Hovers. *The Australian.* https://www.theaustralian.com.au/business/media/abc-executives-staff-spend-20m-on-travel-as-axe-hovers/news-story/0083a476a9c38ca2f4dfccc6a4c5ffa3

Tandoc, E. C., & Duffy, A. (2016). Keeping Up with the Audiences: Journalistic Role Expectations in Singapore. *International Journal of Communication, 10*, 3338–3358. https://primoa.library.unsw.edu.au/permalink/f/11jha62/TN_wos000390936900001

The Newcastle Sun. (1938, May 28). ABC Ideals. *The Newcastle Sun*, p. 4. https://trove.nla.gov.au/newspaper/article/166711374?searchTerm=ABC%20privilege&searchLimits=

Thilmany, J. (2004). Better Housekeeping of Legacy Knowledge. *Mechanical Engineering, 126*(10), 22. http://search.proquest.com/docview/230173378/

Thomas, A. (1980). *Broadcast and be Damned: The ABC's First Two Decades.* Melbourne University Press.

Thornhill, A., & Gibbons, A. (1995). The Positive Management of Redundancy Survivors: Issues and Lessons. *Employee Counselling Today, 7*(3), 5–12. https://doi.org/10.1108/13665629510091060

Tiffen, R. (2014). *Rupert Murdoch: A Reassessment.* NewSouth Publishing.

Tingle, L. (2020, March 18). Coronavirus Messaging from Political Leaders Making a Much-Needed Improvement. Analysis. ABC News. *Australian*

Broadcasting Corporation. https://www.abc.net.au/news/2020-03-18/coronavirus-messaging-from-political-leaders-making-improvement/12067290

Toffler, A. (1984). *Future Shock*. Bantam Books.

Topsfield, J. (2020, March 20). Brendan Murphy: The Public Face of Australia's Fight Against COVID-19. *The Sydney Morning Herald*. https://www.smh.com.au/national/brendan-murphy-the-public-face-of-australia-s-fight-against-covid-19-20200320-p54c87.html

Tracey, M. (1998, reprinted 2002). *The Decline and Fall of Public Service Broadcasting*. Oxford University Press.

Turner, M. M., Boudewyns, V., Kirby-straker, R., & Telfer, J. (2013). A Double Dose of Fear: A Theory-Based Content Analysis of News Articles Surrounding the 2006 Cough Syrup Contamination Crisis in Panama. *Risk Management, 15*(2), 79–99. https://doi.org/10.1057/rm.2012.13

University of Oxford/Reuters Institute for the Study of Journalism. (2016). Digital News Report. Australia. *University of Oxford/Reuters Institute for the Study of Journalism*.http://www.digitalnewsreport.org/survey/2016/australia-2016/

Van der Meer, T., & Verhoeven, P. (2013). Public Framing Organizational Crisis Situations: Social Media Versus News Media. *Public Relations Review, 39*(3), 229–231. https://doi.org/10.1016/j.pubrev.2012.12.001

Varatharajan, P. (2017). A Political Radio Poetics: Ouyang Yu's Poetry and Its Adaptation on ABC Radio National's Poetica. *Cultural Studies Review, 23*(2), 18–34. http://dx.doi.org.wwwproxy1.library.unsw.edu.au/10.5130/csr.v23i2.5050

Varona, A. E. (2009). Toward a Broadband Public Interest Standard. *Administrative Law Review, 61*(1), 1–135. https://primoa.library.unsw.edu.au/permalink/f/11jha62/TN_gale_legal197493069

Venger, O., & Matthews, J. (2019). The Use of Experts in Journalistic Accounts of Media Events: A Comparative Study of the 2005 London Bombings in British, American, and Russian Newspapers. *Journalism, 20*(10), 1343–1359. https://doi.org/10.1177/1464884919830479

Vignal Lambret, C., & Barki, E. (2018). Social Media Crisis Management: Aligning Corporate Response Strategies with Stakeholders' Emotions Online. *Journal of Contingencies and Crisis Management, 26*(2), 295–305. https://doi.org/10.1111/1468-5973.12198

Vine, D. (1988, July 11). Parochialism or Patriotism? *The Canberra Times*, p. 26. https://trove.nla.gov.au/newspaper/article/102031858?searchTerm=ABC%20patriotism&searchLimits=

Vujnovic, M., Singer, J. B., Paulussen, S., Heinonen, A., Reich, Z., Quandt, T., Hermida, A., & Domingo, D. (2010). Exploring the Political-Economic

Factors of Participatory Journalism: Views of Online Journalists in 10 Countries. *Journalism Practice: The Future of Journalism, 4*(3), 285–296. https://doi.org/10.1080/17512781003640588

Vulliamy, E. (1999, March 1). "Neutrality" and the Absence of Reckoning: A Journalist's Account. *Journal of International Affairs, 52*(2), 604. https://primoa.library.unsw.edu.au/permalink/f/11jha62/TN_jstor_archive_1424358055

Wang, L., & Gordon, P. (2011). Trust and Institutions: A Multilevel Analysis. *Journal of Socio—Economics, 40*(5), 583–593. https://doi.org/10.1016/j.socec.2011.04.015

Ward, L. (2005). Stand Up for Who You Are. *The Safety & Health Practitioner, 23*(9), 37–40. http://search.proquest.com/docview/200971662/

Washbrook, C. (2011, July 8). James Murdoch's statement on the Closure of the News of the World. *Media Spy*. http://www.mediaspy.org/report/2011/07/08/james-murdochs-statement-on-the-closure-of-the-news-of-the-world/

Watson, T., & Hickman, M. (2012). *Dial M for Murdoch: News Corporation and the Corruption of Britain*. Allen Lane.

Weber, E. (2010). Democratic Political Leadership. In R. A. Couto *Political and Civic Leadership: A Reference Handbook* (pp. 105–110). SAGE Publications, Inc. https://doi.org/10.4135/9781412979337.n13

Wells, S. W. W. (1959). Impartial. *Notes and Queries, 6*(9), 353–354. https://doi.org/10.1093/nq/6.9.353

West Australian, The. (1936. February 26). Newsprint industry. An Australian Project. Sir Keith Murdoch Interviewed. *The West Australian*.https://trove.nla.gov.au/newspaper/article/32978504?searchTerm=keith%20murdoch

Western Argus, The. (1937, October 19). ABC Policy Defended by Chairman. Listeners Do Not Want To Be Patronised. *The Western Argus*, p. 17. https://trove.nla.gov.au/newspaper/article/34959094?searchTerm=ABC%20POLICY%20DEFENDED%20BY%20CHAIRMAN.%20Listeners%20Do%20Not%20Want%20To%20Be%20Patronised

Whitlam, E. G. (1972, November 13). Australian Federal Election Speeches. Gough Whitlam. Australian Labor Party. *Museum of Democracy Old Parliament House*. Blacktown. https://electionspeeches.moadoph.gov.au/speeches/1972-gough-whitlam

Whitlam, N. (2020, April 25–26). Downfall Not for Reasons He Thinks. *The Australian*. Inquirer, p. 16.

Williamson, D. (2013). *Rupert*. Currency Press. Sydney.

Work, W., & Boileau, D. M. (1985). Television Debates. *Communication Education, 34*(4), 369–375. https://doi.org/10.1080/03634528509378631

Worrall, L. (2000). Surviving Redundancy: The Perceptions of UK Managers. *Journal of Managerial Psychology., 15*(5-6), 460–472.

Worrall, L., Cooper, C. L., & Campbell-Jamison, F. (2000). The Impact of Organizational Change on the Work Experiences and Perceptions of Public Sector Managers. *Personnel Review, 29*(5), 613–636. http://dx.doi.org.www-proxy1.library.unsw.edu.au/10.1108/00483480010296429

Worthington, B., & Snape, J. (2020, March 18). Large Indoor Gatherings Banned, Schools to Stay Open, Scott Morrison Tells Australians Not to Leave the Country in Face of Coronavirus Pandemic. *Australian Broadcasting Corporation.* https://www.abc.net.au/news/2020-03-18/coronavirus-australia-live-updates-covid19-latest-news-anzac-day/12064922

Youmans, W. L., & York, J. C. (2012). Social Media and the Activist Toolkit: User Agreements, Corporate Interests, and the Information Infrastructure of Modern Social Movements. *Journal of Communication, 62*(2), 315–329. https://doi.org/10.1111/j.1460-2466.2012.01636.x

Younger, R. M. (2003). *Keith Murdoch: Founder of a Media Empire.* Harper Collins.

Zaczek, Z. (2020, March 17). 'We had PLENTY of Warning': Infection Expert Unloads on Scott Morrison and His Government for Not Closing Australia's Borders MONTHS Ago to Stop the Spread of the Coronavirus. *The Daily Mail Australia.* https://www.dailymail.co.uk/news/article-8116681/Coronavirus-Bill-Bowtell-unloads-Scott-Morrison-government-COVID-19-response.html

Zaller, J. (1999). *A Theory of Media Politics: How the Interests of Politicians, Journalists, and Citizens Shape the News.* University of Chicago Press.

CHAPTER 6

Political Influences on the ABC: The Loss of the Greater Good

6.1 Organisational Politicking at the ABC

Belief in the essential absence of political interference in the ABC can be summarised in two quotes, separated by context and time. The quotes speak of two key aspects of the institution—its manager and its board. Former World War II Labor Prime Minister, John Curtin said: "The only contact that I have ever had with the ABC is in securing the release of its general manager from the army so that he could carry out the important task of managing the ABC" (The West Australian, 1945)[1]. Here he was speaking of Charles Moses. Then in 2005, former ABC senior broadcaster Kerry O'Brien said: "if you believe in the need for a strong, genuinely independent public broadcaster of integrity then a fundamental part of that process has to be the integrity of the appointment of the board. It has to be free of political influence and seen to be free of political influence" (Simon, 2005).[2]

Institutional theory identified factors at the state or meso level that could influence and shape the activities of political actors working in institutional settings. These actors worked within an organisational setting that was composed of routines, norms, conventions and collections of formal or informal procedures. The political economy shaped the ways in which these routines were evolved in the institutional setting and in turn constrained how the organised interests of actors in that setting could be mobilised (Amenta & Ramsey, 2010).[3] Within the institutional setting, the perspective of the

V. Small, *Strangling Aunty: Perilous Times for the Australian Broadcasting Corporation*,
https://doi.org/10.1007/978-981-16-0776-9_6

actors was located around sets of moral, or cognitive, templates that guided interpretation of events, understanding and action (Hall & Taylor, 1996).[4] This perspective of how events were interpreted and acted upon was explored in the examination of the staff culture in Chap. 3.

In this chapter the focus is around activities and influences within and without public broadcasters, their funding, their business models and the challenge of whether they had to continue to provide comprehensive services or were restricted to specialised areas in digital media. The ABC had always had political influences; its very genesis was political. Its activities also "involve subjective judgements about cultural and social values and are not adequately handled by economic benefit cost analysis" (Brown, 1996).[5] Further, public broadcasters were especially challenged when they were constrained by traditional expectations of broadcasting yet operated in an environment of "pluralism and diversity" (Ariño & Ahlert, 2004).[6] Where once the ABC spoke of looking "to engage not only with small communities of interest but to also bring the nation together around content that will generate critical mass" (Scott, 2010)[7] in the decade since there had been a critical shift in its institutional narrative where the ABC had drifted from the masses to its niche groups and now spoke of "offering personalised services to our diverse audiences" (Anderson, 2020).[8] It was this fundamental and rapid drift which had been critical to new understandings of the role, or "job", of Australia's primary public broadcaster and helped explain the institutional confusion of looking after the greater good of the citizens of Australia, while chasing special interests.

This chapter will take a far broader definition of politics—to mean activities within and around an organisation that prevail upon accretions of power (Amenta & Ramsey, 2010; Hall & Taylor, 1996) and, in this case, those that dictate the situation of the ABC. It will also incorporate the influences of government politics and the realpolitik of having to manage realities and expectations with the pragmatics of funding constraints. Politics (and its good friend 'political influence') are not easy to define (Alexander, 2014).[9] This chapter will explore the concept of "politics" in two ways—firstly in the liberal political theory in which the ABC was grounded and secondly, political influences in a more general sense and how the ABC had managed, organised and re-structured its funding and content changes in human capital. These happened either of its own volition, or under duress. All have impacted upon the production of meaningful, communicative texts in the Australian public sphere.

This book is examining how the ABC has held an élite, privileged institutional *field* in Australian society and how Aunty's voice is being strangled by dual challenges: those from outside and those it places on itself, and examples where it had failed to navigate the tensions between them. To simply examine pressures from political parties into a 'left' and 'right' binaried discussion of "Liberal versus Labor" would narrow and curtail a broader examination of all influences and their consequences on the ABC. A binaried view would also create irrelevance for the theoretical framework of this book when the *field* of the ABC has been nuanced with privilege and more recent pressures of the risky future of public broadcasting in Australia (McGuinness, 2000;[10] Grattan, 2014[11]). Whether the ABC had always been subjected to heavy-handed political influence was contested, anyway. Former ABC Deputy General Manager, Clement Semmler, from 1965 to 1977 who launched the investigative current affairs program Four Corners in 1961, said "the periodic outcries that have gone on down the years about political interference with the ABC amuse me to the point of hilarity" (Semmler, 1981).[12] He said there was always political pressure from both sides, but that good management knew how to keep them "at arm's length" (Ibid.). This signalled that Semmler was mindful of the need for ABC leaders to manage pressures from both within and without the institution. This research had also found that there had been neglect, probably benign, by many governments and certainly a failure to value and protect the ABC. There had also been a failure by its institutional leadership to prepare for the certainty of funding cuts and the drift to digitisation. In addition, there needed to be greater attention paid to the internal and external pressures generally, protect the institution's competitive advantage and demonstrate the agility require to pivot within a digital field (García-Gutiérrez & Martínez-Borreguero, 2016;[13] Orvos, 2019[14]).

Liberal political theory holds that the media enhances the role of democracy, it stems from Enlightenment values of liberty of the individual, freedom of religion, freedom of association, the rule of law and the public's right to know. There is also the argument expressed by former Australian Liberal Senator Cory Bernardi, that:

> The ABC has grown exponentially over the years. And now it's basically encroaching into the newspapers of the 21st century, which is the online space. (Grattan, 2014)[15]

He added that the ABC should not be publicly funded to compete with online commercial media, rather it should be privatised with only television and radio remaining with the ABC as a publicly-supported outfit (Grattan quoting C. Bernardi Ibid.). This is a frequent threat directed at the ABC which all too easily dismisses it as "right-wing attacks" without conducting any public self-analysis; and if the analysis is to be genuine it needs to be with the stakeholders (all taxpaying Australians). Political pressures for the ABC to become more commercially-oriented are part of this concern (Brown & Althaus, 1996),[16] but while the ABC had little choice in the drift to digital media, it also had to reconcile budget constraints. Yet at the same time the shift had failed to transfer the ABC's biggest asset—its strong *cultural capital*. This is the over-riding matter of this book which asks the questions: where did it go? And, why was it not protected? Over-riding all of this, the ABC has to contend with the fact that the concept of "public" was never fully explained in terms of the social role of broadcasting (Scannell, 1997).[17] It is Australian society that will decide how much it values and needs the ABC, the puzzling lack is that it has never formalised its expectations, nor have its successive governments elected to represent them. Governments have used the ABC's independence as an avoidance device, resulting in a form of benign neglect and without providing specific policy feedback. The challenge, now that the ABC is so threatened and weakened by this non-interference and abandonment—is will that discussion ever take place? Or, has the ABC simply been taken for granted? A democracy that yearns to thrive on free and open discussion and information would surely need to examine its oldest national broadcaster if were to re-invest and uphold its future. As Paddy Scannell (1997) pointed out not only broadcasters were confused on the future of public service media, so too were politicians and academics (Scannell Ibid.). Then there is the public.

Australia has a representative democracy. This is guaranteed for all Australians in The Constitution (1901). As part of the role of the mythical, ethereal Fourth Estate in Australia, the media gives voices to the constituents of that democracy and holds power to account. This is exemplified through the reporting of parliament and the courts; and, as an organisation established to provide for all Australians, the ABC is well-provisioned with legal documents and policy that described these requirements. The professional media, especially the ABC, should provide the knowledge and information that the electorate needs to take an informed political opinion to the ballot box. The situation inspired (at least) three questions on political influences on the ABC:

1. If everyone is now accountable to the strident voices on social media and its attendant professional media outfits, such as the ABC, how accountable are these media outfits now to their non-social media audiences and publics (again, what is its institutional definition of public)?

2. Further, if the greater good is a utilitarian view that: "we morally ought to always maximize the aggregate happiness of all" (Kahane et al., 2015),[18] is there still an "all", a single public, or would it be better now described as coalitions of the private? If so, are these private constituents representative of the whole?
3. If the ABC and its fellow media organisations in the emergent commercial digital *field* aim to serve "the public", have they defined their public jointly, or disparately? Do they each serve a different public and forgotten John Doe and Jane Doe? And, by the way—who is J/Doe?
4. Is it unrealistic to expect accountability and broadly representative content from the ABC now it has drifted to the emergent commercial digital *field* that serves niches and notches?

The ethical theory of utilitarianism developed by the philosophers and economists Jeremy Bentham in 1789 and then by John Stuart Mills in 1831 has been described as having "a radically impartial view" (Kahane et al., Ibid.)[19] of providing happiness not only for the instigator but for as many others as possible. The greater good and its attendant 'service' and 'to serve' as the central planks of public service have been analysed earlier in this book but need to be brought forward here to consider political influences on the ABC's public service role and pressures from meddling politicians and sinister commercial operators. This seems like a void argument when the whole concept of the role of 'public' has never been defined, especially its interface with 'broadcasting'.

However, the political influence of social media is never considered. It should be. Activists know it well. Research has found that political influence on social media is "centralized and cliquish" (Choi, 2014) and that they tended to be emotional rather than cognitive, but views expressed in anger held more sway than analysis (Choi, 2014).[20] Research also showed that the use of SNS (social networking services, SNS) increased political participation collectively, but not necessarily political engagement, and endowed users more with psychological empowerment that anything else (Halpern et al., 2017).[21] Other trends showed that people were reliant on their SNS networks for news and information rather than actively sourcing it themselves (Weeks et al., 2017),[22] others were more interested in entertainment than news (Prior, 2009 in Weeks et al., 2017) and yet another cohort were referred to as "prosumers" who were persuasive and influential (Weeks et al., 2017) in gathering support for their preferred issues on SNS. This all had a major impact on individuals' understanding of a civil society (Choi, 2014; Barnidge, 2015) who were now located in an "egocentric public sphere" (Barnidge, Ibid.) [23] in which disagreement is encouraged (Ibid.) selfish-good outweighed greater good, and self-referential insularity had created a lack of diversity. The research literature also said that there was a higher degree of trust in news from media organisations (Web 1.0) rather than on SNS (Web 2.0), thereby challenging whether social media is a valid and accurate measure of the public sphere and public opinion (Ceron, 2015),[24] as it seemed to now be regarded.

Controversial Conservative British and passionately anti-public ownership politician, Enoch Powell, once said politicians who complained about the media were like sailors who complained about the sea (Soley, 2005).[25] There was similar symbiosis, discomfiture and inescapability for politicians in relation to media activities—and the ABC. The role of the ABC as a political actor was described by ABC former Managing Director, Geoffrey Whitehead, as having "highly-politicised ways" (Whitehead, 1988)[26] . Concerns also centred on whether the ABC's liberty to "do its own thing" could continue to be indulged by its paymaster—the state and accompanying taxpayers (Berg & Davidson, 2018).[27] The piper called the tune but Aunty, led by staff culture, danced to a different tune—the impact of which was analysed in Chap. 3.

The ABC faced the dangerous peril of loss of independence and Aunty's voice if funding were to be withdrawn and privatisation put on the table as actionable. The concerning aspect of this was multivarious. The reality of this eventuality may be that Aunty's protectors would panic, but the citizens of Australia, who had been trained to find free news, information and opinion online anywhere, might not be so protective. In a world where strident voices on social media are shouting for, and gaining, attention, where social media sponsors a proliferation of commentators and "Dr Google" advice has ascendancy and has been granted credibility, will Aunty's voice be resonant enough to compete, to cope, to survive? Will the public care to defend the ABC when it no longer "sees" itself in ABC content, not in the superficial terms of identity, but in terms of policy analysis, relevant, general issues and nuanced debate on Australia's place in the world—'all for all'?

Pope Francis described the current state of affairs in Western society as an "incivility of clash" (Spadaro, 2020). He said we live in a world where there is a "dictatorship of relativism" and there is no good or evil because "the empire of God is not given to this world" and therefore "no one is the evil one" (Ibid.).[28] It becomes a challenge for Aunty to cope where her authority has also been relativised and is no longer valued as the ultimate, representative, legitimate media brand in the Australian public sphere. For example, where education is a cornerstone of the development of a society and economy, the ABC once segued with formal school education in providing and supplementing this to Australians. The ABC once ruled the media in children's education with "little competition as an originator and broadcaster of distinctive children's programming" (Rutherford & Brown, 2013).[29]

Commercial media has never controlled, manifestly, the élite media *field* and now that media is merging knowledge and facts for opinions, insinuating knowledge and feelings melded with other major online enterprises—they are actually being priced out of the emergent commercial digital market. This then would give rise to the need for a stronger role than ever for a public broadcaster to provide and re-describe the public sphere with clear and reputably sourced information and for Aunty to educate multicultural, multi-faith, multi-identity Australia as to who it is. In this scenario, Aunty's task had barely begun. The ABC used to answer the call to tell Australians who they were. That challenge has collapsed into what are referred to as the "culture wars" where Australians were at loggerheads, social media encouraged calls for violence and harm, rejection of laws, humiliation, vilification and name-calling. It would seem that never before has there been a greater need for a public broadcaster to unify by seeking informed, dignified, general consensus—and inspire mutually beneficial change.

The model of the ABC—the BBC—had prided itself with its fierce independence from government. Its first Chairman, Lord Reith said famously asserted this in response to British Government criticism of the BBC: "We're doing this thing, not you" (Blain, 1977).[30] Graham Perkin, former Editor of *The Age* in Melbourne, was quoted by former ABC staff member Ellis Blain (1977)[31] as having said in 1975 that:

> The important thing for a journalist is to be aware of his own bias and to counter it in his professional activity. It is part of his training. (Blain, 1977)

The ABC journalist had a serious role in asserting the political neutrality of the organisation by separating himself/herself/themself from personal bias or personal causes to uphold the probity of the information they distributed, as a duty to public service. This had a 'halo' effect of upholding the accountability of all institutions and actors, enhancing public service and amplifying the greater good.

In 2019 the former Royal Commissioner, Kenneth Hayne, made the first speech since the handing down of his findings into the Royal Commission into Misconduct in the Banking, Superannuation and Financial Services Industry. In this speech in July (2019) at the University of

Melbourne Law School he was scathing of political institutions for being beholden to vested interests, sloganizing their policies and therefore responsible for a fall in public trust in them (Bagshaw, 2019).[32] Justice Hayne, a professorial fellow at the school and former High Court Judge, also pointed out that the increasing calls for royal commissions in Australia were linked, in showing institutions were not working for the public, as tasked: "We need to grapple closely with what these calls are telling us about the state of our democratic institutions, … Trust in all sorts of institutions, governmental and private, have been damaged or destroyed" (Bagshaw, Ibid.).

Justice Hayne also pointed out in his address that one of the causes of this was "political, and other commentary, focuses on what divides us rather than what unites us" (Loc. Cit.). In 1979, former ABC Board member (called a commissioner then) Richard Harding presaged the current political influences on the ABC, as well as reflecting on those of his time: "the democrat encourages independent broadcasting, without interference, and his support should not waver if some of the values thereby expressed are antipathetic to his own" (Harding, 1979).[33] He cautioned: "Policy ideas seem often to be framed for only partisan or sectional advantage with little articulation of how or why their implementation would contribute to the ***greater good*** (this author's italics)" (Harding Ibid.).

Allied with this has been a manifest public surge in scepticism in both institutions and leaders. Chancellor of Western Sydney University, Peter Shergold (2017), expressed it as:

> Today I witness the structures of representative and responsible government assailed from all sides. Across the Westminster countries and beyond, I perceive declining trust both in democratic institutions and political leadership; a relentless 24-7 social media that undermines respectful political discourse; the emergence of celebrity-driven populism that seeks to persuade the public that there are simple answers to the wickedly complex problems of public policy to which there are no definitive solutions; and the beguiling appeal of authoritarian ideologies that challenge the tenets of secular liberal democracy and take psychopathic form in religious fundamentalism, fanatical terrorism and bloody warfare. (Ibid.)[34]

All public institutions, and their leaders, should have the guiding light as "the public good". It existed to counteract the selfish, narrow interests of privately-owned business, the profit motive of investors and shareholders and the manifest ideologies that seek to isolate individuals and deprecate others in hierarchies of worthiness. The ideal of the public good draws all together as equals in the Commonwealth of Australia. Public service entities, therefore, were tasked with the challenge of belonging to *field* that opposed self-interest and self-promotion. It could be argued that the Commonwealth of Australia was formed in promotion of this public good, so that all shared in the common wealth of Australia, (notwithstanding the dispersed and separate state-based education systems, public health systems and their public hospitals).

Since Federation governments and legislators have tried to grow that shared identity and shared equality—chiefly through economic means but also in important symbolic ways. However, this has been tested by a loss of appetite for public institutions. In addition, they all scrambled for relevance, compromised by funding cuts, funding conditions, accusations of irrelevance; and, opinions that private enterprise managed money better (although the Hayne banking royal commission found differently on that point). This is an ongoing debate in society and a focal point of election campaigns in Australia—what money will be promised to new public services and what will be re-allocated. The ABC forms part of this political decision-making and in the jostling for money with the others. Managerialism[35] has been criticised as having political motivations in Ireland's public service (Lynch et al., 2012)[36] and an ideology and practice that "in the public sector, will deliver more with less, and in the private sector, will ensure competitiveness in the global market-place" (Pollitt, 2016).[37]

As a public institution, the ABC has tried to adapt to changing circumstances through its regularly traumatised independence, and since the 1980s the advent of managerialism. In this process it had also been accused of irrelevance and bias, and debates about its partiality were sometimes underscored by criticisms from the Federal Government. Even only five years after ABC Radio was launched a Queensland newspaper pointed out: "A.B.C. attacked. CRUEL, COWARDLY BIAS" was a shouted headline in *The Cairns Post* (The Cairns Post, 1937).[38] In 2014, the then Prime Minister, Tony Abbott, said the ABC was "unpatriotic" over its coverage of Edward Snowden's intelligence leaks and asylum-seeker abuse allegations. Without qualifying who the "lot of people" were that he referred to he said: "A lot of people feel at the moment that the ABC instinctively takes everyone's side but Australia's" (Bourke, 2014). In 2016, Gavin Morris, the ABC's then Director of News said:

> I think the point where politicians or corporations or the powerful stop calling the ABC biased is the point where we're not probably doing our job. They call it bias but I call it independence. It's the job we were put here to do. (Quinn, 2016)[39]

This is another example over differences between government and the ABC over exactly what constitutes *independence*—ranging from firstly, benign neglect as described earlier or, secondly, defined in terms of its opposite—direct meddling. This thesis/antithesis approach was no longer serving the institution and there needed to be a middle ground where governments actively support the ABC—help the institution to help itself. However, a third way to create relevance (longevity) seems to have been developed by the ABC which had defined independence as—to put it crudely—upsetting people. There was a need for an adequate interpretation of the principles which underly the philosophy of independence from government. Further, the ABC was wholly dependent on both the government and the people. As an example of the pressures on this fine line of independence, the ABC had been subject to frequent editorial reviews. The seventh was in 2014 on ABC Radio Current Affairs' coverage of the Australia China Free Trade Agreement found that: "the coverage provided by the programs was both fair and impartial and that the key protagonists on both sides of the labour market debate were well-represented across the four-month period" (Cavanagh, 2015).[40] The nature of cultivating audiences, enculturating them and giving them the *cultural capital* to understand the ABC's independence also infiltrated the many quality assurance reports and editorial reviews that had taken place (notably Mansfield, 1997;[41] Committee of Review of the ABC, 1981[42]). The socalled Dix Inquiry (Committee of Review of the ABC, 1981) brought about the ABC's Charter and Corporatisation, while the Mansfield Inquiry recommended outsourcing television production, ending overseas broadcasting and accelerating conversion to digital, all of which were largely accomplished.

In 1976, the then Federal Leader of the Opposition, Gough Whitlam (his government had been dismissed 11 November 1975), told a lunchtime protest outside Parliament House in Canberra against the introduction of community broadcasting (*The Canberra Times*, 1976)[43] that only the ABC provided the public with "comprehensive and fearless discussions" and that the Liberal Government lead by former Prime Minister Malcolm Fraser "wanted to replace these with the pop and pap of commercial broadcasting and television". The newspaper report said "about four busloads" of protesters were at the meeting, most of whom were ABC staff who had travelled from Sydney. The protest was against legislation before Parliament that was considered would interfere with the independence of the ABC. The *Act to amend the Broadcasting and Television Act 1942–1975* was passed but subsequently repealed in 2015. Its aim was "to allow the permanent licensing of stations, and guidelines were issued which referred to three types of licences—educational, special interest and community" (Jolly, 2014),[44] in other words to support the development of community broadcasting (Ibid.).[45] In 1941, responding to government criticism and changes to the broadcaster the commission said: "The commission had always stressed the point that discussion of controversial subjects, provided the varying points of view were put by authoritative speakers, was a stimulus to thought and an essential and valuable element in democratic communities" (*The Newcastle Morning Herald and Miners' Advocate*, 1941).[46]

It is not unusual for ABC management to speak to the public through other media. In 1948 the then Chairman of the Australian Broadcasting Commission, Richard Boyer, said in a letter to the editor of *The Sydney Morning Herald* (1948):[47]

> It is not only our duty, but also a point of honour for the commission and all our staff to serve all sections of the community, of whatever shade of political opinion, with scrupulous fairness, and within the limits of human frailty this has been achieved.
>
> If ever the national service became a direct instrument of Government, it should, in my opinion, be abolished; but while it serves the whole community impartially as a clearing ground for our controversies and a centre of national unity, it should have the support of, all interests. (Ibid.)[48]

In contrast with the 2016 bias accusation, in 1936, it was accused of "becoming haughty and BBC".[49]

How has it strayed from this noble path? Originally, according to Commissioner James Kitto the broadcaster's aim was "to foster and build-up a national spirit" (*The Telegraph*, 1936).[50] Although specifically addressing concerns about ABC public concerts, the intention and context of the statement also described the broadcaster's wider view of its role in the Commonwealth. The BBC (role model's) motto was from The Bible: "nation shall speak peace unto nation" (Micah 4:3):[51] "nation shall not lift up a sword against nation, neither shall they learn war anymore". The preceding clause is perhaps better known: "and they shall beat their swords into ploughshares, and their spears into pruninghooks" (Ibid.).[52] Many stories of The Bible spoke to inspire tribes of people to collaborate instead of wage war, and this became the original mission of the BBC. Born (2005)[53] said the BBC was formed on the basis that the airwaves were also

Image 6.1 Dame Enid Lyons, federal politician and ABC board member 1951–1962. Photographer: Athol Smith, F.R.P.S Melbourne. 1950. Courtesy of the National Archives of Australia. ABC publicity photos. Item 3062, series SP1011/1. Item ID 5410755. Sydney

public property. She said that there had been a "distaste" for American commercial broadcasting and the BBC was devised to bring the British people together, develop a genuine public opinion and support an "inclusive, participatory and enlightened democracy" (Born, 2005).[54] Born (2005) said there were three central measures for the BBC: Universality of access, universality culturally and socially with national and regional programs and universality of genre (Ibid.). Yet universalities are now under threat: the ABC, Australia's SBS, the BBC, The Canadian Broadcasting Corporation, with an apparent deterioration of their utility for 'the greater good'. Historically, the ABC had paid attention to its public role and public good in wanting to provide impartial news and information. More importantly, it had a founding vision of supporting Australian culture, institutions and interests (Image 6.1). Accusations of political interference at the ABC have had a long history. In the appointment of Dame Enid Lyons (widow of Australian Conservative Prime Minister Joseph Lyons who launched the ABC) to the ABC Board in 1951 the then Deputy (Labor) Opposition Leader, Arthur Calwell, said it was "clearly a case of political patronage" (The Canberra Times, 1951) by the Liberal Government. Board "stacking" concerns had occurred from time to time and discussed elsewhere in this book. When a University of Melbourne professor criticised the ABC news service for deteriorating standards of English, Dame Enid did not defend it. She replied: "English has slipped so badly that it is almost impossible to get a well-written letter unless it is from a literary person… we should see that our work is without spot, or blemish" (The Sydney Morning Herald, 1953) (see Image 6.1). Dame Enid explained how she was animated as both a politician and (later) ABC board member on the importance of public service—but aimed for the good of the people. She said in her 1943 maiden speech to parliament (House of Representatives): "The foundation of a nation's greatness is in the homes of its people" (Lyons, 1943). She was quoting the late King George V.

6.2 A Changing Australian Society, the Decline of ABC Privilege—And Change Confusion

In order to analyse the political influences on the ABC they had to be placed in the context of changed Australian societal values and dispositions since the institution's launch and the ebbs and flows of values and processes on all institutions over time. There were similarities between then and now. 1932 was the time of the worst of The Great Depression when Australian unemployment was high—said to be 30%, but this was unreliable to compare with today because of the vast changes in data collection and definitions of unemployment (Gruen & Clark, 2010).[55] Australia's novel Coronavirus pandemic in 2020 saw unemployment rise to 6.2% in April 2020 (in March 2019 it was 5.2%)[56] and compared with levels similar in September 2015. There were massive job losses, but the figure only reflected the numbers registering for unemployment benefits and looking for work. In other ways Australia was a different place since 1932.

Liberal educations were changed vastly. Liberal education, as separate from professional and industrial education, began in Ancient Greece (Dewey, 1916).[57] The aim was to educate individuals of the free and élite social class of Ancient Greece who would become the leaders, compared with the unfree others who were wanted for manual labour and belonged to the group that would be expected to make the lower order contributions to the society (Ibid.). Liberal education aims to develop the whole person in a manner where they have a set of capabilities to deal with the range of demands placed upon them by competing political entities in society and a concern for the legitimation of conditions for supporting democracy (Levinson, 1999).[58]

Today the pursuit of liberal education has undergone a revolution in tertiary institutions which now incorporated neo-Marxist ideology as part of the liberal arts university curriculum. This ideology aimed to expose hidden capitalist power imbalances and structures that were said to have created and perpetuated inequities and inequalities in society between groups and between individuals. This unequal distribution of power in Western societies was said to be based on gender, sexuality, whiteness, culture, élitism, privilege and ethnicity. This was explained as intersectionality. It was said to be depicted in the media where there were "discrepancies between the liberal values of freedom and equality that leaders proclaimed and the unjust concentrations and abuses of power that made those values a myth" (Griffin, 2006).[59] In this framework, it was therefore extrapolated that inequities and inequalities were not just expressed but maintained through communication practices—and the media in particular. This belief had led to a range of changes in legislation, government policies, the overhaul of human resources departments as well as in community and individual behaviours. Josef Stalin said writers were "engineers of the human soul"[60] and referencing this Chinese President Xi Jinping described the power, privilege and efficacy of teachers using the same metaphor (Hongjie & Jacob, 2017).[61] Both leaders invested belief in the power of the writer (and their teacher) to manage change, presumably on their behalf. Such was the understood influence of the teacher in Cambodia/Kampuchea that Pol Pot (1975–1979) eradicated as many teachers and university lecturers as possible (Khlock, 2003).

The impact of intersectionality in analysing Western society and its institutions had resulted in analysing that male power was couched in terms of the pejoratives "white male privilege", "toxic masculinity" and "privileged old white men"; which all implied misogyny, homophobia and malignance. The noun "privilege" had been re-versioned from what the ABC once embraced as part of its *cultural capital* into a deprecating term to mean "unworthy and malicious". This book challenges that in terms of the ABC which institutionally has a right to describe itself as privileged—privileged with the task of furthering the common good. This compares with its dictionary definition: "special right or advantage, to grant a special favour" (Australian Contemporary Dictionary, 1970[62]) and "an opportunity to do something special or enjoyable" (Cambridge English Dictionary)[63] to the later usage of "the existence of economic and social privileges associated with rank or status; the fact of there being such privileges within a society" (Oxford English Dictionary).[64] The popular phrase "white male privilege" describes any man, or woman, or person, with an identified advantage believed to have been obtained to the unquantified, detriment and disadvantage of others. The word's morphology has evolved to "attaining something not deserved by abusive, bad people". The ABC was always privileged for the good of the people.

The changed meaning of the word bears consideration in the context of this book because the ABC began in a privileged *field*. It started as a "white boys club" and was redolent with men—"white male privilege"—even, "old white male privilege"—yet, with one consistent female board member. The fact that the ABC was so highly valued and defended by a completely disparate range of groups and tribes and people in Australian society, many with a more radical bias, is a strange, almost bizarre inconsistency, but analytically important counterpoint to arguments that describe the destructive consequences of all male leadership as "toxic masculinity". The ABC is an outstanding, treasured exception to the assertion that all male leadership is toxic and going forward the institution needed to embrace that and discern the benefits and privilege it accrued from that. The consequences of its almost exclusive white male origins, its focus on upholding privilege to benefit all Australians, actually advanced Australia's liberal democracy and identity for close to 90 years. The ultimate ideological conundrum for Australia is that the privileged, élite ABC is valued by a diverse cohort of Australians of all backgrounds, ideologies and genders—and, moreover, these are the same ABC activists who lobby for its survival, yet condemn 'white male privilege' from whence the ABC originated.

The original leaders of the ABC had a very different usage of the now pejorative 'privilege'. In 1938, the broadcaster was proud to consider itself 'privileged'—it defined it in terms of 'having ideals'. For example, ABC board member James Kitto, who was also a representative of the Postmaster-General's Department which controlled the ABC, released a statement to the press defending the ABC's ideals amidst accusations that its content of classical musical and erudite lectures was too élitist:

> Man does not live by bread alone, and even a Commission which caters for the entertainment of the multitude must be allowed the privilege of having ideals, even if—as happens with the best of us—they do not always work out in 'practice'.[65]

In a very separate definition of 'privilege' in 1946, Liberal Prime Minister, Robert Menzies told the ABC if it were to broadcast parliamentary proceedings (which it did subsequently) it would give the ABC "a privilege which went far beyond any now enjoyed by those newspapers reporting Parliament. Newspaper reports were only partially privileged" (*Daily Mercury*, 1946).[66] Granted, Menzies was referring to parliamentary *legal* privilege as an immunity under law where matters can be debated freely without threat or interference from the law. However, it is linked to the privilege of freedom of speech—another privilege. The media can report parliament because of 'qualified privilege' provided the content is not used in a malicious context (this would then be abuse and violation of 'privilege'). Allied with this, the 'privilege' for journalists in court reporting was that they would not be sued for reporting defamatory remarks made in the courtroom, as long as it was balanced and accurate reporting. This privilege belonged to the tradition of open courts, although a trial could be held in camera—meaning there was no media present (or if they were there, they could not report it).

Then in another meaning of 'privilege' on a completely different level again, in 1953 ABC staff were reported to have lost a 'privilege' with a charge of one shilling a week imposed on morning and afternoon teas that had been previously provided free by the organisation (*The West Australian*, 1953).[67] By the 1980s that privilege had been restored and Tea Ladies had been re-employed. They served hot tea from a voluminous catering-size tea pot, instant coffee and assorted biscuits (and Chelsea buns for someone's birthday) to very grateful, distracted staff at their desks every morning at the ABC's news offices in Kings Cross, Sydney. These women also dispensed emotional labour through their constancy and reassurance in what was a usually highly-stressed finite, deadline-bounded environment. The 'privilege' of their presence was later taken away—again, to save money. So, 'privilege' has the meaning of being a benefit—possibly a highly valued one and not taken for granted (such as the former ABC Tea Ladies)—but one that could be withdrawn as a punishment or, in this instance, to save money. Inmates of correctional facilities, too, experience these types of 'privileges' and understand their loss or denial.

Therefore, the evolved use of the word 'privilege', as an undeserved and unjust advantage, clouds society's judgement on political motives on one level, as well as legal, academic and intellectual achievements, and even the role and ideology of the ABC as an élite, privileged institution in Australian public life. Inversions of the word privilege as a form of insult have created demoralisation, guilt, anger and fear in society, accentuated by social media. Most specifically, it has forced the ABC to turn its back on its founding principles. Where is privileged Aunty to turn when privilege is a bad thing? For example, the ABC published an opinion piece on its News website headed: "ATARs measure privilege, not academic merit, and it starts in kindergarten"[68] (Schultz, 2019). The article stated:

> The fact is that ATARs measure privilege, not academic merit, and it starts in kindergarten. What we believe we can conclude from an ATAR is flawed as our society drifts further away from egalitarianism. (Ibid.)[69]

Of most importance to the ABC's founding argument is that privilege could be viewed as a form of egalitarianism in providing opportunities for creating and enlarging the greater good, just as the ABC was privileged in 1932. It took hold of this privilege to create a unique and treasured national institution. The ABC sprang from privilege, not abuse of power, yet this is no longer recognised and appreciated because privilege had become a form of self-loathing. Aunty was beside herself on this point. In 2017 social scientist Hugh Mackay observed that Australia was headed: "in the direction of becoming a more fragmented, more individualistic, more competitive, more aggressive, less co-operative and therefore more anxious society" (Mackay, 2017).[70] He said:

> The IT revolution that has led us to confuse data transmission with communication, altered our perceptions of privacy and identity, and—above all—made it easier than ever to remain apart from each other. (Mackay, Ibid.)

Mackay (2017) also warned that there were great pressures on the stability and cohesion of society and that: "unless we resist it, the pressure will steadily increase the risk of fragmentation and social isolation" (Mackay Loc. Cit.). He described a growing emphasis on "what's in it for me?" coupled with a loss of community and compassion, and an abandonment of civic responsibility. Humans are social creatures and it is in human nature to cooperate, rather than attack each other. Mackay (2017) said, once people started attacking each other violently, the whole society suffered because of the prioritised belief that because they had been treated badly they were justified to enact revenge, yet: "revenge is a way of bringing us both down to the same level of bad behaviour" (Ibid.). Mackay (2017) echoed this belief in describing a "culture of compassion" in his Australia Day address two years later: "I regard compassion as the only truly rational response to an understanding of what it means to be human" (Mackay, 2019).[71]

The ABC acted out its *cultural capital* of Australian society in a privileged social space through such things as its participatory programs and online engagement where it relied on the 'taste' (Bourdieu, 1984) [72] of its educated audience. It had been tasked to talk to its imagined stable and cohesive society.[73] This research argues that the ABC passed on its "code" through programming that began from pre-school years (with Play School) through to Triple J (Australian youth radio) and other programs that retained the demographic as it aged. Even the re-launch of the radio station Double J (once an AM station) in 2014 attracted a community wanting to re-live its mis-spent youth through retro music[74]. The ABC had been an organisation that educated and inculcated generations of Australians' with its communication content and mode. It had also pre-empted these needs through its content innovation coupled with a respect for nationhood.[75]

6.3 Bias? Or, Whose Bias?

This book situates the ABC in a rapidly changing world and analyses how a public institution had met and responded to the trials and eruptions of what managers claimed with confidence to be "digital disruption". This book argued that the phrase is an understatement and in poor Aunty's case it is more "digital disorder", "digital disorientation" and "digital derangement". This is because of the vast changes to social narratives, cultural expectations, devaluing or replacing values, and new existential threats that challenged beliefs and institutions. Australian society had held faith with its key institutions: the ABC, the rule of law and ethics, governments, the rest of the public service, governments and (once) churches on which it had been built. The ABC had been one of the institutional struts of the functioning democracy; a system which relied on all institutions referencing each other to safeguard the interests of its citizens. As part of this process the ABC had a uniquely designated institutional role to educate, inform and entertain. It is not so long ago that the printed newspaper in nineteenth-century Australia was once a daily, central, manifest ritual and form of information, then in the twentieth century ABC radio news bulletins (and commercial bulletins) followed. In the twenty-first century, however, the impact of digital communications and the internet had reconceived news as information that was malleable and interpretable. Individual, online contributions to the news were as meaningful (perhaps more so) than that of institutional actors. But research into BBC content, for example, already found that outsourced content had lead to a decline in quality because "consumer sovereignty" had displaced the "producer elite" (Deakin et al., 2009). All the institutions had been dislodged, including the ABC. There was no longer one respected source for anything in particular and all institutions had been challenged to prove themselves constantly, even those operating under the rule of law, public accountability and received ethical expectations. Shergold (2017) said the internet: "an invention founded on a libertarian ethos is now a vehicle for conveying "alternative facts" and fear in real time" (Shergold, Ibid.).[76]

The ABC, subjected to this ideological, information warfare, had been accused of partiality and offensive content by trying to keep up and be 'liked' in its new commercial *field*. In addition, to regular complaints over the decades that political parties have "stacked" the ABC board (Seccombe, 2018),[77] there were other claims that it had ill-advisedly used public money on content that was of partisan interests rather than those of general public concern. Rural Australians, in particular, had felt under-represented with the decline in reporting on issues pertinent to them and the diminution of staff placements and offices in regional areas meaning Aunty could not cover issues which had national consequence, such as droughts, crop yields, herding, agricultural exports and emerging markets, floods, bushfires, domestic violence and rural mental health (Echo Net Daily, 2020).[78] Australians who worked in the mining (and related industries), another substantial Australian exporter and employer, had also felt relegated to enemy territory, and worse, irrelevance when many country towns had large populations of mine workers and ancillary industries. A key finding of a Commonwealth Scientific and Industrial Research Organisation (CSIRO) (2017) was that citizens regarded mining as: "central to Australia and contributing substantially to Australia's economy and standard of living" (CSIRO, 2017).

Outsourcing of some ABC television production had given rise to allegations of bias and these were tricky for the ABC to defend, contain or source. The outsourcing of all ABC outside broadcasts was likely which included coverage of "Anzac Day, New Year's Eve, election days and sports events" (Wilson, 2021). Outsourcing of content had been underway for at least a decade. No longer was Aunty able to afford to keep her watchful eye on proceedings. In the big picture of all content, Aunty was challenged as to whether she had opened herself to more bias allegations—or, was merely reflecting reality and "providing alternative understandings" (O'Donnell, 2018). All the while academics had pointed to a poor definition of bias, anyway, that was "more likely to remain a political weapon, than a tool for understanding how the media shapes our experience of crucial events" (Lukin, 2006). Putting that dilemma to one side, accusations of partiality, stem from a variety of matters in dealing with reduced funding and digital media. Aunty had transformed herself into a public service media organisation embracing user-created content, found to be cheap and readily available. There was the novel belief that the audience preferred the sound of its own voice, instead of Aunty's antiquated utterances. The troubling side to this shift towards social media voices, aside from the ABC's loss of long-held institutional authority, was described in the psychology research where it was understood social media fed narcissism and prevented the individual engaging in a negative assessment of themselves and their views by creating a buffer of curated content (Andreassen et al., 2017).[79] The connection between news and social media was that social media "has become ubiquitous over the last several years" (Singh et al., 2018)[80] and it was now integrated through hyperlinks with news media (Fu & Shumate, 2017).[81]

The ultimate irony of the role of the professional journalist was that having a personally enhanced social media account yielded background knowledge for the journalist, media businesses, tracking audiences and on-selling them to marketers; but, resulted in accusations of bias. The ABC's drift to the social media space detracted from its distinctiveness and impartiality when it lost its own voice to speak and analyse for the benefit of the greater good. The ABC's new focus on audience-provided/driven content had brought claims that it was too responsive to individuals and online activism (Minear & Adams, 2017),[82] where the main issues could be overwhelmed by unknown segments of the ABC audience who, as an unfiltered cohort, could skew the professional judgement of presenters and content makers. Social media leaders, such as the ABC, showed readiness to accept the views of social media followers but might actually mean their institutional "search for one 'true self' leads to identity conflict and feelings of insecurity" (Gilani et al.. 2020) and permitted audiences to constantly reshape the institution's identity. Gilani et al. (2020) cautioned: "social media has arguably been used as a means of manipulating voting behavior in various national elections and supplying so-called 'fake news'" (Ibid.). One instance where Aunty out-sourced her practice to social media followers and followed their advice was the changing of the playing of Triple J's Hottest 100 from Australia Day[83] on 26 January to 25 and 27 January because the ABC youth station had been: "heavily involved in the growing dialogue around Indigenous recognition and perspectives on 26 January" (Donoughue, 2017),[84] and because Australia Day events "celebrate genocide" (Donoughue Ibid.). The focus of conflict here was that Australia Day marked the landing of the First Fleet in Sydney Cove in 1788 and seen as an historical event, where the opposite view saw the day as the beginning of unending damage. Philosopher Michel Foucault (1976) said there was no separation of history from the present because there was a continuity such that the past continued to influence the present: "...it has to take account of the fact that discourse has not only a meaning or a truth, but a history, and a specific history that does not refer it back to the laws of an alien development" (Ibid., p. 127). The ABC was relying on postmodernist thinking to re-define an historical event. This redefinition was of cultural interest but contestable and was not situated by the ABC within a broader analysis or understanding. The ABC defended the day-change on the basis of an online survey which said: "your comments will be used by triple j to help shape our decision, alongside the perspectives and learnings from other stakeholders we have spoken to" (ABC, 2017), and this was an example of the impact of an unfiltered, social media audience driving ABC broadcasting practice. However, the point to be made here is that the ABC had the tools (including archived content) and institutional maturity to assess the complexities of the matter and construct a path of mutual understanding, rather than resort to lazy thinking that jumped to a mutually-exclusive "only one or other" response.[85] Educating Australians on the underlying issues that backgrounded this contentious day—racism, the imbalance of power and historical trauma—could have been immense towards creating a better, more enlightened, 'all for all' Australia.

The vexed question of bias and even more pressing: whose bias? through the changing and morphing of facts passed around digital media all called into question how professional journalists were faring in managing political pressures from this (often anonymous) digital disorder. In terms of ethics, the Roy Morgan Survey of the Professions for 2017 found that only 20% of Australians thought newspaper journalists were "high" or "very high" for ethics. The respondents said 17% for television presenters had "high" or "very high" ethics and talkback radio announcers were 14%. Separate research—the *ABC Talks* survey—that found of the respondents split into party affiliations with 54% answering "somewhat" or "a lot" to the question: "How much do you trust each of the following?" (Hanrahan, 2019):[86] Liberal National Party voters trusted journalists "somewhat" or "a lot" 42%, while Australian Labor Party voters trusted journalists "somewhat" or "a lot" 67%, while all participants trusted 54%. By way of comparison doctors and nurses had 98% trust while celebrities were at the bottom of the trust scale. The digitisation of news and content meant that everything was monetised and valued in the digital space. The activity of the ABC amongst this cohort and how it was dealing with its (new) mobile audiences was of special interest to this research and will be developed in the next section.

6.4 The Wild Goose Chase: Online Media and Audience Politics

The discussion now considers further what had happened to the public broadcaster in a media industry that was digitised, monetised, firewalled and platformed. This section will identify the outside political actors in the external economy who are not just politicians, but the digital companies such as Google, which mobilise political pressures from disparate constitutions through the filtering of information. The ABC now used Google as well as the services of citizen journalists who conveyed additional pressures to the way information was created and presented. In the pressure to streamline operations the ABC had been able to segue content from one platform to another which had obtained efficiencies, for example in having one reporter to cover one news event for all relevant ABC content seekers and platforms was a great achievement in cutting costs. Once posted, content became subjected to data supplied from the audience on pay per clicks, hits, conversion rates and moved up the ranking algorithm in an environment of abundance it achieved greater prominence. Google had championed this form of information sharing and marketing and the ABC was now part of this. This was not sinister in and of itself, but it did raise complications (at best) for a *public service* media outfit. Proposed changes in legislation mean that Google and Facebook would have to pay the ABC for content, and the government had said it may be allowed to keep the revenue. The institution said it would spend it on coverage of regional and rural Australia "telling local stories and celebrating unique Australian stories" (Meade & AAP, 2020).[87]

Once there was a scarcity on the airwaves in the broadcasting spectrum and a 1927 royal commission had shown that rural Australians were poorly served by the then Class A and Class B radio licence holders, both sides of politics agreed there was a need for a national service in what "may well have been the only occasion on which political opponents found themselves in accord about the ABC" (Blain, 1977).[88] Hence, the ABC as a service to all Australians was launched, although hamstrung for the first 25 years with no technical services because these were supplied by the Postmaster-General's Department who had an underwhelmingly short time horizon for the ABC always referring to it with "the clear inference that the ABC could be expected to be superseded at any time" (Blain, 1977).[89] Ellis Blain, a former ABC staff member explained humorously: "the menace of a ham-fisted ex-telephone linesman taking control of the mixing during a play or symphony concert was an ever-present hazard" (Blain, Ibid.).[90]

Now, communication is facilitated by satellites, cables and advanced technologies. Where once public service media could remain aloof from the concerns of commercial media, it had drifted into utterly close proximity and over-lapping activities. PSM outfits now had to find their way in market-driven economies where media policy was influenced by overarching commercial considerations, efficiencies and monetised content. The pressures to operate on a more commercial level had been weighing on the broadcaster for a long time; and at least since the 1980s. As former Managing Director Mark Scott said in an address to the National Press Club in 2016 the ABC had: "been in the business of finding efficiencies for many years" (Scott, 2016).[91] Public service broadcasters' exclusive days are over in an "information blitz" (Cushion, 2012);[92] even their nomenclatures including the word "broadcasting" (ABC, BBC) are now redundant and where 'Media' is apt.

The ABC's active engagement with its audiences on social media lends itself to more intimate engagement with individuals (and presumed) ABC audience members. It was a new environment introduced during the management of Mark Scott (2006–2016) where staff were "dedicating themselves to bringing Australian stories to Australians everywhere" (Scott, Ibid.).[93] Where once broadcasters were told that while they were speaking to a multitude and needed to counteract the motivation to give a public address on radio by counter-intuitively imagining one other person, now, journalists literally do engage with that one other person, who has a meme profile photo yet possibly conceals themselves behind a fictitious name. In addition, it may be a bot to which they communicate, so they could enter into part of a dangerous exchange with algorithms. This happens in the context of a crowd of innumerable voyeurs watching on. That special intimacy, although still present in radio, had been changed dramatically with this pseudo-personal engagement of online that seeks approval and supports the individual.

Live streaming from radio studios means radio had become another visual, theatrical performance space where imagination was no longer required because the broadcaster could be filmed during the program. Strangely, perhaps it is a marvel of the magic of radio that the intimacy of the "one listener" relationship had sustained radio as a valued linear medium, in spite of this new "intimacy" through social media. The re-packaging of radio, augmented by online engagement, has not only re-shaped the communication and delivery of the information, it has impacted on the quality of information and communications in a world where media is consumed "in my time, not yours", "whenever I want" and "for as long as I want". Editors no longer arbitrate immediacy and relevance; the audience has that power. The "top of the clock" deadline is now for reference only.

The added conundrum with meeting these small, individualised, personalised, niche audience needs is that it is precarious, even dangerous, to extrapolate on the whole. The assumed public of social media does not actually represent the public at large. Further, the presumed egalitarianism of social media has actually compromised and curtailed democracies (Sunstein, 2018;[94] Ceron & Memoli, 2016[95]), where all voices were supposed to be equally platformed and regarded, but in truth that was not the case. The concept of egalitarianism and universal access of online media was compromised in that not everyone used social media, not everyone used apps, not everyone was online at all times all day and all night engaged continuously. Of importance to this analysis it means the audience was no longer wedded or tied to ABC content, as of days of old. The notion of the public broadcast had been upended and heavily contested because digitisation carried an in-built assumption that increasing connections always had positive results and the more, the better for the individual. This also applies to the collection and pursuit of followers on social media regarded as a new measure of relevance, endorsement, support and engagement (with content), yet the challenge and downside is that in a leader-follower relationship, the power is actually shifted to the follower (Gilani et al., 2020). Media digitisation was regarded as the all-encompassing universe that kept expanding and reflective of the actual universe that expands. This is a problematic assumption for media (Zollman, 2012)[96] however, because of fragmentation. Allied with this is the erroneous idea that people already know the news, anyway, because they follow individuals and organisations on social media, when Prior (2007)[97] said in his book *Post-Broadcast Democracy* that 'digital disruption' had actually caused a decline in interest in political news. Prior (2007) said because users exercised free choice and preferred entertainment (Ibid.) personal preferences motivated their interests to be entertained, not necessarily informed. This created cause for concern in democracies that want to prepare their electorates for a free, fair and informed vote.

Further to that, for those who access news and information online, there were the legacy audiences who still listened to a humble radio in the kitchen, or the television set in what was once referred to quaintly as "the TV room" (now re-purposed by architects as "the media room"). Nonetheless, the rituals of timetabled, appointment news, radio and television, for example, no longer dominated Australians' lives and the public sphere. The audience could migrate online, elsewhere, or nowhere. The days of the radio and television sets as having designated, 'privileged' positions as honoured guests in a home with all seating facing them poised to give full attention and a coffee table at a low height so as not to compete, are no longer mandatory or needed. That way of life has been replaced by portable devices.

The ABC had migrated content to iView, in line with this change so audiences could access content on demand in personally scheduled viewing anytime, anywhere. This then also presented a shift in the audience and its abandonment of the daily itinerary of linear news consumption, its expectations and requirements. For example, the 07.45 am radio news bulletin once consisted of a strict to the second 10 minutes of national/international news and five minutes of state news. At Midday there was a ten-minute radio bulletin, then at 10.00 pm another fifteen-minute bulletin. Audiences were disciplined by the ABC to set their clocks and watches by the news and the rigid format in which it would be presented. This was an extraordinary form of social control that created a loyal and dedicated audience as a result. Once timing was everything, now it was nothing because the audience dipped in and dipped out online. There it was tempted by an abundance of content, where research said it only found news serendipitously—news was "stumbled upon" (Yadamsuren et al., 2017).[98] This had been a major shift for Aunty to accommodate. Online news content was also driven in some areas by the richness of the individual's *cultural capital* who would pursue "quality news" in favour of popular news (Ohlsson et al., 2017)[99] and where "low levels of trust tend to prefer non-mainstream news sources like social media, blogs, and digital-born providers, and are more likely to engage in various forms of online news participation" (Fletcher & Park, 2017).[100] Users then become reliant and trusting, but also discerning, on how the spaces they entered were managed and curated.

6.5 Searching for Shades of Media Grey: Poor Aunty Is "white"

There had been an historical shift away from a singular focus on an Anglo-Australian culture at the ABC with successive immigration policies delivering Aunty a highly diverse cultural profile to its audience. In addition to this shift, there was now a curious self-consciousness and inadequacy within Australian culture, or specifically, its whiteness, being encouraged by the ABC. For example, in 2019 Chair Ita Buttrose said "much of the media is white" (Duke, 2019).[101] Presumably, this was a reference to whiteness studies in Western culture where the literature described how 'white' saw itself as the norm and others classified (and by implication marginalised) racially in Western cultures (Chambers, 1997).[102] Whiteness studies had their origins in African American scholarship. There was a large body of extant literature and research on whiteness and reviewing it is beyond the scope and relevance of this research and more appropriate to audience studies. However, earlier whiteness theory examined how race subordination, racial domination and economic exploitation were used as a justification (in the US context) for slavery and colonialisation (Harris, 1993). These were all implied but problematised with Buttrose' use of the word "white"[103] as a new difficulty for the ABC. It should be noted here that privilege was not an exclusive attribute of 'white' culture. There was also entrenched privilege identified in Asian countries (Li et al., 2004) where, similarly, privilege was organised around power and economics (Pinches, 1999)[104] and other academic literature said black élites in the continent of Africa were also extremely powerful and dominant in their societies and cultures (Kagwanja & Southall, 2009;[105] Branch & Cheeseman, 2008[106]). Élitism and privilege were not something exceptional to Australia, nor were they Western inventions. They had been human inventions. In addition, the blinkered nature of social media, to which the ABC belonged, was self-referential and created online cultures that lacked diversity. In a society challenged with calls for diversity it was ironic that the ABC's strong presence on social media meant it actually belonged to a space that corralled opinion and curtailed diversity. This might occasion the ABC to make a critical examination of its online activities and give clarity to the implied cultural problems at the ABC as to how they manifested. If the ABC wanted to truly engage in diversity (of opinion, of beliefs, of cultures) it could benefit from a firmer grasp on academic understandings of online audiences—most people were "lurkers", much fewer were contributors, and only "a small percentage of users are highly involved in creating and distributing content" (Weeks et al., 2017). This then had powerful implications for the important role of the national public service media as a creator and distributor in terms of: "political participation, perceptions of opinion leadership, attempts at political persuasion, and, ultimately, the democratic process at large" (Weeks et al., 2017). This book suggests those matters of great import for the ABC, as they had been both historically and within its legislative framework.

However, as Buttrose' statement alluded to ABC staff, this was significant for at least two reasons. First, it showed that Buttrose supported what management literature described as 'the ideology of efficiency'. Her words not only reflected the need for measurable improvement but "an ideology of managerial control to produce uniformity of service. It is an ideology of the market" (Stacey & Griffin, 2006).[107] Second, and a significant complicating point here, was that the ABC's *field* was established by an Anglo and Celtic (white, but the two define themselves as ethnically separate), largely male organisation with a vision to be 'all to all'—and it was hugely successful and universally loved for it. Also, this original ABC model and Buttrose's complaint do not stand up in the era of intersectionality where research by Alfrey and Twine (2017) has found that gender fluid white or Asian women who identify as LGBTIQ+ have a greater sense of belonging in the workplace compared with heterosexual women (Ibid. Alfrey & Twine, 2017),[108] for example. Buttrose' criticism of the ABC (media) revealed how highly problematised and ironicised the ABC was because of perceptions of its "white male privilege" from Australian-British origins that saw it grow into a paramount Australian institution that became highly regarded, widely respected and loved—by all. Also, the issue of the backgrounds and identities of staff had been a longstanding one. The near-same complaint about "Anglocentricity" was made by former Managing Director Brian John almost a quarter of a century earlier: "I don't think that we're pluralist enough and that's a problem … it means that we're old-fashioned" (*The Canberra Times*, 1995).[109]

Under current understandings of society, it would appear that the ABC, then has become 'all to all' in spite of itself and loved nonetheless. Adding to this complexity was that Australia's nationhood had been challenged due to a range of linked, questionable and as yet still highly argued and unresolved factors—it was a British colony, colonised by negating, abusing and killing original inhabitants, used as a convict dumping ground for the recidivists of Britain and Ireland and the dispossessed and starved of Ireland and separated slowly from Britain. It fought two world wars in the names of the Kings of England and welcomed influxes of diverse immigrants, subsequently, and after removing a White Australia Policy of immigration that operated from Federation in 1901–1973 became one of the most diverse and successful multicultural democracies in the world.

The ABC played no small part in the growth of this one Australian nation. To explain the ABC's success in its *field*, within the context and detractions of a 'white' heritage and within a Bourdieusian theoretical framework[110] it achieved its élite, privileged status by plotting and planting a *field* for itself offering a point of difference—unique, quality Australian content. Australians of all background were alert to that corporate policy and identified with the organisation on this point of cultural difference with other media—quality and broad representation—telling Australians about themselves. Once content that impacted on the lives of all Australians was prioritised. The ABC's success in achieving this was so immense that this achievement became invisible, ethereal in Australian life. Or, to explain its *field* colloquially—it "owned it". An American colloquialism explaining confident control would have Aunty say: "I've got this". That was the ABC. Even though it failed to meet the mark of entire dedication to multiculturalism, hence the establishment of the Special Broadcasting Service in 1975, it made the early choice of appealing to the many rather than the few and, on that basis, it was a success.

Further to this point on the management complaints about a lack of staff racial-ethnic diversity, ABC policies since the 1970s, beginning with acknowledgement of the Racial Discrimination Act 1975,[111] had addressed this by embracing Corporate Social Responsibility (CSR). Policies, including CSR, have swept through other corporates like wildfire and examples of these abound in "integration", "innovation" and "stakeholder engagement" through "sensible, responsible, sustainable, affordable" policies promoting standards of excellence on matters as diverse as gender, ethnicity, quotas and the environment, and any other areas corporates in which they aspire to improve their public standing by showing an alertness to viewed injustice. The literature identified CSR as problematic because it was considered "an umbrella concept" (Arena et al., 2017).[112] It was also a controversial area because companies had also been accused of creating and acting on CSR policies that consisted of over-reach to the point of corporate incoherence (Kasturi Rangan et al., 2015).[113]

The ABC's late 2019 online diversity survey for on-air staff was an example of its CSR. In 2019, the ABC had already launched its Diversity and Inclusion Plan (ABC, 2019).[114] Then, the survey asked staff to give details of their ethnicity, sexuality, "gender identity" and other categories of personal information. In an email to staff, ABC Talent Manager, Meagan Loader, said: "WE NEED YOU (her emphasis) to please provide us some info about yourself, including things like your ethnicity, gender identity, sexuality and what languages you speak" (Kenny, 2019).[115] The email also said the information given would be confidential, non-identifiable and privacy would be protected. Loader described the email as an "all-of-ABC Talent Project" (Kenny, Ibid.)[116] to "attract, develop and retain our on-air talent" and "pull together more detailed information about who we have on air" (Loc. Cit.).[117] The email explained: "this information has never been captured by the ABC. We'll use it to help guide priority areas for future talent development, to ensure we look and sound like modern Australia" (Kenny, Ibid.).[118] A former human rights commissioner, Tim Wilson, was quoted saying that he was concerned about the ABC's intentions and that the survey was "disturbing" (Kenny, 2019).[119]

Yet, earlier that year in July 2019, the ABC reported on a Radio National Drive program (RN Drive) headlined online: "Millions wasted on diversity and inclusion programs, says report"[120] and described how a report by the Diversity Council in Australia showed that about 1/3 of programs on diversity were "either never or rarely effective" (Karvalas, 2019).[121] The research literature said millions of dollars have been wasted by businesses, charities and the public service on diversity surveys. Diversity Council Chief Executive Officer, Lisa Annese, said the council had surveyed 15% of the labour market and that "creating change at work is really difficult" (Karvalas, Ibid.)[122] as is changing organisational culture, and that includes any change, because "they fail to diagnose a business need" or "may be lax in designing the change" and "very few initiatives get properly evaluated" (Loc. Cit.).[123] The Diversity Council survey found that two groups were lagging in workplace representation: people with disability and Aboriginal and Torres Strait Island people (Loc. Cit.).[124]

Then in October 2019, ABC Chair, Ita Buttrose, made her "too white" statement and said that ABC staff should be more representative of the Australian population (Caisley & Vitorovich, 2019)[125] and, because of that, the ABC might need to introduce quotas for Asian or Middle Eastern staff members. The ABC did struggle, at first, to be culturally/ethnically representative because of the cohort from which it drew its staff. Much later, in 1964 an example occurred that showed it was trying to be 'all to all' when it showed a documentary, made by a BBC producer that local media observed was "without a white star" (*The Canberra Times*, 1964)[126] in which Australian Aborigines were interviewed. The documentary was called "A Changing Race". Since then the ABC had done much more to represent all Australians, without such tokenism and had become an industry leader in advocating the causes of indigenous Australians in a background of policy-makers who were failing indigenous communities by creating a situation that was "shameful and absurd" (ABC, 2016).[127] Buttrose said: "We're made up of many different cultures and nationalities and at the end of the day, most of us call ourselves Australians and we have to reflect that and we don't always do that" (Caisley & Vitorovich, 2019).[128] Further, she asked rhetorically: "do we have enough Asian representation? Should we have more? Should we have some Asians on the board? Do we have enough Middle Eastern representation? Should we have some Middle Eastern representatives on the board? You know, all of these things. I think the issues not just for the ABC, these issues for everybody in any corporate leadership role in Australia" (Caisley & Vitorovich, Ibid.).[129] Buttrose (Loc. Cit.) said the ABC would be releasing a five-year plan in 2020 and presumably the Australia Talks in 2019 online survey of Australians and what mattered to them was a precursor to inform and direct that new policy plan.

Issues of representation have been examined in other jurisdictions. In the US in 1947 the Commission on Freedom of the Press was formed to inquire into the proper function of the media in a democracy and according to Ruggles (1993)[130] the commission's report gave priority to a need to diversify journalism education because "democracy would not work effectively if news media fail to represent diverse social groups, not only weaknesses and vices, but their "common humanity"" (Ruggles, Ibid.).[131] Then, in the 1960s Robert Maynard, who founded the Maynard Institute for Journalism Education, said there were five "fault lines" which journalists needed to know how to portray: "race, gender, class, generation and geography" (Biswas & Izard, 2010).[132] These were "considered as prisms through which people may better see themselves and, indeed, the world" (Biswas & Izard, Ibid.).[133] However, Buttrose' stated lack of representation of the diversity of Australian ethnicities, cultures and religions in the profession of journalism, and at the ABC, goes much deeper than mandating quotas and investigating the personal and intimate profiles of existing staff. If policy change mandating the recruitment of quoted numbers of groups and ethnicities would make the ABC better, it begged two questions—how has the lack of this diversity policy damaged its historical coverage of issues for the good of the nation? and; second, who had gate-kept the shortlists of candidates that gave rise to manifest 'whiteness' at the ABC? Or, perhaps, in truth, it provoked the real issue. There was not a diversity of candidates in the first place because of dwindling career opportunities in the professional media.

Research conducted by the University of Melbourne in 2018 by the Multicultural Youth Australia Project Team (Wyn et al., 2018)[134] found that there were barriers to young migrant Australians aged 15–25 to study at university (and potentially study journalism to become journalists). In the research cohort, more than ¾ of the sample surveyed was born overseas. These barriers included: financial difficulty and academic ability, while family expectations and family responsibilities were onerous for many. The study said: "qualitative research highlighted the gendered ways in which multicultural young people experience family responsibilities and mobility, which may contribute to these different experiences of belonging" (Wyn et al., Ibid.)[135]—and, ergo, working at the national broadcaster. The top five countries of origin of those surveyed (born outside Australia) were: New Zealand (25.6%), Afghanistan (6.9%), The Philippines (4.5%), Myanmar (4.4%) and Iran (3.8%).[136] Other research found that migrants to Australia had a strong chance of finding a job, but struggled to hold onto a good job (where their educational qualifications suit the position) because of their visa status (Junankar & Mahuteau, in Junanker, 2016).[137]

In addition to all that, one has to consider the high unemployment rate for journalists, anyway. The loss of jobs in the last decade in newsrooms, and since the Coronavirus pandemic in particular (with the drop in advertising), had been staggering with all media organisations looking at shedding staff (including the ABC) and as for recruiting trainees, the hopes were even slimmer. Pew Research in the US found that newsrooms had terminated half their staff positions since 2008 (Grieco, 2020).[138] Added to that the novel Coronavirus pandemic has triggered the closure of 157 newsrooms temporarily or forever since early 2019 (Meade, 2020)[139] but that was combined with the impact of digital journalism and the widespread bushfires in south-eastern Australia from late 2019–2020 (Meade, Ibid.) with the dramatic impact on business and its advertising output—coupled later with the Coronavirus impact on business.

Journalism, or media studies, was not so attractive degree as a standalone degree when one could end-up with a subject mix offering employers no specific professionally accredited skills that translated directly into qualifications for a workplace (like those achieved by teachers, pharmacists, accountants, lawyers, medical practitioners et al.) and there was no work, or shrinking workplaces, at the end of the road. It would be unusual for a migrant family to encourage their young to become journalists when migrants wanted to establish themselves, build a life and grow solid futures. High unemployment areas were simply not attractive to migrants who were, anecdotally, known to be hard workers wanting good jobs and financial stability and security for their families. Many migrants flee precarity for more certainty. In addition, many came from countries where free speech was suppressed and punished and, if refugees, they may be fleeing persecution, so therefore they would not encourage their children into what they knew to be vulnerable employment.

In addition, journalism was not a popular study choice for university studies. The main areas favoured by Australian university students were management and commerce (Parr, 2015)[140] where female students outnumbered male students by 100/72 (Larkins, 2018)[141] with more women pursuing higher degrees (Ibid.).[142] This was part of a worldwide trend (Ibid.).[143] In addition, more females studied "society and culture, health, management and commerce" while males studied "information technology, engineering and related technologies" (Ibid.).[144] So, proportionately, more women would be studying journalism than men. Over-riding this was the fact that disadvantaged people and Indigenous were under-represented at university (Larkins, ibid; University of Notre Dame Australia, nd)[145] [146] (which segued with the research conducted by the Diversity Council (2019). In addition, if there were more female candidates for journalism jobs, so this gender bias would call attention to itself at some point, especially if CSR quotas were in place seeking equal representation. A Federal Government-commissioned review into Australia's migrants, led by Shergold et al. (2019), released a report in November 2019: "Investing in Refugees Investing in Australia" (Shergold, Ibid.).[147] Its recommendations included: "a university sponsored visa offering post-graduate or post-doctoral places to academically qualified refugees", and that the Federal Government could assist refugees by "funding a digital platform to help refugees connect directly with volunteers" such as "study support to a university student" (Loc. Cit.).[148] The terms of reference for the report quoted the Settlement Services Advisory Council:

> Investment in migration and settlement is for the prosperity of all Australians. To fully realise the returns of migration, and to deliver a stronger nation through a more diverse workforce, requires enabling the most to be achieved by every person who comes to Australia. (Ibid.)[149]

As previously indicated, in 2019, the ABC ran an "Australia Talks" online survey with the University of Melbourne which allowed the audience with access to a computer and the internet an opportunity to contribute. It was reported that 50,000 people responded.[150] ABC Chair Ita Buttrose said the findings were a "goldmine"[151] and she made the point that the survey found that Australians said political correctness "had gone too far".[152] After Buttrose made the statement, it prompted one Federal Liberal Party Senator, Concetta Fierravanti-Wells (NSW), to call for a merger of the ABC with the multicultural Special Broadcasting Service (SBS) (80% funded by the Federal Government and the remainder from advertising revenue[153]) established in 1978 (it began in 1975 with two experimental radio stations). SBS' Charter required it: "to provide multilingual and multicultural radio, television and digital media services that inform, educate and entertain all Australians and, in doing so, reflect Australia's multicultural society" (SBS, 1991).[154] In a 'careful what you wish for' response to Buttrose, Fierravanti-Wells said a merger would save taxpayers:

> Hundreds of millions of dollars.[155] ... I believe that the public broadcasters should produce content for all Australians irrespective of who they are and where they come from. ... If you really want to talk about diversity and the ABC, I think the time has come to have that discussion. (Caisley & Vitorovich, 2019)[156]

It was as if Buttrose' statement on the ABC had curtailed the organisation's own future by stating it was unrepresentative of Australians and implying it was in breach of its own Charter of 'all to all'. So, it was not surprising that the blending of the two broadcasters seemed a logical and sequitur point for a politician to make in response. Even more importantly, in terms of the original governance and Institutional Logics of the ABC it was contradictory being white and hyper-masculinised—and a success. It was an extraordinary and delightful contradiction of current opinions of Australianness and everything conflated with that—that Aunty was originally white masculine yet her sex was female, and then everyone grew to love her because of him.

6.6 Government Meddling

Although governments say they never meddled with the ABC (and ABC managers were inclined to confirm that in this research), there was an instance between 1965 and 1969 when the Department of External Affairs meddled in the ABC's reporting of an attempted coup in Indonesia. The type of departmental interference manifested in "guidance" from the department plus a threat to take over Radio Australia (Najjarine & Cottle, 2003)[157] to be placed under the control of both the department and the Postmaster-General's Department following push-back over the meddling from the ABC. The Minister for External Affairs, Paul Hasluck, wrote in 1964:

> What is required is that the Government should have the authority, through the Secretary of my Department, to direct the Australian Broadcasting Commission as to the contents of its news services, to the end that Radio Australia would not have the right to broadcast, unless in an approved form, any item which bears directly on the conduct of Australian foreign relations in Asia (…). (Ibid.)[158]

This was all rebuffed by the ABC management and board; however, it was later agreed Radio Australia could accept the department's advice on sensitive matters (Najjarine & Cottle, Ibid.).[159] This interference came about for several reasons: to control the message, concern that Radio Australia was basing its reports "relying on some garbled account by a newspaper correspondent" (Ibid.),[160] and also the government realised that Radio Australia had: "high signal strength and massive listening audience in the archipelago (including the highest echelons of power in Indonesia) was a resource that should be exploited wisely and cooperatively"[161] because "its signal strength was often much stronger than local stations" (Najjarine & Cottle, ibid.).[162] Radio Australia had already been under the control of the government once before in the 1950s and was influential during World War II when media censorship was heavy generally. However, Radio Australia had for some time been seen to have a pro-Indonesian bias (Wood, 2018),[163] or at other times insulting Indonesia (Najjarine & Cottle, ibid.). The situation between Radio Australia and the government was described as an "almost tug of war" (Ibid.)[164] with the government wanting to use it as a means of spreading the Australian perspective to South East Asia.

In the 1960s and 1970s former Head of the ABC's Jakarta Bureau, Errol Hodge, said the Department of External Affairs was pressuring Radio Australia to be used as part of its foreign policy (Hodge, 1996).[165] Then in 1980 the ABC's Jakarta correspondent Warwick Beutler was expelled from Indonesia for Radio Australia broadcasting news about the occupation of East Timor (Hamilton, 2013).[166] There was also blow-back in 1986 from an article in *The Sydney Morning Herald* which was considered inflammatory—an exposé—in 1986 on Indonesian President Suharto. Hodge said the ABC re-established an office in Jakarta in 1991 only after it was "frozen out of Indonesia for 11 years" (Hodge, 1996).[167] Inglis (2006)[168] related an exchange in 1987 between the late Prime Minister Bob Hawke with the late ABC Chairman Bob Somervaille. Hawke was complaining about a Four Corners program which was at the time investigating 'friends of the government'. Hawke referred to Four Corners as "a nest of vipers" angered that "public funds should be used to underwrite people whose purpose is to undermine the fabric of society". Inglis (2006) said Somervaille replied calmly: "I hear what you say, prime minister. But I know you would be the last person to want me to interfere in ABC programming."

The ABC had early experience with meddlers and 1937 was a challenging year for the national broadcaster. The Commission was that year approaching the end of its term. The year began with an attack by the Keith Murdoch owned News (Adelaide) in an article that accused the institution of catering to sectional interests. The article "ABC out of touch with public tastes" (*The News*, 1937)[169] was losing listeners to "B" class radio licence stations (commercial) because "night after night, the owner of a wireless set is threatened with boredom by long and learned dissertations on subjects that have a purely sectional interest" and playing too much classical music (Ibid.). The lambasting article concluded: "the Government, therefore, would be well advised to select as its new members men and women whose life's training has been calculated to teach them what the public really wants. This can be learned only in one school-that of experience" (Ibid.).[170] This was the first fearful acknowledgment that the ABC was acquiring far too much *cultural capital* and establishing itself as an Australian cultural icon—and also accused of not matching public expectations, which had been a recurrent claim made against the institution.

But Keith Murdoch was not the only newspaper proprietor to observe the ABC's growing cultural influence. Later that year, the ABC was accused of playing sub-standard music at a public concert, where a music critic from *The Daily Telegraph* (the paper closed in 1954 and is not the current Murdoch (News Limited) Sydney newspaper of the same name) complained that the Polish violinist Bronislaw Huberman's performance of a classical piece was "a sop" to "cajole" the audience with "pot boilers" and implied that the ABC had asked Huberman to play to an inferior standard (*The Daily Telegraph*, 1937).[171] The Australian Broadcasting Commission's General Manager, Charles Moses, responded with vigour: "the Commission only requests from these artists that they give programmes of the same high standard as they give in cities like London, Vienna, and New York".

However, according to Inglis (1983), Huberman, one of the most renowned violinists of his era, was part of a group of musicians the ABC was bringing to Australia "some of the best European musicians" (Inglis, 1983).[172] Huberman said in his defence and somewhat avoiding the accusation: "my only discussions with the Commission on my programmes have been with a view to arranging the order of the concerts in the broadcasting schedule to ensure that each half of each programme would subsequently be heard on the air" (*The Canberra Times*, 1938).[173] In 1938, Moses, defended the large number of horse-races broadcast on the ABC as meeting Australians' needs because "it is possible that the majority of Australian listeners take a great interest in racing and the Broadcasting Commission had a service to perform giving them the facilities they desire" (*The Canberra Times, ibid.*).[174] He added: "sport played a far more important part in the life of the community in Australia than in England where the BBC gave only about six race broadcasts a year" (Ibid.).

In 1944, the Parliamentary Standing' Committee on Broadcasting said that the public was "well satisfied" with ABC News bulletins (*The Courier Mail*, 1946)[175] while, the ABC was accused in parliament of not considering the public by Labor Party member for Eden-Monaro, Allan Fraser: "To give the national programme over last night, during the principal listening hour, to specialised discussions of the Radio in Education conference is a remarkable illustration of A.B.C. contempt for listeners' entertainment requirements" (Ibid.).[176] Allan Fraser reminded the ABC that: "Although the man who pays the piper is supposed to call the tune, listeners who pay the radio licence fees are not allowed to do it on the A.B.C." (*The Courier Mail, 1946*).[177] In 1951, *The Age* said that at a meeting with the ABC's Chair Richard Boyer and general manager, Charles Moses and the ABC Celebrity Concert Season subscribers the ABC should stop "wrongly using public funds for orchestral concerts" (The Age, 1951) and instead spend its money on improving broadcasts. The meeting resolved to elect an advisory committee.

In 1953, the then Chair of the ABC, Richard Boyer, stated at the Television Royal Commission that at the time because of bandwidth limitation there was only room for one national television channel in Australia. He said: "only a national station could at all times of the day consider the public good" (Goulburn Evening Post, 1953).[178] Thirty years later the role of the ABC in acting in the public good was confirmed by the Chair Ken Myer in 1983 when he defended the ABC in regard to the broadcast that year of a Four Corners program by Chris Masters "The Big League" that resulted in the hugely consequential Street Royal Commission into corruption allegations within NSW Rugby League. It resulted in the Chief Magistrate of NSW being sent to jail and ended the career of the NSWRL President Kevin Humphreys. In response Mr Myer said: "This confirms that the role of the ABC is to throw attention to matters of public interest where truth has been obscured or the public has not been fully informed" (*The Canberra Times*, 1983).[179]

Pressuring and contesting the ABC's public engagement is not new. But stronger political influences on the ABC emerged in 1976. This was corroborated in the literature and published interviews with members of the Malcolm Fraser-led Liberal Government: "political pressure was seldom referred to in the ABC before 1976" (Blain, 1977).[180] In order to build audience affection and institutional support as a counterbalance to political pressure and funding cuts, in 1985 the ABC hired Michael Robinson as Sales and Marketing Director to help the public "feel good" about the ABC.[181] Over time there had been 'fits and starts' in accusations of bias from politicians. A strong comment was made in 2014, when the ABC was accused by the former Liberal Prime Minister of Australia, Tony Abbott, of not being on Australia's side. The criticism was aimed at two matters—the ABC's supportive coverage of Edward Snowden in publishing leaks obtained from phone tapping of the Indonesian President and his wife in 2009; and, the ABC's support for asylum-seeker claims of abuse by the Australian Navy. In the first matter, Mr Abbott referred to Snowden as a "traitor". The then Communications Minister, Malcolm Turnbull, described the ABC's activity in publishing Snowden's efforts as "an error of judgement" (ABC, 2013)[182] while the ABC Managing Director, Mark Scott, defended the ABC for co-publishing the leaks with *The Guardian* newspaper and directed blame at News Corporation for launching a "concentrated attack on the ABC" (ABC, 2013). Interviewees for this book said a constant concern of Scott's during his time managing the ABC—was the believed relentlessness of attacks on the ABC from Rupert Murdoch-owned media.

Evidence of this claimed nastiness was provided by the Murdoch-owned *The Australian* when it published a page one article headlined: "Odd couple: friendship that underpinned a spy story" (Brook, 2013).[183] The layout of this front-page is no longer available via the newspaper's website but was retrieved via a screenshot posted by the media news website, *Mumbrella*. It bears analysis here because photos of Mark Scott and *The Guardian* Editor-in-Chief Alan Rusbridger were positioned above six photos of terrorists described as "thwarted by Australian intelligence agencies". The positioning of the two stories so closely implied an association between Scott, Rusbridger and the terrorists which was not only false but seriously misleading. The layout and headings implied that Scott and Rusbridger were complicit with these terrorists. In addition, the first paragraph of the article said they had a "bromance" (a close but non-sexual relationship between two men). The news article asked: "would the unique and controversial journalistic alliance between the ABC and the Guardian Australia have occurred without such warm relations between the two executives?". The article then said Scott and Rusbridger were a "mutual admiration society". The article said the two were seen having breakfast together when Rusbridger was in Sydney in November 2013. In response Scott said: "some sections seem obsessed by us. There seems to be a never-ending number of stories they want to run about the ABC. … There is some people in News Corp who have a deep ideological opposition to public broadcasting and the ABC" (ABC, 2013).[184]

The second disappointment with the ABC expressed by then Prime Minister Abbott concerned a report by the ABC's Indonesia Correspondent, George Roberts, who had a video that showed asylum-seekers with burns; they said they had suffered because of physical abuse by the Australian Navy where: "asylum seekers were beaten and told to hold on to parts of a hot engine on a boat being towed back to Indonesia (Roberts, 2014).[185] The ABC reported that: "Navy personnel had held the asylum seeker's hand on an exhaust pipe" (ABC, 2013).[186] The injuries were said to have been passed on to Indonesian police; and a Somali asylum-seeker was reported by the ABC to have said: "Australian Navy personnel punched some passengers and others were forced to hold onto the hot metal" (Ibid.). However, Scott and Kate Torney, Director News, subsequently issued a statement saying that "what the video did not do was establish how those injuries occurred … the ABC's initial reporting needed to be more precise on that point. We regret if our reporting led anyone to mistakenly assume that the ABC supported the asylum seekers' claims" (Scott & Torney, 2014).[187] Later the Royal Australian Navy said that the burns suffered by the asylum-seekers were as a result of them trying to light a fire on board their vessel. Navy notations recorded: "Burn associated with attempt to light fire in engine room" (ABC, 2013).

An Australian Defence Force statement said its Investigative Service "found that the allegations [that asylum seekers' hands were held to hot pipes] were not substantiated, and that there was no requirement for further investigation unless new additional information was forthcoming. The ADF personnel involved in the operations behaved professionally under difficult circumstances. The safety and wellbeing of all persons involved in Operation Sovereign Borders activities is paramount" (ABC, Ibid.). Acting Chief of the Defence Force, Air Marshal Mark Binskin, said he had "every confidence in the dedication of our people and their ethical approach to the conduct of operations in difficult and often dangerous conditions" (Wroe et al., 2014)[188] while Chief of Navy, Vice-Admiral Ray Griggs, was reported by the media to have said on Twitter: "Based on everything I know there is no basis to these allegations—none" (Wroe et al., Ibid.). When challenged by Twitter users to deny the allegations outright it was reported by the newspaper that he responded: "I just did!!!!" (Op. Cit.). The Australia Defence Association executive director, Neil James, explained that the allegations were not possible because: "when the Australians arrived at the scene, the engine of the asylum-seeker boat was already cold" (Leys & Nicholson, 2014)[189] and it was later admitted by the asylum-seekers in an ABC 7.30 programme "there had been a previous attempt to sabotage the engine" (Solomons & Roberts, 2014).[190]

Both the then Immigration Minister, Scott Morrison, and then Foreign Minister, Julie Bishop, demanded the ABC apologise to the Navy. Bishop said: "I thought the ABC would do the right thing and having acknowledged that their reporting was substandard at best that they would apologise, … if the ABC refuses to do that, well I think that is a reflection on the ABC. It has been a very unfortunate incident" (Knott, 2014).[191] Communications Minister, Malcolm Turnbull, said: "this has caused enormous offence" (Knott, ibid.). Knott (2014) said the "head of ABC news content Gaven Morris had sent a memo to senior staff reminding reporters and editors not to "embellish" or add "any flourish" to asylum seekers' claims of mistreatment" (Ibid.). Other media (Blair, 2014) revealed that the ABC's national reporting team turned to social media to investigate the veracity of the report through a Facebook post. The media reported the Facebook post stated that the journalist had been: "tasked with finding some navy personnel who might be willing to speak to us in a background capacity—not on the record. It follows the story our Jakarta guy ran on the asylum seekers burns claims. My boss feels the allegations are likely to be untrue. Do you know of any people with navy or defence force affiliations who might be able to put us in touch with someone. … I wouldn't want to approach anyone who didn't feel comfortable talking" (Blair, 2014).[192] The news article said that there were no initial helpful responses, but quoted one reply comment on Facebook: "Jeez, Alison, if your boss had doubts about this, why didn't she seek clarification before running with the story and besmirching the reputation of the whole Australian Navy?" (Blair, ibid.).

Newspaper columnist, Miranda Devine, posted on her newspaper blog that Australians were a "community fed up with the continual undermining of Australia's national interest by the Left and its media boosters" (Devine, 2014).[193] On the other hand, Flinders University Senior Lecturer, Ben Wadham, said that the ABC report showed "the media acting as a fourth estate, which is especially important in a climate of government-driven clandestine military operations" (Wadham, 2014).[194] It was after these incidents that the ABC set up a Fact Checking Unit. It was scrapped in May 2016 by Managing Director, Michelle Guthrie, although already planned for ending after Federal Budget cuts to the ABC by former Managing Director, Mark Scott who left the organisation April 2016. Prime Minister Kevin Rudd had given the ABC an additional AUD60 million over three years that included funding for the Fact Checking unit but the new administration of Scott Morrison reduced it to AUD41.4 million over the next three years. This was an effective ABC budget cut of AUD18.6 million.

Then in 2017 in a content monetisation by stealth situation, RMIT, a Melbourne University, was named the joint funding partner and would provide "researchers, premises and technical support" (Meade, 2017).[195] A promotional link to RMIT was attached to the ABC Fact Checking Unit's website. The ABC Fact Check website described itself within this context: "the ABC is a publicly funded, independent media organisation, and therefore RMIT ABC Fact Check is accountable to the Australian Parliament ... we do not check the work of journalists, from the ABC or elsewhere" (ABC News).[196] Dean of the School of Media and Communication, Professor Martyn Hook, said "the public broadcaster and the university would share resources to bring the badly needed service back to life ... in a time of 'post-truth', 'alternative facts' and 'fake news', it is ever more critical to hold public figures to account and ensure that public discourse—the basis of democracy—is based in fact, ... RMIT is thrilled to join with the ABC to relaunch Fact Check and support this crucial public service"(Meade, Ibid.). As a result of the joint ABC project, RMIT now taught fact-checking as a compulsory first year subject for media students. Aunty had become the rope in a tug of war between the ABC checking on its facts and a preference for social media to guide practice.

In 2018, the ABC had to re-edit an article published online that likened two Australian News Limited journalists (a Murdoch-owned media enterprise) to the Norwegian mass murderer Anders Breivik. The article 'Western Civilization and Conservative Hysteria' on the ABC's Religion and ethics website (2018)[197] was critical of upset expressed by *The Australian*'s Foreign Editor, Greg Sheridan, and *The Australian* Columnist, Chris Kenny, over a decision by the Australian National University, Canberra to end talks with the Ramsey Centre for Western Civilisation for a proposed undergraduate degree in Western civilisation. The Ramsey Centre was established by a benefactor Paul Ramsey who bequeathed AUD3 billion from his estate to the establishment of the centre. It was intended to be non-partisan.

The offending comment in the article, by University of Sydney Professor of Modern History A. Dirk Moses, "do members of the right-wing commentariat think that Western countries are succumbing to a poisonous cocktail of multiculturalism, Muslim immigration, political correctness and cultural Marxism that dilutes the white population and brainwashes young people at school and university? It seems that, much like Anders Breivik[198] and Steve Bannon,[199] they do" (Hevesi, 2018).[200] The article was later re-edited to remove Anders Breivik's name with the comment: "Note: This article has been edited to remove a reference to Anders Breivik" (Moses, 2018). The ABC said it made the change after it found the article was not in line with its own editorial guidelines and that "the item was an opinion piece from an external contributor" (Doctor, 2018)[201] "the reference was removed because it was not consistent with the ABC's editorial standards" (Hevesi Ibid.). Professor Moses then said he "did not intend to imply anyone was a mass murderer (obviously)", and that "some people have overreached themselves with their incendiary rhetoric" (Buckingham Jones & Urban, 2018)[202] .

In 2011, managing director Mark Scott had introduced the current complaints handling process at the ABC—Audience and Consumer Affairs (ACA) managed by ABC editorial director Alan Sunderland. Its creation saw the end of the Independent Complaints Review Panel (ICRP), established in 1991, which was set up in response to claims of bias directed at ABC news and current affairs reporting of the 1991 Gulf war. Then Labor Prime Minister Bob Hawke said the ABC coverage was: "loaded, biased and disgraceful" (Inglis, 2002). Then Minister for Communications, Kim Beazley, publicly proposed in February 1991 that the ABC should be made "more publicly accountable' for complaints about bias" (Inglis, Ibid.).

Former ABC journalist Geoffrey Luck (2018)[203] said he would be ashamed to now work at the broadcaster. He said the ABC was so "seduced" by technology that "its policy is to have journalists report live every possible story" (Luck, Ibid.) which led to trivialisation of news and distortion of news values (recency, frequency, proximity etc.) where once live crosses were reserved for major breaking news. Luck said the use of adjectives—once banned in news copy—now abounded in news reports and headlines were adding bias and personal opinion.

Luck (2018) pinpointed the decline in reporting standards to the failure to apply the same editorial standards to ABC current affairs as well as those already applied to ABC news because current affairs came later and not held to the same account by management: "fact, analysis, opinion and political barrow-pushing—together at times with undergraduate clowning—became inseparably confused" (Luck, 2018).[204] In addition, the public is now concerned about the rise of "groupthink" on the ABC with discussion panel programs presenting a uniform line-up of similar views. Luck said (Ibid.): "At the heart of the community's frustration with the ABC is its refusal to enforce its charter. For more than 30 years it has been fighting to escape accountability for its news and current affairs broadcasts" including that it "watered down its internal self-regulatory system so that only the most egregious breaches can be upheld" (Luck, ibid.).

Luck (2018) argued that the ABC Board was not fulfilling its duty under the ABC Act: "to ensure that the gathering and presentation by the corporation of news and information is accurate and impartial according to the recognised standards of objective journalism" (Australian Government, 2017).[205] He said there was a need to "establish an independent external body—call it an ombudsman—to handle all complaints about breaches of the ABC charter, its code of practice and editorial guidelines" (Luck, Ibid.). The community's simmering disquiet with the public broadcaster's decline in credibility has been trying for years to find its expression in policy terms. The recent populist clamour to "sell off the ABC" can be seen as a final incoherent shout from the frustrated, disappointed and those unwilling to help and wait for Aunty to reclaim her precious *cultural capital.*

Then in November 2018, the Australia/Israel and Jewish Affairs Council, the leading body representing the Australian Jewish community, made a submission to the Senate Standing Committee on Environment and Communications' inquiry into Allegations of Political interference in the ABC (including the termination of the Managing Director, Michelle Guthrie, conduct of the Chair and Board, and governance of the ABC) motivated by what it observed to be: "the inadequate complaints procedure at the ABC" (AIJAC, Ibid.). The submission was condemning:

> Complete editorial independence is all but impossible without adequate external oversight of ABC content by a party widely considered neutral and impartial, that is, not on the ABC payroll or part of a politically-motivated review or inquiry. (AIJAC Staff, 2018)[206]

As well, "the need for the ABC complaints process to be reformed" (Ibid.). The council stated: "complete editorial independence is all but impossible without adequate external oversight of ABC content by a party widely considered neutral and impartial, that is, not on the ABC payroll or part of a politically-motivated review or inquiry" (Ibid.).

The report by the Senate Standing Committee released in April 2019 (Commonwealth of Australia, 2019)[207] found:

4.88 The committee believes that political interference or the prospect of political interference, and all that that entails, is experienced to varying degrees throughout the ABC.

Concluding comments

4.89 Recent and unprecedented events in the ABC have raised questions about the

Australian Government's interference and attempted interference in the public

broadcaster whose independence was enshrined in legislation more than 85 years ago.

4.90 While Australians have considerable trust in the ABC, this trust is not blind.

Should Australian Governments continue to undermine and erode the independence

and integrity of the corporation, the ABC's status as a trusted institution will be

significantly diminished. (Commonwealth of Australia, Ibid.)

The AIJAC expressed disappointment with the ABC's Audience and Consumer Affairs outfit because "confidence in the handling of editorial complaints at the ABC has diminished" (AIJAC Staff, Ibid.)[208] and further that "the ACA is a team within the ABC so it still answerable to both senior ABC management and the ABC board. And like all organisations, public or private, the ABC has its own interests when it comes to complaints handling and other related matters" (AIJAC Staff, Ibid.). It raised the salient point that is revealed by the ABC but any 'in house' investigations of any organisation. That is, in the case of the ABC, it seeks to interpret the ABC's obligations as narrowly as possible, protect its reputation, maintain staff morale, and preserve outsourced content arrangements.

6.7 Accenting the High(er) Political Ground in the *Field*

Another way in which the ABC had controlled the educated *field* had been through the use of the spoken word—initially, the use of educated British accents and higher, more formal registers of English usage—and minimal adjectives and adverbs. This had been a means of demonstrating authority and accuracy, believed initially to be more impressive through a modulated English accent. It set itself apart from the *hoi polloi* of other radio by emulating the BBC's tone and voice. Popular and long-serving ABC television newsreader, James Dibble's opportunity to read news at the ABC only arrived in 1946 when it was decided to widen the remit of accents on the radio and allow "educated Australian" accents instead of exclusive British accents (Veitch, 2010).[209] The first newsreaders wore dinner suits until the early 1940s, a further reinforcement of this formality in presentation and élite agency in the *field*, even though radio was then unseen and attire irrelevant unless performed before an audience. The first Chairman, William Cleary, said that the ABC preferred to employ announcers with "good public-school educations" (*The News*, 1941).[210] There was also talk among staff at the time that there was a need for an "establishment background" in order to gain promotions. The appointments of grammar school educated and Royal Military College Sandhurst graduate General Manager, Charles Moses, and ABC Talks Editor, Gladys Owen, daughter of Supreme Court Judge Sir Langer Meade Loftus Owen, provided staff with ongoing cause for concern that the institution was high-brow and élitist sounding (*The Advertiser*, 1939).[211] Yet, it was Moses and Owens' appointments that helped establish the privileged rules and practices of the ABC *field*.

Overlaying this duty to build an Australian culture, the ABC was also conceived as an antipodean hybrid of the BBC to the point of encouraging the use of British accents by its presenters on radio because of the struggle to find good Australian speaking voices (The News, 1941),[212] therefore ultimately delivering content that was "imperial in their focus and their accents British in their timbre" (Davis, 1988).[213] This is an example of what Bourdieu would describe as embodied *cultural capital*. It was so clearly a part of the purview of the organisation that it was supported specifically by "distributing the BBC's booklet on pronunciation" (Davis, Ibid.) to staff. The expectations of the ABC in having a British accent forced it into a strangely conflicted identity because of this concurrent emphasis to broadcast Australian culture. Its role stipulated that it must be of 'public benefit', as is the BBC. At the same time, however, it accrued *cultural capital* by identifying and linking correct English with that spoken with the accent of what was then "the mother country", and the colonial power, not the Australia accent. From the outset, the organisation was "a thoroughly imperial artefact" (Inglis, 1983)[214] and the early emphasis on the educated British accent and pronunciations was formative in identifying this *habitus* (Bourdieu) or daily dispositions that buttressed *cultural capital* for the ABC. Such was the primacy given to British culture that even the ABC's flagship current affairs television program "Four

Corners" was conceived in 1961 referencing the models of "the quality English Sunday papers" (Pullan, 1986)[215] and its BBC role model "Panorama" because it was believed that "striving for ratings was a sure way to trivialize programming" (Pullan Ibid.).[216] In a digital ecology, striving for ratings/followers/hits/likes/comments/audiences had become everything.

Participatory didacticism in the grand orchestral 17 second "Majestic Fanfare" played at the start of the 7.45 am news bulletin on ABC Radio News in each capital city Monday to Friday once signalled Australia's public life. This had given the ABC a unique platform to educate Australians about what had described and believed to bound unbiased, serious news. It provided an aural cue to the listener to anticipate a "high" standard (orchestral music is linked with "high" culture) of information. It has become what Bourdieu (Bourdieu, 1977) would describe as symbolic support for the news bulletin and gives gravitas and "value" to the information accentuated by participatory orchestral support. Composed in 1935 by British musician, Charles Williams, "The Majestic Fanfare" was first used to introduce broadcasts of Federal Parliament. Then in 1952, the theme was used to announce radio bulletins—and later television news bulletins. In terms or creating *cultural capital*, radio newsreaders—originally only men in what was considered a man's job—manifested *cultural capital.* Music of the parliament was appropriated to lead the news of the nation. It was a success.

By 1939, the ABC was allowed to rebroadcast BBC news, the copyright of which was owned by Australian Associated Press (AAP) and of which Sir Keith Murdoch was Chairman all the while educating Australians that the institution was 'one of us'. Much later (2019) the ABC converted the implied to the stated to remind its audience there was still an "us" through its promotional language. Yet its drift to the digital commercial field meant that the role it once occupied could no longer be taken that for granted in shifting, drifting times. An example of a significant challenge for the ABC "us" occurred after 1939. World War II created a significant problem for the Australian workforce and for the ABC. ABC male staff who served during World War II and were given leave from their ABC positions created a shortage of presenters and technicians. Their replacements were possibly younger men, older men, men with ongoing health complications—but what was of most concern at the time was that their replacements could be women. Not long after the war had started Thomas Bearup wrote to the commissioners about this troubling shift on the horizon, that would stir up received accents, register and timbre of accents from male to female:

> I think we must look in the face the possibility that within a measurable space of time public opinion might strongly object to youthful male voices coming from the loud speakers and we may have to use women announcers, or men well over military age. (Thomas, 1980, quoting the ABC, 1941)[217]

Women were able to make significant inroads to the broadcaster at this juncture, notwithstanding. The ABC also learned it could gain audience support by creating a new 'type' of voice, apart from a woman's voice. It broadcast the voices of the men serving overseas who were invited to tape messages that would be played on ABC radio back home. This was an earlier, morale-building iteration of "yours"—but for the benefit of the "ours"—and ushered in the development of the range of voices on the ABC—Aunty's voice was permitted rich and representative vocalisation.

Another aspect of the ABC's élite *field* and voice was that it eschewed and disdained a role for itself as a publicist, or purveyor of public relations. There was clear institutional individuation between itself and the promotion of celebrity or sectional/business interests. One senior staff member was quite clear on what the ABC was, and was not, in that regard. The late well-known Melbourne radio broadcaster Elizabeth Bond (who presented a top-rating morning program on 3LO and retired in 1979) told her producer: "Don't ask me to interview an actor to promote a show. Don't ask me to interview a publisher to promote a book. We're national broadcasting, not a PR company" (Nicholson & Nattrass, 2003).[218]

6.8 The Politics of Supporting War

The significant role of the ABC at times of national crisis had been paramount. It had not only conveyed official messages 'all to all' but seen itself as invested in a positive outcome for the nation in a crisis. It had taken 'service to country' very seriously and in dominating the élite *field* it had ascendancy and authority to speak and analyse. During World War II, the ABC played a significant role, hand in glove with the government, in lifting morale, staying "on message" by being party to the suppression of news and information (censorship), strengthening national identity and raising money to support the war effort. This had to be situated in the context of Australians who enlisted: they were British subjects and each signed a declaration upon enlistment that they would serve God, King and Country—"resist His Majesty's enemies and cause His Majesty's peace to be kept and maintained" (Australian Military Forces Mobilization Attestation Form, 1941 & Defence Act 1903[219]). The ABC's war efforts, even challenged with staff losses through enlistment, were immense and in October 1939 set up the People's Patriotic Concert Committee to organise ABC orchestras and bands to perform at People's Patriotic Concerts (*The Advertiser*, 1939)[220] each month in each state, and each month at each army camp. These concerts prioritised Australian composers, other broadcasts promoted Australian authors. In 1941 the Australia listener was paying AU£1 per year for a radio licence and half of this went to the ABC (the other half was given to the Postmaster General's Department) (ABC, 1941). Nonetheless, the ABC made a substantial contribution to the lifting national spirit and morale among troops and the general public: "the Commission felt called upon to try, subject to its wartime responsibilities and its revenue limits, to meet its obligation to assist in the growth of Australian cultural life by maintaining high standards in musical programmes, dramatic productions, educational broadcasts for both adults and children, Celebrity Orchestral and Young People's concerts, talks for discussion groups, and generally" (ABC, 1941). ABC staff also raised money for the war effort. If the significance is to be measured in monetary terms, by 1940 and after six concerts, the ABC had raised a net £494/15/5 or AUD41,945.87 (Reserve Bank, 2020).[221] Profits were distributed to the Camp Comforts Fund, The Red Cross and to army camps to purchase radios for the troops (*The Advertiser*, 1939)—building the ABC audience in innovative ways.

The ABC was intrinsic to the Australian war effort at a time of national crisis with existential fears of imminent invasion by Japan. But the ABC tried as best as it was permitted to maintain content balance even then. There were concerns that because the concert programs favoured Australian and British composers, cultural propaganda had infiltrated taste. So, the ABC had decided that German (an enemy and ally of Japan) music could be played as long as there was no living German composer who would be owed royalties (Inglis, 1983).[222] Under government instruction, propaganda became part of the ABC's manner of programming and delivery with the Federal Attorney-General and Minister for External Affairs, Dr H.V. Evatt, ordering ABC Chairman, William Cleary (who passed this message on to his staff) that ABC content would have to "carry subtle propaganda promoting "Australia first"" (Inglis, 1983).[223]

There have been historic pressures on the ABC to promote and prioritise Australian interests, where other media have not been so easily prevailed upon by political influence, unless commercially viable.

During World War II the ABC was shifted from the control of the Postmaster-General's Department to the Department of Information and "virtually every spoken word had to be scripted and approved before it was read" (Inglis, 1983).[224] For the first of the ABC concerts, the Prime Minister, Robert Menzies, addressed the more than 50,000 troops (*The Advertiser*, 1939)[225] in the six state camps around Australia via an ABC radio broadcast:

> Quite sincerely, I welcome this opportunity of saying a few things to you. They are not said merely formally, or officially, but personally. I am your Prime Minister, to be sure, and, I hope, an earnest and patriotic citizen, but I am talking to thousands of men whose earnestness and patriotism are—such that they have become the living bulwark of Australia. (*Daily Telegraph & North Murchison & Pilbara Gazette*, 1939)[226]

The previous quote indicated ABC Radio had become a powerful tool and that a politician had identified it as a 'personal' medium to speak to individuals. Among many other war efforts, the ABC also ran a "Patriotic Poem Contest" (*The Chronicle*, 1941)[227] and provided specific content and broadcast programs that "helped to keep the men of the A.I.F. and R.A.A.F. in touch with news from home" (ABC, 1941).[228]

In 1940, the ABC General Manager, (Major) Charles Moses, took temporary leave from the ABC to take up a post as company commander with the 8th Battalion in Singapore (Thomas Bearup became acting General Manager). Captain Moses escaped a Japanese ambush, ended up in Jakarta, became seriously ill after being hit by a taxi and was later mentioned in dispatches when his next unit the 2/7th Cavalry Regiment fought in Sananandа, Papua New Guinea (Petersen, 2012).[229] Similarly, the ABC encouraged its employees to serve in the defence forces releasing a new policy that offered full ABC salaries for the duration of their service[230] but, as indicated earlier, the consequence was "depleted by enlistments" (ABC Annual Report 1940–41) and it fell to remaining staff to carry additional duties and roles. According to Inglis (1983)[231] about 40 ABC employees entered the defence forces from 1939 to 1940. Even with the loss of staff, there was 149,855 hours broadcast that financial year (reported in the 1939–1940 ABC Annual Report) and this increased by 12.68% the following year (1940–1941 ABC Annual Report). This research was unable to discover the number of ABC staff employed during the war years.

In 1942, the next Prime Minister, John Curtin, gave a national address describing the "Battle for Australia" broadcast on the ABC and warning in evocative language against a lack of patriotism and that the:

> Mortal crime is a weakening in our purpose and therefore our unity. Whosoever is guilty of that crime or of bringing it about in others, of him let it be said it would be better that a mill stone was hung about his neck and that he was cast into the sea. (*The News*, 1942)[232]

The speech was impactful and had substantial reach because in 1939 "Australia was then fifth among the countries of the world in the number of wireless listeners per hundred of population" (1939–1940 ABC Annual Report).[233] Australians were listening—and "yours" was a resounding "ours". Curtin said the fall of Singapore was "Australia's Dunkirk".[234] However, military history has shown there was not really a strong similarity between Dunkirk and Singapore. The historical irony is that the British Army was rescued from Dunkirk, then in Singapore the British Army became prisoners of the Japanese. Analyses of the Australian "invasion" crisis have described the "Battle for Australia" and Japanese invasion story as a fabrication, with belief now that Japan had no intention of invading Australia (*The Age*, 2002,[235] quoting former principal historian of the Australian War Memorial, Peter Stanley[236]). Rather, Japan envisaged Australia as just outside its economic circle in the Pacific—"the raw materials of the South Seas" (2006)[237]—and attempted to isolate and weaken the nation to gain control and leverage (*The Age*, Ibid.) in the region. Australia knew this. However, they did not want to let the Japanese know they had learned this after the US intercepted and decoded Japanese war communications (Ibid.).

Leaving the historical, geo-political, military strategy analysis aside, the Australian media—the ABC—were complicit in perpetuating the Curtin "Battle for Australia" story on behalf of the Federal Government. Onerous censorship and control on all media meant that to all intents and purposes, it was a national emergency. So, the Australian public was convinced and unquestioning of the veracity of this message because the media resonated this received truth. The ABC told them so. The effectiveness of radio in circulating this message was powerful and recalls what Bertolt Brecht said in 1930 (Silberman, 2016): “The public was not waiting for the radio, but rather the radio was waiting for the public”.[238] This researcher’s late father told this researcher he remembered clearly, at age 13, that when his family heard the Curtin speech on the home wireless in rural New South Wales, his family was shocked into silence. He told me that living in rural Australia, the scale of the invasion threat as deeply concerning to rural Australians who dealt with other regular perils of floods, droughts, bushfires, pests and isolation. He said the next thing he remembered was that he and his parents dug an air-raid shelter at the end of the house paddock, as did many others in rural Australia. They stocked it with tinned food. Clearly, ABC Radio delivered a message that was received, understood and acted upon.

This researcher’s mother, who was then a young girl in rural New South Wales at the time, was told that she saw her mother cry when the family listened to Curtin’s speech on the “wireless” and within six weeks, her third son (this researcher’s uncle) had enlisted in the AIF and was sent to New Guinea. This researcher’s mother said after her brother had been sent on active service, her mother would sit by the radio every night and listen with tears in her eyes to the evening news on the ABC. It was understood she had a poignant expectation she would hear good news about her son’s welfare and his return home. Both this researchers’ parents; youths in the war, agreed that they, their families and their rural communities, all reliant and utterly trusting of the ABC, were convinced of this danger and reacted accordingly, patriotically and stoically. If it was heard on the ABC, this researcher’s father would reflect, “then it was so”. This researcher’s late father said part of his family’s war effort also involved responding to instructions heard on ABC Radio to take part in a government drive to gather all the aluminium saucepans they could spare. They took them to ‘the collection train’ at the railway station to be sent off to help the war effort. He said that new saucepans became hard to purchase because of the diversion of iron-making towards war materiel, which was corroborated in newspapers published at the time.[239] Fears of invasion later resonated among Australians with radio news of the bombing of Darwin (there were actually many, but un-reported) and a Japanese submarine sinking ships in Sydney Harbour, so it was not hard for people to remain worried and supportive of the national war effort with this described, imminent threat. The ABC bound communities together in this crisis and a rare trust was invested in the broadcaster.

6.9 Axings and Dispatchings

During the time Michelle Guthrie was the Managing Director there was concern that recruitment favoured younger staff and older staff were being encouraged to leave. An anonymous ABC producer was quoted:

> The contempt of managers for older experienced staff has become a culture which has flowed out into the work floor and there's now a generational divide. (Meade, 2018)[240]

There were anonymous concerns in the media that "experienced staff are ditched for inexperienced staff who take longer to do a job because they don't know how to do it, and they have no one to learn from" (Meade Ibid.).[241] The news report said that: "Since 2014, more than 1100 ABC staff have been retrenched—that's one quarter of the workforce—and most of the retrenchments were older, experienced staff"[242] (Loc. Cit.). Other concerns about Guthrie's term of office involved claims refuted by the ABC's Chief Finance and Strategy Officer, Louise Higgins, that Guthrie was "invisible"—"if Guthrie is not 'visible' it's because she has her head down working and it is very unfair criticism" (Meade, Ibid.).[243] However, a former ABC executive was quoted saying that her non-appearance due to family reasons at the first Budget Estimates Meeting after the Federal Budget was handed down was considered a serious mistake because: "Estimates was the time when Michelle should have been very visible and the organisation should have seen her" (Ibid.).[244] Another staff member said: "She had one job" (Ibid.).[245]

Head of the ABC branch Union of the Community and Public Sector Union, Sinddy Ealy, said "the ABC's culture has changed since 2014 and too much corporate memory has been ripped out" (Ibid.):

> Many staff are fighting hard to resist attempts to dumb down the content and the quality of the ABC but it's hard to stand up to a leadership that is intent on silencing dissent within the organisation. (Loc. Cit.)[246]

One outstanding instance of political position-taking occurred during the leadership of Guthrie and Chairman Justin Milne. In 2018, such was the concern of bias in ABC content that Milne resigned and Guthrie was dismissed. The focus of concern was that the Federal Government had expressed its unease at the perceived bias of two ABC reporters: Economics

Correspondent Emma Alberici and Political Editor Andrew Probyn. Guthrie gave the board a copy of a Milne's private email to her. Three days later she was sacked by the board (24 September 2018). The Milne email stated:

> After two glasses of red of course there's an agenda. They fricken hate her. She keeps sticking it to them with a clear bias against them. We clear her as ok. We r tarred with her brush. I just think it's simple. Get rid of her. My view is we need to save the corporation not Emma. There is no g'tee they will lose the next election [sic]. (Pha, 2018)[247]

Guthrie said she had also had a personal conversation with Milne who told her to "shoot Probyn" (Pha, ibid.) because he had caused the displeasure of Prime Minister Malcolm Turnbull. Guthrie stated on the public record:

> I reiterated the need to maintain public trust and the ABC couldn't be responding or be seen to be responding to pressure from the government of the day. In response, Mr Milne continued to yell at me and berate me and wouldn't let me finish the call. (Pha, Ibid.)

An ABC Radio Producer was quoted: "the ABC is now run by managers who have never been content makers" (Meade, 2018)[248] and an anonymous staff member told the Federal Parliament: "quality News and Current Affairs coverage appears to have gone out the window (Anonymous ND).[249] Staff had been upset that there was a de-emphasis of news content after Mark Scott ended the state editions of the *730* current affairs television program; then, Guthrie had cancelled the political analysis program *Lateline* and reduced radio current affairs programming (Meade, 2018).[250] There was concern that radio content had been reduced to "all froth and bubble" (Meade, 2018) with a de-emphasis on music, religious and documentary content. In addition, ABC management was accused of being "morally and spiritually bankrupt" for cancelling the ABC television science program *Catalyst* (Meade, 2016).[251] The television current affairs program, *Foreign Correspondent*, was experiencing ongoing cuts and reductions.

The public service media outfit told a Senate inquiry on the Economic and Cultural Value of Australian Content that since 2014 its drama content had dropped 20%, factual programming 60% and documentary 13.5%

(Meade, 2018).[252] It was reported that Screen Producers Australia told the inquiry that "if the trend continued, the ABC would no longer be the home of Australian stories" (Meade, Ibid.). All the while the ABC expanded into new digital spaces and platforms tracking down conversations about stories that it believed mattered to all Australians, and diverted funds to pay for its television news channel, News Channel, which had a reach of 4.4 million viewers each week.[253] On this it was difficult to obtain an exact figure on the cost of the outfit and it was revealed in 2011 that the costs were conflated with other costs (Simons, 2011).[254] When the service was launched, Sky News executive, Angelos Frangopoulos, said the ABC would take funding from its existing services, yet the same service was available on commercial television (Dow Jones, 2010).[255] The News Channel Limited was described as a controlled entity in the ABC Annual Report 2017.[256] The ABC had four controlled entities, all incorporated in Australia except ABC AustraliaPlus (Shanghai) Cultural Development Co., Ltd which is incorporated in the People's Republic of China (ABC Annual Report, ibid).

Political influences on the ABC were not always focused on money and could have policy changes as their impetus as part of government pressure on the ABC to be more relevant. In 2016, staff were reported to have expressed concern to Guthrie about the loss of experienced program-makers and their content through redundancies (Meade, 2016)[257] as the ABC's Radio National was shifted to talk only, no more music programs. It was reported that Guthrie challenged this by raising her voice to assembled staff and asking: "what they would do" and to "justify their massive budget when their reach is so low" (Meade, 2016). She then added: "I hate to break it to you but this is a very small decision for me" (Meade, ibid.). The changes were part of the ABC's "digital pivot strategy" (Knott, 2016)[258] aimed at "keeping the broadcaster relevant" (Ibid.), with one ABC senior executive quoted: "RN hasn't grown its audience in 10 years, yet they would prefer it to remain a cul de sac. They think digital strategy is when you upgrade an alarm clock" (Knott, 2016). In reply, an ABC radio executive said "Radio National had been the most innovative and sophisticated part of the ABC. … The real agenda here is to take a huge chunk of resources out of RN and dumb it down" (Meade, 2016).[259] A large group of artists and musicians wrote an open letter to Guthrie and the ABC Board about the loss of music:

> We are deeply concerned about listeners in regional, rural and remote areas where the internet and digital radio access is problematic at best. Many of these listeners rely on linear broadcasting. (Meade, 2016)

Again, there is the fervent belief that everyone is online at all times, and if not, they should be, or, perhaps they are old and/or incompetent with technology and redundant audiences anyway. Yet, none of these accusations may apply and there are other reasons, as ABC staff pointed out in anonymous comments. Access is still highly problematic and challenges Aunty's charter to be 'all to all' where there are gaps in access to digital devices and consistent, existent Broadband. It had become a city-based assumption that all of Australia was widely and profoundly connected in real time. But the corollary, and fallacy was that it might not be possible to have national conversations with everyone, at once, ever again, in the new deeply-fragmented, haphazard emergent commercial digital *field*. It was reported that Guthrie had told staff that the ABC had focus on building an audience of "15–30 and 30–50-year-olds, who had left it in droves" (Manning, 2018).[260] The challenge with this for the ABC was trying to grow an audience where "digital media are part of the taken-for-granted social and cultural fabric of learning, play, and social communication" (Ito, in Metzger & Flanagin, 2008).[261]

The ABC was now part of the media complex of digital education including: "reflected in expressions of identity, how individuals express independence and creativity, and in their ability to learn, exercise judgment, and think systematically" (Ito, in Letzger & Flanagin, ibid.). Guthrie said the new ABC focus was based on a reconceptualisation of the institution: "I think of the ABC much more as an ecosystem than a standalone organisation and I do think the future will be much more of a partnership model" (Meade, 2017).[262] Part of the reconceptualisation of the ABC in partnerships. But, this should involve considerations of valuing, transposing and translating its *cultural capital* into the emergent digital commercial *field* and enforcing it in the commercial *field*. Abandoning that process, relegated the ABC to just another voice in the noisy, shouty commercial *field* and failed to build on its heritage and legacy of being a respected and esteemed educator of the citizens, to which it served.

Swirling around the politics of Guthrie's leadership were personalised staff rumours that she was Rupert Murdoch and Liberal Prime Minister Malcolm Turnbull's choice for the role (Manning, 2018) where she had worked previously for Murdoch at Star TV in Asia and Google. Guthrie rejected the accusations that her work for Murdoch made her "a Murdoch hatchet woman" and she rejected accusations that she had been "Googlising" the ABC (Meade, ibid.). But to place all of this perspective, the ABC had been subjected to accusations of lapses in quality, historically, as examples in this book provided. For example, there was another complicated incident in 1945, when ABC Chairman William Cleary resigned because of "open clashes between Senator Amour and Mr Cleary regarding the quality of programmes presented by the ABC" (*Northern Star*, 1945).[263] However, perhaps when the Chairman of the Parliamentary Committee on Broadcasting (Senator Amour) said, "I know nothing about it" (*The Canberra Times*, 1945)[264] in regard to Cleary's resignation, he was speaking the truth. While Cleary complained later at a government inquiry that there had been political interferences from Canberra, it may not have been the trigger event that actually caused his resignation without immediate explanation. The inquiry was told that ministers were demanding programs be cancelled and that their ministerial announcements be read on air (*The Newcastle Sun*, 1945),[265] which was the source of the political interference, described as clashes over quality.

In an anonymous article by "a staff correspondent" published in *The Sydney Morning Herald* (1945), Cleary's role at the ABC was described as an "aloof leadership" in a satirical, vilifying and personal article. Cleary was said to be "a machine" who would not brook interruption at meetings, was cut "off from the public" and had "iron control over his feelings" (*The Sydney Morning Herald*, Ibid.).[266] To balance this, *The Sun* (1945) newspaper published an article in praise of Cleary. It said his resignation was "a great loss to the cause of Australia's cultural development" and his leadership was one that showed "wise and consistent endeavour to combine entertainment with that duty which is laid on all such bodies as the ABC" (*The Sun*, 1945).[267] While the Communist newspaper *The Tribune* was more entertainingly blunt when it said: "for a long time. Mr Cleary has been waging a lone fight against the efforts of wowsers, tory extremists and sectarian influences to strangle free expression on the air" (*The Tribune*, 1945).[268] He was later praised by the board for his efforts during his time as Chairman during which he set up what would become a heritage of symphony orchestras in each state. The Board said:

> Cleary had seen the service' grow from a small beginning to a national asset of incalculable possibilities. It was largely through his instrumentality that there had developed in Australia an increasing demand for good music. (*The Canberra Times*, 1945)[269]

The ABC had built its *cultural capital* on music. The lack of valuing and failure of policy to capture and transfer that *cultural capital* into the digital *field* has become a core, implied, concern of staff, artists and their audiences.

6.10 Aunty's Voice: Supporting a Free, Democratic Society

The freedom of the media to publish was one of the freedoms of a liberal democracy. A clumsy truism, perhaps, but certainly a complicated one because it permitted the peoples' capacity to 'upset the apple-cart' with accompanied rights and freedoms. These included civil liberties, freedom to vote, freedom of religious expression, freedom of speech, freedom to protest peacefully, debate policies and ideas, and provide a "critique of ruling powers and prevalent ideologies, policies, and institutions" (Zafirovski, 2017).[270] Media freedom supported these with implied unfettered access to information to inform the citizenry. On the other hand, the world had changed, as had its institutions, and media consumers pursued content that fitted with their own world-view. The literature concluded that professional media influence was not as powerful as it was believed. Media influence still took place—albeit now in more "circuitous ways" (Curran & Seaton, 2018).[271] The great challenge for public service media is how to manage themselves in an emergent, commercial media field. Quentin Dempster, former ABC broadcaster, was critical of the ongoing commercialisation for the ABC in a farewell interview. He said it began with the Labor Government of Prime Minister, Bob Hawke, and later emphasised by Liberal Prime Minister Malcolm Turnbull who wanted the ABC to work under efficiency dividends (Parker, 2014).[272] Dempster said this was measuring the success of the ABC in commercial terms when it was not a profit-making private enterprise: "the functional role of a public broadcaster is to look at their audience as citizens in a democracy, not as consumers" (Parker, ibid.).

The first edition of Australia's only national daily newspaper was launched in 1964 by Rupert Murdoch explaining that the newspaper was created "because you want it; because the nation needs it" (*The Australian*, 1964).[273] In many ways this was the opposite of the launch of the ABC in 1932 in that Australians did not necessarily know they wanted or needed a national broadcaster, but grew to love it. They had no inkling of the eventual extent and remit of the institution and how important it was to become. The creation of the ABC was also a way for the government to centralise control of the new medium of radio. It was not simply the unleashing of a new means of communication, as in the case of *The Australian* newspaper. It was part of the government's communications strategy and policy. It would support the development of nationhood. Commercial media had also always had elevated ambitions of its purpose: for instance, in 1831, the first edition of *The Sydney Morning Herald* said: "our editorial management style shall be conducted upon principles of candour, honesty, and honour" (*The Sydney Morning Herald*, 1831)[274] then 23 years later the first edition of Melbourne's *The Age* newspaper proclaimed: "the newspaper has become the great teacher of the age" (*The Age*, 1854).[275]

However, apart from sharing statements aiming for the greater good and intrinsic worth the ABC was also quite different to all of that. Newspapers were business enterprises and commercial organisations tracked down advertisers to pay for their incomes, their news and profits. The ABC was an extension of the government, a property of the state, unique in the Australian media ecology and separate in the food chain (the government's multicultural broadcaster, Special Broadcasting Service, SBS, now accepted paid commercial advertising with government funding, so its content had become monetised by businesses). The ABC was engaged in a constant quest to attend to the expectations of political control, and pursue its understanding of independence in the emergent commercial *field* where it walks that scary tightrope of 'all to all'.

The relationship between the ABC and successive Australian Governments had usually been nuanced over the decades, with the ABC managing the torment of funding cuts, the resentment of political interference, a restive and reactive staff culture, and appeasement of those who controlled the purse strings. That the ABC had managed to develop and persevere, in spite of and because of these, was a substantial tribute to how in spite of its institutional complexities it had sustained itself as a national public service. Yet, what formed a vital and unacknowledged part of this survival had been the continuation of its legacy role, now devalued in a digitised and monetised world, where anything old is actually old and research had found ageism flourished on social media (McNamara & Williamson, 2019). Aunty was the eldest member of the Australian professional media, but faced the challenge of trying to put on a youthful appearance while putting a value on her *reputation* and *capital* in the emergent commercial *field*. ABC content was now subjected to the same consumer algorithms of online success as commercial media, but there was diminished evidence of attempts to sustain the institution's inherent, historical value.

6.11 Raiding the News

On 4 June 2019 the ABC found itself in awkward proximity and in the same boat as its mortal enemy, Rupert Murdoch, when it had been raided by Federal Police the day after his newspaper. The Australian Federal Police (AFP) raided the Canberra home of News Corporation Sunday newspaper Political Editor Annika Smethurst. They alleged that there had been an unauthorised leak of "national security information" to her including "official secrets" in a story she wrote in April 2018. It was reported that the AFP spent seven hours at her home (ABC, 2019)[276] investigating content on her mobile phone, her computer and the rest of her home (Ferguson, 2019).[277] Smethurst's report under contention was published on 29 April 2018 and included photographs of government documents. Smethurst's report also claimed that "the Home Affairs and Defence departments were considering giving spy agencies greater surveillance powers" (ABC, 2019)[278] and that "the new espionage powers that would see the Australian Signals Directorate monitor Australian citizens for the first time" (Ferguson, 2019).[279] News Corporation stated that the raid "demonstrates a dangerous act of intimidation towards those committed to telling uncomfortable truths. The raid was outrageous and heavy handed" (Ferguson, Ibid.)[280] and that "what's gone on this morning sends clear and dangerous signals to journalists and newsrooms across Australia. This will chill public interest reporting" (Loc. Cit.).[281]

The next day the AFP raided the ABC. This time AFP officers were searching for leaked documents that informed a 2017 series of reports "The Afghan Files" (ABC, 2019).[282] These news reports covered allegations of unlawful killings by Australian troops in Afghanistan. The reports were derived from "hundreds of pages of secret Defence documents leaked to the ABC" (Knowles et al., 2019)[283] and according to the ABC "gave an unprecedented insight into the operations of Australia's élite special forces, detailing incidents of troops killing unarmed men and children and accusing Australian forces of having a "warrior culture"" (Oakes & Clark, 2017).[284] The AFP team spent eight hours at ABC headquarters in Sydney pursuing relevant content. ABC journalists Dan Oakes and Sam Clark, as well as the ABC's director of News, Gaven Morris, were named on the search warrant which stated that the search was: "in relation to allegations of publishing classified material, contrary to provisions of the Crimes Act 1914" and "relates to a referral received on 11 July 2017 by the Chief of the Defence Force and the then-Acting Secretary for Defence" (Knowles et al., 2019).[285] The AFP seizure included "124 files on two USB sticks" (McKinnell, 2020).[286]

The AFP gave an undertaking that the material would remain sealed until the legal proceedings have been resolved. ABC Editorial Director, Craig McMurtrie, said the raid was a "very unwelcome and serious development" (Knowles et al., 2019)[287] and that "there was no public interest defence in the section of the Crimes Act under which the ABC was being pursued" (Koziol, 2019).[288] Morris said "journalism is not a crime" (Knowles et al., 2019).[289] He was reported by the ABC to have tweeted:

> For the record,@DanielMOakes and @sclark_melbs are two of @abcnews' finest journalists. Honest and committed to telling the truth in the Australian public's interests. Just like @annikasmethurst. I'm proud of the difficult work they all do. (Knowles et al., Ibid.)[290]

Media, Entertainment and Arts Alliance President, Marcus Strom, said:

> These raids are all about intimidating journalists and intimidating whistle blowers so that mistakes made by the Government, including potential crimes, by the military, remain covered up, remain secret, and don't fall in to the public domain. (Knowles et al. Loc. Cit.)[291]

The ABC's Managing Director, David Anderson, said the raid was "an attempt to intimidate journalists for doing their jobs. … This is at odds with our expectation that we live in an open and transparent society" (McKinnell, 2020).[292] The whistle-blower used by the ABC, David William McBride, a military lawyer, had already been charged under the Defence Act and the Crimes Act for leaking documents and for making public admissions of his involvement with the ABC report (Wootton, 2019).[293] A statement from Home Affairs Minister Peter Dutton said he was "not notified prior to the execution of the warrants. … The AFP's actions have been independent and impartial at all times" and "conduct their investigations and carry out their operations independent from the Government" and that he was only alerted when the search warrants were executed (Knowles et al., 2019).[294] A legal challenge by the ABC on the validity of the warrants was dismissed in 2020 by the Federal Court and the ABC ordered to pay costs. ABC head of investigative journalism John Lyons said: "It is a bad day for Australian journalism. ... After 18 months, we still have two journalists that face possible criminal charges" (McKinnell, 2020).[295] Gaven Morris said:

> It's clear that the way public-interest journalism is able to be undertaken in this country is a mess. ... I think fundamentally the court has ruled the AFP has the right to enter a newsroom and fossick around in confidential files. This should send a chill down all our citizens' spines. (Trask, 2020)[296]

Australian journalist Tony Koch said in an opinion piece that the raid on the ABC was a show by the AFP for their "political masters" to please them and appear to be a relevant force (Koch, 2019).[297] The ABC (and Smethurst) were being prosecuted under Part 6 of the Crimes Act—unauthorised disclosure of information by Commonwealth officers—public servants—but not the journalists and editors involved in publication as well as Part 7, section 79 of the act, related to "official secrets" where "any person who receives or communicates a secret document without permission has committed an indictable offence and faces up to seven years imprisonment" (Koziol, 2019).[298] Sections 6 and 7 of the Crimes Act were since repealed and the offences now come under the Criminal Code, nonetheless the AFP can prosecute based on the law at the time of the search warrants (Koziol, ibid.).[299] It was claimed that alleged breaches of national security laws in the passing on of the documents to the ABC (and The Australian) were referred to the AFP by senior public servants (Loc. Cit.).[300] The raids were an example of the "two ... central forces that shape the development of the news media"—"the commercial and the political" (Miekle, 2009).[301]

The literature agreed that media freedom and democracy were two key tools in the fight against political corruption (Bhattacharyya & Hodler, 2015)[302] and maintaining a vigilant watch on power. According to McChesney (2008) "journalism in any meaningful sense cannot survive without a viable democracy" (McChesney, 2008).[303] However, the media reaction showed that a dichotomy between authoritarianism and media freedom was over-simplified and misleading (Fenton, 2014)[304] because the media was dominated by powerful élite voices and under constant contestation because democracy. The media are: "subject to social forces and indeed social movements that may challenge established and vested interests" (Fenton, ibid.)[305] where "much news is about the violation of values" (Gans, 2004)[306] anyway, where "government is the primary source of pressure" (Gans, Ibid.).[307] The type of stories reported by the ABC in the case of "The Afghan Files" represented what Gans (2004) described as "moral disorder news" where the publication of these reports was aimed at punishing those who deviated from societal values (Gans, ibid.).[308] While "the assumptions and routines of what is known as 'objective journalism', made it exceedingly easy for officials to manipulate day to day news content" (Hallin, 1989)[309] (as was the case in the Vietnam War) it was only those times when media stepped out of familiar reporting rubrics into accessing unnamed sources and publishing secret information that it had fallen foul of government control and hence subjection to harsh legal censure.

However, Schudson (1978) said that journalists had "no systemic means of policing their own intellectual narrowness" and that they should remain open to the changes in society (Schudson, 1978)[310] and were not an insulated profession because most of the trust journalists invested in their sacred role in society sprang from the myth of the Fourth Estate that enveloped democracy and holding power to account. However, they now competed with the "rise of amateurism"—anyone can be a journalist and call them self as such (Blach-Ørsten & Burkal, 2014).[311] Online citizen and professional journalists were now able to interact in new ways building networks of trust (Nah & Chung, 2012)[312] where there also existed "an information and communication marketplace that sustains the commodification and mass consumption of adversarial, anti-establishment news" (Greer & McLaughlin, 2010)[313] and the "romanticised individualism" (Markham, 2011)[314] of citizen journalism.

As discussed in a previous chapter, there was no professional body that registered journalists, prescribed training and standards, nor called them to account, yet many other professions were governed by rules. While there were media university degrees, there were no professionally prescribed subjects, nor professionally directed expectations of course study—these were chosen by the universities who told journalists and the industry what they should know. The rise of social media amateurs within the ranks of professional journalists meant that news journalism was not playing the fundamentally professional role in society that it once did. Journalism was now in peril (Blach-Ørsten & Burkal Ibid.).[315] Journalists had to re-assert their professionalism on a daily basis without the struts of professional standards provided by those who practiced medicine or law, for example (Loc. Cit.).[316] However, contradicting this pessimism was the view that because so many people read blogs and believed their content: "the journalistic profession must make room for bloggers on the news scene and give up some of their power" (Robinson & De Shano, 2011).[317] This made it a highly contested and volatile *field* for the reputation of the ABC which had always considered itself the authoritative voice of Australian news, issues, entertainment and events. It left the ABC with the choice "if you can't beat them, join them" but meant sacrificing *cultural capital* in the drift to belong.

Henry Mayer, the late Professor of Government, The University of Sydney and described as "founding father of the study of mass communication in Australia" (Goot & Inglis, 2014)[318] wrote in 1964 that the Australian press media was riven with a "Janus view" (Mayer, 1964)[319] of the world—it must look to its mythical Fourth Estate role as well as keeping its other eye on the realities of its business. In the case of the ABC this metaphor could be extended to include the ABC with one eye on its Federal Government budget allocation and the other on its "business". To put Mayer's "Janus" criticism in context, Mayer was also concerned that it meant the press avoided acknowledging and navigating conflicts of objectives (Mayer, Ibid.).[320] It also meant that the media, in particular the ABC, would be called to account more frequently with its shift in *field*, movement in boundaries of professional practice, new liberties in expression and inevitable clashes with political actors, funders and operatives both within and without the institution.

This chapter discussed concerns about the quality of ABC content with staff loses and departure of institutional knowledge and processes that supported an independent and neutral information outlet. It also examined the case where both the ABC and its nemesis News Corporation were subjected to government raids on their offices or staff homes to retrieve confidential, sensitive data supplied to both the media businesses. It described the role of institutional actors in promoting major change was having a negative impact on the long-established norms and practices of the ABC and how management had demonstrated opinions that contradicted pursuit of 'the greater good' for the chase of online audiences. There had been no public attention paid to the ABC's cultural and reputational capital and how to transpose it into the emergent commercial field. This had detracted from the ABC's role to serve as a public service by pretending to be an important player in a crowded, commercial sandpit.

Attending to the intangible greater good of a common future may not be an easy fit with institutional and managerial expectations of KPIs (key performance indicators) and financial objectives. It had been explicated through the analysis of extant the literature, documented observations and events a decline in ABC journalistic standards. The downturns in democratic rights and freedoms are germane to these shifts. Revisions of previous practice are overlooked in favour of shifts in institutional priorities and the prevalence of social media as a research tool. Ultimately, it has meant that journalists had a new understanding of public, public interest and the greater good consisting of sometimes disparate groups, tribes and special interests. This has had serious ramifications for the very role of a public broadcaster, supported by universal taxpayer funding and federal legislation. The ABC was not answerable to consumers, yet it had placed itself in that invidious, untenable position. This chapter raised four key points. First, how a free, robust ABC required commitment ipso facto from state actors (political leaders) to supply the state enterprise with adequate money to fulfil its role and government policy support to strengthen its institutional function. Second, how the ABC lacked a decisive, consistent management that understood the value of the ABC's *cultural* and *reputational capital*, and, following from that did not demonstrate a strong grasp on how the institution should now operate in the dangerous, emergent, digital environment. Fourth, the priority to quest for relevance by pursuing fickle, virtual audiences—described in the literature as being creators of content, self-directed (Livingston, 2004) and engaged in a performer/audience relationship (Litt, 2012)—was demanding the ABC re-shape its institutional practice (and content, just as these "prosumers" did). Yet, when Aunty did that she relinquished her cultural leadership role to become just another member of this parochial and self-serving "prosumer" group. Compounding this dilemma, the research literature found when journalists became part of the social media marketplace, respect from audiences diminished (Banjac & Hanusch, 2020). All these matters had compromised the national media outfit. In summary, the institution's activities demonstrated that it had not organised an ensemble approach to meet the changed definition, activities and identities of "audience" and had provided no means to install and reassert its *cultural capital* and *reputational capital* in these rabble-rousing social spaces.

Notes

1. West Australian, The. (1945). Paper attacked. "Blatant inaccuracies". ABC and Mr Churchill. *The West Australian.* 2 March 1945, p. 4. Retrieved from: https://trove.nla.gov.au/newspaper/article/44999578?searchTerm=inaccuracies%20ABC&searchLimits=.
2. Simon, M. (2005). Fear and Loathing at the ABC. *The Monthly.* May 2005. pp. 28–38. Retrieved from: https://search.informit.com.au/documentSummary;dn=200511241;res=IELAPA>.
3. Amenta, E. & Ramsey, K.M. (2010). Institutional Theory. In Handbook of Politics: State and Society in Global Perspective (Eds. K.T. Leicht & J.C. Jenkins). Springer. New York, NY. Retrieved: DOI: https://doi.org/10.1007/978-0-387-68930-2_2 (pp. 15–39).
4. Hall, P.A. and Taylor, R.C. (1996). Political science and the three new institutionalisms. *Political Studies. Discussion Paper.* 44:5. pp. 936–957. Retrieved from: http://search.proquest.com/docview/1008864601/.
5. Brown, A. (1996). Public service broadcasting in four countries: Overview. *The Journal of Media Economics.* 9:1. pp. 77–81. Retrieved from: https://doi.org/info:doi/.
6. Ariño, M. & Ahlert, C. (2004) Beyond broadcasting: the digital future of public service broadcasting. *Prometheus.* 22:4. pp. 393–410. Retrieved from: DOI: https://doi.org/10.1080/0810902041231311678.
7. Scott, M. (2010). New opportunities, new obligations: Public broadcasting in the era of choice. Commonwealth Broadcasting Association Conference. 20 April 2010. *Australian Broadcasting Corporation.* Retrieved from: http://about.abc.net.au/speeches/new-opportunities-new-obligations-public-broadcasting-in-the-era-of-choice/.
8. Anderson, D. (2020). Connecting and Uniting All Australians: National Press Club address. *Australian Broadcasting Corporation.* 8 July 2020. Retrieved from: https://about.abc.net.au/speeches/connecting-and-uniting-all-australians-national-press-club-address/.
9. Alexander, J. (2014). Notes towards a definition of politics. *Philosophy.* 89:348. pp. 273–300. Retrieved from: https://doi.org/10.1017/S0031819113000855.
10. McGuinness, P.P. (2000). The future of the Australian Broadcasting Corporation. *Quadrant.* 44:12. Dec 2000. pp. 2–4. Retrieved from: https://search-informit-com-au.wwwproxy1.library.unsw.edu.au/documentSummary;dn=733687171221108;res=IELLCC.
11. Grattan, M. (2014). What future for the ABC? *Public Administration Today.* 37:January/March 2014. pp. 22–23. Retrieved from: https://search-informit-com-au.wwwproxy1.library.unsw.edu.au/fullText;dn=20141588;res=AGISPT.

12. Semmler, C. (1981). *The ABC - Aunt Sally and Sacred Cow.* Melbourne University Press. Melbourne. p. 22.
13. García-Gutiérrez, I. & Martínez-Borreguero, F.J. (2016). The Innovation Pivot Framework: Fostering Business Model Innovation in Startups. *Research Technology Management.* *59*:5. pp. 48–56. Retrieved from: https://doi.org/10.1080/08956308.2016.1208043.
14. Orvos, J. (2019). *Achieving Business Agility : Strategies for Becoming Pivot Ready in a Digital World* (1st ed. 2019.). Apress. Retrieved from: https://primoa.library.unsw.edu.au/permalink/f/jhud33/UNSW_ALMA51274521450001731.
15. Grattan, M. (2014). What future for the ABC? *Public Administration Today.* 37:January/March 2014. pp. 22–23. Retrieved from: https://search-informit-com-au.wwwproxy1.library.unsw.edu.au/fullText;dn=20141588;res=AGISPT.
16. Brown, A., & Althaus, C. (1996). Public Service Broadcasting in Australia. *Journal of Media Economics.* 9:1. p. 31. Retrieved from: https://doi-org.wwwproxy1.library.unsw.edu.au/10.1207/s15327736me0901_4.
17. Scannell, P. (1989). Public service broadcasting and modern public life. *Media, Culture & Society.* 11:2. pp. 135–166. Retrieved from: https://doi.org/10.1177/016344389011002002.
18. Kahane, G., Everett, J.A.C., Earp, B.D., Farias, M. & Savulescu, J., (2015). "'Utilitarian' judgments in sacrificial moral dilemmas do not reflect impartial concern for the greater good." Cognition. Vol: 143. pp. 193–209. Retrieved from: https://doi.org/10.1016/j.cognition.2014.10.005.
19. Ibid.
20. Choi, S. (2014). Flow, Diversity, Form, and Influence of Political Talk in Social-Media-Based Public Forums. *Human Communication Research.* 40:2. pp. 209–237. Retrieved from: https://doi.org/10.1111/hcre.12023.
21. Halpern, D., Valenzuela, S., & Katz, J. E. (2017). We Face, I Tweet: How Different Social Media Influence Political Participation through Collective and Internal Efficacy. *Journal of Computer-Mediated Communication*, *22*(6), 320–336. Retrieved from: https://doi.org/10.1111/jcc4.12198.
22. Weeks, B.E., Ardèvol-Abreu, A., Gil de Zúñiga, H. (2017). Online Influence? Social Media Use, Opinion Leadership, and Political Persuasion, *International Journal of Public Opinion Research.* 29:2. Summer 2017. pp. 214–239. Retrieved from: https://doi-org.wwwproxy1.library.unsw.edu.au/10.1093/ijpor/edv050.

23. Barnidge, M. (2015). The role of news in promoting political disagreement on social media. *Computers In Human Behavior.* 52. pp. 211–218. Retrieved from: https://doi.org/10.1016/j.chb.2015.06.011.
24. Ceron, A. (2015). Internet, News, and Political Trust: The Difference Between Social Media and Online Media Outlets. *Journal of Computer-Mediated Communication.* 20:5. pp. 487–503. Retrieved from: https://doi.org/10.1111/jcc4.12129\.
25. Soley, C. (2005). The public is sick of us both. *British Journalism Review.* 16:1. pp. 35–39. Retrieved from: https://doi.org/10.1177/0956474805053357. p. 35.
26. Whitehead, G. (1988). *Inside the ABC: Geoffrey Whitehead's Personal Account.* Penguin Books Victoria. p. 111.
27. Berg, C. & Davidson, S. (2018). *Against Public Broadcasting: Why We Should Privatise The ABC and How To Do It.* Connor Court Publishing. Brisbane.
28. Spadaro SJ, A. (2020) Defy the Apocalypse. *La Civiltà Cattolica.* 20 January 2020. Retrieved from: https://www.laciviltacattolica.com/defy-the-apocalypse/.
29. Rutherford, L., & Brown, A. (2013). The Australian Broadcasting Corporation's multiplatform projects: Industrial logics of children's content provision in the digital television era. *Convergence.* 19:2. pp. 201–221. Retrieved from: https://doi.org/10.1177/1354856512457749.
30. Blain, E. (1977). *Life with Aunty: 40 years with the ABC.* Methuen Australia. Sydney. p. 17.
31. Blain, E. (1977). *Life with Aunty: Forty Years with the ABC.* Methuen of Australia. Sydney. p. 75.
32. Bagshaw, Eryk. (2019). Kenneth Hayne: Trust in politics has been destroyed. *The Sydney Morning Herald.* 7 August. https://www.smh.com.au/politics/federal/kenneth-hayne-trust-in-politics-has-been-destroyed-20190807-p52evf.html.
33. Harding, R. (1979). *Outside Interference: The Politics of Australian Broadcasting.* Sun Books. Melbourne. p. vii.
34. Shergold, P. (2017). Re-imagining public service [online]. *The Australian Journal of Social Issues.* 52:1. pp. 4–12. Retrieved from: https://search-informit-com-au.wwwproxy1.library.unsw.edu.au/documentSummary;dn=035171807770944;res=IELAPA.
35. Managerialism is a term devised in 1990 by Emeritus Professor Christopher Pollitt at the Public Governance Institute, Katholieke Universiteit Leuven, Belgium. His book was *Managerialism and the Public Services (1990)* in which he identified managerialism as an ideology linked with practices.

36. Lynch, K., Devine, D. & Grummell, B. (2012). New Managerialism in Education. In *New Managerialism in Education*. Palgrave Macmillan. Retrieved from: https://doi.org/10.1057/9781137007230.
37. Pollitt, C. (2016). Managerialism Redux? *Financial Accountability & Management*. 32:4. pp. 429–447. Retrieved from: https://doi.org/10.1111/faam.12094.
38. Cairns Post, The. (1937). ABC Attacked. CRUEL, COWARDLY BIAS. *The Cairns Post*. 10 September 1937. p. 11. Retrieved from: https://trove.nla.gov.au/newspaper/article/41816337?searchTerm=CRUEL%2C%20COWARDLY%20BIAS.
39. Quinn, K. (2016). ABC news director Gaven Morris says 'bias' is part of the job. *The Sydney Morning Herald*. 5 January 2016. Retrieved from: https://www.smh.com.au/entertainment/tv-and-radio/lunch-with-gaven-morris-abc-director-of-news-20160104-glz8q3.html.
40. Cavanagh, P. (2015). ABC Radio Current Affairs Coverage of The China-Australia Free Trade Agreement. Editorial Review No. 7. *Australian Broadcasting Corporation*. December 2015. Retrieved from: https://about.abc.net.au/wp-content/uploads/2016/02/ABC-Editorial-Review-No-7.pdf.
41. Parliament of Australia. (1996). The Mans*field* Review of The ABC. Retrieved from: https://www.aph.gov.au/Parliamentary_Business/Committees/Senate/Foreign_Affairs_Defence_and_Trade/Completed_inquiries/1996-99/radio/report/c04.
42. Committee of Review of the Australian Broadcasting Commission (aka the Dix Inquiry). (1981). The ABC in Review: National Broadcasting in the 1980s. *Analysis and Policy Observation*. 30 May 1981. Retrieved from: https://apo.org.au/node/41206.
43. *Canberra Times, The*. (1976). "Protest rally calls for public decision on ABC". The Canberra Times. 1 December 1976. p. 7. Retrieved from: https://trove.nla.gov.au/newspaper/article/131798632?searchTerm=Protest%20rally%20calls%20for%20public%20decision%20on%20ABC&searchLimits=.
44. Jolly, R. (2014). Media of the people: broadcasting community media in Australia. *Parliament House Australia*. 2 April 2014. Retrieved from: https://www.aph.gov.au/About_Parliament/Parliamentary_Departments/Parliamentary_Library/pubs/rp/rp1314/Media.
45. Jolly, R. (2014). Media of the people: broadcasting community media in Australia. *Parliament House Australia*. 2 April 2014. Retrieved from: https://www.aph.gov.au/About_Parliament/Parliamentary_Departments/Parliamentary_Library/pubs/rp/rp1314/Media.
46. Newcastle Morning Herald and Miners' Advocate, The. (1941). Number to be Increased. The Newcastle Morning Herald and Miners'

Advocate. 20 March 1941, p. 8. Retrieved from: https://trove.nla.gov.au/newspaper/article/140434400?searchTerm=abc%20employees%20number&searchLimits=#.

47. Sydney Morning Herald, The. (1948). "Impartiality of A.B.C. – Duty to Public." Letters to the Editor. *The Sydney Morning Herald*. 18 September 1948. p. 2. Retrieved from: https://trove.nla.gov.au/newspaper/article/18085248?searchTerm=Impartiality%20of%20A.B.C.%20%E2%80%93%20Duty%20to%20Public&searchLimits=.
48. Ibid.
49. Telegraph, The. (Brisbane). 1936. "Becoming haughty: ABC criticised: Artists now public servants. *The Telegraph*. 28 March 1936. p. 10. https://trove.nla.gov.au/newspaper/article/182665568?searchTerm=ABC%20public&searchLimits=.
50. Telegraph, The. (Brisbane). (1936). "Thinking Nationally: Mr Kitto outlines ABC policy: Giving the public the best." *The Telegraph*. 27 June 1936. p. 7. https://trove.nla.gov.au/newspaper/article/183377190?searchTerm=ABC%20public&searchLimits=.
51. King James Bible. The Book of Micah (4:3). *The King James Bible*. Retrieved from: https://biblehub.com/kjv/micah/4.htm.
52. Ibid.
53. Born, G. (2005). *Uncertain Vision: Birt, Dyke and the Reinvention of the BBC*. Vintage. Great Britain.
54. Born, G. (2005). *Uncertain Vision: Birt, Dyke and the Reinvention of the BBC*. Vintage. Great Britain. p. 28.
55. Gruen, D., & Clark, C. (2010). Nineteenth Colin Clark Lecture: November 2009 What have we Learnt?: The Great Depression in Australia from the Perspective of Today. *Economic Analysis and Policy*. 40:1. pp. 3–20. Retrieved from: https://doi.org/10.1016/S0313-5926(10)50001-8.
56. Australian Bureau of Statistics (2020). 6202.0 – Labour Force, Australia, Apr 2020. *Australian Bureau of Statistics*. Retrieved from: https://www.abs.gov.au/ausstats/abs@.nsf/mf/6202.0.
57. Dewey, J. (1916, re-publ. 2004). *Democracy and Education*. Dover Publications. Mineola, New York.
58. Levinson, M. (1999). *The Demands of Liberal Education*. Oxford University Press. Oxford.
59. Griffin, E. (2006). *A First Look at Communication Theory*. McGraw-Hill, New York. p. 30.
60. Riha, T. Ed. (1969). *Readings in Russian Civilization Volume III: Soviet Russia, 1917–1963*. 2nd Edition. University of Chicago Press. London & Chicago. p. 695.

61. Hongjie, C. & Jacob, W.J. Eds. (2017). *Trends in Chinese Education.* Chapter 15. L. Yunchan. "An examination of the "engineer of human souls" metaphor." Routledge. London & New York. p. 289.
62. Australian Contemporary Dictionary, The. (1970). Collins. Sydney. Ibid., p. 384.
63. Cambridge Dictionary (2020). Retrieved from: https://dictionary.cambridge.org/dictionary/english/privilege.
64. Oxford English Dictionary. (2020). Retrieved from: https://www-oed-com.wwwproxy1.library.unsw.edu.au/view/Entry/151624.
65. Newcastle Sun, The. (1938). ABC Ideals. *The Newcastle Sun.* 28 May 1938. p. 4. Retrieved from: https://trove.nla.gov.au/newspaper/article/166711374?searchTerm=ABC%20privilege&searchLimits=.
66. Daily Mercury (Mackay). (1946). Broadcasting Parliament. ABC Privilege. *Daily Mercury (Mackay).* 29 June 1946. p. 4. Retrieved from: https://trove.nla.gov.au/newspaper/article/171153794?searchTerm=ABC%20privilege&searchLimits=.
67. West Australian, The. (1953). ABC staff has lost a privilege. *The West Australian.* 3 October 1953. p. 3. Retrieved from: https://trove.nla.gov.au/newspaper/article/52932388?searchTerm=ABC%20privilege&searchLimits=.
68. Schultz, T. (2019). "ATARs measure privilege, not academic merit, and it starts in kindergarten." 22 December 2019. Retrieved from: https://www.abc.net.au/news/2019-12-22/atar-measure-privilege-not-academic-merit/11817974.
69. Schultz, T. (2019). "ATARs measure privilege, not academic merit, and it starts in kindergarten." *Australian Broadcasting Corporation.* 22 December 2019. Retrieved from: https://www.abc.net.au/news/2019-12-22/atar-measure-privilege-not-academic-merit/11817974.
70. Mackay, H. (2017). Hugh Mackay: the state of the nation starts in your street. Edited version of the Gandhi Oration, delivered at the University of New South Wales on January 30, 2017. *The Conversation.* 2 February 2017. Retrieved from: https://theconversation.com/hugh-mackay-the-state-of-the-nation-starts-in-your-street-72264.
71. Mackay, H. (2019). Australia Day Address 2019. Delivered 23 January 2019. Retrieved from: https://www.australiaday.com.au/events/australia-day-address/2019-speaker-hugh-mackay/.
72. Bourdieu, P. (1984). *Distinction: A Social Critique of the Judgement of Taste.* Routledge and Kegan Paul. USA. p. 2.
73. As Bourdieu (1984) observed: "a work of art has meaning and interest for someone who possesses the cultural competence, that is, the code into which it is encoded" (Bourdieu, 1984).

74. Bourdieu (1984) said "cultural needs are the product of upbringing and education" (Ibid.).
75. The ABC's once unique, bespoke *field* in the media would map accurately on Bourdieu's *fields* because *fields* have "invariant laws of functioning" (Bourdieu, 1984). This has been supported in the *field* similarly by Institutional Logics with the oversight and organisation by ABC managers and their departments engaged in what French Sociologist Luc Boltanski (2011) described as "a token situation", meaning managers actively engaged in fostering token work in progress, to which is ascribed meaning and value for the institution. It is a situation where symbolic forms "are logically arranged and laden with values" (Boltanski Ibid.). The institutional growth of the ABC has been overseen by these processes and interactions.
76. Ibid.
77. Seccombe, M. (2018). ABC Board Stacking Rife. The Saturday Paper. Retrieved from: https://www.thesaturdaypaper.com.au/news/media/2018/10/06/abc-board-stacking-rife/15387480006958#hrd.
78. Echo Net Daily (2020). Liberal–National party cuts to ABC risk Australian lives. 26 June 2020. Retrieved from: https://www.echo.net.au/2020/06/liberal-national-party-cuts-to-abc-condemned-by-mp-elliot/.
79. Andreassen, C., Pallesen, S., & Griffiths, M. (2017). The relationship between addictive use of social media, narcissism, and self-esteem: Findings from a large national survey. *Addictive Behaviors.* 64. pp. 287–293. Retrieved from: https://doi.org/10.1016/j.addbeh.2016.03.006.
80. Singh, S., Farley, S., & Donahue, J. (2018). Grandiosity on display: Social media behaviors and dimensions of narcissism. *Personality and Individual Differences.* 134. pp. 308–313. Retrieved from: https://doi.org/10.1016/j.paid.2018.06.039.
81. Fu, J.S. & Shumate, M. (2017) News media, social media, and hyperlink networks: An examination of integrated media effects. *The Information Society.* 33:2. pp. 53–63. Retrieved from: DOI: 10.1080/01972243.2016.1271379.
82. Minear, T., & Adams, C. (2017). Oz day heat on ABC. *The Herald Sun.* 28 November 2017. Retrieved from: http://www.heraldsun.com.au/news/abc-under-fire-for-politicising-australia-day-by-moving-triple-js-hottest-100-countdown/news-story/3a7e2e553ec4fca81538bb734ccb88fd.
83. Australia Day commemorates the day in 1788 when British Captain Arthur Philip and the First Fleet of British and Irish convicts sailed into Port Jackson and raised the British flag in what was to be known as Sydney Cove. It is a national public holiday in Australia.

84. Donoughue, P. (2017). The Hottest 100 won't be held on Australia Day next year, triple j says. *Australian Broadcasting Corporation*. 27 November 2017. Retrieved from: https://www.abc.net.au/news/2017-11-27/hottest-100-wont-be-held-on-australia-day-triple-j-says/9197014.
85. Australian Broadcasting Corporation. (2017). How do you feel about the date of the Hottest 100? Triple J. *Australian Broadcasting Corporation*. 2 August 2017. Retrieved from: https://www.abc.net.au/triplej/news/musicnews/h100-survey/8764540.
86. Hanrahan, C. (2019). Australia Talks: The most and least trusted professions revealed. *Australian Broadcasting Corporation*. Retrieved from: https://www.abc.net.au/news/2019-11-27/the-professions-australians-trust-the-most/11725448.
87. Meade, A. and AAP (2020). ABC can keep Google and Facebook payments for news, Coalition says. The Guardian. 8 December 2020. Retrieved from: https://www.theguardian.com/media/2020/dec/08/abc-can-keep-google-and-facebook-payments-for-news-coalition-says.
88. Blain, E. (1977). *Life with Aunty: 40 years with the ABC*. Methuen, Australia. Sydney. p. 166.
89. Ibid., p. 15.
90. Loc. Cit.
91. Scott, M. (2016). *A Media Odyssey: Speeches of an ABC Managing Director 2006–2016*. ABC Books. Sydney. p. 7.
92. Cushion, S. (2012). *The Democratic Value of News: Why Public Service Media Matter*. Palgrave Macmillan. UK & US. p. 1.
93. Scott, M. (2016). *A Media Odyssey: Speeches of an ABC Managing Director 2006–2016*. ABC Books. Sydney. p. 129.
94. Sunstein, C. (2018). *#Republic : Divided Democracy in the Age of Social Media*. Princeton University Press. Princeton. Retrieved from: https://doi.org/10.1515/9781400890521.
95. Ceron, A., & Memoli, V. (2016). Flames and Debates: Do Social Media Affect Satisfaction with Democracy? *Social Indicators Research*. 126:1. pp. 225–240. Retrieved from: https://doi.org/10.1007/s11205-015-0893-x.
96. Zollman, K. (2012). Social network structure and the achievement of consensus. *Politics, Philosophy & Economics*. 11:1. pp. 26–44. Retrieved from: https://doi.org/10.1177/1470594X11416766.
97. Prior, M. (2007) (Reprinted 2014). *Post-Broadcast Democracy: How media choice increases inequality in political involvement and polarises elections*. Cambridge University Press. Cambridge.
98. Yadamsuren, B., & Erdelez, S., Marchionini, G. (2017). *Incidental exposure to online news*. Morgan & Claypool. Retrieved from: http://ieeexplore.ieee.org.wwwproxy1.library.unsw.edu.au/document/7791114.

99. Ohlsson, J., Lindell, J., & Arkhede, S. (2017). A matter of cultural distinction: News consumption in the online media landscape. *European Journal of Communication (London)*. 32:2. pp. 116–130. Retrieved from: https://doi.org/10.1177/0267323116680131.
100. Fletcher, R., & Park, S. (2017). The Impact of Trust in the News Media on Online News Consumption and Participation. *Digital Journalism*. 5:10. pp. 1281–1299. Retrieved from: https://doi.org/10.1080/21670811.2017.1279979.
101. Duke, J. (2019). 'Much of the media is white and we're not all white': ABC chair Ita Buttrose says media needs greater ethnic diversity. *The Sydney Morning Herald*. 8 October 2019. Retrieved from: https://www.smh.com.au/politics/federal/much-of-the-media-is-white-and-we-re-not-all-white-abc-chair-ita-buttrose-says-media-needs-greater-ethnic-diversity-20191008-p52yk5.html.
102. Chambers, R. (1997). 'The unexamined'. In M. Hill (ed.). *Whiteness: A Critical Reader.* New York University Press. London.
103. Harris, C. I. (1993). Whiteness as property. *Harvard Law Review.* 106:8. (June 1993). pp. 1707–1791. Retrieved from: https://doi.org/10.2307/1341787.
104. Pinches, M. (1999). In M. Pinches, (ed.). *Culture and Privilege in Capitalist Asia*. Routledge. London & New York. p. 13.
105. Kagwanja, P., & Southall, R. (2009). Introduction: Kenya - A democracy in retreat? *Journal of Contemporary African Studies: Kenya's Uncertain Democracy: The Electoral Crisis of 2008.* 27:3. pp. 259–277. Retrieved from: https://doi.org/10.1080/02589000903216930.
106. Branch, D., & Cheeseman, N. (2009). DEMOCRATIZATION, SEQUENCING, AND STATE FAILURE IN AFRICA: LESSONS FROM KENYA. *African Affairs.* 108:430. pp. 1–26. Retrieved from: https://doi.org/10.1093/afraf/adn065.
107. Stacey, R. & Griffin, D. (2006). *Complexity and the Experience of Managing in Public Sector Organizations.* Routledge. London & New York. p. 18.
108. Alfrey, L., & Twine, F. W. (2017). Gender-Fluid Geek Girls: Negotiating Inequality Regimes in the Tech Industry. *Gender & Society.* 31:1. pp. 28–50. Retrieved from: https://doi.org/10.1177/0891243216680590.
109. The Canberra Times. (1995). ABC too Anglocentric, needs more multiculturalism: Johns. *The Canberra Times.* 1 August 1995. p. 4. Retrieved from: https://trove.nla.gov.au/newspaper/article/130554848?searchTerm=British%20accent%20ABC.
110. "Social identity is defined and asserted through difference" (Bourdieu 1984).

111. Australian Broadcasting Corporation. (2020). Corporate Responsibility. About the ABC. *Australian Broadcasting Corporation*. Retrieved from: https://about.abc.net.au/how-the-abc-is-run/what-guides-us/corporate-responsibility/.
112. Arena, M., Azzone, G., Mapelli, F. (2017). What drives the evolution of Corporate Social Responsibility strategies? An institutional logics perspective. *Journal of Cleaner Production*. Vol 171. pp. 345–355. Retrieved from: https://www.sciencedirect.com/science/article/abs/pii/S0959652617322576. p. 345.
113. Kasturi Rangan, V., Chase, L. & Karim, S. (2015). The Truth About CSR. *Harvard Business Review*. January-February 2015. Retrieved from: https://hbr.org/2015/01/the-truth-about-csr.
114. Australian Broadcasting Corporation. (2019). Diversity and Inclusion Plan 2019–2020. *Australian Broadcasting Corporation*. Retrieved from: http://about.abc.net.au/wp-content/uploads/2019/11/ABC-Diversity-Inclusion-Plan-201922.pdf.
115. Kenny, C. (2019). ABC staff 'diversity' survey seeks ethnic, gender, sexuality data. *The Australian*. 9 December 2019. Retrieved from: https://www.theaustralian.com.au/nation/aunty-staff-diversity-survey-seeks-ethnic-gender-sexuality-data/news-story/2b661d9c40c198bda7217bbd57616dfc.
116. Ibid.
117. Ibid.
118. Ibid.
119. Ibid.
120. Karvalas, P. (2019). Millions wasted on diversity and inclusion programs, says report. RN Drive. ABC Radio. *Australian Broadcasting Corporation*. Retrieved from: https://www.abc.net.au/radionational/programs/drive/millions-wasted-on-diversity-and-inclusion-programs,-says-report/11339938.
121. Ibid.
122. Ibid.
123. Ibid.
124. Ibid.
125. Caisley, O. & Vitorovich, L. (2019). Ita Buttrose: Media too white and politically correct. *The Australian*. Business Review. 8 October 2019. Retrieved from: https://www.theaustralian.com.au/business/media/ita-buttrose-media-too-white-and-politically-correct/news-story/c9a7abf43db53543802b832ef3690265.
126. The Canberra Times. (1964). ABC Features: Australian Film Without a White. *The Canberra Times*. 26 August 1964, p. 21. Retrieved from: https://trove.nla.gov.au/newspaper/article/105840424?searchTerm=ABC%20white%20australia&searchLimits=.

127. Australian Broadcasting Corporation. (2016). Indigenous Policy. ABC AM. *Australian Broadcasting Corporation.* 7 July 2016. Retrieved from: https://www.abc.net.au/radio/programs/am/20160707-am05-indigenouspolicy/7576144.
128. Ibid.
129. Ibid.
130. Ruggles, R. M. (1993). "History of Standard 12: Establishing Requirements for Pluralizing Education," in *Pluralizing Journalism Education: A Multicultural Handbook.* Ed. C. Martindale. Greenwood Press. Westport, CT. pp. 17–23.
131. Ruggles, R. M. (1993). "History of Standard 12: Establishing Requirements for Pluralizing Education," in *Pluralizing Journalism Education: A Multicultural Handbook.* Ed. C. Martindale. Greenwood Press. Westport, CT. pp. 17–23.
132. Biswas, M and Izard, R. (2010). 2009 Assessment of the Status of Diversity Education in Journalism and Mass Communication Programs. *Journalism and Mass Communication Editor.* 64:4. pp. 378–394. Retrieved from: https://doi.org/10.1177/107769580906400403 Citing P. 378.
133. Ibid. p. 380.
134. Wyn, J., Khan, R., Dadvand, B. (2018). Multicultural Youth Australia Census Status Report. 2017/18. Youth Research Centre. *Melbourne Graduate School of Education Research Unit in Public Cultures School of Culture and Communication University of Melbourne.* Retrieved from: https://education.unimelb.edu.au/__data/assets/pdf_file/0011/2972036/MY-Aust-Report-17-18.pdf.
135. Ibid. p. 2.
136. Ibid. p. 4.
137. Junankar P.N. (Raja)., Mahuteau S. (2005) Do Migrants Get Good Jobs? New Migrant Settlement in Australia. *Economics of Immigration.* Palgrave Macmillan. London. Retrieved from: https://doi-org.wwwproxy1.library.unsw.edu.au/10.1057/9781137555250_6.
138. Grieco, E. (2020). U.S. newspapers have shed half of their newsroom employees since 2008. *Pew Research Center.* 20 April 2020. Retrieved from: https://www.pewresearch.org/fact-tank/2020/04/20/u-s-newsroom-employment-has-dropped-by-a-quarter-since-2008/.
139. Meade, A. (2020). More than 150 Australian newsrooms shut since January 2019 as Covid-19 deepens media crisis. Australian Media. *The Guardian.* 18 May 2020. Retrieved from: https://www.theguardian.com/media/2020/may/18/more-than-150-australian-newsrooms-shut-since-january-2019-as-covid-19-deepens-media-crisis.

140. Parr, N. (2015). Who goes to university? The changing profile of our students. *The Conversation*. Retrieved from: https://theconversation.com/who-goes-to-university-the-changing-profile-of-our-students-40373.
141. Larkins, F. P. (2018) Male students remain underrepresented in Australian universities. Should we be concerned? L.H. Martin Institute. Insights. Retrieved from: https://melbourne-cshe.unimelb.edu.au/__data/assets/pdf_file/0012/2894718/Gender-Enrolment-Trends-F-Larkins-Sep-2018.pdf.
142. Ibid.
143. Ibid.
144. Larkins, F. P. (2018).
145. Ibid.
146. University of Notre Dame Australia, The. (n.d.). Underrepresented groups. Nulungu Research Institute. Retrieved from: https://www.notredame.edu.au/research/nulungu/projects/olt-transition-to-higher-education/key-findings/underrepresented-groups
147. Shergold, P., Benson, K., & Piper, M. (2019). Investing in Refugees Investing in Australia. Department of Home Affairs. *Commonwealth of Australia*. Retrieved from: https://www.homeaffairs.gov.au/reports-and-pubs/files/review-integration-employment-settlement-outcomes-refugees-humanitarian-entrants.pdf.
148. Ibid., pp. 71–72.
149. Ibid., p. iii.
150. Ibid.
151. Ibid.
152. Ibid.
153. SBS first accepted advertising in 1997.
154. SBS Charter. (1991). Special Broadcasting Services Act. *Special Broadcasting Services*. Retrieved from: https://www.sbs.com.au/aboutus/corporate.
155. Ibid.
156. Caisley, O. & Vitorovich, L. (2019). Ita Buttrose: Media too white and politically correct. *The Australian*. 8 October 2019. Retrieved from: https://www.theaustralian.com.au/business/media/ita-buttrose-media-too-white-and-politically-correct/news-story/c9a7abf43d-b53543802b832ef3690265.
157. Najjarine, K. & Cottle, D. (2003). The Department of External Affairs, the ABC and Reporting of the Indonesian Crisis 1965–1969. *Australian Journal of Politics and History*. 49:1. pp. 48–60. Retrieved from: https://onlinelibrary-wiley-com.ezproxy1.library.usyd.edu.au/doi/epdf/10.1111/1467-8497.00280.

158. Ibid., p. 55. Quoting E. Hodge, Radio Wars: Truth, Propaganda and the Struggle for Radio Australia. p. 87.
159. Ibid.
160. Ibid., p. 56. Quoting Memorandum to Secretary, Department of External Affairs from the Minister. 4 June 1965. NAA: A1838/2, 3034/10/18/1. "Indonesia-Relations with Australia-Indonesian Reactions to Radio Australia Commentaries".
161. Ibid., p. 49.
162. Ibid., p. 51.
163. Wood, B. (2018). *Submission to the Review of Australian Broadcasting Services in the Asia Pacific*. 3 August 2018. Retrieved form: https://www.communications.gov.au/sites/default/files/submissions/bradley_wood.pdf.
164. Ibid., p. 50.
165. Hodge, E. (1996). "Constraints on Reporting Indonesia." In A. Lucas (Ed.) Half a Century of Indonesian- Australian Interaction. *Flinders University Asian Studies Monograph*. 6. Flinders Press. Adelaide. pp. 46–59.
166. Hamilton, W. (2013). Rights and Wrongs of ABC spy reports. *Eureka Street*. 23:23. Nov 2013. pp. 4–6. Retrieved from: https://search.informit.com.au/documentSummary;dn=730862220180851;res=IELAPA.
167. Hodge, E. (1996). "Constraints on Reporting Indonesia." In A. Lucas (Ed.) Half a Century of Indonesian- Australian Interaction. *Flinders University Asian Studies Monograph*. 6. Flinders Press. Adelaide. p. 51.
168. Inglis, K. (2006). *Whose ABC? The Australian Broadcasting Corporation, 1983–2006*. Black Inc Books. Sydney. p. 155.
169. News, The. (1937). ABC out of touch with public taste. *The News, Adelaide*. 29 January 1937, p. 6. Retrieved from: https://trove.nla.gov.au/newspaper/article/131403633?searchTerm=ABC%20out%20of%20touch%20with%20public%20taste.%20.
170. Ibid.
171. Daily Telegraph, The. (1937). ABC Denies Sops to Public. *The Daily Telegraph, Sydney*. 30 June 1937. p. 2. Retrieved from: https://trove.nla.gov.au/newspaper/article/247141344?searchTerm=ABC%20Denies%20Sops%20to%20Public.%20.
172. Inglis, K. (1983). *This is the ABC: The Australian Broadcasting Commission 1932–1983*. Melbourne University Press. Melbourne. p. 50.
173. Ibid.
174. Canberra Times, The. (1938). Race Broadcasts. ABC and Public Demand. *The Canberra Times*. 19 January 1938, p. 3. Retrieved from: https://trove.nla.gov.au/newspaper/article/2450534?searchTerm=ABC%20and%20Public%20Demand.%20.

175. Courier-Mail, The. (1946). "ABC needs to consider public". *The Courier-Mail.* 25 January, 1946. p. 3. Retrieved from: https://trove.nla.gov.au/newspaper/article/50256156?searchTerm=ABC%20needs%20to%20consider%20public.
176. Courier-Mail, The. (1946). "ABC needs to consider public". *The Courier-Mail.* 25 January, 1946. p. 3. Retrieved from: https://trove.nla.gov.au/newspaper/article/50256156?searchTerm=ABC%20needs%20to%20consider%20public.
177. Ibid.
178. Goulburn Evening Post. (1953). ABC Chairman's view on TV. *Goulburn Evening Post.* 12 June 1953, p. 3. Retrieved from: https://trove.nla.gov.au/newspaper/article/104558411?searchTerm=ABC%20Chairman%E2%80%99s%20view%20on%20TV.
179. Canberra Times, The. (1983). ABC's role defended by Myer. *The Canberra Times.* 2 August 1983. p. 1. Retrieved from: https://trove.nla.gov.au/newspaper/article/116420987?searchTerm=This%20confirms%20that%20the%20role%20of%20the%20ABC%20is%20to%20throw%20attention%20to%20matters%20of%20public%20interest%20where%20truth%20has%20been%20obscured%20or%20the%20public%20has%20not%20been%20fully%20informed.
180. Blain, E. (1977). *Life with Aunty: 40 year with the ABC.* Methuen Australia. Sydney. p. 17.
181. Tate, A. (1985). "An adman moves into the ABC". *The Canberra Times.* Good Weekend Section.
    24 March, 1985. p. 65. Retrieved from: https://trove.nla.gov.au/newspaper/article/122505247?searchTerm=An%20adman%20moves%20into%20the%20ABC.
182. Australian Broadcasting Corporation. (2013). ABC's Mark Scott defends publishing spy story, hits back at News Corp. ABC Online. *Australian Broadcasting Corporation.* Retrieved from: https://www.abc.net.au/news/2013-12-03/abc27s-mark-scott-hits-back-at-australian-over-bromance-spy-st/5131014.
183. Brook, S. (2013). "Odd couple: friendship that underpinned a spy story". *The Australian.* p. 1. Retrieved from: https://mumbrella.com.au/wp-content/uploads/2013/12/Screen-Shot-2013-12-03-at-12.58.36-PM.png.
184. Australian Broadcasting Corporation. (2013). ABC's Mark Scott defends publishing spy story, hits back at News Corp. 3 December 2013. *Australian Broadcasting Corporation.* Retrieved from: https://www.abc.net.au/news/2013-12-03/abc27s-mark-scott-hits-back-at-australian-over-bromance-spy-st/5131014.

185. Roberts, G. (2014). "Acting Prime Minister Warren Truss defends Navy amid claims asylum seekers beaten and burned." 18 February 2014. *Australian Broadcasting Corporation*. Retrieved from: https://www.abc.net.au/news/2014-01-22/australian-navy-accused-of-beating-burning-asylum-seekers/5211996.
186. Australian Broadcasting Corporation. (2014). Asylum seeker suffered burnt hand during attempt to light fire on boat, Navy member says. *Australian Broadcasting Corporation*. 7 August 2014. Retrieved from: https://www.abc.net.au/news/2014-08-06/asylum-seeker-with-burnt-hands-tried-to-light-fire-navy-says/5653048.
187. Scott, M. & Torney, K. (2014). ABC Statement. 4 February 2014. *Australian Broadcasting Corporation*. Retrieved from: https://about.abc.net.au/press-releases/abc-statement/.
188. Wroe, D., Bachelard, M. & Snow, D. (2014). Asylum seekers' burns claims baseless, say Australian defence chiefs. *The Sydney Morning Herald*. 23 January 2014. Retrieved from: https://www.smh.com.au/politics/federal/asylum-seekers-burns-claims-baseless-say-australian-defence-chiefs-20140122-3196l.html.
189. Leys, N. & Nicholson, B. (2014). ABC sticking to its story as 'abuse' doubts mount. *The Australian*. 24 January 2014. Retrieved from: https://www.theaustralian.com.au/national-affairs/immigration/abc-sticking-to-its-story-as-abuse-doubts-mount/news-story/32f146bf9912a4dc77a3340cdd56b2cb.
190. Solomons, M & Roberts, G. (2014). Asylum seekers describe boat turn-back at centre of burns allegations. *Australian Broadcasting Corporation*. 25 March 2014. Retrieved from: https://www.abc.net.au/news/2014-03-24/asylum-seekers-describe-boat-turn-back/5342210.
191. Knott, M. (2014). ABC admits errors in navy burns report on asylum seeker claims. *The Sydney Morning Herald*. 5 February 2014. Retrieved from: https://www.smh.com.au/politics/federal/abc-admits-errors-in-navy-burns-report-on-asylum-seeker-claims-20140204-31zft.html.
192. Blair, T. (2014). ABC staff disquiet over story about the Australian navy torturing asylum seekers. *The Daily Telegraph*. 29 January 2014. Retrieved from: https://www.dailytelegraph.com.au/news/nsw/abc-staff-disquiet-over-story-about-the-australian-navy-torturing-asylum-seekers/news-story/1da3c4cebec9dcc5a0c4cb8066bb8a29.
193. Devine, M. (2014). Why does the ABC hate our navy? Miranda Devine Blog Posts. *The Daily Telegraph*. 28 January 2014. Retrieved from: https://www.dailytelegraph.com.au/blogs/miranda-devine/why-does-the-abc-hate-our-navy/news-story/939fe6616bc645bfa0b78532bf319ff3.

194. Wadham, B, (2014). **With Navy's record of abuse, asylum boat claims can't be ignored.** ***The Conversation.*** **10 February 2014. Retrieved from:** https://theconversation.com/with-navys-record-of-abuse-asylum-boat-claims-cant-be-ignored-22941.
195. Meade, A. (2017). ABC's Fact Check unit relaunched in partnership with RMIT. *The Guardian*. 14 February 2017. Retrieved from: https://www.theguardian.com/media/2017/feb/14/abcs-fact-check-unit-relaunched-in-partnership-with-rmit.
196. Australian Broadcasting Corporation. (n.d.). About Fact Check. *Australian Broadcasting Corporation*. Retrieved from: https://www.abc.net.au/news/factcheck/about/.
197. Moses. A.D. (2018). Western Civilization and Conservative Hysteria. Thursday 7 June 2018. ABC Religion and Ethics. *Australian Broadcasting Corporation*. Retrieved from: https://www.abc.net.au/religion/western-civilization-and-conservative-hysteria/10094662.
198. Breivik, a far-right terrorist, murdered 77 people in Norway on 22 July, 2011.
199. Bannon was a former chief strategist to US President Donald Trump and was associated with the right-wing website Breitbart News. He was dismissed from his White House role in August 2017 due to disagreements with Trump.
200. Hevesi, B. (2018). Your ABC of hate: Outrage as the taxpayer-funded broadcaster compares two respected journalists to Norwegian mass murderer Anders Breivik. *Daily Mail Australia*. 8 June 2018. Retrieved from: https://www.dailymail.co.uk/news/article-5819227/The-ABC-forced-comparing-journalists-Norwegian-mass-murderer-Anders-Breivik.html.
201. Doctor, D. (2018). ABC article likens senior editor at The Oz to Norwegian mass murderer. *Bandt*. 8 June 2018. Retrieved from: https://www.bandt.com.au/abc-article-likens-editor-oz-norwegian-mass-murderer/.
202. Buckingham Jones, S. & Urban, R. (2018). ABC retracts mass-murder slur over ANU row. *The Australian*. 8 June 2018. Retrieved from: https://www.theaustralian.com.au/business/media/abc-retracts-massmurder-slur-over-anu-row/news-story/28d3ba406b1d7733231c73559ab88e0d.
203. Luck, G. (2018). The rot set in with current affairs, and ABC news has since lost its bearings. *The Australian*. 30 June 2018. Retrieved from: https://www.theaustralian.com.au/news/inquirer/the-rot-set-in-with-current-affairs-and-abc-news-has-since-lost-its-bearings/news-story/06202187428fc0e6b2a14b60f940c8de.

204. Luck, G. (2018). The rot set in with current affairs, and ABC news has since lost its bearings. *The Australian*. 30 June 2018. Retrieved from: https://www.theaustralian.com.au/news/inquirer/the-rot-set-in-with-current-affairs-and-abc-news-has-since-lost-its-bearings/news-story/06202187428fc0e6b2a14b60f940c8de.
205. Australian Government. (2017). Australian Broadcasting Corporation Amendment (Fair and Balanced) Bill 2017. Federal Register of Legislation. *Australian Government*. Retrieved from: https://www.legislation.gov.au/Details/C2017B00228/Explanatory%20Memorandum/Text.
206. AIJAC Staff (2018). Submission to Senate Standing Committee on Environment and Communications' inquiry into Allegations of Political interference in the ABC (including the termination of the Managing Director, Michelle Guthrie, conduct of the Chair and Board, and governance of the ABC). *Australia/Israel and Jewish Affairs Council*. 26 November 2018. Retrieved from: https://aijac.org.au/resource/aijac-inquiry-abc-bias-israel/.
207. Commonwealth of Australia. (2019). Allegations of political interference in the Australian Broadcasting Corporation. The Senate. *Commonwealth of Australia*. April 2019. Retrieved from: https://apo.org.au/sites/default/files/resource-files/2019-04/apo-nid227951.pdf.
208. AIJAC Staff. Ibid.
209. Veitch, H. (2010). The modest face of the ABC: James Dibble 1923–2010. *The Sydney Morning Herald*. 15 December 2010. Retrieved from: https://www.smh.com.au/national/the-modest-face-of-the-abc-20101214-18wpw.html.
210. The News. (1941). Abhors Affected Accent, says A.B.C. Chairman. *The News*. 11 September 1941. p. 3. Retrieved from: https://trove.nla.gov.au/newspaper/article/131982061?searchTerm=ABC%20accent.
211. Thomas, A. (1980). *Broadcast and be Damned: The ABC's first two decades*. Melbourne University Press. Melbourne. p. 56.
212. The News. (1941). Abhors Affected Accent, says A.B.C. Chairman. *The News*. 11 September 1941. p. 3. Retrieved from: https://trove.nla.gov.au/newspaper/article/131982061?searchTerm=ABC%20accent.
213. Davis, G. (1988). *Breaking up the ABC*. Allen and Unwin. Sydney.
214. Inglis, K. (1983). *This is the ABC: The Australian Broadcasting Commission 1932–1983*. Melbourne University Press. Melbourne. p. 19.
215. Pullan, R. (1986). *Four Corners: Twenty-Five Years*. ABC Enterprises. Sydney. p. 16.
216. Pullan, R. (1986). *Four Corners: Twenty-Five Years*. ABC Enterprises. Sydney. p. 20.

217. Thomas, A. (1980). *Broadcast and be Damned: The ABC's First Two decades.* Melbourne University Press. Melbourne. p. 97.
218. Nicholson, J. & Nattrass, S. (2003). Pioneer was courageous voice at ABC. *The Sydney Morning Herald.* Retrieved from: https://www.smh.com.au/national/pioneer-was-courageous-voice-at-abc-20030111-gdg37y.html.
219. Australian Government. (1903). Defence Act. Superseded. *Australian Government.* Retrieved from: https://www.legislation.gov.au/Details/C1903A00020.
220. Advertiser, The (Adelaide). (1939). A.B.C. Concerts To Aid Patriotic Funds. The Advertiser (Adelaide). 13 October 1939. p. 20. Retrieved from: https://trove.nla.gov.au/newspaper/article/49819562?searchTerm=ABC%20patriotic&searchLimits=.
221. Reserve Bank of Australia (2019). Pre-Decimal Inflation Calculator. Retrieved from: https://www.rba.gov.au/calculator/annualPreDecimal.html.
222. Inglis, K. (1983). *This is the ABC. The Australian Broadcasting Commission 1932–1983.* Melbourne University Press. p. 86.
223. Inglis, K. (1983). This is the ABC. The Australian Broadcasting Commission 1932–1983. Melbourne University Press. Melbourne. p. 96
224. Inglis, K. (1983). *This is the ABC. The Australian Broadcasting Commission 1932–1983.* Melbourne University Press. Melbourne. p. 78.
225. Advertiser, The (Adelaide). (1939). Concerts for Patriotic Funds. *The Advertiser.* 28 October, 1939. p. 9. Retrieved from: https://trove.nla.gov.au/newspaper/article/49822564?searchTerm=ABC%20patriotic&searchLimits=exactPhrase|||anyWords|||notWords|||requestHandler|||dateFrom=1939-01-01|||dateTo=1939-12-31|||sortby.
226. Daily Telegraph and North Murchison and Pilbara Gazette (WA). (1939). Australian Army. Mr. Menzies Speaks. Sixth Division For Overseas. "A Fight To The Last". *Daily Telegraph and North Murchison and Pilbara Gazette.* 10 November 1939. p. 1. Retrieved from: https://trove.nla.gov.au/newspaper/article/211798157?searchTerm=ABC%20broadcast%20troops%20Menzies&searchLimits=.
227. Chronicle, The (1941). More ABC Patriotic Poems. The Chronicle. 15 May 1941, p. 37. Retrieved from: https://trove.nla.gov.au/newspaper/article/92414948?searchTerm=ABC%20patriotic&searchLimits=.
228. Australian Broadcasting Commission. Annual Report (1940–41). ABC Research Archives. *Australian Broadcasting Commission.* p. 11.
229. Petersen, N. (2012) Sir Charles Moses. *Australian Dictionary of Biography.* Vol. 18. Melbourne University Press. Retrieved from: http://adb.anu.edu.au/biography/moses-sir-charles-joseph-15044.

230. Daily News, The (Perth). (1939). ABC Encourages Soldiers. *The Daily News.* 18 January 1939. p. 9. Retrieved from: https://trove.nla.gov.au/newspaper/article/82568934?searchTerm=ABC%20soldiers&searchLimits=dateFrom=1939-01-01|||dateTo=1939-12-31.
231. Inglis, K. (1983). *This is the ABC. The Australian Broadcasting Commission 1932–1983.* Melbourne University Press. Melbourne. p. 81.
232. News, The (Adelaide). (1942). Curtin says Battle for Australia has opened. *The News.* 16 February, 1942. p. 3. Retrieved from: https://trove.nla.gov.au/newspaper/article/131950874/11347070.
233. Australian Broadcasting Commission. Annual Report (1940–41). ABC Research Archives. *Australian Broadcasting Commission.* p. 38.
234. The Battle of Dunkirk was a defining and failed battle by the British against the Germans who had invaded and occupied France early in World War II. It was defining because the retreat from Dunkirk gave way to the German air assault of Britain—"The Battle of Britain". As Britain retreated from French shores it then had to defend its own shores against German invasion.
235. Age, The. (2002). Japanese invasion a myth: historian. *The Age.* Retrieved from: https://www.theage.com.au/national/japanese-invasion-a-myth-historian-20020601-gdu9c8.html.
236. Grey, J. (2008) *A Military History of Australia.* Cambridge University Press. Cambridge. p. 171
237. Higgs, R. (2006). How U.S. Economic Warfare Provoked Japan's Attack on Pearl Harbor. 1 May, 2006. The Independent Institute. Quoting G. Morgenstern (1953) "The Actual Road to Pearl Harbor," in *Perpetual War for Perpetual Peace*, (Ed. H. E. Barnes). p. 329. Article retrieved from: https://www.independent.org/news/article.asp?id=1930#2.
238. Silberman, M. (Ed). (2016) *Bertolt Brecht on Film and Radio. Diaries, Letters and Essays.* Bloomsbury Publishing. London.
239. Horsham Times, The. (1940). Discarded Waste Material. *The Horsham Times.* 12 July 1940, p. 8. Retrieved from: https://trove.nla.gov.au/newspaper/article/73150738?searchTerm=saucepans%20war%20effort&searchLimits=.

     This was part of a waste collection program by the government for recycling purposes. It included old tyres, rags and paper.
240. Meade, A. (2018). The ABC in turmoil: 'Frankly, we are all spooked about everything in here.' *The Guardian.* 1 August 2018. Retrieved from: https://www.theguardian.com/media/2018/aug/01/the-abc-in-turmoil-frankly-we-are-all-spooked-about-everything-in-here.
241. Meade, A. (2018). The ABC in turmoil: 'Frankly, we are all spooked about everything in here.' *The Guardian.* 1 August 2018. Retrieved from: https://www.theguardian.com/media/2018/aug/01/the-abc-in-turmoil-frankly-we-are-all-spooked-about-everything-in-here.

242. Meade, A. (2018). The ABC in turmoil: 'Frankly, we are all spooked about everything in here.' *The Guardian*. 1 August 2018. Retrieved from: https://www.theguardian.com/media/2018/aug/01/the-abc-in-turmoil-frankly-we-are-all-spooked-about-everything-in-here.
243. Meade, A. (2018). The ABC in turmoil: 'Frankly, we are all spooked about everything in here.' *The Guardian*. 1 August 2018. Retrieved from: https://www.theguardian.com/media/2018/aug/01/the-abc-in-turmoil-frankly-we-are-all-spooked-about-everything-in-here.
244. Meade, A. (2018). The ABC in turmoil: 'Frankly, we are all spooked about everything in here.' *The Guardian*. 1 August 2018. Retrieved from: https://www.theguardian.com/media/2018/aug/01/the-abc-in-turmoil-frankly-we-are-all-spooked-about-everything-in-here.
245. Meade, A. (2018). The ABC in turmoil: 'Frankly, we are all spooked about everything in here.' *The Guardian*. 1 August 2018. Retrieved from: https://www.theguardian.com/media/2018/aug/01/the-abc-in-turmoil-frankly-we-are-all-spooked-about-everything-in-here.
246. Meade, A. (2018). The ABC in turmoil: 'Frankly, we are all spooked about everything in here.' *The Guardian*. 1 August 2018. Retrieved from: https://www.theguardian.com/media/2018/aug/01/the-abc-in-turmoil-frankly-we-are-all-spooked-about-everything-in-here.
247. Pha, A. (2018). Your ABC: Your democracy . *The Guardian* (Sydney). 1842. 3 October 2018: 1:12. Retrieved from: https://search-informit-com-au.wwwproxy1.library.unsw.edu.au/documentSummary;dn=931380458882186;res=IELAPA ISSN: 1325-295X.
248. Meade, A. (2018). The ABC in turmoil: 'Frankly, we are all spooked about everything in here.' *The Guardian*. 1 August 2018. Retrieved from: https://www.theguardian.com/media/2018/aug/01/the-abc-in-turmoil-frankly-we-are-all-spooked-about-everything-in-here.
249. Anonymous (ND). "I've worked at the ABC for many years." Parliament House. Australian Government. Retrieved from: http://www.aph.gov.au/DocumentStore.ashx?id=89b8ca48-d04e-4b87-85a2-a856a09e5ab3.
250. Meade, A. (2018). The ABC in turmoil: 'Frankly, we are all spooked about everything in here.' *The Guardian*. 1 August 2018. Retrieved from: https://www.theguardian.com/media/2018/aug/01/the-abc-in-turmoil-frankly-we-are-all-spooked-about-everything-in-here.
251. Meade, A. (2016). ABC bosses 'morally and spiritually bankrupt' for axing Catalyst, RN presenter says. *The Guardian*. 30 November 2016. Retrieved from: https://www.theguardian.com/media/2016/nov/30/abc-bosses-morally-and-spiritually-bankrupt-for-axing-catalyst-rn-presenter-says.

252. Meade, A. (2018). ABC reduces factual programming hours by 60% since 2014. *The Guardian*. 13 April 2018. Retrieved from: https://www.theguardian.com/media/2018/apr/13/abc-reduces-factual-programming-hours-by-60-since-2014.
253. Australian Broadcasting Corporation. (2018). ABC Efficiency Paper: Yours, Now and into the Future. *Australian Broadcasting Corporation*. Retrieved from: https://about.abc.net.au/wp-content/uploads/2018/02/FINAL_a11y_ABC_Efficiency_Paper_A4_Final-Ammended.pdf.
254. Simons, M. (2011). Simons: ABC News 24 runs on the smell of an oily rag. *Crikey*. 15 August 2011. Retrieved from: https://www.crikey.com.au/2011/08/15/cost-of-abc-news-24/.
255. Dow Jones Institutional News (2010). Australian public broadcaster launches 24-hour TV news. *Dow Jones*. July 22 2010. Retrieved from: https://login.wwwproxy1.library.unsw.edu.au/login?qurl=https%3A%2F%2Fsearch.proquest.com%2Fdocview%2F2169244539%3Faccountid%3D12763.
256. Australian Broadcasting Corporation. (2017). Annual Report. Australian Broadcasting Corporation. Retrieved from: https://about.abc.net.au/wp-content/uploads/2017/10/ABC7171_AR_2017_Vol2_tagged_v5.pdf.
257. Meade, A. (2016). Jaws drop at ABC as Michelle Guthrie defends Radio National cuts. *The Guardian*. 9 December 2016. Retrieved from: https://www.theguardian.com/media/2016/dec/09/jaws-drop-at-abc-as-michelle-guthrie-defends-radio-national-cuts.
258. Knott, M. (2016). 'If they don't like it they should leave': tensions escalate between ABC management and staff. *The Age*. 5 December 2016. Retrieved from: https://www.theage.com.au/politics/federal/if-they-dont-like-it-they-should-leave-tensions-escalate-between-abc-management-and-staff-20161205-gt47na.html.
259. Meade, A. (2016). Jaws drop at ABC as Michelle Guthrie defends Radio National cuts. *The Guardian*. 9 December 2016. Retrieved from: https://www.theguardian.com/media/2016/dec/09/jaws-drop-at-abc-as-michelle-guthrie-defends-radio-national-cuts.
260. Manning, P. (2018). **Despite her good intentions, Michelle Guthrie was never the right fit for the ABC. *The Conversation*. 25 September 2018. Retrieved from:** https://theconversation.com/despite-her-good-intentions-michelle-guthrie-was-never-the-right-fit-for-the-abc-103755.
261. Ito, M. (2008) "Foreword." *Digital Media, Youth, and Credibility*. Edited by M. J. Metzger & A. J. Flanagin. The John D. and Catherine T. MacArthur Foundation Series on Digital Media and Learning. Cambridge, MA: The MIT Press, 2008. vii–ix. Retrieved from: doi: 10.1162/dmal.9780262562324.vii.

262. Meade, A. (2017). ABC's Michelle Guthrie: I was never a 'Murdoch hatchet woman'. *The Guardian.* 10 June 2017. Retrieved from: https://www.theguardian.com/media/2017/jun/10/abcs-michelle-guthrie-i-was-never-a-murdoch-hatchet-woman.
263. Northern Star, The. (1945). ABC Chairman Resigns. *The Northern Star, Lismore.* 27 February 1945. p. 5. Retrieved from: https://trove.nla.gov.au/newspaper/article/99264583?searchTerm=chairman%20ABC&searchLimits=exactPhrase|||anyWords|||notWords|||requestHandler|||dateFrom=1944-01-01|||dateTo=1946-12-31||||l-advstate=National||||l-advstate=ACT||||l-advstate=New+South+Wales|||sortby.
264. Canberra Times, The. (1945). MYSTERY OF A.B.C. RESIGNATION. *The Canberra Times.* 28 February 1945, p. 2. Retrieved from: https://trove.nla.gov.au/newspaper/article/2618006?searchTerm=chairman%20ABC&searchLimits=exactPhrase|||anyWords|||notWords|||requestHandler|||dateFrom=1944-01-01|||dateTo=1946-12-31||||l-advstate=National||||l-advstate=ACT||||l-advstate=New+South+Wales|||sortby.
265. Newcastle Sun, The. (1945). Politics and the ABC. Editorial. *The Newcastle Sun.* 17 April 1945, p. 6. Retrieved from: https://trove.nla.gov.au/newspaper/article/156641758?searchTerm=Politics%20and%20the%20ABC.
266. Sydney Morning Herald, The (1945). The Man who Never Lost his Temper. *The Sydney Morning Herald.* 28 February 1945. p. 7. Retrieved from: https://trove.nla.gov.au/newspaper/article/27928682?browse=ndp%3Abrowse%2Ftitle%2FS%2Ftitle%2F35%2F1945%2F02%2F28%2Fpage%2F991342%2Farticle%2F27928682.
267. Sun, The. (1945). The ABC and Politics. *The Sun.* 27 February 1945. p. 4. Retrieved from: https://trove.nla.gov.au/newspaper/article/231705224?searchTerm=Politics%20and%20the%20ABC.
268. Tribune, The. (1945). "Cleary' s Resignation Blow To ABC". The Tribune. 1 March 1945, p. 6. Retrieved from: https://trove.nla.gov.au/newspaper/article/208690996?searchTerm=chairman%20ABC&searchLimits=exactPhrase|||anyWords|||notWords|||requestHandler|||dateFrom=1944-01-01|||dateTo=1946-12-31||||l-advstate=National||||l-advstate=ACT||||l-advstate=New+South+Wales|||sortby.
269. Canberra Times, The. (1945). ABC Ex-Chairman Eulogised. *The Canberra Times.* 25 April 1945. p. 2. Retrieved from: https://trove.nla.gov.au/newspaper/article/2624992?searchTerm=chairman%20ABC&searchLimits=exactPhrase|||anyWords|||notWords|||requestHandler|||dateFrom=1944-01-01|||dateTo=1946-12-31||||l-advstate=National||||l-advstate=ACT||||l-advstate=New+South+Wales|||sortby.
270. Zafirovski, M. (2017). *Identifying a free society conditions and indicators.* Brill. Boston. p. 60.

271. Curran, J, & Seaton, J. (2018). *Power without Responsibility: Press, Broadcasting and the Internet in Britain*. 8th Ed. Routledge. London, New York. p. 157.
272. Parker, S. (2014). Quentin Dempster's parting shot at commercialisation of the ABC. *The Sydney Morning Herald*. Retrieved from: https://www.smh.com.au/politics/federal/quentin-dempsters-parting-shot-at-commercialisation-of-the-abc-20141129-11wk7z.html.
273. The Australian. (1964). First edition. *The Australian*. 15 July 1964. p. 1.
274. The Sydney Morning Herald. (1831). First edition. *The Sydney Morning Herald*. 18 April 1831. p. 2.
275. The Age. (1854). First edition. *The Age*. 17 October 1854. p. 4.
276. Australian Broadcasting Corporation. (2019). Scott Morrison defends Federal Police raid on journalist Annika Smethurst's Canberra home. *Australian Broadcasting Corporation*. 5 June 2019. Retrieved from: https://www.abc.net.au/news/2019-06-05/scott-morrison-defends-raid-on-journalist-annika-smethurst-home/11180186.
277. Ferguson, R. (2019). News Corp: Police raid on journalist's home 'dangerous act of intimidation'. *The Australian*. 4 June 2019. Retrieved from: https://www.theaustralian.com.au/business/media/police-raid-home-of-news-corp-journalist/news-story/910d9cf3e9097c647c2800581f86502f.
278. Australian Broadcasting Corporation. (2019). Scott Morrison defends Federal Police raid on journalist Annika Smethurst's Canberra home. *Australian Broadcasting Corporation*. 5 June 2019. Retrieved from: https://www.abc.net.au/news/2019-06-05/scott-morrison-defends-raid-on-journalist-annika-smethurst-home/11180186.
279. Ferguson, R. (2019). News Corp: Police raid on journalist's home 'dangerous act of intimidation'. *The Australian*. 4 June 2019. Retrieved from: https://www.theaustralian.com.au/business/media/police-raid-home-of-news-corp-journalist/news-story/910d9cf3e9097c647c2800581f86502f.
280. Ferguson, R. (2019). News Corp: Police raid on journalist's home 'dangerous act of intimidation'. *The Australian*. 4 June 2019. Retrieved from: https://www.theaustralian.com.au/business/media/police-raid-home-of-news-corp-journalist/news-story/910d9cf3e9097c647c2800581f86502f
281. Ferguson, R. (2019). News Corp: Police raid on journalist's home 'dangerous act of intimidation'. *The Australian*. 4 June 2019. Retrieved from: https://www.theaustralian.com.au/business/media/police-raid-home-of-news-corp-journalist/news-story/910d9cf3e9097c647c2800581f86502f.

282. Oakes, D. & Clark, S. (2017). The Afghan Files. ABC News. *Australian Broadcasting Corporation.* Retrieved from: https://www.abc.net.au/news/2019-06-05/abc-raided-by-australian-federal-police-afghan-files-stories/11181162.
283. Knowles, L., Worthington, E., & Blumer, C. (2019). ABC raid: AFP leave Ultimo building with files after hours-long raid over Afghan Files stories. *Australian Broadcasting Corporation.* 6 June 2019. Retrieved from: https://www.abc.net.au/news/2019-06-05/abc-raided-by-australian-federal-police-afghan-files-stories/11181162.
284. Oakes, D. & Clark, S. (2017). The Afghan Files. ABC News. *Australian Broadcasting Corporation.* Retrieved from: https://www.abc.net.au/news/2019-06-05/abc-raided-by-australian-federal-police-afghan-files-stories/11181162.
285. Knowles, L., Worthington, E., & Blumer, C. (2019). ABC raid: AFP leave Ultimo building with files after hours-long raid over Afghan Files stories. *Australian Broadcasting Corporation.* 6 June 2019. Retrieved from: https://www.abc.net.au/news/2019-06-05/abc-raided-by-australian-federal-police-afghan-files-stories/11181162.
286. McKinnell, J. (2020). AFP warrants used to raid ABC valid, Federal Court rules. 17 February 2020. *Australian Broadcasting Corporation.* Retrieved from: https://www.abc.net.au/news/2020-02-17/afp-warrants-used-to-raid-abc-valid-court-rules/11971018.
287. Knowles, L., Worthington, E., & Blumer, C. (2019). ABC raid: AFP leave Ultimo building with files after hours-long raid over Afghan Files stories. *Australian Broadcasting Corporation.* 6 June 2019. Retrieved from: https://www.abc.net.au/news/2019-06-05/abc-raided-by-australian-federal-police-afghan-files-stories/11181162.
288. Koziol, M. (2019). Journalists in the firing line after AFP changes statement on media raids [online]. *Australasian Policing.* 11:2. July 2019. p. 21. Retrieved from: https://search-informit-com-au.wwwproxy1.library.unsw.edu.au/documentSummary;dn=614670160682088;res=IELHSS.
289. Knowles, L., Worthington, E., & Blumer, C. (2019). ABC raid: AFP leave Ultimo building with files after hours-long raid over Afghan Files stories. *Australian Broadcasting Corporation.* 6 June 2019. Retrieved from: https://www.abc.net.au/news/2019-06-05/abc-raided-by-australian-federal-police-afghan-files-stories/11181162.
290. Knowles, L., Worthington, E., & Blumer, C. (2019). ABC raid: AFP leave Ultimo building with files after hours-long raid over Afghan Files stories. *Australian Broadcasting Corporation.* 6 June 2019. Retrieved from: https://www.abc.net.au/news/2019-06-05/abc-raided-by-australian-federal-police-afghan-files-stories/11181162.

291. Knowles, L., Worthington, E., & Blumer, C. (2019). ABC raid: AFP leave Ultimo building with files after hours-long raid over Afghan Files stories. *Australian Broadcasting Corporation.* 6 June 2019. Retrieved from: https://www.abc.net.au/news/2019-06-05/abc-raided-by-australian-federal-police-afghan-files-stories/11181162.
292. McKinnell, J. (2020). AFP warrants used to raid ABC valid, Federal Court rules. 17 February 2020. *Australian Broadcasting Corporation.* Retrieved from: https://www.abc.net.au/news/2020-02-17/afp-warrants-used-to-raid-abc-valid-court-rules/11971018.
293. Wootton, H. (2019). Police raid on ABC 'unconstitutional'. *The Australian Financial Review.* 2 August 2019. Retrieved from: https://www.afr.com/companies/media-and-marketing/police-raid-on-abc-unconstitutional-20190801-p52czc.
294. Knowles, L., Worthington, E., & Blumer, C. (2019). ABC raid: AFP leave Ultimo building with files after hours-long raid over Afghan Files stories. *Australian Broadcasting Corporation.* 6 June 2019. Retrieved from: https://www.abc.net.au/news/2019-06-05/abc-raided-by-australian-federal-police-afghan-files-stories/11181162.
295. McKinnell, J. (2020). AFP warrants used to raid ABC valid, Federal Court rules. 17 February 2020. *Australian Broadcasting Corporation.* Retrieved from: https://www.abc.net.au/news/2020-02-17/afp-warrants-used-to-raid-abc-valid-court-rules/11971018.
296. Trask, S. (2020). ABC case against AFP raids dismissed. *Australian Associated Press General News Wire.* 16 February 2020. Retrieved from: https://search-proquest-com.wwwproxy1.library.unsw.edu.au/docview/2355696022?rfr_id=info%3Axri%2Fsid%3Aprimo.
297. Koch, T. (2019). AFP media raids more sinister than many thought. *The Sydney Morning Herald.* 15–16 June 2019. p. 34.
298. Koziol, M. (2019). Journalists in the firing line after AFP changes statement on media raids [online]. *Australasian Policing.* 11:2. July 2019. p. 21. Retrieved from: https://search-informit-com-au.wwwproxy1.library.unsw.edu.au/documentSummary;dn=614670160682088;res=IELHSS.
299. Koziol, M. (2019). Journalists in the firing line after AFP changes statement on media raids [online]. *Australasian Policing.* 11:2. July 2019. p. 21. Retrieved from: https://search-informit-com-au.wwwproxy1.library.unsw.edu.au/documentSummary;dn=614670160682088;res=IELHSS.
300. Koziol, M. (2019). Journalists in the firing line after AFP changes statement on media raids [online]. *Australasian Policing.* 11:2. July 2019. p. 21. Retrieved from: https://search-informit-com-au.wwwproxy1.library.unsw.edu.au/documentSummary;dn=614670160682088;res=IELHSS.

301. Miekle, G. (2009). *Interpreting News.* Palgrave Macmillan. New York. p. 4.
302. Bhattacharyya, S., & Hodler, R. (2015). Media freedom and democracy in the fight against corruption. *European Journal Of Political Economy.* 39:C. pp. 13–24. Retrieved from: https://doi.org/10.1016/j.ejpoleco.2015.03.004.
303. McChesney, R.M. (2008). The Political Economy of Media: Enduring Dilemmas. *Monthly Review Press.* New York. p. 34.
304. Fenton, N. (2014). Defending whose democracy? media freedom and media power. *Nordicom Review.* 35. pp. 31–44. Retrieved from: https://www.nordicom.gu.se/sites/default/files/kapitel-pdf/fenton.pdf.
305. Fenton, N. (2014). Defending whose democracy? media freedom and media power. *Nordicom Review.* 35. pp. 31–44. Retrieved from: https://www.nordicom.gu.se/sites/default/files/kapitel-pdf/fenton.pdf p. 33.
306. Gans, H.J. (2004). *Deciding What's News: A Study of CBS Evening News, NBC Nightly News, Newsweek and Time.* 25th Anniversary Edition. Northwestern University Press. Evanston, Illinois. p. 40.
307. Gans, H.J. (2004). *Deciding What's News: A Study of CBS Evening News, NBC Nightly News, Newsweek and Time.* 25th Anniversary Edition. Northwestern University Press. Evanston, Illinois. p. 270.
308. Gans, H.J. (2004). *Deciding What's News: A Study of CBS Evening News, NBC Nightly News, Newsweek and Time.* 25th Anniversary Edition. Northwestern University Press. Evanston, Illinois. p. 293.
309. Hallin, D.C. (1989). *The "Uncensored War": The Media and Vietnam.* University of California Press, Berkeley. p. 25.
310. Schudson, M. (1978). *Discovering the News: A social History of American Newspapers.* Basic Books Inc. USA. p. 219.
311. Blach-Ørsten, M. & Burkal, R. (2014). Credibility and the Media as a Political Institution. *Nordicom Review.* 35. (2014) Special Issue. Retrieved from: https://content.sciendo.com/view/journals/nor/35/s1/nor.35.issue-s1.xml.
312. Nah, S., & Chung, D. S. (2012). When citizens meet both professional and citizen journalists: Social trust, media credibility, and perceived journalistic roles among online community news readers. *Journalism.* 13:6. pp. 14–730. Retrieved from: https://doi.org/10.1177/1464884911431381.
313. Greer, C. &McLaughlin, E. (2010). We Predict a Riot?: Public Order Policing, New Media Environments and the Rise of the Citizen Journalist. *British Journal of Criminology.* 50:6. pp. 1041–1059. Retrieved from: https://doi.org/info:doi/.
314. Markham, T. (2011). Hunched over their laptops: phenomenological perspectives on citizen journalism. (Essay). *Review of Contemporary Philosophy. 10.* Retrieved from: https://doi.org/info:doi/.

315. Blach-Ørsten, M. & Burkal, R. (2014). Credibility and the Media as a Political Institution. *Nordicom Review* 35. (2014) Special Issue. Retrieved from: https://content.sciendo.com/view/journals/nor/35/s1/nor.35.issue-s1.xml.
316. Blach-Ørsten, M. & Burkal, R. (2014). Credibility and the Media as a Political Institution. *Nordicom Review* 35. (2014) Special Issue. Retrieved from: https://content.sciendo.com/view/journals/nor/35/s1/nor.35.issue-s1.xml.
317. Robinson, S. & De Shano, C. (2011). 'Anyone can know': Citizen journalism and the interpretive community of the mainstream press. *Journalism: Theory, Practice, and Criticism.* 12:8. pp. 963–982. Retrieved from: https://doi.org/info:doi/.
318. Goot, M. & Inglis, K.S. (2014). Mayer, Henry (1919–1991). *Australian Dictionary of Biography.* Retrieved from: http://adb.anu.edu.au/biography/mayer-henry-17251.
319. Mayer, H. (1964). *The Press in Australia.* Lansdowne Press. Hong Kong. p. 48.
320. Mayer, H. (1964). *The Press in Australia.* Lansdowne Press. Hong Kong. p. 50.

References

ABC. (2013). Guidelines for Personal Use of Social Media. [online]. Document: D11/22627. http://about.abc.net.au/wp-content/uploads/2014/10/PersonalUseOfSocialMediaINS1.pdf

ABC. (2016, February). *ABC Submission to the House of Representatives Standing Committee on Communications and the Arts.* Inquiry Into the Importance of Public and Commercial Broadcasting, Online Content and Live Production to Rural and Regional Australia, Including the Arts, News and Other Services. [online]. *ABC.* http://d3n8a8pro7vhmx.cloudfront.net/abcfriends/legacy_url/2756/ABC_Submission_Reps_Feb2016_Sub009.pdf?1563515036

ABC. (2017). How do you feel about the date of the Hottest 100? *Triple J. Australian Broadcasting Corporation.* 2 August 2017. Retrieved from: https://www.abc.net.au/triplej/news/musicnews/h100-survey/87645

ABC. (2018, June). *The Cost of Being the ABC: Delivering the Best and Most Efficient Public Broadcasting.* http://www.abc.net.au/cm/lb/9944818/data/the-cost-of-being-the-abc-data.pdf

Advertiser, The (Adelaide). (1939). A.B.C. Concerts To Aid Patriotic Funds. The Advertiser (Adelaide). 13 October 1939, p. 20. Retrieved from: https://trove.nla.gov.au/newspaper/article/49819562?searchTerm=ABC%20patriotic&searchLimits=

Age, The. (1854, October 17). First Edition. *The Age*, p. 4

Age, The. (1951). Misusing Public Money, A.B.C. Told. The Age (Melbourne). 11 December, 1951, p. 3. Retrieved from: https://trove.nla.gov.au/newspaper/article/205663971?searchTerm=wrongly%20using%20public%20funds%20for%20orchestral%20concerts

Age, The. (2002). Japanese Invasion a Myth: Historian. *The Age*.https://www.theage.com.au/national/japanese-invasion-a-myth-historian-20020601-gdu9c8.html

AIJAC Staff. (2018, November 26). Submission to Senate Standing Committee on Environment and Communications' Inquiry Into Allegations of Political Interference in the ABC (Including the Termination of the Managing Director, Michelle Guthrie, conduct of the Chair and Board, and governance of the ABC). *Australia/Israel and Jewish Affairs Council*. https://aijac.org.au/resource/aijac-inquiry-abc-bias-israel/

Alexander, J. (2014). Notes Towards a Definition of Politics. *Philosophy, 89*(348), 273–300. https://doi.org/10.1017/S0031819113000855

Alfrey, L., & Twine, F. W. (2017). Gender-Fluid Geek Girls: Negotiating Inequality Regimes in the Tech Industry. *Gender & Society, 31*(1), 28–50. https://doi.org/10.1177/0891243216680590

Amenta, E., & Ramsey, K. M. (2010). Institutional Theory. In K. T. Leicht & J. C. Jenkins (Eds.), *Handbook of Politics: State and Society in Global Perspective*. Springer. https://doi.org/10.1007/978-0-387-68930-2_2

Andreassen, C., Pallesen, S., & Griffiths, M. (2017). The Relationship Between Addictive Use of Social Media, Narcissism, and Self-Esteem: Findings from a Large National Survey. *Addictive Behaviors, 64*, 287–293. https://doi.org/10.1016/j.addbeh.2016.03.006

Arena, M., Azzone, G., & Mapelli, F. (2017). What Drives the Evolution of Corporate Social Responsibility Strategies? An Institutional Logics Perspective. *Journal of Cleaner Production, 171*, 345–355. https://www.sciencedirect.com/science/article/abs/pii/S0959652617322576

Ariño, M., & Ahlert, C. (2004). Beyond Broadcasting: The Digital Future of Public Service Broadcasting. *Prometheus, 22*(4), 393–410. https://doi.org/10.1080/0810902042000331311678

Australian Broadcasting Commission. Annual Report. (1940–41). ABC Research Archives. *Australian Broadcasting Commission.*

Australian Broadcasting Commission. (1941). Annual Report (1940–41). Year ended 30 June 1941. Accessed with permission of the ABC.

Australian Contemporary Dictionary, The. (1970). *Collins*. Sydney.

Bagshaw, E. (2019, August 7). Kenneth Hayne: Trust in Politics Has Been Destroyed. *The Sydney Morning Herald*. https://www.smh.com.au/politics/federal/kenneth-hayne-trust-in-politics-has-been-destroyed-20190807-p52evf.html

Banjac, S. & Hanusch, F. (2020). A question of perspective: Exploring audiences' views of journalistic boundaries. *New Media & Society*, 1–19. https://doi.org/10.1177/1461444820963795

Barnidge, M. (2015). The Role of News in Promoting Political Disagreement on Social Media. *Computers in Human Behavior, 52*, 211–218. https://doi.org/10.1016/j.chb.2015.06.011

Berg, C., & Davidson, S. (2018). *Against Public Broadcasting: Why We Should Privatise the ABC and How to Do It*. Connor Court Publishing. West End.

Bhattacharyya, S., & Hodler, R. (2015). Media Freedom and Democracy in the Fight Against Corruption. *European Journal of Political Economy, 39*(C), 13–24. https://doi.org/10.1016/j.ejpoleco.2015.03.004

Biswas, M., & Izard, R. (2010). 2009 Assessment of the Status of Diversity Education in Journalism and Mass Communication Programs. *Journalism and Mass Communication Editor, 64*(4), 378–394. https://doi.org/10.1177/107769580906400403

Blach-Ørsten, M., & Burkal, R. (2014). Credibility and the Media as a Political Institution. *Nordicom Review, 35*. Special Issue. https://content.sciendo.com/view/journals/nor/35/s1/nor.35.issue-s1.xml

Blain, E. (1977). *Life with Aunty: 40 Year with the ABC*. Methuen Australia.

Blair, T. (2014, January 29). ABC Staff Disquiet Over Story About the Australian Navy Torturing Asylum Seekers. *The Daily Telegraph*. https://www.dailytelegraph.com.au/news/nsw/abc-staff-disquiet-over-story-about-the-australian-navy-torturing-asylum-seekers/news-story/1da3c4cebec9dcc5a0c4cb8066bb8a29

Born, G. (2005). *Uncertain Vision: Birt, Dyke and the Re-invention of the BBC*. Vintage.

Bourdieu, P. (1977). *Outline of a Theory of Practice* (R. Nice, Trans.). Cambridge University Press.

Bourdieu, P. (1984). *Sociology in Question*. Sage Publications.

Bourke, L. (2014, February 4). Prime Minister Tony Abbott Says ABC Not on Australia's Side in Interview with 2GB. *ABC News Online*. https://www.abc.net.au/news/2014-01-29/tony-abbott-steps-up-criticism-of-abc/5224676

Branch, D., & Cheeseman, N. (2008). Democratization, Sequencing, And State Failure in Africa: Lessons from Kenya. *African Affairs, 108*(430), 1–26. https://doi.org/10.1093/afraf/adn065

Brook, S. (2013). Odd Couple: Friendship That Underpinned a Spy Story. *The Australian*,p. 1. https://mumbrella.com.au/wp-content/uploads/2013/12/Screen-Shot-2013-12-03-at-12.58.36-PM.png

Brown, A. (1996). Public Service Broadcasting in Four Countries: Overview. *The Journal of Media Economics, 9*(1), 77–81.

Brown, A., & Althaus, C. (1996). Public Service Broadcasting in Australia. *Journal of Media Economics, 9*(1). Retrieved from: https://doi-org.wwwproxy1.library.unsw.edu.au/10.1207/s15327736me0901_4

Buckingham Jones, S., & Urban, R. (2018, June 8). ABC Retracts Mass-Murder Slur Over ANU Row. *The Australian*. https://www.theaustralian.com.au/business/media/abc-retracts-massmurder-slur-over-anu-row/news-story/28d3ba406b1d7733231c73559ab88e0d

Cairns Post, The. (1937, September 10). ABC Attacked. CRUEL, COWARDLY BIAS. *The Cairns Post*, p. 11. https://trove.nla.gov.au/newspaper/article/41816337?searchTerm=CRUEL%2C%20COWARDLY%20BIAS

Caisley, O., & Vitorovich, L. (2019, October 8). Ita Buttrose: Media Too White and Politically Correct. *The Australian*. Business Review. https://www.theaustralian.com.au/business/media/ita-buttrose-media-too-white-and-politically-correct/news-story/c9a7abf43db53543802b832ef3690265

Canberra Times, The. (1951). Dame enid lyons appointed to ABC. 14 July 1951, p. 4. Retrieved from Trove.

Canberra Times, The. (1964, August 26). ABC Features: Australian Film Without a White. *The Canberra Times*, p. 21. https://trove.nla.gov.au/newspaper/article/105840424?searchTerm=ABC%20white%20australia&searchLimits=

Canberra Times, The. (1983, August 2). ABC's Role Defended by Myer. *The Canberra Times*, p. 1. https://trove.nla.gov.au/newspaper/article/116420987?searchTerm=This%20confirms%20that%20the%20role%20of%20the%20ABC%20is%20to%20throw%20attention%20to%20matters%20of%20public%20interest%20where%20truth%20has%20been%20obscured%20or%20the%20public%20has%20not%20been%20fully%20informed

Canberra Times, The. (1938). Race Broadcasts. ABC and Public Demand. The Canberra Times. 19 January 1938, p. 3. Retrieved from: https://trove.nla.gov.au/newspaper/article/2450534?searchTerm=ABC%20and%20Public%20Demand.%20

Cavanagh, P. (2015, December). *ABC Radio Current Affairs Coverage of The China-Australia Free Trade Agreement*. Editorial Review No. 7. *Australian Broadcasting Corporation*. https://about.abc.net.au/wp-content/uploads/2016/02/ABC-Editorial-Review-No-7.pdf

Ceron, A. (2015). Internet, News, and Political Trust: The Difference Between Social Media and Online Media Outlets. *Journal of Computer-Mediated Communication, 20*(5), 487–503. https://doi.org/10.1111/jcc4.12129\

Ceron, A., & Memoli, V. (2016). Flames and Debates: Do Social Media Affect Satisfaction with Democracy? *Social Indicators Research, 126*(1), 225–240. https://doi.org/10.1007/s11205-015-0893-x

Chambers, R. (1997). The Unexamined. In M. Hill (Ed.), *Whiteness: A Critical Reader*. New York University Press.

Choi, S. (2014). Flow, Diversity, Form, and Influence of Political Talk in Social-Media-Based Public Forums. *Human Communication Research, 40*(2), 209–237. https://doi.org/10.1111/hcre.12023

Committee of Review of the Australian Broadcasting Commission (aka the Dix Inquiry). (1981). The ABC in Review: National Broadcasting in the 1980s. *Analysis and Policy Observation.* 30 May 1981. Retrieved from: https://apo.org.au/node/41206

Commonwealth Scientific and Industrial Research Organisation. (2017). Australian attitudes toward mining: latest results. Retrieved from: https://www.csiro.au/en/work-with-us/industries/mining-resources/australian-attitudes-to-mining-2017

Chronicle, The. (1941, May 15). More ABC Patriotic Poems. *The Chronicle*, p. 37. https://trove.nla.gov.au/newspaper/article/92414948?searchTerm=ABC%20patriotic&searchLimits=

Courier Mail, The. (1946, January 25). ABC Needs to Consider Public. *The Courier-Mail*, p. 3. https://trove.nla.gov.au/newspaper/article/50256156?searchTerm=ABC%20needs%20to%20consider%20public

Curran, J., & Seaton, J. (2018). *Power Without Responsibility: Press, Broadcasting and the Internet in Britain* (8th ed.). Routledge.

Cushion, S. (2012). *The Democratic Value of News: Why Public Service Media Matter.* Palgrave Macmillan.

Daily Mercury (Mackay). (1946, June 29). Broadcasting Parliament. ABC Privilege. *Daily Mercury (Mackay)*, p. 4. https://trove.nla.gov.au/newspaper/article/171153794?searchTerm=ABC%20privilege&searchLimits=

Daily Telegraph and North Murchison and Pilbara Gazette (WA). (1939, November 10). Australian Army. Mr. Menzies Speaks. Sixth Division For Overseas. "A Fight To The Last". *Daily Telegraph and North Murchison and Pilbara Gazette*, p. 1. https://trove.nla.gov.au/newspaper/article/211798157?searchTerm=ABC%20broadcast%20troops%20Menzies&searchLimits=

Daily Telegraph, The. (1937, June 30). ABC Denies Sops to Public. *The Daily Telegraph, Sydney*, p. 2. https://trove.nla.gov.au/newspaper/article/247141344?searchTerm=ABC%20Denies%20Sops%20to%20Public.%20

Davis, G. (1988). *Breaking Up the ABC.* Allen and Unwin.

Deakin, S., Lourenço, A. & Pratten, S. (2009). No "third way" for economic organization? Networks and quasi-markets in broadcasting. *Industrial and Corporate Change, 18*(1), 51–75. https://doi.org/10.1093/icc/dtn042

Devine, M. (2014, January 28). Why Does the ABC Hate Our Navy? Miranda Devine Blog Posts. *The Daily Telegraph.* https://www.dailytelegraph.com.au/blogs/miranda-devine/why-does-the-abc-hate-our-navy/news-story/939fe6616bc645bfa0b78532bf319ff3

Dewey, J. (1916, re-publ. 2004). *Democracy and Education.* Dover Publications.

Doctor, D. (2018, June 8). ABC Article Likens Senior Editor at The Oz to Norwegian Mass Murderer. *Bandt.* https://www.bandt.com.au/abc-article-likens-editor-oz-norwegian-mass-murderer/

Donoughue, P. (2017, November 27). The Hottest 100 Won't Be Held on Australia Day Next Year, Triple J Says. *Australian Broadcasting Corporation.* https://www.abc.net.au/news/2017-11-27/hottest-100-wont-be-held-on-australia-day-triple-j-says/9197014

Dow Jones Institutional News. (2010, July 22). Australian Public Broadcaster Launches 24-Hour TV News. *Dow Jones.* https://login.wwwproxy1.library.unsw.edu.au/login?qurl=https%3A%2F%2Fsearch.proquest.com%2Fdocview%2F2169244539%3Faccountid%3D12763

Echo Net Daily. (2020, June 26). Liberal–National Party Cuts to ABC Risk Australian Lives. https://www.echo.net.au/2020/06/liberal-national-party-cuts-to-abc-condemned-by-mp-elliot/

Fenton, N. (2014). Defending Whose Democracy? Media Freedom and Media Power. *Nordicom Review, 35*, 31–44. https://www.nordicom.gu.se/sites/default/files/kapitel-pdf/fenton.pdf

Ferguson, R. (2019, June 4). News Corp: Police Raid on Journalist's Home 'Dangerous Act of Intimidation'. *The Australian.* Retrieved https://www.theaustralian.com.au/business/media/police-raid-home-of-news-corp-journalist/news-story/910d9cf3e9097c647c2800581f86502f

Fletcher, R., & Park, S. (2017). The Impact of Trust in the News Media on Online News Consumption and Participation. *Digital Journalism, 5*(10), 1281–1299. https://doi.org/10.1080/21670811.2017.1279979

Foucault, M. (1976). *Trans. A.M. Sheridan Smith. The Archaeology of Knowledge & the Discourse on Language.* Pantheon Book. New York.

Fu, J. S., & Shumate, M. (2017). News Media, Social Media, and Hyperlink Networks: An Examination of Integrated Media Effects. *The Information Society, 33*(2), 53–63. https://doi.org/10.1080/01972243.2016.1271379

Gans, H. J. (2004). *Deciding What's News: A Study of CBS Evening News, NBC Nightly News, Newsweek and Time.* 25th Anniversary Edition. Northwestern University Press.

García-Gutiérrez, I., & Martínez-Borreguero, F. J. (2016). The Innovation Pivot Framework: Fostering Business Model Innovation in Startups. *Research Technology Management, 59*(5), 48–56. https://doi.org/10.1080/08956308.2016.1208043

Gilani, P., Bolat, E., Nordberg, D., & Wilkin, C. (2020). Mirror, mirror on the wall: Shifting leader–follower power dynamics in a social media context. Leadership. London, England. 16(3), 343–363. https://doi.org/10.1177/1742715019889817

Goot, M., & Inglis, K. S. (2014). Mayer, Henry (1919–1991). *Australian Dictionary of Biography.* http://adb.anu.edu.au/biography/mayer-henry-17251

Goulburn Evening Post. (1953, June 12). ABC Chairman's view on TV. *Goulburn Evening Post*, p. 3. https://trove.nla.gov.au/newspaper/article/104558411?searchTerm=ABC%20Chairman%E2%80%99s%20view%20on%20TV

Grattan, M. (2014, January/March). What Future for the ABC? *Public Administration Today, 37*, 22–23. https://search-informit-com-au.www-proxy1.library.unsw.edu.au/fullText;dn=20141588;res=AGISPT

Greer, C., & McLaughlin, E. (2010). We Predict a Riot?: Public Order Policing, New Media Environments and the Rise of the Citizen Journalist. *British Journal of Criminology, 50*(6), 1041–1059.

Grieco, E. (2020, April 20). U.S. Newspapers Have Shed Half of Their Newsroom Employees Since 2008. *Pew Research Center*. https://www.pewresearch.org/fact-tank/2020/04/20/u-s-newsroom-employment-has-dropped-by-a-quarter-since-2008/

Griffin, E. (2006). *A First Look at Communication Theory*. McGraw-Hill.

Gruen, D., & Clark, C. (2010). Nineteenth Colin Clark Lecture: November 2009 What Have We Learnt? The Great Depression in Australia from the Perspective of Today. *Economic Analysis & Policy, 40*(1). https://doi.org/10.1016/S0313-5926(10)50001-8

Hall, P. A., & Taylor, R. C. (1996). Political Science and the Three New Institutionalisms. *Political Studies. Discussion Paper, 44*(5), 936–957. http://search.proquest.com/docview/1008864601/

Hallin, D. C. (1989). *The "Uncensored War": The Media and Vietnam*. University of California Press.

Halpern, D., Valenzuela, S., & Katz, J. E. (2017). We Face, I Tweet: How Different Social Media Influence Political Participation Through Collective and Internal Efficacy. *Journal of Computer-Mediated Communication, 22*(6), 320–336. https://doi.org/10.1111/jcc4.12198

Hamilton, W. (2013, November). Rights and Wrongs of ABC Spy Reports. *Eureka Street, 23*(23), 4–6. https://search.informit.com.au/documentSummary;dn=730862220180851;res=IELAPA

Hanrahan, C. (2019). Australia Talks: The Most and Least Trusted Professions Revealed. *Australian Broadcasting Corporation*. https://www.abc.net.au/news/2019-11-27/the-professions-australians-trust-the-most/11725448

Harding, R. (1979). *Outside Interference: The Politics of Australia Broadcasting*. Sun Books.

Harris, C. I. (1993). Whiteness as Property. *Harvard Law Review, 106*(8), 1707–1791. https://doi.org/10.2307/1341787

Hevesi, B. (2018, June 8). Your ABC of Hate: Outrage as the Taxpayer-Funded Broadcaster Compares Two Respected Journalists to Norwegian Mass Murderer Anders Breivik. *Daily Mail Australia*. https://www.dailymail.co.uk/news/article-5819227/The-ABC-forced-comparing-journalists-Norwegian-mass-murderer-Anders-Breivik.html

Hodge, E. (1996). Constraints on Reporting Indonesia. In A. Lucas (Ed.), *Half a Century of Indonesian- Australian Interaction. Flinders University Asian Studies Monograph* (Vol. 6, pp. 46–59). Flinders Press. Adelaide.

Hongjie, C., & Jacob, W. J. (Eds.). (2017). Trends in Chinese Education. Chap. 15 in L. Yunchan (Ed.), *An Examination of the "Engineer of Human Souls" Metaphor*. Routledge.

Inglis, K. (1983). *The is the ABC: The Australian Broadcasting Commission 1932–1983*. Melbourne University Press.

Inglis, K. (2002, November 27). The Media—Aunty at Seventy: A Health Report on the ABC. [online]. *Analysis and Policy Observatory*. Retrieved March 4, 2020, from https://apo.org.au/node/6627

Inglis, K. (2006). *Whose ABC? The Australian Broadcasting Corporation 1983–2006*. Black Inc.

Ito, M. (2008) "Foreword." Digital Media, Youth, and Credibility. Edited by M. J. Metzger & A. J. Flanagin. The John D. and Catherine T. MacArthur Foundation Series on Digital Media and Learning. Cambridge, MA: The MIT Press, 2008. vii–ix. Retrieved from: https://doi.org/10.1162/dmal.9780262562324.vii.

Junankar P. N. (Raja). & Mahuteau S. (2005). Do Migrants Get Good Jobs? New Migrant Settlement in Australia. *Economics of Immigration*. Palgrave Macmillan. London. Retrieved from: https://doi-org.wwwproxy1.library.unsw.edu.au/10.1057/9781137555250_6

Junankar, P. N. (Raja). (2016). Economics of Immigration. Chapter: Do Migrants Get Good Jobs in Australia? The Role of Ethnic Networks in Job Search. P. N. (Raja). Junanker & S. Mahuteau, pp. 251–272. Palgrave Macmillan UK. London.

Kagwanja, P., & Southall, R. (2009). Introduction: Kenya—A Democracy in Retreat? *Journal of Contemporary African Studies: Kenya's Uncertain Democracy: The Electoral Crisis of 2008, 27*(3), 259–277. https://doi.org/10.1080/02589000903216930

Kahane, G., Everett, J. A. C., Earp, B. D., Farias, M., & Savulescu, J. (2015). 'Utilitarian' Judgments in Sacrificial Moral Dilemmas Do Not Reflect Impartial Concern for the Greater Good. *Cognition, 143*, 193–209. https://doi.org/10.1016/j.cognition.2014.10.005

Karvalas, P. (2019). Millions Wasted on Diversity and Inclusion Programs, Says Report. RN Drive. ABC Radio. *Australian Broadcasting Corporation*. https://www.abc.net.au/radionational/programs/drive/millions-wasted-on-diversity-and-inclusion-programs,-says-report/11339938

Kasturi Rangan, V., Chase, L., & Karim, S. (2015, January–February). The Truth About CSR. *Harvard Business Review*. https://hbr.org/2015/01/the-truth-about-csr

Kenny, C. (2019, December 9). ABC Staff 'Diversity' Survey Seeks Ethnic, Gender, Sexuality Data. *The Australian*. https://www.theaustralian.com.au/nation/aunty-staff-diversity-survey-seeks-ethnic-gender-sexuality-data/news-story/2b661d9c40c198bda7217bbd57616dfc

Khlok, V. R. (2003). The Re-establishment of Cambodian Education System after the Pol Pot Regime: The Study of Vietnamization and Re-Khmerizaion. *Kyōikugaku kenkyū, 70*(3), 383–392. https://doi.org/10.11555/kyoiku1932.70.383

Knott, M. (2014, February 5). ABC Admits Errors in Navy Burns Report on Asylum Seeker Claims. *The Sydney Morning Herald*. https://www.smh.com.au/politics/federal/abc-admits-errors-in-navy-burns-report-on-asylum-seeker-claims-20140204-31zft.html

Knott, M. (2016, December 5). 'If They Don't Like It They Should Leave': Tensions Escalate Between ABC Management and Staff. *The Age*. https://www.theage.com.au/politics/federal/if-they-dont-like-it-they-should-leave-tensions-escalate-between-abc-management-and-staff-20161205-gt47na.html

Knowles, L., Worthington, E., & Blumer, C. (2019, June 6). ABC Raid: AFP leave Ultimo Building with Files After Hours-Long Raid Over Afghan Files Stories. *Australian Broadcasting Corporation*. https://www.abc.net.au/news/2019-06-05/abc-raided-by-australian-federal-police-afghan-files-stories/11181162

Koziol, M. (2019, July). Journalists in the Firing Line After AFP Changes Statement on Media Raids [online]. *Australasian Policing, 11*(2), 21. https://search-informit-com-au.wwwproxy1.library.unsw.edu.au/documentSummary;dn=614670160682088;res=IELHSS

Larkins, F. P. (2018). Male Students Remain Underrepresented in Australian Universities. Should We Be Concerned? L.H. Martin Institute. Insights. https://melbourne-cshe.unimelb.edu.au/__data/assets/pdf_file/0012/2894718/Gender-Enrolment-Trends-F-Larkins-Sep-2018.pdf

Levinson, M. (1999). *The Demands of Liberal Education*. Oxford University Press.

Leys, N., & Nicholson, B. (2014, January 24). ABC Sticking to Its Story as 'Abuse' Doubts Mount. *The Australian*. https://www.theaustralian.com.au/national-affairs/immigration/abc-sticking-to-its-story-as-abuse-doubts-mount/news-story/32f146bf9912a4dc77a3340cdd56b2cb

Li, K., Li, S., Guan, Y. (2004). Institutionalised Corruption and Privilege in Asian Economies: A General Equilibrium Analysis. *Malaysian Journal of Economic Studies. Kuala Lumpur, 41*(1 & 2), 21–37. https://www.proquest.com/openview/13006f139d179947802a1871624c767f/1?pq-origsite=gscholar&cbl=46814

Litt, E. (2012). Knock, Knock. Who's There? The Imagined Audience. *Journal of Broadcasting & Electronic Media, 56*(3), 330–345. https://doi.org/10.1080/08838151.2012.705195

Livingstone, S. (2004). The challenge of changing audiences: Or, what is the audience researcher to do in the Internet age? *European Journal of Communication, 19*(1), pp. 75–86. https://doi.org/10.1177/0267323104040695

Lukin, A. (2006). What is Media 'Bias'? A Case Study of Al Jazeera's Reporting of the Iraq War. *Journal of Policing, Intelligence and Counter Terrorism, 1*(1), 65–80. https://doi.org/10.1080/18335300.2006.9686879

Luck, G. (2018, June 30). The Rot Set in with Current Affairs, and ABC News Has Since Lost Its Bearings. *The Australian*. https://www.theaustralian.com.au/news/inquirer/the-rot-set-in-with-current-affairs-and-abc-news-has-since-lost-its-bearings/news-story/06202187428fc0e6b2a14b60f940c8de

Lynch, K., Devine, D., & Grummell, B. (2012). New Managerialism in Education. In *New Managerialism in Education*. Palgrave Macmillan. https://doi.org/10.1057/9781137007230

Lyons, E. (1943). Governor-General's Speech Address-In-Reply. 29 September, 1943. Parliament of Australia. Retrieved from: https://www.aph.gov.au/About_Parliament/Parliamentary_Departments/Parliamentary_Library/Publications_Archive/archive/women/43Lyons

Mackay, H. (2017, February 2). Hugh Mackay: The State of the Nation Starts in Your Street. Edited Version of the Gandhi Oration, Delivered at the University of New South Wales on January 30, 2017. *The Conversation*. https://theconversation.com/hugh-mackay-the-state-of-the-nation-starts-in-your-street-72264

Mackay, H. (2019, January 23). Australia Day Address 2019. https://www.australiaday.com.au/events/australia-day-address/2019-speaker-hugh-mackay/

Manning, P. (2018, September 25). Despite Her Good Intentions, Michelle Guthrie Was Never the Right Fit for the ABC. *The Conversation*. https://theconversation.com/despite-her-good-intentions-michelle-guthrie-was-never-the-right-fit-for-the-abc-103755

Mansfield, B. (1997). *The Challenge of a Better ABC: The Review of the Role and Functions of the ABC*. Australian Government Publishing Service.

Markham, T. (2011). Hunched Over Their Laptops: Phenomenological Perspectives on Citizen Journalism. (Essay). *Review of Contemporary Philosophy, 10*.

Mayer, H. (1964). *The Press in Australia*. Lansdowne Press.

McChesney, R. W. (2008). *The Political Economy of Media: Enduring Issues, Emerging Dilemmas*. Monthly Review Press.

McGuinness, P. P. (2000, December). The Future of the Australian Broadcasting Corporation. *Quadrant, 44*(12), 2–4. https://search-informit-com-au.wwwproxy1.library.unsw.edu.au/documentSummary;dn=733687171221108;res=IELLCC

McKinnell, J. (2020, February 17). AFP Warrants Used to Raid ABC Valid, Federal Court Rules. *Australian Broadcasting Corporation*. https://www.abc.net.au/news/2020-02-17/afp-warrants-used-to-raid-abc-valid-court-rules/11971018

McNamara, T. K., & Williamson, J. B. (2019). *Ageism: past, present, and future. Routledge, Taylor and Francis Group*. Abingdon, Oxon.

Meade, A., & AAP. (2020, December 8). ABC Can Keep Google and Facebook Payments for News, Coalition Says. *The Guardian*. https://www.theguardian.com/media/2020/dec/08/abc-can-keep-google-and-facebook-payments-for-news-coalition-says

Metzger, M. J., & Flanagin, A. J. (2008). *The John D. and Catherine MacArthur Foundation Series on Digital Media and Learning* (pp. vii–ix). Cambridge, MA: The MIT Press. Retrieved from: https://doi.org/10.1162/dmal.9780262562324.vii

Miekle, G. (2009). *Interpreting News*. Palgrave Macmillan.

Minear, T., & Adams, C. (2017, November 28). Oz Day Heat on ABC. *The Herald Sun*. http://www.heraldsun.com.au/news/abc-under-fire-for-politicising-australia-day-by-moving-triple-js-hottest-100-countdown/news-story/3a7e2e553ec4fca81538bb734ccb88fd

Moses, A. D. (2018, June 7). Western Civilization and Conservative Hysteria. ABC Religion and Ethics. *Australian Broadcasting Corporation*. https://www.abc.net.au/religion/western-civilization-and-conservative-hysteria/10094662

Nah, S., & Chung, D. S. (2012). When Citizens Meet Both Professional and Citizen Journalists: Social Trust, Media Credibility, and Perceived Journalistic Roles Among Online Community News Readers. *Journalism, 13*(6), 14–730. https://doi.org/10.1177/1464884911431381

Najjarine, K., & Cottle, D. (2003). The Department of External Affairs, the ABC and Reporting of the Indonesian Crisis 1965–1969. *Australian Journal of Politics and History, 49*(1), 48–60. https://onlinelibrary-wiley-com.ezproxy1.library.usyd.edu.au/doi/epdf/10.1111/1467-8497.00280

Newcastle Sun, The. (1945, April 17). Politics and the ABC. Editorial. *The Newcastle Sun*, p. 6. https://trove.nla.gov.au/newspaper/article/156641758?searchTerm=Politics%20and%20the%20ABC.

News, The (Adelaide). (1942, February 16). Curtin Says Battle for Australia Has Opened. *The News*, p. 3. https://trove.nla.gov.au/newspaper/article/131950874/11347070

News, The. (1937, January 29). ABC Out of Touch with Public Taste. *The News, Adelaide*, p. 6. https://trove.nla.gov.au/newspaper/article/131403633?searchTerm=ABC%20out%20of%20touch%20with%20public%20taste.%20

News, The. (1941, September 11). Abhors Affected Accent, Says A.B.C. Chairman. *The News*, p. 3. https://trove.nla.gov.au/newspaper/article/131982061?searchTerm=ABC%20accent

Nicholson, J., & Nattrass, S. (2003). Pioneer Was Courageous Voice at ABC. *The Sydney Morning Herald*.https://www.smh.com.au/national/pioneer-was-courageous-voice-at-abc-20030111-gdg37y.html

Northern Star, The. (1945, February 27). ABC Chairman Resigns. *The Northern Star, Lismore*, p. 5. https://trove.nla.gov.au/newspaper/article/99264583?searchTerm=chairman%20ABC&searchLimits=exactPhrase|||anyWords|||notWords|||requestHandler|||dateFrom=1944-01-01|||dateTo=1946-12-31|||l-advstate=National|||l-advstate=ACT|||l-advstate=New+South+Wales|||sortby

Oakes, D., & Clark, S. (2017). The Afghan Files. *ABC News. Australian Broadcasting Corporation.* https://www.abc.net.au/news/2019-06-05/abc-raided-by-australian-federal-police-afghan-files-stories/11181162

O'Donnell, V. (2018). Is the ABC really biased? Opinion. 30 June 2018. *The Sydney Morning Herald.* Retrieved from: https://www.smh.com.au/national/is-the-abc-really-biased-20180629-p4zoh5.html

Ohlsson, J., Lindell, J., & Arkhede, S. (2017). A Matter of Cultural Distinction: News Consumption in the Online Media Landscape. *European Journal of Communication (London), 32*(2), 116–130. https://doi.org/10.1177/0267323116680131

Orvos, J. (2019). *Achieving Business Agility: Strategies for Becoming Pivot Ready in a Digital World* (1st ed.). Apress. https://primoa.library.unsw.edu.au/permalink/f/jhud33/UNSW_ALMA51274521450001731

Parker, S. (2014, November 29). Quentin Dempster's Parting Shot at Commercialisation of the ABC. *The Sydney Morning Herald.* https://www.smh.com.au/politics/federal/quentin-dempsters-parting-shot-at-commercialisation-of-the-abc-20141129-11wk7z.html

Parr, N. (2015). Who Goes to University? The Changing Profile of Our Students. *The Conversation.*https://theconversation.com/who-goes-to-university-the-changing-profile-of-our-students-40373

Petersen, N. (2012). Moses, Sir Charles Joseph (1900–1988). *Australian Dictionary of Biography, 18.* Melbourne University Press. http://adb.anu.edu.au/biography/moses-sir-charles-joseph-15044

Pha, A. (2018, October 3). Your ABC: Your Democracy. *The Guardian (Sydney), 1842*(1), 12. https://search-informit-com-au.wwwproxy1.library.unsw.edu.au/documentSummary;dn=931380458882186;res=IELAPA

Pinches, M. (1999). In M. Pinches (Ed.), *Culture and Privilege in Capitalist Asia.* Routledge.

Pollitt, C. (2016). Managerialism Redux? *Financial Accountability & Management, 32*(4), 429–447. https://doi.org/10.1111/faam.12094

Prior, M. (2007) (Reprinted 2014). *Post-Broadcast Democracy: How media choice increases inequality in political involvement and polarises elections.* Cambridge University Press. Cambridge.

Prior, M. (2009). Improving media effects research through better measurement of news exposure. *The Journal of Politics, 71*, 893–908. https://doi.org/10.1017/S0022381609090781

Pullan, R. (1986). *Four Corners: Twenty-Five Years.* ABC Enterprises.

Quinn, K. (2016, January 5). ABC News Director Gaven Morris Says 'Bias' Is Part of the Job. *The Sydney Morning Herald*. https://www.smh.com.au/entertainment/tv-and-radio/lunch-with-gaven-morris-abc-director-of-news-20160104-glz8q3.html

Reserve Bank of Australia. (2019). Pre-Decimal Inflation Calculator. https://www.rba.gov.au/calculator/annualPreDecimal.html

Reserve Bank of Australia. (2020). Pre-Decimal Inflation Calculator. *Reserve Bank of Australia* https://www.rba.gov.au/calculator/annualPreDecimal.html

Roberts, G. (2014, February 18). Acting Prime Minister Warren Truss Defends Navy Amid Claims Asylum Seekers Beaten and Burned. *Australian Broadcasting Corporation*. https://www.abc.net.au/news/2014-01-22/australian-navy-accused-of-beating-burning-asylum-seekers/5211996

Robinson, S., & De Shano, C. (2011). 'Anyone can Know': Citizen Journalism and the Interpretive Community of the Mainstream Press. *Journalism: Theory, Practice, and Criticism, 12*(8), 963–982.

Ruggles, R. M. (1993). History of Standard 12: Establishing Requirements for Pluralizing Education. In C. Martindale (Ed.), *Pluralizing Journalism Education: A Multicultural Handbook* (pp. 17–23). Greenwood Press.

Rutherford, L., & Brown, A. (2013). The Australian Broadcasting Corporation's Multiplatform Projects: Industrial Logics of Children's Content Provision in the Digital Television Era. *Convergence, 19*(2), 201–221. https://doi.org/10.1177/1354856512457749

SBS Charter. (1991). Special Broadcasting Services Act. Special Broadcasting Services. Retrieved from: https://www.sbs.com.au/aboutus/corporate.

Scannell, P. (1997). Public Service Broadcasting and Modern Public Life. In T. O'Sullivan & Y. Jewkes (Eds.), *The Media Studies Reader*. Arnold.

Schudson, M. (1978). *Discovering the News: A social History of American Newspapers*. Basic Books Inc.

Schultz, T. (2019, December 22). ATARs Measure Privilege, Not Academic Merit, and It Starts in Kindergarten. https://www.abc.net.au/news/2019-12-22/atar-measure-privilege-not-academic-merit/11817974

Scott, M. (2010, April 20). *New Opportunities, New Obligations: Public Broadcasting in the Era of Choice*. Commonwealth Broadcasting Association Conference. *Australian Broadcasting Corporation*.http://about.abc.net.au/speeches/new-opportunities-new-obligations-public-broadcasting-in-the-era-of-choice/

Scott, M. (2016). *A Media Odyssey: Speeches of an ABC Managing Director 2006–2016*. ABC Books.

Scott, M., & Torney, K. (2014, February 4). ABC Statement. *Australian Broadcasting Corporation*.https://about.abc.net.au/press-releases/abc-statement/

Seccombe, M. (2018). ABC Board Stacking Rife. *The Saturday Paper*. https://www.thesaturdaypaper.com.au/news/media/2018/10/06/abc-board-stacking-rife/15387480006958#hrd

Semmler, C. (1981). *The ABC—Aunt Sally and Sacred Cow*. Melbourne University Press.

Shergold, P. (2017). Re-Imagining Public Service [online]. *The Australian Journal of Social Issues, 52*(1), 4–12. https://search-informit-com-au.wwwproxy1.library.unsw.edu.au/documentSummary;dn=035171807770944;res=IELAPA

Shergold, P., Benson, K., & Piper, M. (2019). Investing in Refugees Investing in Australia. Department of Home Affairs. *Commonwealth of Australia*.https://www.homeaffairs.gov.au/reports-and-pubs/files/review-integration-employment-settlement-outcomes-refugees-humanitarian-entrants.pdf

Silberman, M. (Ed.). (2016). *Bertolt Brecht on Film and Radio. Diaries, Letters and Essays*. Bloomsbury Publishing.

Simon, M. (2005, May). Fear and Loathing at the ABC. *The Monthly*, 28–38. https://search.informit.com.au/documentSummary;dn=200511241;res=IELAPA

Singh, S., Farley, S., & Donahue, J. (2018). Grandiosity on Display: Social Media Behaviors and Dimensions of Narcissism. *Personality and Individual Differences, 134*, 308–313. https://doi.org/10.1016/j.paid.2018.06.039

Soley, C. (2005). The Public Is Sick of Us Both. *British Journalism Review, 16*(1), 35–39. https://doi.org/10.1177/0956474805053357

Solomons, M., & Roberts, G. (2014, March 25). Asylum Seekers Describe Boat Turn-Back at Centre of Burns Allegations. *Australian Broadcasting Corporation*. https://www.abc.net.au/news/2014-03-24/asylum-seekers-describe-boat-turn-back/5342210

Spadaro, S. J. A. (2020, January 20). Defy the Apocalypse. *La Civilta Cattolica*. https://www.laciviltacattolica.com/defy-the-apocalypse/

Stacey, R., & Griffin, D. (2006). *Complexity and the Experience of Managing in Public Sector Organizations*. Routledge.

Sun, The. (1945, February 27). The ABC and Politics. *The Sun*, p. 4. https://trove.nla.gov.au/newspaper/article/231705224?searchTerm=Politics%20and%20the%20ABC.

Sunstein, C. R. (2018). *#Republic: Divided Democracy in the Age of Social Media*. Princeton University Press. https://doi.org/10.1515/9781400890521

Sydney Morning Herald, The. (1831, April 18). First edition. *The Sydney Morning Herald*, p. 2.

Sydney Morning Herald, The. (1948, September 18). "Impartiality of A.B.C.—Duty to Public." Letters to the Editor. *The Sydney Morning Herald*, p. 2. https://trove.nla.gov.au/newspaper/article/18085248?searchTerm=Impartiality%20of%20A.B.C.%20%E2%80%93%20Duty%20to%20Public&searchLimits=

Sydney Morning Herald, The. (1953). A.B.C. Hears critics of news broadcasts. 25 November, 1953, p. 6. Retrieved from: Trove.

The Australian. (1964). First edition. *The Australian*. 15 July 1964.

Trask, S. (2020, February 16). ABC Case Against AFP Raids Dismissed. *Australian Associated Press General News Wire*. https://search-proquest-com.wwwproxy1.library.unsw.edu.au/docview/2355696022?rfr_id=info%3Axri%2Fsid%3Aprimo

Tribune, The. (1945, March 1). Cleary' s Resignation Blow To ABC. *The Tribune*, p. 6. https://trove.nla.gov.au/newspaper/article/208690996?searchTerm=chairman%20ABC&searchLimits=exactPhrase|||anyWords|||notWords|||requestHandler|||dateFrom=1944-01-01|||dateTo=1946-12-31|||l-advstate=National|||l-advstate=ACT|||l-advstate=New+South+Wales|||sortby

University of Notre Dame Australia, The. (nd). Underrepresented groups. Nulungu Research Institute. Retrieved from: https://www.notredame.edu.au/research/nulungu/projects/olt-transition-to-higher-education/key-findings/underrepresented-groups

Veitch, H. (2010, December 15). The Modest Face of the ABC: James Dibble 1923–2010. *The Sydney Morning Herald*. https://www.smh.com.au/national/the-modest-face-of-the-abc-20101214-18wpw.html

Wadham, B. (2014, February 10). With Navy's Record of Abuse, Asylum Boat Claims Can't Be Ignored. *The Conversation*. https://theconversation.com/with-navys-record-of-abuse-asylum-boat-claims-cant-be-ignored-22941

Weeks, B.E., Ardèvol-Abreu, A., Gil de Zúñiga, H. (2017). Online Influence? *Social Media Use, Opinion Leadership, and Political Persuasion, International Journal of Public Opinion Research, 29*(2). Summer 2017, 214–239. Retrieved from: https://doi-org.wwwproxy1.library.unsw.edu.au/10.1093/ijpor/edv050

West Australian, The. (1945, March 2). Paper Attacked. "Blatant Inaccuracies". ABC and Mr Churchill. *The West Australian*, p. 4. https://trove.nla.gov.au/newspaper/article/44999578?searchTerm=inaccuracies%20ABC&searchLimits=

West Australian, The. (1953, October 3). ABC Staff Has Lost a Privilege. *The West Australian*, p. 3. https://trove.nla.gov.au/newspaper/article/52932388?searchTerm=ABC%20privilege&searchLimits=

Whitehead, G. (1988). *Inside the ABC: Geoffrey Whitehead's Personal Account*. Penguin Books Victoria.

Wilson, C. (2021). ABC may outsource outside broadcasting as technology ages and budget cuts bite. 12 May 2021. Crikey.com. Retrieved from: https://www.crikey.com.au/2021/05/12/abc-outsource-outside-broadcasting-technology-ages-budget-cuts/

Wood, B. (2018, August 3). *Submission to the Review of Australian Broadcasting Services in the Asia Pacific*. https://www.communications.gov.au/sites/default/files/submissions/bradley_wood.pdf

Wootton, H. (2019, August 2). Police Raid on ABC 'Unconstitutional'. *The Australian Financial Review*. https://www.afr.com/companies/media-and-marketing/police-raid-on-abc-unconstitutional-20190801-p52czc

Wroe, D., Bachelard, M., & Snow, D. (2014, January 23). Asylum Seekers' Burns Claims Baseless, Say Australian Defence Chiefs. *The Sydney Morning Herald*. https://www.smh.com.au/politics/federal/asylum-seekers-burns-claims-baseless-say-australian-defence-chiefs-20140122-3196l.html

Wyn, J., Khan, R., & Dadvand, B. (2018). Multicultural Youth Australia Census Status Report. 2017/18. Youth Research Centre. *Melbourne Graduate School of Education Research Unit in Public Cultures School of Culture and Communication University of Melbourne*. https://education.unimelb.edu.au/__data/assets/pdf_file/0011/2972036/MY-Aust-Report-17-18.pdf

Yadamsuren, B., Erdelez, S., & Marchionini, G. (2017). *Incidental Exposure to Online News*. Morgan & Claypool. http://ieeexplore.ieee.org.wwwproxy1.library.unsw.edu.au/document/7791114

Zafirovski, M. (2017). *Identifying a Free Society Conditions and Indicators*. Brill.

Zollman, K. (2012). Social Network Structure and the Achievement of Consensus. *Politics, Philosophy & Economics, 11*(1), 26–44. https://doi.org/10.1177/1470594X11416766

CHAPTER 7

Future Options

The ABC now had "conversations" with its audiences, as did all commercial media, and in so doing has forsaken the élite authorial voice, its *cultural capital*, that spoke with a consistent attentiveness to the Australian public interest. It now pursued inconsistent conversations and erratic narratives, just like many of its commercial and "prosumer" rivals in the *field*. It had a muddled understanding of its voice yet wanted to remain the voice of Australia, of its 1932 conservative founders, of the government and of the citizens. At its highest function, it existed to protect the integrity of the democratic state and to animate, inspire and enlighten its people. It has one job. But belonging now as it did to the service industries it must now consider its audiences "wants" in the delivery of content as never before.[1] The audience directs the content. Where once Aunty gave Australians' their medicine "because it was good for them", because they needed it, and Australians obligingly took their medicine because it trusted Aunty. Aunty now had to pander to the "needs" and moods of a fractious, free-willed cohort as well as 'group think'.

In examining the ABC's future, this text analysed aspects of its past as an indication of the ABC's current situation and dilemmas for Aunty that jeopardise her fate. This book had analysed a public service broadcaster as a case study drawing on intersections of Bourdieu's *field* theories and Institutional Logics theory where actors in the *field* had been analysed in relation to their cultural and political construction, as well as their choices

V. Small, *Strangling Aunty: Perilous Times for the Australian Broadcasting Corporation*,
https://doi.org/10.1007/978-981-16-0776-9_7

in defining the norms of the organisation: "this is the way we do things". Bourdieu described this as *habitus*. The role of symbols was important in both Institutional Logics analysis and Bourdieu's frameworks where social and professional networks were formed by key actors towards creating an institutional culture, historically. Examples of these were outlined, specifically, in Chap. 1. Early management was attentive to its role in building *cultural capital* by fostering a range of cultural interchanges, for example dinner parties with conductors, taking major visiting overseas artists to restaurants for supper and holding barbecues and cricket matches for dignitaries. ABC management cultivated key literary and artistic figures both from overseas and locally. Nowadays, with the rise of managerialism, such behaviour would be considered a waste of money and resources, and possibly violate corporate social responsibility policies, which would even identify it as exclusionary practice. Yet, it was from these social activities that ABC management "oiled the wheels" and helped the ABC accrue its *cultural* and *reputational capital*.

History is a superlative teacher and much ignored and over-looked in a digital era that quests for the novel, where past experience and contextualisation is disregarded in favour of faddish ideas, reactive social media comments and disruptive content innovation. Contemporary Western society is haunted on two fronts: by the future, with its attendant fear of missing out (FOMO), and fear of the past (FOP) which carries the imperative to repudiate that which is considered 'old'. But as historians know, legacy information can be powerful tools in learning about the present and, as such, this chapter will consider how the ABC's past had shaped the present. The past's shaping of the ABC meant the institution evolved and "acted beyond its institutional broadcasting remit" (Wilson et al., 2010)[2] to become the nation's primary purveyor of news and culture. Until prevailing attitudes were rid of the aberrant belief that the future shaped the present, history would be repeatable. Maybe lamentably so.

This book has examined the dignity of public service, the privilege taken to serve, without guilt or self-consciousness, and service for the greater good as an élite activity, which belonged exclusively to the ABC. It discussed how service was a privileged activity that the ABC has undertaken in an élite *field* of media. In a state of digital disorder and audience fragmentation, it becomes harder for governments to circulate national messages, where audiences are in pursuit of pockets and pitches of information. The role for a national broadcaster had never been more important to act against this fragmentation in the digital realm. However, the

ABC had moved into that emergent digital commercial *field* without regard for the high net worth of its own *cultural capital* acquired in its old *field* that gave it legitimacy, ascendancy, trust and authority among Australian media and as a valued public service provider. It has failed to create policy and leadership that moves this valued capital into the contemporary digital field. The ABC had failed to treasure what had been described in public management literature as its "public value" (Moore, 1995) and there had been an absence of "leadership meta-strategy" (Behn, 1991) in the unrolling of digitisation and staff cutbacks where a related need was identified: "educating the public is an essential element of leadership for cutback management" (Behn, 1980).

Murdock (2004)[3] said where once the state sought to shore up for its citizens "information rights", "knowledge rights", "deliberative rights" (viewing, listening to or contributing to debates), "representation rights" and "participation rights" public service media should now look to lead and be the heart of a "digital commons" where they linked with other public and civil organisations to become "defined by its shared refusal of commercial enclosure and its commitment to free and universal access, reciprocity, and collaborative activity" (Murdock ibid.). He said public service media had the capacity to counter the fragmentation of the internet caused by the binaries of "them" and "us" by providing this central hub where ideas can be debated fruitfully and, in so doing, reclaiming the public trust (ibid.) through enlarging public capacity to understand the many sides of issues, possible actions and their consequences. A neutral, impartial public service information provider within a constitutional democracy is placed, ideally, to serve that social need and scrutinise the trend of conformity through popularity.

This book has concluded that Aunty is neither a PSB nor PSM—in the digitised era she is a public service provider (PSP) in an emergent commercial *field*. It disputed the assertion by James Murdoch (2009) that media had "analogue attitudes in a digital age" (Murdoch, 2009). Rather, the media field had collapsed and reformed into a heavily monetised domain but the unique *cultural capital* and *reputational capital* of the ABC needed to be 'counted and bundled' for the transition as well. ABC cultural and reputation capital was built on analogue but could be transitioned to the emergent digital *field*. The ABC had been let down by governments. They had failed to fund it to an adequate extent, but also—and even more significant—both sides of politics caused erratic funding patterns, which impeded ABC planning and strategic goals. This was confirmed in the so-named Dix Report (Committee of Review of the Australian Broadcasting Commission, 1981): "many people ascribe the ABC's failures to reduced resources—both financial and staff—as a result of Government policies. This view was put strongly by the Commission itself, its management, and to a lesser extent, its staff" (Ibid.). Governments from both sides of politics had failed to provide timely, adequate and appropriate feedback in developing and crafting policy that would "future proof" the ABC. Then, ABC management, had failed to provide effective leadership and interface with government in building the ABC in a digital era. In some instances it had evaded its agency. It had tolerated a restive staff culture. The ABC board that was supposed to work with government had not created the most effective policy to preserve the ABC—and possibly, there was poor interface at times between the management and its board. In addition, the rush to include social media as a main source of "selling" promoting and gathering news and information had provided none of the promised enrichments and instead left ABC news output distracted and depleted by the inadequacies of social media, in particular the propensity of social networks for hearsay and disinformation. The ABC as a whole was now disengaged with the government and, at times, adversarial. These matters have all resulted in a diminishment of credibility, independence and agency as a national institution. Staff freely expressed opinion on management and governments online and sourced or 'liked' information from unfiltered social media, sometimes of unknown origins—and with unknown intent. The ABC did not engage in either self-reflection, or scepticism of social media voices (be they actual people, anonymous people or nation states seeking to destabilise debate). Instead, the ABC collectively had been unable to deal with criticism and deflected attention by blame-shifting to the federal government or accusing fault-finding actors of speaking on behalf, and at the behest, of Rupert Murdoch. As this book analysed, historically feelings between Murdoch media outlets and the ABC was an "ancient hatred" and, in the past, the ABC had weathered it, 'cocked a snook' at it—and pressed on with its charter in spite of it.

Educating the people had been a central plank of the ABC. The ABC's 1939–1940 Annual Report announced the launch of broadcasting to schools which was said to "Conduce to the building of a better educated democracy" [4] at a time when the spoken word had power to change. The ABC was now challenged by competitors in the same digital field where content was distributed on platforms that pretended to be real news; while the ABC was tasked to grow public value for its content and "coevolve with other organizations to meet its goals. As in a biological ecosystem, a PSO ecosystem" (Chen et al., 2020). The ABC had inserted itself in the middle of the current confusion that challenged all players with nagging questions: who were these new online operators, what information did they supply; and, did they contribute to a healthy, vibrant democracy? This book is an effort to bring clarity to controversy, and promote informed, respectful discussion and support for the ABC in describing the role it could play in the media world. It invites debate on how the ABC can evolve to meet the challenges of the ameliorating term "digital disruption" that could more adequately be expressed as "digital disorder" and (sometimes) "digital derangement".

The central problem investigated here has been how the public broadcaster, the ABC, originating and creating its *cultural capital* and *reputational capital* in old media had transitioned to digital media. The Dix Report (Committee of Review of the Australian Broadcasting Commission, 1981) identified a strong growth in the institution's reputation in the 1960s to "initiate robust, mass-oriented current affairs journalism" (Loc. Cit.). Ultimately, the research found it was struggling and being strangled—both by itself and outside actors—and that its core value of universality had been downplayed and compromised in favour of niche pursuits. This book takes a researched, knowledge-based approach to the topics chosen for inquiry.

The ABC can re-build itself as the élite media organisation and return to being a standard-setter, a flag-bearer for its new *field* within the emergent commercial media *field*. The scope of the challenges was surmountable, but they were also urgent. Before the ABC's shift and drift to commercial digital field, there needed to be a plan for relocating Aunty—as a vital national resource. If such planning had occurred, the ABC in its new field would have continued to benefit the greater good and demonstrate an 'all to all' public service, as a continuum from the past. The pressure to pursue niche markets and youth audiences through 'rabbit holes' of entertainment content needed to be restrained by institutional assertiveness and confident "build it and they will come" mind set. Instead of which, the ABC had demonstrated a "hope for the best" approach. It was part of a strategy that the national broadcaster needed to employ that would have worked on the push and pull factors of their established content and audiences transitioning to a new sandpit. The institution needed to take regard of how to transition the status quo to more innovative practices. Instead, the ABC appeared to define the two as distinct and untranslatable. Former Prime Minister Paul Keating eulogised at the funeral of the former head of the Commonwealth Bank (who lead the bank when it was government-owned but moving to privatisation), Donald Sanders: "we owe Don an enormous thanks for transitioning this massive institution to a thing of such value today" (Cockburn, 2020).[5] Keating had identified that Sanders was aware of the Commonwealth Bank's public value and that he had done, in what public management literature would describe, put strategies in place to "exploit the potential of (their) political and organisational settings for creating public value" (Moore, 1995). This book and its research were not advocating privatisation in drawing on this particular comment from Keating about the Commonwealth Bank. Rather, it had analysed the ABC as a public institution which had shifted into a commercial in a drifting push-pull content environment, as had the Commonwealth Bank in terms of banking deregulation in past decades. Commonwealth Bank management had to pivot and preserve the institution, and did so successfully to ensure the continuation and growth of the outfit. There had been a recent growth in the body of literature on innovation in the public service (Osborne et al., 2020; Chen et al., 2020; Skålén et al., 2018; amongst others) after a paucity of research on the topic was identified in 2008 (Windrum & Koch, 2008). While innovation in public sector broadcasting was still "understudied" (Evans, 2018) the emphasis in content had become storytelling rather than packaged news and "the outcome of a novel means for conveying a story" (Evans, ibid.). To achieve this there was a need for the removal of organizational boundaries "first drawn to facilitate the operation of existing processes... and they impede the creation of new processes" (Christensen & Overdorf, 2000) but where entrepreneurial "managers must understand precisely what types of change the existing organization is capable and incapable of handling" (Christensen & Overdorf, ibid.). The ABC had also engaged in a status quo versus innovation stand-off, exemplified in staff backlash, as if the two were mutually exclusive. Yet this did not take into account public accountability and established practices that had built respect for the institution in the past and of which staff was mindful. The word innovation had been mostly used in a generic context and was possibly "often ill-defined or unquestioned" (Evans, ibid.). Research had found it was not a simplified, blanket topic and advised public service managers attend to six types of innovation: "mission, policy, management, partner, service, and citizen" (Chen et al., 2020).

This book and its research make 14 key points about the ABC:

1. It had been forgotten that the ABC had built its *cultural capital* on educating and creating nationhood music. This was described in Chap. 1 where the creation of ABC's early audiences was located in its role in the *field* of Australian culture and national loyalty. Allied with this, the lack of valuing and failure of policy to capture and transfer that *cultural capital* into the digital *field* had become a core, implied, concern of governments, staff, artists and their audiences/ the Australian taxpayer. ABC management assumed the *cultural capital* and *reputational capital* of all ABC content was a resource would last forever. But in times of heightened austerity—and especially after the novel coronavirus had damaged the Australian economy, governments will be scrutinising the public's value for money in all of its activities. It is this situation, alone (the first pandemic in Australia since the 1919 Spanish 'Flu, before the time of the ABC), that added urgency to the ABC's need to revalue, revise and re-assess its role and policies in the digital realm.
2. The ABC needed to tackle its management's reactive, staccato planning around budgets by encouraging stronger interface with governments and to then better inform and manage staff, and identify 'public value' more clearly in its allocation of resources and strategic goals in commercial digital media. This was analysed in *Chap. 2* where management culture had been accused of apparent secrecy. But this research had found it could possibly be better described as a lack of consultation with other stakeholders. In addition, there had been recurrent criticism of ABC board members and managing directors that they lacked experience in public broadcasting, with a concomitant deficit of skills and capacities to plan for a public cultural institution. Overlaying this had been the influx of a managerial emphasis on corporate efficiencies, management performance and KPIs led by the rise of the Master of Business Administration degree and its focus on a generic approach to the running of all organisations as if they were all the same, maybe with a few tweaks. It was of some concern that this model did not apply to a national public cultural institution and that generic styles of managing have not served the ABC and the public's best interests. The ABC now resides in a commercial *field* where there is a perpetual quest for a better product and its institutional strategy needed to prepare for that.

3. *Chapter 3* investigated how staff culture had worked against the organisation, especially in recent years. Even though Former Managing Director Brian Johns said, "it's the only organisation where everyone from the messenger boy up knows how to run the place",[6] there is quite a clear line between good intentions and sabotage. Management needed a more finessed control of staff to prevent the undermining of its management, governments (who superintend funding) and policies by providing clearer vision on how the ABC would sustain itself and hold its distinctive ground in the commercial field. The public image (sometimes referred to as "the optics") of all this disorder was that it appeared the ABC did not know what it was doing. This was the last thing Aunty needed, especially when money was tight and the internet offered such abundance. Idiosyncratic and reactive staff culture was a consequence of the failure in the leadership, especially as digitisation emerged as the way of the future. Further to this, there was a need for order between management and staff, obtained by political engagement on all levels to provide legitimacy for management and a conviction and consistency of content. A significant gain in staff influence in running the ABC was identified as occurring when the first staff-elected representative was allowed to sit on the ABC Board in 1983.
4. Former Prime Minister Kevin Rudd attempted to reinforce the independence and integrity of the ABC Board "above and beyond the reach of frontline culture warriors" (Lewis, 2009, quoting Rudd)[7] by introducing a new format for electing board members overseen by an independent panel to address concerns about the implied "reward" system for board seats. This had unravelled (Knott & Hunter, 2014)[8] and was described in *Chap. 3*. Rudd's feared "culture warriors" were nonetheless still active and appointments to the Board were seen as rewards for other service, when instead shrewd experience in or with public broadcasting might have been preferred. It had been identified that both management and the Board needed apolitical expertise and depth of broadcasting knowledge.
5. The research for this book had revealed there was some merit in re-embracing what would now be regarded as "old school" methods of journalism which also meant in the first instance, a closer alignment with ABC editorial policies[9], the charter and practice, as discussed in *Chap. 4*. "Aunty" once had substantial political capital through its

investment in in-house staff training, the mentoring of journalists by senior journalists and adequate resourcing for 'meaty' investigative journalism. Staff cuts and creeping commercialisation of all media have depleted and disillusioned this pursuit. The ABC also once emphasised the sourcing of authoritative and credible, independent news that was of matter to the general public. Many staff acquired *cultural capital* and 'political capital' over the years giving them agency in the journalism *field* and the results had manifested in Walkley Awards and other peer recognition. These awards occurred because there were baseline expectations of accuracy and impartiality. No opinion or emotive language was used and there was a quality and exactitude of writing that communicated the central issue that served the public's right to know. The journalist was not central and stepped back, placing the news or revelation in central focus. This writing was supported, in large amount, by teams of skilled editors who crafted and upheld quality broadcasting. The *reputational capital* they accrued for the ABC, anonymously, was indispensable to this process. But as the ABC had found out, quality costs money. It has since found out that it was not valued manifestly in the emergent commercial field. Internet oligopolies managed content and shaped opinion to pursue their own policies and agendas, chased and pillaged free content and curated echo chambers for political views. In the face of drifting, fickle audiences and the overwhelming shift of news to online technology, the infiltration of entertainment and opinion as news, and the necessity of celebrity journalism, Aunty's standards were being undermined and threatened to choke Aunty's voice.

6. The ABC's shift to the digital commercial field meant it had become even more vulnerable to funding cuts and privatisation—through sameness with other media and failure to transpose its *cultural capital* and *reputational capital* in the emergent commercial digital *field*. There had been divergence with various digital online ABC platforms and convergence through content integration and removal of duplication; the two complemented each other but at other times had served to undermine the ABC's core broadcasting systems of radio and television. This was partly attributed to the aberrant media belief that everyone was online and already knew the news (or their version of the news), so what was the point? This aspect was revised in *Chap. 6*. This view also promoted a mob psychology approach to

the news—a 'common narratives' style rather than clear scrutiny of events accompanied by insightful analysis, when clarification and 'unpacking' was needed in the public interest. It had been observed that "cultural clashes of online, radio and TV journalists can be a complicating factor" (Sehl et al., 2019, quoting Singer, 2004; Erdal, 2008, 2009; van den Bulck & Tambuyzer, 2013).[10]

7. Coupled with this had been the drift towards opinion in ABC news platforms and the activities of its journalists online revealed how ABC journalists' opinions had become important and marketable for the organisation. This was discussed in *Chaps. 1, 4, 5 and 6*. Aunty's priority was to digitise; there was also government pressure to do so, with the expectations of an easing of costs after initial outlays. The move to digital was vital in order for Aunty to remain innovative and relevant. But in that process she forgot to reversion and apply her standards of credibility and disrespect for hearsay and it had engaged in a drift to commercial conventions. As former ABC journalist and presenter Kerry O'Brien said: "People's desire for knowledge has not changed in the digital age, nor has their need to be able to trust their sources. If anything in the echo chamber of social media when we simply don't know who to trust anymore the need for demonstrable integrity is greater than ever."[11] Consequently, this book argued that the ABC's voice could be threatened with strangulation by digitised opinion. While the ABC's embrace of technological change had been impressive and beneficial to many citizens (although mistaken city-based assumptions persisted that all Australians could access the internet), maximising reach was constrained by government funding as well as the infiltration of opinion, or position-taking in reporting, as evidenced in the coverage of the Pell trial, analysed in *Chap. 3*. There had been a considerable impact on news from the ascendancy of diverse opinion over simple fact. Staff shortages had become a problem in supplying consistently factual reporting. It should be remembered, though, journalists, at best, had always presented a mediated truth. Now, however, their mediation is re-mediated with opinions.

The ABC needed to stake out its own field within the digital field—this would have involved, initially, major policy re-writes, government input and support and management and staff collaboration. While James Murdoch (2009) claimed the BBC was over-asserting itself in a "land grab" in British media, this book asserts that the ABC should have embarked on that strategy in Australia, instead it had collapsed itself into the commercial territory and was desperately trying to 'fit in' and 'be liked'. Cries from Aunty that she was being bullied by commercial media were lacking credence given that she was in direct competition with the digital commercial operators. Both Nine Entertainment (now the largest media provider in Australia after its takeover of Fairfax News) and News Corporation had said that the ABC entered their *field* and offered similar content. This was not a complaint that the ABC should have dismissed as more attacks by Rupert Murdoch. The public media outfit had made a serious encroachment on the commercial digital field and two separate commercial media organisations have observed this and complained about it, publicly. The ABC also erred in not planning strategically to protect its élite content and leaving it open to this attack. Commercial media businesses rely on accruing and shepherding audiences to sell to advertisers, guided by the behemoth internet organisations—but also have to compete with content that is funded by the public. This situation required the ABC to apply consideration to commercial media complaints that the ABC was violating the Federal Government's competitive neutrality policy. In 1996 the Australian Government articulated its policy on competitive neutrality:

> Competitive neutrality requires that government business activities should not enjoy net competitive advantages over their private sector competitors simply by virtue of public sector ownership. (Australian Government, 1996)[12]

In 2018, the "Competitive Neutrality of the National Broadcasters" inquiry into both the ABC and SBS found that:

> The ABC does not have a formal competitive neutrality policy and it is not clear how the ABC considers competitive neutrality in decision-making. (Australian Government, 2018)[13]

So, it was up in the air. But that:

> The Panel considers the National Broadcasters are not causing significant distortions to the competitive process beyond the public interest"

although "Rapid market changes are resulting in an increase in the instances in which the National Broadcasters are 'rubbing up' against a range of domestic private sector competitors. (ibid.)

8. Following this, governments have used the ABC's "independence" and lack of a clear ABC definition, as an avoidance device, resulting in what this research found had been a form of benign neglect. Governments have failed to provide specific policy, objectives feedback and clear direction on the role of the ABC. The only time the ABC was re-assessed was when it caused trouble. There was an absence of positive reinforcement and, as a consequence, the ABC responds by showing cavalier contempt for the governments. This response failed to dignify the ABC as an iconic Australian media entity, its institutional actors, the public it served and the government. The technological changes actually required an entire re-writing of ABC policies and charter in explaining and delineating exactly what was meant by "local" and how its public funding would serve all Australians and their 'right to know'. The ABC was losing the brand by not articulating how serving particular interest groups served the whole. The research had identified the ABC offered shouting matches as the replacement for debate and reasoned, referenced, constructed arguments that intellectually and factually challenged power structures.

In 2019, SBS reported that Australian Prime Minister, Scott Morrison, said "public servants must be accountable to the many" quiet Australians "who they will never meet or hear from and not noisy lobbyists" (SBS News, 2019).[14] This was a veiled instruction to public service as well as public media that it existed for all. PSM policy direction needed to reflect this "voice for the voiceless" role as affirmed in as UNESCO statement in 2012 where it described PSM as an: "educational and cultural vehicle, especially for disadvantaged communities" (UNESCO, 2012)[15] as well it should maintain editorial independence, contribute to "capacity building" (Loc. Cit.) and above all be a model for best practice, a standard-setter for PSM as well as the wider media environment. Public service media outfits should lead and be the heart of a "digital commons" offering a differentiated set of services, not followers and conformers. The role of the ABC as a public service provider was analysed in *Chap. 3.* The desire to belong should not be so overwhelming that standards needed to be forsaken. Murdock (2004) said PSM should link with other public and civil organisations to become "defined by its shared refusal of commercial enclosure and its commitment to free and universal access, reciprocity, and collaborative activity" (Murdock ibid.).[16] PSM could counter the fragmentation and the thought control of the major internet companies, including the social media outfits, by providing sourced valuable news that drew on and built extensions to its *cultural capital* and *reputational capital.* In 2005, British academic Georgina Born said the BBC was in crisis because it needed re-invention.[17] The ABC too.

9. Funding cuts are an onerous pressure for cultural institutions and with a 100% reliance on the government and its public in an economic climate of reduced funding meant the ABC was even more vulnerable. Where at least other cultural outfits might benefit from benefactors, philanthropists and fund-raisers' benevolence, the ABC is not in that category of the Arts and performance. As discussed in *Chap. 3*, starting in 1975 these cuts had very slowly, then more rapidly, nobbled the ABC and it had been battling ever since (Blain, 1977).[18] Funding contractions have forced public service media outfits into "cultural anorexia" (Tracey, 1998)[19] exemplified by the ABC's low level of Australian-produced content and minimal involvement in the education of young Australians. There was also a newly merged media cultural cringe—from a Western perspective—and that problematised any analysis and assertion of Australia, its history, its geopolitics, its cultures—its shared future. For example, further questions arose from the analysis of managing the ABC in *Chap. 3*. These included: how much did the ABC need to run core valued services? And, was there a problem with management in diverting its resource allocation into the television channel ABC (24 hour) News, which had low ratings[20] amongst other free-to-air channels? More to the point, had it come at the expense of other core and valued services?

   The pink elephant in the room was: why is SBS separate? Both outfits could still have dedicated staff and unique platforms, branding and frequencies but with the same senior managers. For instance, the SBS Board and executive have investigated a merger of back-office functions with the ABC but the ABC had been less than enthusiastic (Mason & Roddan, 2020).[21] However, when former ABC Managing Director, Mark Scott, was finishing his term (2016) he said a merger between the two "could save $40 million a year" (McMahon, 2020).[22] This was flagging the duplication that occurred. Senior management and the board could move towards a more productive organisational design where cost savings were made in back-room areas as well as clearer allocation of resources to high value content and less to services that mimicked commercial media, for example the ABC News 24-hour news channel. It was a hotly disputed topic. In 2020 when the service was launched, the then Sky News (subscription service) Chief Executive Officer, Angelos Frangopoulos, said the ABC channel would reduce funding and quality from the ABC's existing services and mean taxpayers would be forced to pay for "needless duplication of services already available to Australians". (Leslie, 2010)[23]

10. The ABC now operated under commercial definitions of public while pursuing its own version of independence as analysed in *Chap. 6*. There was an urgent need for the government and ABC management and board to define the ABC's "independence" and its "public" in the emergent digital commercial *field* and articulate this in policy. Simply "upsetting people" as a foolish understanding of the meaning of independence and public benefit and are not adequate for a national media institution reaching out to the general populace. As an old-timer, Aunty does know better and can hold power to account in a more powerful way. Causing upset to corporates, politicians, groups and other individuals was a consequence of solid public journalism, but not the objective of public journalism. Its aim was to inform and educate—and this will then confronted the abuse of power or, at least, apply a standard tape measure to it and allow the public to decide.
11. There was a disconnect between university generic journalism teaching and specific newsrooms. This had consequences. For example, there was a mismatch between ABC practice, policies and performance and serious topics and issues identified for reporting (see *Chap. 4*). Social media, as discussed earlier in the book, played a major role now in prioritising what internet companies wanted to sell and they were ahead of the game, with news media tagging along behind trying to play "keepy uppy" (a game of keeping the ball in the air)—especially in the choice of social media issues covered. In addition, in the discussions about a lack of diversity on

the ABC which strangled Aunty's voice by privileging the strident voices from social media. Another area of diversity for the ABC to address was the paucity of attention paid to the need for a more *educationally* diverse range of people recruited to the ABC, especially those who had read the evidentiary sciences, agriculture, accounting, economics and history. Business or finance news for example played an important role in educating the Australian citizens on the state of their economy and the impact and roles of business and export/import income. Economics helped describe the state of average earnings and there was no disjointure in the two. Business manoeuvrings were Australians' business because it flowed through to jobs, for example and how government subsidies were spent. Coverage of dialogues between business and government, unions and government, and social welfare groups and government played an important part in positioning relevant issues in the public sphere for general consideration. The ABC needed to consider recruiting a broad base of new staff/graduates and not assume all university education met public information needs. For instance, an ABC cadet journalist said tellingly when they began intensive ABC training: "I learnt more in those six days than I did over four years at uni" (ABC News, 2018).[24]

Given that the cadets recruited were the best of the graduating class, that was making a very serious observation about the value of journalism degrees. The same cadet said: "One of the key pieces of advice I heard over our training week was that at the ABC we are both journalists and public servants—we have a duty to our audiences in a way that commercial and private media outlets don't" (ibid., 2018). In contrast with that statement, this research had found that staff culture was very strong, highly defensive and reactive and could be damaging of the ABC's reputation when management and government were ridiculed publicly by institutional actors. It was a unique culture for both public service in general and commercial media, where the online expression of opinions about bosses was a sacking offence. The juxtaposition in the observations made by the ABC cadet and "duty to audience" and the reality of staff culture which conceived the public audience as something more individual than general, raised the question of what processes the trainee staff underwent when joining the mainstream workforce that changed this perspective, because adherence or awareness of a strong staff culture was not evidenced in the cadet training. Another cadet journalist was quoted: "working with ABC News makes me feel proud and that I am truly working in the public interest" (Loc. Cit.). A former ABC journalist was critical of ABC newsroom staffing in general: "today, we are largely served a diet of inexperienced 20-somethings who are supervised largely by 30- or 40-somethings who lack the years on the road needed to spot a different and important angle to a story, to see through the government or corporate spin and to actually find and break an original yarn" (Waters, 2020).[25]

12. Creating staff redundancies was a "particularly damaging form of organizational change" (Worrall, 2000) and needed reassessment. This was another example of quick-change management that had taken place at the ABC. As described earlier, collaboration between management, stakeholders and staff within frameworks and strategies and attending to government policy might provide a more fruitful outcome for 'public value' than simply eliminating people without context, or simply for cheaper outsourcing. While there was limited research on ABC redundancies and Australian public service redundancies, the Australian workforce overall had been identified as one where "mature age workers are perceived as 'not likely to change', 'not open to new skills', unable to 'catch up on computer literacy' and more likely to 'get sick'" (Patterson, 2004).[26] Compounding this negativity towards older workers, the workforce was geared to early retirement (ibid.) and there was a media bias against ageing (Hatch, 2005).[27] Australia had a "rapidly ageing workforce" (Kossen & Pedersen, 2008)[28] and European research had identified that most organisations did not identify an ageing worker with know how (legacy knowledge) as providing higher productivity. So, from a cost benefit analysis, older workers' productivity did not replenish rising labour costs. Nonetheless, the passing on of know-how in cultural institutions might require a second look, when precious *cultural capital* needs to be preserved for the greater good, and this was an area where further research would shed light.
13. The co-creation of content with online contributors, commentators and audience members (prosumers) was now problematised and complicated. This was addressed in *Chaps. 1, 4 and 6.* The journalist was the primary definer of how an event was to be

depicted and made selections and choices based on the authority of the writer.[29] This was now under threat from the contributions of 'citizen journalists', commentators and self-appointed experts and the close involvement of journalists with social media and opinions. Hawkins (2013)[30] argued that the ABC perpetuated its role through re-enactment and participation.[31] However, this re-enactment was tested and randomised when content was co-created with audience contributors. It confronted Aunty's impartiality. Greater emphasis needed to be re-directed away from ratings towards quality public journalism, for the greater good. Co-creation of content with commercial operators created new marketing pressures for Aunty to perform that were potentially anathema to journalism that catered 'all to all'. As a former (unnamed) ABC journalist said: "*ABC News* contains daily examples of stories that are of no interest to the majority of the potential audience" (Waters, ibid.).

14. The ABC needed to revisit its role as a contributor to Australian education, especially its former 'cradle to grave' approach to the public. Stronger collaborations with universities, contributing to bespoke media courses could benefit the institution, as could other major players benefit such as Nine Entertainment and News Corporation. Greater emphasis needed to be applied in ways of creating content for the public good, rather than finding new ways to market and platform novel content as the priority. Sensation content ultimately had a short shelf-life, or spoke to a narrowly defined public. The ABC needed to reconsider what an ABC education for young Australians would look like and develop it in policy and practice. Australians needed to be able to see themselves again in Aunty's looking glass. Her television channel for kids was now combined with adult comedy, as a cost saving measure, yet the two are separate citizen audiences. The special genre of children's education was mutually exclusive from adult entertainment.

Conclusion

This book investigated how the ABC had come to define itself through the analysis of words and symbols to re-legitimise and reproduce itself culturally and symbolically over the decades while also preserving its élite privilege. It now tried to do the same but in a rambunctious commercial *field*. It had also analysed the role of institutional actors in shaping the

ABC's current situation. As a normative publicly-funded cultural institution it was given the opportunity to form and shape national interests and values remote from the profit motive of shareholder ambitions. That mission had not changed; but its *field* had. The ABC had reified the public sphere. However, part of this drift to the digital commercial *field* had seen the departure from and loss of the ABC's *cultural* and *reputational capital.*[32] Encouraging conversations, participation and collaborations in the digital field, it had hoped to sustain its relevance and ensure its survival but this had brought it into conflict with its mission. This book outlined what that *field* once looked like and how it was carved out for the ABC in Australia through the establishment of the institution, under the "care" of the Postmaster General's Department and then its Charter, and the accretions of symbolic power it enjoyed over decades of dedicated public service from staff and management.

Latterly, the ABC had been accused of bias with "frequent allegations of bias in reporting, inappropriate programming, political appointments to the ABC Board and mismanagement of funds" (Jolly, 2014).[33] The ABC said in 2016–2017, there were 2348 complaints of editorial bias with 6.9% upheld in cases and a further 11.3% resolved after the complaint was corrected (ABC, 2017).[34] By 2018–2019 there were 5675 complaints, 3104 regarded as complaints of editorial bias, and 3.3% upheld and another 7.7% resolved.[35] And while, historically, complaints were nothing new to the ABC, fortified by the old belief that "if we're offending everyone we must be getting it right" which followed the first claims of the BBC's first Director-General, John Reith in 1927 that "there are some people whom it is one's duty to offend!" (Ramachandran, 2003)[36]—but achieving balance and impartiality was more difficult in a volatile digital commercial media *field* for public broadcasters. This was because they were embracing two separate roles—public service to the Commonwealth and popularising itself in niche markets filled with opinion. That dual identity had been punishing for Aunty.

There was the defeatist view of Liberal Democrat Senator David Leyonhjelm that: "Public broadcasters around the world are inherently left-wing. I'm not sure there is an organisational remedy to it" (Ferguson, 2018).[37] It was more complex than that. In times of fiscal thrift, offending everyone was perhaps not the best goal, rather creating loyal audiences was the primary ambition—it pleased the people and the government that paid public money to fund the public service. In order to drill down into an accusation of bias and how the ABC was fulfilling its public role of 'all to all', in Chap. 3 this book conducted a thematic analysis of the ABC's online content coverage of the Cardinal George Pell trials following accusations of biased coverage and reporting. Ultimately, the thematic analysis of online content found that the merger of opinion, shoulder to shoulder with news reports combined with the use of creative writing in court reporting was challenging for the ABC in presenting unbiased news. As such, sustaining impartial news became an uphill battle. The loss of trained rounds people in sufficient number, with their fine legacy knowledge of courts and procedures, also proved to be damaging to the overall ABC output. There needed to be renewed investment in human capital to address the needs when reporting the major institutions of Australian society. The ABC news pages were for news, a given, but the inclusion of comment and opinion with provocative, damning headlines in the sidebar tainted the ABC's coverage, and incorporating outside contributors' photographs was also hugely problematic to impartiality. The audience makes the assumption that opinions, incorporated on news pages and unchallenged by other commentators, have the imprimatur and endorsement of the ABC. This was an issue for all news organisations as they pursued fleeting, skittish online audiences who relished curated newsfeeds based on popularity and sensation.

There was some concession of potential bias by the infiltration of opinion by Managing Director, David Anderson, who said: "the make-up of the broadcaster's panel shows—which also include weekday current affairs discussion program *The Drum*—could negatively affect public perception ... that we haven't accurately reflected what would be the views of the country for whatever reason" (Duke, 2017).[38] However, to stay popular and craft new audiences, the ABC pursued Search Engine Marketing (SEM) buying AdWord ranking with Google for searches on ABC news reports for the wedding of HRH Prince Harry and Meghan the Duchess of Sussex in May 2018: "We spend on SEM purely to ensure our audience can easily find ABC coverage of significant news, television or radio programs or events" (Duke, 2018).[39] While the ABC had always had an important role in supporting the British Royal Family, these matters had become a bone of contention with commercial media. Anderson said:

> I think that in a media landscape where you have prolific and unprecedented choice in all media ... we have a duty to tell the Australian people through search what we have as their public broadcaster and what effectively the taxpayer has invested in, and I think that's going to become more prevalent into the future. (Duke, 2019)[40]

The ABC was located in a world where the concept of media freedom and ideas were under attack and asserting national cultures and nationhood had never been more vital. It could be argued that covering royal events was part of that as Australia was a member of the Commonwealth Heads of Government (The Commonwealth) that met biennially, and Her Majesty Queen Elizabeth II was Head of the Commonwealth. The ABC had also taken positive steps in covering indigenous Australian culture with the founding in 1993 of Screen Australia's Indigenous Department to develop Aboriginal and Torres Strait Islander stories and talent, funding AUD35 million for Australian indigenous content (ABC, 2018).[41] The range of cultural matters the ABC was compelled to cover was extensive in a vast, intricate multicultural nation, yet, it was also tasked with bringing Australians together. Overall, however, it must be mindful that "it is not enough to represent a diversity of viewpoints or cultures in terms of content produced, without attending to diversity and inclusion at the level of practice" (Born, 2012).[42]

In terms of media liberties, the ABC had more relative freedom than media in other democratic countries, for example India. It was asserted by Al Jazeera that India had become one of the "riskiest countries for journalists" (Al Jazeera, 2020)[43] "for reporting on COVID-19 or exercising freedom of opinion and expression" (ibid.). Reporting in other nations had also become problematic, especially in reporting the activities of governments and business actors. Filipina Executive Editor Maria Ressa was found guilty and sentenced to jail for 'cyber libel' of a Filipino businessman and criticism of the government of The Philippines, President Roderigo Duterte. There were at least seven other cases that had been filed against Ressa and her website Rappler (Al Jazeera, 2020).[44] The Foreign Correspondents Association of The Philippines said it was "a menacing blow to press freedom". Overall, the 2020 World Press Freedom Index had dropped Australia's ranking to 26 from 21 (19 in 2018) in a ranking with 180 countries (Reporters Sans Frontières, 2020).[45] The RSF said the drop was caused by Federal police raids in June 2019 on the home of a News Corporation journalist and the ABC, and the matter was outlined in Chap. 6. Australia had implied freedom of the media; it was not enshrined in law. The ABC was funded to defend the pursuit of truth, perhaps not as adequately as in the past, but in an information-overloaded, fact-sparse media scape, its role had become fundamental to the democracy.

The nub of the growing onslaught against the ABC was that it was using public funds to compete in a commercial digital *field*. Blame for "The

Troubles" at the ABC was directed at right-wing voices and Rupert Murdoch and then the problem seemed to be put away until it re-emerged. There was an absence of any public self-analysis of how shifting the ABC from its own unique *field* into the digital commercial sphere might have 'upped the ante' in terms of competition and flak from competitors. Where once the ABC's competitors snarled and snapped from afar (a separate sand-pit) they were now all clambering on top of each other in the same field and had become difficult to ignore. There had been no apparent thought given by management and its policy on how the ABC would preserve its *cultural capital* in that drift to the commercial domain without slipping into the sameness of commercial media. The ABC needed to locate itself within that field by bringing with it its own almost 90 years worth of hard earned *cultural capital* that commercial interests were unable to offer.

Counter-arguments that ABC audiences with expectations and memories of yore (Aunty's quality solid contributions to the public sphere) were redundant audiences have been damaging to the brand overall and insulting to future generations of Australian citizens. The ABC had cultural and intellectual capital in the bank, and it needed to transition that into fulfilling its charter. Quality was ageless and mattered to all generations. Educating its youth would be a solid starting point in re-engaging youth audiences (as it once did with The Argonauts, described in Chap. 5). It could consider supporting regional youth orchestras or bands as part of its education program. The literature argued that there had developed a deep disconnect between youth and the politics of their nation. There was a need for what was described as a vaccine for liberal democracies that were being infected by political disengagement (Kelso, 2007;[46] Snell, 2010[47]), and where moral beliefs were a predictor of this disengagement (Snell ibid.). For instance, research of young Greek Cypriots had shown they "associate politics with corruption and economic interests" (Christodoulou et al., 2017).[48] Some blame for this rests with political parties; and Flinders (2015) said it was important for political parties to avoid becoming as passé as Kodak, the US photo company launched in 1888 which filed for bankruptcy in 2012 after digital cameras had taken hold of the market. But the same message could be sent to public service media, in terms of their content and their need to pivot. Former UK Conservative MP, Douglas Carswell, said political institutions in the UK had not kept up with "an increasingly diverse society … that exists to some extent beyond the reach of the public" (Flinders, 2015).[49] It was the difficult job of the ABC to track these audiences down, as it had in the past, capture their attention and keep them. This was now a complicated set of problems for the ABC because its fellow inhabitants in the commercial field hunted for the fresh too. In addition to that commercial business models generally eschewed the "rusted on" clients (audiences), preferring to churn for the new—as if the two are antithetical.

Chasing a youth audience was problematic and complicated for an organisation like the ABC. While youth was less interested in traditional politics it was very interested in shaping the world into a better place (the aims of the liberal democracy), and while possibly less educated in the ABC's *cultural capital* in so far that they may not have given routine attention to the once 15-minute 7.45 am radio news bulletin, been exposed to Radio for Schools, Bananas in Pyjamas, nor Play School (The Argonauts, long gone), they too deserved a comprehensive attempt at an ABC education. The process of conversion (to the ABC) through the skilled use of technology was a way of gathering audiences and a well-established practice of the ABC over decades. Yet, the ABC had become as subservient to technology, as its audiences. By allowing audiences to create content was certainly cheap. But surely this was insulting to youth audiences who deserved as much attention and quality as previous generations of ABC audiences. Youth too can be invited (convinced) that it could be more supportive of the ABC through evidence of its contributions to democracy and informed debate. To abandon this objective in pursuit of the new had also left its "old" audience high and dry who "grew up" with the ABC—and were well educated by it. This was analysed in *Chap. 5* in describing the power of collective youth education in "The Argonauts". In an era of contested truth—based on the idea of controlling the narrative—what is the ABC's truth and through what ethical framework did it speak in its emergent commercial field? In 1948, the ABC's Chairman, Richard Boyer asserted that Australia was in the midst of "the greatest confusion of mind we have seen for many centuries…" and that the nation "could stand a lot of bad politics but it could not afford to lose its ethical, and spiritual basis." (South Coast Times & Wollongong Argus, 1948).

Ultimately, its current confusion showed Aunty's marketing had failed to engage with the essential need to preserve its *cultural capital* that it accrued by educating 'cradle to grave' audiences of Australians. It has instead chosen to create distractions and blame-shift from this fundamental oversight at a time when fact and information quality was challenged, and democracy under erosion. Highly motivated internet users did not represent the ABC's audience, even though the powerful views and comments from the strident voices seemed compellingly representative and imperative. And it would appear that promoting this noise did not convert as easily into media ranking and ratings as it would appear; where audiences seek summative guidance to make informed decisions. Politicians who chopped and changed government policy based on these voices were slowly realising this. The ABC once understood that as a pillar of Australian democracy it needed to be relevant by keeping one eye on those ratings, but another eye on 'everything else' to fulfill its charter, because ratings did not construe engagement and eyeballs jump around. Similarly, the 'anti-establishment' and 'anti-politics groups' were being treated as one 'anti-something' movement, when in fact they were looking at either doing away with politics, doing away with institutions (of which the ABC forgets it is one too) or doing it their way. Yet these disparate groups are not representative of the whole when "one of the central findings of mass surveys and polling data in advanced liberal democracies around the world is a commitment to democratic principles" (Flinders, 2015).[50]

The ABC was now spending public funds in pursuit of private opinions to create conversations and garner stories from contributors. Age demographics, assumed knowledge of digital technology, assumed knowledge of expertise and assumed expectations surrounding all of that are irrelevant. While quality is quality and the ABC once understood that it spoke to all Australians, in an undifferentiated sense, digitisation has complicated that, but not made it impossible when values are pursued that further the greater good, as discussed in Chap. 3. The ABC said in its 2018 Annual Report that "values matter because they anchor communities in times of disruption. They provide security, stability and dependability" (Milne & Guthrie, 2018).[51] But this understanding had been perplexed over the decades by what former ABC broadcaster Paul Collins (in M. Fraser & J. O'Reilly, 1996) said: "there is not so much an editorial bias as a lack of editorial direction" and that "important areas of the ABC are influenced by journalists and broadcasters of a progressive stamp" (Ibid.).[52] Media is a marketplace of ideas of which the ABC was now a part in the commercial as well as the public sense. It represented public interests in a new media space that, largely, (and anomalously for the ABC) prioritised income and popularity.

The ABC's "conversations" with its audiences were like those carried on by commercial and digital media but in replicating this activity in the same manner had forsaken its authorial voice, its *cultural capital* of the Australian public interest—of which no other media could lay claim. This form of struggle for domination of the *field* made the ABC distinctive from other media outlets, yet other media outlets did not allow staff the same capacity to express personal views. Insubordination was not entertained in the commercial *field*. This was another point of contention and difference for the ABC now that it inhabited the commercial *field*. Commercial media relied on a compliant, (publicly) willing staff culture; in the digital commercial field ABC staff contributors were misfits on this point.

ABC staff culture and defensiveness emerged in the 1970s with the beginnings of serious funding cuts to the organisation and its battle for survival was challenged even further in the 1980s with the emergence of incompatible managerialism that demanded efficiencies, targets, synergies, key performance indicators (KPIs) and dividends—the same as private enterprises. Overlaying these objectives on publicly funded enterprises made an awkward, clunky fit. What, for example, was a KPI for public goodwill? The public management literature would describe ABC staff culture as having "the tooth fairy syndrome" where staff retrenchments were viewed in disbelief and something reversible where a change of government would bring a revised and improved budget to re-instate all the lost jobs. Yet, Behn (1980) said to bring the staff into the reality that the organisation was in decline "leadership for cutback management requires convincing the members of the agency of accepting that unpleasant reality" (Behn, ibid.). The robustness of the push-back from staff culture towards management showed there no evidence management was driving the strategic change, or any attempts to bring the folk on-board were effective. The ABC's future held many challenges, including the relentlessness of the economic rationalism to which it was subjected. Former Managing Director Geoffrey Whitehead (1988) said that by mid-1988 public broadcasters around the world had been forced into free market economic policies. This involved new emphases on management performance and economies of scale. Whitehead (1988) said this resulted in a decline in "excellence in program-making".[53] The signs were troubling amid the rapaciousness of digital media. Schiller (1993) sounded a pessimistic note about this, that the future of media would be at the pleasure of informational technology:

> It will be an almost exclusively privatized social landscape. The public and the public's interest, if not entirely excluded from consideration, will at best be given marginal attention.[54]

This privatised media content control had signalled the erosion of understandings of the public good, commonwealth and the Commonwealth and public service. This had an apparent knock-on effect of undermining the ABC's *cultural capital* achieved through the hard efforts and determination of its initial actors operating in a patriarchal, privileged, élite environment. That these attributes were so castigated in the media meant the ABC and its successful past were confronted, severely. Digitisation and the drift from its *field* without transplanting its *cultural capital* had accelerated a decline in the organisation's role because of digitised confusion as to the roles of opinion, commentators and information—and their merger into one amorphous online content. Overlaying this, the restrictions on management of an embedded staff culture, and a management unable to change the culture or provide clear direction to reassure staff and dissipate this resistance had resulted in a situation where staff publicly professed a greater knowledge of what was best for the ABC and its audiences than management, its board and its policies. This situation made every change at the ABC moot.

The loss of *cultural capital* meant that for all the outstanding work the ABC had done and does, including its contributions to understandings of Australianness and Australian's self-worth, it had been called to serve to a higher standard: it still had to manage legacy memory of that capital, its charter and the ABC Act. Any detraction or error was magnified. This was another important aspect of its once unique *field*—the ABC was special and privileged ensconced in its own content *field*, but its necessary shift to the digital, commercial media *field* meant it drifted from its comfort zone, special sandpit and safe distance but without preserving its capital. The drift actually necessitated a revision of its policies to "protect the brand". Its greatest challenge was that when it removed itself from its exclusive *field* and merged with commercial digital content interests chasing ratings, hits, 'likes', subscribers, comments, shares, followers and social media algorithms—these preferenced disorder in the institution and uproar. This occurred because it was chasing the same commercial audiences that the private media already had in their sights—but algorithms do not preference public good and public service. Aunty should not be in cahoots with the commercial objectives of the participants in this *field*, in that regard. She had behaved as if she should and could compete with these sorts and expected to retain her *cultural capital*. She lived on the perfumed memory of her esteemed *cultural capital* and reputation but long ago needed to cherish her wealth, not simply cash in her treasures—nor forget them.

7.1 Aunty's Woes

Threats of introducing licence fees and forcing it to find external income to pay for the ABC were contentious matters for all public service media. Research showed that in Europe where PSMs were funded by subscriptions and paid advertising, their "quality and attractiveness" had declined (Collins et al., 2001)[55] especially in Europe where "mass media are becoming de-massified" (ibid.). In 1996 Jonathan Davis (1996) warned that short of taking public service broadcasting "intelligentsia out and shot" (Davis, 1996)—it would be starved of funds by the government to bring it under control.[56] Two other factors that Davis said prevailed upon PSM were a growing political preference for the marketplace to take care of more activities, and that in tight times money would (definitely) be cut from public spending (Davis, ibid.).

While this book argued that a greater support for Australia's public service broadcaster was the best way of reviving a jaded PSM industry, with Aunty shouting herself hoarse for attention in an ecology of fake news and strident voices. There was the counter argument. Professor of Media and Communications at *Goldsmiths*, University of London, Des Freedman (2019) said that referencing the BBC's institutional structures and "intimate relationship with élite power" (Freedman, 2019) had actually constrained the BBC from being a stronger watchdog, weakened its independence[57] and "undermined its ability to act as a reliable and independent check on power" (Freedman, 2019).[58] An intimate relationship with élite power by ABC actors was not evident from this research; rather it was found that there was a self-effacement about the power of the ABC concomitant with concerns that the power of a range of other institutions was more evident, and that these had failed society, with specific instances provided of where it needed to be addressed. Of course, the problem and inconsistency with this repudiation of ABC power is that the organisation was founded by an élite privileged, powerful group. It was this group and their links with powerful institutional actors that made it the huge success that was so esteemed. The ABC's denial of its own power can be seen as a loss of confidence and institutional insecurity. In psychological terms it could be self-fulfilling. Confidence can embolden the worth of inestimable capital—its absence can also devalue it.

This book argued that it was precisely that acquisition of those élite privileges in its own *field* that gave the ABC its reputation for quality, independent media and bestowed on it a once respected, envied status and voice in Australian society and media at large. But this advantage, cultivated through hard work, serious relationship networking and clever experimentation in genres, had been eroded by drifting content values as it shifted *field* to mingle and compete with the wilds and wants of commercial digital media. In addition, both academics and governments had failed to conduct assessments of the media activities carried out by public broadcasters (Born, 2012). So, the ABC suffered from a lack of meaningful, sincere feedback. This book identified an unacknowledged matter that challenged the ABC—benign neglect. Instead of governments telling the ABC what it did not want; they, the public and its democratically-elected representatives, who paid for the ABC on their behalf, needed to present serious requests and considered assessments and policies to support strategic initiatives. The ABC had suffered from a lack of positive attention. It also should be noted that *any* attention by governments/politicians was couched by the ABC as interference. As a public enterprise undergoing a content/audience revolution it needed attention, support and advice—its importance demanded critical, contructive engagement. The ABC had responded to government demands to digitise with innovation and initiative, yet there had been a repeated failure by all governments to assess the broadcaster's responses and its new ventures in media. Government accusations, historically, of ABC bias and counter-claims of interference are political terms and they have not been helpful in creating any useful alignments for the greater good, nor demonstrating fine management of staff culture. However, it helped explain how governments had used the ABC's independence as an excuse to challenge the broadcaster, rather than a reason to assess and measure its digital efficacy—and grow the institution. This was partly because in the Australian media there was the decades-old situation that:

> Government intervention, when present, occurs only to reconcile divergent corporate interests or to provide subsidies for projects not yet commercially viable. (Schiller, 1993)[59]

Governments only intervened, largely, to sort out competition issues when private media lobbied for change and improvement of their own business activities. There had been a conflation of this fact with over-reach statements that Rupert Murdoch runs the Australian Government. Governments also intervened to fund projects, conduct inquiries, order royal commissions, check on their expenditure (Senate Estimates

Committee) or the unique (but short-lived) move by former Prime Minister, Kevin Rudd, to attempt to create a more representative and politically-independent ABC Board.

Distinguished Professor at the Australian National University's Crawford School of Public Policy and former Vice Chancellor of the University of Melbourne, Glyn Davis, said the ABC had been riven with contradictions and challenges from the off (Davis, 1988).[60] So, the ABC in crisis in the twenty-first century, was nothing new. History told us so. It had been challenged from its first day of broadcasting in 1932 (Davis, ibid.). The ABC has had to innovate but had also been warned in the literature presciently that it must also try not "to jump on every bandwagon that rolls by" (Harding, 1979).[61] Its history was riven with investigations and inquiries into its utility "as both public pastime and political priority" (Wilson et al., 2010).[62] So, to speak of an ABC crisis as if it were novel is wrong. Aunty had been perennially challenged—especially since the 1970s funding cuts, the 1980s managerialism and then the beginnings of digitisation in the 90s. To frame the outfit as in crisis also denied the hard, dedicated work and invaluable legacy knowledge that had sustained the organisation. It had ridden out a continuum of "crises" where the ABC "expects and receives a great deal of criticism, much of it biased or unfounded, from outsiders" (Harding, ibid.).[63]

By 1980 Managing Director David Hill said if the organisation did not change it would not last another ten years (Davis, 1988).[64] Davis (1988) said the funding problems for the ABC in 1970s were the starting point for an unresolved, ongoing crisis. It was because at this point that Liberal Prime Minister Malcolm Fraser had "set out to tame the ABC" (Harding, 1979) whereas prior to that Labor Prime Minister Gough Whitlam's attempts to control the ABC were "maladroit" (Harding ibid.) and his Minister for Media, Moss Cass, had harmed the ABC because he "overidentified" (Loc. Cit.) with it. Harding (1979) said both Fraser and Whitlam believed the ABC was duplicating roles internally and subsequent coalition government inquiries triggered institutional instability, poor selection of board members, rapid turnover in senior staff (Davis, 1988) and erratic ABC leadership. It was hard to see one side of politics taking all the blame for ABC funding cuts when the figures showed they were bipartisan and not definitively along one party's line. This book had not analysed budgets and expenditure in the light of government spending and the state of the economy. It contributes to the literature in conducting academic analysis and research into the ABC's case looking from an institutional leadership and field perspective. This is placed in the context of history, shifting cultures, declining support for institutions and technological changes.

The ABC has become defensive, self-reflexive to criticism while in constant search for the next innovation racing headlong through digitisation, and as Born (2006) said in regard to the BBC that technological changes have been of "such radical transformation that the concept and practice of public service broadcasting demand to be re-conceived". This is another area where government assessment has been found wanting. The ABC has raced forward without sufficient self-understanding to embrace new paradigms of digital media, without re-configuring and re-conceptualising its role in a media-abundant ecology. Born (2005) said there was a new emphasis everywhere of building communities but the corollary of that was "the social fabric no longer comprises—if it ever did—a cohesive, unified culture built on shared norms, values and tradition".[65] She said the challenges of digital communication for public service broadcasters have lacked consideration of political philosophy, specifically "the politics of difference" (Born Loc. Cit.)[66] in changing democracies.

Born (2005) took issue with two themes put forward by the UK Government to challenge the BBC—and they are equally applicable to the ABC. The first theme she rejected was the government's argument that public broadcasting existed only because of market failure role and therefore new multiple choices; public broadcasting was redundant. There has been a strong argument in Australian government policy of 'market failure' where it is said that the ABC is only needed in areas which commercial media cannot supply. Second, Born (2005) rebuffed the UK Government view that the public broadcaster was expected to be a complicit facilitator with the government in breaching 'the digital divide' with all government services shifted to online ("e-government" and "the information society"). Both these arguments describe the end of public broadcasting and failure to acknowledge its established *cultural capital* and how it could best preserve, translate and develop those for the national interest in a digital *field*.

Born (2006) offered a nuanced understanding of the role of public broadcasters for the future as defending and defining the "politics of difference" while also maintaining their "universal" channels (Born, 2012). To bring Born's (2012) proposition locally, it means the ABC could support its traditional media while also working the digital platforms, as complementary. The media ecology is riven with abuse and uncivil engagement over the key issues of Australian society. The ABC can uphold deliberative democracy in conducting debates and discussion in preference to the performative theatrics of some emerging content. The ABC can reach many more audiences with digital channels, but in Australia there is an extraordinary ignorance of the many remote communities struggling with digital connectivity. Radio through the airwaves can sometimes still be the most convenient means of learning the news. There is another concern that issues now become immersed in what have been described as 'the culture wars' where "absolute moral truths contend with those who place moral authority in individual judgment" (Thomson, 2015)[67] and there is a media assumption that people will want to belong to one camp or its opposite. Yet this presumed polarisation of people is not born out in the research which has found that people are more inclined to be "ambivalent, internally inconsistent" and "moderate" in their "political and religious beliefs" (Thomson, ibid.)[68] and that there is much more overlap in society than diametric opposition. Australians do not learn or enjoy much by having themselves depicted at perpetual war with each other. Nation-building requires common ground while the term 'democracy' itself has become contested and there are diverse understandings of its meaning (Dahlgren, 2013) and "there is no universal template".[69]

Born (2006), quoting Tambini (1999), also questioned whether these newly constituted groups on digital media were representative "of interest and identity groups".[70] Further, the late first female Chairman of the ABC, Professor Dame Leonie Kramer (Dame Leonie was styled Chairman, the correct use of the word meaning "the person presiding over the chair"), cautioned prophetically in 1983 that while there was the "ABC's importance as a pioneer of public affairs programs, … the future will benefit more from its less conspicuous, but less transient work" (Kramer, 1983).[71] It also merits salutary mention here that when asked her thoughts about the ABC Staff Association's opposition to her appointment she replied: "I don't take them very seriously" (Anthony, 1982). Public service broadcasting's *field* of Enlightenment values—science, scepticism, individualism and reason, according to Tracey (2002) "has been placed in its coffin".[72] In its place was content driven by audiences which often presented a rough assemblage of beliefs, values and feelings delivered by commentators but without the expert curation of the general public need and interest. More concerning is that there are implicit expectations (found to be erroneous expectations in academic research) that the audience will divide into mutually hating tribes because of a perceived, binaried world. This "clash" might help create income for digital information businesses, but it was of questionable value to a public broadcaster. The ABC has shifted its model role in its élite *field* by deploying semi-commercialisation and its key institutional actors have acceded to this in favour of what is perceived to be with will/want of the people (aggregated audiences/segments). This is a markedly changed objective from its original purpose of developing an informed public sphere.

In 2020 ABC Chair Ita Buttrose released a statement: "What would Australia look like without the ABC?" (Buttrose, 2020)[73] confirming that "the ABC has not only helped shape Australia" but also adding: "we are the national voice that unites us". Buttrose said: "without the ABC we would have a balkanised and parochial bunch of broadcasters that are in danger of being compromised by profit and more intent on dividing than unifying" (Buttrose, ibid.). Regrettably, this is exactly the plight of the ABC faced with a lack of awareness, robust policies and understanding of the new *field* in which it operates. While the preceding comment was positioned as a caution for what might be, in effect, it described what is. In predicting what the world would be like without the ABC the statement said: "why would anyone want to diminish that and make us less than who we are?" It avoided another of the critical factors in the deteriorated status of the ABC—the neglect of the ABC by its own actors and leadership in the rush to the digital commercial *field* combined with the inadvertent setting up of partisan echo chambers that can never reach a consensus. The statement also clarified that the ABC budget was increasing, but at a reduced amount than requested and anticipated. The overall financial loss was of the magnitude of an expected AUD83.75 million over 2020–2022.

The statement concluded that: "the ABC is essential in generating and preserving Australia's democratic culture" (Loc. Cit.). This is also a central argument of this book. However, with the qualification that the ABC had now problematised the spaces where Australians "share our identity, how we tell our stories, how we listen to each other, how we ask for help and how we give it". On one hand, telling stories is vital for mental health and there are numerous organisations that work purposefully to do that (Reach. out, 2020)[74] and there are valid psychological reasons for telling stories as they are an essential source of identity (Ibarra & Lineback, 2005).[75] Oral history is rich in information (High, 2010).[76] But in a media context this is slightly different, and there are diverse examples of content that confounded people in the rush to tell stories that are absent of editorial authority. In Russia, research found that lesbians were telling stories into a political environment where there was a dangerous (for them) expectation of heterosexuality (Bingham, 2017).[77] In Canada, while the media tells stories about health, there was an absence of media coverage of socio-economic influences identified by governments in policies as causing these health issues (Hayes et al., 2007)[78] and in regard to Australia's Aboriginal and Torres Strait Islander's, journalists from indigenous newspapers have complained that "news stories do not always have to be about 'conflict'" (Sheridan-Burns & McKee, 1999).[79] Further in journalists' storytelling:

> There is ample research suggesting that journalists' often idealistic imagination of their work does not fully materialize in practice or is actually contradicted by their own performance in places. (Hoxha et al., 2018)[80]

Where once the ABC described Australia to itself through its top-down independence, mediating debate and establishing citizenship, now its bottom-up dependency on audiences telling the ABC the stories that mattered has created a dynamic shift. It has presented an awkwardness for the ABC to give a singular, national voice. It has handed over the narrative of Australia and Australianness to its audiences. Research had found Web 2.0 damaging to democracy (Ceron & Memoli, 2016)[81] because it devalued politics and encouraged scepticism (ibid.). Instead of creating a "two-way virtuous circle" (Norris, 2000)[82] of debate, discussion and enlightenment, the ABC has joined the "vicious circle" of the commercial *field* which cannibalises content and people and is self-referential and seeking culprits rather than outward-looking and civic-minded.

Digital media is a complex constellation, offering cross-media globalised content, linking a range of groups and interests that in the "old" days of broadcasting would not collide so forcefully. The opportunities for communication are rich in the use of digital media, but the new belief that the audience knows more, and the audience's needs greater that the common good and they had to be interactive is at all times caused a diminution of the ABC's confidence and assertiveness in platforming its own content through its own ideas and research. That the audience creates, plays with and alters content as part of the belief in a Creative Commons (founded by Lawrence Lessig in 2001 who set up a business where people can access content for free), means the ABC can provide enormously valuable assets allowing audiences perspectives and insights into mainstream events. Attending this challenge, however, is that professional public media is not staffed adequately to be everywhere at once and multi-tasking is now an employees priority, rather than exception. It is understood, that this is not a concern because content deficits can be augmented with the mainstream commercial product and/or—better—audience contributions. In terms of editorial decision-making and authorial choice, it was strangling Aunty's voice.

Policy discussion and pressures on Aunty moved abruptly from the thrill of media convergence in the 2005s to market failure argument in the 2018s, with barely a pause for thought of what went wrong in between. There has been a gap in the analysis of how public broadcasters were to function effectively in the changed media world where assumptions were made and models created in the past that were in opposition to commercial operators who had their own field. There is also division in the academy. On the one hand Born (2006) argued that PSMs, like the BBC, have shown "an awareness of the need to plan subtly the complementarity between services",[83] Tracey (1988) said there were forces at work that have been "beating away at the intellectual plausibility structures of public broadcasting"[84] for some time. One thing that is certain is that Aunty, the alternative media, is no longer the substitute point of difference. She belongs to her new shouty commercial field.

Tracey (1988) said in the evolving media environment "the fundamental problem which public broadcasters face lies in the shakiness of the very idea of a public good and public interest".[85] This is largely due to a lack of definitions of 'public good' and 'public interest' in the ABC Charter and the ABC Act (1983). There needs to be a new language and discourse surrounding public broadcasting in order to ensure its continuation.[86] In the commercial entertainment world creating discord and division, which has become the norm of reality television for example, is a standard formulaic procedure to draw in viewers and advertisers. However, in one of the world's most multicultural societies, a migrant nation, this is stretching Australian's capacity to cohere when repeatedly content separates and divides. Australians invest in an ABC to bind the nation culturally (as it did from 'the off') to support the struts of the democratic process. Antonio Spadaro SJ (2020) wrote that the head of the Catholic Church, Pope Francis I, said aggressive engagements in the public sphere were all part of "a piecemeal war" and a crude over-simplification of issues: "the world is not divided between good and evil, between wrong and right".[87] Spadaro (2020) said this approach had become dangerous because it reinforced: "there are those who campaign for the need to press down the accelerator, who tend to build a ghetto of a few 'pure' against the 'others', that is, the widespread mass of evil doers".[88] Deciding good from evil is an overwhelming and over-reaching task for a Fourth Estate, and it is not its job to do so; ideally, it presents facts and matters of import for audiences/voters to assess. It has one job to do, but it is the hardest job.

The ABC now offers what commercial media offers and it is an overarching point to consider because we have always bundled everyone under the heading of "media", anyway, but now it is convenient to do so—and Australia loses its unique asset, the ABC, in the new media melée. The media has become a merged field of content on the internet but this plurality of presence should not mean all media is the same. The ABC is charged with supplying the people what they *need*—to make informed decisions as citizens of a modern nation state supported by institutions based on the ancient Athenian elected representative government (demos) and the rule of law (nomos) (Blackwell, 2003).[89] Commercial media supplies the *want*—it exists to sell audiences to advertisers who create 'the want' (of the product, service, place). The objectives of public service media and commercial media are mutually exclusive in that regard. Importantly, the ABC has a longstanding relationship with its public—the general public—with whom it holds a trust to deliver what is in the public good and public interest, to make Australia a better, robust democracy—to give it what it needs. Apart from ABC management sloganeering, self-analysis of public service broadcasting in a digital environment, even if only shared internally, appears wanting.

Allied to this successive, Australian governments have not made it easy for the public broadcaster, requiring it to fulfil efficiency reviews and audits and address inquiries into a range of gripes and shortfalls. The ABC is being managed and assessed by governments at times now, as if it were a commercial entity. This has created confusion and eroded vision. Funding is highly contested and the ABC has had to manage the realities of fewer dollars, fewer staff—and reduced content—but ramped up competition. It has at times been let down by partial board members and managing directors who have failed to grasp what a public broadcaster does and is. The ABC has also let itself down by creating a sharply reactive staff culture that makes policy- and decision-making at times impossible to implement. The ABC staff has failed to address these issues that are part of the ABC's strangulation of its voice, instead choosing to become defensive and demonise Rupert Murdoch, as if he and his people were standing permanently outside each ABC building with a cudgel waiting to attack staff. This over-simplification is also unhelpful in unpacking the complexities within the ABC. European research has found, for example, that public service media was also being scrutinised more than ever by commercial media operators, as well as by regulators (Moe, 2008).[90] The impact of this more intense gaze on the ABC will be summarised next.

7.2 Jumping at Shadows

The ABC has abandoned the élite *field* it once occupied, yet "broadcasting is likely to remain central to our everyday lives and thus central to public service remits" (Moe, ibid.). Politicians talk about privatising the ABC because the content drift has created general confusion. Then, the ABC takes these comments as hostile, aggressive and "coming from Murdoch", but from a *cultural capital* point of view the ABC's account is also being run down by itself. It is as if it is still reacting against/proving former Labor Prime Minister Paul Keating's 1985 accusation that the ABC was "the most self-indulgent and self-interested outfit in the country" (The Canberra Times, 1985) .[91]

Chapter 5 explained how the 'ancient hatred' between the ABC and the Murdochs began with Rupert Murdoch's father, the Australian media baron, Sir Keith Murdoch. He and the cohort of Australian newspapers were so alarmed that the new medium of radio—and the ABC—would take away newspaper readers, advertisers and sales that they tried to prevent its establishment. That failed but they established their own radio stations anyway as a counter-move. Generalised, reactive statements about an "evil" Murdoch—who becomes an existential threat prepared to destroy everything ABC—do nothing to solve the challenges the ABC faces and furthermore, are not effective because the ABC never launches counter-attacks to address and contradict, very specifically, these complaints or assaults. It has been identified in this research that a real, ongoing problem for ABC management has been their incapacity/unwillingness to address accusations of bias from wherever they emanate, with contra evidence of impartial content. Instead it allows the staff to deflect all complaints as nastiness from the Murdoch media—and leave it at that. If it were a simple case of spite, it would be easy to rebuff the complaint.

The ABC has abandoned its exclusive, prestigious, élite *field* and moved into the commercial *field* without enough policy backup. That was a considerable shift and content drift, an onerous task given that the ABC has moved into an area that is a private media monopoly environment. There has been strong push-back from those who already "own" and literally own that *field*, including Nine Entertainment (the biggest player) and Murdoch media outlets. The ABC monopolised its own *field*; now in the chase for ratings and 'likes', and so on, and ambitions for greater relevance, management and its staff have failed to see the mine *field* into which bewildered Aunty has been walked. Poor Aunty. The commercial rationale behind the attacks needs to be scrutinised in the construct of how a private business (News Corporation, News Limited aka Murdoch media enterprises) operates in pursuing and hunting down its competition. That is how the business world functions, especially in the hyper-competitive world of international media.

Yet, the ABC staff and management take every attack personally displaying a naïveté of the commercial world, but also an ignorance of how to help Aunty address these challenges. In addition, many ABC staff are typically not earning the wages and salaries of commercial media employees, so there is an emotional investment made by ABC employees in working for the corporation. This is what used to be called "doing it for love, not money" and may help explain why staff take attacks so seriously. But McChesney (2008) said: "The days when journalism was a public service directed at the entire population—obviously never entirely accurate—are long gone".[92] Nonetheless, in analysing the ABC's plight there is a need to examine ways forward in which the ABC can again garner public participation. It has a vital role to fulfil in education and needs to be supported in reclaiming that position. First, it needs to relieve itself of the pressure/torment of chasing audiences online without first re-valuing its biggest asset—its *cultural capital* and how to deploy it—and through policy and closer governance have a tighter grip on not just editorial policies, but editorial direction and interface. The ABC has slipped into the same danger zone with Australian politicians in believing that social media expressions are the full, complete and definitive utterance of public opinion.

Overlaying this is the increasingly problematised role of the Fourth Estate—now a somewhat dated concept with the boom in online access to information for anyone, anywhere, anytime; the common use of the phrase "Google it" to find out information and with many people, including bloggers, now describing themselves as 'journalists'. People with smartphones and apps are now journalists, photographers and filmmakers. The whole definition of the role of a professional journalist barely exists, with all journalists now online and morphing their online entities into social media accounts, apps, questing after sources of news, opinions and comments. Professional journalists strived for trust with their audiences through distance; sometimes reports were exaggerated or just plain wrong, but among the more respected content there was always an effort to eschew opinion and let the facts speak for themselves—notwithstanding the contended position that journalists actually reconstruct reality (Hoxha et al., 2018).[93] Irrespective of this, the ABC has given itself a comprehensive remit and part of its performance criteria, the ABC's 2019–2020 Outcome 1 was to:

> Provide radio, television and digital media services to satisfy diverse audience needs, nationally and internationally, including programs of wide appeal and more specialised interest. It will provide distinctive radio programs that serve all local and regional communities throughout Australia; television programs that contribute to the diversity, quality and innovation of the industry generally; and will engage audiences through digital media services, including on broadband and mobile platforms.[94]

The ABC has developed a loyal following for trust in accuracy and relevance—trust to be a faithful and exacting 'watchdog' on the corridors of power. Former ABC senior journalist Kerry O'Brien pointed out in his memoirs that the impact of digitisation had been such that over his career he noticed that "even ordinary journalism was well-resourced and now often isn't".[95]

7.3 The Way Ahead

The ABC received AUD1.048 billion from the Federal Government for its annual income in 2019–2020. In addition, it was given AUD43,699 million for its enhanced news gathering program which had been established to "bolster local and regional news gathering services, including the establishment of outer-suburban bureaux, a National Reporting Team, state-based digital news, the ABC Fact Check Unit and improving live-linking capacity in the regions".[96] Former Managing Director Geoffrey Whitehead (1988), considered controversial and ultimately rejected by ABC staff and dismissed by Chairman David Hill, had *three* points to make about his future concerns for the ABC that remain relevant today:

1. Governments exercise a political role at the ABC.

   This is because governments "create the overall climate" (Whitehead, 1988)[97] on the ABC Board due to their role of making appointments, and that in turn the boards' appointments of

Managing Directors are tainted by this. Former Managing Director Geoffrey Whitehead said he was troubled by political appointees and questions about the role of government in the ABC (ibid.).[98] Those concerns endure.

2. The ABC staff control ABC management and this power is unaccountable.

   The role of activists within unions at the ABC was a concern for Whitehead (1988), who also questioned the representativeness of staff-elected directors when the first staff-elected member of the board, Tom Molomby, was elected by fewer than 20% of all staff eligible to vote. Referring to a *The Australian Financial Review* article in 1984 "The ABC—Who is in Charge?", he said it pointed out that editorial freedom was the choice of the ABC editor, not the ABC journalist and the article queried the ABC journalist's role when they over-ran management decisions. The article said there was a need for clarity on the line of authority.[99] Whitehead (1988) pointed out that management was accountable to the board and the board and management accountable to parliament. But staff and its unions were not accountable in either context. He recommended guidelines of various roles would mean "the whole would be more fully accountable to the people through parliament".[100]

3. The ABC deserves respect from other media and acknowledgment of its rightful place as a public broadcaster.

   The ABC is part of a wider media ecology and there needed to be respect from the commercial media for the role and responsibilities of the national broadcaster. Reciprocally, the ABC needs to revisit its privileged separateness in terms of content. In one of the rare forthright analyses of the ABC by a former managing director and its institutional role, Whitehead (1988) said there was a concern that if ratings for the ABC slipped too low then the government would reconsider its significant spending on it when so few were part of the audience. Associated with this was that governments failed to appraise themselves of the real cost of running such a large organisation. He said the ABC played a role in the "wider national interest or social role of broadcasting" (ibid.).[101]

Ultimately, Whitehead (1988) believed these recommended changes and considerations would give audiences "a clear choice from a full range of programs" (ibid.).[102]

Nick Davies (2009) said it would be easy to blame a political conspiracy on the collapse in authoritative media generally and "the overbearing power of media proprietors" (ibid.).[103] However, he said there was also something bigger at play, where the reality was that the media system was confronted with "the logic of commerce randomly overwhelming the requirements of reporting" (Loc. Cit.).[104] Given the Australian Government's major expenses are Social Security and Welfare (35%), then Health, Education and Defence, the need to fund and re-pay the future massive debts caused by the novel coronavirus economic crisis and massive government spending on welfare in support for individuals, businesses, global vaccinations and testing may see money taken from other public expenditure. The ABC was not an essential service in profile with other institutional cohorts, yet it can claim a role in being the emergency broadcaster for local communities during natural disasters as part of an arrangement with Federal, State and Territory authorities. The government's focus on essential services was described in the 2019–2020 Budget:

> Protecting the strength of our economy and setting Australia up for continued economic success is central to our plan for the welfare of every single Australian and their future. Prime Minister of Australia The Hon Scott Morrison MP[105]

The Federal Government's Budget for 2019–2020 was headlined: "Our plan for a stronger economy" with the objectives of "returning the budget to surplus, delivering more jobs providing lower taxes, and, guaranteeing essential services like Medicare, schools, hospitals and roads".[106] These priorities, however, were subjected to unparalleled upheaval and disarray with the novel COVID-19 virus pandemic in 2020–21 (and beyond) and the economic challenges it presented Australia.

Funding issues will loom large at the national broadcaster in the future with the huge diversions of money made by the Federal Government to stem the worst consequences of an economic crisis with the shutdown of Australia (and the world) to contain the novel coronavirus in 2020–21. Economic emphases at the time were small businesses and welfare recipients with mass unemployment and isolation, lockdown orders eventuating in a widespread shutdown of society and business, exempting essential services. Prime Minister Scott Morrison said the government's spend was "unprecedented".[107] The Reserve Bank of Australia Governor Philip Lowe said the novel coronavirus had become "a major economic problem, which is having deep ramifications for financial systems around the world".[108] Such was the extraordinary rapidity of the disintegration of the global financial situation; Lowe had said just over five weeks earlier (5 February) that the novel coronavirus was "a short-term economic speedbump".[109]

Looking to the future, the ABC faces the challenge of whether it will remain a comprehensive service or a complementary service, delivering content that commercial media cannot afford to supply or would not run (addressing market failure). Its charter tells it to be comprehensive but funding cuts diminish its capacity such that it now surveys a curtailed consignment. The genuine romance and fascination of being a broadcaster, showcasing creativity, excellence and honesty and communicating 'all to all' is no longer seen to be relevant in the digital age of boutique audiences, niche communication platforms and abundant commentators. Theatrics, re-tweeted grabs and mocking memes have taken the place of serious information. Platformed, networked digital media means everyone's opinion is as worthy and credible as the next. The ABC has gone from being an organisation broadcasting culture (music, literature, academic and educational talks) that was tasked with growing a national identity with a dominant Anglo, Saxon and Celtic Australia to an audience which consists of 270 ethnicities (Powell, nd) and is one of the most stable and culturally and ethnically diverse nations in the world. The ABC's success in meeting that challenge demanded that this becomes a prevailing, not incidental consideration. It still attends to its old linear broadcasting of radio and television in the hope of its retirement. But in an abundant media environment, the "old" broadcasting can play a complementary role rather than be retired as a legacy burden to be eliminated as soon as the imagined legacy audience 'dies away'.

The ABC's discovery of audiences through interaction and conversations will only become more immersive and rapid with the spread of 5G. Feedback is ubiquitous and the audiences that supply this form of feedback expect immediate responses. Instead of broadcasting from a voice to an ear, the ABC now relies on audience participation in a "karaoke-isation" of news in the belief that passing everyone the metaphorical microphone enriches news and provides even more valuable news by incorporating personal interpretations of events. The ABC has relinquished its *cultural capital*, its umpire's voice, in favour of the voices of the town hall in the belief that those voices understand the public good, the greater good better. Stories can inform public good, and certainly enrich insights, but it is mistaken if viewed as informative as a carefully curated, researched reporting—and of profound consequence to the commonwealth. The fundamental problem with taking the particular as representative of the general is that it is at odds with the theory of public broadcasting that "had an 'ideological effect'" (Stuart Hall, 1977 in S. Dawes, 2017)[110] and "served dominant class interests" (Curran, 1990 in S. Dawes, 2017). The ABC had been careful and responsible in the way it informed people; this was its strength, as was its "explicit focus on maintaining editorial standards and the curbing of corporate power" (Dawes, ibid.).

To address the future shortfalls in funding the ABC Section of the Community and Public Sector Union (2008) was critical that the ABC had "shifted towards commissioning programs that involve less research and do not require specialist program makers" (ibid.).[111] Beyond this and to ensure its future, the ABC should re-establish its value as a public service broadcasting service. It "must be clearly defined, clearly efficient, and clearly consistent in applying its principles" (Collins et al., 2001),[112] policies and Charter. ABC Management has to be demonstrably proactive on that front, not just pronounce or allude to standards but craft policy to "future proof" the organisation that will fortify its relevance to Australia. Wilson et al. (2010)[113] concluded there were three means by which the ABC could remain relevant and innovative:

> 1. Deployment of new media platforms to enhance the delivery of content to audiences: content that accords with an existing social and political remit, and especially that which fails to find a home in the market
> 2. Use of digital technologies to engage with audiences in new ways; and,
> 3. Become "engaged to facilitate cultural activity that is not directly related to its role of producing or procuring content for broadcast". (Wilson et al., ibid.)

The authors said regarding the third suggestion the ABC had been innovative but not productive. The ABC is now far more stop-start with innovation than in previous years when it backed its own hunches. Aunty is now very cautious and self-conscious. Survey details where media were defined in terms of content and platform in 2018 by the communications company Edelman found trust in the Australian media was the second lowest of 28 countries surveyed (Gordon, 2018).[114] In addition, 7/10 Australians were deterred by concerns that 'fake news' was being circulated to confuse and change public opinion. The survey found trust in "journalism"—a more specific subset of the media—had actually increased—but this was qualified as news from traditional media and online-only news media (59 from 54 the previous year). The emerging theme from the Edelman report was "The Battle for Truth" (2018; Edelman Trust Barometer, 2018).[115] The survey also showed that 50% people were disengaged with the news. A survey by the Australian National University in 2016 found record low levels of interest in the 2016 election (McAllister et al., 2016).[116] While a Roy Morgan survey in May 2018 found that the ABC was the most trusted media outlet and only "9 per cent distrust the ABC (Levine, 2018)".[117] The Media Net Trust Survey engaged with 1111 Australians. It showed that "Australians told us that their trust of the ABC is driven by its lack of bias and impartiality, quality journalism and ethics" (Levine, ibid.). And, a 2020 Reuters Institute for the Study of Journalism, Oxford University survey found that traditional news media outlets (especially the BBC) were still a prominent means of people obtaining information (Naughton, 2020).[118]

To analyse the accuracy or veracity of claims one can look to the extremes and then try to find rational arguments from common ground. Analysing the situation of the ABC is complex and understanding its role has provided several points worthy of discussion and conflict. The calls for the privatisation of the ABC have been ongoing. It has already happened by stealth, anyway. In 1988, for example, the ABC decided to contract out production of some television programs. The ABC has also since then sold its outside broadcast facilities. In 1985 when the then Treasurer, Paul Keating, was asked about privatising the ABC, he replied: "we are as protective of the ABC's public position as we are of the Commonwealth Bank" (*The Canberra Times*, 1985).[119] The Commonwealth Bank was then a fully government-owned public enterprise. Established in 1911, by 1988 Keating was favouring partial privatisation and the bank was fully privatised in stages up to 1995.

In a book sponsored by the Friends of the ABC, Frank Brennan SJ, Jesuit priest and Professor of Law at the Australian National University, argued: "I am prepared to concede that the ABC has a bias in favour of those whose views and tastes would find no expression on commercial media" (Fraser & O'Reilly, 1996),[120] and that Australians needed to also be "especially cautious when politicians chant, 'Whoever pays the piper calls the tune'" (Fraser & O'Reilly, ibid.). He also pointed out it was a capacity of the ABC to provide freedom of speech unencumbered by commercial considerations of whether the content would "sell". In the same text, former ABC investigative journalist Chris Masters (Fraser & O'Reilly, 1996) revealed: "Sometimes I feel we at the ABC are compelled towards subjects like Aboriginal affairs because we know our commercial colleagues will give them scant attention" (ibid.).[121] Senior ABC broadcaster Robin Williams (Fraser & O'Reilly, 1996) blamed the then crisis at the ABC on "the reluctance to ask for taxes to pay for public services, and a revolution in the technology of our communication" (ibid.)[122]. In a situation where the role of a broadcaster and its impact on culture is one that society is "yet to understand how that relationship works" (Williams, 1996).

The ABC's 2018 tagline "#yours" reflected the organisation's repositioning. This re-branding covered social media and the broadband world at large. When the digitally evolved organisation began as a radio broadcaster in 1932 (as a result of failure of the Federal Government to provide enough radio licences (Semmler, 1981)) its original mission was also animated by the perceived need for an unbiased source of information "improved and freed from all the evils, real or imaginary, of private enterprise" (*The Sydney Morning Herald*, 1931).[123] In the framework of Institutional Logics there has been a shift in language to personalise the ABC as an institution/object that is everybody's; it no longer distinguishes itself from private media, as it did originally. In embracing the immersive and intrusive world of the media that perpetuates itself in lives dominated by hand phones and devices, the ABC is a pronoun; its institutional language tells us it belongs to us and is connected to Australians. The following photograph puts the ABC's role into historical perspective as one that was not just connecting Australians, but building bridges with our regional, Commonwealth neighbours (Image 7.1). Australia's Colombo Plan was launched in 1951 to give economic and technological aid to Asian members of the Commonwealth. The ABC's role was to build diplomatic ties—chiefly through radio—and there were fears of the spread of Communism in the region (Oakman, 2010). The ABC supported government concerns and efforts by sponsoring radio education in Australia.

An expanding range of modes, platforms, programming, content and presenters reiterates the important role the broadcaster has occupied in sharing, educating and reflecting Australian media and culture. This is overseen by ABC policies that describe the broadcaster as an all-encompassing quintessentially Australian entity talking to *all* Australians. Its charter stipulates this embrace is demonstrated through choice of content. This role is manifested in digital format with a vast range of participatory programs on radio, television and online. Channels are now live-streamed. Immediacy is

Image 7.1 Lord Mayor of Sydney, Alderman Harry Jensen, showing artwork in his Sydney Town Hall office to VD Madgulkar (All India Radio, Poona) right, and Abu Bakar bin Ahmad (Brunei Radio), left, participants in a three months' rural broadcasting course in 1960. It was organised by the ABC under the Federal Government's Colombo Plan. Courtesy of the National Archives of Australia. Photographer, John Tanner. 1960. Series: A1501, A2456/3. Item ID: 8890053. Canberra

uppermost. In 2018, the ABC iView on-demand internet television portal carried the slogan "Never miss a moment". Even with the personalised intimacy implied by #yours, in 2019 it promoted its news and current affairs online via its meta-description on the iView URL as "Australia's Most Trusted News and Analysis" (ABC, 2020).[124] However, the then Communications Minister, Stephen Conroy, warned in 2008: "with the expected proliferation of internet-based services, traditional broadcasting may not continue to hold the same degree of influence it had in an analogue world" (Conroy, 2008).[125] And so, it has come to pass.

"Fake news" is a historically enduring American phrase popularised by former US President Donald Trump. The role of the ABC is providing a bulwark against this erosion of truth and supplying standards of objective information seems clear. The debate and focus on whether the ABC was remaining relevant to all Australians was ongoing. The organisation's then Managing Director, Michelle Guthrie in 2016, when she was a few days new to the role, told staff that:

> We must extend our reach and our relevance into areas where we are under-represented. That means more diversity in both our staff and our content. We must collaborate more, with a clear focus on serving the audience, regardless of platform or device. (Guthrie, 2016)

It is part of an ongoing discernment of relevance by public broadcasters which Miragliotta and Errington (2012) have described as "power centres in their own right" (Miragliotta & Errington, ibid.).[126] This was articulated in the 1962 UK Pilkington Report on the British broadcast policy which said in regard to the BBC it had both agency and ascendancy over content:

> The broadcaster must explore it and choose from it first. This might be called "giving a lead": but it is not the lead of the autocratic or arrogant. It is the proper exercise of responsibility by public authorities duly constituted as trustees for the public interest. (UK Government, 1962)[127]

The arrival of digital technology is now responsible for a wider menu of new information and entertainment options. But, even with this, *The Canberra Times* newspaper pointed out in an editorial about the ABC: the "broadly worded public charter is open to nit-picking by those with ideological wheelbarrows to push" (*The Age*, 2016).[128] Watson (2014) described the ABC as "an irrelevant item of mega fauna" (ibid., p. 8) faced with low audiences and concomitant accusations of irrelevance. Yet, more significantly, these concerns about relevance are being watered down with new understandings of how the ABC hybridises itself (Burns & Hawkins, 2013) to meet changing, niche markets through its activities in digital media. Freed from commercial pressures to attract advertisers and make profits, it can experiment and inhabit digital media in innovative ways.

Miragliotta and Errington (2012) argued that "classical market failure arguments that formerly sustained the sector have been substantially weakened" (Miragliotta & Errington, 2012)[129] and that public broadcasters were in fact "more nimble than their neo-liberal critics had imagined" (ibid.)[130] and that the ABC had "improved prospects for the ABC are based on both the subjective nature of market failure and the status of the ABC as a resilient political institution" (Loc. Cit.).[131] This resilience has been sustained mostly because of the *cultural capital* it had built up in the education *field*, now augmented and extended online. However, this is challenged through a lack of preparedness for what lay ahead in digitisation and competing in areas of opinion-making which have also been influencing ABC editorial content and public statements by key institutional actors. There has been a failure of some ABC senior leaders to develop policy and strategy around changing technology. iView has been financially costly (although successful with viewers) and there have been other criticisms of a lack of sharing of back-end facilities with SBS (data and operating syntax that can be shared) to save money.

The prospect of commercial sponsorship for the ABC was challenging. Molomby (1991) said such a discussion "distorts and undermines program priorities".[132] Sponsorship was fraught. He said the Public Broadcasting Service in the US was limited to being educational because sponsors could suddenly withdraw support (for a range of reasons). Molomby (1991) pointed out that the size of the likely audience was also a factor in attracting sponsors. In addition, non-sponsored programs would be pushed to the unfavourable times for broadcast. The prospect of selling the ABC was not possible because it would have to be making profits in order for it to be a viable media purchase and in the current environment all media struggle to survive. In fact, if the ABC were put out to the market it would be making a loss because it served areas of the market (regional areas, such as major Australian country towns and remote rural areas) that did not "make money" for commercial media. On the other hand, there is always a market for loss-making activities where business sees an opportunity for plundering the worthwhile parts of a business and merging them with their existing activities.

In 1985 the British Government set up a committee to find out the best ways of funding the BBC (the Peacock Committee[133]). In 1986, the Report of the Committee on Financing the BBC rejected the idea of funding the BBC with advertising and advised that the licence fee arrangement should remain. Secretary of State for the Home Department Douglas Hurd said:

> The committee argues that, since spectrum is still scarce, and there is as yet no way in which the consumer can pay direct for the programme of his choice, the introduction of advertising would reduce the effective range of choice open to viewers and listeners. (Peacock Committee, in D. Hurd, 1986)[134]

However, the "committee recommends that the BBC should have the option to privatise Radios 1 and 2 and local radio in whole or in part and that the IBA regulation of radio should be replaced by a looser regime".[135] It also left the option open for subscription to the BBC as a revenue raiser. The BBC is funded mostly by a licence fee of GBP154.50 (AUD302) a year paid by every television-owning household in the UK. The penalty for not paying can range from a fine to a prison sentence. Prime Minister Boris Johnson has said his government was considering decriminalising the failure to pay fees but without providing any other funding options for the BBC.[136] The argument is that there were so many digital alternatives, charging fees for using television sets is outdated. Molomby (1991) remarked that when the ABC travelled overseas for meetings "the committee made the observation, in every country we encountered expressions of amazement—even from NBC and ABC in the United States—that the British should be thinking of changing their system, which is almost universally admired".

In preparation for this future financial loss, the BBC announced it was cutting 450 jobs from its News division and staff would be following a "story-led" model, assigned to stories rather than programs.[137] The ABC has 1/8 funding of the BBC while serving as much as 1/3 the population of the UK.[138] John Reith, General Manager/Managing Director of the British Broadcasting Company from 1922 to 1927, later the first Director-General of the BBC, empowered the organisation with three precepts: the BBC was to "inform, educate and entertain". The ABC was modelled on this aspiration of public broadcasting. In fact, so lofty were these objectives that they were enshrined in stone in the hallway of what is known as BBC Headquarters, Broadcasting House, London, in a Latin inscription:

> DEO OMNIPOTENTI—Templum hoc artivm et mvsarvm anno domini MCMXXXI rectore Johanni Reith Primi Dedicant Gvbernatores precantes

vt messem bonam bona proferat sementis vt immvnda omnia et inimica paci expellantvr vt qvaecvnqve pvlchra svnt et sincera qvaecvnqve bonae famae ad haec avrem inclinans popvlvs virtvtis at sapientiae semitam insistat.

ALMIGHTY GOD—This Temple of the Arts and Muses is dedicated by the first Governors in the year 1931, John Reith being Director-General. It is their prayer that good seed sown may bring forth a good harvest, that all things hostile to peace or purity may be banished from this house, and that the people, inclining their ear to whatsoever things are beautiful and honest and of good report, may tread the path of wisdom and uprightness.

The statue over the front entrance is of Prospero and Ariel (from Shakespeare's *The Tempest*). Ariel represents the free spirit of the air—broadcasting. Inside there is another statue "The Sower", a metaphorical representation of the role of broadcasting, where seeds will fall (hopefully) on fertile ground. These lofty ambitions and precepts helped form the ABC. The Canadian Broadcasting Corporation has parted company with the public funding or licence model. Established in 1936, it was allowed to accept paid advertising on national radio (Radio 2) in 2013 for four minutes per hour. A statement by CBC radio management said: "The revenue from advertising has allowed us to avoid more significant cuts to programming and the services we offer" (Weisblott, 2013).[139] In addition, the music FM stations would also be seeking sponsorship. Radio 1 was to remain free of advertising.

The ABC has set a standard for educating Australians by providing access to information and arts by acting as a gatekeeper and educator of what constitutes Australianness and, as a corollary, what constitutes the Australian élite where "certain conditions of existence are designated" (Bourdieu, 1984)[140] and re-enacted. Manifestations of this occur in such contemporary examples as programs on ABC Radio National that encouraged talkback on a radio network aiming to "contribute to the development of an enlightened society" (Whitehead, 1988).[141] Allied with this was the ABC's role, as set up by the government, to be a source of public good in providing public interest news and information. The final report in 2019 by the Australian Competition and Consumer Commission: "Digital Platforms Inquiry" said it was necessary "that stable and adequate funding be provided to the ABC and SBS" (Australian Competition and Consumer Commission, 2019).[142] The ACCC report also noted that the slide in local and regional reporting by media outlets was a result of the impact of the decline in classified advertising in newspapers "and the shift in display advertising to digital platforms" (ibid.).[143]

7.4 What Else Ails Aunty?: An Uncommonly Precarious World

We are now living in an age of precarity habituated by "the precariat" (Standing, 2011).[144] The neologism precariat was first described by Guy Standing (2011) merging precarious with proletariat and describing a new class of people precariously employed and underpaid which had serious implications for their economic and mental wellbeing. He described it as a "dangerous class" (Standing, 2018)[145] because of their loss of identity, eroded rights and general decline in social democracy (Standing, ibid.). Standing (2011) described precariousness as the absence of a "secure identity or sense of development achieved through work and lifestyle" (ibid.).[146] It was a phenomenon identified by the French philosopher Henri Lefebvre as 'ambiguity' (Lefebvre, 1991)[147] leading to social instability and uncertainty. Standing (2018) also said there was an auxiliary loss of the commons—which are land or resources that the community owns:

> In the neoliberal era, the commons—natural, social, civil, cultural, and intellectual—have been plundered via enclosure, commodification, privatization, and colonization. This rent-seeking is an injustice and should be reversed. (Standing, ibid.)

The ABC—as a publicly owned asset—forms part of this commons, but has been pushed to straddle the divide between public and private and market and state-owned by commercialising operations, with the continued threat of privatisation, licence fees or subscription fees. It is precarious. In Australia, the commons cover a gamut from the air we breathe—to the ABC. This is another reason why Aunty does not belong in the commercial *field* without appropriate policy, safeguards and vigilance.

Since moving to the commercial *field*, the ABC has treated its *cultural capital* as an inexhaustible resource. But like other assets mistaken as inexhaustible, such as the natural environment, this is not the case. The ABC has been a custodian of a commonwealth and asset of the Commonwealth of Australia and like all benefits and privileges should be passed on in the same, if not better condition, for the next generation.[148] This book has argued that the ABC's precarity became inevitable in the push to be a competitive digital media player. It is abandoning its commoners—it has actually left the commons and stands vulnerable and unprotected.[149]

As a consequence of this, workers (in the case of this analysis, ABC staff subjected to casualised, temporary and short-term contract work, as discussed in Chap. 3, and ongoing budgetary cuts/restraints) become submissive (ibid.)[150] yet also reactive and fearful; they know the rules of the game and play the game accordingly or get sidelined. Precarity invades the overall job market in Australia where a Parliamentary Library Report said 25% (Gilfillan, 2018)[151] were casually employed while the Australian Council of Trade Unions (ACTU) said it was closer to half of workers engaged in "non-standard forms of employment" (AAP Fact Check, 2018).[152] The level of casualisation is challenged by the Business Council of Australia which said that "the level of casualisation hasn't changed for about 20 years" (ibid.).[153] Casualised work often causes variability in wage payments—this can be due to unpredictable hours of work, loss of entitlements and inaccuracies in paying people—what is referred to colloquially as 'wage theft'. In 2019, it was revealed that the ABC was found to have underpaid 2500 of its casual workers amounting to AUD22.9 million and further the Community and Public Sector Union (CPSU) said "the ABC was aware that casual staff were being underpaid but ignored formal complaints from staff and their unions" (ACTU, 2019).[154] The ABC is often accused of being able to evade the normal rules of economics by operating independently of the profit motive (News Corporation commentators have made this accusation many times). Yet, Aunty is subjected to the torment of her own precarity, such as "paying the piper", and like all prudent Aunties, operating within her budget (whatever the triennial budget looks like at the time) and, in the instance of underpayment, having to hunt about for spare money owed to staff.

At a societal level, non-profit organisations have a positive role, including the ABC, and the acknowledgement of the precarity of groups or individuals in society can "contribute to pluralism by creating centers of influence outside the state and provide vehicles through which disenfranchised groups may organize" (DiMaggio & Anheier, 1990).[155] The ABC then becomes an aggregator of the disenfranchised and a harbour for those who perceive an injustice. Yet this focus on growing a social media presence contributes to the precarity of Aunty's voice because it locates its sympathies with specially identified groups who are seen as society's victims. She is accused of drifting from 'all to all' to 'all for some'. Precarity also refers to the way social media is used (Heidkamp & Kergel, 2017)[156] and the instability it then imparts to people's sense of identity, isolation, anxiety and psychological insecurity about the world that seems beyond hope—or at least beyond the capacity of people to control because of their existential fears harvested from social media and the manifestly gloomy predictions that infiltrate media platforms.

7.5 Looking After Aunty's Future

The 1981 so-called Dix Report—completed by the Committee of Review of the Australian Broadcasting Commission (1981) and chaired by Alex Dix—has been often cited to this author in the course of interviewing and researching for this book as being significantly damaging to the ABC. It was of especial concern to former ABC staff members. It was controversial. One aspect of the report was that the ABC should **not** be looking to serve niche markets, rather it should serve the entire population. Acting against this, there was now talk among politicians that the ABC should be looking to serve only the unprofitable "failed" markets. Ironically, the ABC would appear to be talking itself into that new way of thinking merely through chasing audiences under the marketing umbrella concept #yours and "boutiqueing" its content, rather than looking to an entire Australian nation, as it once did. The advice of the Dix Report (Committee of Review of the Australian Broadcasting Commission, 1981) was for the ABC to rationalise, re-organise and change its structural (resource) arrangements. Over time, these had happened in fits and starts. The Dix Report (Ibid.) also made recommendations on ABC board structure with: "members to represent broadcasting/communications, cultural, technical, financial, managerial or other interests and expertise appropriate to the oversight of a major public broadcasting organisation" (Ibid.). A more recent text that called for the ABC to be privatised (Berg & Davidson, 2018)[157] pointed out that any government changes had to be demonstrably preferable to the status quo. Given that the ABC had abandoned its exclusive the élite *field* in which it was once the star player and now jostled for attention with commercial and any other online entities without safeguards on its reputation, it now faced the difficult task of regaining its former status, but amongst a galaxy of "stars".

In 1979 the literature warned that the ABC had been weakened (Harding, 1979)[158] because commercial media organisations had been allowed to become too strong. In addition, there were calls for vigorous and committed ethnic broadcasting (Harding, ibid.).[159] The ABC then was described as having a "phoney independence" (Loc. Cit.) because of its dependence on Federal Governments. In May 2018, ABC finance executive Louise Higgins told a Senate Estimates Committee hearing that the ABC faced two main challenges:

> First, like our commercial peers here and abroad, the ABC faces production costs that are escalating faster than inflation, driven by the giant content budgets of Facebook, Apple, Amazon, Netflix and Google. Second, we must maintain traditional broadcast services for our large and loyal audiences, at the same time as modernising our technology platforms so that digital audiences can access ABC content wherever, however and whenever they want it. (Meade, 2018)[160]

In 1932, Sir Noman Angell, English Nobel Peace Prize winner and British Labour Party Member of Parliament, said:

> The responsible authority of the BBC was placed in something of the position of a judge. Not "what'll sell the paper" but "what ought the public to know in order to be in a position to judge both sides" and form sound judgments in moral, literary, social and political questions, became, in theory at least, the standard. Let us hope that that standard has not been abandoned. (Angell, 1933)[161]

That situation for the BBC then is as applicable to the ABC now. Aunty needs to 'resume her knitting'. Aunty needs to reclaim the status of her élite media *field* because abandoning the *field* has not been to her advantage. Her voice is now strangled in the fierce competition of commercial media. Former Managing Director Mark Scott (2014) confirmed this shift in the ABC's *field* that critics of the ABC, positioned in the commercial *field*, were unhappy "because of the commercial impact they feel the ABC has on their own operation" (Scott, 2014).[162] This has been so. News Corporation complaints about the ABC often centre on the fact that it gets special treatment as a publicly funded operation. Yet, the Australian Competition and Consumer Commission (2019) said in a report that Federal Government policy to fund the ABC (and SBS) was aimed at meeting the "potential under-provision of public interest journalism" (ACCC, 2019).[163]

In addition, Managing Director Michelle Guthrie (quoted in A. Meade & C. Wahlquist, 2018) said there were concerns that the ABC was being pushed into a corner to be "the market failure organisation it was never intended to be" (Meade & Wahlquist, ibid.).[164] Market failure is where commercial media is unable to supply or service segments of the market because they were not profitable.

Guthrie's comment was prompted by an opinion article by the President of NSW Young Liberals, Harry Stutchbury (2018)[165], in *The Sydney Morning Herald* the previous day calling for the ABC to be privatised. The article suggested the ABC should have a reduced budget as its funding would be better spent on meeting the "market failure" of the Australian media that has occurred in "remote parts of rural Australia": "a publicly funded national broadcaster crowds out its private competitors and is an indulgence we can no longer afford" (Stutchbury, ibid.).

In his maiden speech to parliament in 2015, Senator James McGrath said that the ABC should be privatised and replaced with a "rural and regional broadcasting corporation". He added: "I want to support the ABC. I like the ABC, yet while it continues to represent only inner-city leftist views, and funded by our taxes, it is in danger of losing its social licence to operate" (Knott, 2015).[166] Irrespective of these political positions, the ABC is strangling itself and de-legitimising itself with the strident voices and opinions that are now encouraged to dominate its content and platforms.

In 1981, former deputy General Manager of the ABC Clement Semmler said:

> Trivialisation, indeed, is the pitfall which down the years so often besets ABC public affairs programmes. It is one of the dangers inherent in the system of competition with commercial stations for ratings. Too often the discussion of current, social and economic issues, which constitute the stuff of politics, comes to be treated as an inferior form of entertainment which has to be tarted up to arouse a jaded or apathetic audience. It is indeed a variation of Gresham's Law: the good currency of the thought-provoking treatment of public issues is driven out of circulation by the bad currency of the easily-accepted popular stereotype of the trivialisation of such issues. (Semmler, 1981)[167]

He quoted British Labor politician Richard Crossman that this media tendency to trivialise matters needed to be balanced by:

> Treatment in depth sufficiently strong and persuasive to revive the faith and improve the understanding of that minority of activists, participators and

opinion-formers upon whose quality the vitality of any democracy depends. (Semmler, ibid.)[168]

Semmler (1981) said the ABC needed a more clearly stated policy on programs (Loc. Cit.)[169] "disciplinary control"[170] and "tighter control"[171] with "vested interests and rivalries"[172] between the then separate divisions of News and Current Affairs (now one division). He said that the ABC should not be setting up politicians as "criminals or liars", with a "snippety treatment of them that personalises politics" with a tendency for the "sensational rather than the thoughtful treatment of political and social issues" in a belief there was a need for "jolting the viewer or listener" (Semmler, ibid.).[173] He said "the best way to finance a public broadcaster system was by a licence fee".[174] In the same decade, former ABC Chairman Ken Myer also suggested something similar as he resigned in 1986 criticising the former Labor Prime Minister Bob Hawke that his government's funding by annual appropriation "was strangling the ABC" (Inglis, 2006)[175] and it should either be funded by licence fees or sold off.

Since 1932, Aunty has knitted the fabric of Australian society with deftness, skill and originality because of her focus on making her contribution to political, cultural, democratic and economic life. She made Australia worldly with her patterns of music and challenging, enriching, provocative words and images. She wove the colours of Australia's nationhood and asserted everyone's right to belong. It is time for her to reclaim her *field*. Her voice was accorded and committed to her in 1932, it is hers. #yours is a diverting social media activity for the ABC, but every single person has a story to tell that summarises the national struggle and social media already provides vast facility for that with Facebook. These tribes can be aggregated and located within the abundant special cause 'community-fields' created by the major internet organisations that invite and encourage their self-referencing. Social media is a powerful tool for media and society, but it is not the engine room and it is to the media's detriment—and the greater good's loss—to gauge their corralled comments as public opinion. It can also be safely assumed that among those 25 million Australians—there will be much concordance yet it seems identifying division, hatred and strident voices is easier and more marketable. Finding common ground to strengthen reports by giving individual stories context and national relevance is by far the greater challenge. Curating the voices of Australians takes an expert voice and it was what Aunty once did best. She owned the élite *field* that she was privileged to occupy.

The end of the age of media scarcity has not brought the richness promised, rather it has seen major internet companies become so enlarged and glutted by the free content they have harvested from professional news media outlets, they have aggrandised on the hard work of professionals. Those people have now lost their jobs—the threatened closure of Australian Associated Press in 2020 being an alarming example of this. The Federal Government signalled in 2020 that it would legislate to make these reapers pay. The border reivers[176] of the Scottish Highlands are back, this time on digital terrain. Linked with this, social media has brought about the demise of the media professional. Aunty has upgraded to digital technology but collapsed her information model into that easy, cheap content. The consequences of that choice were not thought through and it has eroded a credible, resourced news and information service. Now, however, unlike in the 1920s when the Australian Broadcasting Company accepted restricted advertising and announced its inclusion in its content quite clearly with "our advertising session is about to commence" and closed after five minutes with "that is the end of our advertising session" (Walker, 1973),[177] Aunty has merged herself with commercial social media and all other media proprietors. When audiences are monetised, it is hard to know where the advertising begins and ends because it attaches cookies and traces people, as marketable items, on the internet. Aunty is now part of the complicated commercial *field*. While the ABC does not publish paid advertising, there have been many other means for her to embrace commercialism, even adding to the profit-making vibrancy on a privatised social media is one example.

As an adjunct to this shift, the separate role for a national broadcaster in Australia in such a media environment, which is opinion rich but quality and fact challenged, has never been more important. In a liberal democracy a public service media organisation is needed to provide quality, objectivity, 'public interest' issues and perspective. This balances the strident voices of social media that provoke knee-jerk government policy or staffing reactions which may not necessarily benefit the Commonwealth of Australia, but rather serve to keep one group happy, maybe, for a short while. The ABC needs to counter the divisive misinformation of social media and anti-democratic views trying to stifle civil discussion being churned out of bot factories, bot farms, click farms and troll farms. These have the specific intent of destabilising democratic governments, distorting public debate and significantly abusing Australian's right to know. It is deliberate and dangerous misinformation fed into the public sphere which is eroding confidence in Australia's democratic institutions and public service institutions. The national security implications of this is a very lightly understood issue by the media in its bolt to embrace social media and chase opinions, 'likes' and organisational/career status. Aunty's authentic, older, public service voice needs to regain its confidence and reclaim its former élite privileged *field* voice to be heard distinctively above the rabble-raising, trolling and fake social media accounts that serve to divide Australians and stir up hatred.

The ABC also needs institutional leaders who will address the means of putting a value on Aunty's own, unique authority. The public investment in the ABC has been a long-term one, and Australians have paid well and paid willingly. This needs acknowledgement by governments and the ABC with committed policy and funding to bolster the liberal democracy. These are demanding and testing times for Aunty and her precious voice where:

> Incompetence and aimlessness, corruption and disloyalty, panic and ultimate disaster, must come to any people which is denied an assured access to the facts. No one can manage to live on pap. Neither can a people. (Lippman, in E. Diamond, 1975)[178]

Democracy is not built only on assent; it is not just turning up at a polling booth to cast a compulsory vote. It is not passive. It has to be grounded in knowledge, debate and an active, enlivened vision for the best interests of society and the nation. The ABC is the best placed institution in Australia to reclaim its invisible, yet invaluable, asset and support and supply that imperative and urgent need. This book has sought to describe and defend the oldest and only fully publicly funded broadcaster in Australia where there have been lapses identified in governments, institutional leaders, staff, strategies, policies and mindsets. The book has outlined the powerful impact of staff culture on the organisation which has confounded, frustrated and constrained management. Leaders have had to find ways to mollify staff who believe they know better. This book has outlined how the definition of public service and service for the greater good has been forgotten such that staff are failing to recognise fellow public servants elsewhere and their mutually shared neutral role in a crisis and in a constitutional democracy.

This book has also given examples of how in taking the important shift to digitisation, the ABC has forgotten to cherish and safeguard its *cultural capital* and plan institutional policies carefully for a transition to new formats. It has been driven by a discerned need to 'go find' audiences rather than support existing audiences. It has mistakenly seen it as an or/other situation. These policies and revisions would have been unique in the Australian media but would have set the organisation on a firmer footing in digital media. It has had *cultural capital* which no amount of media wealth could buy. Instead, it has prioritised the shift from its *field* without a valuation of its assets, and re-investing them, to its detriment. Convergence has offered exciting opportunities for the ABC, and social media offers more opportunities for promotion and corralling interest and stories. Yet, the old media—and the practices of the old media—are still a significant contributor to information consumption and "plays a vital role in modern journalism" (Grinberg, 2018).[179] This book has described how governments have failed to give effective feedback on the ABC's digital transitions, leaving the institution muddling around in its undefined independence—except when accusations of bias are raised. This has added to institutional fear in the ABC, or at least an erosion of confidence. Governments, of both political parties, have also pushed the ABC closer towards a market approach, then largely left it to fend for itself in the commercial digital *field*.

7.6 Conclusion

> I believe it is possible to enter into the singularity of object without renouncing the ambition of drawing out universal propositions. (Pierre Bourdieu, 1979)[180]

This book sought to "enter into the singularity" (Bourdieu, ibid.) of the ABC by addressing two gaps in the academic literature. The first, Cunningham (2013) identified, was that the majority of literature on the ABC had provided commentary or looked at its history to defend or attack it and, instead of this, he asserted that an analysis interrogating the ABC's "innovation track record" may provide a more detailed understanding of the ABC (Cunningham, 2013).[181] The second gap in the literature that this book sought to attend was an identified absence of research focused on practices in and around media (Couldry, 2004),[182] especially that of the field of Institutional Logics. Therefore, it is intended that this book will contribute to the body of work analysing Institutional Logics in symphony orchestras (Glynn, 2000; Glynn & Lounsbury, 2005),[183] book publishers (Thornton & Ocasio, 1999; Thornton, 2001, 2002) and banking

(Marquis & Lounsbury, 2007). It is the objective of this book to contribute to the discussion about the future directions of Australia's only fully publicly funded broadcaster.

In undertaking this research, three central assumptions were made: first, that the ABC has been a central force for good in discourses on Australia's nationhood and identity and a strut of the civil democracy; second, that organisational changes, or mindsets, in preparation for and during digitisation have not stood the ABC in good stead; and third, that as a reasonable sequitur the perilous times of the ABC can also be attributed to failure to plan and understand the critical need to preserve its cultural and national status in transitioning to public service media. The purpose of this book was to test the claim that when the ABC controlled its own élite *field* of media it was more effective in holding power to account because it had legitimate power and authority through its cultural capital. It occupied its own privileged *field*.

This book has merged two methodologies in order to provide a framework of analysis of the ABC. It has used aspects of Bourdieu's *field*, *habitus*, *cultural capital* theories and merges them with Institutional Logics theory (Friedland & Alford, 1991 in W.W. Powell & P.J. DiMaggio, 1991; Thornton et al., 2012). Through this theoretical framework, this book has argued that the key informal social and professional networks assembled by the ABC in 1932 were a significant group of actors who worked hard and built associations through their élite cultural privilege to enrich Aunty, enrich the intonation and articulation in her voice and complement commercial media; these actors then built the organisation's Institutional Logics chiefly through social connections, music, orchestras and bands as embodiments of *social capital* and *cultural capital;* yet that institutional entity is now threatened with a headlong clash with Media Logics[184]—the theory that the media has inherent rules of the game describing how content is made, consumed and iterated—and this was because of the destructive tension between the ABC's digital activities in the emergent commercial *field*.

The organisation's shift in *field* from its own, élite cultural *field* to the contested, commercial, digitised *field* of news, opinion, commentating, experts and strident voices, occurred in the belief that the ABC could live off its reputation built on what Bourdieu (1984) described as bourgeois power systems.[185] Yet a new-found, aberrant belief manifesting that bourgeois power systems are toxic and unwanted has damaged the ABC brand—because it was also an élite, privileged organisation—and valued as such because it was Australia's most respected and loved broadcaster. It was precisely because it *was* élite and privileged that it became valued. This ideological shift has confused Aunty no end, what is she to think? The central problem that was investigated in this book was how the ABC originated and created its *cultural capital* in "old" traditional analogue media and whether it has transitioned with its *cultural capital* intact to "new" digital media. Ultimately, this research has found Aunty's unique voice, Australia's unique voice, is being strangled because of an infiltration of opinion and a perceived lack of attendance in its policy to the needs of all Australians. Its declining interest as an educator of Australians was also debilitating, but this must be seen in tandem with funding and staff cuts since the 1970s by both political parties which have reduced the organisation's capacity, eloquence and robustness.

This book has observed the ABC through a lens on select aspects of leadership, actors and policies using Institutional Logics. It examined management and leadership practices and symbols through language (Thornton et al., 2012)[186] and Bourdieu's *field* theory. Ultimately, it sought to analyse how institutional actors have addressed cultural challenges through management of staff and staff culture. It found that an embedded staff culture has made change difficult. It has also found that savage staff cuts have eroded confidence in remaining staff and the concomitant devaluation of a legacy institution in that process unsettled staff into being defensive, siloed and unsupportive of each other. It became difficult to plan when funding was so changeable. This book analysed how language used by key actors has shaped perceptions and legitimated practices in the ABC to promote particular discourses about and within the organisation. The language of denial and siege has infiltrated management levels stifling self-reflection and affective rebuttal. Management either rejects any criticism or ignores it; instead, giving staff undeclared authority to speak on behalf of the ABC, and projecting any organisational problems towards the accusers (including, but not limited to, Federal Government(s), Rupert Murdoch, "the right wing", conservatives and an unspecified, existential group of naysayers).

This book has argued that the ABC's survival had been supported by paying close attention to its charter and developing policies that underpinned its institutional *habitus* and its future will depend upon being able to address criticism more fluently, nimbly and ably and also to push-back against criticism. If ever there was a time to be the victim, this is not Aunty's time and victimhood is unbecoming. On the other hand, this research has found the public service media outfit fails to acknowledge or demonstrate understanding of the ramifications of operating in a commercial digital *field*, where the play can get even nastier and rules get ignored. That the ABC perceives attacks coming personally from media owned by Rupert Murdoch should not be a surprise now that they are all chasing the same audiences in the same *field*. The ABC might actually might prepare itself for these attacks becoming more frequent and stronger. Funding into the future will continue to create apprehensions, with political threats of privatisation looming on the margins. This book speaks to how the ABC's legitimate power can be reclaimed and must be reclaimed. Digital changes have brought opportunities but had also caused some loss of public goodwill and decline in its credibility.

This book has provided a different academic perspective on how the ABC has functioned as a uniquely Australian 100% taxpayer-funded public service media enterprise, in a media ecology of innovation and commercialisation, the impact of digitisation and the interface with social media on the organisation. It has questioned the validity of the ABC's marketing claim to be "yours" and "ours", because such logics would generally be beyond the purview of an institution that was tasked with being 'all to all'. The ABC had already made an extraordinary and responsible contribution to Australian life in undertaking to be "everyone's", such that a devoted kinship was developed—the ABC became Australia's "Aunty". The ABC contends with arguments about perceived biases, about offering free, yet publicly made news in a commercial *field* where content costs. It chases splintering audiences, finding that divisive opinions now form part of the institution's fragmented content requirements. Ultimately, it also faces the challenge of all public broadcasters as to whether their time has expired since meeting and fulfilling the needs of the early twentieth century. This book has aimed to shed light on how the ABC has managed its transition from being a unique public service broadcaster (PSB) to a public service media (PSM) outlet and found that its *cultural capital* had been sacrificed in the rush to be popular and 'liked' in digital media. The ABC guided by the agency of its management has to expend time and institutional thought to re-build her *cultural capital.* Governments need to support these efforts.

This book sought to reposition understandings of political influences on the ABC, not necessarily through partisanship and blow-by-blow encounters and personalised stories and observations, but rather in considering issues that impinge upon the capacity of the ABC in digital times.

These case studies have revealed that ideologies, not necessarily political views, have influenced content. This book, therefore, argues for a more empowered, nuanced, proactive role and mindset for the ABC to rise to the needs of a media field where there are serious voids in neutrality and fact. As a consequence, this book has argued that the ABC has not only shifted its *field* but also abandoned its *cultural capital* through the infiltration of opinion in lieu of fact and point-of-view content sharing. While the ABC Charter and The ABC Act overlay the expectations on the content-maker reflexively to normalise ABC *habitus*, these roles are also under re-definition, and this can be an opportunity for the ABC in a digitally disorienting *field* in reclaiming its *habitus*/"this is what *we* do" (and do well); it can re-define "public".

The ABC has failed to plan and value its heritage and institutional memory pressured through technological haste to digitise and funding cuts. There have been lapses in management, policy gaps and the outstanding need to create a vigorous, vital presence in the digital space. Management and staff brook no criticisms and label them as efforts to destroy the ABC, yet criticise of the activities of commercial media go almost unremarked. In the rush to digitise, governments, the ABC Board and ABC management all failed to plan. They forgot to assess what was being jettisoned, apply closer discernment to what needed to be preserved and maintained, and identify strategies for change that would preserve its élite status in this gigantic drift and shift.

This book used a socio-constructivist approach to examine how the precipitous shift/drift in *field* and content has had unplanned, dire consequences. Management needed to apply marketing analytics to re-assess its product differentiation for its new *field*. It also needed to analyse carefully the integration of crowd-sourced content, although temptingly cheap, and its impact on the perceptions of the public broadcaster that confuse a public which is neither online all the time nor interacting at all times, nor finds slanging matches or personalised abuse especially enlightening. Aunty's wedded and welded audiences are there, but not there, and that new fickleness has caused some grief and private soul-searching for Aunty. This book examined the new model of the ABC in that transition that has strangled Aunty's voice, with staff expressing opinions online and being publicly supported, or put at arm's length by management where there has been a overall lack of consistency and mismatch between policy and practice. Policy raises expectations yet its execution is laissez faire, free-form or not evident.

This work is an effort to bring clarity to controversy and support for the ABC in describing the sort of media world to which it may continue to contribute. There is no single trope or potted explanation of the ABC because there has been a confluence of forces exerted on the institution over time and it is only through revived robustness of the corporation and the legacy affection of Australians that it survives. This book seeks a revised understanding of the impact and meaning of 'privilege' and how its activation among key ABC élite actors has shaped, educated and inspired Australians for decades through the national broadcaster. The national broadcaster brought Australians together at critical moments in its history; it provided comfort in its authority and exactitude. This book has conducted a prosopographical analysis of select actors among the Australian élite and how their contribution has developed a powerful status for the ABC. This book promotes the position of esteemed scholar Paddy Scannell (1989)[187] that public broadcasting is, and can continue to be, a "public good and social right" (Ibid.). It is the intention of this book to contribute to that discussion about Australia's only fully publicly funded broadcaster in its role as a public servant, providing service to the Commonwealth of Australia, how that future may be adapted in a perilous ecology of high-pressure, profit-driven media and online chaos and how she may retain and reclaim with pride her unique, measured, innovative voice.

The ABC now sees itself in a battle against the forces of destruction, but that approach has not served the ABC well and has created a counter-productive and defensive approach to criticism, where counter-criticism, or push-back with a quality product resplendent with *cultural capital*, could have been a more fitting riposte. However, it is also conflicted with commercial outfits because it has had to abandon its once somewhat aloof, sniffy attitude to other media towards acceptance, collaboration and worse—equality. Sharing around the *cultural capital* in the commercial marketplace has been beneficial for the recipients that have worked with the ABC—but may only result in much benefit for Aunty. The ABC's success and embeddedness in Australian national life can be credited entirely to its control of its own élite, privileged *field* in which it accumulated invaluable Bourdieusian *cultural capital*. It is this that endeared it to Australian national life; all Australians were included because it was good for us, Aunty said so, and because she had educated us in Australianness, we believed her.

The ABC has interviewed the powerful and powerless and allowed the public to decide. She has presented to us moments of great national significance with candour and inclusiveness. That sensitised public has not gone away in the mish-mash of tameless online audiences and their attendant chaos. The ABC's role has been of significant and lasting national consequence. It has only ever been relativised with commercial media, not dependent on it and certainly should never be engaged in armed skirmishes contesting a *field* where even the respected commercial outfits monetise their audiences to survive. In these pushy, intrusive, competitive digital times brimming with wants, there is even greater need for a viable, vocal—and yes, a virile and muscular Aunty, once sovereign queen and matriarch of her institutional *field*.

Notes

1. Ibid., p. 608.
2. Wilson, C. K., Hutchinson, J., & Shea, P. (2010). Public service broadcasting, creative industries, and innovation infrastructure: The case of ABC's pool. *Australian Journal of Communication*. 37:3. pp. 15–32. Retrieved from: https://primoa.library.unsw.edu.au/permalink/f/11jha62/TN_informit_apaft201102742.
3. Murdock, G. (2004). Building the Digital Commons: Public Broadcasting in the Age of the Internet. University of Montreal. The 2004 Spry Memorial Lecture. November 2004. Vancouver. Retrieved from: https://www.researchgate.net/publication/254750526_BUILDING_THE_DIGITAL_COMMONS_PUBLIC_BROADCASTING_IN_THE_AGE_OF_THE_INTERNET, p. 18.
4. *ABC Annual Report* 1939–1940. p. 11.
5. Cockburn, G. (2020). Keating hails one of the greats. *The Australian*. NCA Newswire. 8 December 2020. p. 2.
6. Hooks, B. (1995). Johns knows his ABC. *The Canberra Times*. 11 September 1995. p. 29. Retrieved from: https://trove.nla.gov.au/newspaper/article/127280233?searchTerm=ABC%20staff%20culture&searchLimits=.
7. Lewis, S. (2009). Rudd vows bipartisan ABC board. 17 March 2009. *News.com.au*. Retrieved from https://www.news.com.au/national/rudd-vows-bipartisan-abc-board/news-story/ceac18bd56ef5ff51aed0b9b58140d1b?sv=8d7361759668930309443ad4dee66a24.
8. Knott, M. & Hunter, F. (2014). Partisan appointments to ABC, SBS selection panel crushed Rudd's dream. *The Sydney Morning Herald*. 4 July 2014. Retrieved from: https://www.smh.com.au/politics/federal/partisan-appointments-to-abc-sbs-selection-panel-crushes-rudds-dream-20140704-zsvkz.html.

9. *Australian Broadcasting Corporation*. (2011). Editorial Policies. Retrieved from http://about.abc.net.au/wp-content/uploads/2012/06/EditorialPOL2011.pdf.
10. Sehl, A., Cornia, A., Graves, L., & Nielsen, R. K. (2019). Newsroom Integration as an Organizational Challenge. *Journalism Studies*. 20:9. pp. 1238–1259. Retrieved from: https://doi.org/10.1080/1461670X.2018.1507684.
11. Meade, A. (2018). 'It was magic': Kerry O'Brien on ABC bosses, battles and why it's no bed of lefties. *The Guardian*. P&I Guest Writers. 13 November 2018. Retrieved from: https://johnmenadue.com/amanda-meade-it-was-magic-kerry-obrien-on-abc-bosses-battles-and-why-its-no-bed-of-lefties-the-guardian/.
12. Australian Government. (1996). COMMONWEALTH COMPETITIVE NEUTRALITY POLICY STATEMENT. June 1996. Retrieved from: https://www.pc.gov.au/about/core-functions/competitive-neutrality/commonwealth-competitive-neutrality-policy-statement-1996.pdf.
13. Australian Government. (2018). Inquiry into the Competitive Neutrality of the National Broadcasters—report by the Expert Panel. 12 December 2018. Retrieved from: https://www.communications.gov.au/documents/inquiry-competitive-neutrality-national-broadcasters-report-expert-panel.
14. SBS News. (2019). Public servants must be accountable to the 'quiet Australians': PM. SBS News. 19 August 2019. Retrieved from: https://www.sbs.com.au/news/public-servants-must-be-accountable-to-the-quiet-australians-pm.
15. UNESCO. (2012). Public Service Broadcasting. 15 February 2012. Retrieved from: http://www.unesco.org/new/en/communication-and-information/media-development/public-service-broadcasting/.
16. Murdock, G. (2004). Building the Digital Commons: Public Broadcasting in the Age of the Internet. University of Montreal. *The 2004 Spry Memorial Lecture*. November 2004. Vancouver. Retrieved from: https://www.researchgate.net/publication/254750526_BUILDING_THE_DIGITAL_COMMONS_PUBLIC_BROADCASTING_IN_THE_AGE_OF_THE_INTERNET. p. 18.
17. Op. Cit.
18. Blain, E. (1977). *Life with Aunty. 40 Years with the ABC*. Methuen Australia. p. 162, Inglis, K. (1983). *This is the ABC. The Australian Broadcasting Commission. 1932–1983.* Melbourne University Press. Melbourne. p. 389.
19. Tracey, M. (1998). *The Decline and Fall of Public Broadcasting*. Oxford University Press. Oxford. p. 266.

20. Although it was reported to experience a jump to a record high in ratings at the start of the novel coronavirus pandemic in March 2020 by Mumbrella (Burrowes, T. 2020). News bulletins top week's ratings while ABC News channel attracts record audience share. *Mumbrella*. 29 March 2020. Retrieved from: https://mumbrella.com.au/news-bulletins-top-weeks-ratings-while-abc-news-channel-attracts-record-audience-share-622928.
21. Mason, M., & Roddan, M. (2020). SBS delves deeper into back-office mergers than ABC. The Australian Financial Review. 13 July 2020. Retrieved from: https://www.afr.com/companies/media-and-marketing/sbs-delves-deeper-into-back-office-mergers-than-abc-20200708-p55a2c.
22. McMahon, A. (2020). The ABC and SBS are vital but can be strengthened. Opinion. *Independent Australia*. 4 September 2020. Retrieved from: https://independentaustralia.net/business/business-display/the-abc-and-sbs-are-vital-but-can-be-strengthened,14275.
23. Leslie, T. (2010). Sky falls on ABC's news channel. ABC News. 21 January 2020. Retrieved from: https://www.abc.net.au/news/2010-01-21/sky-falls-on-abcs-news-channel/1217718.
24. ABC News. (2018). Backstory: What ABC News cadets learnt in their first week. *ABC News*. 6 February 2018. Retrieved from: https://www.abc.net.au/news/about/backstory/news-coverage/2018-02-06/what-abc-news-cadets-learnt-in-their-first-week/9400864.
25. Waters, J. (2020). ABC News needs to find a new way to chase ratings. Opinion. Independent Australia. 5 September 2020. Retrieved from: https://independentaustralia.net/business/business-display/abc-news-needs-to-find-a-new-way-to-chase-ratings,14279.
26. Patterson, R. (2004). "The Eradication of Compulsory Retirement and Age Discrimination in the Australian Workplace: A Cause for Celebration and Concern". Elder Law Review. 10:3. p. 65. Retrieved from: http://classic.austlii.edu.au/au/journals/ElderLawRw/2004/10.html.
27. Hatch, L. R. (2005). "Gender and Ageism". *Generations*. 3. pp. 19–24. Retrieved from: https://www.ingentaconnect.com/content/asag/gen/2005/00000029/00000003/art00005.
28. Kossen, C., & Pedersen, C. (2008). Older workers in Australia: The myths, the realities and the battle over workforce 'flexibility'. *Journal of Management and Organization*. 14:1. pp. 73–84. Retrieved from: https://login.wwwproxy1.library.unsw.edu.au/login?qurl=https%3A%2F%2Fwww.proquest.com%2Fscholarly-journals%2Folder-workers-australia-myths-realities-battle%2Fdocview%2F233254008%2Fse-2%3Faccountid%3D12763.
29. Bourdieu (1983) said the *field* of cultural production "is the site of struggles in which what is at stake is the power to impose the dominant defini-

tion of the writer and therefore to delimit the population of those entitled to take part in the struggle to define the writer" (ibid.).

30. Hawkins, G. (2013). Enacting public value on the ABC's Q&A: From normative to performative approaches. Media International Australia. 146:1. February. pp. 82–92. Retrieved from: https://doi.org/10.1177/1329878X1314600112.
31. Situated within Bourdieu's (1977) theory of *cultural capital.*
32. Described by Bourdieu (1986) as: "the aggregate of the actual or potential resources which are linked to possession of a durable network of more or less institutionalized relationships of mutual acquaintance or recognition" (Bourdieu ibid.). The ABC has not survived by "explicitly demanding" attention (Bourdieu, 1984) but by giving access to informed social positions (ibid.) from the centre of the social world (ibid.).
33. Jolly, R. (2014). The ABC: an overview. Executive summary. *Parliament of Australia.* Retrieved from: https://www.aph.gov.au/About_Parliament/Parliamentary_Departments/Parliamentary_Library/pubs/rp/rp1415/ABCoverview#_Toc395086063.
34. Australian Broadcasting Corporation. (2017). Annual Report. *Australian Broadcasting Corporation.* Retrieved from: https://parlinfo.aph.gov.au/parlInfo/search/display/display.w3p;query=Id:%22publications/tabledpapers/c076fdb2-284f-4459-80d1-0af26c9821ff%22.
35. Australian Broadcasting Corporation. (2019). Annual Report. *Australian Broadcasting Corporation.* Retrieved from: https://about.abc.net.au/wp-content/uploads/2019/10/ABC-Annual-Report-201819v2.pdf.
36. Ramachandran, V. S. (2003). The Emerging Mind. The Reith Lectures 2003. *British Broadcasting Corporation.* Retrieved from: https://www.bbc.co.uk/radio4/reith2003/.
37. Ferguson, R. (2018). ABC 'biased' against complaints. *The Australian.* 12 December 2018. Retrieved from: https://www.theaustralian.com.au/nation/nation/abc-biased-against-complaints/news-story/ad79435959f5925c56b29f12fbc78f1b#:~:text=The%20ABC%20has%20*field*ed%20more,only%20upheld%20one%20of%20them.
38. Duke, J. (2017). ABC boss to push for more diversity of views among panel-show guests. *The Sydney Morning Herald.* 17 June 2019. Retrieved from: https://www.smh.com.au/business/companies/abc-boss-to-push-for-more-diversity-of-views-among-panel-show-guests-20190616-p51y7k.html.
39. Duke, J. (2018). ABC planning to pay for ranking in Google 'royal wedding' searches. The Sydney Morning Herald. 18 May 2018. Retrieved from: https://www.smh.com.au/business/companies/abc-planning-to-pay-for-ranking-in-google-royal-wedding-searches-20180518-p4zg3w.html.

40. Duke, J. (2019). ABC boss to push for more diversity of views among panel-show guests. *The Sydney Morning Herald*. 17 June 2019. Retrieved from: https://www.smh.com.au/business/companies/abc-boss-to-push-for-more-diversity-of-views-among-panel-show-guests-20190616-p51y7k.html.
41. Australian Broadcasting Corporation. (2018). Equity and Diversity Annual Report. *Australian Broadcasting Corporation*. Retrieved from: https://parlinfo.aph.gov.au/parlInfo/search/display/display.w3p;page=0;query=australian%20broadcasting%20corporation%20report%202017-2018;rec=0;resCount=Default.
42. Born, G. (2012). in C. J. Emden & D. Midgley (Eds.) Beyond Habermas: Democracy, Knowledge, and the Public Sphere. Ch. 7. "Mediating The Public Sphere: Digitization, Pluralism, and Communicative Democracy". Berghahn. London & New York. pp. 119–146. Retrieved from: https://www.academia.edu/attachments/38605631/download_file?st=MTU5NzAzMjYxNSwxMjEuMjIzLjE0Ni4xNzQsMTY1OTI4OTc2&s=profile.
43. Al Jazeera (2020). 'Decisive measures' in Beijing as coronavirus cases spike: Live blog. *Al Jazeera*. 15 June 2020. Retrieved from: https://www.aljazeera.com/news/2020/06/measures-beijing-coronavirus-cases-spike-live-200614233622226.html.
44. Al Jazeera (2020). Maria Ressa found guilty in blow to Philippines' press freedom. *Al Jazeera*. 15 June 2020. Retrieved from: https://www.aljazeera.com/news/2020/06/philippine-court-rappler-maria-ressa-guilty-cyberlibel-200614210221502.html.
45. Reporters San Frontières. (2020). 2020 World Press Freedom Index. *RSF Reporters Without Borders*. Retrieved from: https://rsf.org/en/ranking.
46. Kelso, A. (2007). Parliament and Political Disengagement: Neither Waving nor Drowning. *Political Quarterly*. 78:3. pp. 364–373. Retrieved from: https://doi.org/10.1111/j.1467-923X.2007.00865.x.
47. Snell, P. (2010). Emerging Adult Civic and Political Disengagement : A Longitudinal Analysis of Lack of Involvement With Politics. *Journal of Adolescent Research*. 25:2. pp. 258–287. Retrieved from: https://doi.org/info:doi/.
48. Christodoulou, I., Pashias, C. Theocharides, S. & Davou, B. (2017) Investigating the roots of political disengagement of young Greek Cypriots. *Contemporary Social Science*. 12:3–4. pp. 376–392. Retrieved from: DOI: 10.1080/21582041.2017.1384562.
49. Flinders, M. (2015). The General Rejection? Political Disengagement, Disaffected Democrats and 'Doing Politics' Differently. *Parliamentary*

Affairs. 68(Suppl1). pp. 241–254. Retrieved from: https://doi.org/10.1093/pa/gsv038.

50. Flinders, M. (2015). The General Rejection? Political Disengagement, Disaffected Democrats and 'Doing Politics' Differently. *Parliamentary Affairs, 68*(suppl1). pp. 241–254. Retrieved from: https://doi.org/10.1093/pa/gsv038.
51. Milne, J. & Guthrie, M. (2018) ABC Annual Report. Welcome. *Australian Broadcasting Corporation.* Retrieved from: https://about.abc.net.au/wp-content/uploads/2018/10/AP18_Vol1_FINALnew.pdf. p. 3.
52. Fraser, M. & O'Reilly, J. (1996). *Save Our ABC: Maintaining Australia's National Broadcaster.* Hyland House. South Melbourne. pp. 89–90.
53. Whitehead, G. (1988). *Inside the ABC: Geoffrey Whitehead's Personal Account.* Penguin Books Victoria. p. 181.
54. Schiller, H. I. (1993). "Public Way or Private Road?" *The Nation.* 257:2. 12 July 1993. pp. 64–66. Retrieved from: http://search.proquest.com/docview/231453434/.
55. Collins, R., Hoskins, C., McFadyen, S., & Finn, A. (2001). Public Service Broadcasting Beyond 2000: Is There a Future for Public Service Broadcasting? *Canadian Journal of Communication.* 26:1. pp. 3–15. Retrieved from: https://doi.org/info:doi/.
56. Davis, J. (1996). "Public Service TV in Crisis". *Broadcast.* 44. 1 Nov. 1996. EMAP Maclaren Ltd. (Archive: 1973–2000). pp. 16–17. Retrieved from: https://login.wwwproxy1.library.unsw.edu.au/login?qurl=https%3A%2F%2Fsearch.proquest.com%2Fdocview%2F1705116138%3Faccountid%3D12763.
57. Freedman, D. (2019). "Public Service" and the Journalism Crisis: Is the BBC the Answer? *Television & New Media.* 20:3. pp. 203–218. Retrieved from: https://doi.org/10.1177/1527476418760985.
58. Freedman, D. (2019). "Public Service" and the Journalism Crisis: Is the BBC the Answer? *Television & New Media.* 20:3. pp. 203–218. Retrieved from: https://doi.org/10.1177/1527476418760985.
59. Schiller, H. I. (1993). "Public Way or Private Road?" *The Nation.* 257:2. 12 July 1993. pp. 64–66. Retrieved from: http://search.proquest.com/docview/231453434/.
60. Davis, G. (1988). *Breaking Up the ABC.* Allen and Unwin. Crows Nest.
61. Harding, R. (1979). *Outside Interference: The Politics Of Australia Broadcasting.* Sun Books. Melbourne. p. 193.
62. Wilson, C. K., Hutchinson, J., & Shea, P. (2010). Public service broadcasting, creative industries, and innovation infrastructure: The case of ABC's pool. *Australian Journal of Communication.* 37:3. pp. 15–32.

Retrieved from: https://primoa.library.unsw.edu.au/permalink/f/11jha62/TN_informit_apaft201102742.

63. Harding, R. (1979). *Outside Interference: The politics of Australia broadcasting*. Sun Books. Melbourne. p. 69.
64. Davis, G. (1988). *Breaking Up the ABC*. Allen and Unwin. Crows Nest. p. ix.
65. Born, G. (2006). Digitising Democracy. *The Political Quarterly*. pp. 102–123. Retrieved from http://search.proquest.com/docview/227288047. p. 102.
66. Born, G. (2006). Digitising Democracy. *The Political Quarterly*. pp. 102–123. Retrieved from http://search.proquest.com/docview/227288047. p. 103.
67. Thomson, I. T. (2015). *Culture Wars and Enduring American Dilemmas*. Project MUSE. Baltimore, Md. p. 1.
68. Thomson, I. T. (2015). *Culture Wars and Enduring American Dilemmas*. Project MUSE. Baltimore, MD. p. 1.
69. Dahlgren, P. (2013). *The Political Web: Media, Participation and Alternative Democracy* (pp. 1–195). Palgrave Macmillan. Retrieved from: https://doi.org/10.1057/9781137326386.
70. Born, G. (2006). Digitising Democracy. *The Political Quarterly*. pp. 102–123. Retrieved from http://search.proquest.pcom/docview/227288047. p. 107.
71. Kramer, L. (1983). This Is the ABC: The Australian Broadcasting Commission, 1932–1983 by Ken S. Inglis. *The Australian Book Review*. 56. November 1983. Melbourne University Press. Melbourne. p. 121.
72. Tracey, M. (1998, reprinted 2002). *The Decline and Fall of Public Service Broadcasting*. Oxford University Press. Oxford. p. 260.
73. Buttrose, I. (2020). What would Australia look like without the ABC? ABC Australian Broadcasting Corporation Media Centre. *Australian Broadcasting Corporation*. 26 June 2020. Retrieved from: http://about.abc.net.au/statements/what-would-australia-look-like-without-the-abc/.
74. Reach.out (2020). The Importance of Sharing Your Stories. *Reach.out*. Retrieved from: https://au.reachout.com/articles/the-importance-of-sharing-your-story.
75. Ibarra, H. & Lineback, K. (2005). What's your story? *Harvard Business Review*. January 2005. Retrieved from: https://au.reachout.com/articles/the-importance-of-sharing-your-story.
76. High, S. (2010). Telling Stories: A Reflection on Oral History And New Media. *Oral History*. 38:1. pp. 101–112. Retrieved from: https://primoa.library.unsw.edu.au/permalink/f/11jha62/TN_jstor_archive_840650320.

77. Bingham, N. (2017). "Telling our stories": Print media interpretations of Moscow lesbians' life stories in 2004 and 2005. *Journal of Lesbian Studies: Contemporary Lesbian Relationships.* 21:1. pp. 120–131. https://doi.org/10.1080/10894160.2016.1191305.
78. Hayes, M., Ross, I., Gasher, M., & Gutstein, D. (2007). Telling stories: News media, health literacy and public policy in Canada. *Social Science & Medicine.* 64:9. pp. 1842–1852. Retrieved from: https://doi.org/10.1016/j.socscimed.2007.01.015.
79. Sheridan-Burns, Lynette and McKee, Alan (1999). Reporting on Indigenous Issues: some practical suggestions for improving journalistic practice in the coverage of indigenous affairs. *Australian Journalism Review: AJR.* 21:2. pp. 103–116. Retrieved from: https://eprints.qut.edu.au/14959/1/14959.pdf.
80. Hoxha, A., Hanitzsch, T., Frère, M. S., & Meyer, C. (2018). How conflict news comes into being: Reconstructing 'reality' through telling stories. *Media, War & Conflict.* 11:1. pp. 46–64. Retrieved from: https://doi.org/10.1177/1750635217727313.
81. Ceron, A. & Memoli, V. (2016). Flames and Debates: DO Social Media Affect Satisfaction with Democracy? *Soc Indic Res* (2016). 126. pp. 225–240. Retrieved from: DOI 10.1007/s11205-015-0893-x.
82. Norris, P. (2000). *A Virtuous Circle: Political Communications in Post-industrial Societies.* Cambridge University Press. Cambridge. p. 318.
83. Born, G. (2006). Digitising Democracy. *The Political Quarterly.* pp. 102–123. Retrieved from http://search.proquest.com/docview/227288047. p. 111.
84. Tracey, M. (1998, reprinted 2002). *The Decline and Fall of Public Service Broadcasting.* Oxford University Press. Oxford. p. 260.
85. Tracey, M. (1998, reprinted 2002). *The Decline and Fall of Public Service Broadcasting.* Oxford University Press. Oxford. p. 260.
86. Tracey, M. (1998, reprinted 2002). *The Decline and Fall of Public Service Broadcasting.* Oxford University Press. Oxford. p. 260.
87. Spadaro, A. (2020). Defy the Apocalypse. *La Civiltà Cattolica.* 20 January 2020. Retrieved from: https://www.laciviltacattolica.com/defy-the-apocalypse/#_ftn5.
88. Spadaro, A. (2020). Defy the Apocalypse. *La Civiltà Cattolica.* 20 January 2020. Retrieved from: https://www.laciviltacattolica.com/defy-the-apocalypse/#_ftn5.
89. Christopher W. Blackwell, "Athenian Democracy: a brief overview," in Adriaan Lanni, Ed., "Athenian Law in its Democratic Context" (Center for Hellenic Studies On-line Discussion Series). Republished in C.W. Blackwell, ed. *Dēmos: Classical Athenian Democracy* (Eds. A. Mahoney and R. Scaife). *The Stoa.* Retrieved from: http://www.stoa.

org/demos/article_democracy_overview@page=all&greek Encoding=UnicodeC.html.

90. Moe, H. (2008). Public Service Media Online? Regulating Public Broadcasters' Internet Services—A Comparative Analysis. *Television & New Media*. 9:3. pp. 220–238. Retrieved from: https://doi.org/10.1177/1527476407307231.
91. Canberra Times, The. (1985). Keating blasts 'indulgence' of the ABC. *The Canberra Times*. 3 August 1985. p. 3. Retrieved from: https://trove.nla.gov.au/newspaper/article/122525482?searchTerm=ABC%20 privatise&searchLimits=.
92. McChesney, R. M. (2008). *The Political Economy of Media: Enduring Dilemmas*. Monthly Review Press. New York. p. 47.
93. Hoxha, A., Hanitzsch, T., Frère, M. S., & Meyer, C. (2018). How conflict news comes into being: Reconstructing 'reality' through telling stories. *Media, War & Conflict*. 11:1. pp. 46–64. Retrieved from: https://doi.org/10.1177/1750635217727313.
94. Australian Government, The. (2019). *Australian Broadcasting Corporation Budget Statements*. Budget 2019–2020. Portfolio Budget Statements 2019–2020. Budget Related Paper No. 1.3. Communications and the Arts Portfolio. *The Australian Government*. Retrieved from: https://www.communications.gov.au/file/48093/download?token=oJLIQtx0. p. 77.
95. O'Brien, K. (2018). *A Memoir*. Allen and Unwin, Sydney. p. 827.
96. Australian Broadcasting Corporation. ABC 2016–2019 funding. 3 May 2016. *Australian Broadcasting Corporation*. Retrieved from: http://about.abc.net.au/press-releases/abc-2016-2019-funding/.
97. Whitehead, G. (1988). *Inside the ABC: Geoffrey Whitehead's Personal Account*. Penguin Books Victoria. pp. 172–173.
98. Whitehead, G. (1988). *Inside the ABC: Geoffrey Whitehead's Personal Account*. Penguin Books Victoria. pp. 172–173.
99. Whitehead, G. (1988). *Inside the ABC: Geoffrey Whitehead's Personal Account*. Penguin Books Victoria. pp. 176–177.
100. Whitehead, G. (1988). *Inside the ABC: Geoffrey Whitehead's Personal Account*. Penguin Books Victoria. p. 180.
101. Whitehead, G. (1988). *Inside the ABC: Geoffrey Whitehead's Personal Account*. Penguin Books Victoria. p. 179.
102. Whitehead, G. (1988). *Inside the ABC: Geoffrey Whitehead's Personal Account*. Penguin Books Victoria. p. 180.
103. Davies, N. (2009). *Flat Earth News*. Vintage Books. London. p. 394.
104. Davies, N. (2009). *Flat Earth News*. Vintage Books. London. p. 394.

105. Australian Government (2019). Budget 2019–2020. *Australian Government.* Retrieved from: https://budget.gov.au/2019-20/content/overview.htm.
106. Australian Government (2019). Budget 2019–2020. *Australian Government.* Retrieved from: https://budget.gov.au/2019-20/content/services.htm.
107. Martin, S. (2020). What Australia's $189 bn coronavirus economic rescue package means for you. *The Guardian.* 22 March 2020. Retrieved from: https://www.theguardian.com/business/2020/mar/22/what-australias-189bn-coronavirus-economic-rescue-package-means-for-you.
108. Hutchens, G. (2020). The coronavirus' economic fallout has its own momentum as RBA makes extraordinary intervention. Analysis. *Australian Broadcasting Corporation.* 20 March 2020. Retrieved from: https://www.abc.net.au/news/2020-03-20/coronavirus-rba-makes-extraordinary-intervention/12070586.
109. Janda, M. & Taylor, D. (2020). Reserve Bank governor Philip Lowe sees coronavirus and bushfires as short-term economic speedbumps. *Australian Broadcasting Corporation.* 5 February 2020. Retrieved from: https://www.abc.net.au/news/2020-02-05/rba-lowe-sees-coronavirus-and-bushfire-economic-speedbumps/11931822.
110. Dawes S. (2017). Broadcasting Regulation, History and Theory. In: *British Broadcasting and the Public-Private Dichotomy.* Palgrave Macmillan, Cham. https://doi-org.wwwproxy1.library.unsw.edu.au/10.1007/978-3-319-50097-3_1. pp. 3–19.
111. ABC Section of the Community and Public Sector Union. (2008). *Towards a Digital Future: Submission to Review of ABC and SBS.* December 2008. *ABC Section of the Community and Public Sector Union.* Retrieved from: https://iloveabc.org.au/wp-content/uploads/2018/11/Towards-a-Digital-Future-2008-1.pdf.
112. Collins, R., Hoskins, C., McFadyen, S., & Finn, A. (2001). Public service broadcasting beyond 2000: Is there a future for public service broadcasting? *Canadian Journal of Communication.* 26:1. Retrieved from: doi: http://dx.doi.org.wwwproxy1.library.unsw.edu.au/10.22230/cjc.2001v26n1a119. p. 3.
113. Wilson, C. K., Hutchinson, J., & Shea, P. (2010). Public service broadcasting, creative industries, and innovation infrastructure: The case of ABC's pool. *Australian Journal of Communication.* 37:3. pp. 15–32. Retrieved from: https://primoa.library.unsw.edu.au/permalink/f/11jha62/TN_informit_apaft201102742.
114. Gordon, J. (2018). Australians are losing their trust in 'the media', but not in journalism. RMIT ABC Fact Check. 19 November 2018. *Australian Broadcasting Corporation.* Retrieved from: https://www.abc.

net.au/news/2018-09-10/fact-checking-the-new-workplace-skill/10209210.

115. Edelman Trust Barometer. (2018). Global Report. *Edelman.* Retrieved from: https://www.edelman.com/sites/g/files/aatuss191/files/2018-10/2018_Edelman_Trust_Barometer_Global_Report_FEB.pdf.
116. McAllister, I; Cameron, S & Sheppard, J. 2016 Australian Election Study. School of Politics and International Relations. *Australian National University.* Retrieved from: https://politicsir.cass.anu.edu.au/news/2016-australian-election-study.
117. Levine, M. (2018). ABC most trusted | Facebook most distrusted. *Roy Morgan.* June 26 2018. Finding No. 7641. Retrieved from: http://www.roymorgan.com/findings/7641-media-net-trust-june-2018-201806260239.
118. Naughton, J. (2020). Reports of social media's influence on voters are greatly exaggerated. *The Guardian.* 16 February 2020. Retrieved from: https://www.theguardian.com/commentisfree/2020/feb/15/reports-of-social-media-influence-on-voters-are-greatly-exaggerated.
119. The Canberra Times. (1985). Keating blasts 'indulgence' of the ABC. *The Canberra Times.* 3 August 1985. p. 3. Retrieved from: https://trove.nla.gov.au/newspaper/article/122525482?searchTerm=ABC%20privatise&searchLimits=.
120. Fraser, M. and O'Reilly, J. (Eds.). (1996). *Save our ABC: The case for maintaining Australia's national broadcaster.* F. Brennan. "By Law Established". Hyland House Publishing. Melbourne. p. 28.
121. Fraser, M. and O'Reilly, J. (Eds.). (1996). *Save our ABC: The case for maintaining Australia's national broadcaster.* C. Masters. "Cheques are not balances". Hyland House Publishing. Melbourne. p. 31.
122. Fraser, M. and O'Reilly, J. (Eds.). (1996). *Save our ABC: The case for maintaining Australia's national broadcaster.* R. Williams. "Too close a shave". Hyland House Publishing. Melbourne. pp. 50.
123. Sydney Morning Herald, The. (1931). Broadcasting. *The Sydney Morning Herald.* 16 November 1931. p. 8. Retrieved from: https://trove.nla.gov.au/newspaper/article/16823317?searchTerm=%22improved%20and%20freed%20from%20all%20the%20evils%2C%20real%20or%20imaginary%2C%20of%20private%20enterprise%22.
124. Australian Broadcasting Corporation. (2020). iView landing page. *Australian Broadcasting Corporation.* Retrieved from: https://iview.abc.net.au › category › news (Now a dead link. See updated landing page: https://iview.abc.net.au.)
125. Conroy, S. (2008). ABC and SBS: Towards a digital future. Discussion paper. Foreword. *Australian Government, Department of Broadband, Communications and the Digital Economy.* October 2008. Retrieved

from: https://www.ames.net.au/-/media/files/policy/7_abc_and_sbs_towards_a_digital_future_low_resolution.pdf?la=en.

126. Miragliotta, N. and Errington, W. (2012). The Rise and Fall and Rise Again of Public Broadcasting? The Case of the Australian Broadcasting Corporation. *Australian Journal of Public Administration*. 71. pp. 55–64. Doi:https://doi.org/10.1111/j.1467-8500.2012.00755.x. p. 59
127. UK Government. (1962) Report of the committee on broadcasting. The Pilkington Report on Broadcasting. London. UK Government. Retrieved from: https://api.parliament.uk/historic-hansard/lords/1962/jul/18/the-pilkington-report-on-broadcasting. p. 18.
128. The Age. (2016, 2014). Cultural relevance not as easy as ABC. *The Age*. First published 2014. 3 May 2016. Retrieved from: https://www.theage.com.au/national/act/cultural-relevance-not-as-easy-as-abc-20160503-gokn6d.html.
129. Miragliotta, N., & Errington, W. (2012). The Rise and Fall and Rise Again of Public Broadcasting? The Case of the Australian Broadcasting Corporation. *Australian Journal of Public Administration*. 71:1. pp. 55–64. https://doi.org/10.1111/j.1467-8500.2012.00755.x. p. 56.
130. Miragliotta, N., & Errington, W. (2012). The Rise and Fall and Rise Again of Public Broadcasting? The Case of the Australian Broadcasting Corporation. *Australian Journal of Public Administration*. 71:1. Pp. 55–64. https://doi.org/10.1111/j.1467-8500.2012.00755.x. p. 60.
131. Miragliotta, N., & Errington, W. (2012). The Rise and Fall and Rise Again of Public Broadcasting? The Case of the Australian Broadcasting Corporation. *Australian Journal of Public Administration*. 71:1. pp. 55–64. https://doi.org/10.1111/j.1467-8500.2012.00755.x.
132. Molomby. (1991). *Is There a Moderate on the Roof?: ABC Years*. W. Heinemann. Australia. p. 308.
133. Hurd, D. (1986). BBC Financing (Peacock Report). Hurd presentation to House of Commons debate 3 July 1986. *UK Parliament*. Vol. 100 cc1180–1193. Retrieved from: https://api.parliament.uk/historic-hansard/commons/1986/jul/03/bbc-financing-peacock-report.
134. Ibid.
135. Ibid.
136. Associated Press. (2020). UK Government, At Odds with Media, Set to Review BBC Funding. *Voice of America News*. 5 February 2020. Retrieved from: https://www.voanews.com/europe/uk-government-odds-media-set-review-bbc-funding.
137. Reuters. (2020). Britain's BBC to Cut 450 Newsroom Jobs in Cost-Cutting Drive. *Reuters*. 29 January 2020. Retrieved from: https://www.voanews.com/europe/britains-bbc-cut-450-newsroom-jobs-cost-cutting-drive.

138. ABC. (2018). The Cost of Being the ABC: Delivering the Best and Most Efficient Public Broadcasting. June 2018. Retrieved from: http://www.abc.net.au/cm/lb/9944818/data/the-cost-of-being-the-abc-data.pdf.
139. Weisblott, M. 2013. CBC music radio stations will now have a word or two from their sponsors. *Canada.com*. Retrieved from: https://o.canada.com/business/cbc-radio-commercial-advertising-approved.
140. Bourdieu, P. (1984). (Transl. R. Nice). *Distinction: A Social Critique of the Judgement of Taste*. Harvard University Press. Massachusetts. p. 20.
141. Whitehead, G. (1988). *Inside the ABC: Geoffrey Whitehead's Personal Account*. Penguin Books. Victoria. p. 62.
142. Australian Competition and Consumer Commission. (2019). Digital Platforms Inquiry. Final Report. June 2019. *Australian Competition and Consumer Commission*. Retrieved from: https://www.accc.gov.au/system/files/Digital%20platforms%20inquiry%20-%20final%20report.pdf.
143. Ibid.
144. Standing, G. (2011). *The Precariat: The New Dangerous Class*. Bloomsbury Academic. Oxford.
145. Standing, G. (2018). The Precariat: Today's Transformative Class? [online]. *Great Transition Initiative* (October 2018). Retrieved from: https://www.greattransition.org/publication/precariat-transformative-class.
146. Standing, G. (2011). *The precariat: The new dangerous class*. Bloomsbury Academic. Oxford. p. 16.
147. Lefebvre, H. (1991). (Transl. D. Nicholson-Smith). *The Production of Space*. Blackwell. Oxford, UK and Cambridge, USA.
148. Quoting Bourdieu and Wacquant, Masquelier. (2018). Said precarity had become a "'privileged engine of economic activity'" but in order for precarity "to become such a central economic principle … (it) had to be made inevitable. It had to be naturalized".
149. Bourdieu (1998) Said: "*La précarité est aujourd'hui partout*/ Precariousness is everywhere today" in which he was scathing of economists for being complicit in creating the model of precarious employment (Bourdieu ibid.). He referred specifically to "the institutions of cultural production and diffusion" (Loc. Cit.) such as the media as being especially impacted upon by precariousness: "the de-structuring of existence, which is deprived among other things of its temporal structures, and the ensuing deterioration of the whole relationship to the world, time and space … the whole world of production, material and cultural, public and private, is thus carried along by a process of intensification of insecurity" (ibid.).
150. Bourdieu, P. (Transl. R. Nice). (1998). "Job Insecurity is Everywhere Now". *Acts of Resistance: Against the myths of our time*. Polity Press.

Cambridge. (Paper delivered at the Intervention at the Rencontres Européennes contre la Précarité, Grenoble, 12–13 Dec. 1997). Retrieved from: https://monoskop.org/images/1/1d/Pierre_Bourdieu_Acts_of_Resistance-_Against_the_New_Myths_of_Our_Time_1998.pdf. p. 84.

151. Gilfillan, G. (2018). 'Trends in use of non-standard forms of employment', by Statistics and Mapping Section. *Parliament of Australia*. 10 December 10, 2018. Retrieved from: https://www.aph.gov.au/About_Parliament/Parliamentary_Departments/Parliamentary_Library/pubs/rp/rp1819/NonStandardEmployment.
152. *AAP FactCheck* (2018). Investigation: Has the level of casual employment in the Australian workforce not changed for two decades? *The Herald Sun*. Retrieved from: https://www.heraldsun.com.au/blogs/andrew-bolt/more-abc-staff-less-value/news-story/e6f8bc5271a1f93606b916a39bddd1b8.
153. *AAP FactCheck* (2018). Investigation: Has the level of casual employment in the Australian workforce not changed for two decades? *The Herald Sun*. Retrieved from: https://www.heraldsun.com.au/blogs/andrew-bolt/more-abc-staff-less-value/news-story/e6f8bc5271a1f93606b916a39bddd1b8.
154. *Australian Council of Trade Unions*. (2019). Report shows ABC wage theft from casuals of $22.9 million. 21 October 2019. Retrieved from: https://www.google.com/search?client=safari&rls=en&q=ABC+staff+casual&ie=UTF-8&oe=UTF-8.
155. DiMaggio, P. & Anheier, H. (1990). The Sociology of Non-profit Organizations and Sectors. *Annual Review of Sociology*. 1990.16. pp. 137–159. p. 151.
156. Heidkamp, B. & Kergel, D. (2017). "Media Change—Precarity Within and Precarity Through the Internet" (Chap. 2). *Precarity within the Digital Age Media Change and Social Insecurity*. Springer. Wiesbaden. Retrieved from: https://link-springer-com.wwwproxy1.library.unsw.edu.au/content/pdf/10.1007%2F978-3-658-17678-5.pdf. p. 10.
157. Berg, C. & Davidson, S. (2018). *Against Public Broadcasting: Why We Should Privatise the ABC and How to Do It*. Connor Court Publishing. West End. Queensland.
158. Harding, R. (1979). *Outside Interference: The politics of Australia broadcasting*. Sun Books. Melbourne.
159. Harding, R. (1979). *Outside Interference: The politics of Australia broadcasting*. Sun Books. Melbourne. p. 187.
160. Meade, A. (2018). ABC has shed 1,012 jobs since 2014, Senate estimates told. *The Guardian*. 24 May 2018. Retrieved from: https://www.theguardian.com/media/2018/may/24/abc-has-shed-1012-jobs-since-2014-senate-estimates-told.

161. Angell, N. (1933). *From Chaos to Control.* Halley Stewart Lecture 1932. Unwin Brothers Limited. Woking. p. 190.
162. Scott, M. (2014). #ourabc. Speech to Faculty of Creative Industries. Queensland University of Technology. 15 August 2014. In M. Scott. (2016). *A Media Odyssey: Speeches of an ABC Managing Director 2006–2016.* ABC Books. p. 125.
163. ACCC. (2019). Digital Platforms Enquiry. Final Report. *ACCA.* June 2019. Retrieved from: https://www.accc.gov.au/system/files/Digital%20platforms%20inquiry%20-%20final%20report.pdf. p. 19.
164. Meade, A. & Wahlquist, C. (2018). Australians don't want ABC used as a 'punching bag', Michelle Guthrie says. *The Guardian.* 19 June 2018. Retrieved from: https://www.theguardian.com/media/2018/jun/19/australians-dont-want-abc-used-as-a-punching-bag-michelle-guthrie-says.
165. Stutchbury, H. (2018). The ABC is an indulgence we can no longer afford. *The Sydney Morning Herald.* 18 June 2018. Retrieved from: https://www.smh.com.au/business/companies/the-abc-is-an-indulgence-we-can-no-longer-afford-20180618-p4zm6y.html.
166. Knott, M. (2015). Everyone from Coalition thinks ABC's Q&A is biased to the left, says LNP senator James McGrath. *The Age.* 28 May 2015. Retrieved from: https://www.theage.com.au/politics/federal/everyone-from-coalition...ed-to-the-left-says-lnp-senator-james-mcgrath-20150527-ghatyw.html. Dead link. Now available at: https://www.smh.com.au/politics/federal/everyone-from-coalition-thinks-abcs-qa-is-biased-to-the-left-says-lnp-senator-james-mcgrath-20150527-ghatyw.html
167. Semmler, C. (1981). *The ABC—Aunt Sally and Sacred Cow.* Melbourne University Press. Melbourne. p. 109.
168. Ibid., p. 109.
169. Ibid., p. 108.
170. Ibid., p. 110.
171. Ibid., p. 110.
172. Ibid., p. 111.
173. Ibid., p. 109.
174. Ibid., p. 184.
175. Inglis, K. (2006). *Whose ABC? The Australian Broadcasting Corporation 1983–2006.* Black Inc Books. Melbourne. p. 120.
176. Border Reivers were Scottish and English who raided and rampaged on the Anglo-Scottish border for centuries up to the sixteenth century, they stole irrespective of nationality, everyone was prey. The word comes from Middle English Scots *reifen*—to pillage and plunder.

177. Walker, R. R. (1973). *The Magic Spark: Fifty Years of Radio in Australia*. The Hawthorn Press. Melbourne. p. 21.
178. Diamond, E. (1975). *The Tin Kazoo: Television, Politics and the News*. MIT Press. Cambridge, MA. p. xi. Quoting Walter Lippman.
179. Grinberg, D. B. (2018). Why Traditional Media Still Matters in Today's Digital Age. *Medium*. 15 March 2018. Retrieved from: https://medium.com/@DBGrinberg/why-traditional-media-still-matters-in-todays-digital-age-f81350674e2f.
180. Bourdieu, P. (1979). Transl. R. Nice. (1984). *Distinction: A Social Critique of the Judgement Of Taste*. Harvard University Press. Cambridge, MA. Preface to the English Language Edition. p. i.
181. Cunningham, S. (2013). *Hidden Innovation: Policy, Industry and the Creative Sector*. University of Queensland Press. Brisbane.
182. Couldry, N. (2004). "Theorising Media as 'practice'." *Social Semiotics*. 14:2. pp. 115–132. Doi: 10.1080/1035033042000238295. p. 117.
183. Glynn, M., & Lounsbury, M. (2005). From the Critics' Corner: Logic Blending, Discursive Change and Authenticity in a Cultural Production System. *The Journal of Management Studies*. 42:5. pp. 1031–1055. https://doi.org/10.1111/j.1467-6486.2005.00531.x.
184. Media Logic (originally no 's') was developed by Altheide, D.L. & Snow, R.P. (1979) Media Logic. Sage Publications. Beverly Hills.
185. Bourdieu, P. Transl. R. Nice. (1984). *Distinction: A Social Critique of The Judgement Of Taste*. Harvard University Press. Cambridge, MA.
186. Thornton, P. H., Ocasio, W., & Lounsbury, M. (2012). *The Emergence and Evolution of field-Level Logics*. DOI:10.1093/acprof:oso/9780199601936.003.0007.
187. Scannell, P. (1989). Public service broadcasting and modern public life. *Media, Culture & Society*. 11(2). pp. 135–166. https://doi.org/10.1177/016344389011002002.

References

2018 Edelman Trust Barometer. (2018). *Global Report*. Edelman. https://www.edelman.com/sites/g/files/aatuss191/files/2018-10/2018_Edelman_Trust_Barometer_Global_Report_FEB.pdf

AAP FactCheck. (2018). Investigation: Has the Level of Casual Employment in the Australian Workforce Not Changed for Two Decades? *The Herald Sun*. https://www.heraldsun.com.au/blogs/andrew-bolt/more-abc-staff-less-value/news-story/e6f8bc5271a1f93606b916a39bddd1b8

ABC. (2016, February). *ABC Submission to the House of Representatives Standing Committee on Communications and the Arts*. Inquiry Into the Importance of Public and Commercial Broadcasting, Online Content and Live Production to Rural and Regional Australia, Including the Arts, News and Other Services.

[online]. *ABC*. http://d3n8a8pro7vhmx.cloudfront.net/abcfriends/legacy_url/2756/ABC_Submission_Reps_Feb2016_Sub009.pdf?1563515036

ABC. (2018, June). *The Cost of Being the ABC: Delivering the Best and Most Efficient Public Broadcasting*. http://www.abc.net.au/cm/lb/9944818/data/the-cost-of-being-the-abc-data.pdf

ABC. (2020, April). *Interview ABC News24. Strapline: "Pell Released. George Pell Freed from Prison After High Court ruling"*. https://www.youtube.com/watch?v=7x29VznAZOE

ABC News. (2018, February 6). Backstory: What ABC News Cadets Learnt in Their First Week. *ABC News*. https://www.abc.net.au/news/about/backstory/news-coverage/2018-02-06/what-abc-news-cadets-learnt-in-their-first-week/9400864

ACCC. (2019, June). *Digital Platforms Enquiry*. Final Report. ACCA. https://www.accc.gov.au/system/files/Digital%20platforms%20inquiry%20-%20final%20report.pdf

Age, The. (2016, 2014, May 3). Cultural Relevance Not as Easy as ABC. *The Age*. First Published 2014. https://www.theage.com.au/national/act/cultural-relevance-not-as-easy-as-abc-20160503-gokn6d.html

Angell, N. (1933). *From Chaos to Control*. Halley Stewart Lecture 1932. Unwin Brothers Limited. Woking.

Anthony, S. (1982). Leonie Kramer takes on a new challenge at the ABC. *The Australian Women's Weekly*. 27 January 1982, p. 13. Retrieved from: https://trove.nla.gov.au/newspaper/article/52620089?searchTerm=Leonie%20kramer%20ABC

Australian Broadcasting Corporation. (2017). Annual Report. *Australian Broadcasting Corporation*. Retrieved from: https://parlinfo.aph.gov.au/parlInfo/search/display/display.w3p;query=Id:%22publications/tabled-papers/c076fdb2-284f-4459-80d1-0af26c9821ff%22

Australian Competition and Consumer Commission. (2019, June). Digital Platforms Inquiry. Final Report. *Australian Competition and Consumer Commission*. https://www.accc.gov.au/system/files/Digital%20platforms%20inquiry%20-%20final%20report.pdf

Australian Council of Trade Unions. (2019, October 21). Report Shows ABC Wage Theft from Casuals of $22.9 Million. https://www.google.com/search?client=safari&rls=en&q=ABC+staff+casual&ie=UTF-8&oe=UTF-8

Australian Government. (1996, June). Commonwealth Competitive Neutrality Policy Statement. https://www.pc.gov.au/about/core-functions/competitive-neutrality/commonwealth-competitive-neutrality-policy-statement-1996.pdf

Australian Government. (2019). Budget 2019–2020. *Australian Government*. https://budget.gov.au/2019-20/content/overview.htm

Behn, R. D. (1980). Leadership in an era of retrenchment. *Public Administration Review, 40*(6), 603. https://doi.org/10.2307/3110316

Behn, R. D. (1991). *Leadership Counts: Lessons for Public Managers from the Massachusetts Welfare, Training, and Employment Program*. Harvard University Press. Cambridge, Mass.

Berg, C., & Davidson, S. (2018). *Against Public Broadcasting: Why We Should Privatise the ABC and How to Do It*. Connor Court Publishing. West End.

Bingham, N. (2017). "Telling Our Stories": Print Media Interpretations of Moscow Lesbians' Life Stories in 2004 and 2005. *Journal of Lesbian Studies: Contemporary Lesbian Relationships, 21*(1), 120–131. https://doi.org/10.1080/10894160.2016.1191305

Blackwell, C. W. (2003). Athenian Democracy: A Brief Overview. In A. Lanni (Ed.), *Athenian Law in its Democratic Context* (Center for Hellenic Studies On-line Discussion Series). Republished in C.W. Blackwell, ed. *Dēmos: Classical Athenian Democracy* (Eds. A. Mahoney & R. Scaife). *The Stoa*. http://www.stoa.org/demos/article_democracy_overview@page=all&greekEncoding=UnicodeC.html

Blain, E. (1977). *Life with Aunty: 40 Year with the ABC*. Methuen Australia.

Born, G. (2005). *Uncertain Vision: Birt, Dyke and the Re-invention of the BBC*. Vintage.

Born, G. (2006). Digitising Democracy. *The Political Quarterly*, pp. 102–123. http://search.proquest.com/docview/227288047

Born, G. (2012). In C. J. Emden & D. Midgley (Eds.), *Beyond Habermas: Democracy, Knowledge, and the Public Sphere. Ch. 7. "Mediating The Public Sphere: Digitization, Pluralism, and Communicative Democracy"* (pp. 119–146). Berghahn. https://www.academia.edu/attachments/38605631/download_file?st=MTU5NzAzMjYxNSwxMjEuMjIzLjE0Ni4xNzQsMTY1OTI4OTc2&s=profile

Bourdieu, P. (1977). *Outline of a Theory of Practice* (R. Nice, Trans.). Cambridge University Press.

Bourdieu, P. (1979). *Distinction: A Social Critique of The Judgement of Taste* (R. Nice (1984), Trans.). Harvard University Press. Preface to the English Language Edition.

Bourdieu, P. (1984). *Sociology in Question*. Sage Publications.

Bourdieu, P. (1998). *On Television and Journalism* (P. Parkhurst Ferguson, Trans.). Pluto Press.

British Broadcasting Corporation. Royal Charter. (1927). History of the BBC. *British Broadcasting Corporation*. https://web.archive.org/web/20170622230610/http://downloads.bbc.co.uk/bbctrust/assets/files/pdf/regulatory_framework/charter_agreement/archive/1927.pdf

Burns, M., & Hawkins, G. (2013). Investigating Public Service Media as Hybrid Arrangements. *Media International Australia, 146*(1), 79–81. https://doi.org/10.1177/1329878X1314600111

Buttrose, I. (2020, June 26). What Would Australia Look Like Without the ABC? ABC Media Centre. *Australian Broadcasting Corporation*. http://about.abc.net.au/statements/what-would-australia-look-like-without-the-abc/

Ceron, A., & Memoli, V. (2016). Flames and Debates: Do Social Media Affect Satisfaction with Democracy? *Social Indicators Research, 126*(1), 225–240. https://doi.org/10.1007/s11205-015-0893-x

Chen, J., Walker, R.M. & Sawhney, M. (2020). Public service innovation: a typology. *Public Management Review, 22*(11), 1674–1695. https://doi.org/10.1080/14719037.2019.1645874

Christensen, C. M. & Overdorf, M. (2000). Meeting the Challenge of Disruptive Change. *Harvard Business Review*. Retrieved from: https://hbr.org/2000/03/meeting-the-challenge-of-disruptive-change

Christodoulou, I., Pashias, C., Theocharides, S., & Davou, B. (2017). Investigating the roots of political disengagement of young Greek Cypriots. *Contemporary Social Science, 12*(3–4), 376–392. https://doi.org/10.1080/21582041.2017.1384562

Cockburn, G. (2020, December 8). Keating Hails One of the Greats. *The Australian*. NCA Newswire.

Collins, R., Hoskins, C., McFadyen, S., & Finn, A. (2001). Public Service Broadcasting Beyond 2000: Is There a Future for Public Service Broadcasting? *Canadian Journal of Communication, 26*(1), 3–15. http://dx.doi.org.wwwproxy1.library.unsw.edu.au/10.22230/cjc.2001v26n1a119

Committee of Review of the Australian Broadcasting Commission. (1981). "The ABC in review: national broadcasting in the 1980s". (aka The Dix Report). Committee of Review of the Australian Broadcasting Commission. 30 May, 1981. *Commonwealth of Australia*. Retrieved from: https://apo.org.au/node/41206

Conroy, S. (2008, October). ABC and SBS: Towards a Digital Future. Discussion Paper. Foreword. *Australian Government, Department of Broadband, Communications and the Digital Economy*. https://www.ames.net.au/-/media/files/policy/7_abc_and_sbs_towards_a_digital_future_low_resolution.pdf?la=en

Couldry, N. (2004). Theorising Media as Practice. *Social Semiotics, 14*(2), 115–132. https://doi.org/10.1080/1035033042000238295

Cunningham, S. (2013). *Hidden Innovation: Policy, Industry and the Creative Sector*. University of Queensland Press.

Curran, J. (1990). 'The New Revisionism in Mass Communication Research: A Reappraisal'. *European Journal of Communication, 5*(2), 135–164. https://doi.org/10.1177/0267323190005002002

Dahlgren, P. (2013). *The Political Web: Media, Participation And Alternative Democracy* (pp. 1–195). Palgrave Macmillan. https://doi.org/10.1057/9781137326386

Davies, N. (2009). *Flat Earth News.* Vintage Books.
Davis, G. (1988). *Breaking Up the ABC.* Allen and Unwin.
Davis, J. (1996, November 1). Public Service TV in Crisis. *Broadcast, 44*, 16–17. EMAP Maclaren Ltd. (Archive: 1973–2000). https://login.wwwproxy1.library.unsw.edu.au/login?qurl=https%3A%2F%2Fsearch.proquest.com%2Fdocview%2F1705116138%3Faccountid%3D12763
Diamond, E. (1975). *The Tin Kazoo: Television, Politics and the News.* MIT Press.
DiMaggio, P., & Anheier, H. (1990). The Sociology of Non-profit Organizations and Sectors. *Annual Review of Sociology, 16*, 137–59. https://www.jstor.org/stable/2083266
Duke, J. (2017). ABC boss to push for more diversity of views among panel-show guests. *The Sydney Morning Herald.* 17 June 2019. Retrieved from: https://www.smh.com.au/business/companies/abc-boss-to-push-for-more-diversity-of-views-among-panel-show-guests-20190616-p51y7k.html
Duke, J. (2018, May 18). ABC Planning to Pay for Ranking in Google 'Royal Wedding' Searches. *The Sydney Morning Herald.* https://www.smh.com.au/business/companies/abc-planning-to-pay-for-ranking-in-google-royal-wedding-searches-20180518-p4zg3w.html
Edelman Trust Barometer. (2018). Global Report. Edelman. Retrieved from: https://www.edelman.com/sites/g/files/aatuss191/files/2018-10/2018_Edelman_Trust_Barometer_Global_Report_FEB.pdf
Evans, S. K. (2018). Making Sense of Innovation. *Journalism Studies, 19*(1), 4–24. London, England. https://doi.org/10.1080/1461670X.2016.1154446
Flinders, M. (2015). The General Rejection? Political Disengagement, Disaffected Democrats and 'Doing Politics' Differently. *Parliamentary Affairs, 68*(Suppl1), 241–254. https://doi.org/10.1093/pa/gsv038
Fraser, M., & O'Reilly, J. (1996). *Save Our ABC: Maintaining Australia's National Broadcaster.* Hyland House. South Melbourne.
Fraser, M., & O'Reilly, J. (Eds.). (1996). *Save Our ABC: The Case for Maintaining Australia's National Broadcaster.* Hyland House.
Freedman, D. (2019). "Public Service" and the Journalism Crisis: Is the BBC the Answer? *Television & New Media, 20*(3), 203–218. https://doi.org/10.1177/1527476418760985
Gilfillan, G. (2018, December 10). 'Trends in Use of Non-Standard Forms of Employment', by Statistics and Mapping Section. *Parliament of Australia.* https://www.aph.gov.au/About_Parliament/Parliamentary_Departments/Parliamentary_Library/pubs/rp/rp1819/NonStandardEmployment
Glynn, M. (2000, May–June). When Cymbals Become Symbols: Conflict Over Organizational Identity Within a Symphony Orchestra. *Organization Science, 11*(3). Special Issue: Cultural Industries: Learning from Evolving Organizational Practices, pp. 285–298. https://www.jstor.org/stable/2640262

Glynn, M., & Lounsbury, M. (2005). From the Critics' Corner: Logic Blending, Discursive Change and Authenticity in a Cultural Production System. *The Journal of Management Studies., 42*(5), 1031–1055. https://doi.org/10.1111/j.1467-6486.2005.00531.x

Gordon, J. (2018, November 19). Australians Are Losing Their Trust in 'The Media', But Not in Journalism. RMIT. ABC Fact Check. *Australian Broadcasting Corporation.* https://www.abc.net.au/news/2018-09-10/fact-checking-the-new-workplace-skill/10209210

Grinberg, D. B. (2018, March 15). Why Traditional Media Still Matters in Today's Digital Age. *Medium.* https://medium.com/@DBGrinberg/why-traditional-media-still-matters-in-todays-digital-age-f81350674e2f

Guthrie, M. (2016). Email to staff, 2 May.

Hall, S. (1977). 'Culture, the Media and the "Ideological Effect"', in J. Curran, M. Gurevitch & J. Woollacott (Eds.), *Mass Communication and Society.* Arnold. London.

Harding, R. (1979). *Outside Interference: The Politics of Australia Broadcasting.* Sun Books.

Hatch, L. R. (2005). Gender and Ageism. *Generations, 3,* 19–24. https://www.ingentaconnect.com/content/asag/gen/2005/00000029/00000003/art00005

Hawkins, G. (2013). Enacting Public Value on the ABC's Q&A: From Normative to Performative Approaches. *Media International Australia, 146*(1), 82–92. https://doi.org/10.1177/1329878X1314600112

Hayes, M., Ross, I., Gasher, M., & Gutstein, D. (2007). Telling Stories: News Media, Health Literacy and Public Policy in Canada. *Social Science & Medicine, 64*(9), 1842–1852. https://doi.org/10.1016/j.socscimed.2007.01.015

Heidkamp, B. & Kergel, D. (2017). "Media Change—Precarity Within and Precarity Through the Internet" (Chap. 2). Precarity within the Digital Age Media Change and Social Insecurity. Springer. Wiesbaden. Retrieved from: https://link-springer-com.wwwproxy1.library.unsw.edu.au/content/pdf/10.1007%2F978-3-658-17678-5.pdf

High, S. (2010). Telling Stories: A Reflection on Oral History and New Media. *Oral History, 38*(1), 101–112. https://primoa.library.unsw.edu.au/permalink/f/11jha62/TN_jstor_archive_840650320

Hoxha, A., Hanitzsch, T., Frère, M. S., & Meyer, C. (2018). How Conflict News Comes Into Being: Reconstructing 'Reality' Through Telling Stories. *Media, War & Conflict, 11*(1), 46–64. https://doi.org/10.1177/1750635217727313

Hurd, D. (1986). BBC Financing (Peacock Report). Hurd presentation to House of Commons debate 3 July 1986. UK Parliament. Vol. 100 cc1180–1193. Retrieved from: https://api.parliament.uk/historic-hansard/commons/1986/jul/03/bbc-financing-peacock-report

Ibarra, H., & Lineback, K. (2005, January). What's your story? *Harvard Business Review*. https://au.reachout.com/articles/the-importance-of-sharing-your-story

Inglis, K. (2006). *Whose ABC? The Australian Broadcasting Corporation 1983–2006*. Black Inc.

Kelso, A. (2007). Parliament and Political Disengagement: Neither Waving Nor Drowning. *Political Quarterly, 78*(3), 364–373. https://doi.org/10.1111/j.1467-923X.2007.00865.x

Knott, M. (2015, May 28). Everyone from Coalition Thinks ABC's Q&A Is Biased to the Left, Says LNP Senator James McGrath. *The Age*. https://www.theage.com.au/politics/federal/everyone-from-coalition...ed-to-the-left-says-lnp-senator-james-mcgrath-20150527-ghatyw.html

Knott, M., & Hunter, F. (2014, July 4). Partisan Appointments to ABC, SBS Selection Panel Crushed Rudd's Dream. *The Sydney Morning Herald*. https://www.smh.com.au/politics/federal/partisan-appointments-to-abc-sbs-selection-panel-crushes-rudds-dream-20140704-zsvkz.html

Kossen, C., & Pedersen, C. (2008). Older Workers in Australia: The Myths, the Realities and the Battle Over Workforce 'Flexibility'. *Journal of Management and Organization, 14*(1), 73–84. https://login.wwwproxy1.library.unsw.edu.au/login?qurl=https%3A%2F%2Fwww.proquest.com%2Fscholarly-journals%2Folder-workers-australia-myths-realities-battle%2Fdocview%2F233254008%2Fse-2%3Faccountid%3D12763

Kramer, L. (1983). This Is the ABC: The Australian Broadcasting Commission, 1932–1983 by Ken S. Inglis. *Australian Book Review, 56*. Melbourne University Press.

Lefebvre, H. (1991). *The Production of Space* (D. Nicholson-Smith, Trans.). Blackwell.

Leslie, T. (2010, January 21). Sky Falls on ABC's News Channel. *ABC News*. https://www.abc.net.au/news/2010-01-21/sky-falls-on-abcs-news-channel/1217718

Levine, M. (2018, June 26). ABC Most Trusted | Facebook Most Distrusted. *Roy Morgan*. Finding No. 7641. http://www.roymorgan.com/findings/7641-media-net-trust-june-2018-201806260239

Lewis, S. (2009, March 17). Rudd Vows Bipartisan ABC Board. *News.com.au*. https://www.news.com.au/national/rudd-vows-bipartisan-abc-board/news-story/ceac18bd56ef5ff51aed0b9b58140d1b?sv=8d7361759668930309443ad4dee66a24

Marquis, C. & Lounsbury, M. (2007). Vive La Resistance: Competing Logics and the Consolidation of US Community Banking. *Academy of Management Journal, 50*, 799–820. https://doi.org/10.5465/AMJ.2007.26279172

Mason, M., & Roddan, M. (2020, July 13). SBS Delves Deeper Into Back-Office Mergers than ABC. *The Australian Financial Review*. https://www.afr.com/

companies/media-and-marketing/sbs-delves-deeper-into-back-office-mergers-than-abc-20200708-p55a2c

McAllister, I., Cameron, S., & Sheppard, J.. (2016). *Australian Election Study. School of Politics and International Relations.* Australian National University. https://politicsir.cass.anu.edu.au/news/2016-australian-election-study

McChesney, R. W. (2008). *The Political Economy of Media: Enduring Issues, Emerging Dilemmas.* Monthly Review Press.

McMahon, A. (2020, September 4). The ABC and SBS Are Vital But Can Be Strengthened. Opinion. *Independent Australia.* https://independentaustralia.net/business/business-display/the-abc-and-sbs-are-vital-but-can-be-strengthened,14275

Meade, A., & Wahlquist, C. (2018, June 19). Australians Don't Want ABC Used as a 'Punching Bag', Michelle Guthrie Says. *The Guardian.* https://www.theguardian.com/media/2018/jun/19/australians-dont-want-abc-used-as-a-punching-bag-michelle-guthrie-says

Milne, J., & Guthrie, M. (2018). ABC Annual Report. Welcome. *Australian Broadcasting Corporation.* https://about.abc.net.au/wp-content/uploads/2018/10/AP18_Vol1_FINALnew.pdf

Miragliotta, N., & Errington, W. (2012). The Rise and Fall and Rise Again of Public Broadcasting? The Case of the Australian Broadcasting Corporation. *Australian Journal of Public Administration, 71*(1), 55–64. https://doi.org/10.1111/j.1467-8500.2012.00755.x

Moe, H. (2008). Public Service Media Online? Regulating Public Broadcasters' Internet Services—A Comparative Analysis. *Television & New Media, 9*(3), 220–238. https://doi.org/10.1177/1527476407307231

Molomby, T. (1991). *Is There a Moderate on the Roof? ABC Years.* William Heinemann.

Moore, M. H. (1995). *Creating Public Value: Strategic Management in Government.* Harvard University Press. Cambridge, Mass.

Murdock, G. (2004, November). Building the Digital Commons: Public Broadcasting in the Age of the Internet. University of Montreal. *The 2004 Spry Memorial Lecture.* https://www.researchgate.net/publication/254750526_BUILDING_THE_DIGITAL_COMMONS_PUBLIC_BROADCASTING_IN_THE_AGE_OF_THE_INTERNET

Murdoch, J. (2009). THE ABSENCE OF TRUST. 2009 Edinburgh International Television Festival. *MacTaggart Lecture.* 29 August 2009. Retrieved from: https://www.abc.net.au/mediawatch/transcripts/0937_mactaggart.pdf

Naughton, J. (2020, February 16). Reports of Social Media's Influence on Voters Are Greatly Exaggerated. *The Guardian.* https://www.theguardian.com/commentisfree/2020/feb/15/reports-of-social-media-influence-on-voters-are-greatly-exaggerated

Norris, P. (2000). *A Virtuous Circle: Political Communications in Post-industrial Societies*. Cambridge University Press.

Oakman, D. (2010). *Facing Asia: A History of the Colombo Plan*. ANC Press. Canberra.

Osborne, S., Brandsen, T., Mele, V., Nemec, J., van Genugten, M. & Flemig, S. (2020). Risking innovation. Understanding risk and public service innovation-evidence from a four nation study. *Public Money & Management*. *40*(1), 52–62. https://doi.org/10.1080/09540962.2019.1621051

Patterson, R. (2004). The Eradication of Compulsory Retirement and Age Discrimination in the Australian Workplace: A Cause for Celebration and Concern. *Elder Law Review, 10*(3), 65. http://classic.austlii.edu.au/au/journals/ElderLawRw/2004/10.html

Powell, M. J. (nd). People of Australia Ethnic groups. *Britannica*. Retrieved from: https://www.britannica.com/place/Australia/Manufacturing

Powell, W. W. & DiMaggio, P. J. (1991). The New Institutionalism and Organisational Analysis. Chapter 10. R. Friedland and R.R. Alford. "Bringing Society Back" In *Symbols, Practices and Institutional Contradictions*. University of Chicago Press. Chicago.

Ramachandran, V. S. (2003). The Emerging Mind. The Reith Lectures 2003. *British Broadcasting Corporation*. https://www.bbc.co.uk/radio4/reith2003/

Reach.out. (2020). The Importance of Sharing Your Stories. *Reach.out*. https://au.reachout.com/articles/the-importance-of-sharing-your-story

Reporters Sans Frontières. (2020). 2020 World Press Freedom Index. Reporters Sans Frontières. https://rsf.org/en/ranking

SBS News. (2019). Public servants must be accountable to the 'quiet Australians': PM. SBS News. 19 August 2019. Retrieved from: https://www.sbs.com.au/news/public-servants-must-be-accountable-to-the-quiet-australians-pm

Scannell, P. (1989). Public Service Broadcasting and Modern Public Life. *Media, Culture & Society, 11*(2), 135–166. https://doi.org/10.1177/016344389011002002

Schiller, H. I. (1993, July 12). Public Way or Private Road? *The Nation, 257*(2), 64–66. http://search.proquest.com/docview/231453434/

Sehl, A., Cornia, A., Graves, L., & Nielsen, R. K. (2019). Newsroom Integration as an Organizational Challenge. *Journalism Studies, 20*(9), 1238–1259. https://doi.org/10.1080/1461670X.2018.1507684

Semmler, C. (1981). *The ABC—Aunt Sally and Sacred Cow*. Melbourne University Press.

Sheridan-Burns, L., & McKee, A. (1999). Reporting on Indigenous Issues: Some Practical Suggestions for Improving Journalistic Practice in the Coverage of Indigenous Affairs. *Australian Journalism Review: AJR, 21*(2), 103–116. https://eprints.qut.edu.au/14959/1/14959.pdf

Skålén, P., Karlsson, J., Engen, M. & Magnusson, P.R. (2018). Understanding Public Service Innovation as Resource Integration and Creation of Value Propositions. *Australian Journal of Public Administration, 77*(4), 700–714. https://doi.org/10.1111/1467-8500.12308

Snell, P. (2010). Emerging Adult Civic and Political Disengagement: A Longitudinal Analysis of Lack of Involvement With Politics. *Journal of Adolescent Research, 25*(2), 258–287.

South Coast Times and Wollongong Argus. (1948). Church Festival. A.B.C. Chief Stresses Spiritual Values. 13 May 1948, p. 14. Retrieved from: https://trove.nla.gov.au/newspaper/article/142229895?searchTerm=ABC%20values

Spadaro, S. J. A. (2020, January 20). Defy the Apocalypse. *La Civilta Cattolica*. https://www.laciviltacattolica.com/defy-the-apocalypse/

Standing, G. (2011). *The Precariat: The New Dangerous Class*. Bloomsbury Academic. https://doi.org/10.5040/9781849664554

Standing, G. (2018, October). The Precariat: Today's Transformative Class? [online]. *Great Transition Initiative*. https://www.greattransition.org/publication/precariat-transformative-class

Stutchbury, H. (2018, June 18). The ABC Is an Indulgence We Can No Longer Afford. *The Sydney Morning Herald*. https://www.smh.com.au/business/companies/the-abc-is-an-indulgence-we-can-no-longer-afford-20180618-p4zm6y.html

Sydney Morning Herald, The. (1931, November 16). Broadcasting. *The Sydney Morning Herald*, p. 8. https://trove.nla.gov.au/newspaper/article/16823317?searchTerm=%22improved%20and%20freed%20from%20all%20the%20evils%2C%20real%20or%20imaginary%2C%20of%20private%20enterprise%22

Terjesen, S., Aguilera, R. V., & Lorenz, R. (2014). Legislating a Woman's Seat on the Board: Institutional Factors Driving Gender Quotas for Boards of Directors. *Journal of Business Ethics, 128*(2), 233–251. https://doi.org/10.1007/s10551-014-2083-1

Thomson, I. T. (2015). *Culture Wars and Enduring American Dilemmas*. Project MUSE. Baltimore, Md.

Thornton, P. (2001). Personal versus market logics of control: A historically contingent theory of the risk of acquisition. *Organization Science, 12*(3), 294–311. https://doi.org/10.1287/orsc.12.3.294.10100

Thornton, P. (2002). The rise of the corporation in a craft industry: Conflict and conformity in institutional logics. *Academy of Management Journal, 45*, 81–101. https://doi.org/10.2307/3069286

Thornton, P., & Ocasio, W. (1999). Institutional Logics and the Historical Contingency of Power in Organizations: Executive Succession in the Higher Education Publishing Industry, 1958–1990. *American Journal of Sociology, 105*(3), 801–843. https://doi.org/10.1086/210361

Tracey, M. (1998, reprinted 2002). *The Decline and Fall of Public Service Broadcasting*. Oxford University Press.

UK Government. (1962). *Report of the Committee on Broadcasting. The Pilkington Report on Broadcasting* (p. 18). UK Government. https://api.parliament.uk/historic-hansard/lords/1962/jul/18/the-pilkington-report-on-broadcasting

UNESCO. (2012, February 15). *Public Service Broadcasting*. http://www.unesco.org/new/en/communication-and-information/media-development/public-service-broadcasting/

Walker, R. R. (1973). *The Magic Spark: Fifty Years of Radio in Australia*. The Hawthorn Press.

Waters, J. (2020, September 5). ABC News Needs to Find a New Way to Chase Ratings. Opinion. *Independent Australia*. https://independentaustralia.net/business/business-display/abc-news-needs-to-find-a-new-way-to-chase-ratings,14279

Watson, D. (2014, March). The Conservative Crusade Against the *ABC. The Monthly*. https://www.themonthly.com.au/issue/2014/march/1393592400/don-watson/conservative-crusade-against-abc#mtr

Weisblott, M. (2013). CBC Music Radio Stations Will Now Have a Word or Two From Their Sponsors. *Canada.com*. https://o.canada.com/business/cbc-radio-commercial-advertising-approved

Whitehead, G. (1988). *Inside the ABC: Geoffrey Whitehead's Personal Account*. Penguin Books Victoria.

Williams, R. (1996). *Normal Service Won't Be Resumed: The Future of Public Broadcasting*. Allen and Unwin. Sydney.

Wilson, C. K., Hutchinson, J., & Shea, P. (2010). Public Service Broadcasting, Creative Industries, and Innovation Infrastructure: The Case of ABC's Pool. *Australian Journal of Communication, 37*(3), 15–32. https://primoa.library.unsw.edu.au/permalink/f/11jha62/TN_informit_apaft201102742

Windrum, P., & Koch, P. (2008). Innovation in public sector services: Entrepreneurship, creativity and management. ProQuest Ebook Central https://ebookcentral.proquest.com

Worrall, L. (2000). Surviving Redundancy: The Perceptions of UK Managers. *Journal of Managerial Psychology., 15*(5-6), 460–472.

References

2018 Edelman Trust Barometer. (2018). *Global Report*. Edelman. https://www.edelman.com/sites/g/files/aatuss191/files/2018-10/2018_Edelman_Trust_Barometer_Global_Report_FEB.pdf

Aagaard, P. (2016). How to Make the Mix Matter: A Case Study of Post-Transformational Leadership in Hybrid Public Management. *International Journal of Public Administration, 39*(14), 1171–1179. https://doi.org/10.1080/01900692.2015.1072211

AAP FactCheck. (2018). Investigation: Has the Level of Casual Employment in the Australian Workforce Not Changed for Two Decades? *The Herald Sun*. https://www.heraldsun.com.au/blogs/andrew-bolt/more-abc-staff-less-value/news-story/e6f8bc5271a1f93606b916a39bddd1b8

ABC. (2013). Guidelines for Personal Use of Social Media. [online]. Document: D11/22627. http://about.abc.net.au/wp-content/uploads/2014/10/PersonalUseOfSocialMediaINS1.pdf

ABC. (2014). GUIDELINES FOR PERSONAL USE OF SOCIAL MEDIA. [online]. Document: D11/22627. Retrieved from: http://about.abc.net.au/wpcontent/uploads/2014/10/PersonalUseOfSocialMediaINS1.pdf. NOTE: now a dead link.

ABC. (2018, June). *The Cost of Being the ABC: Delivering the Best and Most Efficient Public Broadcasting*. http://www.abc.net.au/cm/lb/9944818/data/the-cost-of-being-the-abc-data.pdf

V. Small, *Strangling Aunty: Perilous Times for the Australian Broadcasting Corporation*,
https://doi.org/10.1007/978-981-16-0776-9

ABC. (2020, April). *Interview ABC News24. Strapline: "Pell Released. George Pell Freed from Prison After High Court ruling"*. https://www.youtube.com/watch?v=7x29VznAZOE

ABC. (n.d., June 1). *Frank Dixon*. Australian Broadcasting Corporation. https://www.abc.net.au/news/2017-06-01/frank-dixon/8576568

ABC MediaWatch. (2018, February 19). Taxing Times. *ABC*. https://www.abc.net.au/mediawatch/episodes/taxing-times-at-the-abc/9972348

ABC. (2017). How do you feel about the date of the Hottest 100? *Triple J. Australian Broadcasting Corporation*. 2 August 2017. Retrieved from: https://www.abc.net.au/triplej/news/musicnews/h100-survey/87645

ABC. (2010, September 15). *Interview with John Menadue on the Role of The Australian in the Federal Election Campaign*. Radio 2BL Sydney, Australian Broadcasting Corporation, Broadcast.

ABC Alumni. (n.d.). New Campaign Underway to Rebuild ABC International Service. *ABC Alumni*.https://www.abcalumni.net/news-and-views/our-voice-to-the-world

ABC Online. (2020, March 15). Dr Norman Swan Recommends 'Severe' Shutdowns. *Australian Broadcasting Corporation*.https://www.abc.net.au/news/2020-03-15/dr-norman-swan-recommends-proactive-national-lockdown/12057956

ABC News. (2018, February 6). Backstory: What ABC News Cadets Learnt in Their First Week. *ABC News*. https://www.abc.net.au/news/about/backstory/news-coverage/2018-02-06/what-abc-news-cadets-learnt-in-their-first-week/9400864

Abdel-Magied, Y. (2017). What Are They so Afraid of? I'm Just a Young Brown Muslim Woman Speaking my Mind. *The Guardian*. 6 July 2017. Retrieved from: https://www.theguardian.com/australia-news/2017/jul/06/what-are-they-so-afraid-of-im-just-a-young-brown-muslim-woman-speaking-my-mind

Abebe, M., & Tangpong, C. (2017). Founder-CEOs and Corporate Turnaround Among Declining Firms: Founder CEOs and Turnaround. *Corporate Governance an International Review, 26*(3). https://doi.org/10.1111/corg.12216

ACCC. (2019, June). *Digital Platforms Enquiry*. Final Report. ACCA. https://www.accc.gov.au/system/files/Digital%20platforms%20inquiry%20-%20final%20report.pdf

Accetti, C. I., Mulieri, A., Buchstein, H., Castiglione, D., Disch, L., Frank, J., & Urbinati, N. (2016). Debating Representative Democracy. *Contemporary Political Theory, 15*(2), 205–242. https://doi.org/10.1057/cpt.2015.57

Advertiser, The. (1937, October 16). Vigorous Defence of ABC Policy "We Remain Serene Under Sneers" Not Gods, says Mr Cleary Broadcast at Opening of New Station. *The Advertiser, Adelaide*, p. 26. https://trove.nla.gov.au/

newspaper/article/36379142?searchTerm=%22a%20banquet%20of%20interests%2C%20from%20which%20we%20hope%20you%20will%20never%20turn%20away%20unsatisfied%22&searchLimits=

Advertiser, The. (1941, October 21). Newspapers and Radio: Ownership of Stations Defended, p. 8. https://trove.nla.gov.au/newspaper/article/44962736?searchTerm=Newspapers%20radio%20stations

Advertiser, The. (Adelaide). (1944, September 11). Haydn Beck's Resignation: ABC Manager's Explanation. *The Advertiser*, p. 6. https://trove.nla.gov.au/newspaper/article/43219618?searchTerm=Haydn%20Beck%E2%80%99s%20resignation

Advertiser, The. (1946, 19 June). ABC Service. *The Advertiser, Adelaide*, p. 8. https://trove.nla.gov.au/newspaper/article/35700411?searchTerm=ABC%20service

Advertiser, The (Adelaide). (1939). A.B.C. Concerts To Aid Patriotic Funds. The Advertiser (Adelaide). 13 October 1939, p. 20. Retrieved from: https://trove.nla.gov.au/newspaper/article/49819562?searchTerm=ABC%20patriotic&searchLimits=

Age, The. (1854, October 17). First Edition. *The Age*, p. 4

Age, The. (1951). Misusing Public Money, A.B.C. Told. The Age (Melbourne). 11 December, 1951, p. 3. Retrieved from: https://trove.nla.gov.au/newspaper/article/205663971?searchTerm=wrongly%20using%20public%20funds%20for%20orchestral%20concerts

Age, The. (2002). Japanese Invasion a Myth: Historian. *The Age*.https://www.theage.com.au/national/japanese-invasion-a-myth-historian-20020601-gdu9c8.html

Age, The. (2016, 2014, May 3). Cultural Relevance Not as Easy as ABC. *The Age*. First Published 2014. https://www.theage.com.au/national/act/cultural-relevance-not-as-easy-as-abc-20160503-gokn6d.html

AIJAC Staff. (2018, November 26). Submission to Senate Standing Committee on Environment and Communications' Inquiry Into Allegations of Political Interference in the ABC (Including the Termination of the Managing Director, Michelle Guthrie, conduct of the Chair and Board, and governance of the ABC). *Australia/Israel and Jewish Affairs Council*. https://aijac.org.au/resource/aijac-inquiry-abc-bias-israel/

Al Jazeera. (2020, June 15). 'Decisive Measures' in Beijing as Coronavirus Cases Spike: Live Blog. *Al Jazeera*. https://www.aljazeera.com/news/2020/06/measures-beijing-coronavirus-cases-spike-live-200614233622226.html

Alberici, E. (2018). Why Many Big Companies Don't Pay Corporate Tax. *Australian Broadcasting Corporation*. Posted 14 February 2018. Retrieved February 16, 2018, from https://www.abc.net.au/news/2018-02-14/why-many-big-companies-dont-pay-corporate-tax/9443840

Alexander, J. (2014). Notes Towards a Definition of Politics. *Philosophy, 89*(348), 273–300. https://doi.org/10.1017/S0031819113000855

Alexander, P. (2021). Australia Post's worst nightmare: Christine Holgate to head delivery rival Global Express. *The Conversation*. 10 May 2021. Retrieved from: https://theconversation.com/australia-posts-worst-nightmare-christine-holgate-to-head-delivery-rival-global-express-160606

Alcock, J., & Docwra, G. (2005, October). A Simulation Analysis of the Market Effect of the Australian Broadcasting Corporation. *Information Economics and Policy, 17*(4), 407–427. https://www-sciencedirect-com.ezproxy1.library.usyd.edu.au/science/article/pii/S0167624505000193

Alford, J., & O'Flynn, J. (2009). Making Sense of Public Value: Concepts, Critiques and Emergent Meanings. *International Journal of Public Administration, 32*, 171–191.

Alfrey, L., & Twine, F. W. (2017). Gender-Fluid Geek Girls: Negotiating Inequality Regimes in the Tech Industry. *Gender & Society, 31*(1), 28–50. https://doi.org/10.1177/0891243216680590

Altheide, D. L. (1996). *Qualitative Media Analysis (Qualitative Research Methods. 38)*. Sage Publications.

Altheide, D. L. (2002). *Creating Fear: News and the Construction of Crisis*. Aldine de Gruyter. New York.

Altheide, D. & Schneider, C. (2013). Process of qualitative document analysis. In D. Altheide & C. Schneider. Qualitative Media Analysis. Pp. 38–74. SAGE Publications. London. p. 41. Retrieved from: https://doi.org/10.4135/9781452270043.

Alvarez, P. C., Andujar, C. S. D. B., Curiel, E. H., & Serrano, N. L. (2012). Journalism and Social Media: How Spanish Journalists are Using Twitter. *Estudios Sobre el Mensaje Periodistico, 18*(1), 31–53. https://doi.org/10.5209/revULESMP.2012.v18.n1.39353

Alysen, B. (2012). *The Electronic Reporter: Broadcast Journalism in Australia*. UNSW Press.

Amans, P., Mazars-Chapelon, A., & Villesèque-Dubus, F. (2015). Budgeting in Institutional Complexity: The Case of Performing Arts Organizations. *Management Accounting Research, 27*, 47–66. https://doi.org/10.1016/j.mar.2015.03.001

Amenta, E., & Ramsey, K. M. (2010). Institutional Theory. In K. T. Leicht & J. C. Jenkins (Eds.), *Handbook of Politics: State and Society in Global Perspective*. Springer. https://doi.org/10.1007/978-0-387-68930-2_2

Anand, B., & Attea, K. (2003). In M. Monaghan & S. Prideaux (Eds.) (2016), *State Crime and Immorality: The Corrupting Influence of the Powerful* (p. 140). Polity Press.

Andén-Papadopoulos, K. (2008). The Abu Ghraib Torture Photographs: News Frames, Visual Culture, and the Power of Images. *Journalism, 9*(1), 5–30. https://doi.org/10.1177/1464884907084337

Anderson, B. (1983). *Imagined Communities: Reflections on the Origin and Spread of Nationalism*. Verso.

Anderson, D. (2019). ABC Annual Report 2019. *ABC*.https://about.abc.net.au/wp-content/uploads/2019/10/ABC-Annual-Report-201819v2.pdf

Anderson, N., & Schlunke, K. E. (2008). *Cultural Theory in Everyday Practice*. Oxford University Press.

Andreassen, C., Pallesen, S., & Griffiths, M. (2017). The Relationship Between Addictive Use of Social Media, Narcissism, and Self-Esteem: Findings from a Large National Survey. *Addictive Behaviors, 64*, 287–293. https://doi.org/10.1016/j.addbeh.2016.03.006

Andrejevic, M. (2013). Public Service Media Utilities: Rethinking Search Engines and Social Networking as Public Goods. *Media International Australia, Incorporating Culture & Policy, 146*, 123–132. http://web.a.ebscohost.com.wwwproxy1.library.unsw.edu.au/ehost/pdfviewer/pdfviewer?vid=2&sid=68647279-624f-4ba5-9fda-d25caae82e74%40sdc-v-sessmgr02

Andrews, R., Boyne, G. A., & Walker, R. M. (2012). Overspending in Public Organizations: Does Strategic Management Matter? *International Public Management Journal, 15*(1), 39–61. https://doi.org/10.1080/10967494.2012.684017

Angell, N. (1922). *The Press and the Organisation of Society*. The Labour Publishing Company Limited.

Angell, N. (1933). *From Chaos to Control*. Halley Stewart Lecture 1932. Unwin Brothers Limited. Woking.

Anstead, N., & O'Loughlin, B. (2015). Social Media Analysis and Public Opinion: The 2010 UK General Election. *Journal of Computer-Mediated Communication, 20*(2), 204–220. https://doi.org/10.1111/jcc4.12102

Anthony, S. (1982). Leonie Kramer Takes on a New Challenge at the ABC. *The Australian Women's Weekly*. 27 January 1982, p. 13. Retrieved from: https://trove.nla.gov.au/newspaper/article/52620089?searchTerm=Leonie%20kramer%20ABC

Arena, M., Azzone, G., & Mapelli, F. (2017). What Drives the Evolution of Corporate Social Responsibility Strategies? An Institutional Logics Perspective. *Journal of Cleaner Production, 171*, 345–355. https://www.sciencedirect.com/science/article/abs/pii/S0959652617322576

Arendt, H. (1968). *The Origins of Totalitarianism*. Harvest Book.

Argus, The. (1937, April 15). Higher Costs Expected. Newspaper Industry. President's Review. Future of Paper Making. *The Argus, Melbourne*, p. 12. https://trove.nla.gov.au/newspaper/article/11056793?searchTerm=The%20complete%20supremacy%20of%20newspapers%20as%20an%20advertising%20medium%20was%20unchallenged%20and%20was%20candidly%20admitted%20by%20all%20leading%20advertisers%20throughout%20the%20country

Argus, The. (1944, September 7). Resignation of Mr Haydn Beck: ABC Methods Criticised. *The Argus*, p. 7. https://trove.nla.gov.au/newspaper/article/11360062?searchTerm=haydn%20beck%20ABC&searchLimits=exactPhrase|||anyWords|||notWords|||requestHandler|||dateFrom=1940-01-01|||dateTo=1945-12-31|||sortby

Ariño, M., & Ahlert, C. (2004). Beyond Broadcasting: The Digital Future of Public Service Broadcasting. *Prometheus, 22*(4), 393–410. https://doi.org/10.1080/0810902041233l311678

Aristotle. (2007). *On Rhetoric* (G. A. Kennedy, Trans.). Book 1. Chapter 1, pp. 31–32, 2nd ed. Oxford University Press.

Arora, N. D. (2010). *Political Science for Civil Services Main Examination.* McGraw Hill.

Arsenault, A., & Castells, M. (2008). Switching Power: Rupert Murdoch and the Global Business of Media Politics: A Sociological Analysis. *International Sociology, 23*(4), 488–513. https://doi.org/10.1177/0268580908090725

Artwick, C. (2013). Reporters on Twitter. *Digital Journalism, 1*(2), 212–228. https://doi.org/10.1080/21670811.2012.744555

Arunchand, C. H., & Ramanathan, H. N. (2013). Organizational Culture and Employee Morale: A Public Sector Enterprise Experience. *Journal of Strategic Human Resource Management, 2*(1), 1–8. http://search.proquest.com/docview/1478029898/

Ashbolt, A. (1986). Keynote 4: The Age of Cultural Confusion [online]. In W. Bourne, (Ed.), *Proceedings: Sixth National Conference of the Australian Society for Music Education. Australia Makes Music; Action for a Changing Society* (pp. 38–43). Australian Society for Music Education. https://primoa.library.unsw.edu.au/permalink/f/11jha62/TN_informit444911808726330

Askeland, H., Espedal, G., Jelstad Løvaas, B., & Sirris, S. (Eds.). (2020). *Understanding Values Work: Institutional Perspectives in Organizations and Leadership.* eBook. Springer International. https://primoa.library.unsw.edu.au/primo-explore/fulldisplay?docid=UNSW_ALMA51279111340001731&context=L&vid=UNSWS&lang=en_US&search_scope=SearchFirst&adaptor=Local%20Search%20Engine&tab=default_tab&query=any,contains,institutional%20leadership&offset=0

Atherton, B. (2012, November 13). Pell Accuses Press of Exaggerating Catholic Abuse. *ABC.* https://www.abc.net.au/news/2012-11-13/pell-accuses-press-of-exaggerating-catholic-abuse/4369214

Auletta, K. (2009). *Googled: The End of the World As We Know It.* Virgin Books.

Aufderheide, P., Boyles, J. L., & Bieze, K. (2013). Copyright, Free Speech, and The Public's Right to Know. *Journalism Studies, 14*(6), 875–890. https://doi.org/10.1080/1461670X.2012.739320

Auger, G. (2013). Fostering Democracy Through Social Media: Evaluating Diametrically Opposed Nonprofit Advocacy Organizations' Use of Facebook, Twitter, and YouTube. *Public Relations Review, 39*, 369–376. https://doi.org/10.1016/j.pubrev.2013.07.013

Australia Post. (n.d.). Heritage Strategy Australia Post Heritage Places. *Corporate Infrastructure Services Division – CRE.* Retrieved from: https://auspost.com.au/content/dam/auspost_corp/media/documents/heritage-strategy.pdf

Australian Broadcasting Corporation Annual Report. (2019). *ABC*. https://about.abc.net.au/wp-content/uploads/2019/10/ABC-Annual-Report-201819v2.pdf

Australian Broadcasting Corporation. (2006). ABC Managing Director to leave the Corporation. 20 January 2006. Retrieved from: https://about.abc.net.au/press-releases/abc-managing-director-to-leave-the-corporation/

Australian Broadcasting Corporation. (2015). Mark Scott confirms he will step down as ABC Managing Director in 2016. 14 September 2015. Retrieved from: https://www.abc.net.au/news/2015-09-14/mark-scott-abc-managing-director-announces-he-will-step-down/6774236

Australian Broadcasting Commission. Annual Report. (1940–41). ABC Research Archives. *Australian Broadcasting Commission*.

Australian Broadcasting Commission. (1941). Annual Report (1940–41). Year ended 30 June 1941. Accessed with permission of the ABC.

Australian Contemporary Dictionary, The. (1970). *Collins*. Sydney.

Australian Public Service Commission. (2010). Empowering Change: Fostering Innovation in the Australian Public Service—report by the Management Advisory Committee. P. iii. In: Creed, A. (2011). Organisational Behaviour, Oxford University Press. ProQuest Ebook Central. http://ebookcentral.proquest.com/lib/unsw/detail.action?docID=1985999.

Australian Rationalist. (2016). Destroying the ABC.100. Autumn, pp. 40–41. https://search-informit-com-au.wwwproxy1.library.unsw.edu.au/fullText;dn=20190613012323;res=AGISPT

Australian Associated Press. (2018, October 2). ABC Board Lacks Media Experience: Analyst. *The Newcastle Herald*. https://www.newcastleherald.com.au/story/5678912/abc-board-lacks-media-experience-analyst/send-us-your-news/

Australian Broadcasting Corporation. (2017). Annual Report. *Australian Broadcasting Corporation*. Retrieved from: https://parlinfo.aph.gov.au/parlInfo/search/display/display.w3p;query=Id:%22publications/tabled-papers/c076fdb2-284f-4459-80d1-0af26c9821ff%22

Australian Broadcasting Corporation. (2019a, March 4). Guilty: The Conviction of Cardinal Pell. Four Corners. *Australian Broadcasting Corporation*. https://www.abc.net.au/4corners/guilty:-the-conviction-of-cardinal-pell/10869116

Australian Broadcasting Corporation. (2019b, August 21). Victorian Chief Justice Says Pell "Is Not to Be Made a Scapegoat". *Australian Broadcasting Corporation*. https://www.abc.net.au/news/2019-08-21/judge-says-pell-isnt-to-be-made-scapegoat/11434086

Australian Broadcasting Corporation. (2020). Cardinal Pell. *Corrections and Clarifications*. 2 November 2020. Retrieved from: https://www.abc.net.au/news/corrections/2020-11-02/cardinal-pell/12839220

Australian Broadcasting Corporation. (2021, January 4). Julian Assange's Extradition to the US Rejected by UK Court Over Mental Health Fears. https://www.abc.net.au/news/2021-01-04/julian-assange-wont-be-extradited-to-the-us-uk-court-rules/13030240

Australian Broadcasting Corporation. (2021). Personal Use of Social Media Guidelines. ABC People and Culture. March 2021. Retrieved from: https://about.abc.net.au/wp-content/uploads/2021/03/Final-Personal-use-social-media-guidelines.pdf

Australian Broadcasting Corporation. (2017). Annual Report. *Australian Broadcasting Corporation*. Retrieved from: https://parlinfo.aph.gov.au/parlInfo/search/display/display.w3p;query=Id:%22publications/tabled-papers/c076fdb2-284f-4459-80d1-0af26c9821ff%22

Australian Broadcasting Corporation Media Centre. (2010). New Social Media Reporter for ABC News In Canberra. 13 December 2010. Retrieved from: http://about.abc.net.au/press-releases/new-social-media-reporter-for-abc-news-in-canberra/ Please note: Link removed.

Australian Broadcasting Commission. Annual Report. (1932–33). ABC Research Archives. *Australian Broadcasting Commission*.

Australian Broadcasting Commission. Annual Report. (1939–1940). ABC Research Archives. *Australian Broadcasting Commission*.

Australian Broadcasting Corporation. (2011, September 20). *MPs Angered over Gillard Satire Sex Scene*. https://www.abc.net.au/news/2011-09-20/mps-angered-over-gillard-satire-sex-scene/2908158

Australian Broadcasting Corporation. (2020, March 16). Q and A. Transcript. Australian Broadcasting Corporation. https://www.abc.net.au/qanda/2020-16-03/12040520

Australian Broadcasting Corporation News. (2020, March 14). Coronavirus: Dr. Norman Swan Recommends Proactive National Lockdown. *Australian Broadcasting Corporation. You Tube*. https://www.youtube.com/watch?v=znJ9RD8gYsQ

Australian Bureau of Statistics. (2019, November). Average Weekly Earnings, Australia. 6302.0.

Australian Financial Review, The. (2020, April 8). Pell's Acquittal Is Justice Served. *The Australian Financial Review*.https://www.afr.com/politics/federal/pell-s-acquittal-is-justice-served-20200407-p54hzs

Australian Broadcasting Corporation Annual Report. (2018). *ABC*. https://about.abc.net.au/reports-publications/2017-18-annual-report/

Australian Broadcasting Corporation Annual Report. (2019). *ABC*. https://about.abc.net.au/wp-content/uploads/2019/10/ABC-Annual-Report-201819v2.pdf

Australian Competition and Consumer Commission. (2019, June). Digital Platforms Inquiry. Final Report. *Australian Competition and Consumer*

Commission. https://www.accc.gov.au/system/files/Digital%20platforms%20inquiry%20-%20final%20report.pdf

Australian Communications and Media Authority. (2020). 2019 Investigations. https://www.acma.gov.au/investigations-tv-broadcasters#outcome-of-our-2019-investigations

Australian Council of Trade Unions. (2019, October 21). Report Shows ABC Wage Theft from Casuals of $22.9 Million. https://www.google.com/search?client=safari&rls=en&q=ABC+staff+casual&ie=UTF-8&oe=UTF-8

Australian Government. (1996, June). Commonwealth Competitive Neutrality Policy Statement. https://www.pc.gov.au/about/core-functions/competitive-neutrality/commonwealth-competitive-neutrality-policy-statement-1996.pdf

Australian Financial Review, The. (2019, January 1). Sydney's Record-Breaking $5.8 Million Fireworks Display Welcomes 2019. https://www.afr.com/politics/sydneys-recordbreaking-58-million-fireworks-display-welcomes-2019-20190101-h19l95

Australian Government. (2019). Budget 2019–2020. *Australian Government*. https://budget.gov.au/2019-20/content/overview.htm

AUSTRALIAN PARLIAMENT. (2003, October 15). *Fortieth Parliament First Session—Sixth Period*. https://parlinfo.aph.gov.au/parlInfo/download/chamber/hansards/2003-10-15/toc_pdf/2939-2.pdf;fileType=application%2Fpdf#search=%22chamber/hansards/2003-10-15/0000%22

Australian Strategic Policy Institute (2020). Covid-19 Disinformation & Social Media Manipulation. 27 October 2020. Retrieved from: https://www.aspi.org.au/report/covid-19-disinformation

Australian, The. (2020, February 11). Editorial. Time to End Free Lunch for Google and Facebook. *The Australian*. https://www.theaustralian.com.au/commentary/editorials/time-to-end-free-lunch-for-google-and-facebook/news-story/f84c88b4dd86f54b5cc4397ba07d9cc7

Bagshaw, E. (2019, August 7). Kenneth Hayne: Trust in Politics Has Been Destroyed. *The Sydney Morning Herald*. https://www.smh.com.au/politics/federal/kenneth-hayne-trust-in-politics-has-been-destroyed-20190807-p52evf.html

Baghramian, M., & Carter, J. A. (2015. September). Relativism. *Stanford Encyclopedia of Philosophy*. https://plato.stanford.edu/entries/relativism/

Bailey, R. (2018). When Journalism and Satire Merge: The Implications for Impartiality, Engagement and 'Post-Truth' Politics—A UK Perspective on the Serious Side of US TV Comedy. *European Journal of Communication, 33*(2), 200–213. https://doi.org/10.1177/0267323118760322

Banjac, S. & Hanusch, F. (2020). A Question of Perspective: Exploring Audiences' views of Journalistic Boundaries. *New Media & Society*, 1–19. https://doi.org/10.1177/1461444820963795

Barnidge, M. (2015). The Role of News in Promoting Political Disagreement on Social Media. *Computers in Human Behavior, 52*, 211–218. https://doi.org/10.1016/j.chb.2015.06.011

Bainbridge, A. (2018, October 9). ABC Crisis Shows Need for Independent and Democratised Public Broadcaster [online]. *Green Left Weekly*. 1198, p. 10. https://search-informit-com-au.ezproxy1.library.usyd.edu.au/documentSummary;dn=935516978501507;res=IELHSS

Banet-Weiser, S. (2012). Authentic(tm): The Politics of Ambivalence in a Brand Culture, New York University Press. ProQuest Ebook Central. https://ebookcentral.proquest.com/lib/unsw/detail.action?docID=865546.

Banerjee, I., & Seneviratne, K. (2006). *Public Service Broadcasting in the Age of Globalization*. Asian Media Information and Communication Centre. Nanyang Technological University.

Bandler, J., & Merzon, A. (2020). Cybercrime Investigations: The Comprehensive Resource for Everyone (1st ed.). CRC Press. Taylor and Francis Group. Boca Raton, FL.

Bardoel, J. (2007). in J. Bardoel & G. F. Lowe (2007). From Public Service Broadcasting to Public Service Media: The Core Challenge. *From Public Service Broadcasting to Public Service Media*, 9–26. Nordicom. Göteburg.

Barley, S. R., & Tolbert, P. S. (1997). Institutionalization and Structuration: Studying the Links Between Action and Institution. *Organization Studies, 18*(1), 93–117. https://doi.org/10.1177/017084069701800106

Barratt, S. (2018). Reinforcing Sexism and Misogyny: Social Media, Symbolic Violence and the Construction of Femininity-as-Fail. *Journal of International Women's Studies, 19*(3), 16–31. http://search.proquest.com/docview/2057939820/

Barrett, A. W., & Barrington, L. W. (2005). Is a Picture Worth a Thousand Words?: Newspaper Photographs and Voter Evaluations of Political Candidates. *Harvard International Journal of Press/Politics, 10*(4), 98–113. https://doi.org/10.1177/1081180X05281392

Barrett, A. W., & Barrington, L. W. (2005). Is a Picture Worth a Thousand Words?: Newspaper Photographs and Voter Evaluations of Political Candidates. *Harvard International Journal of Press/Politics, 10*(4), 98–113. https://doi.org/10.1177/1081180X05281392

Barrier Miner, Broken Hill. (1938, July 5). How ABC learns of Public Opinion. *The Barrier Miner*, p. 4. https://trove.nla.gov.au/newspaper/article/47976010?searchTerm=How%20ABC%20learns%20of%20public%20opinion

Barry, P. (2013). *Breaking News: Sex, Lies and the Murdoch Succession*. Allen and Unwin.

Barry, P. (2018, June 25). MediaWatch. *Australian Broadcasting Corporation*. https://www.abc.net.au/mediawatch/episodes/privatising-the-abc/9972184

Barsamian, D. (2001). *The Decline and Fall of Public Broadcasting* (2nd ed.). Southend Press.

Barthes, R. (1977). *Image Music Text* (S. Heath, Trans.). Fontana Books.

Baumann, M. (2010). @twitter Discloses Business Model #promotedtweets RT. *Information Today, 27*(6), 1–46. http://search.proquest.com/docview/357026026/

Beachy, R. N. (2003, January 24). IP Policies and Serving the Public. *Editorial. Science, 299*(5606), 473. https://libkey.io/libraries/757/articles/13426582/full-text-file?utm_source=api_231

Beaglehole, P. (2018). What Matters?: Talking Value in Australian Culture. *Transnational Literature, 11*(1). http://search.proquest.com/docview/2164085415/

Beazley, M. J. (2016, August). Institutional Leadership Amongst Equals. *Judicial Officers Bulletin, 28*(7), 65–69. https://search-informit-com-au.wwwproxy1.library.unsw.edu.au/documentSummary;dn=268275964401160;res=IELAPA

Beharrell, P., Davis, H., Eldridge, J, Hewitt, J., Oddie, J., & Philo, G. (1976). Bad News. In *Theory and Society* (vol. 3, p. 3). Glasgow University Media Group. Routledge & Kegan Paul.

Behn, R. D. (1980). Leadership in an Era of Retrenchment. *Public Administration Review, 40*(6), 603. https://doi.org/10.2307/3110316

Behn, R. D. (1991). *Leadership Counts: Lessons for Public Managers from the Massachusetts Welfare, Training, and Employment Program*. Harvard University Press. Cambridge, Mass.

Bell, C. (1997). *Ritual: Perspectives and Dimensions*. Oxford University Press.

Bennett, W. (1998). 1998 Ithiel De Sola Pool Lecture: The UnCivic Culture: Communication, Identity, and the Rise of Lifestyle Politics. *PS: Political Science and Politics, 31*(4), 741–761. https://doi.org/10.2307/420711

Benington, J. (2011). From Private Choice to Public Value? In J. Benington & M. Moore (Eds.). *Public Value: Theory and Practice* (pp. 31–51). Palgrave Macmillan. London.

Bennett, L. (2018, September 24). Fairfax Calls Out ABC for Running YouTube Ads. *AdNews*. https://www.adnews.com.au/news/fairfax-calls-out-abc-for-running-youtube-ads

Bennett, W. (1998). 1998 Ithiel De Sola Pool Lecture: The UnCivic Culture: Communication, Identity, and the Rise of Lifestyle Politics. *PS: Political Science and Politics, 31*(4), 741–761. https://doi.org/10.2307/420711

Bennett, W. L., & Livingston, S. (2018). The Disinformation Order: Disruptive Communication and the Decline of Democratic Institutions. *European Journal of Communication, 33*(2), 122–139. https://doi.org/10.1177/0267323118760317

Bennis, W. (2007). The Challenges of Leadership in the Modern World: Introduction to the Special Issue. (Author Abstract). *The American Psychologist, 62*(1), 2–5. https://doi.org/10.1037/0003-066X.62.1.2

Benns, M. (2019). GetUp told to pull advert defending ABC—by ABC. *The Daily Telegraph*. Online. 8 May 2019. Retrieved from Factiva.

Benson, R. (2012). Murdoch in the United States: Kingmaker or Ringmaster? *Global Media and Communication, 8*(1), 4–7. https://www.researchgate.net/publication/330508663_Murdoch_in_the_United_States_Kingmaker_or_Ringmaster_Global_Media_and_Communication_8_1_2012_4-7/citation/download

Benson, R., & Neveu, E. (2005). *Bourdieu and the Journalistic Field*. Polity Press.

Berg, C., & Davidson, S. (2018). *Against Public Broadcasting: Why We Should Privatise the ABC and How to Do It*. Connor Court Publishing. West End.

Berger, A. A. (1998). *Media Research Techniques* (2nd ed.). Sage Publications. http://ebookcentral.proquest.com/lib/unsw/detail.action?docID=997016

Berger, P., & Luckmann, T. (1967). *The Social Construction of Reality*. New York: Doubleday Anchor. Retrieved from http://www.perflensburg.se/Berger%20social-construction-of-reality.pdf

Bernstein, C. (2011, September 7). Is Phone-Hacking Scandal Murdoch's Watergate? *Newsweek*. https://www.newsweek.com/carl-bernstein-phone-hacking-scandal-murdochs-watergate-68411

Bhattacharyya, S., & Hodler, R. (2015). Media Freedom and Democracy in the Fight Against Corruption. *European Journal of Political Economy, 39*(C), 13–24. https://doi.org/10.1016/j.ejpoleco.2015.03.004

Biggart, N. W., & Hamilton, G. G. (1987). An Institutional Theory of Leadership. *The Journal of Applied Behavioral Science, 23*(4), 429–441. https://doi.org/10.1177/002188638702300401

Bikramjit, R., & Bandyopadhyay, S. (2018). *Contemporary Issues in Social Media Marketing*. Routledge.

Bingemann, M. (2017, May 18). ABC Part of Our Problem, Says Fairfax Boss Greg Hywood. *The Australian*. https://www.theaustralian.com.au/business/media/print/abc-part-of-our-problem-says-fairfax-boss-greg-hywood/news-story/ecb28edeb8303c10a28b1816ecce41a7

Bingham, N. (2017). "Telling Our Stories": Print Media Interpretations of Moscow Lesbians' Life Stories in 2004 and 2005. *Journal of Lesbian Studies: Contemporary Lesbian Relationships, 21*(1), 120–131. https://doi.org/10.1080/10894160.2016.1191305

Binns, A. (2017). Fair Game? Journalists' Experiences of Abuse Online. *Journal of Applied Journalism & Media Studies*, 6. 183–206. https://doi.org/10.1386/ajms.6.2.183_1.

Biswas, M., & Izard, R. (2010). 2009 Assessment of the Status of Diversity Education in Journalism and Mass Communication Programs. *Journalism and Mass Communication Editor, 64*(4), 378–394. https://doi.org/10.1177/107769580906400403

Bixiao He (2021). Haunted by the State. *Media History, 27*(2), 224–236. https://doi.org/10.1080/13688804.2020.1717939

Blach-Ørsten, M., & Burkal, R. (2014). Credibility and the Media as a Political Institution. *Nordicom Review, 35*. Special Issue. https://content.sciendo.com/view/journals/nor/35/s1/nor.35.issue-s1.xml

Blackiston, H. (2019, November 8). *Q&A After 'Openly Feminist' Broadside Episode*. Mumbrella. https://mumbrella.com.au/abc-launches-investigation-into-qa-after-openly-feminist-broadside-episode-605744

Blackwell, C. W. (2003). Athenian Democracy: A Brief Overview. In A. Lanni (Ed.), *Athenian Law in its Democratic Context* (Center for Hellenic Studies On-line Discussion Series). Republished in C.W. Blackwell, ed. *Dēmos: Classical Athenian Democracy* (Eds. A. Mahoney & R. Scaife). *The Stoa*. http://www.stoa.org/demos/article_democracy_overview@page=all&greekEncoding=UnicodeC.html

Blain, E. (1977). *Life with Aunty: 40 Year with the ABC*. Methuen Australia.

Blankenship, J. C. (2016). LOSING THEIR "MOJO"? Mobile Journalism and the Deprofessionalization of Television News Work. *Journalism Practice, 10*(8), 1055–1071. https://doi.org/10.1080/17512786.2015.1063080

Blair, T. (2014, January 29). ABC Staff Disquiet Over Story About the Australian Navy Torturing Asylum Seekers. *The Daily Telegraph*. https://www.dailytelegraph.com.au/news/nsw/abc-staff-disquiet-over-story-about-the-australian-navy-torturing-asylum-seekers/news-story/1da3c4cebec9dcc5a0c4cb8066bb8a29

Blease, C. (2015). Too Many 'Friends,' Too Few 'Likes'? Evolutionary Psychology and 'Facebook Depression'. *Review of General Psychology, 19*, 1–13. https://doi.org/10.1037/gpr0000030

Blood, G., & May, C. (2018, January 17). Australian Sport History. *Clearinghouse for Sport and Physical Activity*. https://www.clearinghouseforsport.gov.au/knowledge_base/organised_sport/value_of_sport/australian_sport_history

Bogle, A. (2020, June 19). Why China Is Being Blamed for Cyber Attacks on Australia, and What Its Hackers Might be Looking For. *ABC News Online*. https://www.abc.net.au/news/2020-06-19/why-would-china-launch-cyber-attack-against-australia/12374990

Bolino, M. C., & Turnley, W. H. (2003). Going the Extra Mile: Cultivating and Managing Employee Citizenship Behavior. *Academy of Management Executive, 17*(3), 60–73. https://doi.org/10.5465/AME.2003.10954754

Bolino, M. C., Turnley, W. H., & Bloodgood, J. M. (2002). Citizenship Behavior and the Creation of Social Capital in Organizations. *Academy of Management Review, 27*, 505–522.

Bollmer, G. (2016). *Inhuman Networks: Social Media and the Archaeology of Connection, Bloomsbury Academic & Professional*. ProQuest Ebook Central. https://ebookcentral.proquest.com/lib/unsw/detail.action?docID=4542880

Bolt, A. (2018, June 18). *"I Agree': Paul Barry Admits the ABC Is Biased. Quoting Chas Licciardello, Outsiders, Sky News*. https://www.heraldsun.com.au/blogs/andrew-bolt/i-agree-paul-barry-admits-the-abc-is-biased/news-story/7afa1bfe14cb3b119891d7b02aed0b46

Bolt, A. (2020a). Andrew Bolt George Pell Blog. *The Daily Telegraph*. https://www.dailytelegraph.com.au/blogs/andrew-bolt/George%20Pell

Bolt, A. (2020b, April 7). High Court: Pell Innocent. Andrew Bolt Blog Posts. *Herald Sun*. https://www.heraldsun.com.au/blogs/andrew-bolt/high-court-pell-innocent/news-story/655c1462896c6ac287391203137d7d8b

Bolter, J. D. (2019, May 19). Social Media Are Ruining Political Discourse. *The Atlantic*. https://www.theatlantic.com/technology/archive/2019/05/why-social-media-ruining-political-discourse/589108/

Bolton, G. C. (1967). *Dick Boyer: An Australian Humanist*. Australian National University Press. Canberra.

Bonk, K. (2008). *Strategic Communications for Nonprofits: A Step-by-Step Guide to Working with the Media* (2nd Ed.). Jossey-Bass. San Francisco.

Bonyhady, N. (2019, May 29). 'We Might be Biased': More Diverse Views Needed at ABC, Says Buttrose. *The Sydney Morning Herald*. https://www.smh.com.au/entertainment/tv-and-radio/we-might-be-bi…e-diverse-views-needed-at-abc-says-buttrose-20190529-p51sj2.html

Boorstin, D. J. (1987) (orig. pub. 1961). *The Image: A Guide to Pseudo-Events in America*. Atheneum. New York.

Born, G. (2005). *Uncertain Vision: Birt, Dyke and the Re-invention of the BBC*. Vintage.

Born, G. & Prosser, T. (2001). Culture and Consumerism: Citizenship, Public Service Broadcasting and the BBC's Fair Trading Obligations. *The Modern Law Review, 64*(5). September 2001. Retrieved from: https://onlinelibrary-wiley-com.wwwproxy1.library.unsw.edu.au/doi/pdfdirect/10.1111/1468-2230.00345

Boseley, M. (2020, June 11). Four Chris Lilley Shows Removed from Netflix Australia Library. *The Guardian*. https://www.theguardian.com/tv-and-radio/2020/jun/11/four-chris-lilley-shows-removed-from-netflix-australia-library

Booth, P. (2020). The Future of Public Service Broadcasting and the Funding and Ownership of the BBC. *Economic Affairs (Harlow), 40*(3), 324–343. https://doi.org/10.1111/ecaf.12419

Born, G. (2005). *Uncertain Vision: Birt, Dyke and the Re-invention of the BBC*. Vintage.

Born, G. (2006). Digitising Democracy. *The Political Quarterly*, pp. 102–123. http://search.proquest.com/docview/227288047

Born, G. (2012). In C. J. Emden & D. Midgley (Eds.), *Beyond Habermas: Democracy, Knowledge, and the Public Sphere. Ch. 7. "Mediating The Public Sphere: Digitization, Pluralism, and Communicative Democracy"* (pp. 119–146). Berghahn. https://www.academia.edu/attachments/38605631/download_file?st=MTU5NzAzMjYxNSwxMjEuMjIzLjE0Ni4xNzQsMTY1OTI4OTc2&s=profile

Boswell, J. (1851). *Life of Johnson, Volume 3 1776–1780*. T. Nelson & Sons.

Bottery, M., & Herrington, N. (2016). Not so Simple: The Threats to Leadership Sustainability. *Management in Education, 30*(3), 97–101. https://doi.org/10.1177/0892020616653059

Bourdieu, P. (1977). *Outline of a Theory of Practice* (R. Nice, Trans.). Cambridge University Press.

Bourdieu, P. (1979). *Distinction: A Social Critique of The Judgement of Taste* (R. Nice (1984), Trans.). Harvard University Press. Preface to the English Language Edition.

Bourdieu, P. (1980). (Trans. R. Nice) The Aristocracy of Culture. *Media, Culture and Society, 2*(3), 225–254. https://doi.org/10.1177/016344378000200303

Bourdieu, P. (1983). The Forms of Capital. In J. G. Richardson (Ed.), *Handbook of Theory and Research for the Sociology of Education* (pp. 241–258). Greenwood Press. New York.

Bourdieu, P. (1984). *Sociology in Question*. Sage Publications.

Bourdieu, P. (1985). The Social Space and the Genesis of Groups. *Theory and Society, 14*(6), 723–744. Elsevier, Amsterdam. https://doi.org/10.1007/BF00174048

Bourdieu, P. (1990). *The Logic of Practice* (R. Nice, Trans.). Stanford University Pres, Stanford.

Bourdieu, P. (1990). *In Other Words: Essays Towards a Reflexive Sociology* (M. Adamson, Trans.). Stanford University Press. Stanford, CA.

Bourdieu, P. (1991). *Language and Symbolic Power* (J. Thompson, Ed., G. Raymond & M. Adamson, Trans.). Harvard University Press.

Bourdieu, P. (1993). *The Field of Cultural Production: Essays on Art and Literature*. Columbia University Press. New York.

Bourdieu, P. (R. Johnson, Ed.). (1993). *The Field of Cultural Production: Essays on Art and Literature*. Cambridge: Polity Press.

Bourdieu, P. (1994). Structures, '*Habitus*', Power: Basis for a Theory of Symbolic Power. Chap. 4 in N. Dirks, G. Eley, & S. Ortner (Eds.), *Culture/Power/History: A Reader in Contemporary Social Theory*. Princeton Uni. Press.

Bourdieu, P. (1996).*The Rules of Art. Genesis and Structure of the Literary Field* (S. Emanuel, Trans.). Stanford University Press. Stanford.

Bourdieu, P. (1998). *On Television and Journalism* (P. Parkhurst Ferguson, Trans.). Pluto Press.

Bourdieu, P. (2005). *The Social Structures of the Economy* (C. Turner, Trans.). Polity Press.

Bourdieu, P. (2010). Ed. G. Sapiro. *Sociology is a Martial Art: Political Writings of Pierre Bourdieu*. The New Press. New York & London.

Bourdieu, P. (2017, Orig. 1998). *The Forms of Capital. Handbook of Theory and Research for the Sociology of Education* (J. G. Richardson, Ed.). Greenwood Press.

Bourdieu, P., & Wacquant, L. (1992). *An Invitation to Reflexive Sociology*. University of Chicago Press.

Bourgonje, P., Moreno-Schneider, J., Srivastava, A., & Rehm, B. G. (2018). Automatic Classification of Abusive Language and Personal Attacks in Various Forms of Online Communication. In G. Rehm and T. Declerck (Eds.), *Language Technology Lab* (pp. 180–191) Berlin, Germany. Retrieved from: https://doi.org/10.1007/978-3-319-73706-5_15.

Bourke, L. (2014, February 4). Prime Minister Tony Abbott Says ABC Not on Australia's Side in Interview with 2GB. *ABC News Online*. https://www.abc.net.au/news/2014-01-29/tony-abbott-steps-up-criticism-of-abc/5224676

Bourke, L. (2016, July 28). Furious George Pell Demands Victoria Police Investigation as ABC Airs Abuse Claims. *The Sydney Morning Herald*. https://www.smh.com.au/national/furious-george-pell-demands-victoria-police-investigation-as-abc-airs-abuse-claims-20160728-gqfb41.html

Bowling, M. (2020, April 15). Cardinal Pell Describes Reaction to Prosecutors, Reporters and Police in First Television Interview. *The Catholic Leader*. https://catholicleader.com.au/news/cardinal-pell-describes-reaction-to-prosecutors-reporters-and-police-in-first-television-interview

Bowman, D. (2005, June 15). Radical Giant of Australian Broadcasting. *The Sydney Morning Herald*. https://www.smh.com.au/national/radical-giant-of-australian-broadcasting-20050615-gdliic.html

Bowden, T., & Borchers, W. (2006). *50 Years Aunty's Jubilee! Celebrating 50 Years of ABC-TV*. ABC Books.

Boyce, G., Curran, J., & Wingate, P. (1978). Newspaper History: From the 17th Century to the Present Day. In G. Boyce (Ed.), *The Fourth Estate: The Reappraisal of the Concept*. Constable and Sage Publications.

Boyne, G. A., & Walker, R. M. (2004). Strategy Content and Public Service Organizations. *Journal of Public Administration Research and Theory, 14*(2), 231–252. https://doi.org/10.1093/jopart/muh015

Bozeman, B., & Straussman, J. D. (1990). *Public Management Strategies: Guidelines for Managerial Effectiveness*. Jossey-Bass, Inc. San Francisco, CA.

Brady, J. (2006, May 18). 'Red Rupert', The Pragmatist. Brady on Media. *Forbes Magazine*. http://www.forbes.com/2006/05/17/brady-on-media-cx_jb_0518rupert.html

Branch, D., & Cheeseman, N. (2008). Democratization, Sequencing, And State Failure in Africa: Lessons from Kenya. *African Affairs, 108*(430), 1–26. https://doi.org/10.1093/afraf/adn065

Brems, C., Temmerman, M., Graham, T., & Broersma, M. (2017). Personal Branding on Twitter. *Digital Journalism, 5*(4), 443–459. https://doi.org/10.1080/21670811.2016.1176534

Brereton, A. (2016, January 1). Former ABC Managing Director Brian Johns Dies Aged 79. *The Guardian*. https://www.theguardian.com/media/2016/jan/01/brian-johns-a-great-australian-who-positioned-the-abc-for-the-digital-age#:~:text=Former%20ABC%20managing%20director%20Brian%20Johns%20has%20died%20of%20cancer,of%20digital%20news%20and%20entertainment

Braun, J., & Gillespie, T. (2011). Hosting The Public Discourse, Hosting The Public. *Journalism Practice,* 5(4), 383–398. https://doi.org/10.1080/17512786.2011.557560

Braunstein, R. (2018). Boundary-Work and the Demarcation of Civil from Uncivil Protest in the United States: Control, Legitimacy, and Political Inequality. *Theory and Society,* 47(5), 603–633. https://doi.org/10.1007/s11186-018-9329-3

Brevini, B. (2013). *Public Service Broadcasting Online: A Comparative European Policy Study of PSB 2.0.* Palgrave Macmillan.

Brewster, Z. W., Brauer, J. R., & Lynn, M. (2018). Morality at Work: Do Employees' Moral Commitments Inhibit Service Disparities and Reactive Workplace Behaviors? *Social Currents,* 5(3), 244–263. https://doi.org/10.1177/2329496517725330

Briggs, G. (2006, July 17–Aug 1). Right Angles [The ABC Board and the Appointment of Keith Windschuttle]. *Big Issue Australia, 258,* 12–15. https://search-informit-com-au.wwwproxy1.library.unsw.edu.au/documentSummary;dn=200609050;res=IELAPA

British Broadcasting Corporation. (2009, May 25). Police Examine Sex Abuse Report. *British Broadcasting Corporation.* http://news.bbc.co.uk/2/hi/uk_news/northern_ireland/8066994.stm

British Broadcasting Corporation. News. (2011, July 13). The Cloyne Report: A Detailed Guide. https://www.bbc.com/news/uk-northern-ireland-14143822

British Broadcasting Corporation. (2017, August 10). The Anzac Post, Outrage and a Debate About Race. https://www.bbc.com/news/world-australia-40712832

British Broadcasting Corporation. (2020). BBC issues staff with new social media guidance. 29 October 2020. Retrieved from: https://www.bbc.com/news/entertainment-arts-54723282

British Broadcasting Corporation. Royal Charter. (1927). History of the BBC. *British Broadcasting Corporation.* https://web.archive.org/web/20170622230610/http://downloads.bbc.co.uk/bbctrust/assets/files/pdf/regulatory_framework/charter_agreement/archive/1927.pdf

Bromell, D. (2019). Ethical Competencies for Public Leadership: Pluralist Democratic Politics in Practice (1st Ed. 2019.). Springer International Publishing. Cham. Imprint. Springer.

Bromley, M. & Neal, R. (2009). "Farewell old friend or bye-bye bully boy? The Closure of 'mediation' and Challenging the 'free press' Paradigm." *Media International Australia.* August 132. Retrieved from: https://www.researchgate.net/deref/http%3A%2F%2Fdx.doi.org%2F10.1177%2F1329878X0913200105

Brook, S. (2013). Odd Couple: Friendship That Underpinned a Spy Story. *The Australian,* p. 1. https://mumbrella.com.au/wp-content/uploads/2013/12/Screen-Shot-2013-12-03-at-12.58.36-PM.png

Brook, S. (2017, November 20). Waste Not, Want Not the Message for ABC Silos. *The Australian.* https://login.wwwproxy1.library.unsw.edu.au/login?qurl=https%3A%2F%2Fsearch.proquest.com%2Fdocview%2F1990857104%3Facco

Brown, A. (1996). Public Service Broadcasting in Four Countries: Overview. *The Journal of Media Economics, 9*(1), 77–81.

Brown, R. S. (2010). Sampling. In P. Peterson, E. Baker, & B. McGaw (Eds.), *International Encyclopedia of Education* (pp. 142–146, 3rd ed.). Elsevier. https://doi.org/10.1016/B978-0-08-044894-7.00294-3.

Brown, A., & Althaus, C. (1996). Public Service Broadcasting in Australia. *Journal of Media Economics, 9*(1). Retrieved from: https://doi-org.wwwproxy1.library.unsw.edu.au/10.1207/s15327736me0901_4

Brown, A., & Althaus, C. (2009). Public Service Broadcasting in Australia. *The Journal of Media Economics, 9*(1), 31–46. https://doi-org.wwwproxy1.library.unsw.edu.au/10.1207/s15327736me0901_4

Brudholm, T., & Johansen, B. S. (2018). *Hate, Politics, Law: Critical Perspectives on Combating Hate.* Oxford University Press. Oxford.

Bruns, A. (2012). Journalists and Twitter: How Australian News Organisations Adapt to a New Medium. *Media International Australia, Incorporating Culture & Policy, 144*, 97–107. https://primoa.library.unsw.edu.au/permalink/f/11jha62/TN_scopus2-s2.0-84864412059

Bryson, J. M. (1995). *Strategic Planning for Public and Nonprofit Organizations: A Guide to Strengthening and Sustaining Organizational Achievement* (Rev. ed.). Jossey-Bass Publishers. San Francisco, CA.

Bucci, N. (2020). George Pell's Lawyer Calls for Investigation Into Claim Bribes Paid to Influence Sexual Assault Case. *The Guardian.* https://www.theguardian.com/australia-news/2020/oct/05/george-pells-lawyer-calls-for-investigation-into-claim-bribes-paid-to-influence-sexual-assault-case

Buchanan, J. (1965). An Economic Theory of Clubs. *Economica, 32*, 125. New series, 1–14. https://doi.org/10.2307/2552442

Buckingham Jones, S., & Urban, R. (2018, June 8). ABC Retracts Mass-Murder Slur Over ANU Row. *The Australian.* https://www.theaustralian.com.au/business/media/abc-retracts-massmurder-slur-over-anu-row/news-story/28d3ba406b1d7733231c73559ab88e0d

Burden, P. (2008). *News of the World? Fake Sheikhs and Royal Trappings.* Eye Books.

Burgess, K, (2020, March 17). Coronavirus: The Australian Army is Being Subbed in to Help Make Face Masks. *The Sydney Morning Herald.* https://www.canberratimes.com.au/story/6684074/the-australian-army-is-being-subbed-in-to-help-make-face-masks/

Burns, J. F. (2012, July 24). Phone-Hacking Charges Seen as Chill on British Journalism. *The New York Times.* https://www.nytimes.com/2012/07/25/world/europe/two-ex-editors-for-murdoch-to-be-charged-for-phone-hacking.html

Burns, M., & Hawkins, G. (2013). Investigating Public Service Media as Hybrid Arrangements. *Media International Australia, 146*(1), 79–81. https://doi.org/10.1177/1329878X1314600111

Burrowes, T. (2016, January 1). Former ABC Managing Director Brian Johns was 'a Man Ahead of His Time'. *Mumbrella*. https://mumbrella.com.au/former-abc-boss-brian-johns-was-a-man-ahead-of-his-time-337460

Burrowes, T. (2018, January 1). Charlie Pickering Apologises for ABC New Year Countdown 'Kill a Police Officer' Autocue Blunder. *Mumbrella*. Retrieved January 3, 2020, from https://mumbrella.com.au/presenter-charlie-pickering-apologises-kill-police-officer-autocue-blunder-491598

Burrowes, T. (2019, May 19). ABC Wins the Election Ratings While Ten Slumps to 3.6%. *Mumbrella*. https://mumbrella.com.au/abc-wins-the-election-ratings-while-ten-slumps-to-3-6-580222

Burrows, R., Nettleton, S., Pleace, N., Loader, B., & Muncer, S. (2000). Virtual Community Care? Social Policy and the Emergence of Computer Mediated Social Support. *Information, Communication & Society, 3*, 95–121. https://doi.org/10.1080/136911800359446

Buttrose, I. (2020, June 26). What Would Australia Look Like Without the ABC? ABC Media Centre. *Australian Broadcasting Corporation*. http://about.abc.net.au/statements/what-would-australia-look-like-without-the-abc/

Butler, J. (1990). *Gender Trouble: Feminism and the Subversion of Identity*. Routledge.

Buttrose, C. (1984). *Words and Music: Press Barons, Prima Donnas and Coping with the ABC*. Angus and Robertson Publishers.

Cadzow, J. (2018). "Culture Clash". Good Weekend. *The Sydney Morning Herald, 6*(The Culture Issue), 18–24.

Cai, Z., Parker, S., Chen, Z., & Lam, W. (2019). How Does the Social Context Fuel the Proactive Fire? A Multilevel Review and Theoretical Synthesis. *Journal of Organizational Behaviour, 40*(2), 209–230.

Cairns Post, The. (1937, September 10). ABC Attacked. CRUEL, COWARDLY BIAS. *The Cairns Post*, p. 11. https://trove.nla.gov.au/newspaper/article/41816337?searchTerm=CRUEL%2C%20COWARDLY%20BIAS

Cairns Post, The. (1939, September 27). Giving the News. Broadcasting and News. Papers. *The Cairns Post*, p. 5. https://trove.nla.gov.au/newspaper/article/42203333?searchTerm=A.B.C.%20British%20Official%20Wireless

Caisley, O., & Vitorovich, L. (2019, October 8). Ita Buttrose: Media Too White and Politically Correct. *The Australian*. Business Review. https://www.theaustralian.com.au/business/media/ita-buttrose-media-too-white-and-politically-correct/news-story/c9a7abf43db53543802b832ef3690265

Calcutt, L. (2018, June 18). ABC Will Never Be Sold. *Ninenews.com*. https://www.9news.com.au/national/malcolm-turnbull-rules-out-privatising-abc-after-liberal-conference-vote/7220faa9-ebf1-4961-be43-e0ddd32a0afb

Calvet, R., Montoya, M. I., Garcia, I., Franquet, I., Calvet, R., Villa Montoya, M., & Bergillos Garcia, I. (2013). Public Service Broadcasting's Participation in the Reconfiguration of Online News Content. *Journal of Computer-Mediated Communication, 18*(3), 378–397. https://doi.org/10.1111/jcc4.12014

Canberra Times, The. (1936, July 2). ABC ARTISTS. All Will Visit Canberra. *The Canberra Times*, p. 2. https://trove.nla.gov.au/newspaper/article/2420561?searchTerm=ABC%20ARTISTS.%20All%20will%20visit%20Canberra

Canberra Times, The. (1938). Race Broadcasts. ABC and Public Demand. *The Canberra Times*. 19 January 1938, p. 3. Retrieved from: https://trove.nla.gov.au/newspaper/article/2450534?searchTerm=ABC%20and%20Public%20Demand.%20

Canberra Times, The. (1942, January 19). The Department of Information. Editorial. *The Canberra Times*, p. 2. https://trove.nla.gov.au/newspaper/article/2575300?searchTerm=Keith%20Murdoch%20extraordinary%20blunder%20was%20made%20in%20the%20blunderbuss%20

Canberra Times, The. (1951). Dame Enid Lyons Appointed to ABC. 14 July 1951, p. 4. Retrieved from Trove.

Canberra Times, The. (1964, August 26). ABC Features: Australian Film Without a White. *The Canberra Times*, p. 21. https://trove.nla.gov.au/newspaper/article/105840424?searchTerm=ABC%20white%20australia&searchLimits=

Canberra Times, The. (1976, October 8). 'Support' for ABC Staff Campaign, p. 3. https://trove.nla.gov.au/newspaper/article/110829449?searchTerm=ABC%20staff&searchLimits=

Canberra Times, The. (1977, October 24). 'Interference' to ABC 'Insidious'. *The Canberra Times*, p. 7. https://trove.nla.gov.au/newspaper/article/110874090?searchTerm=ABC%20ghost&searchLimits=

Canberra Times, The. (1979, November 8). Sport Call to ABC. Parliament. *The Canberra Times*, p. 12. https://trove.nla.gov.au/newspaper/article/110966616?searchTerm=ABC%20sport%20station&searchLimits=

Canberra Times, The. (1980, April 17). ABC's Structure, Waste Studied. *The Canberra Times*, p. 3. https://trove.nla.gov.au/newspaper/article/110591023?searchTerm=ABC%20waste

Canberra Times, The. (1981, May 28). ABC National Sports Coverage Lacks Resources. *The Canberra Times*, p. 28. https://trove.nla.gov.au/newspaper/result?q=ABC+sport&s=20

Canberra Times, The. (1983, August 2). ABC's Role Defended by Myer. *The Canberra Times*, p. 1. https://trove.nla.gov.au/newspaper/article/116420987?searchTerm=This%20confirms%20that%20the%20role%20of%20the%20ABC%20is%20to%20throw%20attention%20to%20matters%20of%20public%20interest%20where%20truth%20has%20been%20obscured%20or%20the%20public%20has%20not%20been%20fully%20informed

Canberra Times, The. (1985, June 11). 'Phantom Army' Found in ABC. *The Canberra Times*, p. 7. https://trove.nla.gov.au/newspaper/article/122515191?searchTerm=ABC%20phantom%20army&searchLimits=

Cannane, S. (2017, October 28). *After Over 70 Years in Journalism and Publishing, Sir Harry Evans Is Still Irked by Bad Writing*. Correspondents Report. *ABC News Online*. https://www.abc.net.au/news/2017-10-28/does-writing-still-matter-in-the-digital-age/9091716

Carbado, D., Crenshaw, K., Mays, V., & Tomlinson, B. (2013). *Intersectionality:* Mapping the Movements of a Theory. *Du Bois Review: Social Science Research on Race, 10*(2), 303–312. https://doi.org/10.1017/S1742058X13000349

Carey, J. (1996). Where Journalism Education Went Wrong. Conference Presentation Middle Tennessee State University. Retrieved from: https://lindadaniele.wordpress.com/2010/08/11/carey-where-journalism-education-went-wrong/

Carpentier, N. (2014). Participation as a Fantasy: A Psychoanalytical Approach to Power-Sharing Fantasies. In L. Kramp, N. Carpentier, A. Hepp, I. Tomanic-Trivundza, H. Nieminen, R. Kunelius, T. Olsson, E. Sundin & R. Kilborn (Eds.), *Everyday Media Agency in Europe, Chapter: Participation as a Fantasy: A Psychoanalytical Approach to Power-Sharing Fantasies* (pp. 319–330). Edition Lumière. Section 4:5. https://www.researchgate.net/publication/268980799_Participation_as_a_Fantasy_A_Psychoanalytical_Approach_to_Power-Sharing_Fantasies

Carr, D., & Bard, M. (2018). Even a Celebrity Journalist Can't Have an Opinion: Post-Millennials' Recognition and Evaluation of Journalists and News Brands on Twitter. *Electronic News, 12*(1), 3–22. https://doi.org/10.1177/1931243117710280.

Carson, A., Martin, A. J., & Ratcliff, S. (2020). Negative Campaigning, Issue Salience and Vote Choice: Assessing the Effects of the Australian Labor Party's 2016 "Mediscare" Campaign. *Journal of Elections, Public Opinion and Parties, 30*(1), 83–104. https://doi.org/10.1080/17457289.2018.1563093

Castells, M. (2008). The New Public Sphere: Global Civil Society, Communication Networks, and Global Governance. *The Annals of the American Academy of Political and Social Science, 616*, 78–93. www.jstor.org/stable/25097995

Castells, M. (2012). *Networks of Outrage and Hope: Social Movements in the Internet Age*. Polity Press.

Carson, A. (2020, June 10). Cutting the ABC Cuts Public Trust. *La Trobe University*. News Articles. https://www.latrobe.edu.au/news/articles/2020/opinion/cutting-the-abc-cuts-public-trust

Catholic Archdiocese of Melbourne. (n.d.) Melbourne Response. *Catholic Archdiocese of Melbourne*.https://www.cam.org.au/en-us/Safeguarding-Children-Young-People-and-Vulnerable-Persons/Melbourne-Response

Cavanagh, P. (2015, December). *ABC Radio Current Affairs Coverage of The China-Australia Free Trade Agreement*. Editorial Review No. 7. *Australian Broadcasting Corporation*. https://about.abc.net.au/wp-content/uploads/2016/02/ABC-Editorial-Review-No-7.pdf

Celep, A., & Mosher-William, R. (2016). Internal Culture, External Impact: How a Change-Making Culture Positions Foundations to Achieve Transformational Change. *The Foundation Review, 8*(1), 116–129. https://doi.org/10.9707/1944-5660.1288

Centeno, D. (2018). Social Media Stakeholder Co-creation of Celebrities as Human Brands. Chap. 5. in B. Rishi & S. Bandyopadhyay (Eds.), *Contemporary Issues in Social Media Marketing*. Routledge.

Central Queensland Herald (Rockhampton). (1934, August 9). Sydney Letter: Obligations of Broadcasting. Pronouncement by New ABC Chairman, p. 8. https://trove.nla.gov.au/newspaper/article/70566782?searchTerm=ABC%20board%20members&searchLimits=exactPhrase|||anyWords|||notWords|||requestHandler|||dateFrom=1932-01-01|||dateTo=1935-12-31|||sortby

Centre for Media Transition. (2020, January). News in Australia Impartiality and Commercial Influence. [online]. https://www.acma.gov.au/sites/default/files/2020-01/News%20in%20Australia_Impartiality%20and%20commercial%20influence_Review%20of%20literature%20and%20research.pdf

Ceron, A. (2015). Internet, News, and Political Trust: The Difference Between Social Media and Online Media Outlets. *Journal of Computer-Mediated Communication, 20*(5), 487–503. https://doi.org/10.1111/jcc4.12129\

Ceron, A., & Memoli, V. (2016). Flames and Debates: Do Social Media Affect Satisfaction with Democracy? *Social Indicators Research, 126*(1), 225–240. https://doi.org/10.1007/s11205-015-0893-x

Chadwick, P. (2012, September 4–7). Adapting a Public Broadcaster's Self-Regulation for the Convergence Era. [online]. *RIPE@2012 Conference*, Sydney. http://about.abc.net.au/wp-content/uploads/2012/10/AdaptingAPublicBroadcastersSelfRegulationForTheConvergenceEraRIPE2012.pdf

Chakvetadze, L., Dautova, R., & Shakurova, A. (2016). Gender Stereotypes, Mass Media and Migrants *Journal of Organizational Culture, Communications and Conflict, 20*, 39–45. http://search.proquest.com/docview/1827843344/

Chalaby, J. K. (1997). No Ordinary Press Owner: Press Barons as a Weberian Ideal Type. *Media, Culture and Society, 19*(4), 621–641. Retrieved from: https://doi.org/10.1177/016344397019004007.

Chalaby, J. K. (1998). *The Invention of Journalism*. Macmillan Press.

Chambers, R. (1997). The Unexamined. In M. Hill (Ed.), *Whiteness: A Critical Reader*. New York University Press.

Chambers, G., & Brown G. (2018). Former Premiers Take Aim at Bloated Public Sector. *The Australian*. 29 January, 2018. Retrieved from https://www.theaustralian.com.au/nation/politics/former-premiers-take-aim-at-bloated-public-sector/news-story/4798c1ce6d315bcb77296b9f1303ef73

Chapman, R. (Ed.). (2009) *Culture Wars: An Encyclopedia of Issues, Viewpoints, and Voices (Two-Volume Set)*. M. E. Sharpe Incorporated. ProQuest Ebook Central.

Chapman, C., Getha-Taylor, H., Holmes, M. H., Jacobson, W. S., Morse, R. S., & Sowa, J. E. (2016, March). How Public Service Leadership Is Studied: An Examination of a Quarter Century of Scholarship. *Public Administration, 94*(1), 111–128. https://onlinelibrary-wiley-com.wwwproxy1.library.unsw.edu.au/doi/pdfdirect/10.1111/padm.12199

Chaucer, G. (1476, orig.). The Canterbury Tales: The Knight's Tale, p. 3. [online]. http://art3idea.psu.edu/metalepsis/texts/knights_tale.pdf

Chemers, M. (2014). In H. Gray-Hoehn. (2020). Chapter 6: "Talking the Talk: Communication as the Essential Element of Leadership". In K. M. S. Bezio & G. R. Goethals (Eds.), *Leadership, Populism, and Resistance* (Jepson Studies in Leadership Series). Monograph Book. Elgar Online.

Chen, J., Walker, R.M. & Sawhney, M. (2020). Public Service Innovation: A Typology. *Public Management Review, 22*(11), 1674–1695. https://doi.org/10.1080/14719037.2019.1645874

Chenoweth, N. (2001). *Virtual Murdoch: Reality Wars on the Information Highway*. Secker & Warburg.

Chenoweth, N. (2012, February 1). Aunty Faces Cuts, Job Losses and Old Scores: Media. *The Australian Financial Review*. Melbourne, p. 21. https://search-proquest-com.wwwproxy1.library.unsw.edu.au/docview/1753219424?rfr_id=info%3Axri%2Fsid%3Aprimo

Chenoweth, N. (2014). Aunty Faces Cuts, Job Losses and Old Scores: Media. *The Australian Financial Review*. 1 February 2014. p. 21. Retrieved from: https://search-proquest-com.wwwproxy1.library.unsw.edu.au/docview/1753219424?rfr_id=info%3Axri%2Fsid%3Aprimo

Chessell, J. (2010, February 4). "News Corporation on 'Cusp of Digital Dynasty': Murdoch. *The Australian*.http://www.theaustralian.com.au/business/news-corporation-on-the-cusp-of-digital-dynasty-murdoch/story-e6frg8zx-1225826521766

Choi, S. (2014). Flow, Diversity, Form, and Influence of Political Talk in Social-Media-Based Public Forums. *Human Communication Research, 40*(2), 209–237. https://doi.org/10.1111/hcre.12023

Chong, D., & Bogdan, E. (2010). Plural Public Funding and Canada's Contemporary Art Market System. *Cultural Trends: Centre/Periphery: Devolution/Federalism: New Trends in Cultural Policy, 19*(1-2), 93–107. https://doi.org/10.1080/09548961003696096

Christensen, C. M. & Overdorf, M. (2000). Meeting the Challenge of Disruptive Change. *Harvard Business Review*. Retrieved from: https://hbr.org/2000/03/meeting-the-challenge-of-disruptive-change

Christodoulou, I., Pashias, C., Theocharides, S., & Davou, B. (2017). Investigating the roots of political disengagement of young Greek Cypriots. *Contemporary Social Science, 12*(3–4), 376–392. https://doi.org/10.1080/21582041.2017.1384562

Chronicle, The. (1941, May 15). More ABC Patriotic Poems. *The Chronicle*, p. 37. https://trove.nla.gov.au/newspaper/article/92414948?searchTerm=ABC%20patriotic&searchLimits=

Christodoulou, I., Pashias, C., Theocharides, S., & Davou, B. (2017). Investigating the roots of political disengagement of young Greek Cypriots. *Contemporary Social Science, 12*(3–4), 376–392. https://doi.org/10.1080/21582041.2017.1384562

Chung, L. (2018, September 24). Michelle Guthrie Sacked: Why More Trouble Lies Ahead for ABC. *Nine.com.au.* https://finance.nine.com.au/business-news/why-more-trouble-lies-ahead-for-abc/846781d2-7df0-46fd-808d-0a8818bff342

Clark, M. (1995, orig. published 1962). *History of Australia* (p. 537). Melbourne: Melbourne University Press.

Clark, A. (2016, January 4). Johns Had Lasting Impact on ABC and SBS: Obituary. *The Australian Financial Review.*http://ezproxy.library.usyd.edu.au/login?url=https://search-proquest-com.ezproxy2.library.usyd.edu.au/docview/1752885352?accountid=14757

Clarke, M. (2018, February 2). ASIO Takes Custody of Secret Cabinet Documents, Obtained by the ABC. *ABC Online.* https://www.abc.net.au/news/2018-02-01/asio-takes-custody-of-cabinet-documents/9386328

Clarke, J., & Bromley, M. (Eds.). (2011). *International News in the Digital Age: East-West Perceptions of a New World Order.* Taylor & Francis Group. ProQuest Ebook Central. http://ebookcentral.proquest.com/lib/unsw/detail.action?docID=957408

Clarke, N. (2011). An Integrated Conceptual Model of Respect in Leadership. *The Leadership Quarterly, 22*(2), 316–327. https://www-sciencedirect-com.wwwproxy1.library.unsw.edu.au/science/article/pii/S1048984311000208

Clayton, R. (2020). Australia Post chief executive Christine Holgate resigns 'with immediate effect'. *ABC News.* 2 November 2020. Retrieved from: https://www.abc.net.au/news/2020-11-02/australia-post-ceo-christine-holgate-resigns/12839502

Clements, C., & Washbush, J. B. (1999). The Two Faces of Leadership: Considering the Dark Side of Leader-Follower Dynamics. *The Journal of Workplace Learning, 11*(5), 170–176. https://doi.org/10.1108/13665629910279509

CNN Editorial Research. (2020, April 26). UK Phone Hacking Scandal Fast Facts. *CNN.* https://edition.cnn.com/2013/10/24/world/europe/uk-phone-hacking-scandal-fast-facts/index.html

Coady, C. A. J. (2008, March). *ABC Editorial Policies: Short Looks at Some Big Concepts That Govern the ABC.* Australian Broadcasting Corporation, p. 2.

http://about.abc.net.au/wp-content/uploads/2012/06/KeyWordsMarch2008.pdf

Coates, B. (2010). Cracking Into the Panes of Corporate Denial. *Business Renaissance Quarterly*, *5*(3), 23–46. http://ezproxy.library.usyd.edu.au/login?url=https://search-proquest-com.ezproxy2.library.usyd.edu.au/docview/814814238?accountid=14757

Cockburn, G. (2020, December 8). Keating Hails One of the Greats. *The Australian*. NCA Newswire.

Coë, C., & Moore, H. (2019, December 11). ABC Finds They Were Right to Pull a Controversial Q&A from iView Where a Radical Feminist Called for the Killing of Male Rapists—But the Writer Isn't Happy. https://www.dailymail.co.uk/news/article-7779533/ABC-finishes-investigation-radical-female-Q-panel-advocated-killing-rapists.html

Cohen, B. C. (1963). *The Press and Foreign Policy*. Princeton University Press.

Cohen, S. (2002). *Folk Devils and Moral Panics* (3rd ed.). First published 1972. Routledge: London & New York.

Cohen, S. (2011). Whose Side Were We On? The Undeclared Politics of Moral Panic Theory. *Crime Media Culture*, *7*(3), 237–243. https://doi.org/10.1177/1741659011417603

Cokley, J., & Ranke, A. (2010). There's a "Long Tail" in Journalism Education, Too. In B. Franklin & D. Mensing. (2010). *Journalism Education, Training and Employment*. 1st Ed. Routledge. New York.

Cola, M., & Prario, B. (2012, March). New Ways of Consumption: The Audiences of Public Service Media in Italy and Switzerland. *Media, Culture & Society*, *34*(2), 181–194. https://journals-sagepub-com.wwwproxy1.library.unsw.edu.au/doi/pdf/10.1177/0163443711430757

Coleman, P. (2007). Hulme, Sir Alan Shallcross (1907–1989). *Australian Dictionary of Biography*. National Centre of Biography. Australian National University. http://adb.anu.edu.au/biography/hulme-sir-alan-shallcross-12666/text22827

Colliander, J. (2019). "This Is Fake News": Investigating the Role of Conformity to Other Users' Views When Commenting on and Spreading Disinformation in Social Media. *Computers in Human Behavior*, *97*, 202–215. https://doi.org/10.1016/j.chb.2019.03.032

Collins, P. (2011, August). The Commercialisation of the ABC. *Eureka Street*, *21*(15), 27–28. https://search-informit-com-au.wwwproxy1.library.unsw.edu.au/documentSummary;dn=380461935545072;res=IELAPA

Collins, R., Hoskins, C., McFadyen, S., & Finn, A. (2001). Public Service Broadcasting Beyond 2000: Is There a Future for Public Service Broadcasting? *Canadian Journal of Communication*, *26*(1), 3–15. http://dx.doi.org.wwwproxy1.library.unsw.edu.au/10.22230/cjc.2001v26n1a119

Collins, B., & Zadrozny, B. (2021, 9 January). Twitter Permanently Suspends Donald Trump. *NBC News.* https://www.nbcnews.com/tech/tech-news/twitter-permanently-bans-president-donald-trump-n1253588

Collins, C., Neal, J., & Neal, Z. (2014). Transforming Individual Civic Engagement into Community Collective Efficacy: The Role of Bonding Social Capital. *American Journal of Community Psychology, 54,* 328–336. https://doi.org/10.1007/s10464-014-9675-x

Colman, A. (2006). *A Dictionary of Psychology.* Oxford University Press. https://archive.org/details/dictionaryofpsyc00colm_0/page/77/mode/2up

Committee of Review of the Australian Broadcasting Commission. (1981). "The ABC in review: national broadcasting in the 1980s". (aka The Dix Report). Committee of Review of the Australian Broadcasting Commission. 30 May, 1981. *Commonwealth of Australia.* Retrieved from: https://apo.org.au/node/41206

Commonwealth of Australia. (2018, February). Select Committee on the Future of Public Interest Journalism Report. *Commonwealth of Australia.* https://www.aph.gov.au/Parliamentary_Business/Committees/Senate/Future_of_Public_Interest_Journalism/PublicInterestJournalism/~/media/Committees/journalism_ctte/Report/c06.pdf

Commonwealth of Australia. (2018). Select Committee on the Future of Public Interest Journalism. The Senate. *Commonwealth of Australia.* https://www.aph.gov.au/Parliamentary_Business/Committees/Senate/Future_of_Public_Interest_Journalism/PublicInterestJournalism/~/media/Committees/journalism_ctte/Report/report.pdf

Commonwealth Scientific and Industrial Research Organisation. (2017). Australian Attitudes Toward Mining: Latest Results. Retrieved from: https://www.csiro.au/en/work-with-us/industries/mining-resources/australian-attitudes-to-mining-2017

Conboy, M. (2013). *Journalism Studies: The Basics.* Routledge.

Connors, J. (2018, November 30). Opening statement (public hearing, Canberra, 30 November 2018). *Inquiry into Allegations of Political Interference in the ABC.* Tabled by: Dr. Jane Connors. https://www.aph.gov.au/Parliamentary_Business/Committees/Senate/Environment_and_Communications/ABCInterferenceAllegations/Additional_Documents?docType=Tabled%20Documents

Conroy, S. (2008, October). ABC and SBS: Towards a Digital Future. Discussion Paper. Foreword. *Australian Government, Department of Broadband, Communications and the Digital Economy.* https://www.ames.net.au/-/media/files/policy/7_abc_and_sbs_towards_a_digital_future_low_resolution.pdf?la=en

Coombs, W. T. (2012). *Ongoing Crisis Communication: Planning, Managing, and Responding* (p. 37). Sage Publications.

Cooper, S. (2009, Feb-Mar). Murdoch's Boyer Lectures: [Why was Rupert Murdoch chosen to give the 2008 ABC Boyer Lectures?] [online]. *Arena Magazine* (Fitzroy, Vic), *99*, 5–6. Retrieved from: ISSN: 1039–1010.

Cooper, M. (2014). The Long History and Increasing Importance of Public-Service Principles for 21st Century Public Digital Communications Networks. *Journal on Telecommunications & High Technology Law, 12*(1, Spring), 1–54. https://primoa.library.unsw.edu.au/primo-explore/fulldisplay?docid=TN_gale_legal388675657&context=PC&vid=UNSWS&lang=en_US&search_scope=SearchFirst&adaptor=primo_central_multiple_fe&tab=default_tab&query=any,contains,history%20public%20service&offset=0

Cooke, M. (2007). Our Digital Aunty—The ABC's New Media Future. *Metro Magazine: Media & Education Magazine, 154*, 120–124. https://search.informit.org/doi/10.3316/INFORMIT.003683049332154

Corbett, J., Webster, J., & Jenkin, T. (2018). Unmasking Corporate Sustainability at the Project Level: Exploring the Influence of Institutional Logics and Individual Agency. *Journal of Business Ethics, 147*(2), 261–286. https://doi.org/10.1007/s10551-015-2945-1.

Cotter, C. (2010). *News Talk*. Cambridge University Press. Cambridge. https://doi.org/10.1017/CBO9780511811975

Couldry, N. (2003). *Media Rituals: A Critical Approach*. Routledge.

Couldry, N. (2004). Theorising Media as Practice. *Social Semiotics, 14*(2), 115–132. https://doi.org/10.1080/1035033042000238295

County Court of Victoria at Melbourne Criminal Division. (2019, March 13). DPP v Pell (Sentence). His Honour Chief Judge Kidd. https://content.countycourt.vic.gov.au/sites/default/files/documents/2019-03/dpp-v-pell-sentence-2019-vcc-260.pdf

Courier Mail, The. (1934, July 25). Educational Broadcasts: Policy of the A.B.C, p. 20. https://trove.nla.gov.au/newspaper/article/36733653?searchTerm=Educational%20broadcasts%3A%20Policy%20of%20the%20A.B.C

Courier Mail, The. (1934, July 25). Educational Broadcasts: Policy of the A.B.C, p. 20. https://trove.nla.gov.au/newspaper/article/36733653?searchTerm=Educational%20broadcasts%3A%20Policy%20of%20the%20A.B.C

Courier Mail, The. (1946, January 25). ABC Needs to Consider Public. *The Courier-Mail*, p. 3. https://trove.nla.gov.au/newspaper/article/50256156?searchTerm=ABC%20needs%20to%20consider%20public

Courier Mail, The. (1953, June 29). Serve the Democratic Processes. "ABC Is Consistently, Violently Criticised". *The Courier-Mail, Brisbane*, p. 5. https://trove.nla.gov.au/newspaper/article/50541530?searchTerm=ABC%20serve

Craig, G. (2016). *Performing Politics: Media Interviews, Debates and Press Conferences*. Polity Press.

Cranston, M. (2019, September 25). 'It Disturbs Me': RBA Boss Hits Out at CEO Salaries. *The Australian Financial Review*. https://www.afr.com/

policy/economy/it-disturbs-me-rba-boss-hits-out-at-ceo-salaries-20190924-p52ul7

Creed, A. (2011). Organisational Behaviour, Oxford University Press. ProQuest Ebook Central. http://ebookcentral.proquest.com/lib/unsw/detail.action?docID=1985999.

Creed, P. (2013). *Ethics, Norms and the Narratives of War: Creating and Encountering the Enemy Other*. Taylor and Francis.

Crocker, P. (1989). *Radio Days: A Personal View of Australia's Radio Heyday* (p. 75). Simon and Schuster. Brookvale.

Crenshaw, K. W. (1989). "Demarginalizing the Intersection of Race and Sex: A Black Feminist Critique of Antidiscrimination Doctrine, Feminist Theory and Antiracist Politics." University of Chicago Legal Forum 1989. 139–67. Retrieved from: https://heinonline.org

Crikey. (2019, May 30). Ita Buttrose Picks a Side—And It Isn't the ABC's. Tips and Rumours. *Crikey.com*. https://www.crikey.com.au/2019/05/30/tips-ita-buttrose-abc/

Crisp, L. (2011). The Saddest of Days. The Deal. *The Australian Business Magazine, 4*, 9.

Crowe, D. (2020, April 16). Murdoch Wanted Him Out Because He Was 'His Own Man', Turnbull Claims. *The Sydney Morning Herald*. https://www.smh.com.au/politics/federal/murdoch-wanted-him-out-because-he-was-his-own-man-turnbull-claims-20200416-p54kbc.html

Cryle, D. (2008). *Murdoch's Flagship: 25 Years of The Australian Newspaper*. Melbourne University Press.

Cunningham, S. (2013). *Hidden Innovation: Policy, Industry and the Creative Sector*. University of Queensland Press.

Cunningham, S., & Bridgstock, R. (2012, November). Say Goodbye to the Fries: Graduate Careers in Media, Cultural and Communication Studies. *Media International Australia, 145*(1), 6–17. https://primoa.library.unsw.edu.au/permalink/f/11jha62/TN_wos000312972100002

Cunningham, S., & Turner, G. (2010). *The Media and Communications in Australia*. 3rd Ed. Allen & Unwin. Crows News, Sydney.

Cunningham, S., & Craig, D. (2018, May 9). We Must Not Punish Content Creators in Our Rush to Regulate Social Platforms. *The Conversation*. https://theconversation.com/we-must-not-punish-content-creators-in-our-rush-to-regulate-social-platforms-96270

Curran, J. (Ed.). (1978). *The British Press: A Manifesto*. Acton Society Press Group. The Macmillan Press Ltd.

Curran, J. (1990). 'The New Revisionism in Mass Communication Research: A Reappraisal'. *European Journal of Communication, 5*(2), 135–164. https://doi.org/10.1177/0267323190005002002

Curran, J. (1991). *Mass Media and Democracy: A Reappraisal. Mass Media and Society* (J. Curran & M. Gurevitch, Eds.) (pp. 82–117). Edward Arnold.

Curran, J. (2011). *Media and Democracy.* Routledge.

Curran, J., & Seaton, J. (1997). *Power Without Responsibility: The Press and Broadcasting in Britain* (5th ed.). Routledge.

Curran, J., & Seaton, J. (2018). *Power Without Responsibility: Press, Broadcasting and the Internet in Britain* (8th ed.). Routledge.

Curson, P., & McCracken, K. (2014). An Australian Perspective of the 1918–1919. Influenza Pandemic. *NSW Public Health Bulletin, 17*(7–8), 103–107. https://www.phrp.com.au/wp-content/uploads/2014/10/NB06025.pdf

Cushion, S. (2012). *The Democratic Value of News: Why Public Service Media Matter.* Palgrave Macmillan.

Cut, M. (2017). Digital Natives and Digital Immigrants—How Are They Different. *Digital Reflections.* https://medium.com/digital-reflections/digital-natives-and-digital-immigrants-how-are-they-different-e849b0a8a1d3

Cyert, R. M., & J. G. March. (1963). *A Behavioral Theory of the Firm.* Prentice Hall. Englewood Cliffs, NJ.

Çıdam, Ç. (2016). Public Space, Material Worlds, and Democratic Aspirations. *Contemporary Political Theory, 15*(4), 417–426. https://doi.org/10.1057/s41296-016-0011-0

de Smaele, H., Geenen, E., & De Cock, R. (2017). Visual Gatekeeping – Selection of News Photographs at a Flemish Newspaper. *Nordicom Review, 38*(2), 57–70. https://doi.org/10.1515/nor-2017-0414

D'Ambrosia, R. D. (2009, January). Treating the Internet-Informed Patient. *Orthopedics. Thorofare, 32*(1). https://search.proquest.com/docview/220412297?pq-origsite=gscholar&fromopenview=true

Dahlgren, P. (2013). *The Political Web: Media, Participation And Alternative Democracy* (pp. 1–195). Palgrave Macmillan. https://doi.org/10.1057/9781137326386

Daily Examiner, The. (1945, March 30). Reason for Resignation of ABC Chairman. *Daily Examiner, Grafton,* p. 3. https://trove.nla.gov.au/newspaper/article/193817668?searchTerm=chairman%20ABC&searchLimits=exactPhrase|||anyWords|||notWords|||requestHandler|||dateFrom=1944-01-01|||dateTo=1946-12-31|||l-advstate=National|||l-advstate=ACT|||l-advstate=New+South+Wales|||sortby

Daily Mercury (Mackay). (1946, June 29). Broadcasting Parliament. ABC Privilege. *Daily Mercury (Mackay),* p. 4. https://trove.nla.gov.au/newspaper/article/171153794?searchTerm=ABC%20privilege&searchLimits=

Daily Telegraph, The. (1935, October 9). Announcer May Be ABC Head: Moses Likely Appointee. *The Daily Telegraph,* p. 1. https://trove.nla.gov.au/newspaper/article/246584742?searchTerm=ABC%20sport%20Moses&searchLimits=

Daily Telegraph and North Murchison and Pilbara Gazette (WA). (1939, November 10). Australian Army. Mr. Menzies Speaks. Sixth Division For

Overseas. "A Fight To The Last". *Daily Telegraph and North Murchison and Pilbara Gazette*, p. 1. https://trove.nla.gov.au/newspaper/article/211798157?searchTerm=ABC%20broadcast%20troops%20Menzies&searchLimits=

Daily Telegraph, The. (1937, June 30). ABC Denies Sops to Public. *The Daily Telegraph, Sydney*, p. 2. https://trove.nla.gov.au/newspaper/article/247141344?searchTerm=ABC%20Denies%20Sops%20to%20Public.%20

Daily Telegraph, The. (1948, December 4). *A.B.C. WON'T PAY FOR SPORT*, p. 5. https://trove.nla.gov.au/newspaper/article/248351380?searchTerm=ABC%20sport

Dailey, D., & Starbird, K. (2014). *Journalists as Crowdsourcerers: Responding to Crisis by Reporting with a Crowd Computer Supported Cooperative Work* (CSCW) (Vol. 23, pp. 445–481). https://doi.org/10.1007/s10606-014-9208-z

Dal Bo', E. (2006). Regulatory Capture: A Review. *Oxford Review of Economic Policy, 22*(2), 203–225. https://doi.org/10.1093/oxrep/grj013

Dalton, K. (2017, May). Missing in Action: The ABC and Australia's Screen Culture. Platform Papers. *Quarterly Essays on the Performing Arts from Currency House, 51*. Currency House.

Daly, J. (2020, January 6). How Social Licence and Clean Energy Will Change the Mining Industry by 2030. WA Country Hour. *Australian Broadcasting Corporation*. https://www.abc.net.au/news/rural/2020-01-06/how-social-license-and-clean-energy-change-mining-2030/11839044

Dalzell, S. (2019, October 23). 'There Will Be Job Losses': ABC Managing Director Confirms Staff To Go Following Budget Freeze [online]. ABC News. *Australian Broadcasting Corporation*. https://www.abc.net.au/news/2019-10-23/abc-boss-confirms-staff-to-go-following-budget-cuts/11629336

Dalzell, S. (2019, October 23). 'There Will Be Job Losses': ABC Managing Director Confirms Staff To Go Following Budget Freeze [online]. ABC News. *Australian Broadcasting Corporation*. https://www.abc.net.au/news/2019-10-23/abc-boss-confirms-staff-to-go-following-budget-cuts/11629336

Dandira, M. (2012). Dysfunctional Leadership: Organizational Cancer. *Business Strategy Series, 13*(4), 187–192. https://doi.org/10.1108/17515631211246267

Das, R., & Graefer, A. (2017). Regulatory Expectations of Offended Audiences: The Citizen Interest in Audience Discourse. *Communication, Culture & Critique, 10*(4), 626–640. https://doi.org/10.1111/cccr.12179

Datta, D. K., Guthrie, J. P., Basuil, D., & Pandey, A. (2010). Causes and Effects of Employment Downsizing: A Review and Synthesis. *Journal of Management, 36*, 281–348. https://doi.org/10.1177/0149206309346735

Dávid, G., & Furkó, B. (2015). The Journey Metaphor in Mediatized Political Discourse. *Acta Universitatis Sapientiae, Philologica, 7*(2), 7–20. https://doi.org/10.1515/ausp-2015-0043

Davis, J. (1996, November 1). Public Service TV in Crisis. *Broadcast, 44*, 16–17. EMAP Maclaren Ltd. (Archive: 1973–2000). https://login.wwwproxy1.library.unsw.edu.au/login?qurl=https%3A%2F%2Fsearch.proquest.com%2Fdocview%2F1705116138%3Faccountid%3D12763

Davey, M. (2019, February 27). Inside the Pell Trial: We Sat in Court for Months, Forbidden from Reporting a Word. *The Guardian*. https://www.theguardian.com/australia-news/2019/feb/27/inside-the-pell-trial-we-sat-in-court-for-months-forbidden-from-reporting-a-word

Davidson, H. (2015, June 23). Abbott Asks the ABC 'Whose Side Are You On?' Over Zaky Mallah's Q&A Appearance. *The Guardian*. https://www.theguardian.com/australia-news/2015/jun/23/abbott-asks-the-abc-whose-side-are-you-on-over-zaky-mallahs-qa-appearance

Davis, G. (1988). *Breaking Up the ABC*. Allen and Unwin.

Davies, N. (2009). *Flat Earth News*. Vintage Books.

Davies, N. (2014). *Hack Attack: How the Truth Caught Up With Rupert Murdoch*. Chatto & Windus.

Davies, N. (2009). *Flat Earth News*. Vintage Books.

Dawkins, R. (1976). *The Selfish Gene*. Oxford University Press. Oxford.

Dawson, J. (1985). The ABC Pseudo-Crisis. 1 May 1985. *P. 4. Filmnews*. Sydney. Retrieved from: https://trove.nla.gov.au/newspaper/article/213877547?searchTerm=ABC

Deakin, S., Lourenço, A. & Pratten, S. (2009). No "third way" for Economic Organization? Networks and Quasi-markets in Broadcasting. *Industrial and Corporate Change, 18*(1), 51–75. https://doi.org/10.1093/icc/dtn042

Debell, G. (2015). Malcolm Fraser: Realist to Radical and the Great Asia Project. *Australian Journal of International Affairs, 69*(6), 625–636. https://doi.org/10.1080/10357718.2015.1081147

Deitchman, S. (2013). Enhancing Crisis Leadership in Public Health Emergencies. *Disaster Medicine and Public Health Preparedness, 7*(5), 534–540. https://doi.org/10.1017/dmp.2013.81

Delgado, R., & Stefancic, J. (2014). Hate Speech in Cyberspace. *Wake Forest Law Review., 49*(2), 319–343.

Demaria, A. (2015). Employer's Requirement to Post a Social Media Disclaimer Passes NLRB Muster. *Management Report for Nonunion Organizations, 38*(1), 3–4. https://doi.org/10.1002/mare.30020

Dempster, Q. (2000). *Death Struggle: How Political Malice and Boardroom Powerplays are Killing the ABC*. Allen and Unwin.

DeNardis, L. (2014). The global war for internet governance. Yale University Press. New Haven.

Denhardt, J. V., & Denhardt, R. B. (2007). *The New Public Service: Serving, Not Steering*. M.E. Sharpe.

Department of Communications. (2015, July 1). Context and Decisions Regarding the Appearance of Mr Zaky Mallah on the ABC's Q&A Program on 22 June 2015. https://www.abc.net.au/news/2015-07-03/report-finds-q&a-did-investigate-zaky-mallah-before-appearance/6593810

Derrida, J. (1992). *Positions*. University of Chicago Press.

Derrida, J. (1998). *Of Grammatology* (G. C. Spivak, Trans., First published 1967). John Hopkins University Press.

Derrida, J. (2005). *Rogues*. Stanford University Press.

Devenney, M., Howarth, D., Norval, A. J., Stavrakakis, Y., Marchart, O., Biglieri, P., & Perelló, G. (2016). Ernesto Laclau. *Contemporary Political Theory, 15*(3), 304–335. https://doi.org/10.1057/cpt.2016.8

Devine, M. (2014, January 28). Why Does the ABC Hate Our Navy? Miranda Devine Blog Posts. *The Daily Telegraph*. https://www.dailytelegraph.com.au/blogs/miranda-devine/why-does-the-abc-hate-our-navy/news-story/939fe6616bc645bfa0b78532bf319ff3

Dewey, J. (1916, re-publ. 2004). *Democracy and Education*. Dover Publications.

Diakopoulos, N. (2019). *Automating the News: How Algorithms Are Rewriting the Media*. Harvard University Press. ProQuest Ebook Central. http://ebookcentral.proquest.com/lib/unsw/detail.action?docID=5761259

Diamond, E. (1975). *The Tin Kazoo: Television, Politics and the News*. MIT Press.

Dickens, C. (1836). *Pickwick Papers*. The Project Gutenberg EBook 2016. https://www.gutenberg.org/files/580/580-h/580-h.htm#link2HCH0032

Dickinson, H., Needham, C., Mangan, C., & Sullivan, H. E. (2019). *Reimagining the Future Public Service Workforce*. Springer Books.

Diefenbach, T. (2009). New Public Management in Public Sector Organizations: The Dark Sides of Managerialistic 'Enlightenment'. *Public Administration (London), 87*(4), 892–909. https://doi.org/10.1111/j.1467-9299.2009.01766.x

DiMaggio, A. (2009). *When Media Goes to War: Hegemonic Discourse, Public opinion and the Limits of Dissent*. Monthly Review Press.

DiMaggio, P. (1987). *Managers of the Arts: Careers and Opinions of Senior Administrators of U.S. Art Museums, Symphony Orchestras, Resident Theaters, and Local Arts Agencies*. Research Division Report #20 National Endowment for the Arts. Seven Locks Press Publishers. Washington, DC.

DiMaggio, P. (2018). Our Faith-Based Economy. *Distinktion: Journal of Social Theory, 19*(3), 328–335. https://doi.org/10.1080/1600910X.2018.1452769

DiMaggio, P., & Anheier, H. (1990). The Sociology of Non-profit Organizations and Sectors. *Annual Review of Sociology, 16*, 137–59. https://www.jstor.org/stable/2083266

DiMaggio, P. J., & Powell, W. W. (1983). The Iron Cage Revisited: Institutional Isomorphism and Collective Rationality in Organizational Fields. *American Sociological Review, 48*(2), 147–160. https://doi.org/10.2307/2095101

Dinh, J., Lord, R., Gardner, W., Meuser, J., Liden, R., & Hu, J. (2014). Leadership Theory and Research in the New Millennium: Current Theoretical Trends and Changing Perspectives. *Leadership Quarterly, 25*(1), 36–62. https://doi.org/10.1016/j.leaqua.2013.11.005

Dixon, F. (1975). *Inside the ABC: A Piece of Australian History.* The Hawthorn Press.

Doctor, D. (2018, June 8). ABC Article Likens Senior Editor at The Oz to Norwegian Mass Murderer. *Bandt.* https://www.bandt.com.au/abc-article-likens-editor-oz-norwegian-mass-murderer/

Dodd, A., Pasandaran, C.C., Green, S., Octavianto, A.W., & Mardjianto F.X.L.D. Proyek Sepaham. (2017). An Experiment in Crosscultural and Collaborative Journalism Education. *Asia Pacific Media Educator, 27*(1), 67–84. Retrieved from: https://doi.org/10.1177/1326365X17701790.

Donnan, P. (2020, May 4). Pell-Mell and Reform Paths in Catholic Media. *John Menadue Pearls and Irritations.* Public Policy Journal. https://johnmenadue.com/peter-donnan-pell-mell-and-reform-paths-in-catholic-media/

Donoughue, P. (2017, November 27). The Hottest 100 Won't Be Held on Australia Day Next Year, Triple J Says. *Australian Broadcasting Corporation.* https://www.abc.net.au/news/2017-11-27/hottest-100-wont-be-held-on-australia-day-triple-j-says/9197014

Dor, D. (2003). On Newspaper Headlines as Relevance Optimizers. *Journal of Pragmatics, 35*(5), 695–721. https://doi.org/10.1016/S0378-2166(02)00134-0

Dorey, P. (2015). The Legacy of Thatcherism—Public Sector Reform. *Observatoire de la société britannique* [En ligne]. 17. https://doi.org/10.4000/osb.1759

Dorsman, S. J., Bekkers, V. J. J. M., & Edwards, A. R. (2015). Trust the Experts!' Risk Definitions in Dutch Online Forums About the 'Swine Flu'. *Information, Communication & Society, 18*(10), 1217–1237. https://doi.org/10.1080/1369118X.2015.1036767

Downs, A. (1957). *An economic theory of democracy.* HarperCollins. New York.

Dowsley, A., & Deery, A. (2020, April 13). Freed George Pell Faces New Abuse Claims. *The Herald Sun.* https://global-factiva-com.ezproxy2.library.usyd.edu.au/ha/default.aspx#./!?&_suid=1586834573152009674286763378881

Dow Jones Institutional News. (2010, July 22). Australian Public Broadcaster Launches 24-Hour TV News. *Dow Jones.* https://login.wwwproxy1.library.unsw.edu.au/login?qurl=https%3A%2F%2Fsearch.proquest.com%2Fdocview%2F2169244539%3Faccountid%3D12763

Drori, G., Delmestri, S., & Oberg, G. (2016). The Iconography of Universities as Institutional Narratives. *Higher Education, 71*(2), 163–180. https://doi.org/10.1007/s10734-015-9894-6

Drozdek, A. (2015). Media Ethics. In *International Encyclopedia of the Social & Behavioral Sciences: Second Edition* (pp. 42–47). Elsevier Inc. https://doi.org/10.1016/B978-0-08-097086-8.11017-7

Dubie, D. (2003). Retaining Crucial Skills. *Network World, 20*(15), 43. http://search.proquest.com/docview/215974301/

Dubois, E., Gruzd, A., Jacobson, J., Chen, W., & Quan-Haase, A. (2020). Journalists' Use of Social Media to Infer Public Opinion: The Citizens' Perspective. *Social Science Computer Review, 38*(1), 57–74. https://doi.org/10.1177/0894439318791527

Dudley-Nicholson, J. (2020, March 5). AAP Demise a 'Wake-Up Call' Over Tech Giants. *The Australian*. https://www.theaustralian.com.au/business/media/aap-demise-a-wakeup-call-over-tech-giants/news-story/380efd106480aa0eaa5e3b871e2f5bfa

Dugan, J. P. (2011). Pervasive Myths in Leadership Development: Unpacking Constraints on Leadership Learning. *Journal of Leadership Studies, 5*(2), 79–84. https://doi.org/10.1002/jls.20223

Duke, J. (2017). ABC boss to push for more diversity of views among panel-show guests. *The Sydney Morning Herald*. 17 June 2019. Retrieved from: https://www.smh.com.au/business/companies/abc-boss-to-push-for-more-diversity-of-views-among-panel-show-guests-20190616-p51y7k.html

Duke, J. (2018, May 18). ABC Planning to Pay for Ranking in Google 'Royal Wedding' Searches. *The Sydney Morning Herald*. https://www.smh.com.au/business/companies/abc-planning-to-pay-for-ranking-in-google-royal-wedding-searches-20180518-p4zg3w.html

Duke, J. (2020, January 3). ABC Under 'Growing' Cost Pressure as Bushfire Emergency Broadcasts Surge. *The Sydney Morning Herald*. https://www.smh.com.au/business/companies/abc-under-growing-cost-pressure-as-bushfire-emergency-broadcasts-surge-20200103-p53ohp.html

Duke, J., Carmody, B., & Koziol, M. (2018, September 24). Michelle Guthrie: The Inside Story Behind Her Sacking. *The Sydney Morning Herald*. https://www.smh.com.au/business/companies/michelle-guthrie-the-inside-story-behind-her-sacking-20180924-p505ok.html

Dukes, K. N., & Gaither, S. E. (2017). Black Racial Stereotypes and Victim Blaming: Implications for Media Coverage and Criminal Proceedings in Cases of Police Violence against Racial and Ethnic Minorities. *Journal of Social Issues, 73*(4), 789–807. https://doi.org/10.1111/josi.12248

Dumas, D. (2020, April 5). Bondi Beach: How the Australian Icon Became a Coronavirus Hotspot. *The Guardian*. https://www.theguardian.com/australia-news/2020/apr/05/bondi-beach-how-the-australian-icon-became-a-coronavirus-hotspot

Dunstan, J., Longbottom, J., Farnsworth, S., & King, C. (2020, May 7). George Pell 'Surprised' by Royal Commission Finding He Was Told of Ridsdale Abuse.

ABC News. https://www.abc.net.au/news/2020-05-07/royal-commission-findings-on-cardinal-george-pell-released/12217362Dur:7'09"

Dwyer, D. E., Howard, R., Downie, J., & Cunningham, A. L. (1988, July). The "Grim Reaper" Campaign. *The Medical Journal of Australia, 149*(1), 49–50. https://onlinelibrary-wiley-com.wwwproxy1.library.unsw.edu.au/doi/abs/10.5694/j.1326-5377.1988.tb120487.x

Dwyer, T., & Martin, F. (2017). Sharing News Online. *Digital Journalism, 5*(8), 1080–1100. https://doi.org/10.1080/21670811.2017.1338527. Quoting CNNIC 2016; Newman et al. 2016; Pew Research Center 2016.

Dynel, M., Chovanec, M., & Chovanec, J. (2015). *Participation in Public and Social Media Interactions* (p. 49). John Benjamins Publishing Company. https://primoa.library.unsw.edu.au/permalink/f/jhud33/UNSW_ALMA51236854060001731

Easton, S. (2019, May 8). Mike Mrdak: Public Servants Must Ditch the Business Jargon, Stop Being Scared of Citizens. *The Mandarin*. https://www.themandarin.com.au/108114-mike-mrdak-public-servants-must-ditch-the-business-jargon-stop-being-scared-of-citizens/

Echo Net Daily. (2020, June 26). Liberal–National Party Cuts to ABC Risk Australian Lives. https://www.echo.net.au/2020/06/liberal-national-party-cuts-to-abc-condemned-by-mp-elliot/

Eddie, R. (2020, February 14). High Court Sets the Date for George Pall's Final Appeal. *The Sydney Morning Herald*. https://www.smh.com.au/national/high-court-sets-the-date-for-george-pell-s-final-appeal-20200214-p540ub.html

Edelman Trust Barometer. (2018). Global Report. Edelman. Retrieved from: https://www.edelman.com/sites/g/files/aatuss191/files/2018-10/2018_Edelman_Trust_Barometer_Global_Report_FEB.pdf

Edwards, E. D., & Fuller, T. (2020). *Graphic Violence: Illustrated Theories about Violence, Popular Media, and Our Social Lives* (First edition.). Routledge. New York.

Edwards, M., Halligan, J, Horrigan, B., & Nicoll, G. (2012). *Public Sector Governance in Australia*. Australian National University EPress. Griffin Press. https://press-files.anu.edu.au/downloads/press/p190701/pdf/book.pdf

Egan, T. (2019, October 25). Why Doesn't Mark Zuckerberg Get It? The Facebook Co-Founder's Speech at Georgetown Was a Profile in Cowardice. Opinion. *The New York Times*. https://www.nytimes.com/2019/10/25/opinion/facebook-mark-zuckerberg.html?action=click&module=Opinion&pgtype=Homepage

Eisenstein, E. (1979). *The Printing Press as an Agent of Change: Communications and Cultural Transformations in Early Modern Europe*. 1. Cambridge University Press.

Elliott, G., Sainsbury, M., & Overington, C. (2010, July 24). ABC Picks Sides While the 'Editor-in-Chief' Watches On. [online]. *The Australian*. https://

www.theaustralian.com.au/national-affairs/abc-picks-sides-while-the-editor-in-chief-watches-on/news-story/59e747a64f4d496c33e661f4ab25a6e2

Ellison, S. (2010). *War at The Wall Street Journal: How Rupert Murdoch bought an American icon*. Text Publishing. Melbourne.

Enchin, H. (1993, April 12). CBC Seeks Niche in New TV Markets: Network Stresses Role as Public Broadcaster. *The Globe and Mail*. http://search.proquest.com/docview/346810951/

Entman, R. M. (2004). *Projections of Power: Framing News, Public Opinion, and U.S. Foreign Policy*. University of Chicago Press.

Enus, A., Petersen, J., Abo, S., Brennan, F., Francis, P., & Levey, P. (2016). The Pope Says Cardinal George Pell Should Not Face a Trial by Media, Following Allegations Against Him, Aired on Australian Television. In *World News Australia*. RMIT Publishing. https://primoa.library.unsw.edu.au/permalink/f/11jha62/TN_informit_tvnewsTSM201608010257

Epitropaki, O., & Martin, R. (2004). Implicit Leadership Theories in Applied Settings: Factor Structure, Generalizability, and Stability Over Time. *Journal of Applied Psychology, 89*(2), 293–310. http://ovidsp.ovid.com/ovidweb.cgi?T=JS&PAGE=reference&D=ovftg&NEWS=N&AN=00004565-200404000-00008

Erbschloe, M. (2017). *Social Media Warfare: Equal Weapons for All*. Taylor & Francis. E-book. https://ebookcentral.proquest.com/lib/unsw/reader.action?docID=4856182

Ernst, H. (2010). Whither Advocacy Journalism? *World Future Review, 2*(6), 43–46. https://doi.org/10.1177/194675671000200606

Evans, H. (1984). *Good Times, Bad Times. Hodder and Stoughton*. London.

Evans, H. (1986, March). How the ABC Lost the Public. *Quadrant, 30*(3), 28–29, 31–32. https://search-informit-com-au.wwwproxy1.library.unsw.edu.au/documentSummary;dn=329495072963761;res=IELLCC

Evans, H. (2015, April 28). How Thatcher and Murdoch Made Their Secret Deal. *The Guardian*. https://www.theguardian.com/uk-news/2015/apr/28/how-margaret-thatcher-and-rupert-murdoch-made-secret-deal

Evans, S. K. (2018). Making Sense of Innovation. *Journalism Studies, 19*(1), 4–24. London, England. https://doi.org/10.1080/1461670X.2016.1154446

Evening Standard. (2013, February 8). Duchess of York and 16 Other Phone-Hack Victims Get Apologies. *Evening Standard*. https://www.standard.co.uk/news/uk/duchess-of-york-and-16-other-phone-hack-victims-get-apologies-8487104.html

Event Brief of Q4 2008 News Corporation Earnings Conference Call - Final. (2008, Aug 05). *Fair Disclosure Wire*. Retrieved from: https://www.proquest.com/wire-feeds/event-brief-q4-2008-news-corporation-earnings/docview/466169731/se-2?accountid=8194

Examiner, The. (1941). Broadcast of News: Newspapers' Attitude. *The Examiner*, p. 5. https://trove.nla.gov.au/newspaper/article/25898225?searchTerm=The%20newspapers%20rejected%20as%20unjustified%20any%20suggestion%20that%20their%20attitude%20was%20monopolistic

Fairfax, J. (1991). *My Regards to Broadway*. Angus and Robertson.

Fairfax, J. (1992). *My Regards to Broadway*. Angus and Robertson. Pymble.

Fairhurst, G. (2008). Discursive Leadership: A Communication Alternative to Leadership Psychology. *Management Communication Quarterly, 21*(4), 510–521. https://doi.org/10.1177/0893318907313714

Fallows, J. (2003, August 30, September). The Age of Murdoch. *The Weekend Australian*. Also in *The Atlantic*. https://www.theatlantic.com/magazine/archive/2003/09/the-age-of-murdoch/302777/

Fardouly, J., & Holland, E. (2018). Social Media Is Not Real Life: The Effect of Attaching Disclaimer-Type Labels to Idealized Social Media Images on women's Body Image and Mood. *New Media & Society, 20*(11), 4311–4328. https://doi.org/10.1177/1461444818771083

FarmOnline, & AAP. (2020, June 24). ABC Life Becomes ABC Local as National Broadcaster Restructured. [online]. *FarmOnline*. https://www.farmonline.com.au/story/6804883/regional-focus-boost-for-abc-in-major-restructure/

Faruqi, O. (2020, June 25). Closing ABC Life Is More About Politics and Appeasement Than Good Outcomes. *The Guardian*. https://www.theguardian.com/commentisfree/2020/jun/25/closing-abc-life-is-more-about-politics-and-appeasement-than-good-outcomes

Fasoli, F., Maass, A., & Carnaghi, A. (2015). Labelling and Discrimination: Do Homophobic Epithets Undermine Fair Distribution of Resources? *The British Journal of Social Psychology, 54*(2), 383–393. https://doi.org/10.1111/bjso.12090

Fayol, H. (1949). *General and Industrial Management*. Pitman. Quoted in Maughan, M. (2014). *Organisational Behaviour*. Palgrave Macmillan.

Feldman, E. (2014). Legacy Divestitures: Motives and Implications. *Organization Science, 25*(3), 815–832. https://doi.org/10.1287/orsc.2013.0873

Fenton, N. (2014). Defending Whose Democracy? Media Freedom and Media Power. *Nordicom Review, 35*, 31–44. https://www.nordicom.gu.se/sites/default/files/kapitel-pdf/fenton.pdf

Ferguson, J. (2018, March 30). George Pell Committal: Extraordinary Scenes Inside Court 22. *The Australian*. https://www.theaustralian.com.au/nation/inquirer/george-pell-committal-extraordinary-scenes-inside-court-22/news-story/bf3e7f5bafed31e451d3b1680a1776fb

Ferguson, R. (2019, June 4). News Corp: Police Raid on Journalist's Home 'Dangerous Act of Intimidation'. *The Australian*. Retrieved https://www.theaustralian.com.au/business/media/police-raid-home-of-news-corp-journalist/news-story/910d9cf3e9097c647c2800581f86502f

Ferguson, R., & Vitorovich, L. (2020, June 2). US Protests: Police Attack Channel 7 News Team as Donald Trump Walks from White House. *The Australian*. https://www.theaustralian.com.au/business/media/us-protests-police-attack-channel-7-news-team-as-donald-trump-walks-from-white-house/news-story/e326fa536c5b2d15ccca4659ca9ec917

Fifth Estate, The. (2021, January 16). On the Australia Fires and What Comes Next. Environment. Our View. https://www.thefifthestate.com.au/urbanism/environment/on-the-australia-fires-and-what-comes-next/

Finkelstein, R. (2012, February 28). Report of The Independent Inquiry Into The Media and Media Regulation. Report to the Minister for Broadband, Communications and the Digital Economy. *Australian Government*. http://www.abc.net.au/mediawatch/transcripts/1205_finkelstein.pdf

Fisher, C. (2016). The Advocacy Continuum: Towards a Theory of Advocacy in Journalism. *Journalism, 17*(6), 711–726. https://doi.org/10.1177/1464884915582311

Fishman, J. M., & Marvin, C. (2003). Portrayals of Violence and Group Difference in Newspaper Photographs: Nationalism and Media. *Journal of Communication, 53*(1), 32–44. https://doi.org/10.1111/j.1460-2466.2003.tb03003.x

Fiske, J. (1982). *Studies in Communication*. Methuen.

Fiske, J. (1989). Moments of Television: Neither the Text Nor the Audience. In E. Seiter, H. Borchers, G. Kreutzner, & E.-M. Warth (Eds.), *Remote Control: Television Audiences and Cultural Power*. Routledge.

Fitzell, J. (1970). Dealing with the Elephant in the Room. Career Insights: Management Insights. *Professionals Australia*.http://www.professionalsaustralia.org.au/australian-government/blog/dealing-with-the-elephant-in-the-room/

Fitzpatrick, S. M. (2000). Sensational News. *Forum for Applied Research and Public Policy, 15*(3), 95–96. http://search.proquest.com/docview/235135227/

Fitzsimmons, J. A., & Fitzsimmons, M. J. (2004). *Service Management: Operations, Strategy, and Information Technology* (4th ed.). McGraw-Hill.

Flanagan, M. (2014, February 8). Rupert Murdoch's Attack on 'Our ABC' Like a Mediaeval Siege. [online]. *The Sydney Morning Herald, The*. https://www.smh.com.au/opinion/rupert-murdochs-attack-on-our-abc-like-a-mediaeval-siege-20140207-32746.html

Fleck, N., Michel, G., & Zeitoun, V. (2014). Brand Personification through the Use of Spokespeople: An Exploratory Study of Ordinary Employees, CEOs, and Celebrities Featured in Advertising. *Psychology & Marketing, 31*(1), 84–92. https://doi.org/10.1002/mar.20677

Fletcher, R., (2018). *The Rise of Populism and the Consequences for News and Media Use*. Digital News Report. Reuters Institute & University of Oxford. http://www.digitalnewsreport.org/survey/2019/the-rise-of-populism-and-the-consequences-for-news-and-media-use/

Fletcher, R., & Park, S. (2017). The Impact of Trust in the News Media on Online News Consumption and Participation. *Digital Journalism, 5*(10), 1281–1299. https://doi.org/10.1080/21670811.2017.1279979

Fleuriet, C.A., & Lee Williams, M. (2015). Improving Institutional Credibility: Communication as the Centerpiece of Planning in the Age of Accountability. *Educational Planning, 22*(1), 67. Buffalo, N.Y. ISSN: 1537-873X

Flew, T. (2006). The Social Contract and Beyond in Broadcast Media Policy. *Television & New Media, 7*(3), 282–305. https://doi.org/10.1177/1527476404270606

Flew, T., & Goldsmith, B. (2013, August 8). Fact Check: Does Murdoch Own 70% of Newspapers in Australia? *The Conversation*. https://theconversation.com/factcheck-does-murdoch-own-70-of-newspapers-in-australia-16812

Flinders, M. (2015). The General Rejection? Political Disengagement, Disaffected Democrats and 'Doing Politics' Differently. *Parliamentary Affairs, 68*(Suppl1), 241–254. https://doi.org/10.1093/pa/gsv038

Flint, J. (2020, June 11). Race Protests: Gone with The Wind, Little Britain and Comedies by Chris Lilley Pulled by Streaming Services. *The Australian*. https://www.theaustralian.com.au/business/the-wall-street-journal/rhett-forced-to-give-a-damn-about-race-as-gone-with-the-wind-pulled/news-story/10dac76431771e180aa62754329f9db4

Flores, R. (2002). Press Headlines on the Internet: An Aspectual Analysis. *Signos Literarios y Linguisticos,* 4(1), 45–57. http://search.proquest.com/docview/85615892/

Floyd, J. ""The True" in Journalism" in J. Katz, J. E. & Mays, K. K. (2019). *Journalism and Truth in an Age of Social Media*. Oxford University Press. https://doi.org/10.1093/oso/9780190900250.001.0001

Foreign Policy. Editorial. (2010, March/April). iWar. *Foreign Policy, 178*(1). https://www-jstor-org.wwwproxy1.library.unsw.edu.au/stable/20684986?seq=1#metadata_info_tab_contents

Foucault, M. (1976). *Trans. A.M. Sheridan Smith. The Archaeology of Knowledge & the Discourse on Language*. Pantheon Book. New York.

Foucault, M. (1983, October–November). *Discourse and Truth: The Problematization of Parrhesia* (J. Pearson, Ed.). Taken from a Series of Lectures. University of California. https://foucault.info/parrhesia/

Fouskas, V. K. (2013). Athens Has No Voice: On the Closure of Greece's Public Broadcasting Corporation (ERT). *Debatte: Journal of Contemporary Central and Eastern Europe, 21*(1), 107–111. https://doi.org/10.1080/0965156X.2013.836858

Frank, J. (1961). *The Beginnings of the English Newspaper, 1620–60*. Harvard University Press.

Franklin, B., & Mensing, D. (2010). *Journalism Education, Training and Employment*. 1st Ed. Routledge. New York.

Fraser, F. (2014). Orchestrating the Metropolis the Creation of the Sydney Symphony Orchestra as a Modern Cultural Institution. *History Australia, 11*(2), 196–221. https://doi.org/10.1080/14490854.2014.11668522

Fraser, M., & O'Reilly, J. (1996). *Save Our ABC: Maintaining Australia's National Broadcaster.* Hyland House. South Melbourne.

Fraser, M., & O'Reilly, J. (Eds.). (1996). *Save Our ABC: The Case for Maintaining Australia's National Broadcaster.* Hyland House.

Freedman, D. (2019). "Public Service" and the Journalism Crisis: Is the BBC the Answer? *Television & New Media, 20*(3), 203–218. https://doi.org/10.1177/1527476418760985

Friedland, R. (2013). The Gods of Institutional Life: Weber's Value Spheres and the Practice of Polytheism. *Critical Research on Religion, 1*(1), 15–24. https://doi.org/10.1177/2050303213476104

Friedland, R. (2018). Moving Institutional Logics Forward: Emotion and Meaningful Material Practice. *Organization Studies, 39*(4), 515–542. https://doi.org/10.1177/0170840617709307

Friedland, R., & Alford, R. R. (1991). Bringing Society Back. In W. W. Powell & P. J. DiMaggio (Eds.), *Symbols, Practices and Institutional Contradictions (The New Institutionalism in Organisational Analysis).* University of Chicago Press. Chicago, IL.

Friedland, R., & Alford, R. R. (1991). Bringing Society Back, in: W.W. Powell & P.J. DiMaggio (Eds). Symbols, Practices and Institutional Contradictions. The New Institutionalism in Organizational Analysis. Chicago, IL. University of Chicago Press.

Friedman, R. A. (2009). The Role of Psychiatrists Who Write for Popular Media: Experts, Commentators, or Educators? *The American Journal of Psychiatry, 166*(7), 757–759. https://doi.org/10.1176/appi.ajp.2009.08121847

Friends of the ABC (Vic). (2008, December). *Submission: ABC and SBS: Towards a Digital Future.* https://me.abcfriendsvic.org.au/wp-content/uploads/2016/03/abc_review-fabc_submapp08.pdf

Furedi, F. (2006). *Culture of Fear Revisited: Risk-Taking and the Morality of Low Expectation* (4th ed.). Continuum.

Fu, J. S., & Shumate, M. (2017). News Media, Social Media, and Hyperlink Networks: An Examination of Integrated Media Effects. *The Information Society, 33*(2), 53–63. https://doi.org/10.1080/01972243.2016.1271379

Fukuyama, F. (2018). *Identity: The Demand for Dignity and the Politics of Resentment.* Farrar, Straus & Giroux.

Funnell, A. (2020, January 31). Is This the End of the Liberal International Order? And What Might Take Its Place? ABC Radio National. Future Tense. ABC Radio Online. https://www.abc.net.au/news/2020-01-31/liberal-international-order-under-threat-china-us/11905652

Funston, A. (1997). The ABC and Citizenship [online]. *Overland, 147*(Winter), 59–62. https://search-informit-com-au.wwwproxy1.library.unsw.edu.au/documentSummary;dn=971111828;res=IELAPA

Galston, W. (2018, 17 April). *The Populist Challenge to Liberal Democracy.* [online]. Brookings Institute. https://www.brookings.edu/research/the-populist-challenge-to-liberal-democracy/

Galtung, J. (1998). The Peace Movement: An Exercise in Micro-Macro Linkages. *International Social Science Journal, 50*(157), 401–405. https://doi.org/10.1111/1468-2451.00153

Gamson, J. (2015). Celebrity. In A. Drozdek. (2015). Media Ethics. *In International Encyclopedia of the Social & Behavioral Sciences, 15*, 42–47.

Gamson, W., Croteau, D., Hoynes, W., & Sasson, T. (1992). Media Images and the Social Construction of Reality. *Annual Review of Sociology, 18*, 373–393. http://search.proquest.com/docview/199734271/

Gans, H. J. (2003). *Democracy and the News.* Oxford University Press.

Gans, H. J. (2004). *Deciding What's News: A Study of CBS Evening News, NBC Nightly News, Newsweek and Time.* 25th Anniversary Edition. Northwestern University Press.

Gans, H. J. (2004). *Deciding What's News: A Study of CBS Evening News, NBC Nightly News, Newsweek and Time.* 25th Anniversary Edition. Northwestern University Press.

García-Gutiérrez, I., & Martínez-Borreguero, F. J. (2016). The Innovation Pivot Framework: Fostering Business Model Innovation in Startups. *Research Technology Management, 59*(5), 48–56. https://doi.org/10.1080/08956308.2016.1208043

Gardels, N. (1995). Is There a Liberal Bias in the Media? *New Perspectives Quarterly, 12*(2). http://search.proquest.com/docview/196967275/

Gardeström, E. (2017). Losing Control. *Journalism Studies, 18*(4), 511–524. 511–524. https://doi.org/10.1080/1461670X.2015.1073117

Garnham, P. (1986). 'The media and the public sphere'. In P. Golding, G. Murdock & P. Schiesinger (Eds.), *Communicating Politics: Mass Communication and the Political Process.* Leicester University Press. Leicester.

Garrett, D. (2012). The Accidental Entrepreneur—How ABC Music Became More Than Broadcasting. Doctor of Philosophy thesis. Faculty of Creative Arts. *University of Wollongong.* https://ro.uow.edu.au/theses/3680

Gasher, M., & McIntosh, A. (2019). *Media convergence* (English ed.). *Historica Canada.* http://search.proquest.com/docview/2315251385/

Gentzkow, M., Glaeser, E. L., & Goldin, C. (2006). The Rise of the Fourth Estate. How Newspapers Became Informative and Why It Mattered. In E. L. Glaeser & C. Goldin (Eds.), *Corruption and Reform: Lessons from America's Economic History.* University of Chicago Press.

George, P. (1989). Behind the Lines: The Personal Story of an ABC Foreign Correspondent. ABC Books. Sydney.

George, G., Dahlander, L., Graffin, S., & Sim, S. (2016). Reputation and Status: Expanding the Role of Social Evaluations in Management Research. *Academy of Management Journal*, 59(1), 1–13. Retrieved from: https://doi.org/10.5465/amj.2016.4001

Georgetown University. (2018). What is a Jesuit? Retrieved from: https://www.georgetown.edu/news/the-jesuit-mission-seeking-god-in-all-things/#:~:text=What%20is%20a%20Jesuit%3F,seek%20God%20in%20all%20things

Ghosn, N. (2015). The Decline of Public Broadcasting in France. *E-journal of Intermedia, 2*(1, Spring), 143–157. https://search-proquest-com.www-proxy1.library.unsw.edu.au/docview/1810112560?rfr_id=info%3Axri%2Fsid%3Aprimo

Gilani, P., Bolat, E., Nordberg, D., & Wilkin, C. (2020). Mirror, Mirror on the Wall: Shifting Leader–Follower Power Dynamics in a Social Media Context. *Leadership, 16*(3), 343–363. London, England. https://doi.org/10.1177/1742715019889817

Gilfillan, G. (2018, December 10). 'Trends in Use of Non-Standard Forms of Employment', by Statistics and Mapping Section. *Parliament of Australia*. https://www.aph.gov.au/About_Parliament/Parliamentary_Departments/Parliamentary_Library/pubs/rp/rp1819/NonStandardEmployment

Gillin, J. (2013, April 8). Bill Adair: Fact-Checking 'Is a Good Investment'. *The Poynter Institute*. https://www.poynter.org/reporting-editing/2013/bill-adair-fact-checking-is-a-good-investment/

Girard, R., & Grayson, R. (2016). Belonging. *Contagion: Journal of Violence, Mimesis, and Culture, 23*(1), 1–12. https://doi.org/10.14321/contagion.23.1.0001

Giustini, D. (2005). How Google is Changing Medicine. *British Medical Journal, 331*(7531), 1487–1488. https://doi.org/10.1136/bmj.331.7531.1487

Given, J. (1998). *The Death of Broadcasting? Media's Digital Future*. Communications Law Centre. UNSW Press.

Gizbert, R. (2020, August 8). Murdoch's Misinformation: COVID-19, China and Climate Change. *The Listening Post. Al Jazeera*. https://www.aljazeera.com/programmes/listeningpost/2020/08/murdoch-misinformation-covid-19-china-climate-change-200808072643503.html (now a dead link)

Gleeson, C. (2013/14). Social Media and the Courts [online]. *Bar News: The Journal of the NSW Bar Association* (Summer), 54–59. https://search-informit-com-au.wwwproxy1.library.unsw.edu.au/documentSummary;dn=125912803397523;res=IELHSS

Glynn, M. (2000, May–June). When Cymbals Become Symbols: Conflict Over Organizational Identity Within a Symphony Orchestra. *Organization Science*,

11(3). Special Issue: Cultural Industries: Learning from Evolving Organizational Practices, pp. 285–298. https://www.jstor.org/stable/2640262

Glynn, M. (2000, May–June). When Cymbals Become Symbols: Conflict Over Organizational Identity Within a Symphony Orchestra. *Organization Science, 11*(3). Special Issue: Cultural Industries: Learning from Evolving Organizational Practices, pp. 285–298. https://www.jstor.org/stable/2640262

Glynn, M., & Lounsbury, M. (2005). From the Critics' Corner: Logic Blending, Discursive Change and Authenticity in a Cultural Production System. *The Journal of Management Studies., 42*(5), 1031–1055. https://doi.org/10.1111/j.1467-6486.2005.00531.x

Goebbels, J. (1941). "Churchill's Lie Factory," (12 January, 1941). Original: "Aus Churchills Lügenfabrik," Die Zeit ohne Beispiel. Zentralverlag der NSDAP. Munich. pp. 364–369. Jewish Virtual Library. Joseph Goebbels: On the "Big Lie". Retrieved from: https://www.jewishvirtuallibrary.org/joseph-goebbels-on-the-quot-big-lie-quot

Goffman, E. (1961). *Encounters: Two Studies in the Sociology of Interaction*. Bobbs-Merrill. Indianapolis. IN.

Goggin, G. (Ed.). (2004). *Virtual Nation: The Internet in Australia*. UNSW Press.

Golant, B., Sillince, J., Harvey, C., & Maclean, M. (2015). Rhetoric of Stability and Change: The Organizational Identity Work of Institutional Leadership. *Human Relations, 68*(4), 607–631. https://doi.org/10.1177/0018726714532966

Goldman, S. (2019, 03). Jews Must Not Embrace Powerlessness. *Commentary, 147*, 37–39. https://www.commentarymagazine.com/articles/sharon-goldman/jews-must-not-embrace-powerlessness/

Goodall, H. (2012). Media's Influence on Gender Stereotypes. *Media Asia, 39*(3), 160–163. https://doi.org/10.1080/01296612.2012.11689932

Gordon, J. (2013, May 22). State Liberals Propose Privatising ABC, SBS. *The Sydney Morning Herald*. https://www.smh.com.au/politics/federal/state-liberals-propose-privatising-abc-sbs-20130521-2jz5d.html

Gordon, J. (2018, November 19). Australians Are Losing Their Trust in 'The Media', But Not in Journalism. RMIT. ABC Fact Check. *Australian Broadcasting Corporation*. https://www.abc.net.au/news/2018-09-10/fact-checking-the-new-workplace-skill/10209210

Gottschalk, S. (2018). The Infantilization of Western Culture. *The Conversation*. https://theconversation.com/the-infantilization-of-western-culture-99556

Goulburn Evening Penny Post. (1924, July 17). "AUSTRALIANS SPORTS MAD". English Visitor's Opinion. *We Don't Walk Enough*, p. 2. https://trove.nla.gov.au/newspaper/article/99288972?searchTerm=australians%20sports%20mad

Goot, M., & Inglis, K. S. (2014). Mayer, Henry (1919–1991). *Australian Dictionary of Biography*. http://adb.anu.edu.au/biography/mayer-henry-17251

Goulburn Evening Post. (1953, June 12). ABC Chairman's view on TV. *Goulburn Evening Post*, p. 3. https://trove.nla.gov.au/newspaper/article/104558411?searchTerm=ABC%20Chairman%E2%80%99s%20view%20on%20TV

Gordon, J. (2018, November 19). Australians Are Losing Their Trust in 'The Media', But Not in Journalism. RMIT. ABC Fact Check. *Australian Broadcasting Corporation*. https://www.abc.net.au/news/2018-09-10/fact-checking-the-new-workplace-skill/10209210

Grant, E. (1973). Medieval Explanations and Interpretations of the Dictum that 'Nature Abhors a Vacuum'. *Traditio*, *29*, 327–355. https://doi.org/10.1017/S0362152900009004

Grattan, M. (2014, January/March). What Future for the ABC? *Public Administration Today*, *37*, 22–23. https://search-informit-com-au.www-proxy1.library.unsw.edu.au/fullText;dn=20141588;res=AGISPT

Grattan, M. (2017, April 26). Abdel-Magied Anzac Row Is a Storm Over Not Much. *The Conversation*. https://theconversation.com/abdel-magied-anzac-row-is-a-storm-over-not-much-76708

Grattan, M. (2018, June 19). ABC Contributes as Much to the Economy as it Costs the Taxpayer: Michelle Guthrie. *The Conversation*.https://theconversation.com/abc-contributes-as-much-to-the-economy-as-it-costs-the-taxpayer-michelle-guthrie-98553

Gray-Hoehn, H. (2020). In K. Bezio & G. Goethals (Eds.), *Leadership, Populism, and Resistance*. Edward Elgar Publishing.

Greenleaf, R. (1977). *Servant Leadership: A Journey Into the Nature of Legitimate Power and Greatness*. Paulist Press.

Greenwald, R. (2004). *Outfoxed: Rupert Murdoch's War on Journalism*. Brave New Films.

Greenwood, R., Oliver, C., Suddaby, R., & Sahlin-Andersson, K. (2012). *The SAGE Handbook of Organizational Institutionalism. SAGE Publications. ProQuest Ebook Central*. https://ebookcentral.proquest.com/lib/unsw/detail.action?docID=1024020

Greer, A. (2012). Commons and Enclosure in the Colonization of North America. *The American Historical Review*, *117*(2), 365–386. https://doi.org/10.1086/ahr.117.2.365

Greer, A., & Hoggett, P. (1999). Public Policies, Private Strategies and Local Public Spending Bodies. *Public Administration*, *77*(2), 235–256. https://doi.org/10.1111/1467-9299.00152

Greer, A., & Hoggett, P. (2000). Contemporary Governance and Local Public Spending Bodies. *Public Administration, 78*(3), 513–529. https://doi.org/10.1111/1467-9299.00216

Greer, C., & McLaughlin, E. (2010). We Predict a Riot?: Public Order Policing, New Media Environments and the Rise of the Citizen Journalist. *British Journal of Criminology, 50*(6), 1041–1059.

Gregory, P. J. (2005). *Court Reporting in Australia.* Cambridge University Press. Cambridge; New York.

Grensing-Pophal, L. (2010, January–February). Social Media: Journalism's Friend or Foe?. *Econtentmag.com.* http://www.econtentmag.com/Articles/Editorial/Feature/Social-Media-Journalisms-Friend-or-Foe-61147.htm

Grieco, E. (2020, April 20). U.S. Newspapers Have Shed Half of Their Newsroom Employees Since 2008. *Pew Research Center.* https://www.pewresearch.org/fact-tank/2020/04/20/u-s-newsroom-employment-has-dropped-by-a-quarter-since-2008/

Griffen-Foley, B. (2001). The Battle of Melbourne: The rise and fall of the Star. *Journal of Australian Studies, 25*, 69. Retrieved from: https://doi.org/10.1080/14443050109387690

Griffin, E. (2006). *A First Look at Communication Theory.* McGraw-Hill.

Griffith, C. (1996, August). The ABC and Multimedia: A New Media Form [online]. *Media International Australia,* 81, 49–53. https://search-informit-com-au.wwwproxy1.library.unsw.edu.au/documentSummary;dn=078935934053890;res=IELLCC

Grinberg, D. B. (2018, March 15). Why Traditional Media Still Matters in Today's Digital Age. *Medium.* https://medium.com/@DBGrinberg/why-traditional-media-still-matters-in-todays-digital-age-f81350674e2f

Grossman, L. (2010, December 15). Mark Zuckerberg: Person of the Year. [online]. *Time Magazine.* http://content.time.com/time/specials/packages/article/0,28804,2036683_2037183_2037185-1,00.html

Gruber, D., Smerek, R., Thomas-Hunt, M., & James, E. (2015). The Real-Time Power of Twitter: Crisis Management and Leadership in an Age of Social Media. *Business Horizons, 58*(2), 163–172. https://doi.org/10.1016/j.bushor.2014.10.006

Gruen, D., & Clark, C. (2010). Nineteenth Colin Clark Lecture: November 2009 What Have We Learnt? The Great Depression in Australia from the Perspective of Today. *Economic Analysis & Policy, 40*(1). https://doi.org/10.1016/S0313-5926(10)50001-8

Guardian Staff. (2018, September 24). ABC in Turmoil: Who Said What on Boss Michelle Guthrie's Sacking. *The Guardian.* https://www.theguardian.com/media/2018/sep/24/abc-in-turmoil-who-said-what-on-boss-michelle-guthries-sacking

Guardian, The. (2019, July 10). Scott Morrison Prays at Hillsong Conference—Video. *The Guardian*. https://www.theguardian.com/australia-news/video/2019/jul/10/scott-morrison-discusses-freedom-of-religion-during-hillsong-conference-video

Guillot, C. (2013, October 1). The Wisdom of the Crowd. *Internal Auditor, 70*(5), 44. http://search.proquest.com/docview/1464388029/

Guler, A.Y. (2020, April 14). One Coronavirus Patient Can Infect Up to 400. *Anadolu Agency*. https://www.aa.com.tr/en/latest-on-coronavirus-outbreak/one-coronavirus-patient-can-infect-up-to-400/1804349

Gulyas, A. (2013). The Influence of Professional Variables On Journalists' Uses And Views Of Social Media: *A Comparative Study of Finland, Germany, Sweden and the United Kingdom. Digital Journalism, 1*(2). https://doi.org/10.1080/21670811.2012.744559

Gustafson, K. L., & Kenix, L. J. (2016). Visually Framing Press Freedom and Responsibility of a Massacre: Photographic and Graphic Images in Charlie Hebdo"s Newspaper Front Pages Around the World. *Visual Communication Quarterly, 23*(3), 147–160. https://doi.org/10.1080/15551393.2016.1190623

Guterres, A. (2018, September 23). Secretary-General's Address to the General Assembly. *UN Secretary General*. https://www.un.org/sg/en/content/sg/statement/2018-09-25/secretary-generals-address-general-assembly-delivered-trilingual

Guthrie, B. (2010). *Man Bites Murdoch: Four Decades in Print, Six Days in Court*. Melbourne University Press.

Guthrie, M. (2016). Email to staff, 2 May.

Habermas, J. (1962, repr. 1991). *The Structural Transformation of the Public Sphere: An Inquiry Into a Category of Bourgeois Society* (T. Burger, Trans.). MIT Press.

Habermas, J. (1989, origin. publ. 1961). (Trans. T. Burger). *The Structural Transformation of the Public Sphere*. Polity Press. Great Britain.

Habermas, J. (2006, March 9). Acceptance Speech for the Bruno Kreisky Prize for the Advancement of Human Rights. In A. Keen. (2007) (Ed.), *The Cult of the Amateur: How Today's Internet Is Killing Our Culture*. Doubleday/Currency.

Haigh, G. (2011). Why, Oh Why, Must They Be Such Tightwads? *The Australian Rationalist, 87*(Summer), 5–8. https://primoa.library.unsw.edu.au/permalink/f/11jha62/TN_informit_apaft201103405

Hall, P. A., & Taylor, R. C. (1996). Political Science and the Three New Institutionalisms. *Political Studies. Discussion Paper, 44*(5), 936–957. http://search.proquest.com/docview/1008864601/

Hall, S. (1973). *Encoding and Decoding in the Television Discourse*. Centre for Contemporary Cultural Studies, University of Birmingham.

Hall, S. (1977). 'Culture, the Media and the "Ideological Effect"'. In J. Curran, M. Gurevitch & J. Woollacott (Eds.), *Mass Communication and Society*. Arnold. London.

Hall, E.T. (1959, republished 1980). *The Silent Language*. Anchor Books.

Hall, E. (2016, 15 June). "The Drum Wednesday June 15". The Drum. Retrieved via Wikipedia 15 February 2017. Link removed.

Hall, L. J., & Donaghue, N. (2013). 'Nice girls don't carry knives': Constructions of ambition in media coverage of Australia's first female prime minister. *British Journal of Social Psychology, 52*(4), 631–647. https://doi.org/10.1111/j.2044-8309.2012.02114.x

Halligan, J. (2001, September). *Contribution of the Australian Public Service to Public Administration and Management.* Edited version of a paper Presented to The Australian Public Service: 100 Years of Change, the Centenary Conference of the Institute of Public Administration (ACT Division), Rydges Lakeside (2001: Canberra). [online]. *Canberra Bulletin of Public Administration, 101*, 20–25. https://search-informit-com-au.wwwproxy1.library.unsw.edu.au/documentSummary;dn=200116077;res=IELAPA

Hallin, D. C. (1989). *The "Uncensored War": The Media and Vietnam.* University of California Press.

Halpern, D., Valenzuela, S., & Katz, J. E. (2017). We Face, I Tweet: How Different Social Media Influence Political Participation Through Collective and Internal Efficacy. *Journal of Computer-Mediated Communication, 22*(6), 320–336. https://doi.org/10.1111/jcc4.12198

Halton, J. (2004, March–April). A Healthy Public Sector—Vital to Australia's Health? Peter Wilenski Memorial Lecture, 20 February 2004. *Australian Quarterly, 76*(2), 19–24. https://www-jstor-org.wwwproxy1.library.unsw.edu.au/stable/pdf/20638245.pdf?refreqid=excelsior%3Ab09ce3da49e5285ebaec51142ff95634

Halverstadt, A., & Kerman, B. (2017). End-Game Evaluation: Building a Legacy of Learning in a Limited-Life Foundation. *The Foundation Review, 9*(1), 78–91, 109. https://doi.org/10.9707/1944-5660.1352

Hamilton, W. (2013, November). Rights and Wrongs of ABC Spy Reports. *Eureka Street, 23*(23), 4–6. https://search.informit.com.au/documentSummary;dn=730862220180851;res=IELAPA

Hanrahan, C. (2019). Australia Talks: The Most and Least Trusted Professions Revealed. *Australian Broadcasting Corporation.* https://www.abc.net.au/news/2019-11-27/the-professions-australians-trust-the-most/11725448

Hanitzsch, T. (2004). Journalists as Peacekeeping Force? Peace Journalism and Mass Communication Theory. *Journalism Studies, 5*(4), (Quoting Galtung 1998, p. 8.). https://doi.org/10.1080/14616700412331296419

Hansen, H. (1998). Core Values Key to Attracting and Retaining the Most Qualified Staff. *Bowman's Accounting Report, 12*(12), 12–15. http://search.proquest.com/docview/206573843/

Hanusch, F. (2013). Moulding Industry's Image: Journalism Education's Impact on Students' Professional Views. *Media International Australia (8/1/07-Current), 146*, 48–59. https://doi-org.wwwproxy1.library.unsw.edu.au/10.1177/1329878X1314600108

Hanusch, F. (2017). Web Analytics and the Functional Differentiation of Journalism Cultures: Individual, Organizational and Platform-Specific Influences on Newswork. *Information, Communication & Society, 20*(10), 1571–1586. https://doi.org/10.1080/1369118X.2016.1241294

Harcourt, C., Edwards, J., & Philpot, R. (1988, August 1). On the "Grim Reaper" Campaign. *The Medical Journal of Australia, 149*(3), 162, 164. https://onlinelibrary-wiley-com.wwwproxy1.library.unsw.edu.au/doi/epdf/10.5694/j.1326-5377.1988.tb120551.x

Harcup, T. (2014). *A Dictionary of Journalism*. Oxford University Press. https://www-oxfordreference-com.ezproxy1.library.usyd.edu.au/view/10.1093/acref/9780199646241.001.0001/acref-9780199646241.

Hardaker, R. (2020, September 8). Ita and the ABC: Out with the Old and in with the New. *Crikey.com*. https://www.crikey.com.au/2020/09/08/ita-buttrose-abc-new-staff-hires/

Harding, R. (1979). *Outside Interference: The Politics of Australia Broadcasting*. Sun Books.

Hardinge, B. (2020, April 2). The Cost of Misinformation: Social Media in a Pandemic and Representative Democracy. Asia and the Pacific Policy Society. *Policy Forum*. https://www.policyforum.net/the-cost-of-misinformation/

Hardy, J. A. (2017). Re-conceptualising Precarity: Institutions, Structure and Agency. *Employee Relations, 39*(3), 263–273. https://doi.org/10.1108/ER-06-2016-0111

Harris, C. I. (1993). Whiteness as Property. *Harvard Law Review, 106*(8), 1707–1791. https://doi.org/10.2307/1341787

Harsányi, G., & Carbon, C. (2015). How Perception Affects Racial Categorization: On the Influence of Initial Visual Exposure on Labelling People as Diverse Individuals or Racial Subjects. *Perception, 44*(1), 100–102. https://doi.org/10.1068/p7854

Hartley, J. (1982). *Understanding News*. Methuen.

Hartley, J. (2008). *Television Truths*. Blackwell Publishing.

Harvey, C., & Chia, R. (2010). Dominant Corporate Agents and the Power Elite in France and Britain. *Organization Studies, 31*(3), 327–348. https://journals-sagepub-com.wwwproxy1.library.unsw.edu.au/doi/pdf/10.1177/0170840609357377

Hasan, M. (2011, July 11). Is There a More Sickening Sight Than Leaders Sucking Up to the Sun King? *New Statesman, 140*(23). http://ezproxy.library.usyd.edu.au/login?url=https://search-proquest-com.ezproxy1.library.usyd.edu.au/docview/876179782?accountid=14757

Hassan, N., Adair, B., Hamilton, J. T., Li, C., Tremayne, M., Yang, J., & Yu, C. (2015, July). The Quest to Automate Fact-Checking. In *Proceedings of the 2015 Computation+ Journalism Symposium*. http://ranger.uta.edu/~cli/pubs/2015/claimbuster-cj15-hassan.pdf

Hastings, A., & Matthews, P. (2015). Bourdieu and the Big Society: Empowering the Powerful in Public Service Provision? *Policy & Politics, 43*(4), 545–560. https://doi.org/10.1332/030557314X14080105693951

Hatch, L. R. (2005). Gender and Ageism. *Generations, 3*, 19–24. https://www.ingentaconnect.com/content/asag/gen/2005/00000029/00000003/art00005

Hawkins, G. (1997). The ABC and the Mystic Writing Pad. *Media International Australia, 83*, 11–17. https://doi.org/10.1177/1329878X9708300104

Hawkins, G. (2013). Enacting Public Value on the ABC's Q&A: From Normative to Performative Approaches. *Media International Australia, 146*(1), 82–92. https://doi.org/10.1177/1329878X1314600112

Hawkins, G. (1997). The ABC and the Mystic Writing Pad. *Media International Australia, 83*, 11–17. https://doi.org/10.1177/1329878X9708300104

Hayes, M., Ross, I., Gasher, M., & Gutstein, D. (2007). Telling Stories: News Media, Health Literacy and Public Policy in Canada. *Social Science & Medicine, 64*(9), 1842–1852. https://doi.org/10.1016/j.socscimed.2007.01.015

Heanue, S. (2020, March 13). Top Australian Army General to Head Military Taskforce to Manage Coronavirus Outbreak. *Australian Broadcasting Corporation*. https://www.abc.net.au/news/2020-03-13/coronavirus-military-taskforce/12051722

Heidkamp, B., & Kergel, D. (2017). "Media Change—Precarity Within and Precarity Through the Internet" (Chap. 2). Precarity within the Digital Age Media Change and Social Insecurity. Springer. Wiesbaden. Retrieved from: https://link-springer-com.wwwproxy1.library.unsw.edu.au/content/pdf/10.1007%2F978-3-658-17678-5.pdf

Henderson, G. (2020, April 11). George Pell: Fairness Trampled by Social Media Mob. *The Australian*. https://www.theaustralian.com.au/inquirer/george-pell-fairness-trampled-by-social-media-mob/news-story/187e8e447ea804fa35748de1d58e452c

Henderson, G. (2018, August 6). Michelle Guthrie Needs a Fact Checker; Barrie Cassidy's Mea Culpa. *The Australian*. https://www.theaustralian.com.au/business/media/michelle-guthrie-needs-a-fact-checker-barrie-cassidys-mea-cuple/news-story/a5d429bb48fd7b4380baa2e442732fcc

Henderson, G. (2019, November 8). ABC Delays and Bungles Handling of Q&A 'Call to Violence' Episode. *The Australian*. https://www.theaustralian.com.au/commentary/abc-delays-and-bungles-handling-of-qa-call-to-violence-episode/news-story/b11bb0bc356b056297d2a0ffb922a290

Henriques-Gomez, L. (2019, November 5). Let's Burn Stuff: Q&A Panellists Debate Violence and Shattering the Status Quo. *The Guardian*. https://www.theguardian.com/australia-news/2019/nov/05/lets-burn-stuff-qa-panellists-debate-violence-and-shattering-the-status-quo

Henttonen, K., Johanson, J., & Janhonen, M. (2014). Work-Team Bonding and Bridging Social Networks, Team Identity and Performance Effectiveness. *Personnel Review, 43*(3), 330–349. http://dx.doi.org.wwwproxy1.library.unsw.edu.au/10.1108/PR-12-2011-0187

Herald, The. (1943, August 16). Senator Keane and the Newspapers. *The Herald*, p. 7. https://trove.nla.gov.au/newspaper/article/246273154?searchTerm=Keane%20ensure%20that%20news%20of%20national%20interest%20is%20impartially%20presented

Hermida, A. (2012, March). Tweets And Truth: Journalism as a Discipline of Collaborative Verification. *Journalism Practice*, 1–10. https://doi.org/10.1080/17512786.2012.667269

Hesmondhalgh, D. (2013). *The Cultural Industries*. 3rd Edition. SAGE. London.

Hetherington, A. (1985). *News, Newspapers and Television*. The Macmillan Press.

Hevesi, B. (2018, June 8). Your ABC of Hate: Outrage as the Taxpayer-Funded Broadcaster Compares Two Respected Journalists to Norwegian Mass Murderer Anders Breivik. *Daily Mail Australia*. https://www.dailymail.co.uk/news/article-5819227/The-ABC-forced-comparing-journalists-Norwegian-mass-murderer-Anders-Breivik.html

Hewett, J. (2020, July 30). Losing Friends and Influencing People. *The Australian Financial Review*. https://global-factiva-com.wwwproxy1.library.unsw.edu.au/redir/default.aspx?P=sa&an=AFNR000020200801eg7u0000e&cat=a&ep=ASE

High, S. (2010). Telling Stories: A Reflection on Oral History and New Media. *Oral History, 38*(1), 101–112. https://primoa.library.unsw.edu.au/permalink/f/11jha62/TN_jstor_archive_840650320

Higgins, K. (2011). "A fresh page in news evolution". NIE Supplement for Schools. The Sunday Telegraph. 28 August, 2011. Pp. 114–115.

Higton, M. (2012). *A theology of Higher Education*. Oxford Scholarship Online. Chapter 8. https://www-oxfordscholarship-com.wwwproxy1.library.unsw.edu.au/view/10.1093/acprof:oso/9780199643929.001.0001/acprof-9780199643929-chapter-9?rskey=MxVQlf&result=5

Hillman, E. L. (2009, June). Heller, Citizenship, and the Right to Serve in the Military. *Hastings Law Journal, 60*(6), 1269–1283. https://heinonline-org.wwwproxy1.library.unsw.edu.au/HOL/P?h=hein.journals/hastlj60&i=1309.

Hodge, E. (1996). Constraints on Reporting Indonesia. In A. Lucas (Ed.), *Half a Century of Indonesian- Australian Interaction. Flinders University Asian Studies Monograph* (Vol. 6, pp. 46–59). Flinders Press. Adelaide.

Höijer, B. (2011). Social Representations Theory: A New Theory for Media Research. *Nordicom Review, 32*(2), 3–16. https://doi.org/10.1515/nor-2017-0109

Holmes, J. (2019). *On Aunty*. Melbourne University Press. Carlton, Victoria.

Holman, C. D. J., Bucens, M. R., & Sesnan, T. M. K. (1987). AIDS and the Grim Reaper Campaign. *The Medical Journal of Australia, 147*(6), 306–306.

Hongjie, C., & Jacob, W. J. (Eds.). (2017). Trends in Chinese Education. Chap. 15 in L. Yunchan (Ed.), *An Examination of the "Engineer of Human Souls" Metaphor*. Routledge.

Horski, E. (1998). Grounded in Love: An Investigation of the Fundamental Ignatian Teaching on Discernment Within the Tradition of Askesis. *School of Theology and Seminary Graduate Papers/Theses, 1173*. https://digitalcommons.csbsju.edu/sot_papers/1173

Horne, D. (2001). *Looking for Leadership: Australia in the Howard Years*. Viking.

Houghton, D. (2011). Groupthink. In B. Badie, D. Berg-Schlosser, & L. Morlino (Eds.), *International Encyclopedia of Political Science* (pp. 1058–1060). SAGE Publications. Thousand Oaks, CA. https://doi.org/10.4135/9781412959636.n244.

Høyer, S., & Pöttker, H. (Eds.). (2005). *Diffusion of the News Paradigm*. Nordicam. Göteborg University. https://www.nordicom.gu.se/sv/system/tdf/publikationer-hela-pdf/diffusion_of_the_news_paradigm_1850-2000.pdf?file=1&type=node&id=10239&force=0

Howell, A., Ulan, J., & Powell, R. (2014). Essentialist Beliefs, Stigmatizing Attitudes, and Low Empathy Predict Greater Endorsement of Noun Labels Applied to People with Mental Disorders. *Personality and Individual Differences, 66*. https://doi.org/10.1016/j.paid.2014.03.008

Hoxha, A., Hanitzsch, T., Frère, M. S., & Meyer, C. (2018). How Conflict News Comes Into Being: Reconstructing 'Reality' Through Telling Stories. *Media, War & Conflict, 11*(1), 46–64. https://doi.org/10.1177/1750635217727313

Hurd, D. (1986). BBC Financing (Peacock Report). Hurd presentation to House of Commons debate 3 July 1986. UK Parliament. Vol. 100 cc1180–1193. Retrieved from: https://api.parliament.uk/historic-hansard/commons/1986/jul/03/bbc-financing-peacock-report

Hua, D. (2016). *Harnessing the Opportunities of Digital Disruption: The ABC Story. 2nd Annual Digital Disruption X 2016*. Retrieved from: https://www.iqpc.com/media/1002146/55636.pdf

Humphries, B. (1991). *Selected Poems and Other Creatures*. Angus and Robertson.

Hunter, F. (2019, October 21). ABC Boss' Pay Passes $1 Million for First Time. *The Sydney Morning Herald*. https://www.smh.com.au/politics/federal/abc-boss-pay-passes-1-million-for-first-time-20191021-p532o3.html

Hurst, D. (2020, June 19). Cyber-Attack Australia: Sophisticated Attacks from 'State-Based Actor', PM Says. *The Guardian*. https://www.theguardian.com/australia-news/2020/jun/19/australia-cyber-attack-attacks-hack-state-based-actor-says-australian-prime-minister-scott-morrison

Hunt, E. (2016, August 19). Julia Gillard attacks ABC's decision to finance sitcom At Home with Julia. *The Guardian*. https://www.theguardian.com/world/2016/aug/19/julia-gillard-attacks-abcs-decision-to-finance-sitcom-at-home-with-julia

Hunt, E., & Evershed, N. (2016, July 1). George Christensen the Most Abused MP on Twitter, Election Analysis Shows. *The Guardian*. https://www.theguardian.com/australia-news/2016/jul/01/australian-election-2016-turnbull-shorten-coalition-greens-labor-politics-live

Hyland, A. (2015, November 27). Mark Scott's ABC Exit Interview: 'I Had No Idea of the Scale of the Challenge'. *The Australian Financial Review*. https://www.afr.com/life-and-luxury/abcs-mark-scott-on-success-and-his-legacy-20151019-gkcgi8

Ibarra, H., & Lineback, K. (2005, January). What's your story? *Harvard Business Review*. https://au.reachout.com/articles/the-importance-of-sharing-your-story

Ignatius, D. (2019, April 12). Is Julian Assange a Journalist, or Is He Just an Accused Thief? *The Washington Post*. https://www.washingtonpost.com/opinions/is-julian-assange-a-journalist-or-is-he-just-an-accused-thief/2019/04/11/38afac3c-5c9c-11e9-9625-01d48d50ef75_story.html

IGADF Afghanistan Inquiry Report. (2020, November 10). Inspector General of the Australian Defence Force Afghanistan Inquiry Report. *Australian Government*. https://afghanistaninquiry.defence.gov.au/sites/default/files/2020-11/IGADF-Afghanistan-Inquiry-Public-Release-Version.pdf

Imamova, N. (2015). Social Media and Online Public Debate In Central Asia: A Journalist's Perspective. *Demokratizatsiya, 23*(3), 359–376. http://search.proquest.com/docview/1699511722/

Indeed.com. (2020, July). Australian Broadcasting Corporation (ABC) Salaries in Australia. *Indeed.com*. https://au.indeed.com/cmp/Australian-Broadcasting-Corporation-%28abc%29/salaries

Inglis, K. (1983). *The is the ABC: The Australian Broadcasting Commission 1932–1983*. Melbourne University Press. Melbourne.

Inglis, K. (2002, November 27). The Media—Aunty at Seventy: A Health Report on the ABC. [online]. *Analysis and Policy Observatory*. Retrieved March 4, 2020, from https://apo.org.au/node/6627

Inglis, K. (2006). *Whose ABC? The Australian Broadcasting Corporation 1983–2006*. Black Inc.

Ireland, R. (2005). ABC of Collaborative Planning Forecasting and Replenishment. *The Journal of Business Forecasting, 24*(2), 3–4. http://search.proquest.com/docview/226915396/

Irish Times, The. (2011, July 20). Taoiseach's Speech on Cloyne Motion. https://www.irishtimes.com/news/taoiseach-s-speech-on-cloyne-motion-1.880466

Ito, M. (2008) "Foreword." Digital Media, Youth, and Credibility. Edited by M. J. Metzger & A. J. Flanagin. The John D. and Catherine T. MacArthur Foundation Series on Digital Media and Learning. Cambridge, MA: The MIT Press, 2008. vii–ix. Retrieved from: https://doi.org/10.1162/dmal.9780262562324.vii.

Jackson, P. (2008). Pierre Bourdieu, the 'Cultural Turn' and the 'Practice' of International History. *Review of International Studies, 34*(1), 155–181. https://doi.org/10.1017/S026021050800795X

Jackson, D., & Moloney, K. (2016). Inside Churnalism. *Journalism Studies, 17*(6), 763–780. https://doi.org/10.1080/1461670X.2015.1017597

Jackson, J. (2017, January 13). BBC Sets Up Team to Debunk Fake News. *BBC News*. https://www.theguardian.com/media/2017/jan/12/bbc-sets-up-team-to-debunk-fake-news

Jackson, S. (2020, April 20). ABC Statement on Dr Norman Swan. *Australian Broadcasting Corporation*. https://about.abc.net.au/correcting-the-record/abc-statement-on-dr-norman-swan/

Jackson, S., & Vitorovich, L. (2020, April 1). Seven Looks to Cut Pay,Jobs to Survive Crisis. *The Australian*. https://www.theaustralian.com.au/business/media/seven-looks-to-cut-pay-jobs-to-survive-crisis/news-story/2c57ae3d681c821ed258549c0b95746a

James, O., Jilke, S., Petersen, C., & Van de Walle, S. (2016). Citizens' Blame of Politicians for Public Service Failure: Experimental Evidence About Blame Reduction through Delegation and Contracting. *Public Administration Review, 76*(1), 83–93. https://doi.org/10.1111/puar.12471

Jane, E. A. (2018). Gendered Cyberhate as Workplace Harassment and Economic Vandalism. *Feminist Media Studies, 18*(4), 575–591. https://doi.org/10.1080/14680777.2018.1447344

Jaques, C., Islar, M., & Lord, G. (2019). Post-Truth: Hegemony on Social Media and Implications for Sustainability Communication. *Sustainability, 11*(7), 2120. https://doi.org/10.3390/su11072120

Javeline, D., Hellmann, J. J., Castro Cornejo, R., & Shufeldt, G. (2013). Expert Opinion on Climate Change and Threats to Biodiversity. *BioScience, 63*(8), 666–673. https://doi.org/10.1525/bio.2013.63.8.9

Jelenchick, L. A., Eickhoff, J. C., & Moreno, M. A. (2013). Facebook Depression? Social Networking Site Use and Depression in Older Adolescents. *The Journal of Adolescent Health: Official Publication of the Society for Adolescent Medicine, 52*(1), 128–130. Retrieved from: https://doi.org/10.1016/j.jadohealth.2012.05.008

Jenkins, S. (2011, July 8). News of the World Was Not Such a Steal for Murdoch. *The Guardian*.http://www.guardian.co.uk/commentisfree/2011/jul/08/news-of-the-world-rupert-murdoch?intcmp=239

Jensen, K. B. (2010). *Media Convergence: The Three Degrees of Network, Mass and Interpersonal Communication*. Taylor & Francis Group. ProQuest Ebook Central. http://ebookcentral.proquest.com/lib/unsw/detail.action?docID=481099.

Jensen, A. (2019). Interdisciplinary Arts and Health Practice with an Institutional Logics Perspective. *Arts & Health, 11*(3), 219–231. https://doi.org/10.1080/17533015.2018.1443950

Jerit, J. (2009). Understanding the Knowledge Gap: The Role of Experts and Journalists. *The Journal of Politics, 71*(2), 442–456. https://doi.org/10.1017/S0022381609090380

Jewish Messenger, The. (1897, January 2). Quoted in *The New York Times*. Good-Will to Men. *The New York Times*, p. 3.

Jo Nova. (2019). Australia Votes 2019: Shock! Climate Action Bombs. Pollsters Crash. Skeptics Win. *Joanne Nova*. Blog. http://joannenova.com.au/2019/05/it-was-a-climate-election-and-the-skeptics-won-australia-2019/

Johnson, B. (2005, May 26). I Won't Pay to be Abused by the BBC. Comment. *The Telegraph*. https://www.telegraph.co.uk/comment/personal-view/3617184/I-wont-pay-to-be-abused-by-the-BBC.html

Johnson, C. (2013). From Brand Congruence to the 'Virtuous Circle': Branding and the Commercialization of Public Service Broadcasting. *Media Culture and Society*. http://journals.sagepub.com/doi/full/10.1177/0163443712472088

Johnson, K. A. (2020). I Got a New Puppy! The Impact of Personal, Opinion, and Objective Tweets on a Journalist's and a News Organization's Perceived Credibility. *Journalism Practice, 14*(1), 48–66. https://doi.org/10.1080/17512786.2019.1597637

Johnson, L. (1988). *The Unseen Voice: A Cultural Study of Early Australian Radio* (Vol. 3, 2017th ed.). Routledge Library Editions.

Johnson, R., Venus, M., Lanaj, K., Mao, C., Chang, C., & Johnson, R. (2012). Leader Identity as an Antecedent of the Frequency and Consistency of Transformational, Consideration, and Abusive Leadership Behaviors. *The Journal of Applied Psychology, 97*(6), 1262–1272. https://doi.org/10.1037/a0029043

Jolly, R. (2014, August 11). *The ABC: An Overview*. https://www.aph.gov.au/About_Parliament/Parliamentary_Departments/Parliamentary_Library/pubs/rp/rp1415/ABCoverview

Jones, E. (2002, June). Menzies' Razor Gang: Public Service Retrenchment in 1951 [online]. *Canberra Bulletin of Public Administration, 104*, 33–36. https://search-informit-com-au.wwwproxy1.library.unsw.edu.au/fullText;dn=20023710;res=AGISPT

Jones, S. (2010). Negotiating Authentic Objects and Authentic Selves. *Journal of Material Culture, 15*(2), 181–203. https://doi.org/10.1177/1359183510364074

Jones, P. K., & Pusey, M. (2010). Political Communication and 'Media System': The Australian Canary. *Media, Culture & Society, 32*(3), 451–471. https://doi.org/10.1177/0163443709361172

Jones, T. (2020, June 11). Netflix Removes Most of Chris Lilley's Shows. *Gizmodo*. https://www.gizmodo.com.au/2020/06/chris-lilley-netflix-blackface/

Josephi, B. (2000). Newsroom Research: Its Importance for Journalism Studies. *Australian Journalism Review, 22*(2), 75–87. https://primoa.library.unsw.edu.au/permalink/f/11jha62/TN_informit_apaft200204995

Juddery, B. (1976, December 3). Disquiet and Despondency in the ABC. *The Canberra Times*, p. 2. https://trove.nla.gov.au/newspaper/article/131798978?searchTerm=ABC%20BAPH

Jütting, J. (2003). "Institutions and Development: A Critical Review". OECD Development Centre Working Papers. 210. OECD Publishing. https://doi.org/10.1787/341346131416

Juries Victoria. (2020, April 6). Attending for Jury Service. *Juries Victoria*. https://www.juriesvictoria.vic.gov.au/individuals/attending-for-jury-service

Junankar, P. N. (Raja). (2016). Economics of Immigration. Chapter: Do Migrants Get Good Jobs in Australia? The Role of Ethnic Networks in Job Search. P. N. (Raja). Junanker & S. Mahuteau, pp. 251–272. Palgrave Macmillan UK. London.

Junankar P. N. (Raja)., & Mahuteau S. (2005). Do Migrants Get Good Jobs? New Migrant Settlement in Australia. *Economics of Immigration*. Palgrave Macmillan. London. Retrieved from: https://doi-org.wwwproxy1.library.unsw.edu.au/10.1057/9781137555250_6

Kacała, T. (2015). Military Leadership in the Context of Challenges and Threats Existing in Information Environment. *Journal of Corporate Responsibility and Leadership, 2*(1), 9–21. https://doi.org/10.12775/JCRL.2015.001

Kagwanja, P., & Southall, R. (2009). Introduction: Kenya—A Democracy in Retreat? *Journal of Contemporary African Studies: Kenya's Uncertain Democracy: The Electoral Crisis of 2008, 27*(3), 259–277. https://doi.org/10.1080/02589000903216930

Kahane, G., Everett, J. A. C., Earp, B. D., Farias, M., & Savulescu, J. (2015). 'Utilitarian' Judgments in Sacrificial Moral Dilemmas Do Not Reflect Impartial Concern for the Greater Good. *Cognition, 143*, 193–209. https://doi.org/10.1016/j.cognition.2014.10.005

Kakutani, M. (2018). *The Death of Truth*. William Collins.

Kamto, M. (1997). Reaffirming Public-Service Values and Professionalism. *International Review of Administrative Sciences, 63*(3), 295–308. https://doi.org/10.1177/002085239706300302

Karinthy, F. (1929). Chain (short story). In: Everything is Different. Budapest. Cited in: F. Karinthy. (2011). Chain-links. In The Structure and Dynamics of Networks. Vol. 9781400841356. Pp. 21–26.

Karp, P. (2020, April 1). Scott Morrison Prays for Australia and Commits Nation to God Amid Coronavirus Crisis. *The Guardian*. https://www.theguardian.com/australia-news/2020/apr/01/scott-morrison-prays-for-australia-and-commits-nation-to-god-amid-coronavirus-crisis

Karvelas, P. (2007, August 14). 'Kick Swan Out' for Democrats Donation. *The Australian*. https://web.archive.org/web/20071203213618/http://www.theaustralian.news.com.au/story/0,25197,22241106-11949,00.html

Karvalas, P. (2019). Millions Wasted on Diversity and Inclusion Programs, Says Report. RN Drive. ABC Radio. *Australian Broadcasting Corporation*. https://www.abc.net.au/radionational/programs/drive/millions-wasted-on-diversity-and-inclusion-programs,-says-report/11339938

Kasturi Rangan, V., Chase, L., & Karim, S. (2015, January–February). The Truth About CSR. *Harvard Business Review*. https://hbr.org/2015/01/the-truth-about-csr

Katz-Gerro, T. (2012). Do Individuals Who Attend the Arts Support Public Funding of the Arts? Evidence from England and the USA. *Journal of Policy Research in Tourism, Leisure and Events*, *4*(1), 1–27. https://doi.org/10.1080/19407963.2011.597507

Keen, A. (2007). *The Cult of the Amateur*. Doubleday Currency.

Kelling, K., & Thomas, R. J. (2018). The Roles and Functions of Opinion Journalists. *Newspaper Research Journal*, *39*(4), 398–419. https://doi.org/10.1177/0739532918806899

Kenny, C. (2018). ABC Chairman Justin Milne Has to Go Over Push to sack Emma Alberici. *The Australian*.https://www.theaustralian.com.au/business/media/abc-chairman-justin-milne-has-to-go-over-push-to-sack-emma-alberici/news-story/e326ac54ba0a027e70231f3edc3152b3

Kenny, C. (2019, December 9). ABC Staff 'Diversity' Survey Seeks Ethnic, Gender, Sexuality Data. *The Australian*. https://www.theaustralian.com.au/nation/aunty-staff-diversity-survey-seeks-ethnic-gender-sexuality-data/news-story/2b661d9c40c198bda7217bbd57616dfc

Kenny, C. (2020, June 29). Cue the Violins: ABC Needs to Put Its Trivial Troubles Into Perspective. *The Australian*. https://www.theaustralian.com.au/business/media/abc-crybabies-need-to-put-their-trivial-troubles-into-perspective/news-story/af90438cc7f3d09c5767c8004da51170

Kelso, A. (2007). Parliament and Political Disengagement: Neither Waving Nor Drowning. *Political Quarterly*, *78*(3), 364–373. https://doi.org/10.1111/j.1467-923X.2007.00865.x

Kelling, K., & Thomas, R. J. (2018). The Roles and Functions of Opinion Journalists. *Newspaper Research Journal, 39*(4), 398–419. https://doi.org/10.1177/0739532918806899

Keshet, Y., & Popper-Giveon, A. (2018). The Undisciplined Patient in Neoliberal Society: Conscious, Informed and Intuitive Health Behaviours. *Health, Risk & Society, 20*(3-4), 182–199. https://doi.org/10.1080/13698575.2018.1432757

Kester, L., Schwartz, N., Seufert, T., & Zumbach, J. (2008). *Beyond Knowledge: The Legacy of Competence: Meaningful Computer-Based Learning Environments* (1st ed.). Springer.

Khlok, V. R. (2003). The Re-establishment of Cambodian Education System after the Pol Pot Regime: The Study of Vietnamization and Re-Khmerizaion. *Kyōikugaku kenkyū, 70*(3), 383–392. https://doi.org/10.11555/kyoiku1932.70.383

Kidd, J., & Staff. (2014, November 25). ABC Cuts: Managing Director Mark Scott Announces More Than 400 Jobs To Go. *ABC News.* https://www.abc.net.au/news/2014-11-24/mark-scott-announces-abc-job-cuts/5913082?nw=0

Kierkegaard, S. (1941). *Concluding Unscientific Postscript* (W. Lowrie & J. Campbell, Trans.). Princeton Legacy Library.

Kieran, M. (1998). *Media Ethics.* Routledge. London.

Kim, M. N. (2018). The Role of Chief Editor in Managerial System of Editorial Board. *Upravlencheskoe Konsul'tirovanie, 6*, 182–189. https://doaj.org/article/6dc6b7258546412bbececb6622d09299

King, L. (2018, July 20). Rupert Murdoch, Mischief-Maker on a Global Scale. *Inside Sources.* https://www.insidesources.com/rupert-murdoch-mischief-maker-global-scale/

Kirby, M. (2002). Law and Media: Adversaries or Allies in Safeguarding Freedom? *Southern Cross University Law Review, 6*, 1–7. https://primoa.library.unsw.edu.au/permalink/f/11jha62/TN_informit_agis20033704

Klapdor, M., & Arthur, D. (2017). Welfare—What Does It Cost? *Parliament of Australia.* https://www.aph.gov.au/About_Parliament/Parliamentary_Departments/Parliamentary_Library/pubs/BriefingBook45p/WelfareCost

Klikauer, T. (2018). Media and Capitalism [Review of *Media and Capitalism*]. *Critical Sociology, 44*(6), 969–981. SAGE Publications. https://doi.org/10.1177/0896920518774091

Knight, L. (2011, July 7). News of the World: Counting the cost. *BBC News.* http://www.bbc.co.uk/news/business-14044052

Knott, M. (2014, February 5). ABC Admits Errors in Navy Burns Report on Asylum Seeker Claims. *The Sydney Morning Herald.* https://www.smh.com.au/politics/federal/abc-admits-errors-in-navy-burns-report-on-asylum-seeker-claims-20140204-31zft.html

Knott, M., & Hunter, F. (2014, July 4). Partisan Appointments to ABC, SBS Selection Panel Crushed Rudd's Dream. *The Sydney Morning Herald*. https://www.smh.com.au/politics/federal/partisan-appointments-to-abc-sbs-selection-panel-crushes-rudds-dream-20140704-zsvkz.html

Knott, M. (2015, May 28). Everyone from Coalition Thinks ABC's Q&A Is Biased to the Left, Says LNP Senator James McGrath. *The Age*. https://www.theage.com.au/politics/federal/everyone-from-coalition...ed-to-the-left-says-lnp-senator-james-mcgrath-20150527-ghatyw.html

Knott, M. (2016, December 5). 'If They Don't Like It They Should Leave': Tensions Escalate Between ABC Management and Staff. *The Age*. https://www.theage.com.au/politics/federal/if-they-dont-like-it-they-should-leave-tensions-escalate-between-abc-management-and-staff-20161205-gt47na.html

Knott, M., & Samios, Z. (2020, January 15). James Murdoch Breaks Ranks Over 'Climate Change Denial'. *The Sydney Morning Herald*.https://www.smh.com.au/national/james-murdoch-breaks-ranks-over-climate-change-denial-20200115-p53rie.html

Knowles, L., Worthington, E., & Blumer, C. (2019, June 6). ABC Raid: AFP leave Ultimo Building with Files After Hours-Long Raid Over Afghan Files Stories. *Australian Broadcasting Corporation*. https://www.abc.net.au/news/2019-06-05/abc-raided-by-australian-federal-police-afghan-files-stories/11181162

Knox, D. (2017, April 8). New-Look ABC News Ditches News 24. *TV Tonight Blog*. https://tvtonight.com.au/2017/04/new-look-abc-news-ditches-news-24.html

Kobre, S. (1955). *News Behind the Headlines: Background Reporting of Significant Social Problems* (p. iv+204). University of California. http://hdl.handle.net/2027/uc1.b3552959

Kornberger, M. (2009). *The brand society: How brands transform management and lifestyle*. Cambridge University Press. Cambridge.

Kornbluh, K. (2018, September/October). The Internet's Lost Promise: And How America Can Restore It. *Foreign Affairs, 97*(5), 33–38. New York. http://search.proquest.com/docview/2094371395/

Kossen, C., & Pedersen, C. (2008). Older Workers in Australia: The Myths, the Realities and the Battle Over Workforce 'Flexibility'. *Journal of Management and Organization, 14*(1), 73–84. https://login.wwwproxy1.library.unsw.edu.au/login?qurl=https%3A%2F%2Fwww.proquest.com%2Fscholarly-journals%2Folder-workers-australia-myths-realities-battle%2Fdocview%2F233254008%2Fse-2%3Faccountid%3D12763

Kovach, B., & Rosenstiel, T. (2007). *The Elements of Journalism: What Newspeople Should Know and the Public Should Expect* (1st Rev. Ed.). Three Rivers Press.

Koziol, M. (2019, July). Journalists in the Firing Line After AFP Changes Statement on Media Raids [online]. *Australasian Policing, 11*(2), 21. https://

search-informit-com-au.wwwproxy1.library.unsw.edu.au/documentSummary;dn=614670160682088;res=IELHSS

Koziol, M. (2020). ABC News Boss Warns Staff Against Focus on 'Inner City Left-Wing Elites'. *The Sydney Morning Herald*. 25 October 2020. Retrieved from: https://www.smh.com.au/national/abc-news-boss-warns-staff-against-focus-on-inner-city-left-wing-elites-20201023-p56849.html

Kramer, L. (1983). This Is the ABC: The Australian Broadcasting Commission, 1932–1983 by Ken S. Inglis. *Australian Book Review, 56*. Melbourne University Press.

Krause, N. M., Wirz, C. D., Scheufele, D. A., & Xenos, M. A. (2019, August). Fake News A New Obsession with an Old Phenomenon? In J. E. Katz & K. K. Mays (Eds.), *Journalism and Truth in an Age of Social Media*. Oxford Scholarship Online. https://doi.org/10.1093/oso/9780190900250.001.0001

Kress, G. (1985). *Linguistic Processes in Sociocultural Practice*. Deakin University Press.

Krstić, A., & Đurđević, B. (2017). Social Media Marketing. *Marketing (Beograd. 1991), 48*(4), 254–260. https://doaj.org/article/9fdc5a48a7a945fdb1de61e44404bd8c

Krygier, M. (1997). The Uses of Civility. *ABC Boyer Lecture*. 23 November 1997. Retrieved from: https://www.abc.net.au/radionational/programs/boyerlectures/lecture-3-the-uses-of-civility/3460218

Kuehn, B. M. (2013). More Than One-Third of US Individuals Use the Internet to Self-Diagnose. *JAMA, 309*(8), 756–757. https://doi.org/10.1001/jama.2013.629

Kumar, P., & Zattoni, A. (2018, January). Internal Culture and Outside Influence in Corporate Governance. *Corporate Governance: An International Review, 26*(1), 2–3. https://primoa.library.unsw.edu.au/primo-explore/search?query=any,contains,internal%20culture&tab=default_tab&search_scope=SearchFirst&vid=UNSWS&offset=0

Kurtulmuş, B. E. (2019). *The Dark Side of Leadership*. iBooks. Springer. https://doi.org/10.1007/978-3-030-02038-5_1

Kušen, E., Strembeck, M., & Conti, M. (2019). *Influence and Behavior Analysis in Social Networks and Social Media* (M. Kaya & R. Alhajj, Eds.). Springer. ProQuest Ebook Central. http://ebookcentral.proquest.com/lib/unsw/detail.action?docID=5613405

Kuypers, J. A. (2002). *Press Bias and Politics: How Media Frame Controversial Issues*. Praegar Publishers.

Labor Daily, The. (1938). Clean Sweep for ABC. *The Labor Daily*, 5. 15 June, 1938. Retrieved from: https://trove.nla.gov.au/newspaper/article/236409865?searchTerm=ABC%20commissioner%20kitto&searchLimits=

Lackey, D., & AAP. (2020, April 7). High-Profile George Pell Supporter Accuses the ABC of Acting as a 'Cheer Squad' to Have the Cardinal Jailed in a VERY

Fiery Interview on the Public Broadcaster. *The Daily Mail.* https://www.dailymail.co.uk/news/article-8195489/George-Pell-supporter-accuses-ABC-acting-cheer-squad-cardinal-jailed.html

Laclau, E. (1990). *New Reflections on the Revolution of Our Time.* Verso.

Laclau, E., & Mouffe, C. (1985). *Hegemony and Socialist Strategy: Towards a Radical Democratic Politics.* Verso. London.

Laffont, J.-J., & Tirole, J. (1991, November). The Politics of Government Decision-Making: A Theory of Regulatory Capture. *The Quarterly Journal of Economics, 106*(4), 1089–1127. https://www.jstor.org/stable/2937958

Lakoff, G. (2008). *The Political Mind: Why You Can't Understand 21st Century American Politics with an 18th Century Brain.* Viking.

Lallo, M. (2018, December 2). Most-Watched Programs of 2018 Revealed. *The Sydney Morning Herald.* https://www.smh.com.au/entertainment/tv-and-radio/most-watched-programs-of-2018-revealed-20181130-p50jdk.html

Lallo, M. (2019, December 1). Nine Network Tops 2019 Ratings Ending Seven's 12-Year Winning Streak. *The Sydney Morning Herald.* https://www.smh.com.au/culture/tv-and-radio/nine-network-tops-2019-ratings-ending-seven-s-12-year-winning-streak-20191129-p53fd3.html

Lallo, M. (2020, March 1). ABC Workers Face Anxious Wait Over Job, Program Cuts. [online]. *The Herald Sun.* https://www.heraldsun.com.au/blogs/andrew-bolt/more-abc-staff-less-value/news-story/e6f8bc5271a1f93606b916a39bddd1b8

Langer, J. (1998). *Tabloid Television: Popular Journalism and the 'Other News'.* Taylor & Francis Group. ProQuest Ebook Central. https://ebookcentral.proquest.com/lib/unsw/detail.action?docID=165718.

Larkins, F. P. (2018). Male Students Remain Underrepresented in Australian Universities. Should We Be Concerned? L.H. Martin Institute. Insights. https://melbourne-cshe.unimelb.edu.au/__data/assets/pdf_file/0012/2894718/Gender-Enrolment-Trends-F-Larkins-Sep-2018.pdf

Lariscy, R., Avery, E., Sweetser, K., & Howes, P. (2009). An Examination of the Role of Online Social Media in Journalists' Source Mix. *Public Relations Review, 35*(3), 314–316. https://doi.org/10.1016/j.pubrev.2009.05.008

Larsson, S. (2014). Battling Mainstream Media, Commentators and Organized Debaters: Experiences from Citizens' Online Opinion Writing in Sweden. *NORDICOM Review: Nordic Research on Media and Communication, 35*(2), 77+. https://link-gale-com.ezproxy2.library.usyd.edu.au/apps/doc/A396138825/AONE?u=usyd&sid=AONE&xid=f8ac48fc

Lau, T., Wang, H. C., & Chuang, C. C. (2011, May). A Definition of Service as Base for Developing Service Science. *2011 International Joint Conference on Service Science,* 49–53. Conference Paper. https://doi.org/10.1109/IJCSS.2011.18

Lawrence-Lightfoot, S. (1999). *Respect: An Exploration.* Perseus Books.

Law, J. (2009). MBWA. In: *A Dictionary of Business and Management* (5th Ed.). Oxford University Press. Oxford.

Lawrence, T. B., & Suddaby, R. (2006). Institutions and Institutional Work. In S. R. Clegg, C. Hardy, W. R. Nord, & T. Lawrence (Eds.), *Handbook of Organization Studies*. Sage. Thousand Oaks, CA.

Lawrence, R. G., & Schafer, M. L. (2012). Debunking Sarah Palin: Mainstream News Coverage of 'Death Panels'. *Journalism, 13*(6), 766–782. https://doi.org/10.1177/1464884911431389

Lawson, K. (2019, May 20). Election 2019: Why the Opinion Polls Were Always Wrong. *The Canberra Times*. https://www.canberratimes.com.au/story/6132185/why-the-opinion-polls-were-always-wrong-and-how-we-should-have-spotted-it/

Lazer, D. M. J., Baum, M. A., Benkler, Y., Berinsky, A. J., Greenhill, K. M., Menczer, F., Metzger, M., Nyhan, B., Pennycook, G., Rothschild, D., Schudson, M., Sloman, S. A., Sunstein, C. R., Thorson, E. A., Watts, D. J., & Zittrain, J. L. (2018). The Science of Fake News. *Science, 359*(6380), 1094–1096. https://doi.org/10.1126/science.aao2998

Leary, M. R. (1995). *Self-Presentation: Impression Management and Interpersonal Behavior*. Brown & Benchmark.

Leaderonomics.com. (2018, March 29). The Pitfalls of Servant Leadership. https://leaderonomics.com/leadership/the-pitfalls-of-servant-leadership

Lee, A. J. (1976). *The Origins of the Popular Press in England. 1855–1914*. Croom Helm.

Lee, H., & Lee, J.-M. (2017). Viewing Presidential Televised Debates and Civic Engagement in Korea. *International Area Studies Review, 20*(4), 334–348. https://doi.org/10.1177/2233865917726438

Lefebvre, H. (1991). *The Production of Space* (D. Nicholson-Smith, Trans.). Blackwell.

Leftwich, A., & Sen, K. (2010). 'Beyond Institutions: Institutions and Organisations in the Politics and Economics of Poverty Reduction - a Thematic Synthesis of Research Evidence'. IPPG Research Consortium on Improving Institutions for Pro-Poor Growth, University of Manchester. Retrieved from: https://gsdrc.org/document-library/beyond-institutions-institutions-and-organisations-in-the-politics-and-economics-of-poverty-reduction-a-thematic-synthesis-of-research-evidence/

Le Grand, C. (2019, November 28). 'Down the Gurgler': ABC Doyen Blasts Olympic Boycott, Questions Commitment to Sport. *The Sydney Morning Herald*. https://www.smh.com.au/sport/down-the-gurgler-abc-doyen-blasts-olympic-boycott-questions-commitment-to-sport-20191128-p53f68.html

Leroy, D. (1980, June). Public Broadcasting. *Journal of Communication, 30*(3), 2159. https://onlinelibrary-wiley-com.wwwproxy1.library.unsw.edu.au/doi/epdf/10.1111/j.1460-2466.1980.tb02002.x

Leslie, T. (2010, January 21). Sky Falls on ABC's News Channel. *ABC News*. https://www.abc.net.au/news/2010-01-21/sky-falls-on-abcs-news-channel/1217718

Letamendia, A. (2017). Towards the Aestheticisation of the Resistances in the Digital Age? A Critical Approach. Chap. 9 in *Precarity within the Digital Age Media Change and Social Insecurity*. Springer. https://link-springer-com.wwwproxy1.library.unsw.edu.au/content/pdf/10.1007%2F978-3-658-17678-5.pdf

Leveson, B. H., Sir. (2012). *An Inquiry Into the Culture, Practices and Ethics of the Press Executive Summary and Recommendations (aka the Leveson Inquiry)*. The Right Honourable Lord Justice Leveson. https://assets.documentcloud.org/documents/526073/leveson-summary.txt

Levine, L. W. (1988). Highbrow/Lowbrow. Harvard University Press. Cambridge Mass.

Levine, M., & Forrence, J. (1990). Regulatory Capture, Public Interest, and the Public Agenda: Toward a Synthesis. *Journal of Law, Economics, & Organization, 6*, 167–198. www.jstor.org/stable/764987

Levine, M. (2018, June 26). ABC Most Trusted | Facebook Most Distrusted. *Roy Morgan*. Finding No. 7641. http://www.roymorgan.com/findings/7641-media-net-trust-june-2018-201806260239

Levinson, M. (1999). *The Demands of Liberal Education*. Oxford University Press.

Lewis, S. (2000, December 2). Swan Stands Aside While Labor Party Implodes. *The Australian Financial Review Weekend*. https://www.afr.com/politics/swan-stands-aside-while-labor-party-implodes-20001202-jl3ic

Lewis, J. (2006). News and the Empowerment of Citizens. *European Journal of Cultural Studies, 9*(3), 303–319. https://doi.org/10.1177/1367549406066075

Lewis, S. (2009, March 17). Rudd Vows Bipartisan ABC Board. *News.com.au*. https://www.news.com.au/national/rudd-vows-bipartisan-abc-board/news-story/ceac18bd56ef5ff51aed0b9b58140d1b?sv=8d736175966893030944 3ad4dee66a24

Lewis, R., Rowe, M., & Wiper, C. (2017). Online Abuse of Feminists as An Emerging Form of Violence Against Women and Girls. *British Journal of Criminology, 57*(6), 1462–1481. https://academic-oup-com.wwwproxy1.library.unsw.edu.au/bjc/article/57/6/1462/2623986

Leys, N., & Nicholson, B. (2014, January 24). ABC Sticking to Its Story as 'Abuse' Doubts Mount. *The Australian*. https://www.theaustralian.com.au/national-affairs/immigration/abc-sticking-to-its-story-as-abuse-doubts-mount/news-story/32f146bf9912a4dc77a3340cdd56b2cb

Liao, S. H., Hsian, P. Y., & Wu, G. L. (2014). Mining User Knowledge for Investigating the Facebook Business Model: The Case of Taiwan Users. *Applied Artificial Intelligence, 28*(7), 712–736. https://doi.org/10.1080/08839514.2014.927695

Li, K., Li, S., Guan, Y. (2004). Institutionalised Corruption and Privilege in Asian Economies: A General Equilibrium Analysis. *Malaysian Journal of Economic Studies. Kuala Lumpur, 41*(1 & 2), 21–37. https://www.proquest.com/openview/13006f139d179947802a1871624c767f/1?pq-origsite=gscholar&cbl=46814

Lieberman, D. (2007, August 6). Murdoch Grew Up on 'Ritual Feuding with Other Media'. [online]. *USA Today*. https://abcnews.go.com/Business/story?id=3434589&page=1

Lin, X., Spence, P., & Lachlan, K. (2016). Social Media and Credibility Indicators: The Effect of Influence Cues. *Computers in Human Behavior, 63*, 264–271. https://doi.org/10.1016/j.chb.2016.05.002

Line, M. B. (1992). How to Demotivate Staff: A Brief Guide. *Library Management, 13*(1), 4. http://dx.doi.org.wwwproxy1.library.unsw.edu.au/10.1108/01435129210009832

Lincoln, J. R. (1995). Book Review. (Eds. W. W. Powell & P. DiMaggio): The New Institutionalism in Organizational Analysis. *Social Forces, 73*(3), 1147–1148. https://doi.org/10.1093/sf/73.3.1147

Lindenberg, S. (1998). The Cognitive Turn in Institutional Analysis: Beyond NIE, and NIS? *Journal of Institutional and Theoretical Economics, 154*(4), 716–727. Zeitschrift Für Die Gesamte Staatswissenschaft. https://primoa.library.unsw.edu.au/permalink/f/11jha62/TN_cdi_webofscience_primary_000165539200010CitationCount

Littlemore, S. (1996). The Media and Me. ABC Books for the Australian Broadcasting Corporation. Sydney.

Littlefield, R. S., & Quenette, A. M. (2007). Crisis Leadership and Hurricane Katrina: The Portrayal of Authority by the Media in Natural Disasters. *Journal of Applied Communication Research, 35*(1), 26–47. https://doi.org/10.1080/00909880601065664

Litt, E. (2012). Knock, Knock. Who's There? The Imagined Audience. *Journal of Broadcasting & Electronic Media, 56*(3), 330–345. https://doi.org/10.1080/08838151.2012.705195

Liu, H. (2020). *Redeeming Leadership. Chapter: Undoing Leadership*. Bristol University Press. https://www.jstor.org/stable/j.ctvtv93zk

Livingstone, S. (2004). The Challenge of Changing Audiences: Or, What is the Audience Researcher to do in the Internet age? *European Journal of Communication, 19*(1), pp. 75–86. https://doi.org/10.1177/0267323104040695

Livingston, J., Holland, E., & Fardouly, J. (2020). Exposing Digital Posing: The Effect of Social Media Self-Disclaimer Captions on Women's Body Dissatisfaction, Mood, and Impressions of the User. *Body Image, 32*, 150–154. https://doi.org/10.1016/j.bodyim.2019.12.006

Lisners, J. (2012). *The Rise and Fall of the Murdoch Empire*. Blake Publishing. London.

Lisners, J. (2013). *The Rise and Fall of the Murdoch Empire*. John Blake.

Loseke, D. R. (2007). The Study of Identity as Cultural, Institutional, Organizational, and Personal Narratives: Theoretical and Empirical Integrations. *The Sociological Quarterly, 48*(4), 661–688. https://doi.org/10.1111/j.1533-8525.2007.00096.

Low, S., & Smith, N. (2013). *The Politics of Public Space*. Taylor and Francis. https://primoa.library.unsw.edu.au/permalink/f/jhud33/UNSW_ALMA51175562100001731

Luck, G. (2018, June 30). The Rot Set in with Current Affairs, and ABC News Has Since Lost Its Bearings. *The Australian*. https://www.theaustralian.com.au/news/inquirer/the-rot-set-in-with-current-affairs-and-abc-news-has-since-lost-its-bearings/news-story/06202187428fc0e6b2a14b60f940c8de

Lukin, A. (2006). What is Media 'Bias'? A Case Study of Al Jazeera's Reporting of the Iraq War. *Journal of Policing, Intelligence and Counter Terrorism, 1*(1), 65–80. https://doi.org/10.1080/18335300.2006.9686879

Lumsden, K., & Harmer, E. (2019). *Online Othering: Exploring Digital Violence and Discrimination on the Web*. Cham: Springer International Publishing: Imprint: Palgrave Macmillan. https://doi.org/10.1007/978-3-030-12633-9

Lunt, P., & Livingstone, S. (2012). *Media Regulation. Governance and the Interest of Citizens and Consumers*. Sage Publications Ltd. London.

Lupton, D. A. (1992). From Complacency to Panic: AIDS and Heterosexuals in the Australian Press July 1986 to June 1988. *Health Education Research, 7*(1), 9–20. https://academic-oup-com.wwwproxy1.library.unsw.edu.au/her/article/7/1/9/687273

Lutz, E. (2019, September 16). James Murdoch Suggests His Dad's Empire Is Ruining America. *Vanity Fair*. https://www.vanityfair.com/news/2019/09/james-murdoch-fox-news-empire

Luzung, A. (2004/2005). Contempt by Publication: Improving the Law on Court Reporting by the Media [online]. *Reform,* 85(Summer), 27–30, 59. https://search-informit-com-au.wwwproxy1.library.unsw.edu.au/fullText;dn=20051670;res=AGISPT

Lynch, J. (2002). Impunity in Journalism. *Media Development, Xlix*(2), 30–32. http://waccglobal.org/en/20022GimpunityGandGtheGmedia/693GImpunityGinGjournalism.html

Lynch, J. (2014, November 22). ABC Redirected Funds, Says Lib MP. *The Australian Financial Review*, p. 5.

Lynch, K., Devine, D., & Grummell, B. (2012). New Managerialism in Education. In *New Managerialism in Education*. Palgrave Macmillan. https://doi.org/10.1057/9781137007230

Lyons, E. (1943). Governor-General's Speech Address-In-Reply. 29 September, 1943. *Parliament of Australia*. Retrieved from: https://www.aph.gov.au/

About_Parliament/Parliamentary_Departments/Parliamentary_Library/Publications_Archive/archive/women/43Lyons

Lysak, S., Cremedas, M., & Wolf, J. (2012). Facebook and Twitter in the Newsroom: How and Why Local Television News is Getting Social With Viewers? *Electronic News, 6*(4), 187–207. https://doi.org/10.1177/1931243112466095

M2 Presswire. (2016). Optus Partners with ABC Commercial to Revolutionise Retail Employee Wellbeing. http://search.proquest.com/docview/1815277669/

MacInnis, F. (2005, April). Towards a New Definition of Service. *Chief Executive, 197*. https://primoa.library.unsw.edu.au/permalink/f/11jha62/TN_cdi_proquest_reports_212103313

Machimbarrena, J. M., Calvete, E., Fernández-González, L., Álvarez-Bardón, A., Álvarez-Fernández, L., & González-Cabrera, J. (2018). Internet Risks: An Overview of Victimization in Cyberbullying, Cyber Dating Abuse, Sexting, Online Grooming and Problematic Internet Use. *International Journal of Environmental Research and Public Health, 15*(11). https://doi.org/10.3390/ijerph15112471

Mackay, H. (2002). *Media Mania: Why Our Fear of Modern Media Is Misplaced*. UNSW Press.

Mackay, H. (2010). *What Makes Us Tick? The Ten Desires That Drive Us*. Hachette.

Mackay, H. (2017, February 2). Hugh Mackay: The State of the Nation Starts in Your Street. Edited Version of the Gandhi Oration, Delivered at the University of New South Wales on January 30, 2017. *The Conversation*. https://theconversation.com/hugh-mackay-the-state-of-the-nation-starts-in-your-street-72264

Mackay, H. (2019, January 23). Australia Day Address 2019. https://www.australiaday.com.au/events/australia-day-address/2019-speaker-hugh-mackay/

Macmullan, T. (2005). Challenges to Cultural Diversity: Absolutism, Democracy, and Alain Locke's Value Relativism. *The Journal of Speculative Philosophy, 19*(2), 129–139. https://doi.org/10.1353/jsp.2005.0013

Madison, J, (1788). *Popular Basis of Political Authority. The Founders' Constitution, 1*(2). Document 19. The University of Chicago Press. http://press-pubs.uchicago.edu/founders/documents/v1ch2s19.html

Magsaysay, J. F., & Hechanova, M. R. M. (2017). Building an Implicit Change Leadership Theory. *Leadership & Organization Development Journal, 38*(6), 834–848. http://dx.doi.org.wwwproxy1.library.unsw.edu.au/10.1108/LODJ-05-2016-0114

Mahler, J., & Rutenberg, J. (2019, April 3). How Rupert Murdoch's Empire of Influence Remade the World. *The New York Times Magazine*. https://www.nytimes.com/interactive/2019/04/03/magazine/rupert-murdoch-fox-news-trump.html

Malsch, B., & Gendron, Y. (2013). Re-Theorizing Change: Institutional Experimentation and the Struggle for Domination in the *field* of Public Accounting. *Journal Of Management Studies, 50*(5), 870–899. https://doi.org/10.1111/joms.12006

Mann, S. (2004). "Sousveillance"—Inverse Surveillance in Multimedia Imaging. *ACM Multimedia 2004—Proceedings of the 12th ACM International Conference on Multimedia*. Pp. 620–627. Retrieved from: https://primoa.library.unsw.edu.au/permalink/f/11jha62/TN_scopus2-s2.0-13444291148

Manning, P. (2018, September 25). Despite Her Good Intentions, Michelle Guthrie Was Never the Right Fit for the ABC. *The Conversation*. https://theconversation.com/despite-her-good-intentions-michelle-guthrie-was-never-the-right-fit-for-the-abc-103755

Manz, C., Skaggs, B., Pearce, C., & Wassenaar, C. (2015). Serving One Another: Are Shared and Self-Leadership the Keys to Service Sustainability? *Journal of Organizational Behaviour, 36*(4), 607–612. https://doi.org/10.1002/job.1991

Manne, R. (2007, December–2008, January). New Teeth for Aunty: Reinvigorating the National Broadcaster. *The Monthly*, p. 40. https://www.themonthly.com.au/monthly-essays-robert-manne-new-teeth-aunty-reinvigorating-national-broadcaster-749#mtr

Manne, R. (2012, June). Murdoch and Company. *The Monthly*. https://www.themonthly.com.au/issue/2012/june/1338434837/robert-manne/murdoch-company

Mansfield, B. (1997). *The Challenge of a Better ABC: The Review of the Role and Functions of the ABC*. Australian Government Publishing Service.

Mannix, T. (1987, April 6). Two Million Australians risk AIDS. *The Canberra Times*, p. 1. https://trove.nla.gov.au/newspaper/article/118183464?searchTerm=grim%20reaper%20buttrose&searchLimits=

Mao, F. (2019, May 16). 2019 Election: Why Politics Is Toxic for Australia's Women. *British Broadcasting Corporation*. https://www.bbc.com/news/world-australia-48197145

March, J. C., & Simon, H. A. (1958). *Organizations*. Wiley. New York.

Margetts, J., Brown, M., & Staff. (2016, February 5). Cardinal George Pell 'Too Ill' to Travel from Rome for Child Sex Abuse Inquiry. *Australian Broadcasting Corporation*. https://www.abc.net.au/news/2016-02-05/cardinal-george-pell-too-ill-to-child-sex-abuse-inquiry-lawyers/7140584

Markham, T. (2011). Hunched Over Their Laptops: Phenomenological Perspectives on Citizen Journalism. (Essay). *Review of Contemporary Philosophy, 10*.

Marks, K. (2017, August 10). The Anzac Post, Outrage and a Debate About Race. *BBC News*. https://www.bbc.com/news/world-australia-40712832

Marozzi, M. (2015). Measuring Trust in European Public Institutions. *Social Indicators Research, 123*(3), 879–895. https://doi.org/10.1007/s11205-014-0765-9

Marquand, D. (2004). *Decline of the Public: The Hollowing Out of Citizenship*. Polity Press.

Marquis, C., & Lounsbury, M. (2007). Vive La Resistance: Competing Logics and the Consolidation of US Community Banking. *Academy of Management Journal, 50*, 799–820. https://doi.org/10.5465/AMJ.2007.26279172

Marshak, R. J. (2006). *Covert Processes at Work: Managing the Five Hidden Dimensions of Organizational Change*. Berrett-Koehler Publishers. San Francisco, CA.

Martinoli, A. (2016). Digital Media Audience—New Expectations, New Habits. *In Medias Res, 5*(8), 1269–1284. https://doaj.org/article/c7caa3920f984aceb4e9c611dbae7c9c

Martin, F. (2002). Beyond Public Service Broadcasting? ABC Online and the User/Citizen. *Southern Review: Communication, Politics & Culture, 35*(1), 42–62. https://search-informit-com-au.wwwproxy1.library.unsw.edu.au/documentSummary;dn=743199784542203;res=IELAPA

Martin, F., & Dwyer, T. (2019). *Sharing News Online. Commendary Cultures and Social Media News Ecologies*. Chapter 5. Palgrave Macmillan.

Marwick, A. E. (2013). *Status Update: Celebrity, Publicity, and Branding in the Social Media Age*. Yale University Press. https://primoa.library.unsw.edu.au/permalink/f/1gq3lal/UNSW_ALMA51219826020001731

Marr, D. (2013). *The Prince: Faith, Abuse, George Pell*. Quarterly Essay 51. Black Inc.

Massola, J. (2015, June 23). 'Whose side are you on?' Tony Abbott lashes ABC's Q&A program. *The Sydney Morning Herald*. https://www.smh.com.au/politics/federal/whose-side-are-you-on-tony-abbott-lashes-abcs-qa-program-20150623-ghvd0l.html

Massaka, I. (2017). Selected Issues of E-Democracy and Political E-Participation. *Historia i Polityka., 18*(25), 9–18. https://doi.org/10.12775/HiP.2016.028

Masquelier, C. (2019). Bourdieu, Foucault and the Politics of Precarity. *Distinktion: Journal of Social Theory, 20*(2), 135–155. https://doi.org/10.1080/1600910X.2018.1549999

Mason, M. (2020, May 7). Seven Axes 50 Sales Staff in Cost Cutting Effort. *The Australian Financial Review*. https://www.afr.com/companies/media-and-marketing/seven-axes-50-sales-staff-in-cost-cutting-effort-20200507-p54qoq

Mason, M., & Roddan, M. (2020, July 13). SBS Delves Deeper Into Back-Office Mergers than ABC. *The Australian Financial Review*. https://www.afr.com/companies/media-and-marketing/sbs-delves-deeper-into-back-office-mergers-than-abc-20200708-p55a2c

Masaeli, N., & Farhadi, H. (2021). Prevalence of Internet-based Addictive Behaviors during COVID-19 Pandemic: A Systematic Review. *Journal of Addictive Diseases*, 1–27. https://doi.org/10.1080/10550887.2021.1895962

Matei, S. A., Bertino, E., & Russell, M. (2015). Introduction. In S. Matei, M. Russell, & E. Bertino (Eds.), *Transparency in Social Media. Computational Social Sciences*. Springer International Publishing AG. https://doi.org/10.1007/978-3-319-18552-1

Maurer, M., Dumitrescu, D., & Bucy, E. P. (2016). Nonverbal Influence During Televised Debates: Integrating CRM in Experimental Channel Studies. *American Behavioral Scientist, 60*(14), 1799–1815. https://doi.org/10.1177/0002764216676250

Mayer, H. (1964). *The Press in Australia*. Lansdowne Press.

McAllister, I., Cameron, S., & Sheppard, J.. (2016). *Australian Election Study. School of Politics and International Relations*. Australian National University. https://politicsir.cass.anu.edu.au/news/2016-australian-election-study

McCarthy, J. (2018, December 6). 'Catholic Church Has a Lot to Answer For': Philip Wilson's Conviction Overturned. *The Sydney Morning Herald*. https://www.smh.com.au/national/nsw/catholic-church-has-a-lot-to-answer-for-philip-wilson-s-conviction-overturned-20181206-p50kqg.html

McCarthy, J. W., & Karsh, M. (2007, March). Jesuits and Ecology—For the Greater Glory of God! *Forestry Chronicle, 83*(2), 162–163. https://pubs.cif-ifc.org/doi/pdf/10.5558/tfc83159-2

McCauley, D. (2018, May 25). ABC Spends Up on Google, Facebook Ads. *The Australian*. https://www.theaustralian.com.au/business/media/abc-spends-up-on-google-facebook-ads/news-story/5e6a36fcf3463cb5522fec4a5bcf0918

McCauley, D., Bagshaw, E., & Harris, R. (2020, March 16). Australia Prepares for 50,000 to 150,000 Coronavirus Deaths. *The Sydney Morning Herald*. https://www.smh.com.au/politics/federal/australia-prepares-for-50-000-to-150-000-coronavirus-deaths-20200316-p54amn.html

McChesney, R. W. (1997). *The Mythology of Commercial Broadcasting and the Contemporary Crisis of Public Broadcasting*. University of Wisconsin-Madison.

McChesney, R. W. (2008). *The Political Economy of Media: Enduring Issues, Emerging Dilemmas*. Monthly Review Press.

McChesney, R. W. (2012). Farewell to Journalism? Time for a Rethinking. *Journalism Studies, 13*(5-6), 682–694. https://doi.org/10.1080/1461670X.2012.679868

McDowell, D. H. (1975). *The Development and Educational Role of Schools of Arts in England: And Their Influence on the Development and Educational Role of Schools of Arts in Australia*. Masters Thesis. http://handle.unsw.edu.au/1959.4/61038

McGuire, J., Rhodes, G., & Palus, C. (2008). Inside Out: Transforming Your Leadership Culture. *Leadership in Action, 27*, 3–7. https://doi.org/10.1002/lia.1226

McGarity, T. O., & Wagner, W. E. (2008). Bending Science: How Special Interests Corrupt Public Health Research. *Environmental Health Perspectives, 116*(11), A500–A500. First Harvard University Press. Cambridge. Mass.

McGoldrick, A. (2000). Peace Journalism—an Introduction. In Friedrich-Ebert-Stiftung (Ed.), *Medien im Konflikt—Mittäter oder Mediatoren? The Media in Conflicts—Accomplices or Mediators?* (pp. 95–100). FES. Bonn.

McGuinness, P. P. (2000, December). The Future of the Australian Broadcasting Corporation. *Quadrant, 44*(12), 2–4. https://search-informit-com-au.www-proxy1.library.unsw.edu.au/documentSummary;dn=733687171221108;res=IELLCC

McHugh, B. (2014, February 17). The Term 'Social Licence to Operate' Brought Into Question by Report. *Australian Broadcasting Corporation*. https://www.abc.net.au/news/rural/2014-02-17/social-licence-to-operate-a-poorly-defined-concept/5264162

McIlroy, T., & Cranston, M. (2019, October 18). Australia's Best Paid Bureaucrat Rakes in $2.5m. *The Australian Financial Review*. https://www.afr.com/politics/federal/australia-s-best-paid-bureaucrat-rakes-in-2-5m-20191017-p531hy

McKnight, D. (1998, May). Broadcasting and the Enemy Within: Political Surveillance and the ABC, 1951–64. *Media International Australia, Incorporating Culture & Policy, 87*, 35–48. https://search-informit-com-au.wwwproxy1.library.unsw.edu.au/documentSummary;dn=093749146204159;res=IELLCC

McKnight, D. (2012). *Rupert Murdoch: An Investigation of Political Power*. Allen and Unwin.

McKinnell, J. (2020, February 17). AFP Warrants Used to Raid ABC Valid, Federal Court Rules. *Australian Broadcasting Corporation*. https://www.abc.net.au/news/2020-02-17/afp-warrants-used-to-raid-abc-valid-court-rules/11971018

McLuhan, M. (1973) (1964). *Understanding Media*. Abacus. London.

McMahon, A. (2020, September 4). The ABC and SBS Are Vital But Can Be Strengthened. Opinion. *Independent Australia*. https://independentaustralia.net/business/business-display/the-abc-and-sbs-are-vital-but-can-be-strengthened,14275

McMurtrie, C. (2020, April 11). Why the ABC's Reporting of the George Pell Case Wasn't a Witch-Hunt. *Australian Broadcasting Corporation*. https://www.abc.net.au/news/about/backstory/news-coverage/2020-04-11/why-the-abc-reporting-of-the-pell-case-was-not-a-witch-hunt/12137620

McNair, B. (1994). *News and Journalism in the UK*. Routledge.

McNally, P. (2012, April 26). Murdoch: 'Nonsense' That Editors 'Agree with Everything' I Say. *The Guardian*.https://www.journalism.co.uk/news/murdoch-nonsense-that-editors-agree-with-everything-i-say/s2/a548964/

McNamara, T. K., & Williamson, J. B. (2019). *Ageism: Past, Present, and Future. Routledge, Taylor and Francis Group*. Abingdon, Oxon.

McPhee, S. (2020). Coronavirus Australia: Human Biosecurity Emergency Declared. *News.com.au*. https://www.news.com.au/national/politics/coronavirus-australia-human-biosecurity-emergency-declared/news-story/cd7fbff78297c076c8bb774595459c59

Mellet, K. (2011). Online Marketing. *Communications, 88*(1), 103–111. https://doi.org/10.3917/commu.088.0103

Meade, A. (2015, July 23). ABC Shops to Close with Loss of 300 Jobs, Mark Scott Says. *The Guardian*. https://www.theguardian.com/media/2015/jul/23/abc-shops-to-close-with-loss-of-300-jobs-mark-scott-says?CMP=share_btn_link

Meade, A. (2018a, August 21). Michelle Guthrie Says Abuse of ABC Staff Unacceptable After Presenter Cries on Air. *The Guardian*. https://www.theguardian.com/media/2018/aug/21/michelle-guthrie-says-abuse-of-abc-staff-unacceptable-after-presenter-cries-on-air

Meade, A. (2018b, August 1). The ABC in Turmoil: 'Frankly, We Are All Spooked About Everything in Here.' *The Guardian*. https://www.theguardian.com/media/2018/aug/01/the-abc-in-turmoil-frankly-we-are-all-spooked-about-everything-in-here

Meade, A. (2019). ABC Managing Director Rejects Accusations he is Making Funding an Election Issue. *The Guardian*. 8 May 2019. Retrieved from: https://www.theguardian.com/media/2019/may/08/abc-managing-director-rejects-accusations-he-is-making-funding-an-election-issue

Meade, A., & Wahlquist, C. (2018, June 19). Australians Don't Want ABC Used as a 'Punching Bag', Michelle Guthrie Says. *The Guardian*. https://www.theguardian.com/media/2018/jun/19/australians-dont-want-abc-used-as-a-punching-bag-michelle-guthrie-says

Meade, A., & AAP. (2020, December 8). ABC Can Keep Google and Facebook Payments for News, Coalition Says. *The Guardian*. https://www.theguardian.com/media/2020/dec/08/abc-can-keep-google-and-facebook-payments-for-news-coalition-says

MediaWatch. (2020, April 20). Pell—The final verdict. *Australian Broadcasting Corporation*. https://www.abc.net.au/mediawatch/episodes/pell/12166274

Media Entertainment and Arts Alliance. (2020, February 24). Assange Case 'An Attack on Truth': WikiLeaks Editor. *Media Entertainment and Arts Alliance*. https://www.meaa.org/news/assange-case-an-attack-on-truth-wikileaks-editor/

Mercury, The. (1939, September 21). News Broadcasts. Free Use of B.B.C. Bulletins To Be Continued. *The Mercury*, p. 11. https://trove.nla.gov.au/newspaper/

article/25773673?searchTerm=The%20Commission%20may%20broadcast%20up%20to%20a%20maximum%20of%2015%20news%20flashes%20weekly%20

Mercury, The. (1944, September 7). Haydn Beck Resigns ABC Post. *The Mercury*, p. 14. https://trove.nla.gov.au/newspaper/article/26036060?searchTerm=haydn%20beck%20ABC&searchLimits=exactPhrase|||anyWords|||notWords|||requestHandler|||dateFrom=1940-01-01|||dateTo=1945-12-31|||sortby

Mergel, I., & Greeves, B. (2013). *Social Media in the Public Sector Field Guide: Designing and Implementing Strategies and Policies.* Jossey-Bass.

Merrill-Brown. (2005). Carnegie Corporation Report Tracks Changes in Media Consumption by 18-34-Year-Olds; Report Survey Data Reveal That Young Adults Surf the Internet for News, Abandoning Newspapers and Traditional Media. *Business Wire.* https://www.businesswire.com/news/home/20050504005525/en/Carnegie-Corporation-Report-Tracks-Media-Consumption-18-34-Year-Olds

Merriam, S. B. (2010). Qualitative Case Studies. In P. Peterson, E. Baker, & B. McGaw (Eds.), *International Encyclopedia of Education* (3rd ed., pp. 457, 456–462). Elsevier. https://doi.org/10.1016/B978-0-08-044894-7.01532-3

Metzger, M. J., & Flanagin, A. J. (2008). *The John D. and Catherine MacArthur Foundation Series on Digital Media and Learning* (pp. vii–ix). Cambridge, MA: The MIT Press. Retrieved from: https://doi.org/10.1162/dmal.9780262562324.vii

Meusburger, P., Glückler, J., & el Meskioui, M. (2013). *Knowledge and the Economy.* Imprint. Springer. https://primoa.library.unsw.edu.au/permalink/f/jhud33/UNSW_ALMA51206680440001731

Meyer, E. L. (2011, November 3). Media Codes of Ethics: The Difficulty of Defining Standards. A Report to the *Center for International Media Assistance.* https://new.waccglobal.org/wp-content/uploads/2020/05/10-Media-Codes-of-Ethics-CIMA2011.pdf

Meyer, J. W., & Rowan, B. (1977). Institutionalized Organizations: Formal Structure as Myth and Ceremony. *American Journal of Sociology, 83*(2), 340–363. https://doi.org/10.1086/226550

Michaels, S. (2009). Matching Knowledge Brokering Strategies to Environmental Policy Problems and Settings. *Environmental Science & Policy.* https://doi.org/10.1016/j.envsci.2009.05.002

Michael, G., & Agur, C. (2018). The Bully Pulpit, Social Media, and Public Opinion: A Big Data Approach. *Journal of Information Technology & Politics, 15*(3), 262–277. https://doi.org/10.1080/19331681.2018.1485604

Miekle, G. (2009). *Interpreting News.* Palgrave Macmillan.

Miles, R., Snow, C., Meyer, A., & Coleman, H. (1978). Organizational Strategy, Structure, and Process. *The Academy of Management Review, 3*(3), 546–562. www.jstor.org/stable/257544

Mill, J. S. (1859). *On Liberty*. The Walter Scott Publishing Co., Ltd. http://www.gutenberg.org/files/34901/34901-h/34901-h.htm

Mill, J. S. (1863). *On Liberty* (2nd ed.). Tickner and Fields.

Miller, C. (2012). Twitter Trumps Science in Trawler Ban. Frontiers in Ecology and the Environment. *Ecological Society of America, 10*(9), 460–460. Wiley. https://www.jstor.org/stable/41811850

Miller, M. (2019, April 2). Heavy Hearts as the Printing Presses Stop Running. *The Australian*. https://www.theaustralian.com.au/commentary/heavy-hearts-as-the-printing-presses-stop-running/news-story/0dad850f021a215cc3d132821d86ab2a

Milne, J. (2017, November 15). Hector Crawford Oration 2017: ABC Chairman Justin Milne. *Australian Broadcasting Corporation*. https://about.abc.net.au/speeches/hector-crawford-oration-2017/

Milne, J., & Guthrie, M. (2018). ABC Annual Report. Welcome. *Australian Broadcasting Corporation*. https://about.abc.net.au/wp-content/uploads/2018/10/AP18_Vol1_FINALnew.pdf

Mintz, A., & Wayne, C. (2016). The Polythink Syndrome and Elite Group Decision-making. *Political Psychology, 37*(S1), 3.

Mills, T. (2014). George Pell's Truck Driver Analogy Veers into Hostile Territory. *The Age*. 22 August 2014. Retrieved from: https://www.theage.com.au/national/victoria/george-pells-truck-driver-analogy-veers-into-hostile-territory-20140822-1076i4.html

Minear, T., & Adams, C. (2017, November 28). Oz Day Heat on ABC. *The Herald Sun*. http://www.heraldsun.com.au/news/abc-under-fire-for-politicising-australia-day-by-moving-triple-js-hottest-100-countdown/news-story/3a7e2e553ec4fca81538bb734ccb88fd

Missingham, R. (2009). Encouraging the Digital Economy and Digital Citizenship. *The Australian Library Journal, 58*(4), 386–399. https://doi.org/10.1080/00049670.2009.10735927

Mitchell, C. (2019, May 27). ABC Gave Us Groupthink on Steroids. *The Australian*. https://www.theaustralian.com.au/commentary/abc-gave-us-groupthink-on-steroids/news-story/da95e8a9d851509bf8538df28c630c15

Miragliotta, N., & Errington, W. (2012). The Rise and Fall and Rise Again of Public Broadcasting? The Case of the Australian Broadcasting Corporation. *Australian Journal of Public Administration, 71*(1), 55–64. https://doi.org/10.1111/j.1467-8500.2012.00755.x

Moe, H. (2008). Public Service Media Online? Regulating Public Broadcasters' Internet Services—A Comparative Analysis. *Television & New Media, 9*(3), 220–238. https://doi.org/10.1177/1527476407307231

Molomby, T. (1991). *Is There a Moderate on the Roof? ABC Years*. William Heinemann.

Monaghan, M. & Prideaux, S. (2016). *State Crime and Immorality: The Corrupting Influence of the Powerful.* Polity Press. Bristol & Chicago.

Moore, M. H. (1995). *Creating Public Value: Strategic Management in Government.* Harvard University Press. Cambridge, Mass.

Moore, M. H., & Benington, J. (2011). Conclusions: Looking Ahead. In M. H. Moore & J. Benington (Eds.), *Public Value: Theory and Practice* (pp. 256–274). Palgrave Macmillan. London.

Moore, C. B., Payne, G. T., Autry, C. W., & Griffis, S. E. (2018). Project Complexity and Bonding Social Capital in Network Organizations. *Group & Organization Management, 43*(6), 936–970. https://doi.org/10.1177/1059601116650556

Morgan, S. (2018). Influencers. *The Missouri Review, 41*(4), 5–10. https://doi.org/10.1353/mis.2018.0040

Morlet, A., Guinan, J. J., Diefenthaler, I., & Gold, J. (1988, March). The Impact of the "Grim Reaper" National AIDS Educational Campaign on the Albion Street (AIDS) Centre and the AIDS Hotline. *The Medical Journal of Australia, 148*(6), 282–287. https://onlinelibrary-wiley-com.wwwproxy1.library.unsw.edu.au/doi/abs/10.5694/j.1326-5377.1988.tb117836.x

Morning Bulletin, The. (1939, September 21). Newspapers Permit Broadcast of Copyright News. Free Use Allowed of B.B.C. Bulletins. *The Morning Bulletin*, p. 7 https://trove.nla.gov.au/newspaper/article/56046160?searchTerm=A.A.P.%20country%20newspapers

Morton, R. (2020, June 25–26). Exclusive: New Govt Report Targets ABC. [online]. *The Saturday Paper, 306.* https://www.thesaturdaypaper.com.au/news/politics/2020/06/27/exclusive-new-govt-report-targets-abc/159318000010021

Monk, P. (2016). Reason in Western Civilisation. *Australian Rationalist, 100*(Autumn), 5–6. https://primoa.library.unsw.edu.au/permalink/f/11jha62/TN_informit_agis20190613012326

Monk, S. (2019, December). Truth v. Fake News. In *Southern Cross.* pp. 17–19. Anglican Media Sydney.

Mønsted, B., Sapieżyński, P., Ferrara, E., & Lehmann, S. (2017). Evidence of Complex Contagion of Information in Social Media: An Experiment Using Twitter Bots. *PloS One.* https://journals.plos.org/plosone/article/file?id=10.1371/journal.pone.0184148&type=printable

Moses, A. D. (2018, June 7). Western Civilization and Conservative Hysteria. ABC Religion and Ethics. *Australian Broadcasting Corporation.* https://www.abc.net.au/religion/western-civilization-and-conservative-hysteria/10094662

Morahan-Martin, J. (2005). Internet Abuse. *Social Science Computer Review, 23*(1): 39–48. https://doi.org/10.1177/0894439304271533

Murphy, J., Link, M. W., Childs, J. H., Tesfaye, C. L., Dean, E., Stern, M., Pasek, J., Cohen, J., Callegaro, M., & Harwood, P. (2014). Social Media in Public

Opinion Research. *Public Opinion Quarterly, 78*(4), 788–794. https://doi.org/10.1093/poq/nfu053

Murphy, K. (2020, June 23). ABC Board Elects to Take 10% Pay Cut Amid Coronavirus Economic Slump. *The Guardian*. https://www.theguardian.com/media/2020/jun/23/abc-board-elects-to-take-10-pay-cut-amid-coronavirus-economic-slump

Mutch, A. (2003). Communities of 'Practice' and '*Habitus*': A Critique. *Organization Studies, 24*(3), 383–401. M. Maclean. https://journals-sagepub-com.wwwproxy1.library.unsw.edu.au/doi/pdf/10.1177/0170840603024003909

Murray, J. (1994, July–December). The Institutional Origins of ABC Censorship in the 1930s [online]. *Australian Journalism Review, 16*(2), 125–131. https://search-informit-com-au.wwwproxy1.library.unsw.edu.au/documentSummary;dn=960808235;res=IELAPA

Munt, S. R. (2017). Argumentum Ad Misericordiam: The Cultural Politics of Victim Media. *Feminist Media Studies, 17*(5), 866–883. https://doi.org/10.1080/14680777.2016.1259176

Murdock, G. (2004, November). Building the Digital Commons: Public Broadcasting in the Age of the Internet. University of Montreal. *The 2004 Spry Memorial Lecture*. https://www.researchgate.net/publication/254750526_BUILDING_THE_DIGITAL_COMMONS_PUBLIC_BROADCASTING_IN_THE_AGE_OF_THE_INTERNET

Murray, A. (2006a, March 24). Australia: Australian Broadcasting Corporation Board Must be Appointed on Merit. *US Fed News Service* Including *US State News, HT Digital Streams Limited*. http://search.proquest.com/docview/470140665/.

Murray, L. (2006b, May 23). Scott of the ABC: A Family Affair of Service. *The Sydney Morning Herald*. https://www.smh.com.au/national/scott-of-the-abc-a-family-affair-of-service-20060523-gdnlkg.html

Murphy, J., Link, M. W., Childs, J. H., Tesfaye, C. L., Dean, E., Stern, M., Pasek, J., Cohen, J., Callegaro, M., & Harwood, P. (2014). Social Media in Public Opinion Research. *Public Opinion Quarterly, 78*(4), 788–794. https://doi.org/10.1093/poq/nfu053

Muller, D. (2019). Outrage, Polls and Bias: 2019 Federal Election Showed Australian Media Need Better Regulation. Opinion. Mumbrella. 22 May 2019. Retrieved from: https://mumbrella.com.au/outrage-polls-and-bias-2019-federal-election-showed-australian-media-need-better-regulation-580713 Comment by Jennifer 27 May 19.

Mudde, C. & Kaltwasser, C. R. in M. Freeden & M. Stears. Eds. (2013). Populism. The Oxford Handbook of Political Ideologies. Retrieved from: https://www-oxfordhandbooks-com.wwwproxy1.library.unsw.edu.au/view/10.1093/oxfordhb/9780199585977.001.0001/oxfordhb-9780199585977-e-026

Murdoch, K. (Intro. M. McKernan). (2010). *The Gallipoli Letter*. Allen and Unwin.

Murdoch, R. In J. Kaye & S. Quinn. (2005). *Funding Journalism in the Digital Age: Business Models, Strategies, Issues and Trends*. Peter Lang.

Musgrove, N. (1961, April 19). Accent on Michael Charlton. *The Australian Women's Weekly*, p. 53. https://trove.nla.gov.au/newspaper/article/55473519?searchTerm=Michael%20Charlton%20ABC

Myer, R. (2020, February 7). News Corp in 'Dangerous Times' as Audience and Revenues Drop in Print and Digital. *The New Daily*. https://thenewdaily.com.au/finance/finance-news/2020/02/07/news-corp-rupert-murdoch/

Murdoch, J. (2009). THE ABSENCE OF TRUST. 2009 Edinburgh International Television Festival. *MacTaggart Lecture*. 29 August 2009. Retrieved from: https://www.abc.net.au/mediawatch/transcripts/0937_mactaggart.pdf

Nadkarni, A., & Hofmann, S. G. (2012). Why Do People Use Facebook? *Personality and Individual Differences*, *52*, 243–249. https://psycnet.apa.org/doi/10.1016/j.paid.2011.11.007

Nah, S., & Chung, D. S. (2012). When Citizens Meet Both Professional and Citizen Journalists: Social Trust, Media Credibility, and Perceived Journalistic Roles Among Online Community News Readers. *Journalism*, *13*(6), 14–730. https://doi.org/10.1177/1464884911431381

Najjarine, K., & Cottle, D. (2003). The Department of External Affairs, the ABC and Reporting of the Indonesian Crisis 1965–1969. *Australian Journal of Politics and History*, *49*(1), 48–60. https://onlinelibrary-wiley-com.ezproxy1.library.usyd.edu.au/doi/epdf/10.1111/1467-8497.00280

Name-Correa, A. J., & Yildirim, H. (2018). A Capture Theory of Committees. *Public Choice*, *177*(1), 135–154. https://doi.org/10.1007/s11127-018-0593-6

Nathan, J. (2019). *Report on Antisemitism in Australia 2019*. Executive Council of Australian Jewry. https://sydney.edu.au/content/dam/corporate/documents/sydney-law-school/research/centres-institutes/antisemitism-report-2019.pdf

National Commission of Audit. (2014). Executive Summary. Second Phase Report. https://www.ncoa.gov.au/report/phase-two/executive-summary

Nature. (1978, October 26). The Public's Right to Know, *275*, 682. https://doi-org.wwwproxy1.library.unsw.edu.au/10.1038/275682a0

Nash, C. (2013, October). Journalism as a Research Discipline. *Pacific Journalism Review*, *19*(2), 123–135. https://primoa.library.unsw.edu.au/permalink/f/11jha62/TN_informit605741818647699

Naughton, J. (2020, February 16). Reports of Social Media's Influence on Voters Are Greatly Exaggerated. *The Guardian*. https://www.theguardian.com/commentisfree/2020/feb/15/reports-of-social-media-influence-on-voters-are-greatly-exaggerated

Neil, A. (1996). *Full Disclosure*. Macmillan.

Nelson, K. E. (2003). The Melbourne Philharmonic Society Under Contract to the Australian Broadcasting Commission: Preservation and Triumph [online].

Context: Journal of Music Research, 25(Autumn), 25–33. http://search.proquest.com/docview/200101339/

Nelson, R. R., & Winter, S. G. (1982). *An Evolutionary Theory of Economic Change*. Belknap Press of Harvard University Press. Cambridge, Mass.

Nerone, J., & Barnhurst, K. G. (2001). Beyond Modernism: Digital Design, Americanization and the Future of Newspaper Form. *New Media & Society, 3*(4), 467–482. https://doi.org/10.1177/14614440122226191

Nerone, J., & Barnhurst, K. G. (2003). US Newspaper Types, the Newsroom, and the Division of Labor, 1750-2000. *Journalism Studies, 4*(4), 435–449. https://doi.org/10.1080/1461670032000136541

Newcastle Morning Herald and Miners' Advocate, The. (1935, June 6). ABC Appointment: Professor Wallace Retires. *Newcastle Morning Herald and Miners' Advocate*, p. 7. https://trove.nla.gov.au/newspaper/article/139259689?searchTerm=ABC%20commissioner%20kitto&searchLimits=

Newman, L., Biedrzycki, K., & Baum, F. (2012). Digital Technology Use among Disadvantaged Australians: Implications for Equitable Consumer Participation in Digitally-Mediated Communication and Information Exchange with Health Services. *Australian Health Review, 36*(2), 125–129. https://doi.org/10.1071/AH11042

Newman, N. with Fletcher, R., Levy, D. A. L., & Kleis Nielsen, R. (2016). Digital News Report. [online]. *Reuters Institute & Oxford University*.http://media.digitalnewsreport.org/wp-content/uploads/2018/11/Digital-News-Report-2016.pdf?x89475

news.sky.com. (2020, August 1). Rupert Murdoch's Son James Quits News Corporation Board after 'Disagreements over Editorial Content'. *Sky News*. https://news.sky.com/story/rupert-murdochs-son-james-quits-news-corporation-board-after-disagreements-over-editorial-content-12040255

News.com.au. (2018, January 1). Charlie Pickering Says Sorry for 'Kill a Police Officer' Gaffe. *News.com.au*. https://www.news.com.au/entertainment/tv/charlie-pickering-says-sorry-for-kill-a-police-officer-gaffe/news-story/a3415b2110377584ca71e9a083ba3829

NewsMail. (2018, November 24). ABC Goes to War with The Chaser Boys. *News Mail*. https://www.news-mail.com.au/news/abc-executive-criticises-chaser-after-satirists-co/3584319/

News, The. (1937, January 29). ABC Out of Touch with Public Taste. *The News, Adelaide*, p. 6. https://trove.nla.gov.au/newspaper/article/131403633?searchTerm=ABC%20out%20of%20touch%20with%20public%20taste.%20

News, The. (1941, September 11). Abhors Affected Accent, Says A.B.C. Chairman. *The News*, p. 3. https://trove.nla.gov.au/newspaper/article/131982061?searchTerm=ABC%20accent

News, The (Adelaide). (1942, February 16). Curtin Says Battle for Australia Has Opened. *The News*, p. 3. https://trove.nla.gov.au/newspaper/article/131950874/11347070

News, The (Adelaide). (1954, September 14). ABC Sport Policy Examined. *The News*, p. 36. https://trove.nla.gov.au/newspaper/article/130986285?searchTerm=ABC%20sport&searchLimits=

Newcastle Sun, The. (1945, April 17). Politics and the ABC. Editorial. *The Newcastle Sun*, p. 6. https://trove.nla.gov.au/newspaper/article/156641758?searchTerm=Politics%20and%20the%20ABC.

Nicholson, P. (2016). Balance in Redress: Too Slow? Too Rule-Bound? Too Confusing to the Public? The Scottish Legal Complaints Commission Is Consulting on Whether to Seek Radical Changes to Its Complaint Handling Procedures. *The Journal of the Law Society of Scotland, 61*(2). https://primoa.library.unsw.edu.au/permalink/f/11jha62/TN_gale_legal446198366

Nicol, J. W., & Gordon, L. J. (2018). Preparing for Leadership in General Practice: A Qualitative Exploration of How GP Trainees Learn about Leadership. *Education for Primary Care, 29*(6), 327–335. https://doi.org/10.1080/14739879.2018.1528896

Nicholls, P. (2011). *A Business and Labour History of Britain Case Studies of Britain in the Nineteenth and Twentieth Centuries* (M. Richardson & P. Nicholls, Eds.). Palgrave Macmillan.

Nicholson, J., & Nattrass, S. (2003). Pioneer Was Courageous Voice at ABC. *The Sydney Morning Herald*.https://www.smh.com.au/national/pioneer-was-courageous-voice-at-abc-20030111-gdg37y.html

Nine.com.au. (2018, May 23). Emma Alberici Under Fire Again as PM Files Complaints to the ABC. https://finance.nine.com.au/business-news/emma-alberici-abc-complaints-prime-minister-malcolm-turnbull/4dc648ae-6f69-4f2b-b5fd-8d655c9d84f2

Nine.com.au. (2020). Coronavirus: PM Says Aged Care Facilities May Be Put in 'Lock Down' If COVID-19 Outbreak Worsens. A Current Affair. *Channel 9*. https://9now.nine.com.au/a-current-affair/coronavirus-update-prime-minister-scott-morrison-says-covid19-outbreak-may-lead-to-aged-care-facilities-in-lock-down/2b70072b-758b-4e5e-8144-7f2c9241b8f1

Nolan, D. (2006). Media, Citizenship and Governmentality: Defining "The Public" of Public Service Broadcasting. *Social Semiotics, 16*(2), 225–242. https://doi.org/10.1080/10350330600667501

North, D. (1990). *Institutions, Institutional Change and Economic Performance*. Political Economy of Institutions and Decisions. Cambridge University Press. https://doi.org/10.1017/CBO9780511808678

Northouse, P. G. (2010). *Leadership: Theory and Practice* (5th ed.). Sage Publications. Thousand Oaks.

Northouse, P. G. (2013). *Leadership: Theory and Practice* (6th ed.). Sage Publications.

Northridge, M. (2009). Serving the Public Good. *American Journal of Public Health, 99*(3), 393. https://search-proquest-com.wwwproxy1.library.unsw.edu.au/docview/215089511?rfr_id=info%3Axri%2Fsid%3Aprimo

Norington, B. (2020, April 18). Cash for Coronavirus: ABC 'Guru' Norman Swan After Money to Turn Spin Doctor. *The Australian*. https://www.theaustralian.com.au/business/media/cash-for-coronavirus-abc-guru-norman-swan-after-money-to-turn-spin-doctor/news-story/804333e72f653d5891e3706035a50563

Northern Star, The. (1945, February 27). ABC Chairman Resigns. *The Northern Star, Lismore*, p. 5. https://trove.nla.gov.au/newspaper/article/99264583?searchTerm=chairman%20ABC&searchLimits=exactPhrase|||anyWords|||notWords|||requestHandler|||dateFrom=1944-01-01|||dateTo=1946-12-31|||l-advstate=National|||l-advstate=ACT|||l-advstate=New+South+Wales|||sortby

Northern Standard, The. (1950, March 31). Will be Scrapped. *The Northern Standard*, p. 6. https://trove.nla.gov.au/newspaper/article/49475143?searchTerm=ABC%20news%20service

Norris, P. (2000). *A Virtuous Circle: Political Communications in Post-industrial Societies*. Cambridge University Press.

Norman, J. (2018, June 16). Liberal Party Members Vote to Privatise ABC and Move Australia's Israel Embassy to Jerusalem. *ABC Online*. https://www.abc.net.au/news/2018-06-16/liberal-members-vote-to-privatise-abc-move-embassy-to-jerusalem/9877524

NSW Nurses and Midwives' Association. (2018, March 5). Turnbull Pressures ABC on Tax Coverage. Tax Justice. *The Lamp*, p. 20. https://thelamp.com.au/workplace-issues/unions/turnbull-pressures-abc-on-tax-coverage/

Nyhan, B., & Reifler, J. (2015, July). The Effect of Fact-Checking on Elites: A 'Field' Experiment on U.S. State Legislators. *American Journal of Political Science, 59*(3), 628–640. https://ore.exeter.ac.uk/repository/bitstream/handle/10871/21568/Nyhan%20Reifler%20AJPS.pdf?sequence=1

Nygren, G., Leckner, S., & Tenor, C. (2018). Hyperlocals and Legacy Media: Media Ecologies in Transition. *Nordicom Review, 39*(1), 33–49. https://doi.org/10.1515/nor-2017-0419

Oakes, D., & Clark, S. (2017). The Afghan Files. *ABC News. Australian Broadcasting Corporation*. https://www.abc.net.au/news/2019-06-05/abc-raided-by-australian-federal-police-afghan-files-stories/11181162

Oakman, D. (2010). *Facing Asia: A History of the Colombo Plan*. ANC Press. Canberra.

O'Brien, K. (2018). *Kerry O'Brien: A Memoir*. Allen and Unwin.

O'Brien, K. (2019, July 1). 'Don't Ever Again Allow Politicians to Diminish the Public Broadcaster'. Logies Speech. Induction into the Hall of Fame. *Crikey.com*.https://www.crikey.com.au/2019/07/01/kerry-obrien-logies-speech/

O'Carroll, L. (2014, June 30). Phone Hacker Glenn Mulcaire Bankrupt Over Tax on News of the World Earnings. *The Guardian*. https://www.theguardian.com/uk-news/2014/jun/30/phone-hacker-glenn-mulcaire-bankrupt-news-world

O'Donnell, V. (2018). Is the ABC Really Biased? Opinion. 30 June 2018. *The Sydney Morning Herald*. Retrieved from: https://www.smh.com.au/national/is-the-abc-really-biased-20180629-p4zoh5.html

O'Dwyer, E. (2011, May 14). A Bit Weird and Getting Paid for It. *The Sydney Morning Herald*. https://www.smh.com.au/entertainment/tv-and-radio/a-bit-weird-and-getting-paid-for-it-20110514-1en2c.html

OECD. (2011). *Regulatory Policy and Governance: Supporting Economic Growth and Serving the Public Interest*. OECD Publishing. https://doi.org/10.1787/9789264116573-en

Ohlsson, J., Lindell, J., & Arkhede, S. (2017). A Matter of Cultural Distinction: News Consumption in the Online Media Landscape. *European Journal of Communication (London)*, *32*(2), 116–130. https://doi.org/10.1177/0267323116680131

O'Keeffe, A., & Greene, C. (2019, December 11). International Public Broadcasting: A Missed Opportunity for Projecting Australia's Soft Power. *Lowy Institute*. https://www.lowyinstitute.org/publications/international-public-broadcasting-missed-opportunity-projecting-australia-s-soft-power

Olson, M. (1965). *The Logic of Collective Action: Public Goods and Theory of Groups*. Harvard University Press. Cambridge, Mass.

O'Mahen, P. (2016). A Big Bird Effect? The Interaction Among Public Broadcasting, Public Subsidies, and Political Knowledge. *European Political Science Review*, 8(2), 311–332. https://www-cambridge-org.wwwproxy1.library.unsw.edu.au/core/services/aop-cambridge-core/content/view/8EC8052F26A223A76ED7D07A386E10D5/S175577391500003Xa.pdf/big_bird_effect_the_interaction_among_public_broadcasting_public_subsidies_and_political_knowledge.pdf

O'Mallon, F. (2020, May 4). ABC Lost More Than $350m Per Year: Report. *The West Australian*. https://thewest.com.au/politics/abc-lost-more-than-350m-per-year-report-ng-s-2008375

Oreskes, N., & Conway, E. (2010). Defeating the Merchants of Doubt. *Nature*, *465*, 686–687. https://doi.org/10.1038/465686a

Orr, G. D. (2010, June). The Australian Experience of Electoral Bribery: Dealing in Electoral Support. *Australian Journal of Politics & History*, p. 232. https://www.researchgate.net/publication/47456681

Orwell, G. (1949). *1984*. Secker & Warburg.

Orwell, G. (1946) (2021). *Politics and the English Language*. Renard Press. London.

Orvos, J. (2019). *Achieving Business Agility: Strategies for Becoming Pivot Ready in a Digital World* (1st ed.). Apress. https://primoa.library.unsw.edu.au/permalink/f/jhud33/UNSW_ALMA51274521450001731

Osborne, P. (2019). Department Boss Blindsided by Morrison Axe. Australian Associated Press. *The Canberra Times*. 5 December, 2019. Retrieved from: https://www.canberratimes.com.au/story/6527946/department-boss-blindsided-by-morrison-axe/

Osborne, S., Brandsen, T., Mele, V., Nemec, J., van Genugten, M., & Flemig, S. (2020). Risking Innovation. Understanding Risk and Public Service Innovation-Evidence from a Four Nation Study. *Public Money & Management*. *40*(1), 52–62. https://doi.org/10.1080/09540962.2019.1621051

O'Sullivan, P. B. (2005). Masspersonal Communication: An Integrative Model Bridging the Mass-Personal Divide. In Annual Meeting of the International Communication Association. New York City, New York. Retrieved from: http://ilstu.academia.edu/PatrickBOSullivan/Papers/457584/Masspersonal_communication_Rethinking_the_mass_interpersonal_divide.

Ouellette, L. (2008). Makeover Television, Governmentality and the Good Citizen. *Continuum*, *22*(4), 471–484.

Owen, D. (2018). The Past Decade and Future of Political Media: The Ascendance of Social Media. In *Towards a New Enlightenment? A Transcendent Decade*. Madrid: BBVA. Retrieved from: https://www.bbvaopenmind.com/en/articles/the-past-decade-and-future-of-political-media-the-ascendance-of-social-media/.

Oxford English Dictionary. (2021). https://www-oed-com.wwwproxy1.library.unsw.edu.au/view/Entry/141512?redirectedFrom=personnel&

Oxford University Press. (2016). Word of the Year 2016. https://languages.oup.com/word-of-the-year/2016/

Packham, B. (2019, December 11). Lowy Institute Slams Loss of Soft Power Airwaves in Pacific. *The Australian*. https://www.theaustralian.com.au/nation/politics/lowy-institute-slams-loss-of-soft-power-airwaves-in-pacific/news-story/518c5a6072055012c972828724e104a7

Paletz, D. L., & Entman, R. M. (1981). *Media Power Politics*. Free Press.

Palfreyman, R. (1993, November). Opening the Airwaves: Cultural Squeeze for National Broadcasting? *Current Affairs Bulletin*, *70*(6), 19–25. https://hdl.handle.net/10070/89994

Park, C. M. (2010). Public Attitudes toward Government Spending in the Asia-Pacific Region. *Japanese Journal of Political Science*, *11*(1), 77–97. https://doi.org/10.1017/S1468109909990144

Parliament of Australia. (2019). Amendments to *Australian Broadcasting Corporation Act 1983* To: Amend the Australian Broadcasting Corporation (ABC) Charter. [online]. https://www.aph.gov.au/Parliamentary_Business/Bills_Legislation/Bills_Search_Results/Result?bId=r6382

Paas F., van Gog T., Kirschner F., Marcus N., Ayres P., & Sweller J. (2008). Interdisciplinary Perspectives on Cognitive Load Research as a Key to Tackle Challenges of Contemporary Education. In J. Zumbach, N. Schwartz, T. Seufert, & L. Kester (Eds.), *Beyond Knowledge: The Legacy of Competence*. Springer. Dordrecht. https://doi-org.wwwproxy1.library.unsw.edu.au/10.1007/978-1-4020-8827-8_2

Parker, S. (2014, November 29). Quentin Dempster's Parting Shot at Commercialisation of the ABC. *The Sydney Morning Herald*. https://www.smh.com.au/politics/federal/quentin-dempsters-parting-shot-at-commercialisation-of-the-abc-20141129-11wk7z.html

Parr, N. (2015). Who Goes to University? The Changing Profile of Our Students. *The Conversation*.https://theconversation.com/who-goes-to-university-the-changing-profile-of-our-students-40373

Pascoe, M. (2020, August 12). Michael Pascoe: More Job Losses Are a Safe Bet After Network Ten's Dark Day. *The New Daily*.https://thenewdaily.com.au/finance/finance-news/2020/08/12/network-ten-michael-pascoe/#:~:text=Michael%20Pascoe%3A%20More%20job%20losses,after%20Network%20Ten's%20dark%20day&text=A%20well%2Dknown%20TV%20star,as%20income%20falls%20below%20costs.

Passmore, A. (2013, June 3). The Other Culture Shock: The Internal Culture at CUs. *Credit Union Journal, 17*(22), 16. https://search-proquest-com.wwwproxy1.library.unsw.edu.au/docview/1362107663?rfr_id=info%3Axri%2Fsid%3Aprimo

Paas F., van Gog T., Kirschner F., Marcus N., Ayres P., & Sweller J. (2008). Interdisciplinary Perspectives on Cognitive Load Research as a Key to Tackle Challenges of Contemporary Education. In J. Zumbach, N. Schwartz, T. Seufert, & L. Kester (Eds.), *Beyond Knowledge: The Legacy of Competence*. Springer. Dordrecht. https://doi-org.wwwproxy1.library.unsw.edu.au/10.1007/978-1-4020-8827-8_2

Paterson, T., Harms, P., & Tuggle, C. (2018). Revisiting the Rigor–Relevance Relationship: An Institutional Logics Perspective. *Human Resource Management, 57*(6), 1371–1383. https://doi.org/10.1002/hrm.21911

Patrick, A. (2018, April 10). Emma Alberici Anti-Tax Cut Article Contained Nine Errors. *The Australian Financial Review*. https://www.afr.com/policy/tax-and-super/emma-alberici-antitax-cut-article-contained-nine-errors-20180410-h0ykfs

Patrick, A. (2020, April 4). I'm Worried About the Panic Out There: David Isaacs, Germ Expert. *The Australian Financial Review*. https://global-factiva-com.ezproxy2.library.usyd.edu.au/ha/default.aspx#./!?&_suid=158630818658503136619040135381

Patterson, R. (2004). The Eradication of Compulsory Retirement and Age Discrimination in the Australian Workplace: A Cause for Celebration and

Concern. *Elder Law Review, 10*(3), 65. http://classic.austlii.edu.au/au/journals/ElderLawRw/2004/10.html

Patriarche, G., & Dufrasne, M. (2014). Penser la diversité des pratiques médiatiques: Le réseau comme catégorie conceptuelle pour la recherche sur les audiences et les publics. *Réseaux, 187*(5), 195–232. https://doi.org/10.3917/res.187.0195

Paulson, M. (2002, April 8). World Doesn't Share US View of Scandal: Clergy Sexual Abuse Reaches Far, Receives an Uneven Focus. *The Boston Globe.* http://archive.boston.com/globe/spotlight/abuse/print/040802_world.htm

Pearlman, J. (2007, August 30). SBS Not Dumbing Down, Says Boss. *The Sydney Morning Herald.* https://www.smh.com.au/entertainment/sbs-not-dumbing-down-says-boss-20070830-gdqzj9.html

Pearlman, A. (2008). Ethics in Journalism—Accuracy, Honesty, and Credibility. *Journal of the American Society of Echocardiography, 21*(5), 507–508. https://doi.org/10.1016/j.echo.2008.03.008

Pentina, I., & Tarafdar, M. (2014). From "Information" to "Knowing": Exploring the Role of Social Media in Contemporary News Consumption. *Computers in Human Behavior, 35*, 221–223. https://doi.org/10.1016/j.chb.2014.02.045

Percy, K. (2019, March 26). George Pell Trial Suppression Orders Breached by News Organisations, Victorian Prosecutor Alleges. *Australian Broadcasting Corporation.* https://www.abc.net.au/news/2019-03-26/journalists-accused-of-breaking-george-pell-suppression-order/10939980

Perry, J. L., & Rainey, H. G. (1988). The Public-Private Distinction in Organization Theory: A Critique and Research Strategy. *The Academy of Management Review, 13*(2), 182–201. Published by: Academy of Management. http://www.jstor.org/stable/258571

Persily, N. (2017, April). The 2016 U.S. Election: Can Democracy Survive the Internet? *Journal of Democracy, 28*(2), 63–76. https://muse.jhu.edu/article/653377

Petersen, N. (1993). *News Not Views: The ABC, the Press, & Politics. 1932–1947.* Hale and Iremonger.

Petersen, N. (2009). A Biography of Sir Charles Moses. *Global Media Journal, 3*(1). https://www.hca.westernsydney.edu.au/gmjau/archive/v3_2009_1/3vi1_neville_petersen.html

Petersen, N. (2012). Moses, Sir Charles Joseph (1900–1988). *Australian Dictionary of Biography, 18.* Melbourne University Press. http://adb.anu.edu.au/biography/moses-sir-charles-joseph-15044

Pew Research Centre. (2012). Millennials Confident. Connected. Open to Change. https://www.pewresearch.org/wp-content/uploads/sites/3/2010/10/millennials-confident-connected-open-to-change.pdf

Pha, A. (2018, October 3). Your ABC: Your Democracy. *The Guardian (Sydney), 1842*(1), 12. https://search-informit-com-au.wwwproxy1.library.unsw.edu.au/documentSummary;dn=931380458882186;res=IELAPA

Phillips, M., & Magdalinski, T. (2008). Sport in Australia. In B. Houlihan (Ed.), *Sport and Society: A Student Introduction*. Sage Publications.

Pinches, M. (1999). In M. Pinches (Ed.), *Culture and Privilege in Capitalist Asia*. Routledge.

Pitt, H. (2020, March 17). 'It Made a Powerful Impact': ABC Chair Says AIDS Campaign Worked. *The Sydney Morning Herald*. https://www.smh.com.au/national/it-made-a-powerful-impact-abc-chair-says-aids-campaign-worked-20200316-p54an2.html

Pircher Verdorfer, A. (2019). The Paradox of Serving: Can Genuine Servant Leadership Gain Followers' Respect for the Leader? Evidence from Germany and Lithuania. *German Journal of Human Resource Management, 33*(2), 113–136. https://doi.org/10.1177/2397002218793840

Plato. (375BC, revised Ed. 2002). *The Republic*. http://www.idph.net

Pollitt, C. (2016). Managerialism Redux? *Financial Accountability & Management, 32*(4), 429–447. https://doi.org/10.1111/faam.12094

Posetti, J., & Ping, L. (2012). The Twitterisation of ABC's Emergency and Disaster Communication. *The Australian Journal of Emergency Management, 27*(1), 34–39. https://search-informit-com-au.wwwproxy1.library.unsw.edu.au/documentSummary;dn=046926063833158;res=IELAPA

Poterba, J. M., & von Hagen, J. (1999). Introduction to "Fiscal Institutions and Fiscal Performance". In *Fiscal Institutions and Fiscal Performance* (pp. 1–12). University of Chicago Press. Chicago.

Potter, M. R., Olejarski, A. M., & Pfister, S. M. (2014). Capture Theory and the Public Interest: Balancing Competing Values to Ensure Regulatory Effectiveness. *International Journal of Public Administration, 37*, 638–645. https://doi.org/10.1080/01900692.2014.903266

Potuchek, J. L. (1997). Who Supports the Family?: Gender and Breadwinning in Dual-Earner Marriages. Stanford University Press, Stanford CA.

Powe, J. (2010, November). Public Service Leadership in Times of Significant Change and Uncertainty. *The International Journal of Leadership in Public Services, 6*(4). https://www-emerald-com.wwwproxy1.library.unsw.edu.au/insight/content/doi/10.5042/ijlps.2010.0631/full/pdf?title=when-the-going-gets-tough-public-service-leadership-in-times-of-significant-change-and-uncertainty

Powell, M. J. (nd). People of Australia Ethnic groups. *Britannica*. Retrieved from: https://www.britannica.com/place/Australia/Manufacturing

Powell, W. W., & DiMaggio, P. J. (1991). The New Institutionalism and Organisational Analysis. Chapter 10. R. Friedland and R.R. Alford. "Bringing Society Back" In *Symbols, Practices and Institutional Contradictions*. University of Chicago Press. Chicago.

Powers, M., & Vera-Zambrano, S. (2018). How Journalists Use Social Media in France and the United States: Analyzing Technology Use Across Journalistic Fields. *New Media & Society, 20*(8), 2728–2744. https://doi.org/10.1177/1461444817731566

President of the Council of State. (2013, September 5). Temporary Injunction. President of the Council of State 17 June 2013. http://www.ste.gr/portal/page/portal/StE/ProsfatesApofaseis

Prior, M. (2007) (Reprinted 2014). *Post-Broadcast Democracy: How Media Choice Increases Inequality in Political Involvement and Polarises Elections*. Cambridge University Press. Cambridge.

Prior, M. (2009). Improving Media Effects Research through Better Measurement of News Exposure. *The Journal of Politics, 71*, 893–908. https://doi.org/10.1017/S0022381609090781

Price, S. (2014, July 9). Public Broadcasting Under Threat. *Green Left Weekly, 1015*(3). https://primoa.library.unsw.edu.au/permalink/f/11jha62/TN_informit441816198109046

Prosser Scully, R. (2019, May 20). How Did Pollsters Get the Australian Election Result So Wrong? *New Scientist*. https://www.newscientist.com/article/2203837-how-did-pollsters-get-the-australian-election-result-so-wrong/#ixzz6IKLZ24Mq

Pullan, R. (1986). *Four Corners: Twenty-Five Years*. ABC Enterprises.

Pureza, A. P., & Lee, K. (2020). Corporate Social Responsibility Leadership for Sustainable Development: An Institutional Logics Perspective in Brazil. *Corporate Social Responsibility and Environmental Management, 27*(3), 1410–1424. https://doi.org/10.1002/csr.1894

Quinn, K. (2016, January 5). ABC News Director Gaven Morris Says 'Bias' Is Part of the Job. *The Sydney Morning Herald*. https://www.smh.com.au/entertainment/tv-and-radio/lunch-with-gaven-morris-abc-director-of-news-20160104-glz8q3.html

Quinn, B. (2020, June 1). Assange Misses Court Hearing Amid Calls in Australia for His Release. *The Guardian*. https://www.theguardian.com/media/2020/jun/01/julian-assange-misses-court-hearing-amid-calls-in-australia-for-his-release

QSRweb.com. (2015, February 11). *How Customers' Expectations Defines Your Brand*. [online]. Cengage Learning, Inc. https://link-gale-com

Quadrant. (2016, February 6). The ABC's Cardinal Sins. *Quadrant*. https://quadrant.org.au/abcs-cardinal-sins/

Queensland Times. (1937, February 9). ABC Changes? Younger Commissioners Likely. *Queensland Times*, p. 6. https://trove.nla.gov.au/newspaper/article/117630789?searchTerm=ABC%20commissioner%20kitto&searchLimits=

Radioinfo.com.au. (2020). RIP ABC 0745 News Bulletin. https://www.radioinfo.com.au/news/rip-abc-0745-news-bulletin

Radio Info. (2016, July 22). Top 20 Percent of ABC Staff Paid $124 Million: *Senate Estimates*. https://www.radioinfo.com.au/news/top-20-percent-abc-staff-paid-124-million-senate-estimates

Ramachandran, V. S. (2003). The Emerging Mind. The Reith Lectures 2003. *British Broadcasting Corporation*. https://www.bbc.co.uk/radio4/reith2003/

Rao, H., & Giorgi, S. (2006). Code Breaking: How Entrepreneurs Exploit Cultural Logics to Generate Institutional Change. Research in Organizational Behavior, 27, 269–304. https://doi.org/10.1016/S0191-3085(06)27007-2.

Rashkin, H., Choi, E., Jang, J.Y., Volkova, S., & Choi, Y. (2017). Truth of Varying Shades: Analyzing Language in Fake News and Political Fact-Checking. Proceedings of the 2017 Conference on Empirical Methods in Natural Language Processing (2931–2937). Copenhagen, Denmark, September 7–11, 2017. Retrieved from: https://www.aclweb.org/anthology/D17-1317/

Rayner, J., Lawton, A., & Williams, H. (2012). Organizational Citizenship Behavior and the Public Service Ethos: Whither the Organization? *Journal of Business Ethics, 106*, 117–130. https://link-springer-com.wwwproxy1.library.unsw.edu.au/content/pdf/10.1007/s10551-011-0991-x.pdf

Rayner, M. (1997). Democracy and the Good Life. *Leading and Managing, 3*(4, Summer), 237–244. https://search-informit-com-au.wwwproxy1.library.unsw.edu.au/fullText;dn=89267;res=AEIPT

Razavi, H. (2020, May 20). Notes on a Pandemic: How Society Has Responded to Covid-19. *Australian Book Review Magazine, 421*. https://www.australianbookreview.com.au/abr-online/current-issue/788-commentary/6441-notes-on-a-pandemic-how-society-has-responded-to-covid-19-by-hessom-razavi

Reddick, C. G., & Aikins, S. K. (2012). Web 2.0 Technologies and Democratic Governance. In C. Reddick & S. Aikins (Eds.), *Web 2.0 Technologies and Democratic Governance. Public Administration and Information Technology* (Vol. 1). Springer. https://doi-org.wwwproxy1.library.unsw.edu.au/10.1007/978-1-4614-1448-3_1

Reay, T., Zilber, T. B., Langley, A., & Tsoukas, H. (2019). *Institutions and Organizations*. Oxford University Press. Oxford. https://doi.org/10.1093/oso/9780198843818.001.0001

Reach.out. (2020). The Importance of Sharing Your Stories. *Reach.out*. https://au.reachout.com/articles/the-importance-of-sharing-your-story

Reddan, F. (2017, April). Serving the Public Good. *Accountancy Ireland, 49*(2), 21–22. https://www.charteredaccountants.ie/docs/default-source/Publishing/accountancy-ireland-archive/accountancy-ireland-april-2017.pdf?sfvrsn=4

Reed, M. (2012). Masters of the Universe: Power and Elites in Organization Studies. *Organization Studies, 33*(2), 203–221. https://journals-sagepub-com.wwwproxy1.library.unsw.edu.au/doi/pdf/10.1177/0170840611430590

Regencia, T. (2020, June 15). Maria Ressa Found Guilty in Blow to Philippines' Press Freedom. *Al Jazeera*. https://www.aljazeera.com/news/2020/06/philippine-court-rappler-maria-ressa-guilty-cyberlibel-200614210221502.html

Remeikis, A. (2018, September 30). ABC Board Must Get Back to Work and 'Do Better', Scott Morrison Says. *The Guardian*. https://www.theguardian.com/media/2018/sep/30/abc-board-must-get-back-to-work-and-do-better-scott-morrison-says

Reporters Sans Frontières. (2020). 2020 World Press Freedom Index. Reporters Sans Frontières. https://rsf.org/en/ranking

Reporters Sans Frontières. (2020). 2020 World Press Freedom Index. Reporters Sans Frontières. https://rsf.org/en/ranking

Reserve Bank of Australia. (2019). Pre-Decimal Inflation Calculator. https://www.rba.gov.au/calculator/annualPreDecimal.html

Reserve Bank of Australia. (2020). Pre-Decimal Inflation Calculator. *Reserve Bank of Australia* https://www.rba.gov.au/calculator/annualPreDecimal.html

Reuters. (n.d.). Handbook of Journalism. Standards and Values. *Reuters*. http://handbook.reuters.com/index.php?title=Standards_and_Values

Richardson, A. (2017). Bearing Witness While Black: Theorizing African American Mobile Journalism after Ferguson. *Digital Journalism, 5*(6), 673–698. Retrieved from: https://doi.org/10.1080/21670811.2016.1193818

Rickard, J. (2003). Symposium: Choral Music in Melbourne—"Messiahs," "Elijahs" and All that Jazz: Melbourne Musical Taste Between the Wars. *Context*, 35–39. http://search.proquest.com/docview/1465088/

Ritchie, E. (2019, December 30). ABC's Own Calls Out Drop in News, Sport Coverage. *The Australian*. https://www.theaustralian.com.au/nation/abcs-own-call-out-drop-in-news-sport-coverage/news-story/590d680302572167e1c3991432144398

Roberts, G. (2014, February 18). Acting Prime Minister Warren Truss Defends Navy Amid Claims Asylum Seekers Beaten and Burned. *Australian Broadcasting Corporation*. https://www.abc.net.au/news/2014-01-22/australian-navy-accused-of-beating-burning-asylum-seekers/5211996

Robertson, A. (1970, June 3). ABC Censorship Move Stirs New Staff Challenge. *The Tribune*, p. 4. https://trove.nla.gov.au/newspaper/article/237505888?searchTerm=ABC%20staff%20culture&searchLimits=

Robertson, J. (2015, June 26). ABC Offices in Security Lockdown After Threats Following Q&A Zaky Mallah Episode. *The Sydney Morning Herald*. https://www.smh.com.au/politics/federal/abc-offices-in-security-lockdown-after-threats-following-qa-zaky-mallah-episode-20150626-ghy48b.html

Robertson, A. (2019, September 28). How Did CEO Pay Get to 500 Times the Wages of Ordinary Workers? Analysis. *Australian Broadcasting Corporation*. https://www.abc.net.au/news/2019-09-28/how-did-ceo-pay-get-to-500-times-the-wages-of-ordinary-workers/11556394

Robertson, J., & Meade, A. (2017, May 9). Fairfax Boss Greg Hywood was Paid as Much as $7.2m in 2016. *The Guardian*. https://www.theguardian.com/media/2017/may/09/fairfax-boss-greg-hywood-paid-more-2016

Robinson, S., & De Shano, C. (2011). 'Anyone can Know': Citizen Journalism and the Interpretive Community of the Mainstream Press. *Journalism: Theory, Practice, and Criticism, 12*(8), 963–982.

Robinson, N. (2015, July 1). Q&A guest Zaky Mallah Hits Back with New Gang-Bang Tweets. *The Australian*. https://www.theaustralian.com.au/business/media/qa-guest-zaky-mallah-hits-back-with-new-gangbang-tweets/news-story/fe0701f40bc64bc45b2053194949d81c

Robinson, E. (2016, December 30). Why Journalists Love Twitter—Tweets Make Lazy Political Journalism Easier Than Ever. *Current Affairs*. https://www.currentaffairs.org/2016/11/why-journalists-love-twitter

Robinson, S. L. (1996). Trust and Breach of the Psychological Contract. *Administrative Science Quarterly, 41*(4), 574–599. https://doi.org/10.2307/2393868

Robbins, S., Judge, T. A., Edwards, M., Sandiford, P., Fitzgerald, M., & Hunt, J. (2019). *Organisational Behaviour* (9th ed.). EBook. Pearson Education Australia. http://ebookcentral.proquest.com/lib/unsw/detail.action?docID=5220538

Roe, I. (2020, February 7). Distrust, Transparency Issues Blamed for Democracy Disengagement. PM. *ABC*. https://www.abc.net.au/radio-australia/programs/pm/distrust,-transparency-issues-blamed-for-democracy-disengagement/11945204

Rogstad, I. D. (2014). Political News Journalists in Social Media: Transforming Political Reporters Into Political Pundits? *Journalism Practice, 8*(6), 688–703. https://doi.org/10.1080/17512786.2013.865965

Rogers, J., O'Boyle, N., Preston, P., & Fehr, F. (2014). The Significance of Small Differences: Cultural Diversity and Broadcasting in Ireland. *European Journal of Communication, 29*(4), 399–415. https://doi.org/10.1177/0267323114530367

Rogers, S., Sedghi, A., & Evans, L. (2011, July 19). James and Rupert Murdoch at the Culture, Media and Sport Select Committee—Live Transcript. http://www.guardian.co.uk/news/datablog/2011/jul/19/james-rupert-murdoch-live-transcript

Rojek, C. (2012). Demand Side Factors. Ch. 7. In *Fame Attack: The Inflation of Celebrity and Its Consequences* (pp. 98–122). Bloomsbury Academic. London. http://dx.doi.org/10.5040/9781849661386.ch-007

Roy Morgan. (2019, July 22). ABC Still Most Trusted—Facebook Improves. *Finding 8064*. http://www.roymorgan.com/findings/8064-abc-remains-most-trusted-media-201907220424

Royal Commission into Institutional Responses to Child Sexual Abuse. (2017). Final Report. Royal Commission into Institutional Responses to Child Sexual Abuse. https://www.childabuseroyalcommission.gov.au/

Ross, D. (2020a, January 1). Tex Perkins Upsets Viewers of ABC New Year's Eve Performance. *The Australian*. https://www.theaustralian.com.au/business/media/tex-perkins-upsets-viewers-of-abc-new-years-eve/news-story/4931060d16f89e4d805001eefa3b967b

Ross, D. (2020b, January 2). Maurice Newman Demands ABC Apologise Over Tex Perkins Obscene Gesture at NY Eve Performance. *The Australian*. https://www.theaustralian.com.au/business/media/tex-perkins-upsets-viewers-of-abc-new-years-eve/news-story/4931060d16f89e4d805001eefa3b967b?fbclid=IwAR1VwTKDvN3FGbGzJVjUzUxgWBtF4ktC5cznayJisQAtXylsxAmo1Qhbo5Y

Rowland, M. (2016). Media Concentration and Public Concern in Australia. ABC Fact Check. *Australian Broadcasting Corporation*.https://cdn.theconversation.com/static_files/files/22/68437-2016-11-22-media-concentration-and-public-concern-in-australia-Research_-_Media_concentration_and_public_concern_in_Australia.pdf?1518059940

Ruggles, R. M. (1993). History of Standard 12: Establishing Requirements for Pluralizing Education. In C. Martindale (Ed.), *Pluralizing Journalism Education: A Multicultural Handbook* (pp. 17–23). Greenwood Press.

Russell, F. M., Hendricks, M. A., Choi, H., & Stephens, E. C. (2015). Who Sets the News Agenda on Twitter? *Digital Journalism, 3*(6), 925–943. https://doi.org/10.1080/21670811.2014.995918

Rudd, K. (20yp://kevinrudd.com/2019/02/04/the-complacent-country/

Rutherford, L., & Brown, A. (2013). The Australian Broadcasting Corporation's Multiplatform Projects: Industrial Logics of Children's Content Provision in the Digital Television Era. *Convergence, 19*(2), 201–221. https://doi.org/10.1177/1354856512457749

Ryan, P. (1986, December 6). How Sir Keith Built, and Lost, a Newspaper. *The Sydney Morning Herald*, p. 11. https://global-factiva-com.wwwproxy1.library.unsw.edu.au/ha/default.aspx#./!?&_suid=159677667635208788332424849641

Sainsbury, M. (2007). Media. The Australian. 6 December 2007.

Salter, D. (2007). *The Media We Deserve: Underachievement in The Fourth Estate*. Melbourne University Press.

Sammartino, S. (2014). *The Great Fragmentation: And Why the Future of All Business Is Small* (1st ed.). John Wiley & Sons.

Samios, Z. (2021). ABC to relocate 300 Ultimo staff to Parramatta. *The Sydney Morning Herald*. 16 June 2021. Retrieved from: https://www.smh.com.au/politics/federal/abc-to-relocate-300-staff-to-parramatta-20210616-p581eh.html.

Sanchez Perry, H. (2017). Intersectionality as an Institution: Changing the Definition of Feminism. *DePaul Journal of Women, Gender and the Law*, 7(1), 140–174. https://via.library.depaul.edu/jwgl/vol7/iss1/4

Sanders, P. (2020). In K. Bezio & G. Goethals (Eds.), *Leadership, Populism, and Resistance*. Edward Elgar Publishing.

Sanderson, W. (2000, November 27). "Preferential Treatment". 7.30 Program. *ABC Television*. Broadcast. http://www.abc.net.au/7.30/stories/s217353.htm

Sanford, D. (1983). Impartial Perception. *Philosophy*, *58*(225), 392–395. www.jstor.org/stable/3750775

Santana, A. D., & Hopp, T. (2016). Tapping Into a New Stream of (Personal) Data: Assessing Journalists' Different Use of Social Media. *Journalism & Mass Communication Quarterly*, *93*(2), 383–408. https://doi.org/10.1177/1077699016637105

Santoro, S. (2013). Senate. Official Hansard. Parliamentary Debates. *Commonwealth of Australia*.

Saul, J. R. (1993). *Voltaire's Bastards: The Dictatorship of Reason in the West*. Penguin Books.

Sawers, P. (2015, February 7). How NewsWhip Helps Newsrooms Track the Web's Top-Trending Stories. https://venturebeat.com/2015/02/07/how-newswhip-helps-newsrooms-track-the-webs-top-trending-stories/

SBS Charter. (1991). Special Broadcasting Services Act. Special Broadcasting Services. Retrieved from: https://www.sbs.com.au/aboutus/corporate.

SBS News. (2019). Public servants must be accountable to the 'quiet Australians': PM. SBS News. 19 August 2019. Retrieved from: https://www.sbs.com.au/news/public-servants-must-be-accountable-to-the-quiet-australians-pm

Scannell, P. (1989). Public Service Broadcasting and Modern Public Life. *Media, Culture & Society*, *11*(2), 135–166. https://doi.org/10.1177/016344389011002002

Scannell, P. (1997). Public Service Broadcasting and Modern Public Life. In T. O'Sullivan & Y. Jewkes (Eds.), *The Media Studies Reader*. Arnold.

Scannell, P. (2005). In G. Ferrell Lowe & P. Jauert (Eds.), *The Meaning of Broadcasting in the Digital Era. Cultural Dilemmas in Public Service Broadcasting* (pp. 141–142). Ripe@2005. Nordicom. Göteborg. Retrieved from: https://www.diva-portal.org/smash/get/diva2:1534711/FULLTEXT01.pdf#page=15

Scannell, P. (2019). *Why Do People Sing? On Voice*. Polity Press.

Scannell, P. (Ed.). (1991). Broadcast Talk. In *Introduction: The Relevance of Talk*. Sage Publications.

Schein, E. H. (2010). *Organizational Culture and Leadership* (4th Ed.). The Jossey-Bass Business & Management Series, 2(4). Wiley.

Schiffrin, A. (2017). Disinformation and Democracy: The Internet Transformed Protest but Did Not Improve Democracy. *Journal of International Affairs, 71*(1). Fall 2016–Winter 2017. Pp. 117–125. Retrieved from: http://search.proquest.com/docview/2054916939/

Schifferes, S., Newman, N., Thurman, N., Corney, D., Goker, A. S., & Martin, C. (2014). Identifying and Verifying News Through Social Media: Developing a User-Centred Tool for Professional Journalists. *Digital Journalism, 2*(3), 406–418. https://doi.org/10.1080/21670811.2014.892747

Schiller, H. I. (1993, July 12). Public Way or Private Road? *The Nation, 257*(2), 64–66. http://search.proquest.com/docview/231453434/

Schlesinger, P., & Tumber, H. (1994). *Reporting Crime: The Media Politics of Criminal Justice*. Clarendon Press. New York. Oxford University Press. Oxford.

Schirato, T., & Yell, S. (1997). *Communication and Cultural Literacy: An Introduction*. Allen and Unwin.

Schroeder, R. (2018). Social Theory after the Internet: Media, Technology, and Globalization. UCL Press. London. https://doi.org/10.14324/111.9781787351226

Schudson. (2005). "The Virtues of an Unlovable Press" Intro. *Political Quarterly, 1*(76), 23–32. https://doi.org/10.1111/j.1467-923X.2006.00745.x

Schudson, M. (1978). *Discovering the News: A social History of American Newspapers*. Basic Books Inc.

Schudson, M. (2008). *Why Democracies Need an Unlovable Press*. Polity Press.

Schultz, J. (1998). *Reviving the Fourth Estate: Democracy, Accountability and the Media*. Cambridge University Press.

Schultz, T. (2019, December 22). ATARs Measure Privilege, Not Academic Merit, and It Starts in Kindergarten. https://www.abc.net.au/news/2019-12-22/atar-measure-privilege-not-academic-merit/11817974

Schulz, A. Levy, D. A. L., & Kleis Nielsen, R. (2019, September). Old, Educated, and Politically Diverse: The Audience of Public Service News. *Reuters Institute Report*. https://reutersinstitute.politics.ox.ac.uk/sites/default/files/2019-09/The_audience_of_public_service_news_FINAL.pdf

Schultz, A., & Napier-Raman, K. (2020, July 16). What Does the Governor-General Do—And How Much Does It Cost the Country? *The Mandarin and Crikey*. https://www.themandarin.com.au/136189-what-does-the-governor-general-do-and-how-much-does-it-cost-the-country/?utm_source=TheJuice&utm_medium=email&utm_source=newsletter; crikey.com.au

Schubert, M., & Canberra Bureau. (2007, August 14). Costello Attacks Swan Over Democrats Money. *The Age*. https://www.theage.com.au/national/costello-attacks-swan-over-democrats-money-20070814-ge5kuv.html

Schwartz, J. (2008). The Choice Between Tweedledum and Tweedledee: Australian Media Coverage of the 2007 Federal Election Campaign. *Metro: Media & Education Magazine*. Pp. 110–121. Retrieved from: https://search-informit-com-au.wwwproxy1.library.unsw.edu.au/documentSummary;dn=516965508581790;res=IELLCC

Scott, W. R. (1994). Conceptualizing Organizational Fields: Linking Organizations and Societal Systems. In H.-U. Derlien, U. Gerhardt, & F. W. Scharpf (Eds.), *Systems Rationality and Partial Interests* (pp. 203–221). Nomos Verlagsgesselschaft.

Scott, B. (2000). Consulting on the inside: an internal consultant's guide to living and working inside organizations. Alexandria, VA: American Society for Training & Development.

Scott, W. R. (2001). *Institutions and Organizations* (2nd ed.). Sage in S. Yousafzai, S.

Scott, W. R. (2008). Institutions and organizations: ideas and interests (3rd ed.). Sage Publications. Thousand Oaks, Calif.

Scott, M. (2009, September 9). Commonwealth Broadcasting Association Lecture 2009. *ABC Speeches*. https://about.abc.net.au/speeches/association-lecture-2009/

Scott, M. (2010, April 20). *New Opportunities, New Obligations: Public Broadcasting in the Era of Choice*. Commonwealth Broadcasting Association Conference. *Australian Broadcasting Corporation*.http://about.abc.net.au/speeches/new-opportunities-new-obligations-public-broadcasting-in-the-era-of-choice/

Scott, M. (2015, June 26). ABC Is a Public Broadcaster, Not a State Broadcaster. *The Sydney Morning Herald*. https://www.smh.com.au/opinion/abc-is-a-public-broadcaster-not-a-state-broadcaster-20150625-ghxt5m.html

Scott, M. (2016). *A Media Odyssey: Speeches of an ABC Managing Director 2006–2016.* ABC Books.

Scott, M. (2018). *On Us.* Melbourne University Press.

Scott, M., & Torney, K. (2014, February 4). ABC Statement. *Australian Broadcasting Corporation*. https://about.abc.net.au/press-releases/abc-statement/

Seccombe, M. (2014, November 29–December 5). What Mark Scott Is Really Doing with the ABC Cuts. *The Saturday Paper, 40.* https://www.thesaturdaypaper.com.au/news/media/2014/11/29/what-mark-scott-really-doing-with-the-abc-cuts/14171796001308

Seccombe, M. (2016, December 3–9). Senior ABC Staff Say Michelle Guthrie 'Out of Her Depth'. *The Saturday Paper, 137.* https://www.thesaturdaypaper.com.au/news/media/2016/12/03/senior-abc-staff-say-michelle-guthrie-out-her-depth/14806836004053

Seccombe, M. (2018). ABC Board Stacking Rife. *The Saturday Paper*. https://www.thesaturdaypaper.com.au/news/media/2018/10/06/abc-board-stacking-rife/15387480006958#hrd

Seccombe, M. (2020, May 9–15). Hundreds Facing the Sack with ABC Cuts. *The Saturday Paper, 300*. https://www.thesaturdaypaper.com.au/news/politics/2020/05/09/hundreds-facing-the-sack-with-abc-cuts/15889464009792

Sehl, A. (2020). Public Service Media in a Digital Media Environment: Performance from an Audience Perspective. *Media and Communication, 8*(3), 359–372. https://doi.org/10.17645/mac.v8i3.3141.

Sehl, A., Cornia, A., Graves, L., & Nielsen, R. K. (2019). Newsroom Integration as an Organizational Challenge. *Journalism Studies, 20*(9), 1238–1259. https://doi.org/10.1080/1461670X.2018.1507684

Selznick, P. (1949). *TVA and the Grass Roots* (p. 146). University of California Press. Quoting Key, V. O. Politics and Administration. In L. D. White (Ed.) (1942), *The Future of Government in the United States*. University of Chicago Press.

Selznick, P. (1957). *Leadership in Administration*. University of California Press.

Semetko, H., & Valkenburg, P. (2000). Framing European Politics: A Content Analysis of Press and Television News. *Journal of Communication, 50*(2, Spring), 93–109. https://doi.org/10.1111/j.1460-2466.2000.tb02843.x

Semmler, C. (1981). *The ABC—Aunt Sally and Sacred Cow*. Melbourne University Press.

Shanahan, L. (2019, November 17). ABC Staff Push for Climate Group. *The Australian*. https://www.theaustralian.com.au/business/media/abc-staff-propose-climate-group/news-story/50af6696dbff695d103f9fba77f1ed05

Shand, W. (2015). *Exploring Institutional Change: The Contribution of Co-Production to Shaping Institutions*. International Institute for Environment and Development, Chapter 2, pp. 6–8. www.jstor.org/stable/resrep18045.4

Shergold, P. (2017). Re-Imagining Public Service [online]. *The Australian Journal of Social Issues, 52*(1), 4–12. https://search-informit-com-au.wwwproxy1.library.unsw.edu.au/documentSummary;dn=035171807770944;res=IELAPA

Shah, C. (2017). Social Information Seeking Leveraging the Wisdom of the Crowd. In *The Information Retrieval Series* (Vol. 38). Springer. https://primoa.library.unsw.edu.au/permalink/f/jhud33/UNSW_ALMA51227992500001731

Shani, G., & Westphal, J. D. (2016). Persona Non Grata? Determinants and Consequences of Social Distancing From Journalists Who Engage in Negative Coverage of Firm Leadership. *Academy of Management Journal, 59*(1), 302–329. https://doi.org/10.5465/amj.2013.1162

Shapiro, I., Brin, C., Bédard-Brûlé, I., & Mychajlowycz, K. (2013). Verification as a Strategic Ritual: How Journalists Retrospectively Describe Processes for Ensuring Accuracy. *Journalism Practice, 7*(6), 657–673. https://doi.org/10.1080/17512786.2013.765638, Quoting W. Lippmann [1920] 1995. Liberty and the News. New Brunswick, NJ: Transaction Publishers.

Sharman, R. (2019). The Psychological Reason Why Some Can't Believe the Evidence Against George Pell and Michael Jackson. *Australian Broadcasting Corporation*. 13 March, 2019. Retrieved from: https://www.abc.net.au/news/2019-03-13/george-pell-michael-jackson-cognitive-dissonance/10892948

Shaw, S. J. (1959). Colonial Newspaper Advertising: A Step Toward Freedom of the Press. *Business History Review (pre-1986), 33*(000003), p. 409. http://search.proquest.com/docview/205528871/

Shawcross, W. (1997). *Murdoch: The Making of a Media Empire*. Touchstone.

Shergold, P. (2017). Re-Imagining Public Service [online]. *The Australian Journal of Social Issues, 52*(1), 4–12. https://search-informit-com-au.wwwproxy1.library.unsw.edu.au/documentSummary;dn=035171807770944;res=IELAPA

Shergold, P., Benson, K., & Piper, M. (2019). Investing in Refugees Investing in Australia. Department of Home Affairs. *Commonwealth of Australia*.https://www.homeaffairs.gov.au/reports-and-pubs/files/review-integration-employment-settlement-outcomes-refugees-humanitarian-entrants.pdf

Sheridan-Burns, L., & McKee, A. (1999). Reporting on Indigenous Issues: Some Practical Suggestions for Improving Journalistic Practice in the Coverage of Indigenous Affairs. *Australian Journalism Review: AJR, 21*(2), 103–116. https://eprints.qut.edu.au/14959/1/14959.pdf

Sheridan, G. (2020, April 16). ABC's Groupthink on George Pell a Sin Against Journalism. *The Australian*. https://www.theaustralian.com.au/commentary/abcs-groupthink-on-george-pell-a-sin-against-journalism/news-story/ba3a43fe6ca1d4625a3857884dfaad2c

Shiffrin, S. (1994). The Politics of The Mass Media and Free Speech Principle. *Indiana Law Journal, 69*(3, Article 2), 689–721. Law Library. Indiana University. https://primoa.library.unsw.edu.au/permalink/f/11jha62/TN_gale_legal15296131

Sigal, L. V. (1973). *Reporters and Officials: The Organization and Politics of Newsmaking*. D. C. Heath. Lexington, Mass.

Silberman, M. (Ed.). (2016). *Bertolt Brecht on Film and Radio. Diaries, Letters and Essays*. Bloomsbury Publishing.

Similar Web. (2020). Top Websites Ranking. https://www.similarweb.com/top-websites/australia

Simon, M. (2005, May). Fear and Loathing at the ABC. *The Monthly*, 28–38. https://search.informit.com.au/documentSummary;dn=200511241;res=IELAPA

Simons, M. (2017, May 29). Trump, Fake News, and Shrinking Newsrooms: Does Journalism Still Matter in 2017? *The Guardian*. https://www.theguardian.com/media/2017/may/29/trump-fake-news-and-shrinking-newsrooms-does-journalism-still-matter-in-2017

Simpson, J. (2020, January 3). Aunty's Radio Rules the Waves, But ABC TV Is Listing Badly. *The Australian*. https://www.theaustralian.com.au/commentary/auntys-radio-rules-the-waves-but-abc-tv-is-listing-badly/news-story/a0d3ecd28922d461b984cb7ccfe073cc

Simões, R. B., & Silveirinha, M. J. (2019). Framing Street Harassment: Legal Developments and Popular Misogyny in Social Media. *Feminist Media Studies*, 1–17. https://doi.org/10.1080/14680777.2019.1704816

Simons, M. (2008, January 30). No New Logo for the ABC But Rebranding on the Cards. *Crikey.com*. https://www.crikey.com.au/2008/01/30/no-new-logo-for-the-abc-but-rebranding-on-the-cards/

Simon, R. & Sykes Wylie, M. (2021). Comment by S. Turkle. Technology: Tool for Therapeutic Connection, or a Hindrance? Psychotherapy Networker. Posted: 11 Jun 2021. Retrieved from: https://www.psychotherapynetworker.org/blog/details/521/technology-tool-for-therapeutic-connection-or-a-hindrance?_ga=2.195534188.1776400064.1626134387-711596993.1626134387

Simons, M. (2006). 'Leaked KPMG Report: ABC Efficient but Underfunded.' *Crikey*. 21 November, 2016. Retrieved from: https://www.crikey.com.au/2006/11/21/leaked-kpmg-report-abc-efficient-but-underfunded/

Simons, M. (2016, September). Is Michelle Guthrie Tuned in to the ABC? *The Monthly*. https://www.themonthly.com.au/issue/2016/september/1472652000/margaret-simons/michelle-guthrie-tuned-abc#mtr

Sinclair, A. (2007). *Leadership for the Disillusioned: Moving Beyond Myths and Heroes to Leading That Liberates*. Allen and Unwin.

Singh, S., Farley, S., & Donahue, J. (2018). Grandiosity on Display: Social Media Behaviors and Dimensions of Narcissism. *Personality and Individual Differences, 134*, 308–313. https://doi.org/10.1016/j.paid.2018.06.039

Singer, P. W., & Brooking, E. T. (2018). *Likewar: The Weaponization of Social Media*. Houghton, Miffler, Harcourt.

Sinnig, J. (2020). *The Role of Origin of Fame in Influencer Branding: A Comparative Analysis of German and Russian Consumers* (1st ed.). Springer Fachmedien Wiesbaden. Imprint: Springer Gabler.

Skålén, P., Karlsson, J., Engen, M. & Magnusson, P.R. (2018). Understanding Public Service Innovation as Resource Integration and Creation of Value Propositions. *Australian Journal of Public Administration, 77*(4), 700–714. https://doi.org/10.1111/1467-8500.12308

Skog, D.A., Wimelius, H., & Sandberg, J. (2018). Digital Disruption. *Business & Information Systems Engineering (60)*5, 431–437. https://doi.org/10.1007/s12599-018-0550-4

Skidmore, P. (1995). Telling Tales: Media Power, Ideology and the Reporting of Child Sexual Abuse in Britain. In D. Kidd-Hewitt & R. Osborne (Eds.), *Crime and the Media: A Post-modern Spectacle*. Pluto Press.

Sloan, R., & Warner, R. (2016). Unauthorized Access: The Crisis in Online Privacy and Security (Edition 1). In *Unauthorized Access: The Crisis in <b>Online</b> Privacy and <b>Security</b> (Edition 1)* (1st ed.). CRC Press. https://doi.org/10.1201/b15148

Small, V., & Warn, J. (2020, June). Impacts on Food Policy from Traditional and Social Media Framing of Moral Outrage and Cultural Stereotypes. *Agriculture and Human Values, 37*(2), 295–309. Springer. The Agriculture, Food, & Human Values Society (AFHVS). https://doi.org/10.1007/s10460-019-09983-6

Smith-Spark, L. (2011, July 7). Firms Reconsider ad Deals Over Newspaper Phone Hacking Scandal. *CNN*. http://edition.cnn.com/2011/BUSINESS/07/06/uk.phonehacking.ads/index.html

Smith's Weekly. (1935, December 21). Sir Keith Murdoch's Little War. A Fight Between Broadcasting Commission and Daily Press. ABC Plans Comprehensive News Service. *Smith's Weekly*, p. 4. https://trove.nla.gov.au/newspaper/article/234617298?searchTerm=Keith%20Murdoch%20ABC&searchLimits=

Smith, L. (2020). 2020 versus 1919: Is COVID-19 as bad as the 'Spanish' Flu? Analysis. The University of Sydney. *News and Opinion*. 27 May 2020. Retrieved from: https://www.sydney.edu.au/news-opinion/news/2020/05/27/2020-versus-1919--is-covid-19-as-bad-as-the--spanish--flu-.html

Smith, Z. (2020a, April 14). 'Unjust' to Take Accusations as Gospel. *The Herald-Sun*. https://www.pressreader.com/australia/herald-sun/20200414/281547998017480

Smith, Z. (2020b, April 14). Pell Attacks System. *The Herald Sun*. https://global-factiva-com.ezproxy2.library.usyd.edu.au/ha/default.aspx#./!?&_suid=158683457315200967428676337888l

Smith, M. A., Himelboim, I., Rainie, L., & Shneiderman, B. (2015). The Structures of Twitter Crowds and Conversations. In S. Matei, M. Russell, & E. Bertino (Eds.), *Transparency in Social Media. Computational Social Sciences*. Springer.

Smolkin, R. (2006). Adapt or Die: As Newspaper Companies Confront a Challenging Future, They Are Increasingly Viewing Their Trademark Print Product as the Engine Driving a Diverse "Portfolio" That Embraces Other "Platforms" Such as Web Sites and Niche Publications. Is This a Strategy for Survival? *American Journalism Review, 28*(3). https://go.gale.com/ps/anonymous?id=GALE%7CA147375836&sid=googleScholar&v=2.1&it=r&linkaccess=abs&issn=10678654&p=AONE&sw=w

Snell, P. (2010). Emerging Adult Civic and Political Disengagement: A Longitudinal Analysis of Lack of Involvement With Politics. *Journal of Adolescent Research, 25*(2), 258–287.

Soley, C. (2005). The Public Is Sick of Us Both. *British Journalism Review, 16*(1), 35–39. https://doi.org/10.1177/0956474805053357

Solomons, M., & Roberts, G. (2014, March 25). Asylum Seekers Describe Boat Turn-Back at Centre of Burns Allegations. *Australian Broadcasting Corporation*. https://www.abc.net.au/news/2014-03-24/asylum-seekers-describe-boat-turn-back/5342210

Sommerville, C. J. (1996). *The News Revolution in England: Cultural Dynamics of Daily Information*. Oxford University Press.

Sotiriadou, P., & Brouwers, J. (2012). A Critical Analysis of the Impact of the Beijing Olympic Games on Australia's Sport Policy Direction. *International Journal of Sport Policy and Politics: Olympic and Paralympic Policy, 4*(3), 321–341. https://doi.org/10.1080/19406940.2012.656687

South Coast Times and Wollongong Argus. (1948). Church Festival. A.B.C. Chief Stresses Spiritual Values. 13 May 1948, p. 14. Retrieved from: https://trove.nla.gov.au/newspaper/article/142229895?searchTerm=ABC%20values

Soysal, Z. (2019). Truth in Journalism. In J. E. Katz & K. K. Mays (Eds.), *Journalism and Truth in an Age of Social Media*. Oxford University Press. https://doi.org/10.1093/oso/9780190900250.001.0001

Soutphommasane, T. (2018, July 19). Cultural Backlash and the Rise of Populism. Speech to *Sydney Ideas*, The University of Sydney. https://www.humanrights.gov.au/about/news/speeches/cultural-backlash-and-rise-populism

Spadaro, S. J. A. (2020, January 20). Defy the Apocalypse. *La Civilta Cattolica*. https://www.laciviltacattolica.com/defy-the-apocalypse/

Sparks, G.G. (2013). *Media Effects Research: A Basic Overview*. 4th Edition. Wadsworth. Cengage Learning. Boston, MA.

Spath, R., Strand, V., & Bosco-Ruggiero, S. (2013). What Child Welfare Staff Say about Organizational Culture. *Child Welfare, 92*(11), 9–31. http://search.proquest.com/docview/1509394964/

Spaulding, S., Nair, D., & Nelson, A. (2020). *Russia's Attacks on Democratic Justice Systems*. Center for Strategic and International Studies. https://www.csis.org/features/russias-attacks-democratic-justice-systems

Spears, L. C. (2002). Tracing the Past, Present and Future of Servant Leadership. In L. C. Spears & M. Lawrence (Eds.), *Focus on Leadership: Servant Leadership for the 21st Century*. John Wiley & Sons.

Special Broadcasting Service. (2018, October 4). Liberals to Again Debate Selling the ABC. *SBS*. https://www.sbs.com.au/news/liberals-to-again-debate-selling-the-abc

Speers, D. (2020, March 15). Scott Morrison's 'F-Word' Misread the Public Mood on the Coronavirus Pandemic. ABC News Online. Analysis. *Australian Broadcasting Corporation*. https://www.abc.net.au/news/2020-03-15/coronavirus-scott-morrison-footy-next-information-campaign/12054174

Spigelman, J. (2012, September 6). Public Broadcasting, Public Value. [online]. The Drum. Analysis. *ABC*. https://www.abc.net.au/news/2012-09-05/spigelman-public-broadcasting-public-value/4244468

Spigelman, J. (2013). The ABC and Australia's Media Landscape. *Media International Australia, Incorporating Culture & Policy, 146*, 12–24. https://primoa.library.unsw.edu.au/permalink/f/11jha62/TN_informit182288913833846

Spitznagel, E. (2013, November 14). Q&A: Chris Lilley on Drag, Blackface, Teenage Girls & Confrontational Comedy. *Esquire*. https://www.esquire.com/entertainment/interviews/a25930/chris-lilley-interview/

Stacey, R., & Griffin, D. (2006). *Complexity and the Experience of Managing in Public Sector Organizations*. Routledge.

Standing, G. (2011). *The Precariat: The New Dangerous Class*. Bloomsbury Academic. https://doi.org/10.5040/9781849664554

Standing, G. (2018, October). The Precariat: Today's Transformative Class? [online]. *Great Transition Initiative*. https://www.greattransition.org/publication/precariat-transformative-class

Statham, P. (2007). Journalists as Commentators on European Politics. *European Journal of Communication, 22*(4), 461–477. London. https://doi.org/10.1177/0267323107083063

Stelzer, I. (2018). *The Murdoch Method. Notes on Running an Empire*. Atlantic Books.

Stephens, M. (2007). *A History of News* (3rd ed.). Oxford University Press.

Stephens, M. (2009, June). *Beyond News: The Case for Wisdom Journalism*. Joan Shorenstein Center on the Press, Politics and Public Policy, *DP Series*. D-53. Harvard Kennedy School. https://shorensteincenter.org/beyond-news-the-case-for-wisdom-journalism-mitchell-stephens/

Stiehm, J. H. (2002). *U.S. Army War College: Military Education in a Democracy*. Temple University Press.

Stigler, G. J. (1971). The Theory of Economic Regulation. *The Bell Journal of Economics and Management Science, 2*(1, Spring), 3–21. https://www.jstor.org/stable/3003160

Stieglitz, S., & Dang-Xuan, L. (2013). Emotions and Information Diffusion in Social Media—Sentiment of Microblogs and Sharing Behavior. *Journal of Management Information Systems, 29*(4), 217–248. https://doi.org/10.2753/MIS0742-1222290408

Stove, D. (1992). A New Religion. *Philosophy, 67*(260), 233–240, 234. www.jstor.org/stable/3751453

Streitfeld, D. (2017, May 20). 'The Internet Is Broken': @ev Is Trying to Salvage It. *The New York Times*. https://www.nytimes.com/2017/05/20/technology/evan-williams-medium-twitter-internet.html

Strekalova, Y. A. (2017). Health Risk Information Engagement and Amplification on Social Media: News About an Emerging Pandemic on Facebook. *Health Education & Behavior, 44*(2), 332–339. https://journals-sagepub-com.wwwproxy1.library.unsw.edu.au/doi/pdf/10.1177/1090198116660310

Strzelecki, A. (2020). Google Medical Update: Why Is the Search Engine Decreasing Visibility of Health and Medical Information Websites? *International Journal of Environmental Research and Public Health*, 17(4). https://doi.org/10.3390/ijerph17041160

Stutchbury, H. (2018, June 18). The ABC Is an Indulgence We Can No Longer Afford. *The Sydney Morning Herald*. https://www.smh.com.au/business/companies/the-abc-is-an-indulgence-we-can-no-longer-afford-20180618-p4zm6y.html

Stuever, H. (2018, January 12). Letterman Sits Down with Obama, But Both Men Seem Rusty and Off Their Game. *The Washington Post*. https://www.washingtonpost.com/entertainment/tv/letterman-sits-down-with-obama-but-both-men-seem-rusty-and-off-their-game/2018/01/11/2b6dc8c0-f70c-11e7-a9e3-ab18ce41436a_story.html

Styles, A. (2016, July 3). Federal Election 2016: ABC Wins Election Night Coverage Despite Leigh Sales' 'Delirium'. *The Sydney Morning Herald*. https://www.smh.com.au/entertainment/tv-and-radio/federal-election-2016-abc-wins-election-night-coverage-despite-leigh-sales-delirium-20160703-gpxlti.html

Styles, J. (2002, April). *The ABC: Unique Unto Itself. The Institute of Public Affairs Review: A Quarterly Review of Politics and Public Affairs*. Institute of Public Affairs. https://search.informit.org/doi/10.3316/ielapa.200203149

Suddaby, R. (2010). Challenges for Institutional Theory. *Journal of Management Inquiry, 19*(1), 14–20. https://doi.org/10.1177/1056492609347564

Sun, The. (1935, June 17). Kitto's Praise for Public Service. *The Sun*, p. 9. https://trove.nla.gov.au/newspaper/article/230251698?searchTerm=ABC%20commissioner%20kitto&searchLimits=

Sun, The. (1939, December 30). New ABC Critics Answered. *The Sun*, p. 3. https://trove.nla.gov.au/newspaper/article/231500394?searchTerm=ABC%20commissioner%20kitto&searchLimits=

Sun, The. (1945, February 27). The ABC and Politics. *The Sun*, p. 4. https://trove.nla.gov.au/newspaper/article/231705224?searchTerm=Politics%20and%20the%20ABC.

Sun, The. (1946, October 16). Suspension of ABC Staff Chief. *The Sun*, p. 5. https://trove.nla.gov.au/newspaper/article/229551981?searchTerm=ABC%20staff&searchLimits=

Sunderland, A. (2016, July 14). 2016 ABC Federal Election Report of the Chairman, Election Coverage Review Committee. *ABC*. http://about.abc.net.au/wp-content/uploads/2016/11/2016FederalElectionECRCRPT.pdf

Sunstein, C. R. (2018). *#Republic: Divided Democracy in the Age of Social Media*. Princeton University Press. https://doi.org/10.1515/9781400890521

Sunstein, C. R. (2009). *Republic.com 2.0*. Princeton University Press. *Princeton. EBook*. http://ebookcentral.proquest.com/lib/unsw/detail.action?docID=581662

Supreme Court of Victoria. (2019). George Pell V. The Queen. *Supreme Court of Victoria*.https://www.supremecourt.vic.gov.au/case-summaries/court-of-appeal-proceedings/george-pell-v-the-queen

Swan, W. (2001, February 26). Grievance Debate. Australian Labor Party: Queensland. *House of Representatives Hansard*, p. 24394. https://parlinfo.aph.gov.au/parlInfo/search/display/display.w3p;db=CHAMBER;id=chamber/hansardr/2001-02-26/0129;query=Id:%22chamber/hansardr/2001-02-26/0000%22

Swan, N. (2020, March 16). Norman Swan Answers Your Coronavirus Questions on Pregnancy, Asthma, Pools and Schools. ABC News Breakfast Program and ABC News 24. *Australian Broadcasting Corporation*. Televised, Broadcast and Online. https://www.abc.net.au/news/2020-03-16/coronavirus-questions-on-pregnancy-asthma-pools-and-schools/12058926

Swannie, B. J. (2019, July 4). In Australia, Criticising a Judge Can Land You in Jail. This Is a Danger for Democracy. *The Conversation*. https://theconversation.com/in-australia-criticising-a-judge-can-land-you-in-jail-this-is-a-danger-for-democracy-119296

Swartz, N. P. (2012, Winter). 'Dumbing Down' the CBC News. *Humanist Perspectives, 183*, p. 18. Retrieved from: http://search.proquest.com/docview/1268836316/.

Swinehart, K., & Graber, K. (2012). Tongue-Tied Territories: Languages and Publics in Stateless Nations. *Language and Communication, 32*(2), 95–97. https://doi.org/10.1016/j.langcom.2011.05.007

Swindall, C. (2011). *Engaged Leadership: Building a Culture to Overcome Employee Disengagement* (2nd ed.). John Wiley and Sons.

Switzer, T. (2013, May). 'Why the ABC should be privatised'. *Quadrant*. https://quadrant.org.au/magazine/2013/05/why-the-abc-should-be-privatised/

Sydney Morning Herald, The. (1932, March 10). Broadcasting: The Appointment of Commissioners: Proposed Legislation, p. 11. https://trove.nla.gov.au/newspaper/article/29946918?searchTerm=Broadcasting%3A%20The%20Appointment%20of%20Commissioners%3A%20Proposed%20Legislation.%20

Sydney Morning Herald, The. (1944, September 12). "Mr Moses Most Unfair" Haydn Beck's Reply. *The Sydney Morning Herald*, p. 4. https://trove.nla.gov.au/newspaper/article/17920452?searchTerm=haydn%20beck%20ABC&searchLimits=exactPhrase|||anyWords|||notWords|||requestHandler|||dateFrom=1940-01-01|||dateTo=1945-12-31|||sortby

Sydney Morning Herald, The. (1945a, April 17). How Much Freedom for the ABC?, p. 2. *The Sydney Morning Herald*.https://trove.nla.gov.au/newspaper/article/27932662?searchTerm=chairman%20ABC&searchLimits=exactPhrase|||anyWords|||notWords|||requestHandler|||dateFrom=1944-01-01|||dateTo=1946-12-31||||l-advstate=National|||l-advstate=ACT|||l-advstate=New+South+Wales|||sortby

Sydney Morning Herald, The. (1945b, March 30). Mr Cleary Talks of Clashes, p. 4. *The Sydney Morning Herald*.https://trove.nla.gov.au/newspaper/articl

e/17937290?searchTerm=chairman%20ABC&searchLimits=exactPhrase|||anyWords|||notWords|||requestHandler|||dateFrom=1945-01-31|||dateTo=1945-04-30|||l-advstate=National|||l-advstate=ACT|||l-advstate=New+South+Wales|||sortby

Sydney Morning Herald, The. (1976, December 9). Sir Henry Spells Out Views on ABC. *The Sydney Morning Herald*, p. 10. https://trove.nla.gov.au/newspaper/article/131800175?searchTerm=henry%20bland%20ABC%20orchestras

Sydney Morning Herald, The. (2003, October 11). ABC Loses Points in Alston's 'Bias' Plea. *The Sydney Morning Herald*. https://www.smh.com.au/national/abc-loses-points-in-alstons-bias-plea-20031011-gdhkgd.html

Sydney Morning Herald, The. (1831, April 18). First edition. *The Sydney Morning Herald*, p. 2.

Sydney Morning Herald, The. (1931, November 16). Broadcasting. *The Sydney Morning Herald*, p. 8. https://trove.nla.gov.au/newspaper/article/16823317?searchTerm=%22improved%20and%20freed%20from%20all%20the%20evils%2C%20real%20or%20imaginary%2C%20of%20private%20enterprise%22

Sydney Morning Herald, The. (1941, July 11). Broadcasting of News: Views of ABC Chairman. *The Sydney Morning Herald*, p. 4. https://trove.nla.gov.au/newspaper/article/17752645?searchTerm=Broadcasting%20of%20news%3A%20views%20of%20ABC%20Chairman

Sydney Morning Herald, The. (1948, September 18). "Impartiality of A.B.C.—Duty to Public." Letters to the Editor. *The Sydney Morning Herald*, p. 2. https://trove.nla.gov.au/newspaper/article/18085248?searchTerm=Impartiality%20of%20A.B.C.%20%E2%80%93%20Duty%20to%20Public&searchLimits=

Sydney Morning Herald, The. (1953). A.B.C. Hears Critics of News Broadcasts. 25 November, 1953, p. 6. Retrieved from: Trove.

Tabakoff, N. (2019, December 27). ABC Executives, Staff Spend $20m on Travel as Axe Hovers. *The Australian*. https://www.theaustralian.com.au/business/media/abc-executives-staff-spend-20m-on-travel-as-axe-hovers/news-story/0083a476a9c38ca2f4dfccc6a4c5ffa3

Tandoc, E. C., & Duffy, A. (2016). Keeping Up with the Audiences: Journalistic Role Expectations in Singapore. *International Journal of Communication, 10*, 3338–3358. https://primoa.library.unsw.edu.au/permalink/f/11jha62/TN_wos000390936900001

Telegraph, The (Brisbane). Empire Broadcasting: Early Inauguration. [online]. 13 July 1932, p. 10. Retrieved from: https://trove.nla.gov.au/newspaper/article/181268000?searchTerm=abc%20inaugural&searchLimits=exactPhrase|||anyWords|||notWords|||requestHandler|||dateFrom=1932-06-01|||dateTo=1932-07-31|||sortby.

Tengblad, S. (2012). *The Work of Managers Towards a Practice Theory of Management*. Oxford University Press.

Terjesen, S., Aguilera, R. V., & Lorenz, R. (2014). Legislating a Woman's Seat on the Board: Institutional Factors Driving Gender Quotas for Boards of Directors.

Journal of Business Ethics, 128(2), 233–251. https://doi.org/10.1007/s10551-014-2083-1

Thakur, R. (2019, September 2). Cardinal Pell's Guilty Verdict Is Deeply Troubling. *John Menadue: Pearls and Irritations.* https://johnmenadue.com/ramesh-thakur-cardinal-pells-guilty-verdict-is-deeply-troubling/

The Australian. (1964). First edition. *The Australian.* 15 July 1964, p. 1.

The Newcastle Sun. (1938, May 28). ABC Ideals. *The Newcastle Sun*, p. 4. https://trove.nla.gov.au/newspaper/article/166711374?searchTerm=ABC%20privilege&searchLimits=

Thierer, A. (2013). The Perils of Classifying Social Media Platforms as Public Utilities. *CommLaw Conspectus, 21*(2), 297–297. https://primoa.library.unsw.edu.au/permalink/f/11jha62/TN_gale_legal401032615

Thilmany, J. (2004). Better Housekeeping of Legacy Knowledge. *Mechanical Engineering, 126*(10), 22. http://search.proquest.com/docview/230173378/

Thomas, A. (1980). *Broadcast and be Damned: The ABC's First Two Decades.* Melbourne University Press.

Thomas, D. R. (2016). Digital Disruption: A Transformation in Graduate Management Online Education. In A. Khare, B. Stewart, & R. Schatz (Eds.), *Phantom Ex Machina* (223–233). Springer. Retrieved from: https://doi.org/10.1007/978-3-319-44468-0_15

Thomson, P. (2005). Bringing Bourdieu to Policy Sociology: Codification, Misrecognition and Exchange Value in the UK Context. *Journal of Education Policy, 20*(6), 741–758. https://doi.org/10.1080/02680930500238929

Thomson, I. T. (2015). *Culture Wars and Enduring American Dilemmas.* Project MUSE. Baltimore, Md.

Thompson, R. (2011). Radicalization and the Use of Social Media. *Journal of Strategic Security, 4*(4), 167–190. https://doi.org/10.5038/1944-0472.4.4.8

Thornhill, A., & Gibbons, A. (1995). The Positive Management of Redundancy Survivors: Issues and Lessons. *Employee Counselling Today, 7*(3), 5–12. https://doi.org/10.1108/13665629510091060

Thornton, P. (2002). The Rise of the Corporation in a Craft Industry: Conflict and Conformity in Institutional Logics. *Academy of Management Journal, 45*(1), 81–101.

Thornton, P. H. (2001). Personal Versus Market Logics of Control: A Historically Contingent Theory of the Risk of Acquisition. *Organization Science, 12*(3), 294–311.

Thornton, P. H. (2004). *Markets from Culture: Institutional Logics and Organizational Decisions in Higher Education Publishing.* Stanford University Press.

Thornton, P., & Ocasio, W. (1999). Institutional Logics and the Historical Contingency of Power in Organizations: Executive Succession in the Higher

Education Publishing Industry, 1958–1990. *American Journal of Sociology, 105*(3), 801–843. https://doi.org/10.1086/210361

Thornton, P. H., & Ocasio, W. (2008). Institutional Logics. In R. Greenwood, C. Oliver, K. Sahlin-Andersson, & R. Suddaby (Eds.), *The Sage Handbook of Organisational Institutionalism*. Sage.

Thornton, P. H., Ocasio, W., & Lounsbury, M. (2012a). *The Emergence and Evolution of Field-Level Logics*. https://doi.org/10.1093/acprof:oso/9780199601936.003.0007.

Thornton, P. H., Ocasio, W., & Lounsbury, M. (2012b). *Introduction to the Institutional Logics Perspective: A New Approach to Culture, Structure and Processes*. Oxford: Oxford University Press.

Tibbitts, C. (n.d.). Casualties of War. *The Australian War Memorial*.https://www.awm.gov.au/wartime/article2

Tiffen, R. (1989). *News and Power*. Allen & Unwin.

Tiffen, R. (2014). *Rupert Murdoch: A Reassessment*. NewSouth Publishing.

Tingle, L. (2020, March 18). Coronavirus Messaging from Political Leaders Making a Much-Needed Improvement. Analysis. ABC News. *Australian Broadcasting Corporation*. https://www.abc.net.au/news/2020-03-18/coronavirus-messaging-from-political-leaders-making-improvement/12067290

Toffler, A. (1984). *Future Shock*. Bantam Books.

Tomlinson, M., O'Reilly, D., Wallace, M., Edwards, G., Elliott, C., Iszatt-White, M., & Schedlitzki, D. (2013). Developing Leaders as Symbolic Violence: Reproducing Public Service Leadership Through the (Misrecognized) Development of Leaders' Capitals. *Management Learning, 44*(1), 81–97. https://doi.org/10.1177/1350507612472151

Tomlinson, M., O'Reilly, D., Wallace, M., Edwards, G., Elliott, C., Iszatt-White, M., & Schedlitzki, D. (2013). Developing Leaders as Symbolic Violence: Reproducing Public Service Leadership Through the (Misrecognized) Development of Leaders' Capitals. *Management Learning, 44*(1), 81–97. https://doi.org/10.1177/1350507612472151

Tomevska, S. (2021). Philip Wilson, former Catholic Archbishop of Adelaide, farewelled at St Francis Xavier's Cathedral. *ABC News*. 3 February 2021. Retrieved from: https://www.abc.net.au/news/2021-02-03/former-adelaide-catholic-archbishop-philip-wilson-funeral-held/13116352

Tong, K. (2020). Funding for Small-to-Medium Art Music Organisations in Brisbane (Queensland, Australia): A Case Study. *Music Education Research, 22*(5), 495–504. https://doi.org/10.1080/14613808.2020.1840538

Tonioni, F., D'Alessandris, L., Lai, C., Martinelli, D., Corvino, S., Vasale, M., & Bria, P. (2012). Internet Addiction: Hours Spent Online, Behaviors and Psychological Symptoms. *General Hospital Psychiatry, 34*(1), 80–87. https://doi.org/10.1016/j.genhosppsych.2011.09.013

Topsfield, J. (2020, March 20). Brendan Murphy: The Public Face of Australia's Fight Against COVID-19. *The Sydney Morning Herald*. https://www.smh.

com.au/national/brendan-murphy-the-public-face-of-australia-s-fight-against-covid-19-20200320-p54c87.html

Topsfield, J. (2021).'No sense of momentum': Poll finds drop in support for Australia becoming a republic. *The Sydney Morning Herald*. 25 January 2021. Retrieved from: https://www.smh.com.au/national/no-sense-of-momentum-poll-finds-drop-in-support-for-australia-becoming-a-republic-20210125-p56wpe.html

Torii, A. (2017). Effects of Public Broadcasting on the Competition Among Private Broadcasters and the Total Surplus. *Journal of Media Business Studies, 14*(2), 116–145. https://www-tandfonline-com.wwwproxy1.library.unsw.edu.au/doi/pdf/10.1080/16522354.2017.1290023?needAccess=true

Toronto Star. (2002, August 21). Australian Archbishop Accused of Child Abuse. *Toronto Star*, p. 3. https://search-proquest-com.wwwproxy1.library.unsw.edu.au/docview/438492151?rfr_id=info%3Axri%2Fsid%3Aprimo

Toscano, N., & Lee, J. (2015, May 21). Cardinal George Pell Denies Allegations of Involvement in Abuse Cover-Up. *The Sydney Morning Herald*. https://www.smh.com.au/national/cardinal-george-pell-denies-allegations-of-involvement-in-abuse-coverup-20150520-gh67ml.html

Tracey, M. (1998, reprinted 2002). *The Decline and Fall of Public Service Broadcasting*. Oxford University Press.

Tracey, M. (2002). *The Decline and Fall of Public Service Broadcasting*. Oxford University Press. Oxford.

Trask, S. (2020, February 16). ABC Case Against AFP Raids Dismissed. *Australian Associated Press General News Wire*. https://search-proquest-com.wwwproxy1.library.unsw.edu.au/docview/2355696022?rfr_id=info%3Axri%2Fsid%3Aprimo

Tribune, The. (1945, March 1). Cleary' s Resignation Blow To ABC. *The Tribune*, p. 6. https://trove.nla.gov.au/newspaper/article/208690996?searchTerm=chairman%20ABC&searchLimits=exactPhrase|||anyWords|||notWords|||requestHandler|||dateFrom=1944-01-01|||dateTo=1946-12-31|||l-advstate=National|||l-advstate=ACT|||l-advstate=New+South+Wales|||sortby

Truth, The. (1948, June 13). Tale of Table-Thumping in A.B.C. Chief's Office. *The Truth*, p. 8. https://trove.nla.gov.au/newspaper/article/169378780?searchTerm=ABC%20staff%20McCarthy&searchLimits=

Truu, M. (2019, November 8). Minister for Communications Paul Fletcher Said the Decision to Investigate Monday Night's Q&A Program Was "Appropriate". *SBS News*. https://www.sbs.com.au/news/abc-announces-probe-into-feminist-q-a-episode-after-audience-complaints

Tuchman, G. (1978, January). Making News: A Study in the Construction of Reality. *Social Forces, 59*(4). https://doi.org/10.2307/2578016

Tucker, J. A., Theocharis, Y., Roberts, M. E., & Barberá, P. (2017). From Liberation to Turmoil: Social Media and Democracy. *Journal of Democracy, 28*(4), 46–59. https://doi.org/10.1353/jod.2017.0064

Turkle, S. (1995). *Life on the Screen: Identity in the Age of the Internet.* Simon & Schuster. New York.

Turner, G. (2000). 'Media Wars' Journalism, Cultural and Media Studies in Australia. *Journalism, 1*(3), 353–365. https://doi.org/10.1177/146488490000100305

Turner, G. (2020). Dealing with Diversity: Australian Television, Homogeneity and Indigeneity. *Media International Australia, 174*(1), 20–28. https://doi.org/i1.o0r.gl/107.171/1737/2193829787X8X1919886699481

Turner, M. M., Boudewyns, V., Kirby-straker, R., & Telfer, J. (2013). A Double Dose of Fear: A Theory-Based Content Analysis of News Articles Surrounding the 2006 Cough Syrup Contamination Crisis in Panama. *Risk Management, 15*(2), 79–99. https://doi.org/10.1057/rm.2012.13

Uldam, J. (2016). Corporate Management of Visibility and the Fantasy of the Post-Political: Social Media and Surveillance. *New Media & Society, 18*(2), 201–219. https://doi.org/10.1177/1461444814541526

Ulin, J. (2009). *The Business of Media Distribution: Monetizing Film, TV and Video Content in an Online World.* Focal. Elsevier E-Book. https://primoa.library.unsw.edu.au/permalink/f/jhud33/UNSW_ALMA5118 1866550001731

UK Government. (1962). *Report of the Committee on Broadcasting. The Pilkington Report on Broadcasting* (p. 18). UK Government. https://api.parliament.uk/historic-hansard/lords/1962/jul/18/the-pilkington-report-on-broadcasting

UNESCO. (2012, February 15). *Public Service Broadcasting.* http://www.unesco.org/new/en/communication-and-information/media-development/public-service-broadcasting/

University of New England. (2020). Sir Robert Madgwick and His Legacy. Our Values and Culture. *University of New England.*https://www.une.edu.au/about-une/our-values-and-culture/sir-robert-madgwick

University of Oxford/Reuters Institute for the Study of Journalism. (2016). Digital News Report. Australia. *University of Oxford/Reuters Institute for the Study of Journalism.*http://www.digitalnewsreport.org/survey/2016/australia-2016/

University of Notre Dame Australia, The. (nd). Underrepresented groups. Nulungu Research Institute. Retrieved from: https://www.notredame.edu.au/research/nulungu/projects/olt-transition-to-higher-education/key-findings/underrepresented-groups

Ursell, G. (2003). Creating Value and Valuing Creation in Contemporary UK Television: or "Dumbing Down" the Workforce. *Journalism Studies., 4*(1), 31–46. https://doi.org/10.1080/14616700306501

USA Today. (2004, June 19). Religion. *USW Today.* https://usatoday30.usatoday.com/news/religion/2004-06-19-church-abuse_x.htm

Uscinski, J. E., & Butler, R. W. (2013). The Epistemology of Fact Checking. *Critical Review—A Journal of Politics and Society, 25*(2), 162–180. https://www.tandfonline.com/doi/abs/10.1080/08913811.2013.843872

van Acker, E. (2003). Media Representations of Women Politicians in Australia and New Zealand: High Expectations, Hostility or Stardom. *Policy and Society, 22*(1), 116–136. https://doi.org/10.1016/S1449-4035(03)70016-2

Van den Bulck, H., & Moe, H. (2018). Public Service Media, Universality and Personalisation through Algorithms: Mapping Strategies and Exploring Dilemmas. *Media, Culture & Society, 40*(6), 875–892. https://doi.org/10.177/016344371773407

Van der Meer, T., & Verhoeven, P. (2013). Public Framing Organizational Crisis Situations: Social Media Versus News Media. *Public Relations Review, 39*(3), 229–231. https://doi.org/10.1016/j.pubrev.2012.12.001

van Dijk, T. (1992). Discourse and the Denial of Racism. *Discourse & Society, 3*(1), 87–118. https://doi.org/10.1177/0957926592003001005

van Dierendonck, D., & Patterson, K. (Eds.). (2010). *Servant Leadership: Developments in Theory and Research*. Palgrave Macmillan.

Van Der Houwen, F., & Sliedrecht, K. (2016). The Form and Function of Formulations: Co-Constructing Narratives in Institutional Settings. *Journal of Pragmatics, 105*. http://search.proquest.com/docview/2061520159/

Vallone, R., Ross, L., & Lepper, M. R. (1985). The Hostile Media Phenomenon: Biased Perception and Perceptions of Media Bias in Coverage of the Beirut Massacre. *Journal of Personality and Social Psychology, 49*(3), 577–585. https://doi.org/10.1037/0022-3514.49.3.577

Vakkayil, J. (2008). Learning and Organizations: Towards Cross-Metaphor Conversations. *Learning Inquiry, 2*(1), 13–27. https://doi.org/10.1007/s11519-008-0025-5

Vanstone, A. (2019, October 28). Media Members Have Lead Roles, Too. *The Sydney Morning Herald*, p. 21. Dow Jones Global Factiva.

Varatharajan, P. (2017). A Political Radio Poetics: Ouyang Yu's Poetry and Its Adaptation on ABC Radio National's Poetica. *Cultural Studies Review, 23*(2), 18–34. http://dx.doi.org.wwwproxy1.library.unsw.edu.au/10.5130/csr.v23i2.5050

Varga, R. (2018, September 26). Spigelman Hits Out Over Guthrie Sacking. *The Australian*. https://www.theaustralian.com.au/business/media/abc-former-chairman-james-spigelman-hits-out-over-guthrie-sacking/news-story/9951e4c9f27ef10813f0ecd1abca7e3a

Varona, A. E. (2009). Toward a Broadband Public Interest Standard. *Administrative Law Review, 61*(1), 1–135. https://primoa.library.unsw.edu.au/permalink/f/11jha62/TN_gale_legal197493069

Varpio, L, O'Brien, B., Hu, W., ten Cate, O., Durning, S. J., van der Vleuten, C., Gruppen, L., Irby, D., Humphrey-Murto, S., & Hamstra, S. J. (2017). Exploring the Institutional Logics of Health Professions Education Scholarship Units. *Medical Education, 51*(7), 755.

Veitch, H. (2010, December 15). The Modest Face of the ABC: James Dibble 1923–2010. *The Sydney Morning Herald*. https://www.smh.com.au/national/the-modest-face-of-the-abc-20101214-18wpw.html

Venger, O., & Matthews, J. (2019). The Use of Experts in Journalistic Accounts of Media Events: A Comparative Study of the 2005 London Bombings in British, American, and Russian Newspapers. *Journalism, 20*(10), 1343–1359. https://doi.org/10.1177/1464884919830479

Vignal Lambret, C., & Barki, E. (2018). Social Media Crisis Management: Aligning Corporate Response Strategies with Stakeholders' Emotions Online. *Journal of Contingencies and Crisis Management, 26*(2), 295–305. https://doi.org/10.1111/1468-5973.12198

Vine, D. (1988, July 11). Parochialism or Patriotism? *The Canberra Times*, p. 26. https://trove.nla.gov.au/newspaper/article/102031858?searchTerm=ABC%20patriotism&searchLimits=

Vine, P. (2017). When Is a Journalist Not a Journalist? Negotiating a New Form of Advocacy Journalism Within the Environmental Movement [online]. *Pacific Journalism Review,* 23(1), 43-54. https://doi.org/10.24135/pjr.v23i1.212

Visentin, L. (2020, November 2). 'Deep Regret': Christine Holgate to Forgo Payout as Australia Post Chief. *The Sydney Morning Herald*. https://www.smh.com.au/politics/federal/christine-holgate-to-resign-as-australia-post-chief-20201102-p56ask.html

Visontay, E. (2019, May 15). Where's Their Work? *The Australian*. https://www.theaustralian.com.au/nation/politics/federal-election-2019-campaign-day-35-scott-morrison-bill-shorten-hunt-for-votes/news-story/f0e7301ad5f058fec20a72fd6d9d1264

Vitorovitch, L., & Shanahan. L. (2020, March 3). AAP's Newswire to Close in June. *The Australian*. https://www.theaustralian.com.au/business/media/aaps-newswire-to-close-in-june/news-story/91ae9b35935ced854f8dddadd0616f84

Vitorovitch, L., & Swan, D. (2020, March 5). Guardian Hypocrisy Over AAP Shutdown. *The Australian*. https://www.theaustralian.com.au/business/media/accc-reviewing-aap-demise-says-rod-sims/news-story/78a2380813fc8574680b81e5ec570ec3

Voelz, G. J. (2015). (Rep.) *The Rise of iWar: Identity, Information, and the Individualization of Modern Warfare*. Strategic Studies Institute, US Army War College. www.jstor.org/stable/resrep11804

Von Clausewitz, C. (J. J. Graham, Trans.). (1874). *On War*. The Project Gutenberg EBook. http://www.gutenberg.org/files/1946/1946-h/1946-h.htm

Vosoughi, S., Roy, D., & Aral, S. (2018). The Spread of True and False News Online. *Science, 359*(6380), 1446–1151. https://doi.org/10.1126/science.aap9559

Voxted, S. (2017). 100 Years of Henri Fayol. *Management Revue, 28*(2), 256–274. https://doi.org/10.5771/0935-9915-2017-2-256

Vujnovic, M., Singer, J. B., Paulussen, S., Heinonen, A., Reich, Z., Quandt, T., Hermida, A., & Domingo, D. (2010). Exploring the Political-Economic Factors of Participatory Journalism: Views of Online Journalists in 10 Countries. *Journalism Practice: The Future of Journalism, 4*(3), 285–296. https://doi.org/10.1080/17512781003640588

Vulliamy, E. (1999, March 1). "Neutrality" and the Absence of Reckoning: A Journalist's Account. *Journal of International Affairs, 52*(2), 604. https://primoa.library.unsw.edu.au/permalink/f/11jha62/TN_jstor_archive_1424358055

Wade, L. (2011). Journalism, Advocacy and the Social Construction of Consensus. *Media, Culture & Society, 33*(8), 1166–1184. https://doi.org/10.1177/0163443711418273

Wadham, B. (2014, February 10). With Navy's Record of Abuse, Asylum Boat Claims Can't Be Ignored. *The Conversation*. https://theconversation.com/with-navys-record-of-abuse-asylum-boat-claims-cant-be-ignored-22941

Waisbord, S. (2018). The Elective Affinity Between Post-Truth Communication and Populist Politics. *Communication Research and Practice: Special Issue: ANZCA 2017—Communication Worlds: Access, Voice, Diversity. Engagement, 4*(1), 17–34. https://doi.org/10.1080/22041451.2018.1428928. Guest Editor: F. Martin.

Wallace, D. M., Raver Luning, C., Rosenstein, J. E., Ledford, A., & Cyr-Roman, B. (2020). A Culture of Respect: Leader Development and Preventing Destructive Behavior. *Industrial and Organizational Psychology, 13*(2), 225–229. https://doi.org/10.1017/iop.2020.46

Wallach, B. (2005). *Understanding the Cultural Landscape*. The Guilford Press.

Walker, T. (2018, October 17). Shifting the Australian Embassy in Israel to Jerusalem Would Be a Big, Cynical Mistake. *ABC News Online*. https://www.abc.net.au/news/2018-10-17/australian-embassy-jerusalem-big-cynical-mistake/10388108

Walker, R. R. (1973). *The Magic Spark: Fifty Years of Radio in Australia*. The Hawthorn Press.

Wander, F. (Ed.). (2013). The Servant Leader. Chap. 10 in *Transforming IT Culture* (pp. 123–136). Wiley.

Wang, L., & Gordon, P. (2011). Trust and Institutions: A Multilevel Analysis. *Journal of Socio—Economics, 40*(5), 583–593. https://doi.org/10.1016/j.socec.2011.04.015

Wanous, J. P., Reichers, A. E., & Austin, J. T. (2004). Cynicism about Organizational Change: An Attribution Process Perspective. *Psychological*

Reports, 94(3, Suppl), 1421–1434. https://doi.org/10.2466/pr0.94.3c.1421-1434

Warburton, J. W. (1963). Schools of Arts. *The Australian Quarterly, 35*(4), 72–80. https://doi.org/10.2307/20633919

Ward, L. (2005). Stand Up for Who You Are. *The Safety & Health Practitioner, 23*(9), 37–40. http://search.proquest.com/docview/200971662/

Ward, T. (2009). The Heart of What It Means to Be Australian. *Soccer & Society, 10*(5), 532–543. https://doi.org/10.1080/14660970902955463

Ward, S. J. A. (2014). Radical Media Ethics: Ethics for a Global Digital World. *Digital Journalism, 2*(4), 455–471. https://doi.org/10.1080/21670811.2014.952985

Wardle, C. (2019, September 1). Misinformation Has Created a New World Disorder. *Scientific American*. https://www.scientificamerican.com/article/misinformation-has-created-a-new-world-disorder/

Wardle, C., & Derakhshan, H. (2017). *Information Disorder: Toward an Interdisciplinary Framework for Research and Policy Making*. Council of Europe. https://rm.coe.int/information-disorder-toward-an-interdisciplinary-framework-for-researc/168076277c

Washbrook, C. (2011, July 8). James Murdoch's statement on the Closure of the News of the World. *Media Spy*. http://www.mediaspy.org/report/2011/07/08/james-murdochs-statement-on-the-closure-of-the-news-of-the-world/

Watson, T., & Hickman, M. (2012). *Dial M for Murdoch: News Corporation and the Corruption of Britain*. Allen Lane.

Walker, R. R. (1973). *The Magic Spark: Fifty Years of Radio in Australia*. The Hawthorn Press.

Waters, J. (2020, September 5). ABC News Needs to Find a New Way to Chase Ratings. Opinion. *Independent Australia*. https://independentaustralia.net/business/business-display/abc-news-needs-to-find-a-new-way-to-chase-ratings,14279

Waters, R., & Murphy, H. (2021, January 16). Donald Trump, Twitter and the Messy Fight Over Free Speech. *The Financial Times*. The Big Read. Social Media. https://www.ft.com/content/78a3ed8c-d930-4bf5-9f6e-1b6b4751090f

Waters, S. (2018). The Effects of Mass Surveillance on Journalists' Relations with Confidential Sources: A Constant Comparative Study. *Digital Journalism, 6*(10), 1294–1313. https://doi.org/10.1080/21670811.2017.1365616

Waterhouse-Watson, D. (2016). News Media on Trial: Towards a Feminist Ethics of Reporting Footballer Sexual Assault Trials. *Feminist Media Studies, 16*(6), 952–967. https://doi.org/10.1080/14680777.2016.1162827

Watson, D. (2014, March). The Conservative Crusade Against the ABC. *The Monthly*. https://www.themonthly.com.au/issue/2014/march/1393592400/don-watson/conservative-crusade-against-abc#mtr

Warren, M. (2005). What Separation of Powers? (Australia). *Monash University Law Review, 31*(1). (Contribution posted 2019). https://doi.org/10.26180/5db7f780d5393

Warren, A. M., Sulaiman, A., & Ismawati Jaafar, N. (2014). Social Media Effects on Fostering Online Civic Engagement and Building Citizen Trust and Trust in Institutions. *Government Information Quarterly, 31*, 291–301. www.elsevier.com/locate/govinf

Watson, D. (2014, March). The Conservative Crusade Against the *ABC. The Monthly.* https://www.themonthly.com.au/issue/2014/march/1393592400/don-watson/conservative-crusade-against-abc#mtr

Weaver, D. (Ed.). (1998). *The Global Journalist: News People Around the World.* Hampton Press.

Weber, E. (2010). Democratic Political Leadership. In R. A. Couto *Political and Civic Leadership: A Reference Handbook* (pp. 105–110). SAGE Publications, Inc. https://doi.org/10.4135/9781412979337.n13

Weeks, B.E., Ardèvol-Abreu, A., & Gil de Zúñiga, H. (2017). Online Influence? *Social Media Use, Opinion Leadership, and Political Persuasion, International Journal of Public Opinion Research, 29*(2). Summer 2017, 214–239. Retrieved from: https://doi-org.wwwproxy1.library.unsw.edu.au/10.1093/ijpor/edv050

Weinert, E. (2019). Host of Internet Forum Not Liable for Abuse Online—Status Quo But for How Much Longer? *Entertainment Law Review, 30*(5), 162–163. https://primoa.library.unsw.edu.au/permalink/f/11jha62/TN_gale_legal592533264

Weisblott, M. (2013). CBC Music Radio Stations Will Now Have a Word or Two From Their Sponsors. *Canada.com.* https://o.canada.com/business/cbc-radio-commercial-advertising-approved

Wells, S. W. W. (1959). Impartial. *Notes and Queries, 6*(9), 353–354. https://doi.org/10.1093/nq/6.9.353

Werner, W. (2004). "What Does This Picture Say?" Reading the Intertextuality of Visual Images. *International Journal of Social Education, 19.* https://eric.ed.gov/?id=EJ718728

West Australian, The. (1936. February 26). Newsprint industry. An Australian Project. Sir Keith Murdoch Interviewed. *The West Australian.*https://trove.nla.gov.au/newspaper/article/32978504?searchTerm=keith%20murdoch

West Australian, The. (1945, March 2). Paper Attacked. "Blatant Inaccuracies". ABC and Mr Churchill. *The West Australian*, p. 4. https://trove.nla.gov.au/newspaper/article/44999578?searchTerm=inaccuracies%20ABC&searchLimits=

West Australian, The. (1953, October 3). ABC Staff Has Lost a Privilege. *The West Australian*, p. 3. https://trove.nla.gov.au/newspaper/article/52932388?searchTerm=ABC%20privilege&searchLimits=

West, K., & Lloyd, J. (2017). The Role of Labelling and Bias in the Portrayals of Acts of "Terrorism": Media Representations of Muslims vs. *Non-Muslims.*

Journal of Muslim Minority Affairs, 37(2), 211–222. https://doi.org/10.1080/13602004.2017.1345103

West, A. (2020). Did a Former Vatican Official Pay a Bribe to Tilt the George Pell Trial? *ABC.* The Religion and Ethics Report. https://www.abc.net.au/radionational/programs/religionandethicsreport/could-former-vatican-staffer-have-bribed-to-tilt-the-pell-case/12738792

Westmore, P. (2018, October 20). Media: Internal Strife at Fortress ABC [online]. *News Weekly.* 3031, p. 13. https://search.informit.com.au/documentSummary;dn=988136489334664;res=IELAPA

Western Argus, The. (1937, October 19). ABC Policy Defended by Chairman. Listeners Do Not Want To Be Patronised. *The Western Argus*, p. 17. https://trove.nla.gov.au/newspaper/article/34959094?searchTerm=ABC%20POLICY%20DEFENDED%20BY%20CHAIRMAN.%20Listeners%20Do%20Not%20Want%20To%20Be%20Patronised

Whetstone, J. T. (2002). Personalism and Moral Leadership: The Servant Leader with a Transforming Vision. *Business Ethics: A European Review, 11*(4), 385–392. https://doi.org/10.1111/1467-8608.00298

White, D., & Lynch, J. (2014, November 20). Turnbull Takes on ABC, SBS. [online]. *The Australian Financial Review.* http://search.proquest.com/docview/1748835968/

Whitehead, G. (1988). *Inside the ABC: Geoffrey Whitehead's Personal Account.* Penguin Books Victoria.

Whitlam, E. G. (1972, November 13). Australian Federal Election Speeches. Gough Whitlam. Australian Labor Party. *Museum of Democracy Old Parliament House.* Blacktown. https://electionspeeches.moadoph.gov.au/speeches/1972-gough-whitlam

Whitlam, N. (2020, April 25–26). Downfall Not for Reasons He Thinks. *The Australian.* Inquirer, p. 16.

Williams, K. (2010). *Read All About It: A History of the British Newspaper.* Routledge.

Williams, M. (2006). *Virtually Criminal: Crime, Deviance and Regulation Online.* Routledge.

Williams, R. (1996). Normal Service Won't Be Resumed: The Future of Public Broadcasting. Allen & Unwin. Crows Nest. Sydney.

Williamson, D. (2013). *Rupert.* Currency Press. Sydney.

Willem, A., De Vos, A., & Buelens, M. (2010). Comparing Private and Public Sector Employees' Psychological Contracts Do They Attach Equal Importance to Generic Work Aspects? *Public Management Review, 12*(2), 275-302. https://www-tandfonline-com.wwwproxy1.library.unsw.edu.au/doi/pdf/10.1080/14719031003620323?needAccess=true

Wilson. J. (2008, May 13). Will Newspapers Be First Against the Wall? *New Matilda.* http://newmatilda.com/2008/05/13/when-revolution-comes

Wilson, C. K., Hutchinson, J., & Shea, P. (2010). Public Service Broadcasting, Creative Industries, and Innovation Infrastructure: The Case of ABC's Pool. *Australian Journal of Communication, 37*(3), 15–32. https://primoa.library.unsw.edu.au/permalink/f/11jha62/TN_informit_apaft201102742

Wilson, Z. (2019). David Anderson Named ABC Managing Director. *Radio Today.* https://www.radiotoday.com.au/david-anderson-named-abc-managing-director/

Wilson, C. K., Hutchinson, J., & Shea, P. (2010). Public Service Broadcasting, Creative Industries, and Innovation Infrastructure: The Case of ABC's Pool. *Australian Journal of Communication, 37*(3), 15–32. https://primoa.library.unsw.edu.au/permalink/f/11jha62/TN_informit_apaft201102742

Wilson, C. (2021). ABC May Outsource Outside Broadcasting as Technology Ages and Budget Cuts Bite. 12 May 2021. *Crikey.com.* Retrieved from: https://www.crikey.com.au/2021/05/12/abc-outsource-outside-broadcasting-technology-ages-budget-cuts/

Winslow, D. (1999). Rites of Passage and Group Bonding in the Canadian Airborne. *Armed Forces & Society, 25.* http://afs.sagepub.com/content/25/3/429

Wilkie, K. (2017, January 15). Controversial Muslim Activist Yassmin Abdel-Magied is Now Flogging Products and Companies on Instagram as a Paid Social Media 'Influencer'. *The Daily Mail.* https://www.dailymail.co.uk/news/article-7887389/Yassmin-Abdel-Magied-flogging-companies-Instagram-paid-social-media-influencer.html

Windrum, P., & Koch, P. (2008). Innovation in Public Sector Services: Entrepreneurship, Creativity and Management. ProQuest Ebook Central https://ebookcentral.proquest.com

Windschuttle, K. (2000). The Poverty of Cultural Studies. *Journalism Studies, 1*(1), 145–159. https://doi.org/10.1080/146167000361221

Wood, G., & Schaffer, B. (1985). *Labelling in Development Policy: Essays in Honour of Bernard Schaffer.* Sage Publications.

Wood, D., Daley, J., & Chivers, C. (2018). Policy Forum: Economics and Populism Australia Demonstrates the Rise of Populism Is About More than Economics. *The Australian Economic Review, 51*(3), 399–410. https://doi.org/10.1111/1467-8462.12294

Wood, B. (2018, August 3). *Submission to the Review of Australian Broadcasting Services in the Asia Pacific.* https://www.communications.gov.au/sites/default/files/submissions/bradley_wood.pdf

Wooten, M., & Hoffman, A.J. (2008). Organizational Fields: Past, Present and Future. Chap. 4 in R. Greenwood, C. Oliver, R. Suddaby, & K. Sahlin-Andersson (Eds.), *The SAGE Handbook of Organizational Institutionalism.* SAGE Publications.

Wootton, H. (2019, August 2). Police Raid on ABC 'Unconstitutional'. *The Australian Financial Review*. https://www.afr.com/companies/media-and-marketing/police-raid-on-abc-unconstitutional-20190801-p52czc

Work, W., & Boileau, D. M. (1985). Television Debates. *Communication Education, 34*(4), 369–375. https://doi.org/10.1080/03634528509378631

Worrall, L. (2000). Surviving Redundancy: The Perceptions of UK Managers. *Journal of Managerial Psychology., 15*(5-6), 460–472.

Worrall, L., Cooper, C. L., & Campbell-Jamison, F. (2000). The Impact of Organizational Change on the Work Experiences and Perceptions of Public Sector Managers. *Personnel Review, 29*(5), 613–636. http://dx.doi.org.wwwproxy1.library.unsw.edu.au/10.1108/00483480010296429

Worrall, L. (2000). Surviving Redundancy: The Perceptions of UK Managers. *Journal of Managerial Psychology., 15*(5-6), 460–472.

Worthington, B., & Snape, J. (2020, March 18). Large Indoor Gatherings Banned, Schools to Stay Open, Scott Morrison Tells Australians Not to Leave the Country in Face of Coronavirus Pandemic. *Australian Broadcasting Corporation*. https://www.abc.net.au/news/2020-03-18/coronavirus-australia-live-updates-covid19-latest-news-anzac-day/12064922

Worthington, B., & Hitch, G. (2020, June 24). Up to 250 ABC Jobs to Go, ABC Life Brand Scrapped, Flagship Radio News Bulletin Dumped to Tackle $84 Million Budget Cut. [online]. *ABC News*. https://www.abc.net.au/news/2020-06-24/abc-announces-cuts-to-programming-and-jobs-funding/12384972

Wright, B. E., Moynihan, D. P., & Pandey, S. J. (2012). Pulling the Levers: Transformational Leadership, Public Service Motivation, and Mission Valence. *Public Administration Review, 72*(2), 206–215. The American Society for Public Administration. https://doi.org/10.1111/j.1540-6210.2011.02496.x

Wroe, D., Bachelard, M., & Snow, D. (2014, January 23). Asylum Seekers' Burns Claims Baseless, Say Australian Defence Chiefs. *The Sydney Morning Herald*. https://www.smh.com.au/politics/federal/asylum-seekers-burns-claims-baseless-say-australian-defence-chiefs-20140122-3196l.html

Wyn, J., Khan, R., & Dadvand, B. (2018). Multicultural Youth Australia Census Status Report. 2017/18. Youth Research Centre. *Melbourne Graduate School of Education Research Unit in Public Cultures School of Culture and Communication University of Melbourne*. https://education.unimelb.edu.au/__data/assets/pdf_file/0011/2972036/MY-Aust-Report-17-18.pdf

Xie, Q. (2018). Analysis of Intertextuality in English News Headlines. (Report). *Theory and Practice in Language Studies., 8*(8), 1010–1014. https://doi.org/10.17507/tpls.0808.13

Yadamsuren, B., Erdelez, S., & Marchionini, G. (2017). *Incidental Exposure to Online News*. Morgan & Claypool. http://ieeexplore.ieee.org.wwwproxy1.library.unsw.edu.au/document/7791114

Yang, X., Chen, B. C., Maity, M., & Ferrara, E. (2016). Social Politics: Agenda Setting and Political Communication on Social Media. *arXiv.org, 10046*, 330–344. https://doi.org/10.1007/978-3-319-47880-7_20

Youmans, W. L., & York, J. C. (2012). Social Media and the Activist Toolkit: User Agreements, Corporate Interests, and the Information Infrastructure of Modern Social Movements. *Journal of Communication, 62*(2), 315–329. https://doi.org/10.1111/j.1460-2466.2012.01636.x

Younger, R. M. (2003). *Keith Murdoch: Founder of a Media Empire*. Harper Collins.

Younger, E. (2019, April 15). George Pell Media Contempt Case Could Have 'Chilling Effect' on Open Justice, Court Hears. *Australian Broadcasting Corporation*. https://www.abc.net.au/news/2019-04-15/george-pell-guilty-verdict-coverage-media-contempt-case/11002760

Yukl, G. (2010, republished). *Leadership in Organisations* (7th ed.). Pearson.

Zaczek, Z. (2020, March 17). 'We had PLENTY of Warning': Infection Expert Unloads on Scott Morrison and His Government for Not Closing Australia's Borders MONTHS Ago to Stop the Spread of the Coronavirus. *The Daily Mail Australia*. https://www.dailymail.co.uk/news/article-8116681/Coronavirus-Bill-Bowtell-unloads-Scott-Morrison-government-COVID-19-response.html

Zafirovski, M. (2017). *Identifying a Free Society Conditions and Indicators*. Brill.

Zaller, J. (1999). *A Theory of Media Politics: How the Interests of Politicians, Journalists, and Citizens Shape the News*. University of Chicago Press.

Zhou, N. (2017, July 12). I'd Be Tempted to Run Over Yassmin Abdel-Magied, Commentator Says: Radio 2GB Defends Prue MacSween's Comments as 'Light Hearted' and 'Nonliteral' After She Says Abdel-Magied Was Right Not to Feel Safe in Australia. *The Guardian*. https://www.theguardian.com/australia-news/2017/jul/12/conservative-commentator-run-over-yassmin-abdel-magied

Zhou, C. & Xiao, B. (2020). China's Social Credit System is Pegged to be Fully Operational by 2020—But What Will it Look Like? *Australian Broadcasting Corporation*. 2 January 2020. Retrieved from: https://www.abc.net.au/news/2020-01-02/china-social-credit-system-operational-by-2020/11764740

Zineldin, M., & Hytter, A. (2012). Leaders' Negative Emotions and Leadership Styles Influencing Subordinates' Well-being. *The International Journal of Human Resource Management, 23*(4), 748–758. https://doi.org/10.1080/09585192.2011.606114

Zollman, K. (2012). Social Network Structure and the Achievement of Consensus. *Politics, Philosophy & Economics, 11*(1), 26–44. https://doi.org/10.1177/1470594X11416766

Zuo, J. (2003). From Revolutionary Comrades to Gendered Partners: Marital Construction of Breadwinning in Post-Mao Urban China. *Journal of Family Issues, 24*(3), 314–337. https://doi.org/10.1177/0192513X02250888

Index[1]

A

[1] Note: Page numbers followed by 'n' refer to notes.

V. Small, *Strangling Aunty: Perilous Times for the Australian Broadcasting Corporation*,
https://doi.org/10.1007/978-981-16-0776-9

M

N

O

P